P9-DHP-928

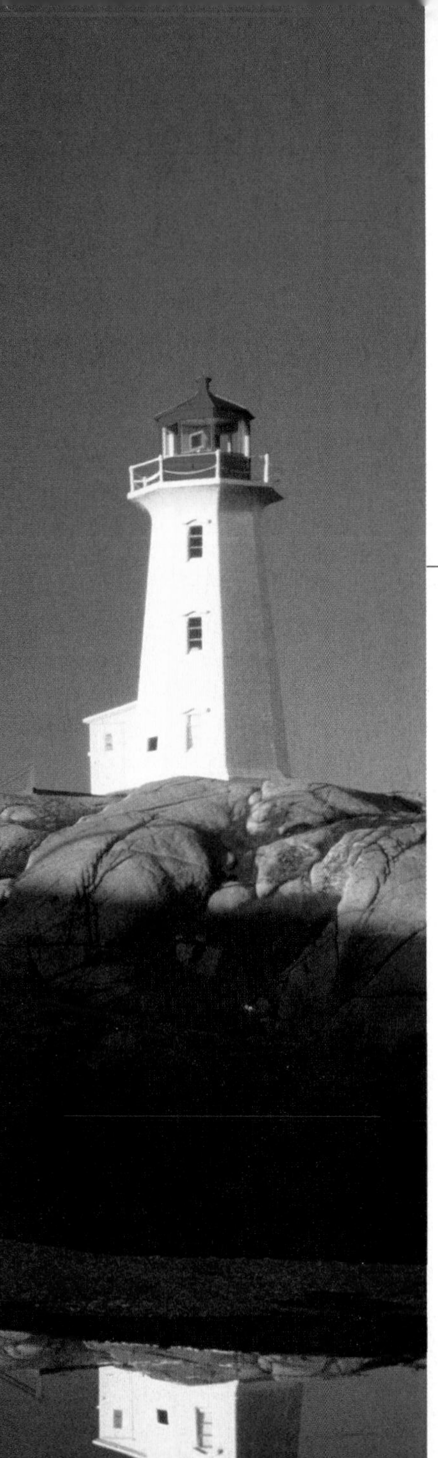

SEVENTH CANADIAN EDITION

MANAGERIAL ACCOUNTING

Ray H. Garrison, D.B.A., CPA
Professor Emeritus
Brigham Young University

Eric W. Noreen, Ph.D., CMA
Professor Emeritus
University of Washington

Peter C. Brewer, Ph.D., CPA
Miami University—Oxford, Ohio

G. Richard Chesley, Ph.D.
Saint Mary's University

Ray F. Carroll, Ph.D., FCGA, CMA, LIFA
Dalhousie University

Contributor
Alan Webb, Ph.D., CA
University of Waterloo

Toronto Montréal Boston Burr Ridge, IL Dubuque, IA Madison, WI New York San Francisco
St. Louis Bangkok Bogotá Caracas Kuala Lumpur Lisbon London Madrid
Mexico City Milan New Delhi Santiago Seoul Singapore Sydney Taipei

The McGraw·Hill Companies

McGraw-Hill Ryerson

Managerial Accounting
Seventh Canadian Edition

ISBN-13: 978-0-07-095168-6

ISBN-10: 0-07-095168-3

2 3 4 5 6 7 8 9 10 TCP 0 9 8 7

Printed and bound in China

Publisher, Business & Economics: Nicole Lukach
Sponsoring Editor: Rhondda McNabb
Marketing Manager: Charlotte Liu
Developmental Editor: Denise Foote
Senior Associate Editor: Christine Lomas
Copy Editor: Shirley Corriveau
Production Coordinator: Janie Deneau
Cover Design: Sharon Lucas
Cover Image Credit: © Garry Black/Masterfile
Page Layout: Bill Renaud
Printer: China Translation and Printing Services Limited

Library and Archives Canada Cataloguing in Publication

Managerial accounting / Ray H. Garrison ... [et al.]. — 7th Canadian ed.

Includes index.
ISBN 0-07-095168-3

1. Managerial accounting—Textbooks. I. Garrison, Ray H.

HF5657.4.M38 2006 658.15'11 C2005-907538-4

Dedication

This book attempts to reflect the dedication of our instructors and colleagues who provided us with the inspiration for our efforts to explain managerial accounting.

GRC and RFC

About the Authors

Ray H. Garrison is emeritus Professor of Accounting at Brigham Young University, Provo, Utah. He received his B.S. and M.S. degrees from Brigham Young University and his D.B.A. degree from Indiana University.

As a certified public accountant, Professor Garrison has been involved in management consulting work with both national and regional accounting firms. He has published articles in *The Accounting Review, Management Accounting*, and other professional journals. Innovation in the classroom has earned Professor Garrison the Karl G. Maeser Distinguished Teaching Award from Brigham Young University.

Eric W. Noreen is Professor Emeritus of Accounting at the University of Washington and was Visiting Price Waterhouse Professor of Management Information & Control at INSEAD, an international graduate school of business located in France, and a professor at the Hong Kong University of Science and Technology.

He received his B.A. degree from the University of Washington and M.B.A. and Ph.D. degrees from Stanford University. A Certified Management Accountant, he was awarded a Certificate of Distinguished Performance by the Institute of Certified Management Accountants.

Professor Noree has served as Associate Editor of *The Accounting Review* and the *Journal of Accounting and Economics*. He has published numerous articles in academic journals as well as won a number of awards for his teaching.

Peter C. Brewer is an Associate Professor in the Department of Accountancy at Miami University, Oxford, Ohio. He holds a B.S. degree in accounting from Penn State University, a M.S. degree in accounting from the University of Virginia, and a Ph.D. from the University of Tennessee. He has published numerous articles in a variety of journals.

Professor Brewer has received Miami University's Richard T. Farmer School of Business Teaching Excellence Award and has been recognized on two occasions by the Miami University Associated Student Government for "making a remarkable commitment to students and their educational development." He is a leader in undergraduate management accounting curriculum innovation and the use of the case method for teaching undergraduate management accounting courses. He is a frequent presenter at various professional and academic conferences and meetings.

G. Richard Chesley is Professor of Accounting at Saint Mary's University in Halifax, Nova Scotia. He is a graduate of Mount Allison University and The Ohio State University, with B. Comm., M.A., and Ph.D. degrees. He has held appointments at Dalhousie University, the University of Pennsylvania, Hong Kong's Lingnan University, Hong Kong Baptist University, and the University of Iowa. Professor Chesley has also conducted lectures and presentations throughout Canada, the United States, and abroad, both east and west. His publications appear in *The Accounting Review*, the *Journal of Accounting Research*, *CA Magazine*, *CMA Management* magazine, and numerous books and proceedings. Research interests include Web-based reporting, non-monetary reporting, accounting regulation, and management accounting practices. In 1996, his efforts were recognized by his peers with the L. S. Rosen Outstanding Educator Award by the Canadian Academic Accounting Association. In 2005, Saint Mary's University recognized his university efforts with its inaugural Exemplary Service Award.

Ray F. Carroll is Associate Professor of Accounting at Dalhousie University in Halifax, Nova Scotia. He is a graduate of Saint Francis Xavier University, where he completed his B.B.A. and B.Ed. degrees, and Dalhousie University, from which he obtained M.B.A. and Ph.D. degrees. Professor Carroll has taught at Hong Kong Baptist University and lectured in various international MBA programs throughout Hong Kong and Mainland China. His recent publications appear in the *Journal of International Business*, *Teaching Business Ethics*, and the *Journal of Intellectual Capital*. He is a Fellow of Certified General Accountants-Canada and a member of the Institute of Management Accountants of Australia. He has served as chairperson of the Canadian Certified General Accountants' National Education Committee and as a member of the American Accounting Association's Globalization Initiatives Committee.

Brief Contents

BONUS CHAPTER AND THREE SUPPLEMENTS ON THE GARRISON ONLINE LEARNING CENTRE

To view and download, go to:
http://www.mcgrawhill.ca/college/garrison/

Contents

Chapter Ten
Standard Costs 427

BONUS CHAPTER AND THREE SUPPLEMENTS ON THE GARRISON ONLINE LEARNING CENTRE

Bonus Chapter 15: "How Well Am I Doing?" Financial Statement Analysis—
Learn more about financial statement analysis and interpreting financial ratios.

Supplement A: Inventory Decisions

Supplement B: Shrinkage and Lost Units

Supplement C: Risk and Uncertainty in Capital Budgeting

To view and download, go to:
http://www.mcgrawhill.ca/college/garrison/

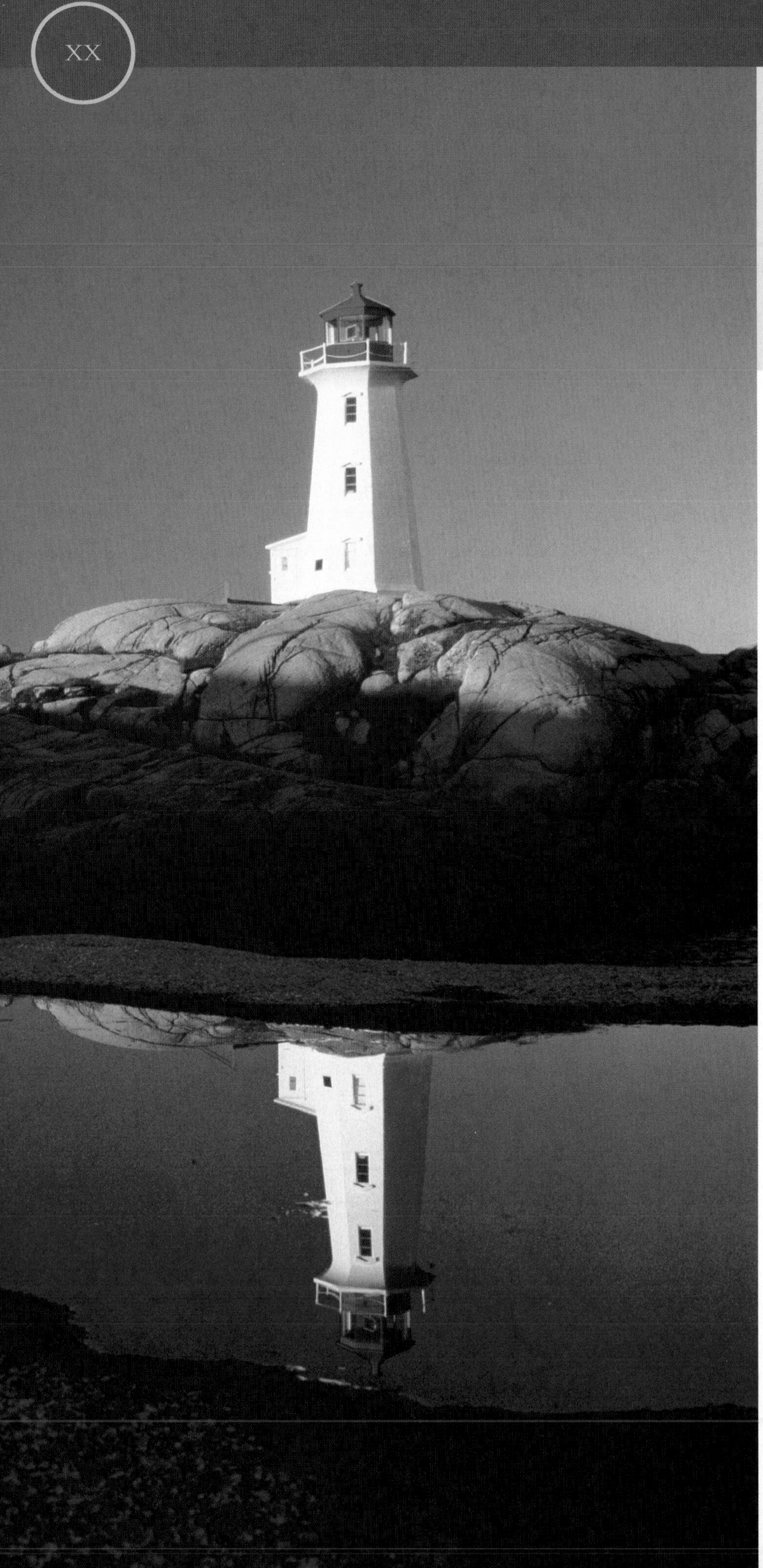

Your guide through

For centuries, the lighthouse has stood as a beacon of guidance for mariners at sea. More than an aid to navigation, the lighthouse symbolizes safety, permanence, reliability, and the comforts of the familiar.

For this reason, we have chosen to illustrate the Canadian seventh edition of our "flagship" accounting publication, **Managerial Accounting** by Garrison, Noreen, Brewer, Chesley, and Carroll, with an image that we feel encapsulates the greatest strengths of this market-leading text.

Garrison is your guide through the challenging waters of managerial accounting. It identifies the three functions managers must perform within their organizations—plan operations, control activities, and make decisions—and explains what accounting information is necessary for these functions, how to collect it, and how to interpret it. To achieve this, the **Managerial Accounting** seventh Canadian edition focuses, now as in the past, on three qualities:

Garrison/Noreen/Brewer/Chesley/Carroll:

the challenging waters of managerial accounting

Relevance. Every effort is made to help students relate the concepts in this book to the decisions made by working managers. With insightful chapter openers, the popular Managerial Accounting in Action segments within the chapters, and stimulating end-of-chapter exercises, a student reading Garrison should never have to ask, "Why am I learning this?"

Balance. Garrison mixes its coverage to include a variety of business types, including not-for-profit, retail, service, and wholesale organizations, as well as manufacturing. In the Canadian seventh edition, service company examples are highlighted with icons in the margins of the text.

Clarity. Generations of students have praised Garrison for the friendliness and readability of its writing, but that's just the beginning. Technical discussions have been simplified, material has been reordered, and the entire book has been carefully retuned to make teaching—and learning—from Garrison as easy as it can be. Key term definitions and icons signifying ethics, writing, and Internet assignments continue to add clarity for both students and professors. In addition, students and professors will work with clear, well-written supplements that employ consistent terminology.

The authors' steady focus on these three core elements has led to tremendous results.

What makes Garrison such a powerful learning tool?

Managerial Accounting is full of pedagogy designed to make studying productive and hassle-free. On the following pages, you will see the kind of engaging, helpful pedagogical features that make Garrison a favourite among both teachers and students.

Service-Related Examples
Owing to the growing number of service-based companies in business today, the Canadian seventh edition uses a helpful icon to distinguish service-related examples in the text.

Spreadsheets
These have become an increasingly common budgeting tool for managerial accountants; therefore, to assist students in understanding how budgets look in a spreadsheet, we've included Microsoft Excel® screen captures pertaining to budgeting.

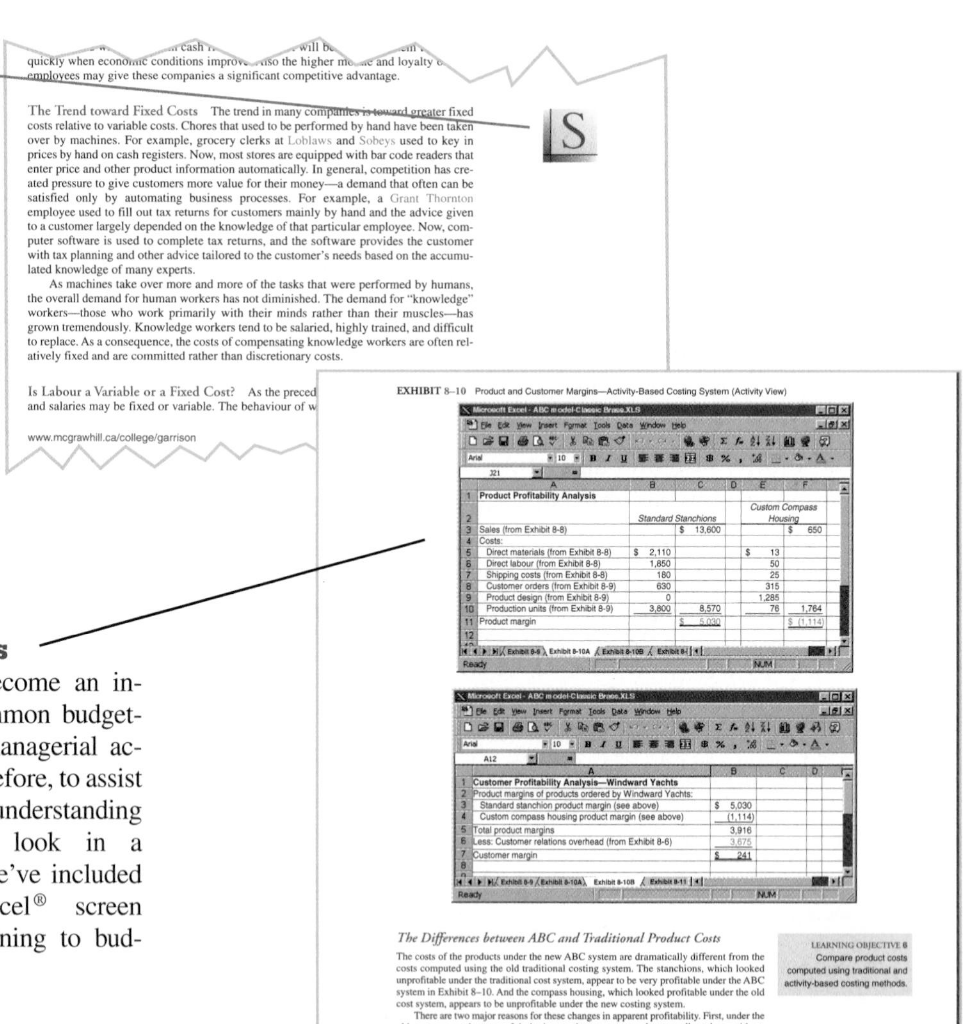

quickly when economic conditions improve. Also the higher morale and loyalty of employees may give these companies a significant competitive advantage.

S

The Trend toward Fixed Costs The trend in many companies is toward greater fixed costs relative to variable costs. Chores that used to be performed by hand have been taken over by machines. For example, grocery clerks at Loblaws and Sobeys used to key in prices by hand on cash registers. Now, most stores are equipped with bar code readers that enter price and other product information automatically. In general, competition has created pressure to give customers more value for their money—a demand that often can be satisfied only by automating business processes. For example, a Grant Thornton employee used to fill out tax returns for customers mainly by hand and the advice given to a customer largely depended on the knowledge of that particular employee. Now, computer software is used to complete tax returns, and the software provides the customer with tax planning and other advice tailored to the customer's needs based on the accumulated knowledge of many experts.

As machines take over more and more of the tasks that were performed by humans, the overall demand for human workers has not diminished. The demand for "knowledge" workers—those who work primarily with their minds rather than their muscles—has grown tremendously. Knowledge workers tend to be salaried, highly trained, and difficult to replace. As a consequence, the costs of compensating knowledge workers are often relatively fixed and are committed rather than discretionary costs.

Is Labour a Variable or a Fixed Cost? As the preced
and salaries may be fixed or variable. The behaviour of w

www.mcgrawhill.ca/college/garrison

EXHIBIT 8–10 Product and Customer Margins—Activity-Based Costing System (Activity View)

	A	B	C	D	E	F
1	**Product Profitability Analysis**					
2		*Standard Stanchions*			*Custom Compass Housing*	
3	Sales (from Exhibit 8-8)		$ 13,600			$ 650
4	Costs:					
5	Direct materials (from Exhibit 8-8)	$ 2,110			$ 13	
6	Direct labour (from Exhibit 8-8)	1,850			50	
7	Shipping costs (from Exhibit 8-8)	180			25	
8	Customer orders (from Exhibit 8-9)	630			315	
9	Product design (from Exhibit 8-9)	0			1,285	
10	Production units (from Exhibit 8-9)	3,800	8,570		76	1,764
11	Product margin		$ 5,030			$ (1,114)

	A	B
1	**Customer Profitability Analysis—Windward Yachts**	
2	Product margins of products ordered by Windward Yachts:	
3	Standard stanchion product margin (see above)	$ 5,030
4	Custom compass housing product margin (see above)	(1,114)
5	Total product margins	3,916
6	Less: Customer relations overhead (from Exhibit 8-6)	3,675
7	Customer margin	$ 241

The Differences between ABC and Traditional Product Costs

LEARNING OBJECTIVE 6
Compare product costs computed using traditional and activity-based costing methods.

The costs of the products under the new ABC system are dramatically different from the costs computed using the old traditional costing system. The stanchions, which looked unprofitable under the traditional cost system, appear to be very profitable under the ABC system in Exhibit 8–10. And the compass housing, which looked profitable under the old cost system, appears to be unprofitable under the new costing system.

There are two major reasons for these changes in apparent profitability. First, under the old cost system, the costs of designing products were spread across all products without regard to whether they actually required design work. Under the new ABC system, these

www.mcgrawhill.ca/college/garrison

FOCUS *on Current Practice*

Given the importance of government budgets, the CICA's Public Sector Accounting Board (PSAB) commissioned a research report to survey the state of the union. The survey looks at the basis of accounting and accounting policies used by Canadian federal, provincial and territorial governments in their budgets and estimates (appropriations) as compared with those adopted in their summary financial statements. Planning, budgeting and reporting are elements of a government's performance management and accountability framework. The report discusses each of these elements. Traditionally, the approach begins with priority setting and planning, followed by the budgeting process and ending with reporting and auditing. The survey findings indicate a clear trend for senior governments in Canada: (1) to move to accrual-based accounting, (2) to prepare a summary budget, and (3) to change certain significant accounting policies to be in line with the recommendations set out in the Public Sector Accounting Handbook.

Source: Excerpted from J.Paul-Emile, "Accounting Bases Used in Canadian Government Budgeting," *CA Magazine*, Toronto, January/February 2005, vol. 138, iss. 1, p. 18. Reproduced by permission from *CA Magazine* produced by the Canadian Institute of Chartered Accountants, Toronto, Canada.

ACTIVITY-BASED BUDGETING

Activity-based budgeting A type of budgeting in which emphasis is placed on budgeting the costs of the activities needed to produce and market the firm's goods and services

In Chapter 8, we saw that activity-based costing has been developed to help provide the manager with more accurate product or service costs. More accurate costs should translate into better decision making and tighter control over costs. Activity-based costing principles can also be applied to budgeting. With **activity-based budgeting**, the emphasis is on budgeting the costs of the activities needed to produce and market the firm's goods and services.

Activity-based budgeting involves several stages. First, the budgeted cost of accomplishing each unit of activity is determined. Recall that an activity is a cost driver, such as machine set-up, a purchase order, a quality inspection, or a maintenance request. Next, sales and production targets are used to estimate the demand for these activities. The unit cost of ... plied by the expected demand to determine the total cost of each ... dget based on activities that drive costs rather than the traditional ... functions and expense classifications.

..., costs within the responsibility centre are classified by activity, ... than simple quantities produced or sold are identified. Activities ... s, materials handling, assembly, shipping, purchasing, and so on ... and costed. These costs are then compiled to present the overall ... ervices if overall results are desired. The activity costing pre... ates how activity budgets are presented.

...ng activity-based costing techniques to budgeting technically ... BC approach. Instead of going from costs of resources, to activ... of outputs, activity-based budgeting goes from outputs to their ... equired activities, and then to the costs of procuring the required ... ce the outputs. Such a reversal can result in inaccuracies in the ... when the resources do not have a simple linear relationship to ... tments may be needed to compensate for the difficulties that this ... cess may cause.[8]

CHAPTER

2

LEARNING OBJECTIVES

After studying Chapter 2, you should be able to:

1. Identify and give examples of each of the three basic cost elements involved in the manufacture of a product.
2. Distinguish between product costs and period costs and give examples of each.
3. Prepare an income statement including the calculation of cost of goods sold.
4. Prepare a schedule of cost of goods manufactured.
5. Explain the difference in the behaviour of variable and fixed costs.
6. Distinguish between direct and indirect costs.
7. Define and give examples of additional cost classifications used in making decisions: differential costs, opportunity costs, and sunk costs.
8. (Appendix 2A) Identify the four types of quality costs and explain how they interact.
9. (Appendix 2A) Prepare and interpret a quality cost report.

COST TERMS, CONCEPTS, AND CLASSIFICATIONS

BUSINESS FOCUS

CONSIDERING THE COSTS

Terri, the owner of a retail florist shop, has been trying to decide for some time whether she should continue to use a local courier service to deliver flowers to customers or buy a delivery truck and use one of her employees to make the deliveries. At a recent family dinner, she brought up the subject of the delivery truck with her brother-in-law, who fancies himself as an expert on all management subjects. He grabbed this opportunity to impress on Terri his understanding of costs.

In rapid-fire succession, Terri's brother-in-law told her that the fees paid to the courier to deliver flowers are a variable cost and a period cost, but the costs of the flowers are product costs rather than period costs, even though the flower costs are also variable costs. On the other hand, the depreciation of the delivery truck would be a fixed cost and a period cost. And while the fuel for the truck would be a variable cost and a differential cost, the wages of the person making the deliveries would be a fixed cost, not a differential cost, and would involve an opportunity cost. At th... Terri excused herself—pleading that she had to help in the kitchen.

Terri felt that her brother-in-law's comments were more c... helpful, but she knew that she could no longer put off the deci... delivery truck. She would have to think carefully about her costs ... what costs should be considered in this decision.

MANAGERIAL ACCOUNTING IN ACTION

The Issue

The Colonial Pewter Company was organized a year ago. The company's only product at present is a reproduction of an eighteenth-century pewter bookend. The bookend is made largely by hand, using traditional metal-working tools. Consequently, the manufacturing process is labour-intensive and requires a high level of skill.

Colonial Pewter has recently expanded its workforce to take advantage of unexpected demand for the bookends as gifts. The company started with a small cadre of experienced pewter workers but has had to hire less experienced workers as a result of the expansion. The president of the company, J.D. Wriston, has called a meeting to discuss production problems. Attending the meeting are Tom Kuchel, the production manager; Janet Warner, the purchasing manager; and Terry Sherman, the corporate controller.

J.D.: I've got a feeling that we aren't getting the production we should out of our new people.

Tom: Give us a chance. Some of the new people have been on board for less than a month.

Janet: Let me add that production seems to be wasting an awful lot of material—particularly pewter. That stuff is very expensive.

Tom: What about the shipment of defective pewter you bought a couple of months ago—the one with the iron contamination? That caused us major problems.

Janet: That's ancient history. How was I to know it was off-grade? Besides, it was a great deal.

J.D.: Calm down everybody. Let's get the facts before we start sinking our fangs into each other.

Tom: I agree. The more facts the better.

J.D.: Okay, Terry, it's your turn. Facts are the con...ller's department.

"Focus on Current Practice"

These helpful boxed features offer a glimpse into how real companies use the managerial accounting concepts discussed in the chapter. Every chapter contains from two to nine of these current examples.

Opening Vignettes

These opening pieces, based on real-world scenarios, introduce the chapter and bring forward the issues, concepts and practices to be discussed in the ensuing pages.

"Managerial Accounting in Action"

These highly praised vignettes depict cross-functional teams working together in real-life settings, working with the products and services that students recognize from their own lives. Students are shown step by step how accounting concepts are implemented in organizations and how these concepts are applied to solve everyday business problems. First, "The Issue" is introduced through a dialogue. The student then walks through the implementation process. Finally, "The Wrap-Up" summarizes the big picture.

What makes Managerial Accounting such a powerful learning tool?

End-of-Chapter Material

Managerial Accounting has earned a reputation for the best end-of-chapter review and discussion material of any text on the market. Most of the exercises, problems, and cases have been revised for the Canadian seventh edition. Other helpful features include:

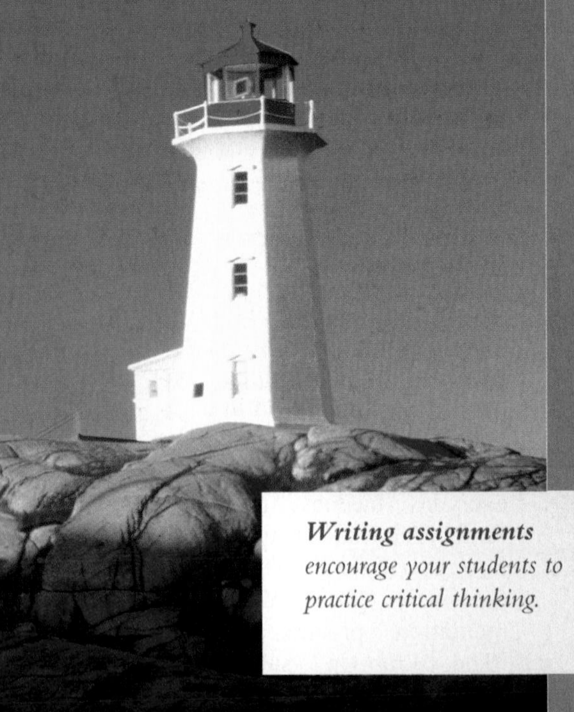

Writing assignments encourage your students to practice critical thinking.

Leeds Architectural Consultants is a service firm, so the names of the accounts it uses are different from the names used in manufacturing firms. Costs of Subcontracted Work is comparable to Direct Materials; Direct Staff Costs is the same as Direct Labour; Studio Overhead is the same as Manufacturing Overhead; and Completed Projects is the same as Finished Goods. Apart from the difference in terms, the accounting methods used by the company are identical to the methods used by manufacturing companies.

Leeds Architectural Consultants uses a job-order costing system and applies studio overhead to Work in Process on the basis of direct staff costs. At the end of January, only one job was still in process. This job (Lexington Gardens Project) had been charged with $6,500 in direct staff costs.

Required:

1. Compute the predetermined overhead rate that was in use during January.
2. Complete the following job cost sheet for the partially completed Lexington Gardens Project.

Job Cost Sheet—Lexington Gardens Project As of January 31	
Costs of subcontracted work	$?
Direct staff costs	?
Studio overhead	?
Total cost to January 31	$?

EXERCISE 3–12 Varying Predetermined Overhead Rates [LO3, LO5]

Kingsport Containers, Ltd, of the Bahamas experiences wide variation in demand for the 200-litre steel drums it fabricates. The leakproof, rustproof steel drums have a variety of uses from storing liquids and bulk materials to serving as makeshift musical instruments. The drums are made to order and are painted according to the customer's specifications—often in bright patterns and designs. The company is well known for the artwork that appears on its drums. Unit product costs are computed on a quarterly basis by dividing each quarter's manufacturing costs (materials, labour, and overhead) by the quarter's production in units. The company's estimated costs, by quarter, for the coming year follow:

	Quarter			
	First	Second	Third	Fourth
Direct materials	$240,000	$120,000	$60,000	$180,000
Direct labour	128,000	64,000	32,000	96,000
Manufacturing overhead	300,000	220,000	180,000	260,000
Total manufacturing costs	$668,000	$404,000	$272,000	$536,000
Number of units to be produced	80,000	40,000	20,000	60,000
Estimated unit product cost	$8.35	$10.10	$13.60	$8.93

Management finds the variation in unit costs to be confusing and difficult to work with. It has been suggested that the problem lies with manufacturing overhead, since it is the largest element of cost. Accordingly, you have been asked to find a more appropriate way of assigning manufacturing overhead cost to units of product. After some analysis, you have determined that the company's overhead costs are mostly fixed and therefore show little sensitivity to changes in the level of production.

Required:

1. The company uses a job-order costing system. How would you recommend that manufacturing overhead cost be assigned to production? Be specific, and show computations.
2. Recompute the company's unit product costs in accordance with your recommendations in (1) above.

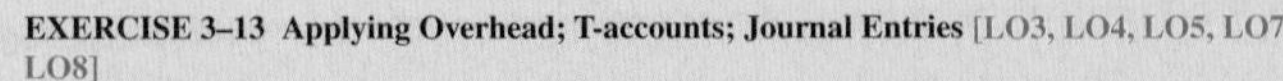

EXERCISE 3–13 Applying Overhead; T-accounts; Journal Entries [LO3, LO4, LO5, LO7, LO8]

Harwood Company is a manufacturer that operates a job-order costing system. Overhead costs are applied to jobs on the basis of machine-hours. At the beginning of the year, management estimated that the company would incur $192,000 in manufacturing overhead costs and work 80,000 machine-hours.

Internet exercises *teach students how to find information online and apply it to managerial accounting situations.* ***Group exercises*** *can be assigned either as homework or as in-class discussion projects*

GROUP AND INTERNET EXERCISES

GROUP EXERCISE 10–34 Standards in an Auto Repair Shop

Make an appointment to meet with the manager of an auto repair shop that uses standards. In most cases, this would be an auto repair shop that is affiliated with a national chain such as Canadian Tire or the service department of a new-car dealer.

Required:

At the scheduled meeting, seek answers to the following questions:

1. How are standards set?
2. Are standards practical or ideal?
3. How are the standards used?
4. Is the actual time taken to complete a task compared to the standard time?
5. What are the consequences of unfavourable variances? Of favourable variances?
6. Do the standards and variances create any potential problems?

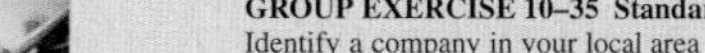

GROUP EXERCISE 10–35 Standards in Practice

Identify a company in your local area that is likely to use standards such as a commercial bakery, commercial printer, chain restaurant, or manufacturer. After verifying that the company uses standards, make an appointment to meet with the manager, controller, or chief financial officer of the organization.

Required:

At the scheduled meeting, seek answers to the following questions:

1. How are standards set?
2. Are standards practical or ideal?
3. How are the standards used?
4. What are the consequences of unfavourable variances? Of favourable variances?
5. Do the standards and variances create any potential problems?

INTERNET EXERCISE 10–36

As you know, the World Wide Web is a medium that is constantly evolving. Sites come and go, and change without notice. To enable the periodic updating of site addresses, this problem has been posted to the textbook Web site (www.mcgrawhill.ca/college/garrison). After accessing the site, enter the Student Centre and select this chapter. Select and complete the Internet Exercise.

While completing the financial reports, Perlman discovered a sizable inventory of outda
that should have been discounted for sale or returned to the manufacturer. She discussed
tion with her management colleagues; the consensus was to ignore reporting this inventor
lete, since reporting it would diminish the financial results and their bonuses.

Required:

1. According to the Standards of Ethical Conduct for Practitioners of Management A
and Financial Management, would it be ethical for Perlman *not* to report the in
obsolete?
2. Would it be easy for Perlman to take the ethical action in this situation?

(CMA

PROBLEM 1–6 Line and Staff Positions [LO2]

Special Alloys Corporation manufactures a variety of specialized metal products for ind
Most of the revenues are generated by large contracts with companies that have g
defence contracts. The company also develops and markets parts to the major automobile companies. It employs many metallurgists and skilled technicians because most of its products are made from highly sophisticated alloys.

The company recently signed two large contracts; as a result, the workload of Wayne Washburn, the general manager, has become overwhelming. To relieve some of this overload, Mark Johnson was transferred from the Research Planning Department to the general manager's office. Johnson, who has been a senior metallurgist and supervisor in the Research Planning Department, was given the title "assistant to the general manager."

Washburn assigned several responsibilities to Johnson in their first meeting. Johnson will oversee the testing of new alloys in the Product Planning Department and be given the authority to make decisions as to the use of these alloys in product development; he will also be responsible for maintaining the production schedules for one of the new contracts. In addition to these duties, he will be required to meet with the supervisors of the production departments regularly to consult with them about production problems they may be experiencing. Washburn expects to be able to manage the company much more efficiently with Johnson's help.

Required:

1. Positions within organizations are often described as having (a) line authority or (b) staff authority. Describe what is meant by these two terms.
2. Of the responsibilities assigned to Mark Johnson as assistant to the general manager, which tasks have line authority and which have staff authority?
3. Identify and discuss the conflicts Mark Johnson may experience in the production departments as a result of his new responsibilities.

(CMA, adapted)

PROBLEM 1–7 Ethics in Business [LO4]

South of the border a prominent nationwide chain of auto repair shops was accused of misleading customers and selling them unnecessary parts and services, from brake jobs to front-end alignments. Lynn Sharpe Paine reported the situation as follows in "Managing for Organizational Integrity," *Harvard Business Review,* March–April, 1994:

> In the face of declining revenues, shrinking market share, and an increasingly competitive market . . . management attempted to spur performance of its auto centers. . . . The automotive service advisers were given product-specific sales quotas—sell so many springs, shock absorbers, alignments, or brake jobs per shift—and paid a commission based on sales. . . . [F]ailure to meet quotas could lead to a transfer or a reduction in work hours. Some employees spoke of the "pressure, pressure, pressure" to bring in sales.
>
> This pressure-cooker atmosphere created conditions under which employees felt that the only way to satisfy top management was by selling products and services to customers that they didn't really need.

Suppose all automotive repair businesses routinely followed the practice of attempting to sell customers unnecessary parts and services.

Required:

1. How would this behaviour affect customers? How might customers attempt to protect themselves against this behaviour?
2. How would this behaviour probably affect profits and employment in the automotive service industry?

Ethics assignments *serve as a reminder that good conduct is just as important as profits in business.*

Focus on the Canadian Seventh Edition

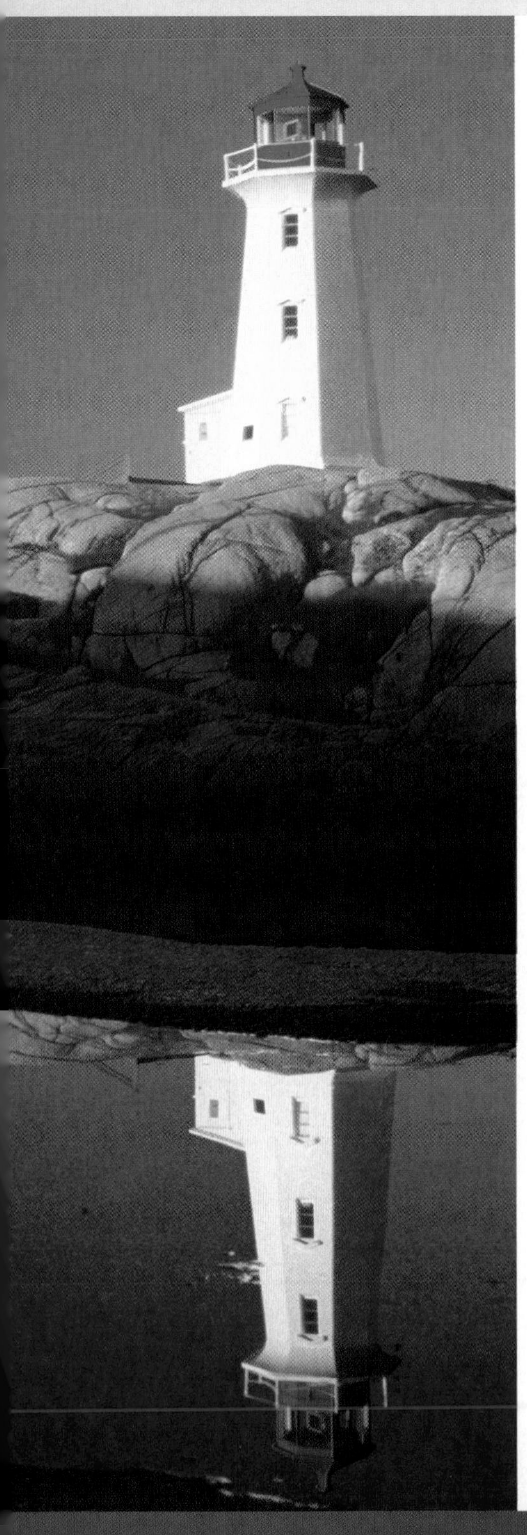

Book Philosophy and Structure

Presenting a textbook on a topic as varied as managerial accounting is a challenge that must have a guiding philosophy.

The authors of the seventh Canadian edition believe in the framework provided by Garrison, Noreen and Brewer in their eleventh U.S. edition. We are able to take this framework and provide a story that reflects the Canadian business and education scene. Our presentation attempts to make readers comfortable with the topic and provide the flexibility needed for the varied philosophies of Canadian users. We have tried to provide a text that can be covered in a single term yet, as our students tell us, a text that provides them with a reference book for later courses in the various programs they select.

We begin the book by describing the key players in managerial accounting and their concerns and areas of interest followed by the developments taking place in the field. Next, we move to two areas that support managerial accounting: costing products and services, and cost behaviour. This focus is seen in Chapters 2 to 8 with Appendix A as a natural addendum if desired. To permit an early view of the relevance of this foundation material, we present a simplified yet powerful analysis for decisions and the development of a cost driver, or base, creating cost behaviour.

In Chapters 9, 10 and 11, we build the first major application of this foundation—predetermined costs described as budgets and standards—and introduce their application. Chapter 12 provides the use of predetermined costing for management control. Control requires a knowledge of costing, cost behaviour and predetermined targets to be effective. The bonus Chapter 15 on financial statement analysis can be used to extend control practices to those exerted by parties external to the organization.

The second major application of costing and cost behaviour is described in Chapters 13 and 14, where we first introduce costing analysis to support short-term decisions, and second, the analysis needed to support long-term decisions by management.

Not everyone can study all chapters, even though all have a place. Each of the chapters provides a selection of problems and applications focusing on manufacturing, service and not-for-profit organizations as well as international businesses so that the text reflects the variety of situations faced in today's business world. Professors will select those topics deemed appropriate for the needs of each course. What isn't covered in a course will serve as a useful reference. Online Chapter 15, for example, may be left to another course or discipline, yet managers will need to know how they are perceived by statement users external to the organization. Thus, not only is this chapter an extension of Chapter 12 on control, it also complements Chapters 13 and 14 on decision analysis because external statements help to control managers and influence their decisions.

One text for a single course cannot do everything Canadian users may want, but it can provide a presentation users can understand and a foundation for later application. Clarity, balance, relevance and accuracy are necessary to the successful use of the text, our ultimate objective.

What's New in the Seventh Edition

The seventh Canadian edition has been reviewed more extensively than at any time in its history in an attempt to make this edition the clearest to date for the reader. The results of these peer reviews and the authors' efforts are reflected in revision and reorganization in nearly every chapter to extend relevant discussions, clarify previous discussions, and present new topics. We believe we have improved an already good text to provide an even greater understanding of the issues.

For example, coverage of cost behaviour, including its relevance and terminology, has been altered. The role of inventory and the treatment of overhead have been explained in connection with cost behaviour. Activity based costing and its connections to management decisions have been clarified.

Additional topics and changes include expanded content on the role of management accounting in serving management's needs. Chapter 1 also features a condensed and clarified discussion of the changing business environment, and standards of ethical conduct for management accountants to reflect the relevance to the current business scene and the requirements of accredited programs.

Chapter 2 reflects the move of the discussion of strategic planning to chapter 9 to provide a guide for the planning described there. The discussion of the cost of goods manufactured has been clarified.

Chapter 8 on activity-based costing includes a discussion of the adjustments and practices needed when these costs are applied to decision situations where the unaltered use of activity costs could be misleading. The appendix to chapter 8 is an especially relevant extension of the discussion of these anomalies.

In addition to coverage of strategic planning, Chapter 9 now also contains an expanded discussion of the business plan to emphasize the interactive nature of business planning. Plus, new materials will help readers further understand detailed schedules, including a new Schedule 7 that relates cash flow to the income statement.

The discussion of balanced scorecards has been removed from chapter 10 and presented in chapter 12 where it provides a natural extension of traditional financial controls.

Chapter 13 features revisions to integrate the various topics in decision analyses. New "Decision Aid" boxes assist the reader with the application of these concepts.

Chapter 14 includes a new discussion of the popular payback method of analysis together with an expanded discussion of post-appraisal of investment projects. An appendix on risk analysis of long-term projects has been added extending the discussion in chapter 6.

Chapter 15 provides a new discussion of sustainability reporting in the Canadian context, a key focus for today's business managers.

In addition, the chapter-opening Business Focus discussions have been updated in nearly all instances, new real-world examples are highlighted in Focus on Current Practice boxes, and most exercises, problems and cases have been revised or replaced to keep this text current.

Decision Criteria

Each chapter contains materials that provide a basis for managerial decisions. All decisions require a comparative base that enables the manager to evaluate the information. The following represents common approaches that management employs to assess the results derived from managerial accounting reports and analyses:

Chapter 1: Professional ethics
2: Financial statement rules, economic cost behaviour, and strategy
3: Chart of accounts, cost comparisons, and reporting periods
4: Cost average comparisons, both historical and current
5: Cost behaviour patterns related to sales and production
6: Cost-volume-profit analyses
7: Internal management profit behaviour
8: Activity cost comparisons
9: Proposed target costs and revenues
10: Standard cost determinations for materials, labour, and overhead
11: Overhead standards
12: Segmented performance results
13: Pricing rules and differential revenues and costs
14: Long-term differential revenues and costs
15: Previous overall results and the performance of other firms
Appendix A: Departmental performance and comparisons

Teaching and Learning with

Managerial Accounting's technology learning solutions complement the textbook every step of the way, giving students the extra help they need while providing instructors with tools for teaching a stimulating and rewarding class.

Lyryx Assessment for Managerial Accounting

A complete online assessment system

Lyryx Assessment for Managerial Accounting is a Web-based teaching and learning tool that has captured the attention of post-secondary institutions across the country, and improved student success in managerial accounting.

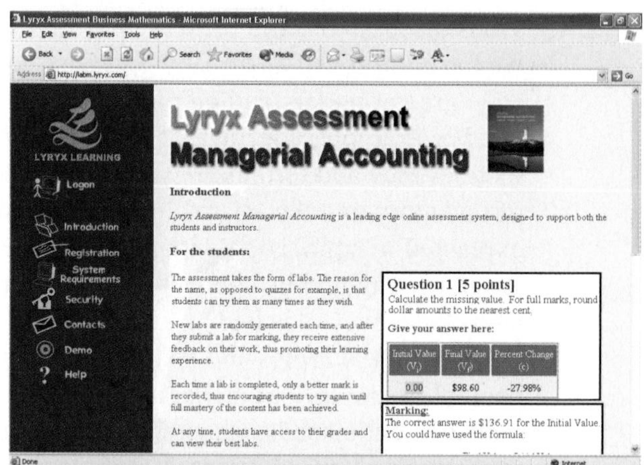

Lyryx Assessment Accounting Labs
Developed specifically for *Managerial Accounting*, Seventh Canadian Edition by Garrison, Noreen, Brewer, Chesley, and Carroll, **Lyryx Assessment** is a leading-edge online assessment system that delivers significant benefits to both students and instructors.

After registering their course with us, instructors can create Labs of their choice by selecting problems from our test bank and setting deadlines. Instructors have access to all the students' marks and can view their best Labs. At any time, instructors can download the class grades for their own programs to analyze individual and class performance.

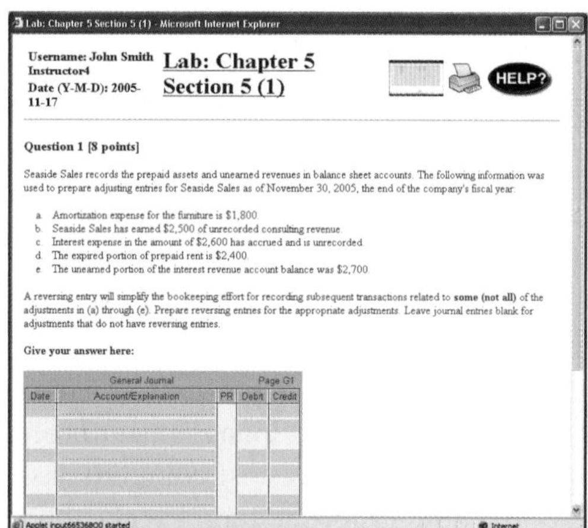

The assessment takes the form of a homework assignment called a Lab, which corresponds to the chapters in the Garrison text. The Labs are algorithmically generated and automatically graded, so students get instant scores and feedback—no need to wait until the next class to find out how well they did!

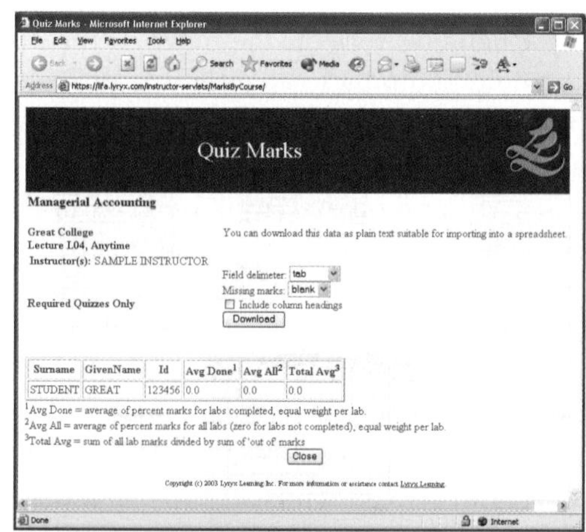

With new Labs randomly generated each time, students have unlimited opportunities to try a type of question. Student motivation is high with these Labs, because they can be tied to assessment, and because they can try as many times as they want prior to the due date, with only their best grade being recorded.

If students are doing their managerial accounting practice and homework, they will improve their performance in the course. Recent research regarding the use of Lyryx has shown when Labs are tied to assessment, even if worth only a small percentage of the total grade for the course, students *will* do their homework—*and more than once. The result is improved student success in managerial accounting!*

Please contact your *i*Learning Sales Specialist
for additional information on the Lyryx Interactive Managerial Accounting system.

Technology

Algorithmic Test Bank

If you've ever thought that no test bank, however well made, could have all the problems you could possibly need, think again. The Algorithmic Test Bank available with Managerial Accounting, 7th Canadian edition, includes a problem generator that replicates the structure of text problems while populating them with fresh numbers. Create unique versions of every homework assignment, every quiz, every test—or use it to provide dozens of similar but distinct problems for students to practise on.

Online Learning Centre

McGraw-Hill Ryerson offers you an online resource that combines the best content with the flexibility and power of the Internet. Organized by chapter, the Garrison Online Learning Centre (OLC) offers the following features to enhance your learning and understanding of Managerial Accounting:

Student Centre

This interactive student component features multiple-choice questions, group and Internet exercises, practice exams, videos, and more.

Instructor Centre

Instructors can access additional problems and solutions, and downloadable supplements including the Instructor's Manual, Solutions Manual, Microsoft® PowerPoint® slides, and Microsoft® Excel® template solutions.

Student Supplements

Student Study Guide

This study aid provides suggestions for studying chapter material, summarizes essential points in each chapter, and tests students' knowledge using self-test questions and exercises.

Microsoft® Excel® Templates

This spreadsheet-based software uses Excel to solve selected problems and cases in the text. These selected problems and cases are identified in the margin of the text with an appropriate icon. The Excel templates are available on the text's Online Learning Centre.

Online Learning Centre (www.mcgrawhill.ca/college/garrison)

The Student Centre of this Web site contains an interactive student component with multiple-choice questions, group and Internet exercises, practice exams, videos, and more.

Instructor Supplements

*i*Learning Sales Specialist

Your Integrated Learning Sales Specialist is a McGraw-Hill Ryerson representative who has the experience, product knowledge, training, and support to help you assess and integrate any of the following products, technology, and services into your course for optimum teaching and learning performance. Whether it's helping your students improve their grades, or putting your entire course online, your *i*Learning Sales Specialist is there to help you do it. Contact your local *i*Learning Sales Specialist today to learn how to maximize all of McGraw-Hill Ryerson's resources!

Instructor's CD-ROM

This all-in-one resource incorporates the Instructor's Manual, Solutions Manual, Computerized Test Bank, Microsoft® PowerPoint® slides, and Microsoft® Excel® templates plus solutions, each described below.

Instructor's Manual

The Instructor's Manual includes chapter overviews, lecture notes, assignment grids plus levels of difficulty and suggested times for assignment materials, chapter-by-chapter lists of service examples, and more.

Solutions Manual

This supplement contains completely worked-out solutions to all assignment material and a general discussion of the use of group exercises. In addition, the manual contains suggested course outlines and a listing of exercises, problems, and cases scaled according to difficulty. This supplement is also available on the text's Online Learning Centre.

Computerized Test Bank

Nearly 2,000 questions are organized by chapter and include true/false, multiple-choice, and essay questions plus computational problems. Use it to make different versions of the same test, change the answer order, edit and add questions, and conduct online testing. Technical support for this software is available. The files are also available in RTF format for printing.

Microsoft® PowerPoint® Slides

Available on the CD and on the text's Web site, these slides offer a great visual complement for your lectures. A complete set of slides covers each chapter.

Microsoft® Excel® Templates

These are the solutions to the Excel templates offered to students in the Online Learning Centre.

Online Learning Centre (www.mcgrawhill.ca/college/garrison)

See the OLC Instructor Centre on page XXIX.

PageOut

Visit www.mhhe.com/pageout to create a Web page for your course using our resources. PageOut is the McGraw-Hill Ryerson Web site development centre. This Web page-generation software is free to adopters and is designed to help faculty create an online course, complete with assignments, quizzes, links to relevant Web sites, and more—all in a matter of minutes.

In addition, content cartridges are available for the course management systems WebCT and Blackboard. These platforms provide instructors with user-friendly, flexible teaching tools. Please contact your local McGraw-Hill Ryerson *i*Learning Sales Specialist for details.

Primis Online

Primis Online gives you access to our resources in the best medium for your students: printed textbooks or electronic e-books. There are over 350,000 pages of content available from which you can create customized learning tools from our online database at www.mhhe.com/primis.

*i*Learning Services Program

McGraw-Hill Ryerson offers a unique *i*Learning Services package designed for Canadian faculty. Our mission is to equip providers of higher education with superior tools and resources required for excellence in teaching. For additional information visit http://www.mcgrawhill.ca/highereducation/iservices.

Reviewers

Ann Bigelow, *University of Western Ontario*
Ralph Cecere, *McGill University*
Elliott Currie, *University of Guelph*
Lynn De Grace, *Concordia University*
Gerry Dupont, *Carleton University*
Richard Farrar, *Conestoga College*
Michael Favere-Marchesi, *Simon Fraser University*
George Gekas, *Ryerson University*
Ilene Gilborn, *Mount Royal College*
Larry Goldsman, *McGill University*
Cliff Grenfell, *CGA*
Masuma Jaffer, *Seneca College*
Kiridaran Kanagaretnam, *McMaster University*
Robert Madden, *St. Francis Xavier University*
Elin Maher, *University of New Brunswick*
Sayed Ahmed Naqi, *Lakehead University*
Mary Oxner, *St. Francis Xavier University*
Pamela Quon, *Athabasca University*
Nancy Tait, *Sir Sanford Fleming College*
Alan Webb, *University of Waterloo*
Keith Whitmore, *Open Learning Agency*

Suggestions have been received from many of our colleagues across Canada and throughout the world who have used the prior editions of **Managerial Accounting.** This is vital feedback that we rely on in each edition. Each of those who have offered comments and suggestions has our thanks.

The efforts of many people are needed to develop and improve a text. Among these people are the reviewers and consultants who point out areas of concern, cite areas of strength, and make recommendations for change. In this regard, the professors named on this page provided feedback that was enormously helpful in preparing the Canadian seventh edition of **Managerial Accounting**.

Acknowledgements

The Canadian seventh edition of **Managerial Accounting** has benefited from the assistance of numerous individuals and groups. This assistance was invaluable in providing us with materials, review comments and suggestions, and technical assistance. Most importantly, we must recognize the significant effort of Alan Webb, Ph.D., CA, University of Waterloo, who thoroughly revised and updated chapter 13. Commissioned reviewers across Canada assisted with suggestions and clarifications that reflect their views of the materials they examined.

Materials were provided by the American Accounting Association, CGA-Canada, SAP Canada, The Accounting Case Institute at Saint Mary's University, CICA, and CMA-Canada. In each case, an acknowledgement is included when the material is used in the textbook. The U.S. authors acknowledge materials provided by the AICPA, the Institute of Certified Management Accountants, and the Chartered Institute of Management Accountants (United Kingdom).

Technical and secretarial assistance was provided by Heather Pace, along with the editorial and technical staff of McGraw-Hill Ryerson Limited. Our book would have been impossible to produce without such help.

Despite the assistance we received, we acknowledge our responsibility for the contents of this book. We appreciate suggestions and questions from our audience.

CHAPTER 1

LEARNING OBJECTIVES

After studying Chapter 1, you should be able to:

1. Identify the major differences and similarities between financial and managerial accounting.
2. Understand the role of management accountants in an organization.
3. Understand the basic concepts underlying just-in-time (JIT), total quality management (TQM), process re-engineering, and the theory of constraints (TOC).
4. Explain the importance of upholding ethical standards.

MANAGERIAL ACCOUNTING AND THE BUSINESS ENVIRONMENT

BUSINESS FOCUS

GLOBALIZATION: OPPORTUNITIES AND THREATS

Advances in communications and transportation technology along with freer trade have placed Canadian companies in a global market. Globalization provides companies with opportunity to pursue new markets leading to increased sales and profits and to reduce costs due to access to more and cheaper supply sources. For some industry sectors, such as retailing, the threat, however, is daunting. The entrance of big box stores such as Wal-Mart into Canada threatens the survival of its competitors. Wal-Mart had global sales of $256 billion in 2003 and if it were a country it would have had more GDP than that of Saudi Arabia. Wal-Mart is known for its ruthless efficiency and meticulous management of the flow of goods from its suppliers to its store shelves. To avoid being a Wal-Mart casualty Canadian companies need accounting information systems that give the latest data on revenues, costs, margins, and consumer trends. Accurate and timely accounting data on production costs and shipping, for example, is needed to help Canadian companies with decisions such as whether they should use overseas or local suppliers. Accounting data can inform managers where they can implement improvements in cost efficiency that will lead to greater profitability. Accounting information can provide the feedback needed to control inventory and shipping costs and the data needed to ensure that labour costs are kept under control and conform to company policies.

Managerial accounting
The phase of accounting concerned with providing information to managers for use in planning and controlling operations and in decision making.

Financial accounting
The phase of accounting concerned with providing information to shareholders, creditors, and others outside the organization.

Managerial accounting is concerned with providing information to managers—that is, people inside an organization who direct and control its operations. In contrast, **financial accounting** is concerned with providing information to shareholders, creditors, and others who are outside an organization. Managerial accounting provides the essential data that helps organizations run more efficiently. Financial accounting provides the scorecard by which a company's past performance is judged.

Managerial accounting is concerned with determining and developing internal accounting information as a tool for helping managers make business decisions that satisfy customers while continuously containing costs and improving efficiencies. This requires managerial accountants to prepare a variety of reports. Some reports compare actual results to plans and to benchmarks focusing on how well managers or business units have performed. Other reports provide timely, frequent updates on key indicators such as orders received, order backlog, capacity utilization, and sales. Reports may also be prepared as needed to help investigate specific problems such as a decline in profitability of a product line or help with the decision of whether to outsource some of the business operations. And yet other reports analyze a developing situation or opportunity. In contrast, financial accounting is geared toward producing a limited set of specific annual and quarterly financial statements in accordance with generally accepted accounting principles (GAAP).

Because it is manager-oriented, any study of managerial accounting must be preceded by some understanding of what managers do, the information managers need, and the general business environment. Accordingly, the purpose of this chapter is to briefly examine these subjects.

THE WORK OF MANAGEMENT AND THE NEED FOR MANAGERIAL ACCOUNTING INFORMATION

Every organization—large and small—has managers. Someone must be responsible for making plans, organizing resources, directing personnel, and controlling operations. This is true of the Bank of Montreal, the Canadian Cancer Society, the University of Waterloo, the United Church, and the Nova Corporation, as well as the local Needs convenience store. In this chapter, we will use a particular organization—Good Vibrations, Inc.—to illustrate the work of management. What we have to say about the management of Good Vibrations, Inc., however, is very general and can be applied to virtually any organization.

Good Vibrations, Inc. runs a chain of retail outlets that sell a full range of music CDs. The chain's stores are concentrated in Pacific Rim cities such as Sydney, Singapore, Hong Kong, Beijing, Tokyo, and Vancouver. The company has found that the best way to generate sales, and income, is to create an exciting shopping environment. Consequently, the company puts a great deal of effort into planning the layout and decor of its stores—which are often quite large and extend over several floors in key downtown locations. Management knows that different types of clientele are attracted to different kinds of music. The international rock section is generally decorated with bold, brightly coloured graphics, and the aisles are purposely narrow to create a crowded feeling much like one would experience at a popular nightclub on Friday night. In contrast, the classical music section is wood-panelled and fully sound insulated, with the rich, spacious feeling of a country club meeting room.

Planning
Selecting a course of action and specifying how the action will be implemented.

Directing and motivating
Mobilizing people to carry out plans and run routine operations.

Controlling
Ensuring that the plan is actually carried out and is appropriately modified as circumstances change.

Managers at Good Vibrations, Inc., like managers everywhere, carry out three major activities—*planning, directing and motivating,* and *controlling.* **Planning** involves selecting a course of action and specifying how the action will be implemented. **Directing and motivating** involve mobilizing people to carry out plans and run routine operations. **Controlling** involves ensuring that the plan is actually carried out and is appropriately modified as circumstances change. Management accounting information plays a vital role in these basic management activities—but most particularly in the planning and control functions.

Planning

The first step in planning is to identify alternatives and then to select from among the alternatives the one that does the best job of furthering the organization's objectives. The basic objective of Good Vibrations, Inc. is to earn profits for the owners of the company by providing superior service at competitive prices in as many markets as possible. To further this objective, every year top management carefully considers a range of options, or alternatives, for expanding into new geographic markets. This year, management is considering opening new stores in Shanghai, Jakarta, and Auckland.

When making this and other choices, management must balance the opportunities against the demands made on the company's resources. Management knows from bitter experience that opening a store in a major new market is a big step that cannot be taken lightly. It requires enormous amounts of time and energy from the company's most experienced, talented, and busy professionals. When the company attempted to open stores in both Beijing and Vancouver in the same year, resources were stretched too thinly. The result was that neither store opened on schedule, and operations in the rest of the company suffered. Therefore, entering new markets is planned very, very carefully.

Among other data, top management looks at the sales volumes, profit margins, and costs of the company's established stores in similar markets. These data, supplied by the management accountant, are combined with projected sales volume data at the proposed new locations to estimate the profits that would be generated by the new stores. In general, virtually all important alternatives considered by management in the planning process have some effect on revenues or costs, and management accounting data are essential in estimating those effects.

After considering all of the alternatives, Good Vibrations, Inc.'s top management decided to open a store in the burgeoning Shanghai market in the third quarter of the year, but to defer opening any other new stores to another year. As soon as this decision was made, detailed plans were drawn up for all parts of the company that would be involved in the Shanghai opening. For example, the Personnel Department's travel budget was increased, since it would be providing extensive on-site training to the new personnel hired in Shanghai.

As in the Personnel Department example, the plans of management are often expressed formally in **budgets**, and the term *budgeting* is applied to generally describe this part of the planning process. Budgets are usually prepared under the direction of the **controller**, who is the manager in charge of the Accounting Department. Typically, budgets are prepared annually and represent management's plans in specific, quantitative terms. In addition to a travel budget, the Personnel Department will be given goals in terms of new hires, courses taught, and detailed breakdowns of expected expenses. Similarly, the manager of each store will be given a target for sales volume, income, expenses, pilferage losses, and employee training. These data will be collected, analyzed, and summarized for management use in the form of budgets prepared by management accountants.

Budget
A detailed plan for the future, usually expressed in formal quantitative terms.

Controller
The manager in charge of the accounting department in an organization.

Directing and Motivating

In addition to planning for the future, managers must oversee day-to-day activities and keep the organization functioning smoothly. This requires the ability to motivate and effectively direct people. Managers assign tasks to employees, arbitrate disputes, answer questions, solve on-the-spot problems, and make many small decisions that affect customers and employees. In effect, directing is that part of the managers' work that deals with the routine and the here and now. Managerial accounting data, such as daily sales reports, are often used in this type of day-to-day decision making.

Controlling

Control
The process of instituting procedures and then obtaining feedback to ensure that all parts of the organization are functioning effectively and moving toward overall company goals.

Feedback
Accounting and other reports that help managers monitor performance and focus on problems and/or opportunities that might otherwise go unnoticed.

Performance report
A detailed report comparing budgeted data to actual data.

In carrying out the **control** function, managers seek to ensure that the plan is being followed. **Feedback**, which signals whether operations are on track, is the key to effective control. In sophisticated organizations, this feedback is provided by detailed reports of various types. One of these reports, which compares budgeted to actual results, is called a **performance report**. Performance reports suggest where operations are not proceeding as planned and where some parts of the organization may require additional attention. For example, before the opening of the new Shanghai store in the third quarter of the year, the store's manager will be given sales volume, income, and expense targets for the fourth quarter of the year. As the fourth quarter progresses, periodic reports will be made in which the actual sales volume, income, and expenses are compared to the targets. If the actual results fall below the targets, top management is alerted that the Shanghai store requires more attention. Experienced personnel can be flown in to help the new manager, or top management may come to the conclusion that plans will have to be revised. As we shall see in following chapters, providing this kind of feedback to managers is one of the central purposes of managerial accounting.

The Results of Managers' Activities

As a customer enters one of the Good Vibrations stores, the results of management's planning, directing and motivating, and control activities will be evident in the many details that make the difference between a pleasant and an irritating shopping experience. The store will be clean, fashionably decorated, and logically laid out. Featured artists' videos will be displayed on TV monitors throughout the store, and the background rock music will be loud enough to send some patrons scurrying for the classical music section. Popular CDs will be in stock, and the latest hits will be available for private listening on earphones. Specific titles will be easy to find. Regional music, such as Cantopop in Hong Kong, will be prominently featured. Checkout clerks will be alert, friendly, and efficient. In short, what the customer experiences doesn't simply happen; it is the result of the efforts of managers who must visualize and fit together the processes that are needed to get the job done. A role of managerial accounting is to inform and facilitate management decisions throughout these processes so that managers' efforts result in the efficient achievement of company goals.

The Planning and Control Cycle

Planning and control cycle
The flow of management activities through planning, directing and motivating, and controlling, and then back to planning again.

The work of management can be summarized in a model such as the one in Exhibit 1–1. The model, which depicts the **planning and control cycle,** illustrates the smooth flow of management activities from planning through directing and motivating, controlling, and then back to planning again. All of these activities involve decision making, so it is depicted as the hub around which the other activities revolve.

Management accounting can help serve the information needs of managers in all phases of the planning and control cycle. The management accountant can prepare detailed reports that managers need to make both day-to-day and long-term decisions. They prepare budgets to help direct resources towards the organization's goals. Later actual costs and revenues are compared with the budgeted figures and reports are prepared to inform management about any significant variances from budget. Management information needs vary from business to business but as you work your way through this book you will be introduced to many of the tools management accountants use to meet these needs. For example, managerial accountants typically provide reports that help answer questions such as the following:

How much does it cost to provide a particular good or service?
How do costs behave when the company operates at different levels of activity?
How can a company reduce costs to help improve profitability?
How many units must be sold to break even?

EXHIBIT 1–1 The Planning and Control Cycle

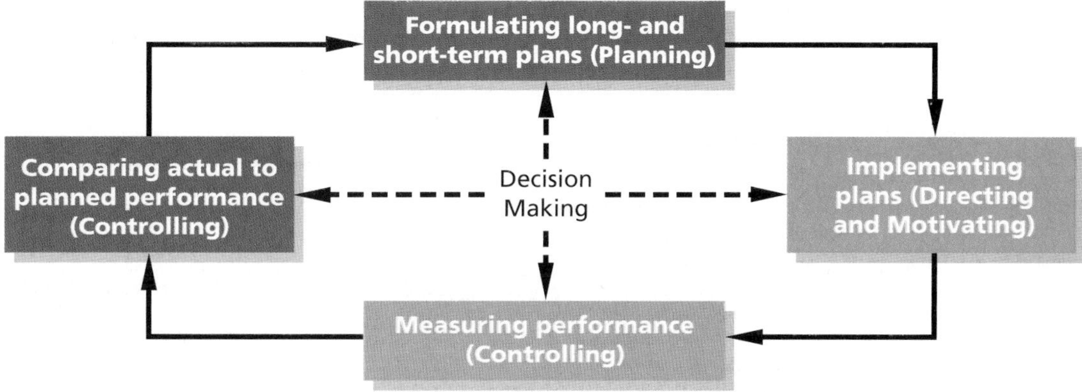

What will our budgets look like at different forecasted levels of activity?
Should the company add or drop a product line?
Should the company outsource some of its operations?
How should management choose when selecting among competing investment proposals?
What new projects should the company invest in and what projects should be abandoned?

COMPARISON OF FINANCIAL AND MANAGERIAL ACCOUNTING

LEARNING OBJECTIVE 1
Identify the major differences and similarities between financial and managerial accounting.

Financial accounting reports are prepared for the use of external parties such as shareholders and creditors, whereas managerial accounting reports are prepared for managers inside the organization. This contrast in basic orientation results in a number of major differences between financial and managerial accounting, even though both financial and managerial accounting rely on the same underlying financial data. These differences are summarized in Exhibit 1–2.

As shown in Exhibit 1–2, in addition to the reports being prepared for different people, financial and managerial accounting also differ in their emphasis between the past and the future, in the type of data provided to users, and in several other ways. These differences are discussed in the following paragraphs.

Emphasis on the Future

Since *planning* is such an important part of the manager's job, managerial accounting has a strong future orientation. In contrast, financial accounting primarily provides summaries of past financial transactions. These summaries may be useful in planning, but only to a point. The future is not simply a reflection of what has happened in the past. Changes are constantly taking place in economic conditions, customer needs and desires, competitive conditions, and so on. All of these changes demand that the manager's planning be based in large part on estimates of what will happen rather than on summaries of what has already happened.

Relevance of Data

Financial accounting data are expected to be objective and verifiable. However, for internal uses the manager wants information that is relevant even if it is not completely objective or

EXHIBIT 1–2 Comparion of Financial and Management Accounting

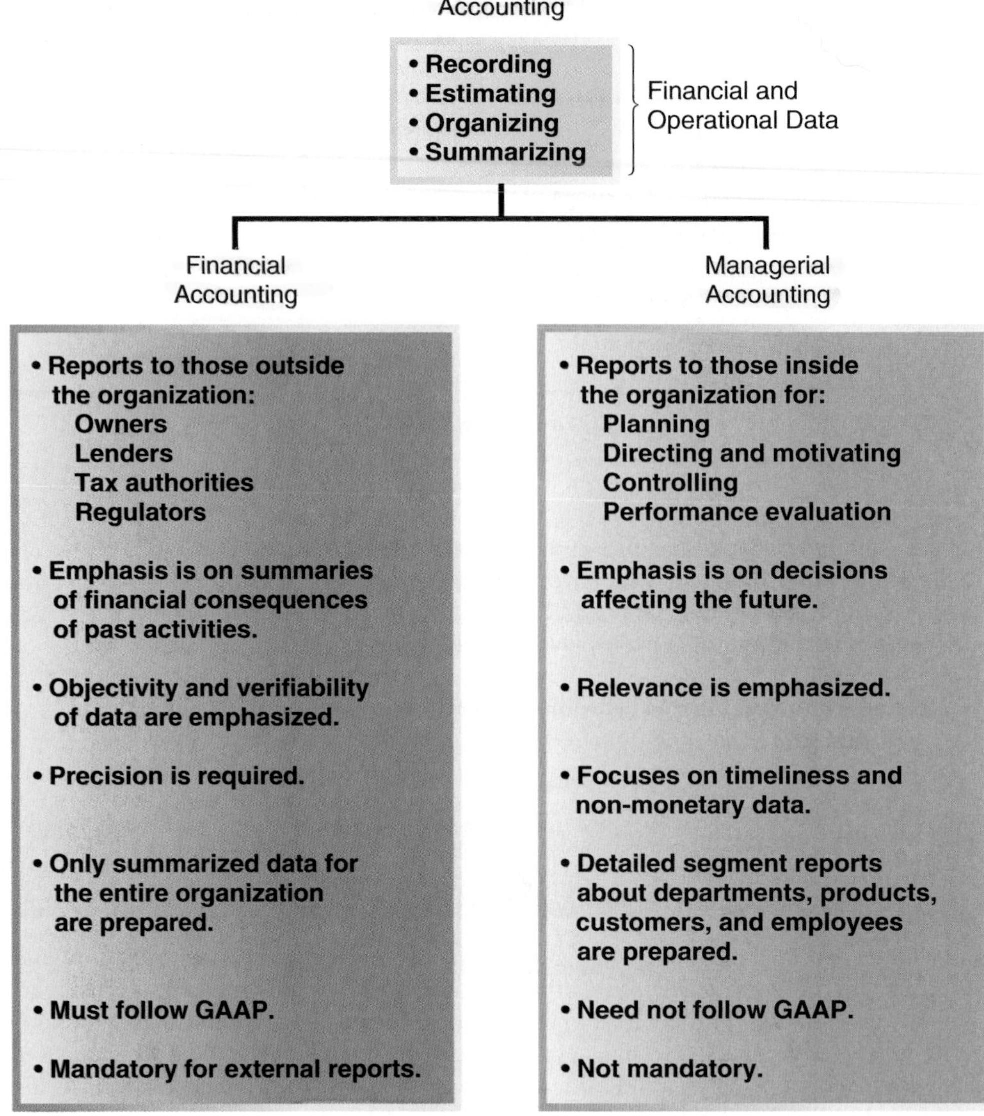

verifiable. By relevant, we mean *appropriate for the problem at hand.* For example, it is difficult to verify estimated sales volumes for a proposed new store at Good Vibrations, Inc., but this is exactly the type of information that is most useful to managers in their decision making. The managerial accounting information system should be flexible enough to provide whatever data are relevant for a particular decision.

Accounting
• Recording
• Estimating
• Organizing
• Summarizing
Financial and Operational Data
Financial Accounting
Managerial Accounting
• Reports to those outside the organization:
Owners
Lenders
Tax authorities
Regulators
• Emphasis is on summaries of financial consequences of past activities.
• Objectivity and verifiability of data are emphasized.
• Precision is required.
• Only summarized data for the entire organization are prepared.
• Must follow GAAP.
• Mandatory for external reports.
• Reports to those inside the organization for:
Planning
Directing and motivating
Controlling
Performance evaluation
• Emphasis is on decisions affecting the future.
• Relevance is emphasized.
• Focuses on timeliness and non-monetary data.
• Detailed segment reports about departments, products, customers, and employees are prepared.
• Need not follow GAAP.
• Not mandatory.

Less Emphasis on Precision

Making sure that dollar amounts are accurate down to the last dollar or penny takes time and effort. While that kind of accuracy is desirable for external reports, most managers would rather have an immediate estimate than wait for a more precise answer. For this reason, managerial accountants often place less emphasis on precision than do financial accountants. In fact, one authoritative source recommends that, as a general rule, no one needs more than three significant digits in the data that are used in decision making.[1] For example, in a decision involving hundreds of millions of dollars, estimates that are

1. *Statements on Management Accounting, Statement Number 5B, Fundamentals of Reporting Information to Managers,* Institute of Management Accountants, Montvale, NJ, p. 6.

rounded off to the nearest million dollars are probably good enough. In addition to placing less emphasis on precision than financial accounting, managerial accounting places more weight on non-monetary data. For example, data about customer satisfaction may be routinely used in managerial accounting reports.

Segments of an Organization

Financial accounting is primarily concerned with reporting for the company as a whole. By contrast, managerial accounting focuses much more on the parts, or **segments,** of a company. These segments may be product lines, customers, sales territories, divisions, departments, or any other categorization of the company's activities that management finds useful. Financial accounting does require some breakdowns of revenues and costs by major segments in external reports, but this is a secondary emphasis. In managerial accounting, segment reporting is the primary emphasis.

Segment
Any part of an organization that can be evaluated independently of other parts and about which the manager seeks financial data. Examples include a product line, a customer, a sales territory, a division, or a department.

Generally Accepted Accounting Principles

Financial accounting statements prepared for external users must be prepared in accordance with generally accepted accounting principles (GAAP). External users must have some assurance that the reports have been prepared in accordance with some common set of ground rules. These common ground rules enhance comparability and help reduce fraud and misrepresentation, but they do not necessarily lead to the type of reports that would be most useful in internal decision making. For example, GAAP requires that land be stated at its historical cost on financial reports. However, if management is considering moving a store to a new location and then selling the land on which the store currently sits, management would like to know the current market value of the land—a vital piece of information that is ignored under GAAP.

Managerial accounting is not bound by generally accepted accounting principles. Managers set their own ground rules concerning the content and form of internal reports. The only constraint is that the expected benefits from using the information should outweigh the costs of collecting, analyzing, and summarizing the data. Nevertheless, as we shall see in subsequent chapters, it is undeniably true that financial reporting requirements have heavily influenced management accounting practice.

Managerial Accounting—Not Mandatory

Financial accounting is mandatory; that is, it must be done. Various outside parties such as the provincial securities commissions and the tax authorities require periodic financial statements. Managerial accounting, on the other hand, is not mandatory. A company is completely free to do as much or as little as it wishes. No regulatory bodies or other outside agencies specify what is to be done or, for that matter, whether anything is to be done at all. Since managerial accounting is completely optional, the important question is always, "Is the information useful?" rather than, "Is the information required?"

ORGANIZATIONAL STRUCTURE

LEARNING OBJECTIVE 2
Understand the role of management accountants in an organization.

Management must accomplish its objectives by working *through* people. Presidents of companies like Good Vibrations, Inc. could not possibly execute all of their companies' strategies alone; they must rely on other people. This is done by creating an organizational structure that permits effective *decentralization* of management decisions.

Decentralization

Decentralization is the delegation of decision-making authority throughout an organization by providing managers at various operating levels with the authority to make

Decentralization
The delegation of decision-making authority throughout an organization by providing managers at various operating levels with the authority to make key decisions relating to their areas of responsibility.

decisions relating to their areas of responsibility. Some organizations are more decentralized than others. Because of Good Vibrations, Inc.'s geographic dispersion and the peculiarities of local markets, the company is highly decentralized.

Good Vibrations, Inc.'s president (also called chief executive officer or CEO) sets the broad strategy for the company and makes major strategic decisions such as opening stores in new markets, but much of the remaining decision-making authority is delegated to managers on various levels throughout the organization. These levels are as follows: The company has a number of retail stores, each of which has a store manager as well as a separate manager for each section such as international rock and classical/jazz. In addition, the company has support departments such as a central Purchasing Department and a Personnel Department. The organizational structure of the company is depicted in Exhibit 1–3.

Organization chart
A visual diagram of a firm's organizational structure that depicts formal lines of reporting, communication, and responsibility between managers.

The arrangement of boxes shown in Exhibit 1–3 is called an **organization chart.** The purpose of an organization chart is to show how responsibility has been divided among managers and to show formal lines of reporting and communication, or *chain of command.* Each box depicts an area of management responsibility, and the lines between the boxes show the lines of formal authority between managers. The chart tells us, for example, that the store managers are responsible to the operations vice-president. In turn, the latter is responsible to the company president, who in turn is responsible to the board of directors. Following the lines of authority and communication on the organization chart, we can see that the manager of the Hong Kong store would ordinarily report to the operations vice-president rather than directly to the president of the company.

Informal relationships and channels of communication often develop outside the formal reporting relationships on the organization chart as a result of personal contacts

EXHIBIT 1–3 Organization Chart, Good Vibrations, Inc.

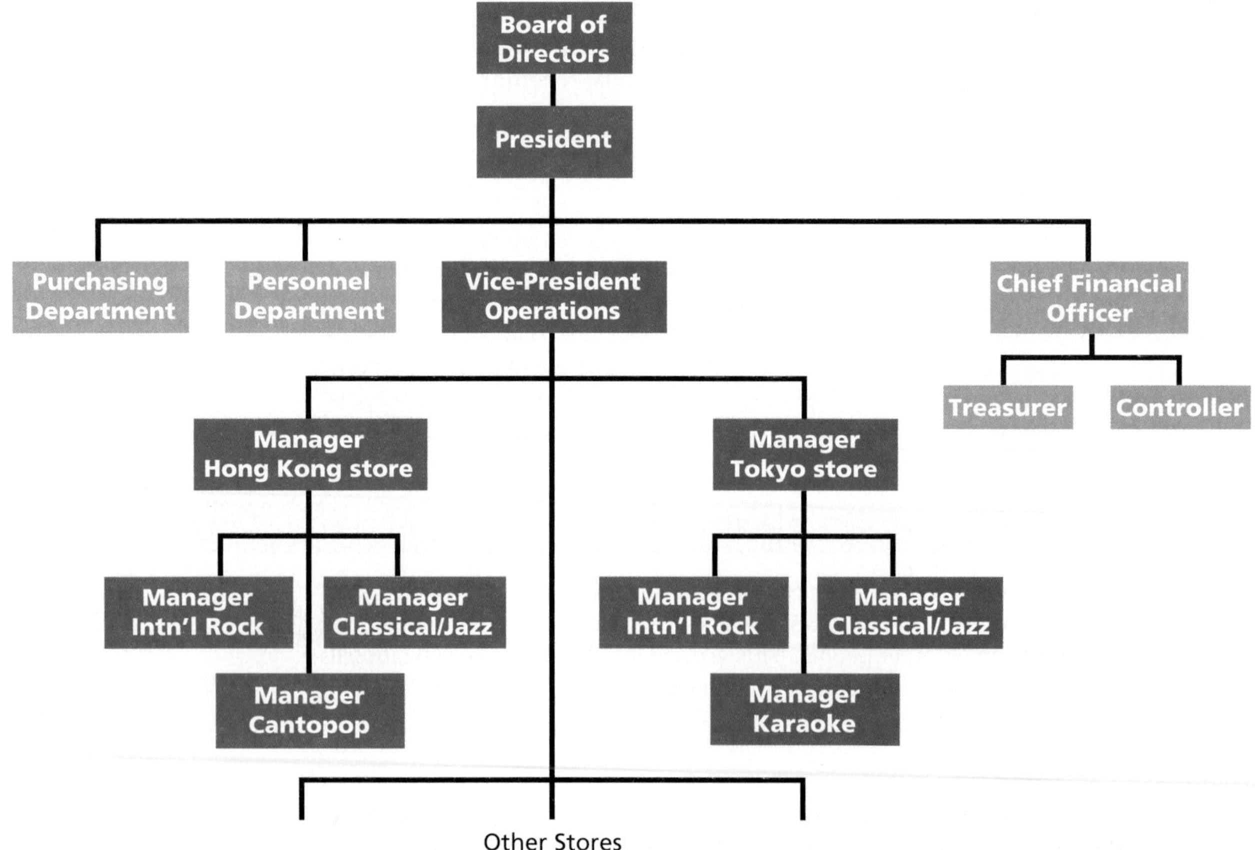

between managers. The informal structure does not appear on the organization chart, but it is often vital to effective operations.

Line and Staff Relationships

An organization chart also depicts *line* and *staff* positions in an organization. A person in a **line** position is *directly* involved in achieving the basic objectives of the organization. A person in a **staff** position, by contrast, is only *indirectly* involved in achieving those basic objectives. Staff positions *support* or provide assistance to line positions or other parts of the organization, but they do not have direct authority over line positions. Refer again to the organization chart in Exhibit 1–3. Since the basic objective of Good Vibrations, Inc. is to sell recorded music at a profit, those managers whose areas of responsibility are directly related to the sales effort occupy line positions. These positions, which are shown in a darker colour in the exhibit, include the managers of the various music departments in each store, the store managers, the operations vice-president, and members of top management.

By contrast, the manager of the central Purchasing Department occupies a staff position, since the only function of the Purchasing Department is to support and serve the line departments by doing their purchasing for them. However, both line and staff managers have authority over the employees in their own departments.

Line
A position in an organization that is directly related to the achievement of the organization's basic objectives.

Staff
A position in an organization that is only indirectly related to the achievement of the organization's basic objectives. Such positions are supportive in nature in that they provide service or assistance to line positions or to other staff positions.

The Controller

In Canada, the manager in charge of the Accounting Department is usually known as the *controller.* The controller is the member of the top-management team who is given the responsibility of providing relevant and timely data to support planning and control activities and of preparing financial statements for external users. Because the controller becomes familiar with all parts of a company's operations by working with managers throughout the company, it is not unusual for the controller's office to be a stepping stone to the top position in a company.

The controller is a highly paid professional who has command over the technical details of accounting and finance, can provide leadership to other professionals in her or his department, and can analyze new and evolving situations. An effective controller is able to work well with top managers from other disciplines and can communicate technical information in a simple and clear manner.

Much of the work under the controller's responsibility involves consulting and business analysis. Many managerial accountants engaged in such activities actually identify themselves as working in finance since very few, if any, of their activities is about debits and credits or preparing journal entries. These managerial accountants see themselves as advisors who work on cross-functional teams throughout the organization.

THE PROFESSIONAL MANAGEMENT ACCOUNTANT

Three professional accounting organizations in Canada have members who make up the ranks of management accountants. *CGA*, *CA*, and *CMA* are the designations used by professional accountants who belong to societies and associations such as the *Certified General Accountants Association,* the *Canadian Institute of Chartered Accountants* (*L'Ordre de CGA* in Québec), and the *Society of Management Accountants.*[2] Members of these three associations work in various fields—industry, commerce, government, education, and public practice—after completing their particular programs of study and passing their professional certification examinations. In the United States, both CPAs and CMAs are professional management accountants. The CPA designation is used by members of

2. Web sites for these three groups contain background information. See http://www.cga-canada.org/, http://www.cica.ca/, and http://www.cma-canada.org/.

the *American Institute of Certified Public Accountants* or various state CPA associations. CMAs are members of the *Institute of Management Accountants*.

Management accounting is not subject to the type of regulation that is evident for financial accounting. However, the Society of Management Accountants of Canada issues *management accounting guidelines* on fundamental areas of practice. Adherence to the guidelines is voluntary, but wide acceptance is expected because of the relevance and expertise used in their preparation. Currently, 60 guidelines have been issued to date on such topics as capital expenditures, internal control, cash management, foreign currency risk management, the annual financial statement audit, managing quality improvements, benchmarking, activity-based costing, incentive plans, value chain analysis, and just-in-time (JIT) production systems. New topics are continually being presented to the accounting community.

THE CHANGING BUSINESS ENVIRONMENT

LEARNING OBJECTIVE 3
Understand the basic concepts underlying just-in-time (JIT), total quality management (TQM), process re-engineering, and the theory of constraints (TOC).

The last two decades have been a period of tremendous turmoil and change in the business environment. Competition in many industries has become worldwide in scope, and the pace of innovation in products and services has accelerated. This has been good news for consumers, since intensified competition has generally led to lower prices, higher quality, and more choices. However, the last two decades have been a period of wrenching change for many businesses and their employees. Globalization and the Internet have added new challenges and opportunities. Many managers have learned that cherished ways of doing business do not work anymore and that major changes must be made in how organizations are managed and in how work gets done.

These changes in the business environment have affected managerial accounting—as we will see throughout the rest of the text. First, however, it is necessary to have an appreciation of the ways in which organizations are transforming themselves to become more competitive. Since the early 1980s, many companies have gone through several waves of improvement programs, starting with *just-in-time* (JIT) and passing on to *total quality management* (TQM), *process re-engineering, lean production, six sigma,* and various other management programs—including in some companies the *theory of constraints* (TOC). When properly implemented, these improvement programs can enhance quality, reduce cost, increase output, eliminate delays in responding to customers, and ultimately increase profits. However, they have not always been wisely implemented, and considerable controversy remains concerning the ultimate value of each of these programs, Nevertheless, the current business environment cannot be properly understood without some appreciation of what these programs attempt to accomplish. Each is worthy of extended study, but we will discuss only those program aspects that are essential for understanding managerial accounting. The details of improvement programs are best handled in operations management courses.

This section on the changing business environment will close with a discussion of the role of international competition and the effect of the Internet on business.

Just-in-Time (JIT)

Just-in-time (JIT)
A production and inventory control system in which materials are purchased and units are produced only as needed to meet actual customer demand.

Traditionally, manufacturers have forecasted demand for their products into the future and then attempted to smooth out production to meet that forecasted demand. At the same time, they have also attempted to keep everyone and everything as busy as possible producing output so as to maximize "efficiency" and (hopefully) reduce costs. Unfortunately, this approach has a number of major drawbacks including accumulating large inventories, long production times, high defect rates, product obsolescence, an inability to meet delivery schedules, and (ironically) high costs. None of this was obvious or companies would have abandoned this approach a long time ago. Managers at Toyota are credited with the insight that an entirely new approach, called *just-in-time*, was needed.

When companies use the the JIT production and inventory control system, they purchase materials and produce units only as needed to meet actual customer demand. In a JIT system, inventories are reduced to the minimum and in some cases are zero. For example, the automotive industry depends on JIT deliveries by thousands of trucks crossing the border safely and efficiently to meet tight production schedules. Since the 9/11 disaster at the World Trade Center in New York, however, it has become increasingly more difficult to meet these deadlines.

FOCUS *on Current Practice*

Companies that are responsive to changes in market conditions and are able to meet the needs of their customers often possess world-class manufacturing execution and operational excellence systems. These companies have often undergone some form of business process re-engineering, just-in-time supply chain management, activity-based costing, continuous improvement, and the integration of manufacturing resource planning (MRP). This enables these companies to deliver quick, top-of-the-line, world-class products, promptly and efficiently to their clientele.

Source: "Open systems: Open market for MES," *Process Engineering*, May 17, 2004, pp. 28.

The JIT approach can be used in both merchandising and manufacturing companies. It has the most profound effects, however, on the operations of manufacturing companies, which maintain three classes of inventories—*raw materials, work (goods) in process,* and *finished goods.* **Raw materials** are the materials that are used to make a product. **Work in process** inventories consist of units of product that are only partially complete and will require further work before they are ready for sale to a customer. **Finished goods** inventories consist of units of product that have been completed but have not yet been sold to customers.

Raw materials
Materials that are used to make a product.

Work in process
Units of product that are only partially complete and will require further work before they are ready for sale to a customer.

Finished goods
Units of product that have been completed but have not yet been sold to customers.

Traditionally, manufacturing companies have maintained large amounts of all three kinds of inventories to act as *buffers* so that operations can proceed smoothly even if there are unanticipated disruptions. Raw materials inventories provide insurance in case suppliers are late with deliveries. Work in process inventories are maintained in case a workstation is unable to operate due to a breakdown or other reason. Finished goods inventories are maintained to accommodate unanticipated fluctuations in demand.

While these inventories provide buffers against unforeseen events, they have a cost. In addition to the money tied up in the inventory, experts argue that the presence of inventories encourages inefficient and sloppy work, results in too many defects, and dramatically increases the amount of time required to complete a product.

Under ideal conditions, a company operating a just-in-time system would purchase only enough materials each day to meet that day's needs. Moreover, the company would have no goods still in process at the end of the day, and all goods completed during the day would have been shipped immediately to customers. As this sequence suggests, "just-in-time" means that raw materials are received just in time to go into production, manufactured parts are completed just in time to be assembled into products, and products are completed just in time to be shipped to customers.

Although few companies have been able to reach this ideal, many companies have been able to reduce inventories to only a fraction of their previous levels. The result has been a substantial reduction in ordering and warehousing costs, and much more effective operations. In a JIT system, the traditional emphasis on keeping everyone busy is abandoned in favour of producing only what customers actually want—even if that means some workers are idle.

FOCUS ***on Current Practice***

Priority Management, located in Vancouver, is a worldwide training organization which provides tools, techniques and training solutions to enhance productivity. The company has 23 franchises shipping directly to clients. In the past, franchise offices would place their orders and expect Priority Management headquarters to always carry the stock. Priority Management was losing money on overstocking of time-sensitive inventory. By adopting a Just-In-Time system, the company has been able to improve their ordering processes and cash flow. By enhancing its database, management has been able to improve data integrity, resulting in more accurate inventory counts and improved customer service. The switch to JIT has positioned the company to more accurately meet the demands of their franchises leading to better served end-clients.

Source: "Costs Go Down, Profits Go Up," www.accpac.com.

JIT Consequences Managers who attempted to implement the JIT approach found that it was necessary to make other major improvements in operations if inventories were to be significantly reduced. First, production would be held up and a deadline for shipping a product would be missed if a key part was missing or was found to be defective. So suppliers had to be able to deliver defect-free goods in just the right quantity and just when needed. This typically meant that the company would have to rely on a few, ultra-reliable suppliers that would be willing to make frequent deliveries in small lots just before the parts and materials would be needed in production. Second, the typical plant layout needed to be improved. Traditionally, similar machines were grouped together in a single location. All of the drill presses would be in one place, all of the lathes in another place, and so on. As a result, work in process had to be moved frequently over long distances—creating delays, difficulties in locating orders, and sometimes damage. In a JIT system, all of the machines required to make a single product or product line are typically brought together in one location—creating what is called a *focused factory* or a *manufacturing cell*. This improved plant layout allows workers to focus all of their efforts on one product from start to finish—creating a sense of ownership and pride in the product and minimizing handling and moving. One company was able to reduce the distance travelled by one product from 5 kilometres to 100 metres. An improved plant layout can dramatically increase *throughput,* which is the total volume of production through a facility during a period, and it can dramatically reduce **throughput time** (also known as **cycle time**), which is the time required to make a product.

Throughput time
The time required to make a completed unit of product, starting with raw materials; also know as *cycle time.*

Cycle time
Same as *throughput time.*

Set-ups
Activities that must be performed whenever production is switched over from making one type of item to another.

Changing over production from one product to another, which involves *set-ups*, also creates problems for JIT. **Set-ups** require activities—such as moving materials, changing machine settings, setting up equipment, and running tests—that must be performed whenever production is switched over from making one item to another. For example, a company that makes side panels for DaimlerChrysler's PT Cruiser must prime and paint the steel panels with the colour specified by DaimlerChrysler. Every time the colour is changed, the spray paint reservoirs must be completely purged and cleaned. This may take hours and results in wasted paint. Because of the time and expense involved in such set-ups, many managers believe set-ups should be avoided and therefore items should be produced only in large batches. Think of this in terms of scheduling your classes. If you have to commute to school and pay for parking, would you rather have two classes more or less back-to-back on the same day or on different days? By scheduling your classes back-to-back on the same day, you will have to commute and pay for parking only once.

Managers follow the same reasoning when they schedule production. If the customer has ordered 400 units, most managers would rather produce all of them in one big batch and incur the set-up costs once rather than in two batches of 200 units each, which incurs the set-up costs twice. Indeed, because of set-up costs, most companies have rules about the minimum size of a batch that can be run. If the customer orders just 25 units, managers will still run the order in a batch of 400 units and keep the other 375 units on hand in inventory in case someone orders the item later. The problem with this line of reasoning is that big batches result in large amounts of inventory—the exact opposite of what JIT attempts to accomplish. In JIT, this problem is attacked directly by reducing set-up time so that it becomes insignificant. Simple techniques such as doing as much of the set-up work as possible in advance off-line rather than waiting until production is shut down are often very effective in reducing set-up time and costs. Reduced set-up times make smaller batches more economical, which in turn makes it easier to respond quickly to the market with exactly the items that customers want.

Defective units create big problems in a JIT environment. If a completed order contains a defective unit, the company must ship the order with less than the promised quantity or it must restart the whole production process to make just one unit. At a minimum, this creates a delay in shipping the order and may generate a ripple effect that delays other orders. For this and other reasons, defects cannot be tolerated in a JIT system. Companies that are deeply involved in JIT tend to become zealously committed to a goal of *zero defects.* Even though it may be next to impossible to attain the zero defect goal, companies have found that they can come very close.

In a traditional company, parts and materials are inspected for defects when they are received from suppliers, and quality inspectors inspect units as they progress along the production line. In a JIT system, the company's suppliers are responsible for the quality of incoming parts and materials. And instead of using quality inspectors, the company's production workers are directly responsible for spotting defective units. A worker who discovers a defect is supposed to punch an alarm button that stops the production flow line and sets off flashing lights. Supervisors and other workers then descend on the workstation to determine the cause of the defect and correct it before any further defective units are produced. This procedure ensures that problems are quickly identified and corrected, but it does require that defects are rare—otherwise there would be constant disruptions to the production process.

Workers on a JIT line must be multiskilled and flexible. They are often expected to operate all of the equipment in a manufacturing cell. In addition, they perform minor repairs and do maintenance work when they would otherwise be idle. In contrast, on a conventional assembly line, a worker performs a single task all of the time every day and all maintenance work is done by a specialized maintenance crew.

Benefits of a JIT System Many companies—large and small—have employed JIT with great success. Among the major companies using JIT are Ford, General Motors, Magna, and Nortel. The main benefits of JIT are the following:

1. Funds that were tied up in inventories can be used elsewhere.
2. Areas previously used to store inventories are made available for other, more productive uses.
3. Throughput time is reduced, resulting in greater potential output and quicker response to customers.
4. Defect rates are reduced, resulting in less waste and greater customer satisfaction.

As a result of benefits such as those cited above, more companies are embracing JIT each year. Most companies find, however, that simply reducing inventories is not enough. To remain competitive in an ever-changing and ever-more competitive business environment, companies must strive for *continuous improvement.*

Total Quality Management (TQM)

Perhaps the most popular approach to continuous improvement is known as *total quality management.* There are two major characteristics of **total quality management (TQM):** (1) a focus on serving customers and (2) systematic problem solving using teams made up of front-line workers. A variety of specific tools are available to aid teams in their problem solving. One of these tools, **benchmarking,** involves studying organizations that are

Total quality management (TQM) An approach to continuous improvement that focuses on customers and using teams of front-line workers to systematically identify and solve problems.

Benchmarking A study of organizations that are among the best in the world at performing a particular task.

among the best in the world at performing a particular task. For example, General Mills studied NASCAR pit crews in action to figure out how to cut the time to change a production line from one product to another from 4.5 hours to just under 12 minutes.[3]

Process Re-Engineering

Process re-engineering An approach to improvement that involves completely redesigning business processes in order to eliminate unnecessary steps, reduce errors, and reduce costs.

Business process A series of steps that are followed in order to carry out some task in a business.

Process re-engineering is a more radical approach to improvement than TQM. Instead of tweaking the existing system in a series of incremental improvements, in **process re-engineering**, a *business process* is diagrammed in detail, questioned, and then completely redesigned in order to eliminate unnecessary steps, to reduce opportunities for errors, and to reduce costs. A **business process** is any series of steps that are followed in order to carry out some task in a business. For example, the steps followed to make a large pineapple and bacon pizza at Godfather's Pizza comprise a business process. The steps followed by your bank when you deposit a cheque are a business process. While process re-engineering is similar in some respects to TQM, its proponents view it as a more sweeping approach to change. One difference is that while TQM emphasizes a team approach involving people who work directly in the processes, process re-engineering is more likely to be imposed from above and to use outside consultants.

Non-value-added activity An activity that consumes resources or takes time but that does not add value for which customers are willing to pay.

Process re-engineering focuses on *simplification* and *elimination of wasted effort.* A central idea of process re-engineering is that *all activities that do not add value to a product or service should be eliminated.* Activities that do not add value to a product or service that customers are willing to pay for are known as **non-value-added activities.** For example, moving large batches of work in process from one workstation to another is a non-value-added activity that can be eliminated by redesigning the factory layout as discussed earlier in the section on JIT. To some degree, JIT involves process re-engineering as does TQM. These management approaches often overlap.[4]

Process re-engineering has been used by many organizations from health care providers to traditional manufacturers to deal with a wide variety of problems. Heroux-Devtek Inc., a Quebec manufacturer of aerospace and industrial products, for example, recently succeeded in increasing military repair and overhaul productivity by about 30% during just one quarter after taking on manufacturing process re-engineering initiatives.[5]

Wal-Mart re-engineered inventory management by giving suppliers access to its inventory system. Suppliers monitor the database and automatically send another shipment when stocks are low. This eliminates the need for purchase orders resulting in much faster delivery time, lower inventory carrying costs, and the prevention of stock-out costs. IBM Credit re-engineered its credit application and approval process by automating the approval process. Re-engineering reduced the number of days to approve a credit application from 25 days to less than 5 days.

Managers must be careful when trying to convert business process improvements into more profits. There are only two ways to increase profits—decrease costs or increase sales. Cutting costs may seem easy—lay off workers who are no longer needed because of the elimination of non-value-added activities. However, employees quickly get the message that process improvements lead to job losses and they will understandably resist further improvement efforts. If improvement is to be ongoing, employees must be convinced that the end result of improvement will be more secure rather than less secure jobs. This can only happen if management uses business process improvements to generate more business rather that to cut the workforce.

The Theory of Constraints

Constraint Anything that prevents an organization or individual from getting more of what is wanted.

A **constraint** is anything that prevents you from getting more of what you want. Every individual and every organization faces at least one constraint, so it is not difficult to find

3. Pallavi Gogoi, "Thinking Outside the Cereal Box," *Business Week*, July 28, 2003, pp. 74–75.
4. Activity-based costing and activity-based management, both of which are discussed in Chapter 8, can be helpful in identifying areas in the company that could benefit from process re-engineering.
5. "Heroux-Devtek Reports Year-End Results," *Canada NewsWire*, June 9, 2004.

examples of constraints. You may not have enough time to study thoroughly for every subject *and* to go out with your friends on the weekend, so time is your constraint. Air Canada has only a limited number of loading gates available at its busy Toronto hub, so its constraint is loading gates. Banff Resorts has only a limited amount of land to develop as home sites and commercial lots at its ski areas, so its constraint is land.

Since a constraint prevents you from getting more of what you want, the **theory of constraints (TOC)** maintains that effectively managing the constraint is a key to success. For example, Air Canada should concentrate on quickly turning around its aircraft on the ground so they do not tie up precious gates. Delays on the ground decrease the number of flights that can be flown out of Toronto and therefore result in lost business.

Theory of constraints (TOC) A management approach that emphasizes the importance of managing constraints.

TOC is based on the insight that effectively managing the constraint is a key to success. As an example, long waiting periods for surgery are a chronic problem in the National Health Service (NHS), the government-funded provider of health care in the United Kingdom. The diagram in Exhibit 1–4 illustrates a simplified version of the steps followed by a patient who is identified for surgery and eventually treated. The number of patients who can be processed through each step in a day is indicated in the exhibit. For example, appointments for outpatient visits can be made for up to 100 referrals from general practitioners in a day.

The constraint, or *bottleneck,* in the system is determined by the step that has the smallest capacity—in this case surgery. The total number of patients processed through the entire system cannot exceed 15 per day—the maximum number of patients who can be treated in surgery. No matter how hard managers, doctors, and nurses try to improve the processing rate elsewhere in the system, they will never succeed in driving down wait lists until the capacity of surgery is increased. In fact, improvements elsewhere in the system—particularly before the constraint—are likely to result in even longer waiting times and more frustrated patients and health care providers. Thus, improvement efforts must be focused on the constraint to be effective. A business process, such as the process for serving surgery patients, is like a chain. If you want to increase the strength of a chain, what is the most effective way to do this? Should you concentrate your efforts on strengthening the strongest link, all the links, or the weakest link? Clearly, focusing your effort on the weakest link will bring the biggest benefit.

Continuing with this analogy, the procedure needed to strengthen the chain is clear. First, identify the weakest link, which is the constraint. Second, don't place a greater strain on the system than the weakest link can handle—if you do, the chain will break. In the case of the NHS, waiting lists become unacceptably long. Third, concentrate improvement efforts on strengthening the weakest link. Find ways to increase the number of surgeries that can be performed in a day. Fourth, if the improvement efforts are successful, eventually the weakest link will improve to the point where it is no longer the weakest link. At that point, the new weakest link (i.e., the new constraint) must be identified, and improvement efforts must be shifted over to that link. This simple sequential process provides a powerful strategy for continuous improvement. The TOC approach is a perfect complement to other improvement tools such as TQM and process re-engineering—it focuses improvement efforts where they are likely to be most effective.

EXHIBIT 1–4 Processing Surgery Patients at an NHS Facility (simplified)*

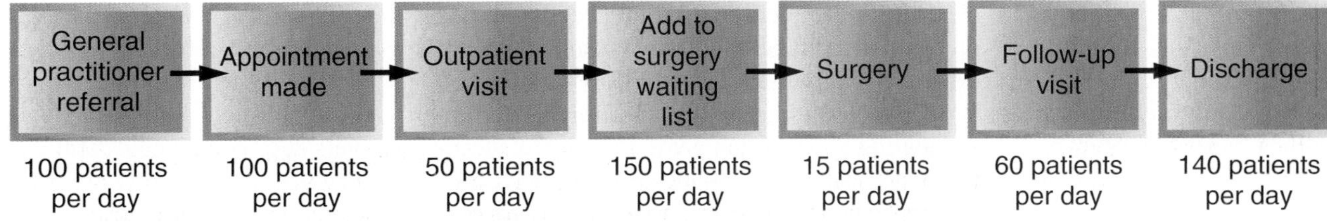

*This diagram originally appeared in the February 1999 issue of the U.K. magazine *Health Management.*

FOCUS *on Current Practice*

At one hospital, the emergency room became so backlogged that its doors were closed to the public and patients were turned away for over 36 hours in the course of a single month. It turned out, after investigation, that the constraint was not the emergency room itself; it was the housekeeping staff. To cut costs, managers at the hospital had laid off housekeeping workers. This created a bottleneck in the emergency room because rooms were not being cleaned as quickly as the emergency room staff could process new patients. Thus, laying off some of the lowest paid workers at the hospital had the effect of forcing the hospital to idle some of its most highly paid staff and most expensive equipment!

Source: Tracey Burton-Houle, "AGI Continues to Steadily Make Advances with the Adaptation of TOC into Healthcare," **www.goldratt.com/toctquarterly/august2002.htm**.

INTERNATIONAL COMPETITION

Over the last several decades, competition has become worldwide in many industries. This has been caused by reductions in tariffs, quotas, and other barriers to free trade; improvements in global transportation systems; and increasing sophistication in international markets. These factors work together to reduce the costs of conducting international trade and make it possible for foreign companies to compete on a more equal footing with local firms.

The movement toward freer trade has been most dramatic in the European Union (EU). The EU has grown from a very small free-trade zone involving a few basic commodities such as coal and steel in the late 1950s to a free-trade zone of 15 European nations involving almost unlimited movement of goods and services across national borders. This vast, largely unified market has a population of over 375 million, as compared with over 268 million in the United States and about 125 million in Japan. Most of the countries in the EU have adopted a common currency called the *euro*, which should make trading within the EU even easier. The euro has replaced traditional currencies such as the French franc, the German mark, and the Italian lira. The North American Free Trade Agreement (NAFTA) trading block, which consists of Canada, the United States, and Mexico, has a combined population in excess of 480 million.

Such reductions in trade barriers have made it easier for agile and aggressive companies to expand outside of their home markets. As a result, very few firms can afford to be complacent. A company may be very successful today in its local market relative to its local competitors, but tomorrow the competition may come from halfway around the globe. As a matter of survival, even firms that are presently doing very well in their home markets must become world-class competitors. On the bright side, the freer international movement of goods and services presents tremendous export opportunities for those companies that can transform themselves into world-class competitors. And, from the standpoint of consumers, heightened competition promises an even greater variety of goods, at higher quality and lower prices.

What are the implications for managerial accounting of increased global competition? It would be very difficult for a firm to become world-class if it plans, directs, and controls its operations and makes decisions using a second-class management accounting system. An excellent management accounting system will not by itself guarantee success, but a poor management accounting system can stymie the best efforts of people in an organization to make the firm truly competitive.

Throughout this text, we will highlight the differences between obsolete management accounting systems that get in the way of success and well-designed management accounting systems that can enhance a firm's performance. It is noteworthy that elements of well-designed management accounting systems have originated in many countries. More and more, managerial accounting has become a discipline that is worldwide in scope.

E-Commerce

Widespread use of the Internet is a fairly new phenomenon, and the impact it will eventually have on business is far from settled. For a few years, it looked like dot-com start-ups would take over the business world—their stock market valuations reached astonishing heights. But, of course, the bubble burst and few of the start-ups are now in business. With the benefit of hindsight, it is now clear that the managers of the dot-com start-ups would have benefited from the use of many of the tools covered in this book, including cost concepts (Chapter 2), cost estimation (Chapter 5), cost-volume-profit analysis (Chapter 6), activity-based costing (Chapter 8), budgeting (Chapter 9), decision making (Chapter 13), and capital budgeting (Chapter 14). While applying these tools to a new company with little operational history would be difficult, it needs to be done. And the investors who plowed billions into dot-com start-ups only to see the money vanish would have been wise to pay attention to cash flows and financial statement analysis.

FOCUS *on Current Practice*

Global competition sometimes comes from unexpected sources. Companies in the former Soviet bloc in Central and Eastern Europe are rapidly raising the quality of their products to Western standards and are beginning to provide stiff competition. The Hungarian company Petofi Printing & Packaging Co., a maker of cardboard boxes, wrappers, and other containers, provides a good example. "Only a few years ago, Petofi's employees drank beer at work. Flies buzzing in open windows got stuck in the paint and pressed into the paperboard. Containers were delivered in the wrong colours and sizes." Under the Communist system, the company's customers didn't dare complain, since there was no other source for their packaging needs.

The company was privatized after the fall of the Soviet system, and the company "began overhauling itself, leapfrogging Western companies with state-of-the-art machinery. It whipped its workforce into shape with a combination of inducements and threats." Now, most of its products are exported. PepsiCo, for example, buys Petofi wrappers for Cheetos and Ruffles snacks and claims that Petofi's quality compares very favourably with Western suppliers. PepsiCo's buyer states, "They have filled the gap between competitive quality and best cost."

Source: Dana Milbank, "New Competitor: East Europe's Industry Is Raising Its Quality and Taking on West," *The Wall Street Journal*, September 21, 1994, pp. A1, A7.

At the time of this writing, it is still not clear if a successful business model will emerge for Internet-based companies. It is generally believed that Amazon.com and eBay may have the best chances of building sustainable e-commerce businesses. If a successful e-commerce business model does emerge, it will be based on attracting enough profitable customers to cover the fixed expenses of the company, as discussed in Chapter 6.

Established brick-and-mortar companies like Bell Canada, The Bay, WestJet, and Wal-Mart will undoubtedly continue to expand into cyberspace—both for business-to-business transactions and for retailing. The Internet has important advantages over more conventional marketplaces for some kinds of transactions, such as mortgage banking. The financial institution does not have to tie up staff filling out forms—that can be done directly by the consumer over the Internet. Data and funds can be sent back and forth electronically—no courier needs to drop by the consumer's home to deliver a cheque.

Global Forces

Traditionally, management accounting practices have differed significantly from one country to another. For example, Spain, Italy, and Greece have relied on less formal management accounting systems than other European countries. According to Professor Norman B. Macintosh, "In Greece and Italy the predominance of close-knit, private, family firms motivated by secrecy, tax avoidance, and largesse for family members along with lack of market competition (price fixing?) mitigated the development of MACS [management accounting and control systems]. Spain also followed this pattern and relied more on personal relationships and oral inquisitions than on hard data for control." At the same time, other western European countries such as Germany, France, and the Netherlands developed relatively sophisticated formal management accounting systems emphasizing efficient operations. In the case of France, these were codified in law. In England, management accounting practice was influenced by economists, who emphasized the use of accounting data in decision making. The Nordic countries tended to import management accounting ideas from both Germany and England.

A number of factors have been acting in recent years to make management accounting practices more similar within Europe and around the world. These forces include intensified global competition, which makes it more difficult to continue sloppy practices; standardized information system software sold throughout the world by vendors such as SAP, PeopleSoft, Oracle, and Baan; the increasing significance and authority of multinational corporations; the global consultancy industry; the diffusion of information throughout academia; and the global use of market-leading textbooks.

PROFESSIONAL ETHICS

A series of high profile scandals in the public and private sectors have raised deep concerns about ethics in business and government.[6] Ethics is important because it is the lubricant that keeps the economy running. As James Surowiecki writes:

> Flourishing economies require a healthy level of trust in the reliability and fairness of everyday transactions. If you assumed every potential deal was a rip-off or that the products you were buying were probably going to be lemons, then very little business would get done. More important, the cost of the transactions that did take place would be exorbitant, since you'd have to do enormous work to investigate each deal and you'd have to rely on the threat of legal action to enforce every contract. For an economy to prosper, what's needed is not a Pollyanish faith that everyone else has your best interests at heart —"caveat emptor" (buyer beware) remains an important truth—but a basic confidence in the promises and commitments that people make about their products and services.[7]

There are good reasons for companies to be concerned about their ethical reputation. A company that is not trusted by its customers, employees, and suppliers will eventually suffer. In the short run, virtue is sometimes its own reward but in the long run business ethics should be taken seriously because the very survival of the company may depend on the level of trust held by its stakeholders.

Professional accounting groups are given the right of association and certain rights of self-government by provincial governments in Canada. One inherent requirement of such rights is an expression of public service in the form of a code of ethics. Each accounting group is then permitted to operate according to the laws of the country, using its code of ethics as an operating guideline.[8]

Typically, these codes contain details of how members should conduct themselves in their dealings with the public, their association, and their fellow members. For example,

---

6. Examples include the Federal sponsorship scandal and other involving businesses such as Enron, WorldCom, Global Crossing, Arthur Andersen and many others. Currently, there are also class action suits outstanding against Nortel alleging that it overstated revenues for the years 2000 and 2001.
7. James Surowiecki, "A Virtuous Cycle," *Forbes*, December 23, 2002, pp. 248–256.
8. The Web sites listed in footnote 2 for Canadian accounting associations provide details about the ethical standards of their members. Also, http://www.ifac.org/ contains ethical expectations for members of the International Federation of Accountants.

accountants must maintain a level of competence appropriate to their designation. Confidentiality is essential because of the importance of the information they analyze. Integrity is maintained by avoiding conflicts of interest with their employers or clients, by communicating the limits of professional competence, and by not accepting favours that would compromise their judgement. Objectivity must be present in communications, so that recipients can receive both favourable and unfavourable information.

Professional accountants must study the full text of their code of ethics because the rules for competence, confidentiality, integrity, and objectivity are complex in real situations. In addition, procedures for resolving complex situations should be known.

Business Codes of Ethics

Some codes of ethics give more extensive guidance than others. The Institute of Management Accountants in the United States, for example, provides quite clear guidance concerning what ethical standards to follow and also gives advice on how to resolve ethical conflict situations. This information is reproduced in Exhibit 1-5.

EXHIBIT 1–5 Standards of Ethical Conduct for Practitioners of Management Accounting and Financial Management

Members of IMA have an obligation to the public, their profession, the organization they serve, and themselves, to maintain the highest standards of ethical conduct. In recognition of this obligation, the IMA has promulgated the following standards of ethical conduct for its members. Members shall not commit acts contrary to these standards nor shall they condone the commission of such acts by others within their organizations.

Competence. Members have a responsibility to:

- Maintain an appropriate level of professional competence by ongoing development of their knowledge and skills.
- Perform their professional duties in accordance with relevant laws, regulations, and technical standards.
- Prepare complete and clear reports and recommendations after appropriate analysis of relevant and reliable information.

Confidentiality. Members have a responsibility to:

- Refrain from disclosing confidential information acquired in the course of their work except when authorized, unless legally obligated to do so.
- Inform subordinates as appropriate regarding the confidentiality of information acquired in the course of their work and monitor their activities to assure the maintenance of that confidentiality.
- Refrain from using or appearing to use confidential information acquired in the course of their work for unethical or illegal advantage either personally or through third parties.

Integrity. Members have a responsibility to:

- Avoid actual or apparent conflicts of interest and advise all appropriate parties of any potential conflict.
- Refrain from engaging in any activity that would prejudice their ability to carry out their duties ethically.
- Refuse any gift, favour, or hospitality that would influence or would appear to influence their actions.
- Refrain from either actively or passively subverting the attainment of the organization's legitimate and ethical objectives.
- Recognize and communicate professional limitations or other constraints that would preclude responsible judgement or successful performance of an activity.
- Communicate unfavourable as well as favourable information and professional judgments or opinions.

continued

EXHIBIT 1–5 (concluded)

- Refrain from engaging in or supporting any activity that would discredit the profession.

Objectivity. Members have a responsibility to:

- Communicate information fairly and objectively.
- Disclose fully all relevant information that could reasonably be expected to influence an intended user's understanding of the reports, comments, and recommendations presented.

Resolution of Ethical Conflict. In applying the standards of ethical conduct, members may encounter problems in identifying unethical behaviour or in resolving an ethical conflict. When faced with significant ethical issues, members should follow the established policies of the organization bearing on the resolution of such conflict. If these policies do not resolve the ethical conflict, such practitioner should consider the following courses of action:

- Discuss such problems with the immediate superior except when it appears that the superior is involved, in which case the problem should be presented initially to the next higher managerial level. If a satisfactory resolution cannot be achieved when the problem is initially presented, submit the issues to the next higher managerial level. If the immediate superior is the chief executive officer, or equivalent, the acceptable reviewing authority may be a group such as the audit committee, executive committee, board of directors, board of trustees, or owners. Contact with levels above the immediate superior should be initiated only with the superior's knowledge, assuming the superior is not involved. Except where legally prescribed, communication of such problems to authorities or individuals not employed or engaged by the organization is not considered appropriate.
- Clarify relevant ethical issues by confidential discussion with an objective advisor (e.g., IMA Ethics Counseling Service) to obtain a better understanding of possible courses of action. — Consult your own attorney as to legal obligations and rights concerning the ethical conflict.
- If the ethical conflict still exists after exhausting all levels of internal review, there may be no other recourse on significant matters than to resign from the organization and to submit an informative memorandum to an appropriate representative of the organization. After resignation, depending on the nature of the ethical conflict, it may also be appropriate to notify other parties.

Source: *Institute of Management Accountants, formerly National Association of Accountants, *Statements on Management Accounting: Objectives of Management Accounting,* Statement No. 1B, New York, NY, June 17, 1982 as revised in 1987 (www.imanet.org).

FOCUS *on Current Practice*

On February 10, 2004, federal Auditor General Sheila Fraser released the hotly anticipated results of her audit of the controversial government advertising and sponsorship program run by the federal Public Works Department.

She found that $100 million was paid to a variety of communications agencies in the form of fees and commissions and said the program was basically designed to generate commissions for these companies rather than to produce any benefit for Canadians.

The program has been in the spotlight since 2002, when Fraser recommended the RCMP investigate how $1.6 million in federal government advertising contracts were handed out to a Montreal ad agency. Officials in Canada's Public Works Department "broke just about every rule in the book" when it came to awarding contracts to Groupaction Inc., Fraser said.

Opposition critics allege the program was used to award lucrative advertising contracts to Liberal party supporters.

Source: "Auditor General Gives Details of 'Scandalous' Sponsorship Program," *CBC News Online*, February 11, 2004.

FOCUS on Current Practice

New Canadian legislation is aimed at preventing the kind of corporate abuse that has occurred in high profile scandals that led to the collapse of Enron Corp. and WorldCom Inc. WorldCom was headed by Bernie Ebbers, a Canadian. The Canadian government has set up nine integrated market enforcement teams in Canada's four major financial centres: Toronto, Vancouver, Montreal, and Calgary. These teams consisting of police officers, lawyers, and other investigators aim to stop corporate fraud in its tracks. Inside traders could go to jail for up to 10 years under new Canadian legislation aimed at preventing the kind of accounting scandals that resulted in the collapse of U.S. corporate giants Enron Corp. and WorldCom Inc. The RCMP and federal partners will receive up to $30 million a year over the next five years to implement this get tough initiative. Effective efforts to deter serious capital market fraud depend on four critical pillars: (1) a strong legal framework, (2) strong investigative processing, (3) timely resources to pursue prosecutions, and (4) appropriate sentencing of those found guilty.

Source: "Federal Strategy to Deter Serious Capital Market Fraud," Department of Justice Canada NewsRoom: http://canada.justice.gc.ca/en/news/nr/2003,doc 30928.html.

Businesses are organizations of people that pursue objectives (sometimes termed *missions*). These organizations have formal relationships among their members as described by the organization chart illustrated earlier in this chapter. However, informal relationships and activities are also present that must be focused on the achievement of the objectives of a wide group of people known as *stakeholders*. Stakeholders are people within and outside the organization who have an interest in the activities of the organization. Employees, shareholders, and creditors have an obvious interest in what the organization does. But so do the public, the customers, the suppliers, and the competitors. All of these stakeholders can benefit from the organization's undertakings and they also can be harmed by these activities.

A code of ethics is prepared by an organization to reflect its value and moral system. The document specifies what is expected of its employees in their dealings with the various stakeholders. Thus, the code reflects what the organization stands for when it interacts through its employees with other stakeholders. For example, the organization may wish to pursue environmental standards in excess of those specified in local laws and regulations. The organization may wish to use the standards of conduct present in its home country rather than those of its host country in its cross-border activities. Through its code of ethics, a business can express what it stands for in its activities as well as provide its members with a guide as to how their activities should be conducted to reflect the values needed to achieve the objectives of the organization.

Codes of Conduct on the International Level

The *IFAC Code of Ethics for Professional Accountants*, revised November 2001 by the International Federation of Accountants (IFAC), governs the activities of *all* professional accountants throughout the world, regardless of whether they are practising as independent public accountants, employed in government service, or employed as internal accountants.[9] In addition to outlining ethical requirements in matters dealing with competence, objectivity, independence, and confidentiality, the IFAC code also outlines the accountant's ethical responsibilities in matters relating to taxes, fees and commissions, advertising and solicitation, the handling of monies, and cross-border activities. Where

9. A copy of this code can be obtained from http://www.ifac.org/.

cross-border activities are involved, the IFAC ethical requirements must be followed if these requirements are stricter than the ethical requirements of the country in which the work is being performed.[10]

SUMMARY

Managerial accounting assists managers in carrying out their responsibilities, which include planning, directing and motivating, and controlling.

Since managerial accounting is geared to the needs of managers rather than to the needs of outsiders, it differs substantially from financial accounting. Managerial accounting is oriented more toward the future, places less emphasis on precision, emphasizes segments of an organization (rather than the organization as a whole), is not governed by generally accepted accounting principles, and is not mandatory.

Most organizations are decentralized to some degree. The organization chart depicts who works for whom in the organization and which units perform staff functions rather than line functions. Accountants perform a staff function—they support and provide assistance to others inside the organization.

The business environment in recent years has been characterized by increasing competition and a relentless drive for continuous improvement. Several approaches have been developed to assist organizations in meeting these challenges—including *just-in-time* (JIT), *total quality management* (TQM), *process reengineering*, and the *theory of constraints* (TOC).

JIT emphasizes the importance of reducing inventories to the barest minimum possible. This reduces working capital requirements, frees up space, reduces throughput time, reduces defects, and eliminates waste.

TQM involves focusing on the customer, and it employs systematic problem solving using teams made up of front-line workers. By emphasizing teamwork, a focus on the customer, and facts, TQM can avoid the organizational infighting that might otherwise block improvement.

Process Re-engineering involves completely redesigning a business process in order to eliminate non-value-added activities and to reduce opportunities for errors. Process Re-engineering relies more on outside specialists than TQM and is more likely to be imposed by top management.

The theory of constraints emphasizes the importance of managing the organization's constraints. Since the constraint is whatever is holding back the organization, improvement efforts usually must be focused on the constraint in order to be really effective.

Ethical standards serve a very important practical function in an advanced market economy. Without widespread adherence to ethical standards, material living standards would fall. Ethics are the lubrication that keep a market economy functioning smoothly. The Standards of Ethical Conduct for Practitioners of Management Accounting and Financial Management provide sound, practical guidelines for resolving ethical problems that might arise in an organization.

GLOSSARY

Visit the Online Learning Centre at http://www.mcgrawhill.ca/college/garrison/ for a review of glossary terms and definitions.

QUESTIONS

1–1 What is the basic difference in orientation between financial and managerial accounting?

1–2 What are the three major activities of a manager?

1–3 Describe the four steps in the planning and control cycle.

10. *IFAC Code of Ethics for Professional Accountants* (New York: International Federation of Accountants, November 2001), section 6. The IFAC document *Codifying Power and Control—Ethical Codes in Action, 1999*, contains vignettes of a number of companies located in France, Italy, Australia, and the United Kingdom, as well as various industries.

1–4 Distinguish between line and staff positions in an organization.
1–5 What are the major differences between financial and managerial accounting?
1–6 Identify the benefits that can result from reducing the setup time for a product.
1–7 What are the major benefits of a JIT system?
1–8 Why is process re-engineering a more radical approach to improvement than total quality management?
1–9 How can process re-engineering undermine employee morale?
1–10 Where does the theory of constraints recommend that improvement efforts be focused?
1–11 Why is adherence to ethical standards important for the smooth functioning of an advanced market economy?

EXERCISES

EXERCISE 1–1 The Roles of Managers and Management Accountants [LO1, LO2]
A number of terms that relate to organizations, the work of management, and the role of managerial accounting are listed below:

Budgets	Controller
Decentralization	Directing and motivating
Feedback	Financial accounting
Line	Managerial accounting
Non-monetary data	Performance report
Planning	Precision
Staff	Chief Financial Officer

Choose the term or terms above that most appropriately complete the following statements:

1. A position on the organization chart that is directly related to achieving the basic objectives of an organization is called a ________ position.
2. When ________, managers oversee day-to-day activities and keep the organization functioning smoothly.
3. The plans of management are expressed formally in ________.
4. ________ consists of identifying alternatives, selecting from among the alternatives the one that is best for the organization, and specifying what actions will be taken to implement the chosen alternative.
5. A ________ position provides service or assistance to other parts of the organization and does not directly achieve the basic objectives of the organization.
6. The delegation of decision-making authority throughout an organization by allowing managers at various operating levels to make key decisions relating to their area of responsibility is called ________.
7. Managerial accounting places less emphasis on ________ and more emphasis on ________ than financial accounting.
8. ________ is concerned with providing information for the use of those who are inside the organization, whereas ________ is concerned with providing information for the use of those who are outside the organization.
9. The accounting and other reports coming to management that are used in controlling the organization are called ________.
10. The manager in charge of the accounting department is generally known as the ________.
11. A detailed report to management comparing budgeted data with actual data for a specific time period is called a ________.
12. The ________ is the member of the top management team who is responsible for providing timely and relevant data to support planning and control activities and for preparing financial statements for external users.

EXERCISE 1–2 The Business Environment [LO3]
A number of terms that relate to just-in-time, total quality management, process re-engineering, and theory of constraints are listed below:

Benchmarking	Setup
Constraint	Business process
Just-In-Time	Frequent

Non-value-added activities	Non-constraint
Process re-engineering	Total quality management

Choose the term or terms above that most appropriately complete the following statements:

1. __________ is an incremental approach to improvement, whereas __________ tends to be a more radical approach that involves completely redesigning business processes.
2. A production system in which units are produced and materials are purchased only as needed to meet actual customer demand is called __________.
3. Increasing the rate of output of a __________ as the result of an improvement effort is unlikely to have much effect on profits.
4. __________ involves studying the business processes of companies that are considered among the best in the world at performing a particular task.
5. The activities involved in getting equipment ready to produce a different product are called a __________.
6. The theory of constraints suggests that improvement efforts should be focused on the company's __________.
7. In process re-engineering, two objectives are to simplify and to eliminate __________.
8. A __________ is any series of steps that are followed in order to carry out some task in a business.

EXERCISE 1–3 Ethics in Business [LO4]

Mary Karston was hired by a popular fast-food restaurant as an order-taker and cashier. Shortly after taking the job, she was shocked to overhear an employee bragging to a friend about shortchanging customers. She confronted the employee who then snapped back: "Mind your own business. Besides, everyone does it and the customers never miss the money." Mary didn't know how to respond to this aggressive stance.

Required:

What would be the practical consequences on the fast-food industry and on consumers if cashiers generally shortchanged customers at every opportunity?

PROBLEMS

PROBLEM 1–4 Preparing an Organization Chart [LO2]

Moncton University is a large private school located in New Brunswick. The university is headed by a president who has five vice presidents reporting to him. These vice presidents are responsible for, respectively, auxiliary services, admissions and records, academics, financial services (controller), and the physical plant.

In addition, the university has managers over several areas who report to these vice presidents. These include managers over central purchasing, the university press, and the university bookstore, all of whom report to the vice president for auxiliary services; managers over computer services and over accounting and finance, who report to the vice president for financial services; and managers over grounds and custodial services and over plant and maintenance, who report to the vice president for physical plant.

The university has four colleges—business, humanities, fine arts, and engineering and quantitative methods—and a law school. Each of these units has a dean who is responsible to the academic vice president. Each college has several departments.

Required:

1. Prepare an organization chart for Moncton University.
2. Which of the positions on your chart would be line positions? Why would they be line positions? Which would be staff positions? Why?
3. Which of the positions on your chart would have need for accounting information? Explain.

S

PROBLEM 1–5 Ethics and the Manager [LO4]

Richmond, Inc., operates a chain of department stores across Canada that has steadily grown to its present size of 44 stores. Two years ago, the board of directors of Richmond approved a large-scale remodelling of its stores to attract a more upscale clientele.

Before finalizing these plans, two stores were remodelled as a test. Linda Perlman, assistant controller, was asked to oversee the financial reporting for these test stores, and she and other management personnel were offered bonuses based on the sales growth and profitability of these stores.

While completing the financial reports, Perlman discovered a sizable inventory of outdated goods that should have been discounted for sale or returned to the manufacturer. She discussed the situation with her management colleagues; the consensus was to ignore reporting this inventory as obsolete, since reporting it would diminish the financial results and their bonuses.

Required:

1. According to the Standards of Ethical Conduct for Practitioners of Management Accounting and Financial Management, would it be ethical for Perlman *not* to report the inventory as obsolete?
2. Would it be easy for Perlman to take the ethical action in this situation?

(CMA, adapted)

PROBLEM 1–6 Line and Staff Positions [LO2]

Special Alloys Corporation manufactures a variety of specialized metal products for industrial use. Most of the revenues are generated by large contracts with companies that have government defence contracts. The company also develops and markets parts to the major automobile companies. It employs many metallurgists and skilled technicians because most of its products are made from highly sophisticated alloys.

The company recently signed two large contracts; as a result, the workload of Wayne Washburn, the general manager, has become overwhelming. To relieve some of this overload, Mark Johnson was transferred from the Research Planning Department to the general manager's office. Johnson, who has been a senior metallurgist and supervisor in the Research Planning Department, was given the title "assistant to the general manager."

Washburn assigned several responsibilities to Johnson in their first meeting. Johnson will oversee the testing of new alloys in the Product Planning Department and be given the authority to make decisions as to the use of these alloys in product development; he will also be responsible for maintaining the production schedules for one of the new contracts. In addition to these duties, he will be required to meet with the supervisors of the production departments regularly to consult with them about production problems they may be experiencing. Washburn expects to be able to manage the company much more efficiently with Johnson's help.

Required:

1. Positions within organizations are often described as having (a) line authority or (b) staff authority. Describe what is meant by these two terms.
2. Of the responsibilities assigned to Mark Johnson as assistant to the general manager, which tasks have line authority and which have staff authority?
3. Identify and discuss the conflicts Mark Johnson may experience in the production departments as a result of his new responsibilities.

(CMA, adapted)

PROBLEM 1–7 Ethics in Business [LO4]

South of the border a prominent nationwide chain of auto repair shops was accused of misleading customers and selling them unnecessary parts and services, from brake jobs to front-end alignments. Lynn Sharpe Paine reported the situation as follows in "Managing for Organizational Integrity," *Harvard Business Review,* March–April, 1994:

> In the face of declining revenues, shrinking market share, and an increasingly competitive market . . . management attempted to spur performance of its auto centers. . . . The automotive service advisers were given product-specific sales quotas—sell so many springs, shock absorbers, alignments, or brake jobs per shift—and paid a commission based on sales. . . . [F]ailure to meet quotas could lead to a transfer or a reduction in work hours. Some employees spoke of the "pressure, pressure, pressure" to bring in sales.
>
> This pressure-cooker atmosphere created conditions under which employees felt that the only way to satisfy top management was by selling products and services to customers that they didn't really need.

Suppose all automotive repair businesses routinely followed the practice of attempting to sell customers unnecessary parts and services.

Required:

1. How would this behaviour affect customers? How might customers attempt to protect themselves against this behaviour?
2. How would this behaviour probably affect profits and employment in the automotive service industry?

PROBLEM 1–8 Ethics; Just-In-Time (JIT) Purchasing [LO3, LO4]

(The situation described below was adapted from a case published by the Institute of Management Accountants' Committee on Ethics.[11])

WIW is a publicly owned corporation that makes various control devices used in manufacturing mechanical equipment. J.B. is the president of WIW, Tony is the purchasing agent, and Diane is J.B.'s executive assistant. All three have been with WIW for about five years. Charlie is WIW's controller and has been with the company for two years.

J.B.: Hi, Charlie, come on in. Diane said you had a confidential matter to discuss. What's on your mind?

Charlie: J.B., I was reviewing our increased purchases from A-1 Warehouse Sales last week and wondered why our volume has tripled in the past year. When I discussed this with Tony he seemed a bit evasive and tried to dismiss the issue by stating that A-1 can give us one-day delivery on our orders.

J.B.: Well, Tony is right. You know we have been trying to implement just-in-time and have been trying to get our inventory down.

Charlie: We still have to look at the overall cost. A-1 is more of a jobber than a warehouse. After investigating orders placed with them, I found that only 10% are delivered from their warehouse and the other 90% are drop-shipped from the manufacturers. The average markup by A-1 is 30%, which amounted to about $600,000 on our orders for the past year. If we had ordered directly from the manufacturers when A-1 didn't have an item in stock, we could have saved about $540,000 ($600,000 × 90%). In addition, some of the orders were late and not complete.

J.B.: Now look, Charlie, we get quick delivery on most items, and who knows how much we are saving by not having to stock this stuff in advance or worry about it becoming obsolete. Is there anything else on your mind?

Charlie: Well, J.B., as a matter of fact, there is. I ordered a Dun & Bradstreet credit report on A-1 and discovered that Mike Bell is the principal owner. Isn't he your brother-in-law?

J.B.: Sure he is. But don't worry about Mike. He understands this JIT approach. Besides, he's looking out for our interests.

Charlie (to himself): This conversation has been enlightening, but it doesn't really respond to my concerns. Can I legally or ethically ignore this apparent conflict of interests?

Required:

1. Would Charlie be justified in ignoring this situation, particularly since he is not the purchasing agent? In preparing your answer, consider the IMA's Standards of Ethical Conduct.
2. State the specific steps Charlie should follow to resolve this matter.

GROUP AND INTERNET EXERCISES

GROUP EXERCISE 1–9 Ethics on the Job

Ethical standards are very important in business, but they are not always followed. If you have ever held a job—even a summer job—describe the ethical climate in the organization where you worked. Did employees work a full day or did they arrive late and leave early? Did employees honestly report the hours they worked? Did employees use their employer's resources for their own purposes? Did managers set a good example? Did the organization have a code of ethics and were employees made aware of its existence? If the ethical climate in the organization you worked for was poor, what problems, if any, did it create?

INTERNET EXERCISE 1–10

As you know, the World Wide Web is a medium that is constantly evolving. Sites come and go, and change without notice. To enable periodic updating of site addresses, this problem has been posted to the textbook Web site (www.mcgrawhill.ca/college/garrison). After accessing the site, enter the Student Centre and select this chapter. Select and complete the Internet Exercise.

11. Neil Holmes, ed., "Ethics," *Management Accounting* 73, no. 8 (February 1992), p. 16. Used with permission from the Institute of Management Accountants (IMA), Montvale, N.J., USA, www.imanet.org.

CHAPTER 2

LEARNING OBJECTIVES

After studying Chapter 2, you should be able to:

1. Identify and give examples of each of the three basic cost elements involved in the manufacture of a product.
2. Distinguish between product costs and period costs and give examples of each.
3. Prepare an income statement including the calculation of cost of goods sold.
4. Prepare a schedule of cost of goods manufactured.
5. Explain the difference in the behaviour of variable and fixed costs.
6. Distinguish between direct and indirect costs.
7. Define and give examples of additional cost classifications used in making decisions: differential costs, opportunity costs, and sunk costs.
8. (Appendix 2A) Identify the four types of quality costs and explain how they interact.
9. (Appendix 2A) Prepare and interpret a quality cost report.

COST TERMS, CONCEPTS, AND CLASSIFICATIONS

BUSINESS FOCUS

CONSIDERING THE COSTS

Terri, the owner of a retail florist shop, has been trying to decide for some time whether she should continue to use a local courier service to deliver flowers to customers or buy a delivery truck and use one of her employees to make the deliveries. At a recent family dinner, she brought up the subject of the delivery truck with her brother-in-law, who fancies himself as an expert on all management subjects. He grabbed this opportunity to impress on Terri his understanding of costs.

In rapid-fire succession, Terri's brother-in-law told her that the fees paid to the courier to deliver flowers are a variable cost and a period cost, but the costs of the flowers are product costs rather than period costs, even though the flower costs are also variable costs. On the other hand, the depreciation of the delivery truck would be a fixed cost and a period cost. And while the fuel for the truck would be a variable cost and a differential cost, the wages of the person making the deliveries would be a fixed cost, not a differential cost, and would involve an opportunity cost. At this point, Terri excused herself—pleading that she had to help in the kitchen.

Terri felt that her brother-in-law's comments were more confusing than helpful, but she knew that she could no longer put off the decision about the delivery truck. She would have to think carefully about her costs and determine what costs should be considered in this decision.

As explained in Chapter 1, the work of management focuses on (1) planning, which includes setting objectives and outlining how to attain these objectives; and (2) control, which includes the steps to take to ensure that objectives are realized. To carry out these planning and control responsibilities, managers need *information* about the organization. From an accounting point of view, this information often relates to the *costs* of the organization.

In managerial accounting, the term *cost* is used in many different ways. The reason is that there are many types of costs, and these costs are classified differently according to the immediate needs of management. For example, managers may want cost data to prepare external financial reports, to prepare planning budgets, or to make decisions. Each different use of cost data demands a different classification and definition of costs. For example, the preparation of external financial reports requires the use of historical cost data, whereas decision making may require current cost data.

In this chapter, we discuss many of the possible uses of cost data and how costs are defined and classified for each use. Our first task is to explain how costs are classified for the purpose of preparing external financial reports—particularly in manufacturing companies. To set the stage for this discussion, we begin the chapter by defining some terms commonly used in manufacturing.

GENERAL COST CLASSIFICATIONS

All types of organizations incur costs—business, non-business, manufacturing, retail, and service. Generally, the kinds of costs that are incurred and the way in which these costs are classified depend on the type of organization involved. Managerial accounting is as applicable to one type of organization as to another. For this reason, we will consider in our discussion the cost characteristics of a variety of organizations—manufacturing, merchandising, and service.

Our initial focus in this chapter is on manufacturing companies, since their basic activities include most of the activities found in other types of business organizations. Manufacturing companies such as Magna, Ford, and Molson are involved in acquiring raw materials, producing finished goods, marketing, distributing, billing, and almost every other business activity. Therefore, an understanding of costs in a manufacturing company can be very helpful in understanding costs in other types of organizations.

LEARNING OBJECTIVE 1
Identify and give examples of each of the three basic cost elements involved in the manufacture of a product.

In this chapter, we develop cost concepts that apply to diverse organizations. For example, these cost concepts apply to fast-food outlets such as KFC, Pizza Hut, and Taco Bell; movie studios such as Disney, Paramount, and United Artists; consulting firms such as Grant Thornton Consulting and KPMG; and your local hospital. The exact terms used in these industries may not be the same as those used in manufacturing, but the same basic concepts apply. With some slight modifications, these basic concepts also apply to merchandising companies such as Wal-Mart, Canadian Tire, Zellers, and the Bay that resell finished goods acquired from manufacturers and other sources. With that in mind, let us begin our discussion of manufacturing costs.

Manufacturing Costs

Most manufacturing companies divide manufacturing costs into three broad categories: direct materials, direct labour, and manufacturing overhead. A discussion of each of these categories follows.

Raw materials
Any materials that go into the final product.

Direct Materials The materials that go into the final product are called **raw materials.** This term is somewhat misleading, since it seems to imply unprocessed natural resources like wood pulp or iron ore. Actually, *raw materials* refers to any materials that are used in the final product, and the finished product of one company can become the raw materials of another company. For example, the plastics produced by Du Pont are a raw material used by Hewlett Packard in its personal computers. One study back in the 1990s of 37 manufacturing industries found that materials averaged about 55% of sales revenues.[1]

Direct materials are those materials that become an integral part of the finished product and that can be physically and conveniently traced to it. This would include, for example, the seats Bombardier purchases from subcontractors to install in its commercial aircraft. Also included is the tiny electric motor Panasonic uses in its CD players to make the CD spin.

Direct materials
Those materials that become an integral part of a finished product and can be conveniently traced to it.

Sometimes it is not worth the effort to trace the costs of relatively insignificant materials to the end products. Such minor items would include the solder used to make electrical connections in a Sony TV or the glue used to assemble an Ethan Allen chair. Materials such as solder and glue are called **indirect materials** and are included as part of manufacturing overhead, which is discussed later in this section.

Indirect materials
Small items of material such as glue and nails. These items may become an integral part of a finished product but are traceable to the product only at great cost or inconvenience.

Direct Labour

The term **direct labour** is reserved for those labour costs that can be easily (i.e., physically and conveniently) traced to individual units of product. Direct labour is sometimes called *touch labour,* since direct labour workers typically touch the product while it is being made. The labour costs of assembly-line workers, for example, would be direct labour costs, as would the labour costs of carpenters, bricklayers, and machine operators.

Direct labour
Those factory labour costs that can be traced easily to individual units of product. Also called *touch labour.*

Labour costs that cannot be physically traced to the creation of products, or that can be traced only at great cost and inconvenience, are termed **indirect labour** and treated as part of manufacturing overhead, along with indirect materials. Indirect labour includes the labour costs of janitors, supervisors, materials handlers, and night security guards. Although the efforts of these workers are essential to production, it would be either impractical or impossible to accurately trace their costs to specific units of product. Hence, such labour costs are treated as indirect labour.

Indirect labour
The labour costs of janitors, supervisors, materials handlers, and other factory workers that cannot be conveniently traced directly to particular products.

In some industries, major shifts are taking place in the structure of labour costs. Sophisticated automated equipment, run and maintained by skilled indirect workers, is increasingly replacing direct labour. In the study of 37 manufacturing industries cited above direct labour averaged 10% of sales revenues. In a few companies, direct labour has become such a minor element of cost that it has disappeared altogether as a separate cost category. More is said in later chapters about this trend and about the impact it is having on cost systems. However, the vast majority of manufacturing and service companies throughout the world continue to recognize direct labour as a separate cost category.

FOCUS *on Current Practice*

S

After filing for bankruptcy protection in 2003 and having pilots agree to a reduced salary, Air Canada attempted to take steps to restructure its business processes hoping to remove itself from bankruptcy protection and improve profits. However, Air Canada was back at the bargaining table in 2003 with its unions. Many unions readily accepted salary cuts. But the Canadian Auto Workers Union chose to bargain and held out until the end. Air Canada has since admitted that the most difficult task in the restructuring process has been reducing labour costs. Many of the current employees were acquired through the acquisition of Canadian Airlines and staff can not readily be discharged without substantial cost to the company.

Source: Deborah Stokes, "Milton says worst over for Air Canada," *National Post*, June 7, 2004, p. FP.

1. Germain Boer and Debra Jeter, "What's New About Modern Manufacturing? Empirical Evidence on Manufacturing Cost Changes," *Journal of Management Accounting Research*, Fall 1993, pp. 61–83.

Manufacturing overhead
All costs associated with manufacturing except direct materials and direct labour.

Manufacturing Overhead **Manufacturing overhead,** the third element of manufacturing costs, includes all costs of manufacturing except direct materials and direct labour. Manufacturing overhead includes items such as indirect materials; indirect labour; maintenance and repairs on production equipment; and heat and light, property taxes, depreciation, and insurance on manufacturing facilities. A company also incurs costs for heat and light, property taxes, insurance, depreciation, and so forth, associated with its selling and administrative functions, but these costs are not included as part of manufacturing overhead. Only those costs associated with *operating the factory* are included in the manufacturing overhead category. Several studies have found manufacturing overhead costs to average about 16% of sales revenues.[2]

Various names are used for manufacturing overhead, such as *indirect manufacturing cost, factory overhead,* and *factory burden.* All of these terms are synonymous with *manufacturing overhead.*

Conversion cost
Direct labour cost plus manufacturing overhead cost.

Prime cost
Direct materials cost plus direct labour cost.

Manufacturing overhead combined with direct labour is called **conversion cost.** This term stems from the fact that direct labour costs and overhead costs are incurred to convert materials into finished products. Direct labour combined with direct materials is called **prime cost.**

The proportion of labour to overhead varies from company to company and even within companies within the same industry. Some automated companies have a large proportion of overhead compared to direct labour costs. Some even classify all labour as overhead. Others, such as those engaged in meat packing, have a large proportion of direct labour. Some companies buy materials partially assembled while others manufacture their subassembled parts to be used by other departments in the manufacturing process. How organizations determine their proportions of materials, labour, and overhead is a significant part of their strategic planning.

Classification of Labour Costs of Manufacturing

The classification of direct labour and indirect labour costs is relatively straightforward. Janitorial wages would usually be classified as overhead because they represent an indirect cost, as would payroll costs for supervisors, security personnel, and maintenance workers. However, the classification of idle time and overtime premiums is somewhat more difficult. For example, if three hours of a production worker's time are idle and each hour costs $12, then $36 of idle time cost usually would be charged to overhead if management felt that the cost was a general cost of all production, as would be the case for a JIT wait situation. If, however, a specific job required idle time such as that caused by waiting for materials as a result of a specification change, then the idle time could be charged to the direct labour costs of a job. Whether the customer will pay for the charge depends on the prevailing market conditions or the contract with the customer.

Overtime premium
The extra hourly wage rate paid to workers who must work above their normal time requirements.

Overtime premiums represent the extra hourly wage rate paid to workers who must work above their normal time requirements. For example, a worker might be paid time and a half for five overtime hours. Thus, if $12 was the base rate, the five hours would have an overtime premium of $6 × 5 hours, or $30. Classification of the overtime as direct labour or overhead depends on the cause of the overtime. A job-specific reason would dictate a direct job cost, whereas a normal overtime cost resulting from general management decisions, such as peak production needs, would dictate an overhead (indirect) charge to all jobs.

Employee benefits such as employment taxes, medical plans, and pension costs of the employer can be 30% to 40% of the base pay. Those employee benefits costs for indirect labour would obviously be classified as indirect overhead. However, the employee benefits for direct labour could justifiably be added to the base direct labour rate to specifically follow their driver: direct labour costs.

---

2. J. Miller, A. DeMeyer and J. Nakane, *Benchmarking Global Manufacturing* (Homewood, IL: Richard D. Irvin, 1992), Chapter 2. The Boer and Jeter article cited above contains a similar finding concerning the magnitude of manufacturing overhead.

Non-Manufacturing Costs

Generally, non-manufacturing costs are subclassified into two categories:

1. Marketing or selling costs.
2. Administrative costs.

Marketing or selling costs include all costs necessary to secure customer orders and get the finished product or service into the hands of the customer. These costs are often called *order-getting and order-filling costs.* Examples of marketing costs include order-getting costs such as those for advertising, sales travel, and sales salaries. Order-filling costs would include shipping, sales commissions, and the costs of finished goods warehouses.

Marketing or selling costs
All costs necessary to secure customer orders and get the finished product or service into the hands of the customer.

Administrative costs include all executive, organizational, and clerical costs associated with the *general management* of an organization rather than with manufacturing, marketing, or selling. Examples of administrative costs include executive compensation, general accounting, secretarial, public relations, and similar costs involved in the overall, general administration of the organization *as a whole.*

Administrative costs
All executive, organizational, and clerical costs associated with the general management of an organization rather than with manufacturing, marketing, or selling.

Managerial accounting concepts and techniques apply just as much to non-manufacturing activities as they do to manufacturing activities. Service organizations, for example, are making increased use of cost concepts in analyzing and costing their services. Banks now use cost analysis in determining the cost of offering such services as chequing accounts, consumer loans, and credit cards, and insurance companies determine costs of servicing customers by geographic location, age, marital status, and occupation. Cost breakdowns of these types provide data for control over selling and administrative functions in the same way that manufacturing cost breakdowns provide data for control over manufacturing functions.

PRODUCT COSTS VERSUS PERIOD COSTS

LEARNING OBJECTIVE 2
Distinguish between product costs and period costs and give examples of each.

In addition to the distinction between manufacturing and non-manufacturing costs, there are other ways to look at costs. For instance, they can also be classified as either *product costs* or *period costs.* To understand the difference between product costs and period costs, we must first refresh our understanding of the matching principle from financial accounting.

Generally, costs are recognized as expenses on the income statement in the period that benefits from the cost. For example, if a company pays for liability insurance in advance for two years, the entire amount is not considered an expense of the year in which the payment is made. Instead, one-half of the cost would be recognized as an expense each year. The reason is that both years—not just the first year—benefit from the insurance payment. The unexpensed portion of the insurance payment is carried on the balance sheet as an asset called *prepaid insurance*. You should be familiar with this type of *accrual* from your financial accounting coursework.

The *matching principle* is based on the accrual concept and states that *costs incurred to generate a particular revenue should be recognized as expenses in the same period that the revenue is recognized.* This means that if a cost is incurred to acquire or make something that will eventually be sold, then the cost should be recognized as an expense only when the sale takes place—that is, when the benefit occurs. Such costs are called *product costs.*

Product Costs

For financial accounting purposes, **product costs** include all of the costs that are involved in acquiring or making a product. In the case of manufactured goods, these costs consist of direct materials, direct labour, and manufacturing overhead. Product costs are viewed as "attaching" to units of product as the goods are purchased or manufactured, and they remain attached as the goods go into inventory awaiting sale. So, initially, product costs

Product costs
All costs that are involved in the purchase or manufacture of goods. In the case of manufactured goods, these costs consist of direct materials, direct labour, and manufacturing overhead. Also called *inventoriable costs.*

are assigned to an inventory account on the balance sheet. When the goods are sold, the costs are released from inventory as expenses (typically called *cost of goods sold*) and matched against sales revenue. Since product costs are initially assigned to inventories, they are also known as **inventoriable costs.**

Inventoriable costs
Same as *product costs*.

We want to emphasize that product costs are not necessarily treated as expenses in the period in which they are incurred. Rather, as explained above, they are treated as expenses in the period in which the related products *are sold*. This means that a product cost such as direct materials or direct labour might be incurred during one period but not treated as an expense until a following period when the completed product is sold.

Period costs
Those costs that are taken directly to the income statement as expenses in the period in which they are incurred or accrued; such costs consist of selling (marketing) and administrative expenses.

Period Costs

Period costs are all of the costs that are not included in product costs. These costs are expensed on the income statement in the period in which they are incurred, using the usual rules of accrual accounting you have already learned in financial accounting. Period costs are not included as part of the cost of either purchased or manufactured goods. Sales commissions and office rent are good examples of these kinds of costs. Neither commissions nor office rent are included as part of the cost of purchased or manufactured goods. Rather, both items are treated as expenses on the income statement in the period in which they are incurred. Thus, they are said to be period costs.

As suggested above, *all selling and administrative expenses are considered to be period costs.* Therefore, advertising, executive salaries, sales commissions, public relations, and other non-manufacturing costs discussed earlier would all be period costs. They will appear on the income statement as expenses in the period in which they are incurred.

FOCUS *on Current Practice*

United Colors of Benetton, an Italian apparel company headquartered in Ponzano, is unusual in that it is involved in all activities in the "value chain" from clothing design through manufacturing, distribution, and ultimate sale to customers in Benetton retail outlets. Most companies are involved in only one or two of these activities. Looking at this company allows us to see how costs are distributed across the entire value chain. A recent income statement from the company contained the following data:

	Millions of Euros	Percent of Revenues
Revenue	2,125	100.0%
Cost of sales	1,199	56.4
Selling, general, and administrative expenses:		
Payroll and related cost	126	5.9
Distribution and transport	45	2.1
Sales commissions	102	4.8
Advertising and promotion	125	5.9
Depreciation and amortization	62	2.9
Other expenses	141	6.6
Total selling, general, and administrative expenses	601	28.3%

Even though this company spends large sums on advertising and runs its own shops, the cost of sales is still quite high in relation to the revenue—56.4% of revenue. And despite the company's lavish advertising campaigns, advertising and promotion costs amounted to only 5.9% of revenue.

Exhibit 2–1 contains a summary of the cost terms that we have introduced so far.

EXHIBIT 2–1 Summary of Cost Terms

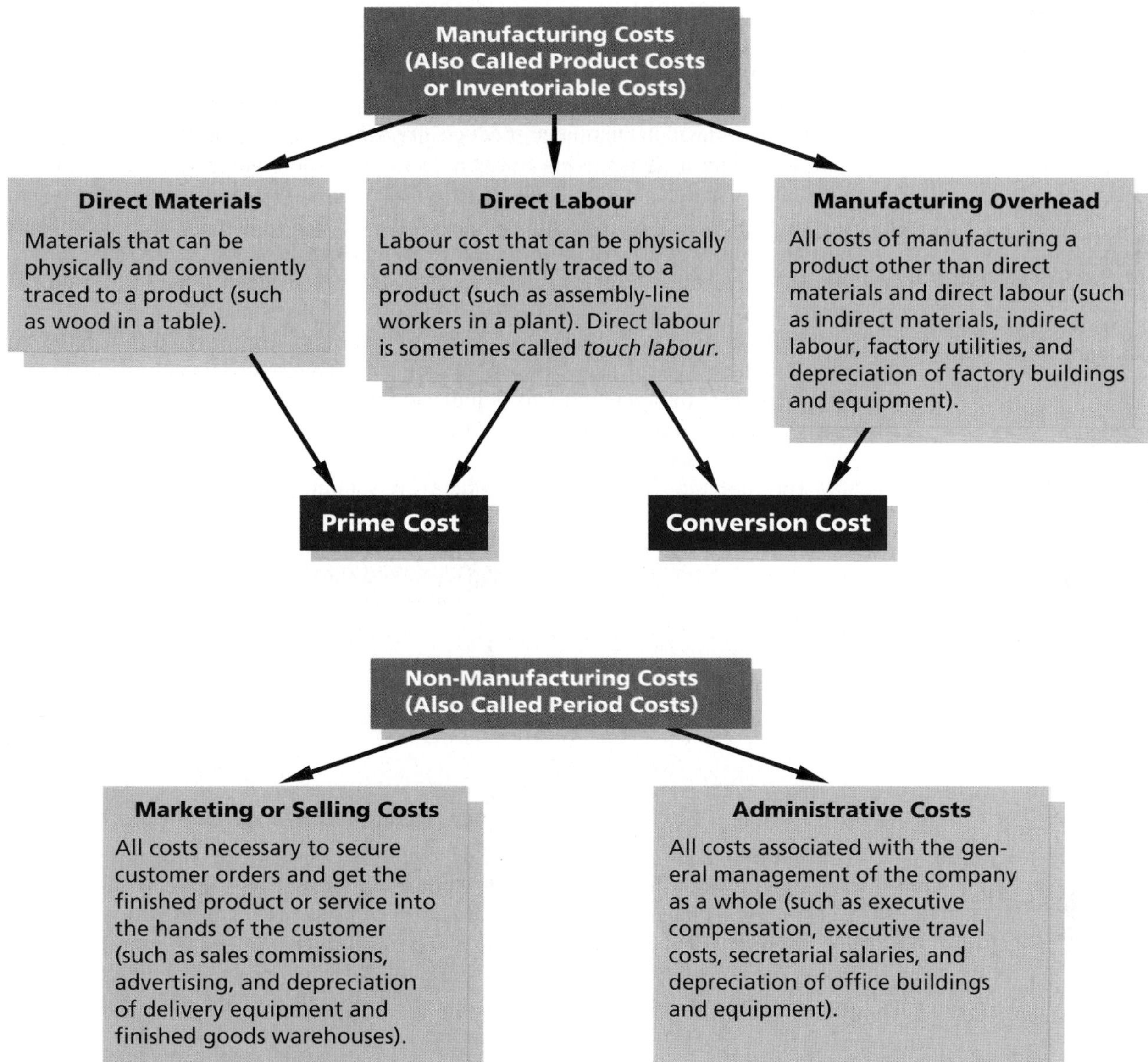

Manufacturing Costs
(Also Called Product Costs
or Inventoriable Costs)
Direct Materials
Materials that can be physically and conveniently traced to a product (such as wood in a table).
Direct Labour
Labour cost that can be physically and conveniently traced to a product (such as assembly-line workers in a plant). Direct labour is sometimes called *touch labour.*
Manufacturing Overhead
All costs of manufacturing a product other than direct materials and direct labour (such as indirect materials, indirect labour, factory utilities, and depreciation of factory buildings and equipment).
Prime Cost
Conversion Cost
Non-Manufacturing Costs
(Also Called Period Costs)
Marketing or Selling Costs
All costs necessary to secure customer orders and get the finished product or service into the hands of the customer (such as sales commissions, advertising, and depreciation of delivery equipment and finished goods warehouses).
Administrative Costs
All costs associated with the general management of the company as a whole (such as executive compensation, executive travel costs, secretarial salaries, and depreciation of office buildings and equipment).

COST CLASSIFICATIONS ON FINANCIAL STATEMENTS

In your prior accounting training, you learned that firms prepare periodic financial reports for creditors, shareholders, and others to show the financial condition of the firm and the firm's earnings performance over some specified interval. The reports you studied were probably those of merchandising companies, such as retail stores, which simply purchase goods from suppliers for resale to customers.

Financial statements prepared by a *manufacturing* company are more complex than the statements prepared by a merchandising company. Manufacturing companies are more complex organizations than merchandising companies because the manufacturing company must produce its goods as well as market them. The production process gives rise to many costs that do not exist in a merchandising company, and somehow these costs must be accounted for on the manufacturing company's financial statements. In this section, we focus our attention on how this accounting is carried out in the balance sheet and income statement.

The Balance Sheet

Raw materials The materials that are used to make a product.

Work in process Consists of units of product that are only partially complete and will require further work before they are ready for sale to a customer.

Finished goods Consist of units of product that have been completed but have not yet been sold to customers.

The balance sheet, or statement of financial position, of a manufacturing company is similar to that of a merchandising company. However, there are differences in the inventory accounts. A merchandising company has only one class of inventory—goods purchased from suppliers that are awaiting resale to customers. By contrast, manufacturing companies have three classes of inventories—**raw materials**, **work in process**, and **finished goods**. The overall inventory figure is usually broken down into these three classes of inventories and provided in a footnote to the financial statements.

We will use two companies—Graham Manufacturing and Reston Bookstore—to illustrate the concepts discussed in this section. Graham Manufacturing is located in Victoria, British Columbia, and makes precision brass fittings for yachts. Reston Bookstore is a small bookstore in Moncton, New Brunswick, specializing in selling books about Maritime Canada.

The footnotes to Graham Manufacturing's annual report reveal the following information concerning its inventories:

Graham Manufacturing Corporation
Inventory Accounts

	Beginning Balance	Ending Balance
Raw Materials	$ 60,000	$ 50,000
Work in Process	90,000	60,000
Finished Goods	125,000	175,000
Total inventory accounts	$275,000	$285,000

Graham Manufacturing's raw materials inventory consists largely of brass rods and brass blocks. The work in process inventory consists of partially completed brass fittings. The finished goods inventory consists of brass fittings that are ready to be sold to customers.

In contrast, the inventory account at Reston Bookstore consists entirely of the costs of books the company has purchased from publishers for resale to the public. In merchandising companies like Reston, these inventories may be called *merchandise inventories*. The beginning and ending balances in this account appear as follows:

Reston Bookstore
Inventory Account

	Beginning Balance	Ending Balance
Merchandise Inventory	$100,000	$150,000

The Income Statement

LEARNING OBJECTIVE 3
Prepare an income statement including the calculation of cost of goods sold.

Exhibit 2–2 compares the income statements of Reston Bookstore and Graham Manufacturing. For purposes of illustration, these statements contain more detail about cost of goods sold than you will generally find in published financial statements.

At first glance, the income statements of merchandising and manufacturing firms like Reston Bookstore and Graham Manufacturing are very similar. The only apparent difference is in the labels of some of the entries that go into the computation of the cost of goods sold figure. In the exhibit, the computation of cost of goods sold relies on the following basic equation for inventory accounts:

EXHIBIT 2–2 Comparative Income Statements: Merchandising and Manufacturing Companies

MERCHANDISING COMPANY
Reston Bookstore

	Sales		$1,000,000
The cost of merchandise inventory purchased from outside suppliers during the period. → Add: Purchases	Cost of goods sold:		
	Beginning merchandise inventory	$100,000	
	Add: Purchases	650,000	
	Goods available for sale	750,000	
	Deduct: Ending merchandise inventory	150,000	600,000
	Gross margin		400,000
	Less operating expenses:		
	Selling expense	100,000	
	Administrative expense	200,000	300,000
	Net income		$ 100,000

MANUFACTURING COMPANY
Graham Manufacturing

	Sales		$1,500,000
The manufacturing costs associated with the goods that were finished during the period. (See Exhibit 2–4 for details.) → Add: Cost of goods manufactured	Cost of goods sold:		
	Beginning finished goods inventory	$125,000	
	Add: Cost of goods manufactured	850,000	
	Goods available for sale	975,000	
	Deduct: Ending finished goods inventory	175,000	800,000
	Gross margin		700,000
	Less operating expenses:		
	Selling expense	250,000	
	Administrative expense	300,000	550,000
	Net income		$ 150,000

Basic Equation for Inventory Accounts

Beginning balance + Additions to inventory = Ending balance + Withdrawals from inventory

The logic underlying this equation, which applies to any inventory account, is illustrated in Exhibit 2-3. At the beginning of the period, the inventory contains a beginning balance. During the period, additions are made to the inventory through purchases or other means. The sum of the beginning balance and the additions to the account is the total amount of inventory available. During the period, withdrawals are made from inventory. Whatever is left at the end of the period after these withdrawals is the ending balance. The sum of the additions to the account and the beginning balance represents the total amount of inventory that is available for use during the period. At the end of the period, all of the inventory that was available must either be in ending inventory or must have been withdrawn from the inventory account.

These concepts are applied to determine the cost of goods sold for a merchandising company like Reston Bookstore as follows:

Cost of Goods Sold in a Merchandising Company

Beginning merchandise inventory + Purchases = Ending merchandise inventory + Cost of goods sold or

$$\text{Cost of goods sold} = \text{Beginning merchandise inventory} + \text{Purchases} - \text{Ending merchandise inventory}$$

The cost of goods sold for a manufacturing company like Graham Manufacturing is determined as follows:

Cost of Goods Sold in a Manufacturing Company

$$\text{Beginning finished goods inventory} + \text{Cost of goods manufactured} = \text{Ending finished goods inventory} + \text{Cost of goods sold}$$

or

$$\text{Cost of goods sold} = \text{Beginning finished goods inventory} + \text{Cost of goods manufactured} - \text{Ending finished goods inventory}$$

To determine the cost of goods sold in a merchandising company like Reston Bookstore, we need to know only the beginning and ending balances in the Merchandise Inventory account and the purchases. Total purchases can be determined easily in a merchandising company by simply adding together all purchases from suppliers.

To determine the cost of goods sold in a manufacturing company like Graham Manufacturing, we need to know the *cost of goods manufactured* and the beginning and ending balances in the Finished Goods inventory account. The **cost of goods manufactured** consists of the manufacturing costs associated with goods that were *finished* during the period. The cost of goods manufactured figure for Graham Manufacturing is derived in Exhibit 2–4, which contains a *schedule of cost of goods manufactured.*

Cost of goods manufactured The manufacturing costs associated with the goods that were finished during the period.

Schedule of Cost of Goods Manufactured

LEARNING OBJECTIVE 4
Prepare a schedule of cost of goods manufactured.

At first glance, the **schedule of cost of goods manufactured** in Exhibit 2–4 appears complex and perhaps even intimidating. However, it is all quite logical. The schedule of cost of goods manufactured contains the three elements of product costs that we discussed earlier—direct materials, direct labour, and manufacturing overhead. The total of these three cost elements is *not* the cost of goods manufactured, however. The reason is that some of the materials, labour, and overhead costs incurred during the period relate to goods that are not yet completed. The costs that relate to goods that are not yet completed are shown in the work in process inventory figures at the bottom of the schedule. Note that the beginning work in process inventory must be added to the manufacturing costs of the period, and the ending work in process inventory must be deducted, to arrive at the cost of goods manufactured.

Schedule of cost of goods manufactured A schedule showing the direct materials, direct labour, and manufacturing overhead costs incurred for a period and assigned to work in process and completed goods.

The direct material cost is not simply the cost of materials purchased during the period—rather it is the cost of materials *used* during the period. The purchases of raw

EXHIBIT 2–3 Inventory Flows

Beginning balance + Additions = Total available − Withdrawals = Ending balance

EXHIBIT 2–4 Schedule of Cost of Goods Manufactured

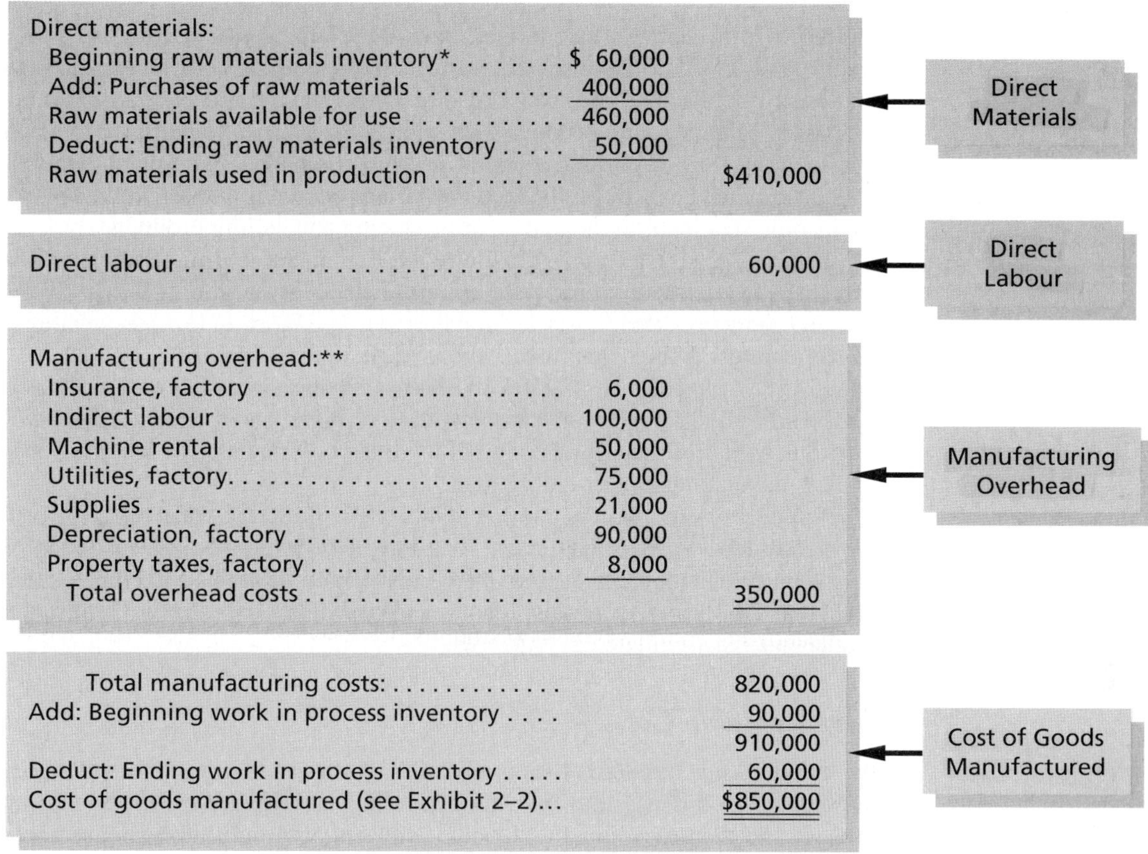

Direct materials:		
Beginning raw materials inventory*	$ 60,000	
Add: Purchases of raw materials	400,000	
Raw materials available for use	460,000	
Deduct: Ending raw materials inventory	50,000	
Raw materials used in production		$410,000
Direct labour		60,000
Manufacturing overhead:**		
Insurance, factory	6,000	
Indirect labour	100,000	
Machine rental	50,000	
Utilities, factory	75,000	
Supplies	21,000	
Depreciation, factory	90,000	
Property taxes, factory	8,000	
Total overhead costs		350,000
Total manufacturing costs:		820,000
Add: Beginning work in process inventory		90,000
		910,000
Deduct: Ending work in process inventory		60,000
Cost of goods manufactured (see Exhibit 2–2)		$850,000

*We assume in this example that the Raw Materials inventory account contains only direct materials and that indirect materials are carried in a separate Supplies account. Using a Supplies account for indirect materials is a common practice among companies. In Chapter 3, we discuss the procedure to be followed if *both* direct and indirect materials are carried in a single account.

**In Chapter 3 we will see that the manufacturing overhead section of the schedule of cost of goods manufactured can be considerably simplified by using what is called a *predetermined overhead rate.*

materials are added to the beginning balance to determine the cost of materials available for use. The ending inventory is deducted from this amount to arrive at the cost of the materials used in production. The sum of the three cost elements—materials, direct labour, and manufacturing overhead—is the total manufacturing cost. This is *not* the same thing, however, as the cost of goods manufactured for the period. The subtle distinction between the total manufacturing cost and the cost of goods manufactured is very easy to miss. Some of the materials, direct labour, and manufacturing overhead costs incurred during the period relate to goods that are not yet completed. As stated above, the *cost of goods manufactured* consists of the manufacturing cost associated with the goods that were *finished* during the period. Consequently, adjustments need to be made to the total manufacturing costs of the period for the partially completed goods that were in process at the beginning and at the end of the period. The costs that relate to goods that are not yet completed are shown in the work in process inventory figures at the bottom of the schedule. Note that the beginning work in process inventory must be added to the manufacturing costs of the period, and the ending work in process inventory must be deducted, to arrive at the cost of goods manufactured.

PRODUCT COSTS—FLOWS

Earlier in the chapter, we defined product costs as consisting of those costs that are involved in either the purchase or the manufacture of goods. For manufactured goods, we stated that these costs consist of direct materials, direct labour, and manufacturing overhead. To understand product costs more fully, it will be helpful at this point to look briefly at the flow of costs in a manufacturing company. By doing so, we will be able to see how product costs move through the various accounts and affect the balance sheet and the income statement in the course of producing and selling products.

Exhibit 2–5 illustrates the flow of costs in a manufacturing company. Raw materials purchases are recorded in the Raw Materials inventory account. When raw materials are used in production, their costs are transferred to the Work in Process inventory account as direct materials. Notice that direct labour cost and manufacturing overhead cost are added directly to Work in Process. Work in Process can be viewed most simply as products on an assembly line. The direct materials, direct labour, and manufacturing overhead costs added to Work in Process in Exhibit 2–4 are the costs needed to complete these products as they move along this assembly line.

Notice from the exhibit that as goods are completed, their cost is transferred from Work in Process to Finished Goods. Here the goods await sale to a customer. As goods are sold, their cost is then transferred from Finished Goods to Cost of Goods Sold. It is at this point that the various materials, labour, and overhead costs that are required to make the product are finally treated as expenses.

Inventoriable Costs

As stated earlier, product costs are often called *inventoriable costs*. The reason is that these costs go directly into inventory accounts as they are incurred (first into Work in Process and then into Finished Goods), rather than going into expense accounts. Thus, they are termed *inventoriable costs. This is a key concept, since such costs can end up on the balance sheet as assets if goods are only partially completed or are unsold at the end of a period.* To illustrate this point, refer again to the data in Exhibit 2–5. At the end of the period, the materials, labour, and overhead costs that are associated with the units in the

EXHIBIT 2–5 Cost Flows and Classifications in a Manufacturing Company

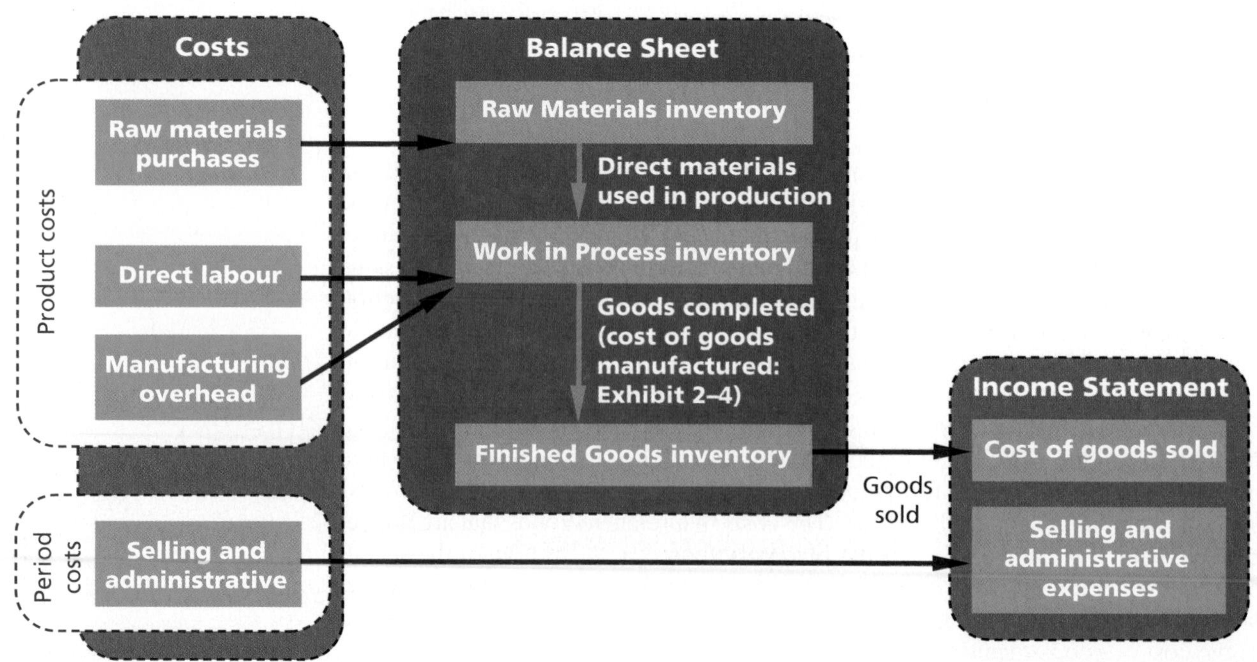

Work in Process and Finished Goods inventory accounts will appear on the balance sheet as part of the company's assets. As explained earlier, these costs will not become expenses until later when the goods are completed and sold.

As shown in Exhibit 2–5, selling and administrative expenses are not involved in the manufacture of a product. For this reason, they are not treated as product costs but rather as period costs that go directly into expense accounts as they are incurred.

An Example of Cost Flows

To provide an example of cost flows in a manufacturing company, assume that a company's annual insurance cost is $2,000. Three-fourths of this amount ($1,500) applies to factory operations, and one-fourth ($500) applies to selling and administrative activities. Therefore, $1,500 of the $2,000 insurance cost would be a product (inventoriable) cost and would be added to the cost of goods produced during the year. This concept is illustrated in Exhibit 2-6, where $1,500 of insurance cost is added into Work in Process. As shown in the exhibit, this portion of the year's insurance cost will not become an expense until the goods that are produced during the year are sold, and the $1,500 will remain as part of the asset, inventory (either as part of Work in Process or as part of Finished Goods), along with the other costs of producing the goods.

By contrast, the $500 of insurance costs that applies to the company's selling and administrative activities will be expensed immediately.

Thus far, we have been mainly concerned with classifications of manufacturing costs for the purpose of determining inventory valuations on the balance sheet and cost of goods sold on the income statement of external financial reports. However, costs are used for many purposes, and each purpose requires a different classification of costs. We will consider several different purposes for cost classifications in the remaining sections of this chapter. To help keep the big picture in mind, we suggest that you refer back to Exhibit 2–7 as you progress through the rest of this chapter.

EXHIBIT 2–6 An Example of Cost Flows in a Manufacturing Company

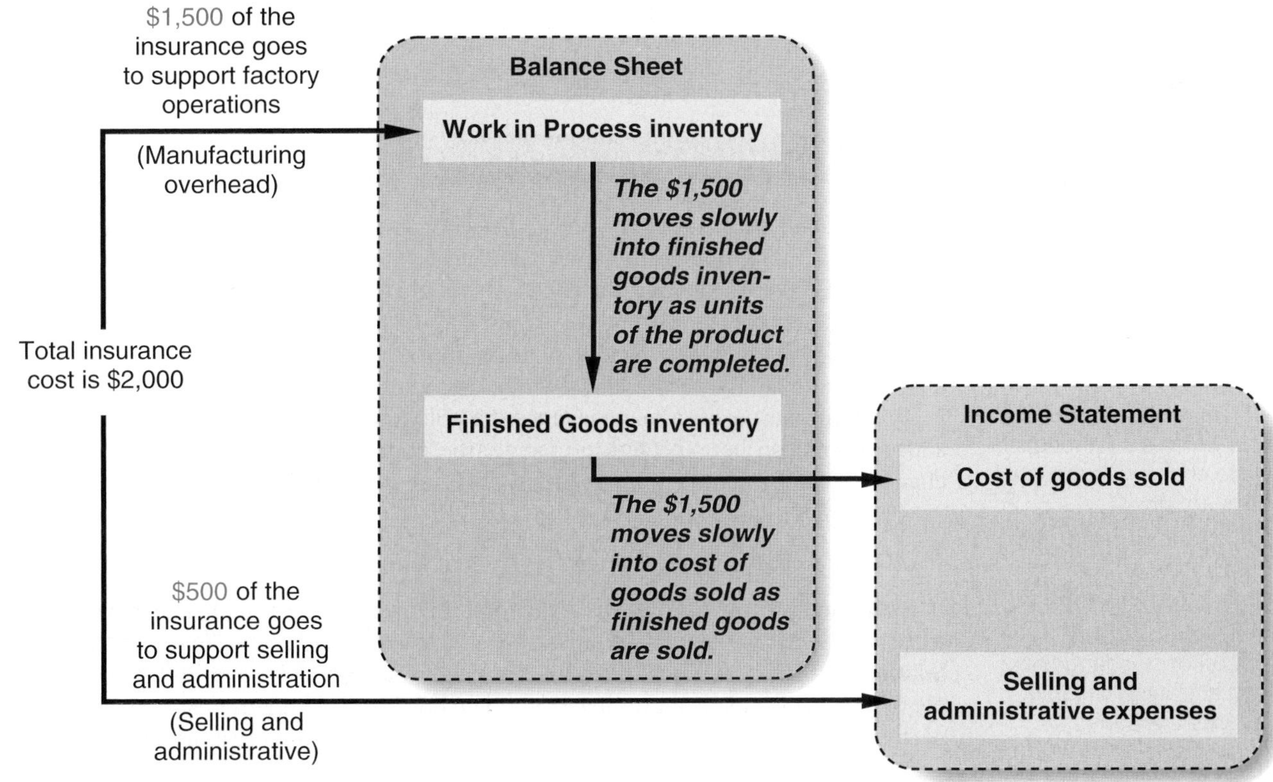

EXHIBIT 2–7 Summary of Cost Classifications

Purpose of Cost Classification	Cost Classifications
Preparing external financial statements	• Product costs (inventoriable) • Direct materials • Direct labour • Manufacturing overhead • Period costs (expensed) • Non-manufacturing costs • Marketing or selling costs • Administrative costs
Predicting cost behaviour in response to changes in activity	• Variable cost (proportional to activity) • Fixed cost (constant in total)
Assigning costs to cost objects such as departments or products	• Direct cost (can easily be traced) • Indirect cost (cannot easily be traced; must be allocated)
Making decisions	• Differential cost (differs between alternatives) • Sunk cost (past cost not affected by a decision) • Opportunity cost (forgone benefit)
Cost of quality (Appendix 2A)	• Prevention costs • Appraisal costs • Internal failure costs • Opportunity cost (forgone benefit)

COST CLASSIFICATIONS FOR PREDICTING COST BEHAVIOUR

LEARNING OBJECTIVE **5**
Explain the difference in the behaviour of variable and fixed costs.

Quite frequently, it is necessary to predict how a certain cost will behave in response to a change in activity. For example, a manager at Aliant Telecom may want to estimate the impact a 5% increase in long-distance calls would have on the company's total electric bill or on the total wages the company pays its long-distance operators. **Cost behaviour** means how a cost will react or respond to changes in the level of business activity. As the activity level rises and falls, a particular cost may rise and fall as well—or it may remain constant. For planning purposes, a manager must be able to anticipate which of these will happen, and if a cost can be expected to change, the manager must know by how much it will change. To help make such distinctions, costs are often categorized as *variable* or *fixed.*

Cost behaviour
The way in which a cost reacts or responds to changes in the level of business activity.

Variable Cost

Variable cost
A cost that varies, in total, in direct proportion to changes in the level of activity. A variable cost is constant per unit.

A **variable cost** is a cost that varies, in total, in direct proportion to changes in the level of activity. The activity can be expressed in many ways, such as units produced, units sold, kilometres driven, beds occupied, lines of print, hours worked, and so forth. A good example of a variable cost is direct materials. The cost of direct materials used during a period will vary, in total, in direct proportion to the number of units that are produced. To illustrate this idea, consider the Nova Bus Corporation. Each bus requires one battery. As the output of buses increases and decreases, the number of batteries used will increase and decrease proportionately. If bus production goes up 10%, then the number of batteries used will also go up 10%. The concept of a variable cost is shown in graphic form in Exhibit 2–8.

It is important to note that when we speak of a cost as being variable, we mean the *total* cost rises and falls as the activity level rises and falls. This idea is presented below, assuming that a battery costs $24:

Number of Buses Produced	Cost per Battery	Total Variable Cost—Batteries
1	$24	$ 24
500	24	12,000
1,000	24	24,000

One interesting aspect of variable cost behaviour is that a variable cost is constant if expressed on a *per unit* basis. Observe from the tabulation above that the per unit cost of batteries remains constant at $24 even though the total amount of cost involved increases and decreases with activity.

There are many examples of costs that are variable with respect to the products and services provided by a company. In a manufacturing company, variable costs include items such as direct materials and some elements of manufacturing overhead such as lubricants, and period costs such as shipping and sales commissions. For the present, we will also assume that direct labour is a variable cost, although as we shall see in Chapter 6, direct labour may act more like a fixed cost in many situations. In a merchandising company, variable costs include items such as cost of goods sold, commissions to salespersons, and billing costs. In a hospital, the variable costs of providing health care services to patients would include the costs of the supplies, drugs, meals, and perhaps nursing services.

When we say that a cost is variable, we ordinarily mean that it is variable with respect to the products and services the organization produces. However, cost can be variable with respect to other activities. For example, the wages paid to employees at a Blockbuster Video outlet will depend on the number of hours the store is open and not strictly on the number of videos rented. In this case, we would say that wage costs are variable with respect to the hours of operation. Nevertheless, when we say that a cost is variable, we ordinarily mean it is variable with respect to the volume of revenue-generating output—in other words, how many units are produced and sold, how many videos are rented, how many patients are treated, and so on.

S

EXHIBIT 2–8 Variable and Fixed Cost Behaviour

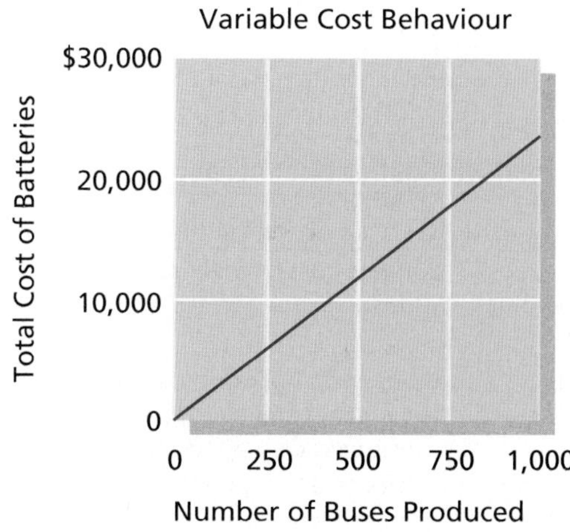

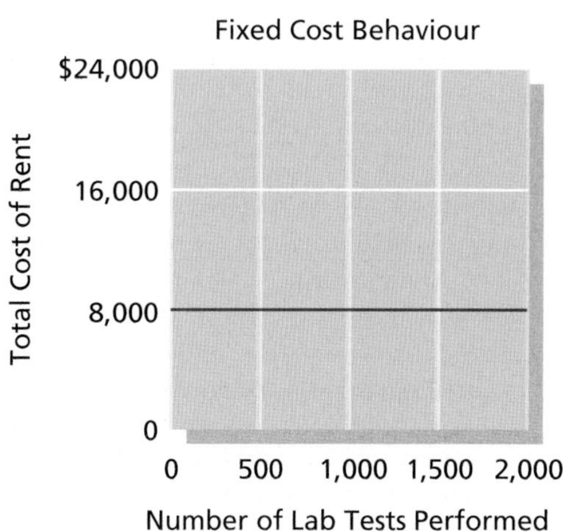

Fixed Cost

Fixed cost
A cost that remains constant, in total, regardless of changes in the level of activity within the relevant range. If a fixed cost is expressed on a per unit basis, it varies inversely with the level of activity.

A **fixed cost** is a cost that remains constant, in total, regardless of changes in the level of activity. Unlike variable costs, fixed costs are not affected by changes in activity. Consequently, as the activity level rises and falls, the fixed costs remain constant in total amount unless influenced by some outside force, such as price changes. Rent is a good example of a fixed cost. Suppose the PEI Clinic rents a machine for $8,000 per month that tests blood samples for the presence of leukemia cells. The $8,000 monthly rental cost will be sustained regardless of the number of tests that may be performed during the month. The concept of a fixed cost is shown in graphic form in Exhibit 2–8.

Very few costs are completely fixed. Most will change if there is a large enough change in activity. For example, suppose that the capacity of the leukemia diagnostic machine at the PEI Clinic is 2,000 tests per month. If the clinic wishes to perform more than 2,000 tests in a month, it would be necessary to rent an additional machine, which would cause a jump in the fixed costs. When we say a cost is fixed, we mean it is fixed within some *relevant range.* The **relevant range** is the range of activity within which the assumptions about variable and fixed costs are valid. For example, the assumption that the rent for diagnostic machines is $8,000 per month is valid within the relevant range of 0 to 2,000 tests per month.

Relevant range
The range of activity within which assumptions about variable and fixed cost behaviour are valid.

Fixed costs can create difficulties if it becomes necessary to express the costs on a per unit basis. This is because if fixed costs are expressed on a per unit basis, they will react *inversely* with changes in activity. In the PEI Clinic, for example, the average cost per test will fall as the number of tests performed increases. This is because the $8,000 rental cost will be spread over more tests. Conversely, as the number of tests performed in the clinic declines, the average cost per test will rise as the $8,000 rental cost is spread over fewer tests. This concept is illustrated in the table below:

Monthly Rental Cost	Number of Tests Performed	Average Cost per Test
$8,000	10	$800
8,000	500	16
8,000	2,000	4

Note that if the PEI Clinic performs only 10 tests each month, the rental cost of the equipment will average $800 per test. But if 2,000 tests are performed each month, the average cost will drop to only $4 per test. More will be said later about the problems created for both the accountant and the manager by this variation in unit costs.

Examples of fixed costs include straight-line depreciation, insurance, property taxes, rent, supervisory salaries, administrative salaries, and advertising.

A summary of both variable and fixed cost behaviour is presented in Exhibit 2–9.

EXHIBIT 2–9 Summary of Variable and Fixed Cost Behaviour

	Behaviour of the Cost (within the relevant range)	
Cost	**In Total**	**Per Unit**
Variable cost	Total variable cost increases and decreases in proportion to changes in the activity level.	Variable costs remain constant per unit.
Fixed cost	Total fixed cost is not affected by changes in the activity level within the relevant range.	Fixed costs decrease per unit as the activity level rises and increase per unit as the activity level falls.

FOCUS *on Current Practice*

On average, the variable cost of physically transporting a telephone call is about 7% of the price a customer pays for a call. It now costs more to bill for the call than to provide it. Then why aren't telephone companies fabulously profitable? In short, they have extremely high fixed costs for equipment, buildings, and personnel. The prices the telephone companies charge to consumers must cover these fixed costs as well as the relatively small variable costs of completing a particular call for a customer.

Source: Scott Wooley, "Meltdown," *Forbes*, July 3, 2000, pp. 70–71.

COST CLASSIFICATIONS FOR ASSIGNING COSTS TO COST OBJECTS

LEARNING OBJECTIVE 6
Distinguish between direct and indirect costs.

Costs are assigned to objects for a variety of purposes including pricing, profitability studies, and control of spending. A **cost object** is anything for which cost data are desired—including products, product lines, customers, jobs, and organizational subunits. For purposes of assigning costs to cost objects, costs are classified as either *direct* or *indirect.*

Cost object
Anything for which cost data are desired.

Direct cost
A cost that can easily and conveniently be traced to the particular cost object under consideration.

Direct Cost

A **direct cost** is a cost that can easily and conveniently be traced to the particular cost object under consideration. The concept of direct cost extends beyond just direct materials and direct labour. For example, if Reebok is assigning costs to its various regional and national sales offices, then the salary of the sales manager in its Tokyo office would be a direct cost of that office.

Indirect cost
A cost that cannot easily and conveniently be traced to the particular cost object under consideration.

Common cost
A common cost is a cost that is common to a number of costing objects but cannot be traced to them individually.

Indirect Cost

An **indirect cost** is a cost that cannot easily and conveniently be traced to the particular cost object under consideration. For example, a Moosehead Breweries factory may produce many varieties of beer. The factory manager's salary would be an indirect cost of a particular variety such as Dry. The reason is that the factory manager's salary is not caused by any one variety of beer but rather is incurred as a consequence of running the entire factory. *To be traced to a cost object such as a particular product, the cost must be caused by the cost object.* The factory manager's salary is called a *common cost* of producing the various products of the factory. A **common cost** is a cost that is common to a number of costing objects but cannot be traced to them individually. A common cost is a particular type of indirect cost.

A particular cost may be direct or indirect, depending on the cost object. While the Moosehead Breweries factory manager's salary is an *indirect* cost of manufacturing Dry beer, it is a *direct* cost of the manufacturing division. In the first case, the cost object is the brand of beer. In the second case, the cost object is the entire manufacturing division.

COST CLASSIFICATIONS FOR DECISION MAKING

LEARNING OBJECTIVE 7
Define and give examples of additional cost classifications used in making decisions: differential costs, opportunity costs, and sunk costs.

Costs are an important feature of many business decisions. In making decisions, it is essential to have a firm grasp of the concepts *differential cost, opportunity cost,* and *sunk cost.*

Differential Cost and Revenue

Decisions involve choosing among alternatives. In business decisions, each alternative will have certain costs and benefits that must be compared to the costs and benefits of the

Differential cost A difference in cost between any two alternatives.

Differential revenue The difference in revenue between any two alternatives.

Incremental cost An increase in cost between two alternatives.

other available alternatives. A difference in costs between any two alternatives is known as a **differential cost.** A difference in revenues between any two alternatives is known as **differential revenue.**

A differential cost is also known as an **incremental cost,** although technically an incremental cost should refer only to an increase in cost from one alternative to another; decreases in cost should be referred to as *decremental costs.* Differential cost is a broader term, encompassing both cost increases (incremental costs) and cost decreases (decremental costs) between alternatives.

The accountant's differential cost concept can be compared to the economist's marginal cost concept. In speaking of changes in cost and revenue, the economist employs the terms *marginal cost* and *marginal revenue.* The revenue that can be obtained from selling one more unit of product is called *marginal revenue*, and the cost involved in producing one more unit of product is called *marginal cost.* The economist's marginal concept is basically the same as the accountant's differential concept applied to a single unit of output.

Differential costs can be either fixed or variable. To illustrate, assume that Nature Way Cosmetics, Inc. is thinking about changing its marketing method from distribution through retailers to distribution by door-to-door direct sale. Present costs and revenues are compared to projected costs and revenues in the following table:

	Retailer Distribution (present)	Direct Sale Distribution (proposed)	Differential Costs and Revenues
Revenues (V)	$700,000	$800,000	$100,000
Cost of goods sold (V)	350,000	400,000	50,000
Advertising (F)	80,000	45,000	(35,000)
Commissions (V)	–0–	40,000	40,000
Warehouse depreciation (F)	50,000	80,000	30,000
Other expenses (F)	60,000	60,000	–0–
Total	540,000	625,000	85,000
Net income	$160,000	$175,000	$ 15,000

V = Variable; F = Fixed.

According to the preceding analysis, the differential revenue is $100,000 and the differential costs total $85,000, leaving a positive differential net income of $15,000 under the proposed marketing plan.

The decision of whether Nature Way Cosmetics should stay with the present retail distribution or switch to door-to-door direct selling could be made on the basis of the net incomes of the two alternatives. As we see in the preceding analysis, the net income under the present distribution method is $160,000, whereas the net income under door-to-door direct selling is estimated to be $175,000. Therefore, the door-to-door direct distribution method is preferred, since it would result in $15,000 higher net income. Note that we would have arrived at exactly the same conclusion by simply focusing on the differential revenues, differential costs, and differential net income, which also show a $15,000 advantage for the direct selling method.

In general, only the differences between alternatives are relevant in decisions. Those items that are the same under all alternatives and that are not affected by the decision can be ignored. For example, in the Nature Way Cosmetics example, the Other Expenses category, which is $60,000 under both alternatives, can be ignored, since it has no effect on the decision. If it was removed from the calculations, the door-to-door direct selling method would still be preferred by $15,000. This is an extremely important principle in management accounting that we will return to in later chapters.

FOCUS *on Current Practice*

In a recent annual report the Bank of Montreal Group of Companies announced the strategic emphasis on improving technology and access channels to enter new markets. To accomplish this, the bank announced agreements with The Great Atlantic and Pacific Tea Company of Canada and Canada Safeway Limited to open in-store branches. In addition, the bank installed 560 new InstaBank Extra printers for ABMs. These activities resulted in minor incremental costs and provided improved technology and new markets without the cost of new full-service branches.

Opportunity Cost

Opportunity cost is the potential benefit that is given up when one alternative is selected over another. To illustrate this important concept, consider the following examples:

Opportunity cost
The potential benefit that is given up when one alternative is selected over another.

Example 1

Vicki has a part-time job that pays her $100 per week while attending college. She would like to spend a week at the beach during spring break, and her employer has agreed to give her the time off, but without pay. The $100 in lost wages would be an opportunity cost of taking the week off to be at the beach.

Example 2

Suppose that the Bay is considering investing a large sum of money in land that may be a site for a future store. Rather than invest the funds in land, the company could invest the funds in high-grade securities. If the land is acquired, the opportunity cost will be the investment income that could have been realized if the securities had been purchased instead.

Example 3

Steve is employed with a company that pays him a salary of $30,000 per year. He is thinking about leaving the company and returning to school. Since returning to school would require that he give up his $30,000 salary, the forgone salary would be an opportunity cost of seeking further education.

Opportunity cost is not usually entered in the accounting records of an organization, but it is a cost that must be explicitly considered in every decision a manager makes. Virtually every alternative has some opportunity cost attached to it. In example 3 above, for instance, if Steve decides to stay at his job, there still is an opportunity cost involved: It is the higher income that could be realized in future years as a result of returning to school.

Sunk Cost

A **sunk cost** is a cost *that has already been incurred* and that cannot be changed by any decision made now or in the future. Since sunk costs cannot be changed by any decision, they are not differential costs. Therefore, they can and should be ignored when making a decision.

Sunk cost
Any cost that has already been incurred and that cannot be changed by any decision made now or in the future.

To illustrate a sunk cost, assume that a company paid $50,000 several years ago for a special-purpose machine. The machine was used to make a product that is now obsolete and is no longer being sold. Even though in hindsight the purchase of the machine may have been unwise, no amount of regret can undo that decision. And it would be folly to continue making the obsolete product in a misguided attempt to "recover" the original cost of the machine. In short, the $50,000 originally paid for the machine has already been incurred and cannot be a differential cost in any future decision. For this reason, such costs are said to be sunk and should be ignored in decisions.

SUMMARY

In this chapter, we have looked at some of the ways in which managers classify costs. How the costs will be used—for preparing external reports, predicting cost behaviour, assigning costs to cost objects, or decision making—will dictate how the costs will be classified.

For purposes of valuing inventories and determining expenses for the balance sheet and income statement, costs are classified as either product costs or period costs. Product costs are assigned to inventories and are considered assets until the products are sold. At the point of sale, product costs become cost of goods sold on the income statement. In contrast, following the usual accrual practices, period costs are taken directly to the income statement as expenses in the period in which they are incurred.

In a merchandising company, product cost is whatever the company paid for its merchandise. For external financial reports in a manufacturing company, product costs consist of all manufacturing costs. In both kinds of companies, selling and administrative costs are considered to be period costs and are expensed as incurred.

For purposes of predicting cost behaviour—how costs will react to changes in activity—managers commonly classify costs into two categories—variable and fixed. Variable costs, in total, are strictly proportional to activity. Thus, the variable cost per unit is constant. Fixed costs, in total, remain at the same level for changes in activity that occur within the relevant range. Thus, the average fixed cost per unit decreases as the number of units increases.

For purposes of assigning costs to cost objects such as products or departments, costs are classified as direct or indirect. Direct costs can conveniently be traced to the cost objects. Indirect costs cannot conveniently be traced to cost objects.

For purposes of making decisions, the concepts of differential costs and revenue, opportunity cost, and sunk cost are of vital importance. Differential cost and revenue are the cost and revenue items that differ between alternatives. Opportunity cost is the benefit that is forgone when one alternative is selected over another. Sunk cost is a cost that occurred in the past and cannot be altered. Differential cost and opportunity cost should be carefully considered in decisions. Sunk cost is always irrelevant in decisions and should be ignored.

These various cost classifications are *different* ways of looking at costs. A particular cost, such as the cost of cheese in a taco served at Taco Bell, could be a manufacturing cost, a product cost, a variable cost, a direct cost, and a differential cost—all at the same time.

Taco Bell can be perceived as a manufacturer of fast food. The cost of the cheese in a taco would be considered a manufacturing cost and, as such, it would also be a product cost. In addition, the cost of the cheese would be considered variable with respect to the number of tacos served and would be a direct cost of serving tacos. Finally, the cost of the cheese used would be a differential cost of making and serving the tacos.

REVIEW PROBLEM 1: COST TERMS

Many new cost terms have been introduced in this chapter. It will take you some time to learn what each term means and how to properly classify costs in an organization. To assist in this learning process, consider the following example: Porter Company manufactures furniture, including tables. Selected costs associated with the manufacture of the tables and the general operation of the company are given below:

1. The tables are made of wood that costs $100 per table.
2. The tables are assembled by workers, at a wage cost of $40 per table.
3. Workers assembling the tables are supervised by a factory supervisor who is paid $25,000 per year.
4. Electrical costs are $2 per machine-hour. Four machine-hours are required to produce a table.

5. The depreciation cost of the machines used to make the tables totals $10,000 per year.
6. The salary of the president of Porter Company is $100,000 per year.
7. Porter Company spends $250,000 per year to advertise its products.
8. Salespersons are paid a commission of $30 for each table sold.
9. Instead of producing the tables, Porter Company could rent its factory space out at a rental income of $50,000 per year.

In the following tabulation, these costs are classified according to various cost terms used in the chapter. *Carefully study the classification of each cost.* If you don't understand why a particular cost is classified the way it is, reread the section of the chapter discussing the particular cost term. The terms *variable cost* and *fixed cost* refer to how costs behave with respect to the number of tables produced in a year.

Solution to Review Problem 1

				Product Cost			To Units of Product			
	Variable Cost	Fixed Cost	Period (selling and administrative) Cost	Direct Materials	Direct Labour	Manufacturing Overhead	Direct	Indirect	Sunk Cost	Opportunity Cost
1. Wood used in a table ($100 per table)	X			X			X			
2. Labour cost to assemble a table ($40 per table) . . .	X				X		X			
3. Salary of the factory supervisor ($25,000 per year)		X				X		X		
4. Cost of electricity to produce tables ($2 per machine-hour)	X					X		X		
5. Depreciation of machines used to produce tables ($10,000 per year)		X				X		X	X*	
6. Salary of the company president ($100,000 per year)		X	X							
7. Advertising expense ($250,000 per year)		X	X							
8. Commissions paid to salespersons ($30 per table sold)	X		X							
9. Rental income forgone on factory space										X†

*This is a sunk cost, since the outlay for the equipment was made in a previous period.

†This is an opportunity cost, since it represents the potential benefit that is lost or sacrificed as a result of using the factory space to produce tables. Opportunity cost is a special category of cost that is not ordinarily recorded in an organization's accounting books. To avoid possible confusion with other costs, we will not attempt to classify this cost in any other way except as an opportunity cost.

REVIEW PROBLEM 2: SCHEDULE OF COST OF GOODS MANUFACTURED AND INCOME STATEMENT

The following information has been taken from the accounting records of Klear-Seal Company for last year:

Selling expenses	$ 140,000
Raw materials inventory, January 1	90,000
Raw materials inventory, December 31	60,000
Utilities, factory	36,000
Direct labour cost	150,000
Depreciation, factory	162,000
Purchases of raw materials	750,000
Sales	2,500,000
Insurance, factory	40,000
Supplies, factory	15,000
Administrative expenses	270,000
Indirect labour	300,000
Maintenance, factory	87,000
Work in process inventory, January 1	180,000
Work in process inventory, December 31	100,000
Finished goods inventory, January 1	260,000
Finished goods inventory, December 31	210,000

Management wants to organize these data into a better format so that financial statements can be prepared for the year.

Required:

1. Prepare a schedule of cost of goods manufactured as in Exhibit 2–3.
2. Compute the cost of goods sold.
3. Using data as needed from (1) and (2) above, prepare an income statement.

Solution to Review Problem 2

1.

KLEAR-SEAL COMPANY
Schedule of Cost of Goods Manufactured
For the Year Ended December 31

Direct materials:		
Raw materials inventory, January 1	$ 90,000	
Add: Purchases of raw materials	750,000	
Raw materials available for use	840,000	
Deduct: Raw materials inventory, December 31	60,000	
Raw materials used in production		$ 780,000
Direct labour		150,000
Manufacturing overhead:		
Utilities, factory	36,000	
Depreciation, factory	162,000	
Insurance, factory	40,000	
Supplies, factory	15,000	
Indirect labour	300,000	
Maintenance, factory	87,000	
Total overhead costs		640,000
Total manufacturing costs		1,570,000
Add: Work in process inventory, January 1		180,000
		1,750,000
Deduct: Work in process inventory, December 31		100,000
Cost of goods manufactured		$1,650,000

2. The cost of goods sold would be computed as follows:

Finished goods inventory, January 1	$ 260,000
Add: Cost of goods manufactured	1,650,000

Goods available for sale		1,910,000
Deduct: Finished goods inventory, December 31		210,000
Cost of goods sold		$1,700,000

3.

KLEAR-SEAL COMPANY
Income Statement
For the Year Ended December 31

Sales		$2,500,000
Less cost of goods sold (above)		1,700,000
Gross margin		800,000
Less selling and administrative expenses:		
Selling expenses	$ 140,000	
Administrative expenses	270,000	
Total expenses		410,000
Net income		$ 390,000

APPENDIX 2A: COST OF QUALITY

LEARNING OBJECTIVE 8
Identify the four types of quality costs and explain how they interact.

Companies that develop a reputation for low-quality products generally lose market share and face declining profits. It does not do much good to have a product with a high-quality design that is made with high-quality materials if the product falls apart on the first use due to poor assemlby. One very important aspect of quality is the absence of defects. Defective products result in high warranty costs, but more importantly, they result in dissatisfied customers. People who are dissatisfied with a product are unlikely to buy the product again. They are also likely to tell others about their bad experiences. One study found that customers who have bad experiences often tell several other people. This is the worst possible sort of advertising. To prevent such problems, companies have been expending a great deal of effort to reduce defects. The objective is to have high *quality of conformance*.

QUALITY OF CONFORMANCE

A product that meets or exceeds its design specifications and is free of defects that mar its appearance or degrade its performance is said to have high **quality of conformance**. Note that if an economy car is free of defects, it can have a quality of conformance that is just as high as a defect-free luxury car. The purchasers of economy cars cannot expect their cars to be as opulently equipped as luxury cars, but they can and do expect them to be free of defects.

Quality of conformance The degree to which a product or service meets or exceeds its design specifications and is free of defects or other problems that mar its appearance or degrade its performance.

Preventing, detecting, and dealing with defects cause costs that are called *quality costs* or the *cost of quality*. The use of the term *quality cost* is confusing to some people. It does not refer to costs such as using a higher-grade leather to make a wallet or using 14K gold instead of gold-plating in jewellery. Instead, the term **quality cost** refers to all of the costs that are incurred to prevent defects or that are incurred as a result of defects occurring.

Quality cost Costs that are incurred to prevent defective products from falling into the hands of customers or that are incurred as a result of defective units.

Quality costs can be broken down into four broad groups. Two of these groups—known as *prevention costs* and *appraisal costs*—are incurred in an effort to keep defective products from falling into the hands of customers. The other two groups of costs—known as *internal failure costs* and *external failure costs*—are incurred because defects are produced despite efforts to prevent them. Examples of specific costs involved in each of these four groups are given in Exhibit 2–10.

EXHIBIT 2–10 Typical Quality Costs

Prevention Costs	Internal Failure Costs
Systems development	Net cost of scrap
Quality engineering	Net cost of spoilage
Quality training	Rework labour and overhead
Quality circles	Reinspection of reworked products
Statistical process control activities	Retesting of reworked products
Supervision of prevention activities	Downtime caused by quality problems
Quality data gathering, analysis, and reporting	Disposal of defective products
Quality improvement projects	Analysis of the cause of defects in production
Technical support provided to suppliers	Re-entering data because of keying errors
Audits of the effectiveness of the quality system	Debugging software errors
Appraisal Costs	***External Failure Costs***
Test and inspection of incoming materials	Cost of field servicing and handling complaints
Test and inspection of in-process goods	Warranty repairs and replacements
Final product testing and inspection	Repairs and replacements beyond the warranty period
Supplies used in testing and inspection	Product recalls
Supervision of testing and inspection activities	Liability arising from defective products
Depreciation of test equipment	Returns and allowances arising from quality problems
Maintenance of test equipment	Lost sales arising from a reputation for poor quality
Plant utilities in the inspection area	
Field testing and appraisal at customer site	

Several things should be noted about the quality costs shown in the exhibit. First, note that quality costs do not relate to just manufacturing; rather, they relate to all of the activities in a company from initial research and development (R&D) through customer service. Second, note that the number of costs associated with quality is very large; therefore, total quality cost can be quite high unless management gives this area special attention. Finally, note how different the costs are in the four groupings. We will now look at each of these groupings more closely.

Prevention Costs

Prevention costs Costs that are incurred to keep defects from occurring.

Generally the most effective way to minimize quality costs while maintaining high-quality output is to avoid having quality problems arise in the first place. This is the purpose of **prevention costs**; such costs relate to any activity that reduces the number of defects in products or services. Companies have learned that it is much less costly to prevent a problem from ever happening than it is to find and correct the problem after it has occurred.

Quality circles Small groups of employees that meet on a regular basis to discuss ways of improving quality.

Note from Exhibit 2–10 that prevention costs include activities relating to quality circles and statistical process control. **Quality circles** consist of small groups of employees that meet on a regular basis to discuss ways to improve the quality of output. Both management and workers are included in these circles. Quality circles are widely used and can be found in manufacturing companies, utilities, health care organizations, banks, and many other organizations.

Statistical process control A charting technique used to monitor the quality of work being done at a workstation for the purpose of immediately correcting any problems.

Statistical process control is a technique that is used to detect whether a process is in or out of control. An out-of-control process results in defective units and may be caused by a miscalibrated machine or some other factor. In statistical process control, workers use charts to monitor the quality of units that pass through their workstations. Using these charts, workers can quickly spot processes that are out of control and that are creating defects. Problems can be immediately corrected and further defects prevented rather than waiting for an inspector to catch the defects later.

Note also from the list of prevention costs in Exhibit 2–10 that some companies provide technical support to their suppliers as a way of preventing defects. Particularly in just-in-time (JIT) systems, such support to suppliers is vital. In a JIT system, parts are delivered from suppliers just in time and in just the correct quantity to fill customer orders. There are no stockpiles of parts. If a defective part is received from a supplier, the part cannot be used and the order for the ultimate customer cannot be filled on time. Hence, every part received from a supplier must be free of defects. Consequently, companies that use JIT often require that their suppliers use sophisticated quality control programs such as statistical process control and that their suppliers certify that they will deliver parts and materials that are free of defects.

Appraisal Costs

Any defective parts and products should be caught as early as possible. **Appraisal costs**, which are sometimes called *inspection costs*, are incurred to identify defective products *before* the products are shipped to customers. Unfortunately, performing appraisal activities doesn't keep defects from happening again, and most managers now realize that maintaining an army of inspectors is a costly (and ineffective) approach to quality control.

Appraisal costs Costs that are incurred to identify defective products before the products are shipped to customers.

Professor John K. Shank of Dartmouth College has aptly stated, "The old-style approach was to say, 'We've got great quality. We have 40 quality control inspectors in the factory.' Then somebody realized that if you need 40 inspectors, it must be a lousy factory. So now the trick is to run a factory without any quality control inspectors; each employee is his or her own quality control person."[3]

Employees in both manufacturing and service functions are increasingly being asked to be responsible for their own quality control. This approach, along with designing products to be easy to manufacture properly, allows quality to be built into products rather than relying on inspection to get the defects out.

Internal Failure Costs

Failure costs are incurred when a product fails to conform to its design specifications. Failure costs can be either internal or external. **Internal failure costs** result from identification of defects during the appraisal process. Such costs include scrap, rejected products, reworking of defective units, and downtime caused by quality problems. It is crucial that defects be discovered before a product is shipped to customers. Of course, the more effective a company's appraisal activities, the greater the chance of catching defects internally and the greater the level of internal failure costs (as compared to external failure costs). Unfortunately, appraisal activities focus on symptoms rather than on causes and they do nothing to reduce the number of defective items. However, appraisal activities do bring defects to the attention of management, which may lead to efforts to increase prevention activities so that the defects do not happen.

Internal failure costs Costs that are incurred as a result of identifying defective products before they are shipped to customers.

External Failure Costs

External failure costs result when a defective product is delivered to a customer. As shown in Exhibit 2–10, external failure costs include warranty repairs and replacements, product recalls, liability arising from legal action against a company, and lost sales arising from a reputation for poor quality. Such costs can devastate profits.

External failure costs Costs that are incurred when a product or service that is defective is delivered to a customer.

In the past, some managers have taken the attitude, "Let's go ahead and ship everything to customers, and we'll take care of any problems under the warranty." This attitude generally results in high external failure costs, customer ill will, and declining market share and profits.

Recent history is replete with customer recalls, especially in the meat packing, automotive and pharmaceutical industries. For example, on October 22, 2002, Health Canada approved an urgent but voluntary vaccine recall. Aventis Pasteur Limited notified all customers who may have had a single dose of the vaccine Menomune®. There was a failure

3. Robert W. Casey, "The Changing World of the CEO," *PPM World* 24, no. 2, 1990, p. 31.

in the vaccine's stability testing in the United States for some lots indicating a potential for reduced protection from disease.

Distribution of Quality Costs

A company's total quality cost is likely to be very high unless management gives this area special attention. Studies show that quality costs for U.S. companies range between 10% and 20% of total sales, whereas experts say that these costs should be more in the 2% to 4% range. How does a company reduce its total quality cost? The answer lies in how the quality costs are distributed. Refer to the graph in Exhibit 2–11, which shows total quality costs as a function of the quality of conformance.

The graph shows that when the quality of conformance is low, total quality cost is high and that most of this cost consists of costs of internal and external failure. A low quality of conformance means that a high percentage of units are defective and hence the company must incur high failure costs. However, as a company spends more and more on prevention and appraisal, the percentage of defective units drops (the percentage of defect-free units increases). This results in lower costs of internal and external failure. Ordinarily, total quality cost drops rapidly as the quality of conformance increases. Thus, a company can reduce its total quality cost by focusing its efforts on prevention and appraisal. The cost savings from reduced defects usually swamp the costs of the additional prevention and appraisal efforts.

The graph in Exhibit 2–11 has been drawn so that the total quality cost is minimized when the quality of conformance is less than 100%. However, some experts and managers contend that the total quality cost is not minimized until the quality of conformance is 100% and there are no defects. Indeed, many companies have found that the total quality costs seem to keep dropping even when the quality of conformance approaches 100% and defect rates are as low as one in a million units. Others argue that eventually total quality cost increases as the quality of conformance increases. However, in most companies, this does not seem to happen until the quality of conformance is very close to 100% and defect rates are very close to zero.

As a company's quality program becomes more refined and as its failure costs begin to fall, prevention activities usually become more effective than appraisal activities. Appraisal can only find defects, whereas prevention can eliminate them. The best way to prevent defects from happening is to design processes that reduce the likelihood of defects and to continually monitor processes using statistical process control methods.

EXHIBIT 2–11 Effect of Quality Costs on Quality of Conformance

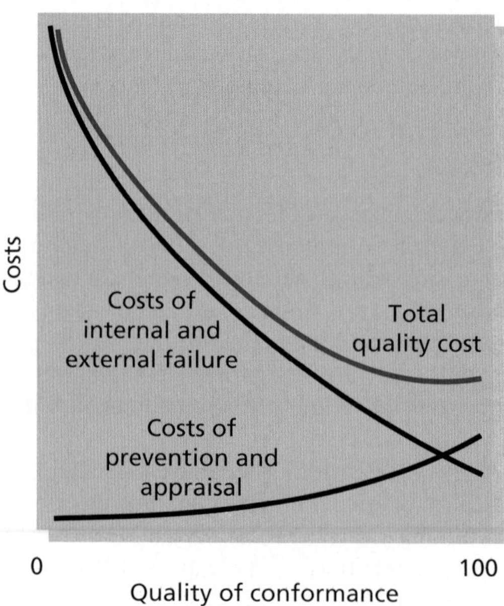

QUALITY COST REPORTS

LEARNING OBJECTIVE 9
Prepare and interpret a quality cost report.

As an initial step in quality improvement programs, companies often construct a *quality cost report* that provides an estimate of the financial consequences of the company's current level of defects. A **quality cost report** details the prevention costs, appraisal costs, and costs of internal and external failures that arise from the company's current level of defective products and services. Managers are often shocked by the magnitude of these costs. A typical quality cost report is shown in Exhibit 2-12.

Quality cost report A report that details prevention costs, appraisal costs, and the costs of internal and external failures.

Several things should be noted from the data in the exhibit. First, note that Ventura Company's quality costs are poorly distributed in both years, with most of the costs being traceable to either internal failure or external failure. The external failure costs are particularly high in year 1 in comparison to other costs.

Second, note that the company increased its spending on prevention and appraisal activities in year 2. As a result, internal failure costs go up in that year (from $2 million in year 1 to $3 million in year 2), but external failure costs drop sharply (from $5.15 million in year 1 to only $2 million in year 2). Because of the increase in appraisal activity in year 2, more defects are being caught inside the company before goods are shipped to

EXHIBIT 2–12 Quality Cost Report

VENTURA COMPANY
Quality Cost Report
For Years 1 and 2

	Year 2		Year 1	
	Amount	**Percent***	**Amount**	**Percent***
Prevention costs:				
Systems development	$ 400,000	0.80%	$ 270,000	0.54%
Quality training	210,000	0.42%	130,000	0.26%
Supervision of prevention activities	70,000	0.14%	40,000	0.08%
Quality improvement projects	320,000	0.64%	210,000	0.42%
Total	1,000,000	2.00%	650,000	1.30%
Appraisal costs:				
Inspection	600,000	1.20%	560,000	1.12%
Reliability testing	580,000	1.16%	420,000	0.84%
Supervision of testing and inspection	120,000	0.24%	80,000	0.16%
Depreciation of test equipment	200,000	0.40%	140,000	0.28%
Total	1,500,000	3.00%	1,200,000	2.40%
Internal failure costs:				
Net cost of scrap	900,000	1.80%	750,000	1.50%
Rework labour and overhead	1,430,000	2.86%	810,000	1.62%
Downtime due to defects in quality	170,000	0.34%	100,000	0.20%
Disposal of defective products	500,000	1.00%	340,000	0.68%
Total	3,000,000	6.00%	2,000,000	4.00%
External failure costs:				
Warranty repairs	400,000	0.80%	900,000	1.80%
Warranty replacements	870,000	1.74%	2,300,000	4.60%
Allowances	130,000	0.26%	630,000	1.26%
Cost of field servicing	600,000	1.20%	1,320,000	2.64%
Total	2,000,000	4.00%	5,150,000	10.30%
Total quality cost	$7,500,000	15.00%	$9,000,000	18.00%

*As a percentage of total sales. We assume that in each year sales totalled $50,000,000.

customers. This results in more cost for scrap, rework, and so forth, but saves huge amounts in warranty repairs, warranty replacements, and other external failure costs.

Third, note that as a result of greater emphasis on prevention and appraisal, *total* quality cost has decreased in year 2. As continued emphasis is placed on prevention and appraisal in future years, total quality cost should continue to decrease. That is, future increases in prevention and appraisal costs should be more than offset by decreases in failure costs. Moreover, appraisal costs should also decrease as more effort is put into prevention.

Quality Cost Reports in Graphic Form

As a supplement to the quality cost report shown in Exhibit 2–12, companies frequently prepare quality cost information in graphic form. Graphic presentations include pie charts, bar graphs, trend lines, and so forth. The data for Ventura Company from Exhibit 2–12 are presented in bar graph form in Exhibit 2–13.

The first bar graph in Exhibit 2–13 is scaled in terms of dollars of quality cost, and the second is scaled in terms of quality cost as a percentage of sales. In both graphs, the data are "stacked" upward. That is, appraisal costs are stacked on top of prevention costs, internal failure costs are stacked on top of the sum of prevention costs plus appraisal costs, and so forth. The percentage figures in the second graph show that total quality cost equals 18% of sales in year 1 and 15% of sales in year 2, the same as reported earlier in Exhibit 2–12.

Data in graphic form help managers to see trends more clearly and to see the magnitude of the various costs in relation to each other. Such graphs are easily prepared using computer graphics packages.

Uses of Quality Cost Information

The information provided by a quality cost report is used by managers in several ways. First, quality cost information helps managers see the financial significance of defects. Managers usually are not aware of the magnitude of their quality costs because these costs

EXHIBIT 2–13 Effect of Quality Costs on Quality of Conformance

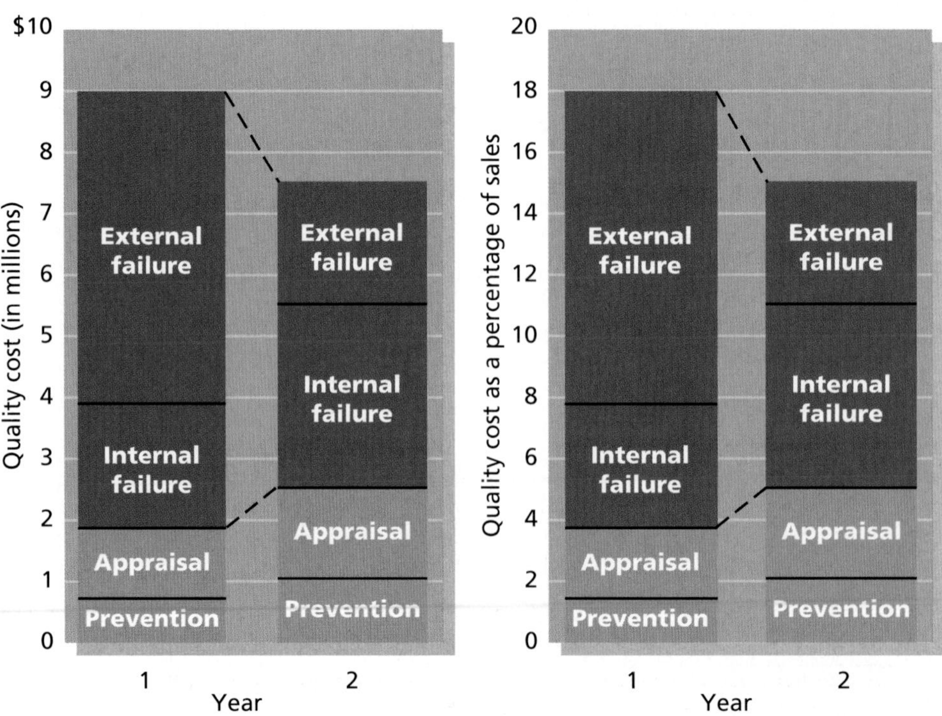

cut across departmental lines and are not normally tracked and accumulated by the cost system. Thus, when first presented with a quality cost report, managers often are surprised by the amount of cost attributable to poor quality.

Second, quality cost information helps managers identify the relative importance of the quality problems faced by the firm. For example, the quality cost report may show that scrap is a major quality problem or that the company is incurring huge warranty costs. With this information, managers have a better idea of where to focus efforts.

Third, quality cost information helps managers see whether their quality costs are poorly distributed. In general, quality costs should be distributed more toward prevention and appraisal activities and less toward failures.

Counterbalancing these uses, three limitations of quality cost information should be recognized. First, simply measuring and reporting quality costs does not solve quality problems. Problems can be solved only by taking action. Second, results usually lag behind quality improvement programs. Initially, total quality cost may even increase as quality control systems are designed and installed. Decreases in these costs may not begin to occur until the quality program has been in effect for a year or more. And third, the most important quality cost, lost sales arising from customer ill will, is usually omitted from the quality cost report because it is difficult to estimate.

Typically, during the initial years of a quality improvement program, the benefits of compiling a quality cost report outweigh the costs and limitations of the reports. As managers gain experience in balancing prevention and appraisal activities, the need for quality cost reports often diminishes.

INTERNATIONAL ASPECTS OF QUALITY

Many of the tools used in quality management today were developed in Japan after World War II. In statistical process control, Japanese companies borrowed heavily from the work of W. Edwards Deming. However, Japanese companies are largely responsible for quality circles, JIT, the idea that quality is everyone's responsibility, and the emphasis on prevention rather than on inspection.

In the 1980s, quality re-emerged as a pivotal factor in the market. Many companies now find that it is impossible to effectively compete without a very strong quality program in place. This is particularly true of companies that wish to compete in the European market.

The ISO 9000 Standards

The International Organization for Standardization (ISO), based in Geneva, Switzerland, has established quality control guidelines known as the **ISO 9000 standards**. Many companies and organizations in Europe will buy only from ISO 9000 standard-certified suppliers. This means that the suppliers must demonstrate to a certifying agency that:

ISO 9000 standards Quality control requirements issued by the International Standards Organization that relate to products sold in European countries.

1. A quality control system is in use, and the system clearly defines an expected level of quality.
2. The system is fully operational and is backed up with detailed documentation of quality control procedures.
3. The intended level of quality is being achieved on a sustained, consistent basis.

The key to receiving certification under the ISO 9000 standards is documentation. It is one thing for a company to say that it has a quality control system in operation, but it is quite a different thing to be able to document the steps in that system. Under ISO 9000, this documentation must be so detailed and precise that if all of the employees in a company were suddenly replaced, the new employees could use the documentation to make the product exactly as it was made by the former employees. Even companies with good quality control systems find that it takes up to two years of painstaking work to develop this detailed documentation. But companies often find that compiling this documentation results in improvements in their quality systems.

The ISO 9000 standards have become an international measure of quality. Although the standards were developed to control the quality of goods sold in European countries, they have become widely accepted elsewhere as well. Companies in North America that export to Europe often expect their own suppliers to comply with the ISO 9000 standards, since these exporters must document the quality of the materials going into their products as part of their own ISO 9000 certification.

The ISO 9000 international quality standard is usually associated with manufacturing firms. However, Industry Canada has issued a document called, "ISO 9000 for Service Companies" that shows how these standards apply also to service sectors such as health services, banking, consulting, the restaurant sector, and the public service. For example, ISO standards can be applied to developing better fire protection and police services.[4]

APPENDIX 2A SUMMARY

Defects cause costs, which can be classified as prevention costs, appraisal costs, internal failure costs, and external failure costs. Prevention costs are incurred to keep defects from happening. Appraisal costs are incurred to ensure that defective products, once made, are not shipped to customers. Internal failure costs are incurred as a consequence of detecting defective products before they are shipped to customers. External failure costs are the consequences (in terms of repairs, servicing, and lost future business) of delivering defective products to customers. Most experts agree that management effort should be focused on preventing defects. Small investments in prevention can lead to dramatic reductions in appraisal costs and costs of internal and external failure.

Quality costs are summarized on a quality cost report. This report shows the type of quality costs being incurred and their significance and trends. The report helps managers understand the importance of quality costs, spot problem areas, and assess the way in which the quality costs are distributed.

GLOSSARY

Visit the Online Learning Centre at http://www.mcgrawhill.ca/college/garrison/ for a review of glossary terms and definitions.

QUESTIONS

2–1 What are the three major elements of product costs in a manufacturing company?

2–2 Distinguish between the following: (a) direct materials, (b) indirect materials, (c) direct labour, (d) indirect labour, and (e) manufacturing overhead.

2–3 Explain the difference between a product cost and a period cost.

2–4 Describe how the income statement of a manufacturing company differs from the income statement of a merchandising company.

2–5 Of what value is the schedule of cost of goods manufactured? How does it tie into the income statement?

2–6 Describe how the inventory accounts of a manufacturing company differ from the inventory account of a merchandising company.

2–7 Why are product costs sometimes called inventoriable costs? Describe the flow of such costs in a manufacturing company from the point of incurrence until they finally become expenses on the income statement.

4. See the Industry Canada Web site at www.strategis.ic.ca.

2–8 Is it possible for costs such as salaries or depreciation to end up as assets on the balance sheet? Explain.

2–9 What is meant by the term *cost behaviour?*

2–10 "A variable cost is a cost that varies per unit of product, whereas a fixed cost is constant per unit of product." Do you agree? Explain.

2–11 How do fixed costs create difficulties in costing units of product?

2–12 Why is manufacturing overhead considered an indirect cost of a unit of product?

2–13 Define the following terms: differential cost, opportunity cost, and sunk cost.

2–14 Only variable costs can be differential costs. Do you agree? Explain.

2–15 (Appendix 2A) Mary Adams is employed by Acme Company. Last week she worked 34 hours assembling one of the company's products and was idle 6 hours due to material shortages. Acme's employees are engaged at their workstations for a normal 40-hour week. Ms. Adams is paid $15 per hour. Allocate her earnings between direct labour cost and manufacturing overhead cost.

2–16 John Olsen operates a stamping machine on the assembly line of Drake Manufacturing Company. Last week Mr. Olsen worked 45 hours. His basic wage rate is $14 per hour, with time and a half for overtime (time worked in excess of 40 hours per week). Allocate Mr. Olsen's wages for the week between direct labour cost and manufacturing overhead cost.

2–17 (Appendix 2A) Costs associated with the quality of conformance can be broken down into four broad groups. What are these four groups and how do they differ?

2–18 (Appendix 2A) In their efforts to reduce the total cost of quality, should companies generally focus on decreasing prevention costs and appraisal costs?

2–19 (Appendix 2A) What is probably the most effective way to reduce a company's total quality costs?

2–20 (Appendix 2A) What are the main uses of quality cost reports?

2–21 (Appendix 2A) Why are managers often unaware of the magnitude of quality costs?

EXERCISES

EXERCISE 2–1 Classifying Manufacturing Costs [LO1]

The PC Works assembles custom computers from components supplied by various manufacturers. The company is very small and its assembly shop and retail sales store are housed in a single facility in a Waterloo industrial park. Listed below are some of the costs that are incurred at the company.

Required:

For each cost, indicate whether it would most likely be classified as direct labour, direct materials, manufacturing overhead, marketing and selling, or an administrative cost.

1. The cost of a hard drive installed in a computer.
2. The cost of advertising in the *Puget Sound Computer User* newspaper.
3. The wages of employees who assemble computers from components.
4. Sales commissions paid to the company's salespeople.
5. The wages of the assembly shop's supervisor.
6. The wages of the company's accountant.
7. Depreciation on equipment used to test assembled computers before release to customers.
8. Rent on the facility in the industrial park.

EXERCISE 2–2 Classification of Costs as Period or Product Cost [LO2]

A product cost is also known as an inventoriable cost. Classify the following costs as either product (inventoriable) costs or period (noninventoriable) costs in a manufacturing company:

1. Depreciation on salespersons' cars.
2. Rent on equipment used in the factory.
3. Lubricants used for maintenance of machines.
4. Salaries of finished goods warehouse personnel.
5. Soap and paper towels used by factory workers at the end of a shift.
6. Factory supervisors' salaries.
7. Heat, water, and power consumed in the factory.
8. Materials used for boxing products for shipment overseas. (Units are not normally boxed.)
9. Advertising costs.

10. Workers' compensation insurance on factory employees.
11. Depreciation on chairs and tables in the factory lunchroom.
12. The wages of the receptionist in the administrative offices.
13. Lease cost of the corporate jet used by the company's executives.
14. Rent on rooms at a British Columbia resort for holding of the annual sales conference.
15. Attractively designed box for packaging the company's product—breakfast cereal.

EXERCISE 2–3 Constructing an Income Statement [LO3]

Last month CyberGames, a computer game retailer, had total sales of $1,450,000, selling expenses of $210,000, and administrative expenses of $180,000. The company had beginning merchandise inventory of $240,000, purchased additional merchandise inventory for $950,000, and had ending merchandise inventory of $170,000.

Required:

Prepare an income statement for the company for the month.

EXERCISE 2–4 Prepare a Schedule of Cost of Goods Manufactured [LO4]

Lompac Products manufactures a variety of products in its factory. Data for the most recent month's operations appear below:

Beginning raw materials inventory	$ 60,000
Purchases of raw materials	$690,000
Ending raw materials inventory	$ 45,000
Direct labour	$135,000
Manufacturing overhead	$370,000
Beginning work in process inventory	$120,000
Ending work in process inventory	$130,000

Required:

Prepare a schedule of cost of goods manufactured for the company for the month.

EXERCISE 2–5 Classification of Costs as Fixed or Variable [LO5]

Below are a number of costs that are incurred in a variety of organizations.

Required:

Classify each cost as being variable or fixed with respect to the number of units of product or services provided by the organization by placing an *X* in the appropriate column.

	Cost Behaviour	
Cost Item	Variable	Fixed
1. X-ray film used in the radiology lab at a private clinic.		
2. The costs of advertising a Madonna rock concert in Toronto.		
3. Rental cost of a McDonald's restaurant building in Hong Kong.		
4. The electrical costs of running a roller coaster at Magic Mountain.		
5. Property taxes on your local cinema.		
6. Commissions paid to salespersons at Nortel.		
7. Property insurance on a Coca-Cola bottling plant.		
8. The costs of synthetic materials used to make Nike running shoes.		
9. The costs of shipping Panasonic televisions to retail stores.		
10. The cost of leasing an ultra-scan diagnostic machine at the Hospital for Sick Children.		

EXERCISE 2–6 Identifying Direct and Indirect Costs [LO6]

Northwest Clinic provides a full range of emergency room care to outpatient clinics.

Required:

For each cost incurred at Northwest clinic, indicate whether it would most likely be a direct cost or an indirect cost of the specified cost object by placing an *X* in the appropriate column.

Cost	Cost object	Direct Cost	Indirect Cost
Ex. Catered food served to patients	A particular patient	X	
1. The wages of pediatric nurses	The pediatric department		
2. Prescription drugs	A particular patient		
3. Heating the hospital	The pediatric department		
4. The salary of the head of pediatrics	The pediatric department		
5. The salary of the head of pediatrics	A particular pediatric patient		
6. Hospital chaplain's salary	A particular patient		
7. Lab tests by outside contractor	A particular patient		
8. Lab tests by outside contractor	A particular department		

EXERCISE 2–7 Differential, Opportunity, and Sunk Costs [LO7]

Northwest Clinic provides a full range of emergency room care to outpatient clinics. The clinic's Radiology Department is considering replacing an old inefficient X-ray machine with a state-of-the-art digital X-ray machine. The new machine would provide higher quality X-rays in less time and at a lower cost per X-ray. It would also require less power and would use a colour laser printer to produce easily readable X-ray images. Instead of investing the funds in the new X-ray machine, the Laboratory Department is lobbying the hospital's management to buy a new DNA analyzer.

Required:

For each of the items below, indicate by placing an *X* in the appropriate column whether it should be considered a differential cost, an opportunity cost, or a sunk cost in the decision to replace the old X-ray machine with a new machine. If none of the categories apply for a particular item, leave all columns blank.

Item	Differential Cost	Opportunity Cost	Sunk Cost
Ex. Cost of X-ray film used in the old machine	X		
1. Cost of the old X-ray machine			
2. The salary of the head of the Radiology Department . . .			
3. The salary of the head of the Pediatrics Department . . .			
4. Cost of the new colour laser printer			
5. Rent on the space occupied by Radiology			
6. The cost of maintaining the old machine			
7. Benefits from a new DNA analyzer			
8. Cost of electricity to run the X-ray machines			

EXERCISE 2–8 Classification of Overtime Cost [LO1]

Several days ago you took your TV set into a shop to have some repair work done. When you later picked up the set, the bill showed a $75 charge for labour. This charge represented two hours of service time—$30 for the first hour and $45 for the second.

When questioned about the difference in hourly rates, the shop manager explained that work on your set was started at 4 o'clock in the afternoon. By the time work was completed two hours later at 6 o'clock, an hour of overtime had been put in by the repair technician. The second hour therefore contained a charge for an "overtime premium," since the company had to pay the repair technician time and a half for any work in excess of eight hours per day. The shop manager further explained that the shop was working overtime to "catch up a little" on its backlog of repairs, but it still needed to maintain a "decent" profit margin on the technicians' time.

Required:

1. Do you agree with the shop's computation of the service charge on your job?
2. Assume that the shop pays its technicians $14 per hour for the first eight hours worked in a day and $21 per hour for any additional time worked in a day. Prepare computations to show how the cost of the repair technician's time for the day (nine hours) should be allocated between direct labour cost and general overhead cost on the shop's books.
3. Under what circumstances might the shop be justified in charging an overtime premium for repair work on your set?

EXERCISE 2–9 (Appendix 2A) Classification of Quality Costs [LO8]

Listed below are a number of costs that are incurred in connection with a company's quality control system.

a. Product testing.
b. Product recalls.
c. Rework labour and overhead.
d. Quality circles.
e. Downtime caused by defects.
f. Cost of field servicing.
g. Inspection of goods.
h. Quality engineering.
i. Warranty repairs.
j. Statistical process control.
k. Net cost of scrap.
l. Depreciation of test equipment.
m. Returns and allowances arising from poor quality.
n. Disposal of defective products.
o. Technical support to suppliers.
p. Systems development.
q. Warranty replacements.
r. Field testing at customer site.
s. Product design.

Required:

1. Classify each of the costs above into one of the following categories: prevention cost, appraisal cost, internal failure cost, or external failure cost.
2. Which of the costs in (1) above are incurred in an effort to keep poor quality of conformance from occurring? Which of the costs in (1) above are incurred because poor quality of conformance has occurred?

EXERCISE 2–10 Preparation of Schedule of Costs of Goods Manufactured and Cost of Goods Sold [LO1, LO3, LO4]

The following cost and inventory data are taken from the accounting records of Mason Company for the year just completed:

Costs incurred:	
Direct labour cost	$70,000
Purchases of raw materials	$118,000
Indirect labour	$30,000
Maintenance, factory equipment	$6,000
Advertising expense	$90,000
Insurance, factory equipment	$800
Sales salaries	$50,000
Rent, factory facilities	$20,000
Supplies	$4,200
Depreciation, office equipment	$3,000
Depreciation, factory equipment	$19,000

	Beginning of the Year	End of the Year
Inventories:		
Raw materials	$7,000	$15,000
Work in process	$10,000	$5,000
Finished goods	$20,000	$35,000

Required:

1. Prepare a schedule of cost of goods manufactured in good form.
2. Prepare the cost of goods sold section of Mason Company's income statement for the year.

EXERCISE 2–11 Classification of Costs as Variable or Fixed and as Selling and Administrative or Product [LO2, LO5]

Below are listed various costs that are found in organizations.

1. Hamburger buns in a Wendy's outlet.
2. Advertising by a dental office.
3. Apples processed and canned by Del Monte.
4. Shipping canned apples from a Del Monte plant to customers.
5. Insurance on a Bausch & Lomb factory producing contact lenses.
6. Insurance on IBM's corporate headquarters.
7. Salary of a supervisor overseeing production of printers at Hewlett-Packard.

8. Commissions paid to Encyclopedia Britannica salespersons.
9. Depreciation of factory lunchroom facilities at a General Electric plant.
10. Steering wheels installed in BMWs.

Required:
Classify each cost as being either variable or fixed with respect to the number of units produced and sold. Also classify each cost as either a selling and administrative cost or a product cost. Prepare your answer sheet as shown below. Place an *X* in the appropriate columns to show the proper classification of each cost.

	Cost Behaviour		Selling and Administrative	Product
Cost Item	Variable	Fixed	Cost	Cost

EXERCISE 2–12 Product Cost Flows; Product versus Period Costs [LO2, LO3]
The Devon Motor Company produces motorcycles. During April, the company purchased 8,000 batteries at a cost of $10 per battery. Devon withdrew 7,600 batteries from the storeroom during the month. Of these, 100 were used to replace batteries in motorcycles used by the company's travelling sales staff. The remaining 7,500 batteries withdrawn from the storeroom were placed in motorcycles being produced by the company. Of the motorcycles in production during April, 90% were completed and transferred from work in process to finished goods. Of the motorcycles completed during the month, 30% were unsold at April 30.

There were no inventories of any type on April 1.

Required:
1. Determine the cost of batteries that would appear in each of the following accounts at April 30:
   a. Raw Materials.
   b. Work in Process.
   c. Finished Goods.
   d. Cost of Goods Sold.
   e. Selling Expense.
2. Specify whether each of the above accounts would appear on the balance sheet or on the income statement at April 30.

EXERCISE 2–13 Classification of Labour Costs [LO1]

Paul Clark is employed by Aerotech Products and assembles a component part for one of the company's product lines. He is paid $14 per hour for regular time and time and a half (i.e., $21 per hour) for all work in excess of 40 hours per week.

Required:
1. Assume that during a given week Paul is idle for five hours due to machine breakdowns and that he is idle for four more hours due to material shortages. No overtime is recorded for the week. Allocate Paul's wages for the week between direct labour cost and manufacturing overhead cost.
2. Assume that during the following week Paul works a total of 48 hours. He has no idle time for the week. Allocate Paul's wages for the week between direct labour cost and manufacturing overhead cost.
3. Paul's company provides an attractive package of employee benefits for its employees. This package includes a retirement program and a health insurance program. Explain two ways that the company could handle the costs of its direct labourers' employee benefits in its cost records.

PROBLEMS

PROBLEM 2–14 Classification of Costs [LO1, LO2, LO5, LO7]
Wollongong Group Ltd. of New South Wales, Australia, acquired its factory building about 10 years ago. For several years the company has rented out a small annex attached to the rear of the building. The company has received a rental income of $30,000 per year on this space. The renter's lease will expire soon, and rather than renewing the lease, the company has decided to use the space itself to manufacture a new product.

Direct materials cost for the new product will total $80 per unit. To have a place to store finished units of product, the company will rent a small warehouse nearby. The rental cost will be

$500 per month. In addition, the company must rent equipment for use in producing the new product; the rental cost will be $4,000 per month. Workers will be hired to manufacture the new product, with direct labour cost amounting to $60 per unit. The space in the annex will continue to be depreciated on a straight-line basis, as in prior years. This depreciation is $8,000 per year.

Advertising costs for the new product will total $50,000 per year. A supervisor will be hired to oversee production; her salary will be $1,500 per month. Electricity for operating machines will be $1.20 per unit. Costs of shipping the new product to customers will be $9 per unit.

To provide funds to purchase materials, meet payrolls, and so forth, the company will have to liquidate some temporary investments. These investments are presently yielding a return of about $3,000 per year.

Required:

Prepare an answer sheet with the following column headings:

Name of the Cost	Variable Cost	Fixed Cost	Product Cost: Direct Materials	Product Cost: Direct Labour	Product Cost: Manufacturing Overhead	Period (selling and administrative) Cost	Opportunity Cost	Sunk Cost

List the different costs associated with the new product decision down the extreme left column (under Name of the Cost). Then place an *X* under each heading that helps to describe the type of cost involved. There may be *X*'s under several column headings for a single cost. (For example, a cost may be a fixed cost, a period cost, and a sunk cost; you would place an *X* under each of these column headings opposite the cost.)

PROBLEM 2–15 Cost Classification [LO2, LO5, LO6]

Listed below are a number of costs typically found in organizations.

1. Property taxes, factory.
2. Boxes used for packaging detergent produced by the company.
3. Salespersons' commissions.
4. Supervisor's salary, factory.
5. Depreciation, executive autos.
6. Wages of workers assembling computers.
7. Insurance, finished goods warehouses.
8. Lubricants for machines.
9. Advertising costs.
10. Microchips used in producing calculators.
11. Shipping costs on merchandise sold.
12. Magazine subscriptions, factory lunchroom.
13. Thread in a garment factory.
14. Billing costs.
15. Executive life insurance.
16. Ink used in textbook production.
17. Employee benefits, assembly-line workers.
18. Yarn used in sweater production.
19. Wages of receptionist, executive offices.

Required:

Prepare an answer sheet with column headings as shown below. For each cost item, indicate whether it would be variable or fixed with respect to the number of units produced and sold; and then whether it would be a selling cost, an administrative cost, or a manufacturing cost. If it is a manufacturing cost, indicate whether it would typically be treated as a direct cost or an indirect cost with respect to units of product. Three sample answers are provided for illustration.

Cost Item	Variable or Fixed	Selling Cost	Administrative Cost	Manufacturing (Product) Cost: Direct	Manufacturing (Product) Cost: Indirect
Direct labour	V			X	
Executive salaries	F		X		
Factory rent	F				X

PROBLEM 2–16 Cost Classification [LO5, LO6]

Various costs associated with the operation of factories are given below:

1. Electricity used in operating machines.
2. Rent on a factory building.
3. Cloth used in drapery production.
4. Production superintendent's salary.
5. Wages of labourers assembling a product.
6. Depreciation of air purification equipment used in furniture production.
7. Janitorial salaries.
8. Peaches used in canning fruit.
9. Lubricants needed for machines.
10. Sugar used in soft-drink production.
11. Property taxes on the factory.
12. Wages of workers painting a product.
13. Depreciation on cafeteria equipment.
14. Insurance on a building used in producing helicopters.
15. Cost of rotor blades used in producing helicopters.

Required:

Classify each cost as either variable or fixed with respect to the number of units produced and sold. Also indicate whether each cost would typically be treated as a direct cost or an indirect cost with respect to units of product. Prepare your answer sheet as shown below:

	Cost Behaviour		To Units of Product	
Cost Item	Variable	Fixed	Direct	Indirect
Example: Factory insurance		X		X

PROBLEM 2–17 Allocating Labour Costs [LO1]

Mark Hansen is employed by Eastern Products, Inc., and works on the company's assembly line. Mark's basic wage rate is $20 per hour. The company's union contract states that employees are to be paid time and a half (i.e., $30 per hour) for any work in excess of 40 hours per week.

Required:

1. Suppose that in a given week Mark works 46 hours. Compute Mark's total wages for the week. How much of this amount would be allocated to direct labour cost? To manufacturing overhead cost?
2. Suppose in another week that Mark works 48 hours but is idle for 3 hours during the week due to machine breakdowns. Compute Mark's total wages for the week. How much of this amount would be allocated to direct labour cost? To manufacturing overhead cost?
3. Eastern Products, Inc., has an attractive package of employee benefits that costs the company $6 for each hour of employee time (either regular time or overtime). During a particular week, Mark works 50 hours but is idle for 2 hours due to material shortages. Compute Mark's total wages and employee benefits for the week. If the company treats all employee benefits as part of manufacturing overhead cost, how much of Mark's wages and employee benefits for the week would be allocated to direct labour cost? To manufacturing overhead cost?
4. Refer to the data in (3) above. If the company treats that part of fringe benefits relating to direct labour as added direct labour cost, how much of Mark's wages and employee benefits for the week will be allocated to direct labour cost? To manufacturing overhead cost?

PROBLEM 2–18 (Appendix 2A) Quality Cost Report [LO8, LO9]

In response to intensive foreign competition, the management of Florex Company has attempted over the past year to improve the quality of its products. A statistical process control system has been installed and other steps have been taken to decrease the amount of warranty and other field costs, which have been trending upward over the past several years. Costs relating to quality and quality control over the last two years are given at the top of the following page.

Sales have been flat over the past few years, at $75,000,000 per year. A great deal of money has been spent in the effort to upgrade quality, and management is anxious to see whether or not the effort has been effective.

	Costs (in thousands)	
	This Year	Last Year
Inspection	$900	$750
Quality engineering	$570	$420
Depreciation of test equipment	$240	$210
Rework labour	$1,500	$1,050
Statistical process control	$180	$0
Cost of field servicing	$900	$1,200
Supplies used in testing	$60	$30
Systems development	$750	$480
Warranty repairs	$1,050	$3,600
Net cost of scrap	$1,125	$630
Product testing	$1,200	$810
Product recalls	$750	$2,100
Disposal of defective products	$975	$720

Required:

1. Prepare a quality cost report that contains data for both this year and last year. Carry percentage computations to two decimal places.
2. Prepare a bar graph showing the distribution of the various quality costs by category.
3. Prepare a written evaluation to accompany the reports you have prepared in (1) and (2) above. This evaluation should discuss the distribution of quality costs in the company, changes in this distribution that you see taking place, the reasons for changes in costs in the various categories, and any other information that would be of value to management.

PROBLEM 2–19 Classification of Various Costs [LO1, LO2, LO5, LO7]

Staci Valek began dabbling in pottery several years ago as a hobby. Her work is quite creative, and it has been so popular with friends and others that she has decided to quit her job with an aerospace firm and manufacture pottery full time. The salary from Staci's aerospace job is $3,800 per month.

Staci will rent a small building near her home to use as a place for manufacturing the pottery. The rent will be $500 per month. She estimates that the cost of clay and glaze will be $2 for each finished piece of pottery. She will hire workers to produce the pottery at a labour rate of $8 per pot. To sell her pots, Staci feels that she must advertise heavily in the local area. An advertising agency states that it will handle all advertising for a fee of $600 per month. Staci's brother will sell the pots; he will be paid a commission of $4 for each pot sold. Equipment needed to manufacture the pots will be rented at a cost of $300 per month.

Staci has already paid the legal and filing fees associated with incorporating her business. These fees amounted to $500. A small room has been located in a tourist area that Staci will use as a sales office. The rent will be $250 per month. A phone installed in the room for taking orders will cost $40 per month. In addition, a recording device will be attached to the phone for taking after-hours messages.

Staci has some money in savings that is earning interest of $1,200 per year. These savings will be withdrawn and used to get the business going. For the time being, Staci does not intend to draw any salary from the new company.

Required:

1. Prepare an answer sheet with the following column headings:

Name of the Cost	Variable Cost	Fixed Cost	Product Cost: Direct Materials	Product Cost: Direct Labour	Product Cost: Manufacturing Overhead	Period (selling and administrative) Cost	Opportunity Cost	Sunk Cost

List the different costs associated with the new company down the extreme left column (under Name of Cost). Then place an *X* under each heading that helps to describe the type of cost involved. There may be *X*'s under several column headings for a single cost. (That is, a cost may be a fixed cost, a period cost, and a sunk cost; you would place an *X* under each of these column headings opposite the cost.)

Under the Variable Cost column, list only those costs that would be variable with respect to the number of units of pottery that are produced and sold.

2. All of the costs you have listed above, except one, would be differential costs between the alternatives of Staci producing pottery or staying with the aerospace firm. Which cost is *not* differential? Explain.

PROBLEM 2–20 Classification of Salary Cost as a Period or Product Cost [LO2]

You have just been hired by Ogden Company to fill a new position that was created in response to rapid growth in sales. It is your responsibility to coordinate shipments of finished goods from the factory to distribution warehouses located in various parts of Canada so that goods will be available as orders are received from customers.

The company is unsure how to classify your annual salary in its cost records. The company's cost analyst says that your salary should be classified as a manufacturing (product) cost; the controller says that it should be classified as a selling expense; and the president says that it doesn't matter which way your salary cost is classified.

Required:

1. Which viewpoint is correct? Why?
2. From the point of view of the reported net operating income for the year, is the president correct in his statement that it doesn't matter which way your salary cost is classified? Explain.

PROBLEM 2–21 Variable and Fixed Costs; Subtleties of Direct and Indirect Costs [LO5, LO6]

Madison Seniors Care Centre is a non-profit organization that provides a variety of health services to the elderly. The centre is organized into a number of departments, one of which is the meals-on-wheels program that delivers hot meals to seniors in their homes on a daily basis. Below are listed a number of costs of the centre and the meals-on-wheels program.

example The cost of groceries used in meal preparation.

a. The cost of leasing the meals-on-wheels van.
b. The cost of incidental supplies such as salt, pepper, napkins, and so on.
c. The cost of gasoline consumed by the meals-on-wheels van.
d. The rent on the facility that houses Madison Seniors Care Centre, including the meals-on-wheels program.
e. The salary of the part-time manager of the meals-on-wheels program.
f. Depreciation on the kitchen equipment used in the meals-on-wheels program.
g. The hourly wages of the caregiver who drives the van and delivers the meals.
h. The costs of complying with health safety regulations in the kitchen.
i. The costs of mailing letters soliciting donations to the meals-on-wheels program.

Required:

For each cost listed above, indicate whether it is a direct or indirect cost of the meals-on-wheels program, whether it is a direct or indirect cost of particular seniors served by the program, and whether it is variable or fixed with respect to the number of seniors served. Use the below form for your answer.

		Direct or Indirect Cost of the Meals-on-Wheels Program		Direct or Indirect Cost of Particular Seniors Served by the Meals-on-Wheels Program		Variable or Fixed with Respect to the Number of Seniors Served by the Meals-on-Wheels Program	
Item	Description	Direct	Indirect	Direct	Indirect	Variable	Fixed
example	The cost of groceries used in meal preparation	X		X		X	

PROBLEM 2–22 (Appendix 2A) Analyzing a Quality Cost Report [LO9]

Mercury, Inc., produces pagers at its plant in Ontario. In recent years, the company's market share has been eroded by stiff competition from overseas. Price and product quality are the two key areas in which companies compete in this market.

A year ago, the company's pagers had been ranked low in product quality in a consumer survey. Shocked by this result, Jorge Gomez, Mercury's president, initiated a crash effort to improve product quality. Gomez set up a task force to implement a formal quality improvement program. Included on this task force were representatives from the Engineering, Marketing, Customer Service, Production, and Accounting departments. The broad representation was needed because Gomez believed that this was a companywide program and that all employees should share the responsibility for its success.

After the first meeting of the task force, Holly Elsoe, manager of the Marketing Department, asked John Tran, production manager, what he thought of the proposed program. Tran replied, "I have reservations. Quality is too abstract to be attaching costs to it and then to be holding you and me responsible for cost improvements. I like to work with goals that I can see and count! I'm nervous about having my annual bonus based on a decrease in quality costs; there are too many variables that we have no control over."

Mercury's quality improvement program has now been in operation for one year. The company's most recent quality cost report is shown below.

MERCURY, INC.
Quality Cost Report
(in thousands)

	This Year	Last Year
Prevention costs:		
Machine maintenance	$ 120	$ 70
Training suppliers	10	0
Quality circles	20	0
Total prevention costs	150	70
Appraisal costs:		
Incoming inspection	40	20
Final testing	90	80
Total appraisal costs	130	100
Internal failure costs:		
Rework	130	50
Scrap	70	40
Total internal failure costs	200	90
External failure costs:		
Warranty repairs	30	90
Customer returns	80	320
Total external failure costs	110	410
Total quality cost	$ 590	$ 670
Total production cost	$4,800	$4,200

As they were reviewing the report, Elsoe asked Tran what he now thought of the quality improvement program. Tran replied. "I'm relieved that the new quality improvement program hasn't hurt our bonuses, but the program has increased the workload in the Production Department. It is true that customer returns are way down, but the pagers that were returned by customers to retail outlets were rarely sent back to us for rework."

Required:

1. Expand the company's quality cost report by showing the costs in both years as percentages of both total production cost and total quality cost. Carry all computations to one decimal place. By analyzing the report, determine if Mercury, Inc.'s quality improvement program has been successful. *List specific evidence to support your answer.*
2. Do you expect the improvement program as it progresses to continue to increase the workload in the Production Department?
3. Jorge Gomez believed that the quality improvement program was essential and that Mercury, Inc., could no longer afford to ignore the importance of product quality. Discuss how Mercury, Inc., could measure the cost of *not* implementing the quality improvement program.

(CMA, adapted)

PROBLEM 2–23 Ethics and the Manager [LO2]

M. K. Gallant is president of Kranbrack Corporation, a company whose stock is traded on a national exchange. In a meeting with investment analysts at the beginning of the year, Gallant had predicted that the company's earnings would grow by 20% this year. Unfortunately, sales have been less than expected for the year, and Gallant concluded within two weeks of the end of the fiscal year that it would be impossible to ultimately report an increase in earnings as large as predicted unless some drastic action was taken. Accordingly, Gallant has ordered that wherever possible, expenditures should be postponed to the new year—including cancelling or postponing orders with suppliers, delaying planned maintenance and training, and cutting back on end-of-year advertising and travel. Additionally, Gallant ordered the company's controller to carefully scrutinize all costs that are currently classified as period costs and reclassify as many as possible as product costs. The company is expected to have substantial inventories of work in process and finished goods at the end of the year.

Required:

1. Why would reclassifying period costs as product costs increase this period's reported earnings?
2. Do you believe Gallant's actions are ethical? Why or why not?

PROBLEM 2–24 Schedule of Cost of Goods Manufactured; Income Statement; Cost Behaviour [LO1, LO2, LO3, LO4, LO5]

Various cost and sales data for Meriwell Company for the just completed year appear in the worksheet below:

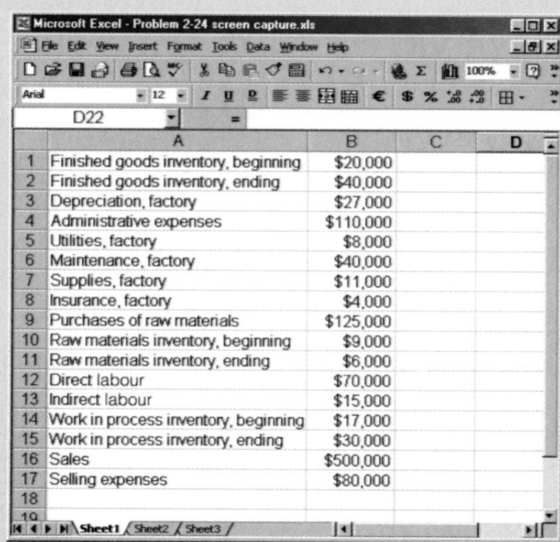

	A	B
1	Finished goods inventory, beginning	$20,000
2	Finished goods inventory, ending	$40,000
3	Depreciation, factory	$27,000
4	Administrative expenses	$110,000
5	Utilities, factory	$8,000
6	Maintenance, factory	$40,000
7	Supplies, factory	$11,000
8	Insurance, factory	$4,000
9	Purchases of raw materials	$125,000
10	Raw materials inventory, beginning	$9,000
11	Raw materials inventory, ending	$6,000
12	Direct labour	$70,000
13	Indirect labour	$15,000
14	Work in process inventory, beginning	$17,000
15	Work in process inventory, ending	$30,000
16	Sales	$500,000
17	Selling expenses	$80,000

Required:

1. Prepare a schedule of cost of goods manufactured.
2. Prepare an income statement.
3. Assume that the company produced the equivalent of 10,000 units of product during the year just completed. What was the average cost per unit for direct materials? What was the average cost per unit for factory depreciation?
4. Assume that the company expects to produce 15,000 units of product during the coming year. What average cost per unit and what total cost would you expect the company to incur for direct materials at this level of activity? For factory depreciation? (In preparing your answer, assume that direct materials is a variable cost and that depreciation is a fixed cost; also assume that depreciation is computed on a straight-line basis.)
5. As the manager responsible for production costs, explain to the president any difference in the average costs per unit between (3) and (4) above.

PROBLEM 2–25 Cost Classification and Cost Behaviour [LO2, LO5, LO6]

The Dorilane Company specializes in producing a set of wood patio furniture consisting of a table and four chairs. The set enjoys great popularity, and the company has ample orders to keep production going at its full capacity of 2,000 sets per year. Annual cost data at full capacity follow:

Factory labour, direct	$118,000
Advertising	$50,000
Factory supervision	$40,000
Property taxes, factory building	$3,500
Sales commissions	$80,000
Insurance, factory	$2,500
Depreciation, office equipment	$4,000
Lease cost, factory equipment	$12,000
Indirect materials, factory	$6,000
Depreciation, factory building	$10,000
General office supplies (billing)	$3,000
General office salaries	$60,000
Direct materials used (wood, bolts, etc.)	$94,000
Utilities, factory	$20,000

Required:

1. Prepare an answer sheet with the column headings shown below. Enter each cost item on your answer sheet, placing the dollar amount under the appropriate headings. As examples, this has been done already for the first two items in the list above. Note that each cost item is classified in two ways: first, as variable or fixed with respect to the number of units produced and sold; and second, as a selling and administrative cost or a product cost. (If the item is a product cost, it should also be classified as either direct or indirect as shown.)

	Cost Behaviour		Selling or Administrative	Product Cost	
Cost Item	Variable	Fixed	Cost	Direct	Indirect*
Factory labour, direct	$118,000			$118,000	
Advertising		$50,000	$50,000		

*To units of product.

2. Total the dollar amounts in each of the columns in (1) above. Compute the average product cost of one patio set.
3. Assume that production drops to only 1,000 sets annually. Would you expect the average product cost of one set to increase, decrease, or remain unchanged? Explain. No computations are necessary.
4. Refer to the original data. The president's brother-in-law has considered making himself a patio set and has priced the necessary materials at a building supply store. The brother-in-law has asked the president if he could purchase a patio set from the Dorilane Company "at cost," and the president agreed to let him do so.
   a. Would you expect any disagreement between the two men over the price the brother-in-law should pay? Explain. What price does the president probably have in mind? The brother-in-law?
   b. Since the company is operating at full capacity, what cost term used in the chapter might be justification for the president to charge the full, regular price to the brother-in-law and still be selling "at cost"?

PROBLEM 2–26 Schedule of Cost of Goods Manufactured; Income Statement [LO1, LO2, LO3, LO4]

Swift Company was organized on March 1 of the current year. After five months of start-up losses, management had expected to earn a profit during August. Management was disappointed, however, when the income statement for August at the top of page 69 also showed a loss.

After seeing the $12,000 loss for August, Swift's president stated, "I was sure we'd be profitable within six months, but our six months are up and this loss for August is even worse than July's. I think it's time to start looking for someone to buy out the company's assets—if we don't, within a few months there won't be any assets to sell. By the way, I don't see any reason to look for a new controller. We'll just limp along with Sam for the time being."

The company's controller resigned a month ago. Sam, a new assistant in the controller's office, prepared the income statement below. Sam has had little experience in manufacturing operations.

SWIFT COMPANY
Income Statement
For the Month Ended August 31

Sales		$450,000
Less operating expenses:		
Indirect labour cost	$ 12,000	
Utilities	15,000	
Direct labour cost	70,000	
Depreciation, factory equipment	21,000	
Raw materials purchased	165,000	
Depreciation, sales equipment	18,000	
Insurance	4,000	
Rent on facilities	50,000	
Selling and administrative salaries	32,000	
Advertising	75,000	462,000
Net operating loss		$ (12,000)

Additional information about the company follows:

a. Some 60% of the utilities cost and 75% of the insurance apply to factory operations. The remaining amounts apply to selling and administrative activities.
b. Inventory balances at the beginning and end of August were:

	August 1	August 31
Raw materials	$8,000	$13,000
Work in process	$16,000	$21,000
Finished goods	$40,000	$60,000

c. Only 80% of the rent on facilities applies to factory operations; the remainder applies to selling and administrative activities.
The president has asked you to check over the income statement and make a recommendation as to whether the company should look for a buyer for its assets.

Required:

1. As one step in gathering data for a recommendation to the president, prepare a schedule of cost of goods manufactured for August.
2. As a second step, prepare a new income statement for August.
3. Based on your statements prepared in (1) and (2) above, would you recommend that the company look for a buyer?

PROBLEM 2–27 Schedule of Cost of Goods Manufactured; Income Statement; Cost Behaviour [LO1, LO2, LO3, LO4, LO5]

Selected account balances for the year ended December 31 are provided below for Superior Company:

Selling and administrative salaries	$110,000
Insurance, factory	$8,000
Utilities, factory	$45,000
Purchases of raw materials	$290,000
Indirect labour	$60,000
Direct labour	?
Advertising expense	$80,000
Cleaning supplies, factory	$7,000
Sales commissions	$50,000
Rent, factory building	$120,000
Maintenance, factory	$30,000

Inventory balances at the beginning and end of the year were as follows:

	Beginning of the Year	End of the Year
Raw materials	$40,000	$10,000
Work in process	?	$35,000
Finished goods	$50,000	?

The total manufacturing costs for the year were $683,000; the goods available for sale totalled $740,000; and the cost of goods sold totalled $660,000.

Required:

1. Prepare a schedule of cost of goods manufactured and the cost of goods sold section of the company's income statement for the year.
2. Assume that the dollar amounts given above are for the equivalent of 40,000 units produced during the year. Compute the average cost per unit for direct materials used and the average cost per unit for rent on the factory building.
3. Assume that in the following year the company expects to produce 50,000 units. What average cost per unit and total cost would you expect to be incurred for direct materials? For rent on the factory building? (Assume that direct materials is a variable cost and that rent is a fixed cost.)
4. As the manager in charge of production costs, explain to the president the reason for any difference in average cost per unit between (2) and (3) above.

PROBLEM 2–28 Income Statement; Schedule of Cost of Goods Manufactured [LO1, LO2, LO3, LO4]

Visic Corporation, a manufacturing company, produces a single product. The following information has been taken from the company's production, sales, and cost records for the just completed year.

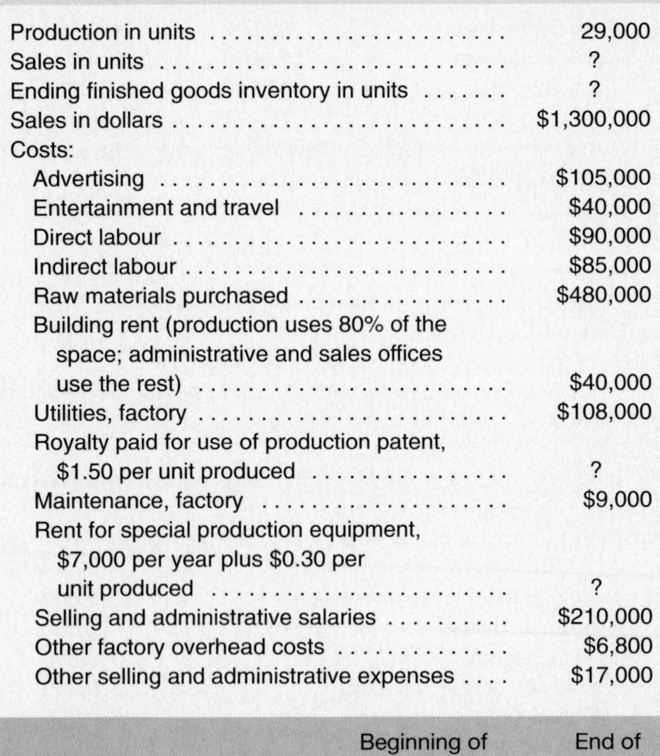

Production in units	29,000
Sales in units	?
Ending finished goods inventory in units	?
Sales in dollars	$1,300,000
Costs:	
Advertising	$105,000
Entertainment and travel	$40,000
Direct labour	$90,000
Indirect labour	$85,000
Raw materials purchased	$480,000
Building rent (production uses 80% of the space; administrative and sales offices use the rest)	$40,000
Utilities, factory	$108,000
Royalty paid for use of production patent, $1.50 per unit produced	?
Maintenance, factory	$9,000
Rent for special production equipment, $7,000 per year plus $0.30 per unit produced	?
Selling and administrative salaries	$210,000
Other factory overhead costs	$6,800
Other selling and administrative expenses	$17,000

	Beginning of the Year	End of the Year
Inventories:		
Raw materials	$20,000	$30,000
Work in process	$50,000	$40,000
Finished goods	$0	?

The finished goods inventory is being carried at the average unit production cost for the year. The selling price of the product is $50 per unit.

Required:

1. Prepare a schedule of cost of goods manufactured for the year.
2. Compute the following:
   a. The number of units in the finished goods inventory at the end of the year.
   b. The cost of the units in the finished goods inventory at the end of the year.
3. Prepare an income statement for the year.

PROBLEM 2–29 Working with Incomplete Data from the Income Statement and Schedule of Cost of Goods Manufactured [LO3, LO4]

Supply the missing data in the following cases. Each case is independent of the others.

	Case			
	1	2	3	4
Direct materials	$4,500	$6,000	$5,000	$3,000
Direct labour	?	$3,000	$7,000	$4,000
Manufacturing overhead	$5,000	$4,000	?	$9,000
Total manufacturing costs	$18,500	?	$20,000	?
Beginning work in process inventory	$2,500	?	$3,000	?
Ending work in process inventory	?	$1,000	$4,000	$3,000
Sales	$30,000	$21,000	$36,000	$40,000
Beginning finished goods inventory	$1,000	$2,500	?	$2,000
Cost of goods manufactured	$18,000	$14,000	?	$17,500
Goods available for sale	?	?	?	?
Ending finished goods inventory	?	$1,500	$4,000	$3,500
Cost of goods sold	$17,000	?	$18,500	?
Gross margin	$13,000	?	$17,500	?
Operating expenses	?	$3,500	?	?
Net operating income	$4,000	?	$5,000	$9,000

CASES

CASE 2–30 Inventory Computations from Incomplete Data [LO3, LO4]

Hector P. Wastrel, a careless employee, left some combustible materials near an open flame in Salter Company's plant. The resulting explosion and fire destroyed the entire plant and administrative offices. Justin Quick, the company's controller, and Constance Trueheart, the operations manager, were able to save only a few bits of information as they escaped from the roaring blaze.

"What a disaster," cried Justin. "And the worst part is that we have no records to use in filing an insurance claim."

"I know," replied Constance. "I was in the plant when the explosion occurred, and I managed to grab only this brief summary sheet that contains information on one or two of our costs. It says that our direct labour cost this year has totalled $180,000 and that we have purchased $290,000 in raw materials. But I'm afraid that doesn't help much; the rest of our records are just ashes."

"Well, not completely," said Justin. "I was working on the year-to-date income statement when the explosion knocked me out of my chair. I instinctively held onto the page I was working on, and from what I can make out, our sales to date this year have totalled $1,200,000 and our gross margin rate has been 40% of sales. Also, I can see that our goods available for sale to customers has totalled $810,000 at cost."

"Maybe we're not so bad off after all," exclaimed Constance. "My sheet says that prime cost has totalled $410,000 so far this year and that manufacturing overhead is 70% of conversion cost. Now if we just had some information on our beginning inventories."

"Hey, look at this," cried Justin. "It's a copy of last year's annual report, and it shows what our inventories were when this year started. Let's see, raw materials was $18,000, work in process was $65,000, and finished goods was $45,000.

"Super," yelled Constance. "Let's go to work."

To file an insurance claim, the company must determine the amount of cost in its inventories as of the date of the fire. You may assume that all materials used in production during the year were direct materials.

Required:
Determine the amount of cost in the Raw Materials, Work in Process, and Finished Goods inventory accounts as of the date of the fire. (Hint: One way to proceed would be to reconstruct the various schedules and statements that would have been affected by the company's inventory accounts during the period.)

CASE 2–31 Missing Data; Income Statement; Schedule of Cost of Goods Manufactured [LO1, LO2, LO3, LO4]

"I was sure that when our battery hit the market it would be an instant success," said Roger Strong, founder and president of Solar Technology, Inc. "But just look at the gusher of red ink for the first quarter. It's obvious that we're better scientists than we are businesspeople." The data to which Roger was referring follow:

SOLAR TECHNOLOGY, INC.
Income Statement
For the Quarter Ended March 31

Sales (32,000 batteries)		$ 960,000
Less operating expenses:		
Selling and administrative salaries	$110,000	
Advertising	90,000	
Maintenance, factory	43,000	
Indirect labour cost	120,000	
Cleaning supplies, factory	7,000	
Purchases of raw materials	360,000	
Rental cost, facilities	75,000	
Insurance, factory	8,000	
Depreciation, office equipment	27,000	
Utilities	80,000	
Depreciation, factory equipment	100,000	
Direct labour cost	70,000	
Travel, salespersons	40,000	1,130,000
Net operating loss		$ (170,000)

"At this rate we'll be out of business within a year," said Cindy Zhang, the company's accountant. "But I've double-checked these figures, so I know they're right."

Solar Technology was organized at the beginning of the current year to produce and market a revolutionary new solar battery. The company's accounting system was set up by Margie Wallace, an experienced accountant who recently left the company to do independent consulting work. The statement above was prepared by Zhang, her assistant.

"We may not last a year if the insurance company doesn't pay the $226,000 it owes us for the 8,000 batteries lost in the warehouse fire last week," said Roger. "The insurance adjuster says our claim is inflated, but he's just trying to pressure us into a lower figure. We have the data to back up our claim, and it will stand up in any court."

On April 3, just after the end of the first quarter, the company's finished goods storage area was swept by fire and all 8,000 unsold batteries were destroyed. (These batteries were part of the 40,000 units completed during the first quarter.) The company's insurance policy states that the company will be reimbursed for the "cost" of any finished batteries destroyed or stolen. Zhang has determined this cost as follows:

$$\frac{\text{Total costs for the quarter}}{\text{Batteries produced during the quarter}} = \frac{\$1{,}130{,}000}{40{,}000 \text{ units}}$$

$$= \$28.25 \text{ per unit}$$

$$8{,}000 \text{ batteries} \times \$28.25 \text{ per unit} = \$226{,}000$$

The following additional information is available on the company's activities during the quarter ended March 31:

a. Inventories at the beginning and end of the quarter were as follows:

	Beginning of the Quarter	End of the Quarter
Raw materials	$0	$10,000
Work in process	$0	$50,000
Finished goods	$0	?

b. Eighty percent of the rental cost for facilities and 90% of the utilities cost relate to manufacturing operations. The remaining amounts relate to selling and administrative activities.

Required:

1. What conceptual errors, if any, were made in preparing the income statement above?
2. Prepare a schedule of cost of goods manufactured for the first quarter.
3. Prepare a corrected income statement for the first quarter. Your statement should show in detail how the cost of goods sold is computed.
4. Do you agree that the insurance company owes Solar Technology, Inc., $226,000? Explain your answer.

GROUP AND INTERNET EXERCISES

GROUP EXERCISE 2–32 Implications of Mass Production

Management accounting systems tend to parallel the manufacturing systems they support and control. Traditional manufacturing systems emphasized productivity (average output per hour or per employee) and cost. This was the result of a competitive philosophy that was based on mass producing a few standard products and "meeting or beating competitors on price." If a company is going to compete on price, it had better be a low-cost producer.

Companies achieved low unit cost for a fixed set of resources by maximizing the utilization of those resources. That is, traditional production strategies were based on the economies of mass production and maximizing output for a given productive capacity. North America has experienced over 100 years of unprecedented economic prosperity in large part because innovators like Henry Ford applied these economic principles with a vengeance.

Competitors, never being completely satisfied with their present condition, were always looking for ways to lower the cost of a product or service even further to gain some temporary cost advantage. Additional productivity gains were achieved by standardizing work procedures, specializing work, and using machines to enhance the productivity of individual workers.

Required:

1. Henry Ford made a now-famous statement that the Model T "could be had in any colour as long as it was black." Explain what he meant by this statement.
2. How would Henry Ford or any other manufacturer with a narrow product line gain even further efficiencies based on the traditional production model described above?
3. Are there any limits to lowering the cost of black Model Ts, black Bic pens, or any high-volume, commodity product? Explain.
4. Once understood, the economies of mass production were applied to most sectors of the American economy. Universities, hospitals, and airlines are prime examples. Describe how the concepts of mass production, standardization, and specialization have been applied to lower the costs of a university education. Of a stay in the hospital.

GROUP EXERCISE 2–33 If Big Is Good, Bigger Must Be Better

Steel production involves a large amount of fixed costs. Since competition is defined primarily in terms of price, North American steel manufacturers (and many of their manufacturing and service industry counterparts) try to gain a competitive advantage by using economies of scale and investment in technology to increase productivity and drive unit costs lower. Their substantial fixed costs are the result of their size.

Required:

1. How are fixed costs and variable costs normally defined?

2. Give examples of fixed costs and variable costs for a steel company. What is the relevant measure of production activity?
3. Give examples of fixed and variable costs for a hospital, university, and auto manufacturer. What is the relevant measure of production or service activity for each of these organizations?
4. Using the examples of fixed and variable costs for steel companies from (2) above, explain the relationship between production output at a steel company and each of the following: total fixed costs, fixed cost per unit, total variable costs, variable cost per unit, total costs, and average unit cost.
5. With an *X* axis (horizontal axis) of tonnes produced and a *Y* axis (vertical axis) of total costs, graph total fixed costs, total variable costs, and total costs against tonnes produced.
6. With an *X* axis of tonnes produced and a *Y* axis of unit costs, graph fixed cost per unit, variable cost per unit, and total (or average) cost per unit against tonnes produced.
7. Explain how costs (total and per unit) behave with changes in demand once capacity has been set.

INTERNET EXERCISE 2–34

As you know, the World Wide Web is constantly evolving. Sites come and go, and change without notice. To enable periodic updating of site addresses, this problem has been posted to the textbook Web site (www.mcgrawhill.ca/college/garrison). After accessing the site, enter the Student Centre and select this chapter. Select and complete the Internet Exercise.

CHAPTER 3

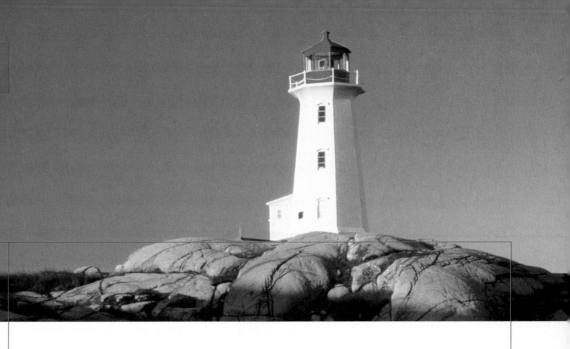

LEARNING OBJECTIVES

After studying Chapter 3, you should be able to:

1. Distinguish between process costing and job-order costing and identify companies that would use each costing method.
2. Identify the documents used in a job-order costing system.
3. Compute predetermined overhead rates and explain why estimated overhead costs (rather than actual overhead costs) are used in the costing process.
4. Record the journal entries that reflect the flow of costs in a job-order costing system.
5. Apply overhead cost to Work in Process using a predetermined overhead rate.
6. Prepare schedules of cost of goods manufactured and cost of goods sold.
7. Compute under- or overapplied overhead cost and prepare the journal entry to close the balance in Manufacturing Overhead to the appropriate accounts.
8. (Appendix 3A) Explain the implications of basing the predetermined overhead rate on activity at capacity rather than on estimated activity for the period.

SYSTEMS DESIGN: JOB-ORDER COSTING

BUSINESS FOCUS

OVERAPPLIED/UNDERAPPLIED

Cris Griffiths Guitar Works of Saint Johns, Newfoundland, focuses on repair work and building custom guitars. Late one night while disassembling yet another guitar, Griffiths had a vision of a single bracing piece instead of the three-dozen separate internal reinforcements acoustic guitars typically have. "It was a simple idea that was easy to flesh out, but turning it from an idea into a corporation was a pretty lengthy process," he recalls. "I often say it took me six minutes to come up with the idea and six years to make it work."

Part of the problem was that using wood to make a one-piece brace was pretty much out of the question. It would take years to whittle down a wood block into a single piece, but Griffiths realized a composite material that could be punched out using injection-molding equipment could perform the same trick. Again, simple enough to conceive but it took three years before he had a solid business plan he could present to investors. Even then, Griffiths didn't have the $100,000 he needed to build a prototype, so he leveraged his existing business to the hilt, effectively putting the future of both companies on the line. Eventually, he convinced investors to pony up some seed money and hit the road. At a Los Angeles trade show in early 2000, his guitar—lo and behold—was a hit, attracting lineups of people wanting to check out the new star.

Production started in mid-2001 and roughly $6 million pumped into the business over the next three years to keep it rolling. In 2003 the company switched to a lean manufacturing operation called the Toyota production system. That has meant a 50% cut in labour costs and manufacturing space as well as a 70% reduction in work-in-progress inventory.

Source: Andy Holloway, "Between the Rock and a Hard Place," *Canadian Business*, Dec. 27, 2004–Jan. 16, 2005, vol. 78, Iss. 1, p. 69.

As discussed in Chapter 2, product costing is the process of assigning costs to the products and services provided by a company. An understanding of this costing process is vital to managers, because the way in which a product or service is costed can have a substantial impact on reported net income, as well as on key management decisions.

The essential purpose of any managerial costing system should be to provide cost data to help managers plan, control, direct, and make decisions. Nevertheless, external financial reporting and tax reporting requirements often heavily influence how costs are accumulated and summarized in managerial reports. This is true of product costing.

Absorption costing
A costing method that includes all manufacturing costs—direct materials, direct labour, and both variable and fixed overhead—as part of the cost of a finished unit of product. This term is synonymous with *full cost.*

Full cost
Same as *absorption costing.*

In this chapter and in Chapter 4, we use an *absorption costing* approach to determine product costs. This was also the method that was used in Chapter 2. In **absorption costing,** *all* manufacturing costs, fixed and variable, are assigned to units of product—units are said to *fully absorb manufacturing costs.* The absorption costing approach is also known as the **full cost** approach. Later, in Chapter 7, we look at product costing from a different point of view called *variable costing,* which is often advocated as an alternative to absorption costing. Chapter 7 also discusses the strengths and weaknesses of the two approaches.

While studying product costing, we must keep in mind that the essential purpose of any costing system is to accumulate costs for managerial use. A costing system is not an end in itself. Rather, it is a managerial tool in that it exists to provide managers with the cost data needed to direct the affairs of organizations.

The design of the costing system depends on cost/benefit trade-offs as assessed by managers. The level of detail and sophistication in a cost accounting system will influence its costs of development and operation. Relevance to management and external regulatory requirements will be the benefit. Usually, more sophistication yields more benefit by providing more relevant information. But when the additional cost of providing added sophistication equals the benefits from the added relevance, the system's designer is at an optimal point in the cost/benefit trade-off and thus the added sophistication should stop.

The nature of systems design is also influenced by the nature of what is to be costed. The explanation provided in the pages that follow will focus on the nature of what is costed rather than the cost/benefit trade-offs. This will enable a description of what physically needs to be considered when the cost/benefit decision must be made. In other words, physical characteristics represent a fundamental consideration to the higher level and more subjective cost/benefit trade-off.

Absorption costing is a popular approach for determining the cost of goods sold and inventories for financial accounting and income taxes. These requirements influence how management determines costs because it may be easier and less expensive for the organization to use a single method of costing for both external and internal purposes.

Costing of products or services represents an approach that focuses on the costing of the efforts that make up the goods or services that are sold by the organization. This emphasis on costing products or services is one of the three common approaches used in managerial accounting. The discussion of costing begins with this focus because of its long tradition and its continued popularity for many types of organizations. After this approach to costing is thoroughly explored in the next few chapters, the alternatives will be studied so that a more complete picture will be available for your study of managerial accounting.

PROCESS AND JOB-ORDER COSTING

In computing the cost of a product or a service, managers are faced with a difficult problem. Many costs (such as rent) do not change much from month to month, whereas production may change frequently, with production going up in one month and then down in another. In addition to variations in the level of production, several different products or services may be produced in a given period in the same facility. Under these conditions, how is it possible to accurately determine the cost of a product or service? In practice, assigning costs to products and services involves an averaging of some type across time periods and across products. The way in which this averaging is carried out will depend heavily on the type of production process involved. Two costing systems are commonly used in manufacturing and in many service companies; these two systems are known as *process costing* and *job-order costing*.

LEARNING OBJECTIVE 1
Distinguish between process costing and job-order costing and identify companies that would use each costing method.

Process Costing

A **process costing system** is used in situations where the company produces many units of a single product (such as frozen orange juice concentrate) for long periods at a time. Examples include producing paper at Bowater, refining aluminum ingots at Alcan, mixing and bottling beverages at Coca-Cola, and making wieners at J.M. Schneider Inc. All of these industries are characterized by an essentially homogeneous product that flows evenly through the production process on a continuous basis.

Process costing system A costing system used in those manufacturing situations where a single, homogeneous product (such as cement or flour) is produced for long periods of time.

The basic approach in process costing is to accumulate costs in a particular operation or department for an entire period (month, quarter, year) and then to divide this total by the number of units produced during the period. The basic formula for process costing is as follows:

$$\frac{\text{Unit cost}}{\text{(per litre, kilogram, bottle)}} = \frac{\text{Total manufacturing cost}}{\text{Total units produced (litres, kilograms, bottles)}}$$

Since one unit of product (litre, kilogram, bottle) is indistinguishable from any other unit of product, each unit is assigned the same average cost as any other unit produced during the period. This costing technique results in a broad, average unit cost figure that applies to homogeneous units flowing in a continuous stream out of the production process.

Job-Order Costing

A **job-order costing system** is used in situations where many *different* products are produced each period. For example, a Levi Strauss clothing factory would typically make many different types of jeans for both men and women during a month. A particular order might consist of 1,000 stonewashed men's blue denim jeans, style number A312, with a 32-inch waist and a 30-inch inseam. This order of 1,000 jeans is called a *batch* or a *job*. In a job-order costing system, costs are traced and allocated to jobs and then the costs of the job are divided by the number of units in the job to arrive at an average cost per unit.

Job-order costing system A costing system used in situations where many different products, jobs, or services are produced each period.

Other examples of situations where job-order costing would be used include large-scale construction projects managed by Bechtel International, commercial aircraft produced by Bombardier, greeting cards designed and printed at Hallmark, and airline meals prepared by Cara. All of these examples are characterized by diverse outputs. Each Bechtel project is unique and different from every other—the company may be simultaneously constructing a dam in Zaire and a bridge in Indonesia. Likewise, each airline orders a different type of meal from Cara's catering service.

Job-order costing is also used extensively in service industries. Hospitals, law firms, movie studios, accounting firms, advertising agencies, and repair shops all use a variation of job-order costing to accumulate costs for accounting and billing purposes. For example, the production of the British Open golf broadcast by TSN would be suitable as a job costing project.

Although the detailed example of job-order costing provided in the following section deals with a manufacturing firm, the same basic concepts and procedures are used by many service organizations. The essential difference for service organizations is the lack of raw materials in the cost of their services. For example, a public accounting firm would have cost elements involving direct labour and overhead but not raw materials, because the firm does not make a physical item. However, to avoid duplicating the discussion that follows, the more comprehensive manufacturing environment will be presented, with the service application addressed in exercises and problems.

The record-keeping and cost assignment problems are more complex when a company sells many different products and services than when it has only a single product. Since the products are different, the costs are typically different. Consequently, cost records must be maintained for each distinct product or job. For example, an attorney in a large criminal law practice would ordinarily keep separate records of the costs of advising and defending each of her clients. And the Levi Strauss factory mentioned earlier would keep separate track of the costs of filling orders for particular styles, sizes, and colours of jeans. Thus, a job-order costing system requires more effort than a process costing system.

In this chapter, we focus on the design of a job-order costing system. In the following chapter, we focus on process costing and also look more closely at the similarities and differences between the two costing methods.

JOB-ORDER COSTING—AN OVERVIEW

LEARNING OBJECTIVE 2
Identify the documents used in a job-order costing system.

To introduce job-order costing, we will follow a specific job as it progresses through the manufacturing process. This job consists of two experimental couplings that Yost Precision Machining has agreed to produce for Loops Unlimited, a manufacturer of roller coasters. The couplings connect the cars on the roller coaster and are a critical component in the performance and safety of the ride. Before we begin our discussion, recall from Chapter 2 that companies generally classify manufacturing costs into three broad categories: (1) direct materials, (2) direct labour, and (3) manufacturing overhead. As we study the operation of a job-order costing system, we will see how each of these three types of costs is recorded and accumulated.

The Issue

Yost Precision Machining is a small company in Nova Scotia that specializes in fabricating precision metal parts that are used in a variety of applications, ranging from deep-sea exploration vehicles to the inertial triggers in automobile air bags. The company's top managers gather every day at 8:00 A.M. in the company's conference room for the daily planning meeting. Attending the meeting this morning are Jean Yost, the company's president; David Cheung, the marketing manager; Debbie Turner, the production manager; and Marcus White, the company controller. The president opened the meeting:

Jean: The production schedule indicates we'll be starting job 2B47 today. Isn't that the special order for experimental couplings, David?

David: That's right, Jean. That's the order from Loops Unlimited for two couplings for their new roller coaster ride for Magic Mountain.

Debbie: Why only two couplings? Don't they need a coupling for every car?

David: That's right. But this is a completely new roller coaster. The cars will go faster and will be subjected to more twists, turns, drops, and loops than on any other existing roller coaster. To hold up under these stresses, Loops Unlimited's engineers had to completely redesign the cars and couplings. They want to thoroughly test the design before proceeding to large-scale production. So they want us to make just two of these new couplings for testing purposes. If the design works, then we'll have the inside track on the order to supply couplings for the whole ride.

Jean: We agreed to take on this initial order at our cost just to get our foot in the door. Marcus, will there be any problem documenting our cost so we can get paid?

Marcus: No problem. The contract with Loops stipulates that they will pay us an amount equal to our cost of goods sold. With our job-order costing system, I can tell you that number on the day the job is completed.

Jean: Good. Is there anything else we should discuss about this job at this time? No? Well then let's move on to the next item of business.

Measuring Direct Materials Cost

Yost Precision Machining will require four G7 connectors and two M46 housings to make the two experimental couplings for Loops Unlimited. If this was a standard product, there would be a *bill of materials* for the product. A **bill of materials** is a document that lists the type and quantity of each item of the materials needed to complete a unit of product. In this case, there is no established bill of materials, so Yost's production staff determined the materials requirements from the blueprints submitted by the customer. Each coupling requires two connectors and one housing, so to make two couplings, four connectors and two housings are required.

Bill of materials A document that shows the type and quantity of each major item of the materials required to make a product.

When an agreement has been reached with the customer concerning the quantities, prices, and shipment date for the order, a *production order* is issued. The Production Department then prepares a *materials requisition form* similar to the form in Exhibit 3–1. The **materials requisition form** is a detailed source document that (1) specifies the type and quantity of materials to be drawn from the storeroom, and (2) identifies the job to which the costs of the materials are to be charged. It serves as a means for controlling the flow of materials into production and also for making entries in the accounting records.

Materials requisition form A detailed source document that specifies the type and quantity of materials that are to be drawn from the storeroom and identifies the job to which the costs of materials are to be charged.

The Yost Precision Machining materials requisition form in Exhibit 3–1 shows that the company's Milling Department has requisitioned two M46 housings and four G7 connectors for job 2B47. This completed form is presented to the storeroom clerk who then issues the necessary raw materials. The storeroom clerk is not allowed to release materials without such a form bearing an authorized signature.

The previous paragraphs used the terms *direct materials* and *raw materials*, which should be clarified. Direct materials represent materials that are directly traced to the product or service. Raw materials are ingredients that are converted into a finished product. Semi-finished materials, or supplies for a service job, could be considered direct materials if they were important enough to be directly traced to the job, but they will not be raw materials. In summary, because raw materials can be direct materials but all direct materials do not need to be raw materials, the terms often appear interchangeably in business terminology.

Job Cost Sheet

After being notified that the production order has been issued, the Accounting Department prepares a *job cost sheet* similar to the one presented in Exhibit 3–2. A **job cost sheet** is a form prepared for each separate job that records the materials, labour, and overhead costs charged to the job.

Job cost sheet A form prepared for each job that records the materials, labour, and overhead costs charged to the job.

EXHIBIT 3–1 Materials Requisition Form

Materials Requisition Number: 14873

Date:

Job Number to Be Charged: 2B47

Department: Milling

Description	Quantity	Unit Cost	Total Cost
M46 Housing	2	$124	248
G7 Conector	4	103	412
			$660

Bill White

Authorized Signature

EXHIBIT 3–2 Job Cost Sheet

JOB COST SHEET

Job Number	Date Initiated
2B47	March 2
Department	**Date Completed**
Milling	
Item	**Units Completed**
For Stock	

Direct Materials		Direct Labour			Manufacturing Overhead		
Req. No.	Amount	Ticket	Hours	Amount	Hours	Rate	Amount
14873	$660	843	5	$45			

Cost Summary		Units Shipped		
		Date	Number	Balance
Direct Materials	$			
Direct Labour	$			
Manufacturing Overhead	$			
Total Cost	$			
Unit Cost	$			

After direct materials are issued, the Accounting Department records their costs directly on the job cost sheet. Note from Exhibit 3–2, for example, that the $660 cost for direct materials shown earlier on the materials requisition form has been charged to job 2B47 on its job cost sheet. The requisition number 14873 is also recorded on the job cost sheet to make it easier to identify the source document for the direct materials charge.

In addition to serving as a means for charging costs to jobs, the job cost sheet also serves as a key part of a firm's accounting records. The job cost sheets form a subsidiary ledger to the Work in Process account. They are detailed records for the jobs in process that add up to the balance in Work in Process.

Measuring Direct Labour Cost

Direct labour cost is handled in much the same way as direct materials cost. Direct labour consists of labour charges that are easily traced to a particular job. Labour charges that cannot be easily traced directly to any job are treated as part of manufacturing overhead. As discussed in Chapter 2, this latter category of labour costs is termed *indirect labour* and includes tasks such as maintenance, supervision, and clean-up.

Time ticket A detailed source document that is used to record an employee's hour-by-hour activities during a day.

Workers use *time tickets* to record the time they spend on each job and task. A completed **time ticket** is an hour-by-hour summary of the employee's activities throughout the day. An example of an employee time ticket is shown in Exhibit 3–3. When working on a specific job, the employee enters the job number on the time ticket and notes the amount of time spent on that job. When not assigned to a particular job, the employee

EXHIBIT 3–3 Employee Time Ticket

Time Ticket No.			Date		
843			March 3		
Employee			Station		
Mary Holden			4		

Started	Ended	Time Completed	Rate	Amount	Job Number
7:00	12:00	5.0	$9	$45	2B47
12:30	2:30	2.0	9	18	2B50
2:30	3:30	1.0	9	9	Maintenance
Totals		8.0		$72	

R.W. Pace
Supervisor

records the nature of the indirect labour task (such as clean-up and maintenance) and the amount of time spent on the task.

At the end of the day, the time tickets are gathered and the Accounting Department enters the direct labour-hours and costs on individual job cost sheets. (See Exhibit 3–2 for an example of how direct labour costs are entered on the job cost sheet.) The daily time tickets are source documents that are used as the basis for labour cost entries into the accounting records.

The system we have just described is a manual method for recording and posting labour costs. Many companies now rely on computerized systems and no longer record labour time by hand on sheets of paper. One computerized approach uses bar codes to enter the basic data into the computer. Each employee and each job has a unique bar code. When an employee begins work on a job, he or she scans three bar codes, using a hand-held device much like the bar code readers at grocery store checkout stands. The first bar code indicates that a job is being started; the second is the unique bar code on the employee's identity badge; and the third is the unique bar code of the job itself. This information is fed automatically via an electronic network to a computer that notes the time and then records all of the data. When the employee completes the task, he or she scans a bar code indicating the task is complete, the bar code on the employee's identity badge, and the bar code attached to the job. This information is relayed to the computer that again

FOCUS *on Current Practice*

Canada's health care system gives Canadian business a striking competitive advantage with respect to labour costs. As Kirstin Downey writes:

> Employers in Canada pay only about $50 a month, or $600 a year, mostly for optional items such as eyeglasses and orthopedic shoes, said Elaine Bernard, executive director of the labour and worklife program at Harvard Law School. "Health care is significantly cheaper for corporations in Canada," she said. U.S. employers pay more than 10 times as much—an average $552 a month per employee for health insurance, according to the Kaiser Family Foundation.

Source: Kirstin Downey, "A Heftier Dose to Swallow Rising Cost of Health Care in U.S. Gives Other Developed Countries an Edge in Keeping Jobs," *Washington Post,* March 6, 2004, pp. E01.

notes the time, and a time ticket is automatically prepared. Since all of the source data is already in computer files, the labour costs can automatically be posted to job cost sheets (or their electronic equivalents). Computers, coupled with technology such as bar codes, can eliminate much of the drudgery involved in routine bookkeeping activities while at the same time increasing timeliness and accuracy.

Application of Manufacturing Overhead

LEARNING OBJECTIVE 3
Compute predetermined overhead rates and explain why estimated overhead costs (rather than actual overhead costs) are used in the costing process.

Manufacturing overhead must be included with direct materials and direct labour on the job cost sheet since manufacturing overhead is also a product cost. However, assigning manufacturing overhead to units of product can be a difficult task. There are three reasons for this.

1. Manufacturing overhead is an *indirect cost.* This means that it is either impossible or difficult to trace these costs to a particular product or job.
2. Manufacturing overhead consists of many different items, ranging from the grease used in machines to the annual salary of the production manager.
3. Even though output may fluctuate due to seasonal or other factors, manufacturing overhead costs tend to remain relatively constant due to the presence of fixed costs.

Given these problems, about the only way to assign overhead costs to products is to use an allocation process. This allocation of overhead costs is accomplished by selecting an *allocation base* that is common to all of the company's products and services. An **allocation base** is a measure such as direct labour-hours (DLH) or machine-hours (MH) that is used to assign overhead costs to products and services.

Allocation base
A measure of activity such as direct labour-hours or machine-hours that is used to assign costs to cost objects.

The most widely used allocation bases are direct labour-hours and direct labour cost, with machine-hours and even units of product (where a company has only a single product) also used to some extent.

The allocation base is used to compute the **predetermined overhead rate** in the following formula:

Predetermined overhead rate
A rate used to charge overhead cost to jobs in production; the rate is established in advance for each period by use of estimates of total manufacturing overhead cost and of the total allocation base for the period.

$$\text{Predetermined overhead rate} = \frac{\text{Estimated total manufacturing overhead cost}}{\text{Estimated total units in the allocation base}}$$

Note that the predetermined overhead rate is based on *estimated* rather than actual figures. This is because the *predetermined* overhead rate is computed *before* the period begins and is used to *apply* overhead cost to jobs throughout the period. The process of assigning overhead cost to jobs is called **overhead application.** The formula for determining the amount of overhead cost to apply to a particular job is:

Overhead application
The process of charging manufacturing overhead cost to job cost sheets and to the Work in Process account.

$$\begin{matrix}\text{Overhead applied to} \\ \text{a particular job}\end{matrix} = \begin{matrix}\text{Predetermined} \\ \text{overhead rate}\end{matrix} \times \begin{matrix}\text{Amount of the allocation} \\ \text{base incurred by the job}\end{matrix}$$

For example, if the predetermined overhead rate is $8 per direct labour-hour, then $8 of overhead is *applied* to a job for each direct labour-hour incurred by the job. When the allocation base is direct labour-hours, the formula becomes:

$$\begin{matrix}\text{Overhead applied to} \\ \text{a particular job}\end{matrix} = \begin{matrix}\text{Predetermined} \\ \text{overhead rate}\end{matrix} \times \begin{matrix}\text{Actual direct labour-hours} \\ \text{charged to the job}\end{matrix}$$

Using the Predetermined Overhead Rate To illustrate the steps involved in computing and using a predetermined overhead rate, let's return to Yost Precision Machining. The company has estimated its total manufacturing overhead costs to be $320,000 for the year and its total direct labour-hours to be 40,000. Its predetermined overhead rate for the year would be $8 per direct labour-hour, as shown as follows:

$$\text{Predetermined overhead rate} = \frac{\text{Estimated total manufacturing overhead cost}}{\text{Estimated total units in the allocation base}}$$

$$\frac{\$320{,}000}{40{,}000 \text{ direct labour-hours}} = \$8 \text{ per direct labour-hour}$$

The job cost sheet in Exhibit 3–4 indicates that 27 direct labour-hours were charged to job 2B47. Therefore, a total of $216 of overhead cost would be applied to the job:

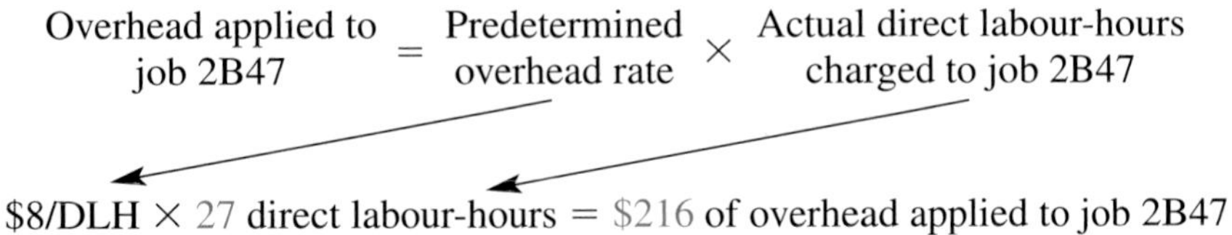

This amount of overhead has been entered on the job cost sheet in Exhibit 3–4. Note that this is *not* the actual amount of overhead caused by the job. There is no attempt to trace actual overhead costs to jobs—if that could be done, the costs would be direct costs, not overhead. The overhead assigned to the job is simply a share of the total overhead that was estimated at the beginning of the year. When a company applies overhead cost to jobs

EXHIBIT 3–4 A Completed Job Cost Sheet

JOB COST SHEET

Job Number	Date Initiated
2B47	March 2
Department	**Date Completed**
Milling	March 8
Item	**Units Completed**
Special order coupling	2
For Stock	

Direct Materials		Direct Labour			Manufacturing Overhead		
Req. No.	Amount	Ticket	Hours	Amount	Hours	Rate	Amount
14873	$ 660	843	5	$ 45	27	$8/DLH	$216
14875	506	846	8	60			
14912	238	850	4	21			
	$1,404	851	10	54			
			27	$180			

Cost Summary		Units Shipped		
		Date	Number	Balance
Direct Materials	$1,404			
Direct Labour	$ 180	March 8		2
Manufacturing Overhead	$ 216			
Total Cost	$1,800			
Unit Cost	$ 900*			

*$1,800 2 units = $900 per unit.

as we have done—that is, by multiplying actual activity times the predetermined overhead rate—it is called a **normal cost system.**

Normal cost system A costing system in which overhead costs are applied to jobs by multiplying a predetermined overhead rate by the actual amount of the allocation base incurred by the job.

The overhead may be applied as direct labour-hours are charged to jobs, or all of the overhead can be applied at once when the job is completed. The choice is up to the company. If a job is not completed at year-end, however, overhead should be applied to value the work in process inventory.

The Need For a Predetermined Rate Instead of using a predetermined rate, a company could wait until the end of the accounting period to compute an actual overhead rate based on the *actual* total manufacturing costs and the *actual* total units in the allocation base for the period. However, managers cite several reasons for using predetermined overhead rates instead of actual overhead rates:

1. Managers would like to know the accounting system's valuation of completed jobs before the end of the accounting period. Suppose, for example, that Yost Precision Machining waits until the end of the year to compute its overhead rate. Then there would be no way for managers to know the cost of goods sold for job 2B47 until the close of the year, even though the job was completed and shipped to the customer in March. The seriousness of this problem can be reduced to some extent by computing the actual overhead more frequently, but that immediately leads to another problem, as discussed below.
2. If actual overhead rates are computed frequently, seasonal factors in overhead costs or in the allocation base can produce fluctuations in the overhead rates. For example, the costs of heating and cooling a production facility in Halifax will be highest in the winter and summer months and lowest in the spring and fall. If an overhead rate were computed each month or each quarter, the predetermined overhead rate would go up in the winter and summer and down in the spring and fall. Two identical jobs, one completed in the winter and one completed in the spring, would be assigned different costs if the overhead rate were computed on a monthly or quarterly basis. Managers generally feel that such fluctuations in overhead rates and costs serve no useful purpose and are misleading.
3. The use of a predetermined overhead rate simplifies record-keeping. To determine the overhead cost to apply to a job, the accounting staff at Yost Precision Machining simply multiplies the direct labour-hours recorded for the job by the predetermined overhead rate of $8 per direct labour-hour.

For these reasons, most companies use predetermined overhead rates rather than actual overhead rates in their cost accounting systems.

Choice of an Allocation Base for Overhead Cost

Cost driver A factor, such as machine-hours, beds occupied, computer time, or flight-hours, that causes overhead costs.

Ideally, an allocation base should be used that is a *cost driver* of overhead cost. A **cost driver** is a factor, such as machine-hours, beds occupied, computer time, or flight-hours, that causes overhead costs. If a base is used to compute overhead rates that does not "drive" overhead costs, then the result will be inaccurate overhead rates and distorted product costs. For example, if direct labour-hours is used to allocate overhead, but in reality overhead has little to do with direct labour-hours, then products with high direct labour-hour requirements will shoulder an unrealistic burden of overhead and will be overcosted.

Most companies use direct labour-hours or direct labour cost as the allocation base for manufacturing overhead. However, as discussed in earlier chapters, major shifts are taking place in the structure of costs in many industries. In the past, direct labour accounted for up to 60% of the cost of many products, with overhead cost making up only a portion of the remainder. This situation has been changing—for two reasons. First, sophisticated automated equipment has taken over functions that used to be performed by direct labour workers. Since the costs of acquiring and maintaining such equipment are classified as overhead, this increases overhead while decreasing direct labour. Second, products are themselves becoming more sophisticated and complex and change more frequently. This increases the need for highly skilled indirect workers such as engineers. As a result of these two trends, direct labour is becoming less of a factor and overhead is becoming more of a factor in the cost of products in many industries.

In companies where direct labour and overhead costs have been moving in opposite directions, it would be difficult to argue that direct labour "drives" overhead costs. Accordingly, in recent years, managers in some companies have used *activity-based costing* principles to redesign their cost accounting systems. Activity-based costing is a costing technique that is designed to more accurately reflect the demands that products, customers, and other cost objects make on overhead resources. The activity-based approach is discussed in more detail in Chapter 8.

We hasten to add that although direct labour may not be an appropriate allocation basis in some industries, in others it continues to be a significant driver of manufacturing overhead. Indeed, most manufacturing companies in North America continue to use direct labour as the primary or secondary allocation base for manufacturing overhead. The key point is that the allocation base used by the company should really drive, or cause, overhead costs, and direct labour is not always an appropriate allocation base.

FOCUS *on Current Practice*

CPI Plastics Group Ltd. of Mississauga, Ontario, has three major operating segments—outdoor living products, film products, and custom products. The company was able to reduce manufacturing labour costs during the first quarter of 2002 by employing a strategy that included increasing consumer products sales while also making improving plant efficiencies. Manufacturing overhead costs, however, rose during the same period due to increased plant electricity costs resulting from deregulation in the electricity market in the Province of Ontario.

Source: CPI Plastics Group Ltd., *First Quarter Report*, ended March 31, 2003.

Computation of Unit Costs

With the application of Yost Precision Machining's $216 manufacturing overhead to the job cost sheet in Exhibit 3–4, the job cost sheet is almost complete. There are two final steps. First, the totals for direct materials, direct labour, and manufacturing overhead are transferred to the Cost Summary section of the job cost sheet and added together to obtain the total cost for the job. Then the total cost ($1,800) is divided by the number of units (2) to obtain the unit cost ($900). As indicated earlier, *this unit cost is an average cost and should not be interpreted as the cost that would actually be incurred if another unit was produced.* Much of the actual overhead would not change at all if another unit was produced, so the incremental cost of an additional unit is something less than the average unit cost of $900.

The completed job cost sheet is now ready to be transferred to the Finished Goods inventory account, where it will serve as the basis for valuing unsold units in ending inventory and determining cost of goods sold.

Summary of Document Flows

The sequence of events discussed above is summarized in Exhibit 3–5. A careful study of the flow of documents in this exhibit will provide a good overview of the overall operation of a job-order costing system.

EXHIBIT 3–5 The Flow of Documents in a Job-Order Costing System

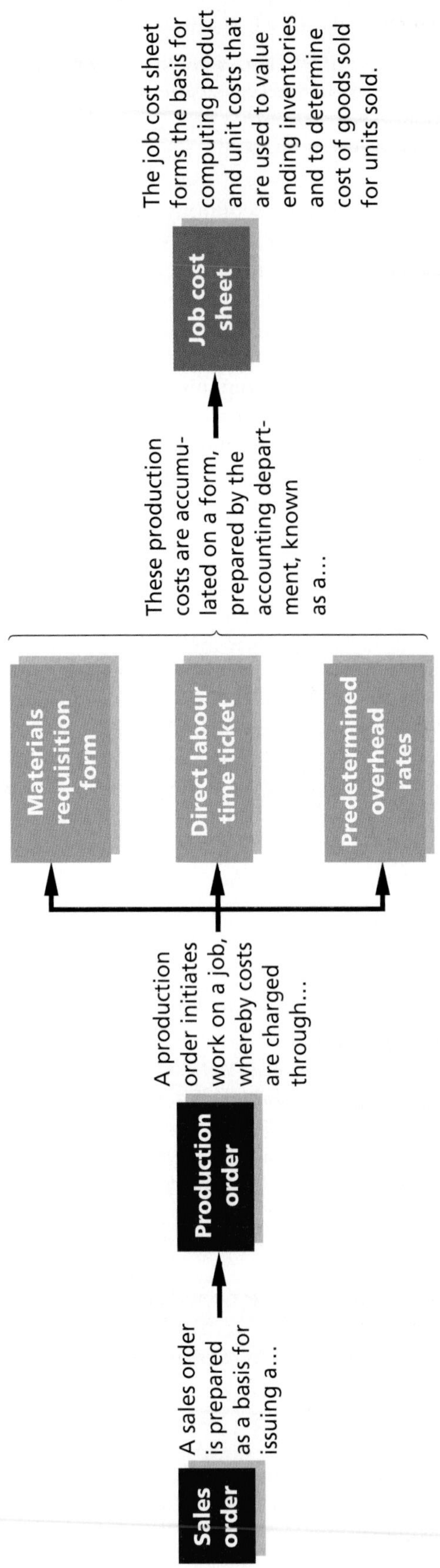

Sales order

A sales order is prepared as a basis for issuing a...

Production order

A production order initiates work on a job, whereby costs are charged through...

Materials requisition form

Direct labour time ticket

Predetermined overhead rates

These production costs are accumulated on a form, prepared by the accounting department, known as a...

Job cost sheet

The job cost sheet forms the basis for computing product and unit costs that are used to value ending inventories and to determine cost of goods sold for units sold.

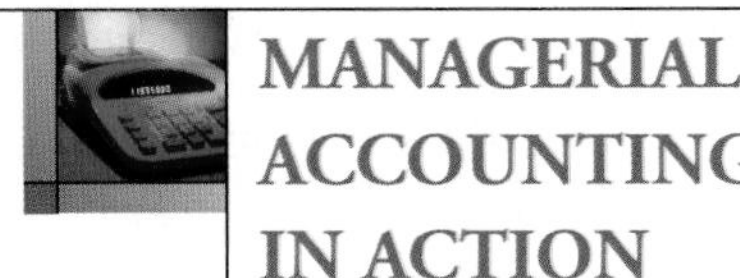

MANAGERIAL ACCOUNTING IN ACTION

The Wrap-Up

In the 8:00 A.M. daily planning meeting on March 9, Jean Yost, the president of Yost Precision Machining, once again drew attention to job 2B47, the experimental couplings:

Jean: I see job 2B47 is completed. Let's get those couplings shipped immediately to Loops Unlimited so they can get their testing program under way. Marcus, how much are we going to bill Loops for those two units?

Marcus: Just a second, let me check the job cost sheet for that job. Here it is. We agreed to sell the experimental units at cost, so we will be charging Loops Unlimited just $900 a unit.

Jean: Fine. Let's hope the couplings work out and we make some money on the big order later.

JOB-ORDER COSTING—THE FLOW OF COSTS

LEARNING OBJECTIVE 4
Record the journal entries that reflect the flow of costs in a job-order costing system.

We are now ready to take a more detailed look at the flow of costs through the company's formal accounting system. To illustrate, we shall consider a single month's activity for Rand Company, a producer of gold and silver commemorative medallions. Rand Company has two jobs in process during April, the first month of its fiscal year. Job A, a special minting of 1,000 gold medallions commemorating the world junior hockey championships held in Halifax, was started during March and had $30,000 in manufacturing costs already accumulated on April 1. Job B, an order for 10,000 silver medallions commemorating the same event, was started in April.

The Purchase and Issue of Materials

On April 1, Rand Company had $7,000 in raw materials on hand. During the month, the company purchased an additional $60,000 in raw materials. The purchase is recorded in journal entry (1) below:

(1)

Raw Materials	60,000	
Accounts Payable		60,000

As explained in Chapter 2, Raw Materials is an asset account. Thus, when raw materials are purchased, they are initially recorded as an asset—not as an expense.

Issue of Direct and Indirect Materials During April, $52,000 in raw materials were requisitioned from the storeroom for use in production. These raw materials include $50,000 of direct materials and $2,000 of indirect materials. Entry (2) records the issue of the materials to the production departments:

(2)

Work in Process	50,000	
Manufacturing Overhead	2,000	
Raw Materials		52,000

The materials charged to Work in Process represent direct materials for specific jobs. As these materials are entered into the Work in Process account, they are also recorded on the appropriate job cost sheets. This point is illustrated in Exhibit 3–6, where $28,000 of the $50,000 in direct materials is charged to job A's cost sheet and the remaining $22,000 is charged to job B's cost sheet. (In this example, all data are presented in summary form and the job cost sheet is abbreviated.)

The $2,000 charged to Manufacturing Overhead in entry (2) represents indirect materials used in production during April. Observe that the Manufacturing Overhead account is separate from the Work in Process account. The purpose of the Manufacturing Overhead account is to accumulate all manufacturing overhead costs as they are incurred during a period.

EXHIBIT 3–6 Raw Materials Cost Flows

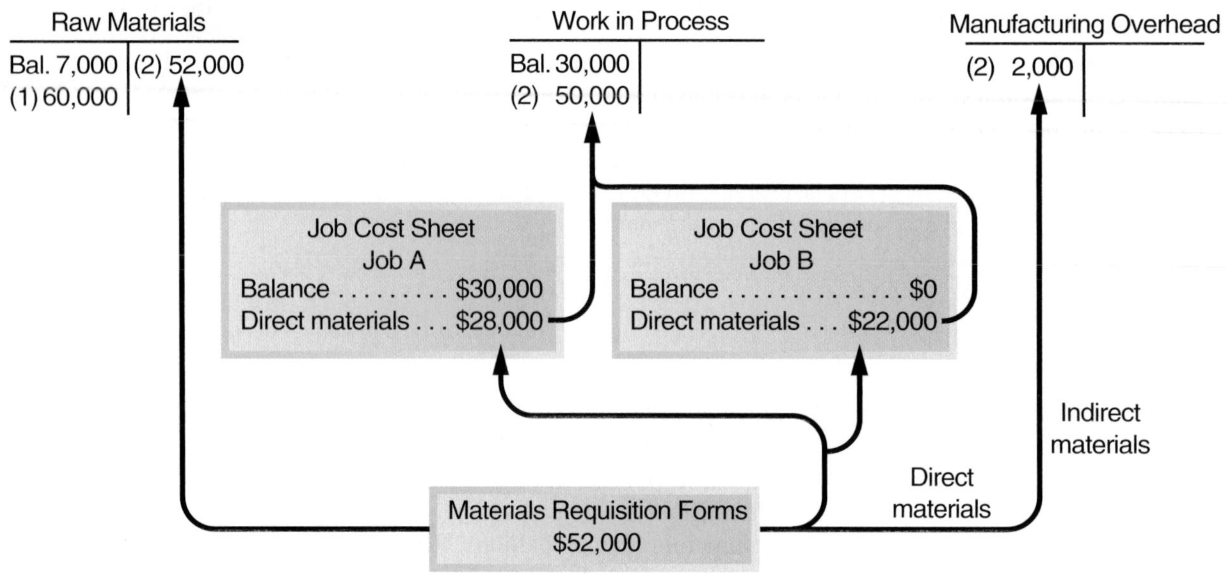

Before leaving Exhibit 3–6, note that the job cost sheet for job A contains a beginning balance of $30,000. We stated earlier that this balance represents the cost of work done during March that has been carried forward to April. Also note that the Work in Process account contains the same $30,000 balance. *The reason the $30,000 appears in both places is that the Work in Process account is a control account and the job cost sheets form a subsidiary ledger. Thus, the Work in Process account contains a summarized total of all costs appearing on the individual job cost sheets for all jobs in process at any given point in time.* (Since Rand Company had only job A in process at the beginning of April, job A's $30,000 balance on that date is equal to the balance in the Work in Process account.)

Issue of Direct Materials Only Sometimes the materials drawn from the Raw Materials inventory account are all direct materials. In this case, the entry to record the issue of the materials into production would be as follows:

Work in Process	XXX	
Raw Materials		XXX

Labour Cost

As work is performed in various departments of Rand Company from day to day, employee time tickets are filled out by workers, collected, and forwarded to the Accounting Department. In the Accounting Department, the tickets are costed according to the various employee wage rates, and the resulting costs are classified as either direct or indirect labour. In April, $60,000 was recorded for direct labour and $15,000 for indirect labout resulting in the following summary entry:

(3)

Work in Process	60,000	
Manufacturing Overhead	15,000	
Salaries and Wages Payable		75,000

Only direct labour is added to the Work in Process account. For Rand Company, this amounted to $60,000 for April.

At the same time that direct labour costs are added to Work in Process, they are also added to the individual job cost sheets, as shown in Exhibit 3–7. During April, $40,000 of direct labour cost was charged to job A and the remaining $20,000 was charged to job B.

EXHIBIT 3–7 Labour Cost Flows

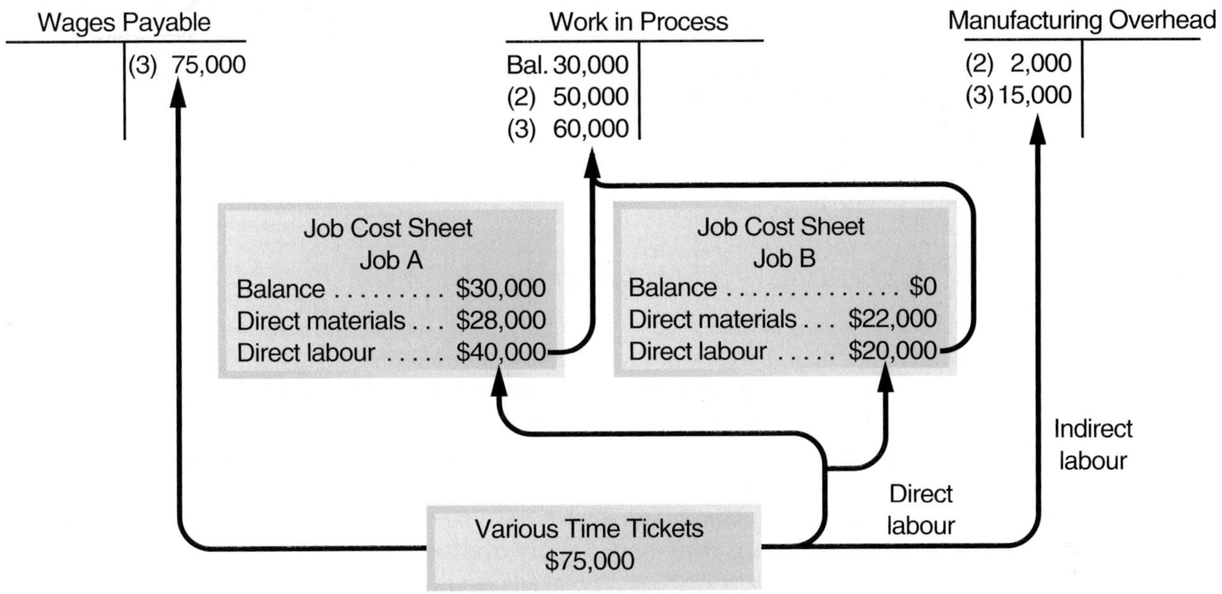

The labour costs charged to Manufacturing Overhead represent the indirect labour costs of the period, such as supervision, janitorial work, and maintenance.

Manufacturing Overhead Costs

Recall that all costs of operating the factory other than direct materials and direct labour are classified as manufacturing overhead costs. These costs are entered directly into the Manufacturing Overhead account as they are incurred. To illustrate, assume that Rand Company incurred the following general factory costs during April:

Utilities (heat, water, and power)	$21,000
Rent on factory equipment	16,000
Miscellaneous factory costs	3,000
Total	$40,000

The following entry records the incurrence of these costs:

(4)

Manufacturing Overhead	40,000	
Accounts Payable		40,000

In addition, let us assume that during April, Rand Company recognized $13,000 in accrued property taxes and that $7,000 in prepaid insurance expired on factory buildings and equipment. The following entry records these items:

(5)

Manufacturing Overhead	20,000	
Property Taxes Payable		13,000
Prepaid Insurance		7,000

Finally, let us assume that the company recognized $18,000 in depreciation on factory equipment during April. The following entry records the accrual of this depreciation:

(6)

Manufacturing Overhead	18,000	
Accumulated Depreciation		18,000

In short, *all* manufacturing overhead costs are recorded directly into the Manufacturing Overhead account as they are incurred day by day throughout a period. It is important to understand that Manufacturing Overhead is a control account for many—perhaps thousands—of subsidiary accounts such as Indirect Materials, Indirect Labour, Factory Utilities, and so forth. As the Manufacturing Overhead account is debited for costs during a period, the various subsidiary accounts are also debited. In the example above and also in the assignment material for this chapter, we omit the entries to the subsidiary accounts for the sake of brevity.

LEARNING OBJECTIVE 5
Apply overhead cost to Work in Process using a predetermined overhead rate.

The Application of Manufacturing Overhead

Since actual manufacturing costs are charged to the Manufacturing Overhead control account rather than to Work in Process, how are manufacturing overhead costs assigned to Work in Process? The answer is, by means of the predetermined overhead rate. Recall from our discussion earlier in the chapter that a predetermined overhead rate is established at the beginning of each year. The rate is calculated by dividing the estimated total manufacturing overhead cost for the year by the estimated total units in the allocation base (measured in machine-hours, direct labour-hours, or some other base). The predetermined overhead rate is then used to apply overhead costs to jobs. For example, if direct labour-hours is the allocation base, overhead cost is applied to each job by multiplying the number of direct labour-hours charged to the job by the predetermined overhead rate.

To illustrate, assume that Rand Company has used machine-hours in computing its predetermined overhead rate and that this rate is \$6 per machine-hour. Also assume that during April, 10,000 machine-hours were worked on job A and 5,000 machine-hours were worked on job B (a total of 15,000 machine-hours). Thus, \$90,000 in overhead cost (15,000 machine-hours × \$6 = \$90,000) would be applied to Work in Process. The following entry records the application of Manufacturing Overhead to Work in Process:

(7)

	Debit	Credit
Work in Process	90,000	
Manufacturing Overhead		90,000

The flow of costs through the Manufacturing Overhead account is detailed in Exhibit 3–8.

The "actual overhead costs" in the Manufacturing Overhead account shown in Exhibit 3–8 are the costs that were added to the account in entries (2)–(6). Observe that the incurrence of these actual overhead costs [entries (2)–(6)] and the application of overhead to Work in Process [entry (7)] represent two separate and entirely distinct processes.

The Concept of a Clearing Account The Manufacturing Overhead account operates as a clearing account. As we have noted, actual factory overhead costs are debited to the accounts as they are incurred day by day throughout the year. At certain intervals during the year, usually when a job is completed, overhead cost is released from the Manufacturing Overhead account and is applied to the Work in Process account by means of the predetermined overhead rate. This sequence of events is illustrated as follows:

Manufacturing Overhead (a clearing account)

Actual overhead costs are charged to the account as these costs are incurred day by day throughout the period. →	→ Overhead is applied to Work in Process using the predetermined overhead rate.

The actual overhead costs incurred and shown as debits in the manufacturing account are a result of many different types of overhead costs. A brief list of some of the different types is presented in the journal entries, numbers 4, 5 and 6, or in the schedule of cost of

EXHIBIT 3–8 The Flow of Costs in Overhead Application

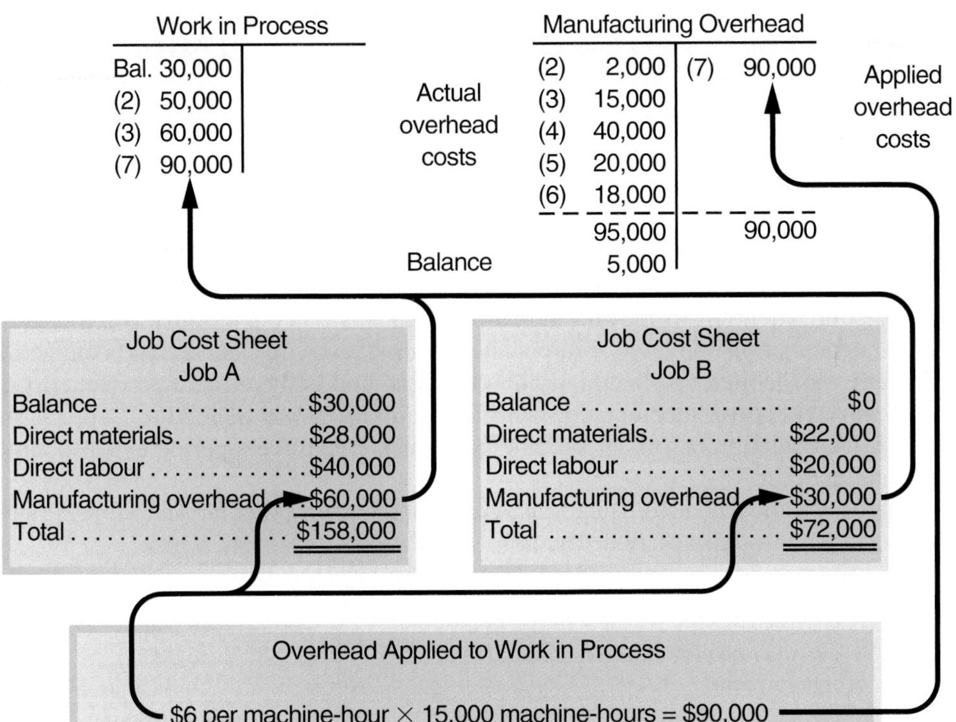

goods manufactured, shown in Exhibit 3–11 on page 96 or previously in Exhibit 2–4 on page 36. The clearing account concept actually represents a general ledger control account for a subsidiary ledger that contains the detailed information on each type of overhead cost.

As we emphasized earlier, the predetermined overhead rate is based entirely on estimates of what overhead costs are *expected* to be, and it is established before the year begins. As a result, the overhead cost applied during a year will almost certainly turn out to be more or less than the overhead cost that is actually incurred. For example, notice from Exhibit 3–8 that Rand Company's actual overhead costs for the period are $5,000 greater than the overhead cost that has been applied to Work in Process, resulting in a $5,000 debit balance in the Manufacturing Overhead account. We will reserve discussion of what to do with this $5,000 balance until a later section in this chapter, Complications of Overhead Application.

For the moment, we can conclude by noting from Exhibit 3–8 that the cost of a completed job consists of the actual materials cost of the job, the actual labour cost of the job, and the overhead cost *applied* to the job. Pay particular attention to the following subtle but important point: *Actual overhead costs are not charged to jobs; actual overhead costs do not appear on the job cost sheet nor do they appear in the Work in Process account. Only the applied overhead cost, based on the predetermined overhead rate, appears on the job cost sheet and in the Work in Process account.* Study this point carefully.

Non-Manufacturing Costs

In addition to manufacturing costs, companies also incur marketing and selling costs. As explained in Chapter 2, these costs should be treated as period expenses and charged directly to the income statement. *Non-manufacturing costs should not go into the Manufacturing Overhead account.* To illustrate the correct treatment of non-manufacturing costs, assume that Rand Company incurred $30,000 of selling and administrative costs during April. The following entry records these salaries:

(8)

Salaries Expense	30,000	
Salaries and Wages Payable		30,000

Assume that depreciation on office equipment during April was $7,000. The entry is as follows:

(9)

Depreciation Expense	7,000	
Accumulated Depreciation		7,000

Pay particular attention to the difference between this entry and entry (6) where we recorded depreciation on factory equipment. In journal entry (6), depreciation on factory equipment was debited to Manufacturing Overhead and is therefore a product cost. In journal entry (9) above, depreciation on office equipment was debited to Depreciation Expense. Depreciation on office equipment is considered to be a period expense rather than a product cost.

Finally, assume that advertising was $42,000 and that other selling and administrative expenses in April totalled $8,000. The following entry records these items:

(10)

Advertising Expense	42,000	
Other Selling and Administrative Expense	8,000	
Accounts Payable		50,000

Because the amounts in entries (8) through (10) all go directly into expense accounts, they will have no effect on product costs. The same will be true of any other selling and administrative expenses incurred during April, including sales commissions, depreciation on sales equipment, rent on office facilities, insurance on office facilities, and related costs.

The distinction between manufacturing overhead costs and non-manufacturing costs such as selling and administrative expenses is sometimes difficult because of the type of cost. For example, depreciation or salaries should be classified as product costs if related to manufacturing but are classified as period costs and expensed if related to non-manufacturing activities. In practice, the classification has to be based on what the firm does to incur the costs. If it sells or markets, then this is not production and the distinction is clear. If, however, it administers, then the distinction depends on what is administered and how important it is to separate production administration from overall administration. For example, if all the company does is produce the Hibernia oil platform, then administration is production (manufacturing) overhead. However, if the company is administering many jobs and marketing new jobs at the same time, it may not be able to distinguish overhead from administrative time on the part of the senior management. Thus, unless costs are needed for a cost-recovery billing, administration salaries expense may be the expeditious way to treat the salaries.

Cost of Goods Manufactured

LEARNING OBJECTIVE **6**
Prepare schedules of cost of goods manufactured and cost of goods sold.

When a job has been completed, the finished output is transferred from the production departments to the finished goods warehouse. By this time, the Accounting Department will have charged the job with direct materials and direct labour cost, and manufacturing overhead will have been applied using the predetermined rate. A transfer of these costs must be made within the costing system that *parallels* the physical transfer of the goods to the finished goods warehouse. The costs of the completed job are transferred out of the Work in Process account and into the Finished Goods account. The sum of all amounts transferred between these two accounts represents the cost of goods manufactured for the period. (This point was illustrated earlier in Exhibit 2–4 in Chapter 2.)

In the case of Rand Company, let us assume that job A was completed during April. The following entry transfers the cost of job A from Work in Process to Finished Goods:

(11)

Finished Goods	158,000	
Work in Process		158,000

The $158,000 represents the completed cost of job A, as shown on the job cost sheet in Exhibit 3–8. Since job A was the only job completed during April, the $158,000 also represents the cost of goods manufactured for the month.

Job B was not completed by month-end, so its cost will remain in the Work in Process account and carry over to the next month. If a balance sheet is prepared at the end of April, the cost accumulated thus far on job B will appear as "Work in process inventory" in the assets section.

Cost of Goods Sold

As units in finished goods are shipped to customers their accumulated cost are transferred from the Finished Goods account into the Cost of Goods Sold account. If a complete job is shipped, as in the case where a job has been done to a customer's specifications, then it is a simple matter to transfer the entire cost appearing on the job cost sheet into the Cost of Goods Sold account. In most cases, however, only a portion of the units involved in a particular job will be immediately sold. In these situations, the unit cost must be used to determine how much product cost should be removed from Finished Goods and charged to Cost of Goods Sold.

For Rand Company, we will assume that 750 of the 1,000 gold medallions in job A were shipped to customers by the end of the month for total sales revenue of $225,000. Since 1,000 units were produced and the total cost of the job from the job cost sheet was $158,000, the unit product cost was $158. The following journal entries would record the sale (all sales are on account):

(12)

Accounts Receivable	225,000	
Sales		225,000

(13)

Cost of Goods Sold	118,500	
Finished Goods		118,500
($158 per unit × 750 units = $118,500)		

With entry (13), the flow of costs through our job-order costing system is completed.

Summary of Cost Flows

To pull the entire Rand Company example together, journal entries (1) through (13) are summarized in Exhibit 3–9. The flow of costs through the accounts is presented in T-account form in Exhibit 3–10.

Exhibit 3–11 presents a schedule of cost of goods manufactured and a schedule of cost of goods sold for Rand Company. Note particularly from Exhibit 3–11 that the manufacturing overhead cost on the schedule of cost of goods manufactured is the overhead applied to jobs during the month—not the actual manufacturing overhead costs incurred. The reason for this can be traced back to journal entry (7) and the T-account for Work in Process that appears in Exhibit 3–10. Under a normal costing system as illustrated in this chapter, applied—not actual—overhead costs are applied to jobs and thus to Work in Process inventory. Note also that the cost of goods manufactured for the month ($158,000) agrees with the amount transferred from Work in Process to Finished Goods for the month, as recorded earlier in entry (11). Also note that this $158,000 figure is used in computing the cost of goods sold for the month.

An income statement for April is presented in Exhibit 3–12. Observe that the cost of goods sold figure on this statement ($123,500) is carried down from Exhibit 3–11.

EXHIBIT 3–9 Summary of Rand Company Journal Entries

	Debit	Credit
(1)		
Raw Materials	60,000	
Accounts Payable		60,000
(2)		
Work in Process	50,000	
Manufacturing Overhead	2,000	
Raw Materials		52,000
(3)		
Work in Process	60,000	
Manufacturing Overhead	15,000	
Salaries and Wages Payable		75,000
(4)		
Manufacturing Overhead	40,000	
Accounts Payable		40,000
(5)		
Manufacturing Overhead	20,000	
Property Taxes Payable		13,000
Prepaid Insurance		7,000
(6)		
Manufacturing Overhead	18,000	
Accumulated Depreciation		18,000
(7)		
Work in Process	90,000	
Manufacturing Overhead		90,000
(8)		
Salaries Expense	30,000	
Salaries and Wages Payable		30,000
(9)		
Depreciation Expense	7,000	
Accumulated Depreciation		7,000
(10)		
Advertising Expense	42,000	
Other Selling and Administrative Expense	8,000	
Accounts Payable		50,000
(11)		
Finished Goods	158,000	
Work in Process		158,000
(12)		
Accounts Receivable	225,000	
Sales		225,000
(13)		
Cost of Goods Sold	118,500	
Finished Goods		118,500

EXHIBIT 3–10 Summary of Cost Flows—Rand Company

Accounts Receivable

	Debit		Credit
	XX*		
(12)	225,000		

Prepaid Insurance

	Debit		Credit
	XX		
		(5)	7,000

Raw Materials

	Debit		Credit
Bal.	7,000	(2)	52,000
(1)	60,000		
Bal.	15,000		

Work in Process

	Debit		Credit
Bal.	30,000	(11)	158,000
(2)	50,000		
(3)	60,000		
(7)	90,000		
Bal.	72,000		

Finished Goods

	Debit		Credit
Bal..	10,000	(13)	118,500
(11)	158,000		
Bal.	49,500		

Accumulated Depreciation

	Debit		Credit
			XX
		(6)	18,000
		(9)	7,000

Manufacturing Overhead

	Debit		Credit
(2)	2,000	(7)	90,000
(3)	15,000		
(4)	40,000		
(5)	20,000		
(6)	18,000		
Bal.	5,000		

Accounts Payable

	Debit		Credit
			XX
		(1)	60,000
		(4)	40,000
		(10)	50,000

Salaries and Wages Payable

	Debit		Credit
			XX
		(3)	75,000
		(8)	30,000

Property Taxes Payable

	Debit		Credit
			XX
		(5)	13,000

Capital Stock

	Debit		Credit
			XX

Retained Earnings

	Debit		Credit
			XX

Sales

	Debit		Credit
		(12)	225,000

Cost of Goods Sold

	Debit		Credit
(13)	118,500		

Salaries Expense

	Debit		Credit
(8)	30,000		

Depreciation Expense

	Debit		Credit
(9)	7,000		

Advertising Expense

	Debit		Credit
(10)	42,000		

Other Selling and Administrative Expense

	Debit		Credit
(10)	8,000		

Explanation of entries:
(1) Raw materials purchased.
(2) Direct and indirect materials issued into production.
(3) Direct and indirect factory labour cost incurred.
(4) Utilities and other factory costs incurred.
(5) Property taxes and insurance incurred on the factory.
(6) Depreciation recorded on factory assets.
(7) Overhead cost applied to Work in Process.
(8) Administrative salaries expense incurred.
(9) Depreciation recorded on office equipment.
(10) Advertising and other expense incurred.
(11) Cost of goods manufactured transferred into finished goods.
(12) Sale of job A recorded.
(13) Cost of goods sold recorded for job A.

*XX = Normal balance in the account (for example, Accounts Receivable normally carries a debit balance).

EXHIBIT 3–11 Schedules of Cost of Goods Manufactured and Cost of Goods Sold

Cost of Goods Manufactured		
Direct materials:		
Raw materials inventory, beginning	$ 7,000	
Add: Purchases of raw materials	60,000	
Total raw materials available	67,000	
Deduct: Raw materials inventory, ending	15,000	
Raw materials used in production	52,000	
Less indirect materials included in manufacturing overhead	2,000	$ 50,000
Direct labour		60,000
Manufacturing overhead applied to work in process		90,000
Total manufacturing costs		200,000
Add: Beginning work in process inventory		30,000
		230,000
Deduct: Ending work in process inventory		72,000
Cost of goods manufactured		$158,000
Cost of Goods Sold		
Finished goods inventory, beginning		$ 10,000
Add: Cost of goods manufactured		158,000
Goods available for sale		168,000
Deduct: Finished goods inventory, ending		49,500
Unadjusted cost of goods sold		118,500
Add: Underapplied overhead		5,000
Adjusted cost of goods sold		$123,500

*Note that the underapplied overhead is added to cost of goods sold. If overhead was overapplied, it would be deducted from costs of goods sold.

EXHIBIT 3–12 Income Statement

RAND COMPANY
Income Statement
For the Month Ending April 30

Sales		$225,000
Less cost of goods sold ($118,500 + $5,000)		123,500
Gross margin		101,500
Less selling and administrative expenses:		
Salaries expense	$30,000	
Depreciation expense	7,000	
Advertising expense	42,000	
Other expense	8,000	87,000
Net income		$ 14,500

COMPLICATIONS OF OVERHEAD APPLICATION

We need to consider two complications relating to overhead application. These are (1) the computation of underapplied and overapplied overhead and (2) the disposition of any balance remaining in the Manufacturing Overhead account at the end of a period.

Underapplied and Overapplied Overhead

LEARNING OBJECTIVE 7
Compute under- or overapplied overhead cost and prepare the journal entry to close the balance in Manufacturing Overhead to the appropriate accounts.

Since the predetermined overhead rate is established before a period begins and is based entirely on estimated data, there generally will be a difference between the amount of overhead cost applied to Work in Process and the amount of overhead cost actually incurred during a period. In the case of Rand Company, for example, the predetermined overhead rate of $6 per hour resulted in $90,000 of overhead cost being applied to Work in Process, whereas actual overhead costs for April proved to be $95,000 (as shown in Exhibit 3–8). The difference between the overhead cost applied to Work in Process and the actual overhead costs of a period is termed either **underapplied** or **overapplied overhead.** For Rand Company, overhead was underapplied because the applied cost ($90,000) was $5,000 less than the actual cost ($95,000). If the tables had been reversed and the company had applied $95,000 in overhead cost to Work in Process while incurring actual overhead costs of only $90,000, then the overhead would have been overapplied.

Underapplied overhead
A debit balance in the Manufacturing Overhead account that arises when the amount of overhead cost actually incurred is greater than the amount of overhead cost applied to Work in Process during a period.

Overapplied overhead
A credit balance in the Manufacturing Overhead account that arises when the amount of overhead cost applied to Work in Process is greater than the amount of overhead cost actually incurred during a period.

What is the cause of underapplied or overapplied overhead? The causes can be complex, and a full explanation will have to wait for Chapters 10 and 11. Nevertheless, the basic problem is that the method of applying overhead to jobs using a predetermined overhead rate assumes that actual overhead costs will be proportional to the actual amount of the allocation base incurred during the period. If, for example, the predetermined overhead rate is $6 per machine-hour, then it is assumed that actual overhead costs incurred will be $6 for every machine-hour that is actually worked. There are at least two reasons why this may not be true. First, much of the overhead often consists of fixed costs. Since these costs are fixed, they do not grow as the number of machine-hours incurred increases. Second, spending on overhead items may or may not be under control. If individuals who are responsible for overhead costs do a good job, those costs should be less than were expected at the beginning of the period. If they do a poor job, those costs will be more than expected. As we indicated above, however, a fuller explanation of the causes of underapplied and overapplied overhead will have to wait for later chapters.

To illustrate what can happen, suppose that two companies—Turbo Crafters and Black & Howell—have prepared the following estimated data for the coming year:

	Company	
	Turbo Crafters	**Black & Howell**
Predetermined overhead rate based on	Machine-hours	Direct materials cost
Estimated manufacturing overhead	$300,000 (a)	$120,000 (a)
Estimated machine-hours	75,000 (b)	—
Estimated direct materials cost	—	$ 80,000 (b)
Predetermined overhead rate, (a) ÷ (b)	$4 per machine-hour	150% of direct materials cost

Note that when the allocation base is dollars—such as direct material cost in the case of Black and Howell—the predetermined overhead rate is a percentage. When dollars are divided by dollars, the result is a percentage.

Now assume that because of unexpected changes in overhead spending and changes in demand for the companies' products, the *actual* overhead cost and the *actual* activity recorded during the year in each company are as follows:

	Company	
	Turbo Crafters	**Black & Howell**
Actual manufacturing overhead costs	$290,000	$130,000
Actual machine-hours	68,000	—
Actual direct material costs	—	$ 90,000

For each company, note that the actual data for both cost and activity differ from the estimates used in computing the predetermined overhead rate. This results in underapplied and overapplied overhead as follows:

	Company	
	Turbo Crafters	Black & Howell
Actual manufacturing overhead costs	$290,000	$130,000
Manufacturing overhead cost applied to Work in Process during the year:		
68,000 *actual* machine-hours × $4	272,000	
$90,000 *actual* direct materials cost × 150%		135,000
Underapplied (overapplied) overhead	$ 18,000	$ (5,000)

For Turbo Crafters, notice that the amount of overhead cost that has been applied to Work in Process ($272,000) is less than the actual overhead cost for the year ($290,000). Therefore, overhead is underapplied. Also notice that the original estimate of overhead in Turbo Crafters ($300,000) is not directly involved in this computation. Its impact is felt only through the $4 predetermined overhead rate that is used.

For Black & Howell, the amount of overhead cost that has been applied to Work in Process ($135,000) is greater than the actual overhead cost for the year ($130,000), and so overhead is overapplied.

A summary of the concepts discussed above is presented in Exhibit 3–13.

Disposition of Under- or Overapplied Overhead Balances

What disposition should be made of any under- or overapplied balance remaining in the Manufacturing Overhead account at the end of a period? Generally, any balance in the account is treated in one of three ways:

1. Closed out to Cost of Goods Sold.
2. Allocated between Work in Process, Finished Goods, and Cost of Goods Sold in proportion to the overhead applied during the current period in the ending balances of these accounts.[1]

EXHIBIT 3–13 Summary of Overhead Concepts

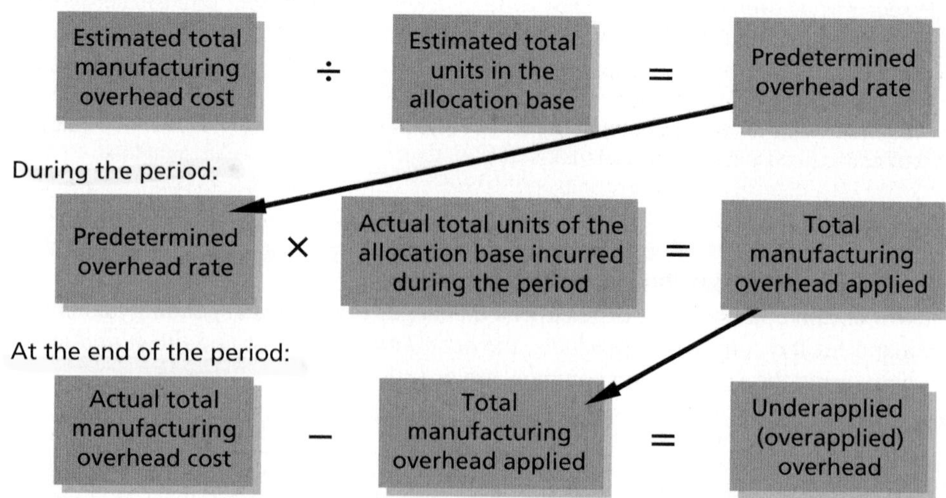

1. Some firms prefer to make the allocation on the basis of the total cost of direct materials, direct labour, and applied manufacturing overhead in each of the accounts at the end of the period. This method is not as accurate as allocating the balance in the Manufacturing Overhead account on the basis of just the overhead applied in each of the accounts during the current period.

3. Carried forward to the next period.

The second method, which allocates the under- or overapplied overhead among ending inventories and Cost of Goods Sold, is equivalent to using an "actual" overhead rate and is for that reason considered by many to be more accurate than the first method. Consequently, if the amount of underapplied or overapplied overhead is material, many accountants would insist that the second method be used. In problem assignments, we will always indicate which method you are to use for disposing of under- or overapplied overhead.

Close Out to Cost of Goods Sold As mentioned above, closing out the balance in Manufacturing Overhead to Cost of Goods Sold is simpler than the allocation method. Returning to the example of Rand Company, the entry to close the $5,000 of underapplied overhead to Cost of Goods Sold would be as follows:

(14)		
Cost of Goods Sold	5,000	
Manufacturing Overhead		5,000

Note that since there is a debit balance in the Manufacturing Overhead account, Manufacturing Overhead must be credited to close out the account. This has the effect of increasing Cost of Goods Sold for April to $123,500:

Unadjusted cost of goods sold [from entry (13)]	$118,500
Add underapplied overhead [entry (14) above]	5,000
Adjusted cost of goods sold	$123,500

After this adjustment has been made, Rand Company's income statement for April will appear as was shown earlier in Exhibit 3–12.

Allocate among Accounts Allocation of under- or overapplied overhead among Work in Process, Finished Goods, and Cost of Goods Sold is more accurate than closing the entire balance into Cost of Goods Sold. The reason is that allocation assigns overhead costs to where they would have gone in the first place had it not been for the errors in the estimates going into the predetermined overhead rate.

Had Rand Company chosen to allocate the underapplied overhead among the inventory accounts and Cost of Goods Sold, it would first be necessary to determine the amount of overhead that had been applied during April in each of the accounts. The computations would have been as follows:

Overhead applied in work in process inventory, April 30	$30,000	33.33%
Overhead applied in finished goods inventory, April 30 ($60,000/1,000 units = $60 per unit) × 250 units	15,000	16.67%
Overhead applied in cost of goods sold, April ($60,000/1,000 units = $60 per unit) × 750 units	45,000	50.00%
Total overhead applied	$90,000	100.00%

Based on the above percentages, the underapplied overhead (i.e., the debit balance in Manufacturing Overhead) would be allocated as in the following journal entry:

Work in Process (33.33% × $5,000)	1,666.50	
Finished Goods (16.67% × $5,000)	833.50	
Cost of Goods Sold (50.00% × $5,000)	2,500.00	
Manufacturing Overhead		5,000.00

Note that the first step in the allocation was to determine the amount of overhead applied in each of the accounts. For Finished Goods, for example, the total amount of overhead applied to job A, $60,000, was divided by the total number of units in job A, 1,000 units, to arrive at the average overhead applied of $60 per unit. Since there were still 250 units from job A in ending finished goods inventory, the amount of overhead applied in the Finished Goods Inventory account was $60 per unit multiplied by 250 units, or $15,000 in total.

If overhead had been overapplied, the entry above would have been just the reverse, since a credit balance would have existed in the Manufacturing Overhead account.

An alternative but less accurate way to allocate under- or overapplied overhead among Work in Process, Finished Goods, and Cost of Goods Sold is to use the entire cost of manufacturing in each account.

Had we chosen to allocate the underapplied overhead in the Rand Company example, the computations and entry would have been:

Work in process inventory, April 30		$ 72,000	36.00%
Finished goods inventory, April 30		49,500	24.75
Cost of goods sold	$118,500		
Less: Work in process inventory, April 1	30,000		
Finished goods inventory, April 1	10,000	78,500	39.25
Total		$200,000	100.00%
Work in Process (36.0% × $5,000)	1,800		
Finished Goods (24.75% × $5,000)	1,237		
Cost of Goods Sold (39.25% × $5,000)	1,963		
Manufacturing Overhead		5,000	

A comparison of the percentages above with those using only overhead suggests that total manufacturing costs and overhead were not in the same proportions in each account. This difference is the inaccuracy in the problem resulting from using total manufacturing costs.

The rationale for deducting the beginning work in process and finished goods inventories from the cost of goods sold is to permit the allocation to be based on costs from the current period. By doing so, the 39.25% in the Rand Company example reflects only costs from April and thus corresponds to the period in which the underapplied overhead occurred. Without this adjustment, cost of goods sold would be assigned the overhead difference based on costs carried over from March and thus bear a disproportionate amount of the under- or overapplied overhead.

Carry the Balance Forward Recall the section earlier in this chapter entitled Application of Manufacturing Overhead. Notice that some firms have large seasonal variations in output while being faced with relatively constant overhead costs. Predetermined overhead was used to even out fluctuations in the cost of overhead caused by seasonal variations in output and seasonal variations in costs (e.g., heating costs). The predetermined overhead rate is computed using estimated total manufacturing costs for a year divided by estimated total units in the base. The result is an average rate. When the average predetermined rate is applied to actual production for the period, the applied overhead is determined. The under- or overapplied overhead is a result of two factors: an actual base that is different from one-twelfth of the annual estimated base and actual overhead costs that do not equal one-twelfth of the total estimated overhead costs. Therefore, for any given month, an under- or overapplied overhead amount would be expected. In some months, it would be positive; in other months, it would be negative. Over the year, these amounts may largely cancel out. If this is the situation, then significant debits and credits could be carried forward to the year-end so that a final disposition can be made either by adjusting Cost of Goods Sold or allocating (sometimes termed *prorating*) the amount to the inventories and Cost of Goods Sold.

The Rand Company example would be treated as follows:

Underapplied Overhead		
[a deferred debit balance on the balance sheet]	5,000	
Manufacturing Overhead		5,000

A General Model of Product Cost Flows

The flow of costs in a product costing system is presented in the form of a T-account model in Exhibit 3–14. This model applies as much to a process costing system as it does to a job-order costing system. Examination of this model can be very helpful in gaining a perspective as to how costs enter a system, flow through it, and finally end up as Cost of Goods Sold on the income statement.

Variations from the General Model of Product Cost Flow

Costing systems can vary from what is reflected by the general model. While the general model is the most complete description, circumstances may make such a complete system too costly. For example, a system variation known as *backflush costing* can permit labour charges to be made directly to manufacturing overhead. Then, overhead is applied to the cost of completed jobs along with raw materials, so that the need to keep work in process records can be avoided. Such a minimal treatment of work in process is justified in a mechanized JIT environment. Cost of completed jobs still reflects the material and overhead (including labour), but the record system reflects the simplified needs of the production environment.

EXHIBIT 3–14 A General Model of Cost Flows

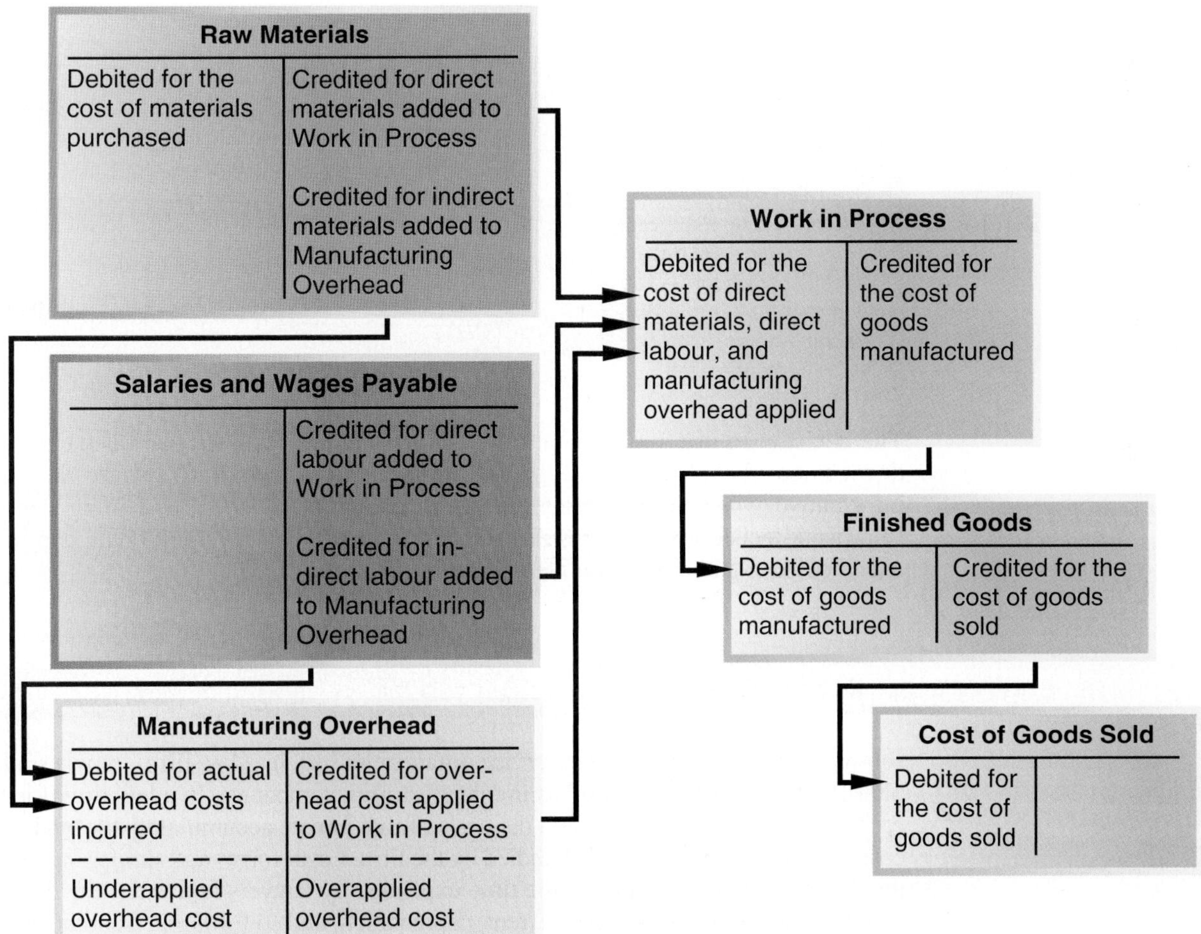

Multiple Predetermined Overhead Rates

Plantwide overhead rate
A single predetermined overhead rate that is used throughout a plant.

Multiple predetermined overhead rates
A costing system in which there are multiple overhead cost pools with a different predetermined rate for each cost pool, rather than a single predetermined overhead rate for the entire company. Frequently, each production department is treated as a separate overhead cost pool.

Our discussion of overhead in this chapter has assumed that there is a single predetermined overhead rate for an entire factory called a **plantwide overhead rate.** This is, in fact, a common practice—particularly in smaller companies. But in larger companies, *multiple predetermined overhead rates* are often used. In a **multiple predetermined overhead rate** system there is usually a different overhead rate for each production department. Such a system, while more complex, is considered to be more accurate, because it can reflect differences across departments in how overhead costs are incurred. For example, overhead might be allocated based on direct labour-hours in departments that are relatively labour-intensive and based on machine-hours in departments that are relatively machine-intensive. When multiple predetermined overhead rates are used, overhead is applied in each department according to its own overhead rate as a job proceeds through the department.

To illustrate, refer to the data in the following table where Cook Company has two departments (A and B) and several jobs in process. Data is provided for two of these jobs (X and Y). If the company uses a plantwide overhead rate of \$12 (\$336, 000 ÷ 28,000 DLH) then the overhead costs applied to Job X and Job Y will be \$8,400 (\$12 × 700 hours + \$12 × 0) and \$12 (\$12 × 0 hours + \$12 × 1 hour) respectively. However, if overhead is applied using department overhead rates then Job X will be assigned \$2,800 (\$4 × 700 direct labour-hours) and Job Y will be assigned \$8,400 (\$12 × 700 machine-hours).

Cook Company	Department A	Department B	Total
Overhead cost	\$84,000	\$252,000	\$336,000
Direct labour-hours	21,000	7,000	28,000 DLH
Machine-hours	7,000	21,000	28,000 MH
Overhead cost driver	21,000 DLH	21,000 MH	
Overhead rate: Plant wide			\$12 per DLH
By department	\$4/DLH	\$12/MH	
Direct labour-hours—**Job X**	700	0	
Direct labour-hours—**Job Y**	0	1	
Machine-hours—Job X	1	0	
Machine-hours—Job Y	0	700	

The decision to use a plantwide rate versus separate rates for each department comes down to cost/benefit. It is cheaper to use a plantwide rate but separate rates are more informative when the activities that drive overhead costs differ among departments. Improved decision making resulting from more accurate overhead data can justify the added costs of gathering separate departmental overhead data.

JOB-ORDER COSTING IN SERVICE COMPANIES

Job-order costing is also used in service organizations such as law firms, movie studios, hospitals, and repair shops, as well as in manufacturing companies. In a law firm, for example, each client represents a "job," and the costs of that job are accumulated day by day on a job cost sheet as the client's case is handled by the firm. Legal forms and similar inputs represent the direct materials for the job; the time expended by lawyers represents the direct labour; and the costs of secretaries, clerks, rent, depreciation, and so forth represent the overhead.

In a movie studio, each film produced by the studio is a "job," and costs for direct materials (costumes, props, film, etc.) and direct labour (actors, directors, and extras) are accounted for and charged to each film's job cost sheet. A share of the studio's overhead costs, such as utilities, depreciation of equipment, salaries of maintenance workers, and so forth, is also charged to each film.

In summary, job-order costing is a versatile and widely used costing method, and may be encountered in virtually any organization that provides there are diverse products or services.

USE OF INFORMATION TECHNOLOGY

Earlier in the chapter, we discussed how bar code technology can be used to record labour time—reducing the drudgery in that task and increasing accuracy. Bar codes have many other uses.

In a company with a well-developed bar code system, the manufacturing cycle begins with the receipt of a customer's order in electronic form. Until very recently, the order would have been received via electronic data interchange (EDI), which involves a network of computers linking organizations. An EDI network allows companies to electronically exchange business documents and other information that extend into all areas of business activity from ordering raw materials to shipping completed goods. EDI was developed in the 1980s and requires significant investments in programming and networking hardware. Recently, EDI has been challenged by a far cheaper Internet-based alternative—XML (Extensible Markup Language), an extension of HTML (Hypertext Markup Language). HTML uses codes to tell your Web browser how to display information on your screen, but the computer doesn't know what the information is—it just displays it. XML provides additional tags that identify the kind of information that is being exchanged. For example, price data might be coded as <price> 14.95 <price>. When your computer reads this data and sees the tags <price> surrounding 14.95, your computer will immediately know that this is a price. XML tags can designate many different kinds of information—customer orders, medical records, bank statements, and so on—and the tags will indicate to your computer how to display, store, and retrieve the information. Office Depot was an early adopter of XML, which it is using to facilitate e-commerce with its big customers.

Once an order has been received via EDI or over the Internet in the form of an XML file, the computer draws up a list of required raw materials and sends out electronic purchase orders to suppliers. When materials arrive at the company's plant from the suppliers, bar codes that have been applied by the suppliers are scanned to update inventory records and to trigger payment for the materials. The bar codes are scanned again when the materials are requisitioned for use in production. At that point, the computer credits the Raw Materials inventory account for the amount and type of goods requisitioned and charges the Work in Process inventory account.

A unique bar code is assigned to each job. This bar code is scanned to update Work in Process records for labour and other costs incurred in the manufacturing process. When goods are completed, another scan is performed that transfers both the cost and quantity of goods from the Work in Process inventory account to the Finished Goods inventory account, or charges Cost of Goods Sold for goods ready to be shipped.

Goods ready to be shipped are packed into containers, which are bar-coded with information that includes the customer number, the type and quantity of goods being shipped, and the order number. This bar code is then used for preparing billing information and for tracking the packed goods until placed on a carrier for shipment to the customer. Some customers require that the packed goods be bar-coded with point-of-sale labels that can be scanned at retail checkout counters. These scans allow the retailer to update inventory records, verify price, and generate a customer receipt.

In short, bar code technology is being integrated into all areas of business activity. When combined with EDI or XML, it eliminates a lot of clerical drudgery and allows companies to capture and exchange more data and to analyze and report information much more quickly and completely and with less error than with manual systems.

The integration of XML and the internal computer system for management reporting is called an *enterprise resource planning system* (ERP system). An ERP system represents a real-time computer system using a single uniform database that is coupled with modules for accounting, logistics, and human resources. Full use of these modules permits an integrated systems response for Internet-based orders in XML, supplier purchases and payables, inventory management, production, sales and receivables, treasury, and capital (fixed) assets management. Major suppliers of such ERP systems include Oracle, SAP, Baan, and J.D. Edwards.[2] Other companies provide certified software that is compatible with these systems. Samples of the overall menus for SAP are shown in Exhibit 3–15.

Operationally, these systems can provide global capabilities to regulate the variety of financial accounting and tax situations and do so in the appropriate language. Combining (better known as *consolidation*) of these different reports is performed by the system, along with drill-down capabilities for investigating details.

EXHIBIT 3-15 Sample SAP menus

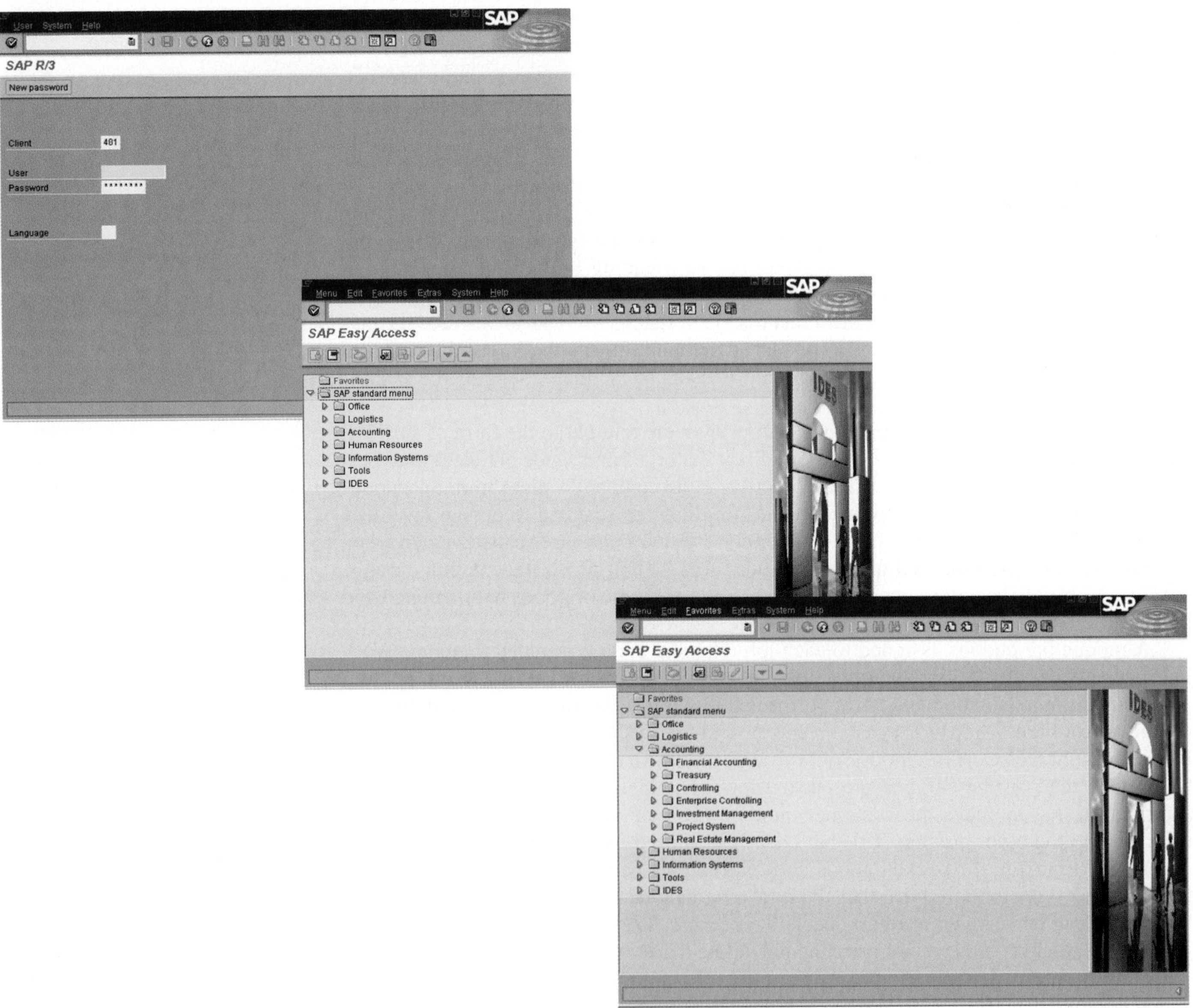

2. Internet sites for these companies provide details about each of their products and services: http://www.oracle.com/, http://www.sap.com/, http://www.baan.com/, and http://www.jdedwards.com/.

Critical to the installation of these systems is a well-specified operating system and well-trained personnel. Configurations for these systems to suit specific industries are provided with the software installation. For example, SAP, the world leader in such software, provides configurations for such industries as defence, apparel, automotive, construction, chemicals, and education, to mention only a few.

ERP systems combined with Web-based software and executive decision support reporting represent the current technology used by progressive organizations in both the commercial and not-for-profit fields. The size of an organization has to be sufficient to support the larger systems mentioned here, but small business software is available to do similar activities in an appropriately simplified way.[3]

INTERNATIONAL JOB COSTING

Studies of the international accounting scene suggest that the general principles of product costing are universally applicable. Nevertheless, differences do exist from country to country in how specific costs are classified. For example, a study of Russian operational accounting and statistical record-keeping, the equivalent of product costing, suggests that the required reporting structure in Russia would assign some cost elements to inventory that we might classify as selling or administrative. Other costs such as the rent on plant facilities would be classified outside of the usual overhead category. If a company was executing a contract with a foreign government, the differences in what is or is not permitted as contract costs would be particularly important. Similarly, what Public Works and Government Services Canada will allow as contract costs is described by the word "prudent" and elaborated in a specific list of costs excluded from product costs.[4] For example, these requirements would permit certain general and selling costs to be included if a prudent person would incur such costs as part of the contract. Thus, while the general principles may be similar, the specifics can vary as a result of government regulations.

FOCUS *on Current Practice*

KPMG conducted a detailed 10-month study of international business costs in 11 countries in North America, Europe and Asia-Pacific: *Canada's costs were the lowest recorded by the study* with business costs approximately 9% below those in the United States. The study compared the after-tax costs of start-up and operation for 12 types of business over a 10-year period. Cost components for business such as labour, utilities, transportation, and taxes and 21 others were measured in 98 cities worldwide.

Calgary	91.4	Kelowna	89.7	Toronto	93.2
Charlottown	87.8	Montreal	91.3	Vancouver	93.6
Edmonton	89.2	Ottawa	92.0	Waterloo Region	91.0
Halifax	88.6	Saskatoon	89.4	Winnipeg	90.5

*Business Costs are expressed as an index with the United States given a baseline index of 100.0. A cost index less than 100 indicates lower cost than the U.S. but a cost index greater that 100 indicates a higher cost than the U.S. For example, Halifax, with an index number of 88.6 has a 11.4.0% cost advantage relative to the U.S.

Source: *Competitive Alternatives, the CEO's Guide to International Business Costs*, http://www.competitivealternatives.com.

3. For background information on ERP, see Gerald Trites, *Enterprise Resource Planning* (Toronto, ON: The Canadian Institute of Chartered Accountants, 2000), and F. Robert Jacobs and D. Clay Whyback, *Why ERP? A Primer on SAP Implementation* (New York, NY: McGraw-Hill/Irwin, 2000).
4. Section 3, General Conditions, DSS-MAS 1031-2, "Contract Cost Principles," *Standard Acquisition Clauses and Conditions Manual*, Public Works and Government Services Canada, 1997.

RECORDED COSTS FOR QUALITY

Deficiencies in quality result in scrap, rework, delays in production, extra inventory, warranty claims, and poor customer relations. Such costs have been estimated at 25% to 35% of total product costs for some companies.

To illustrate the accounting process for defective units, assume that 2,000 units were started for a job, but only 1,900 good units were finished. If raw material, direct labour, and overhead applied amounted to $4,800 at the end of production, then each good unit would have a unit cost of $4,800 ÷ by 1,900, or $2.53 per unit. If management wanted to charge the 100 units to all production instead of the particular 1,900-unit job, the situation could be recorded as follows:

Manufacturing Overhead	240	
Work in Process Inventory		240

Calculations:

$4,800 ÷ 2,000 units = $2.40 per unit

100 defective units would cost 100 × $2.40

The 1,900 good units would cost ($4,800 – $240) = $4,560, or $2.40 per unit.

Any recovery from the 100 units of scrap would be credited to manufacturing overhead or the job costs, depending on the procedure used for the initial recording. If repair or rework was undertaken on the 100 defective units, then material, direct labour, and overhead costs would be charged to the job or the overhead account to be offset by any recovery.

The logic of whether to charge scrap or rework costs to all production or to a specific job is determined by deciding if defect costs were a normal cost of all production (thus a charge to overhead) or a cost of the specific situation surrounding a particular job (thus a charge solely of that job).

Environmentally hazardous scrap or defects can require disposal costs. Such environmental costs can be presented in a manner that they would provide management with evidence of the remediation or disposal requirements for their production processes.

SUMMARY

Job-order costing and process costing are widely used to track costs. Job-order costing is used in situations where the organization offers many different products or services, such as in furniture manufacturing, hospitals, and legal firms. Process costing is used where units of product are homogeneous, such as in flour milling or cement production.

Materials requisition forms and labour time tickets are used to assign direct materials and direct labour costs to jobs in a job-costing system. Manufacturing overhead costs are assigned to jobs through use of a predetermined overhead rate. The predetermined overhead rate is determined before the period begins by dividing the estimated total manufacturing cost for the period by the estimated total allocation base for the period. The most frequently used allocation bases are direct labour-hours and machine-hours. Overhead is applied to jobs by multiplying the predetermined overhead rate by the actual amount of the allocation base used by the job.

Since the predetermined overhead rate is based on estimates, the actual overhead cost incurred during a period may be more or less than the amount of overhead cost applied to production. Such a difference is referred to as under- or overapplied overhead. The under- or overapplied overhead for a period can be (1) closed out to Cost of Goods Sold or

(2) allocated among Work in Process, Finished Goods, and Cost of Goods Sold or (3) carried forward to the end of the year. When overhead is underapplied, manufacturing overhead costs have been understated and therefore inventories and/or expenses must be adjusted upward. When overhead is overapplied, manufacturing overhead costs have been overstated and therefore inventories and/or expenses must be adjusted downward.

REVIEW PROBLEM: JOB-ORDER COSTING

Hogle Company is a manufacturing firm that uses job-order costing. On January 1, the beginning of its fiscal year, the company's inventory balances were as follows:

Raw materials	$20,000
Work in process	15,000
Finished goods	30,000

The company applies overhead cost to jobs on the basis of machine-hours worked. For the current year, the company estimated that it would work 75,000 machine-hours and incur $450,000 in manufacturing overhead cost. The following transactions were recorded for the year:

a. Raw materials were purchased on account, $410,000.
b. Raw materials were requisitioned for use in production, $380,000 ($360,000 direct materials and $20,000 indirect materials).
c. The following costs were incurred for employee services: direct labour, $75,000; indirect labour, $110,000; sales commissions, $90,000; and administrative salaries, $200,000.
d. Sales travel costs were incurred, $17,000.
e. Utility costs were incurred in the factory, $43,000.
f. Advertising costs were incurred, $180,000.
g. Depreciation was recorded for the year, $350,000 (80% relates to factory operations, and 20% relates to selling and administrative activities).
h. Insurance expired during the year, $10,000 (70% relates to factory operations, and the remaining 30% relates to selling and administrative activities).
i. Manufacturing overhead was applied to production. Due to greater than expected demand for its products, the company worked 80,000 machine-hours during the year.
j. Goods costing $900,000 to manufacture according to their job cost sheets were completed during the year.
k. Goods were sold on account to customers during the year at a total selling price of $1,500,000. The goods cost $870,000 to manufacture according to their job cost sheets.

Required:

1. Prepare journal entries to record the preceding transactions.
2. Post the entries in (1) above to T-accounts (do not forget to enter the opening balances in the inventory accounts).
3. Is Manufacturing Overhead underapplied or overapplied for the year? Prepare a journal entry to close any balance in the Manufacturing Overhead account to Cost of Goods Sold. Do not allocate the balance between ending inventories and Cost of Goods Sold.
4. Prepare an income statement for the year and a statement of cost of goods manufactured.

Solution to Review Problem

1.	*a.* Raw Materials	410,000	
	Accounts Payable		410,000
	b. Work in Process	360,000	
	Manufacturing Overhead	20,000	
	Raw Materials		380,000
	c. Work in Process	75,000	
	Manufacturing Overhead	110,000	
	Sales Commissions Expense	90,000	
	Administrative Salaries Expense	200,000	
	Salaries and Wages Payable		475,000

d.	Sales Travel Expense	17,000	
	Accounts Payable		17,000
e.	Manufacturing Overhead	43,000	
	Accounts Payable		43,000
f.	Advertising Expense	180,000	
	Accounts Payable		180,000
g.	Manufacturing Overhead	280,000	
	Depreciation Expense	70,000	
	Accumulated Depreciation		350,000
h.	Manufacturing Overhead	7,000	
	Insurance Expense	3,000	
	Prepaid Insurance		10,000

i. The predetermined overhead rate for the year would be computed as follows:

$$\frac{\text{Estimated manufacturing overhead, \$450,000}}{\text{Estimated machine-hours, 75,000}} = \$6 \text{ per machine-hour}$$

Based on the 80,000 machine-hours actually worked during the year, the company would have applied $480,000 in overhead cost to production: 80,000 machine-hours × $6 = $480,000. The following entry records this application of overhead cost:

	Work in Process	480,000	
	Manufacturing Overhead		480,000
j.	Finished Goods	900,000	
	Work in Process		900,000
k.	Accounts Receivable	1,500,000	
	Sales		1,500,000
	Cost of Goods Sold	870,000	
	Finished Goods		870,000

2.

Accounts Receivable

	Debit		Credit
(k)	1,500,000		

Manufacturing Overhead

	Debit		Credit
(b)	20,000	(i)	480,000
(c)	110,000		
(e)	43,000		
(g)	280,000		
(h)	7,000		
	460,000		480,000
		Bal.	20,000

Sales

	Debit		Credit
		(k)	1,500,000

Cost of Goods Sold

	Debit		Credit
(k)	870,000		

Prepaid Insurance

	Debit		Credit
		(h)	10,000

Accumulated Depreciation

	Debit		Credit
		(g)	350,000

Commissions Expense

	Debit		Credit
(c)	90,000		

Administrative Salary Expense

	Debit		Credit
(c)	200,000		

Raw Materials

	Debit		Credit
Bal.	20,000	(b)	380,000
(a)	410,000		
Bal.	50,000		

Accounts Payable

	Debit		Credit
		(a)	410,000
		(d)	17,000
		(e)	43,000
		(f)	180,000

Sales Travel Expense

	Debit		Credit
(d)	17,000		

Advertising Expense

	Debit		Credit
(f)	180,000		

Work in Process

Bal.	15,000	(j)	900,000
(b)	360,000		
(c)	75,000		
(i)	480,000		
Bal.	30,000		

Salaries and Wages Payable

		(c)	475,000

Depreciation Expense

(g)	70,000		

Insurance Expense

(h)	3,000		

Finished Goods

Bal.	30,000	(k)	870,000
(j)	900,000		
Bal.	60,000		

3. Manufacturing overhead is overapplied for the year. The entry to close it out to Cost of Goods Sold is as follows:

Manufacturing Overhead	20,000	
Cost of Goods Sold		20,000

4.

HOGLE COMPANY
Income Statement
For the Year Ended December 31

Sales		$1,500,000
Less cost of goods sold ($870,000 − $20,000)		850,000
Gross margin		650,000
Less selling and administrative expenses:		
Commissions expense	$ 90,000	
Administrative salaries expense	200,000	
Sales travel expense	17,000	
Advertising expense	180,000	
Depreciation expense	70,000	
Insurance expense	3,000	560,000
Net income		$ 90,000

HOGLE COMPANY
Schedule of Cost of Goods Manufactured and Cost of Goods Sold

Direct Materials:		
Raw materials inventory, January 1	$ 20,000	
Add: Purchases of raw materials	410,000	
Total raw materials available	430,000	
Deduct: Raw materials inventory, December 31	50,000	
Raw materials used in production	380,000	
Less: Indirect materials (below)	20,000	
Direct materials used in production		$360,000
Direct Labour		75,000
Manufacturing Overhead:		
Indirect materials	20,000	
Indirect labour	110,000	
Utilities	43,000	
Depreciation	280,000	
Insurance	7,000	
Actual overhead costs	460,000	
Add: Overapplied overhead	20,000	

continued

Overhead applied to work in process	480,000*
Total manufacturing costs	915,000
Add: Beginning work in process inventory	15,000
	930,000
Deduct: Ending work in process inventory	30,000
Cost of goods manufactured	900,000
Add: Finished goods inventory, January 1	30,000
Goods available for sale	930,000
Deduct: Finished goods inventory, December 31	60,000
Cost of Goods Sold	870,000
Deduct: Overapplied overhead	20,000
Adjusted cost of goods sold	$850,000

*The details of manufacturing overhead may be omitted as shown in Exhibit 3–11. If these are not omitted then the overapplied overhead must be added to actual overhead costs and only the total ($480,000) is added to direct materials and direct labour. The reason is that the schedule of cost of goods manufactured represents a summary of costs flowing through the Work in Process account during a period and therefore must include only overhead applied to production. If a reverse situation had existed and overhead had been underapplied during the period, then the amount of underapplied overhead would have been deducted from actual overhead costs on the schedule. This would have brought the actual overhead costs down to the amount that had been applied to production.

APPENDIX 3A: THE PREDETERMINED OVERHEAD RATE AND CAPACITY

LEARNING OBJECTIVE 8
Explain the implications of basing the predetermined overhead rate on activity at capacity rather than on estimated activity for the period.

Companies typically base their predetermined overhead rates on the estimated, or budgeted, amount of the allocation base for the upcoming period. This is the method that is used in the chapter, but it is a practice that has recently come under severe criticism. An example will be very helpful in understanding why. Prahad Corporation manufactures music CDs for local recording studios. The company has a CD duplicating machine that is capable of producing a new CD every 10 seconds from a master CD. The company leases the CD duplicating machine for $180,000 per year, and this is the company's only manufacturing overhead. With allowances for set-ups and maintenance, the machine is theoretically capable of producing up to 900,000 CDs per year. However, due to weak retail sales of CDs, the company's commercial customers are unlikely to order more than 600,000 CDs next year. The company uses machine time as the allocation base for applying manufacturing overhead. These data are summarized below:

PRAHAD CORPORATION DATA

Total manufacturing overhead cost	$180,000 per year
Allocation base: machine time per CD	10 seconds per CD
Capacity	900,000 CDs per year
Budgeted output for next year	600,000 CDs

If Prahad follows common practice and computes its predetermined overhead rate using estimated, or budgeted, figures, then its predetermined overhead rate for next year would be $0.03 per second of machine time, computed as follows:

$$\frac{\text{Estimated total manufacturing overhead cost, \$180,000}}{\text{Estimated total units in the allocation base, 600,000 CDs} \times \text{10 seconds per CD}} = \text{\$0.03 per second}$$

Since each CD requires 10 seconds of machine time, each CD will be charged for $0.30 of overhead cost.

Critics charge that there are two problems with this procedure. First, if predetermined overhead rates are based on budgeted activity, then the unit product costs will fluctuate, depending on the budgeted level of activity for the period. For example, if the budgeted output for the year was only 300,000 CDs, the predetermined overhead rate would be \$0.06 per second of machine time or \$0.60 per CD rather than \$0.30 per CD. In general, if budgeted output falls, the overhead cost per unit will increase; it will appear that the CDs cost more to make. Managers may then be tempted to increase prices at the worst possible time—just as demand is falling.

Second, critics charge that under the traditional approach, products are charged for resources that they do not use. When the fixed costs of capacity are spread over estimated activity, the units that are produced must shoulder the costs of unused capacity. That is why the applied overhead cost per unit increases as the level of activity falls. The critics argue that products should be charged only for the capacity that they use; they should not be charged for the capacity they do not use. This can be accomplished by basing the predetermined overhead rate on capacity as follows:

$$\frac{\text{Total manufacturing overhead cost at capacity, \$180,000}}{\text{Total units in the allocation base at capacity, 900,000 CDs} \times \text{10 seconds per CD}} = \$0.02 \text{ per second}$$

Since the predetermined overhead rate is \$0.02 per second, the overhead cost applied to each CD would be \$0.20. This charge is constant and would not be affected by the level of activity during a period. If output falls, the charge would still be \$4.00 per CD after adding materials and labour variable costs.

This method will almost certainly result in underapplied overhead. If actual output at Prahad Corporation is 600,000 CDs, then only \$120,000 of overhead cost would be applied to products (\$0.20 per CD × 600,000 CDs). Since the actual overhead cost is \$180,000, there would be underapplied overhead of \$60,000. In another departure from tradition, the critics suggest that the underapplied overhead that results from idle capacity should be separately disclosed on the income statement as the Cost of Unused Capacity—a period expense. Disclosing this cost as a lump sum on the income statement, rather than burying it in Cost of Goods Sold or ending inventories, makes it much more visible to managers.

Official pronouncements do not prohibit basing predetermined overhead rates on capacity for external reports. Nevertheless, basing the predetermined overhead rate on estimated, or budgeted, activity is a long-established practice in industry, and some managers and accountants may object to the large amounts of underapplied overhead that would often result from using capacity to determine predetermined overhead rates. And some may insist that the underapplied overhead be allocated among Cost of Goods Sold and ending inventories—which would defeat the purpose of basing the predetermined overhead rate on capacity.

GLOSSARY

Visit the Online Learning Centre at http:// www.mcgrawhill.ca/college/garrison/ for a review of key terms and definitions.

QUESTIONS

3–1 Why aren't actual overhead costs traced to jobs just as direct materials and direct labour costs are traced to jobs?

3–2 When would job-order costing be used in preference to process costing?

3–3 What is the purpose of the job cost sheet in a job-order costing system?

3–4 What is a predetermined overhead rate, and how is it computed?

3–5 Explain how a sales order, a production order, a materials requisition form, and a labour time ticket are involved in producing and costing products.

3–6 Explain why some production costs must be assigned to products through an allocation process. Name several such costs. Would such costs be classified as *direct* or as *indirect* costs?

3–7 Why do firms use predetermined overhead rates rather than actual manufacturing overhead costs in applying overhead to jobs?

3–8 What factors should be considered in selecting a base to be used in computing the predetermined overhead rate?

3–9 If a company fully allocates all of its overhead costs to jobs, does this guarantee that a profit will be earned for the period?

3–10 What account is credited when overhead cost is applied to Work in Process? Would you expect the amount applied for a period to equal the actual overhead costs of the period? Why or why not?

3–11 What is underapplied overhead? Overapplied overhead? What disposition is made of these amounts at period end?

3–12 Give two reasons why overhead might be underapplied in a given year.

3–13 What adjustment is made for underapplied overhead on the schedule of cost of goods sold? What adjustment is made for overapplied overhead?

3–14 Sigma Company applies overhead cost to jobs on the basis of direct labour cost. Job A, which was started and completed during the current period, shows charges of $5,000 for direct materials, $8,000 for direct labour, and $6,000 for overhead on its job cost sheet. Job B, which is still in process at year-end, shows charges of $2,500 for direct materials and $4,000 for direct labour. Should any overhead cost be added to job B at year-end? Explain.

3–15 A company assigns overhead cost to completed jobs on the basis of 125% of direct labour cost. The job cost sheet for job 313 shows that $10,000 in direct materials has been used on the job and that $12,000 in direct labour cost has been incurred. If 1,000 units were produced in job 313, what is the cost per unit?

3–16 What is a plantwide overhead rate? Why are multiple overhead rates, rather than a plantwide rate, used in some companies?

3–17 What happens to overhead rates based on direct labour when automated equipment replaces direct labour?

3–18 Predetermined overhead rates smooth product costs. Do you agree? Why?

3–19 Explain clearly the rationale for why under- and overapplied overhead for an interim period should be carried to the balance sheet. What conceptual factor is assumed in the argument?

3–20 Why does the calculation of the percentages for prorating the under- or overapplied overhead reduce the costs of goods sold by the opening inventories? What would happen if such a deduction was not made?

3–21 (Appendix A) If the plant is operated at less than capacity and the predetermined overhead rate is based on the estimated total units in the allocation base at capacity, will overhead ordinarily be overapplied or underapplied?

3–22 (Appendix A) Rather than netting underapplied overhead against Cost of Goods Sold or Cost of Goods Sold and ending inventories, some critics suggest an alternative way to disclose underapplied overhead. What is this alternative method?

EXERCISES

EXERCISE 3–1 Process Costing and Job-Order Costing [LO1]

Which method of determining product costs, job-order costing or process costing, would be more appropriate in each of the following situations?

a. An Elmer's glue factory.
b. A textbook publisher such as McGraw-Hill Ryerson.
c. An Exxon oil refinery.
d. A facility that makes Minute Maid frozen orange juice.
e. A Scott paper mill.
f. A custom home builder.
g. A shop that customizes vans.

h. A manufacturer of specialty chemicals.
i. An auto repair shop.
j. A Firestone tire manufacturing plant.
k. An advertising agency.
l. A law office.

EXERCISE 3–2 Job-Order Costing Documents [LO2]
Cycle Gear Corporation has incurred the following costs on job number W456, an order for 20 special sprockets to be delivered at the end of next month.

Direct materials:
On April 10, requisition number 15673 was issued for 20 titanium blanks to be used in the special order. The blanks cost $15.00 each.
On April 11, requisition number 15678 was issued for 480 hardened nibs also to be used in the special order. The nibs cost $1.25 each.
Direct labour:
On April 12, Jamie Unser worked from 11:00 AM until 2:45 PM on Job W456. He is paid $9.60 per hour.
On April 18, Melissa Chan worked from 8:15 AM until 11:30 AM on Job W456. She is paid $12.20 per hour.

Required:
1. On what documents would these costs be recorded?
2. How much cost should have been recorded on each of the documents for Job W456?

EXERCISE 3–3 Compute the Predetermined Overhead Rate [LO3]
Harris Fabrics computes its predetermined overhead rate annually on the basis of direct labour-hours. At the beginning of the year it estimated that its total manufacturing overhead would be $134,000 and the total direct labour would be 20,000 hours. Its actual total manufacturing overhead for the year was $123,900 and its actual total direct labour was 21,000 hours.

Required:
Compute the company's predetermined overhead rate for the year.

EXERCISE 3–4 Prepare Journal Entries [LO4]
Larned Corporation recorded the following transactions for the just completed month.
a. $80,000 in raw materials were purchased on account.
b. $71,000 in raw materials were requisitioned for use in production. Of this amount, $62,000 was for direct materials and the remainder was for indirect materials.
c. Total labour wages of $112,000 were incurred. Of this amount, $101,000 was for direct labour and the remainder was for indirect labour.
d. Additional manufacturing overhead costs of $175,000 were incurred.

Required:
Record the above transactions in journal entries.

EXERCISE 3–5 Apply Overhead [LO5]
Luthan Company uses a predetermined overhead rate of $23.40 per direct labour-hour. This predetermined rate was based on 11,000 estimated direct labour-hours and $257,400 of estimated total manufacturing overhead.

The company incurred actual total manufacturing overhead costs of $249,000 and 10,800 total direct labour-hours during the period.

Required:
Determine the amount of manufacturing overhead that would have been applied to units of product during the period.

EXERCISE 3–6 Applying Overhead; Cost of Goods Manufactured [LO5, LO6, LO8]
The following cost data relate to the manufacturing activities of Chang Company during the just completed year:

The company uses a predetermined overhead rate to apply overhead cost to production. The rate for the year was $25 per machine-hour. A total of 19,400 machine-hours was recorded for the year.

Manufacturing overhead costs incurred:	
Indirect materials	$15,000
Indirect labour	130,000
Property taxes, factory	8,000
Utilities, factory	70,000
Depreciation, factory	240,000
Insurance, factory	10,000
Total actual manufacturing overhead costs incurred	$473,000
Other costs incurred:	
Purchases of raw materials (both direct and indirect)	$400,000
Direct labour cost	$60,000
Inventories:	
Raw materials, beginning	$20,000
Raw materials, ending	$30,000
Work in process, beginning	$40,000
Work in process, ending	$70,000

Required:

1. Compute the amount of under- or overapplied overhead cost for the year.
2. Prepare a schedule of cost of goods manufactured for the year.

EXERCISE 3–7 Prepare T-Accounts [LO7, LO8]

Jurvin Enterprises recorded the following transactions for the just completed month. The company had no beginning inventories.

a. $94,000 in raw materials were purchased for cash.
b. $89,000 in raw materials were requisitioned for use in production. Of this amount, $78,000 was for direct materials and the remainder was for indirect materials.
c. Total labour wages of $132,000 were incurred and paid. Of this amount, $112,000 was for direct labour and the remainder was for indirect labour.
d. Additional manufacturing overhead costs of $143,000 were incurred and paid.
e. Manufacturing overhead costs of $152,000 were applied to jobs using the company's predetermined overhead rate.
f. All of the jobs in progress at the end of the month were completed and shipped to customers.
g. The underapplied or overapplied overhead for the period was closed out to Cost of Goods Sold.

Required:

1. Post the above transactions to T-accounts.
2. Determine the cost of goods sold for the period.

EXERCISE 3–8 Under- and Overapplied Overhead [LO8]

Osborn Manufacturing uses a predetermined overhead rate of $18.20 per direct labour-hour. This predetermined rate was based on 12,000 estimated direct labour-hours and $218,400 of estimated total manufacturing overhead.

The company incurred actual total manufacturing overhead costs of $215,000 and 11,500 total direct labour-hours during the period.

Required:

1. Determine the amount of underapplied or overapplied manufacturing overhead for the period.
2. Assuming that the entire amount of the underapplied or overapplied overhead is closed out to Cost of Goods Sold, what would be the effect of the underapplied or overapplied overhead on the company's gross margin for the period?

EXERCISE 3–9 Departmental Overhead Rates [LO2, LO3, LO5]

White Company has two departments, Cutting and Finishing. The company uses a job-order cost system and computes a predetermined overhead rate in each department. The Cutting Department bases its rate on machine-hours, and the Finishing Department bases its rate on direct labour cost. At the beginning of the year, the company made the following estimates:

	Department	
	Cutting	Finishing
Direct labour-hours	6,000	30,000
Machine-hours	48,000	5,000
Manufacturing overhead cost	$360,000	$486,000
Direct labour cost	$50,000	$270,000

Required:

1. Compute the predetermined overhead rate to be used in each department.
2. Assume that the overhead rates that you computed in (1) above are in effect. The job cost sheet for Job 203, which was started and completed during the year, showed the following:

	Department	
	Cutting	Finishing
Direct labour-hours	6	20
Machine-hours	80	4
Materials requisitioned	$500	$310
Direct labour cost	$70	$150

   Compute the total overhead cost applied to Job 203.
3. Would you expect substantially different amounts of overhead cost to be assigned to some jobs if the company used a plantwide overhead rate based on direct labour cost, rather than using departmental rates? Explain. No computations are necessary.

EXERCISE 3–10 Journal Entries and T-accounts [LO4, LO5, LO7]

The Polaris Company uses a job-order costing system. The following data relate to October, the first month of the company's fiscal year.

a. Raw materials purchased on account, $210,000.
b. Raw materials issued to production, $190,000 ($178,000 direct materials and $12,000 indirect materials).
c. Direct labour cost incurred, $90,000; indirect labour cost incurred, $110,000.
d. Depreciation recorded on factory equipment, $40,000.
e. Other manufacturing overhead costs incurred during October, $70,000 (credit Accounts Payable).
f. The company applies manufacturing overhead cost to production on the basis of $8 per machine-hour. There were 30,000 machine-hours recorded for October.
g. Production orders costing $520,000 according to their job cost sheets were completed during October and transferred to Finished Goods.
h. Production orders that had cost $480,000 to complete according to their job cost sheets were shipped to customers during the month. These goods were sold on account at 25% above cost.

Required:

1. Prepare journal entries to record the information given above.
2. Prepare T-accounts for Manufacturing Overhead and Work in Process. Post the relevant information above to each account. Compute the ending balance in each account, assuming that Work in Process has a beginning balance of $42,000.

EXERCISE 3–11 Applying Overhead in a Service Company [LO2, LO3, LO5]

Leeds Architectural Consultants began operations on January 2. The following activity was recorded in the company's Work in Process account for the first month of operations:

Work in Process

Costs of subcontracted work	230,000	To completed projects	390,000
Direct staff costs	75,000		
Studio overhead	120,000		

Leeds Architectural Consultants is a service firm, so the names of the accounts it uses are different from the names used in manufacturing firms. Costs of Subcontracted Work is comparable to Direct Materials; Direct Staff Costs is the same as Direct Labour; Studio Overhead is the same as Manufacturing Overhead; and Completed Projects is the same as Finished Goods. Apart from the difference in terms, the accounting methods used by the company are identical to the methods used by manufacturing companies.

Leeds Architectural Consultants uses a job-order costing system and applies studio overhead to Work in Process on the basis of direct staff costs. At the end of January, only one job was still in process. This job (Lexington Gardens Project) had been charged with $6,500 in direct staff costs.

Required:

1. Compute the predetermined overhead rate that was in use during January.
2. Complete the following job cost sheet for the partially completed Lexington Gardens Project.

Job Cost Sheet—Lexington Gardens Project As of January 31	
Costs of subcontracted work	$?
Direct staff costs	?
Studio overhead	?
Total cost to January 31	$?

EXERCISE 3–12 Varying Predetermined Overhead Rates [LO3, LO5]

Kingsport Containers, Ltd, of the Bahamas experiences wide variation in demand for the 200-litre steel drums it fabricates. The leakproof, rustproof steel drums have a variety of uses from storing liquids and bulk materials to serving as makeshift musical instruments. The drums are made to order and are painted according to the customer's specifications—often in bright patterns and designs. The company is well known for the artwork that appears on its drums. Unit product costs are computed on a quarterly basis by dividing each quarter's manufacturing costs (materials, labour, and overhead) by the quarter's production in units. The company's estimated costs, by quarter, for the coming year follow:

	Quarter			
	First	Second	Third	Fourth
Direct materials	$240,000	$120,000	$60,000	$180,000
Direct labour	128,000	64,000	32,000	96,000
Manufacturing overhead	300,000	220,000	180,000	260,000
Total manufacturing costs	$668,000	$404,000	$272,000	$536,000
Number of units to be produced	80,000	40,000	20,000	60,000
Estimated unit product cost	$8.35	$10.10	$13.60	$8.93

Management finds the variation in unit costs to be confusing and difficult to work with. It has been suggested that the problem lies with manufacturing overhead, since it is the largest element of cost. Accordingly, you have been asked to find a more appropriate way of assigning manufacturing overhead cost to units of product. After some analysis, you have determined that the company's overhead costs are mostly fixed and therefore show little sensitivity to changes in the level of production.

Required:

1. The company uses a job-order costing system. How would you recommend that manufacturing overhead cost be assigned to production? Be specific, and show computations.
2. Recompute the company's unit product costs in accordance with your recommendations in (1) above.

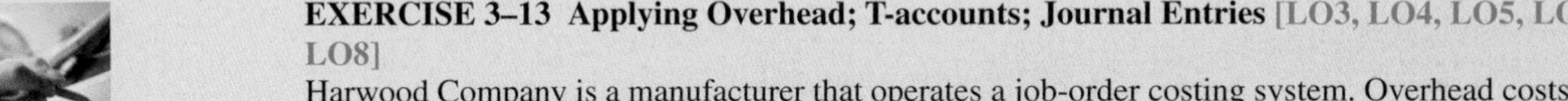

EXERCISE 3–13 Applying Overhead; T-accounts; Journal Entries [LO3, LO4, LO5, LO7, LO8]

Harwood Company is a manufacturer that operates a job-order costing system. Overhead costs are applied to jobs on the basis of machine-hours. At the beginning of the year, management estimated that the company would incur $192,000 in manufacturing overhead costs and work 80,000 machine-hours.

Required:

1. Compute the company's predetermined overhead rate.
2. Assume that during the year the company works only 75,000 machine-hours and incurs the following costs in the Manufacturing Overhead and Work in Process accounts:

Manufacturing Overhead			Work in Process		
(Maintenance)	21,000	?	(Direct materials)	710,000	
(Indirect materials)	8,000		(Direct labour)	90,000	
(Indirect labour)	60,000		(Overhead)	?	
(Utilities)	32,000				
(Insurance)	7,000				
(Depreciation)	56,000				

   Copy the data in the T-accounts above onto your answer sheet. Compute the amount of overhead cost that would be applied to Work in Process for the year and make the entry in your T-accounts.
3. Compute the amount of under- or overapplied overhead for the year and show the balance in your Manufacturing Overhead T-account. Prepare a journal entry to close out the balance in this account to Cost of Goods Sold.
4. Explain why the manufacturing overhead was under- or overapplied for the year.

EXERCISE 3–14 Applying Overhead; Journal Entries; Disposition of Underapplied or Overapplied Overhead [LO4, LO7, LO8]

The following information is taken from the accounts of Latta Company. The entries in the T-accounts are summaries of the transactions that affected those accounts during the year.

Manufacturing Overhead				Work in Process			
(a)	460,000	(b)	390,000	Bal.	15,000	(c)	710,000
Bal.	70,000				260,000		
					85,000		
				(b)	390,000		
				Bal.	40,000		

Finished Goods				Cost of Goods Sold			
Bal.	50,000	(d)	640,000	(d)	640,000		
(c)	710,000						
Bal.	120,000						

The overhead that had been applied to production during the year is distributed among the ending balances in the accounts as follows:

Work in Process, ending	$ 19,500
Finished Goods, ending	58,500
Cost of Goods Sold	312,000
Overhead applied	$390,000

For example, of the $40,000 ending balance in Work in Process, $19,500 was overhead that had been applied during the year.

Required:

1. Identify reasons for entries (a) through (d).
2. Assume that the company closes any balance in the Manufacturing Overhead account directly to Cost of Goods Sold. Prepare the necessary journal entry.
3. Assume instead that the company allocates any balance in the Manufacturing Overhead account to the other accounts in proportion to the overhead applied in their ending balances. Prepare the necessary journal entry, with supporting computations.

EXERCISE 3–15 Applying Overhead; Journal Entries; T-accounts [LO3, LO4, LO5, LO7]
Dillon Products manufactures various machined parts to customer specifications. The company uses a job-order costing system and applies overhead cost to jobs on the basis of machine-hours. At the beginning of the year, it was estimated that the company would work 240,000 machine-hours and incur $4,800,000 in manufacturing overhead costs.

The company spent the entire month of January working on a large order for 16,000 custom-made machined parts. The company had no work in process at the beginning of January. Cost data relating to January follow:

a. Raw materials purchased on account, $325,000.
b. Raw materials requisitioned for production, $290,000 (80% direct materials and 20% indirect materials).
c. Labour cost incurred in the factory, $180,000 (one-third direct labour and two-thirds indirect labour).
d. Depreciation recorded on factory equipment, $75,000.
e. Other manufacturing overhead costs incurred, $62,000 (credit Accounts Payable).
f. Manufacturing overhead cost was applied to production on the basis of 15,000 machine-hours actually worked during the month.
g. The completed job was moved into the finished goods warehouse on January 31 to await delivery to the customer. (In computing the dollar amount for this entry, remember that the cost of a completed job consists of direct materials, direct labour, and *applied* overhead.)

Required:
1. Prepare journal entries to record items (a) through (f) above [ignore item (g) for the moment].
2. Prepare T-accounts for Manufacturing Overhead and Work in Process. Post the relevant items from your journal entries to these T-accounts.
3. Prepare a journal entry for item (g) above.
4. Compute the unit product cost that will appear on the job cost sheet.

EXERCISE 3–16 (Appendix 3A) Overhead Rates and Capacity Issues [LO3, LO5, LO8, LO9]
Security Pension Services helps clients to set up and administer pension plans that are in compliance with tax laws and regulatory requirements. The firm uses a job-order costing system in which overhead is applied to clients' accounts on the basis of professional staff hours charged to the accounts. Data concerning two recent years appear below:

	2005	2004
Estimated professional staff hours to be charged to clients' accounts	4,600	4,500
Estimated overhead cost	$310,500	$310,500
Professional staff hours available	6,000	6,000

"Professional staff hours available" is a measure of the capacity of the firm. Any hours available that are not charged to clients' accounts represent unused capacity.

Required:
1. Marta Brinksi is an established client whose pension plan was set up many years ago. In both 2004 and 2005, only 2.5 hours of professional staff time were charged to Ms. Brinksi's account. If the company bases its predetermined overhead rate on the estimated overhead cost and the estimated professional staff hours to be charged to clients, how much overhead cost would have been applied to Ms. Brinksi's account in 2004? In 2005?
2. Suppose that the company bases its predetermined overhead rate on the estimated overhead cost and the estimated professional staff hours to be charged to clients as in (1) above. Also suppose that the actual professional staff hours charged to clients' accounts and the actual overhead costs turn out to be exactly as estimated in both years. By how much would the overhead be under- or overapplied in 2004? In 2005?
3. Refer back to the data concerning Ms. Brinksi in (1) above. If the company bases its predetermined overhead rate on the estimated overhead cost and the *professional staff hours available*, how much overhead cost would have been applied to Ms. Brinksi's account in 2004? In 2005?
4. Suppose that the company bases its predetermined overhead rate on the estimated overhead cost and the professional staff hours available as in (3) above. Also suppose that the actual

professional staff hours charged to clients' accounts and the actual overhead costs turn out to be exactly as estimated in both years. By how much would the overhead be under- or overapplied in 2004? In 2005?

EXERCISE 3–17 Applying Overhead in a Service Company; Journal Entries [LO4, LO5, LO8]

S

Vista Landscaping uses a job-order costing system to track the costs of its landscaping projects. The company provides garden design and installation services for its clients. The table below provides data concerning the three landscaping projects that were in progress during April. There was no work in process at the beginning of April.

	Project		
	Harris	Chan	James
Designer-hours	120	100	90
Direct materials cost	$4,500	$3,700	$1,400
Direct labour cost	$9,600	$8,000	$7,200

Actual overhead costs were $30,000 for April. Overhead costs are applied to projects on the basis of designer-hours since most of the overhead is related to the costs of the garden design studio. The predetermined overhead rate is $90 per designer-hour. The Harris and Chan projects were completed in April; the James project was not completed by the end of the month.

Required:

1. Compute the amount of overhead cost that would have been charged to each project during April.
2. Prepare a journal entry showing the completion of the Harris and Chan projects and the transfer of costs to the Completed Projects (i.e., Finished Goods) account.
3. What is the balance in the Work in Process account at the end of the month?
4. What is the balance in the Overhead account at the end of the month? What is this balance called?

PROBLEMS

PROBLEM 3–18 Comprehensive Problem [LO3, LO4, LO5, LO7, LO8]

Gold Nest Company of Guandong, China, is a family-owned enterprise that makes birdcages for the South China market. A popular pastime among older Chinese men is to take their pet birds on daily excursions to teahouses and public parks where they meet with other bird owners to talk and play mahjong. A great deal of attention is lavished on these birds, and the birdcages are often elaborately constructed from exotic woods and contain porcelain feeding bowls and silver roosts. Gold Nest Company makes a broad range of birdcages that it sells through an extensive network of street vendors who receive commissions on their sales. The Chinese currency is the renminbi, which is denoted by Rmb. All of the company's transactions with customers, employees, and suppliers are conducted in cash; there is no credit.

The company uses a job-order costing system in which overhead is applied to jobs on the basis of direct labour cost. At the beginning of the year, it was estimated that the total direct labour cost for the year would be Rmb200,000 and the total manufacturing overhead cost would be Rmb330,000. At the beginning of the year, the inventory balances were as follows:

Raw materials	Rmb25,000
Work in process	Rmb10,000
Finished goods	Rmb40,000

During the year, the following transactions were completed:

a. Raw materials purchased for cash, Rmb275,000.
b. Raw materials requisitioned for use in production, Rmb280,000 (materials costing Rmb220,000 were charged directly to jobs; the remaining materials were indirect).
c. Costs for employee services were incurred as follows:

Direct labour	Rmb180,000
Indirect labour	Rmb72,000
Sales commissions	Rmb63,000
Administrative salaries	Rmb90,000

d. Rent for the year was Rmb18,000 (Rmb13,000 of this amount related to factory operations, and the remainder related to selling and administrative activities).
e. Utility costs incurred in the factory, Rmb57,000.
f. Advertising costs incurred, Rmb140,000.
g. Depreciation recorded on equipment, Rmb100,000. (Rmb88,000 of this amount was on equipment used in factory operations; the remaining Rmb12,000 was on equipment used in selling and administrative activities.)
h. Manufacturing overhead cost was applied to jobs, Rmb ___?___.
i. Goods that had cost Rmb675,000 to manufacture according to their job cost sheets were completed during the year.
j. Sales for the year totalled Rmb1,250,000. The total cost to manufacture these goods according to their job cost sheets was Rmb700,000.

Required:

1. Prepare journal entries to record the transactions for the year.
2. Prepare T-accounts for inventories, Manufacturing Overhead, and Cost of Goods Sold. Post relevant data from your journal entries to these T-accounts (don't forget to enter the beginning balances in your inventory accounts). Compute an ending balance in each account.
3. Is Manufacturing Overhead underapplied or overapplied for the year? Prepare a journal entry to close any balance in the Manufacturing Overhead account to Cost of Goods Sold.
4. Prepare an income statement for the year. (Do not prepare a schedule of cost of goods manufactured; all of the information needed for the income statement is available in the journal entries and T-accounts you have prepared.)

PROBLEM 3–19 Cost Flows; T-Accounts; Income Statement [LO3, LO5, LO6, LO7, LO8]
Supreme Videos, Inc., produces short musical videos for sale to retail outlets. The company's balance sheet accounts as of January 1, the beginning of its fiscal year, are given below.

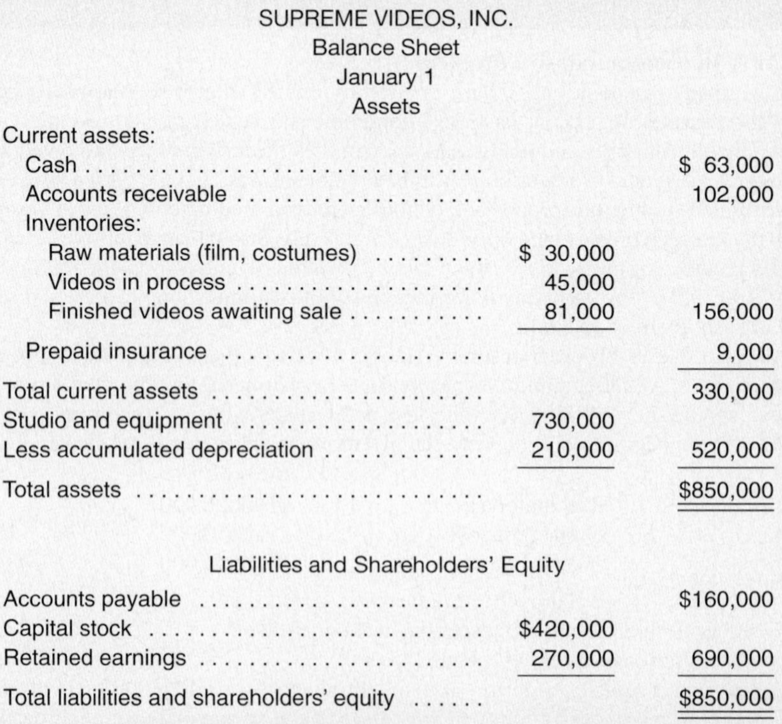

SUPREME VIDEOS, INC.
Balance Sheet
January 1
Assets

Current assets:		
Cash		$ 63,000
Accounts receivable		102,000
Inventories:		
Raw materials (film, costumes)	$ 30,000	
Videos in process	45,000	
Finished videos awaiting sale	81,000	156,000
Prepaid insurance		9,000
Total current assets		330,000
Studio and equipment	730,000	
Less accumulated depreciation	210,000	520,000
Total assets		$850,000

Liabilities and Shareholders' Equity

Accounts payable		$160,000
Capital stock	$420,000	
Retained earnings	270,000	690,000
Total liabilities and shareholders' equity		$850,000

Since the videos differ in length and in complexity of production, the company uses a job-order costing system to determine the cost of each video produced. Studio (manufacturing) overhead is charged to videos on the basis of camera-hours of activity. At the beginning of the year, the company estimated that it would work 7,000 camera-hours and incur $280,000 in studio overhead cost. The following transactions were recorded for the year:

a. Film, costumes, and similar raw materials purchased on account, $185,000.
b. Film, costumes, and other raw materials issued to production, $200,000 (85% of this material was considered direct to the videos in production, and the other 15% was considered indirect).
c. Utility costs incurred in the production studio, $72,000.
d. Depreciation recorded on the studio, cameras, and other equipment, $84,000. Three-fourths of this depreciation related to actual production of the videos, and the remainder related to equipment used in marketing and administration.
e. Advertising expense incurred, $130,000.
f. Costs for salaries and wages were incurred as follows:

Direct labour (actors and directors)	$82,000
Indirect labour (carpenters to build sets, costume designers, and so forth)	$110,000
Administrative salaries	$95,000

g. Prepaid insurance expired during the year, $7,000 (80% related to production of videos, and 20% related to marketing and administrative activities).
h. Miscellaneous marketing and administrative expenses incurred, $8,600.
i. Studio (manufacturing) overhead was applied to videos in production. The company recorded 7,250 camera-hours of activity during the year.
j. Videos that cost $550,000 to produce according to their job cost sheets were transferred to the finished videos warehouse to await sale and shipment.
k. Sales for the year totalled $925,000 and were all on account. The total cost to produce these videos according to their job cost sheets was $600,000.
l. Collections from customers during the year totalled $850,000.
m. Payments to suppliers on account during the year, $500,000; payments to employees for salaries and wages, $285,000.

Required:

1. Prepare a T-account for each account on the company's balance sheet and enter the beginning balances.
2. Record the transactions directly into the T-accounts. Prepare new T-accounts as needed. Key your entries to the letters (a) through (m) above. Find the ending balance in each account.
3. Is the Studio (manufacturing) Overhead account underapplied or overapplied for the year? Make an entry in the T-accounts to close any balance in the Studio Overhead account to Cost of Goods Sold.
4. Prepare an income statement for the year. (Do not prepare a schedule of cost of goods manufactured; all of the information needed for the income statement is available in the T-accounts.)

PROBLEM 3–20 Journal Entries; T-Accounts; Cost Flows [LO4, LO5, LO7]

Almeda Products, Inc., uses a job-order costing system. The company's inventory balances on April 1, the start of its fiscal year, were as follows:

Raw materials	$32,000
Work in process	$20,000
Finished goods	$48,000

During the year, the following transactions were completed:

a. Raw materials were purchased on account, $170,000.
b. Raw materials were issued from the storeroom for use in production, $180,000 (80% direct and 20% indirect).
c. Employee salaries and wages were accrued as follows: direct labour, $200,000; indirect labour, $82,000; and selling and administrative salaries, $90,000.
d. Utility costs were incurred in the factory, $65,000.
e. Advertising costs were incurred, $100,000.
f. Prepaid insurance expired during the year, $20,000 (90% related to factory operations, and 10% related to selling and administrative activities).
g. Depreciation was recorded, $180,000 (85% related to factory assets, and 15% related to selling and administrative assets).
h. Manufacturing overhead was applied to jobs at the rate of 175% of direct labour cost.

i. Goods that cost $700,000 to manufacture according to their job cost sheets were transferred to the finished goods warehouse.
j. Sales for the year totalled $1,000,000 and were all on account. The total cost to manufacture these goods according to their job cost sheets was $720,000.

Required:

1. Prepare journal entries to record the transactions for the year.
2. Prepare T-accounts for Raw Materials, Work in Process, Finished Goods, Manufacturing Overhead, and Cost of Goods Sold. Post the appropriate parts of your journal entries to these T-accounts. Compute the ending balance in each account. (Don't forget to enter the beginning balances in the inventory accounts.)
3. Is Manufacturing Overhead underapplied or overapplied for the year? Prepare a journal entry to close this balance to Cost of Goods Sold.
4. Prepare an income statement for the year. (Do not prepare a schedule of cost of goods manufactured; all of the information needed for the income statement is available in the journal entries and T-accounts you have prepared.)

PROBLEM 3–21 T-accounts; Applying Overhead [LO5, LO7, LO8]

Hudson Company's trial balance as of January 1, the beginning of its fiscal year, is given below:

Cash	$ 7,000	
Accounts Receivable	18,000	
Raw Materials	9,000	
Work in Process	20,000	
Finished Goods	32,000	
Prepaid Insurance	4,000	
Plant and Equipment	210,000	
Accumulated Depreciation		$ 53,000
Accounts Payable		38,000
Capital Stock		160,000
Retained Earnings		49,000
Total	$300,000	$300,000

Hudson Company is a manufacturer that uses a job-order costing system. During the year, the following transactions took place:

a. Raw materials purchased on account, $40,000.
b. Raw materials were requisitioned for use in production, $38,000 (85% direct and 15% indirect).
c. Factory utility costs incurred, $19,100.
d. Depreciation was recorded on plant and equipment, $36,000. Three-fourths of the depreciation related to factory equipment, and the remainder related to selling and administrative equipment.
e. Advertising expense incurred, $48,000.
f. Costs for salaries and wages were incurred as follows:

Direct labour	$45,000
Indirect labour	$10,000
Administrative salaries	$30,000

g. Prepaid insurance expired during the year, $3,000 (80% related to factory operations, and 20% related to selling and administrative activities).
h. Miscellaneous selling and administrative expenses incurred, $9,500.
i. Manufacturing overhead was applied to production. The company applies overhead on the basis of $8 per machine-hour; 7,500 machine-hours were recorded for the year.
j. Goods that cost $140,000 to manufacture according to their job cost sheets were transferred to the finished goods warehouse.
k. Sales for the year totalled $250,000 and were all on account. The total cost to manufacture these goods according to their job cost sheets was $130,000.
l. Collections from customers during the year totalled $245,000.
m. Payments to suppliers on account during the year, $150,000; payments to employees for salaries and wages, $84,000.

Required:

1. Prepare a T-account for each account in the company's trial balance and enter the opening balances shown above.

2. Record the transactions above directly into the T-accounts. Prepare new T-accounts as needed. Key your entries to the letters (a) through (m) above. Find the ending balance in each account.
3. Is manufacturing overhead underapplied or overapplied for the year? Make an entry in the T-accounts to close any balance in the Manufacturing Overhead account to Cost of Goods Sold.
4. Prepare an income statement for the year. (Do not prepare a schedule of cost of goods manufactured; all of the information needed for the income statement is available in the T-accounts.)

PROBLEM 3–22 T-accounts; Overhead Rates; Journal Entries [LO2, LO3, LO4, LO5, LO7]

AOZT Volzhskije Motory of St. Petersburg, Russia, makes marine motors for vessels ranging in size from harbour tugs to open-water icebreakers. (The Russian currency is the ruble, which is denoted by RUR. All currency amounts below are in thousands of RUR.)

The company uses a job-order costing system. Only three jobs—Job 208, Job 209, and Job 210—were worked on during May and June. Job 208 was completed on June 20; the other two jobs were uncompleted on June 30. Job cost sheets on the three jobs are given below:

	Job Cost Sheet		
	Job 208	Job 209	Job 210
May costs incurred:*			
Direct materials	RUR9,500	RUR5,100	RUR —
Direct labour	RUR8,000	RUR3,000	RUR —
Manufacturing overhead	RUR11,200	RUR4,200	RUR —
June costs incurred:			
Direct materials	RUR —	RUR6,000	RUR7,200
Direct labour	RUR4,000	RUR7,500	RUR8,500
Manufacturing overhead	RUR ?	RUR ?	RUR ?

*Jobs 208 and 209 were started during May.

The following additional information is available:

a. Manufacturing overhead is applied to jobs on the basis of direct labour cost.
b. Balances in the inventory accounts at May 31 were:

Raw Materials	RUR30,000
Work in Process	RUR?
Finished Goods	RUR50,000

Required:

1. Prepare T-accounts for Raw Materials, Work in Process, Finished Goods, and Manufacturing Overhead. Enter the May 31 balances given above; in the case of Work in Process, compute the May 31 balance and enter it into the Work in Process T-account.
2. Prepare journal entries for *June* as follows:
   a. Prepare an entry to record the issue of materials into production and post the entry to appropriate T-accounts. (In the case of direct materials, it is not necessary to make a separate entry for each job.) Indirect materials used during June totalled RUR3,600.
   b. Prepare an entry to record the incurrence of labour cost and post the entry to appropriate T-accounts. (In the case of direct labour cost, it is not necessary to make a separate entry for each job.) Indirect labour cost totalled RUR7,000 for June.
   c. Prepare an entry to record the incurrence of RUR19,400 in various actual manufacturing overhead costs for June. (Credit Accounts Payable.) Post this entry to the appropriate T-accounts.
3. What apparent predetermined overhead rate does the company use to assign overhead cost to jobs? Using this rate, prepare a journal entry to record the application of overhead cost to jobs for June (it is not necessary to make a separate entry for each job). Post this entry to appropriate T-accounts.
4. As stated earlier, Job 208 was completed during June. Prepare a journal entry to show the transfer of this job off of the production line and into the finished goods warehouse. Post the entry to appropriate T-accounts.
5. Determine the balance at June 30 in the Work in Process inventory account. How much of this balance consists of costs charged to Job 209? To Job 210?

PROBLEM 3–23 Multiple Departments; Applying Overhead [LO3, LO5, LO8]

High Desert Potteryworks makes a variety of pottery products that it sells to retailers such as Home Depot. The company uses a job-order costing system in which predetermined overhead rates are used to apply manufacturing overhead cost to jobs. The predetermined overhead rate in the Molding Department is based on machine-hours, and the rate in the Painting Department is based on direct labour cost. At the beginning of the year, the company's management made the following estimates:

	Department	
	Molding	Painting
Direct labour-hours	12,000	60,000
Machine-hours	70,000	8,000
Direct materials cost	$510,000	$650,000
Direct labour cost	$130,000	$420,000
Manufacturing overhead cost	$602,000	$735,000

Job 205 was started on August 1 and completed on August 10. The company's cost records show the following information concerning the job:

	Department	
	Molding	Painting
Direct labour-hours	30	85
Machine-hours	110	20
Materials placed into production	$470	$332
Direct labour cost	$290	$680

Required:

1. Compute the predetermined overhead rate used during the year in the Molding Department. Compute the rate used in the Painting Department.
2. Compute the total overhead cost applied to Job 205.
3. What would be the total cost recorded for Job 205? If the job contained 50 units, what would be the unit product cost?
4. At the end of the year, the records of High Desert Potteryworks revealed the following *actual* cost and operating data for all jobs worked on during the year:

	Department	
	Molding	Painting
Direct labour-hours	10,000	62,000
Machine-hours	65,000	9,000
Direct materials cost	$430,000	$680,000
Direct labour cost	$108,000	$436,000
Manufacturing overhead cost	$570,000	$750,000

What was the amount of under- or overapplied overhead in each department at the end of the year?

PROBLEM 3–24 T-Account Analysis of Cost Flows [LO3, LO6, LO8]

Selected ledger accounts of Moore Company are given below for the just completed year:

Raw Materials

Bal. 1/1	15,000	Credits	?
Debits	120,000		
Bal. 12/31	25,000		

Manufacturing Overhead

Debits	230,000	Credits	?

Work in Process

Bal. 1/1	20,000	Credits	470,000
Direct materials	90,000		
Direct labour	150,000		
Overhead	240,000		
Bal. 12/31	?		

Factory Wages Payable

Debits	185,000	Bal. 1/1	9,000
		Credits	180,000
		Bal. 12/31	4,000

Finished Goods

Bal. 1/1	40,000	Credits	?
Debits	?		
Bal. 12/31	60,000		

Cost of Goods Sold

Debits	?		

Required:

1. What was the cost of raw materials put into production during the year?
2. How much of the materials in (1) above consisted of indirect materials?
3. How much of the factory labour cost for the year consisted of indirect labour?
4. What was the cost of goods manufactured for the year?
5. What was the cost of goods sold for the year (before considering under- or overapplied overhead)?
6. If overhead is applied to production on the basis of direct labour cost, what rate was in effect during the year?
7. Was manufacturing overhead under- or overapplied? By how much?
8. Compute the ending balance in the Work in Process inventory account. Assume that this balance consists entirely of goods started during the year. If $8,000 of this balance is direct labour cost, how much of it is direct materials cost? Manufacturing overhead cost?

PROBLEM 3–25 Journal Entries; T-Accounts; Disposition of Underapplied or Overapplied Overhead [LO3, LO4, LO5, LO7, LO8]

Film Specialties, Inc., operates a small production studio in which advertising films are made for TV and other uses. The company uses a job-order costing system to accumulate costs for each film produced. The company's trial balance as of May 1, the start of its fiscal year, is given as follows:

Cash	$ 60,000	
Accounts Receivable	210,000	
Materials and Supplies	130,000	
Films in Process	75,000	
Finished Films	860,000	
Prepaid Insurance	90,000	
Studio and Equipment	5,200,000	
Accumulated Depreciation		$1,990,000
Accounts Payable		700,000
Salaries and Wages Payable		35,000
Capital Stock		2,500,000
Retained Earnings		1,400,000
Total	$6,625,000	$6,625,000

Film Specialties, Inc., uses a Production Overhead account to record all transactions relating to overhead costs and applies overhead costs to jobs on the basis of camera-hours. For the current year, the company estimated that it would incur $1,350,000 in production overhead costs, and film 15,000 camera-hours. During the year, the following transactions were completed:

a. Materials and supplies purchased on account, $690,000.
b. Materials and supplies issued from the storeroom for use in production of various films, $700,000 (80% direct to the films and 20% indirect).
c. Utility costs incurred in the production studio, $90,000.

d. Costs for employee salaries and wages were incurred as follows:

Actors, directors, and camera crew	$1,300,000
Indirect labour costs of support workers	$230,000
Marketing and administrative salaries	$650,000

e. Advertising costs incurred, $800,000.
f. Prepaid insurance expired during the year, $70,000. Of this amount, $60,000 related to the operation of the production studio, and the remaining $10,000 related to the company's marketing and administrative activities.
g. Depreciation recorded for the year, $650,000 (80% represented depreciation of the production studio, cameras, and other production equipment; the remaining 20% represented depreciation of facilities and equipment used in marketing and administrative activities).
h. Rental costs incurred on various facilities and equipment used in production of films, $360,000; and rental costs incurred on equipment used in marketing and administrative activities, $40,000.
i. Production overhead was applied to jobs filmed during the year. The company recorded 16,500 camera-hours.
j. Films that cost $3,400,000 to produce according to their job cost sheets were completed during the year. The films were transferred to the finished films storeroom to await delivery to customers.
k. Sales of films for the year (all on account) totalled $6,000,000. The total cost to produce these films was $4,000,000 according to their job cost sheets.
l. Collections on account from customers during the year, $5,400,000.
m. Cash payments made during the year; to creditors on account, $2,500,000; and to employees for salaries and wages, $2,200,000.

Required:
1. Prepare journal entries to record the year's transactions.
2. Prepare a T-account for each account in the company's trial balance and enter the opening balances given above. Post your journal entries to the T-accounts. Prepare new T-accounts as needed. Compute the ending balance in each account.
3. Is production overhead underapplied or overapplied for the year? Prepare the necessary journal entry to close the balance in Production Overhead to Cost of Films Sold.
4. Prepare an income statement for the year. (Do not prepare a schedule of cost of goods manufactured; all of the information needed for the income statement is available in the T-accounts.)

PROBLEM 3–26 Predetermined Overhead Rate; Disposition of Under- or Overapplied Overhead [LO3, LO8]

Bieler & Cie of Altdorf, Switzerland, makes furniture using the latest automated technology. The company uses a job-order costing system and applies manufacturing overhead cost to products on the basis of machine-hours. The following estimates were used in preparing the predetermined overhead rate at the beginning of the year:

Machine-hours	75,000
Manufacturing overhead cost	Sfr900,000

The currency in Switzerland is the Swiss franc, which is denoted by Sfr.

During the year, a glut of furniture on the market resulted in cutting back production and a buildup of furniture in the company's warehouse. The company's cost records revealed the following actual cost and operating data for the year:

Machine-hours	60,000
Manufacturing overhead cost	Sfr850,000
Inventories at year-end:	
Raw materials	Sfr30,000
Work in process (includes overhead applied of 36,000)	Sfr100,000
Finished goods (includes overhead applied of 180,000)	Sfr500,000
Cost of goods sold (includes overhead applied of 504,000)	Sfr1,400,000

Required:

1. Compute the company's predetermined overhead rate.
2. Compute the under- or overapplied overhead.
3. Assume that the company closes any under- or overapplied overhead directly to Cost of Goods Sold. Prepare the appropriate journal entry.
4. Assume that the company allocates any under- or overapplied overhead to Work in Process, Finished Goods, and Cost of Goods Sold on the basis of the amount of overhead applied that remains in each account at the end of the year. Prepare the journal entry to show the allocation for the year.
5. How much higher or lower will net operating income be if the under- or overapplied overhead is allocated rather than closed directly to Cost of Goods Sold?

PROBLEM 3–27 Schedule of Cost of Goods Manufactured; Overhead Analysis [LO3, LO5, LO6, LO7]

Gitano Products operates a job-order costing system and applies overhead cost to jobs on the basis of direct materials *used in production* (*not* on the basis of raw materials purchased). In computing a predetermined overhead rate at the beginning of the year, the company's estimates were: manufacturing overhead cost, $800,000; and direct materials to be used in production, $500,000. The company has provided the following data in the form of an Excel worksheet:

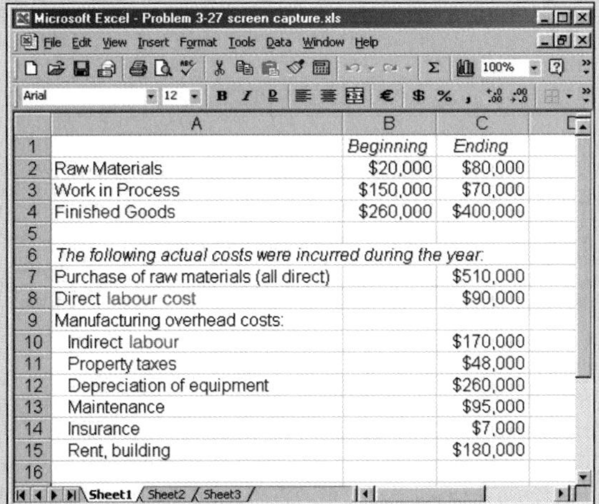

	A	B	C
1		*Beginning*	*Ending*
2	Raw Materials	$20,000	$80,000
3	Work in Process	$150,000	$70,000
4	Finished Goods	$260,000	$400,000
5			
6	*The following actual costs were incurred during the year:*		
7	Purchase of raw materials (all direct)		$510,000
8	Direct labour cost		$90,000
9	Manufacturing overhead costs:		
10	Indirect labour		$170,000
11	Property taxes		$48,000
12	Depreciation of equipment		$260,000
13	Maintenance		$95,000
14	Insurance		$7,000
15	Rent, building		$180,000
16			

Required:

1. *a.* Compute the predetermined overhead rate for the year.
   b. Compute the amount of under- or overapplied overhead for the year.
2. Prepare a schedule of cost of goods manufactured for the year.
3. Compute the Cost of Goods Sold for the year. (Do not include any under- or overapplied overhead in your Cost of Goods Sold figure.) What options are available for disposing of under- or overapplied overhead?
4. Job 215 was started and completed during the year. What price would have been charged to the customer if the job required $8,500 in direct materials and $2,700 in direct labour cost and the company priced its jobs at 25% above the job's cost according to the accounting system?
5. Direct materials made up $24,000 of the $70,000 ending Work in Process inventory balance. Supply the information missing below:

Direct materials	$24,000
Direct labour	?
Manufacturing overhead	?
Work in process inventory	$70,000

PROBLEM 3–28 (Appendix 3A) Predetermined Overhead Rate and Capacity [LO3, LO5, LO8, LO9]

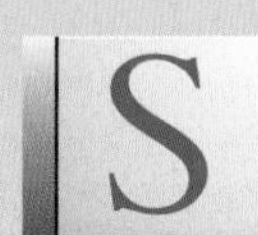

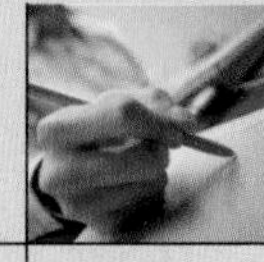

Platinum Tracks, Inc., is a small audio recording studio located in Alberta. The company handles work for advertising agencies—primarily for radio ads—and has a few singers and bands as clients. Platinum Tracks handles all aspects of recording from editing to making a digital master from which CDs can be copied. The competition in the audio recording industry in Alberta has always been tough, but it has been getting even tougher over the last several years. The studio has been losing customers to newer studios that are equipped with more up-to-date equipment and that are able to offer very attractive prices and excellent service. Summary data concerning the last two years of operations follow:

	2005	2004
Estimated hours of studio service	800	1,000
Estimated studio overhead cost	$160,000	$160,000
Actual hours of studio service provided	500	750
Actual studio overhead cost incurred	$160,000	$160,000
Hours of studio service at capacity	1,600	1,600

The company applies studio overhead to recording jobs on the basis of the hours of studio service provided. For example, 40 hours of studio time were required to record, edit, and master the *Verde Baja* music CD for a local Latino band. All of the studio overhead is fixed, and the actual overhead cost incurred was exactly as estimated at the beginning of the year in both 2004 and 2005.

Required:

1. Platinum Tracks computes its predetermined overhead rate at the beginning of each year based on the estimated studio overhead and the estimated hours of studio service for the year. How much overhead would have been applied to the *Verde Baja* job if it had been done in 2004? In 2005? By how much would overhead have been under- or overapplied in 2004? In 2005?
2. The president of Platinum Tracks has heard that some companies in the industry have changed to a system of computing the predetermined overhead rate at the beginning of each year based on the estimated studio overhead for the year and the hours of studio service that could be provided at capacity. He would like to know what effect this method would have on job costs. How much overhead would have been applied using this method to the *Verde Baja* job if it had been done in 2004? In 2005? By how much would overhead have been under- or overapplied in 2004 using this method? In 2005?
3. How would you interpret the under- or overapplied overhead that results from using studio hours at capacity to compute the predetermined overhead rate?
4. What fundamental business problem is Platinum Tracks facing? Which method of computing the predetermined overhead rate is likely to be more helpful in facing this problem? Explain.

PROBLEM 3–29 Multiple Departments; Overhead Rates; Under- or Overapplied Overhead [LO3, LO5, LO8]

Hobart, Evans, and Nix is a small law firm that contains 10 partners and 12 support persons. The firm employs a job-order costing system to accumulate costs chargeable to each client, and it is organized into two departments—the Research and Documents Department and the Litigation Department. The firm uses predetermined overhead rates to charge the costs of these departments to its clients. At the beginning of the year, the firm's management made the following estimates for the year:

	Department	
	Research and Documents	Litigation
Research-hours	24,000	—
Direct lawyer-hours	9,000	18,000
Legal forms and supplies	$16,000	$5,000
Direct lawyer cost	$450,000	$900,000
Departmental overhead cost	$840,000	$360,000

The predetermined overhead rate in the Research and Documents Department is based on research-hours, and the rate in the Litigation Department is based on direct lawyer cost.

The costs charged to each client are made up of three elements: legal forms and supplies used, direct lawyer costs incurred, and an applied amount of overhead from each department in which work is performed on the case.

Case 418-3 was initiated on February 23 and completed on May 16. During this period, the following costs and time were recorded on the case:

	Department	
	Research and Documents	Litigation
Research-hours	26	—
Direct lawyer-hours	7	114
Legal forms and supplies	$80	$40
Direct lawyer cost	$350	$5,700

Required:

1. Compute the predetermined overhead rate used during the year in the Research and Documents Department. Compute the rate used in the Litigation Department.
2. Using the rates you computed in (1) above, compute the total overhead cost applied to Case 418-3.
3. What would be the total cost charged to Case 418-3? Show computations by department and in total for the case.
4. At the end of the year, the firm's records revealed the following actual cost and operating data for all cases handled during the year:

	Department	
	Research and Documents	Litigation
Research-hours	26,000	—
Direct lawyer-hours	8,000	15,000
Legal forms and supplies	$19,000	$6,000
Direct lawyer cost	$400,000	$750,000
Departmental overhead cost	$870,000	$315,000

Determine the amount of under- or overapplied overhead cost in each department for the year.

PROBLEM 3–30 Plantwide versus Departmental Overhead Rates; Under- or Overapplied Overhead [LO3, LO5, LO8]

"Blast it!" said David Wilson, president of Teledex Company. "We've just lost the bid on the Koopers job by $2,000. It seems we're either too high to get the job or too low to make any money on half the jobs we bid."

Teledex Company manufactures products to customers' specifications and operates a job-order costing system. Manufacturing overhead cost is applied to jobs on the basis of direct labour cost. The following estimates were made at the beginning of the year:

	Department			
	Fabricating	Machining	Assembly	Total Plant
Direct labour	$200,000	$100,000	$300,000	$600,000
Manufacturing overhead	$350,000	$400,000	$90,000	$840,000

Jobs require varying amounts of work in the three departments. The Koopers job, for example, would have required manufacturing costs in the three departments as follows:

	Department			
	Fabricating	Machining	Assembly	Total Plant
Direct materials	$3,000	$200	$1,400	$4,600
Direct labour	$2,800	$500	$6,200	$9,500
Manufacturing overhead	?	?	?	?

The company uses a plantwide overhead rate to apply manufacturing overhead cost to jobs.

Required:

1. Assuming use of a plantwide overhead rate:
   a. Compute the rate for the current year.
   b. Determine the amount of manufacturing overhead cost that would have been applied to the Koopers job.
2. Suppose that instead of using a plantwide overhead rate, the company had used a separate predetermined overhead rate in each department. Under these conditions:
   a. Compute the rate for each department for the current year.
   b. Determine the amount of manufacturing overhead cost that would have been applied to the Koopers job.
3. Explain the difference between the manufacturing overhead that would have been applied to the Koopers job using the plantwide rate in question 1 (b) above and using the departmental rates in question 2 (b).
4. Assume that it is customary in the industry to bid jobs at 150% of total manufacturing cost (direct materials, direct labour, and applied overhead). What was the company's bid price on the Koopers job? What would the bid price have been if departmental overhead rates had been used to apply overhead cost?
5. At the end of the year, the company assembled the following *actual* cost data relating to all jobs worked on during the year.

	Department			
	Fabricating	Machining	Assembly	Total Plant
Direct materials	$190,000	$16,000	$114,000	$320,000
Direct labour	$210,000	$108,000	$262,000	$580,000
Manufacturing overhead	$360,000	$420,000	$84,000	$864,000

Compute the under- or overapplied overhead for the year (a) assuming that a plantwide overhead rate is used, and (b) assuming that departmental overhead rates are used.

PROBLEM 3–31 Journal Entries; T-Accounts; Comprehensive Problem; Financial Statements; [LO3, LO4, LO5, LO6, LO7, LO8]

Froya Fabrikker A/S of Bergen, Norway, is a small company that manufactures specialty heavy equipment for use in North Sea oil fields. (The Norwegian currency is the krone, which is denoted by Nkr.) The company uses a job-order costing system and applies manufacturing overhead cost to jobs on the basis of direct labour-hours. At the beginning of the year, the following estimates were made for the purpose of computing the predetermined overhead rate: manufacturing overhead cost, Nkr360,000; and direct labour-hours, 900.

The following transactions took place during the year (all purchases and services were acquired on account):

a. Raw materials were purchased for use in production, Nkr200,000.
b. Raw materials were requisitioned for use in production (all direct materials), Nkr185,000.
c. Utility bills were incurred, Nkr70,000 (90% related to factory operations, and the remainder related to selling and administrative activities).
d. Salary and wage costs were incurred:

Direct labour (975 hours)	Nkr230,000
Indirect labour	Nkr90,000
Selling and administrative salaries	Nkr110,000

e. Maintenance costs were incurred in the factory, Nkr54,000.
f. Advertising costs were incurred, Nkr136,000.
g. Depreciation was recorded for the year, Nkr95,000 (80% related to factory equipment, and the remainder related to selling and administrative equipment).
h. Rental cost incurred on buildings, Nkr120,000 (85% related to factory operations, and the remainder related to selling and administrative facilities).
i. Manufacturing overhead cost was applied to jobs, Nkr __?__.
j. Cost of goods manufactured for the year, Nkr770,000.

k. Sales for the year (all on account) totalled Nkr1,200,000. These goods cost Nkr800,000 to manufacture according to their job cost sheets.

The balances in the inventory accounts at the beginning of the year were:

Raw Materials	Nkr30,000
Work in Process	Nkr21,000
Finished Goods	Nkr60,000

Required:

1. Prepare journal entries to record the preceding data.
2. Post your entries to T-accounts. (Don't forget to enter the beginning inventory balances above.) Determine the ending balances in the inventory accounts and in the Manufacturing Overhead account.
3. Prepare a schedule of cost of goods manufactured.
4. Prepare a journal entry to close any balance in the Manufacturing Overhead account to Cost of Goods Sold. Prepare a schedule of cost of goods sold.
5. Prepare an income statement for the year.
6. Job 412 was one of the many jobs started and completed during the year. The job required Nkr8,000 in direct materials and 39 hours of direct labour time at a total direct labour cost of Nkr9,200. The job contained only four units. If the company bills at a price 60% above the unit product cost on the job cost sheet, what price per unit would have been charged to the customer?

PROBLEM 3–32 Comprehensive Problem: T-Accounts, Job-Order Cost Flows; Financial Statements [LO3, LO5, LO6, LO8]

Chenko Products, Inc., manufactures goods to customers' orders and uses a job-order costing system. A beginning-of-the-year trial balance for the company is given below:

Cash	$ 35,000	
Accounts Receivable	127,000	
Raw Materials	10,000	
Work in Process	44,000	
Finished Goods	75,000	
Prepaid Insurance	9,000	
Plant and Equipment	400,000	
Accumulated Depreciation		$110,000
Accounts Payable		86,000
Salaries and Wages Payable		9,000
Capital Stock		375,000
Retained Earnings		120,000
Total	$700,000	$700,000

The company applies manufacturing overhead cost to jobs on the basis of direct materials cost. The following estimates were made at the beginning of the year for purposes of computing a predetermined overhead rate: manufacturing overhead cost, $510,000; and direct materials cost, $340,000. Summarized transactions of the company for the year are given below:

a. Raw materials purchased on account, $400,000.
b. Raw materials requisitioned for use in production, $370,000 ($320,000 direct materials and $50,000 indirect materials).
c. Salary and wage costs were incurred as follows:

Direct labour	$76,000
Indirect labour	$130,000
Selling and administrative salaries	$110,000

d. Maintenance costs incurred in the factory, $81,000.
e. Travel costs incurred by salespeople, $43,000.
f. Prepaid insurance on the factory expired during the year, $7,000.
g. Utility costs incurred, $70,000 (90% related to factory operations, and 10% related to selling and administrative activities).

h. Property taxes incurred on the factory building, $9,000.
i. Advertising costs incurred, $200,000.
j. Rental cost incurred on special factory equipment, $120,000.
k. Depreciation recorded for the year, $50,000 (80% related to factory assets, and 20% related to selling and administrative assets).
l. Manufacturing overhead cost applied to jobs, $? .
m. Cost of goods manufactured for the year, $890,000.
n. Sales for the year totalled $1,400,000 (all on account); the cost of goods sold totalled $930,000.
o. Cash collections from customers during the year totalled $1,350,000.
p. Cash payments during the year: to employees, $300,000; on accounts payable, $970,000.

Required:

1. Enter the company's transactions directly into T-accounts. (Don't forget to enter the beginning balances into the T-accounts.) Key your entries to the letters (a) through (p) above. Create new T-accounts as needed. Find the ending balance in each account.
2. Prepare a schedule of cost of goods manufactured.
3. Prepare a journal entry to close any balance in the Manufacturing Overhead account to Cost of Goods Sold. Prepare a schedule of cost of goods sold.
4. Prepare an income statement for the year.
5. Job 412 was one of the many jobs started and completed during the year. The job required $8,000 in direct materials and $1,600 in direct labour cost. If the job contained 400 units and the company billed the job at 175% of the unit product cost on the job cost sheet, what price per unit would have been charged to the customer?

CASES

CASE 3–33 Critical Thinking; Interpretation of Manufacturing Overhead Rates [LO3, LO5]

Kelvin Aerospace, Inc., manufactures parts such as rudder hinges for the aerospace industry. The company uses a job-order costing system with a plantwide predetermined overhead rate based on direct labour-hours. On December 16, 2005, the company's controller made a preliminary estimate of the predetermined overhead rate for the year 2006. The new rate was based on the estimated total manufacturing overhead cost of $3,402,000 and the estimated 63,000 total direct labour-hours for 2006:

$$\text{Predetermined overhead rate} = \frac{\$3{,}402{,}000}{63{,}000 \text{ hours}}$$

$$= \$54 \text{ per direct labour-hour}$$

This new predetermined overhead rate was communicated to top managers in a meeting on December 19. The rate did not cause any comment because it was within a few pennies of the overhead rate that had been used during 2005. One of the subjects discussed at the meeting was a proposal by the production manager to purchase an automated milling machine built by Sunghi Industries. The president of Kelvin Aerospace, Harry Arcany, agreed to meet with the sales representative from Sunghi Industries to discuss the proposal.

On the day following the meeting, Mr. Arcany met with Jasmine Chang, Sunghi Industries' sales representative. The following discussion took place:

Arcany: Wally, our production manager, asked me to meet with you since he is interested in installing an automated milling machine. Frankly, I'm skeptical. You're going to have to show me this isn't just another expensive toy for Wally's people to play with.

Chang: This is a great machine with direct bottom-line benefits. The automated milling machine has three major advantages. First, it is much faster than the manual methods you are using. It can process about twice as many parts per hour as your present milling machines. Second, it is much more flexible. There are some up-front programming costs, but once those have been incurred, almost no setup is required to run a standard operation. You just punch in the code for the standard operation, load the machine's hopper with raw material, and the machine does the rest.

Arcany: What about cost? Having twice the capacity in the milling machine area won't do us much good. That centre is idle much of the time anyway.

Chang: I was getting there. The third advantage of the automated milling machine is lower cost. Wally and I looked over your present operations, and we estimated that the automated equipment would eliminate the need for about 6,000 direct labour-hours a year. What is your direct labour cost per hour?

Arcany: The wage rate in the milling area averages about $32 per hour. Employee benefits raise that figure to about $41 per hour.

Chang: Don't forget your overhead.

Arcany: Next year the overhead rate will be $54 per hour.

Chang: So including employee benefits and overhead, the cost per direct labour-hour is about $95.

Arcany: That's right.

Chang: Since you can save 6,000 direct labour-hours per year, the cost savings would amount to about $570,000 a year. And our 60-month lease plan would require payments of only $348,000 per year.

Arcany: That sounds like a no-brainer. When can you install the equipment?

Shortly after this meeting, Mr. Arcany informed the company's controller of the decision to lease the new equipment, which would be installed over the Christmas vacation period. The controller realized that this decision would require a recomputation of the predetermined overhead rate for the year 2006 since the decision would affect both the manufacturing overhead and the direct labour-hours for the year. After talking with both the production manager and the sales representative from Sunghi Industries, the controller discovered that in addition to the annual lease cost of $348,000, the new machine would also require a skilled technician/programmer who would have to be hired at a cost of $50,000 per year to maintain and program the equipment. Both of these costs would be included in factory overhead. There would be no other changes in total manufacturing overhead cost, which is almost entirely fixed. The controller assumed that the new machine would result in a reduction of 6,000 direct labour-hours for the year from the levels that had initially been planned.

When the revised predetermined overhead rate for the year 2006 was circulated among the company's top managers, there was considerable dismay.

Required:

1. Recompute the predetermined rate assuming that the new machine will be installed. Explain why the new predetermined overhead rate is higher (or lower) than the rate that was originally estimated for the year 2006.
2. What effect (if any) would this new rate have on the cost of jobs that do not use the new automated milling machine?
3. Why would managers be concerned about the new overhead rate?
4. After seeing the new predetermined overhead rate, the production manager admitted that he probably wouldn't be able to eliminate all of the 6,000 direct labour-hours. He had been hoping to accomplish the reduction by not replacing workers who retire or quit, but that had not been possible. As a result, the real labour savings would be only about 2,000 hours—one worker. Given this additional information, evaluate the original decision to acquire the automated milling machine from Sunghi Industries.

CASE 3–34 (Appendix 3A) Ethics; Predetermined Overhead Rate and Capacity [LO5, LO8, LO9]

Pat Miranda, the new controller of Vault Hard Drives, Inc., has just returned from a seminar on the choice of the activity level in the predetermined overhead rate. Even though the subject did not sound exciting at first, she found that there were some important ideas presented that should get a hearing at her company. After returning from the seminar, she arranged a meeting with the production manager, J. Stevens, and the assistant production manager, Marvin Washington.

Pat: I ran across an idea that I wanted to check out with both of you. It's about the way we compute predetermined overhead rates.

J.: We're all ears.

Pat: We compute the predetermined overhead rate by dividing the estimated total factory overhead for the coming year by the estimated total units produced for the coming year.

Marvin: We've been doing that as long as I've been with the company.

J.: And it has been done that way at every other company I've worked at, except at most places they divide by direct labour-hours.

Pat: We use units because it is simpler and we basically make one product with minor variations. But, there's another way to do it. Instead of dividing the estimated total factory overhead by the estimated total units produced for the coming year, we could divide by the total units produced at capacity.

Marvin: Oh, the Sales Department will love that. It will drop the costs on all of our products. They'll go wild over there cutting prices.

Pat: That is a worry, but I wanted to talk to both of you first before going over to Sales.

J.: Aren't you always going to have a lot of underapplied overhead?

Pat: That's correct, but let me show you how we would handle it. Here's an example based on our budget for next year.

Budgeted (estimated) production	160,000 units
Budgeted sales	160,000 units
Capacity	200,000 units
Selling price	$60 per unit
Variable manufacturing cost	$15 per unit
Total manufacturing overhead cost (all fixed)	$4,000,000
Administrative and selling expenses (all fixed)	$2,700,000
Beginning inventories	$0

Traditional Approach to Computation of the Predetermined Overhead Rate

$$\frac{\text{Estimated total manufacturing overhead cost, \$4,000,000}}{\text{Estimated total units produced, 160,000}} = \text{\$25 per unit}$$

Budgeted Income Statement

Revenue (160,000 units × $60 per unit)		$9,600,000
Cost of goods sold:		
Variable manufacturing (160,000 units × $15 per unit)	$2,400,000	
Manufacturing overhead applied (160,000 units × $25 per unit)	4,000,000	6,400,000
Gross margin		3,200,000
Administrative and selling expenses		2,700,000
Net operating income		$ 500,000

New Approach to Computation of the Predetermined Overhead Rate Using Capacity in the Denominator

$$\frac{\text{Estimated total manufacturing overhead cost, \$4,000,000}}{\text{Total units at capacity, 200,000}} = \text{\$20 per unit}$$

Budgeted Income Statement

Revenue (160,000 units × $60 per unit)		$9,600,000
Cost of goods sold:		
Variable manufacturing (160,000 units × $15 per unit)	$2,400,000	
Manufacturing overhead applied (160,000 units × $20 per unit)	3,200,000	5,600,000
Gross margin		4,000,000
Cost of unused capacity [(200,000 units − 160,000 units) × $20 per unit]		800,000
Administrative and selling expenses		2,700,000
Net operating income		$ 500,000

J.: Whoa!! I don't think I like the looks of that "Cost of unused capacity." If that thing shows up on the income statement, someone from headquarters is likely to come down here looking for some people to lay off.

Marvin: I'm worried about something else too. What happens when sales are not up to expectations? Can we pull the "hat trick"?

Pat: I'm sorry, I don't understand.

J.: Marvin's talking about something that happens fairly regularly. When sales are down and profits look like they are going to be lower than the president told the owners they were going to be, the president comes down here and asks us to deliver some more profits.

Marvin: And we pull them out of our hat.

J.: Yeah, we just increase production until we get the profits we want.

Pat: I still don't understand. You mean you increase sales?

J.: Nope, we increase production. We're the production managers, not the sales managers.

Pat: I get it. Since you have produced more, the sales force has more units it can sell.

J.: Nope, the marketing people don't do a thing. We just build inventories and that does the trick.

Required:

In all of the questions below, assume that the predetermined overhead rate under the traditional method is $25 per unit, and under the new method it is $20 per unit. Also assume that under the traditional method any under- or overapplied overhead is taken directly to the income statement as an adjustment to Cost of Goods Sold.

1. Suppose actual production is 160,000 units. Compute the net operating incomes that would be realized under the traditional and new methods if actual sales are 150,000 units and everything else turns out as expected.
2. How many units would have to be produced under each of the methods in order to realize the budgeted net operating income of $500,000 if actual sales are 150,000 units and everything else turns out as expected?
3. What effect does the new method based on capacity have on the volatility of net operating income?
4. Will the "hat trick" be easier or harder to perform if the new method based on capacity is used?
5. Do you think the "hat trick" is ethical?

CASE 3–35 Ethics and the Manager [LO3, LO5, LO8]

Terri Ronsin had recently been transferred to the Home Security Systems Division of National Home Products. Shortly after taking over her new position as divisional controller, she was asked to develop the division's predetermined overhead rate for the upcoming year. The accuracy of the rate is of some importance, since it is used throughout the year and any overapplied or underapplied overhead is closed out to Cost of Goods Sold at the end of the year. National Home Products uses direct labour-hours in all of its divisions as the allocation base for manufacturing overhead.

To compute the predetermined overhead rate, Terri divided her estimate of the total manufacturing overhead for the coming year by the production manager's estimate of the total direct labour-hours for the coming year. She took her computations to the division's general manager for approval but was quite surprised when he suggested a modification in the base. Her conversation with the general manager of the Home Security Systems Division, Harry Irving, went like this:

Ronsin: Here are my calculations for next year's predetermined overhead rate. If you approve, we can enter the rate into the computer on January 1 and be up and running in the job-order costing system right away this year.

Irving: Thanks for coming up with the calculations so quickly, and they look just fine. There is, however, one slight modification I would like to see. Your estimate of the total direct labour-hours for the year is 440,000 hours. How about cutting that to about 420,000 hours?

Ronsin: I don't know if I can do that. The production manager says she will need about 440,000 direct labour-hours to meet the sales projections for the year. Besides, there are going to be over 430,000 direct labour-hours during the current year and sales are projected to be higher next year.

Irving: Teri, I know all of that. I would still like to reduce the direct labour-hours in the base to something like 420,000 hours. You probably don't know that I had an agreement with your predecessor as divisional controller to shave 5% or so off the estimated direct labour-hours every year. That way, we kept a reserve that usually resulted in a big boost to net operating income at the end of the fiscal year in December. We called it our Christmas bonus. Corporate headquarters always seemed as pleased as punch that we could pull off such a miracle at the end of the year. This system has worked well for many years, and I don't want to change it now.

Required:

1. Explain how shaving 5% off the estimated direct labour-hours in the base for the predetermined overhead rate usually results in a big boost in net operating income at the end of the fiscal year.
2. Should Terri Ronsin go along with the general manager's request to reduce the direct labour-hours in the predetermined overhead rate computation to 420,000 direct labour-hours?

GROUP AND INTERNET EXERCISES

GROUP EXERCISE 3–36 Talk with a Controller

Look in the yellow pages or contact your local chamber of commerce or local chapter of a professional accounting association to find the names of manufacturing companies in your area. Make an appointment to meet with the controller or chief financial officer of one of these companies.

Required:

Ask the following questions and write a brief report concerning what you found out.

1. Does the company use job-order costing, process costing, or some other method of determining product costs?
2. How is overhead assigned to products? What is the overhead rate? What is the basis of allocation? Is more than one overhead rate used?
3. Are product costs used in making any decisions? If so, what are those decisions and how are product costs used?
4. How are profits affected by changes in production volume? By changes in sales?
5. Has the company recently changed its cost system or is it considering changing its cost system? If so, why? What changes were made or what changes are being considered?

INTERNET EXERCISE 3–37

As you know, the World Wide Web is constantly evolving. Sites come and go, and change without notice. To enable periodic updating of site addresses, this problem has been posted to the textbook Web site (www.mcgrawhill.ca/college/garrison). After accessing the site, enter the Student Centre and select this chapter. Select and complete the Internet Exercise.

CHAPTER 4

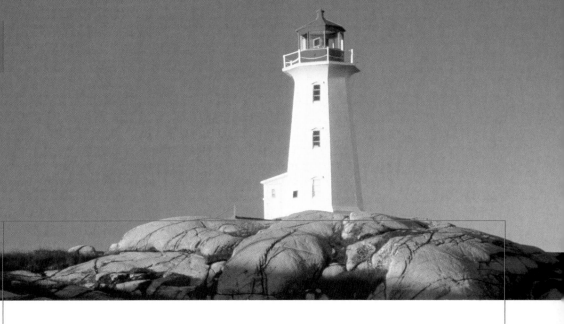

LEARNING OBJECTIVES

After studying Chapter 4, you should be able to:

1. Record the flow of materials, labour, and overhead through a process costing system.
2. Compute the equivalent units of production using the weighted-average method.
3. Prepare a quantity schedule using the weighted-average method.
4. Compute the costs per equivalent unit using the weighted-average method.
5. Prepare a cost reconciliation using the weighted-average method.
6. (Appendix 4A) Explain and compute the equivalent units of production using the FIFO method.
7. (Appendix 4A) Prepare a quantity schedule using the FIFO method.
8. (Appendix 4A) Compute the costs per equivalent unit using the FIFO method.
9. (Appendix 4A) Prepare a cost reconciliation using the FIFO method.

SYSTEMS DESIGN: PROCESS COSTING

BUSINESS FOCUS

COSTING CREAM SODA

Using an old family recipe, Megan started a company in Toronto that produced cream soda. At first the company struggled, but as sales increased, the company expanded rapidly. Megan soon realized that to expand any further, it would be necessary to borrow money. The investment in additional equipment was too large for her to finance out of the company's current cash flows.

Megan was disappointed to find that few banks were willing to make a loan to such a small company, but she finally found a bank that would consider her loan application. However, Megan was informed that she would have to supply up-to-date financial statements with her loan application.

Megan had never bothered with financial statements before—she felt that as long as the balance in the company's chequebook kept increasing, the company was doing fine. She wondered how she was going to determine the value of the cream soda in the work in process and finished goods inventories. The valuation of the cream soda would affect both the cost of goods sold and the inventory balances of her company. Megan thought of perhaps using job-order costing, but her company produces only one product. Raw ingredients were continually being mixed to make more cream soda, and more bottled cream soda was always coming off the end of the bottling line. Megan didn't see how she could use a job-order costing system, since the job never really ended. Perhaps there was another way to account for the costs of producing the cream soda.

As explained in Chapter 3, there are two basic costing systems in use: job-order costing and process costing. A job-order costing system is used in situations where many different jobs or products are worked on each period. Examples of industries that would typically use job-order costing include furniture manufacturers, special-order printers, shipbuilders, and many types of service organizations, such as repair shops and professional accounting services.

Process costing
A costing method used in situations where essentially homogeneous products are produced on a continuous basis.

By contrast, **process costing** is most commonly used in industries that produce essentially homogeneous (i.e., uniform) products on a continuous basis, such as bricks, corn flakes, or paper. Process costing is particularly used in companies that convert basic raw materials into homogeneous products, such as Alcan (aluminum ingots), Kimberly-Clark (toilet paper), Dover Mills (flour), Imperial Oil (gasoline and lubricating oils), and Christie's (crackers). In addition, process costing is often employed in companies that use a form of process costing in their assembly operations, such as Panasonic (video monitors), Hewlett Packard (personal computers), General Electric (refrigerators), Toyota (automobiles), Maytag (washing machines), and Sony (CD players). A form of process costing may also be used in utilities that produce gas, water, and electricity. As suggested by the length of this list, process costing is in very wide use.

Our purpose in this chapter is to extend the discussion of product costing to include a process costing system.

COMPARISON OF JOB-ORDER AND PROCESS COSTING

In some ways, process costing is very similar to job-order costing, and in some ways it is very different. In this section, we focus on these similarities and differences in order to provide a foundation for the detailed discussion of process costing that follows.

Similarities between Job-Order and Process Costing

Much of what was learned in the preceding chapter about costing and cost flows applies equally well to process costing in this chapter. We are not throwing out all that we have learned about costing and starting from scratch with a whole new system. The similarities that exist between job-order and process costing can be summarized as follows:

1. Both systems have the same basic purposes—to assign materials, labour, and overhead costs to products and to provide a mechanism for computing unit costs.
2. Both systems use the same basic manufacturing accounts, including Manufacturing Overhead, Raw Materials, Work in Process, and Finished Goods.
3. The flow of costs through the manufacturing accounts is basically the same in both systems.

As can be seen from this comparison, much of the knowledge that we have already acquired about costing is applicable to a process costing system. Our task now is simply to refine and extend this knowledge to process costing.

Differences between Job-Order and Process Costing

The differences between job-order and process costing arise from two factors. The first is that the flow of units in a process costing system is more or less continuous, and the second is that these units are indistinguishable from one another. Under process costing, it makes no sense to try to identify materials, labour, and overhead costs with a particular order from a customer (as we did with job-order costing), since each order is just one of many that are filled from a continuous flow of virtually identical units from the production line. Under process costing, we accumulate costs *by department,* rather than by order, and assign these costs equally to all units that pass through the department during a period.

A further difference between the two costing systems is that the job cost sheet is not used in process costing, since the focal point of that method is departments. Instead of using job cost sheets, a document known as a **production report** is prepared for each department in which work is done on products. The production report serves several functions. It provides a summary of the number of units moving through a department during a period, and it also provides a computation of unit costs. In addition, it shows what costs were charged to the department and what disposition was made of these costs. The department production report is the key document in a process costing system.

The major differences between job-order and process costing are summarized in Exhibit 4–1.

Production report
A report that summarizes all activity in a department's Work in Process account during a period and that contains three parts: a quantity schedule and a computation of equivalent units, a computation of total and unit costs, and a cost reconciliation.

FOCUS *on Current Practice*

Managers in the Canadian auto parts industry understand the importance of keeping track of manufacturing costs to help access productivity. "Despite the sharp appreciation of the Canadian dollar Canadian suppliers still have a 15% labour-cost advantage over their counterparts in the United States," says Carlos Gomes, Scotiabank's auto industry specialist. The Canadian auto parts industry has boosted productivity (value added per employee) by 3.1% per annum since 1997 to nearly double the annual 1.7% productivity advance by U.S. suppliers. This reflects capital expenditures of more than $11 billion during the past decade, with more than 90% destined to productivity-enhancing machinery and equipment.

Source: "Canadian Suppliers Gain Market Share from Rivals, Despite Stronger Canadian Dollar," *Canada NewsWire*, Toronto, Feb. 27, 2004.

A PERSPECTIVE OF PROCESS COST FLOWS

Before presenting a detailed example of process costing, it will be helpful to see how manufacturing costs flow through a process costing system.

Processing Departments

A **processing department** is part of organization where work is performed on a product and where materials, labour, or overhead costs are added to the product. For example, a potato chip factory operated by Frito-Lay might have three processing departments—one for preparing potatoes, one for cooking, and one for inspecting and packaging. A brick

Processing department
Any location in an organization where work is performed on a product and where materials, labour, or overhead costs are added to the product.

EXHIBIT 4–1 Differences between Job-Order and Process Costing

Job-Order Costing	Process Costing
1. Many different jobs are worked on during each period, with each job having different production requirements.	1. A single product is produced either on a continuous basis or for long periods of time. All units of product are identical.
2. Costs are accumulated by individual job, regardless of the accounting period during which the work is done.	2. Costs are accumulated by department, during an accounting period.
3. The *job cost sheet* is the key document controlling the accumulation of costs by a job.	3. The *department production report* is the key document showing the accumulation and disposition of costs by a department.
4. Unit costs are computed *by job* on the job cost sheet.	4. Unit costs are computed *by department* on the department production report.

factory might have two processing departments—one for mixing and moulding clay into brick form and one for firing the moulded brick. A company can have as many or as few processing departments as are needed to complete a product or service. Some products and services may go through several processing departments, while others may go through only one or two. Regardless of the number of departments involved, all processing departments have two essential features. First, the activity performed in the processing department must be performed uniformly on all of the units passing through it. Second, the output of the processing department must be homogeneous.

The processing departments involved in making a product such as bricks or potato chips would probably be organized in a *sequential* pattern in which units flow in sequence from one department to another. An example of processing departments arranged in a sequential pattern is given in Exhibit 4–2, which illustrates a potato chip processing plant.

A different type of processing pattern, known as *parallel processing,* is required to make some products. Parallel processing is used in those situations where, after a certain point, some units may go through different processing departments than others. For example, Petro-Canada and Shell Canada Limited in their petroleum refining operations input crude oil into one processing department and then use the refined output for further processing into several end products, such as gasoline, heating oil, jet fuel, and lubricants. Each end product may undergo several steps of further processing after the initial refining, some of which may be shared with other end products and some of which may not.

An example of parallel processing is provided in Exhibit 4–3, which shows the process flows in a Coca-Cola bottling plant. In the first processing department, raw materials are mixed to make the basic concentrate. This concentrate can be used to make bottled Coke or it may be sold to restaurants and bars for use in soda fountains. Under the first option, the concentrate is sent on to the bottling department where it is mixed with carbonated water and then injected into sterile bottles and capped. In the final processing department, the bottles are inspected, labels are applied, and the bottles are packed in cartons. If the concentrate is to be sold for use in soda fountains, it is injected into large sterile metal cylinders, inspected, and packaged for shipping. This is just an example of one way in which parallel processing can be set up. The number of possible variations in parallel processing is virtually limitless.

FOCUS *on Current Practice*

Honeytop Speciality Foods, the United Kingdom's leading manufacturer of authentic naan breads, has been instrumental in fuelling the growth of the naan bread market. The company produces innovative fresh, long-life, chilled and frozen naan breads in a wide variety of flavours for leading supermarkets, ready-meals manufacturers, pubs, restaurants, and hotels. Owned by brothers Charles and William Eid, Honeytop combines traditional tandoori food preparation methods with the latest baking technology to ensure consistent quality. Traditionally, the dough is laboriously kneaded and shaped by hand and then slapped onto the inside wall of a ceramic oven, where it sticks and is baked at high heat. With the exception of one step, the 60-minute process is now automated. High-speed machinery measures and mixes the ingredients; rolls, shapes, and flame-bakes the dough; and packages the bread. People, however, are still needed to perform the final step of shaping the naan into a teardrop shape.

Source: "Naan Bread Revolution," *Food Manufacture*, February 2000, pp. 38–39.

The Flow of Materials, Labour, and Overhead Costs

Cost accumulation is simpler in a process costing system than in a job-order costing system. In a process costing system, instead of having to trace costs to hundreds of different jobs, costs are traced to only a few processing departments. In a process costing system, production costs are not identified with specific units or batches of product. Instead, an

EXHIBIT 4–2 Sequential Processing Departments

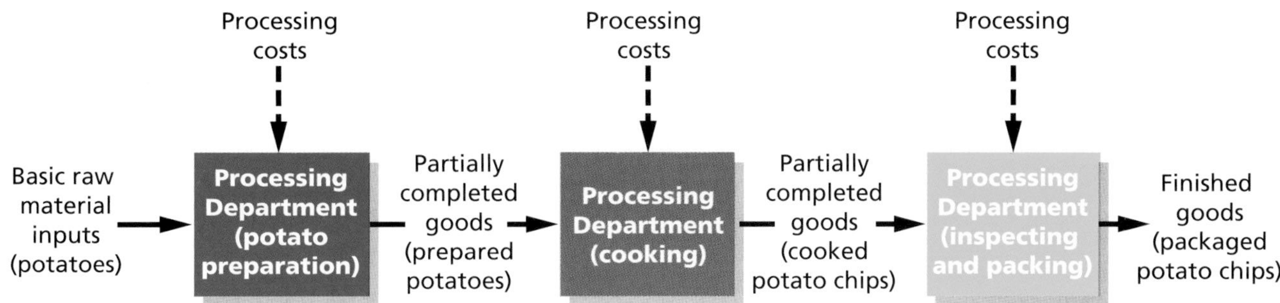

average unit cost is computed by dividing total production costs for the period by the number of units produced during the same period. This is discussed in more detail later in this chapter.

A T-account model of materials, labour, and overhead cost flows in a process costing system is given in Exhibit 4–4. Several key points should be noted from this exhibit. First, note that a separate Work in Process account is maintained for *each processing department.* In contrast, in a job-order costing system there may be only a single Work in Process account for the entire company. Second, note that the completed production of the first processing department (Department A in the exhibit) is transferred into the Work in Process account of the second processing department (Department B), where it undergoes further work. After this further work, the completed units are then transferred into Finished Goods. (In Exhibit 4–4, we show only two processing departments, but a company may have many processing departments.)

Finally, note that materials, labour, and overhead costs can be added in *any* processing department—not just the first. Costs in Department B's Work in Process account would consist of the materials, labour, and overhead costs incurred in Department B plus the costs attached to partially completed units transferred in from Department A (called **transferred-in costs**).

Transferred-in cost
The cost attached to products that have been received from a prior processing department.

EXHIBIT 4–3 Parallel Processing Departments

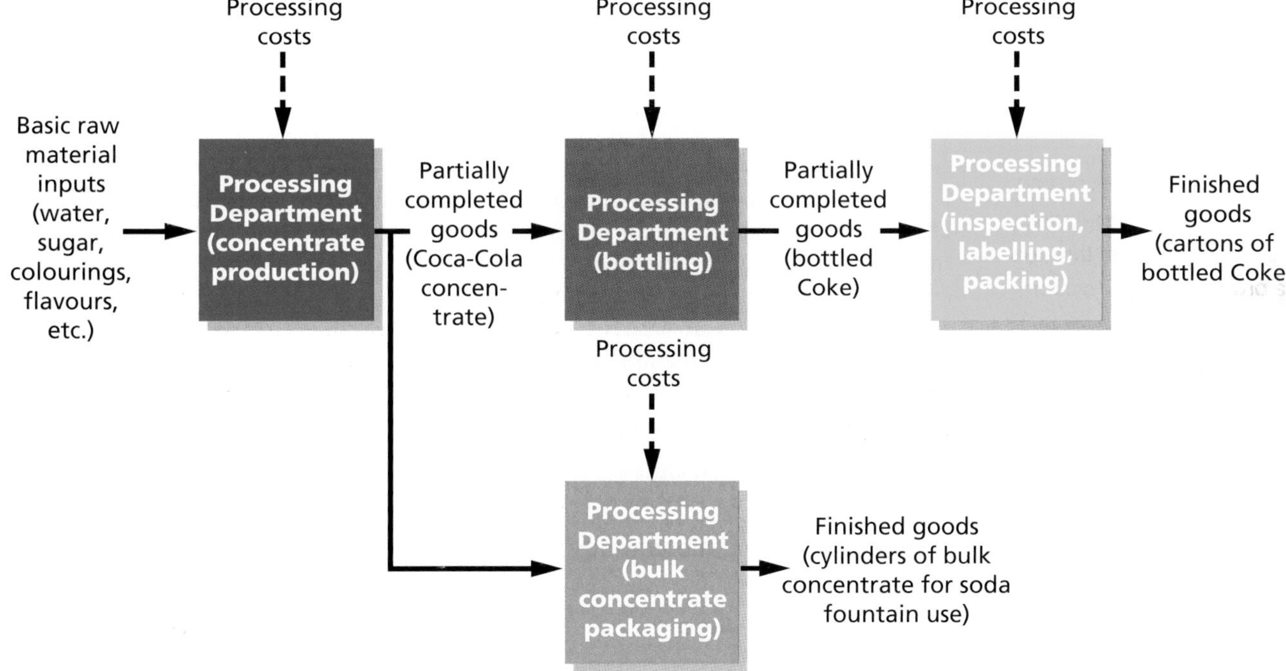

EXHIBIT 4–4 T-Account Model of Process Costing Flows

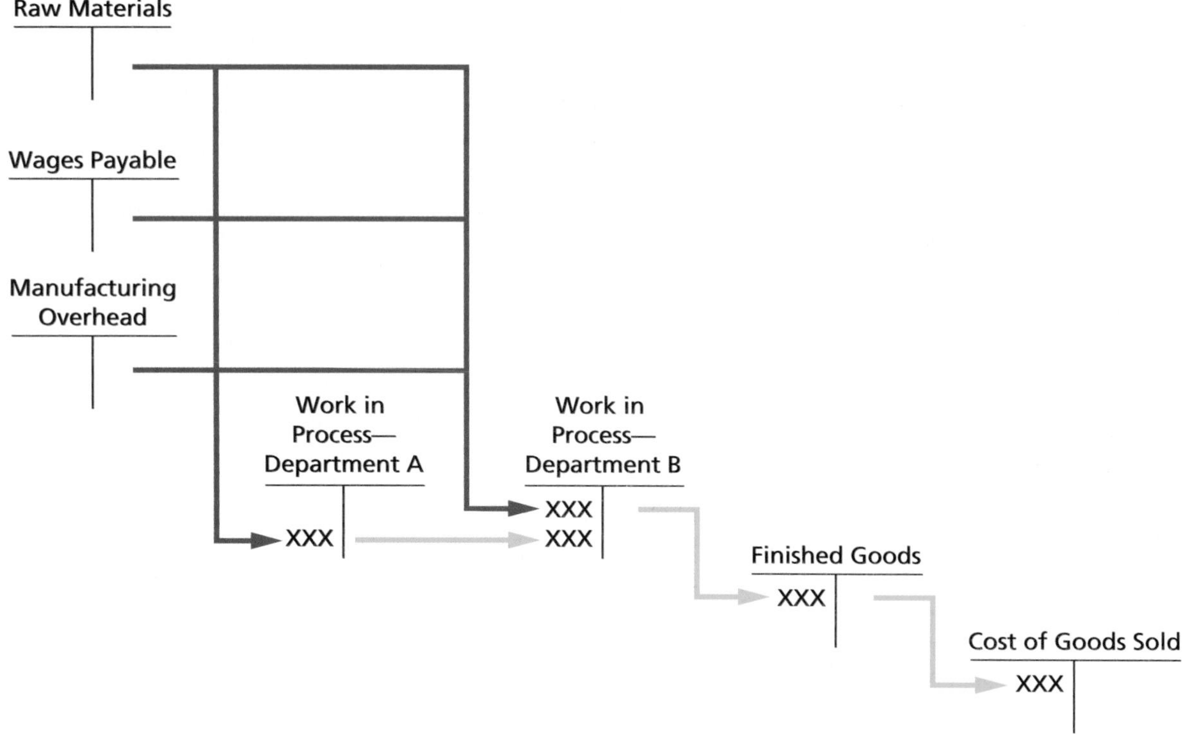

Materials, Labour, and Overhead Cost Entries

To complete our discussion of cost flows in a process costing system, in this section we show journal entries relating to materials, labour, and overhead costs at Megan's Classic Cream Soda, the company mentioned at the beginning of this chapter. Megan's company has two processing departments—Formulating and Bottling. In the Formulating Department, the various ingredients are checked for quality and then mixed and injected with carbon dioxide to create bulk cream soda. In the Bottling Department, bottles are checked for defects, filled with cream soda, capped, visually inspected again for defects, and then packed for shipping.

LEARNING OBJECTIVE 1
Record the flow of materials, labour, and overhead through a process costing system.

Materials Costs As in job-order costing, materials are drawn from the storeroom using a materials requisition form. Materials can be added in any processing department, although it is not unusual for materials to be added only in the first processing department, with subsequent departments adding only labour and overhead costs as the partially completed units move along toward completion.

At Megan's Classic Cream Soda (MCCS), some materials (water, flavourings, sugar, and carbon dioxide) are added in the Formulating Department and other materials (bottles, caps, and packing materials) are added in the Bottling Department The journal entry for placing materials into process in the first department is as follows:

Work in Process—Formulating	XXX	
Raw Materials		XXX

If other materials are subsequently added in another department, as with MCCS, the entry is the following:

Work in Process—Bottling	XXX	
Raw Materials		XXX

Labour Costs In process costing, labour costs are traced to departments not to specific jobs. Since MCCS has two processing departments, Formulating and Bottling, the following journal entry will record the labour costs for a period:

Work in Process—Formulating	XXX	
Work in Process—Bottling	XXX	
Salaries and Wages Payable		XXX

Overhead Costs If production is stable from period to period and if overhead costs are incurred uniformly over the year, actual overhead costs can be charged to products. However, if production levels fluctuate or if overhead costs are not incurred uniformly, charging products with actual overhead costs will result in unit product costs that vary randomly from one period to the next. In such a situation, predetermined overhead rates should be used to charge overhead cost to products, the same as in job-order costing. When predetermined overhead rates are used, each department has its own separate rate with the rates being computed as discussed in Chapter 3. Overhead cost is then applied to units of product as the units move through the various departments. Since predetermined overhead rates are widely used in process costing, we will assume their use throughout the remainder of this chapter.

The following journal entry is used to apply overhead costs to units of product for the Formulating and Bottling Departments:

Work in Process—Formulating	XXX	
Work in Process—Bottling	XXX	
Manufacturing Overhead		XXX

Completing the Cost Flows Once processing has been completed in a department, the product units are transferred to the next department for further processing, as illustrated earlier in the T-accounts in Exhibit 4–4. The following journal entry is used to transfer the costs of partially completed units from the Formulating Department to the Bottling Department:

Work in Process—Bottling	XXX	
Work in Process—Formulating		XXX

After processing has been completed in the final department, the costs of the completed units are then transferred to the Finished Goods inventory account:

Finished Goods	XXX	
Work in Process—Bottling		XXX

Finally, when a customer's order is filled and units are sold, the cost of the units is transferred to Cost of Goods Sold:

Cost of Goods Sold	XXX	
Finished Goods		XXX

To summarize, we stated earlier that the cost flows between accounts are basically the same in a process costing system as they are in a job-order costing system. The only noticeable difference at this point is that a process costing system has a separate Work in Process account for each department.

MANAGERIAL ACCOUNTING IN ACTION

The Issue

Samantha Trivers, president of Double Diamond Skis, was worried about the future of the company. After a rocky start, the company had come out with a completely redesigned ski called The Ultimate, made of exotic materials and featuring flashy graphics. Exhibit 4–5 illustrates how this ski is manufactured. The ski was a runaway best seller—particularly among younger skiers—and had provided the company with much-needed cash for two years. However, last year a dismal snowfall in the Rocky Mountains had depressed sales, and Double Diamond was once again short of cash. Samantha was worried that another bad ski season would force Double Diamond into bankruptcy.

EXHIBIT 4–5 The Production Process at Double Diamond Skis*

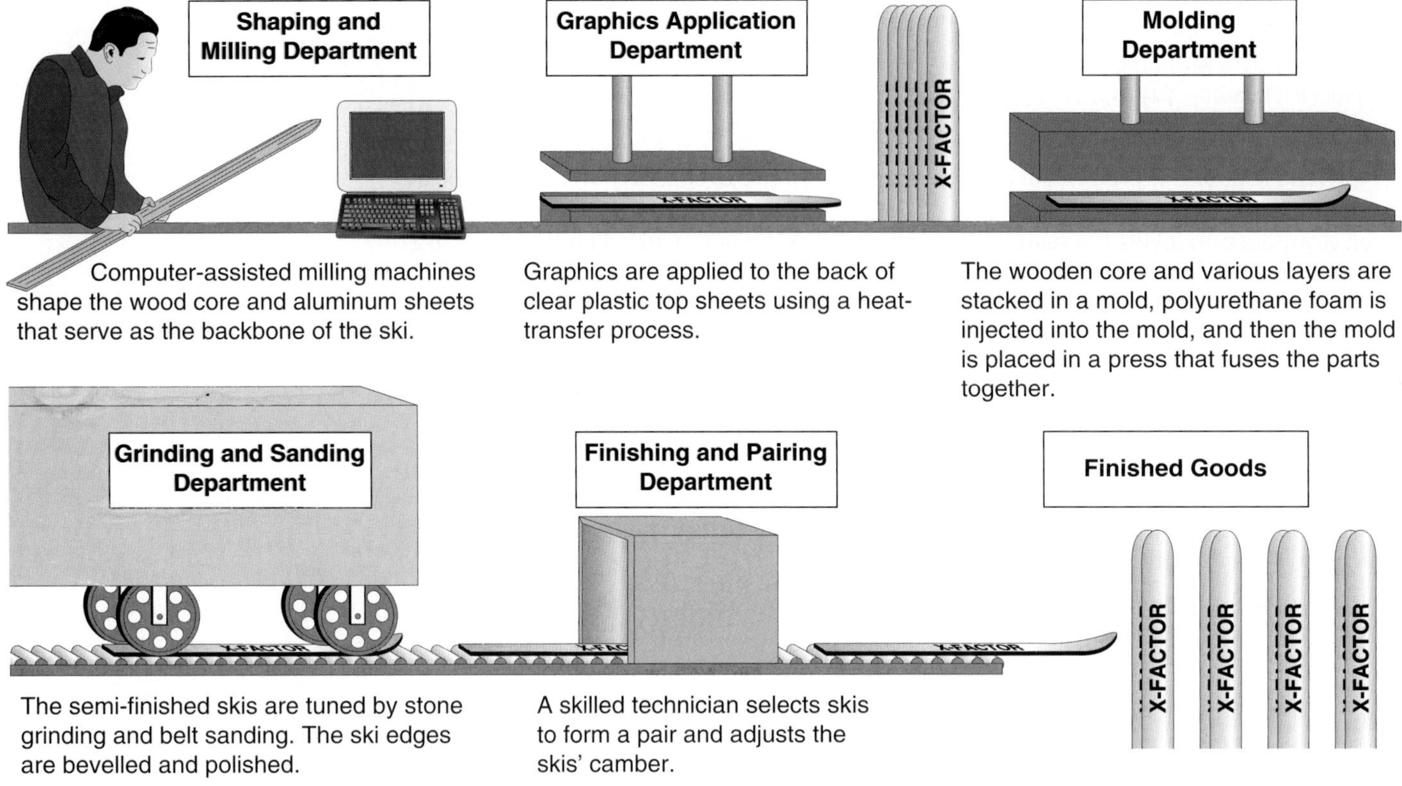

Shaping and Milling Department
Graphics Application Department
X-FACTOR
Molding Department
Computer-assisted milling machines shape the wood core and aluminum sheets that serve as the backbone of the ski.
Graphics are applied to the back of clear plastic top sheets using a heat-transfer process.
The wooden core and various layers are stacked in a mold, polyurethane foam is injected into the mold, and then the mold is placed in a press that fuses the parts together.
Grinding and Sanding Department
Finishing and Pairing Department
Finished Goods
X-FACTOR
The semi-finished skis are tuned by stone grinding and belt sanding. The ski edges are bevelled and polished.
A skilled technician selects skis to form a pair and adjusts the skis' camber.
X-FACTOR

*Adapted from Bill Gout, Jesse James Doquilo, and Studio MD, "Capped Crusaders," *Skiing*, October 1993, pp. 138–144.

Just before starting production of next year's model of The Ultimate, Samantha called Jerry Madison, the company controller, into her office to discuss the reports she would need in the coming year.

Samantha: Jerry, I am going to need more frequent cost information this year. I really have to stay on top of things.

Jerry: What do you have in mind?

Samantha: I'd like reports at least once a month that detail our production costs for each department and for each pair of skis.

Jerry: That shouldn't be much of a problem. We already compiled almost all of the necessary data for the annual report. The only complication is our work in process inventories. They haven't been a problem in our annual reports, since our fiscal year ends at a time when we have finished producing skis for the last model year and haven't yet started producing for the new model year. Consequently, there aren't any work in process inventories to value for the annual report. But that won't be true for monthly reports.

Samantha: I'm not sure why that is a problem, Jerry. But I'm sure you can figure out how to solve it.

EQUIVALENT UNITS OF PRODUCTION

Jerry Madison, the controller of Double Diamond Skis, was concerned with the following problem: After materials, labour, and overhead costs have been accumulated in a department, the department's output must be determined so that unit costs can be computed. In the simplest case average unit cost can be computed by dividing total manufacturing costs by the number of units produced during a given time period. The difficulty is that a department usually has some partially completed units in its ending inventory. It does not seem reasonable to count these partially completed units as equivalent to fully completed units when counting the department's output. Therefore, Madison will mathematically convert those partially completed units into an *equivalent* number of fully completed units. In process costing, this is done using the following formula:

Equivalent units = Number of partially completed units × percentage completion

As the formula states, **equivalent units** is defined as the product of the number of partially completed units and the percentage completion of those units. Equivalent units are the number of complete units that could have been obtained from the materials and effort that went into the partially complete units.

For example, suppose the Moulding Department at Double Diamond has 500 units in its ending work in process inventory that are 60% complete. These 500 partially complete units are equivalent to 300 fully complete units (500 × 60% = 300). Therefore, the ending work in process inventory would be said to contain 300 equivalent units. These equivalent units would be added to any fully completed units to determine the period's output for the department—called the *equivalent units of production.*

Equivalent units of production for a period can be computed in two different ways. In this chapter, we discuss the *weighted-average method.* In Appendix 4A, the *FIFO method* is discussed. The **FIFO method** of process costing is a method in which equivalent units and unit costs relate only to work done during the current period. In contrast, the **weighted-average method** blends together units and costs from the current period with units and costs from the prior period. In the weighted-average method, the **equivalent units of production** for a department are the number of units transferred to the next department (or to finished goods) plus the equivalent units in the department's ending work in process inventory.

Equivalent units
The product of the number of partially completed units and their percentage of completion with respect to a particular cost. Equivalent units are the number of complete whole units one could obtain from the materials and effort contained in partially completed units.

FIFO method
A method of accounting for cost flows in a process costing system in which equivalent units and unit costs relate only to work done during the current period.

Weighted-average method A method of process costing that blends together units and costs from both the current and prior periods.

Equivalent units of production (weighted-average method)
The units transferred to the next department (or to finished goods) during the period plus the equivalent units in the department's ending work in process inventory.

Weighted-Average Method

LEARNING OBJECTIVE 2
Compute the equivalent units of production using the weighted-average method.

Under the weighted-average method, a department's equivalent units are computed as follows:

Weighted-Average Method
(a separate calculation is made for each cost category in each processing department)

Equivalent units of production = Units transferred to the next department or to finished goods
+ Equivalent units in ending work in process inventory

We do not have to make an equivalent units calculation for units transferred to the next department. We can assume that they would not have been transferred unless they were 100% complete with respect to the work performed in the transferring department. However, an equivalent units calculation does need to be made for the partially completed units in ending inventory.

Consider the Shaping and Milling Department at Double Diamond. This department uses computerized milling machines to precisely shape the wooden core and metal sheets that will be used to form the backbone of the ski (see Exhibit 4–5 for an overview of the production process at Double Diamond). The following activity took place in the department in May, several months into the production of the new model of The Ultimate ski:

	Units	Percent Completed	
		Materials	Conversion
Work in process, May 1	200	55%	30%
Units started into production during May	5,000		
Units completed during May and transferred to the next department	4,800	100%*	100%*
Work in process, May 31	400	40%	25%

*It is always assumed that units transferred out of a department are 100% complete with respect to the processing done in that department.

Conversion cost
Direct labour cost plus manufacturing overhead cost.

Note the use of the term *conversion* in the above table. **Conversion cost,** as defined in Chapter 2, is direct labour cost plus manufacturing overhead cost. In process costing, conversion cost is often—but not always—treated as a single element of product cost.

Also note that the May 1 beginning work in process was 55% complete with respect to materials costs and 30% complete with respect to conversion costs. This means that 55% of the materials costs required to complete the units had already been incurred. Likewise, 30% of the conversion costs required to complete the units had already been incurred.

Since Double Diamond's work in process inventories are at different stages of completion in terms of the amounts of materials cost and conversion cost that have been added, two equivalent unit figures must be computed. The equivalent unit computations are given in Exhibit 4–6.

Note from the computations in Exhibit 4–6 that units in the beginning work in process inventory are ignored. The weighted-average method is concerned only with the fact that there are 4,900 equivalent units for conversion cost in ending inventories and in units transferred to the next department—the method is not concerned with the additional fact that some of this work was accomplished in prior periods. This is a key point in the weighted-average method that is easy to overlook.

The weighted-average method blends together the work that was accomplished in prior periods with the work that was accomplished in the current period. In the FIFO method, the units and costs of prior periods are cleanly separated from the units and costs of the current period. Some managers believe the FIFO method is more accurate for this reason. However, the FIFO method is more complex than the weighted-average method and for that reason is covered in Appendix 4A.

Averages, in general, hide the details of the elements that make up the average. For example, the average of $2 + 4$ is 3. The average of $1 + 5$ is 3. If the manager is uninterested in the details of the elements, then the average provides all of the information needed. If costs from one period to the next are approximately equal (for example, $3 + 3$) the average is also a reasonable representation of the results. A third explanation for the use of the average approach is the relative size of the beginning inventory of work in process compared to the current production. For example, if the beginning inventory is only one-tenth the current production, the average (weighted) of $\frac{1}{10}(1) + \frac{9}{10}(5) = 4.60$ is very accurate and very close to a FIFO result. In addition to the advantage of ease of computation, another advantage of the weighted-average method is that it generates very accurate results when costs are relatively stable from one period to the next or when the size of current production dwarfs the beginning inventory.

EXHIBIT 4–6 Equivalent Units of Production: Weighted-Average Method

	Materials	Conversion
Units transferred to the next department.	4,800	4,800
Work in process, May 31:		
400 units × 40% complete with respect to materials	160	
400 units × 25% complete with respect to labour.		100
Equivalent units of production	4,960	4,900

A visual perspective of the computation of equivalent units of production is provided in Exhibit 4–7. The data are for conversion costs in the Shaping and Milling Department of Double Diamond Skis. Study this exhibit carefully before going on.

FOCUS *on Current Practice*

Drug makers now use sophisticated processing systems that help catch errors as they occur rather than after the fact and cost of production reports are used to help inform decisions about expanding capacity. For example, after analyzing its production capacity, Biomedical Corporation announced that it would ship an additional 1.2 million doses of its influenza vaccine, Fluviral(R), to the Canadian market. Fluviral is produced from its two flu vaccine production facilities located in Laval and Quebec City. The Quebec City facility is undergoing expansion to increase its manufacturing capacity to about 50 million doses by 2007. The U.S. government asked Biomedical to consider sending any excess supply to the U.S. under an Investigational New Drug (IND) application. After negotiating with the FDA the company agreed to make production process changes for 2005 and beyond. With the new process in place, including a manufacturing change that is required in the U.S., it is expected that the vaccine will meet FDA approval.

Source: "ID Biomedical to Ship 1.2 Million Doses of Its Flu Vaccine to the Canadian Market," *Canada NewsWire*, Dec. 7, 2004.

PRODUCTION REPORT—WEIGHTED-AVERAGE METHOD

The production report developed in this section contains the information requested by the president of Double Diamond Skis. The purpose of the production report is to summarize for management all of the activity that takes place in a department's Work in Process account for a period. This activity includes the units and costs that flow through the Work in Process account. As illustrated in Exhibit 4–8, a separate production report is prepared for each department.

Earlier, when we outlined the differences between job-order costing and process costing, we stated that the production report takes the place of a job cost sheet in a process costing system. The production report is a key management document and is vital to the proper operation of the system. The production report has three separate (although highly interrelated) parts:

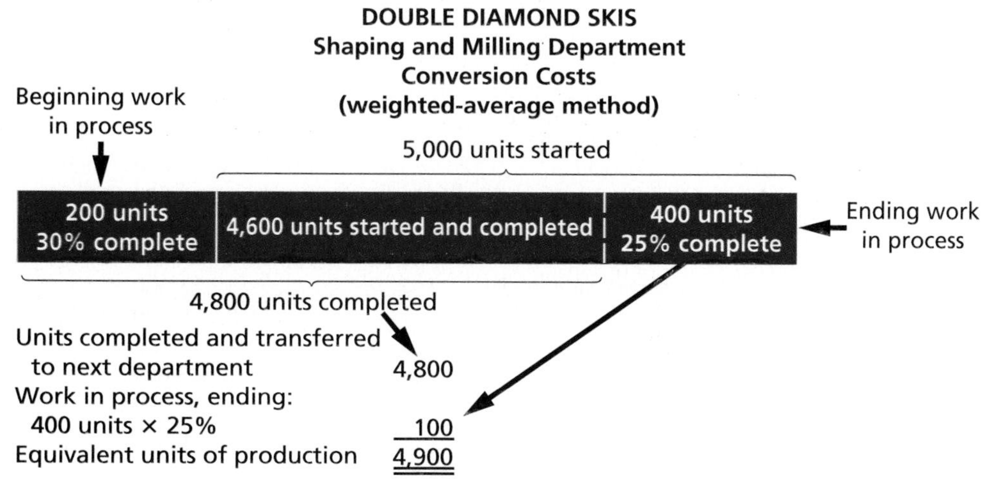

EXHIBIT 4–7 Visual Perspective of Equivalent Units of Production

EXHIBIT 4–8 The Position of the Production Report in the Flow of Costs

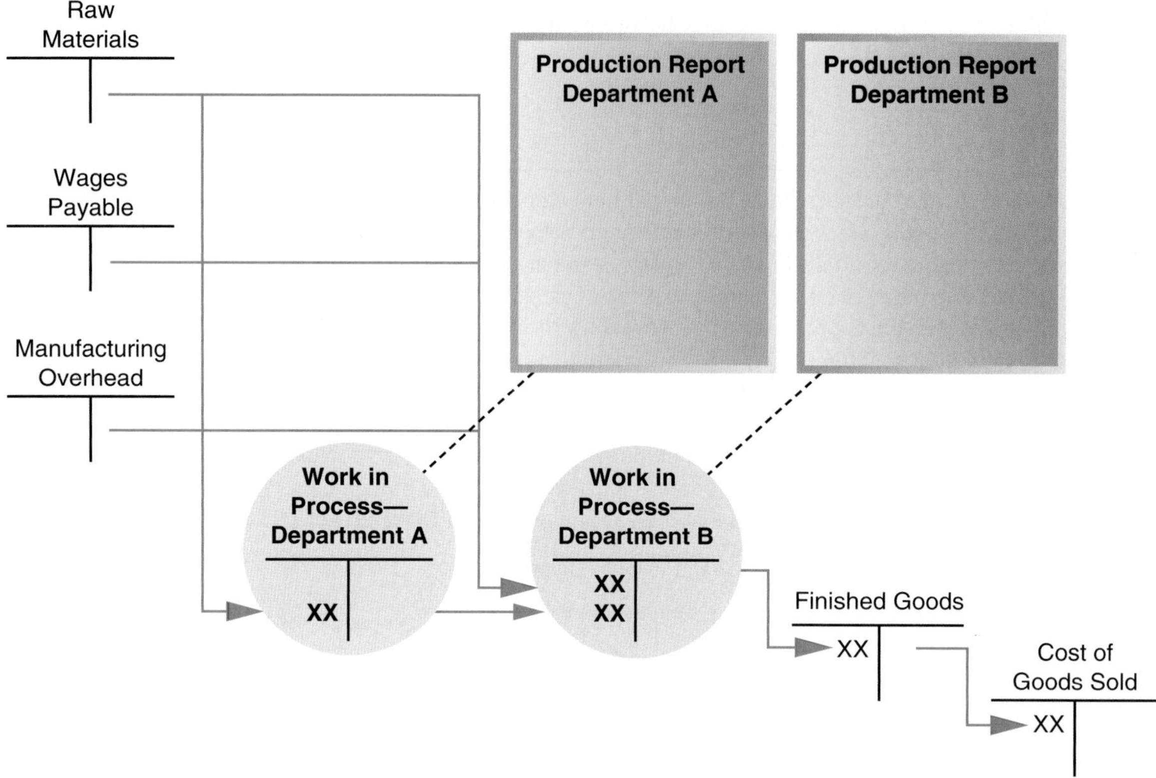

1. A quantity schedule, which shows the flow of units through the department and a computation of equivalent units.
2. A computation of costs per equivalent unit.
3. A reconciliation of all cost flows into and out of the department during the period.

We will use the data on the next page for the May operations of the Shaping and Milling Department of Double Diamond Skis to illustrate the production report. Keep in mind that this report is only one of the five reports that would be prepared for the company since the company has five processing departments.

In this section, we show how a production report is prepared when the weighted-average method is used to compute equivalent units and unit costs. The preparation of a production report under the FIFO method is illustrated in Appendix 4A at the end of this chapter.

Shaping and Milling Department for May Operations	
Work in process, beginning:	
Units in process	200
Stage of completion with respect to materials	55%
Stage of completion with respect to conversion	30%
Costs in the beginning inventory:	
Materials cost	$ 9,600
Conversion cost	5,575
Total cost in process	$ 15,175
Units started into production during May	5,000
Units completed and transferred out	4,800
Costs added to production during May:	
Materials cost	$368,600
Conversion cost	350,900
Total cost added in the department	$719,500

Work in process, ending:		
Units in process		400
Stage of completion with respect to materials	40%	
Stage of completion with respect to conversion	25%	

Step 1: Prepare a Quantity Schedule and Compute the Equivalent Units

LEARNING OBJECTIVE 3
Prepare a quantity schedule using the weighted-average method.

The first part of a production report consists of a **quantity schedule,** which shows the flow of units through a department and a computation of equivalent units. To illustrate, a quantity schedule combined with a computation of equivalent units is given below for the Shaping and Milling Department of Double Diamond Skis:

Quantity schedule
The part of a production report that shows the flow of units through a department during a period and a computation of equivalent units.

	Quantity Schedule	Equivalent Units: Materials	Equivalent Units: Conversion
Units to be accounted for:			
Work in process, May 1 (materials 55% complete; conversion 30% complete)	200		
Started into production	5,000		
Total units to be accounted for	5,200		
Units accounted for as follows:			
Transferred to the next department	4,800	4,800	4,800
Work in process, May 31 (materials 40% complete; conversion 25% complete)	400	160*	100†
Total units and equivalent units of production	5,200	4,960	4,900

*40% × 400 units = 160 equivalent units.
†25% × 400 units = 100 equivalent units.

The quantity schedule shows at a glance how many units moved through the department during the period as well as the stage of completion of any in-process units. In addition to providing this information, the quantity schedule serves as an essential guide in preparing and tying together the remaining parts of a production report.

Step 2: Compute Costs per Equivalent Unit

LEARNING OBJECTIVE 4
Compute the costs per equivalent unit using the weighted-average method.

As stated earlier, the weighted-average method blends together the work that was accomplished in the prior period with the work that was accomplished in the current period. That is why it is called the weighted-average method; it averages together units and costs from both the prior and current periods by adding the cost in the beginning work in process inventory to the current period costs. These computations are shown below for the Shaping and Milling Department for May:

The cost per equivalent unit (EU) that we have computed for the Shaping and Milling Department will be used to apply cost to units that are transferred to the next department, Graphics Application, and will also be used to compute the cost in the ending work in process inventory. For example, each unit transferred out of the Shaping and Milling Department to the Graphics Application Department will carry with it a cost of $149. Since the costs are passed on from department to department, the unit cost of the last department, Finishing and Pairing, will represent the final unit cost of a completed unit of product.

Shaping and Milling Department	Total Cost	Materials		Conversion		Whole Unit
Cost to be accounted for:						
Work in process, May 1	$ 15,175	$ 9,600		$ 5,575		
Cost added in the Shaping and Milling Department	719,500	368,600		350,900		
Total cost (a)	$734,675	$378,200		$356,475		
Equivalent units of production (Step 1 above) (b)		4,960		4,900		
Cost per EU, (a) ÷ (b)		$76.25	+	$72.75	=	$149.00

LEARNING OBJECTIVE 5
Prepare a cost reconciliation using the weighted-average method.

Cost reconciliation
The part of a production report that shows what costs a department has to account for during a period and how those costs are accounted for.

Step 3: Prepare a Cost Reconciliation

The purpose of a **cost reconciliation** is to show how the costs that have been charged to a department during a period are accounted for. Typically, the costs charged to a department will consist of the following:

1. Cost in the beginning work in process inventory.
2. Materials, labour, and overhead costs added during the period.
3. Cost (if any) transferred in from the preceding department.

In a production report, these costs are generally entitled "Cost to be accounted for." They are accounted for in a production report by computing the following amounts:

1. Cost transferred out to the next department (or to Finished Goods).
2. Cost remaining in the ending work in process inventory.

In short, when a cost reconciliation is prepared, the "Cost to be accounted for" from step 2 is reconciled with the sum of the cost transferred out during the period plus the cost in the ending work in process inventory. This concept is shown graphically in Exhibit 4–9. Study this exhibit carefully before going on to the cost reconciliation for the Shaping and Milling Department.

Example of a Cost Reconcilation To prepare a cost reconciliation, *follow the quantity schedule line for line and show the cost associated with each group of units.* This is

EXHIBIT 4–9 Graphic Illustration of the Cost Reconciliation Part of a Production Report

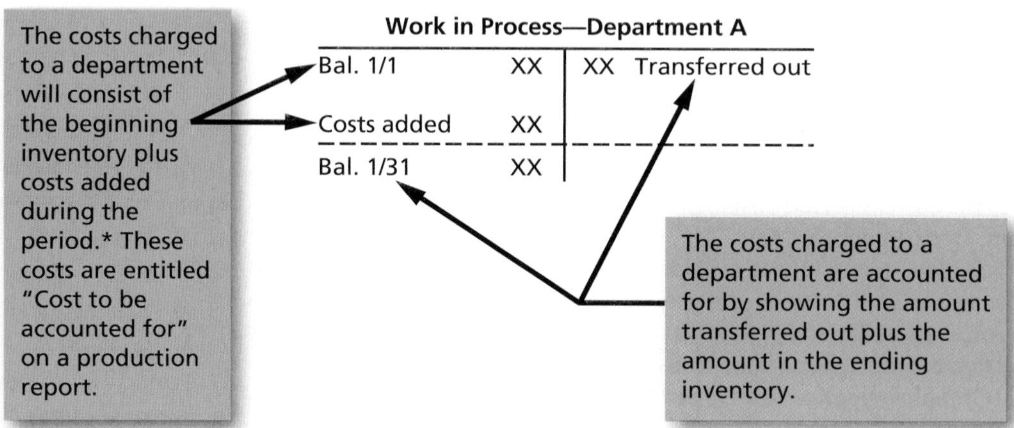

done in Exhibit 4–10 on page 152, where we present a completed production report for the Shaping and Milling Department.

The quantity schedule in the exhibit shows that 200 units were in process on May 1 and that an additional 5,000 units were started into production during the month. Looking at the "Cost to be accounted for" in the middle part of the exhibit, notice that the units in process on May 1 had $15,175 in cost attached to them and that the Shaping and Milling Department added another $719,500 in cost to production during the month. Thus, the department has $734,675 ($15,175 + $719,500) in cost to be accounted for.

This cost is accounted for in two ways. As shown on the quantity schedule, 4,800 units were transferred to the Graphics Application Department, the next department in the production process. Another 400 units were still in process in the Shaping and Milling Department at the end of the month. Thus, part of the $734,675 "Cost to be accounted for" goes with the 4,800 units to the Graphics Application Department, and part of it remains with the 400 units in the ending work in process inventory in the Shaping and Milling Department.

Each of the 4,800 units transferred to the Graphics Application Department is assigned $149 in cost, for a total $715,200. The 400 units still in process at the end of the month are assigned costs according to their stage of completion. To determine the stage of completion, we refer to the equivalent units computation and bring the equivalent units figures down to the cost reconciliation part of the report. We then assign costs to these units, using the cost per equivalent unit figures already computed.

After cost has been assigned to the ending work in process inventory, the total cost that we have accounted for ($ 734,675) agrees with the amount that we had to account for ($734,675). Thus, the cost reconciliation is complete.

As we have seen, process costing produces cost figures for work-in-process, finished goods and costs of goods sold. These numbers appear in external reports where they serve a control purpose because they influence management evaluation. This can create an incentive for managers to make decisions that minimize average costs per unit without actually maximizing profits. By producing more units than can be sold, managers can spread some of the fixed costs over these additional units. The result is excess inventory costs. We deal with this problem in more detail in Chapter 7 where we discuss absorption costing.

MANAGERIAL ACCOUNTING IN ACTION

The Wrap-Up

Jerry: Here's an example of the kind of report I can put together for you every month. This particular report is for the Shaping and Milling Department. It follows a fairly standard format for industries like ours and is called a production report. I hope this is what you have in mind.

Samantha: Yes, the quantity schedule makes sense to me. I can see we had a total of 5,200 units to account for in the department, and 4,800 of those were transferred to the next department while 400 were still in process at the end of the month. What are these "equivalent units"?

Jerry: That's the problem I mentioned earlier. The 400 units still in process are far from complete. When we compute the unit costs, it wouldn't make sense to count them as whole units.

Samantha: I suppose not, so I see what you are driving at. Since those 400 units are only 25% complete with respect to our conversion costs, they should be counted as only 100 units when we compute the unit costs for conversion.

Jerry: That's right. Is the rest of the report clear?

Samantha: Yes, it does seem pretty clear, although I want to work the numbers through on my own to make sure I thoroughly understand the report.

Jerry: Does this report give you the information you wanted?

Samantha: Yes, it does. I can tell how many units are in process, how complete they are, what happened to them, and their costs. While I know the unit costs are averages and are heavily influenced by our volume, they still can give me some idea of how well we are doing on the cost side. Thanks, Jerry.

EXHIBIT 4–10 Production Report—Weighted-Average Method

DOUBLE DIAMOND SKIS
Shaping and Milling Department Production Report
(weighted-average method)

Quantity Schedule and Equivalent Units

	Quantity Schedule	Equivalent Units (EU)	
		Materials	Conversion
Units to be accounted for:			
Work in process, May 1 (materials 55% complete; conversion 30% complete)	200		
Started into production	5,000		
Total units	5,200		
Units accounted for as follows:			
Transferred to the next department	4,800	4,800	4,800
Work in process, May 31 (materials 40% complete; conversion 25% complete)	400	160*	100†
Total units and equivalent units of production	5,200	4,960	4,900

Costs per Equivalent Unit

	Total Cost	Materials		Conversion		Whole Unit
Cost to be accounted for:						
Work in process, May 1	$ 15,175	$ 9,600		$ 5,575		
Cost added in the Shaping and Milling Department	719,500	368,600		350,900		
Total cost (a)	$734,675	$378,200		$356,475		
Equivalent units of production (above) (b)		4,960		4,900		
Cost per EU, (a) ÷ (b)		$ 76.25	+	$ 72.75	=	$149.00

Cost Reconciliation

	Total Cost	Equivalent Units (above)	
		Materials	Conversion
Cost accounted for as follows:			
Transferred to next department:			
4,800 units × $149,00 each	$715,200	4,800	4,800
Work in process, May 31:			
Materials, at $76.25 per EU	12,200	160	
Conversion, at $72.75 per EU	7,275		100
Total work in process, May 31	19,475		
Total cost	$734,675		

*40% × 400 units = 160 equivalent units.
†25% × 400 units = 100 equivalent units.
EU = Equivalent unit.

A Comment about Rounding Errors

If you use a calculator or computer spreadsheet and do not round off the costs per equivalent unit, there shouldn't be any discrepancy between the "Cost to be accounted for" and the "Cost accounted for" in the cost reconciliation. However, if you round off the costs per equivalent unit, the two figures will not always exactly agree. The two figures in the report in Exhibit 4–10 do agree, but this will not always happen. In all of the homework assignments and other materials, we follow two rules: (1) All of the costs per equivalent unit are rounded off to three decimal places as in Exhibit 4–10, and (2) any adjustment needed to reconcile the "Cost accounted for" with the "Cost to be accounted for" is made to the cost "transferred" amount rather than to the ending inventory.

OPERATION COSTING

The costing systems discussed in Chapter 3 and in this chapter represent the two ends of a continuum. On one end, we have job-order costing, which is used by companies that produce many different items—generally to customers' specifications. On the other end, we have process costing, which is used by companies that produce basically homogeneous products in large quantities. Between these two extremes, there are many hybrid systems that include characteristics of both job-order and process costing. One of these hybrids is called *operation costing.*

Operation costing is used in situations where products have some common characteristics and also some individual characteristics. Shoes, for example, have common characteristics in that all styles involve cutting and sewing that can be done on a repetitive basis, using the same equipment and following the same basic procedures. Shoes also have individual characteristics—some are made of expensive leathers and others may be made using inexpensive synthetic materials. In a situation such as this, where products have some common characteristics but also must be handled individually, operation costing may be used to determine product costs.

Operation costing
A hybrid costing system used when products are manufactured in batches and when the products have some common characteristics and some individual characteristics. This system handles materials the same as in job-order costing, and labour and overhead the same as in process costing.

As mentioned above, operation costing is a hybrid system that employs aspects of both job-order and process costing. Products are typically handled in batches when operation costing is in use, with each batch charged for its own specific materials. In this sense, operation costing is similar to job-order costing. However, labour and overhead costs are accumulated by operation or by department, and these costs are assigned to units as in process costing. If shoes are being produced, for example, each shoe is charged the same per unit conversion cost, regardless of the style involved, but it is charged with its specific materials cost. Thus, the company is able to distinguish between styles in terms of materials, but it is able to employ the simplicity of a process costing system for labour and overhead costs.

Examples of other products for which operation costing may be used include electronic equipment (such as semiconductors), textiles, clothing, and jewellery (such as rings, bracelets, and medallions). Products of this type are typically produced in batches, but they can vary considerably from model to model or from style to style in terms of the cost of raw material inputs. Therefore, an operation costing system is well suited for providing cost data.

FLEXIBLE MANUFACTURING SYSTEMS

A plant that uses a flexible manufacturing system (FMS) is heavily automated and its activities are organized around cells, or islands, of automated equipment. The FMS concept is having a major impact on costing in several ways. One of these is through allowing companies to switch their systems from the more costly job-order approach to a less costly process or operation approach. This switching is made possible because FMS is proving to be highly efficient in reducing the set-up time required between products and jobs. With set-up time only a small fraction of previous levels, companies are able to move between products and jobs with about the same speed as if they were working in a continuous, process-type environment. The result is that these companies are able to employ process costing techniques in situations that previously required job-order costing. As the use of FMS grows (and becomes even more efficient), some managers predict that job-order costing will slowly disappear except in a few selected industries.

A further impact of FMS is through its focus on cells rather than on departments. Although production reports are still prepared in FMS settings, these reports are either much broader to include the entire production process (many cells) or much narrower to include only a single cell or workstation. As stated earlier, if JIT is practised, then the production report becomes greatly simplified, regardless of the level at which it is prepared.

SUMMARY

Process costing is used in situations where homogeneous products or services are produced on a continuous basis. Costs flow through the manufacturing accounts in basically the same way in both job-order and process costing systems. A process costing system differs from a job-order system primarily in that costs are accumulated by department (rather than by job) and the department production report replaces the job cost sheet.

To compute unit costs in a department, the department's output in terms of equivalent units must be determined. In the weighted-average method, the equivalent units for a period are the sum of the units transferred out of the department during the period and the equivalent units in the ending work in process inventory at the end of the period.

The activity in a department is summarized in a production report. There are three separate (though highly interrelated) parts to a production report. The first part is a quantity schedule, which includes a computation of equivalent units and shows the flow of units through a department during a period. The second part consists of a computation of costs per equivalent unit, with unit costs being provided individually for materials, labour, and overhead as well as in total for the period. The third part consists of a cost reconciliation, which summarizes all cost flows through a department for a period.

REVIEW PROBLEM 1: PROCESS COST FLOWS AND REPORTS

Luxguard Home Paint Company produces exterior latex paint, which it sells in four-litre containers. The company has two processing departments—Base Fab and Finishing. White paint, which is used as a base for all of the company's paints, is mixed from raw ingredients in the Base Fab Department. Pigments are added to the basic white paint, the pigmented paint is squirted under pressure into four-litre containers, and the containers are labelled and packed for shipping in the Finishing Department. Information relating to the company's operations for April is as follows:

a. Raw materials were issued for use in production: Base Fab Department, $851,000, and Finishing Department, $629,000.
b. Direct labour costs were incurred: Base Fab Department, $330,000, and Finishing Department, $270,000.
c. Manufacturing overhead cost was applied: Base Fab Department, $665,000, and Finishing Department, $405,000.
d. Basic white paint was transferred from the Base Fab Department to the Finishing Department, $1,850,000.
e. Paint that had been prepared for shipping was transferred from the Finishing Department to Finished Goods, $3,200,000.

Required:

1. Prepare journal entries to record items (a) through (e) above.
2. Post the journal entries from (1) above to T-accounts. The balance in the Base Fab Department's Work in Process account on April 1 was $150,000; the balance in the Finishing Department's Work in Process account was $70,000. After posting entries to the T-accounts, find the ending balance in each department's Work in Process account.
3. Prepare a production report for the Base Fab Department for April. The following additional information is available regarding production in the Base Fab Department during April:

Production data for four-litre containers of paint:	
Units (containers) in process, April 1: 100% complete as to materials, 60% complete as to labour and overhead	30,000
Units (containers) started into production during April	420,000
Units (containers) completed and transferred to the Finishing Department	370,000
Units (containers) in process, April 30: 50% complete as to materials, 25% complete as to labour and overhead	80,000
Cost data:	
Work in process inventory, April 1:	
Materials	$ 92,000
Labour	21,000
Overhead	37,000
Total cost	$150,000
Cost added during April:	
Materials	$851,000
Labour	330,000
Overhead	665,000

Solution to Review Problem 1

1.	a. Work in Process—Base Fab Department	851,000	
	Work in Process—Finishing Department	629,000	
	Raw Materials		1,480,000
	b. Work in Process—Base Fab Department	330,000	
	Work in Process—Finishing Department	270,000	
	Salaries and Wages Payable		600,000
	c. Work in Process—Base Fab Department	665,000	
	Work in Process—Finishing Department	405,000	
	Manufacturing Overhead		1,070,000
	d. Work in Process—Finishing Department	1,850,000	
	Work in Process—Base Fab Department		1,850,000
	e. Finished Goods	3,200,000	
	Work in Process—Finishing Department		3,200,000

2.

Raw Materials

Bal.	XXX	(a)	1,480,000

Salaries and Wages Payable

		(b)	600,000

Work in Process—Base Fab Department

Bal.	150,000	(d)	1,850,000
(a)	851,000		
(b)	330,000		
(c)	665,000		
Bal.	146,000		

Manufacturing Overhead

(Various actual costs)	(c)	1,070,000

Work in Process—Finishing Department				Finished Goods	
Bal.	70,000	(e)	3,200,000	Bal.	XXX
(a)	629,000			(e)	3,200,000
(b)	270,000				
(c)	405,000				
(d)	1,850,000				
Bal.	24,000				

LUXGUARD HOME PAINT COMPANY
Production Report—Base Fab Department
For the Month Ended April 30

Quantity Schedule and Equivalent Units

	Quantity Schedule	Equivalent Units (EU) Materials	Labour	Overhead
Units (four-litre containers) to be accounted for:				
Work in process, April 1 (all materials, 60% labour and overhead added last month)	30,000			
Started into production	420,000			
Total units	450,000			
Units (four-litre containers) accounted for as follows:				
Transferred to Finishing Department	370,000	370,000	370,000	370,000
Work in process, April 30 (materials 50% complete; labour and overhead 25% complete)	80,000	40,000*	20,000*	20,000*
Total units and equivalent units of production	450,000	410,000	390,000	390,000

Costs per Equivalent Unit

	Total Cost	Materials	Labour	Overhead	Whole Unit
Cost to be accounted for:					
Work in process, April 1	$ 150,000	$ 92,000	$ 21,000	$ 37,000	
Cost added by the Finishing Department	1,846,000	851,000	330,000	665,000	
Total cost (a)	$1,996,000	$943,000	$351,000	$702,000	
Equivalent units of production (b)	—	410,000	390,000	390,000	
Cost per EU, (a) ÷ (b)	—	$2.30 +	$0.90 +	$1.80 =	$5.00

Cost Reconciliation

	Total Cost	Materials	Labour	Overhead
Cost accounted for as follows:				
Transferred to				
Finishing Department:				
370,000 units × $5.00 each . . .	$1,850,000	370,000	370,000	370,000
Work in process, April 30:				
Materials, at $2.30 per EU	92,000	40,000		
Labour, at $0.90 per EU	18,000		20,000	
Overhead, at $1.80 per EU	36,000			20,000
Total work in process	146,000			
Total cost	$1,996,000			

*Materials: 80,000 units × 50% = 40,000 equivalent units; labour and overhead: 80,000 units × 25% = 20,000 equivalent units.

EU = Equivalent unit.

REVIEW PROBLEM 2: UNITS AND COST ASSIGNMENT

Power Company passes its product through several departments, the last of which is the finishing department. Conversion costs are added evenly throughout the process in this department. One-fourth of direct materials is added at the beginning of the process and the remaining three-fourths are added when the process is 50% complete with respect to conversion costs.

During June, 475,000 units of product were transferred to finished goods. Of these units, 100,000 units were 40% complete with respect to conversion costs at the beginning of the period and 375,000 were started and completed during the period. At the end of June, the work in process inventory comprised 225,000 units that were 30% complete with respect to conversion costs. Total costs to account for include $939,675 for conversion costs and $605,625 for direct materials.

Required:

1. Determine equivalent units of production with respect to conversion costs and with respect to direct materials for the finishing department.
2. Compute the direct conversion cost and the direct materials cost per equivalent unit.
3. Compute the amount of conversion cost and the amount of the direct materials cost assigned to the beginning goods in process inventory, to the units started and completed, and to the ending goods in process inventory.

Solution to Review Problem 2

1.

		Equivalent Units (EU)	
		Materials	Conversion
Units accounted for as follows:			
Transferred to the next department	475,000	475,000	475,000
Work in process, June 30:			
material, 25% complete; labour, 30% complete) . .	225,000	56,250	67,500
Total units accounted for	700,000	531,250	542,500

2.

Conversion cost per equivalent unit = $939,675/542,500 units = $1.73

Direct materials cost per equivalent unit = $605,625/531,250 units = $1.14

3.
Allocation of materials and conversion cost to products:

	Equivalent Units	Per Unit Cost	Allocated Cost
Transferred out:			
Materials	475,000	$1.14	541,500
Conversion costs	475,000	1.73	821,750
			$1,363,250 a)
Goods in Process			
Materials (225,000 × .25)	56,250	$1.14	$ 64,125
Conversion (225,000 × .3)	67,500	1.73	116,775
			$ 180,900 b)
Total cost accounted for: a) + b)			$1,544,150

APPENDIX 4A: FIFO METHOD

The FIFO method of process costing differs from the weighted-average method in two basic ways: (1) the computation of equivalent units, and (2) the way in which costs of beginning inventory are treated in the cost reconciliation report. The FIFO method is generally considered to be more accurate than the weighted-average method, but it is more complex. The complexity is not a problem for computers, but the FIFO method is a little more difficult to understand and to learn than the weighted-average method.

Equivalent Units—FIFO Method

LEARNING OBJECTIVE **6**
Explain and compute the equivalent units of production using the FIFO method.

The computation of equivalent units under the FIFO method differs from the computation under the weighted-average method in two ways.

First, the "units transferred out" figure is divided into two parts. One part consists of the units from the beginning inventory that were completed and transferred out, and the other part consists of the units that were both *started* and *completed* during the current period.

Second, full consideration is given to the amount of work expended during the current period on units in the *beginning* work in process inventory as well as on units in the ending inventory. Thus, under the FIFO method, it is necessary to convert both inventories to an equivalent units basis. For the beginning inventory, the equivalent units represent the work done to *complete* the units; for the ending inventory, the equivalent units represent the work done to bring the units to a stage of partial completion at the end of the period (the same as with the weighted-average method).

The formula for computing the equivalent units of production under the FIFO method is more complex than under the weighted-average method:

FIFO Method
(a separate calculation is made for each cost category in each processing department)

Equivalent units of production = Equivalent units to complete beginning inventory*
+ Units started and completed during the period
+ Equivalent units in ending work in process inventory

$$\text{*Equivalent units to complete beginning inventory} = \text{Units in beginning inventory} \times \left(100\% - \text{Percentage completion of beginning inventory}\right)$$

Or, the equivalent units of production can also be determined as follows:

Equivalent units of production = Units transferred out
+ Equivalent units in ending work in process inventory
− Equivalent units in beginning inventory

To illustrate the FIFO method, refer again to the data for the Shaping and Milling Department at Double Diamond Skis. The department completed and transferred 4,800 units to the next department, the Graphics Application Department, during May. Since 200 of these units came from the beginning inventory, the Shaping and Milling Department must have started and completed 4,600 units during May. The 200 units in the beginning inventory were 55% complete with respect to materials and only 30% complete with respect to conversion costs when the month started. Thus, to complete these units the department must have added another 45% of materials costs (100% – 55%) and another 70% of conversion costs (100% − 30%). Following this line of reasoning, the equivalent units for the department for May would be computed as shown in Exhibit 4–11.

Comparison of Equivalent Units of Production under the Weighted-Average and FIFO Methods

Stop at this point and compare the data in Exhibit 4–11 with the data in Exhibit 4–6 in the chapter, which shows the computation of equivalent units under the weighted-average method. Also refer to Exhibit 4–12, which provides a visual comparison of the two methods.

The essential difference between the two methods is that the weighted-average method blends work and costs from the prior period with work and costs in the current period, whereas the FIFO method cleanly separates the two periods. To see this more clearly, consider the following comparison of the two calculations of equivalent units:

	Materials	Conversion
Equivalent units—weighted-average method	4,960	4,900
Less equivalent units in beginning inventory:		
200 units × 55%	110	
200 units × 30%		60
Equivalent units of production—FIFO method	4,850	4,840

From this comparison, it is evident that the FIFO method removes the equivalent units that were already in beginning inventory from the equivalent units as defined using the weighted-average method. Thus, the FIFO method isolates the equivalent units due to

EXHIBIT 4–11 Equivalent Units of Produciton: FIFO Method

	Materials	Conversion
Work in process, May 1:		
200 units × (100% − 55%)*	90	
200 units × (100% − 30%)*		140
Units started and completed in May	4,600†	4,600†
Work in process, May 31:		
400 units × 40%	160	
400 units × 25%		100
Equivalent units of production	4,850	4,840

*This is the work needed to complete the units in beginning inventory.

†5,000 units started—400 units in ending work in process + 4,600 units started and completed. The FIFO method assumes that the units in beginning inventory are finished first.

EXHIBIT 4–12 Visual Perspective of Equivalent Units of Production

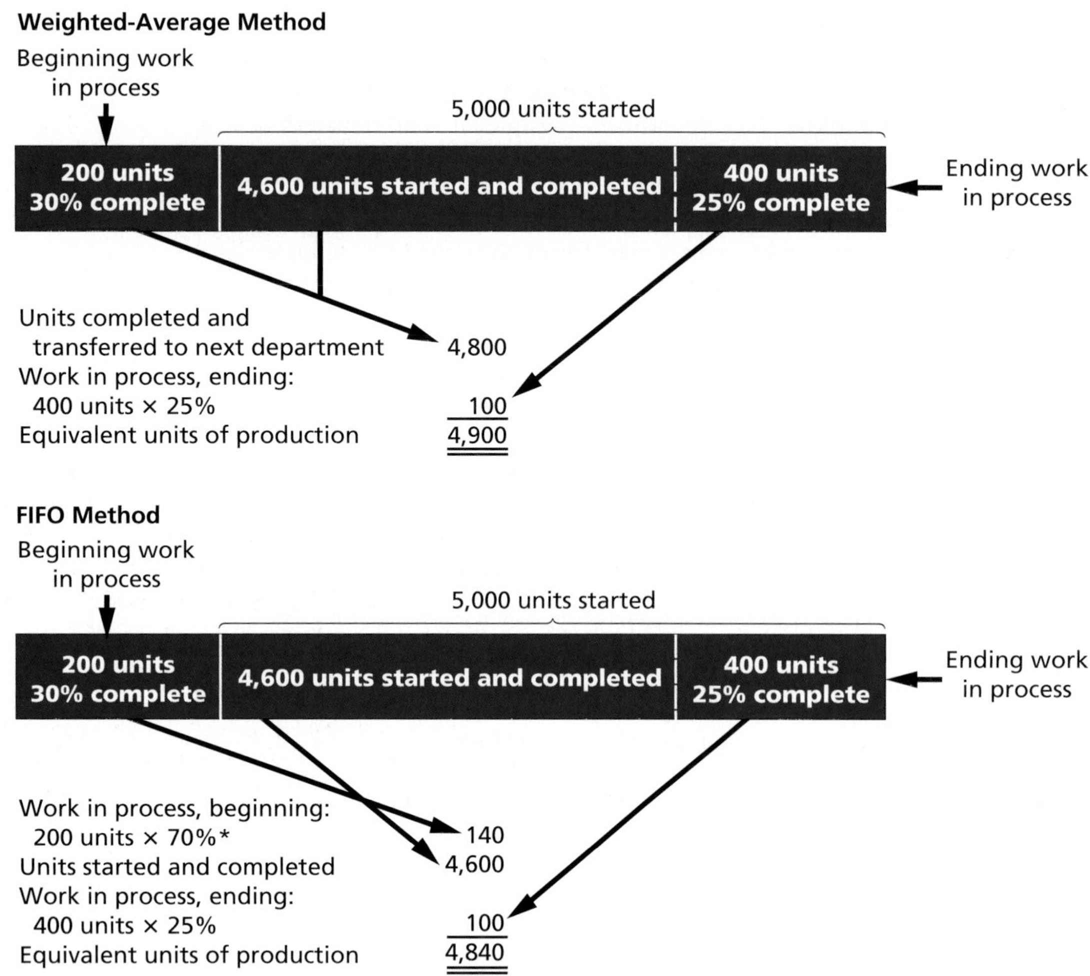

*100% – 30% = 70%. This 70% represents the work needed to complete the units in the beginning inventory.

work performed during the current period. The weighted-average method blends together the equivalent units already in beginning inventory with the equivalent units due to work performed in the current period.

Production Report—FIFO Method

The steps followed in preparing a production report under the FIFO method are the same as those discussed earlier for the weighted-average method. However, since the FIFO method makes a distinction between units in the beginning inventory and units started during the year, the cost reconciliation portion of the report is more complex under the FIFO method than it is under the weighted-average method. To illustrate the FIFO method, we will again use the data for Double Diamond Skis on page 148.

LEARNING OBJECTIVE 7
Prepare a quantity schedule using the FIFO method.

Step 1: Prepare a Quantity Schedule and Compute the Equivalent Units There is only one difference between a quantity schedule prepared under the FIFO method and one prepared under the weighted-average method. This difference relates to units transferred out. As explained earlier in our discussion of equivalent units, the FIFO method divides units transferred out into two parts. One part consists of the units in the beginning inventory, and the other part consists of the units started and completed during the current period. A quantity schedule showing this format for units transferred out is presented in Exhibit 4–13, along with a computation of equivalent units for the month.

We explained earlier that in computing equivalent units under the FIFO method, we must first show the amount of work required *to complete* the units in the beginning inventory. We then show the number of units started and completed during the period, and finally we show the amount of work *completed* on the units still in process at the end of the period. Carefully trace through these computations in Exhibit 4–13.

LEARNING OBJECTIVE 8
Compute the costs per equivalent unit using the FIFO method.

Step 2: Compute the Costs Per Equivalent Unit In computing unit costs under the FIFO method, we use only those costs that were incurred during the current period, and we ignore any costs in the beginning work in process inventory. Under the FIFO method, *unit costs relate only to work done during the current period.*

The costs per equivalent unit (EU) computed in Exhibit 4–13 are used to cost units of product transferred to the next department; in addition, they are used to show the cost attached to partially completed units in the ending work in process inventory.

LEARNING OBJECTIVE 9
Prepare a cost reconciliation using the FIFO method.

Step 3: Prepare a Cost Reconciliation The purpose of cost reconciliation is to show how the costs charged to a department during a period are accounted for. With the FIFO method, two cost elements are associated with the units in the beginning work in process inventory. The first element is the cost carried over from the prior period. The second element is the cost needed *to complete* these units. For the Shaping and Milling Department, $15,175 in cost was carried over from last month. In the cost reconciliation in Exhibit 4–13, we add to this figure the $6,840 in materials cost and $10,150 in conversion cost needed to complete these units. Note from the exhibit that these materials and conversion cost figures are computed by multiplying the costs per equivalent unit for materials and conversion times the equivalent units of work needed *to complete* the items that were in the beginning inventory. (The equivalent units figures used in this computation are brought down from the "Equivalent units" portion of the production report.)

For units started and completed during the month, we simply multiply the number of units started and completed by the total cost per unit to determine the amount transferred out. This would be $683,100 (4,600 units × $148.50 per unit = $683,100) for the department.

Finally, the amount of cost attached to the ending work in process inventory is computed by multiplying the cost per equivalent unit figures for the month times the equivalent units for materials and conversion costs in the ending inventory. Once again, the equivalent units needed for this computation are brought down from the "Equivalent units" portion of the production report.

Exhibit 4–14 summarizes the major similarities and differences between production reports prepared under the weighted-average and FIFO methods.

A Comparison of Costing Methods

In most situations, the weighted-average and FIFO methods will produce very similar unit costs. If there never are any ending inventories, as in an ideal JIT environment, the two methods will produce identical results. The reason for this is that without any ending inventories, no costs can be carried forward into the next period and the weighted-average method will base the unit costs on just the current period's costs—just as in the FIFO method. If there *are* ending inventories, either erratic input prices or erratic production levels would also be required to generate much of a difference in unit costs under the two methods. This is because the weighted-average method will blend the unit costs from the prior period with the unit costs of the current period. Unless these unit costs differ greatly, the blending will not make much difference.

Nevertheless, from the standpoint of cost control, the FIFO method is superior to the

EXHIBIT 4–13 Production Report—FIFO Method

DOUBLE DIAMOND SKIS
Shaping and Milling Department Production Report
(FIFO method)

Quantity Schedule and Equivalent Units

	Quantity Schedule		
Units to be accounted for:			
Work in process, May 1 (materials 55% complete; conversion 30% complete)	200		
Started into production	5,000		
Total units	5,200		
		Equivalent Units (EU)	
		Materials	**Conversion**
Units accounted for as follows:			
Transferred to next department:			
From the beginning inventory*	200	90	140
Started and completed this month†	4,600	4,600	4,600
Work in process, May 31 (materials 40% complete; conversion 25% complete)‡	400	160	100
Total units and equivalent units of production	5,200	4,850	4,840

Costs per Equivalent Unit

	Total Cost	Materials		Conversion		Whole Unit
Cost to be accounted for:						
Work in process, May 1	$ 15,175					
Cost added in the department (a)	719,500	$368,600		$350,900		
Total cost	$734,675					
Equivalent units of production (above) (b)		4,850		4,840		
Costs per EU, (a) ÷ (b)		$76.00	+	$72.50	=	$148.50

Cost Reconciliation

	Total Cost	Equivalent Units (above)	
		Materials	**Conversion**
Cost accounted for as follows:			
Transferred to next department:			
From the beginning inventory:			
Cost in the beginning inventory	$ 15,175		
Cost to complete these units:			
Materials, at $76.00 per EU	6,840	90*	
Conversion, at $72.50 per EU	10,150		140*
Total cost	$ 32,165		
Units started and completed this month, at $148.50 per unit	683,100	4,600†	4,600†
Total cost transferred	$715,265		
Work in process, May 31:			
Materials, at $76.00 per EU	$ 12,160	160‡	
Conversion, at $72.50 per EU	7,250		100‡
Total work in process, May 31	19,410		
Total cost	$734,675		

*Materials: 200 × (100% − 55%) = 90 equivalent units. Conversion: 200 × (100% − 30%) = 140 equivalent units.

†5,000 units started − 400 units in ending inventory = 4,600 units started and completed.

‡Materials: 400 × (40%) = 160 equivalent units. Conversion: 400 × (25%) = 100 equivalent units.
EU = Equivalent units.

EXHIBIT 4–14 A Comparison of Production Report Content

Weighted-Average Method	FIFO Method
Quantity Schedule and Equivalent Units	
1. The quantity schedule includes all units transferred out in a single figure.	1. The quantity schedule divides the units transferred out into two parts. One part consists of units in the beginning inventory, and the other part consists of units started and completed during the current period.
2. In computing equivalent units, the units in the beginning inventory are treated as if they were started and completed during the current period.	2. Only work needed to *complete* units in the beginning inventory is included in the computation of equivalent units. Units started and completed during the current period are shown as a separate figure.
Total and Unit Costs	
1. The "Cost to be accounted for" part of the report is the same for both methods.	1. The "Cost to be accounted for" part of the report is the same for both methods.
2. Costs in the beginning inventory are added in with costs of the current period in computations of costs per equivalent unit.	2. Only costs of the current period are included in computations of costs per equivalent unit.
Cost Reconciliation	
1. All units transferred out are treated the same, regardless of whether they were part of the beginning inventory or started and completed during the period.	1. Units transferred out are divided into two groups: (a) units in the beginning inventory, and (b) units started and completed during the period.
2. Units in the ending inventory have cost applied to them in the same way under both methods.	2. Units in the ending inventory have cost applied to them in the same way under both methods.

weighted-average method. Current performance should be measured in relation to costs of the current period only, and the weighted-average method mixes costs of the current period with costs of the prior period. Thus, under the weighted-average method, the manager's apparent performance is influenced by what happened in the prior period. This problem does not arise under the FIFO method, since it makes a clear distinction between costs of prior periods and costs incurred during the current period. For the same reason, the FIFO method also provides more up-to-date cost data for decision-making purposes.

On the other hand, the weighted-average method is simpler to apply than the FIFO method, but computers can handle the more intricate calculations which are required under FIFO.

GLOSSARY

Visit the Online Learning Centre at http:// www.mcgrawhill.ca/college/garrison/ for a review of key terms and definitions.

QUESTIONS

4–1 Under what conditions would it be appropriate to use a process costing system?

4–2 In what ways are job-order and process costing similar?

4–3 Costs are accumulated by job in a job-order costing system. How are costs accumulated in a process costing system?

4–4 What two essential features characterize any processing department in a process costing system?

4–5 Distinguish between departments arranged in a sequential pattern and departments arranged in a parallel pattern.

4–6 Why is cost accumulation easier under a process costing system than it is under a job-order costing system?

4–7 How many Work in Process accounts are maintained in a company using process costing?

4–8 Assume that a company has two processing departments, Mixing and Firing. Prepare a journal entry to show a transfer of partially completed units from the Mixing Department to the Firing Department.

4–9 Assume again that a company has two processing departments, Mixing and Firing. Explain what costs might be added to the Firing Department's Work in Process account during a period.

4–10 What is meant by the term *equivalent units of production* when the weighted-average method is used?

4–11 What is a quantity schedule, and what purpose does it serve?

4–12 Under process costing, it is often suggested that a product is like a rolling snowball as it moves from department to department. Why is this an apt comparison?

4–13 Watkins Trophies, Inc. produces thousands of medallions made of bronze, silver, and gold. The medallions are identical except for the materials used in their manufacture. What costing system would you advise the company to use?

4–14 Give examples of companies that might use operation costing.

4–15 (Appendix 4A) How does the computation of equivalent units under the FIFO method differ from the computation of equivalent units under the weighted-average method?

4-16 (Appendix 4A) On the cost reconciliation part of the production report, the weighted-average method treats all units transferred out in the same way. How does this differ from the FIFO method of handling units transferred out?

4-17 (Appendix 4A) From the standpoint of cost control, why is the FIFO method superior to the weighted-average method?

4-18 Job-order costing is likely to increase in importance as a result of the widespread use of flexible manufacturing systems. Do you agree with this statement? Explain.

4-19 How does the use of JIT reduce or eliminate the difference in unit costs between FIFO and weighted-average methods of preparing a cost of production report?

EXERCISES

EXERCISE 4–1 Process Costing Journal Entries [LO1]

Quality Brick Company produces bricks in two processing departments—Molding and Firing. Information relating to the company's operations in March follows:

a. Raw materials were issued for use in production: Molding Department, $23,000; and Firing Department, $8,000.
b. Direct labour costs were incurred: Molding Department, $12,000; and Firing Department, $7,000.
c. Manufacturing overhead was applied: Molding Department, $25,000; and Firing Department, $37,000.
d. Unfired, molded bricks were transferred from the Molding Department to the Firing Department. According to the company's process costing system, the cost of the unfired, molded bricks was $57,000.
e. Finished bricks were transferred from the Firing Department to the finished goods warehouse. According to the company's process costing system, the cost of the finished bricks was $103,000.
f. Finished bricks were sold to customers. According to the company's process costing system, the cost of the finished bricks sold was $101,000.

Required:

Prepare journal entries to record items (a) through (f) above.

EXERCISE 4–2 Computation of Equivalent Units—Weighted-Average Method [LO2]
Clonex Labs, Inc., uses a process costing system. The following data are available for one department for October:

		Percent Completed	
	Units	Materials	Conversion
Work in process, October 1 . . .	30,000	65%	30%
Work in process, October 31 . .	15,000	80%	40%

The department started 175,000 units into production during the month and transferred 190,000 completed units to the next department.

Required:
Compute the equivalent units of production for October assuming that the company uses the weighted-average method of accounting for units and costs.

EXERCISE 4–3 (Appendix 4A) Computation of Equivalent Units—FIFO Method [LO6]
Refer to the data for Clonex Labs, Inc., in Exercise 4–2.

Required:
Compute the equivalent units of production for October assuming that the company uses the FIFO method of accounting for units and costs.

EXERCISE 4–4 Preparation of Quantity Schedule—Weighted-Average Method [LO3]
Hielta Oy, a Finnish company, processes wood pulp for various manufacturers of paper products. Data relating to tonnes of pulp processed during June are provided below:

		Percent Completed	
	Tonnes of Pulp	Materials	Labour and Overhead
Work in process, June 1	20,000	90%	80%
Work in process, June 30	30,000	60%	40%
Started into production during June	190,000		

Required:
1. Compute the number of tonnes of pulp completed and transferred out during June.
2. Prepare a quantity schedule for June assuming that the company uses the weighted-average method.

EXERCISE 4–5 (Appendix 4A) Preparation of Quantity Schedule—FIFO Method [LO7]
Refer to the data for Hielta Oy in Exercise 4–4.

Required:
1. Compute the number of tonnes of pulp completed and transferred out during June.
2. Prepare a quantity schedule for June assuming that the company uses the FIFO method.

EXERCISE 4–6 Cost per Equivalent Unit—Weighted-Average Method [LO4]
Superior Micro Products uses the weighted-average method in its process costing system. Data for the Assembly Department for May appear below:

	Materials	Labour	Overhead
Work in process, May 1	$ 18,000	$ 5,500	$ 27,500
Cost added during May	$238,900	$80,300	$401,500
Equivalent units of production	35,000	33,000	33,000

Required:
1. Compute the cost per equivalent unit for materials, for labour, and for overhead.
2. Compute the total cost per equivalent whole unit.

EXERCISE 4–7 Cost Reconciliation—Weighted-Average Method [LO5]

Superior Micro Products uses the weighted-average method in its process costing system. During January, the Delta Assembly Department completed its processing of 25,000 units and transferred them to the next department. The cost of beginning inventory and the costs added during January amounted to $599,780 in total. The ending inventory in January consisted of 3,000 units, which were 80% complete with respect to materials and 60% complete with respect to labour and overhead. The costs per equivalent unit for the month were as follows:

	Materials	Labour	Overhead
Cost per equivalent unit	$12.50	$3.20	$6.40

Required:

1. Compute the total cost per equivalent unit for the month.
2. Compute the equivalent units of materials, labour, and overhead in the ending inventory for the month.
3. Prepare the cost reconciliation portion of the department's production report for January.

EXERCISE 4–8 (Appendix 4A) Cost per Equivalent Unit—FIFO Method [LO8]

Superior Micro Products uses the FIFO method in its process costing system. Data for the Assembly Department for May appear below:

	Materials	Labour	Overhead
Cost added during May	$193,320	$62,000	$310,000
Equivalent units of production	27,000	25,000	25,000

Required:

1. Compute the cost per equivalent unit for materials, labour, and overhead.
2. Compute the total cost per equivalent whole unit.

EXERCISE 4–9 (Appendix 4A) Cost Reconciliation—FIFO Method [LO9]

Jarvene Corporation uses the FIFO method in its process costing system. The following data are for the most recent month of operations in one of the company's processing departments:

Units in beginning inventory	400
Units started into production	3,000
Units in ending inventory	300
Units transferred to the next department	3,100

	Materials	Conversion
Percentage completion of beginning inventory	80%	40%
Percentage completion of ending inventory	70%	60%

The cost of beginning inventory according to the company's costing system was $11,040 and the costs added during the month amounted to $132,730. The costs per equivalent unit for the month were:

	Materials	Conversion
Cost per equivalent unit	$25.40	$18.20

Required:

1. Compute the total cost per equivalent unit for the month.
2. Compute the equivalent units of material and of conversion costs in the ending inventory.
3. Compute the equivalent units of material and of conversion costs that were required to complete the beginning inventory.
4. Determine the number of units started and completed during the month.
5. Prepare the cost reconciliation portion of the department's production report for the month.

EXERCISE 4–10 Process Costing Journal Entries [LO1]

Chocolaterie de Geneve, SA, is located in a French-speaking canton in Switzerland. The company makes chocolate truffles that are sold in popular embossed tins. The company has two processing departments—Cooking and Molding. In the Cooking Department, the raw ingredients for the truffles are mixed and then cooked in special candy-making vats. In the Molding Department, the melted chocolate and other ingredients from the Cooking Department are carefully poured into molds and decorative flourishes are applied by hand. After cooling, the truffles are packed for sale. The company uses a process costing system. The T-accounts below show the flow of costs through the two departments in April (all amounts are in Swiss francs):

Work in Process—Cooking

Balance 4/1	8,000	160,000	Transferred out
Direct materials	42,000		
Direct labour	50,000		
Overhead	75,000		

Work in Process—Molding

Balance 4/1	4,000	240,000	Transferred out
Transferred in	160,000		
Direct labour	36,000		
Overhead	45,000		

Required:

Prepare journal entries showing the flow of costs through the two processing departments during April.

EXERCISE 4–11 Quantity Schedule and Equivalent Units—Weighted-Average Method [LO2, LO3]

Northern Fisheries, Inc., processes salmon for various distributors. Two departments are involved—Cleaning and Packing. Data relating to kilograms of salmon processed in the Cleaning Department during July are presented below:

	Kilograms of Salmon	Percent Completed*
Work in process, July 1	20,000	30%
Started into production during July	380,000	—
Work in process, July 31	25,000	60%

*Labour and overhead only.

All materials are added at the beginning of processing in the Cleaning Department.

Required:

Prepare a quantity schedule and a computation of equivalent units for July for the Cleaning Department assuming that the company uses the weighted-average method of accounting for units.

EXERCISE 4–12 (Appendix 4A) Quantity Schedule and Equivalent Units—FIFO Method [LO6, LO7]

Refer to the data for Northern Fisheries, Inc., in Exercise 4–11.

Required:

Prepare a quantity schedule and a computation of equivalent units for July for the Cleaning Department assuming that the company uses the FIFO method of accounting for units.

EXERCISE 4–13 Equivalent Units and Cost per Equivalent Unit—Weighted-Average Method [LO2, LO4]

Helox, Inc., manufactures a product that passes through two production processes. A quantity schedule for the month of May for the first process follows:

	Quantity Schedule		
Units to be accounted for:			
Work in process, May 1 (materials 100% complete; conversion 40% complete)	5,000		
Started into production	180,000		
Total units to be accounted for	185,000		
		Equivalent Units	
		Materials	Conversion
Units accounted for as follows:			
Transferred to the next department	175,000	?	?
Work in process, May 31 (materials 100% complete; conversion 30% complete)	10,000	?	?
Total units accounted for	185,000	?	?

Costs in the beginning work in process inventory of the first processing department were: materials, $1,500; and conversion cost, $4,000. Costs added during the month were: materials, $54,000; and conversion cost, $352,000.

Required:

1. Assume that the company uses the weighted-average method of accounting for units and costs. Determine the equivalent units for the month for the first process.
2. Compute the costs per equivalent unit for the month for the first process.

EXERCISE 4–14 Cost Reconciliation—Weighted-Average Method [LO5]

(This exercise should be assigned only if Exercise 4–13 is also assigned.) Refer to the data for Helox, Inc., in Exercise 4–13 and to the equivalent units and costs per equivalent unit you have computed there.

Required:

Complete the following cost reconciliation for the first process:

	Total	Equivalent Units	
Cost Reconciliation	Cost	Materials	Conversion
Cost accounted for as follows:			
Transferred to the next department: (? units × $? per unit) . .	$?		
Work in process, May 31:			
Materials, at _____ per EU	?	?	
Conversion, at _____ per EU	?		?
Total work in process, May 31	?		
Total cost accounted for	$?		

EXERCISE 4–15 (Appendix 4A) Quantity Schedule, Equivalent Units, Cost per Equivalent Unit—FIFO Method [LO6, LO7, LO8]

Refer to the data for Helox, Inc., in Exercise 4–13. Assume that the company uses the FIFO cost method.

Required:

1. Prepare a quantity schedule and a computation of equivalent units for the month for the first process.
2. Compute the costs per equivalent unit for the month for the first process.

EXERCISE 4–16 (Appendix 4A) Cost Reconciliation—FIFO Method [LO9]

(This exercise should be assigned only if Exercise 4–15 is also assigned.) Refer to the data for Helox, Inc., in Exercise 4–13 and to the equivalent units and costs per equivalent unit that you computed in Exercise 4–15.

Required:

Complete the following cost reconciliation for the first process:

Cost Reconciliation	Total Cost	Equivalent Units Materials	Equivalent Units Conversion
Cost accounted for as follows:			
Transferred to the next department:			
From the beginning inventory:			
Cost in the beginning inventory	$?		
Cost to complete these units:			
Materials, at _____ per EU	?	?	
Conversion, at _____ per EU	?		?
Total cost from beginning inventory	?		
Units started and completed this month: _____ units × _____ per unit	?	?	?
Total cost transferred to the next department	?		
Work in process, May 31:			
Materials, at _____ per EU	?	?	
Conversion, at _____ per EU	?		?
Total work in process, May 31	?		
Total cost accounted for	$?		

EXERCISE 4–17 Quantity Schedule, Equivalent Units, and Cost per Equivalent Unit—Weighted-Average Method [LO2, LO3, LO4]

Pureform, Inc., manufactures a product that passes through two departments. Data for a recent month for the first department follow:

	Units	Materials	Labour	Overhead
Work in process, beginning	5,000	$4,320	$1,040	$1,790
Units started in process	45,000			
Units transferred out	42,000			
Work in process, ending	8,000			
Cost added during the month		$52,800	$21,500	$32,250

The beginning work in process inventory was 80% complete with respect to materials and 60% complete with respect to labour and overhead. The ending work in process inventory was 75% complete with respect to materials and 50% complete with respect to labour and overhead.

Required:

1. Assume that the company uses the weighted-average method of accounting for units and costs. Prepare a quantity schedule and a computation of equivalent units for the month for the first department.
2. Determine the costs per equivalent unit for the month.

EXERCISE 4–18 (Appendix 4A) Quantity Schedule, Equivalent Units, and Cost per Equivalent Unit—FIFO Method [LO6, LO7, LO8]

Refer to the data for Pureform, Inc., in Exercise 4–17.

Required:

1. Assume that the company uses the FIFO method of accounting for units and costs. Prepare a quantity schedule and a computation of equivalent units for the month for the first processing department.
2. Determine the costs per equivalent unit for the month.

PROBLEMS

PROBLEM 4–19 Step-by-Step Production Report—Weighted-Average Method [LO2, LO3, LO4, LO5]

Builder Products, Inc., manufactures a caulking compound that goes through three processing stages prior to completion. Information on work in the first department, Cooking, is given below for May:

Production data:	
Units in process, May 1; materials 100% complete; labour and overhead 80% complete	10,000
Units started into production during May	100,000
Units completed and transferred out	95,000
Units in process, May 31; materials 60% complete; labour and overhead 20% complete	?
Cost data:	
Work in process inventory, May 1:	
Materials cost	$1,500
Labour cost	$1,800
Overhead cost	$5,400
Cost added during May:	
Materials cost	$154,500
Labour cost	$22,700
Overhead cost	$68,100

Materials are added at several stages during the cooking process, whereas labour and overhead costs are incurred uniformly. The company uses the weighted-average method.

Required:

Prepare a production report for the Cooking Department for May. Use the following three steps in preparing your report:

1. Prepare a quantity schedule and a computation of equivalent units.
2. Compute the costs per equivalent unit for the month.
3. Using the data from (1) and (2) above, prepare a cost reconciliation.

PROBLEM 4–20 (Appendix 4A) Step-by-Step Production Report—FIFO Method [LO6, LO7, LO8, LO9]

Selzik Company makes super-premium cake mixes that go through two processing departments, Blending and Packaging. The following activity was recorded in the Blending Department during July:

Production data:		
Units in process, July 1 (materials 100% complete; conversion 30% complete)		10,000
Units started into production		170,000
Units completed and transferred to Packaging		?
Units in process, July 31 (materials 100% complete; conversion 40% complete)		20,000
Cost data:		
Work in process inventory, July 1:		
Materials cost	$ 8,500	
Conversion cost	4,900	$ 13,400
Cost added during the month:		
Materials cost	139,400	
Conversion cost	244,200	383,600
Total cost		$397,000

All materials are added at the beginning of work in the Blending Department. The company uses the FIFO method.

Required:
Prepare a production report for the Blending Department for July. Use the following three steps as a guide in preparing your report:

1. Prepare a quantity schedule and compute the equivalent units.
2. Compute the costs per equivalent unit for the month.
3. Using the data from (1) and (2) above, prepare a cost reconciliation.

PROBLEM 4–21 Production Report—Weighted-Average Method [LO2, LO3, LO4, LO5]
Sunspot Beverages, Ltd., of Fiji makes blended tropical fruit drinks in two stages. Fruit juices are extracted from fresh fruits and then blended in the Blending Department. The blended juices are then bottled and packed for shipping in the Bottling Department. The following information pertains to the operations of the Blending Department for June. (The currency in Fiji is the Fijian dollar.)

Microsoft Excel - Problem 4-20 screen capture.xls

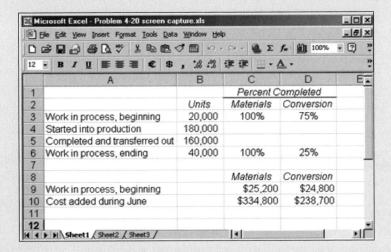

	A	B	C	D
1			*Percent Completed*	
2		*Units*	*Materials*	*Conversion*
3	Work in process, beginning	20,000	100%	75%
4	Started into production	180,000		
5	Completed and transferred out	160,000		
6	Work in process, ending	40,000	100%	25%
7				
8			*Materials*	*Conversion*
9	Work in process, beginning		$25,200	$24,800
10	Cost added during June		$334,800	$238,700
11				
12				

Required:
Prepare a production report for the Blending Department for June assuming that the company uses the weighted-average method.

PROBLEM 4–22 (Appendix 4A) Production Report—FIFO Method [LO6, LO7, LO8, LO9]
Refer to the data for the Blending Department of Sunspot Beverages, Ltd., in Problem 4–21. Assume that the company uses the FIFO method rather than the weighted-average method in its process costing.

Required:
Prepare a production report for the Blending Department for June.

PROBLEM 4–23 Analysis of Work in Process T-Account—Weighted-Average Method [LO2, LO3, LO4, LO5]

Weston Products manufactures an industrial cleaning compound that goes through three processing departments—Grinding, Mixing, and Cooking. All raw materials are introduced at the start of work in the Grinding Department. The Work in Process T-account for the Grinding Department for a recent month is given below:

Work in Process—Grinding Department

Debit		Credit	
Inventory, May 1 (18,000 kilograms, labour and overhead 1/3 complete)	21,800	?	Completed and transferred to mixing (? kilograms)
May costs added:			
Raw materials (167,000 kilograms)	133,400		
Labour and overhead	226,800		
Inventory, May 31 (15,000 kilograms, labour and overhead 2/3 complete)	?		

The May 1 work in process inventory consists of $14,600 in materials cost and $7,200 in labour and overhead cost. The company uses the weighted-average method to account for units and costs.

Required:

1. Prepare a production report for the Grinding Department for the month.
2. What criticism can be made of the unit costs that you have computed on your production report if they are used to evaluate how well costs have been controlled?

PROBLEM 4–24 (Appendix 4A) Analysis of Work in Process T-Account—FIFO Method [LO6, LO7, LO8, LO9]

Superior Brands, Inc., manufactures paint. The paint goes through three processing departments—Cracking, Mixing, and Cooking. Activity in the Cracking Department during a recent month is summarized in the department's Work in Process account below:

Work in Process—Cracking Department

Inventory, April 1 (10,000 litres, labour and overhead 80% complete)	39,000	?	Completed and transferred to mixing (? litres)
April costs added:			
Materials (140,000 litres)	259,000		
Labour and overhead	312,000		
Inventory, April 30 (30,000 litres, labour and overhead 60% complete)	?		

The materials are added at the beginning of work in the Cracking Department. The company uses the FIFO method.

Required:

Prepare a production report for the Cracking Department for the month.

PROBLEM 4–25 Interpreting a Production Report—Weighted-Average Method [LO2, LO3, LO4]

Cooperative San José of southern Sonora state in Mexico makes a unique syrup using cane sugar and local herbs. The syrup is sold in small bottles and is prized as a flavouring for drinks and for use in desserts. The bottles are sold for $12 each. (The Mexican currency is the peso and is denoted by $.) The first stage in the production process is carried out in the Mixing Department, which removes foreign matter from the raw materials and mixes them in the proper proportions in large vats. The company uses the weighted-average method in its process costing system.

A hastily prepared report for the Mixing Department for April appears below:

Quantity Schedule	
Units to be accounted for:	
Work in process, April 1 (materials 90% complete; conversion 80% complete)	30,000
Started into production	200,000
Total units to be accounted for	230,000
Units accounted for as follows:	
Transferred to next department	190,000
Work in process, April 30 (materials 75% complete; conversion 60% complete)	40,000
Total units accounted for	230,000
Total Cost	
Cost to be accounted for:	
Work in process, April 1	$ 98,000
Cost added during the month	827,000
Total cost to be accounted for	$925,000

continued

Cost Reconciliation	
Cost accounted for as follows:	
Transferred to next department	$805,600
Work in process, April 30	119,400
Total cost accounted for	$925,000

Cooperative San José has just been acquired by another company, and the management of the acquiring company wants some additional information about Cooperative San José's operations.

Required:

1. What were the equivalent units for the month?
2. What were the costs per equivalent unit for the month? The beginning inventory consisted of the following costs: materials, $67,800; and conversion cost, $30,200. The costs added during the month consisted of: materials, $579,000; and conversion cost, $248,000.
3. How many of the units transferred to the next department were started and completed during the month?
4. The manager of the Mixing Department, anxious to make a good impression on the new owners, stated, "Materials prices jumped from about $2.50 per unit in March to $3 per unit in April, but due to good cost control I was able to hold our materials cost to less than $3 per unit for the month." Should this manager be rewarded for good cost control? Explain.

PROBLEM 4–26 Comprehensive Process Costing Problem—Weighted-Average Method [LO1, LO2, LO3, LO4, LO5]

Lubricants, Inc., produces a special kind of grease that is widely used by race car drivers. The grease is produced in two processing departments: Refining and Blending. Raw materials are introduced at various points in the Refining Department.

The following incomplete Work in Process account is available for the Refining Department for March:

Work in Process—Refining Department

March 1 inventory (20,000 litres; materials 100% complete; labour and overhead 90% complete)	38,000	?	Completed and transferred to blending (? litres)
March costs added:			
Raw oil materials (390,000 litres)	495,000		
Direct labour	72,000		
Overhead	181,000		
March 31 inventory (40,000 litres; materials 75% complete; labour and overhead 25% complete)	?		

The March 1 work in process inventory in the Refining Department consists of the following cost elements: raw materials, $25,000; direct labour, $4,000; and overhead, $9,000.

Costs incurred during March in the Blending Department were: materials used, $115,000; direct labour, $18,000; and overhead cost applied to production, $42,000. The company uses the weighted-average method in its process costing.

Required:

1. Prepare journal entries to record the costs incurred in both the Refining Department and Blending Department during March. Key your entries to the items (a) through (g) below.
   a. Raw materials were issued for use in production.
   b. Direct labour costs were incurred.
   c. Manufacturing overhead costs for the entire factory were incurred, $225,000. (Credit Accounts Payable.)
   d. Manufacturing overhead cost was applied to production using a predetermined overhead rate.

e. Units that were complete with respect to processing in the Refining Department were transferred to the Blending Department, $740,000.

f. Units that were complete with respect to processing in the Blending Department were transferred to Finished Goods, $950,000.

g. Completed units were sold on account, $1,500,000. The Cost of Goods Sold was $900,000.

2. Post the journal entries from (1) above to T-accounts. The following account balances existed at the beginning of March. (The beginning balance in the Refining Department's Work in Process account is given above.)

Raw Materials	$618,000
Work in Process—Blending Department	$65,000
Finished Goods	$20,000

After posting the entries to the T-accounts, find the ending balance in the inventory accounts and the manufacturing overhead account.

3. Prepare a production report for the Refining Department for March.

PROBLEM 4–27 Equivalent Units; Costing of Inventories; Journal Entries—Weighted-Average Method [LO1, LO2, LO4]

You are employed by Spirit Company, a manufacturer of digital watches. The company's chief financial officer is trying to verify the accuracy of the ending work in process and finished goods inventories prior to closing the books for the year. You have been asked to assist in this verification. The year-end balances shown on Spirit Company's books are as follows:

	Units	Costs
Work in process, December 31 (labour and overhead 50% complete)	300,000	$660,960
Finished goods, December 31	200,000	$1,009,800

Materials are added to production at the beginning of the manufacturing process, and overhead is applied to each product at the rate of 60% of direct labour cost. There was no finished goods inventory at the beginning of the year. A review of Spirit Company's inventory and cost records has disclosed the following data:

		Costs	
	Units	Materials	Labour
Work in process, January 1 (labour and overhead 80% complete)	200,000	$200,000	$315,000
Units started into production	1,000,000		
Cost added during the year:			
Materials cost		$1,300,000	
Labour cost			$1,995,000
Units completed during the year	900,000		

The company uses the weighted-average method.

Required:

1. Determine the equivalent units and costs per equivalent unit for materials, labour, and overhead for the year.
2. Determine the amount of cost that should be assigned to the ending work in process and finished goods inventories.
3. Prepare the necessary correcting journal entry to adjust the work in process and finished goods inventories to the correct balances as of December 31.
4. Determine the cost of goods sold for the year assuming there is no under- or overapplied overhead.

(CPA, adapted)

PROBLEM 4–28 Comprehensive Process Costing Problem—Weighted-Average Method [LO1, LO2, LO3, LO4, LO5]

Hilox, Inc., produces an antacid product that goes through two departments—Cooking and Bottling. The company has recently hired a new assistant accountant, who has prepared the following summary of production and costs for the Cooking Department for May using the weighted-average method.

Cooking Department costs:	
Work in process inventory, May 1: 70,000 litres, materials 60% complete, labour and overhead 30% complete	$ 61,000*
Materials added during May	570,000
Labour added during May	100,000
Overhead applied during May	235,000
Total departmental costs	$966,000
Cooking Department costs assigned to:	
Litres completed and transferred to the Bottling Department: 400,000 litres at ? per litre	$?
Work in process inventory, May 31: 50,000 litres, materials 70% complete, labour and overhead 40% complete	?
Total departmental costs assigned	$?

*Consists of materials, $39,000; labour, $5,000; and overhead, $17,000.

The new assistant accountant has determined the cost per quart transferred to be $2.415, as follows:

$$\frac{\text{Total departmental costs, \$966,000}}{\text{Litres completed and transferred, 400,000}} = \$2.415$$

However, the assistant accountant is unsure how to use this unit cost figure in assigning cost to the ending work in process inventory. In addition, the company's general ledger shows only $900,000 in cost transferred from the Cooking Department to the Bottling Department, which does not agree with the $966,000 figure above.

The general ledger also shows the following costs incurred in the Bottling Department during May: materials used, $130,000; direct labour cost incurred, $80,000; and overhead cost applied to products, $158,000.

Required:

1. Prepare journal entries as follows to record activity in the company during May. Key your entries to the letters (a) through (g) below.
   a. Raw materials were issued to the two departments for use in production.
   b. Direct labour costs were incurred in the two departments.
   c. Manufacturing overhead costs were incurred, $400,000. (Credit Accounts Payable.) The company maintains a single Manufacturing Overhead account for the entire plant.
   d. Manufacturing overhead cost was applied to production in each department using predetermined overhead rates.
   e. Units completed as to processing in the Cooking Department were transferred to the Bottling Department, $900,000.
   f. Units completed as to processing in the Bottling Department were transferred to Finished Goods, $1,300,000.
   g. Units were sold on account, $2,000,000. The Cost of Good Sold was $1,250,000.
2. Post the journal entries from (1) above to T-accounts. Balances in selected accounts on May 1 are given below:

Raw Materials	$710,000
Work in Process—Bottling Department	$85,000
Finished Goods	$45,000

After posting the entries to the T-accounts, find the ending balance in the inventory accounts and the Manufacturing Overhead account.

3. Prepare a production report for the Cooking Department for May.

CASES

CASE 4–29 Ethics and the Manager, Understanding the Impact of Percentage Completion on Profit—Weighted-Average Method [LO2, LO4, LO5]

Gary Stevens and Mary James are production managers in the Consumer Electronics Division of General Electronics Company, which has several dozen plants scattered in locations throughout the world. Mary manages the plant located in Toronto, while Gary manages the plant in Guanzhou, China. Production managers are paid a salary and get an additional bonus equal to 5% of their base salary if the entire division meets or exceeds its target profits for the year. The bonus is determined in March after the company's annual report has been prepared and issued to shareholders.

Shortly after the beginning of the new year, Mary received a phone call from Gary that went like this:

Gary: How's it going, Mary?

Mary: Fine, Gary. How's it going with you?

Gary: Great! I just got the preliminary profit figures for the division for last year and we are within $200,000 of making the year's target profits. All we have to do is pull a few strings, and we'll be over the top!

Mary: What do you mean?

Gary: Well, one thing that would be easy to change is your estimate of the percentage completion of your ending work in process inventories.

Mary: I don't know if I can do that, Gary. Those percentage completion figures are supplied by Tom Winthrop, my lead supervisor, who I have always trusted to provide us with good estimates. Besides, I have already sent the percentage completion figures to corporate headquarters.

Gary: You can always tell them there was a mistake. Think about it, Mary. All of us managers are doing as much as we can to pull this bonus out of the hat. You may not want the bonus cheque, but the rest of us sure could use it.

The final processing department in Mary's production facility began the year with no work in process inventories. During the year, 210,000 units were transferred in from the prior processing department and 200,000 units were completed and sold. Costs transferred in from the prior department totalled $39,375,000. No materials are added in the final processing department. A total of $20,807,500 of conversion cost was incurred in the final processing department during the year.

Required:

1. Tom Winthrop estimated that the units in ending inventory in the final processing department were 30% complete with respect to the conversion costs of the final processing department. If this estimate of the percentage completion is used, what would be the Cost of Goods Sold for the year?
2. Does Gary Stevens want the estimated percentage completion to be increased or decreased? Explain why.
3. What percentage completion would result in increasing reported net operating income by $200,000 over the net operating income that would be reported if the 30% figure were used?
4. Do you think Mary James should go along with the request to alter estimates of the percentage completion?

CASE 4–30 Production Report of Second Department—Weighted-Average Method [LO2, LO3, LO4, LO5]

"I think we goofed when we hired that new assistant controller," said Ruth Scarpino, president of Provost Industries. "Just look at this production report that he prepared for last month for the Finishing Department. I can't make heads or tails out of it."

"He's struggling to learn our system," replied Frank Harrop, the operations manager. "The problem is that he's been away from process costing for a long time, and it's coming back slowly."

"It's not just the format of his report that I'm concerned about. Look at that $25.71 unit cost that he's come up with for April. Doesn't that seem high to you?" said Ms. Scarpino.

"Yes, it does seem high; but on the other hand, I know we had an increase in materials prices during April, and that may be the explanation," replied Mr. Harrop. "I'll get someone else to redo this report and then we may be able to see what's going on."

Provost Industries manufactures a ceramic product that goes through two processing departments—Molding and Finishing. The company uses the weighted-average method in its process costing.

Finishing Department costs:	
Work in process inventory, April 1, 450 units; materials 100% complete; conversion 60% complete	$ 8,208*
Costs transferred in during the month from the preceding department, 1,950 units	17,940
Materials cost added during the month (materials are added when processing is 50% complete in the Finishing Department)	6,210
Conversion costs incurred during the month	13,920
Total departmental costs	$46,278
Finishing Department costs assigned to:	
Units completed and transferred to finished goods, 1,800 units at $25.71 per unit	$46,278
Work in process inventory, April 30, 600 units; materials 0% complete; conversion 35% complete	0
Total departmental costs assigned	$46,278

*Consists of cost transferred in, $4,068; materials cost, $1,980; and conversion cost, $2,160.

Required:

1. Prepare a revised production report for the Finishing Department.
2. Explain to the president why the unit cost on the new assistant controller's report is so high.

CASE 4–31 (Appendix 4A) Production Report of Second Department—FIFO Method [LO6, LO7, LO8, LO9]

Refer to the data for Provost Industries in the preceding case. Assume that the company uses the FIFO method to account for units and costs.

Required:

1. Prepare a production report for the Finishing Department for April.
2. As stated in the case, the company experienced an increase in materials prices during April. Would the effects of this price increase tend to show up more under the weighted-average method or under the FIFO method? Why?

GROUP AND INTERNET EXERCISES

GROUP EXERCISE 4–32 Operation Costing

Operation costing combines characteristics of both job-order costing and process costing. It is used in those situations where the products have some common characteristics and also some individual characteristics. Examples of industries where operation costing may be appropriate include shoes, clothing, jewellery, and semiconductors.

Required:

Select one of the above products and research how the product is made. Construct a flowchart of the production process. Indicate which steps in the production process would use job-order costing and which steps would use process costing.

INTERNET EXERCISE 4–33

As you know, the World Wide Web is a medium that is constantly evolving. Sites come and go, and change without notice. To enable the periodic updating of site addresses, this problem has been posted to the textbook Web site (www.mcgrawhill.ca/college/garrison). After accessing the site, enter the Student Centre and select this chapter. Select and complete the Internet exercise.

CHAPTER 5

LEARNING OBJECTIVES

After studying Chapter 5, you should be able to:

1. Describe how fixed and variable costs behave and how to use them to predict costs.

2. Use a scattergram plot to diagnose cost behaviour.

3. Analyze a mixed cost using the high-low method.

4. Analyze a mixed cost using least squares regression.

5. Prepare an income statement using the contribution format.

6. (Appendix 5A) Elaborate about the least-squares regression method.

COST BEHAVIOUR: ANALYSIS AND USE

BUSINESS FOCUS

COSTLY BEHAVIOUR REQUIRED

Polytech Products of Calgary Alberta is a manufacturer and distributor of heating and cooling systems. During the 1990s, Polytech experienced rapid growth and reported in 2004 that it had 60 employees.

In 2001, management addressed a concern over its information system and implemented a new Microsoft Axapta system by August 2002. The system provides new information, reduces conflicting information in the legacy systems, lessens data entry errors and redundant entries, and improves management controls.

Costs for the new system were of two types, implementation costs for hardware, software and consulting labour of $260,000 and annual operating costs of $25,000.

The management committee needed to know how the installation costs behave so they could assess what benefits are necessary to recover their costs and the types of areas where benefits might be located.

Source: http://www.microsoft.com/resources/casestudies, April 1, 2005.

In our discussion of cost terms and concepts in Chapter 2, we stated that one way in which costs can be classified is by behaviour. *Cost behaviour* refers to how a cost will react or change as changes take place in the level of business activity. An understanding of cost behaviour is the key to many decisions in an organization. Managers who understand how costs behave are better able to predict what costs will be under various operating circumstances. Attempts at decision making without a thorough understanding of the costs involved—and how these costs may change with the activity level—can lead to disaster. For example, a decision to drop a particular product line might result in far less cost savings than managers had assumed—leading to a decline in profits. To avoid such problems, a manager must be able to accurately predict what costs will be at various activity levels. In this chapter, we will find that the key to effective cost prediction lies in understanding cost behaviour patterns.

In this chapter, we briefly review the definitions of variable costs and fixed costs and then discuss the behaviour of these costs in greater depth than we were able to do in Chapter 2. After this review and discussion, we turn our attention to the analysis of mixed costs. We conclude the chapter by introducing a new income statement format—called the *contribution format*—in which costs are organized by behaviour rather than by the traditional functions of production, sales, and administration.

Cost behaviour, as presented in this chapter, introduces the description and analytical techniques needed for all the areas of managerial accounting, that is, costing, budgeting, decision, and control. The descriptions and techniques presented here are simplified so that they are transparent but the ideas are appropriate for analysis of more complex situations that will appear in later chapters. Thus careful study of each of the discussions is important because it will be a foundation for numerous follow-up descriptions. For example, the distinction between total cost and unit cost is a major source of confusion in more complex situations.

TYPES OF COST BEHAVIOUR PATTERNS

In Chapter 2, we mentioned only variable and fixed costs. There is a third behaviour pattern, generally known as a *mixed* or *semivariable* cost. All three cost behaviour patterns—variable, fixed, and mixed—are found in most organizations. The relative proportion of each type of cost present in a firm is known as the firm's **cost structure.** For example an organization might have many fixed costs but few variable or mixed costs. Alternatively, it might have many variable costs but few fixed or mixed costs. A firm's cost structure can have a significant effect on decisions. In this chapter, we will concentrate on gaining a fuller understanding of the behaviour of each type of cost. In the next chapter, we will more fully discuss how cost structure affects decisions.

Cost structure
The relative proportion of fixed, variable, and mixed costs found within an organization.

Variable Costs

LEARNING OBJECTIVE 1
Describe how fixed and variable costs behave and how to use them to predict costs.

We explained in Chapter 2 that a variable cost is a cost whose *total dollar* amount varies in direct proportion to changes in the activity level. Direct proportion signifies that if the activity level doubles, the total dollar amount of the variable costs also doubles. If the activity level increases by only 10%, then the total dollar amount of the variable costs increases by 10% as well.

We also explained in Chapter 2 that a variable cost remains constant if expressed on a *per unit* basis. To provide an example, consider Adventure Rafting, a small company that provides daylong white-water rafting excursions on rivers in the Yukon. The company provides all of the necessary equipment and experienced guides, and it serves gourmet meals to its guests. The meals are purchased from an exclusive caterer for $30 per person for a daylong excursion. If we look at the cost of the meals on a *per person* basis, the cost remains constant at $30. This $30 cost per person will not change, regardless of how

many people participate in a daylong excursion. The behaviour of this variable cost, on both a per unit and a total basis, is tabulated as follows:

Number of Guests	Cost of Meals per Guest	Total Cost of Meals
250	$30	$ 7,500
500	30	15,000
750	30	22,500
1,000	30	30,000

The idea that a variable cost is constant per unit but varies in total with the activity level is crucial to an understanding of cost behaviour patterns. We will rely on this concept again and again in this chapter and in chapters ahead.

Exhibit 5–1 provides a graphic illustration of variable cost behaviour. Note that the graph of the total cost of the meals slants upward to the right. This is because the total cost of the meals is directly proportional to the number of guests. In contrast, the graph of the per unit cost of meals is flat. This is because the cost of the meals per guest is constant at $30 per guest.

Activity base
A measure of whatever causes the incurrence of a variable cost. For example, the total cost of X-ray film in a hospital will increase as the number of X-rays taken increases. Therefore, the number of X-rays is an activity base for explaining the total cost of X-ray film.

The Activity Base For a cost to be variable, it must be variable *with respect to something.* That "something" is its *activity base.* An **activity base** is a measure of whatever causes the incurrence of variable cost. In Chapter 3, we mentioned that an activity base is sometimes referred to as a *cost driver.* Some of the most common activity bases are direct labour-hours, machine-hours, units produced, and units sold. Other activity bases (cost drivers) might include the number of kilometres driven by salespersons, the number of kilograms of laundry processed by a hotel, the number of letters typed by a secretary, and the number of occupied beds in a hospital.

To plan and control variable costs, a manager must be well acquainted with the various activity bases within the firm. People sometimes get the notion that if a cost doesn't vary with production or with sales, then it is not really a variable cost. This is not correct. As suggested by the range of bases or drivers listed above, costs are caused by many different activities within an organization. Whether a cost is considered to be variable depends on whether it is caused by the activity under consideration. For example, if a manager is analyzing the cost of service calls for a product warranty, the relevant activity

EXHIBIT 5–1 Variable Cost Behaviour

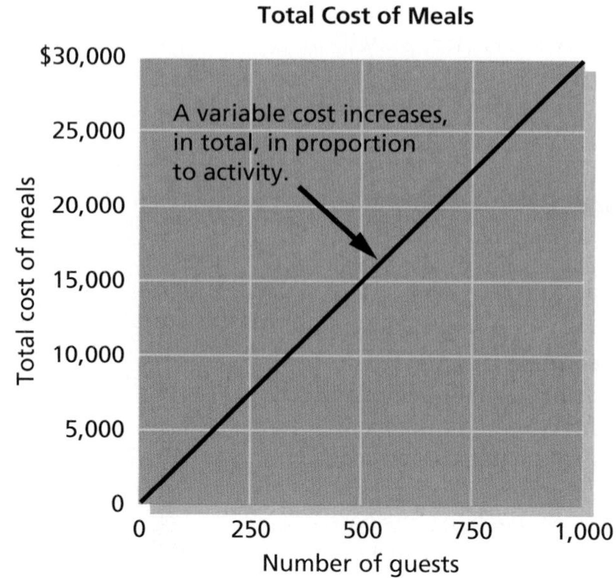

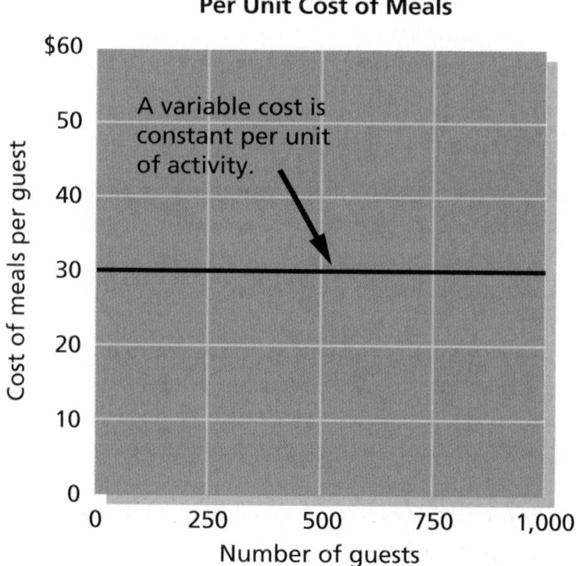

measure will be the number of service calls made. Those costs that vary in total with the number of service calls made are the variable costs of making service calls.

Nevertheless, unless stated otherwise, you can assume that the activity base under consideration is the total volume of goods and services produced or sold by the organization. So, for example, if we ask whether the cost of direct materials at Ford Canada is a variable cost, the answer is yes, since the cost of direct materials is variable with respect to Ford's total volume of production. We will specify the activity base only when it is something other than total production or sales.

Extent of Variable Costs The number and type of variable costs present in an organization will depend in large part on the organization's structure and purpose. A public utility like New Brunswick Power, with large investments in equipment, will tend to have few variable costs. Most of the costs are associated with its plant, and these costs tend to be insensitive to changes in levels of service provided. A manufacturing company like Rocky Mountain Bicycle of British Columbia, by contrast, will often have many variable costs; these costs will be associated with both the manufacture and distribution of its products to customers.

A merchandising company like Canadian Tire or Atlantic Superstore will usually have a high proportion of variable costs in its cost structure. In most merchandising companies, the cost of merchandise purchased for resale, a variable cost, constitutes a very large component of total cost. Service companies, by contrast, have diverse cost structures. Some service companies, such as the restaurant chain Tim Hortons, have fairly large variable costs because of the costs of their raw materials. On the other hand, service companies involved in consulting, auditing, engineering, dental, medical, and architectural activities have very large fixed costs in the form of expensive facilities and highly trained salaried employees.

Some of the more frequently encountered variable costs are listed in Exhibit 5–2. This exhibit is not a complete listing of all costs that can be considered variable. Moreover, some of the costs listed in the exhibit may behave more like fixed than variable costs in some firms. We will see some examples of this later in the chapter. Nevertheless, Exhibit 5–2 provides a useful listing of many of the costs that normally would be considered variable with respect to the volume of output.

FOCUS *on Current Practice*

Some managers are thriftier than others. Kenneth Iverson built Nucor Steel into the most successful U.S. steel company of recent years by developing a whole new approach to steel-making using cost-efficient minimills. Iverson ran his company with few layers of management and a commitment to employees that everyone would be treated alike. Workers were "dissuaded from joining a union by high wages and a series of No's—no management dining rooms, no company yachts, no company planes, no first-class travel for executives, and no support staff to pamper the upper echelons." Iverson ran the largest steel company in the U.S. with only 20 people in his headquarters. "By responding to market signals, focusing on a single major product line, and treating his employees with respect and compassion, Mr. Iverson contributed immensely to the industrial rebirth in this country."

Source: Donald F. Barnett and Robert W. Crandall, "Remembering a Man of Steel," *The Wall Street Journal*, April 23, 2002, p. B4.

True Variable versus Step-Variable Costs

Not all variable costs have exactly the same behaviour pattern. Some variable costs behave in a *true variable* or *proportionately variable* pattern. Other variable costs behave in a *step-variable* pattern.

EXHIBIT 5–2 Examples of Variable Costs

Type of Organization	Costs That Are Normally Variable With Respect to Volume of Output
Merchandising company	Cost of goods (merchandise) sold
Manufacturing company	Manufacturing costs:
	Direct materials
	Direct labour*
	Variable portion of manufacturing overhead:
	Indirect materials
	Lubricants
	Supplies
	Power
Both merchandising and manufacturing companies	Selling, general, and administrative costs:
	Commissions
	Clerical costs, such as invoicing
	Shipping costs
Service organizations	Supplies, travel clerical

*Direct labour may or may not be variable in practice. See the discussion later in this chapter.

True Variable Costs Direct materials is a true or proportionately variable cost because the amount used during a period will vary in direct proportion to the level of production activity. Moreover, any amounts purchased but not used can be stored and carried forward to the next period as inventory.

Step-Variable Costs The wages of maintenance workers are often considered to be a variable cost, but this labour cost doesn't behave in quite the same way as the cost of direct materials. Unlike direct materials, the time of maintenance workers is obtainable only in large chunks. Moreover, any maintenance time not utilized cannot be stored as inventory and carried forward to the next period. If the time is not used effectively, it is gone forever. Furthermore, a maintenance crew can work at a fairly leisurely pace if pressures are light but intensify its efforts if pressures build up. For this reason, small changes in the level of production may have no effect on the number of maintenance people employed by the company.

A resource that is obtainable only in large chunks (such as maintenance workers) and whose cost increases or decreases only in response to fairly wide changes in the activity level is known as a **step-variable cost.** The behaviour of a step-variable cost, contrasted with the behaviour of a true variable cost, is illustrated in Exhibit 5–3.

Step-variable cost
A cost (such as the cost of a maintenance worker) that is obtainable only in large chunks and that increases and decreases only in response to fairly wide changes in the activity level.

Notice that the need for maintenance help changes only with fairly wide changes in volume and that when additional maintenance time is obtained, it comes in large, indivisible chunks. The strategy of management in dealing with step-variable costs must be to obtain the fullest use of services possible for each separate step. Great care must be taken in working with these kinds of costs to prevent "fat" from building up in an organization. There may be a tendency to employ additional help more quickly than needed, and there is a natural reluctance to lay off people when volume declines.

The Linearity Assumption and the Relevant Range

In dealing with variable costs, we have assumed a strictly linear relationship between cost and volume, except in the case of step-variable costs. Economists correctly point out that many costs that the accountant classifies as variable actually behave in a *curvilinear* fashion. The behaviour of a **curvilinear cost** is shown in Exhibit 5–4.

Curvilinear costs
A relationship between cost and activity that is a curve rather than a straight line.

Although many costs are not strictly linear when plotted as a function of volume, a

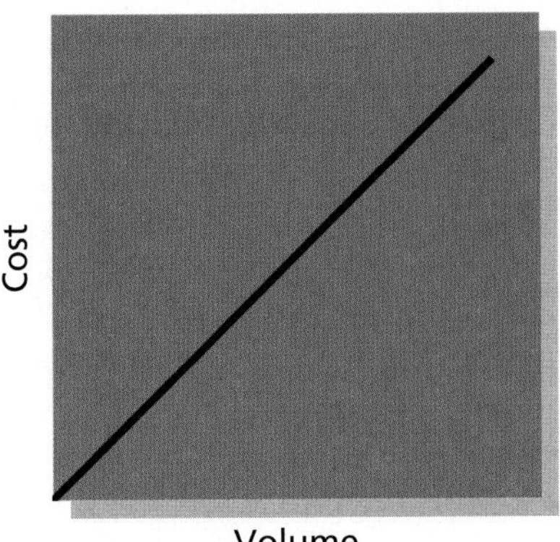

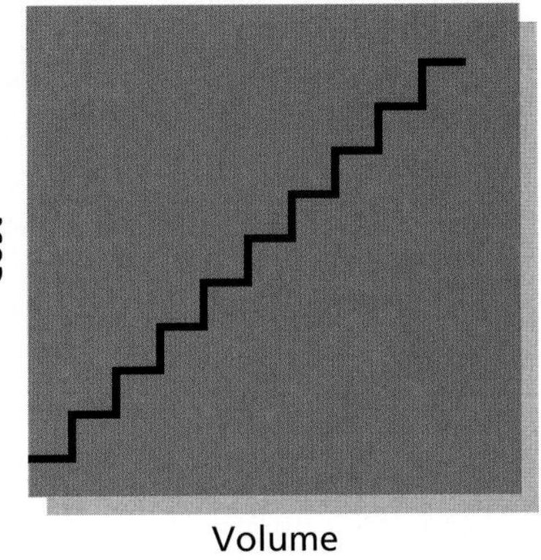

EXHIBIT 5–3 True Variable versus Step-Variable Costs

curvilinear cost can be satisfactorily approximated with a straight line within a narrow band of activity known as the *relevant range*. The **relevant range** is that range of activity within which the assumptions made about cost behaviour by the manager are valid. For example, note that the dashed line in Exhibit 5–4 can be used as an approximation to the curvilinear cost with very little loss of accuracy within the shaded relevant range. However, outside of the relevant range, this particular straight line is a poor approximation to the curvilinear cost relationship. Managers should always keep in mind that a particular assumption made about cost behaviour may be very inappropriate if activity falls outside of the relevant range.

Relevant range
The range of activity within which assumptions about variable and fixed cost behaviour are valid.

Fixed Costs

In our discussion of cost behaviour patterns in Chapter 2, we stated that fixed costs remain constant in total dollar amount within the relevant range of activity. To continue the Adventure Rafting example, assume the company decides to rent a building for $500 per month to store its equipment. The *total* amount of rent paid is the same regardless of the number of guests the company takes on its expeditions during any given month. This cost behaviour pattern is shown graphically in Exhibit 5–5.

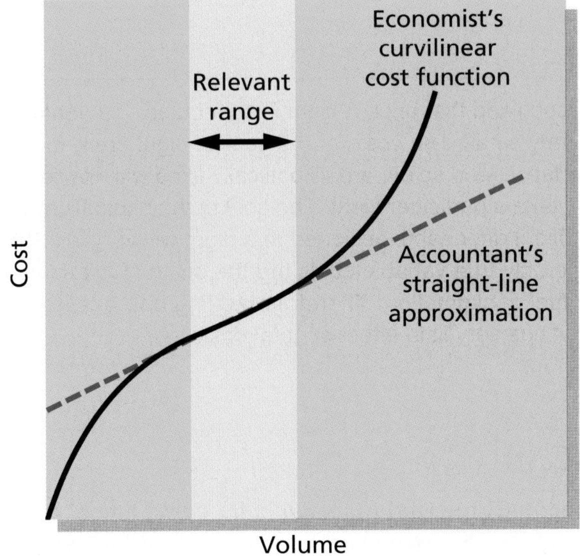

EXHIBIT 5–4 Curvilinear Costs and the Relevant Range

EXHIBIT 5–5 Fixed Cost Behaviour

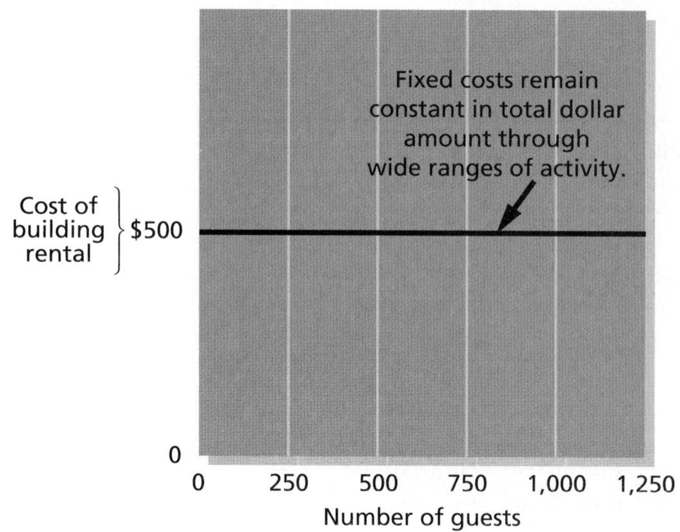

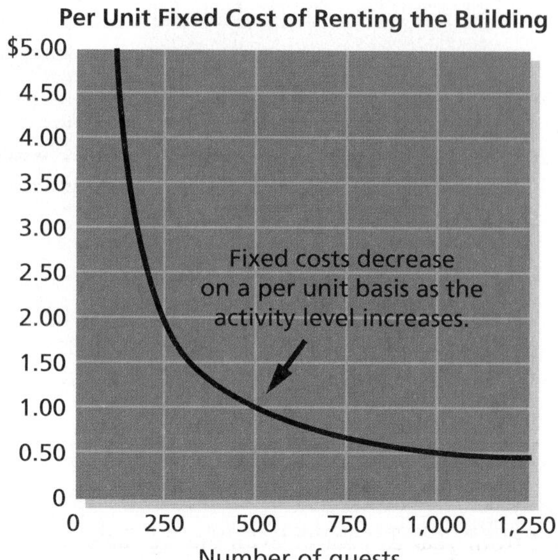

Since fixed costs remain constant in total, the amount of fixed cost computed on a *per unit* basis becomes progressively smaller as the level of activity increases. If Adventure Rafting has only 250 guests in a month, the $500 fixed rental cost would amount to $2 per guest. If there are 1,000 guests, the fixed rental cost would amount to only 50 cents per guest. This aspect of the behaviour of fixed costs is also displayed in Exhibit 5–5. Note that as the number of guests increases, the average unit cost drops, but it drops at a decreasing rate. The first guests have the greatest impact on unit costs.

As we noted in Chapter 2, this aspect of fixed costs can be confusing, although it is necessary in some contexts to express fixed costs on an average per unit basis. We found in Chapter 3, for example, that unit product costs for use in *external* financial statements contain both fixed and variable elements. For *internal* uses, however, fixed costs should not be expressed on a per unit basis because of the potential confusion. Experience has shown that for internal uses, fixed costs are most easily (and most safely) dealt with on a total basis rather than on a per unit basis.

FOCUS ***on Current Practice***

Airlines have long recognized that once a flight is scheduled, the variable cost of filling a seat with a passenger is very small. The costs of the cockpit flight crew, fuel, gate rentals, maintenance, aircraft depreciation, and so on, are all basically fixed with respect to the number of passengers who actually take a particular flight. The cost of the cabin flight crew is a step-variable cost—the number of flight attendants assigned to a flight will vary with the number of passengers on the flight. The only true variable costs are the costs of meals and an almost inconsequential increase in fuel consumption. Therefore, adding one passenger to a flight brings in additional revenue but has very little effect on total cost.

Types of Fixed Costs

Fixed costs are sometimes referred to as *capacity costs*, since they result from outlays made for buildings, equipment, skilled professional employees, and other items needed to provide the basic capacity for sustained operations. For planning purposes, fixed costs can be viewed as being either *committed* or *discretionary.*

Committed Fixed Costs **Committed fixed costs** are those costs that are difficult to adjust and relate to investment in buildings, equipment, and the basic organizational structure of a company. Committed fixed costs are long term in nature and cannot be significantly reduced, even for a short period of time, without seriously impairing a firm's long-run goals or profitability. Examples include depreciation of buildings and equipment, taxes on real estate, insurance, and salaries of top-management and operating personnel.

Committed fixed costs Those fixed costs that are difficult to adjust and that relate to the investment in facilities, equipment, and the basic organizational structure of a firm

Discretionary Fixed Costs **Discretionary fixed costs** are those costs that arise from annual decisions by management to spend in certain fixed cost areas. Examples of discretionary fixed costs include advertising, research and development, and management training programs.

Discretionary fixed costs Those fixed costs that arise from annual decisions by management to spend in certain fixed cost areas, such as advertising and research.

The planning horizon for discretionary fixed costs is fairly short—usually a single year. Management may be able to adjust these fixed costs periodically as circumstances change, since the firm is not locked into a decision regarding these costs. They can be adjusted from year to year or even during the course of a year if circumstances demand that costs be modified.

Caution should be taken to not confuse discretionary costs with unnecessary costs. For example, if a high-tech company such as Nortel were to cut its research and development budget, serious harm could be done to its ability to compete in the future. Similarly, cutting training costs can lead to lower employee morale and a resulting drop in productivity.

Whether a particular cost is regarded as committed or discretionary may depend on management's strategy. For example, during recessions when the level of home building is down, many construction companies lay off most of their workers and virtually disband operations. Other construction companies retain large numbers of employees on the payroll, even though the workers have little or no work to do. While these latter companies may be faced with short-term cash flow problems, it will be easier for them to respond quickly when economic conditions improve. Also the higher morale and loyalty of their employees may give these companies a significant competitive advantage.

The Trend toward Fixed Costs The trend in many companies is toward greater fixed costs relative to variable costs. Chores that used to be performed by hand have been taken over by machines. For example, grocery clerks at Loblaws and Sobeys used to key in prices by hand on cash registers. Now, most stores are equipped with bar code readers that enter price and other product information automatically. In general, competition has created pressure to give customers more value for their money—a demand that often can be satisfied only by automating business processes. For example, a Grant Thornton employee used to fill out tax returns for customers mainly by hand and the advice given to a customer largely depended on the knowledge of that particular employee. Now, computer software is used to complete tax returns, and the software provides the customer with tax planning and other advice tailored to the customer's needs based on the accumulated knowledge of many experts.

As machines take over more and more of the tasks that were performed by humans, the overall demand for human workers has not diminished. The demand for "knowledge" workers—those who work primarily with their minds rather than their muscles—has grown tremendously. Knowledge workers tend to be salaried, highly trained, and difficult to replace. As a consequence, the costs of compensating knowledge workers are often relatively fixed and are committed rather than discretionary costs.

Is Labour a Variable or a Fixed Cost? As the preceding discussion suggests, wages and salaries may be fixed or variable. The behaviour of wage and salary costs will differ from one country to another, depending on labour regulations, labour contracts, and custom. In some countries, such as France, Germany, and Japan, management has little flexibility in adjusting the labour force to changes in business activity. In countries such as Canada and the United Kingdom, management typically has much greater latitude. However, even in these less restrictive environments, managers may choose to treat employee compensation as a fixed cost for several reasons.

First, companies have become much more reluctant to adjust the workforce in response to short-term fluctuations in sales. Most companies realize that their employees are a very valuable asset. More and more, highly skilled and trained employees are required to run a successful business, and these workers are not easy to replace. Trained workers who are laid off may never return, and layoffs undermine the morale of those workers who remain.

In addition, managers do not want to be caught with a bloated payroll in an economic downturn. Therefore, there is an increased reluctance to add workers when sales activity picks up. Many companies are turning to temporary and part-time workers to take up the slack when their permanent, full-time employees are unable to handle all of the demand for the company's products and services. In such companies, labour costs are a curious mixture of fixed and variable costs.

Contract staffing enables an organization to handle increases in workloads without taking on the responsibility and expense of permanent hiring. These costs can be treated as variable costs. However, regular full-time employee staffing costs are properly classified as fixed costs when they are governed by labour union agreements that stipulate fixed annual salary amounts and restrictive layoff policies.

Many major companies have undergone waves of downsizing in recent years in which large numbers of employees—particularly middle managers—have lost their jobs. It may seem that this downsizing proves that even management salaries should be regarded as variable costs, but this would not be a valid conclusion. Downsizing has been the result of attempts to re-engineer business processes and cut costs rather than a response to a decline in sales activity. This underscores an important, but subtle, point: Fixed costs can change—they just do not change in response to small changes in activity.

In summary, we cannot provide a clear-cut answer to the question "Is labour a variable or fixed cost?" It depends on how much flexibility management has and management's strategy. Nevertheless, we will assume in this text that, unless otherwise stated, direct labour is a variable cost. This assumption is more likely to be valid for companies in Canada than in countries where employment laws permit much less flexibility.

FOCUS ***on Current Practice***

By making investments in technology, cutting edge companies have created radically different cost structures from traditional companies. John Labbett, the CFO of Onsale, an Internet auctioneer of discontinued computers, was previously employed at House of Fabrics, a traditional retailer. The two companies have roughly the same total revenues of about $250 million. However, House of Fabrics, with 5,500 employees, has a revenue per employee of about $90,000. At Onsale, with only 200 employees, the figure is $1.18 million per employee. Additionally, Internet companies like Onsale are often able to grow at very little cost. If demand grows, an Internet company may not have to do much more than just add another computer server. If demand grows at a traditional retailer, the company may have to invest in a new building and additional inventory and may have to hire additional employees.

Source: George Donnelly, "New @ttitude," *CFO*, June 1999, pp. 42–54.

Fixed Costs and the Relevant Range

The concept of the relevant range, which was introduced in the discussion of variable costs, is also important in understanding fixed costs—particularly discretionary fixed costs. The levels of discretionary fixed costs are typically decided at the beginning of the year and depend on the support needs of the planned programs such as advertising and training. The scope of these programs will depend, in turn, on the overall anticipated level of activity for the year. At very high levels of activity, programs are usually broadened or expanded. For example, if the company hopes to increase sales by 25%, it would probably plan for much larger advertising costs than if no sales increase was planned. So the *planned* level of activity may affect total discretionary fixed costs. However, once the total discretionary fixed costs have been budgeted, they are unaffected by the *actual* level of activity. For example, once the advertising budget has been decided on and has been spent, it will not be affected by how many units are actually sold. Therefore, the cost is fixed with respect to the *actual* number of units sold.

Discretionary fixed costs are easier to adjust than committed fixed costs. They also tend to be less "lumpy." Committed fixed costs tend to consist of costs of buildings, equipment, and the salaries of key personnel. It is difficult to buy half of a piece of equipment or to hire a quarter of a product-line manager, so the step pattern depicted in Exhibit 5–6 is typical for such costs. The relevant range of activity for a fixed cost is the range of activity over which the graph of the cost is flat, as in Exhibit 5–6. As a company expands its level of activity, it may outgrow its present facilities, or the key management team may need to be expanded. The result, of course, will be increased committed fixed costs as larger facilities are built and as new management positions are created.

One reaction to the step pattern depicted in Exhibit 5–6 is to say that discretionary and committed fixed costs are really just step-variable costs. To some extent this is true, since almost *all* costs can be adjusted in the long run. There are two major differences, however, between the step-variable costs depicted earlier in Exhibit 5–3 and the fixed costs depicted in Exhibit 5–6.

The first difference is that the step-variable costs can often be adjusted quickly as conditions change, whereas once fixed costs have been set, they often cannot be changed easily. A step-variable cost such as maintenance labour, for example, can be adjusted upward or downward by hiring and laying off maintenance workers. By contrast, once a company has signed a lease for a building, it is locked into that level of lease cost for the life of the contract.

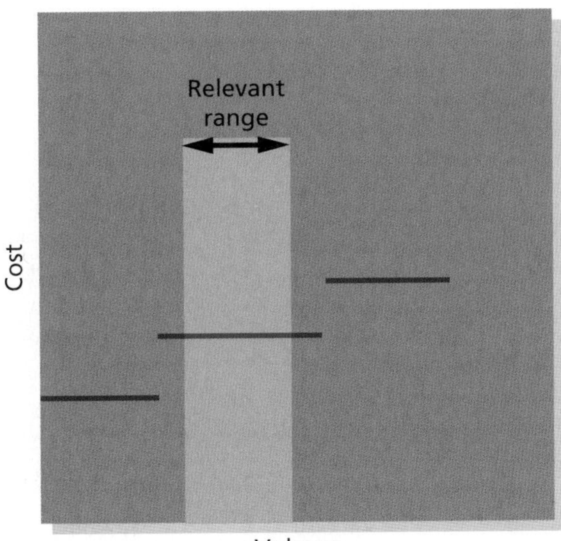

EXHIBIT 5–6 Fixed Costs and the Relevant Range

The second difference is that the *width of the steps* depicted for step-variable costs is much narrower than the width of the steps depicted for the fixed costs in Exhibit 5–6. The width of the steps relates to volume or level of activity. For step-variable costs, the width of a step may be 40 hours of activity or less if one is dealing, for example, with maintenance labour cost. For fixed costs, however, the width of a step may be *thousands* or even *tens of thousands* of hours of activity. In essence, the width of the steps for step-variable costs is generally so narrow that these costs can be treated essentially as variable costs for most purposes. The width of the steps for fixed costs, on the other hand, is so wide that these costs must generally be treated as being entirely fixed within the relevant range.

Mixed Costs

Mixed cost
A cost that contains both variable and fixed cost elements.

A **mixed cost** is one that contains both variable and fixed cost elements. Mixed costs are also known as *semivariable costs*. To continue the Adventure Rafting example, the company must pay a licence fee of $25,000 per year plus $3 per rafting party to the Yukon's Ministry of the Environment. If the company runs 1,000 rafting parties this year, then the total fees paid to the Yukon would be $28,000, made up of $25,000 in fixed cost plus $3,000 in variable cost. The behaviour of this mixed cost is shown graphically in Exhibit 5–7.

Even if Adventure fails to attract any customers and there are no rafting parties, the company will still have to pay the licence fee of $25,000. This is why the cost line in Exhibit 5–7 intersects the vertical cost axis at the $25,000 point. For each rafting party the company organizes, the total cost of the government fees will increase by $3. Therefore, the total cost line slopes upward as the variable cost element is added to the fixed cost element.

Since the mixed cost in Exhibit 5–7 is represented by a straight line, the following equation for a straight line can be used to express the relationship between mixed cost and the level of activity:

$$Y = a + bX$$

In this equation,

Y = The total mixed cost
a = The total fixed cost (the vertical intercept of the line)
b = The variable cost per unit of activity (the slope of the line)
X = The level of activity

EXHIBIT 5–7 Mixed Cost Behaviour

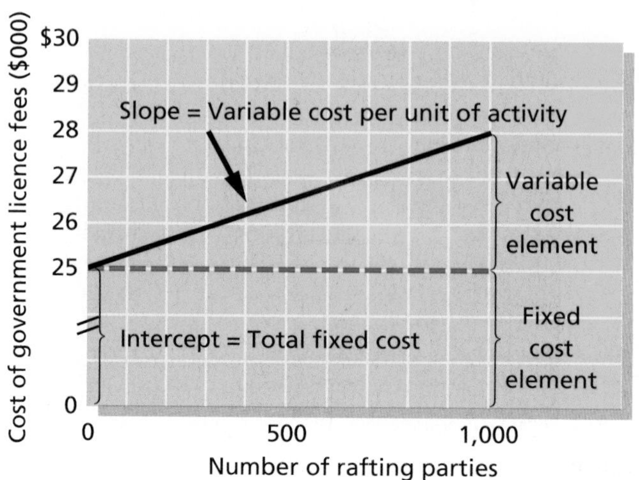

In the case of the Yukon's fees paid by Adventure Rafting, the equation is written as follows:

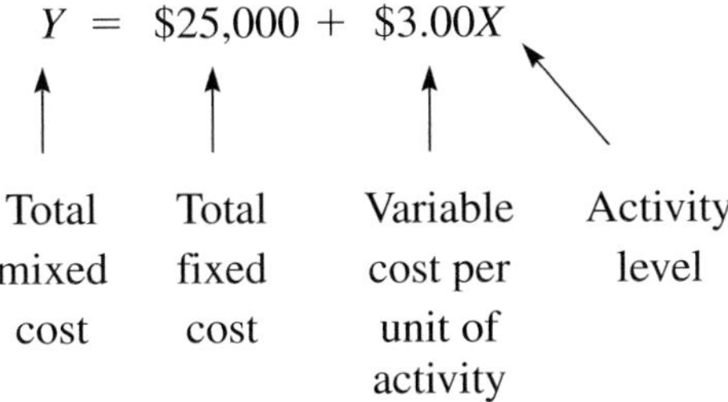

This equation makes it very easy to calculate what the total mixed cost would be for any level of activity within the relevant range. For example, suppose that the company expects to organize 800 rafting parties in the next year. Then the total government fees would be $27,400, calculated as follows:

$$Y = \$25{,}000 + (\$3.00 \text{ per rafting party} \times 800 \text{ rafting parties})$$
$$= \$27{,}400$$

FOCUS *on Current Practice*

A KPMG study of cost competitiveness of 11 countries and 17 industries suggests Canada is the overall cost leader (lowest cost) followed closely by Australia, indicating approximately 8 to 9% less cost than the United States in 2004. Japan, on the other hand, had overall costs approximately 24% higher than the United States. Labour costs, facility costs, transportation, utility, and taxes are all considered using equalized currency rates. Individual cities are also examined with Charlottetown, Halifax, Moncton, and Sherbrooke being among the lowest cost cities in Canada.

Given the wide range of operations around the world, what type of cost calculations would seem appropriate for the analysis?

Source: www.competitivealternatives.com.

THE ANALYSIS OF MIXED COSTS

In practice, mixed costs are very common. For example, the cost of providing X-ray services to patients at the Queen Elizabeth II Health Sciences Centre is a mixed cost. There are substantial fixed costs for equipment depreciation and for salaries for radiologists and technicians, but there are also variable costs for X-ray film, power, and supplies. At Air Canada, maintenance costs are a mixed cost. The company must incur fixed costs for renting maintenance facilities and for keeping skilled mechanics on the payroll, but the costs of replacement parts, lubricating oils, tires, and so forth, are variable with respect to how often and how far the company's aircraft are flown.

The fixed portion of a mixed cost represents the basic, minimum cost of just having a service *ready and available* for use. The variable portion represents the cost incurred for *actual consumption* of the service. The variable element varies in proportion to the amount of service that is consumed.

How does management go about actually estimating the fixed and variable components of a mixed cost? The most common methods used in practice are *account analysis* and the *engineering approach.* These methods are used most often in later chapters of this text.

Account analysis
A method for analyzing cost behaviour in which each account under consideration is classified as either variable or fixed based on the analyst's prior knowledge of how the cost in the account behaves.

Engineering approach
A detailed analysis of cost behaviour based on an industrial engineer's evaluation of the inputs that are required to carry out a particular activity and of the prices of those inputs.

In **account analysis,** each account under consideration is classified as either variable or fixed, based on the analyst's prior knowledge of how the cost in the account behaves. For example, direct materials would be classified as variable and a building lease cost would be classified as fixed because of the nature of those costs. The total fixed cost is the sum of the costs for the accounts that have been classified as fixed. The variable cost per unit is estimated by dividing the sum of the costs for the accounts that have been classified as variable by the total activity.

The **engineering approach** to cost analysis involves a detailed analysis of what cost behaviour should be, based on an industrial engineer's evaluation of the production methods to be used, the materials specifications, labour requirements, equipment usage, efficiency of production, power consumption, and so on. For example, Pizza Hut might use the engineering approach to estimate the cost of serving a particular take-out pizza. The cost of the pizza would be estimated by carefully costing the specific ingredients used to make the pizza, the power consumed to cook the pizza, and the cost of the container in which the pizza is delivered. The engineering approach must be used in those situations where no past experience is available concerning activity and costs. In addition, it is sometimes used together with other methods to improve the accuracy of cost analysis.

Account analysis works best when analyzing costs at a fairly aggregated level, such as the cost of caring for patients in the emergency room (ER) of the Queen Elizabeth II Health Sciences Centre. The costs of drugs, supplies, forms, wages, equipment, and so on, can be roughly classified as variable or fixed and a mixed cost formula for the overall cost of the emergency room can be estimated fairly quickly. However, this method glosses over the fact that some of the accounts may have elements of both fixed and variable costs. For example, the cost of electricity for the ER is a mixed cost. Most of the electricity is used for heating and lighting and is a fixed cost. However, the consumption of electricity increases with activity in the ER, since diagnostic equipment, operating theatre lights, defibrillators, and so on, all consume electricity. The most effective way to estimate the fixed and variable elements of such a mixed cost may be to analyze past records of cost and activity data. These records should reveal whether electrical costs vary significantly with the number of patients, and if so, by how much. The remainder of this section will be concerned with how to conduct such an analysis of past cost and activity data.

MANAGERIAL ACCOUNTING IN ACTION

The Issue

Dr. Derek Chalmers, the chief executive officer of Brentline Hospital, motioned Kinh Nguyen, the chief financial officer of the hospital, into his office.

Derek: Kinh, come on in.

Kinh: What can I do for you?

Derek: Well, for one thing, could you get the government to rescind the bookcase-full of regulations against the wall over there?

Kinh: Sorry, that's a bit beyond my authority.

Derek: Just wishing, Kinh. Actually, I wanted to talk to you about our maintenance expenses. I didn't used to have to pay attention to such things, but these expenses seem to be bouncing around a lot. Over the last half year or so, they have been as low as $7,400 and as high as $9,800 per month.

Kinh: Actually, that's a pretty normal variation in those expenses.

Derek: Well, we budgeted a constant $8,400 a month. Can't we do a better job of predicting what these costs are going to be? And how do we know when we've spent too much in a month? Shouldn't there be some explanation for these variations?

Kinh: Now that you mention it, we are in the process right now of tightening up our budgeting process. Our first step is to break all of our costs down into fixed and variable components.

Derek: How will that help?

Kinh: Well, that will permit us to predict what the level of costs will be. Some costs are fixed and shouldn't change much. Other costs go up and down as our activity goes up and down. The trick is to figure out what is driving the variable component of the costs.

Derek: What about the maintenance costs?

Kinh: My guess is that the variations in maintenance costs are being driven by our overall level of activity. When we treat more patients, our equipment is used more intensively, which leads to more maintenance expense.

Derek: How would you measure the level of overall activity? Would you use patient-days?

Kinh: I think so. Each day a patient is in the hospital counts as one patient-day. The greater the number of patient-days in a month, the busier we are. Besides, our budgeting is all based on projected patient-days.

Derek: Okay, so suppose you are able to break the maintenance costs down into fixed and variable components. What will that do for us?

Kinh: Basically, I will be able to predict what maintenance costs should be as a function of the number of patient-days.

Derek: I can see where that would be useful. We could use it to predict costs for budgeting purposes.

Kinh: We could also use it as a benchmark. Based on the actual number of patient-days for a period, I can predict what the maintenance costs should have been. We can compare this to the actual spending on maintenance.

Derek: Sounds good to me. Let me know when you get the results.

Diagnosing Cost Behaviour with a Scattergram Plot

LEARNING OBJECTIVE **2**
Use a scattergram plot to diagnose cost behaviour.

Kinh Nguyen began his analysis of maintenance costs by collecting cost and activity data for a number of recent months. Those data are as follows:

Month	Activity Level: Patient-Days	Maintenance Cost Incurred
January	5,600	$7,900
February.	7,100	8,500
March	5,000	7,400
April	6,500	8,200
May	7,300	9,100
June	8,000	9,800
July.	6,200	7,800

The first step in analyzing the cost and activity data should be to plot the data on a scattergram. This plot will immediately reveal any non-linearities or other problems with the data. The scattergram of maintenance costs versus patient-days at Brentline Hospital is reproduced in the first panel of Exhibit 5–8. Two things should be noted about this scattergram:

1. The total maintenance cost, Y, is plotted on the vertical axis. Cost is known as the **dependent variable,** since the amount of cost incurred during a period depends on the level of activity for the period. (That is, as the level of activity increases, total cost will also ordinarily increase.)
2. The activity, X (patient-days in this case), is plotted on the horizontal axis. Activity is known as the **independent variable,** since it causes variations in the cost.

Dependent variable
A variable that reacts or responds to some causal factor; total cost is the dependent variable, as represented by the letter Y, in the equation $Y = a + bX$.

Independent variable
A variable that acts as a causal factor; activity is the independent variable, as represented by the letter X, in the equation $Y = a + bX$.

From the scattergram, it is evident that maintenance costs do increase with the number of patient-days. In addition, the scattergram reveals that the relationship between maintenance costs and patient-days is approximately *linear*. In other words, the points lie more or less along a straight line. Such a straight line has been drawn using a ruler in the second panel of Exhibit 5–8. Cost behaviour is said to be **linear** whenever a straight line is a reasonable approximation for the relationship between cost and activity. Note that the data points do not fall exactly on the straight line. This will almost always happen in practice; the relationship is seldom perfectly linear.

Linear cost behaviour
Cost behaviour is linear when a straight line is a reasonable approximation for the relationship between cost and activity.

EXHIBIT 5–8 Scattergram Method of Cost Analysis

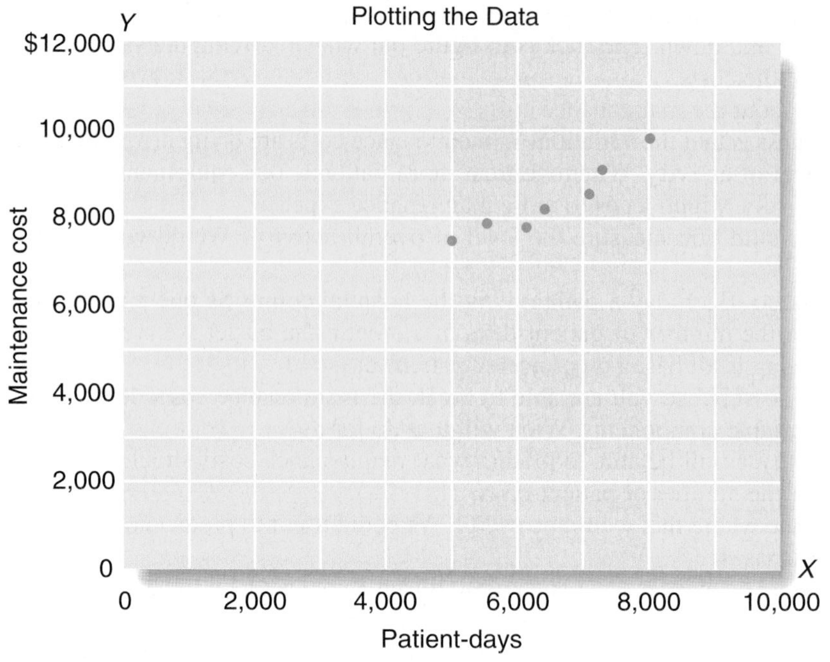

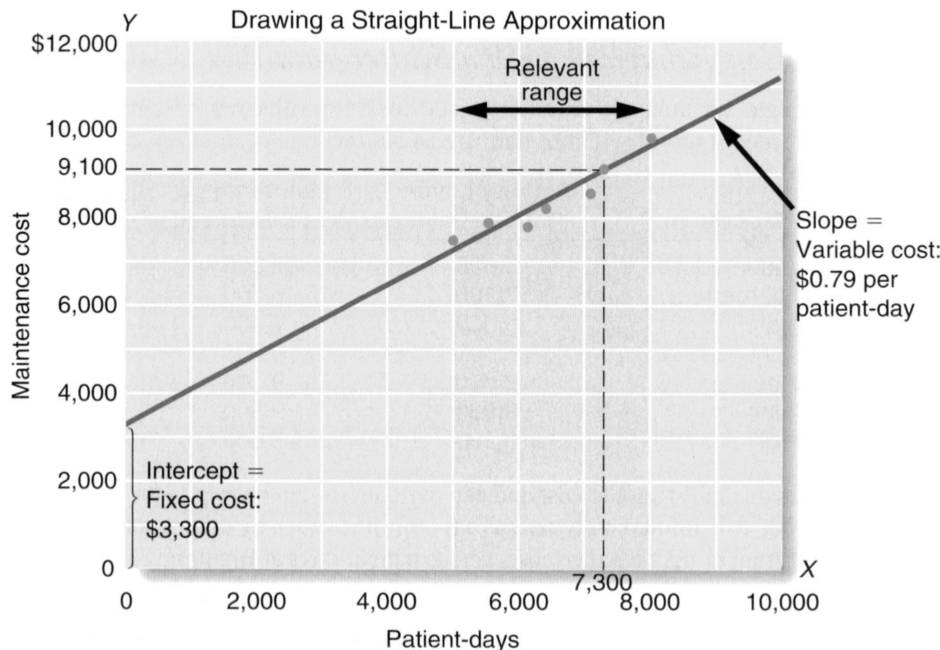

Note that the straight line in Exhibit 5–8 has been drawn through the point representing 7,300 patient-days and a total maintenance cost of $9,100. Drawing the straight line through one of the data points allows the analyst to make a quick estimate of variable and fixed costs. The vertical intercept where the straight line crosses the *Y*-axis—in this case, about $3,300—is the rough estimate of the fixed cost. The variable cost can be quickly estimated by subtracting the estimated fixed cost from the total cost at the point lying on the straight line:

Total maintenance cost for 7,300 patient-days (a point falling on the straight line)	$9,100
Less estimated fixed cost (the vertical intercept)	3,300
Estimated total variable cost for 7,300 patient-days	$5,800

The average variable cost per unit at 7,300 patient-days is computed as follows:

$$\text{Variable cost per unit} = \$5{,}800 \div 7{,}300 \text{ patient-days}$$
$$= \$0.79 \text{ per patient-day (rounded)}$$

Combining the estimate of the fixed cost and the estimate of the variable cost per patient-day, we can write the relationship between cost and activity as follows:

$$Y = \$3{,}300 + \$0.79X$$

where X is the number of patient-days.

We hasten to add that this *is* a quick method of estimating the fixed and variable cost elements of a mixed cost; it is seldom used in practice when significant matters are at stake. However, setting aside the estimates of the fixed and variable cost elements, plotting the data on a scattergram is an essential diagnostic step that is too often overlooked. Suppose, for example, we had been interested in the relationship between total nursing wages and the number of patient-days at the hospital. The permanent, full-time nursing staff can handle up to 7,000 patient-days in a month. Beyond that level of activity, part-time nurses must be called in. The cost and activity data for nurses are plotted on the scattergram in Exhibit 5–9. Looking at that scattergram, it is evident that two straight lines would do a much better job of fitting the data than a single straight line. Up to 7,000 patient-days, total nursing wages are essentially a fixed cost. Above 7,000 patient-days, total nursing wages are a mixed cost. This happens because, as stated above, the permanent, full-time nursing staff can handle up to 7,000 patient-days in a month. Above that level, part-time nurses are called in to help, which adds to the cost. Consequently, two straight lines (and two equations) would be used to represent total nursing wages—one for the relevant range of 5,600 to 7,000 patient-days and one for the relevant range of 7,000 to 8,000 patient-days.

As another example, suppose that Brentline Hospital management is interested in the relationship between the hospital's telephone costs and patient-days. Patients are billed directly for their use of telephones, so those costs do not appear on the hospital's cost records. The telephone costs of concern to management are the charges for the staff's use of telephones. The data for this cost are plotted in Exhibit 5–10. It is evident from that plot that while the telephone costs do vary from month to month, they are not related to patient-days. Something other than patient-days is driving the telephone bills. Therefore, it would not make sense to analyze this cost any further by attempting to estimate a variable cost per patient-day for telephone costs. Plotting the data helps the cost analyst to diagnose such situations.

The High-Low Method

LEARNING OBJECTIVE 3
Analyze a mixed cost using the high-low method.

In addition to the quick method described in the preceding section, more precise methods are available for estimating fixed and variable costs. However, it must be emphasized that fixed and variable costs should be computed only if a scattergram plot confirms that the relationship is approximately linear. In the case of maintenance costs at Brentline Hospital, the relationship does appear to be linear. In the case of telephone costs, there isn't any clear relationship between telephone costs and patient-days, so there is no point in estimating how much of the cost varies with patient-days.

Assuming that the scattergram plot indicates a linear relationship between cost and activity, the fixed and variable cost elements of a mixed cost can be estimated using the *high-low method* or the *least-squares regression method*. The **high-low method** is based on the rise-over-run formula for the slope of a straight line. As discussed above, if the relationship between cost and activity can be represented by a straight line, then the slope of the straight line is equal to the variable cost per unit of activity. Consequently, the following formula from high school algebra can be used to estimate the variable cost:

High-low method
A method of separating a mixed cost into its fixed and variable elements by analyzing the change in cost between the high and low levels of activity.

$$\text{Variable cost} = \text{Slope of the line} = \frac{\text{Rise}}{\text{Run}} = \frac{Y_2 - Y_1}{X_2 - X_1}$$

EXHIBIT 5–9 More than One Relevant Range

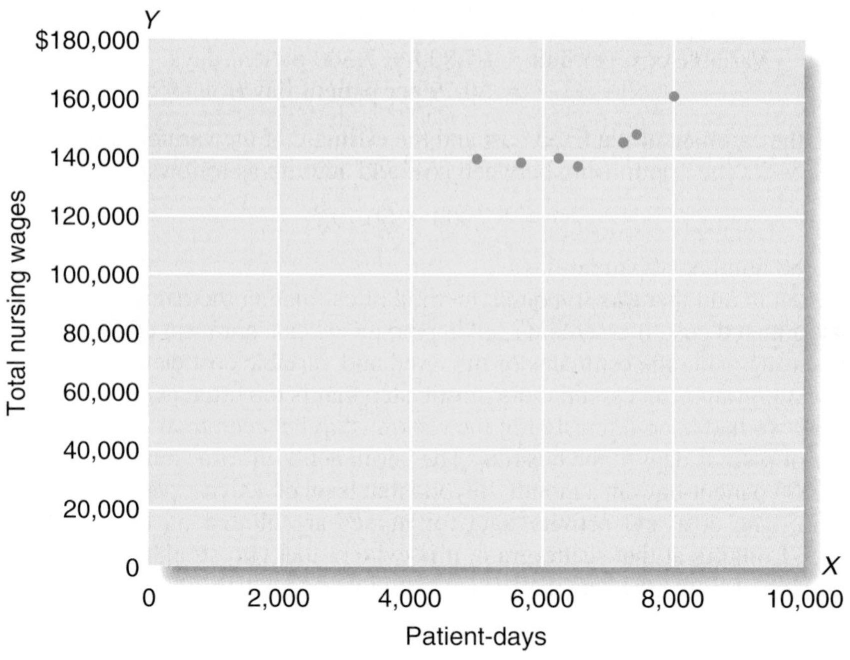

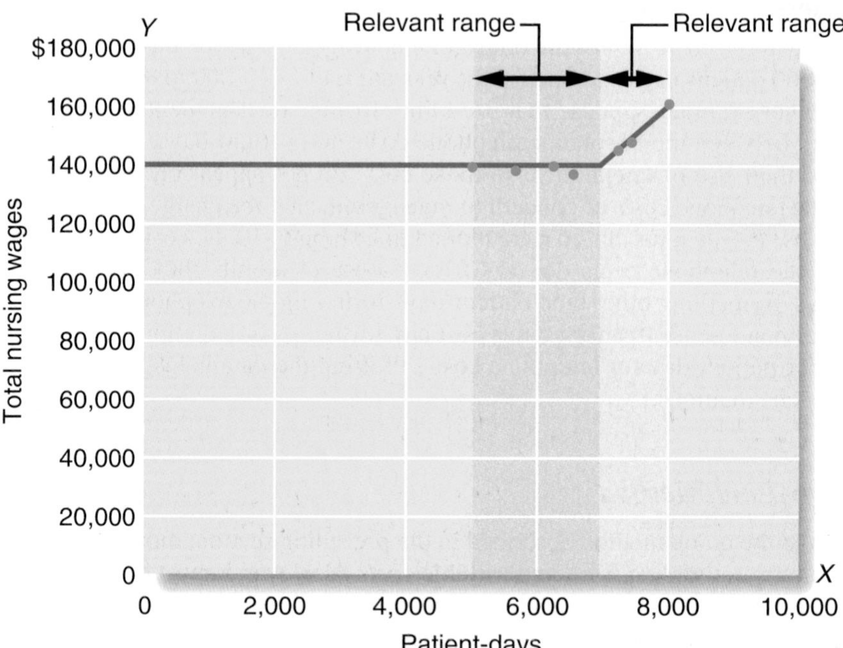

To analyze mixed costs with the high-low method, you begin by identifying the period with the lowest level of activity and the period with the highest level of activity. The period with the lowest activity is selected as the first point in the above formula and the period with the highest activity is selected as the second point. Consequently, the formula becomes:

$$\text{Variable cost} = \frac{Y_2 - Y_1}{X_2 - X_1} = \frac{\text{Cost at the high activity level} - \text{Cost at the low activity level}}{\text{High activity level} - \text{Low activity level}}$$

or

$$\text{Variable cost} = \frac{\text{Change in cost}}{\text{Change in activity}}$$

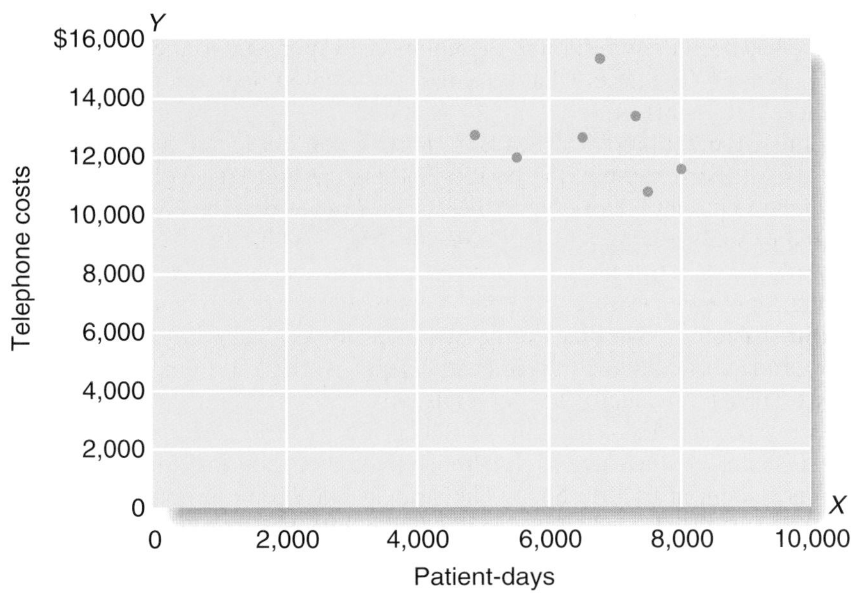

EXHIBIT 5–10 A Diagnostic Scattergram Plot

Therefore, when the high-low method is used, the variable cost is estimated by dividing the difference in cost between the high and low levels of activity by the change in activity between those two points.

Using the high-low method, we first identify the periods with the highest and lowest *activity*—in this case, June and March. We then use the activity and cost data from these two periods to estimate the variable cost component as follows:

	Patient-Days	Maintenance Cost Incurred
High activity level (June)	8,000	$9,800
Low activity level (March)	5,000	7,400
Change	3,000	$2,400

$$\text{Variable cost} = \frac{\text{Change in cost}}{\text{Change in activity}} = \frac{\$2{,}400}{3{,}000 \text{ patient-days}} = \$0.80 \text{ per patient-day}$$

Having determined that the variable rate for maintenance cost is 80 cents per patient-day, we can now determine the amount of fixed cost. This is done by taking total cost at *either* the high or the low activity level and deducting the variable cost element. In the computation below, total cost at the high activity level is used in computing the fixed cost element:

$$\begin{aligned}\text{Fixed cost element} &= \text{Total cost} - \text{Variable cost element}\\ &= \$9{,}800 - (\$0.80 \text{ per patient-day} \times 8{,}000 \text{ patient-days})\\ &= \$3{,}400\end{aligned}$$

Both the variable and fixed cost elements have now been isolated. The cost of maintenance can be expressed as $3,400 per month plus 80 cents per patient-day.

The cost of maintenance can also be expressed in terms of the equation for a straight line as follows:

$$Y = \$3{,}400 + \$0.80X$$

↑ Total maintenance cost (Y)   ↑ Total patient-days (X)

The data used in this illustration are shown graphically in Exhibit 5–11. Notice that a straight line has been drawn through the points corresponding to the low and high levels of activity. In essence, that is what the high-low method does—it draws a straight line through those two points.

Sometimes the high and low levels of activity don't coincide with the high and low amounts of cost. For example, the period that has the highest level of activity may not have the highest amount of cost. Nevertheless, the highest and lowest levels of *activity* are always used to analyze a mixed cost under the high-low method. The reason is that the analyst would like to use data that reflect the greatest possible variation in activity.

The high-low method is very simple to apply, but it suffers from a major (and sometimes critical) defect—it utilizes only two data points. Generally, two points are not enough to produce accurate results in cost analysis work. Additionally, periods in which the activity level is unusually low or unusually high will tend to produce inaccurate results. A cost formula that is estimated solely using data from these unusual periods may seriously misrepresent the true cost relationship that holds during normal periods. Such a distortion is evident in Exhibit 5–11. The straight line should probably be shifted down somewhat so that it is closer to more of the data points. For these reasons, other methods of cost analysis that utilize a greater number of points will generally be more accurate than the high-low method. If a manager chooses to use the high-low method, she or he should do so with a full awareness of the method's limitations.

Fortunately, modern computer software makes it very easy to use sophisticated statistical methods, such as *least-squares regression,* that use all of the data and that are capable of providing much more information than just the estimates of variable and fixed costs. The details of these statistical methods are beyond the scope of this text, but the basic approach is discussed below. Nevertheless, even if the least-squares regression approach is used, it is always a good idea to plot the data in a scattergram. By simply looking at the scattergram, you can quickly verify whether it makes sense to fit a straight line to the data using least-squares regression or some other method.

EXHIBIT 5–11 High-Low Method of Cost Analysis

Activity Level	Patient-Days	Maintenance Cost
High	8,000	$9,800
Low	5,000	$7,400

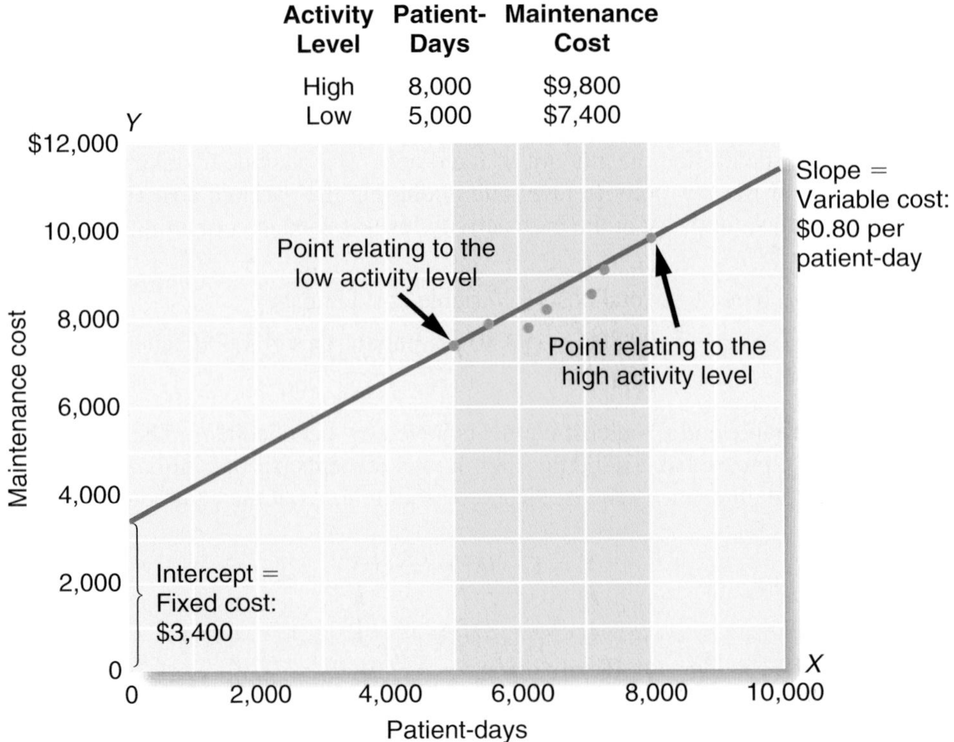

The Least-Squares Regression Method

LEARNING OBJECTIVE 4
Analyze a mixed cost using least squares regression.

The **least-squares regression method** is a method of separating a mixed cost into its fixed and variable components that uses all of the data. A *regression line* of the form $Y = a + bX$ is fitted to the data, where a represents the total fixed cost and b represents the variable cost per unit of activity. The basic idea underlying the least-squares regression method is illustrated in Exhibit 5–12 using hypothetical data points. Notice from the exhibit that the deviations from the plotted points to the regression line are measured vertically on the graph. These vertical deviations are called the *regression errors* and are the key to understanding what least-squares regression does. There is nothing mysterious about the least-squares regression method. It simply computes the regression line that minimizes the sum of these squared errors. The formulas that accomplish this are fairly complex and involve numerous calculations, but the principle is simple.

Least-squares regression method A method of separating a mixed cost into its fixed and variable elements by fitting a regression line that minimizes the sum of the squared errors.

Fortunately, computers are adept at carrying out the computations required by the least-squares regression formulas. The data—the observed values of X and Y—are entered into the computer, and software does the rest. In the case of the Brentline Hospital maintenance cost data, we used a statistical software package on a personal computer to calculate the following least-squares regression estimates of the total fixed cost (a) and the variable cost per unit of activity (b):

$$a = \$3{,}431$$

$$b = \$0.759$$

Therefore, using the least-squares regression method, the fixed element of the maintenance cost is \$3,431 per month and the variable portion is 75.9 cents per patient-day.

In terms of the linear equation $Y = a + bX$, the cost formula can be written as

$$Y = \$3{,}431 + \$0.759X$$

where activity (X) is expressed in patient-days.

While we used statistical software to calculate the values of a and b in this example, the estimates can also be computed using a spreadsheet application such as Microsoft Excel. In Appendix 5A to this chapter, we show how this can be done.

In addition to estimates of the intercept (fixed cost) and slope (variable cost per unit), least-squares regression software ordinarily provides a number of other very useful statistics. One of these statistics is the R^2, which is a measure of "goodness of fit." The R^2 tells us the percentage of the variation in the dependent variable (cost) that is explained by variation in the independent variable (activity). The R^2 varies from 0% to 100%, and the

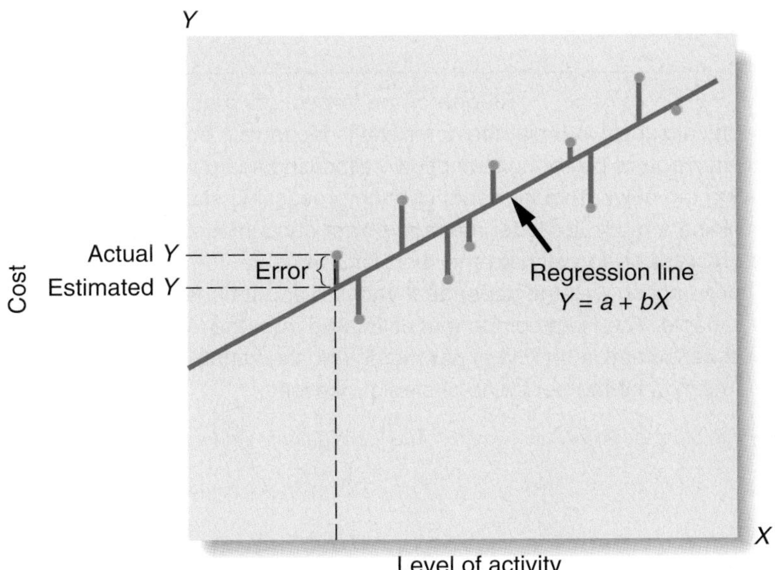

EXHIBIT 5–12 The Concept of Least-Squares Regression

higher the percentage, the better. A regression line that fits the data perfectly would have an R^2 of 1, but R^2 would be 0 in a situation where no fit was achieved by the regression line. In the case of the Brentline Hospital maintenance cost data, the R^2 is 0.90, which indicates that 90% of the variation in maintenance costs is explained by the variation in patient-days. This is reasonably high and is an indication of a good fit. On the other hand, a low R^2 would be an indication of a poor fit. You should always plot the data in a scattergram, but it is particularly important to check the data visually when the R^2 is low. A quick look at the scattergram can reveal that there is little real relationship between the cost and the activity or that the relationship is something other than a simple straight line. In such cases, additional analysis would be required.

MANAGERIAL ACCOUNTING IN ACTION

The Wrap-Up

After completing the analysis of maintenance costs, Kinh Nguyen met with Dr. Derek Chalmers to discuss the results.

Kinh: We used least-squares regression analysis to estimate the fixed and variable components of maintenance costs. According to the results, the fixed cost per month is \$3,431 and the variable cost per patient-day is 75.9 cents.

Derek: Okay, so if we plan for 7,800 patient-days next month, what is your estimate of the maintenance costs?

Kinh: That will take just a few seconds to figure out. [Kinh wrote the following calculations on a pad of paper.]

Fixed costs	\$3,431
Variable costs:	
7,800 patient-days × \$0.759 per patient-day	5,920
Total expected maintenance costs	\$9,351

Derek: Nine thousand, three hundred and fifty-*one* dollars! Isn't that a bit *too* precise?

Kinh: Sure. I don't really believe the maintenance costs will be exactly this figure. However, based on the information we have, this is the best estimate we can come up with.

Derek: Don't let me give you a hard time. Even though it is an estimate, it will be a lot better than just guessing, as we have done in the past. Thanks. I hope to see more of this kind of analysis.

FOCUS *on Current Practice*

The Tata Iron Steel Company Ltd. is one of the largest companies in India. Because of the unreliable electrical supply in India, the company is faced with frequent power shortages and must carefully manage its power consumption—allocating scarce power to the most profitable uses. Estimating the power requirements of each processing station in the steel mill was the first step in building a model to better manage power consumption. Management used simple least-squares regression to estimate the fixed and variable components of the power load. Total power consumption was the dependent variable and tonnes of steel processed was the independent variable. The fixed component estimated from the least-squares regression was the fixed power consumption (in kWhs) per month and the variable component was the power consumption (again in kWhs) per tonne of steel processed.

Source: "How Tata Steel Optimized Its Results," *The Management Accountant* (India), May 1996, pp. 372–76.

Comparing Cost Estimation Methods

The three methods result in slightly different estimates of fixed and variable costs, as summarized in Exhibit 5–13. Results from the scattergram method are based on a judgmental interpretation of the visual fit of the data points. The high-low method uses only two values, corresponding to the lowest and highest sales volumes, which potentially may not be very representative of the actual data. The least-squares regression method gives the most accurate results, because it uses a statistical technique that takes all of the available data points into account.

Cost estimates resulting from any of these methods are good only if the data used for estimation are reliable. A limitation common to all three methods is that they use past data, and estimates will be inaccurate if future cost conditions change.

In summary, analysis of cost behaviour begins with a scatterplot so that the type of cost behaviour can be seen. If the trend appears to be linear, then if the amount of data permits, a linear regression will usually provide the most reasonable answer. If time or data are short, high-low will provide a reasonable approximation of the linear formula needed for subsequent applications. Complex cost behaviours will require engineering studies and/or complex statistical analysis techniques such as multiple regression. Thus, more advanced study or specialized assistance will be necessary.

Multiple Regression Analysis

In the discussion thus far, we have assumed that a single factor such as patient-days drives the variable cost component of a mixed cost. This assumption is acceptable for many mixed costs, but in some situations there may be more than one causal factor driving the variable cost element. For example, shipping costs may depend on both the number of units shipped *and* the weight of the units. In a situation such as this, *multiple regression* is necessary. **Multiple regression** is an analytical method that is used when the dependent variable (i.e., cost) is caused by more than one factor. Although adding more factors, or variables, makes the computations more complex, the principles involved are the same as in the simple least-squares regressions discussed above.

Multiple regression An analytical method required in those situations where variations in a dependent variable are caused by more than one factor.

EXHIBIT 5–13 Comparison of Cost Estimation Methods

Estimation Method	Fixed Cost	Variable Cost
Scattergram	$3,300	$0.79 per patient-day
High-low	$3,400	$0.80 per patient-day
Least-squares regression	$3,431	$0.759 per patient-day

THE CONTRIBUTION FORMAT

LEARNING OBJECTIVE 5
Prepare an income statement using the contribution format.

Once the manager has separated costs into fixed and variable elements, what is done with the data? We have already answered this question somewhat by showing how a cost formula can be used to predict costs. To answer this question more fully will require most of the remainder of this text, since much of what the manager does requires an understanding of cost behaviour. One immediate and very significant application of the ideas we have developed, however, is found in an income statement format known as the **contribution approach.** The unique thing about the contribution approach is that it provides the manager with an income statement geared directly to cost behaviour.

Contribution approach An income statement format that is geared to cost behaviour in that costs are separated into variable and fixed categories rather than being separated according to the functions of production, sales, and administration.

Why Another Income Statement Format?

An income statement prepared using the *traditional approach*, as illustrated in Chapter 2, is not organized in terms of cost behaviour. Rather, it is organized in a "functional" format—emphasizing the functions of production, administration, and sales in the classification and presentation of cost data. No attempt is made to distinguish between the behaviour of costs included under each functional heading. Under the heading Administrative Expense, for example, one can expect to find both variable and fixed costs lumped together.

Although an income statement prepared in the functional format may be useful for external reporting purposes, it has serious limitations when used for internal purposes. Internally, the manager needs cost data organized in a format that will facilitate planning, control, and decision making. As we will see in later chapters, these tasks are much easier when cost data are available in a fixed and variable format. The contribution approach to the income statement was developed in response to this need.

The Contribution Approach

Exhibit 5–14 illustrates the contribution approach to the income statement with a simple example based on assumed data, along with the traditional approach discussed in Chapter 2.

Contribution margin The amount remaining from sales revenues after all variable expenses have been deducted.

Notice that the contribution approach separates costs into fixed and variable categories, first deducting variable expenses from sales to obtain what is known as the *contribution margin.* The **contribution margin** is the amount remaining from sales revenues after variable expenses have been deducted. This amount *contributes* toward covering fixed expenses and then toward profits for the period.

The simplified contribution approach income statement makes a common assumption that can confuse. The variable production expenses assume production equals sales in terms of units. Thus these expenses for production like those for selling and administrative use sales volume as a driver. A more complete income statement would need to show inventory levels so that variable production costs can use production volume activity as the cost driver.

EXHIBIT 5–14 Comparison of the Contribution Income Statement with the Traditional Income Statement

Traditional Approach (costs organized by function)

Sales		$12,000
Less cost of goods sold		6,000*
Gross margin		6,000
Less operating expenses:		
Selling	$3,100*	
Administrative	1,900*	5,000
Operating income		$ 1,000

Contribution Approach (costs organized by behaviour)

Sales		$12,000
Less variable expenses:		
Variable production	$2,000	
Variable selling	600	
Variable administrative	400	3,000
Contribution margin		9,000
Less fixed expenses:		
Fixed production	4,000	
Fixed selling	2,500	
Fixed administrative	1,500	8,000
Operating income		$ 1,000

*Contains both variable and fixed expenses. This is the income statement for a manufacturing company; thus, when the income statement is placed in the contribution format, the cost of goods sold figure is divided between variable production costs and fixed production costs. If this was the income statement for a *merchandising* company (which simply purchases completed goods from a supplier), then the cost of goods sold would be *all* variable.

The contribution approach to the income statement is used as an internal planning and decision-making tool. Its emphasis on costs by behaviour facilitates cost-volume-profit analysis, such as we will be doing in the next chapter. The approach is also very useful in appraising management performance, in segmented reporting of profit data, and in budgeting. Moreover, the contribution approach helps managers organize data pertinent to all kinds of special decisions such as product-line analysis, pricing, use of scarce resources, and make or buy analysis. All of these topics are covered in later chapters.

SUMMARY

As we will see in later chapters, the ability to predict how costs will respond to changes in activity is critical for making decisions, for controlling operations, and for evaluating performance. Three major classifications of costs were discussed in this chapter—variable, fixed, and mixed. Mixed costs consist of a mixture of variable and fixed elements and a mixed cost can be expressed in equation form as $Y = a + bX$, where X is the activity, Y is the cost, a is the fixed cost element, and b is the variable cost per unit of activity. Several methods are available to estimate the fixed and variable cost components of a mixed cost using past records of cost and activity. If the relationship between cost and activity appears to be linear based on a scattergram plot, then the variable and fixed components of the mixed cost can be estimated using the quick method, the high-low method, or the least-squares regression method. The quick method is based on drawing a straight line and then using the slope and the intercept of the straight line to estimate the variable and fixed cost components of the mixed cost. The high-low method implicitly draws a straight line through the points of lowest activity and highest activity. In most situations, the least-squares regression method should be used in preference to both the quick and the high-low methods. Computer software is widely available for using the least-squares method and a variety of useful statistics are automatically produced by most software packages, along with estimates of the intercept (fixed cost) and slope (variable cost per unit). Nevertheless, even when least-squares regression is used, the data should be plotted to confirm that the relationship is really a straight line. To complete the discussion, it should be noted that the tools of plot, account analysis, engineering and least squares can be used to analyze cost behaviour with other activity drivers. Sales and production or service levels represent only two of such drivers. Others will be seen in Chapter 8.

Managers use costs organized by behaviour as a basis for many decisions. To facilitate this use, the income statement can be prepared in a contribution format. The contribution format classifies costs on the income statement by cost behaviour (i.e., variable versus fixed) rather than by the functions of production, administration, and sales.

APPENDIX 5A: LEAST SQUARES REGRESSION CALCULATIONS

LEARNING OBJECTIVE **6**
Elaborate about the least squares method.

The least-squares regression method for estimating a linear relationship is based on the equation for a straight line:

$$Y = a + bX$$

The following formulas are used to calculate the values of the vertical intercept *(a)* and the slope *(b)* that minimize the sum of the squared errors:[1]

$$b = \frac{n(\Sigma XY) - (\Sigma X)(\Sigma Y)}{n(\Sigma X^2) - (\Sigma X)^2}$$

$$a = \frac{(\Sigma Y) - b(\Sigma X)}{n}$$

1. See calculus or statistics books for details concerning how these formulas are derived.

where:

X = The level of activity (independent variable)
Y = The total mixed cost (dependent variable)
a = The total fixed cost (the vertical intercept of the line)
b = The variable cost per unit of activity (the slope of the line)
n = Number of observations
Σ = Sum across all n observations

Carrying out the calculations required by the formulas is tedious at best. Fortunately, statistical software packages are widely available that perform the calculations automatically. Spreadsheet software, such as Microsoft Excel, can also be used to do least-squares regression—although it requires a little more work than specialized statistical packages do.

To illustrate how Excel can be used to calculate the intercept a, the slope b, and the R^2, we will use the Brentline Hospital data for maintenance costs on page 191. The worksheet in Exhibit 5–15 contains the data and the calculations.

As you can see, the X values (the independent variable) have been entered in cells B4 through B10. The Y values (the dependent variable) have been entered in cells C4 through C10. The slope, intercept, and R^2 are computed using the Excel functions INTERCEPT, SLOPE, and RSQ. In each case, you must specify the range of cells for the Y values and for the X values. In the Exhibit 5–15 worksheet, cell B12 contains the formula =INTERCEPT(C4:C10,B4:B10); cell B13 contains the formula =SLOPE(C4:C10,B4:B10); and cell B14 contains the formula =RSQ(C4:C10,B4:B10).

EXHIBIT 5–15 The Least-Squares Regression Worksheet for Brentline Hospital

Microsoft Excel - Appendix 5A.xls

File Edit View Insert Format Tools Data Window Help

Arial 12 | G16 =

	A	B	C	D	E
1		*Patient-*	*Maintenance*		
2		*Days*	*Costs*		
3	*Month*	*X*	*Y*		
4	January	5,600	$7,900		
5	February	7,100	8,500		
6	March	5,000	7,400		
7	April	6,500	8,200		
8	May	7,300	9,100		
9	June	8,000	9,800		
10	July	6,200	7,800		
11					
12	Intercept	$3,431			
13	Slope	$0.759			
14	RSQ	0.90			
15					

Least-squares regression

Ready NUM

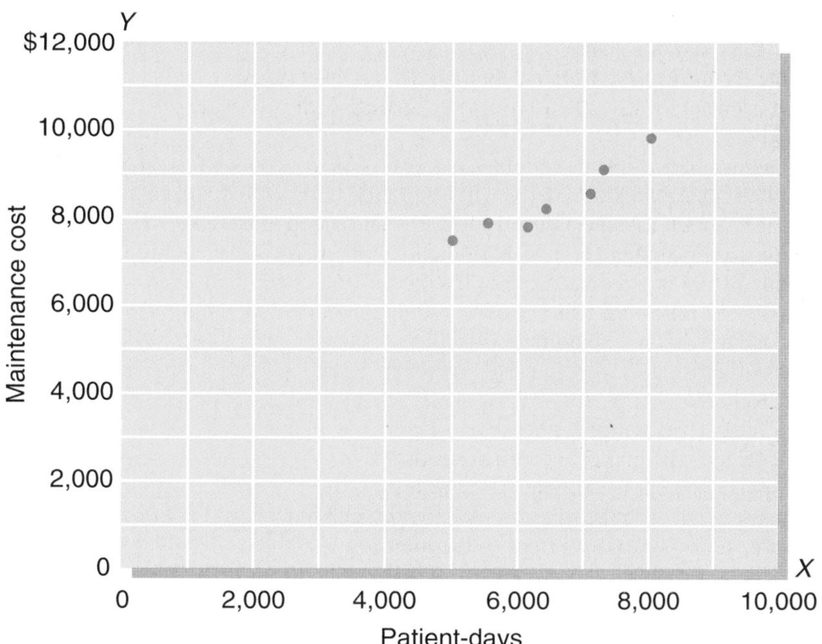

EXHIBIT 5–16 A Scattergram Plot of the Brentline Hospital Data

According to the calculations carried out by Excel, the fixed maintenance cost (the intercept) is $3,431 per month and the variable cost (the slope) is $0.759 per patient-day. Therefore, the cost formula for maintenance cost is:

$$Y = a + bX$$

$$Y = \$3{,}431 + \$0.759X$$

Note that the R^2 (i.e., RSQ) is 0.90, which—as previously discussed—is quite good and indicates that 90% of the variation in maintenance costs is explained by the variation in patient-days.

Plotting the data is easy in Excel. Select the range of values that you would like to plot—in this case, cells B4:C10. Then select the Chart Wizard tool on the toolbar and make the appropriate choices in the various dialogue boxes that appear. When you are finished, you should have a scattergram that looks something like the plot in Exhibit 5–16. Note that the relationship between cost and activity is approximately linear, so it is reasonable to fit a straight line to the data as we have implicitly done with the least-squares regression.

GLOSSARY

Visit the Online Learning Centre at http:// www.mcgrawhill.ca/college/garrison/ for a review of key terms and definitions.

QUESTIONS

5–1 Distinguish between (*a*) a variable cost, (*b*) a fixed cost, and (*c*) a mixed cost.

5–2 What effect does an increase in volume have on the following?

a. Unit fixed costs.

b. Unit variable costs.

c. Total fixed costs.
d. Total variable costs.

5–3 Define the terms (*a*) cost behaviour and (*b*) relevant range.

5–4 What is meant by an *activity base* when dealing with variable costs? Give several examples of activity bases.

5–5 Distinguish between (*a*) a variable cost, (*b*) a mixed cost, and (*c*) a step-variable cost. Chart the three costs on a graph, with activity plotted horizontally and cost plotted vertically.

5–6 Managers often assume a strictly linear relationship between cost and volume. How can this practice be defended in light of the fact that many costs are curvilinear?

5–7 Distinguish between discretionary fixed costs and committed fixed costs.

5–8 Classify the following fixed costs as normally being either committed or discretionary:
a. Depreciation on buildings.
b. Advertising.
c. Research.
d. Long-term equipment leases.
e. Pension payments to the firm's retirees.
f. Management development and training.

5–9 Does the concept of the relevant range apply to fixed costs? Explain.

5–10 What is the major disadvantage of the high-low method?

5–11 What is meant by a regression line? Give the general formula for a regression line. Which term represents the variable cost? The fixed cost?

5–12 What is meant by the term *least-squares regression?*

5–13 What is the difference between ordinary least-squares regression analysis and multiple regression analysis?

5–14 What is the meaning of R^2?

5–15 What is the difference between the contribution approach to the income statement and the traditional approach to the income statement?

5–16 What is the contribution margin?

EXERCISES

EXERCISE 5–1 Fixed and Variable Cost Behaviour [LO1]

Espresso Express operates a number of espresso coffee stands in busy suburban malls. The fixed weekly expense of a coffee stand is $1,200 and the variable cost per cup of coffee served is $0.22.

Required:

1. Fill in the following table with your estimates of total costs and cost per cup of coffee at the indicated levels of activity for a coffee stand. Round off the cost of a cup of coffee to the nearest tenth of a cent.

	Cups of Coffee Served in a Week		
	2,000	2,100	2,200
Fixed cost	?	?	?
Variable cost	?	?	?
Total cost	?	?	?
Cost per cup of coffee served	?	?	?

2. Does the cost per cup of coffee served increase, decrease, or remain the same as the number of cups of coffee served in a week increases? Explain.

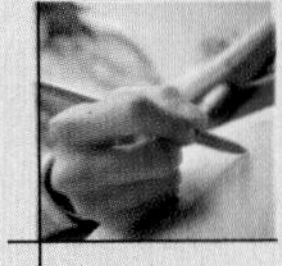

EXERCISE 5–2 High-Low Method; Scattergram Analysis [LO2, LO3]

The following data relating to units shipped and total shipping expense have been assembled by Archer Company, a wholesaler of large, custom-built air-conditioning units for commercial buildings:

Month	Units Shipped	Total Shipping Expense
January	3	$1,800
February	6	$2,300
March	4	$1,700
April	5	$2,000
May	7	$2,300
June	8	$2,700
July	2	$1,200

Required:

1. Using the high-low method, estimate a cost formula for shipping expense.
2. The president of the company has no confidence in the high-low method and would like you to check out your results using a scattergram.
   a. Prepare a scattergram, using the data given above. Plot cost on the vertical axis and activity on the horizontal axis. Use a ruler to fit a straight line to your plotted points.
   b. Using your scattergram, estimate the approximate variable cost per unit shipped and the approximate fixed cost per month with the quick-and-dirty method.
3. Use the formula for a and b shown in Appendix 5A to calculate the slope and intercept for the cost behaviour equation. (Hint: you will need to compute $\sum x$, $\sum y$, $\sum x^*y$, $\sum x^2$)
4. What factors, other than the number of units shipped, are likely to affect the company's total shipping expense? Explain.

EXERCISE 5–3 (Appendix 5A) Least-Square Regression [LO4]

Refer to the data for Archer Company in Exercise 5–2.

Required:

1. Using the least-squares regression method, estimate a cost formula for shipping expense.
2. If you also completed Exercise 5–2, prepare a simple table comparing the variable and fixed cost elements of shipping expense as computed under the quick-and-dirty scattergram method, the high-low method, and the least-squares regression method.

EXERCISE 5–4 High-Low Method [LO3]

The Cabot Hotel in Ingonish, Cape Breton, has accumulated records of the total electrical costs of the hotel and the number of occupancy-days over the last year. An occupancy-day represents a room rented out for one day. The hotel's business is highly seasonal, with peaks occurring during the ski season and in the summer.

Month	Occupancy-Days	Electrical Costs
January	1,736	$4,127
February	1,904	$4,207
March	2,356	$5,083
April	960	$2,857
May	360	$1,871
June	744	$2,696
July	2,108	$4,670
August	2,406	$5,148
September	840	$2,691
October	124	$1,588
November	720	$2,454
December	1,364	$3,529

Required:

1. Using the high-low method, estimate the fixed cost of electricity per month and the variable cost of electricity per occupancy-day. Round off the fixed cost to the nearest whole dollar and the variable cost to the nearest whole cent.
2. What other factors other than occupancy-days are likely to affect the variation in electrical costs from month to month?

EXERCISE 5–5 Contribution Format Income Statement [LO5]

The Alpine House, Inc., is a large retailer of winter sports equipment. An income statement for the company's Ski Department for a recent quarter is presented below:

THE ALPINE HOUSE, INC. Income Statement—Ski Department For the Quarter Ended March 31		
Sales		$150,000
Less cost of goods sold		90,000
Gross margin		60,000
Less operating expenses:		
Selling expenses	$30,000	
Administrative expenses	10,000	40,000
Operating income		$ 20,000

Skis sell, on the average, for $750 per pair. Variable selling expenses are $50 per pair of skis sold. The remaining selling expenses are fixed. The administrative expenses are 20% variable and 80% fixed. The company does not manufacture its own skis; it purchases them from a supplier for $450 per pair.

Required:

1. Prepare an income statement for the quarter using the contribution approach.
2. For every pair of skis sold during the quarter, what was the contribution toward covering fixed expenses and toward earning profits?

EXERCISE 5–6 Cost Behaviour; Contribution Format Income Statement [LO1, LO5]

Harris Company manufactures and sells a single product. A partially completed schedule of the company's total and per unit costs over the relevant range of 30,000 to 50,000 units produced and sold annually is given below:

	Units Produced and Sold		
	30,000	40,000	50,000
Total costs:			
Variable costs	$180,000	?	?
Fixed costs	300,000	?	?
Total costs	$480,000	?	?
Cost per unit:			
Variable cost	?	?	?
Fixed cost	?	?	?
Total cost per unit	?	?	?

Required:

1. Complete the schedule of the company's total and unit costs above.
2. Assume that the company produces and sells 45,000 units during the year at a selling price of $16 per unit. Prepare a contribution format income statement for the year.

EXERCISE 5–7 High-Low Method; Predicting Cost [LO1, LO3]

St. Mark's Elder Care contains 450 beds. The average occupancy rate is 80% per month. In other words, on average, 80% of the beds are occupied by patients. At this level of occupancy, the operating costs are $32 per occupied bed per day, assuming a 30-day month. This $32 figure contains both variable and fixed cost elements.

During June, the occupancy rate was only 60%. A total of $326,700 in operating cost was incurred during the month.

Required:

1. Using the high-low method, estimate:
   a. The variable cost per occupied bed on a daily basis.
   b. The total fixed operating costs per month.

2. Assume an occupancy rate of 70% per month. What amount of total operating cost would you expect the facility to incur?

EXERCISE 5–8 High-Low Method; Predicting Cost [LO1, LO3]

The Lakeshore Hotel's guest-days of occupancy and custodial supplies expense over the last seven months were:

Month	Guest-Days of Occupancy	Custodial Supplies Expense
March	4,000	$7,500
April	6,500	$8,250
May	8,000	$10,500
June	10,500	$12,000
July	12,000	$13,500
August	9,000	$10,750
September	7,500	$9,750

Guest-days is a measure of the overall activity at the hotel. For example, a guest who stays at the hotel for three days is counted as three guest-days.

Required:

1. Using the high-low method, estimate a cost formula for custodial supplies expense.
2. Using the cost formula you derived above, what amount of custodial supplies expense would you expect to be incurred at an occupancy level of 11,000 guest-days?

EXERCISE 5–9 Scattergram Analysis; High-Low Method [LO2, LO3]

Refer to the data for Lakeshore Hotel in Exercise 5–8.

Required:

1. Prepare a scattergram using the data from Exercise 5–8. Plot cost on the vertical axis and activity on the horizontal axis. Using a ruler, fit a line to your plotted points.
2. Using the quick method, what is the approximate monthly fixed cost? The approximate variable cost per guest-day?
3. Scrutinize the points on your graph and explain why the high-low method would or would not yield an accurate cost formula in this situation.

EXERCISE 5–10 Scattergram Analysis [LO2]

Oki Products, Ltd., has observed the following processing costs at various levels of activity over the last 15 months:

Month	Units Produced	Processing Cost
1	4,500	$38,000
2	11,000	$52,000
3	12,000	$56,000
4	5,500	$40,000
5	9,000	$47,000
6	10,500	$52,000
7	7,500	$44,000
8	5,000	$41,000
9	11,500	$52,000
10	6,000	$43,000
11	8,500	$48,000
12	10,000	$50,000
13	6,500	$44,000
14	9,500	$48,000
15	8,000	$46,000

Required:

1. Prepare a scattergram using the above data. Plot cost on the vertical axis and activity on the horizontal axis. Fit a line to your plotted points using a ruler.

2. Using the quick method, what is the approximate monthly fixed cost? The approximate variable cost per unit processed? Show your computations.

EXERCISE 5–11 Cost Behaviour; High-Low Method [LO1, LO3]

Hoi Chong Transport, Ltd., operates a fleet of delivery trucks in Singapore. The company has determined that if a truck is driven 105,000 kilometres during a year, the average operating cost is 11.4 cents per kilometre. If a truck is driven only 70,000 kilometres during a year, the average operating cost increases to 13.4 cents per kilometre. (The Singapore dollar is the currency used in Singapore.)

Required:

1. Using the high-low method, estimate the variable and fixed cost elements of the annual cost of truck operation.
2. Express the variable and fixed costs in the form $Y = a + bX$.
3. If a truck were driven 80,000 kilometres during a year, what total cost would you expect to be incurred?

EXERCISE 5–12 (Appendix 5A) Least-Squares Regression [LO1, LO6]

George Caloz & Frères, located in Grenchen, Switzerland, makes prestige high-end custom watches in small lots. The company has been in operation since 1856. One of the company's products, a platinum diving watch, goes through an etching process. The company has observed etching costs as follows over the last six weeks:

Week	Units	Total Etching Cost
1	4	SFr18
2	3	17
3	8	25
4	6	20
5	7	24
6	2	16
	30	SFr120

The Swiss currency is the Swiss Franc, which is denoted by SFr.

For planning purposes, management would like to know the amount of variable etching cost per unit and the total fixed etching cost per week.

Required:

1. Using the least-squares regression method, estimate the variable and fixed elements of etching cost.
2. Express the cost data in (1) above in the form $Y = a + bX$.
3. If the company processes five units next week, what would be the expected total etching cost?

PROBLEMS

PROBLEM 5–13 Cost Behaviour; High-Low Method; Contribution Format Income Statement [LO1, LO3, LO5]

Morrisey & Brown, Ltd., of Sydney is a merchandising company that is the sole distributor of a product that is increasing in popularity among Australian consumers. The company's income statements for the three most recent months is at the top of the next page.

(Note: Morrisey & Brown, Ltd.'s Australian-formatted income statement has been recast in the format common in Canada. The Australian dollar is denoted here by A$.)

MORRISEY & BROWN, LTD.
Income Statements
For the Three Months Ending September 30

	July	August	September
Sales in units	4,000	4,500	5,000
Sales revenue	A$400,000	A$450,000	A$500,000
Less cost of goods sold	240,000	270,000	300,000
Gross margin	160,000	180,000	200,000
Less operating expenses:			
Advertising expense	21,000	21,000	21,000
Shipping expense	34,000	36,000	38,000
Salaries and commissions	78,000	84,000	90,000
Insurance expense	6,000	6,000	6,000
Depreciation expense	15,000	15,000	15,000
Total operating expenses	154,000	162,000	170,000
Operating income	A$ 6,000	A$ 18,000	A$ 30,000

Required:

1. Identify each of the company's expenses (including cost of goods sold) as either variable, fixed, or mixed.
2. Using the high-low method, separate each mixed expense into variable and fixed elements. State the cost formula for each mixed expense.
3. Redo the company's income statement at the 5,000-unit level of activity using the contribution format.

PROBLEM 5–14 Contribution Format versus Traditional Income Statement [LO5]

Marwick's Pianos, Inc., purchases pianos from a large manufacturer and sells them at the retail level. The pianos cost, on the average, $2,450 each from the manufacturer. Marwick's Pianos, Inc., sells the pianos to its customers at an average price of $3,125 each. The selling and administrative costs that the company incurs in a typical month are presented below:

Costs	Cost Formula
Selling:	
Advertising	$700 per month
Sales salaries and commissions	$950 per month, plus 8% of sales
Delivery of pianos to customers	$30 per piano sold
Utilities	$350 per month
Depreciation of sales facilities	$800 per month
Administrative:	
Executive salaries	$2,500 per month
Insurance	$400 per month
Clerical	$1,000 per month, plus $20 per piano sold
Depreciation of office equipment	$300 per month

During August, Marwick's Pianos, Inc., sold and delivered 40 pianos.

Required:

1. Prepare an income statement for Marwick's Pianos, Inc., for August. Use the traditional format, with costs organized by function.
2. Redo (1) above, this time using the contribution format, with costs organized by behaviour. Show costs and revenues on both a total and a per unit basis down through contribution margin.
3. Refer to the income statement you prepared in (2) above. Why might it be misleading to show the fixed costs on a per unit basis?

PROBLEM 5–15 (Appendix 5A) Least-Squares Regression Method Scattergram; Cost Behaviour [LO1, LO2, LO6]

Professor John Morton has just been appointed chairperson of the Finance Department at Westland University. In reviewing the department's cost records, Professor Morton has found the following total cost associated with Finance 101 over the last several terms:

	A	B	C	D
1	*Term*	*Number of Sections Offered*	*Total Cost*	
2	Fall, last year	4	$10,000	
3	Winter, last year	6	$14,000	
4	Summer, last year	2	$7,000	
5	Fall, this year	5	$13,000	
6	Winter, this year	3	$9,500	
7				

Professor Morton knows that there are some variable costs, such as amounts paid to graduate assistants, associated with the course. He would like to have the variable and fixed costs separated for planning purposes.

Required:

1. Using the least-squares regression method, estimate the variable cost per section and the total fixed cost per term for Finance 101.
2. Express the cost data derived in (1) above in the linear equation form $Y = a + bX$.
3. Assume that because of the small number of sections offered during the Winter Term this year, Professor Morton will have to offer eight sections of Finance 101 during the Fall Term. Compute the expected total cost for Finance 101. Can you see any problem with using the cost formula from (2) above to derive this total cost figure? Explain.
4. Prepare a scattergram and fit a line to the plotted points using the cost formula expressed in (2) above.

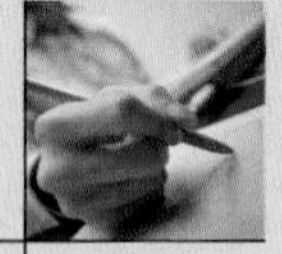

PROBLEM 5–16 Identifying Cost Behaviour Patterns [LO1]

A number of graphs displaying cost behaviour patterns are shown below. The vertical axis on each graph represents total cost, and the horizontal axis represents level of activity (volume).

Required:

1. For each of the following situations, identify the graph below that illustrates the cost behaviour pattern involved. Any graph may be used more than once.
   a. Cost of raw materials used.
   b. Electricity bill—a flat fixed charge, plus a variable cost after a certain number of kilowatt-hours are used.
   c. City water bill, which is computed as follows:

First 1,000,000 litres or less	$1,000 flat fee
Next 10,000 litres	$0.003 per litre used
Next 10,000 litres	$0.006 per litre used
Next 10,000 litres	$0.009 per litre used
Etc.	Etc.

   d. Depreciation of equipment, where the amount is computed by the straight-line method. When the depreciation rate was established, it was anticipated that the obsolescence factor would be greater than the wear and tear factor.
   e. Rent on a factory building donated by the city, where the agreement calls for a fixed fee payment unless 200,000 labour-hours or more are worked, in which case no rent need be paid.

f. Salaries of maintenance workers, where one maintenance worker is needed for every 1,000 hours of machine-hours or less (that is, 0 to 1,000 hours requires one maintenance worker, 1,001 to 2,000 hours requires two maintenance workers, etc.)

g. Cost of raw materials, where the cost starts at $7.50 per unit and then decreases by 5 cents per unit for each of the first 100 units purchased, after which it remains constant at $2.50 per unit.

h. Rent on a factory building donated by the county, where the agreement calls for rent of $100,000 less $1 for each direct labour-hour worked in excess of 200,000 hours, but a minimum rental payment of $20,000 must be paid.

i. Use of a machine under a lease, where a minimum charge of $1,000 is paid for up to 400 hours of machine time. After 400 hours of machine time, an additional charge of $2 per hour is paid up to a maximum charge of $2,000 per period.

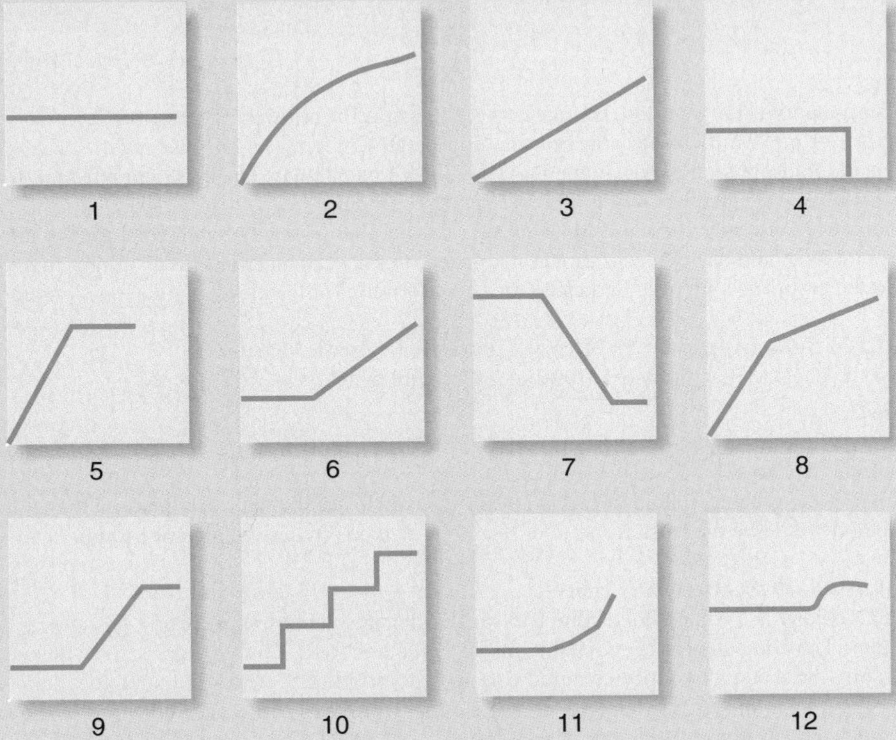

2. How would a knowledge of cost behaviour patterns such as those above be of help to a manager in analyzing the cost structure of his or her company?

(CPA, adapted)

PROBLEM 5–17 High-Low and Scattergram Analysis [LO2, LO3]

Pleasant View Hospital of British Columbia has just hired a new chief administrator who is anxious to employ sound management and planning techniques in the business affairs of the hospital. Accordingly, she has directed her assistant to summarize the cost structure of the various departments so that data will be available for planning purposes.

The assistant is unsure how to classify the utilities costs in the Radiology Department since these costs do not exhibit either strictly variable or fixed cost behaviour. Utilities costs are very high in the department due to a CAT scanner that draws a large amount of power and is kept running at all times. The scanner can't be turned off due to the long warm-up period required for its use. When the scanner is used to scan a patient, it consumes an additional burst of power. The assistant has accumulated data on utilities costs and use of the scanner since the first of the year, shown on p. 212.

The chief administrator has informed her assistant that the utilities cost is probably a mixed cost that will have to be broken down into its variable and fixed cost elements by use of a scattergram. The assistant feels, however, that if an analysis of this type is necessary, then the high-low method should be used, since it is easier and quicker. The controller has suggested that there may be a better approach.

Month	Number of Scans	Utilities Cost
January	60	$2,200
February	70	$2,600
March	90	$2,900
April	120	$3,300
May	100	$3,000
June	130	$3,600
July	150	$4,000
August	140	$3,600
September	110	$3,100
October	80	$2,500

Required:

1. Using the high-low method, estimate a cost formula for utilities. Express the formula in the form $Y = a + bX$. (The variable rate should be stated in terms of cost per scan.)
2. Use the formula for a and b shown in Appendix 5A to calculate the slope and intercept for the cost behaviour equation. (Hint: you will need to compute $\sum x$, $\sum y$, $\sum x^*y$, $\sum x^2$)
3. Prepare a scattergram using the data above. (The number of scans should be placed on the horizontal axis, and utilities cost should be placed on the vertical axis.) Fit a straight line to the plotted points using a ruler and estimate a cost formula for utilities using the quick method.

PROBLEM 5–18 (Appendix 5A) Least-Squares Regression Method [LO6]

Refer to the data for Pleasant View Hospital in Problem 5–17.

Required:

1. Using the least-squares regression method, estimate a cost formula for utilities. (Round the variable cost to two decimal places.)
2. Refer to the graph prepared in part (3) of Problem 5–17. Explain why in this case the high-low method would be the least accurate of the three methods in deriving a cost formula.

PROBLEM 5–19 Scattergram Analysis [LO2]

Molina Company is a value-added computer resaler that specializes in providing services to small companies. The company owns and maintains several autos for use by the sales staff. All expenses of operating these autos have been entered into an Automobile Expense account on the company's books. Along with this record of expenses, the company has also kept a careful record of the number of miles the autos have been driven each month.

The company's records of kilometres driven and total auto expenses over the past 10 months are given below:

Month	Total Kilometres (000)	Total Cost
January	4	$3,000
February	8	$3,700
March	7	$3,300
April	12	$4,000
May	6	$3,300
June	11	$3,900
July	14	$4,200
August	10	$3,600
September	13	$4,100
October	15	$4,400

Molina Company's president wants to know the cost of operating the fleet of cars in terms of the fixed monthly cost and the variable cost per kilometre driven.

Required:

1. Prepare a scattergram using the data given above. Place cost on the vertical axis and activity (kilometres driven) on the horizontal axis. Using a ruler, fit a straight line to the plotted points.

2. Estimate the fixed cost per month and the variable cost per kilometre driven using the quick method.

PROBLEM 5–20 (Appendix 5A) Least-Squares Regression Method [LO6]

Refer to the data for Molina Company in Problem 5–19.

Required:

1. Using the least-squares regression method, estimate the variable and fixed cost elements associated with the company's fleet of autos. (Since the Total Mileage is in thousands of kilometres, the variable cost you compute will also be in thousands of kilometres. The cost can be left in this form, or you can convert it to a per kilometre basis by dividing the cost you get by 1,000.)
2. From the data in (1) above, express the cost formula for auto use in the linear equation form $Y = a + bX$.

PROBLEM 5–21 (Appendix 5A) Least-Squares Regression Analysis; Contribution Format Income Statement [LO5, LO6]

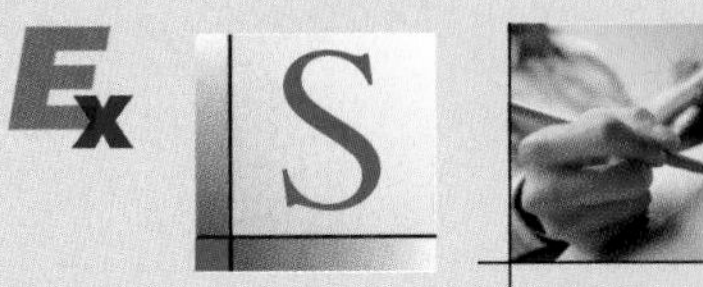

Milden Company has an exclusive franchise to purchase a product from the manufacturer and distribute it on the retail level. As an aid in planning, the company has decided to start using the contribution format income statement internally. To have data to prepare such a statement, the company has analyzed its expenses and developed the following cost formulas:

Cost	Cost Formula
Cost of good sold	$35 per unit sold
Advertising expense	$210,000 per quarter
Sales commissions	6% of sales
Shipping expense	?
Administrative salaries	$145,000 per quarter
Insurance expense	$9,000 per quarter
Depreciation expense	$76,000 per quarter

Management has concluded that shipping expense is a mixed cost, containing both variable and fixed cost elements. Units sold and the related shipping expense over the last eight quarters follow:

Quarter	Units Sold (000)	Shipping Expense
Year 1:		
First	10	$119,000
Second	16	$175,000
Third	18	$190,000
Fourth	15	$164,000
Year 2:		
First	11	$130,000
Second	17	$185,000
Third	20	$210,000
Fourth	13	$147,000

Milden Company's president would like a cost formula derived for shipping expense so that a budgeted income statement using the contribution approach can be prepared for the next quarter.

Required:

1. Using the least-squares regression method, estimate a cost formula for shipping expense. (Since the Units Sold above are in thousands of units, the variable cost you compute will also be in thousands of units. It can be left in this form, or you can convert your variable cost to a per unit basis by dividing it by 1,000.)
2. In the first quarter of Year 3, the company plans to sell 12,000 units at a selling price of $100 per unit. Prepare a contribution format income statement for the quarter.

PROBLEM 5–22 High-Low Method; Cost of Goods Manufactured [LO1, LO3]

Amfac Company manufactures a single product. The company keeps careful records of manufacturing activities from which the following information has been extracted:

	Level of Activity	
	March–Low	June–High
Number of units produced	6,000	9,000
Cost of goods manufactured	$168,000	$257,000
Work in process inventory, beginning	$9,000	$32,000
Work in process inventory, ending	$15,000	$21,000
Direct materials cost per unit	$6	$6
Direct labour cost per unit	$10	$10
Manufacturing overhead cost, total	?	?

The company's manufacturing overhead cost consists of both variable and fixed cost elements. To have data available for planning, management wants to determine how much of the overhead cost is variable with units produced and how much of it is fixed per month.

Required:

1. For both March and June, estimate the amount of manufacturing overhead cost added to production. The company had no under- or overapplied overhead in either month. (Hint: A useful way to proceed might be to construct a schedule of cost of goods manufactured.)
2. Using the high-low method, estimate a cost formula for manufacturing overhead. Express the variable portion of the formula in terms of a variable rate per unit of product.
3. If 7,000 units are produced during a month, what would be the cost of goods manufactured? (Assume that work in process inventories do not change and that there is no under- or overapplied overhead cost for the month.)

PROBLEM 5–23 High-Low Method; Predicting Cost [LO1, LO3]

Sawaya Co., Ltd., of Japan is a manufacturing company whose total factory overhead costs fluctuate considerably from year to year according to increases and decreases in the number of direct labour-hours worked in the factory. Total factory overhead costs (in Japanese yen, denoted ¥) at high and low levels of activity for recent years are given below:

	Level of Activity	
	Low	High
Direct labour-hours	50,000	75,000
Total factory overhead costs	¥14,250,000	¥17,625,000

The factory overhead costs above consist of indirect materials, rent, and maintenance. The company has analyzed these costs at the 50,000-hour level of activity as follows:

Indirect materials (variable)	¥5,000,000
Rent (fixed)	6,000,000
Maintenance (mixed)	3,250,000
Total factory overhead costs	¥14,250,000

To have data available for planning, the company wants to break down the maintenance cost into its variable and fixed cost elements.

Required:

1. Estimate how much of the ¥17,625,000 factory overhead cost at the high level of activity consists of maintenance cost. (Hint: To do this, it may be helpful to first determine how much of the ¥17,625,000 consists of indirect materials and rent. Think about the behaviour of variable and fixed costs!)
2. Using the high-low method, estimate a cost formula for maintenance.
3. What total factory overhead costs would you expect the company to incur at an operating level of 70,000 direct labour-hours?

PROBLEM 5–24 High-Low Method; Predicting Cost [LO1, LO3]
Nova Company's total overhead costs at various levels of activity are presented below:

Month	Machine-Hours	Total Overhead Costs
April	70,000	$198,000
May	60,000	$174,000
June	80,000	$222,000
July	90,000	$246,000

Assume that the total overhead costs above consist of utilities, supervisory salaries, and maintenance. The breakdown of these costs at the 60,000 machine-hour level of activity is:

Utilities (variable)	$ 48,000
Supervisory salaries (fixed)	21,000
Maintenance (mixed)	105,000
Total overhead costs	$174,000

Nova Company's management wants to break down the maintenance cost into its variable and fixed cost elements.

Required:

1. Estimate how much of the $246,000 of overhead cost in July was maintenance cost. (Hint: To do this, it may be helpful to first determine how much of the $246,000 consisted of utilities and supervisory salaries. Think about the behaviour of variable and fixed costs!)
2. Using the high-low method, estimate a cost formula for maintenance.
3. Express the company's *total* overhead costs in the linear equation form $Y = a + bX$.
4. What *total* overhead costs would you expect to be incurred at an operating activity level of 75,000 machine-hours?

CASES

CASE 5–25 (Appendix 5A) Analysis of Mixed Costs and Job-Order Costing [LO1, LO2, LO6]

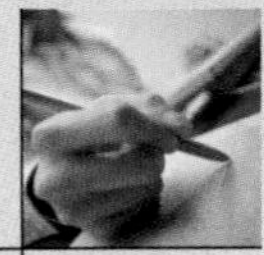

Hokuriku-Seika Co., Ltd., of Yokohama, Japan, is a subcontractor to local manufacturing companies. The company specializes in precision metal cutting using focused high-pressure water jets and high-energy lasers. The company has a traditional job-order costing system in which direct labour and direct materials costs are assigned directly to jobs, but factory overhead is applied to jobs using a predetermined overhead rate with direct labour-hours as the activity base. Management uses this job cost data for valuing cost of goods sold and inventories for external reports. For internal decision making, management has largely ignored this cost data since direct labour costs are basically fixed and management believes overhead costs actually have little to do with direct labour-hours. Recently, management has become interested in activity-based costing (ABC) as a way of estimating job costs and other costs for decision-making purposes.

Management assembled a cross-functional team to design a prototype ABC system. Electrical costs were among the first factory overhead costs investigated by the team. Electricity is used to provide light, to power equipment, and to heat the building in the winter and cool it in the summer. The ABC team proposed allocating electrical costs to jobs based on machine-hours since running the machines consumes significant amounts of electricity. Data assembled by the team concerning actual direct labour-hours, machine-hours, and electrical costs over a recent eight-week period follow. (The Japanese currency is the yen, which is denoted by ¥.)

	Direct Labour-Hours	Machine-Hours	Electrical Costs
Week 1	8,920	7,200	¥ 77,100
Week 2	8,810	8,200	84,400
Week 3	8,950	8,700	80,400
Week 4	8,990	7,200	75,500
Week 5	8,840	7,400	81,100
Week 6	8,890	8,800	83,300
Week 7	8,950	6,400	79,200
Week 8	8,990	7,700	85,500
Total	71,340	61,600	¥646,500

To help assess the effect of the proposed change to machine-hours as the allocation base, the eight-week totals were converted to annual figures by multiplying them by six.

	Direct Labour-Hours	Machine-Hours	Electrical Costs
Estimated annual total (eight-week total above × 6)	428,040	369,600	¥3,879,000

Required:

1. Assume that the estimated annual totals from the above table are used to compute the company's predetermined overhead rate. What would be the predetermined overhead rate for electrical costs if the allocation base is direct labour-hours? Machine-hours?
2. Hokuriku-Seika Co. intends to bid on a job for a shipyard that would require 350 direct labour-hours and 270 machine-hours. How much electrical cost would be charged to this job using the predetermined overhead rate computed in (1) above if the allocation base is direct labour-hours? Machine-hours?
3. Prepare a scattergram in which you plot direct labour-hours on the horizontal axis and electrical costs on the vertical axis. Prepare another scattergram in which you plot machine-hours on the horizontal axis and electrical costs on the vertical axis. Do you agree with the ABC team that machine-hours is a better allocation base for electrical costs than direct labour-hours? Why?
4. Using machine-hours as the measure of activity, estimate the fixed and variable components of electrical costs using least-squares regression.
5. How much electrical cost do you think would actually be caused by the shipyard job in (2) above? Explain.
6. What factors, apart from direct labour-hours and machine-hours, are likely to affect consumption of electrical power in the company?

CASE 5–26 Scattergram Analysis; Selection of an Activity Base [LO2]

Angora Wraps of Pendleton, Alberta, makes fine sweaters out of pure angora wool. The business is seasonal, with the largest demand during the fall, the winter, and Christmas holidays. The company must ramp up production each summer to meet estimated demand.

The company has been analyzing its costs to determine which costs are fixed and variable for planning purposes. Following are data for the company's activity and direct labour costs over the last year.

The number of workdays varies from month to month due to the number of weekdays, holidays, and days of vacation in the month. The paid days include paid vacations (in July) and paid holidays (in November and December). The number of units produced in a month varies depending on demand and the number of workdays in the month.

The company has eight workers who are classified as direct labour.

Month	Thousands of Units Produced	Number of Paid Days	Direct Labour Cost
January	98	20	$14,162
February	76	20	$12,994
March	75	21	$15,184
April	80	22	$15,038
May	85	22	$15,768
June	102	21	$15,330
July	52	19	$13,724
August	136	21	$14,162
September	138	22	$15,476
October	132	23	$15,476
November	86	18	$12,972
December	56	21	$14,074

Required:

1. Plot the direct labour cost and units produced on a scattergram. (Place cost on the vertical axis and units produced on the horizontal axis.)
2. Plot the direct labour cost and number of paid days on a scattergram. (Place cost on the vertical axis and the number of paid days on the horizontal axis.)
3. Which measure of activity—number of units produced or paid days—should be used as the activity base for explaining direct labour cost? Explain

CASE 5–27 Analysis of Mixed Costs in a Pricing Decision [LO1 and LO2, LO3, or LO6]

Maria Chavez owns a catering company that serves food and beverages at parties and business functions. Chavez's business is seasonal, with a heavy schedule during the summer months and holidays and a lighter schedule at other times.

One of the major events Chavez's customers request is a cocktail party. She offers a standard cocktail party and has estimated the cost per guest as follows:

Food and beverages	$15.00
Labour (0.5 hrs. @ $10.00/hr.)	5.00
Overhead (0.5 hrs. @ $13.98/hr.)	6.99
Total cost per guest	$26.99

The standard cocktail party lasts three hours and Chavez hires one worker for every six guests, so that works out to one-half hour of labour per guest. These workers are hired only as needed and are paid only for the hours they actually work.

When bidding on cocktail parties, Chavez adds a 15% markup to yield a price of about $31 per guest. She is confident about her estimates of the costs of food and beverages and labour but is not as comfortable with the estimate of overhead cost. The $13.98 overhead cost per labour hour was determined by dividing total overhead expenses for the last 12 months by total labour hours for the same period. Monthly data concerning overhead costs and labour-hours follow:

Month	Labour-Hours	Overhead Expenses
January	2,500	$ 55,000
February	2,800	59,000
March	3,000	60,000
April	4,200	64,000
May	4,500	67,000
June	5,500	71,000
July	6,500	74,000
August	7,500	77,000

continued

September	7,000	75,000
October	4,500	68,000
November	3,100	62,000
December	6,500	73,000
Total	57,600	$805,000

Chavez has received a request to bid on a 180-guest fund-raising cocktail party to be given next month by an important local charity. (The party would last the usual three hours.) She would like to win this contract because the guest list for this charity event includes many prominent individuals that she would like to land as future clients. Maria is confident that these potential customers would be favourably impressed by her company's services at the charity event.

Required:

1. Estimate the contribution to profit of a standard 180-guest cocktail party if Chavez charges her usual price of $31 per guest. (In other words, by how much would her overall profit increase?)
2. How low could Chavez bid for the charity event in terms of a price per guest and still not lose money on the event itself?
3. The individual who is organizing the charity's fund-raising event has indicated that he has already received a bid under $30 from another catering company. Do you think Chavez should bid below her normal $31 per guest price for the charity event? Why or why not?

(CMA, adapted)

CASE 5–28 (Appendix 5A) Mixed Cost Analysis Using Three Methods [LO2, LO3, LO6]

The Ramon Company manufactures a wide range of products at several locations. The Franklin plant, which manufactures electrical components, has been experiencing difficulties with fluctuating monthly overhead costs. These fluctuations have made it difficult to estimate the level of overhead that will be incurred for a month.

Management wants to be able to estimate overhead costs accurately to better plan its operational and financial needs. A trade publication indicates that for companies manufacturing electrical components, overhead tends to vary with direct labour-hours, but may contain both fixed and variable elements.

A member of the accounting staff has suggested that a good starting place for determining the cost behaviour of overhead costs would be an analysis of historical data. The methods that have been proposed for determining the cost behaviour pattern include high-low, scattergram, and least-squares regression. Data on direct labour-hours and overhead costs have been collected for the past two years. The raw data are as follows:

	Last Year		This Year	
Month	Direct Labour-Hours	Overhead Costs	Direct Labour-Hours	Overhead Costs
January	20,000	$84,000	21,000	$86,000
February	25,000	$99,000	24,000	$93,000
March	22,000	$89,500	23,000	$93,000
April	23,000	$90,000	22,000	$87,000
May	20,000	$81,500	20,000	$80,000
June	19,000	$75,500	18,000	$76,500
July	14,000	$70,500	12,000	$67,500
August	10,000	$64,500	13,000	$71,000
September	12,000	$69,000	15,000	$73,500
October	17,000	$75,000	17,000	$72,500
November	16,000	$71,500	15,000	$71,000
December	19,000	$78,000	18,000	$75,000

All equipment in the Franklin plant is leased under an arrangement calling for a flat fee up to 19,500 direct labour-hours, after which lease charges are assessed on an hourly basis. Lease expense is a major element of overhead cost.

Required:

1. Using the high-low method, estimate the cost formula for overhead in the Franklin plant.
2. Repeat (1) above, this time using the least-squares regression method.
3. Prepare a scattergram using all of the data for the two-year period. Fit a straight line or lines to the plotted points using a ruler. In this part it is not necessary to compute the fixed and variable cost elements.
4. Assume that the Franklin plant works 22,500 direct labour-hours during a month. Estimate the expected overhead cost for the month using the cost formulas developed above with:
   a. The high-low method.
   b. The least-squares regression method.
   c. The scattergram method [read the expected costs directly off the graph prepared in (3) above].
5. Of the three proposed methods, explain which one the Ramon Company should use to estimate monthly overhead costs in the Franklin plant. Explain why the other methods are less desirable.

(CMA, adapted)

GROUP AND INTERNET EXERCISES

GROUP EXERCISE 5–29 Variable and Fixed Costs in Practice

Form a team to investigate how an organization in your area handles variable and fixed costs. It may be in any industry and can be a business, a not-for-profit organization, or a part of the government. Research the organization on the Web and in periodicals to learn what the organization does and how it has performed financially. Make an appointment to meet with the controller, chief financial officer, or with another top manager who is familiar with the financial side of the organization. After meeting with that individual, write a memo in which you discuss the following issues.

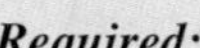

Required:

1. Does the organization distinguish between variable and fixed costs in planning and controlling operations? If not, why not?
2. If the organization does distinguish between variable and fixed costs, how are variable and fixed costs estimated? What activity bases are used? How are these activity bases selected? What method does the company use for estimating the variable cost per unit of activity? How often are these estimates made? Does the company prepare scattergrams of past cost and activity data?
3. If the organization does distinguish between variable and fixed costs, how does this help managers in planning and controlling operations?

INTERNET EXERCISE 5–30

As you know, the World Wide Web is a medium that is constantly evolving. Sites come and go, and change without notice. To enable the periodic updating of site addresses, this problem has been posted to the textbook Web site (www.mcgrawhill.ca/college/garrison). After accessing the site, enter the Student Centre and select this chapter. Select and complete the Internet Exercise.

CHAPTER 6

LEARNING OBJECTIVES

After studying Chapter 6, you should be able to:

1. Explain how changes in activity affect contribution margin and operating income.
2. Prepare and interpret a cost-volume-profit (CVP) graph.
3. Use contribution margin (CM) ratio and variation of other CVP elements to analyze the effect on operating income.
4. Compute the break-even point and the level of sales to achieve a desired target profit.
5. Determine the margin of safety and the degree of operating leverage.
6. Compute the break-even point for a multiple-product company and explain the effects of shifts in the sales mix on contribution margin and the break-even point.
7. (Appendix 6A) Construct cost-volume-profit analysis with uncertainty.

COST-VOLUME-PROFIT RELATIONSHIPS

BUSINESS FOCUS

WHAT HAPPENED TO THE PROFIT?

The hospitality business represents a common place where CVP is applied. The quotation from Chip Conley below illustrates one such application.

Chip Conley is CEO of Joie de Vivre Hospitality, a company that owns and operates 28 hospitality businesses in northern California. Conley summed up the company's experience after the dot.com crash and 9/11 as follows: "In the history of American hotel markets, no hotel market has ever seen a drop in revenues as precipitous as the one in San Francisco and Silicon Valley in the last two years. On average, hotel revenues . . . dropped 40% to 45%. . . . We've been fortunate that our breakeven point is lower than our competition's. . . . But the problem is that the hotel business is a fixed-cost business. So in an environment where you have those precipitous drops and our costs are moderately fixed, our net incomes—well, they're not incomes anymore, they're losses."

Source: Karen Dillon, "Shop Talk," *Inc*, December 2002, pp. 111–114.

Cost-volume-profit (CVP) analysis is a powerful tool that managers have at their command. It helps them understand the interrelationship among cost, volume, and profit in an organization by focusing on interactions among the following five elements:

1. Prices of products.
2. Volume or level of activity.
3. Per unit variable costs.
4. Total fixed costs.
5. Mix of products sold.

Because CVP analysis helps managers understand the interrelationship among cost, volume, and profit, it is a vital tool in many business decisions. These decisions include, for example, what products to manufacture or sell, what pricing policy to follow, what marketing strategy to employ, and what type of production facilities to acquire. Careful study of the elements and assumptions, however, is needed to avoid mistakes and to know when to extend the ideas presented in this chapter to correct for more complex situations. One area of potential confusion left in the discussion to follow is the use of the terms profits and income interchangeably. This confused terminology is not corrected because the older term *profit* is often used to mean *income* by both managers and accountants.

To help understand the role of CVP analysis in business decisions, consider the case of Acoustic Concepts, Inc., a company founded by Prem Narayan.

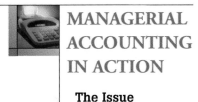

MANAGERIAL ACCOUNTING IN ACTION

The Issue

Prem, a graduate engineering student at the time, started Acoustic Concepts to market a radical new speaker that he had designed for automobile sound systems. The speaker, called the Sonic Blaster, uses an advanced microprocessor chip to boost amplification to awesome levels. Prem contracted with a Taiwanese electronics manufacturer to produce the speaker. With seed money provided by his family, Prem placed an order with the manufacturer for completed units and ran advertisements in auto magazines.

The Sonic Blaster was an almost immediate success, and sales grew to the point that Prem moved the company's headquarters out of his apartment and into rented quarters in a neighbouring industrial park. He also hired a receptionist, an accountant, a sales manager, and a small sales staff to sell the speakers to retail stores. The accountant, Bob Luchinni, had worked for several small companies where he had acted as a business advisor as well as accountant and bookkeeper. The following discussion occurred soon after Bob was hired:

Prem: Bob, I've got a lot of questions about the company's finances that I hope you can help answer.

Bob: The business is in great shape. The loan from your family will be paid off within a few months.

Prem: I know, but I am worried about the risks I've taken on by expanding operations. What would happen if a competitor entered the market and our sales slipped? How far could sales drop without putting us into the red? Another question I've been trying to resolve is how much our sales would have to increase in order to justify the big marketing campaign the sales staff is pushing for.

Bob: Marketing always wants more money for advertising.

Prem: And they are always pushing me to drop the selling price on the speaker. I agree with them that a lower price will boost our volume, but I'm not sure the increased volume will offset the loss in revenue from the lower price.

Bob: It sounds like these questions all are related in some way to the relationships between our selling prices, our costs, and our volume. We shouldn't have a problem coming up with some answers. I'll need a day or two, though, to gather some data.

Prem: Why don't we set up a meeting for three days from now? That would be Thursday.

Bob: That'll be fine. I'll have some preliminary answers for you as well as a model you can use for answering similar questions in the future.

Prem: Good. I'll be looking forward to seeing what you come up with.

THE BASICS OF COST-VOLUME-PROFIT (CVP) ANALYSIS

Bob Luchinni's preparation for the Thursday meeting begins where our study of cost behaviour in the preceding chapter left off—with the contribution income statement. The contribution income statement emphasizes the behaviour of costs and therefore is extremely helpful to a manager in judging the impact on profits of changes in selling price, cost, or volume. Bob will base his analysis on the following contribution income statement he prepared last month:

ACOUSTIC CONCEPTS, INC.
Contribution Income Statement
For the Month of June

	Total	Per Unit
Sales (400 speakers)	$100,000	$250
Less variable expenses	60,000	150
Contribution margin	40,000	$100
Less fixed expenses	35,000	
Operating income*	$ 5,000	

*Operating income less interest expense less income tax expense equals net income.

This contribution income statement was prepared for management's use inside the company and would not ordinarily be made available to those outside the company. Note that this statement reports sales, variable expenses, and contribution margin on both a per unit basis and a total basis. These per unit figures will be very helpful for performing the costs-volume-profit analysis that we will be studying over the next several pages. Also, note that we use operating income as our measure of profit. We ignore income taxes throughout most of this chapter so that we can more easily focus on the central issues of cost-volume-profit analysis.

Contribution Margin

LEARNING OBJECTIVE 1
Explain how changes in activity affect contribution margin and operating income.

As explained in Chapter 5, contribution margin is the amount remaining from sales revenue after variable expenses have been deducted. Thus, it is the amount available to cover fixed expenses and then to provide profits for the period. Notice the sequence here—contribution margin is used *first* to cover the fixed expenses, and then whatever remains goes toward profits. If the contribution margin is not sufficient to cover the fixed expenses, then a loss occurs for the period. To illustrate with an extreme example, assume that by the middle of a particular month Acoustic Concepts has been able to sell only one speaker. At that point, the company's income statement will appear as follows:

	Total	Per Unit
Sales (1 speaker)	$ 250	$250
Less variable expenses	150	150
Contribution margin	100	$100
Less fixed expenses	35,000	
Operating loss	$(34,900)	

For each additional speaker that the company is able to sell during the month, $100 more in contribution margin will become available to help cover the fixed expenses. If a second speaker is sold, for example, then the total contribution margin will increase by $100 (to a total of $200) and the company's operating loss will decrease by $100, to $34,800:

	Total	Per Unit
Sales (2 speakers)	$ 500	$250
Less variable expenses	300	150
Contribution margin	200	$100
Less fixed expenses	35,000	
Operating loss	$(34,800)	

If enough speakers can be sold to generate $35,000 in contribution margin, then all of the fixed costs will be covered and the company will have managed to at least *break even* for the month—that is, to show neither profit nor loss but just cover all of its costs. To reach the break-even point, the company will have to sell 350 speakers in a month, since each speaker sold yields $100 in contribution margin:

	Total	Per Unit
Sales (350 speakers)	$87,500	$250
Less variable expenses	52,500	150
Contribution margin	35,000	$100
Less fixed expenses	35,000	
Operating income	$ –0–	

Computation of the break-even point is discussed in detail later in the chapter; for the moment, note that the **break-even point** is the level of sales at which profit is zero.

Break-even point The level of sales at which profit is zero. The break-even point can also be defined as the point where total sales equals total expenses or as the point where total contribution margin equals total fixed expenses.

Once the break-even point has been reached, operating income will increase by the unit contribution margin for each additional unit sold. If 351 speakers are sold in a month, for example, then we can expect that the operating income for the month will be $100, since the company will have sold 1 speaker more than the number needed to break even:

	Total	Per Unit
Sales (351 speakers)	$87,750	$250
Less variable expenses	52,650	150
Contribution margin	35,100	$100
Less fixed expenses	35,000	
Operating income	$ 100	

If 352 speakers are sold (2 speakers above the break-even point), then we can expect that the operating income for the month will be $200, and so forth. To know what the profits will be at various levels of activity, therefore, it is not necessary for a manager to prepare a whole series of income statements. The manager can simply take the number of units to be sold over the break-even point and multiply that number by the unit contribution margin. The result represents the anticipated operating profits for the period. Or, to estimate the effect of a planned increase in sales on profits, the manager can simply multiply the increase in units sold by the unit contribution margin. The result will be the expected increase in operating profits. To illustrate, if Acoustic Concepts is currently selling 400 speakers per month and plans to increase sales to 425 speakers per month, the anticipated effect on operating profits can be computed as follows:

Increased number of speakers to be sold	25
Contribution margin per speaker	×$100
Increase in operating income	$2,500

These calculations can be verified as follows:

	Sales Volume			
	400 Speakers	425 Speakers	Difference 25 Speakers	Per Unit
Sales	$100,000	$106,250	$6,250	$250
Less variable expenses	60,000	63,750	3,750	150
Contribution margin	40,000	42,500	2,500	$100
Less fixed expenses	35,000	35,000	-0-	
Operating income	$ 5,000	$ 7,500	$2,500	

To summarize these examples, if there were no sales, the company's loss would equal its fixed expenses. Each unit that is sold reduces the loss by the amount of the unit contribution margin. Once the break-even point has been reached, each additional unit sold increases the company's operating profit by the amount of the unit contribution margin.

The simplified income statements for Acoustic Concepts illustrate the fundamentals of cost-volume-profit. Simplifications such as sales driving expenses, fixed expenses remaining fixed even for large changes in sales volumes, and the fact that no limits exist for sales levels are a few assumptions often used in even complex situations. Such simplifications permit a preliminary examination of alternatives. The contribution income statement can always be made more complex using computer spreadsheets so that "what if" analysis can be made more realistic.

FOCUS *on Current Practice*

Embraer is a competitor to Bombardier Inc. Embraer, Empresa Brasileira de Aeronautica SA, has a 100-seat aircraft known as the JB001 that it expects to deliver to Jet Blue, a New York discount carrier.

An analysis of the potential benefits of the new aircraft is provided for the New York to Richmond, Virginia, route. The current fare is suggested to be $200 each way. The new aircraft provides an opportunity to cut the fare to $90 each way and to triple the customers.

Why is Jet Blue excited about the new aircraft? Does cost-volume-profit provide an answer? Should other carriers be concerned?

Source: Sean Silcoff, "Embraer Cracks New Markets," *National Post*, March 29, 2005, pp. FP1 and FP6.

CVP Relationships in Graphic Form

LEARNING OBJECTIVE 2
Prepare and interpret a cost-volume-profit (CVP) graph.

Relationships among revenue, cost, profit, and volume can be expressed graphically by preparing a **cost-volume-profit graph**. A CVP graph highlights CVP relationships over wide ranges of activity and can give managers a perspective that can be obtained in no other way. To help explain his analysis to Prem Narayan, Bob Luchinni decided to prepare a CVP graph for Acoustic Concepts.

Cost-volume-profit (CVP) graph The relationships among revenues, costs, and level of activity in an organization presented in graphic form.

Preparing the CVP Graph In a CVP graph (sometimes called a *break-even chart*), unit volume is commonly represented on the horizontal x-axis and dollars on the vertical y-axis. Preparing a CVP graph involves three steps. These steps are keyed to the graph in Exhibit 6–1.

1. Draw a line parallel to the volume axis to represent total fixed expenses. For Acoustic Concepts, total fixed expenses are $35,000.
2. Choose some volume of sales and plot the point representing total expenses (fixed and variable) at the activity level you have selected. In Exhibit 6–1, Bob Luchinni chose a volume of 600 speakers. Total expenses at that activity level would be as follows:

Fixed expenses	$ 35,000
Variable expenses (600 speakers × $150)	90,000
Total expenses	$125,000

   After the point has been plotted, draw a line through it back to the point where the fixed expenses line intersects the dollars axis.
3. Again choose some volume of sales and plot the point representing total sales dollars at the activity level you have selected. In Exhibit 6–1, Bob Luchinni again chose a volume of 600 speakers. Sales at that activity level total $150,000 (600 speakers × $250). Draw a line through this point back to the origin.

The interpretation of the completed CVP graph is given in Exhibit 6–2. The anticipated profit or loss at any given level of sales is measured by the vertical distance between the total revenue line (sales) and the total expenses line (variable expenses plus fixed expenses).

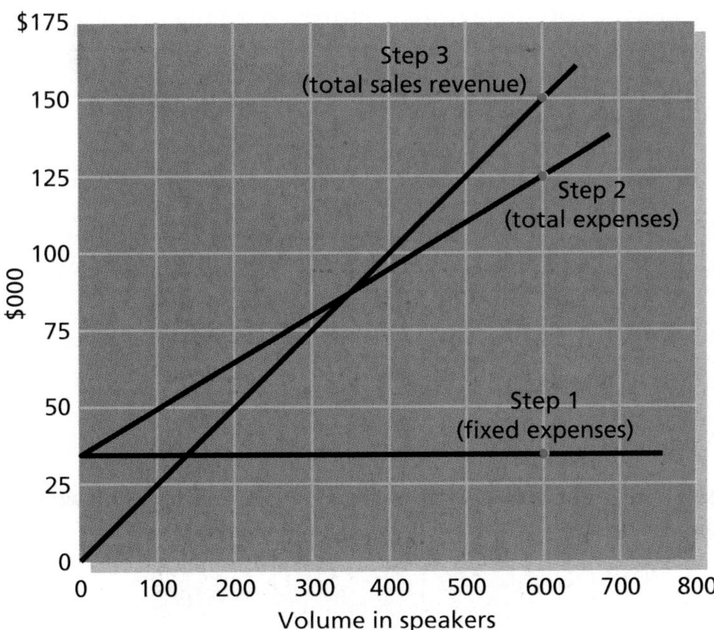

EXHIBIT 6–1 Preparing the CVP graph

EXHIBIT 6–2 The Completed CVP Graph

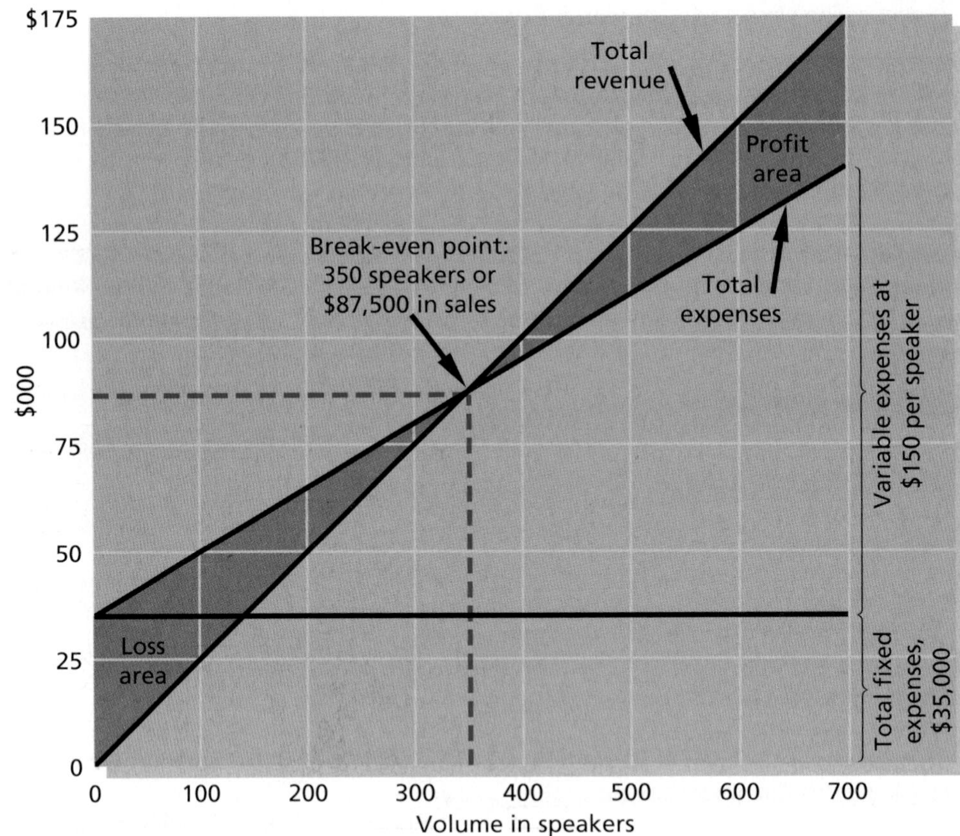

The break-even point is where the total revenue and total expenses lines cross. The break-even point of 350 speakers in Exhibit 6–2 agrees with the break-even point obtained for Acoustic Concepts in earlier computations.

LEARNING OBJECTIVE **3**
Use contribution margin (CM) ratio and variation of other CVP elements to analyze the effect on operating income.

Contribution Margin (CM) Ratio

In the previous section, we explored how cost-volume-profit relationships can be visualized. In this section, we will see how the contribution margin can be used in cost-volume-profit calculations. As the first step, we have added a column to Acoustic Concepts' contribution income statement, in which sales revenues, variable expenses, and contribution margin are expressed as a percentage of sales:

	Total	Per Unit	Percent of Sales
Sales (400 speakers)	$100,000	$250	100%
Less variable expenses	60,000	150	60%
Contribution margin	40,000	$100	40%
Less fixed expenses	35,000		
Operating income	$ 5,000		

Contribution margin (CM) ratio The contribution margin as a percentage of total sales.

The contribution margin as a percentage of total sales is referred to as the **contribution margin (CM) ratio.** This ratio is computed as follows:

$$\text{CM ratio} = \frac{\text{Contribution margin}}{\text{Sales}}$$

For Acoustic Concepts, the computations are:

$$\frac{\text{Total contribution margin, \$40,000}}{\text{Total sales, \$100,000}} = 40\% \quad \text{or} \quad \frac{\text{Per unit contribution margin, \$100}}{\text{Per unit sales, \$250}} = 40\%$$

The CM ratio is extremely useful since it shows how the contribution margin will be affected by a change in total sales. To illustrate, notice that Acoustic Concepts has a CM ratio of 40%. This means that for each dollar increase in sales, total contribution margin will increase by 40 cents ($1 sales × CM ratio of 40%). Operating income will also increase by 40 cents, assuming that fixed costs do not change.

As this illustration suggests, *the effect on operating income of any given dollar change in total sales can be computed in seconds by simply applying the CM ratio to the dollar change.* For example, if Acoustic Concepts plans a $30,000 increase in sales during the coming month, the contribution margin will increase by $12,000 ($30,000 increased sales × CM ratio of 40%). As we noted above, operating income will also increase by $12,000 if fixed costs do not change. This is verified by the following table:

	Sales Volume			
	Present	**Expected**	**Increase**	**Percent of Sales**
Sales	$100,000	$130,000	$30,000	100%
Less variable expenses	60,000	78,000*	18,000	60%
Contribution margin	40,000	52,000	12,000	40%
Less fixed expenses	35,000	35,000	–0–	
Operating income	$ 5,000	$ 17,000	$12,000	

*$130,000 expected sales ÷ $250 per unit = 520 units. 520 units × $150 per unit = $78,000. Alternatively (1 – .40) × $130,000 = $78,000.

Some managers prefer to work with the CM ratio rather than the unit contribution margin. The CM ratio is particularly valuable in those situations where trade-offs must be made between more dollar sales of one product versus more dollar sales of another. Generally speaking, when trying to increase sales, products that yield the greatest amount of contribution margin per dollar of sales should be emphasized.

CM ratio is also helpful when working with a group of products or services where units cannot be sensibly added. For example, selling dolls and doll houses together can be added in dollars but two dolls plus one doll house does not equal three units of doll products. Because companies often work on product lines, this type of problem is often encountered.

Some Applications of CVP Concepts

Bob Luchinni, the accountant at Acoustic Concepts, wanted to demonstrate to the company's president Prem Narayan how the concepts developed on the preceding pages of this text can be used in planning and decision making. Bob gathered the following basic data:

	Per Unit	**Percent of Sales**
Sales price	$250	100%
Less variable expenses	150	60%
Contribution margin	$100	40%

Recall that fixed expenses are $35,000 per month. Bob Luchinni will use these data to show the effects of changes in variable costs, fixed costs, sales price, and sales volume on the company's profitability.

Change in Fixed Cost and Sales Volume Acoustic Concepts is currently selling 400 speakers per month (monthly sales of $100,000). The sales manager feels that a $10,000 increase in the monthly advertising budget would increase monthly sales by $30,000. Should the advertising budget be increased? The following table shows the effect of the proposed change in monthly advertising budget:

	Current Sales	Sales with Additional Advertising Budget	Difference	Percent of Sales
Sales	$100,000	$130,000	$30,000	100%
Less variable expenses	60,000	78,000	18,000	60%
Contribution margin	40,000	52,000	12,000	40%
Less fixed expenses	35,000	45,000*	10,000	
Operating income	$ 5,000	$ 7,000	$ 2,000	

*$35,000 plus additional $10,000 monthly advertising budget = $45,000.

Assuming there are no other factors to be considered, the increase in the advertising budget should be approved since it would lead to an increase in operating income of $2,000. There are two shorter ways to present this solution. The first alternative solution follows:

Alternative Solution 1

Expected total contribution margin:	
$130,000 × 40% CM ratio	$52,000
Present total contribution margin:	
$100,000 × 40% CM ratio	40,000
Incremental contribution margin	12,000
Change in fixed costs:	
Less incremental advertising expense	10,000
Increased operating income	$ 2,000

Since in this case only the fixed costs and the sales volume change, the solution can be presented in an even shorter format, as follows:

Alternative Solution 2

Incremental contribution margin:	
$30,000 × 40% CM ratio	$12,000
Less incremental advertising expense	10,000
Increased operating income	$ 2,000

Incremental analysis
An analytical approach that focuses only on those items of revenue, cost, and volume that will change as a result of a decision.

Notice that this approach does not depend on a knowledge of previous sales. Also notice that it is unnecessary under either shorter approach to prepare an income statement. Both of the solutions above involve an **incremental analysis** in that they consider only those items of revenue, cost, and volume that will change if the new program is implemented. Although in each case a new income statement could have been prepared the incremental approach is simpler and more direct, and focuses attention on the specific items involved in the decision.

In economics, this incremental analysis is often termed *marginal analysis* because of the assumptions used in economics about the behaviour of revenues and costs. Accountants tend to use a more general term, *incremental*, so that less restrictive assumptions about the behaviour of revenues and costs can be made, for example step variable costs.

Change in Variable Costs and Sales Volume Refer to the original data. Recall that Acoustic Concepts is currently selling 400 speakers per month. Management is contemplating the use of higher-quality components, which would increase variable costs (and thereby reduce the contribution margin) by $10 per speaker. However, the sales manager predicts that the higher overall quality would increase sales to 480 speakers per month. Should the higher-quality components be used? The $10 increase in variable costs will decrease the unit contribution margin by $10—from $100 to $90.

Solution

Expected total contribution margin with higher-quality components:	
480 speakers × $90 per speaker	$43,200
Present total contribution margin:	
400 speakers × $100 per speaker	40,000
Increase in total contribution margin	$ 3,200

According to this analysis, the higher-quality components should be used. Since fixed costs will not change, the $3,200 increase in contribution margin shown above should result in a $3,200 increase in operating income.

Change in Fixed Cost, Sales Price, and Sales Volume Refer to the original data and recall again that the company is currently selling 400 speakers per month. To increase sales, the sales manager would like to cut the selling price by $20 per speaker and increase the advertising budget by $15,000 per month. The sales manager argues that if these two steps are taken, unit sales will increase by 50% to 600 speakers per month. Should the changes be made? A decrease of $20 per speaker in the selling price will cause the unit contribution margin to decrease from $100 to $80.

Solution

Expected total contribution margin with lower selling price:	
600 speakers × $80 per speaker	$48,000
Present total contribution margin:	
400 speakers × $100 per speaker	40,000
Incremental contribution margin	8,000
Change in fixed costs:	
Less incremental advertising expense	15,000
Reduction in operating income	$(7,000)

According to this analysis, the changes should not be made. The same solution can be obtained by preparing comparative income statements as shown at the top of page 230. Notice that the effect on operating income is the same as that obtained by the incremental analysis above.

	Present 400 Speakers per Month		Expected 600 Speakers per Month		
	Total	Per Unit	Total	Per Unit	Difference
Sales	$100,000	$250	$138,000	$230	$38,000
Less variable expenses	60,000	150	90,000	150	30,000
Contribution margin	40,000	$100	48,000	$ 80	8,000
Less fixed expenses	35,000		50,000*		15,000
Operating income (loss)	$ 5,000		$ (2,000)		$ (7,000)

*35,000 + Additional monthly advertising budget of $15,000 = $50,000.

Change in Variable Cost, Fixed Cost, and Sales Volume Refer to the original data. As before, the company is currently selling 400 speakers per month. The sales manager would like to place the sales staff on a commission basis of $15 per speaker sold, rather than on flat salaries that now total $6,000 per month. The sales manager is confident that the change will increase monthly sales by 15% to 460 speakers per month. Should the change be made?

Solution

Changing the sales staff from a salaried basis to a commission basis will affect both fixed and variable costs. Fixed costs will decrease by $6,000, from $35,000 to $29,000. Variable costs will increase by $15, from $150 to $165, and the unit contribution margin will decrease from $100 to $85.

Expected total contribution margin with sales staff on commission:	
460 speakers × $85 per speaker	$39,100
Present total contribution margin:	
400 speakers × $100 per speaker	40,000
Decrease in total contribution margin	(900)
Change in fixed costs:	
Add salaries avoided if a commission is paid	6,000
Increase in operating income	$ 5,100

According to this analysis, the change should be made. Again, the same answer can be obtained by preparing comparative income statements:

	Present 400 Speakers per Month		Expected 460 Speakers per Month		Difference: Increase or (Decrease) in Net Income
	Total	Per Unit	Total	Per Unit	
Sales	$100,000	$250	$115,000	$250	$15,000
Less variable expenses	60,000	150	75,900	165	(15,900)
Contribution margin	40,000	$100	39,100	$ 85	(900)
Less fixed expenses	35,000		29,000		6,000
Operating income	$ 5,000		$ 10,100		$ 5,100

Change in Regular Sales Price Refer to the original data where Acoustic Concepts is currently selling 400 speakers per month. The company has an opportunity to make a bulk sale of 150 speakers to a wholesaler if an acceptable price can be worked out. This sale would not disturb the company's regular sales. What price per speaker should be quoted to the wholesaler if Acoustic Concepts wants to increase its monthly profits by $3,000?

Variable cost per speaker	$150
Desired profit per speaker:	
$3,000 ÷ 150 speakers	20
Quoted price per speaker	$170

Notice that no fixed expenses are included in the computation. This is because fixed expenses are not affected by the bulk sale, so all of the additional revenue that is in excess of variable costs goes to increasing the profits of the company.

If Acoustic Concepts had been operating at a loss rather than at a profit, many managers would look at the situation somewhat differently. Instead of a modest profit of $3,000, many managers would attempt to reverse all or part of the company's overall loss by quoting a higher price. To illustrate this point, assume that Acoustic Concepts presently has a loss of $6,000 this month and that the company would like to make enough money on the bulk sale of speakers to turn this loss into a profit of $3,000. Under these circumstances, the quoted price on the 150 new speakers would be computed as shown below:

Variable cost per speaker	$150
Present net loss:	
$6,000 ÷ 150 speakers	40
Desired profit:	
$3,000 ÷ 150 speakers	20
Quoted price per speaker	$210

The $210 price we have computed represents a substantial discount from the $250 regular selling price per speaker. Thus, both the wholesaler and the company would benefit from the bulk order at this price. This will not always happen, however. By attempting to cover all of the company's losses on one special order, a manager may quote such a high price that the order is lost. Any price greater than $150 will help to reduce the company's loss. A manager must always keep such market considerations in mind when deciding on prices.

As noted above, this example assumes that the bulk order will not affect sales to regular customers. There may be serious strategic implications to accepting this bulk order if this assumption does not hold. Will negative consequences result from accepting this bulk order? For example, existing customers may find out about this order and demand the same low price, or they may simply buy from competitors. Will this bulk sale lead to more orders from the new customer? In summary, managers should consider both the short-term and long-range strategic effects before deciding to accept or reject the bulk order.

Importance of the Contribution Margin

As stated in the introduction to this chapter, CVP analysis seeks the most profitable combination of variable costs, fixed costs, selling price, and sales volume. The above examples show that the effect on the contribution margin is a major consideration in deciding on the most profitable combination of these factors. We have seen that profits can sometimes be improved by reducing the contribution margin if fixed costs can be reduced by a greater amount. More commonly, however, we have seen that the way to improve profits is to increase the total contribution margin figure. Sometimes this can be done by reducing the selling price and thereby increasing volume; sometimes it can be done by increasing the fixed costs (such as advertising) and thereby increasing volume; and sometimes it can be done by trading off variable and fixed costs with appropriate changes in volume. Many other combinations of factors are possible.

The size of the unit contribution margin figure (and the size of the CM ratio) will have a significant influence on what steps a company is willing to take to improve profits.

For example, the greater the unit contribution margin, the greater is the amount that a company will be willing to spend in order to increase unit sales. This explains in part why companies with high unit contribution margins (such as auto manufacturers) advertise so heavily, while companies with low unit contribution margins (such as dishware manufacturers) tend to spend much less for advertising.

In short, the effect on the contribution margin is the key to many decisions.

BREAK-EVEN ANALYSIS

LEARNING OBJECTIVE 4
Compute the break-even point and the level of sales to achieve a desired target profit.

CVP analysis is sometimes referred to simply as *break-even analysis*. This is unfortunate because break-even analysis is only one element of CVP analysis—although an important element. Break-even analysis is designed to answer questions such as those asked by Prem Narayan, the president of Acoustic Concepts, concerning how far sales could drop before the company begins to lose money.

Break-Even Computations

Earlier in the chapter, we defined the break-even point to be the level of sales at which the company's profit (operating income) is zero. The break-even point can be computed using either the *equation method* or the *contribution margin method*—the two methods are equivalent.

Equation method
A method of computing the break-even point that relies on the equation Sales = Variable expenses + Fixed expenses + Profits.

The Equation Method The **equation method** centres on the contribution approach to the income statement illustrated earlier in the chapter. The format of this income statement can be expressed in equation form as follows:

$$\text{Profits} = (\text{Sales} - \text{Variable expenses}) - \text{Fixed expenses}$$

Rearranging this equation slightly yields the following equation, which is widely used in CVP analysis:

$$\text{Sales} = \text{Variable expenses} + \text{Fixed expenses} + \text{Profits}$$

At the break-even point, profits are zero. Therefore, the break-even point can be computed by finding that point where sales just equal the total of the variable expenses plus the fixed expenses. For Acoustic Concepts, the break-even point in unit sales, Q, can be computed as follows:

$$\text{Sales} = \text{Variable expenses} + \text{Fixed expenses} + \text{Profits}$$

$$\begin{aligned} \$250Q &= \$150Q + \$35{,}000 + \$0 \\ \$100Q &= \$35{,}000 \\ Q &= \$35{,}000 \div 100 \\ Q &= 350 \text{ speakers} \end{aligned}$$

where:

Q = Number (quantity) of speakers sold
\$250 = Unit sales price
\$150 = Unit variable expenses
\$35,000 = Total fixed expenses

The break-even point in sales dollars can be computed by multiplying the break-even level of unit sales by the selling price per unit:

$$350 \text{ speakers} \times \$250 = \$87,500$$

The break-even in total sales dollars, X, can also be directly computed as follows:

$$\text{Sales} = \text{Variable expenses} + \text{Fixed expenses} + \text{Profits}$$

$$\begin{aligned} X &= 0.60X + \$35,000 + \$0 \\ 0.40X &= \$35,000 \\ X &= \$35,000 \div 0.40 \\ X &= \$87,500 \end{aligned}$$

where:

X = Total sales dollars
0.60 = Variable expenses as a percentage of sales
$35,000 = Total fixed expenses

Firms often have data available only in percentage form, and the approach we have just illustrated must then be used to find the break-even point. Notice that use of percentages in the equation yields a break-even point in sales dollars rather than in units sold. The break-even point in units sold is the following:

$$\$87,500 \div \$250 = 350 \text{ speakers}$$

FOCUS *on Current Practice*

CD is a company set up by two young engineers, George Searle and Humphrey Chen, to allow customers to order music CDs on their cell phones. Suppose you hear a cut from a CD on your car radio that you would like to own. Pick up your cell phone, punch "CD," enter the radio station's frequency, and the time you heard the song, and the CD will soon be on its way to you.

CD charges about $17 for a CD, including shipping. The company pays its supplier about $13, leaving a contribution margin of $4 per CD. Because of the fixed costs of running the service, Searle expects the company to lose $1.5 million on sales of $1.5 million in its first year of operations. That assumes the company sells 88,000 CDs.

What is the company's break-even point? Working backwards, the company's fixed expenses would appear to be about $1,850,000 per year. Since the contribution margin per CD is $4, the company would have to sell over 460,000 CDs per year just to break even!

Source: Peter Kafka, "Play It Again," *Forbes*, July 26, 1999, p. 94.

The Contribution Margin Method The **contribution margin method** is actually just a short-cut version of the equation method already described. The approach centres on the idea discussed earlier that each unit sold provides a certain amount of contribution margin that goes toward covering fixed costs. To find how many units must be sold to break even, divide the total fixed costs by the unit contribution margin:

Contribution margin method A method of computing the break-even point in which the fixed expenses are divided by the contribution margin per unit.

$$\text{Break-even point in units sold} = \frac{\text{Fixed expenses}}{\text{Unit contribution margin}}$$

Each speaker generates a contribution margin of $100 ($250 selling price, less $150 variable expenses). Since the total fixed expenses are $35,000, the break-even point is as follows:

$$\frac{\text{Fixed expenses}}{\text{Unit contribution margin}} = \frac{\$35,000}{\$100} = 350 \text{ speakers}$$

A variation of this method uses the CM ratio instead of the unit contribution margin. The result is the break-even in total sales dollars rather than in total units sold.

$$\text{Break-even point in total sales dollars} = \frac{\text{Fixed expenses}}{\text{CM ratio}}$$

In the Acoustic Concepts example, the calculations are as follows:

$$\frac{\text{Fixed expenses}}{\text{CM ratio}} = \frac{\$35{,}000}{40\%} = \$87{,}500$$

This approach, based on the CM ratio, is particularly useful in those situations where a company has multiple product lines and wishes to compute a single break-even point for the company as a whole. More is said on this point in a later section entitled The Concept of Sales Mix.

Target Operating Profit Analysis

CVP formulas can be used to determine the sales volume needed to achieve a target operating profit. Suppose that Prem Narayan of Acoustic Concepts would like to earn a target operating profit of $40,000 per month. How many speakers would have to be sold?

The CVP Equation One approach is to use the equation method. Instead of solving for the unit sales where operating profits are zero, you instead solve for the unit sales where operating profits are $40,000:

$$\text{Sales} = \text{Variable expenses} + \text{Fixed expenses} + \text{Profits}$$

$$\begin{aligned} \$250Q &= \$150Q + \$35{,}000 + \$40{,}000 \\ \$100Q &= \$75{,}000 \\ Q &= \$75{,}000 \div \$100 \\ Q &= 750 \text{ speakers} \end{aligned}$$

where:

$$\begin{aligned} Q &= \text{Number of speakers sold} \\ \$250 &= \text{Unit sales price} \\ \$150 &= \text{Unit variable expenses} \\ \$35{,}000 &= \text{Total fixed expenses} \\ \$40{,}000 &= \text{Target operating profit} \end{aligned}$$

Thus, the target operating profit can be achieved by selling 750 speakers per month, which represents $187,500 in total sales ($250 × 750 speakers).

The Contribution Margin Approach A second approach involves expanding the contribution margin formula to include the target operating profit:

$$\text{Units sold to attain the target profit} = \frac{\text{Fixed expenses} + \text{Target operating profit}}{\text{Unit contribution margin}}$$

$$\frac{\$35{,}000 \text{ fixed expenses} + \$40{,}000 \text{ target operating profit}}{\$100 \text{ contribution margin per speaker}} = 750 \text{ speakers}$$

This approach gives the same answer as the equation method since it is simply a short-cut version of the equation method. Similarly, the dollar sales needed to attain the target operating profit can be computed as follows:

$$\text{Dollar sales to attain target profit} = \frac{\text{Fixed expenses} + \text{Target operating profit}}{\text{CM ratio}}$$

$$= \frac{\$35{,}000 + \$40{,}000}{0.40}$$

$$= \$187{,}500$$

After-Tax Analysis

Operating profit in the preceding analysis has ignored income taxes and is actually income before taxes. In general, operating income after tax can be computed as a fixed percentage of income before taxes. To calculate the income taxes, we simply multiply the tax rate (t) by the operating income before taxes (B). After-tax profit is equal to profit before taxes times 1 minus the tax rate and is derived as follows:

$$\begin{aligned}\text{Income after taxes} &= \text{Before-tax profit} - \text{Taxes}\\ &= B - t(B)\\ &= B(1 - t)\end{aligned}$$

Dividing both sides by $(1 - t)$, income before taxes is equal to income after taxes divided by 1 minus the tax rate $(1 - t)$:

$$B = \frac{\text{Income after taxes}}{(1 - t)}$$

Using the previous example, assume that the tax rate is 30% and the target operating profit is \$48,000 after taxes. The target profit can be achieved by selling 1,036 speakers. The appropriate formula to use would be:

$$\frac{\text{Fixed expenses} + [(\text{Target after-tax profit})/(1 - \text{tax rate})]}{\text{Contribution margin per unit}}$$

$$\frac{\$35{,}000 + [\$48{,}000/(1 - 0.3)]}{\$100} = 1{,}036 \text{ speakers (rounded)}$$

THE MARGIN OF SAFETY

LEARNING OBJECTIVE 5
Determine the margin of safety and the degree of operating leverage.

The **margin of safety** is the excess of budgeted (or actual) sales over the break-even volume of sales. It states the amount by which sales can drop before losses begin to be incurred. The higher the margin of safety, the lower the risk of not breaking even. The formula for its calculation is as follows:

Margin of safety
The excess of budgeted (or actual) sales over the break-even volume of sales.

$$\text{Margin of safety} = \text{Total budgeted (or actual) sales} - \text{Break-even sales}$$

The margin of safety can also be expressed in percentage form. This percentage is obtained by dividing the margin of safety in dollar terms by total sales:

$$\text{Margin of safety percentage} = \frac{\text{Margin of safety in dollars}}{\text{Total budgeted (or actual) sales}}$$

The calculations for the margin of safety for Acoustic Concepts are as follows:

Sales (at the current volume of 400 speakers) (a)	$100,000
Break-even sales (at 350 speakers)	87,500
Margin of safety (in dollars) (b)	$ 12,500
Margin of safety as a percentage of sales, (b) ÷ (a)	12.5%

This margin of safety means that at the current level of sales and with the company's current prices and cost structure, a reduction in sales of $12,500, or 12.5%, would result in just breaking even.

In a single-product firm like Acoustic Concepts, the margin of safety can also be expressed in terms of the number of units sold by dividing the margin of safety in dollars by the selling price per unit. In this case, the margin of safety is 50 speakers ($12,500 ÷ $250 per speaker = 50 speakers).

MANAGERIAL ACCOUNTING IN ACTION

The Wrap-Up

It is Thursday morning, and Prem Narayan and Bob Luchinni are discussing the results of Bob's analysis.

Prem: Bob, everything you have shown me is pretty clear. I can see what effect some of the sales manager's suggestions would have on our profits. Some of those suggestions are quite good and some are not so good. I also understand that our break-even is 350 speakers, so we have to make sure we don't slip below that level of sales. What really bothers me is that we are selling only 400 speakers a month now. What did you call the 50-speaker cushion?

Bob: That's the margin of safety.

Prem: Such a small cushion makes me very nervous. What can we do to increase the margin of safety?

Bob: We have to increase total sales or decrease the break-even point or both.

Prem: And to decrease the break-even point, we have to either decrease our fixed expenses or increase our unit contribution margin?

Bob: Exactly.

Prem: And to increase our unit contribution margin, we have to either increase our selling price or decrease the variable cost per unit?

Bob: Correct.

Prem: So what do you suggest?

Bob: Well, the analysis doesn't tell us which of these to do, but it does indicate we have a potential problem here.

Prem: If you don't have any immediate suggestions, I would like to call a general meeting next week to discuss ways we can work on increasing the margin of safety. I think everyone will be concerned about how vulnerable we are to even small downturns in sales.

Bob: I agree. This is something everyone will want to work on.

FOCUS *on Current Practice*

The company eToys, which sells toys on the Internet, lost $190 million in 1999 on sales of $151 million. One major cost was advertising: eToys spent about $37 on advertising for each $100 of sales. Other e-tailers were spending even more—in some cases, up to $460 on advertising for each $100 in sales!

eToys does have some advantages over brick-and-mortar stores such as Toys "R" Us. For example, eToys has much lower inventory costs, since it needs to keep on hand only one or two of a slow-moving item, whereas a traditional store has to fully stock its shelves. Also, brick-and-mortar retail spaces in malls and elsewhere cost money—on average, about 7% of sales. However, e-tailers such as eToys have their own disadvantages. Customers can "pick and pack" their own items at a brick-and-mortar outlet, but e-tailers have to pay employees to carry out this task, which costs approximately $33 for every $100 of sales. And the technology to sell on the Net is not free: eToys paid some $29 on its Web site and related technology for every $100 in sales. However, many of these costs of selling on the Net are fixed. Toby Lenk, the CEO of eToys, estimates that the company will pass the break-even point somewhere between $750 million and $950 million in sales—representing less than 1% of the market for toys.

Source: Erin Kelly, "The Last e-Store on the Block," *Fortune*, September 18, 2000, pp. 214–20.

CVP CONSIDERATIONS IN CHOOSING A COST STRUCTURE

As stated in the preceding chapter, *cost structure* refers to the relative proportion of fixed and variable costs in an organization. An organization often has some latitude in trading off between fixed and variable costs. For example, fixed investments in automated equipment can reduce variable labour costs. In this section, we discuss the choice of a cost structure, focusing on the effect of cost structure on profit stability, in which *operating leverage* plays a key role.

Cost Structure and Profit Stability

When a manager has some latitude in trading off between fixed and variable costs, which cost structure is better—high variable costs and low fixed costs, or the opposite? No single answer to this question is possible; there may be advantages either way, depending on the specific circumstances. To show what we mean by this statement, refer to the income statements given below for two blueberry farms. Bogside Farm depends on migrant workers to pick its berries by hand, whereas Sterling Farm has invested in expensive berry-picking machines. Consequently, Bogside Farm has higher variable costs, but Sterling Farm has higher fixed costs:

	Bogside Farm		Sterling Farm	
	Amount	**Percent**	**Amount**	**Percent**
Sales	$100,000	100%	$100,000	100%
Less variable expenses	60,000	60%	30,000	30%
Contribution margin	40,000	40%	70,000	70%
Less fixed expenses	30,000		60,000	
Operating income	$ 10,000		$ 10,000	

The question as to which farm has the better cost structure depends on many factors, including the long-run trend in sales, year-to-year fluctuations in the level of sales, and the attitude of the owners toward risk. If sales are expected to be above $100,000 in the future, then Sterling Farm probably has the better cost structure. The reason is that its CM ratio is higher, and its profits will therefore increase more rapidly as sales increase. To illustrate, assume that each farm experiences a 10% increase in sales without any increase in fixed costs. The new income statements would be as follows:

	Bogside Farm		Sterling Farm	
	Amount	Percent	Amount	Percent
Sales	$110,000	100%	$110,000	100%
Less variable expenses	66,000	60%	33,000	30%
Contribution margin	44,000	40%	77,000	70%
Less fixed expenses	30,000		60,000	
Operating income	$ 14,000		$ 17,000	

Sterling Farm has experienced a greater increase in operating income due to its higher CM ratio even though the increase in sales was the same for both farms.

What if sales drop below $100,000 from time to time? What are the break-even points of the two farms? What are their margins of safety? The computations needed to answer these questions are carried out as follows, using the contribution margin method:

	Bogside Farm	Sterling Farm
Fixed expenses	$ 30,000	$ 60,000
Contribution margin ratio	÷40%	÷70%
Break-even in total sales dollars	$ 75,000	$ 85,714
Total current sales (a)	$100,000	$100,000
Break-even sales	75,000	85,714
Margin of safety in sales dollars (b)	$ 25,000	$ 14,286
Margin of safety as a percentage of sales, (b) ÷ (a)	25.0%	14.3%

This analysis makes it clear that Bogside Farm is less vulnerable to downturns than Sterling Farm. We can identify two reasons for this. First, due to its lower fixed expenses, Bogside Farm has a lower break-even point and a higher margin of safety, as shown by the computations above. Therefore, it will not incur losses as quickly as Sterling Farm in periods of sharply declining sales. Second, due to its lower CM ratio, Bogside Farm will not lose contribution margin as rapidly as Sterling Farm when sales fall off. Thus, Bogside Farm's income will be less volatile. We saw earlier that this is a drawback when sales increase, but it provides more protection when sales drop.

To summarize, without knowing the future, it is not obvious which cost structure is better. Both have advantages and disadvantages. Sterling Farm, with its higher fixed costs and lower variable costs, will experience wider swings in operating income as changes take place in sales, with greater profits in good years and greater losses in bad years. Bogside Farm, with its lower fixed costs and higher variable costs, will enjoy greater stability in operating income and will be more protected from losses during bad years, but at the cost of lower operating income in good years.

FOCUS *on Current Practice*

Both JetBlue and United Airlines use an Airbus 235 to fly from Dulles International Airport near Washington, DC, to Oakland, California. Both planes have a pilot, copilot, and four flight attendants. That is where the similarity ends. Based on 2002 data, the pilot on the United flight earned $16,350 to $18,000 a month compared to $6,800 per month for the JetBlue pilot. United's senior flight attendants on the plane earned more than $41,000 per year; whereas the JetBlue attendants were paid $16,800 to $27,000 per year. Largely because of the higher labor costs at United, its costs of operating the flight were more than 60% higher than JetBlue's costs. Due to intense fare competition from JetBlue and other low-cost carriers, United was unable to cover its higher operating costs on this and many other flights. Consequently, United went into bankruptcy at the end of 2002.

Source: Susan Carey, "Costly Race in the Sky," *The Wall Street Journal*, September 9, 2002, pp. B1 and B3.

Operating Leverage

A lever is a tool for multiplying force. Using a lever, a massive object can be moved with only a modest amount of force. In business, *operating leverage* serves a similar purpose. **Operating leverage** is a measure of how sensitive operating income is to percentage changes in sales. Operating leverage acts as a multiplier. If operating leverage is high, a small percentage increase in sales can produce a much larger percentage increase in operating income.

Operating leverage
A measure of how sensitive operating income is to a given percentage change in sales. It is computed by dividing the contribution margin by operating income.

Operating leverage can be illustrated by returning to the data given above for the two blueberry farms. We previously showed that a 10% increase in sales (from $100,000 to $110,000 for each farm) results in a 70% increase in the operating income of Sterling Farm (from $10,000 to $17,000) and only a 40% increase in the operating income of Bogside Farm (from $10,000 to $14,000). Thus, for a 10% increase in sales, Sterling Farm experiences a much greater percentage increase in profits than does Bogside Farm. Therefore, Sterling Farm has greater operating leverage than Bogside Farm.

The **degree of operating leverage** at a given level of sales is computed by the following formula:

Degree of operating leverage
A measure, at a given level of sales, of how a percentage change in sales volume will affect profits. The degree of operating leverage is computed by dividing contribution margin by operating income.

$$\text{Degree of operating leverage} = \frac{\text{Contribution margin}}{\text{Operating income}}$$

The degree of operating leverage is a measure, at a given level of sales, of how a percentage change in sales volume will affect profits. To illustrate, the degree of operating leverage for the two farms at a $100,000 sales level would be as follows:

$$\text{Bogside Farm: } \frac{\$40{,}000}{\$10{,}000} = 4$$

$$\text{Sterling Farm: } \frac{\$70{,}000}{\$10{,}000} = 7$$

Since the degree of operating leverage for Bogside Farm is 4, the farm's operating income grows four times as fast as its sales. Similarly, Sterling Farm's operating income grows seven times as fast as its sales. Thus, if sales increase by 10%, then we can expect the operating income of Bogside Farm to increase by four times this amount, or by 40%, and the operating income of Sterling Farm to increase by seven times this amount, or by 70%.

	(1) Percent Increase in Sales	(2) Degree of Operating Leverage	(3) Percent Increase in Operating Income (1) × (2)
Bogside Farm	10%	4	40%
Sterling Farm	10%	7	70%

What is responsible for the higher operating leverage at Sterling Farm? The only difference between the two farms is their cost structure. If two companies have the same total revenue and same total expense but different cost structures, then the company with the higher proportion of fixed costs in its cost structure will have higher operating leverage. Referring back to the original example on page 237, when both farms have sales of $100,000 and total expenses of $90,000, one-third of Bogside Farm's costs are fixed but two-thirds of Sterling Farm's costs are fixed. As a consequence, Sterling's degree of operating leverage is higher than Bogside's.[1]

The degree of operating leverage is greatest at sales levels near the break-even point and decreases as sales and profits rise. This can be seen from the tabulation below, which shows the degree of operating leverage for Bogside Farm at various sales levels. (Data used earlier for Bogside Farm are shown in colour.)

Sales	$75,000	$80,000	$100,000	$150,000	$225,000
Less variable expenses	45,000	48,000	60,000	90,000	135,000
Contribution margin (a)	30,000	32,000	40,000	60,000	90,000
Less fixed expenses	30,000	30,000	30,000	30,000	30,000
Operating income (b)	$ -0-	$ 2,000	$ 10,000	$ 30,000	$ 60,000
Degree of operating leverage, (a) ÷ (b)	∞	16	4	2	1.5

Thus, a 10% increase in sales would increase operating profits by only 15% (10% × 1.5) if the company was operating at a $225,000 sales level, as compared to the 40% increase we computed earlier at the $100,000 sales level. The degree of operating leverage will continue to decrease the further the company moves from its break-even point. At the break-even point, the degree of operating leverage will be infinitely large ($30,000 contribution margin ÷ $0 operating income = ∞).

A manager can use the degree of operating leverage to quickly estimate what effect various percentage changes in sales will have on profits, without the necessity of preparing detailed income statements. As shown by our examples, the effects of operating leverage can be dramatic. If a company is near its break-even point, then even small percentage increases in sales can yield large percentage increases in profits. *This explains why management will often work very hard for only a small increase in sales volume.* If the degree of operating leverage is 5, then a 6% increase in sales would translate into a 30% increase in profits.

In summary, we can predict the percentage change in operating income before taxes (OIBT) resulting from a given percentage change in sales. The following equation does this by multiplying the percentage change in sales by the degree of operating leverage:

$$\%\Delta \text{ OIBT} = \%\Delta \text{ Sales} \times \text{Degree of operating leverage}$$

Automation: Risks and Rewards from a CVP Perspective

We have noted in preceding chapters that several factors, including the move toward flexible manufacturing systems and other uses of automation, have resulted in a shift toward greater fixed costs and less variable costs in organizations. In turn, this shift in cost structure has had an impact on the CM ratio, the break-even point, and the degree of operating leverage.

Many benefits can accrue from automation, but certain risks are introduced when a company moves toward greater amounts of fixed costs. These risks suggest that

1. See Richard A. Lord, "Interpreting and Measuring Operating Leverage," *Issues in Accounting Education,* Fall 1995, pp. 317–29, for an extensive discussion of the impact of cost structure on the degree of operating leverage.

management must be careful as it automates to ensure that investment decisions are made in accordance with a carefully devised long-run strategy. This point is discussed further in Chapter 14 where we deal with investment decisions in an automated environment.

INDIFFERENCE ANALYSIS

We have seen that cost-volume-profit analysis is a decision tool that can be used as input for decisions about the profitability of individual products. CVP analysis is also useful for aiding decisions about the comparative profitability of alternative products or methods of production. The analysis focuses on cost behaviour in relation to changes in activity level. Relative profitability depends on activity level. A product with a high level of fixed costs will require a higher sales activity level to generate a profit than will a product with low fixed costs and comparatively high variable costs. Cost-volume-profit analyses facilitate the comparison of alternatives with different fixed and variable cost structures

To illustrate, assume that Goodwin Company has decided to introduce a new product that can be manufactured by either a labour-intensive production (LIP) system or a capital-intensive production (CIP) system. The manufacturing method will not affect the quality of the product. The estimated manufacturing costs of a labour-intensive production system and a capital-intensive production system are as follows:

	Labour-Intensive Production System		Capital-Intensive Production System	
Selling price per unit sold		$30.00		$30.00
Direct material		6.00		5.00
Direct labour-hours (DLH)	0.8 DLH @ $9	7.20	0.5 DLH@ $12	6.00
Variable overhead	0.8 DLH @ $6	4.80	0.5 DLH @ $6	3.00
Variable selling expense		2.00		2.00
Total variable costs		20.00		16.00
Contribution margin		$10.00		$14.00
Fixed overhead*		$1,200,000.00		$2,550,000.00
Fixed selling expenses		$ 600,000.00		$ 600,000.00
Break-even sales		$5,400,000.00		$6,750,000.00
Break-even units		180,000		225,000

*These costs are directly traceable to the new product line. They would not be incurred if the new product was not produced.

We can calculate the point at which Goodwin will be indifferent about using a labour-intensive production system or a capital-intensive production system as follows:

1. Determine the unit CM times the number of units (Q) plus total fixed costs of each alternative.
2. Set up an equation with each alternative on opposite sides of the equal sign.
3. Solve for Q, the indifference point.

$$\$10Q + \$1,800,000 = \$14Q + \$3,150,000$$
$$\$4Q = \$1,350,000$$
$$Q = 337,500 \text{ units}$$

Note from line 2 of the equation that the $4 change in contribution margin is on the left-hand side of the equation, and the $1,350,000 on the right-hand side of the equation is the change in fixed costs. The indifference point can therefore be found quickly by dividing the change in fixed cost by the change in contribution margin for each alternative:

$$\frac{\text{Fixed cost of CIP} - \text{Fixed cost of LIP}}{\text{CM of CIP} - \text{CM of LIP}} = \frac{\$3,150,000 - \$1,8000,000}{\$14 - \$10} = \frac{\$1,350,000}{\$4} = 337,500 \text{ units}$$

At sales below the indifference point of 337,500 units, profitability will be higher for LIP. Sales above the indifference point will generate higher profitability for CIP, because CIP generates a higher contribution margin per unit than LIP does.

STRUCTURING SALES COMMISSIONS

Companies generally compensate salespeople by paying them either a commission based on sales or a salary plus a sales commission. Commissions based on sales dollars can lead to lower profits in a company. To illustrate, consider Pipeline Unlimited, a producer of surfing equipment. Salespeople for the company sell the company's product to retail sporting goods stores throughout North America and the Pacific Basin. Data for two of the company's surfboards, the XR7 and Turbo models, are as follows:

	Model	
	XR7	Turbo
Selling price	$100	$150
Less variable expenses	75	132
Contribution margin	$ 25	$ 18

Which model will salespeople push hardest if they are paid a commission of 10% of sales revenue? The answer is the Turbo, since it has the higher selling price. On the other hand, from the standpoint of the company, profits will be greater if salespeople steer customers toward the XR7 model since it has the higher contribution margin.

To eliminate such conflicts, some companies base salepersons' commissions on contribution margin rather than on selling price alone. The reasoning goes like this: Since contribution margin represents the amount of sales revenue available to cover fixed expenses and profits, a firm's well-being will be maximized when contribution margin is maximized. By tying salespeople's commissions to contribution margin, the sales staff is automatically encouraged to concentrate on the element that is of most importance to the firm. There is no need to worry about what mix of products the salespersons sell because they will strive to sell the mix of products that will maximize the contribution margin. In effect, by maximizing their own compensation, they also maximize the firm's profit, as long as there is no change in fixed expenses.

THE CONCEPT OF SALES MIX

LEARNING OBJECTIVE 6
Compute the break-even point for a multiple-product company and explain the effects of shifts in the sales mix on contribution margin and the break-even point.

Before concluding our discussion of CVP concepts, we will consider the effect of changes in sales mix on a firm's profits.

The Definition of Sales Mix

The term **sales mix** refers to the relative proportions in which a company's products are sold. Managers try to achieve the combination, or mix, that will yield the greatest amount of profits. Most companies have several products, and often these products are not equally profitable; therefore, profits will depend to some extent on the company's sales mix. Profits will be greater if high-margin rather than low-margin items make up a relatively large proportion of total sales.

Changes in the sales mix can cause interesting (and sometimes confusing) variations in a company's profits. A shift in the sales mix from high-margin items to low-margin items can cause total profits to decrease even though total sales may increase. Conversely, a shift in the sales mix from low-margin items to high-margin items can cause the reverse effect—total profits may increase even though total sales decrease. It is one thing to achieve a particular sales volume, but it is quite a different thing to sell the most profitable mix of products.

Sales mix
The relative proportions in which a company's products are sold. Sales mix is computed by expressing the sales of each product as a percentage of total sales.

FOCUS *on Current Practice*

Kodak dominates the film industry in the U.S., selling two out of every three rolls of film. It also processes 40% of all film dropped off for developing. Unfortunately for Kodak, this revenue stream is threatened by digital cameras, which do not use film at all. To counter this threat, Kodak has moved into the digital market with its own line of digital cameras and various services, but sales of digital products undeniably cut into the company's film business. "Chief Financial Officer Robert Brust has 'stress-tested' profit models based on how quickly digital cameras may spread. If half of homes go digital, . . . Kodak's sales would rise 10% a year—but profits would go up only 8% a year. Cost cuts couldn't come fast enough to offset a slide in film sales and the margin pressure from selling cheap digital cameras." The sales mix is moving in the wrong direction, given the company's current cost structure and competitive prices.

Source: Bruce Upbin, "Kodak's Digital Moment," *Forbes*, August 21, 2000, pp. 106–112.

Sales Mix and Break-Even Analysis

If a company sells more than one product, break-even analysis is somewhat more complex than discussed earlier in the chapter. The reason is that different products will have different selling prices, different costs, and different contribution margins. Consequently, the break-even point will depend on the mix in which the various products are sold. To illustrate, consider Sound Unlimited, a small company that imports CD-ROMs from France for use in personal computers. At present, the company distributes the following to retail computer stores: the Le Louvre CD, a multimedia free-form tour of the famous art museum in Paris; and the Le Vin CD, which features the wines and wine-growing regions of France. Both multimedia products have sound, photos, video clips, and sophisticated software. The company's September sales, expenses, and break-even point are shown in Exhibit 6–3.

As shown in the exhibit, the break-even point is $60,000 in sales. This is computed by dividing the fixed costs by the company's *overall* CM ratio of 45%. But $60,000 in sales represents the break-even point for the company only as long as the sales mix does not change. *If the sales mix changes, then the break-even point will also change.* This is illustrated by the results for October in which the sales mix shifted away from the more profitable Le Vin CD (which has a 50% CM ratio) toward the less profitable Le Louvre CD (which has only a 25% CM ratio). These results appear in Exhibit 6–4.

Although sales have remained unchanged at $100,000, the sales mix is exactly the reverse of what it was in Exhibit 6–3, with the bulk of the sales now coming from the less profitable Le Louvre CD. Notice that this shift in the sales mix has caused both the overall CM ratio and total profits to drop sharply from the prior month—the overall CM ratio has dropped from 45% in September to only 30% in October, and operating income has dropped from $18,000 to only $3,000. In addition, with the drop in the overall CM ratio, the company's break-even point is no longer $60,000 in sales. Since the company is now realizing less average contribution margin per dollar of sales, it takes more sales to cover the same amount of fixed costs. Thus, the break-even point has increased from $60,000 to $90,000 in sales per year.

EXHIBIT 6–3 Multiple-Product Break-Even Analysis

SOUND UNLIMITED
Contribution Income Statement
For the Month of September

	Le Louvre CD		Le Vin CD		Total	
	Amount	**Percent**	**Amount**	**Percent**	**Amount**	**Percent**
Sales	$20,000	100%	$80,000	100%	$100,000	100%
Less variable expenses	15,000	75%	40,000	50%	55,000	55%
Contribution margin	$ 5,000	25%	$40,000	50%	45,000	45%
Less fixed expenses					27,000	
Operating income					$ 18,000	

Computation of the break-even point:

$$\frac{\text{Fixed expenses}}{\text{Overall CM ratio}} = \frac{\$27{,}000}{0.45} = \$60{,}000$$

Verification of the break-even:

Break-even sales equals $27,000 ÷ .45 = $60,000. If Sound Unlimited keeps 20:80 sales mix LeLouvre sales = .20 × $60,000 = $12,000 while LeVin = .80 × $60,000 = $48.000. Exhibit 6–4 shows a different result because the sales mix changes.

	Le Louvre CD		Le Vin CD		Total	
	Amount	**Percent**	**Amount**	**Percent**	**Amount**	**Percent**
Sales	$12,000	100%	$48,000	100%	$ 60,000	100%
Less variable expenses	9,000	75%	24,000	50%	33,000	55%
Contribution margin	$ 3,000	25%	$24,000	50%	27,000	45%
Less fixed expenses					27,000	
Operating income					$ –0–	

EXHIBIT 6–4 Multiple-Product Break-Even Analysis: A Shift in Sales Mix (see Exhibit 6–3)

SOUND UNLIMITED
Contribution Income Statement
For the Month of October

	Le Louvre CD		Le Vin CD		Total	
	Amount	**Percent**	**Amount**	**Percent**	**Amount**	**Percent**
Sales	$80,000	100%	$20,000	100%	$100,000	100%
Less variable expenses	60,000	75%	10,000	50%	70,000	70%
Contribution margin	$20,000	25%	$10,000	50%	30,000	30%
Less fixed expenses					27,000	
Operating income					$ 3,000	

Computation of the break-even point:

$$\frac{\text{Fixed expenses}}{\text{Overall CM ratio}} = \frac{\$27{,}000}{0.30} = \$90{,}000$$

In preparing a break-even analysis, some assumption must be made concerning the sales mix. Usually the assumption is that it will not change. However, if the manager knows that shifts in various factors (consumer tastes, market share, and so forth) are causing shifts in the sales mix, then these factors must be explicitly considered in any CVP computations. Otherwise, the manager may make decisions on the basis of outmoded or faulty data.

ASSUMPTIONS OF CVP ANALYSIS

A number of assumptions typically underlie CVP analysis:

1. Selling price is constant throughout the entire relevant range. The price of a product or service will not change as volume changes.
2. Costs are linear throughout the entire relevant range, and they can accurately be divided into variable and fixed elements. The variable element is constant per unit, and the fixed element is constant in total over the entire relevant range.
3. In multiproduct companies, the sales mix is constant.
4. In manufacturing companies, inventories do not change. The number of units produced equals the number of units sold (this assumption is considered further in the next chapter).

While some of these assumptions may be violated in practice, the violations are usually not serious enough to call into question the basic validity of CVP analysis. For example, in most multiproduct companies, the sales mix is constant enough that the results of CVP analysis are reasonably valid.

Perhaps the greatest danger lies in relying on simple CVP analysis when a manager is contemplating a large change in volume that lies outside of the relevant range. For example, a manager might contemplate increasing the level of sales far beyond what the company has ever experienced. However, even in these situations, a manager can adjust the model as we have done in this chapter to take into account anticipated changes in selling prices, fixed costs, and the sales mix that would otherwise violate the assumptions. For example, in a decision that would affect fixed costs, the change in fixed costs can explicitly be taken into account as illustrated earlier in the chapter in the Acoustic Concepts example on page 236.

SUMMARY

CVP analysis involves finding the most favourable combination of variable costs, fixed costs, selling price, sales volume, and mix of products sold. Trade-offs are possible between types of costs, as well as between costs and selling price, and between selling price and sales volume. Sometimes these trade-offs are desirable, and sometimes they are not. CVP analysis provides the manager with a powerful tool for identifying those courses of action that will improve profitability.

The application of CVP analysis can take many forms. The equation for profits and its algebraic adjustments represent a quick way to proceed if units can be added. Contribution margin ratio is an alternative that will yield dollar results if desired. The contribution income statement permits exploration of more complex situations if such is needed. After tax analysis and operating leverage represent variations and short cuts where these issues need to be explored.

The concepts developed in this chapter represent a *way of thinking* rather than a mechanical set of procedures. That is, to put together the optimum combination of costs, selling price, and sales volume, the manager must be trained to think in terms of the unit contribution margin, the break-even point, the CM ratio, the sales mix, and the other concepts developed in this chapter. These concepts are dynamic in that a change in one will trigger changes in others—changes that may not be obvious on the surface.

REVIEW PROBLEM: CVP RELATIONSHIPS

Voltar Company manufactures and sells a telephone answering machine. The company's contribution format income statement for the most recent year is given below:

	Total	Per Unit	Percent of Sales
Sales (20,000 units)	$1,200,000	$60	100%
Less variable expenses	900,000	45	? %
Contribution margin	300,000	$15	? %
Less fixed expenses	240,000		
Operating income	$ 60,000		

Management is anxious to improve the company's profit performance and has asked for several items of information.

Required:

1. Compute the company's CM ratio and variable expense ratio.
2. Compute the company's break-even point in both units and sales dollars. Use the equation method.
3. Assume that sales increase by $400,000 next year. If cost behaviour patterns remain unchanged, by how much will the company's operating income increase? Use the CM ratio to determine your answer.
4. Refer to original data. Assume that next year management wants the company to earn a minimum profit of $90,000. How many units will have to be sold to meet this target profit figure?
5. Refer to the original data. Compute the company's margin of safety in both dollar and percentage form.
6. *a.* Compute the company's degree of operating leverage at the present level of sales.
   b. Assume that, through a more intense effort by the sales staff, the company's sales increase by 8% next year. By what percentage would you expect operating income to increase? Use the operating leverage concept to obtain your answer.
   c. Verify your answer to (*b*) by preparing a new income statement showing an 8% increase in sales.
7. In an effort to increase sales and profits, management is considering the use of a higher-quality speaker. The higher-quality speaker would increase variable costs by $3 per unit, but management could eliminate one quality inspector who is paid a salary of $30,000 per year. The sales manager estimates that the higher-quality speaker would increase annual sales by at least 20%.
   a. Assuming that changes are made as described above, prepare a projected income statement for next year. Show data on a total, per unit, and percentage basis.
   b. Compute the company's new break-even point in both units and dollars of sales. Use the contribution margin method.
   c. Would you recommend that the changes be made?

Solution to Review Problem

1. CM ratio: Variable expense ratio:

$$\frac{\text{Contribution margin, \$15}}{\text{Selling price, \$60}} = 25\% \qquad \frac{\text{Variable expense, \$45}}{\text{Selling price, \$60}} = 75\%$$

2.
$$\text{Sales} = \text{Variable expenses} + \text{Fixed expenses} + \text{Profits}$$
$$\$60Q = \$45Q + \$240{,}000 + \$0$$

$$
\begin{aligned}
\$15Q &= \$240{,}000 \\
Q &= \$240{,}000 \div \$15 \\
Q &= 16{,}000 \text{ units; or at \$60 per unit, \$960,000}
\end{aligned}
$$

Alternative solution:

$$
\begin{aligned}
X &= 0.75X + \$240{,}000 + \$0 \\
0.25X &= \$240{,}000 \\
X &= \$240{,}000 \div 0.25 \\
X &= \$960{,}000\text{; or at \$60 per unit, 16,000 units}
\end{aligned}
$$

3.

Increase in sales	$400,000
Multiply by the CM ratio	× 25%
Expected increase in contribution margin	$100,000

Since the fixed expenses are not expected to change, operating income will increase by the entire $100,000 increase in contribution margin computed above.

4. Equation method:

$$\text{Sales} = \text{Variable expenses} + \text{Fixed expenses} + \text{Profits}$$

$$
\begin{aligned}
\$60Q &= \$45Q + \$240{,}000 + \$90{,}000 \\
\$15Q &= \$330{,}000 \\
Q &= \$330{,}000 \div \$15 \\
Q &= 22{,}000 \text{ units}
\end{aligned}
$$

Contribution margin method:

$$\frac{\text{Fixed expenses} + \text{Target profit}}{\text{Contribution margin per unit}} = \frac{\$240{,}000 + \$90{,}000}{\$15} = 22{,}000 \text{ units}$$

5.

$$\text{Total sales} - \text{Break-even sales} = \text{Margin of safety in dollars}$$

$$\$1{,}200{,}000 - \$960{,}000 = \$240{,}000$$

$$\frac{\text{Margin of safety in dollars, \$240,000}}{\text{Total sales, \$1,200,000}} = 20\%$$

6. *a.*

$$\frac{\text{Contribution margin, \$300,000}}{\text{Operating income, \$60,000}} = 5 \text{ (degree of operating leverage)}$$

b.

Expected increase in sales	8%
Degree of operating leverage	× 5
Expected increase in operating income	40%

c. If sales increase by 8%, then 21,600 units (20,000 × 1.08 = 21,600) will be sold next year. The new income statement will be as follows:

	Total	Per Unit	Percent of Sales
Sales (21,600 units)	$1,296,000	$60	100%
Less variable expenses	972,000	45	75%
Contribution margin	324,000	$15	25%
Less fixed expenses	240,000		
Operating income	$ 84,000		

Thus, the $84,000 expected operating income for next year represents a 40% increase over the $60,000 operating income earned during the current year:

$$\frac{\$84{,}000 - \$60{,}000 = \$24{,}000}{\$60{,}000} = 40\% \text{ increase}$$

Note from the income statement above that the increase in sales from 20,000 to 21,600 units has resulted in increases in *both* total sales and total variable expenses. It is a common error to overlook the increase in variable expenses when preparing a projected income statement.

7. *a.* A 20% increase in sales would result in 24,000 units being sold next year: 20,000 units × 1.20 = 24,000 units.

	Total	Per Unit	Percent of Sales
Sales (24,000 units)	$1,440,000	$60	100%
Less variable expenses . . .	1,152,000	48*	80%
Contribution margin	288,000	$12	20%
Less fixed expenses	210,000†		
Operating income	$ 78,000		

*$45 + $3 = $48; $48 ÷ $60 = 80%.
†$240,000 − $30,000 = $210,000.

Note that the change in per unit variable expenses results in a change in both the per unit contribution margin and the CM ratio.

b.

$$\text{Break-even in unit sales} = \frac{\text{Fixed expenses}}{\text{Contribution margin per unit}}$$

$$= \frac{\$210{,}000}{\$12 \text{ per unit}} = 17{,}500 \text{ units}$$

$$\text{Break-even in sales dollars} = \frac{\text{Fixed expenses}}{\text{Contribution margin ratio}}$$

$$= \frac{\$210{,}000}{0.20} = \$1{,}050{,}000$$

c. Yes, based on these data the changes should be made. The changes will increase the company's operating income from the present $60,000 to $78,000 per year. Although the changes will also result in a higher break-even point (17,500 units as compared to the present 16,000 units), the company's margin of safety will actually be wider than before:

$$\text{Margin of safety in dollars} = \text{Total sales} - \text{Break-even sales}$$
$$\$1{,}400{,}000 - \$1{,}050{,}000 = \$390{,}000$$

As shown in (5) above, the company's present margin of safety is only $240,000. Thus, several benefits will result from the proposed changes.

APPENDIX 6A: COST-VOLUME-PROFIT WITH UNCERTAINTY

LEARNING OBJECTIVE 7
Construct cost-volume-profit analysis with uncertainty.

CVP analysis is often employed to assess what future prospects might be under various arrangements. Given the compactness of the analysis, the CVP formula is a convenient approach to conducting such assessments. Consider the following example:

Novelties Ltd. produces and sells highly faddish products directed toward the teen market. A new product has come onto the market that the company is anxious to produce and sell. Enough capacity exists in the company's plant to produce 15,000 units each month. Variable costs to manufacture and sell one unit would be $1.60, and fixed costs would total $16,000 per month.

The management of Novelties wants to assess the implications of various alternatives. As part of the investigation, management wants an analysis of the operating income if various alternative sales volumes, selling prices, and variable expenses occur. Sales volumes would be 13,500 units or 15,000 units. Selling prices would be $3.50 or $4.00. Variable expenses were estimated as being $1.28 or $1.60, depending on a series of outcomes. First, consider the eight (2 × 2 × 2) possible outcomes:

Alternatives	Variable Expenses	Selling Prices	Sales Volumes	Fixed Expenses	Operating Income
1	$1.28	$3.50	13,500	$16,000	$13,970
2	1.28	3.50	15,000	16,000	17,300
3	1.28	4.00	13,500	16,000	20,720
4	1.28	4.00	15,000	16,000	24,800
5	1.60	3.50	13,500	16,000	9,650
6	1.60	3.50	15,000	16,000	12,500
7	1.60	4.00	13,500	16,000	16,400
8	1.60	4.00	15,000	16,000	20,000

By noticing the repetitions of variable expenses and selling prices, the preceding table can be represented in the form of a tree, commonly termed a *decision tree*, as shown in Exhibit 6–5.

As a manager, one would like alternative 4, with a profit of $24,800. If a manager can force the future components of a profit to be the following—variable expenses, $1.28; selling price, $4.00; and sales volume, 15,000 units—an operating income of $24,800 can be achieved. Unfortunately, managers do not have such a luxury.

Assume that the best the manager can do is assess the chances of each alternative occurring. These chances are commonly called *subjective probabilities* and can represent what the manager believes will occur. Each of the possible chances can also be placed on the tree, as shown in Exhibit 6–6.

Close observation reveals several important and general results to the manager of Novelties. First, the chances for each uncertain factor are expressed in decimal form and sum to one. Second, the chances are multiplied on the tree in the same sequence as the CVP elements. Third, no chance was assigned to fixed expenses because they are known in every case.

The manager notes that if the subjective probabilities are correct, there is only a 2% chance, or 2 chances in 100, of having a profit of $24,800.

EXHIBIT 6–5 A Decision Tree

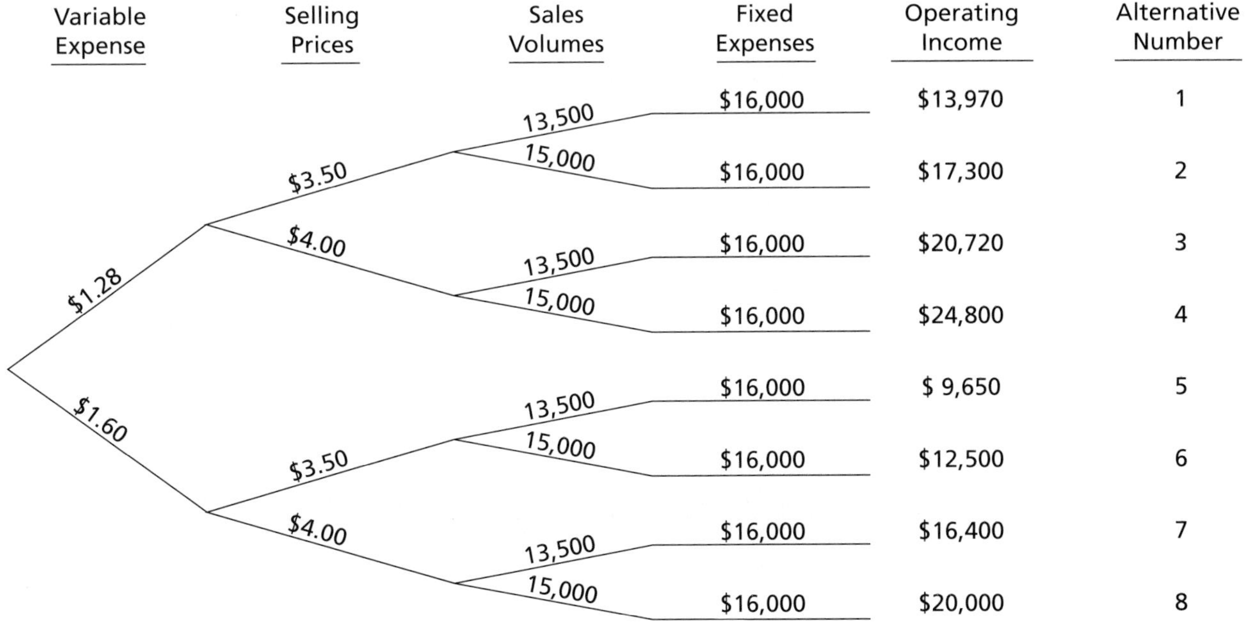

EXHIBIT 6–6 A Decision Tree

Variable Expense Chances	Selling Price Chances	Sales Volume Chances	Product Results	Alternative Number
.60	.70	.90	.60 × .70 × .90 = .38	1
		.10	.60 × .70 × .10 = .04	2
	.30	.90	.60 × .30 × .90 = .16	3
		.10	.60 × .30 × .10 = .02	4
.40	.70	.90	.40 × .70 × .90 = .25	5
		.10	.40 × .70 × .10 = .03	6
	.30	.90	.40 × .30 × .90 = .11	7
		.10	.40 × .30 × .10 = .01	8
			Total 1.00	

To ascertain what Novelties might expect future profits to be, the expected value (often termed a *mean*) is computed as follows:

Alternatives	Profits	Chances	Products	
1	$13,970	.38	$5,308.60	($13,970 × .38)
2	17,300	.04	692.00	($17,300 × .04)
3	20,720	.16	3,315.20	
4	24,800	.02	496.00	
5	9,650	.25	2,412.50	
6	12,500	.03	375.00	
7	16,400	.11	1,804.00	
8	20,000	.01	200.00	
		1.00		
Total expected value			$14,603.30	

The expected value, $14,603.30, is a reasonable estimate of what the profit of Novelties might be for next period, given the data and the chances supplied to the analysis.

The decision tree analysis is very powerful. A computer can facilitate the tedious calculations. However, it is important to note that the number of calculations increases dramatically with both the number of alternatives (e.g., 1.28 or 1.60 for variable expenses) considered (e.g., 3 × 3 × 3 = 27, 4 × 4 × 4 = 64) and the number of factors (e.g., selling prices, sales volumes, etc.) considered in the CVP formulation (e.g., 2 × 2 × 2 × 2 = 16, 2 × 2 × 2 × 2 × 2 = 32). Even a computer can be taxed very quickly.

GLOSSARY

Visit the Online Learning Centre at http://www.mcgrawhill.ca/college/garrison/ for a review of key terms and definitions.

QUESTIONS

6–1 What is meant by a product's CM ratio? How is this ratio useful in planning business operations?

6–2 Often the most direct route to a business decision is an incremental analysis. What is meant by an *incremental analysis*?

6–3 Company A's cost structure includes costs that are mostly variable, whereas Company B's cost structure includes costs that are mostly fixed. In a time of increasing sales, which company will tend to realize the most rapid increase in profits? Explain.

6–4 What is meant by the term *operating leverage*?

6–5 A 10% decrease in the selling price of a product will have the same impact on operating income as a 10% increase in the variable expenses. Do you agree? Why or why not?

6–6 What is meant by the term *break-even point*?

6–7 Name three approaches to break-even analysis. Briefly explain how each approach works.

6–8 In response to a request from your immediate supervisor, you have prepared a CVP graph portraying the cost and revenue characteristics of your company's product and operations. Explain how the lines on the graph and the break-even point would change if (*a*) the selling price per unit decreased, (*b*) fixed costs increased throughout the entire range of activity portrayed on the graph, and (*c*) variable costs per unit increased.

6–9 Al's Auto Wash charges $4 to wash a car. The variable costs of washing a car are 15% of sales. Fixed expenses total $1,700 monthly. How many cars must be washed each month for Al to break even?

6–10 What is meant by the margin of safety?

6–11 Companies X and Y are in the same industry. Company X is highly automated, whereas Company Y relies primarily on labour to make its products. If sales and total expenses in the two companies are about the same, which would you expect to have the lower margin of safety? Why?

6–12 What is meant by the term *sales mix*? What assumption is usually made concerning sales mix in CVP analysis?

6–13 Explain how a shift in the sales mix could result in both a higher break-even point and a lower net income.

6–14 Why do accountants commonly use linear CVP analysis rather than the curvilinear form?

6–15 What effect would a 30% income tax rate have on the CVP formula?

6–16 Why must inventories be assumed to be constant in the CVP formula?

6–17 What would happen to CVP analysis if worker productivity increased on reaching the top of the relevant range?

6–18 Describe how uncertainty can explicitly be considered in CVP analysis.

6–19 Does the concept of relevant range imply more than one break-even point? Explain.

EXERCISES

EXERCISE 6–1 Preparing a Contribution Format Income Statement [LO1]

Whirly Corporation's most recent income statement is shown below:

	Total	Per Unit
Sales (10,000 units)	$350,000	$35.00
Less variable expenses	200,000	20.00
Contribution margin	150,000	$15.00
Less fixed expenses	135,000	
Operating income	$ 15,000	

Required:

Prepare a new contribution format income statement under each of the following conditions (consider each case independently):

1. The sales volume increases by 100 units.

2. The sales volume decreases by 100 units.
3. The sales volume is 9,000 units.

EXERCISE 6–2 Prepare a Cost-Volume-Profit (CVP) Graph [LO2]
Karlik Enterprises has a single product whose selling price is $24 and whose variable cost is $18 per unit. The company's monthly fixed expense is $24,000.

Required:
1. Prepare a cost-volume-profit graph for the company up to a sales level of 8,000 units.
2. Estimate the company's break-even point in unit sales using your cost-volume-profit graph.

EXERCISE 6–3 Computing and Using the CM Ratio [LO3]
Last month when Holiday Creations, Inc., sold 50,000 units, total sales were $200,000, total variable expenses were $120,000, and total fixed expenses were $65,000.

Required:
1. What is the company's contribution margin (CM) ratio?
2. Estimate the change in the company's operating income if it were to increase its total sales by $1,000.

EXERCISE 6–4 Changes in Variable Costs, Fixed Costs, Selling Price, and Volume [LO3]
Data for Hermann Corporation are shown below:

	Per Unit	Percent of Sales
Selling price	$90	100%
Less variable expenses	63	70
Contribution margin	$27	30%

Fixed expenses are $30,000 per month and the company is selling 2,000 units per month.

Required:
1. The marketing manager argues that a $5,000 increase in the monthly advertising budget would increase monthly sales by $9,000. Should the advertising budget be increased?
2. Refer to the original data. Management is considering using higher-quality components that would increase the variable cost by $2 per unit. The marketing manager believes the higher-quality product would increase sales by 10% per month. Should the higher-quality components be used?

EXERCISE 6–5 Compute the Break-Even Point [LO4]
Mauro Products has a single product, a woven basket whose selling price is $15 and whose variable cost is $12 per unit. The company's monthly fixed expenses are $4,200.

Required:
1. Solve for the company's break-even point in unit sales using the equation method.
2. Solve for the company's break-even point in sales dollars using the equation method and the CM ratio.
3. Solve for the company's break-even point in unit sales using the contribution margin method.
4. Solve for the company's break-even point in sales dollars using the contribution margin method and the CM ratio.

EXERCISE 6–6 Compute the Level of Sales Required to Attain a Target Profit [LO4]
Lin Corporation has a single product whose selling price is $120 and whose variable cost is $80 per unit. The company's monthly fixed expense is $50,000.

Required:
1. Using the equation method, solve for the unit sales that are required to earn a target profit of $10,000.
2. Using the contribution margin approach, solve for the dollar sales that are required to earn a target profit of $15,000.

EXERCISE 6–7 Compute the Margin of Safety [LO5]
Molander Corporation is a distributor of a sun umbrella used at resort hotels. Data concerning the next month's budget appear below:

Selling price	$30 per unit
Variable expense ...	$20 per unit
Fixed expense	$7,500 per month
Unit sales	1,000 units per month

Required:
1. Compute the company's margin of safety.
2. Compute the company's margin of safety as a percentage of its sales.

S

EXERCISE 6–8 Compute and Use the Degree of Operating Leverage [LO5]
Engberg Company installs lawn sod in home yards. The company's most recent monthly contribution format income statement follows:

	Amount	Percent of Sales
Sales	$80,000	100%
Less variable expenses	32,000	40%
Contribution margin	48,000	60%
Less fixed expenses	38,000	
Operating income	$10,000	

Required:
1. Compute the company's degree of operating leverage.
2. Using the degree of operating leverage, estimate the impact on net income of a 5% increase in sales.
3. Verify your estimate from part (2) above by constructing a new contribution format income statement for the company assuming a 5% increase in sales.

S

EXERCISE 6–9 Compute the Break-Even Point for a Multiproduct Company [LO6]
Lucido Products markets two computer games: Claimjumper and Makeover. A contribution format income statement for a recent month for the two games appears below:

	Claimjumper	Makeover	Total
Sales	$30,000	$70,000	$100,000
Less variable expenses	20,000	50,000	70,000
Contribution margin	$10,000	$20,000	30,000
Less fixed expenses			24,000
Operating income			$ 6,000

Required:
1. Compute the overall contribution margin (CM) ratio for the company.
2. Compute the overall break-even point for the company in sales dollars.
3. Verify the overall break-even point for the company by constructing a contribution format income statement showing the appropriate levels of sales for the two products.

EXERCISE 6–10 Using a Contribution Format Income Statement [LO1, LO3]
Miller Company's most recent contribution format income statement is shown below:

	Total	Per Unit
Sales (20,000 units)	$300,000	$15.00
Less variable expenses	180,000	9.00
Contribution margin	120,000	$6.00
Less fixed expenses	70,000	
Operating income	$ 50,000	

Required:

Prepare a new contribution format income statement under each of the following conditions (consider each case independently):

1. The sales volume increases by 15%.
2. The selling price decreases by $1.50 per unit, and the sales volume increases by 25%.
3. The selling price increases by $1.50 per unit, fixed expenses increase by $20,000, and the sales volume decreases by 5%.
4. The selling price increases by 12%, variable expenses increase by 60 cents per unit, and the sales volume decreases by 10%.

EXERCISE 6–11 Break-Even Analysis and CVP Graphing [LO2, LO3, LO4]

The Vancouver Symphony Guild is planning its annual dinner-dance. The dinner-dance committee has assembled the following expected costs for the event:

Dinner (per person)	$18
Favours and program (per person)	$2
Band	$2,800
Rental of ballroom	$900
Professional entertainment during intermission	$1,000
Tickets and advertising	$1,300

The committee members would like to charge $35 per person for the evening's activities.

Required:

1. Compute the break-even point for the dinner-dance (in terms of the number of persons who must attend).
2. Assume that last year only 300 persons attended the dinner-dance. If the same number attend this year, what price per ticket must be charged in order to break even?
3. Refer to the original data ($35 ticket price per person). Prepare a CVP graph for the dinner-dance from a zero level of activity up to 600 tickets sold. Number of persons should be placed on the horizontal *(X)* axis, and dollars should be placed on the vertical *(Y)* axis.

EXERCISE 6–12 Break-Even and Target Profit Analysis [LO3, LO4]

Lindon Company is the exclusive distributor for an automotive product that sells for $40 per unit and has a CM ratio of 30%. The company's fixed expenses are $180,000 per year.

Required:

1. What are the variable expenses per unit?
2. Using the equation method:
   a. What is the break-even point in units and sales dollars?
   b. What sales level in units and in sales dollars is required to earn an annual operating income of $60,000?
   c. Assume that by using a more efficient shipper, the company is able to reduce its variable expenses by $4 per unit. What is the company's new break-even point in units and sales dollars?
3. Repeat (2) above using the contribution margin method.

EXERCISE 6–13 Break-Even and Target Profit Analysis [LO3, LO4]

Outback Outfitters sells recreational equipment. One of the company's products, a small camp stove, sells for $50 per unit. Variable expenses are $32 per stove, and fixed expenses associated with the stove total $108,000 per month.

Required:

1. Compute the break-even point in number of stoves and in total sales dollars.
2. If the variable expenses per stove increase as a percentage of the selling price, will it result in a higher or a lower break-even point? Why? (Assume that the fixed expenses remain unchanged.)
3. At present, the company is selling 8,000 stoves per month. The sales manager is convinced that a 10% reduction in the selling price would result in a 25% increase in monthly sales of stoves. Prepare two contribution income statements, one under present operating conditions, and one as operations would appear after the proposed changes. Show both total and per unit data on your statements.
4. Refer to the data in (3) above. How many stoves would have to be sold at the new selling price to yield a minimum operating income of $35,000 per month?

EXERCISE 6–14 Missing Data; Basic CVP Concepts [LO1, LO6]

Fill in the missing amounts in each of the eight case situations below. Each case is independent of the others. (Hint: One way to find the missing amounts would be to prepare a contribution income statement for each case, enter the known data, and then compute the missing items.)

a. Assume that only one product is being sold in each of the four following case situations:

Case	Units Sold	Sales	Variable Expenses	Contribution Margin per Unit	Fixed Expenses	Operating Income (Loss)
1	15,000	$180,000	$120,000	?	$50,000	?
2	?	$100,000	?	$10	$32,000	$8,000
3	10,000	?	$70,000	$13	?	$12,000
4	6,000	$300,000	?	?	$100,000	$(10,000)

b. Assume that more than one product is being sold in each of the four following case situations:

Case	Sales	Variable Expenses	Average Contribution Margin (Percent)	Fixed Expenses	Operating Income (Loss)
1	$500,000	?	20%	?	$7,000
2	$400,000	$260,000	?	$100,000	?
3	?	?	60%	$130,000	$20,000
4	$600,000	$420,000	?	?	$(5,000)

EXERCISE 6–15 Break-Even Analysis; Target Profit; Margin of Safety; CM Ratio [LO1, LO3, LO4, LO5]

Menlo Company manufactures and sells a single product. The company's sales and expenses for last quarter follow:

	Total	Per Unit
Sales	$450,000	$30
Less variable expenses	180,000	12
Contribution margin	270,000	$18
Less fixed expenses	216,000	
Operating income	$ 54,000	

Required:

1. What is the quarterly break-even point in units sold and in sales dollars?
2. Without resorting to computations, what is the total contribution margin at the break-even point?
3. How many units would have to be sold each quarter to earn a target profit of $90,000? Use the contribution margin method. Verify your answer by preparing a contribution format income statement at the target sales level.
4. Refer to the original data. Compute the company's margin of safety in both dollar and percentage terms.
5. What is the company's CM ratio? If sales increase by $50,000 per quarter and there is no change in fixed expenses, by how much would you expect quarterly operating income to increase?

EXERCISE 6–16 Operating Leverage [LO3, LO5]

Magic Realm, Inc., has developed a new fantasy board game. The company sold 15,000 games last year at a selling price of $20 per game. Fixed costs associated with the game total $182,000 per year, and variable costs are $6 per game. Production of the game is entrusted to a printing contractor. Variable costs consist mostly of payments to this contractor.

Required:

1. Prepare a contribution format income statement for the game last year and compute the degree of operating leverage.

2. Management is confident that the company can sell 18,000 games next year (an increase of 3,000 games, or 20%, over last year). Compute:
   a. The expected percentage increase in operating income for next year.
   b. The expected total dollar operating income for next year. (Do not prepare an income statement; use the degree of operating leverage to compute your answer.)

EXERCISE 6–17 Multiproduct Break-Even Analysis [LO6]
Olongapo Sports Corporation is the distributor in the Philippines of two premium golf balls—the Flight Dynamic and the Sure Shot. Monthly sales and the contribution margin ratios for the two products follow:

	Product		
	Flight Dynamic	Sure Shot	Total
Sales	P150,000	P250,000	P400,000
CM ratio	80%	36%	?

Fixed expenses total P183,750 per month. (The currency in the Philippines is the peso, which is denoted by P.)

Required:
1. Prepare a contribution format income statement for the company as a whole. Carry computations to one decimal place.
2. Compute the break-even point for the company based on the current sales mix.
3. If sales increase by P100,000 a month, by how much would you expect operating income to increase? What are your assumptions?

PROBLEMS

PROBLEM 6–18 Basic CVP Analysis; Graphing [LO1, LO2, LO3, LO4]
The Fashion Shoe Company operates a chain of women's shoe shops around the country. The shops carry many styles of shoes that are all sold at the same price. Sales personnel in the shops are paid a substantial commission on each pair of shoes sold (in addition to a small basic salary) in order to encourage them to be aggressive in their sales efforts.

The following worksheet contains cost and revenue data for Shop 48 and is typical of the company's many outlets:

Microsoft Excel - Problem 6-18 screen capture.xls

	A	B	C
1		*Per Pair of Shoes*	
2	Selling price	$ 30.00	
3			
4	Variable expenses:		
5	Invoice cost	$ 13.50	
6	Sales commission	4.50	
7	Total variable expenses	$ 18.00	
8			
9		*Annual*	
10	Fixed expenses:		
11	Advertising	$ 30,000	
12	Rent	20,000	
13	Salaries	100,000	
14	Total fixed expenses	$ 150,000	
15			

Required:

1. Calculate the annual break-even point in dollar sales and in unit sales for Shop 48.
2. Prepare a CVP graph showing cost and revenue data for Shop 48 from a zero level of activity up to 17,000 pairs of shoes sold each year. Clearly indicate the break-even point on the graph.
3. If 12,000 pairs of shoes are sold in a year, what would be Shop 48's operating income or loss?
4. The company is considering paying the store manager of Shop 48 an incentive commission of 75 cents per pair of shoes (in addition to the salesperson's commission). If this change is made, what will be the new break-even point in dollar sales and in unit sales?
5. Refer to the original data. As an alternative to (4) above, the company is considering paying the store manager 50 cents commission on each pair of shoes sold in excess of the break-even point. If this change is made, what will be the shop's operating income or loss if 15,000 pairs of shoes are sold?
6. Refer to the original data. The company is considering eliminating sales commissions entirely in its shops and increasing fixed salaries by $31,500 annually. If this change is made, what will be the new break-even point in dollar sales and in unit sales for Shop 48? Would you recommend that the change be made? Explain.

PROBLEM 6–19 Basics of CVP Analysis; Cost Structure [LO1, LO3, LO4]

Due to erratic sales of its sole product—a high-capacity battery for laptop computers—PEM, Inc., has been experiencing difficulty for some time. The company's contribution format income statement for the most recent month is given below:

Sales (19,500 units × $30 per unit)	$585,000
Less variable expenses	409,500
Contribution margin	175,500
Less fixed expenses	180,000
Operating loss	$ (4,500)

Required:

1. Compute the company's CM ratio and its break-even point in both units and dollars.
2. The president believes that a $16,000 increase in the monthly advertising budget, combined with an intensified effort by the sales staff, will result in an $80,000 increase in monthly sales. If the president is right, what will be the effect on the company's monthly operating income or loss? (Use the incremental approach in preparing your answer.)
3. Refer to the original data. The sales manager is convinced that a 10% reduction in the selling price, combined with an increase of $60,000 in the monthly advertising budget, will cause unit sales to double. What will the new contribution format income statement look like if these changes are adopted?
4. Refer to the original data. The Marketing Department thinks that a fancy new package for the laptop computer battery would help sales. The new package would increase packaging costs by 75 cents per unit. Assuming no other changes, how many units would have to be sold each month to earn a profit of $9,750?
5. Refer to the original data. By automating certain operations, the company could reduce variable costs by $3 per unit. However, fixed costs would increase by $72,000 each month.
   a. Compute the new CM ratio and the new break-even point in both units and dollars.
   b. Assume that the company expects to sell 26,000 units next month. Prepare two contribution format income statements, one assuming that operations are not automated and one assuming that they are. (Show data on a per unit and percentage basis, as well as in total, for each alternative.)
   c. Would you recommend that the company automate its operations? Explain.

PROBLEM 6–20 Basics of CVP Analysis [LO1, LO3, LO4, LO5]

Feather Friends, Inc., distributes a high-quality wooden birdhouse that sells for $20 per unit. Variable costs are $8 per unit, and fixed costs total $180,000 per year.

Required:

Answer the following independent questions:

1. What is the product's CM ratio?
2. Use the CM ratio to determine the break-even point in sales dollars.

3. Due to an increase in demand, the company estimates that sales will increase by $75,000 during the next year. By how much should operating income increase (or operating loss decrease) assuming that fixed costs do not change?
4. Assume that the operating results for last year were:

Sales	$400,000
Less variable expenses	160,000
Contribution margin	240,000
Less fixed expenses	180,000
Operating income	$60,000

   a. Compute the degree of operating leverage at the current level of sales.
   b. The president expects sales to increase by 20% next year. By what percentage should operating income increase?
5. Refer to the original data. Assume that the company sold 18,000 units last year. The sales manager is convinced that a 10% reduction in the selling price, combined with a $30,000 increase in advertising, would cause annual sales in units to increase by one-third. Prepare two contribution income statements, one showing the results of last year's operations and one showing the results of operations if these changes are made. Would you recommend that the company do as the sales manager suggests?
6. Refer to the original data. Assume again that the company sold 18,000 units last year. The president does not want to change the selling price. Instead, he wants to increase the sales commission by $1 per unit. He thinks that this move, combined with some increase in advertising, would increase annual sales by 25%. By how much could advertising be increased with profits remaining unchanged? Do not prepare an income statement; use the incremental analysis approach.

PROBLEM 6–21 Sales Mix; Multiproduct Break-Even Analysis [LO7]
Gold Star Rice, Ltd., of Thailand exports Thai rice throughout Asia. The company grows three varieties of rice—Fragrant, White, and Loonzain. (The currency in Thailand is the baht, which is denoted by B.) Budgeted sales by product and in total for the coming month are shown below:

	Product							
	White		Fragrant		Loonzain		Total	
Percentage of total sales	20%		52%		28%		100%	
Sales	B150,000	100%	B390,000	100%	B210,000	100%	B750,000	100%
Less variable expenses	108,000	72%	78,000	20%	84,000	40%	270,000	36%
Contribution margin	B 42,000	28%	B312,000	80%	B126,000	60%	480,000	64%
Less fixed expenses							449,280	
Operating income							B30,720	

$$\frac{\text{Break-even point}}{\text{in sales dollars}} = \frac{\text{Fixed expenses}}{\text{CM ratio}} = \frac{\text{B449,280}}{0.64} = \text{B702,000}$$

As shown by these data, operating income is budgeted at B30,720 for the month and break-even sales at B702,000.

Assume that actual sales for the month total B750,000 as planned. Actual sales by product are: White, B300,000; Fragrant, B180,000; and Loonzain, B270,000.

Required:
1. Prepare a contribution format income statement for the month based on actual sales data. Present the income statement in the format shown above.
2. Compute the break-even point in sales dollars for the month based on your actual data.
3. Considering the fact that the company met its B750,000 sales budget for the month, the president is shocked at the results shown on your income statement in (1) above. Prepare a brief memo for the president explaining why both the operating results and the break-even point in sales dollars are different from what was budgeted.

PROBLEM 6–22 Break-Even Analysis; Pricing [LO1, LO3, LO4]

Minden Company introduced a new product last year for which it is trying to find an optimal selling price. Marketing studies suggest that the company can increase sales by 5,000 units for each $2 reduction in the selling price. The company's present selling price is $70 per unit, and variable expenses are $40 per unit. Fixed expenses are $540,000 per year. The present annual sales volume (at the $70 selling price) is 15,000 units.

Required:

1. What is the present yearly operating income or loss?
2. What is the present break-even point in units and in dollar sales?
3. Assuming that the marketing studies are correct, what is the *maximum* profit that the company can earn yearly? At how many units and at what selling price per unit would the company generate this profit?
4. What would be the break-even point in units and in sales dollars using the selling price you determined in (3) above (e.g., the selling price at the level of maximum profits)? Why is this break-even point different from the break-even point you computed in (2) above?

PROBLEM 6–23 Interpretive Questions on the CVP Graph [LO2, LO4]

A CVP graph such as the one shown below is a useful technique for showing relationships between an organization's costs, volume, and profits.

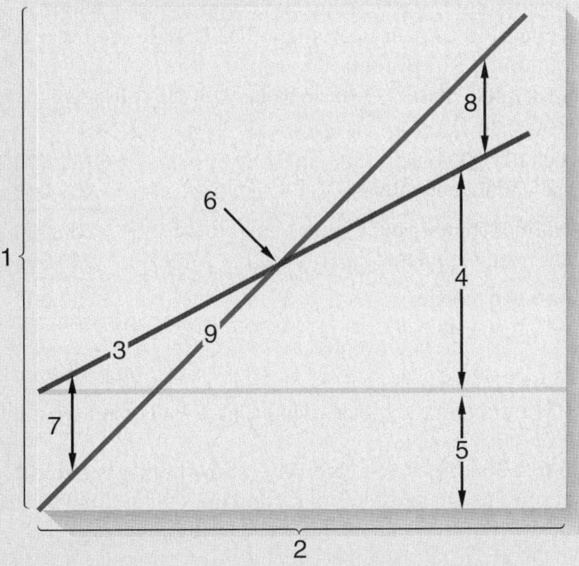

Required:

1. Identify the numbered components in the CVP graph.
2. State the effect of each of the following actions on line 3, line 9, and the break-even point. For line 3 and line 9, state whether the action will cause the line to:

   Remain unchanged.
   Shift upward.
   Shift downward.
   Have a steeper slope (i.e., rotate upward).
   Have a flatter slope (i.e., rotate downward).
   Shift upward *and* have a steeper slope.
   Shift upward *and* have a flatter slope.
   Shift downward *and* have a steeper slope.
   Shift downward *and* have a flatter slope.

   In the case of the break-even point, state whether the action will cause the break-even point to:

   Remain unchanged.
   Increase.
   Decrease.
   Probably change, but the direction is uncertain.

   Treat each case independently.

x. *Example.* Fixed costs are reduced by $5,000 per period.
Answer (see choices above): Line 3: Shift downward.
Line 9: Remain unchanged.
Break-even point: Decrease.

a. The unit selling price is increased from $18 to $20.
b. Unit variable costs are decreased from $12 to $10.
c. Fixed costs are increased by $3,000 per period.
d. Two thousand more units are sold during the period than were budgeted.
e. Due to paying salespersons a commission rather than a flat salary, fixed costs are reduced by $8,000 per period and unit variable costs are increased by $3.
f. Due to an increase in the cost of materials, both unit variable costs and the selling price are increased by $2.
g. Advertising costs are increased by $10,000 per period, resulting in a 10% increase in the number of units sold.
h. Due to automating an operation previously done by workers, fixed costs are increased by $12,000 per period and unit variable costs are reduced by $4.

PROBLEM 6–24 Various CVP Questions: Break-Even Point; Cost Structure; Target Sales [LO1, LO3, LO4, LO5]

Northwood Company manufactures basketballs. The company has a ball that sells for $25. At present, the ball is manufactured in a small plant that relies heavily on direct labour workers. Thus, variable costs are high, totalling $15 per ball.

Last year, the company sold 30,000 of these balls, with the following results:

Sales (30,000 balls)	$750,000
Less variable expenses	450,000
Contribution margin	300,000
Less fixed expenses	210,000
Operating income	$ 90,000

Required:

1. Compute (a) the CM ratio and the break-even point in balls, and (b) the degree of operating leverage at last year's sales level.
2. Due to an increase in labour rates, the company estimates that variable costs will increase by $3 per ball next year. If this change takes place and the selling price per ball remains constant at $25, what will be the new CM ratio and break-even point in balls?
3. Refer to the data in (2) above. If the expected change in variable costs takes place, how many balls will have to be sold next year to earn the same operating income ($90,000) as last year?
4. Refer again to the data in (2) above. The president feels that the company must raise the selling price of its basketballs. If Northwood Company wants to maintain *the same CM ratio as last year,* what selling price per ball must it charge next year to cover the increased labour costs?
5. Refer to the original data. The company is discussing the construction of a new, automated manufacturing plant. The new plant would slash variable costs per ball by 40%, but it would cause fixed costs per year to double. If the new plant is built, what would be the company's new CM ratio and new break-even point in balls?
6. Refer to the data in (5) above.
   a. If the new plant is built, how many balls will have to be sold next year to earn the same operating income ($90,000) as last year?
   b. Assume the new plant is built and that next year the company manufactures and sells 30,000 balls (the same number as sold last year). Prepare a contribution income statement and compute the degree of operating leverage.
   c. If you were a member of top management, would you have been in favour of constructing the new plant? Explain.

PROBLEM 6–25 Graphing; Incremental Analysis; Operating Leverage [LO2, LO3, LO4, LO5]

Angie Silva has recently opened The Sandal Shop in Brisbane, Australia, a store that specializes in fashionable sandals. Angie has just received a degree in business and she is anxious to apply the principles she has learned to her business. In time, she hopes to open a chain of sandal shops. As a first step, she has prepared the following analysis for her new store:

Sales price per pair of sandals	$40
Variable expenses per pair of sandals	16
Contribution margin per pair of sandals . . .	$24
Fixed expenses per year:	
Building rental	$15,000
Equipment depreciation	7,000
Selling	20,000
Administrative	18,000
Total fixed expenses	$60,000

Required:

1. How many pairs of sandals must be sold each year to break even? What does this represent in total sales dollars?
2. Prepare a CVP graph for the store from a zero level of activity up to 4,000 pairs of sandals sold each year. Indicate the break-even point on your graph.
3. Angie has decided that she must earn at least $18,000 the first year to justify her time and effort. How many pairs of sandals must be sold to reach this target profit?
4. Angie now has two salespersons working in the store—one full time and one part time. It will cost her an additional $8,000 per year to convert the part-time position to a full-time position. Angie believes that the change would bring in an additional $25,000 in sales each year. Should she convert the position? Use the incremental approach. (Do not prepare an income statement.)
5. Refer to the original data. During the first year, the store sold only 3,000 pairs of sandals and reported the following operating results:

Sales (3,000 pairs)	$120,000
Less variable expenses	48,000
Contribution margin	72,000
Less fixed expenses	60,000
Operating income	$ 12,000

   a. What is the store's degree of operating leverage?
   b. Angie is confident that with a more intense sales effort and with a more creative advertising program she can increase sales by 50% next year. What would be the expected percentage increase in operating income? Use the degree of operating leverage to compute your answer.

PROBLEM 6–26 Changes in Fixed and Variable Costs; Break-Even and Target Profit Analysis [LO3, LO4]

Neptune Company produces toys and other items for use in beach and resort areas. A small, inflatable toy has come onto the market that the company is anxious to produce and sell. The new toy will sell for $3 per unit. Enough capacity exists in the company's plant to produce 16,000 units of the toy each month. Variable costs to manufacture and sell one unit would be $1.25, and fixed costs associated with the toy would total $35,000 per month.

The company's Marketing Department predicts that demand for the new toy will exceed the 16,000 units that the company is able to produce. Additional manufacturing space can be rented from another company at a fixed cost of $1,000 per month. Variable costs in the rented facility would total $1.40 per unit, due to somewhat less efficient operations than in the main plant.

Required:

1. Compute the monthly break-even point for the new toy in units and in total sales dollars. Show all computations in good form.
2. How many units must be sold each month to make a monthly profit of $12,000?
3. If the sales manager receives a bonus of 10 cents for each unit sold in excess of the break-even point, how many units must be sold each month to earn a return of 25% on the monthly investment in fixed costs?

PROBLEM 6–27 Break-Even and Target Profit Analysis [LO4]

The Shirt Works sells a large variety of tee shirts and sweatshirts. Steve Hooper, the owner, is thinking of expanding his sales by hiring local high school students, on a commission basis, to sell sweatshirts bearing the name and mascot of the local high school.

These sweatshirts would have to be ordered from the manufacturer six weeks in advance, and they could not be returned because of the unique printing required. The sweatshirts would cost Mr. Hooper $8 each with a minimum order of 75 sweatshirts. Any additional sweatshirts would have to be ordered in increments of 75.

Since Mr. Hooper's plan would not require any additional facilities, the only costs associated with the project would be the costs of the sweatshirts and the costs of the sales commissions. The selling price of the sweatshirts would be $13.50 each. Mr. Hooper would pay the students a commission of $1.50 for each shirt sold.

Required:

1. To make the project worthwhile, Mr. Hooper would require a $1,200 profit for the first three months of the venture. What level of sales in units and in dollars would be required to reach this target operating income? Show all computations.
2. Assume that the venture is undertaken and an order is placed for 75 sweatshirts. What would be Mr. Hooper's break-even point in units and in sales dollars? Show computations and explain the reasoning behind your answer.

PROBLEM 6–28 Changes in Cost Structure; Break-Even Analysis; Operating Leverage; Margin of Safety [LO3, LO4, LO5]

Morton Company's contribution format income statement for last month is given below:

Sales (15,000 units × $30 per unit)	$450,000
Less variable expenses	315,000
Contribution margin	135,000
Less fixed expenses	90,000
Operating income	$ 45,000

The industry in which Morton Company operates is quite sensitive to cyclical movements in the economy. Thus, profits vary considerably from year to year according to general economic conditions. The company has a large amount of unused capacity and is studying ways of improving profits.

Required:

1. New equipment has come onto the market that would allow Morton Company to automate a portion of its operations. Variable costs would be reduced by $9 per unit. However, fixed costs would increase to a total of $225,000 each month. Prepare two contribution format income statements, one showing present operations and one showing how operations would appear if the new equipment is purchased. Show an Amount column, a Per Unit column, and a Percent column on each statement. Do not show percentages for the fixed costs.
2. Refer to the income statements in (1) above. For both present operations and the proposed new operations, compute (a) the degree of operating leverage, (b) the break-even point in dollars, and (c) the margin of safety in both dollar and percentage terms.
3. Refer again to the data in (1) above. As a manager, what factor would be paramount in your mind in deciding whether to purchase the new equipment? (Assume that ample funds are available to make the purchase.)
4. Refer to the original data. Rather than purchase new equipment, the marketing manager is thinking about changing the company's marketing strategy. Rather than pay sales commissions, which are currently included in variable expenses, the company would pay salespersons fixed salaries and would invest heavily in advertising. The marketing manager claims this new approach would increase unit sales by 30% without any change in selling price; the company's new monthly fixed expenses would be $180,000; and its operating income would increase by 20%. Compute the break-even point in sales dollars for the company under the new marketing strategy. Do you agree with the marketing manager's proposal?

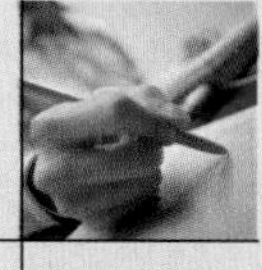

PROBLEM 6–29 Sales Mix; Break-Even Analysis; Margin of Safety [LO5, LO6]

Island Novelties, Inc., of Palau makes two products, Hawaiian Fantasy and Tahitian Joy. Present revenue, cost, and sales data for the two products follow:

	Hawaiian Fantasy	Tahitian Joy
Selling price per unit	$15	$100
Variable expenses per unit	$9	$20
Number of units sold annually	20,000	5,000

Fixed expenses total $475,800 per year. The Republic of Palau uses the U.S. dollar as its currency.

Required:

1. Assuming the sales mix given above, do the following:
   a. Prepare a contribution format income statement showing both dollar and percent columns for each product and for the company as a whole.
   b. Compute the break-even point in dollars for the company as a whole and the margin of safety in both dollars and percent.
2. The company has developed a new product to be called Samoan Delight. Assume that the company could sell 10,000 units at $45 each. The variable expenses would be $36 each. The company's fixed expenses would not change.
   a. Prepare another contribution format income statement, including sales of the Samoan Delight (sales of the other two products would not change).
   b. Compute the company's new break-even point in dollars and the new margin of safety in both dollars and percent.
3. The president of the company examines your figures and says, "There's something strange here. Our fixed costs haven't changed and you show greater total contribution margin if we add the new product, but you also show our break-even point going up. With greater contribution margin, the break-even point should go down, not up. You've made a mistake somewhere." Explain to the president what has happened.

PROBLEM 6–30 Sales Mix; Commission Structure; Multiproduct Break-Even Analysis [LO6]

Carbex, Inc., produces cutlery sets out of high-quality wood and steel. The company makes a standard cutlery set and a deluxe set and sells them to retail department stores throughout the country. The standard set sells for $60, and the deluxe set sells for $75. The variable expenses associated with each set are given below (in cost per set):

	Standard	Deluxe
Production costs	$15.00	$30.00
Sales commissions (15% of sales price)	$9.00	$11.25

The company's fixed expenses each month are:

Advertising	$105,000
Depreciation	$21,700
Administrative	$63,000

Salespersons are paid on a commission basis to encourage them to be aggressive in their sales efforts. Mary Parsons, the financial vice president, watches sales commissions carefully and has noted that they have risen steadily over the last year. For this reason, she was shocked to find that even though sales have increased, profits for the current month—May—are down substantially from April. Sales, in sets, for the last two months are given below:

	Standard	Deluxe	Total
April	4,000	2,000	6,000
May	1,000	5,000	6,000

Required:

1. Prepare contribution format income statements for April and May. Use the following headings:

	Standard		Deluxe		Total	
	Amount	Percent	Amount	Percent	Amount	Percent
Sales						
Etc						

Place the fixed expenses only in the Total column. Do not show percentages for the fixed expenses.

2. Explain why there is a difference in operating income between the two months, even though the same *total* number of sets was sold in each month.
3. What can be done to the sales commissions to optimize the sales mix?
4. *a.* Using April's figures, what was the break-even point for the month in sales dollars?
   b. Has May's break-even point gone up or down from that of April? Explain your answer without calculating the break-even point for May.

PROBLEM 6–31 Break-Even-Even Analysis; Indifference Analysis [LO4]
Production cost and price data for Beltar Company are as follows:

Maximum capacity per year	200,000 units
Variable manufacturing costs	$12/unit
Fixed factory overhead costs	$600,000/year
Variable selling and administrative costs	$5/unit
Fixed selling and administrative costs	$300,000/year
Current sales price	$23/unit

The company's sales for the year just ended totalled 185,000 units. However, a strike at a major supplier has caused a shortage of raw materials, and as a result, the current year's sales will reach only 160,000 units. Top management is planning to reduce fixed costs this year by $59,000, as compared to last year.

Management is also thinking of either increasing the selling price or reducing the variable costs, or both, in order to earn a target operating income that will be the same dollar amount as last year's. The company has already sold 30,000 units this year at $23 per unit, with the variable costs remaining unchanged from last year.

Required:

1. Calculate the contribution margin per unit required on the remaining 130,000 units in order to reach the target operating income.
2. The president of the company is contemplating a significant change in the manufacturing process for next year. This change would increase the capacity to 225,000 units. The change would increase fixed factory overhead to $2,200,000, while reducing the variable manufacturing cost per unit to $3.35. All other costs and revenues would remain unchanged.

   Draft a brief memo to the president explaining the potential benefits and risks of a move to this cost structure. Support your explanation with the necessary numerical analysis. (Hint: Use the previous year's sales and costs as a point of reference to compare the effects on operating income of a 19% increase or a 19% decrease in sales volume under the current and proposed cost structures.)

(CGA, adapted)

CASES

CASE 6–32 Detailed Income Statement; CVP Analysis [LO1, LO3, LO4]
The most recent income statement for Whitney Company appears at the top of page 265.

All variable expenses in the company vary in terms of units sold, except for sales commissions, which are based on sales dollars. Variable manufacturing overhead is 30 cents per unit. There were no beginning or ending inventories. Whitney Company's plant has a capacity of 75,000 units per year.

The company has been operating at a loss for several years. Management is studying several possible courses of action to determine what should be done to make next year profitable.

WHITNEY COMPANY
Income Statement
For the Year Ended December 31

Sales (45,000 units at $10 per unit)			$450,000
Less cost of goods sold:			
Direct materials		$90,000	
Direct labour		78,300	
Manufacturing overhead		98,500	266,800
Gross margin			183,200
Less operating expenses:			
Selling expenses:			
Variable:			
Sales commissions	$27,000		
Shipping	5,400	32,400	
Fixed (advertising, salaries)		120,000	
Administrative:			
Variable (billing and other)		1,800	
Fixed (salaries and other)		48,000	202,200
Operating loss			$ (19,000)

Required:

1. Redo Whitney Company's income statement in the contribution format. Show both a Total column and a Per Unit column on your statement. Leave enough space to the right of your numbers to enter the solution to both parts of (2) below.
2. The president is considering two proposals prepared by members of his staff:
   a. For next year, the vice president would like to reduce the unit selling price by 20%. She is certain that this would fill the plant to capacity.
   b. For next year, the sales manager would like to increase the unit selling price by 20%, increase the sales commission to 9% of sales, and increase advertising by $100,000. Based on marketing studies, he is confident this would increase unit sales by one-third.

   Prepare two contribution income statements, one showing what profits would be under the vice president's proposal and one showing what profits would be under the sales manager's proposal. On each statement, include both Total and Per Unit columns (do not show per unit data for the fixed costs).
3. Refer to the original data. The president believes it would be a mistake to change the unit selling price. Instead, he wants to use less costly raw materials, thereby reducing unit costs by 70 cents. How many units would have to be sold next year to earn a target profit of $30,200?
4. Refer to the original data. Whitney Company's board of directors believes that the company's problem lies in inadequate promotion. By how much can advertising be increased and still allow the company to earn a target profit of 4.5% on sales of 60,000 units?
5. Refer to the original data. The company has been approached by an overseas distributor who wants to purchase 9,500 units on a special price basis. There would be no sales commission on these units. However, shipping costs would be increased by 50% and variable administrative costs would be reduced by 25%. In addition, a $5,700 special insurance fee would have to be paid by Whitney Company to protect the goods in transit. What unit price would have to be quoted on the 9,500 units by Whitney Company to allow the company to earn a profit of $14,250 on total operations? Regular business would not be affected by this special order.

CASE 6–33 Missing Data; Break-Even Analysis; Target Profit; Margin of Safety; Operating Leverage [LO1, LO3, LO4, LO5]

You were employed just this morning by Pyrrhic Company, a prominent and rapidly growing organization. As your initial assignment, you were asked to complete an analysis of one of the company's products for the board of directors meeting later in the day. After completing the analysis, you left your office for a few moments only to discover on returning that a broken sprinkler in the ceiling has destroyed most of your work. Only the following bits remained:

PYRRHIC COMPANY
Actual Income Statement
For the Month Ended June 30

	Total	Per Unit	Percent
Sales (? units)	$?	$?	100%
Less variable expenses	?	?	?%
Contribution margin	?	$?	?%
Less fixed expenses	?		
Operating income	$?		
Break-even point:			
In units	? units		
In dollars	$180,000		
Margin of safety:			
In dollars	$?		
In percentage	20%		
Degree of operating leverage	?		

The computations above are all based on actual results for June. The company's *projected* contribution format income statement for this product for July follows:

PYRRHIC COMPANY
Projected Income Statement
For the Month Ended July 31

	Total	Per Unit	Percent
Sales (33,000 units)	$?	$?	?%
Less variable expenses	?	?	?%
Contribution margin	?	$?	?%
Less fixed expenses	?		
Operating income	$40,500		

To add to your woes, the company's mainframe computer is down so no data are available from that source. You do remember that sales for July are projected to increase by 10% over sales for June. You also remember that June's operating income was $27,000—the same amount as your annual salary from the company. Finally, you remember that the degree of operating leverage is highly useful to the manager as a predictive tool.

Total fixed expenses, the unit selling price, and the unit variable expenses are planned to be the same in June and July.

The board of directors meets in just one hour.

Required:

1. For the June data, do the following:
   a. Complete the June contribution format income statement (all three columns).
   b. Compute the break-even point in units and verify the break-even point in sales dollars that is provided above. Use the contribution margin method.
   c. Compute the margin of safety in dollars and verify the margin of safety percentage that is provided above.
   d. Compute the degree of operating leverage as of June 30.
2. For the July data, do the following:
   a. Complete the July projected contribution format income statement (all three columns).
   b. Compute the margin of safety in dollars and percent and compute the degree of operating leverage. Why has the margin of safety gone up and the degree of operating leverage gone down?
3. Brimming with confidence after having completed (1) and (2) above in less than one hour, you decide to give the board of directors some added data. You know that direct labour accounts for $1.80 of the company's per unit variable expenses. You have learned that direct labour costs may increase by one-third next year. Assuming that this cost increase takes place and that

selling price and other cost factors remain unchanged, how many units will the company have to sell in a month to earn a operating income equal to 20% of sales?

CASE 6–34 Cost Structure; Break-Even; Target Profits [LO3, LO4]

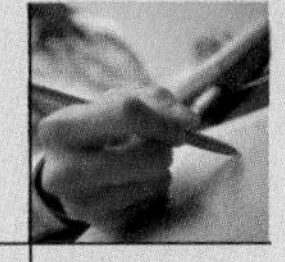

Pittman Company is a small but growing manufacturer of telecommunications equipment. The company has no sales force of its own; rather, it relies completely on independent sales agents to market its products. These agents are paid a commission of 15% of selling price for all items sold.

Barbara Cheney, Pittman's controller, has just prepared the company's budgeted income statement for next year. The statement follows:

PITTMAN COMPANY
Budgeted Income Statement
For the Year Ended December 31

Sales		$16,000,000
Manufacturing costs:		
Variable	$7,200,000	
Fixed overhead	2,340,000	9,540,000
Gross margin		6,460,000
Selling and administrative costs:		
Commissions to agents	2,400,000	
Fixed marketing costs	120,000*	
Fixed administrative costs	1,800,000	4,320,000
Operating income		2,140,000
Less fixed interest cost		540,000
Income before income taxes		1,600,000
Less income taxes (30%)		480,000
Net income		$ 1,120,000

*Primarily depreciation on storage facilities.

As Barbara handed the statement to Karl Vecci, Pittman's president, she commented, "I went ahead and used the agents' 15% commission rate in completing these statements, but we've just learned that they refuse to handle our products next year unless we increase the commission rate to 20%."

"That's the last straw," Karl replied angrily. "Those agents have been demanding more and more, and this time they've gone too far. How can they possibly defend a 20% commission rate?"

"They claim that after paying for advertising, travel, and the other costs of promotion, there's nothing left over for profit," replied Barbara.

"I say it's just plain robbery," retorted Karl. "And I also say it's time we dumped those guys and got our own sales force. Can you get your people to work up some cost figures for us to look at?"

"We've already worked them up," said Barbara. "Several companies we know about pay a 7.5% commission to their own salespeople, along with a small salary. Of course, we would have to handle all promotion costs, too. We figure our fixed costs would increase by $2,400,000 per year, but that would be more than offset by the $3,200,000 (20% × $16,000,000) that we would avoid on agents' commissions."

The breakdown of the $2,400,000 cost follows:

Salaries:	
Sales manager	$ 100,000
Salespersons	600,000
Travel and entertainment	400,000
Advertising	1,300,000
Total	$2,400,000

"Super," replied Karl. "And I noticed that the $2,400,000 is just what we're paying the agents under the old 15% commission rate."

"It's even better than that," explained Barbara. "We can actually save $75,000 a year because that's what we're having to pay the auditing firm now to check out the agents' reports. So our overall administrative costs would be less."

"Pull all of these numbers together and we'll show them to the executive committee tomorrow," said Karl. "With the approval of the committee, we can move on the matter immediately."

Required:

1. Compute Pittman Company's break-even point in sales dollars for next year assuming:
   a. That the agents' commission rate remains unchanged at 15%.
   b. That the agents' commission rate is increased to 20%.
   c. That the company employs its own sales force.
2. Assume that Pittman Company decides to continue selling through agents and pays the 20% commission rate. Determine the volume of sales that would be required to generate the same net income as contained in the budgeted income statement for next year.
3. Determine the volume of sales at which net income would be equal regardless of whether Pittman Company sells through agents (at a 20% commission rate) or employs its own sales force.
4. Compute the degree of operating leverage that the company would expect to have on December 31 at the end of next year assuming:
   a. That the agents' commission rate remains unchanged at 15%.
   b. That the agents' commission rate is increased to 20%.
   c. That the company employs its own sales force.
   Use income *before* income taxes in your operating leverage computation.
5. Based on the data in (1) through (4) above, make a recommendation as to whether the company should continue to use sales agents (at a 20% commission rate) or employ its own sales force. Give reasons for your answer.

(CMA, adapted)

CASE 6–35 Break-Even Analysis with Step Fixed Costs [LO4]

The Pediatric Department at Wymont General Hospital has a capacity of 90 beds and operates 24 hours a day every day. The measure of activity in the department is patient-days, where one patient-day represents one patient occupying a bed for one day. The average revenue per patient-day is $130 and the average variable cost per patient-day is $50. The fixed cost of the department (not including personnel costs) is $454,000.

The only personnel directly employed by the Pediatric Department are aides, nurses, and supervising nurses. The hospital has minimum staffing requirements for the department based on total annual patient-days in Pediatrics. Hospital requirements, beginning at the minimum expected level of activity, follow:

Annual Patient-Days	Aides	Nurses	Supervising Nurses
10,000–14,000	21	11	4
14,001–17,000	22	12	4
17,001–23,725	22	13	4
23,726–25,550	25	14	5
25,551–27,375	26	14	5
27,376–29,200	29	16	6

These staffing levels represent full-time equivalents, and it should be assumed that the Pediatric Department always employs only the minimum number of required full-time equivalent personnel.

Average annual salaries for each class of employee are: aides, $18,000; nurses, $26,000; and supervising nurses, $36,000.

Required:

1. Compute the total fixed costs (including the salaries of aides, nurses, and supervising nurses) in the Pediatric Department for each level of activity shown above (i.e., total fixed costs at the 10,000–14,000 patient-day level of activity, total fixed costs at the 14,001–17,000 patient-day level of activity, etc.).
2. Compute the minimum number of patient-days required for the Pediatric Department to break even.
3. Determine the minimum number of patient-days required for the Pediatric Department to earn an annual "profit" of $200,000.

(CPA, adapted)

CASE 6–36 Break-Evens for Individual Products in a Multiproduct Company [LO4, LO6]
Cheryl Montoya picked up the phone and called her boss, Wes Chan, the vice president of marketing at Piedmont Fasteners Corporation: "Wes, I'm not sure how to go about answering the questions that came up at the meeting with the president yesterday."

"What's the problem?"

"The president wanted to know the break-even point for each of the company's products, but I am having trouble figuring them out."

"I'm sure you can handle it, Cheryl. And, by the way, I need your analysis on my desk tomorrow morning at 8:00 sharp in time for the follow-up meeting at 9:00."

Piedmont Fasteners Corporation makes three different clothing fasteners in its manufacturing facility in Edmonton. Data concerning these products appear below:

	Velcro	Metal	Nylon
Normal annual sales volume	100,000	200,000	400,000
Unit selling price	$1.65	$1.50	$0.85
Variable cost per unit	$1.25	$0.70	$0.25

Total fixed expenses are $400,000 per year.

All three products are sold in highly competitive markets, so the company is unable to raise its prices without losing unacceptable numbers of customers.

The company has an extremely effective just-in-time manufacturing system, so there are no beginning or ending work in process or finished goods inventories.

Required:

1. What is the company's over-all break-even in total sales dollars?
2. Of the total fixed costs of $400,000, $20,000 could be avoided if the Velcro product were dropped, $80,000 if the Metal product were dropped, and $60,000 if the Nylon product were dropped. The remaining fixed costs of $240,000 consist of common fixed costs such as administrative salaries and rent on the factory building that could be avoided only by going out of business entirely.
   a. What is the break-even point in units for each product?
   b. If the company sells exactly the break-even quantity of each product, what will be the overall profit of the company? Explain this result.

CASE 6–37 CVP, Uncertainty (Appendix 6A) [LO7]
Note: Each part is independent.

Part A

Glace Bay has just announced plans to build a library and arts centre complex. To encourage development of creative design concepts, the city has indicated its intention to hold a design competition. The best entry will win the architectural contract, which will generate a revenue of $250,000 before the design costs.

A local firm of architects is considering submitting a proposal. They know that a well thought-out design would greatly enhance their chance of winning. However, such a design is costly. On the other hand, a less costly design proposal has a limited chance of winning.

The architectural firm has two proposals under consideration. Each proposal has the following cost and probabilities associated with it:

	Cost of Design Proposal	Probability of Winning Contract
Proposal A	80,000	60
Proposal B	30,000	30

Design costs are assumed to be incurred at the beginning of the current year. Income taxes are 40%.

Required:

Which proposal would you recommend the architectural firm submit to the design competition? Show all calculations.

(SMAC Adapted)

Part B

New Fashion Inc., is a manufacturer of several clothing lines based on oriental motifs. Aggressive advertising and sales campaigns have resulted in rapid growth up to existing capacity and the owner, Ying Yao, is now considering the purchase of the necessary additional production equipment to start up a new dress line.

Yao's purchasing manager has selected a machine with the following characteristics:

Initial cost per machine	$200,000
Estimated salvage in 5 years	$10,000
Capacity per year	600 units
Capital cost allowance, class B	20%

In an effort to improve its own sagging fortunes, the company selling the machine has offered to sell Yao a second or any subsequent machine required at a 20% discount from the normal single unit cost.

Market research has indicated that annual demand for the new dress line can be established and stabilized at a static figure for a period of five years.

The production manager has estimated that the manufacturing cost for the new dress will be as follows:

Direct Materials	$40 per unit
Direct Labour	6 hours at $10 per hour
Variable overhead	20% of direct labour cost

Required:

1. The sales manager has estimated the probability distribution for annual demand based on a price of $220 as follows:

Demand Level	Probability
800	.20
1,000	.40
1,200	.30
1,400	.10

   Determine the expected contribution before taxes.

2. Not satisfied with the uncertainty of this distribution, the sales manager hired an industrial specialist who had prior information regarding the fashion market. Using his prior information, the specialist predicted the following table of conditional probabilities:

Demand Level	Conditional Probability
800	.1250
1,000	.1875
1,200	.2500
1,400	.4375

Determine the expected contribution margin after receipt of this information.

(SMAC Adapted)

GROUP AND INTERNET EXERCISES

GROUP EXERCISE 6–38 CVP and Collegiate Sports

Revenue from major intercollegiate sports is an important source of funds for many universities. Most of the costs of putting on a football or basketball game are fixed and increase very little as the size of the crowd increases. Thus, the revenue from every extra ticket sold is almost pure profit.

Choose a sport played at your college or university, such as football or basketball, that generates significant revenue. Talk with the business manager of your sports programs before answering the following questions:

Required:

1. What is the maximum seating capacity of the stadium or arena in which the sport is played? During the past year, what was the average attendance at the games? On average, what percentage of the stadium or arena capacity was filled?
2. The number of seats sold often depends on the opponent. The attendance for a game with a traditional rival is usually substantially above the average. Also, games against conference foes may draw larger crowds than other games. As a consequence, the number of tickets sold for a game is somewhat predictable. What implications does this have for the nature of the costs of putting on a game? Are most of the costs really fixed with respect to the number of tickets sold?
3. Estimate the variable cost per ticket sold.
4. Estimate the total additional revenue that would be generated in an average game if all of the tickets were sold at their normal prices. Estimate how much profit is lost because these tickets are not sold.
5. Estimate the ancillary revenue (parking and concessions) per ticket sold. Estimate how much profit is lost in an average game from these sources of revenue as a consequence of not having a sold-out game.
6. Estimate how much additional profit would be generated for your college if every game were sold out for the entire season.

GROUP EXERCISE 6–39 Airline Cost Structure

Airlines provide an excellent illustration of the concept of operating leverage, the sensitivity of a firm's operating profits to changes in demand, and the opportunities and risks presented by such a cost structure. The Uniform System of Accounts required by the Department of Transportation for airlines operating in the United States contains the following cost categories:

- Fuel and oil.
- Flying operations labour (flight crews—pilots, copilots, navigators, and flight engineers).
- Passenger service labour (flight attendants).
- Aircraft traffic and servicing labour (personnel servicing aircraft and handling passengers at gates, baggage, and cargo).
- Promotions and sales labour (reservations and sales agents, advertising and publicity).
- Maintenance labour (maintenance of flight equipment and ground property and equipment).
- Maintenance materials and overhead.
- Ground property and equipment (landing fees, rental expenses, and depreciation for ground property and equipment).
- Flight equipment (rental expenses and depreciation on aircraft frames and engines).
- General overhead (administrative personnel, utilities, insurance, communications, etc.).

Required:

1. Which of the above costs are likely to be affected if an airline adds an airport to its network?
2. Which of the above costs are likely to be affected if an airline schedules one more flight out of an airport that the airline already serves?
3. Which of the above costs are likely to be variable with respect to the number of passengers who actually fly on a particular scheduled flight?
4. Are airline profits likely to be affected very much by their load factors? Why? (The load factor refers to the percentage of scheduled seats filled by paying passengers.)

INTERNET EXERCISE 6–40

As you know, the World Wide Web is a medium that is constantly evolving. Sites come and go, and change without notice. To enable the periodic updating of site addresses, this problem has been posted to the textbook Web site (www.mcgrawhill.ca/college/garrison). After accessing the site, enter the Student Centre and select this chapter. Select and complete the Internet exercise.

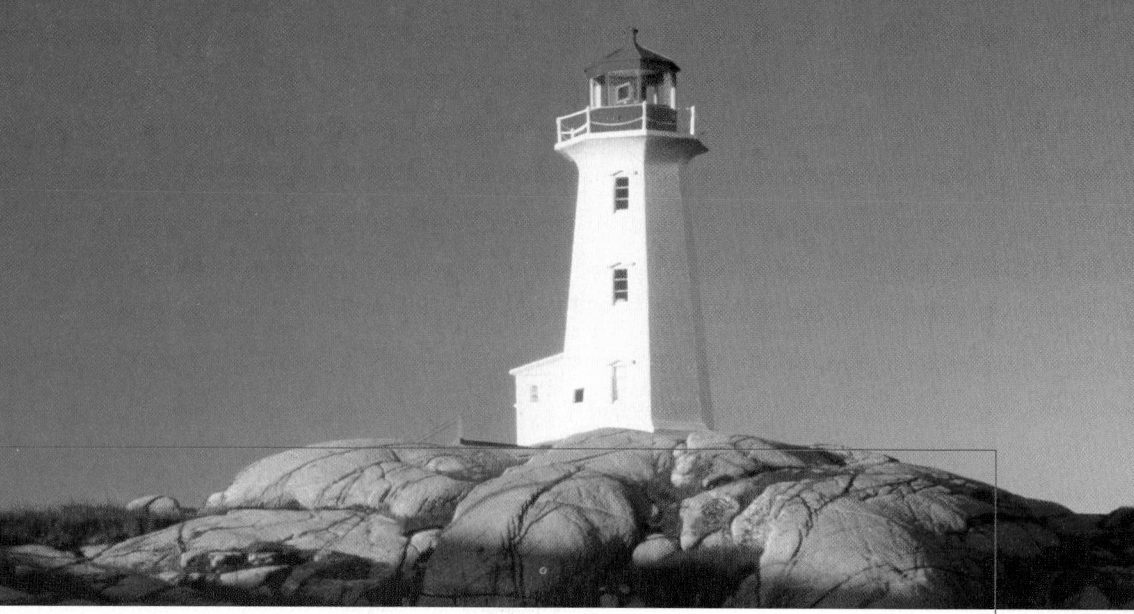

CHAPTER 7

LEARNING OBJECTIVES

After studying Chapter 7, you should be able to:

1. Explain how variable costing differs from absorption costing and compute unit product costs under each method.
2. Prepare income statements using both variable and absorption costing.
3. Reconcile variable costing and absorption costing operating incomes and explain why the two amounts differ.
4. Explain the advantages and disadvantages of both variable and absorption costing.
5. Explain how the use of JIT reduces the difference in reported operating income under the variable and absorption costing methods.

VARIABLE COSTING: A TOOL FOR MANAGEMENT

BUSINESS FOCUS

MANIPULATING PROFITS

Tina Xu is employed as an investment analyst in Toronto. She has just received the current annual report of Andersen Transformers Limited and is puzzled by several items in the report.

Andersen Transformers' ending inventory was 40% higher than the previous year's amount and operating income had risen, even though sales had remained relatively stable.

How can building inventories increase profits without any increases in sales? As we will see in this chapter, absorption costing—the most widely used method of determining product costs—can be used to manipulate profits in just this way.

Two general approaches are used for costing products for the purposes of valuing inventories and cost of goods sold. One approach, called *absorption costing,* was discussed in Chapter 3. Absorption costing is generally used for external financial reports. The other approach, called *variable costing,* is preferred by some managers for internal decision making and must be used when an income statement is prepared in the contribution format. Ordinarily, absorption costing and variable costing produce different figures for net operating income, and the difference can be quite large. In addition to showing how these two methods differ, we will consider the arguments for and against each costing method and we will show how management decisions can be affected by the costing method chosen.

In Chapters 5 and 6, the presentations generally assumed inventories were insignificant or that production equals sales. This assumption is reasonable in some situations as shall be presented later in this chapter. However, inventories can be important to income results in other situations. The explanations to follow will show what is involved when production does not equal sales and thus production is a cost driver rather than sales. Also the analysis will include the elements of production costs rather than using only the total production costs.

OVERVIEW OF ABSORPTION AND VARIABLE COST

LEARNING OBJECTIVE 1
Explain how variable costing differs from absorption costing and compute unit product costs under each method.

In the last two chapters, we learned that the contribution format income statement and cost-volume-profit (CVP) analysis are valuable management tools. Both of these tools emphasize cost behaviour and require that managers carefully distinguish between variable and fixed costs. Absorption costing assigns both variable and fixed costs to products—mingling them in a way that makes it difficult for managers to distinguish between them. In contrast, variable costing focuses on *cost behaviour*, clearly separating fixed from variable costs. One of the strengths of variable costing is that it harmonizes fully with both the contribution approach and the CVP concepts discussed in the preceding chapters.

Absorption Costing

In Chapter 3, we learned that **absorption costing** treats *all* costs of production as product costs, regardless of whether they are variable or fixed. The cost of a unit of product under the absorption costing method therefore consists of direct materials, direct labour, and *both* variable and fixed overhead. Thus, absorption costing allocates a portion of fixed manufacturing overhead cost to each unit of product, along with the variable manufacturing costs. Because absorption costing includes all costs of production as product costs, it is frequently referred to as the **full cost method**.

Absorption costing
A costing method that includes all manufacturing costs—direct materials, direct labour, and both variable and fixed manufacturing overhead—in the cost of a unit of product. Absorption costing is also referred to as the *full cost method.*

Full cost method
Same as *absorption costing.*

Variable Costing

Under **variable costing,** only those costs of production that vary with output are treated as product costs. This would generally include direct materials, direct labour, and the variable portion of manufacturing overhead. Fixed manufacturing overhead is not treated as a product cost under this method. Rather, fixed manufacturing overhead is treated as a period cost and, like selling and administrative expenses, it is charged off in its entirety against revenue each period. Consequently, the cost of a unit of product in inventory or in cost of goods sold under the variable costing method contains no element of fixed overhead cost.

Variable costing
A costing method that includes only variable manufacturing costs—direct materials, direct labour, and variable manufacturing overhead—in the cost of a unit of product.

Direct costing Same as *variable costing.*

Marginal costing Same as *variable costing.*

Variable costing is sometimes referred to as **direct costing** or **marginal costing.** The term *direct costing* was popular for many years, but it is slowly disappearing from day-to-day use. The term *variable costing* is more descriptive of the way in which product costs are computed when a contribution income statement is prepared.

To complete this summary comparison of absorption and variable costing, we need to consider briefly the handling of selling and administrative expenses. These expenses are rarely treated as product costs, regardless of the costing method in use. Thus, under either absorption or variable costing, selling and administrative expenses are always treated as period costs and deducted from revenues as incurred.

The concepts discussed so far in this section are illustrated in Exhibit 7–1, which shows the classification of costs under both absorption and variable costing.

EXHIBIT 7–1 Cost Classifications—Absorption versus Variable Costing

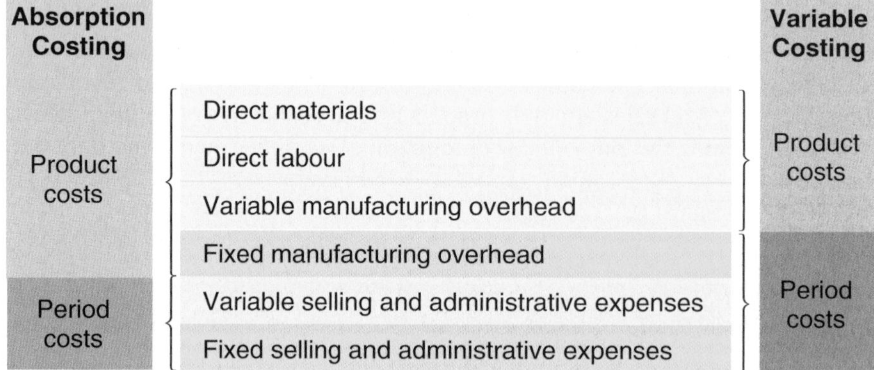

Unit Cost Computations

To illustrate the computation of unit costs under both absorption and variable costing, consider Boley Company, a small company that produces a single product and has the following cost structure:

Number of units produced each year	6,000
Variable costs per unit:	
Direct materials	$ 2
Direct labour	4
Variable manufacturing overhead	1
Variable selling and administrative expenses	3
Fixed costs per year:	
Fixed manufacturing overhead	30,000
Fixed selling and administrative expenses	10,000

Required:

1. Compute the unit product cost under absorption costing.
2. Compute the unit product cost under variable costing.

Solution

Absorption Costing	
Direct materials	$ 2
Direct labour	4
Variable manufacturing overhead	1
Total variable production cost	7
Fixed manufacturing overhead ($30,000 ÷ 6,000 units of product)	5
Unit product cost	$12

Variable Costing

Direct materials	$ 2
Direct labour	4
Variable manufacturing overhead	1
Unit product cost	$ 7

(The $30,000 fixed manufacturing overhead in variable costing will be charged off in total against income as a period expense along with the selling and administrative expenses.)

Under the absorption costing method, notice that *all* production costs, variable and fixed, are included when determining the unit product cost. Thus, if the company sells a unit of product and absorption costing is being used, then $12 (consisting of $7 variable cost and $5 fixed cost) will be deducted on the income statement as cost of goods sold. Similarly, any unsold units will be carried as inventory on the balance sheet at $12 each.

Under the variable costing method, notice that only the variable production costs are included in product costs. Therefore, if the company sells a unit of product, only $7 will be deducted as cost of goods sold, and unsold units will be carried in the balance sheet inventory account at only $7 each.

INCOME COMPARISON OF ABSORPTION AND VARIABLE COSTING

LEARNING OBJECTIVE **2**
Prepare income statements using both variable and absorption costing.

Income statements prepared under the absorption and variable costing approaches are shown in Exhibit 7–2. In preparing these statements, we use the data for Boley Company presented earlier, along with other information about the company as given below:

Units in beginning inventory	–0–
Units produced	6,000
Units sold	5,000
Units in ending inventory	1,000
Selling price per unit	$ 20
Selling and administrative expenses:	
Variable per unit	3
Fixed per year	10,000

	Absorption Costing	Variable Costing
Unit product cost:		
Direct materials	$ 2	$ 2
Direct labour	4	4
Variable manufacturing overhead	1	1
Fixed manufacturing overhead ($30,000 ÷ 6,000 units)	5	—
Unit product cost	$12	$ 7

Several points can be made about the financial statements in Exhibit 7–2:

Fixed manufacturing overhead cost deferred in inventory
The portion of the fixed manufacturing overhead cost of a period that goes into inventory under the absorption costing method as a result of production exceeding sales.

1. Under the absorption costing method, if there is an ending inventory the fixed manufacturing costs associated with the inventory will be carried forward as a balance sheet account, inventory, rather than being treated as a period cost. Such a deferral of costs is known as **fixed manufacturing overhead cost deferred in inventory.** The process involved can be explained by referring to the data for Boley Company. During the

EXHIBIT 7–2 Comparison of Absorption and Variable Costing—Boley Company

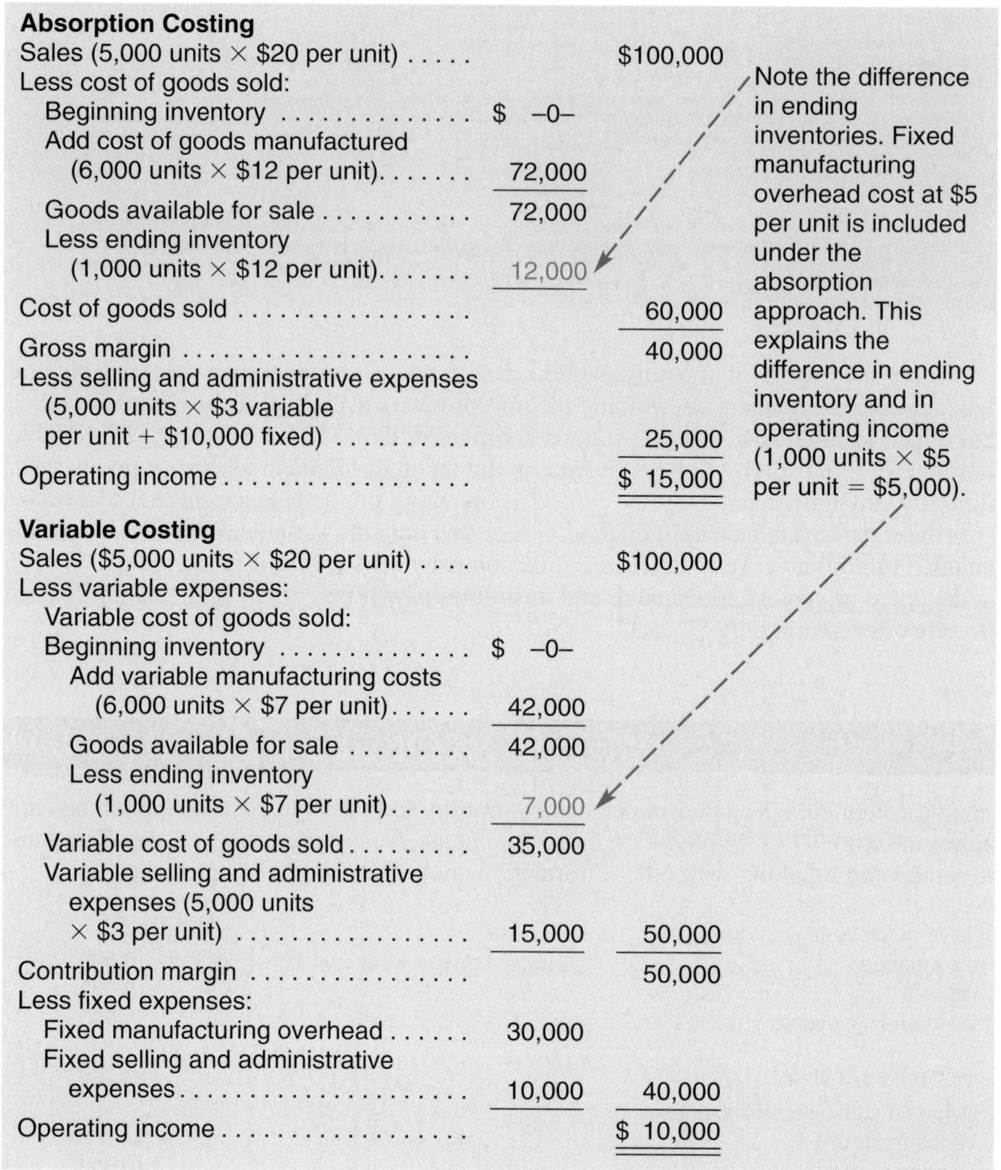

Absorption Costing		
Sales (5,000 units × $20 per unit)		$100,000
Less cost of goods sold:		
Beginning inventory	$ –0–	
Add cost of goods manufactured (6,000 units × $12 per unit).	72,000	
Goods available for sale	72,000	
Less ending inventory (1,000 units × $12 per unit).	12,000	
Cost of goods sold		60,000
Gross margin		40,000
Less selling and administrative expenses (5,000 units × $3 variable per unit + $10,000 fixed)		25,000
Operating income		$ 15,000
Variable Costing		
Sales ($5,000 units × $20 per unit)		$100,000
Less variable expenses:		
Variable cost of goods sold:		
Beginning inventory	$ –0–	
Add variable manufacturing costs (6,000 units × $7 per unit).	42,000	
Goods available for sale	42,000	
Less ending inventory (1,000 units × $7 per unit).	7,000	
Variable cost of goods sold.	35,000	
Variable selling and administrative expenses (5,000 units × $3 per unit)	15,000	50,000
Contribution margin		50,000
Less fixed expenses:		
Fixed manufacturing overhead	30,000	
Fixed selling and administrative expenses.	10,000	40,000
Operating income		$ 10,000

Note the difference in ending inventories. Fixed manufacturing overhead cost at $5 per unit is included under the absorption approach. This explains the difference in ending inventory and in operating income (1,000 units × $5 per unit = $5,000).

current period, Boley Company produced 6,000 units but sold only 5,000 units, thus leaving 1,000 unsold units in the ending inventory. Under the absorption costing method, each unit produced was assigned $5 in fixed overhead cost (see the unit cost computations above). Therefore, each of the 1,000 units going into inventory at the end of the period has $5 in fixed manufacturing overhead cost attached to it, or a total of $5,000 for the 1,000 units. *This fixed manufacturing overhead cost of the current period is deferred in inventory to the next period, when, hopefully, these units will be taken out of inventory and sold.* The deferral of $5,000 of fixed manufacturing overhead costs can be seen clearly by analyzing the ending inventory under the absorption costing method:

Variable manufacturing costs: 1,000 units × $7	$ 7,000
Fixed manufacturing overhead costs: 1,000 units × $5	5,000
Total inventory value	$12,000

In summary, under absorption costing, of the $30,000 in fixed manufacturing overhead costs incurred during the period, only $25,000 (5,000 units sold × $5) has been included in cost of goods sold. The remaining $5,000 (1,000 units *not* sold × $5) has been deferred in inventory to the next period.

2. Under the variable costing method, the entire $30,000 in fixed manufacturing overhead costs has been treated as an expense of the current period (see the bottom portion of the variable costing income statement).
3. The ending inventory figure under the variable costing method is $5,000 lower than it is under the absorption costing method. The reason is that under variable costing, only the variable manufacturing costs are assigned to units of product and therefore included in inventory:

Variable manufacturing costs: 1,000 units × $7	$7,000

   The $5,000 difference in ending inventories explains the difference in operating income reported between the two costing methods. Operating income is $5,000 *higher* under absorption costing since, as already explained, $5,000 of fixed manufacturing overhead cost has been deferred in inventory to the next period under that costing method.
4. The absorption costing income statement makes no distinction between fixed and variable costs; therefore, it is not well suited for CVP computations, which are important for good planning and control. To generate data for CVP analysis, it would be necessary to spend considerable time reworking and reclassifying costs on the absorption statement.
5. The variable costing approach to costing units of product blends very well with the contribution approach to the income statement, since both concepts are based on the idea of classifying costs by behaviour. The variable costing data in Exhibit 7–2 could be used immediately in CVP computations.

Careful reading of the previous two sections, unit cost calculations and income comparisons of absorption and variable costing, may have created confusion when the fixed overhead unit cost was calculated. Chapter 3, Exhibit 3-13 and Appendix 3A, suggest the use of a predetermined overhead rate. Such a rate would be applicable to the unit cost of fixed overhead and the unit cost of variable overhead used here. However, in the examples in this chapter we used actual overhead rates rather than predetermined ones in order to reduce unneeded discussion. What is illustrated about the effects of inventory on the difference in operating income will hold regardless of the use of actual or predetermined overhead rates. Later chapters will show full treatment of predetermined overhead rates to prove this assertion.

Essentially, the difference between the absorption costing method and the variable costing method centres on timing. Advocates of variable costing say that fixed manufacturing costs should be expensed immediately in total, whereas advocates of absorption costing say that fixed manufacturing costs should be charged against revenues bit by bit as units of product are sold. Any units of product not sold under absorption costing result in fixed costs being inventoried and carried forward as *assets* to the next period. We will defer discussing the arguments presented by each side in this dispute until after we have a better understanding of the two methods. Nevertheless, as we will see in the discussion of Emerald Isle Knitters, the use of absorption costing can sometimes produce strange effects on income statements.

MANAGERIAL ACCOUNTING IN ACTION

The Issue

Emerald Isle KNITTERS

Mary O'Meara is the owner and manager of Emerald Isle Knitters, Ltd. of Galway, Republic of Ireland. The company is very small, with only 10 employees. Mary started the company three years ago with cash loaned to her by a local bank. The company manufactures a traditional wool fisherman's sweater from a pattern Mary learned from her grandmother. Like most apparel manufacturers, Emerald Isle Knitters sells its product to department stores and clothing store chains rather than to retail customers.

The sweater was an immediate success, and the company sold all of the first year's production. However, in the second year of operations, one of the company's major customers cancelled its order due to bankruptcy, and the company ended the year with large stocks of unsold sweaters. The third year of operations was a great year in contrast to that disastrous second year. Sales rebounded dramatically, and all of the unsold production carried over from the second year was sold by the end of the third year.

Shortly after the close of the third year, Mary met with her accountant Sean MacLafferty to discuss the results for the year. (Note: In Ireland, the unit of currency is the euro, which is denoted by the symbol €.)

Mary: Sean, the results for this year look a lot better than for last year, but I am frankly puzzled why this year's results aren't even better than the income statement shows.

Sean: I know what you mean. The net income for this year is just €90,000. Last year it was €30,000. That is a huge improvement, but it seems that profits this year should have been even higher and profits last year should have been much less. We were in big trouble last year. I was afraid we might not even break even—yet we showed a healthy €30,000 profit. Somehow it doesn't seem quite right.

Mary: I wondered about that €30,000 profit last year, but I didn't question it since it was the only good news I had received for quite some time.

Sean: In case you're wondering, I didn't invent that profit last year just to make you feel better. Our auditor required that I follow certain accounting rules in preparing those reports for the bank. This may sound heretical, but we *could* use different rules for our own internal reports.

Mary: Wait a minute, rules are rules—especially in accounting.

Sean: Yes and no. For our internal reports, it might be better to use different rules than we use for the reports we send to the bank.

Mary: As I said, rules are rules. Still, I'm willing to listen if you want to show me what you have in mind.

Sean: It's a deal.

Immediately after the meeting with Mary, Sean put together the data and financial reports that appear in Exhibit 7–3. To make the principles clearer, Sean simplified the data so that the illustrations all use round figures.

EXTENDED COMPARISON OF INCOME DATA

LEARNING OBJECTIVE 3
Reconcile variable costing and absorption costing operating incomes and explain why the two amounts differ.

The basic data appear in the first part of Exhibit 7–3, on page 279, and the absorption costing income statements as reported to the bank for the last three years appear in the first part on page 280. Sean decided to try using the variable costing approach to see what effect that might have on operating income. The variable costing income statements for the last three years appear in the lower part on page 280.

Note that Emerald Isle Knitters maintained a steady rate of production per year of 25,000 sweaters. However, sales varied from year to year. In year 1, production and sales were equal. In year 2, production exceeded sales due to the cancelled order. In year 3, sales recovered and exceeded production. As a consequence, inventories did not change during year 1, inventories increased during year 2, and inventories decreased during year 3. *The change in inventories during the year is the key to understanding how absorption costing differs from variable costing.* Note that when inventories increase in year 2, absorption costing operating income exceeds variable costing operating income. When inventories decrease in year 3, the opposite occurs—variable costing operating income exceeds absorption costing operating income. And when there is no change in inventories, as in year 1, there is no difference in operating income between the two methods. Why is this? The reasons are discussed below and are briefly summarized in Exhibit 7–4.

1. When production and sales are equal, as in year 1 for Emerald Isle Knitters, operating income will generally be the same regardless of whether absorption or variable costing

is used. The reason is as follows: The *only* difference that can exist between absorption and variable costing operating income is the amount of fixed manufacturing overhead recognized as expense on the income statement. When everything that is produced in the year is sold, all of the fixed manufacturing overhead assigned to units of product under absorption costing become part of the year's cost of goods sold. Under variable costing, the total fixed manufacturing overhead flows directly to the income statement as an expense. So under either method, when production equals sales (and hence there is no change in inventories), all of the fixed manufacturing overhead incurred during the year flows through to the income statement as expense. Therefore, the operating income under the two methods is the same.

2. When production exceeds sales (see year 2 in Exhibit 7–3), the operating income reported under absorption costing will generally be greater than the operating income reported under variable costing. This occurs because under absorption costing, part of the fixed manufacturing overhead costs of the current period is deferred in inventory. In year 2, for example, €30,000 of fixed manufacturing overhead costs (5,000 units × €6 per unit) has been applied to units in ending inventory. These costs are excluded from cost of goods sold.

   Under variable costing, however, *all* of the fixed manufacturing overhead costs of year 2 have been charged immediately against income as a period cost. As a result, the operating income for year 2 under variable costing is €30,000 *lower* than it is under absorption costing. Exhibit 7–5 contains a reconciliation of the variable costing and absorption costing operating income figures.

3. When production is less than sales (see year 3 in Exhibit 7–3), the operating income reported under the absorption costing approach will generally be less than the

EXHIBIT 7–3 Absorption and Variable Costing Data—Emerald Isle Knitters, Ltd.

Basic Data	
Selling price per unit sold	€ 20
Variable manufacturing cost per unit produced	7
Fixed manufacturing overhead costs per year	150,000
Variable selling and administrative expenses per unit sold	1
Fixed selling and administrative expenses per year	90,000

	Year 1	**Year 2**	**Year 3**	**Three Years Together**
Units in beginning inventory	–0–	–0–	5,000	–0–
Units produced	25,000	25,000	25,000	75,000
Units sold	25,000	20,000	30,000	75,000
Units in ending inventory	–0–	5,000	–0–	–0–

Unit Product Costs	**Year 1**	**Year 2**	**Year 3**
Under variable costing (variable manufacturing costs only)	€ 7	€ 7	€ 7
Under absorption costing:			
Variable manufacturing costs	€ 7	€ 7	€ 7
Fixed manufacturing overhead costs (€150,000 spread over the number of units produced in each year)	6	6	6
Total absorption cost per unit	€13	€13	€13

continued

EXHIBIT 7–3 *concluded*

	Year 1		Year 2		Year 3		Three Years Together	
Absorption Costing								
Sales		€500,000		€400,000		€600,000		€1,500,000
Less cost of goods sold:								
Beginning inventory	€ –0–		€ –0–		€ 65,000		€ –0–	
Add cost of goods manufactured (25,000 units × €13 per unit)	325,000		325,000		325,000		975,000	
Goods available for sale	325,000		325,000		390,000		975,000	
Less ending inventory (5,000 units × €13 per unit)	€ –0–		65,000		€ –0–		€ –0–	
Cost of goods sold		325,000		260,000		390,000		975,000
Gross margin		175,000		140,000		210,000		525,000
Less selling and administrative expenses		115,000*		110,000*		120,000*		345,000
Operating income		€ 60,000		€ 30,000		€ 90,000		€ 180,000

*The selling and administrative expenses are computed as follows:
Year 1: 25,000 units × €1 per unit variable + €90,000 fixed = €115,000.
Year 2: 20,000 units × €1 per unit variable + €90,000 fixed = €110,000.
Year 3: 30,000 units × €1 per unit variable + €90,000 fixed = €120,000.

	Year 1		Year 2		Year 3		Three Years Together	
Variable Costing								
Sales		€500,000		€400,000		€600,000		€1,500,000
Less variable expenses:								
Variable cost of goods sold:								
Beginning inventory	€ –0–		€ –0–		€ 35,000		€ –0–	
Add variable manufacturing costs (25,000 units × €7 per unit)	175,000		175,000		175,000		525,000	
Goods available for sale	175,000		175,000		210,000		525,000	
Less ending inventory (5,000 units × €7 per unit)	€ –0–		35,000		€ –0–		€ –0–	
Variable cost of goods sold	175,000*		140,000*		210,000*		525,000	
Variable selling and administrative expenses (€1 per unit sold)	25,000	200,000	20,000	160,000	30,000	240,000	75,000	600,000
Contribution margin		300,000		240,000		360,000		900,000
Less fixed expenses:								
Fixed manufacturing overhead	150,000		150,000		150,000		450,000	
Fixed selling and administrative expenses	90,000	240,000	90,000	240,000	90,000	240,000	270,000	720,000
Operating income		€ 60,000		€ –0–		€120,000		€ 180,000

*The variable cost of goods sold could have been computed more simply as follows:
Year 1: 25,000 units sold × €7 per unit = €175,000.
Year 2: 20,000 units sold × €7 per unit = €140,000.
Year 3: 30,000 units sold × €7 per unit = €210,000.

Relationship between Production and Sales for the Period	Effect on Inventories	Relationship between Absorption and Variable Costing Net Operating Incomes
Production = Sales	No change in inventories	Absorption costing operating income = Variable costing operating income
Production > Sales	Inventories increase	Absorption costing operating income > Variable costing operating income*
Production < Sales	Inventories decrease	Absorption costing operating income < Variable costing operating income†

*Operating income is higher under absorption costing, since fixed manufacturing overhead cost is *deferred* in inventory under absorption costing as inventories increase.
†Operating income is lower under absorption costing, since fixed manufacturing overhead cost is *released* from inventory under absorption costing as inventories decrease.

EXHIBIT 7–4
Comparative Income Effects—Absorption and Variable Costing

operating income reported under the variable costing approach. This happens because inventories are drawn down and fixed manufacturing overhead costs that were previously deferred in inventory under absorption costing are released and charged against income (known as **fixed manufacturing overhead cost released from inventory**). In year 3, for example, the €30,000 in fixed manufacturing overhead costs deferred in inventory under the absorption approach from year 2 to year 3 is released from inventory because these units were sold. As a result, the cost of goods sold for year 3 contains not only all of the fixed manufacturing overhead costs for year 3 (since all that was produced in year 3 was sold in year 3) but €30,000 of fixed manufacturing overhead costs from year 2 as well.

Fixed manufacturing overhead cost released from inventory The portion of the fixed manufacturing overhead cost of a prior period that becomes an expense of the current period under the absorption costing method as a result of sales exceeding production.

By contrast, under variable costing only the fixed manufacturing overhead costs of year 3 have been charged against year 3. The result is that operating income under variable costing is €30,000 *higher* than it is under absorption costing. Exhibit 7–5 contains a reconciliation of the variable costing and absorption costing operating income figures for year 3.

4. Over an *extended* period of time, the operating income figures reported under absorption costing and variable costing will tend to be the same. The reason is that over the long run, sales cannot exceed production, nor can production much exceed sales. The shorter the time period, the more the operating income figures will tend to differ.

	Year 1	Year 2	Year 3
Variable costing operating income	€60,000	€ –0–	€120,000
Add fixed manufacturing overhead costs deferred in inventory under absorption costing (5,000 units × €6 per unit)	–0–	30,000	–0–
Deduct fixed manufacturing overhead costs released from inventory under absorption costing (5,000 units × €6 per unit)	–0–	–0–	(30,000)
Absorption costing operating income	€60,000	€30,000	€ 90,000

EXHIBIT 7–5
Reconciliation of Variable Costing and Absorption Costing—Operating Income Data from Exhibit 7–3

MANAGERIAL ACCOUNTING IN ACTION

The Wrap-Up

After checking all of his work, Sean took the exhibits he had prepared to Mary's office where the following conversation took place:

Sean: I have some calculations I would like to show you.

Mary: Will this take long? I have only a few minutes before I have to meet with the buyer from Irish Yarn.

Sean: Well, we can at least get started. These exhibits should help explain why our operating income didn't increase this year as much as you thought it should have.

Mary: This first exhibit (i.e., Exhibit 7–3) looks like it just summarizes our income statements for the last three years.

Sean: Not exactly. There are actually two sets of income statements on this exhibit. The absorption costing income statements are the ones I originally prepared and we submitted to the bank. Below the absorption costing income statements is another set of income statements.

Mary: Those are the ones labelled Variable Costing.

Sean: That's right. You can see that the operating incomes are the same for the two sets of income statements in our first year of operations, but they differ for the other two years.

Mary: I'll say! The variable costing statements indicate that we just broke even in the second year instead of earning a €30,000 profit. And the increase in operating income between the second and third years is €120,000 instead of just €60,000. I don't know how you come up with two different operating income figures, but the variable costing operating income seems to be much closer to the truth. The second year was almost a disaster. We barely sold enough sweaters to cover all of our fixed costs.

Sean: You and I both know that, but the accounting rules view the situation a little differently. If we produce more than we sell, the accounting rules require that we take some of the fixed cost and assign it to the units that end up in inventories at year-end.

Mary: You mean that instead of appearing on the income statement as an expense, some of the fixed costs wind up on the balance sheet as inventories?

Sean: Precisely.

Mary: I thought accountants were conservative. Since when was it conservative to call an expense an asset?

Sean: We accountants have been debating whether fixed production costs are an asset or an expense for over 50 years.

Mary: It must have been a *fascinating* debate.

Sean: I have to admit that it ranks right up there with watching grass grow in terms of excitement level.

Mary: I don't know what the arguments are, but I can tell you for sure that we don't make any money by just producing sweaters. If I understand what you have shown me, I can increase my operating income under absorption costing by simply making more sweaters—we don't have to sell them.

Sean: Correct.

Mary: So all I have to do to enjoy the lifestyle of the rich and famous is to hire every unemployed knitter in Ireland to make sweaters I can't sell.

Sean: We would have a major cash flow problem, but our operating income would certainly go up.

Mary: Well, if the banks want us to use absorption costing, so be it. I don't know why they would want us to report that way, but if that's what they want, that's what they'll get. Is there any reason why we can't use this variable costing method ourselves? The statements are easier to understand, and the operating income figures make more sense to me. Can't we do both?

Sean: I don't see why not. Making the adjustment from one method to the other is very simple.

Mary: Good. Let's talk about this some more after I get back from the meeting with Irish Yarn.

EFFECT OF CHANGES IN PRODUCTION ON OPERATING INCOME

In the Emerald Isle Knitters example in the preceding section, production was constant and sales fluctuated over the three-year period. Since sales fluctuated, the data Sean MacLafferty presented in Exhibit 7–3 allowed us to see the effect of changes in sales on operating income under both variable and absorption costing.

To further investigate the differences between variable and absorption costing, Sean next put together the hypothetical example in Exhibit 7–6. In this hypothetical example, sales are constant and production fluctuates (the opposite of Exhibit 7–3). The purpose of Exhibit 7–6 is to illustrate for Mary O'Meara the effect of changes in *production* on operating income under both variable and absorption costing.

Variable Costing

Operating income is *not* affected by changes in production under variable costing. Notice from Exhibit 7–6 that operating income is the same for all three years under the variable costing approach, although production exceeds sales in one year and is less than sales in another year. In short, a change in production has no effect on operating income when variable costing is in use.

Absorption Costing

Operating income *is* affected by changes in production when absorption costing is in use, however. As shown in Exhibit 7–6, operating income under the absorption approach goes up in year 2, in response to the increase in production for that year, and then goes down in year 3, in response to the drop in production for that year. Note particularly that operating income goes up and down between these two years *even though the same number of units is sold in each year.* The reason for this effect can be traced to the shifting of fixed

EXHIBIT 7–6 Sensitivity of Costing Methods to Changes in Production—Hypothetical Data

Basic Data			
Selling price per unit sold			€ 25
Variable manufacturing cost per unit produced			10
Fixed manufacturing overhead costs per year			300,000
Variable selling and administrative expenses per unit sold			1
Fixed selling and administrative expenses per year			200,000
	Year 1	**Year 2**	**Year 3**
Units in beginning inventory	–0–	–0–	10,000
Units produced	40,000	50,000	30,000
Units sold	40,000	40,000	40,000
Units in ending inventory	–0–	10,000	–0–
Unit Product Costs			
Under variable costing (variable manufacturing costs only)	€10.00	€10.00	€10.00
Under absorption costing			
Variable manufacturing costs	€10.00	€10.00	€10.00
Fixed manufacturing overhead costs (€300,000 total spread over the number of units produced in each year)	7.50	6.00	10.00
Total absorption cost per unit	€17.50	€16.00	€20.00

continued

EXHIBIT 7–6 *concluded*

	Year 1		Year 2		Year 3	
Absorption Costing						
Sales (40,000 units)		€1,000,000		€1,000,000		€1,000,000
Less cost of goods sold:						
Beginning inventory	€ –0–		€ –0–		€160,000	
Add cost of goods manufactured	700,000*		800,000*		600,000*	
Goods available for sale	700,000		800,000		760,000	
Less ending inventory	–0–		160,000†		–0–	
Cost of goods sold		700,000		640,000		760,000
Gross margin		300,000		360,000		240,000
Less selling and administrative expenses (40,000 units × €1 per unit + €200,000)		240,000		240,000		240,000
Operating income		€ 60,000		€ 120,000		€ –0–

*Cost of goods manufactured:

Year 1: 40,000 units × €17.50 per unit = €700,000.

Year 2: 50,000 units × €16.00 per unit = €800,000.

Year 3: 30,000 units × €20.00 per unit = €600,000.

†Ending inventory, year 2: 10,000 units × €16 per unit = €160,000.

	Year 1		Year 2		Year 3	
Variable Costing						
Sales (40,000 units)		€1,000,000		€1,000,000		€1,000,000
Less variable expenses:						
Variable cost of goods sold:						
Beginning inventory	€ –0–		€ –0–		€100,000	
Add variable manufacturing costs at €10 per unit produced	400,000		500,000		300,000	
Goods available for sale	400,000		500,000		400,000	
Less ending inventory	–0–		100,000†		–0–	
Variable cost of goods sold	400,000		400,000		400,000	
Variable selling and administrative expenses	40,000	440,000	40,000	440,000	40,000	440,000
Contribution margin		560,000		560,000		560,000
Less fixed expenses:						
Fixed manufacturing overhead	300,000		300,000		300,000	
Fixed selling and administrative expenses	200,000	500,000	200,000	500,000	200,000	500,000
Operating income		€ 60,000		€ 60,000		€ 60,000

*Ending inventory, year 2: 10,000 units × €10 per unit = €100,000.

manufacturing overhead costs between periods under the absorption costing method as a result of changes in inventory.

As shown in Exhibit 7–6, production exceeds sales in year 2, resulting in an increase of 10,000 units in inventory. Each unit produced during year 2 has €6 in fixed manufacturing overhead costs attached to it (see the unit cost computations at the top of Exhibit 7–6). Therefore, €60,000 (10,000 units × €6) of the fixed manufacturing overhead costs of year 2 are not charged against that year but rather are added to the inventory account (along with the variable manufacturing costs). The operating income of year 2 rises sharply, because of the deferral of these costs in inventories, even though the same number of units is sold in year 2 as in the other years.

The reverse effect occurs in year 3. Since sales exceed production in year 3, that year is forced to cover all of its own fixed manufacturing overhead costs as well as the fixed manufacturing overhead costs carried forward in inventory from year 2. A substantial drop in operating income during year 3 results from the release of fixed manufacturing overhead costs from inventories, despite the fact that the same number of units is sold in that year as in the other years.

The variable costing and absorption costing operating incomes are reconciled in Exhibit 7–7. This exhibit shows that the differences in operating income can be traced to the effects of changes in inventories on absorption costing operating income. Under absorption costing, fixed manufacturing overhead costs are deferred in inventory when inventories increase and are released from inventory when inventories decrease.

EXHIBIT 7–7
Reconciliation of Variable Costing and Absorption Costing—Operating Income Data from Exhibit 7–6

	Year 1	Year 2	Year 3
Variable costing operating income	€60,000	€ 60,000	€60,000
Add fixed manufacturing overhead costs deferred in inventory under absorption costing (10,000 units × €6 per unit)	–0–	60,000	–0–
Deduct fixed manufacturing overhead costs released from inventory under absorption costing (10,000 units × €6 per unit)	–0–	–0–	(60,000)
Absorption costing operating income	€60,000	€120,000	€ 0

FOCUS ***on Current Practice***

Albert J. Dunlap, who relishes the nickname "Chainsaw Al," left Sunbeam Corporation under a cloud after three years as CEO. Dunlap was hired to turn around Sunbeam with his well-known cost-cutting and disregard for the sensibilities of existing employees.

Three years later, Dunlap had been fired by the board of directors amid well-publicized concerns about his aggressive accounting practices. In addition to questionable accounting practices, Dunlap left a legacy of excess inventories. Dunlap's successors complain that eliminating those excess inventories has required the company to keep production levels well under capacity. Since Sunbeam, like almost all other companies, uses absorption costing to prepare its external financial reports, liquidating these excess inventories depresses the company's profits.

The aggressive accounting practices at Sunbeam have been characterized as a disaster such as those seen at Enron and WorldCom. The aftermath included the bankruptcy and reorganization of Sunbeam, the permanent banning of Mr. Dunlap as an executive of a public company, a fine of $500,000 by the SEC, and a $15 million personal settlement of a shareholder lawsuit.

Sunbeam was reorganized to become American Household Inc. which was recently sold for $746 million.

Sources: Michael Schroeder, "Dunlap Settles Fraud Charges with the SEC," *Wall Street Journal*, September 5, 2002, p. C1. Dennis K. Berman and Henny Sender, "Jarden is set to Acquire American Household; Consumer-Products Firm is to pay $746 million for Successor to Sunbeam," *The Wall Street Journal*, September 20, 2004, p. A6.

CHOOSING A COSTING METHOD

The Impact on the Manager

LEARNING OBJECTIVE 4
Explain the advantages and disadvantages of both variable and absorption costing.

Like Mary O'Meara, opponents of absorption costing argue that shifting fixed manufacturing overhead cost between periods can be confusing and can lead to misinterpretations and even to faulty decisions. Look again at the data in Exhibit 7–6; a manager might wonder why operating income went up substantially in year 2 under absorption costing when sales remained the same as in the prior year. Was it a result of lower selling costs, or more efficient operations, or was some other factor involved? The manager is unable to tell, looking simply at the absorption costing income statement. Then in year 3, operating income drops sharply, even though again the same number of units is sold as in the other two years. Why would income rise in one year and then drop in the next? The figures seem erratic and contradictory and can lead to confusion and a loss of confidence in the integrity of the statement data.

By contrast, the variable costing income statements in Exhibit 7–6 are clear and easy to understand. Sales remain constant over the three-year period covered in the exhibit, so both contribution margin and operating income also remain constant. The statements are consistent with what the manager would expect to happen under the circumstances, so they tend to generate confidence rather than confusion.

Under variable costing, essentially revenue drives operating income. Under absorption costing both revenue and production drive operating income. The two drivers create confusion for the user of operating income because it is difficult to perceive income without selling the production, something absorption costing does.

To avoid mistakes when absorption costing is used, readers of financial statements should be alert to changes in inventory levels. Under absorption costing, if there is an increase in inventories, fixed manufacturing overhead costs are deferred in inventories and operating income is elevated. If there is a decrease in inventories, fixed manufacturing overhead costs are released from inventories and operating income is depressed. Thus, fluctuations in operating income can be due to changes in inventories rather than to changes in sales.

FOCUS *on Current Practice*

While managers can artificially increase operating income under absorption costing by producing more than is really necessary and building up inventories, a few unscrupulous managers have stepped over the line into the area of outright fraud. By claiming inventories that don't exist, an unethical manager can produce instant profits and dress up the balance sheet. Since the value of ending inventories is subtracted from the cost of goods available for sale in order to arrive at the cost of goods sold, phantom inventories directly reduce cost of goods sold. Phantom inventories also beef up the balance sheet by increasing assets.

Auditors attempt to uncover such fraud by physically verifying the existence of inventory reported on the balance sheet. This is done by counting random samples of perhaps 5% to 10% of reported inventory items. However, this audit approach is not always effective.

Jed Connelly, the top American executive at Nissan North America, admits: "We had a lot of excess production that we had to force on the market." Nissan liked to run its factories at capacity, regardless of how well the cars were selling, because under its bookkeeping rules (presumably absorption costing), the factories would then generate a profit. As a consequence, Nissan dealers had to slash prices and offer big rebates to sell their cars. According to *Fortune* magazine, "Years of discounting and distress sales seriously undercut the value of the Nissan brand. While Toyota stood for quality, customers came to Nissan to get a better deal."

In 1999 after Renault of France purchased a 44% interest in Nissan, a major turn around was accomplished under the direction of the new CEO from Renault, Carlos Ghosn. Employee layoffs, factory closures, elimination of product models and new designs have made Nissan number two in Japan and a company with the highest operating margin of large volume carmakers.

Despite the success since 1999, the new Nissan factory in the United States has reported production quality problems for the North American segment that need to be addressed, a task directed by the CEO Carlos Ghosn.

Thus cost and quality are important issues for firms that extend beyond the accounting incentives of absorption costing.

Source: Alex Taylor III, "The Man Who Wants to Change Japan Inc.," *Fortune*, December 20, 1999, pp. 189–198; "The $10 Billion Man: Face Value," *The Economist*, London, February 26, 2005, vol. 374, p. 76.

CVP Analysis and Absorption Costing

Absorption costing is widely used for both internal and external reports. Many firms use the absorption approach exclusively because of its focus on *full* costing of units of product. A weakness of the method, however, is its inability to dovetail well with CVP analysis.

To illustrate, refer again to Exhibit 7–3. Let us compute the break-even point for Emerald Isle Knitters. To obtain the break-even point, we divide total fixed costs by the contribution margin per unit:

Selling price per unit	€ 20
Variable costs per unit	8
Contribution margin per unit	€ 12
Fixed manufacturing overhead costs	€150,000
Fixed selling and administrative costs	90,000
Total fixed costs	€240,000

$$\frac{\text{Total fixed costs}}{\text{Contribution margin per unit}} = \frac{€240{,}000}{€12} = 20{,}000 \text{ units}$$

The break-even point is 20,000 units. Notice from Exhibit 7–3 that in year 2, the firm sold exactly 20,000 units, the break-even volume. Under the contribution approach, using variable costing, the firm does break even in year 2, showing zero operating income. *Under absorption costing, however, the firm shows a positive operating income of €30,000 for year 2.* How can this be? How can absorption costing produce a positive operating income when the firm sold exactly the break-even volume of units?

The answer lies in the fact that €30,000 in fixed manufacturing overhead costs were deferred in inventory during year 2 under absorption costing and therefore did not appear as charges against income. By deferring these fixed manufacturing overhead costs in inventory, the income statement shows a profit even though the company sold exactly the break-even volume of units. Absorption costing runs into similar kinds of difficulty in other areas of CVP analysis, which assumes that variable costing is being used.

Absorption break-even analysis would require the analysis of two drivers, sales and production. By determining various levels for each driver, a zero operating income could be determined. But like the truism from mathematics, a single equation does not provide a unique solution when there are two unknowns. Various possible sales and production levels that can create a break-even operating income would be what break-even means here. For example see year three of Exhibit 7-6 where 40,000 units were sold and 30,000 units were produced. Operating income is zero, or break-even.

Decision Making

A basic problem with absorption costing is that fixed manufacturing overhead costs appear to be variable with respect to the number of units sold, but they are not. For example, in Exhibit 7–3, the absorption unit product cost is €13, but the variable portion of this cost is only €7. Since the product costs are stated in terms of a per unit figure, managers may mistakenly believe that if another unit is produced, it will cost the company €13.

The misperception that absorption unit product costs are variable can lead to many managerial problems, including inappropriate pricing decisions and decisions to drop products that are in fact profitable. These problems with absorption costing product costs will be discussed more fully in later chapters.

External Reporting and Income Taxes

Practically speaking, absorption costing is required for external reports in the United States and is the predominant method used in Canada. In Canada, accounting standards for external reporting require a company to assign to work in process and finished goods the laid-down cost of materials plus the cost of direct labour and the applicable share of overhead expenses properly charged to production.[1] This implies that both variable and absorption costing are possible in Canada. For income tax purposes in Canada, *Interpretation Bulletin 473* permits both variable and absorption costing for the purposes of determining taxable income.[2]

Even if a company uses absorption costing for its external reports, a manager can, as Mary O'Meara suggests, use variable costing statements for internal reports. No particular accounting problems are created by using *both* costing methods—the variable costing method for internal reports and the absorption costing method for external reports. As we demonstrated earlier in Exhibits 7–5 and 7–7, the adjustment from variable costing operating income to absorption costing operating income is a simple one that can be made easily at year-end. Computer systems such as those described in Chapter 3 can make the conversion as long as the information is contained in the supporting data base.

Top executives of publicly held corporations are typically evaluated based on the earnings reported in the external financial reports presented to shareholders. This creates a problem for top executives who might otherwise favour using variable costing for internal reports. They may feel that since they are evaluated based on absorption costing reports, decisions should also be based on absorption costing data.

FOCUS *on Current Practice*

Absorption costing is the norm for external financial reports around the world. After the fall of communism, accounting methods changed in Russia to bring them into closer agreement with accounting methods in the West. One result was the adoption of absorption costing.

Source: Adolf J.H. Enthoven, "Russia's Accounting Moves West," *Strategic Finance*, July 1999, pp. 32–37.

Advantages of Variable Costing and the Contribution Approach

As stated earlier, even if the absorption approach is used for external reporting purposes, variable costing, together with the contribution margin format income statement, is an

1. *Canadian Institute of Chartered Accountants' Handbook*, section 3030, "Inventories," paragraph 06.
2. Robert E. Beam and Stanley N. Laiken, *Introduction to Federal Income Taxation in Canada*, 17th ed. (North York, ON: CCH Canadian Limited, 1996), p. 149.

appealing alternative for internal reports. The advantages of variable costing can be summarized as follows:

1. The data that are required for CVP analysis can be taken directly from a contribution margin format income statement. These data are not available on a conventional income statement based on absorption costing.
2. Under variable costing, the profit for a period is not affected by changes in inventories. Other things remaining equal (i.e., selling prices, costs, sales mix, etc.), profits move in the same direction as sales when variable costing is in use.
3. Managers often assume that unit product costs are variable costs. This is a problem under absorption costing, since unit product costs are a combination of both fixed and variable costs. Under variable costing, unit product costs do not contain fixed costs.
4. The impact of fixed costs on profits is emphasized under the variable costing and contribution approach. The total amount of fixed costs appears explicitly on the income statement. Under absorption costing, the fixed costs are mingled together with the variable costs and are buried in cost of goods sold and in ending inventories.
5. Variable costing data make it easier to estimate the profitability of products, customers, and other segments of the business. With absorption costing, profitability is obscured by arbitrary allocations of fixed costs. These issues will be discussed in later chapters.
6. Variable costing ties in with cost control methods such as standard costs and flexible budgets, which will be covered in later chapters.

With all of these advantages, one might wonder why absorption costing continues to be used almost exclusively for external reporting and why it is the predominant choice for internal reports as well. This is partly due to tradition, but absorption costing is also attractive to many accountants and managers because they believe it better matches costs with revenues. Advocates of absorption costing argue that *all* manufacturing costs must be assigned to products in order to properly match the costs of producing units of product with the revenues from the units when they are sold. The fixed costs of depreciation, taxes, insurance, supervisory salaries, and so on, are just as essential to manufacturing products as are the variable costs.

Advocates of variable costing argue that fixed manufacturing costs are not really the costs of any particular unit of product. These costs are incurred in order to have the *capacity* to make products during a particular period and will be incurred even if nothing is made during the period. Moreover, whether a unit is made or not, the fixed manufacturing costs will be exactly the same. Therefore, variable costing advocates argue that fixed manufacturing costs are not part of the costs of producing a particular unit of product and thus the matching principle dictates that fixed manufacturing costs should be charged to the current period.

Another downside of absorption or full costing is that it can be used by an unethical manager to deliberately mislead others. This is possible because reported profits are affected by inventory build-ups or drawdowns if fixed costs are included in inventory. During periods of inventory build-up, less than a year's fixed costs will be expensed and during years in which inventory is reduced, more than a year's fixed costs will be expensed. An unethical manager whose bonus is based on operating income, for example, could make profits appear higher by simply building up inventory levels, since there is a direct relationship between ending inventory and operating income. Those responsible for performance evaluation should look beyond the bottom line to identify such abuses.

One restriction on the unethical use of absorption costing to increase operating income by building ending inventories is the application of the generally accepted accounting principle of lower of cost or market. The ending inventory has to be examined for its saleability by determining its market value. If market is below cost then a loss is recorded in the income statement of the current period. Thus if the excess inventory could not be sold, a write-down is expected which would reduce but not necessarily eliminate the operating income resulting from the inventory buildup. Whether the result would make absorption operating income equal to variable operating income is a question of the specifics and thus unlikely to be exactly equal.

At any rate, absorption costing is a generally accepted method for preparing mandatory external financial reports. Probably because of the cost and possible confusion of maintaining two separate costing systems—one for external reporting and one for internal reporting—most companies use absorption costing for both external and internal reports.

There may also be important strategic reasons for using absorption costing. Senior management, for example, may fear that variable costing will result in an overemphasis on contribution margin and lead to insufficient attention to the management of fixed costs. Decision makers may focus too much on short-run profitability and bring long-run harm to the company. For example, long-term profitability will suffer if managers, lured by the attractiveness of high contribution margins, set product prices too low because of blindness to the existence of fixed costs. This is a particular risk in those industries in which the trend has been for cost structures to shift away from variable costs. Judging from the dominant use of absorption costing, it appears that managers have generally concluded that the incremental benefits of variable costing information are outweighed by these strategic factors and the additional costs of maintaining parallel systems.

Variable Costing and the Theory of Constraints

The theory of constraints (TOC), which was introduced in Chapter 1, focuses on managing the constraints in a company as the key to improving profits. For reasons that will be discussed in Chapter 13, this requires careful identification of the variable costs of each product. Consequently, companies involved in TOC use a form of variable costing.

One difference is that, in the TOC approach, direct labour is generally considered to be a fixed cost. As discussed in earlier chapters, in many companies, direct labour is not really a variable cost. Even though direct labour workers may be paid on an hourly basis, many companies have a commitment—sometimes enforced in labour contracts or by law—to guarantee workers a minimum number of paid hours. In TOC companies, there are two additional reasons to consider direct labour to be a fixed cost.

First, direct labour is not usually the constraint. In the simplest cases, the constraint is a machine. In more complex cases, the constraint is a policy (such as a poorly designed compensation scheme for salespersons) that prevents the company from using its resources more effectively. If direct labour is not the constraint, there is no reason to increase it. Hiring more direct labour would increase costs without increasing the output of saleable products and services.

Second, TOC emphasizes continuous improvement to maintain competitiveness. Without committed and enthusiastic employees, sustained continuous improvement is virtually impossible. Since layoffs often have devastating effects on employee morale, managers involved in TOC are extremely reluctant to lay off employees.

For these reasons, most managers in TOC companies believe that direct labour in their companies behaves much more like a committed fixed cost than a variable cost. Hence, in the modified form of variable costing used in TOC companies, direct labour is not included as a part of product costs.

IMPACT OF JIT INVENTORY METHODS

LEARNING OBJECTIVE 5
Explain how the use of JIT reduces the difference in reported operating income under the variable and absorption costing methods.

As discussed in this chapter, variable and absorption costing will produce different operating income figures whenever the number of units produced is different from the number of units sold—in other words, whenever there is a change in the number of units in inventory. We have also learned that the absorption costing operating income figure can be erratic, sometimes moving in a direction that is opposite from the movement in sales.

When companies use just-in-time (JIT) methods, these problems are reduced. The erratic movement of operating income under absorption costing and the difference in operating income between absorption and variable costing occur because of changes in the number of units in inventory. Under JIT, goods are produced to customers' orders and the goal is to eliminate finished goods inventories entirely and reduce work in process inventory to almost nothing. If there is very little inventory, then changes in inventories will be very small and both variable and absorption costing will show basically the same operating income figure. In that case, absorption costing operating income will move in the same direction as movements in sales.

Of course, the cost of a unit of product will still be different between variable and absorption costing, as explained earlier in the chapter. But when JIT is used, the differences in operating income will largely disappear.

SUMMARY

Variable and absorption costing are alternative methods of determining unit product costs. Under variable costing, only those production costs that vary with output are treated as product costs. This includes direct materials, variable overhead, and ordinarily, direct labour. Fixed manufacturing overhead is treated as a period cost and charged off against revenue as it is incurred, the same as selling and administrative expenses. By contrast, absorption costing treats fixed manufacturing overhead as a product cost, along with direct materials, direct labour, and variable overhead.

Since absorption costing treats fixed manufacturing overhead as a product cost, a portion of fixed manufacturing overhead is assigned to each unit as it is produced. If units of product are unsold at the end of a period, then the fixed manufacturing overhead cost attached to the units is carried with them into the inventory account and deferred to the next period. When these units are later sold, the fixed manufacturing overhead cost attached to them is released from the inventory account and charged against revenues as a part of cost of goods sold. Thus, under absorption costing, it is possible to defer a portion of the fixed manufacturing overhead cost of one period to the next period through the inventory account.

Unfortunately, this shifting of fixed manufacturing overhead cost between periods can cause operating income to fluctuate erratically and can result in confusion and unwise decisions on the part of management. To guard against mistakes when they interpret income statement data, managers should be alert to any changes that may have taken place in inventory levels or in unit product costs during the period.

Practically speaking, variable costing cannot be used externally for financial reporting purposes in certain jurisdictions. However, it may be used internally for planning purposes. The variable costing approach dovetails well with CVP concepts that are often indispensable in profit planning and decision making.

REVIEW PROBLEM: CONTRASTING VARIABLE AND ABSORPTION COSTING

Dexter Company produces and sells a single product, a wooden hand loom for weaving small items such as scarves. Selected cost and operating data relating to the product for two years are given below:

Selling price per unit	$ 50	
Manufacturing costs:		
Variable per unit produced:		
Direct materials	11	
Direct labour	6	
Variable overhead	3	
Fixed per year	120,000	
Selling and administrative costs:		
Variable per unit sold	5	
Fixed per year	70,000	
	Year 1	**Year 2**
Units in beginning inventory	–0–	2,000
Units produced during the year	10,000	6,000
Units sold during the year	8,000	8,000
Units in ending inventory	2,000	–0–

Required:

1. Assume that the company uses absorption costing.
   a. Compute the unit product cost in each year.
   b. Prepare an income statement for each year.
2. Assume that the company uses variable costing.
   a. Compute the unit product cost in each year.
   b. Prepare an income statement for each year.
3. Reconcile the variable costing and absorption costing operating incomes.

Solution to Review Problem

1. *a.* Under absorption costing, all manufacturing costs, variable and fixed, are included in unit product costs:

	Year 1	Year 2
Direct materials	$11	$11
Direct labour	6	6
Variable manufacturing overhead	3	3
Fixed manufacturing overhead		
($120,000 ÷ 10,000 units)	12	
($120,000 ÷ 6,000 units)		20
Unit product cost	$32	$40

b. The absorption costing income statements follow:

	Year 1		Year 2	
Sales (8,000 units × $50 per unit)		$400,000		$400,000
Less cost of goods sold:				
Beginning inventory	$ –0–		$ 64,000	
Add cost of goods manufactured				
(10,000 units × $32 per unit)	320,000			
(6,000 units × $40 per unit)			240,000	
Goods available for sale	320,000		304,000	
Less ending inventory (2,000 units × $32 per unit; 0 units)	64,000	256,000	–0–	304,000
Gross margin		144,000		96,000
Less selling and administrative expenses		110,000*		110,000*
Operating income		$ 34,000		$ (14,000)

*Selling and administrative expenses:

Variable (8,000 units × $5 per unit)	$ 40,000
Fixed per year	70,000
Total	$110,000

2. *a.* Under variable costing, only the variable manufacturing costs are included in unit product costs:

	Year 1	Year 2
Direct materials	$11	$11
Direct labour	6	6
Variable manufacturing overhead	3	3
Unit product cost	$20	$20

b. The variable costing income statements follow. Notice that the variable cost of goods sold is computed in a simpler, more direct manner than in the examples provided earlier. On a variable costing income statement, either approach to computing the cost of goods sold followed in this chapter is acceptable.

	Year 1		Year 2	
Sales (8,000 units × $50 per unit)		$400,000		$400,000
Less variable expenses:				
Variable cost of goods sold (8,000 units × $20 per unit)	$160,000		$160,000	
Variable selling and administrative expenses (8,000 units × $5 per unit)	40,000		40,000	
Contribution margin.		200,000		200,000
Less fixed expenses:				
Fixed manufacturing overhead	120,000		120,000	
Fixed selling and administrative expenses	70,000	190,000	70,000	190,000
Operating income		$ 10,000		$ 10,000

3. The reconciliation of the variable and absorption costing operating incomes follows:

	Year 1	Year 2
Variable costing operating income	$10,000	$10,000
Add fixed manufacturing overhead costs deferred in inventory under absorption costing (2,000 units × $12 per unit)	24,000	
Deduct fixed manufacturing overhead costs released from inventory under absorption costing (2,000 units × $12 per unit)		24,000
Absorption costing operating income	$34,000	$(14,000)

GLOSSARY

Visit the Online Learning Centre at http://www.mcgrawhill.ca/college/garrison/ for a review of key terms and definitions.

QUESTIONS

7–1 What is the basic difference between absorption costing and variable costing?

7–2 Are selling and administrative expenses treated as product costs or as period costs under variable costing?

7–3 Explain how fixed manufacturing overhead costs are shifted from one period to another under absorption costing.

7–4 What arguments can be advanced in favour of treating fixed manufacturing overhead costs as product costs?

7–5 What arguments can be advanced in favour of treating fixed manufacturing overhead costs as period costs?

7–6 If production and sales are equal, which method would you expect to show the higher operating income, variable costing or absorption costing? Why?

7–7 If production exceeds sales, which method would you expect to show the higher operating income, variable costing or absorption costing? Why?

7–8 If fixed manufacturing overhead costs are released from inventory under absorption costing, what does this tell you about the level of production in relation to the level of sales?

7–9 Scott Company had $5,000,000 in sales and reported a $300,000 loss in its annual report to shareholders. According to a CVP analysis prepared for management's use, $5,000,000 in sales is the break-even point for the company. Did the company's inventory level increase, decrease, or remain unchanged? Explain.

7–10 Under absorption costing, how is it possible to increase operating income without increasing sales?

7–11 How is the use of variable costing limited?

7–12 Develop a reason from financial accounting theory that would support a recommendation to use absorption costing for financial reporting purposes.

7-13 Brûlé Company produces both absorption costing and variable costing income statements. Brûlé's income statement for the year ended March 31, 2002, showed that its actual sales revenues, total gross profit, and total contribution margin were very close to the budgeted figures. However, its operating income was substantially greater than the budgeted amount. Explain how this can happen.

7–14 How does the use of JIT inventory methods reduce or eliminate the difference in reported operating income between absorption and variable costing?

7-15 Would absorption costing or variable costing make any difference in operating income for a public accounting firm in costing its jobs? For a dentist? Discuss.

EXERCISES

EXERCISE 7–1 Variable and Absorption Costing Unit Product Costs [LO1]

Ida Sidha Karya Company is a family-owned company located in the village of Gianyar on the island of Bali in Indonesia. The company produces a handcrafted Balinese musical instrument called a gamelan that is similar to a xylophone. The sounding bars are cast from brass and hand-filed to attain just the right sound. The bars are then mounted on an intricately hand-carved wooden base. The gamelans are sold for 850 (thousand) rupiahs. (The currency in Indonesia is the rupiah, which is denoted by Rp.) Selected data for the company's operations last year follow (all currency values are in thousands of rupiahs):

Units in beginning inventory	0
Units produced	250
Units sold	225
Units in ending inventory	25
Variable costs per unit:	
Direct materials	Rp100
Direct labour	Rp320
Variable manufacturing overhead	Rp40
Variable selling and administrative	Rp20
Fixed costs:	
Fixed manufacturing overhead	Rp60,000
Fixed selling and administrative	Rp20,000

Required:

1. Assume that the company uses absorption costing. Compute the unit product cost for one gamelan.
2. Assume that the company uses variable costing. Compute the unit product cost for one gamelan.

EXERCISE 7–2 Variable Costing Income Statement; Explanation of Difference in Operating Income [LO2]

Refer to the data in Exercise 7–1 for Ida Sidha Karya Company. An absorption costing income statement prepared by the company's accountant appears below (all currency values are in thousands of rupiahs):

Required:

1. Determine how much of the ending inventory of Rp17,500 consists of fixed manufacturing overhead cost deferred in inventory to the next period.

2. Prepare an income statement for the year using the variable costing method. Explain the difference in operating income between the two costing methods.

Sales (225 units × Rp850 per unit)		Rp191,250
Less cost of goods sold:		
Beginning inventory	Rp 0	
Add cost of goods manufactured		
(250 units × Rp _?_ per unit)	175,000	
Goods available for sale	175,000	
Less ending inventory		
(25 units × Rp _?_ per unit)	17,500	157,500
Gross margin		33,750
Less selling and administrative expenses:		
Variable selling and administrative	4,500	
Fixed selling and administrative	20,000	24,500
Operating income		Rp 9,250

EXERCISE 7–3 Reconciliation of Absorption and Variable Costing Operating Incomes [LO3]

Jorgansen Lighting, Inc., manufactures heavy-duty street lighting systems for municipalities. The company uses variable costing for internal management reports and absorption costing for external reports to shareholders, creditors, and the government. The company has provided the following data:

	Year 1	Year 2	Year 3
Inventories:			
Beginning (units)	200	170	180
Ending (units)	170	180	220
Variable costing operating income	$1,080,400	$1,032,400	$996,400

The company's fixed manufacturing overhead per unit was constant at $560 for all three years.

Required:

1. Determine each year's absorption costing operating income. Present your answer in the form of a reconciliation report such as the one shown in Exhibit 7–5.
2. In Year 4, the company's variable costing operating income was $984,400 and its absorption costing operating income was $1,012,400. Did inventories increase or decrease during Year 4? How much fixed manufacturing overhead cost was deferred or released from inventory during Year 4?

EXERCISE 7–4 Evaluating Absorption and Variable Costing as Alternative Costing Methods [LO4]

The questions below pertain to two different scenarios involving a manufacturing company. In each scenario, the cost structure of the company is constant from year to year. Selling prices, unit variable costs, and total fixed costs are the same every year. However, unit sales and/or unit production levels may vary from year to year.

Required:

1. Consider the following data for scenario A:

	Year 1	Year 2	Year 3	Year 4
Variable costing operating income	$510,600	$510,600	$510,600	$510,600
Absorption costing operating income	$577,290	$636,518	$471,082	$361,500

a. Were unit sales constant from year to year? Explain.

b. What was the relation between unit sales and unit production levels in each year? For each year, indicate whether inventories grew or shrank.

2. Consider the following data for scenario B:

	Year 1	Year 2	Year 3	Year 4
Variable costing operating income	$770,600	$640,600	$380,600	$510,600
Absorption costing operating income	$603,745	$603,745	$603,745	$603,745

   a. Were unit sales constant from year to year? Explain.
   b. What was the relation between unit sales and unit production levels in each year? For each year, indicate whether inventories grew or shrank.
3. Given the patterns of operating income in scenarios A and B above, which costing method, variable costing or absorption costing, do you believe provides a better reflection of economic reality? Explain.

EXERCISE 7–5 Variable and Absorption Costing Unit Product Costs and Income Statements [LO1, LO2]

Lynch Company manufactures and sells a single product. The following costs were incurred during the company's first year of operations:

Variable costs per unit:	
Manufacturing:	
Direct materials	$6
Direct labour	$9
Variable manufacturing overhead	$3
Variable selling and administrative	$4
Fixed costs per year:	
Fixed manufacturing overhead	$300,000
Fixed selling and administrative	$190,000

During the year, the company produced 25,000 units and sold 20,000 units. The selling price of the company's product is $50 per unit.

Required:

1. Assume that the company uses the absorption costing method:
   a. Compute the unit product cost.
   b. Prepare an income statement for the year.
2. Assume that the company uses the variable costing method:
   a. Compute the unit product cost.
   b. Prepare an income statement for the year.

EXERCISE 7–6 Variable Costing Income Statement; Reconciliation [LO2, LO3]

Whitman Company has just completed its first year of operations. The company's accountant has prepared an absorption costing income statement for the year:

WHITMAN COMPANY Income Statement		
Sales (35,000 units at $25 per unit)		$875,000
Less cost of goods sold:		
Beginning inventory	$ 0	
Add cost of goods manufactured (40,000 units at $16 per unit)	640,000	
Goods available for sale	640,000	
Less ending inventory (5,000 units at $16 per unit)	80,000	560,000
Gross margin		315,000
Less selling and administrative expenses		280,000
Operating income		$ 35,000

The company's selling and administrative expenses consist of $210,000 per year in fixed expenses and $2 per unit sold in variable expenses. The $16 per unit product cost given above is computed as follows:

Direct materials	$ 5
Direct labour	6
Variable manufacturing overhead	1
Fixed manufacturing overhead ($160,000 ÷ 40,000 units)	4
Unit product cost	$16

Required:

1. Redo the company's income statement in the contribution format using variable costing.
2. Reconcile any difference between the operating income on your variable costing income statement and the operating income on the absorption costing income statement above.

EXERCISE 7–7 Inferring Costing Method; Unit Product Cost [LO1, LO4]

Sierra Company incurs the following costs to produce and sell a single product.

Variable costs per unit:	
Direct materials	$9
Direct labour	$10
Manufacturing overhead	$5
Selling and administrative expenses	$3
Fixed costs per year:	
Fixed manufacturing overhead	$150,000
Fixed selling and administrative expenses	$400,000

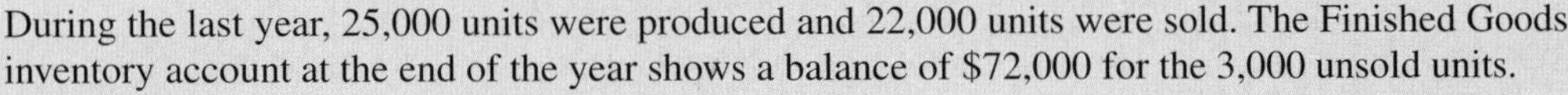

During the last year, 25,000 units were produced and 22,000 units were sold. The Finished Goods inventory account at the end of the year shows a balance of $72,000 for the 3,000 unsold units.

Required:

1. Is the company using absorption costing or variable costing to cost units in the Finished Goods inventory account? Show computations to support your answer.
2. Assume that the company wishes to prepare financial statements for the year to issue to its shareholders.
   a. Is the $72,000 figure for Finished Goods inventory the correct amount to use on these statements for external reporting purposes? Explain.
   b. At what dollar amount *should* the 3,000 units be carried in the inventory for external reporting purposes?

EXERCISE 7–8 Variable Costing Unit Product Cost and Income Statement; Break-Even [LO1, LO2]

Chuck Wagon Grills, Inc., makes a single product—a handmade specialty barbecue grill that it sells for $210. Data for last year's operations follow:

Units in beginning inventory	0
Units produced	20,000
Units sold	19,000
Units in ending inventory	1,000
Variable costs per unit:	
Direct materials	$ 50
Direct labour	80
Variable manufacturing overhead	20
Variable selling and administrative	10
Total variable cost per unit	$ 160
Fixed costs:	
Fixed manufacturing overhead	$700,000
Fixed selling and administrative	285,000
Total fixed costs	$985,000

Required:

1. Assume that the company uses variable costing. Compute the unit product cost for one barbecue grill.
2. Assume that the company uses variable costing. Prepare an income statement for the year using the contribution format.
3. What is the company's break-even point in terms of the number of barbecue grills sold?

EXERCISE 7–9 Absorption Costing Unit Product Cost and Income Statement [LO1, LO2]
Refer to the data in Exercise 7–8 for Chuck Wagon Grills. Assume in this exercise that the company uses absorption costing.

Required:

1. Compute the unit product cost for one barbecue grill.
2. Prepare an income statement for the year.

PROBLEMS

PROBLEM 7–10 Variable and Absorption Costing Unit Product Costs and Income Statements; Explanation of Difference in Operating Income [LO1, LO2, LO3]
High Country, Inc., produces and sells many recreational products. The company has just opened a new plant to produce a folding camp cot. The following cost and revenue data relate to May, the first month of the plant's operation:

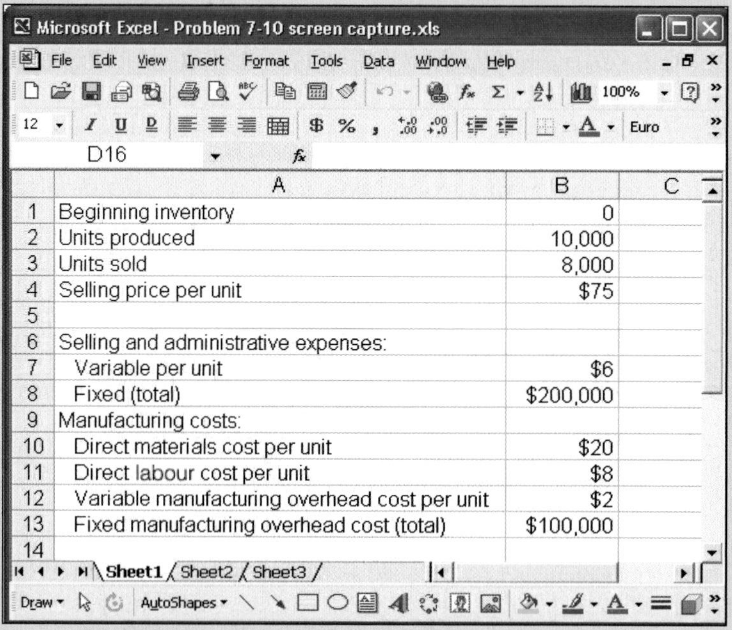
Microsoft Excel - Problem 7-10 screen capture.xls

	A	B
1	Beginning inventory	0
2	Units produced	10,000
3	Units sold	8,000
4	Selling price per unit	$75
5		
6	Selling and administrative expenses:	
7	Variable per unit	$6
8	Fixed (total)	$200,000
9	Manufacturing costs:	
10	Direct materials cost per unit	$20
11	Direct labour cost per unit	$8
12	Variable manufacturing overhead cost per unit	$2
13	Fixed manufacturing overhead cost (total)	$100,000
14		

Management is anxious to see how profitable the new camp cot will be and has asked that an income statement be prepared for May.

Required:

1. Assume that the company uses absorption costing.
   a. Determine the unit product cost.
   b. Prepare an income statement for May.
2. Assume that the company uses the contribution approach with variable costing.
   a. Determine the unit product cost.
   b. Prepare an income statement for May.
3. Explain the reason for any difference in the ending inventory balance under the two costing methods and the impact of this difference on reported operating income.

PROBLEM 7–11 Variable Costing Income Statement; Reconciliation [LO2, LO3]

During Heaton Company's first two years of operations, the company reported absorption costing operating income as follows:

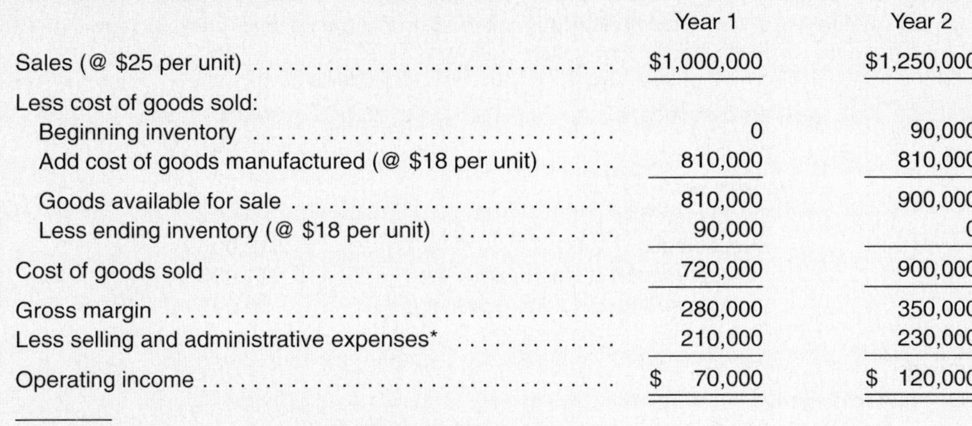

	Year 1	Year 2
Sales (@ $25 per unit)	$1,000,000	$1,250,000
Less cost of goods sold:		
Beginning inventory	0	90,000
Add cost of goods manufactured (@ $18 per unit)	810,000	810,000
Goods available for sale	810,000	900,000
Less ending inventory (@ $18 per unit)	90,000	0
Cost of goods sold	720,000	900,000
Gross margin	280,000	350,000
Less selling and administrative expenses*	210,000	230,000
Operating income	$ 70,000	$ 120,000

*$2 per unit variable; $130,000 fixed each year.

The company's $18 unit product cost is computed as follows:

Direct materials	$ 4
Direct labour	7
Variable manufacturing overhead	1
Fixed manufacturing overhead ($270,000 ÷ 45,000 units)	6
Unit product cost	$18

Production and cost data for the two years are:

	Year 1	Year 2
Units produced	45,000	45,000
Units sold	40,000	50,000

Required:

1. Prepare a variable costing income statement for each year.
2. Reconcile the absorption costing and the variable costing operating income figures for each year.

PROBLEM 7–12 Absorption and Variable Costing; Production Constant, Sales Fluctuate [LO1, LO2, LO3, LO4]

Tami Tyler opened Tami's Creations, Inc., a small manufacturing company, at the beginning of the year. Getting the company through its first quarter of operations placed a considerable strain on Ms. Tyler's personal finances. The following income statement for the first quarter was prepared by a friend who has just completed a course in managerial accounting at a local university.

TAMI'S CREATIONS, INC.
Income Statement
For the Quarter Ended March 31

Sales (28,000 units)		$1,120,000
Less variable expenses:		
Variable cost of goods sold*	$462,000	
Variable selling and administrative	168,000	630,000
Contribution margin		490,000
Less fixed expenses:		
Fixed manufacturing overhead	300,000	
Fixed selling and administrative	200,000	500,000
Operating loss		$ (10,000)

*Consists of direct materials, direct labour, and variable manufacturing overhead.

Ms. Tyler is discouraged over the loss shown for the quarter, particularly since she had planned to use the statement as support for a bank loan. Another friend, a CGA, insists that the company should be using absorption costing rather than variable costing, and argues that if absorption costing had been used the company would probably have reported at least some profit for the quarter.

At this point, Ms. Tyler is manufacturing only one product, a swimsuit. Production and cost data relating to the swimsuit for the first quarter follow:

Units produced	30,000
Units sold	28,000
Variable costs per unit:	
Direct materials	$3.50
Direct labour	$12.00
Variable manufacturing overhead	$1.00
Variable selling and administrative	$6.00

Required:

1. Complete the following:
   a. Compute the unit product cost under absorption costing.
   b. Redo the company's income statement for the quarter using absorption costing.
   c. Reconcile the variable and absorption costing operating income (loss) figures.
2. Was the CGA correct in suggesting that the company really earned a "profit" for the quarter? Explain.
3. During the second quarter of operations, the company again produced 30,000 units but sold 32,000 units. (Assume no change in total fixed costs.)
   a. Prepare an income statement for the quarter using variable costing.
   b. Prepare an income statement for the quarter using absorption costing.
   c. Reconcile the variable costing and absorption costing operating income figures.

PROBLEM 7–13 Comprehensive Problem with Labour Fixed [LO1, LO2, LO3, LO4]
Far North Telecom, Ltd., of Ontario, has organized a new division to manufacture and sell specialty cellular telephones. The division's monthly costs are shown below:

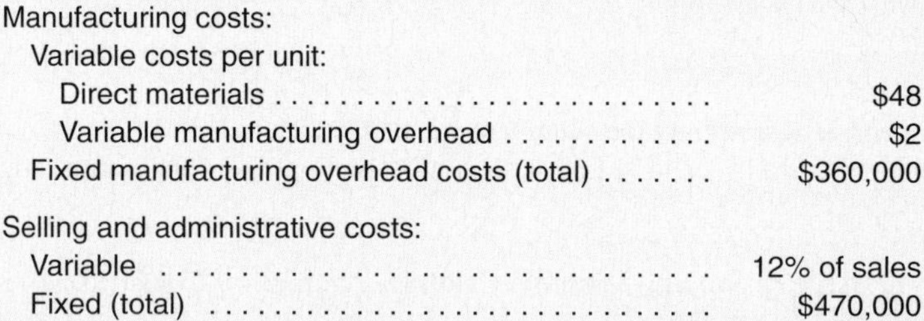

Manufacturing costs:	
Variable costs per unit:	
Direct materials	$48
Variable manufacturing overhead	$2
Fixed manufacturing overhead costs (total)	$360,000
Selling and administrative costs:	
Variable	12% of sales
Fixed (total)	$470,000

Far North Telecom regards all of its workers as full-time employees and the company has a long-standing no layoff policy. Furthermore, production is highly automated. Accordingly, the company includes its labour costs in its fixed manufacturing overhead. The cellular phones sell for $150 each. During September, the first month of operations, the following activity was recorded:

Units produced	12,000
Units sold	10,000

Required:

1. Compute the unit product cost under:
   a. Absorption costing.
   b. Variable costing.
2. Prepare an income statement for September using absorption costing.
3. Prepare an income statement for September using variable costing.
4. Assume that the company must obtain additional financing in order to continue operations. As a member of top management, would you prefer to rely on the statement in (2) above or in (3) above when meeting with a group of prospective investors?

5. Reconcile the absorption costing and variable costing operating income figures in (2) and (3) above.

PROBLEM 7–14 Prepare and Reconcile Variable Costing Statements [LO1, LO2, LO3, LO4]

Denton Company manufactures and sells a single product. Cost data for the product are given below:

Variable costs per unit:	
Direct materials	$ 7
Direct labour	10
Variable manufacturing overhead	5
Variable selling and administrative	3
Total variable cost per unit	$ 25
Fixed costs per month:	
Fixed manufacturing overhead	$315,000
Fixed selling and administrative	245,000
Total fixed cost per month	$560,000

The product sells for $60 per unit. Production and sales data for July and August, the first two months of operations, follow:

	Units Produced	Units Sold
July	17,500	15,000
August	17,500	20,000

The company's Accounting Department has prepared absorption costing income statements for July and August as presented below:

	July	August
Sales	$900,000	$1,200,000
Less cost of goods sold:		
Beginning inventory	0	100,000
Add cost of goods manufactured	700,000	700,000
Goods available for sale	700,000	800,000
Less ending inventory	100,000	0
Cost of goods sold	600,000	800,000
Gross margin	300,000	400,000
Less selling and administrative expenses	290,000	305,000
Operating income	$ 10,000	$ 95,000

Required:

1. Determine the unit product cost under:
   a. Absorption costing.
   b. Variable costing.
2. Prepare variable costing income statements for July and August using the contribution approach.
3. Reconcile the variable costing and absorption costing operating income figures.
4. The company's Accounting Department has determined the company's break-even point to be 16,000 units per month, computed as follows:

$$\frac{\text{Fixed cost per month, \$560,000}}{\text{Unit contribution margin, \$35 per unit}} = 16{,}000 \text{ units}$$

"I'm confused," said the president. "The accounting people say that our break-even point is 16,000 units per month, but we sold only 15,000 units in July, and the income statement they prepared shows a $10,000 profit for that month. Either the income statement is wrong or the break-even point is wrong." Prepare a brief memo for the president, explaining what happened on the July income statement.

PROBLEM 7–15 Variable Costing Income Statements; Sales Constant, Production Varies; JIT Impact [LO1, LO2, LO3, LO4, LO5]

"This makes no sense at all," said Bill Sharp, president of Essex Company. "We sold the same number of units this year as we did last year, yet our profits have more than doubled. Who made the goof—the computer or the people who operate it?" The statements to which Mr. Sharp was referring are shown below (absorption costing basis):

	Year 1	Year 2
Sales (20,000 units each year)	$700,000	$700,000
Less cost of goods sold	460,000	400,000
Gross margin	240,000	300,000
Less selling and administrative expenses	200,000	200,000
Operating income	$ 40,000	$100,000

The statements above show the results of the first two years of operation. In the first year, the company produced and sold 20,000 units; in the second year, the company again sold 20,000 units, but it increased production as shown below:

	Year 1	Year 2
Production in units	20,000	25,000
Sales in units	20,000	20,000
Variable manufacturing cost per unit produced	$8	$8
Variable selling and administrative expense per unit sold	$1	$1
Fixed manufacturing overhead costs (total)	$300,000	$300,000

Essex Company applies fixed manufacturing overhead costs to its only product on the basis of *each year's production.* (Thus, a new fixed manufacturing overhead rate is computed each year, as in Exhibit 7–6.)

Required:

1. Compute the unit product cost for each year under:
   a. Absorption costing.
   b. Variable costing.
2. Prepare a variable costing income statement for each year, using the contribution approach.
3. Reconcile the variable costing and absorption costing operating income figures for each year.
4. Explain to the president why, under absorption costing, the operating income for Year 2 was higher than the operating income for Year 1, although the same number of units was sold in each year.
5. *a.* Explain how operations would have differed in Year 2 if the company had been using JIT inventory methods.
   b. If JIT had been in use during Year 2, what would the company's operating income have been under absorption costing? Explain the reason for any difference between this income figure and the figure reported by the company in the statements above.

PROBLEM 7–16 Incentives Created by Absorption Costing; Ethics and the Manager [LO2, LO4]

Carlos Cavalas, the manager of Echo Products' Brazilian Division, is trying to decide what production schedule to set for the last quarter of the year. The Brazilian Division had planned to sell 3,600 units during the year, but by September 30 only the activity shown at the top of page 303 had been reported. The division can rent warehouse space to store up to 1,000 units. The minimum inventory level that the division should carry is 50 units. Mr. Cavalas is aware that production must be at least 200 units per quarter in order to retain a nucleus of key employees. Maximum production capacity is 1,500 units per quarter.

Demand has been soft, and the sales forecast for the last quarter is only 600 units. Due to the nature of the division's operations, fixed manufacturing overhead is a major element of product cost.

	Units
Inventory, January 1	0
Production	2,400
Sales	2,000
Inventory, September 30	400

Required:

1. Assume that the division is using variable costing. How many units should be scheduled for production during the last quarter of the year? (The basic formula for computing the required production for a period in a company is: Expected sales + Desired ending inventory − Beginning inventory = Required production.) Show computations and explain your answer. Will the number of units scheduled for production affect the division's reported income or loss for the year? Explain.
2. Assume that the division is using absorption costing and that the divisional manager is given an annual bonus based on divisional operating income. If Mr. Cavalas wants to maximize his division's operating income for the year, how many units should be scheduled for production during the last quarter? [See the formula in (1) above.] Explain.
3. Identify the ethical issues involved in the decision Mr. Cavalas must make about the level of production for the last quarter of the year.

PROBLEM 7–17 Prepare and Interpret Income Statements; Changes in Both Sales and Production; JIT [LO1, LO2, LO3, LO4, LO5]

Starfax, Inc., manufactures a small part that is widely used in various electronic products such as home computers. Operating results for the first three years of activity were as follows (absorption costing basis):

	Year 1	Year 2	Year 3
Sales	$800,000	$640,000	$800,000
Cost of goods sold:			
Beginning inventory	0	0	200,000
Add cost of goods manufactured	580,000	600,000	560,000
Goods available for sale	580,000	600,000	760,000
Less ending inventory	0	200,000	140,000
Cost of goods sold	580,000	400,000	620,000
Gross margin	220,000	240,000	180,000
Less selling and administrative expenses	190,000	180,000	190,000
Operating income (loss)	$ 30,000	$ 60,000	$ (10,000)

In the latter part of Year 2, a competitor went out of business and in the process dumped a large number of units on the market. As a result, Starfax's sales dropped by 20% during Year 2 even though production increased during the year. Management had expected sales to remain constant at 50,000 units; the increased production was designed to provide the company with a buffer of protection against unexpected spurts in demand. By the start of Year 3, management could see that inventory was excessive and that spurts in demand were unlikely. To reduce the excessive inventories, Starfax cut back production during Year 3, as shown below:

	Year 1	Year 2	Year 3
Production in units	50,000	60,000	40,000
Sales in units	50,000	40,000	50,000

Additional information about the company follows:

a. The company's plant is highly automated. Variable manufacturing costs (direct materials, direct labour, and variable manufacturing overhead) total only $2 per unit, and fixed manufacturing overhead costs total $480,000 per year.
b. Fixed manufacturing overhead costs are applied to units of product on the basis of each year's production. (That is, a new fixed manufacturing overhead rate is computed each year, as in Exhibit 7–6.)
c. Variable selling and administrative expenses were $1 per unit sold in each year. Fixed selling and administrative expenses totalled $140,000 per year.
d. The company uses a FIFO inventory flow assumption.

Starfax's management can't understand why profits doubled during Year 2 when sales dropped by 20% and why a loss was incurred during Year 3 when sales recovered to previous levels.

Required:

1. Prepare variable costing income statements for each year using the contribution approach.
2. Refer to the absorption costing income statements above.
   a. Compute the unit product cost in each year under absorption costing. (Show how much of this cost is variable and how much is fixed.)
   b. Reconcile the variable costing and absorption costing operating income figures for each year.
3. Refer again to the absorption costing income statements. Explain why operating income was higher in Year 2 than it was in Year 1 under the absorption approach, in light of the fact that fewer units were sold in Year 2 than in Year 1.
4. Refer again to the absorption costing income statements. Explain why the company suffered a loss in Year 3 but reported a profit in Year 1 although the same number of units was sold in each year.
5. *a.* Explain how operations would have differed in Year 2 and Year 3 if the company had been using JIT inventory methods.
   b. If JIT had been used during Year 2 and Year 3, what would the company's operating income (or loss) have been in each year under absorption costing? Explain the reason for any differences between these income figures and the figures reported by the company in the statements above.

CASES

CASE 7–18 Absorption and Variable Costing; Uneven Production; Break-Even Analysis; JIT Impact [LO2, LO3, LO4, LO5]

"Now this doesn't make any sense at all," said Flora Fisher, financial vice president for Warner Company. "Our sales have been steadily rising over the last several months, but profits have been going in the opposite direction. In September we finally hit $2,000,000 in sales, but the bottom line for that month drops off to a $100,000 loss. Why aren't profits more closely correlated with sales?"

The statements to which Ms. Fisher was referring are shown on page 305 (absorption costing basis):

Hal Taylor, a recent graduate from Saint Mary's University who has just been hired by Warner Company, has stated to Ms. Fisher that the contribution approach, with variable costing, is a much better way to report profit data to management. Sales and production data for the last quarter follow:

	July	August	September
Production in units	85,000	80,000	60,000
Sales in units	70,000	75,000	80,000

Additional information about the company's operations is given below:

a. Five thousand units were in inventory on July 1.
b. Fixed manufacturing overhead costs total $1,680,000 per quarter and are incurred evenly throughout the quarter. This fixed manufacturing overhead cost is applied to units of product on the basis of a budgeted production volume of 80,000 units per month.

c. Variable selling and administrative expenses are $6 per unit sold. The remainder of the selling and administrative expenses on the statements above are fixed.
d. The company uses a FIFO inventory flow assumption. Work in process inventories are insignificant and can be ignored.

"I know production is somewhat out of step with sales," said Carla Vorhees, the company's controller. "But we had to build inventory early in the quarter in anticipation of a strike in September. Since the union settled without a strike, we then had to cut back production in September in order to reduce the excess inventories. The income statements you have are completely accurate."

WARNER COMPANY Monthly Income Statements	July	August	September
Sales (@ $25 per unit)	$1,750,000	$1,875,000	$2,000,000
Less cost of goods sold:			
Beginning inventory	80,000	320,000	400,000
Cost applied to production:			
Variable manufacturing costs (@ $9 per unit)	765,000	720,000	540,000
Fixed manufacturing overhead	595,000	560,000	420,000
Cost of goods manufactured	1,360,000	1,280,000	960,000
Goods available for sale	1,440,000	1,600,000	1,360,000
Less ending inventory	320,000	400,000	80,000
Cost of goods sold	1,120,000	1,200,000	1,280,000
Underapplied or (overapplied) fixed overhead cost	(35,000)	—	140,000
Adjusted cost of goods sold	1,085,000	1,200,000	1,420,000
Gross margin	665,000	675,000	580,000
Less selling and administrative expenses	620,000	650,000	680,000
Operating income (loss)	$ 45,000	$ 25,000	$ (100,000)

Required:

1. Prepare a variable costing income statement for each month using the contribution approach.
2. Compute the monthly break-even point under variable costing.
3. Explain to Ms. Fisher why profits have moved erratically over the three-month period shown in the absorption costing statements and why profits have not been more closely related to changes in sales volume.
4. Reconcile the variable costing and absorption costing operating income (loss) figures for each month. Show all computations, and show how you derived each figure used in your reconciliation.
5. Assume that the company had decided to introduce JIT inventory methods at the beginning of September. (Sales and production during July and August were as shown above.)
   a. How many units would have been produced during September under JIT?
   b. Starting with the next quarter (October, November, and December), would you expect any difference between the income reported under absorption costing and under variable costing? Explain why there would or would not be any difference.
   c. Refer to your computations in (2) above. How would JIT help break-even analysis "make sense" under absorption costing?

CASE 7–19 Ethics and the Manager; Absorption Costing Income Statements [LO2, LO4]

Guochang Li was hired as chief executive officer (CEO) in late November by the board of directors of ContactGlobal, a company that produces an advanced global positioning system (GPS) device. The previous CEO had been fired by the board of directors due to a series of shady business practices including shipping defective GPS devices to dealers.

Guochang felt that his first priority was to restore employee morale—which had suffered during the previous CEO's reign. He was particularly anxious to build a sense of trust between himself and the company's employees. His second priority was to prepare the budget for the coming year, which the board of directors wanted to review in their December 15 meeting.

After hammering out the details in meetings with key managers, Guochang was able to put together a budget that he felt the company could realistically meet during the coming year. That budget appears below:

Basic budget data	
Units in beginning inventory	0
Units produced	400,000
Units sold	400,000
Units in ending inventory	0
Variable costs per unit:	
Direct materials	$ 57.20
Direct labour	15.00
Variable manufacturing overhead	5.00
Variable selling and administrative	10.00
Total variable cost per unit	$ 87.20
Fixed costs:	
Fixed manufacturing overhead	$ 6,888,000
Fixed selling and administrative	4,560,000
Total fixed costs	$11,448,000

CONTACTGLOBAL
Budgeted Income Statement
(absorption method)

Sales (400,000 units × $120 per unit)		$48,000,000
Less cost of goods sold:		
Beginning inventory	$ 0	
Add cost of goods manufactured (400,000 units × $94.42 per unit)	37,768,000	
Goods available for sale	37,768,000	
Less ending inventory	0	37,768,000
Gross margin		10,232,000
Less selling and administrative expenses:		
Variable selling and administrative (400,000 units × $10 per unit)	4,000,000	
Fixed selling and administrative	4,560,000	8,560,000
Operating income		$ 1,672,000

The board of directors made it clear that this budget was not as ambitious as they had hoped. The most influential member of the board stated that "managers should have to stretch to meet profit goals." After some discussion, the board decided to set a profit goal of $2,000,000 for the coming year. To provide strong incentives, the board agreed to pay out very substantial bonuses to top managers of $10,000 to $25,000 each if this profit goal was eventually met. The bonus would be all-or-nothing. If actual operating income turned out to be $2,000,000 or more, the bonus would be paid. Otherwise, no bonus would be paid.

Required:

1. Assuming that the company does not build up its inventory (i.e., production equals sales) and its selling price and cost structure remain the same, how many units of the GPS device would have to be sold to meet the operating income goal of $2,000,000?
2. Verify your answer to (1) above by constructing a revised budget and budgeted absorption costing income statement that yields an operating income of $2,000,000.
3. Unfortunately, by October of the next year it had become clear that the company would not be able to make the $2,000,000 target profit. In fact, it looked like the company would wind up

the year as originally planned, with sales of 400,000 units, no ending inventories, and a profit of $1,672,000.

Several managers who were reluctant to lose their year-end bonuses approached Guochang and suggested that the company could still show a profit of $2,000,000. The managers pointed out that at the present rate of sales, there was enough capacity to produce tens of thousands of additional GPS devices for the warehouse and thereby shift fixed manufacturing overhead costs to another year. If sales are 400,000 units for the year and the selling price and cost structure remain the same, how many units would have to be produced in order to show a profit of at least $2,000,000 under absorption costing?

4. Verify your answer to (3) above by constructing an absorption costing income statement.
5. Do you think Guochang Li should approve the plan to build ending inventories in order to attain the target profit?
6. What advice would you give to the board of directors concerning how they determine bonuses in the future?

CASE 7–20 The Case of the Plummeting Profits; JIT Impact [LO2, LO3, LO4, LO5]

"These statements can't be right," said Ben Yoder, president of Rayco, Inc. "Our sales in the second quarter were up by 25% over the first quarter, yet these income statements show a precipitous drop in operating income for the second quarter. Those accounting people have fouled something up." Mr. Yoder was referring to the following statements (absorption costing basis):

RAYCO, INC.
Income Statements
For the First Two Quarters

	First Quarter		Second Quarter	
Sales		$480,000		$600,000
Less cost of goods sold:				
Beginning inventory	$ 80,000		$140,000	
Add cost of goods manufactured	300,000		180,000	
Goods available for sale	380,000		320,000	
Less ending inventory	140,000		20,000	
Cost of goods sold	240,000		300,000	
Add underapplied overhead	—	240,000	72,000	372,000
Gross margin		240,000		228,000
Less selling and administrative expenses		200,000		215,000
Operating income		$ 40,000		$ 13,000

After studying the statements briefly, Mr. Yoder called in the controller to see if the mistake in the second quarter could be located before the figures were released to the press. The controller stated, "I'm sorry to say that those figures are correct, Ben. I agree that sales went up during the second quarter, but the problem is in production. You see, we budgeted to produce 15,000 units each quarter, but a strike on the west coast among some of our suppliers forced us to cut production in the second quarter back to only 9,000 units. That's what caused the drop in operating income."

Mr. Yoder was confused by the controller's explanation. He replied, "This doesn't make sense. I ask you to explain why operating income dropped when sales went up and you talk about production! So what if we had to cut back production? We still were able to increase sales by 25%. If sales go up, then operating income should go up. If your statements can't show a simple thing like that, then it's time for some changes in your department!"

Budgeted production and sales for the year, along with actual production and sales for the first two quarters, are given below:

The company's plant is heavily automated, and fixed manufacturing overhead amounts to $180,000 each quarter. Variable manufacturing costs are $8 per unit. The fixed manufacturing overhead is applied to units of product at a rate of $12 per unit (based on the budgeted production shown above). Any under- or overapplied overhead is closed directly to cost of goods sold for the quarter. The company had 4,000 units in inventory to start the first quarter and uses the FIFO inventory flow assumption. Variable selling and administrative expenses are $5 per unit.

	Quarter			
	First	Second	Third	Fourth
Budgeted sales (units)	12,000	15,000	15,000	18,000
Actual sales (units)	12,000	15,000	—	—
Budgeted production (units)	15,000	15,000	15,000	15,000
Actual production (units)	15,000	9,000	—	—

Required:

1. What characteristic of absorption costing caused the drop in operating income for the second quarter and what could the controller have said to explain the problem?
2. Prepare a variable costing income statement for each quarter using the contribution approach.
3. Reconcile the absorption costing and the variable costing operating income figures for each quarter.
4. Identify and discuss the advantages and disadvantages of using the variable costing method for internal reporting purposes.
5. Assume that the company had introduced JIT (just-in-time) at the beginning of the second quarter. (Sales and production during the first quarter remain the same.)
   a. How many units would have been produced during the second quarter under JIT?
   b. Starting with the third quarter, would you expect any difference between the operating income reported under absorption costing and under variable costing? Explain why there would or would not be any difference.

GROUP AND INTERNET EXERCISES

GROUP EXERCISE 7–21 Who Needs Customers? I Can Make Money without Them
Tough times always seem to bring out the worst in people. When companies are desperate to stay in business or to report more favourable earnings to Bay Street, some managers just can't seem to resist the temptation to manipulate reported profits. Unfortunately, inventory is sometimes a tempting source of such manipulations. It is important to know how such earnings distortions can occur, whether they result from intentional actions or innocent miscalculations.

Required:

1. What product costing method is used for external financial reporting purposes?
2. Excluding inflation and changes in the selling prices of products, how could a company with the same sales as last year report significantly higher profits without cutting any costs? Could a company with sales below the break-even point report profits? Explain.
3. Are all such "fictitious" profits an attempt to distort profits and mislead investors and creditors?
4. Could the reverse situation occur? That is, could lower accounting profits be reported even though the company is not economically worse off?

GROUP EXERCISE 7–22 Changing Cost Structures and Product Costing
As companies automate their operations with advanced manufacturing technology and information technology, cost structures are becoming more fixed with higher proportions of overhead.

Required:

1. What implications does this trend hold for arguments favouring absorption costing? What implications does this trend hold for arguments favouring variable costing?
2. If absorption costing continues to be used for external financial reporting, what impact will inventory buildups or inventory liquidations have on future reported earnings compared with the effects they have had on past reported earnings?

3. Most companies evaluate and compensate top management, in part, on the basis of operating income. Would top management have a preference for basing its evaluations on variable costing or full absorption costing? Explain.

INTERNET EXERCISE 7–23

Go to the Web site of Petro-Canada and obtain the annual financial statements for 2004. These may also be obtained from www.Sedar.com. Examine the balance sheet and the associated footnotes for inventories. Describe what you can determine about the method of costing for inventories. Would absorption or variable costing make any significant difference to the operating income of Petro-Canada?

Examine footnote number 26 which describes how the financial results would look under U.S. GAAP. Did absorption costing influence the results of U.S. operating income?

INTERNET EXERCISE 7–24

As you know, the World Wide Web is a medium that is constantly evolving. Sites come and go, and change without notice. To enable the periodic updating of site addresses, this problem has been posted to the textbook Web site (www.mcgrawhill.ca/college/garrison). After accessing the site, enter the Student Centre and select this chapter. Select and complete the Internet Exercise.

CHAPTER 8

LEARNING OBJECTIVES

After studying Chapter 8, you should be able to:

1. Explain activity-based costing and how it differs from a traditional costing system.
2. Assign costs to cost pools using a first-stage allocation.
3. Compute activity rates for cost pools.
4. Assign costs to a cost object using a second-stage allocation.
5. Prepare a report showing activity-based costing margins from an activity view.
6. Compare product costs computed using traditional and activity-based costing methods.
7. (Appendix 8A) Prepare an action analysis report using activity-based costing data and interpret the report.

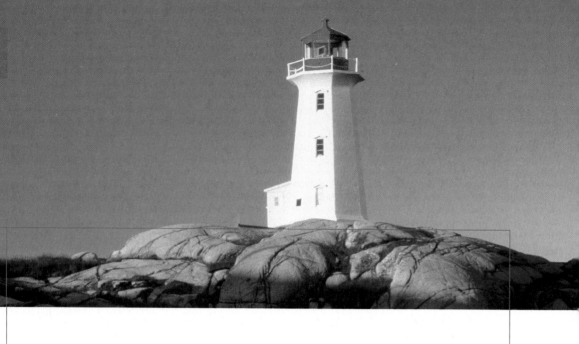

ACTIVITY-BASED COSTING: A TOOL TO AID DECISION MAKING

BUSINESS FOCUS

SHEDDING LIGHT ON PRODUCT PROFITABILITY

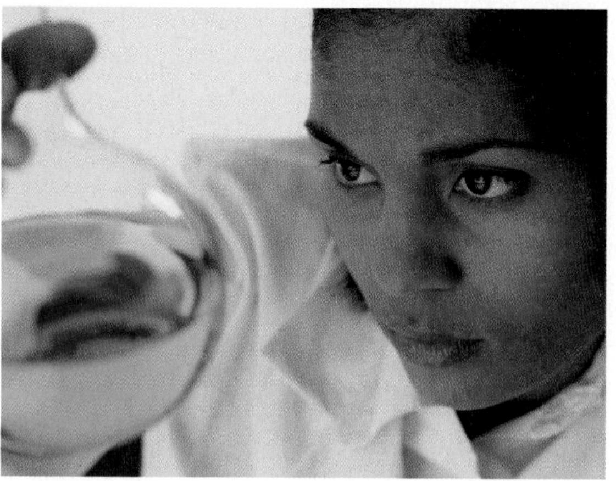

Reichhold, Inc., one of the world's leading suppliers of synthetic materials, adopted activity-based costing to help shed light on the profitability of its various products. Reichhold's prior cost system used one allocation base, reactor hours, to assign overhead costs to products. The ABC system uses four additional activity measures—preprocess preparation hours, thin-tank hours, filtration hours, and waste disposal costs per batch—to assign costs to products. Reichhold has rolled out ABC to all 19 of its North American plants because the management team believes that ABC helps improve the company's "capacity management, cycle times, value-added pricing decisions, and analysis of product profitability."

Source: Edward Blocher, Betty Wong, and Christopher McKittrick, "Making Bottom-Up ABC Work at Reichhold, Inc.," *Strategic Finance*, April 2002, pp. 51–55.

The cost accounting systems described in Chapters 2, 3, and 4 were designed primarily to provide unit product costs for external reporting purposes. Variable costing, which was described in Chapter 7, is intended to provide managers with product costs and other information for decisions that do not affect fixed costs and capacity. Another method called *activity-based costing* has been embraced by a wide variety of organizations. **Activity-based costing (ABC)** is a costing method that is designed to provide managers with cost information for strategic and other decisions that potentially affect capacity and therefore "fixed" costs. Activity-based costing is ordinarily used as a supplement to, rather than as a replacement for, the company's usual costing system. Most organizations that use activity-based costing have two costing systems—the official costing system that is used for preparing external financial reports and the activity-based costing system that is used for internal decision making and for managing activities.[1]

Activity-based costing (ABC) A costing method based on activities that is designed to provide managers with cost information for strategic and other decisions that potentially affect capacity and therefore fixed costs.

In practice, companies interpret activity-based costing differently. Because of this variation, we focus our attention in this chapter on what we consider to be "the best practice"—those techniques that provide managers with the most useful information for making strategic decisions. We will assume that the ABC system is used as a supplement to, rather than as a replacement for, the company's formal cost accounting system. The cost accounting methods described in Chapters 2, 3, and 4 would continue to be used to determine product costs for external financial reports. Activity-based costing would be used to determine product and other costs for special management reports.

Enterprise resource planning (ERP) software systems provide the opportunity to classify costs both by activity and in the traditional way. Exhibit 8–1 shows part of the menu screen for SAP, displaying the costing alternatives. This menu shows three different classifications: by cost elements, by cost centre, and by activity if configurations are carried out. The advantage of ERP systems for managers is that they can be assured by ERP that the ABC classification shown in this chapter balances with the traditional general cost accounting system.

Thus, "different costs for different purposes," a theme of managerial accounting, is facilitated by ERP computer programs. However, some companies find the configuration

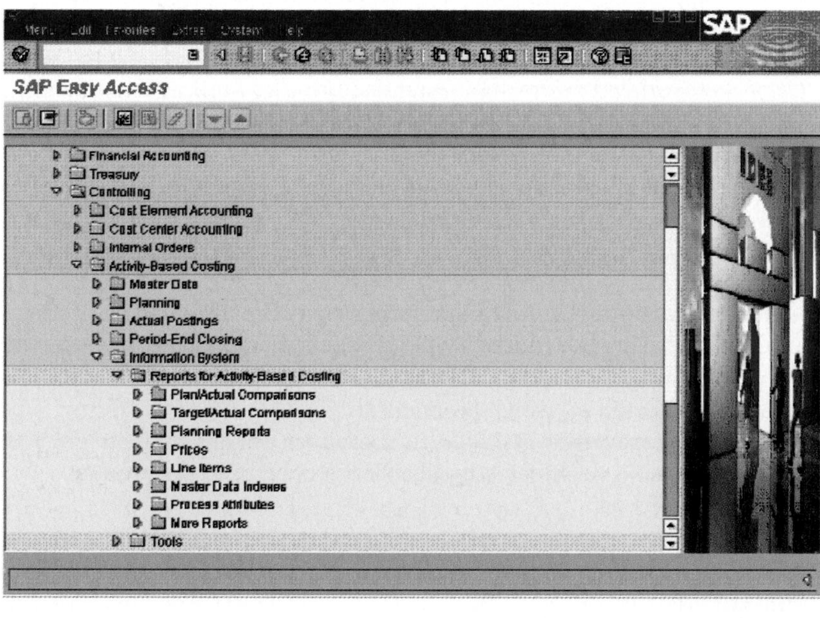

EXHIBIT 8–1 SAP Costing Menu

1. Daniel E. O'Leary, "ABB Industries: Implementing SAP's ABC, *Journal of Emerging Technologies in Accounting*, vol. 2, 2005, pp. 73–85, describes the system's development and implementation issues of SAP's–ABC module and the ultimate integration of ABC with the financial statements produced by SAP software.

of an ABC system for their organizations a challenge that they are not willing to meet, presumably because costs outweigh benefits.[2]

LEARNING OBJECTIVE 1
Explain activity-based costing and how it differs from a traditional costing system.

In the traditional cost accounting systems described in Chapters 2, 3, and 4, the objective is to value inventories and cost of goods sold for external financial reports in accordance with generally accepted accounting principles (GAAP). In activity-based costing, the objective is to understand overhead and the profitability of products and customers and to manage overhead. As a consequence of these differences in objectives, "best practice" activity-based costing differs in a number of ways from traditional cost accounting. In activity-based costing:

1. Non-manufacturing as well as manufacturing costs may be assigned to products.
2. Some manufacturing costs may be excluded from product costs.
3. A number of **overhead cost pools** are used, each of which is allocated to products and other costing objects using its own unique measure of activity.
4. The allocation bases often differ from those used in traditional costing systems.
5. The overhead rates, or *activity rates,* may be based on the level of activity at capacity rather than on the budgeted level of activity.

Overhead cost pool A group of overhead cost elements (see page 319).

As we will see later in the chapter, these differences from traditional cost accounting systems can dramatically impact the apparent costs of products and the profitability of products and customers. But first, we will briefly discuss the reasons for these departures from traditional cost accounting practices.[3]

HOW COSTS ARE TREATED UNDER ACTIVITY-BASED COSTING

Non-Manufacturing Costs and Activity-Based Costing

In traditional cost accounting, only manufacturing costs are assigned to products. Selling, general, and administrative expenses are treated as period expenses and are not assigned to products. However, many of these non-manufacturing costs are also part of the costs of producing, selling, distributing, and servicing products. For example, commissions paid to salespersons, shipping costs, and warranty repair costs can easily be traced to individual products. In this chapter, we will use the term *overhead* to refer to non-manufacturing costs as well as to indirect manufacturing costs. In activity-based costing, products are assigned all of the overhead costs—non-manufacturing as well as manufacturing—that they can reasonably be supposed to have caused. In essence, we will be determining the entire cost of a product rather than just its manufacturing cost. The focus in Chapters 2, 3, and 4 was on determining just the manufacturing cost of a product.

Manufacturing Costs and Activity-Based Costing

In traditional cost accounting, *all* manufacturing costs are assigned to products—even manufacturing costs that are not caused by the products. For example, a portion of the factory security guard's wages would be allocated to each product even though the guard's wages are totally unaffected by which products are made or not made during a period. In activity-based costing, a cost is assigned to a product only if there is good reason to believe that the cost would be affected by decisions concerning the product.

---

2. For a review of the literature documenting some of the reasons given by firms for not adopting ABC, see Tom Kennedy and John Affleck-Graves, "The Impact of Activity-Based Costing Techniques on Firm Performance," *Journal of Management Accounting Research*, vol. 13, 2001, pp. 19–45.
3. T. Colwyn Jones and D. Dugdale, "The ABC bandwagon and the juggernaut of modernity," Accounting, Organizations and Society, vol. 27, 2002, pp. 121–1263, provide an interesting, if lengthy, history of various schools of thought about ABC. Many of the implicit lessons from the study are contained in the materials to follow.

Plantwide Overhead Rate Our discussion in Chapter 3 assumed that a single overhead rate, called a *plantwide overhead rate,* was being used throughout an entire factory and that the allocation base was most often direct labour-hours or machine-hours. This simple approach to overhead assignment can result in distorted unit product costs when it is used for decision-making purposes.

When cost systems were developed in the 1800s, cost and activity data had to be collected by hand and all calculations were done with paper and pen. Consequently, the emphasis was on simplicity. Companies often established a single *overhead cost pool* for an entire facility or department, as described in Chapter 3. Direct labour was the obvious choice as an allocation base for overhead costs. Direct labour-hours were already being recorded for purposes of determining wages and direct labour time spent on tasks was often closely monitored. In the labour-intensive production processes of that time, direct labour was a large component of product costs—larger than it is today. Moreover, managers believed direct labour and overhead costs were highly correlated. (Two variables, such as direct labour and overhead costs, are highly correlated if they tend to move together.) And finally, most companies produced a very limited variety of products that required similar resources to produce, so in fact there was probably little difference in the overhead costs attributable to different products. Under these conditions, it was not cost-effective to use a more elabourate costing system.

Conditions have changed. Many companies now sell a large variety of products and services that consume significantly different overhead resources. Consequently, a costing system that assigns essentially the same rate of overhead cost to every product may no longer be adequate. Additionally, many managers now believe that overhead costs and direct labour are no longer highly correlated and that other factors drive overhead costs.

On an economywide basis, direct labour and overhead costs have been moving in opposite directions for a long time. As a percentage of total cost, direct labour has frequently been declining, whereas overhead has been increasing.[4] Many tasks that used to be done by hand are now done with automated equipment—a component of overhead. Furthermore, product diversity has increased. Companies are creating new products and services at an ever-accelerating rate that differ in volume, batch size, and complexity. Managing and sustaining this product diversity requires many more overhead resources, such as production schedulers and product design engineers, and many of these overhead resources have no obvious connection with direct labour. Finally, computers, bar code readers, and other technology have dramatically reduced the costs of collecting and manipulating data—making more complex (and accurate) costing systems such as activity-based costing much less expensive to build and maintain.

Nevertheless, direct labour remains a viable base for applying overhead to products in some companies—particularly for external reports. Direct labour is an appropriate allocation base for overhead when overhead costs and direct labour are highly correlated. And indeed, most companies throughout the world continue to base overhead allocations on direct labour or machine-hours. However, if factorywide overhead costs do not move in tandem with factorywide direct labour or machine-hours, some other means of assigning overhead costs must be found or product costs will be distorted.

Departmental Overhead Rates Rather than use a plantwide overhead rate, many companies have a system in which each department has its own overhead rate. The nature of the work performed in a department will determine the department's allocation base. For example, overhead costs in a machining department may be allocated on the basis of the machine-hours incurred in that department. In contrast, the overhead costs in an assembly department may be allocated on the basis of direct labour-hours incurred in that department.

4. Germain Böer provides some data concerning these trends in "Five Modern Management Accounting Myths," *Management Accounting*, January 1994, pp. 22–27. Data maintained by the U.S. Department of Commerce show that since 1849, on average, material cost has been fairly constant at 55% of sales. Labour cost has always been less important than direct materials and declined steadily from 23% of sales in 1849 to about 10% in 1987. Overhead grew from about 18% of sales in 1947 to about 33% of sales 50 years later.

Unfortunately, even departmental overhead rates will not correctly assign overhead costs in situations where a company has a range of products that differ in volume, batch size, or complexity of production.[5] The reason is that the departmental approach usually relies on volume as the factor in allocating overhead cost to products. For example, if a machining department's overhead is applied to products on the basis of machine-hours, it is assumed that the department's overhead costs are caused by, and are directly proportional to, machine-hours. However, the department's overhead costs are probably more complex than this and are caused by a variety of factors, including the range of products processed in the department, the number of batch set-ups that are required, the complexity of the products, and so on. Activity-based costing is a technique that is designed to reflect these diverse factors more accurately when costing products. It attempts to accomplish this goal by identifying the major *activities* such as batch set-ups, purchase order processing, and so on, that consume overhead resources and thus cause costs. An activity is any event that causes the consumption of overhead resources. The costs of carrying out these activities are assigned to the products that cause the activities.

Application of Activity-Based Costing

Activity-based costing is used in a wide variety of organizations. Service organizations such as consultants employ ABC because of their large overhead costs relative to their labour costs and the variety of services requiring varying overheads. Not-for-Profit organizations including health care services employ ABC because of the significance of overhead and the disparate nature of their operations. Restaurants and food processors have varying products and the need to know what overhead is associated with each type. Hotels and financial institutions interested in costing customer services can employ ABC to improve the accuracy of costs over what the average resulting from the use of plantwide or departmental overhead assignment would provide. While not all these organizations will use ABC, those with the need for accurate costs for their varying products or services and who have well understood operations can employ ABC to their advantage.[6]

FOCUS ***on Current Practice***

LogiCan Technologies Inc. of Edmonton, Alberta, is described as a robotized, customization operation servicing high-tech customers around the world. Using 200 employees to generate $38 million in sales, it can produce and deliver dozens of high-tech items such as monitors, radios, and modems within 72 hours anywhere in the world. Robotics provide the ability to compete because the labour component is less than 10% of the product cost.

Source: Diane Francis, *"Finding Chances on the Run," Financial Post*, January 8, 2005, pp. FP1 and FP6.

The Costs of Idle Capacity in Activity-Based Costing

In traditional cost accounting, predetermined overhead rates are computed by dividing budgeted overhead costs by a measure of budgeted activity such as budgeted direct labour-hours. This practice results in applying the costs of unused, or idle, capacity to products, and it results in unstable unit product costs as discussed in Appendix 3A. If budgeted activity falls, the overhead rate increases because the fixed components of overhead are spread over a smaller base, resulting in increased unit product costs.

5. See Robin Cooper and Robert S. Kaplan, "How Cost Accounting Distorts Product Costs," *Management Accounting,* April 1988, pp. 20–27.
6. Tom Kennedy and John Affleck-Graves, "The Impact of Activity-Based Costing Techniques on Firm Performance," *Journal of Management Accounting Research*, vol. 13, 2001, pp. 19–45.

In contrast to traditional cost accounting, in activity-based costing, products are charged for the costs of capacity they use—not for the costs of capacity they don't use. In other words, the costs of idle capacity are not charged to products. This results in more stable unit costs and is consistent with the objective of assigning only those costs to products that are actually caused by the products. Instead of assigning the costs of idle capacity to products, in activity-based costing these costs are considered to be period costs that flow through to the income statement as an expense of the current period. This treatment highlights the cost of idle capacity rather than burying it in inventory and cost of goods sold.[7]

DESIGNING AN ACTIVITY-BASED COSTING SYSTEM

Experts agree on several essential characteristics of any successful implementation of activity-based costing. First, the initiative to implement activity-based costing must be strongly supported by top management. Second, the design and implementation of an ABC system should be the responsibility of a cross-functional team rather than of the Accounting Department. The team should include representatives from each area that will use the data provided by the ABC system. Ordinarily, this would include representatives from marketing, production, engineering, and top management, as well as technically trained accounting staff. An outside consultant who specializes in activity-based costing may serve as an advisor to the team.

The reason for insisting on strong top-management support and a multifunction team approach is rooted in the fact that it is difficult to implement changes in organizations unless those changes have the full support of those who are affected. Activity-based costing changes "the rules of the game" since it changes some of the key measures that managers use for their decision making and for evaluating individuals' performance. Unless the managers who are directly affected by the changes in the rules have a say, resistance will be inevitable. In addition, designing a good ABC system requires intimate knowledge of many parts of the organization's overall operations. This knowledge can come only from the people who are familiar with those operations.

Top managers must support the initiative for two reasons. First, without leadership from top management, some managers may not see any reason to change. Second, if top managers do not support the ABC system and continue to play the game by the old rules, their subordinates will quickly get the message that ABC is not important and they will abandon the ABC initiative. Time after time, when accountants have attempted to implement an ABC system on their own without top-management support and active cooperation from other managers, the results have been ignored.

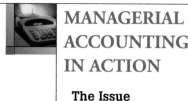

MANAGERIAL ACCOUNTING IN ACTION

The Issue

Classic Brass Inc. makes finely machined brass fittings for a variety of applications including stanchions, cleats, and helms for luxury yachts. The president of the company, John Towers, recently attended a management conference at which activity-based costing was discussed. Following the conference, he called a meeting of the top managers in the company to discuss what he had learned. Attending the meeting were the production manager Susan Ritcher, the marketing manager Tom Olafson, and the accounting manager Mary Goodman.

John: I'm glad we could all get together this morning. I just attended a conference that dealt with some issues that we have all been wondering about for some time.

7. Several *Statements on Management Accounting* issued by the Institute of Management Accountants, Montvale, New Jersey (http://www.imanet.org/), deal with implementing activity-based costing, including: *Statement 4T, Implementing Activity-Based Costing; Statement 4CC, Implementing Activity-Based Management; and Statement 4EE, Tools and Techniques for Implementing ABC/ABM*. Many of these studies are also available from the Society of Management Accountants of Canada, a joint sponsor of some of the research (http://www.cma-canada.org/).

Susan: Did anyone at the conference explain why my equipment always breaks down at the worst possible moment?

John: Sorry, Susan, I guess that must be bad karma.

Tom: Did the conference tell you why we've been losing all those bids lately on our high-volume routine work?

John: Tom, you probably weren't expecting this answer, but, yes, there may be a simple reason why we've been losing those bids.

Tom: Let me guess. We've been losing the bids because we have more competition.

John: Yes, the competition has a lot to do with it. But, Tom, we may have been shooting ourselves in the foot.

Tom: How so? I don't know about anyone else, but my salespeople have been hustling like crazy to get more business for the company.

Susan: Wait a minute, Tom, my production people have been turning in tremendous improvements in defect rates, on-time delivery, and so on.

John: Whoa, everybody. Calm down. I don't think anyone is to blame for losing the bids. Tom, when you talk with our customers, what reasons do they give for taking their business to our competitors? Is it a problem with the quality of our products or our on-time delivery?

Tom: No, they don't have any problem with our products or with our service—our customers readily admit we're among the best in the business.

Susan: Darn right!

John: Then what's the problem?

Tom: Price. The competition is undercutting our prices on the high-volume work.

John: Why are our prices too high?

Tom: Our prices aren't too high. Theirs are too low. Our competitors must be pricing below their cost.

John: Tom, why do you think that?

Tom: Well, if we charged the prices on high-volume work that our competitors are quoting, we'd be pricing below *our* cost, and I know we are just as efficient as any competitor.

Susan: Tom, why would our competitors price below their cost?

Tom: They are out to grab market share.

Susan: Does that make any sense? What good does more market share do if they are pricing below their cost?

John: I think Susan has a point, Tom. Mary, you're the expert with the numbers. Can you suggest another explanation?

Mary: I was afraid you would ask that. Those unit product cost figures our department reports to you are primarily intended to be used to value inventories and to determine cost of goods sold for our external financial statements. I am awfully uncomfortable about using them for bidding. In fact, I have mentioned this several times, but no one was interested.

John: Now I'm interested. Mary, are you telling us that the product cost figures we have been using for bidding are wrong? Perhaps the competition isn't pricing below our cost—we just don't know what our cost is?

Mary: Yes, that could be the problem. I just wish someone had listened earlier.

John: Does everyone agree with Mary that this is a problem we should work on?

Tom: Sure, if it means we can win more bids.

John: Okay, I want each of you to appoint one of your top people to a special team to investigate how we cost products.

Susan: Isn't this something Mary can handle with her staff?

John: Perhaps she could, but you know more about your operations than she does and besides, I want to make sure you agree with the results of the study and use them. Mary, do you agree?

Mary: Absolutely.

After studying the existing cost accounting system at Classic Brass and reviewing articles in professional and trade journals, the special team decided to implement an activity-based costing system. Like most other ABC implementations, the new ABC system would supplement, rather than replace, the existing cost accounting system, which would continue to be used for external financial reports. The new ABC system would be used to prepare special reports for management decisions such as bidding on new business.

The accounting manager drew the chart appearing in Exhibit 8–2 to explain the general structure of the ABC model. **Cost objects** such as products generate activities. For example, a customer order for a brass cupholder requires the activity of preparing a production order. Such an activity consumes resources. A production order uses a sheet of paper and takes time to fill out. And consumption of resources causes costs. The greater the number of sheets used to fill out production orders and the greater the amount of time devoted to filling out such orders, the greater the cost. Activity-based costing attempts to trace through these relationships to identify how products and customers affect costs.

Cost Object
The specific product or service to be costed.

EXHIBIT 8–2 The Activity-Based Costing Model

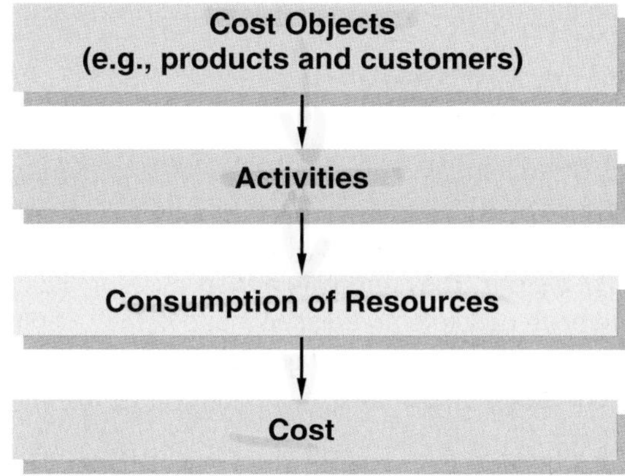

As in most other companies, the ABC team at Classic Brass felt that the company's traditional cost accounting system adequately measured the direct material and direct labour costs of products since these costs are directly traced to products. Therefore, the ABC study would be concerned solely with the other costs of the company—manufacturing overhead and selling, general, and administrative costs.

The team felt it was important to carefully plan how it would go about implementing the new ABC system at Classic Brass. Accordingly, the implementation process was broken down into the following six basic steps:

1. Identify and define activities and **activity cost pools**.
2. Whenever possible, directly trace overhead costs to activities and cost objects.
3. Assign costs to activity cost pools.
4. Calculate activity rates.
5. Assign costs to cost objects using the activity rates and activity measures.
6. Prepare management reports.

Activity Cost Pool
A group of cost elements directly associated with a specific type of activity.

Step 1: Identify and Define Activities and Activity Cost Pools

The first major step in implementing an ABC system is to identify the activities that will form the foundation for the system. This can be difficult and time-consuming, and involves a great deal of judgement. A common procedure is for the individuals on the ABC implementation team to interview people who work in overhead departments and ask them to describe their major activities. Ordinarily, this results in a very long list of activities.

The numbers to be used by the team for the first set of ABC reports were based on the most recent actual cost numbers. This approach permits the team to check its new analysis against totals available from the traditional system. Once the new ABC results are tested, the ABC costs can be used by Classic Brass to collect both budget and actual information.

FOCUS *on Current Practice*

The company art.com™ sells prints and framed prints over the Web. An ABC study identified the following 12 activities carried out by the company:

1. Service customers
2. Web site optimization
3. Merchandise inventory selection and management
4. Purchasing and receiving
5. Customer acquisition and retention—paid-for marketing
6. Customer acquisition and retention—revenue share marketing (affiliate group)
7. Sustain information system
8. Sustain business—administration
9. Sustain business—production
10. Maintain facility—administrative
11. Maintain facility—production
12. Sustain business—executive

For example, the activity "merchandise inventory selection and management" involves scanning, describing, classifying, and linking each inventory item to search options. "Staff must carefully manage each change to the database, which is similar to adding and removing inventory items from the shelf of a store. They annotate added inventory items and upload them into the system, as well as remove obsolete and discontinued items. . . . The number of inventory items for an e-tailer is typically much greater than for a brick-and-mortar [store], which is a competitive advantage, but experience shows managing a large inventory consumes substantial resources."

Source: Thomas L. Zeller, David R. Kublank, and Philip G. Makris, " How art.com™ Uses ABC to Succeed," *Strategic Finance*, March 2001, pp. 25–31. Reprinted with permission from the IMA, Montvale, NJ, USA, http://www.imanet.org/.

The length of the list of activities poses a problem. On the one hand, the greater the number of activities tracked in the ABC system, the more accurate the costs are likely to be. On the other hand, it is costly to design, implement, maintain, and use a complex system involving large numbers of activities. Consequently, the original lengthy list of activities is usually reduced to a handful by combining similar activities. For example, several actions may be involved in handling and moving raw materials—from receiving raw materials on the loading dock to sorting them into the appropriate bins in the storeroom. All of these activities might be combined into a single activity called *materials handling*.

Unit-level activities Activities that arise as a result of the total volume of goods and services that are produced and that are performed each time a unit is produced.

Batch-level activities Activities that are performed each time a batch of goods is handled or processed, regardless of how many units are in a batch. The amount of resource consumed depends on the number of batches run rather than on the number of units in the batch.

A useful way to think about activities and how to combine them is to organize them into five general levels: *unit-level, batch-level, product-level, customer-level,* and *organization-sustaining* activities. These levels are described as follows:[8]

1. **Unit-level activities** are performed each time a unit is produced. The costs of unit-level activities should be proportional to the number of units produced. For example, providing power to run processing equipment would be a unit-level activity since power tends to be consumed in proportion to the number of units produced.
2. **Batch-level activities** are performed each time a batch is handled or processed, regardless of how many units are in the batch. For example, tasks such as placing

8. Robin Cooper, "Cost Classification in Unit-Based and Activity-Based Manufacturing Cost Systems," *Journal of Cost Management*, Fall 1990, pp. 4–14.

purchase orders, setting up equipment, and arranging for shipments to customers are batch-level activities. They are incurred once for each batch (or customer order). Costs at the batch level depend on the number of batches processed rather than on the number of units produced, the number of units sold, or other measures of volume. For example, the cost of setting up a machine for batch processing is the same regardless of whether the batch contains one item or thousands of items.

3. **Product-level activities** relate to specific products and typically must be carried out regardless of how many batches are run or units of product are produced or sold. For example, activities such as designing a product, advertising a product, and maintaining a product manager and staff are all product-level activities.
4. **Customer-level activities** relate to specific customers and include activities such as sales calls, catalogue mailings, and general technical support that are not tied to any specific product.
5. **Organization-sustaining activities** are carried out regardless of which customers are served, which products are produced, how many batches are run, or how many units are made. This category includes activities such as heating the factory, cleaning executive offices, providing a computer network, arranging for loans, preparing annual reports to shareholders, and so on.

Product-level activities Activities that relate to specific products that must be carried out regardless of how many units are produced and sold or batches run.

Customer-level activities Activities that are carried out to support customers but that are not related to any specific product.

Organization-sustaining activities Activities that are carried out regardless of which customers are served, which products are produced, how many batches are run, or how many units are made.

When combining activities in an ABC system, activities should be grouped together at the appropriate level. Batch-level activities should not be combined with unit-level activities, or product-level activities with batch-level activities, and so on. In general, it is best to combine only those activities that are highly correlated with each other within a level. Activities are correlated with each other if they tend to move in tandem. For example, the number of customer orders received is likely to be highly correlated with the number of completed customer orders shipped, so these two batch-level activities (receiving and shipping orders) can usually be combined with little loss of accuracy.

At Classic Brass, the ABC team, in consultation with top managers, selected the following *activity cost pools* and *activity measures*:

Activity Cost Pools at Classic Brass

Activity Cost Pool	Activity Measure
Customer orders	Number of customer orders
Product design...............	Number of product designs
Production units..............	Machine-hours
Customer relations	Number of active customers
Other	Not applicable

An **activity cost pool** is a "bucket" in which costs are accumulated that relate to a single activity measure in the ABC system. For example, the Customer Orders cost pool will be assigned all costs of resources that are consumed by taking and processing customer orders, including costs of processing paperwork and any costs involved in setting up machines for specific orders. The measure of activity for this cost pool is simply the number of customer orders received. This is a batch-level activity, since each order generates work that occurs regardless of whether the order is for one unit or a thousand units. The number of customer orders received is an example of an *activity measure.* An **activity measure** is an allocation base in an activity-based costing system. The term *cost driver* is also used to refer to an activity measure. The activity measure should "drive" the cost being allocated.

Activity cost pool A "bucket" in which costs are accumulated that relate to a single activity measure in the activity-based costing system.

Activity measure An allocation base in an activity-based costing system; ideally, a measure of the amount of activity that drives the costs in an activity cost pool; also called a *cost driver*.

Activity measures are often very rough measures of resource consumption. Probably the least accurate type of activity measure is known as a *transaction driver*. **Transaction drivers** are simple counts of the number of times an activity occurs, such as the number of bills sent out to customers. This activity measure is satisfactory when all bills take about the same amount of time to prepare. However, if some bills are simple to prepare and others are very complex, a more accurate type of activity measure known as a *duration driver* may be used. **Duration drivers** are measures of the amount of time required to perform an activity, such as the time spent preparing individual bills. In general, duration drivers are more accurate measures of the consumption of resources than transaction

Transaction driver A simple count of the number of times an activity occurs.

Duration driver A measure of the amount of time required to perform an activity.

drivers, but they take more effort to record. For that reason, transaction drivers are often used in practice.

The Product Design cost pool will be assigned all costs of resources consumed in designing products. The activity measure for this cost pool is the number of products designed. This is a product-level activity, since the amount of design work on a new product does not depend on the number of units ultimately ordered or batches ultimately run.

The Production Units cost pool will be assigned all costs of resources consumed as a consequence of the number of units produced, including the costs of miscellaneous factory supplies, power to run machines, and some equipment depreciation. This is a unit-level activity since each unit requires some of these resources. The activity measure for this cost pool is machine-hours.

The Customer Relations cost pool will be assigned all costs associated with maintaining relations with customers, including the costs of sales calls and the costs of entertaining customers. The activity measure for this cost pool is the number of customers the company has on its active customer list. The Customer Relations cost pool represents a customer-level activity.

The Other cost pool will be assigned all overhead costs that are not associated with customer orders, product design, production units, or customer relations. These costs mainly consist of organization-sustaining costs and the costs of unused, idle capacity. These costs will *not* be assigned to products since they represent resources that are *not* consumed by products.

It is unlikely that any other company would use exactly the same activity cost pools and activities that were selected by Classic Brass. Because of the amount of judgement involved, the number and definitions of the activity cost pools and activity measures used by companies vary considerably.

THE MECHANICS OF ACTIVITY-BASED COSTING

After the ABC system had been designed, the team was ready to begin the process of actually computing the costs of products, customers, and other objects of interest.

Step 2: Whenever Possible, Directly Trace Overhead Costs to Activities and Cost Objects

The second step in implementing an ABC system is to directly trace as many overhead costs as possible to the ultimate cost objects. At Classic Brass, the ultimate cost objects are products, customer orders, and customers. The company's annual manufacturing overhead and selling, general, and administrative costs are listed in Exhibit 8–3. In the ABC system at Classic Brass, all of these costs are considered to be "overhead" and will be assigned to cost objects where appropriate.

One of these overhead costs—shipping—can be traced directly to customer orders. Classic Brass is directly billed for each customer order it ships, so it is a simple matter to trace these costs to the customer orders. Customers do not pay these actual shipping costs; instead, they pay a standard shipping charge that can differ substantially from the actual bill that Classic Brass receives from the freight company.

No other overhead costs can be directly traced to products, customer orders, or customers. Consequently, the remainder of the overhead costs are assigned to cost objects using the ABC system.

LEARNING OBJECTIVE 2
Assign costs to cost pools using a first-stage allocation.

Step 3: Assign Costs to Activity Cost Pools

Most overhead costs are originally classified in the company's basic accounting system according to the departments in which they are incurred. For example, salaries, supplies, rent, etc., incurred by the Marketing Department are charged to that department. In some

EXHIBIT 8–3
Annual Overhead Costs (both Manufacturing and Non-Manufacturing) at Classic Brass

Production Department:		
Indirect factory wages	$500,000	
Factory equipment depreciation	300,000	
Factory utilities	120,000	
Factory building lease	80,000	$1,000,000
Shipping costs*		40,000
General Administrative Department:		
Administrative wages and salaries	400,000	
Office equipment depreciation	50,000	
Administrative building lease	60,000	510,000
Marketing Department:		
Marketing wages and salaries	250,000	
Selling expenses	50,000	300,000
Total overhead costs		$1,850,000

*Shipping costs can be traced directly to customer orders.

cases, some or all of these costs can be directly traced to one of the activity cost pools in the ABC system—the third step in implementing activity-based costing. For example, if the ABC system has an activity called *purchase order processing,* then all of the costs of the Purchasing Department could probably be traced to that activity. To the extent possible, costs should be traced directly to the activity cost pools. However, it is quite common for an overhead department to be involved in several of the activities that are tracked in the ABC system. In such situations, the costs of the department are divided among the activity cost pools via an allocation process called *first-stage allocation.* The **first-stage allocation** in an ABC system is the process by which overhead costs are assigned to activity cost pools.

First-stage allocation The process by which overhead costs are assigned to activity cost pools in an activity-based costing system.

The immediate problem is to figure out how to divide, for example, the $500,000 of indirect factory wages at Classic Brass shown in Exhibit 8–3 among the various activity cost pools in the ABC system. The point of activity-based costing is to determine the resources consumed by cost objects. Since indirect factory worker time is a resource, we need some way of estimating the amount of indirect factory worker time that is consumed by each activity in the ABC system. Often, the best way to get this kind of information is to ask the people who are directly involved. Members of the ABC team interview indirect factory workers (e.g., supervisors, engineers, quality inspectors, etc.) and ask them what percentage of time they spend dealing with customer orders, with product design, with processing units of product (i.e., order size), and with customer relations. These interviews are conducted with considerable care. Those who are interviewed must thoroughly understand what the activities encompass and what is expected of them in the interview. In addition, departmental managers are interviewed to determine how the non-personnel costs should be distributed across the activity cost pools. In each case, the key question is, "What percentage of the available resource is consumed by this activity?" For example, the production manager would be asked, "What percentage of the available machine capacity is consumed as a consequence of the number of units processed (i.e., size of orders)?"

The results of the interviews at Classic Brass are displayed in Exhibit 8–4 on page 323. For example, factory equipment depreciation is distributed 20% to Customer Orders, 60% to Production Units, and 20% to the Other cost pool. The resource in this instance is machine time. According to the estimate made by the production manager, 60% of the total available time was used to actually process units to fill orders. Each customer order requires setting up, which also requires machine time. This activity consumes 20% of the total available machine time and is entered under the Customer Orders column. The remaining 20% of available machine time represents idle time and is entered under the Other column.

Exhibit 8–4 and many of the other exhibits in this chapter are presented in the form of Excel spreadsheets. All of the calculations required in activity-based costing can be done by hand. Nevertheless, setting up the activity-based costing system on a spreadsheet or using special ABC software can save a lot of work—particularly in situations involving many activity cost pools and in organizations that periodically update their ABC systems.

We will not go into the details of how all of the percentages in Exhibit 8–4 were determined. However, note that 100% of the factory building lease has been assigned to the Other cost pool. Classic Brass has a single production facility. It has no plans to expand or to sublease any excess space. The cost of this production facility is treated as an organization-sustaining cost since there is no way to avoid even a portion of this cost if a particular product or customer was dropped. (Remember that organization-sustaining costs are assigned to the Other cost pool and are not allocated to products.) In contrast, some companies have separate facilities for manufacturing specific products. The costs of these separate facilities could be directly traced to the specific products.

Once the percentage distributions in Exhibit 8–4 have been established, it is a simple matter to allocate costs to the activity cost pools. The results of this first-stage allocation are displayed in Exhibit 8–5. Each cost is allocated across the activity cost pools by multiplying it by the percentages in Exhibit 8–4. For example, the indirect factory wages of $500,000 are multiplied by the 25% entry under Customer Orders in Exhibit 8–4 to arrive at the $125,000 entry under Customer Orders in Exhibit 8–5. Similarly, the indirect factory wages of $500,000 are multiplied by the 40% entry under Product Design in Exhibit 8–4 to arrive at the $200,000 entry under Product Design in Exhibit 8–5. All of the entries in Exhibit 8–5 are computed in this way.

Now that the first-stage allocations to the activity cost pools have been completed, the fourth step is to compute the activity rates.

Step 4: Calculate Activity Rates

LEARNING OBJECTIVE 3
Compute activity rates for cost pools.

The activity rates that will be used for assigning overhead costs to products and customers are computed in Exhibit 8–6. The ABC team determined the total activity for each cost pool that would be required to produce the company's present product mix and to serve its present customers. These numbers are listed in Exhibit 8–6. For example, the ABC team found that 200 new product designs are required each year to serve the company's present customers. The activity rates are computed by dividing the *total* cost for each activity by its *total* activity. For example, the $315,000 total annual cost for the Customer Orders cost pool is divided by the total of 1,000 customer orders per year to arrive at the activity rate of $315 per customer order. Similarly, the $257,000 *total* cost for the Product Design cost pool is divided by the *total* number of designs (i.e., 200 product designs) to determine the activity rate of $1,285 per design. Note that activity rates are not computed for the Other category of costs. This is because the Other cost pool consists of organization-sustaining costs and costs of idle capacity that are not allocated to products and customers. Overall profits must be large enough to cover these unallocated costs. Also note that the activity rates represent *average* costs. For example, the average cost of a customer order is $315.

The entries in Exhibit 8–6 indicate that on average a customer order consumes resources that cost $315; a product design consumes resources that cost $1,285; a unit of product consumes resources that cost $19 per machine-hour; and maintaining relations with a customer consumes resources that cost $3,675. Note that these are *average* figures. Some members of the ABC design team at Classic Brass argued that it would be unfair to charge all new products the same $1,285 product design cost regardless of how much design time they actually require. After discussing the pros and cons, the team concluded that it would not be worth the effort at the present time to keep track of actual design time spent on each new product. They felt that the benefits of increased accuracy would not be great enough to justify the higher cost of implementing and maintaining the more detailed costing system. Similarly, some team members were uncomfortable assigning the same $3,675 cost to each customer. Some customers are undemanding—ordering standard products well in advance of their needs. Others are very demanding and consume large amounts of marketing and administrative staff time. These are generally customers who

EXHIBIT 8–4
Results of Interviews: Distribution of Resource Consumption across Activity Cost Pools

	Customer Orders	Product Design	Production Units	Customer Relations	Other	Totals
	Activity Cost Pools					
Production Department:						
Indirect factory wages	25%	40%	20%	10%	5%	100%
Factory equipment depreciation	20%	0%	60%	0%	20%	100%
Factory utilities	0%	10%	50%	0%	40%	100%
Factory building lease	0%	0%	0%	0%	100%	100%
Shipping costs*	NA	NA	NA	NA	NA	NA
General Administrative Department:						
Administrative wages and salaries	15%	5%	10%	30%	40%	100%
Office equipment depreciation	30%	0%	0%	25%	45%	100%
Administrative building lease	0%	0%	0%	0%	100%	100%
Marketing Department:						
Marketing wages and salaries	20%	10%	0%	60%	10%	100%
Selling expenses	10%	0%	0%	70%	20%	100%

*Shipping costs are not included in this and subsequent spreadsheets because they are directly traced to customer orders rather than being allocated using the ABC system. NA = Not applicable.

EXHIBIT 8–5
First-Stage Allocations to Activity Cost Pools

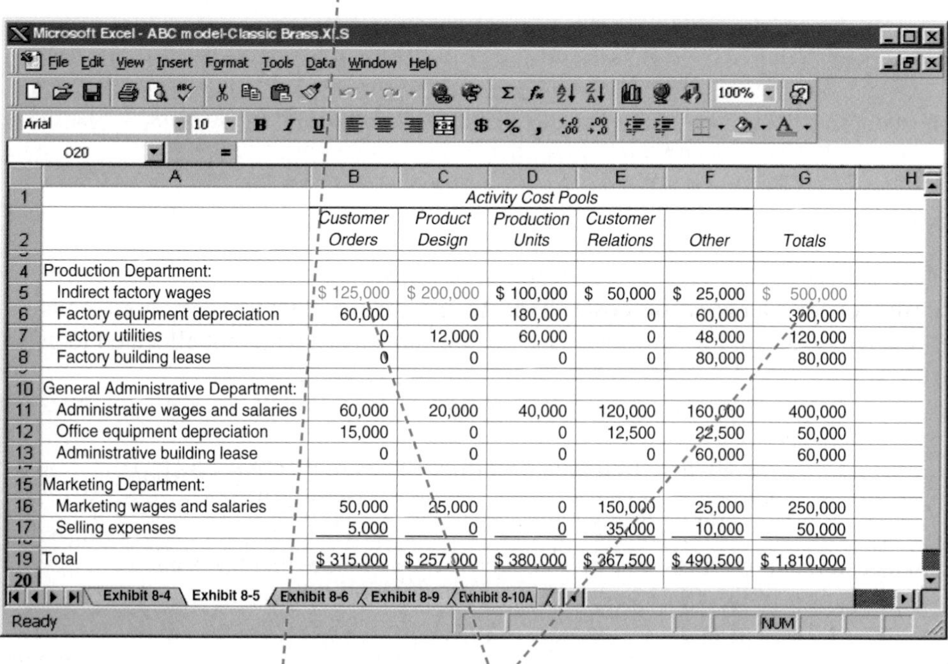

	Customer Orders	Product Design	Production Units	Customer Relations	Other	Totals
	Activity Cost Pools					
Production Department:						
Indirect factory wages	$ 125,000	$ 200,000	$ 100,000	$ 50,000	$ 25,000	$ 500,000
Factory equipment depreciation	60,000	0	180,000	0	60,000	300,000
Factory utilities	0	12,000	60,000	0	48,000	120,000
Factory building lease	0	0	0	0	80,000	80,000
General Administrative Department:						
Administrative wages and salaries	60,000	20,000	40,000	120,000	160,000	400,000
Office equipment depreciation	15,000	0	0	12,500	22,500	50,000
Administrative building lease	0	0	0	0	60,000	60,000
Marketing Department:						
Marketing wages and salaries	50,000	25,000	0	150,000	25,000	250,000
Selling expenses	5,000	0	0	35,000	10,000	50,000
Total	$ 315,000	$ 257,000	$ 380,000	$ 367,500	$ 490,500	$ 1,810,000

Exhibit 8–4 shows that Customer Orders consume 25% of the resources represented by the $500,000 of indirect factory wages.

25% × $500,000 = $125,000

Other entries in the spreadsheet are computed in a similar fashion.

EXHIBIT 8–6 Computation of Activity Rates

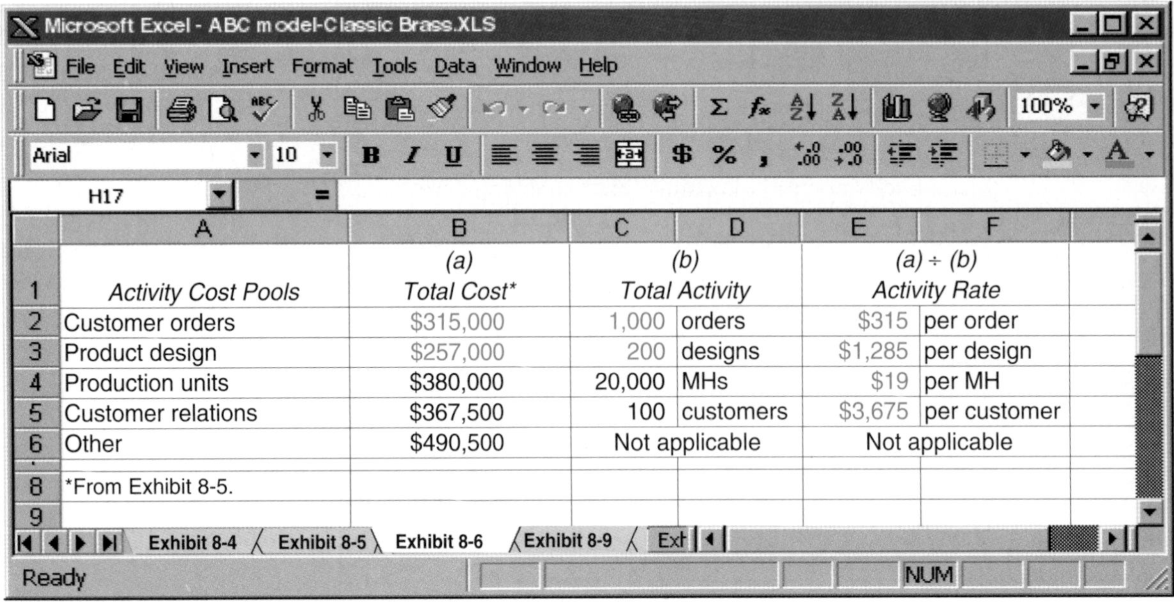

Activity Cost Pools	(a) Total Cost*	(b) Total Activity		(a) ÷ (b) Activity Rate	
Customer orders	$315,000	1,000	orders	$315	per order
Product design	$257,000	200	designs	$1,285	per design
Production units	$380,000	20,000	MHs	$19	per MH
Customer relations	$367,500	100	customers	$3,675	per customer
Other	$490,500	Not applicable		Not applicable	

*From Exhibit 8-5.

order customized products, who tend to order at the last minute, and who change their minds. While everyone agreed with this observation, the data that would be required to measure individual customers' demands on resources were not currently available. Rather than delay implementation of the ABC system, the team decided to defer such refinements to a later date.

Before proceeding, it would be helpful to get a better idea of the overall process of assigning costs to products and other cost objects in an ABC system. Exhibit 8–7 provides a visual perspective of the ABC system at Classic Brass. We recommend that you carefully go over this exhibit. In particular, note that the Other category, which contains organization-sustaining costs and costs of idle capacity, is not allocated to products or customers.

EXHIBIT 8–7 The Activity-Based Costing Model at Classic Brass

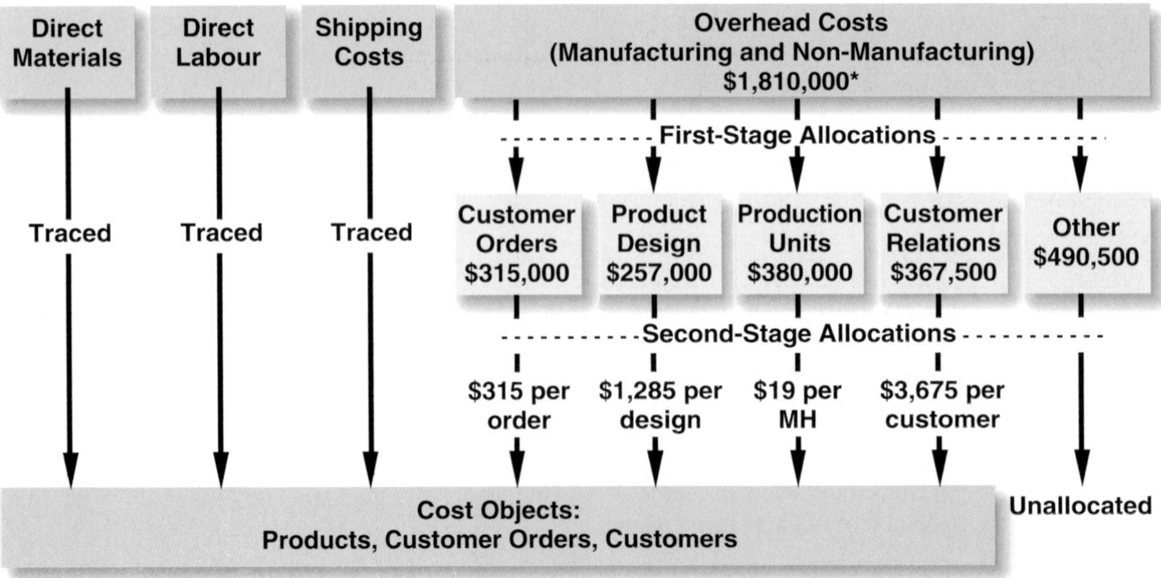

*Total overhead cost of $1,850,000 less $40,000 of shipping costs directly traced to customer orders.

Step 5: Assign Costs to Cost Objects

LEARNING OBJECTIVE 4
Assign costs to a cost object using a second-stage allocation.

The fifth step in the implementation of activity-based costing is called *second-stage allocation.* In the **second-stage allocation,** activity rates are used to apply costs to products and customers. At Classic Brass, the ABC system might be used to apply activity costs to all of the company's products, customer orders, and customers. For purposes of illustration, we will consider only one customer—Windward Yachts. This customer ordered two different products—stanchions and a compass housing. The stanchions are a standard product that does not require any design work. In contrast, the compass housing is a custom product that requires extensive designing. Data concerning these two products appear in Exhibit 8–8. Direct materials and direct labour costs are the same under the old traditional cost accounting system and the new ABC system. However, the two systems handle overhead very differently.

Second-stage allocation The process by which activity rates are used to apply costs to products and customers in activity-based costing.

The overhead calculations for the stanchions and compass housings are carried out in Exhibit 8–9. Let's examine the ABC overhead calculations for the stanchions. For each activity cost pool, the amount of activity is multiplied by the activity rate to arrive at the amount of overhead cost applied to the product. For example, since the stanchions involve 2 orders and the activity rate is $315 per order, the total Customer Order cost applied to the stanchions is $630 (2 × $315). Because the stanchion is a standard product that does not require a new design, no Product Design costs are assigned to this product. Also note that none of the Customer Relations costs have been allocated to the stanchions. A customer-level cost is assigned to customers directly; it is not assigned to products. Note how this procedure for assigning overhead costs differs from traditional costing. Instead of just a single overhead cost pool and a single predetermined overhead rate based on direct labour or machine-hours, now there are several cost pools and predetermined overhead rates.

The same procedure is followed in Exhibit 8–9 to determine the overhead cost for the custom compass housing.

Step 6: Prepare Management Reports

LEARNING OBJECTIVE 5
Prepare a report showing activity-based costing margins from an activity view.

In Exhibit 8–10 on page 327, the overhead costs computed in Exhibit 8–9 are combined with direct materials, direct labour, and shipping cost data. For each of the products, these combined costs are deducted from sales to arrive at product margins. Under the ABC system, the stanchions show a profit of $5,030, whereas the compass housing shows a loss of $1,114.

Note from Exhibit 8–10 that the new ABC system also includes a profitability analysis of Windward Yachts, the customer that ordered the stanchions and the custom compass housing. Such customer analyses can be accomplished easily by adding together the product margins for each of the products a customer has ordered and then subtracting the average charge of $3,675 for Customer Relations.

EXHIBIT 8–8
Data Concerning the Products Ordered by Windward Yachts

Standard Stanchions
1. This is a standard design that does not require any new design resources.
2. Four hundred units were ordered during the year, comprising two separate orders.
3. Each stanchion required 0.5 machine-hours, for a total of 200 machine-hours.
4. The selling price per unit was $34, for a total of $13,600.
5. Direct materials for 400 units totalled $2,110.
6. Direct labour for 400 units totalled $1,850.
7. Shipping costs for the two orders totalled $180.

Custom Compass Housing
1. This is a custom product that requires new design resources.
2. There was only one order for a single unit during the year.
3. The compass housing required 4 machine-hours.
4. The selling price was $650.
5. Direct materials were $13.
6. Direct labour was $50.
7. Shipping costs were $25.

EXHIBIT 8–9 Computation of Overhead Costs

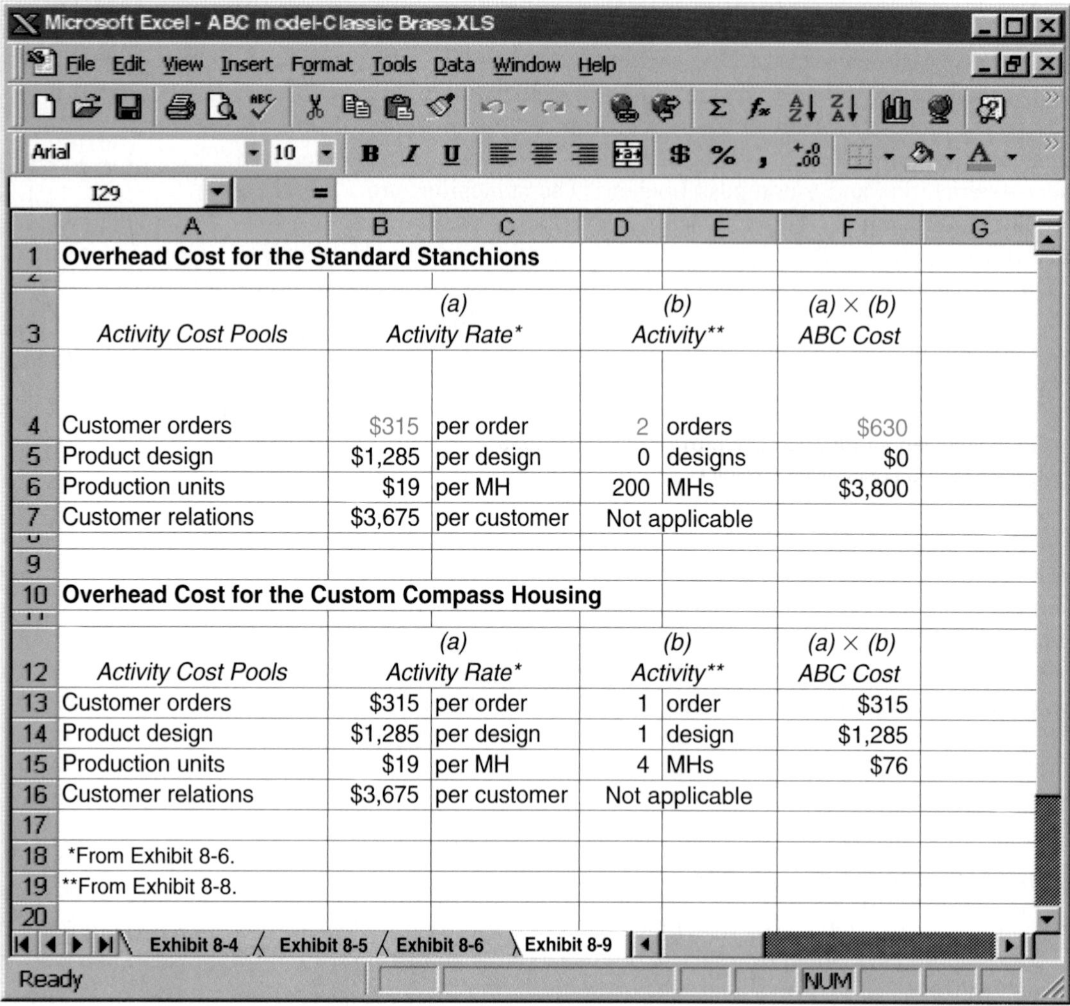

	A	B	C	D	E	F
1	**Overhead Cost for the Standard Stanchions**					
3	*Activity Cost Pools*	*(a) Activity Rate**		*(b) Activity***		*(a) × (b) ABC Cost*
4	Customer orders	$315	per order	2	orders	$630
5	Product design	$1,285	per design	0	designs	$0
6	Production units	$19	per MH	200	MHs	$3,800
7	Customer relations	$3,675	per customer	Not applicable		
10	**Overhead Cost for the Custom Compass Housing**					
12	*Activity Cost Pools*	*(a) Activity Rate**		*(b) Activity***		*(a) × (b) ABC Cost*
13	Customer orders	$315	per order	1	order	$315
14	Product design	$1,285	per design	1	design	$1,285
15	Production units	$19	per MH	4	MHs	$76
16	Customer relations	$3,675	per customer	Not applicable		
18	*From Exhibit 8-6.					
19	**From Exhibit 8-8.					

COMPARISON OF TRADITIONAL AND ABC PRODUCT COSTS

Now that the product margins have been computed using activity-based costing, it would be interesting to compare them to the product margins computed using the company's traditional cost system.

Product Margins Computed Using the Traditional Cost System

The costs of the two products ordered by Windward Yachts are computed under the company's traditional cost accounting system in Exhibit 8–11 on page 328. The company's traditional system uses a plantwide predetermined overhead rate based on machine-hours. Since the total manufacturing overhead cost is $1,000,000 (see Exhibit 8–3) and the total machine time is 20,000 machine-hours (see Exhibit 8–6), the predetermined manufacturing overhead rate for the company is $50 per machine-hour ($1,000,000 ÷ 20,000 machine-hours = $50 per machine-hour). From Exhibit 8–11, we see that when this predetermined manufacturing overhead rate is used to determine product costs, the stanchions show a loss of $360, whereas the compass housing shows a profit of $387.

EXHIBIT 8–10 Product and Customer Margins—Activity-Based Costing System (Activity View)

Microsoft Excel - ABC model-Classic Brass.XLS

	A	B	C	D	E	F
1	**Product Profitability Analysis**					
2		*Standard Stanchions*			*Custom Compass Housing*	
3	Sales (from Exhibit 8-8)		$ 13,600			$ 650
4	Costs:					
5	Direct materials (from Exhibit 8-8)	$ 2,110			$ 13	
6	Direct labour (from Exhibit 8-8)	1,850			50	
7	Shipping costs (from Exhibit 8-8)	180			25	
8	Customer orders (from Exhibit 8-9)	630			315	
9	Product design (from Exhibit 8-9)	0			1,285	
10	Production units (from Exhibit 8-9)	3,800	8,570		76	1,764
11	Product margin		$ 5,030			$ (1,114)

Exhibit 8-9 | Exhibit 8-10A | Exhibit 8-10B | Exhibit 8-

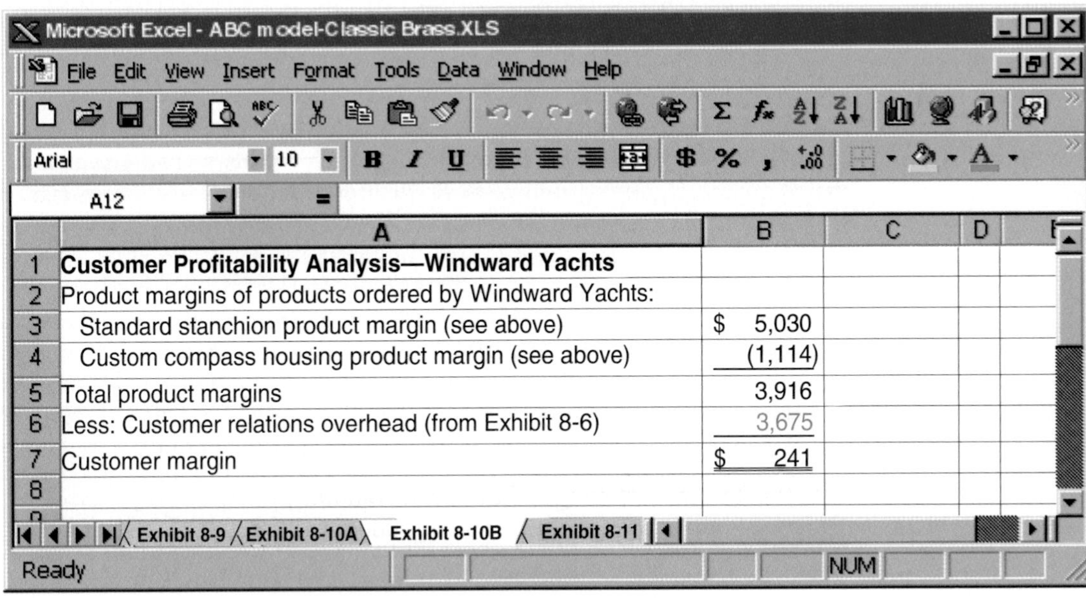

Microsoft Excel - ABC model-Classic Brass.XLS

	A	B
1	**Customer Profitability Analysis—Windward Yachts**	
2	Product margins of products ordered by Windward Yachts:	
3	Standard stanchion product margin (see above)	$ 5,030
4	Custom compass housing product margin (see above)	(1,114)
5	Total product margins	3,916
6	Less: Customer relations overhead (from Exhibit 8-6)	3,675
7	Customer margin	$ 241

Exhibit 8-9 | Exhibit 8-10A | Exhibit 8-10B | Exhibit 8-11

The Differences between ABC and Traditional Product Costs

LEARNING OBJECTIVE 6
Compare product costs computed using traditional and activity-based costing methods.

The costs of the products under the new ABC system are dramatically different from the costs computed using the old traditional costing system. The stanchions, which looked unprofitable under the traditional cost system, appear to be very profitable under the ABC system in Exhibit 8–10. And the compass housing, which looked profitable under the old cost system, appears to be unprofitable under the new costing system.

There are two major reasons for these changes in apparent profitability. First, under the old cost system, the costs of designing products were spread across all products without regard to whether they actually required design work. Under the new ABC system, these

EXHIBIT 8–11
Product Margins—Traditional Cost Accounting System

	Standard Stanchions		Custom Compass Housing	
Sales (from Exhibit 8–8)		$13,600		$650
Cost:				
Direct materials (from Exhibit 8–8)	$ 2,110		$ 13	
Direct labour (from Exhibit 8–8)	1,850		50	
Manufacturing overhead (see below)	10,000	13,960	200	263
Product margin*		$ (360)		$387

In the traditional costing system used at Classic Brass, manufacturing overhead is applied based on machine-hours. The predetermined rate is $50 per machine-hour, determined as follows:

$$\text{Predetermined manufacturing overhead rate} = \frac{\text{Total estimated manufacturing overhead}}{\text{Total estimated machine-hours}}$$

$$= \frac{\$1{,}000{,}000}{20{,}000 \text{ machine-hours}} = \$50 \text{ per machine-hour}$$

Referring back to Exhibit 8–8, the standard stanchions require 200 machine-hours in total and the custom compass housing requires 4 machine-hours. Therefore, $10,000 (200 machine-hours × $50 per machine-hour) of manufacturing overhead would be charged to the standard stanchions and $200 (4 machine-hours × $50 per machine-hour) to the custom compass housing.

*In a traditional costing system, the product margins do not include any non-manufacturing costs such as shipping costs.

costs are assigned only to products that actually require design work. Consequently, under the ABC system, design costs have been shifted from standard products like stanchions, which do not require any design work, to custom products like the compass housing.

Second, the Customer Orders costs, which are batch-level costs, were applied on the basis of machine-hours, a unit-level base, under the old cost system. Therefore, under the old cost system, high-volume products absorbed the bulk of these batch-level costs, even though they caused no more of these costs than low-volume products that are ordered as frequently. Under the new cost system, these batch-level costs are assigned as a lump sum to each customer order. Consequently, the new cost system shifts these costs from high-volume orders like the stanchions to low-volume orders like the compass housing.

When there are batch-level or product-level costs, activity-based costing will ordinarily shift costs from high-volume products produced in large batches to low-volume products produced in small batches. This cost shifting will usually have a greater impact on the *per unit* costs of low-volume products than on the per unit costs of high-volume products. For example, suppose that a total of $100 in batch-level cost is shifted from a high-volume, 100-unit product to a low-volume, 1-unit product. This shifting of cost will decrease the cost of the high-volume product by $1 per unit, on average, but will increase the cost of the low-volume product by $100 for the single unit. In summary, implementing activity-based costing will typically shift costs from high-volume to low-volume products, but the effects will be much more dramatic on the per unit costs of the low-volume products. The per unit costs of the low-volume products will increase far more than the per unit costs of the high-volume products will decrease.

It is important to remember another major difference between the costs of products as computed under the new ABC system at Classic Brass and product costs as computed under the old traditional cost system. Under a traditional system, only manufacturing costs are assigned to products, while under the new ABC system at Classic Brass, non-manufacturing costs are assigned to products as well as the manufacturing costs. In addition, the organization-sustaining manufacturing costs and the costs of idle capacity are *not* assigned to products under the ABC system, whereas they *are* assigned to products under the old traditional costing system. For these reasons, the term *product cost* in this chapter has a different meaning than it had in Chapters 2, 3, and 4. In the context of an ABC system such as the one implemented at Classic Brass, product costs include the costs of *all* resources consumed by the product, whether or not they are manufacturing costs.

FOCUS *on Current Practice*

The Hospice of Central Ontario (HCO) provides all medical needs to terminally ill patients, including nursing care, medical equipment, medications, and palliative treatments so that patients can be at home with their families during their last days. HCO was being squeezed by increasing costs, without any compensating increases in reimbursements from insurance companies. As the first step in negotiating a better reimbursement plan, management decided to use ABC to get a better understanding of its costs. The following activity rates were computed:

Activity Cost Pool	Total Cost	Total Activity	Activity Rate
Pre-referral	$ 24,611	74 referrals*	$332.58 per referral
Referral.	10,873	74 referrals*	$146.93 per referral
Admission.	1,960	46 admissions	$ 42.61 per admission
Post-admission.	3,649	46 admissions	$ 79.33 per admission
Post-death	1,476	46 deaths	$ 32.09 per death
Bereavement	12,670	46 deaths	$275.43 per death
Medical services.	5,588	2,080 service calls	$ 2.69 per service call
Reception	8,597	3,200 calls	$ 2.69 per call
Accounting/finance. . . .	13,566	5,553 patient-days*	$ 2.44 per patient-day
Management	17,107	5,553 patient-days*	$ 3.08 per patient-day
Information systems . . .	6,191	5,553 patient-days*	$ 1.11 per patient-day
Billing	2,899	192 billings	$ 15.10 per billing
Volunteer services	3,378	75 volunteers	$ 45.04 per volunteer
Total	$112,565		

*Referrals and patient-days are weighted by the stage of the disease. For example, the actual number of patient-days is 3,593, but a day for a patient whose death is imminent is counted as equivalent to three patient-days for a patient in slow decline due to the more intensive care such patients receive.

The ABC system was then used to estimate the average cost per patient-day for patients in various stages of their diseases:

Stage of Disease	Cost per Patient-Day
Slow decline	$27.39
Rapid decline	$29.84
Imminent death.	$62.88
Death	$381.57

This was a definite eye-opener for the hospice's management. The hospice's old cost system did not distinguish between costs at various stages of a disease and indeed would have given an answer of a flat $31.33 per patient-day ($112,565 ÷ 3,593 unweighted patient-days), regardless of the stage of the disease. This new information helped management to negotiate more favourable reimbursement rates from insurance companies.

Source: Sidney J. Baxendale and Victoria Dornbusch, "Activity-Based Costing for a Hospice," *Strategic Finance*, March 2000, pp. 65–70. Reprinted with permission from the IMA, Montvale, NJ, USA, http://www.imanet.org/.

MANAGERIAL ACCOUNTING IN ACTION

The Wrap-Up

The ABC design team presented the results of its work in a meeting attended by all of the top managers of Classic Brass, including the president John Towers, the production manager Susan Ritcher, the marketing manager Tom Olafson, and the accounting manager Mary Goodman. The ABC team brought with them to the meeting copies of the chart showing the ABC design (Exhibit 8–7), the calculations showing the product margins for the stanchions and compass housing under the company's old cost accounting system (Exhibit 8–11), and the spreadsheets showing the ABC analysis of the same products (Exhibit 8–10). After the formal presentation by the ABC team, the following discussion took place:

John: I would like to personally thank the ABC team members for all of the work they have done and for an extremely interesting presentation. I am now beginning to wonder about a lot of the decisions we made in the past using our old cost accounting system.

Mary: I hope I don't have to remind anyone that I have been warning everyone for quite some time about this problem.

John: No, you don't have to remind us, Mary. I guess we just didn't understand the problem before.

John: Tom, why did we accept this order for standard stanchions in the first place if our old cost accounting system was telling us it was a big money loser?

Tom: Windward Yachts, the company that ordered the stanchions, has asked us to do a lot of custom work like the compass housing in the past. To get that work, we felt we had to accept their orders for money-losing standard products.

John: According to this ABC analysis, we had it all backwards. We are losing money on the custom products and making a fistful on the standard products.

Susan: I never did believe we were making a lot of money on the custom jobs. You ought to see all of the problems they create for us in production.

Tom: I hate to admit it, but the custom jobs always seem to give us headaches in marketing, too.

John: Why don't we just stop soliciting custom work? This seems like a no-brainer to me. If we are losing money on custom jobs like the compass housing, why not suggest to our customers that they go elsewhere for that kind of work?

Tom: Wait a minute, we would lose a lot of sales.

Susan: So what—we would save a lot more costs.

Mary: Maybe yes, maybe no. Some of the costs would not disappear if we were to drop all of those products.

Tom: Like what?

Mary: Well Tom, part of your salary is included in the costs of the ABC model.

Tom: Where? I don't see anything listed that looks like my salary.

Mary: Tom, when the ABC team interviewed you, they asked you what percentage of your time was spent in handling customer orders and how much was spent dealing with new product design issues. Am I correct?

Tom: Sure, but what's the point?

Mary: I believe you said that about 10% of your time is spent dealing with new products. As a consequence, 10% of your salary was allocated to the Product Design cost pool. If we were to drop all of the products requiring design work, would you be willing to take a 10% pay cut?

Tom: I trust you're joking.

Mary: Do you see the problem? Just because 10% of your time is spent on custom products doesn't mean that the company would save 10% of your salary if the custom products were dropped. Before we take a drastic action like dropping the custom products, we should identify which costs are really relevant.

John: I think I see what you are driving at. We wouldn't want to drop a lot of products just to find that our costs really haven't changed much. It is true that dropping the products would free up resources like Tom's time, but we had better be sure we have some good use for those resources *before* we take such an action.

As this discussion among the managers of Classic Brass illustrates, caution should be exercised before taking an action based on an ABC analysis such as the one in Exhibit 8–10. The product and customer margins computed in that exhibit are a useful starting point for further analysis, but managers need to know what costs are really affected before taking any action such as dropping a product or customer or changing the prices of products or services. The appendix to this chapter shows how an *action analysis report* can be constructed to help managers make such decisions. An **action analysis report** provides more detail about costs and how they might adjust to changes in activity than the ABC analysis presented in Exhibit 8–10.

Action analysis report
A report showing what costs have been assigned to a cost object, such as a product or customer, and how difficult it would be to adjust the cost if there is a change in activity.

Classic Brass demonstrates the potential improvements in information available for strategic decisions that can result from ABC, as summarized in Exhibit 8-10. The results show that, given the two products, the standard high-volume product makes the profit, while the intensive custom product loses profits because the extra costs involved are not being recovered in the selling price. The traditional costing system demonstrated in Exhibit 8-11 shows the opposite results: losses for the standard product and profits for the custom one.

The misleading results presented by the traditional system occur because of the use of a single overhead rate to assign overhead solely on volume, in this case, machine-hours. Because the standard product is standardized and has a high volume, most of the overhead is assigned to it. Such an assignment ignores the substantial overhead resulting from design and order-taking activities associated with the custom product that are not captured in an accurate way by machine-hours.

The discussion of the results shown in the Managerial Accounting in Action feature demonstrates that care is needed when using the results, because changing the focus on custom products may affect the ability to gain the benefits from the standard product. Also, all costs do not necessarily react in the manner portrayed by ABC. The salary allocated to custom products may not disappear if the custom products were eliminated. Chapter 13 will elaborate on the strategic analysis of such interactions so that a clearer picture can emerge.

TARGETING PROCESS IMPROVEMENTS

Activity-based costing can be used to identify areas that would benefit from process improvements. Indeed, managers often cite this as the major benefit of activity-based costing.[9] **Activity-based management (ABM)** is used in conjunction with activity-based costing to improve processes and reduce costs. Activity-based management is used in organizations as diverse as manufacturing companies, hospitals, and the Canadian Coast Guard.[10] When "forty percent of the cost of running a hospital involves storing, collecting and moving information," there is obviously a great deal of room for eliminating waste and for improvement.[11]

Activity-based management (ABM)
A management approach that focuses on managing activities as a way of eliminating waste and reducing delays and defects.

The first step in any improvement program is to decide what to improve. The theory of constraints approach discussed in Chapter 1 is a powerful tool for targeting the area in an organization where improvement will yield the greatest benefit. Activity-based management provides another approach. The activity rates computed in activity-based costing can provide valuable clues concerning where there is waste and scope for improvement in an organization. For example, managers at Classic Brass were surprised at the high cost of customer orders. Some customer orders are for less than $100 worth of products, and

9. Dan Swenson, "The Benefits of Activity-Based Cost Management to the Manufacturing Industry," *Journal of Management Accounting Research* 7, Fall 1995, pp. 168–80.
10. William T. Bonner, "Stormy Waters and the Canadian Coast Guard," *CMA Magazine*, February 1998, pp. 21–26, and Michael Senyshen, "ABC/M in the Federal Government," *CGA Magazine*, December 1997, p. 19.
11. Kambiz Foroohar, "Rx: Software," *Forbes*, April 7, 1997, p. 114.

yet it costs, on average, $315 to process an order according to the activity rates calculated in Exhibit 8–6. This seemed like an awful lot of money for an activity that adds no value to the product. As a consequence, the customer order processing activity was targeted for improvement using TQM and process re-engineering as discussed in Chapter 1.

Benchmarking provides a systematic approach to identifying the activities with the greatest room for improvement. For example, the Marketing Resources Group of a the telephone company performed an ABC analysis of the activities carried out in the Accounting Department.[12] Managers computed the activity rates for the activities of the Accounting Department and then compared these rates to the costs of carrying out the same activities in other companies. Two benchmarks were used: (1) a sample of Fortune 100 companies, which are the largest 100 companies in the United States; and (2) a sample of "world-class" companies that had been identified by a consultant as having the best accounting practices in the world. These comparisons follow:

Activity	Activity Measure	Telephone Company	Fortune 100 Benchmark	World-Class Benchmark
Processing accounts receivable	Number of invoices processed	$3.80 per invoice	$15.00 per invoice	$4.60 per invoice
Processing accounts payable	Number of invoices processed	$8.90 per invoice	$7.00 per invoice	$1.80 per invoice
Processing payroll cheques	Number of cheques processed	$7.30 per cheque	$5.00 per cheque	$1.72 per cheque
Managing customer credit	Number of customer accounts	$12.00 per account	$16.00 per account	$5.60 per account

It is clear from this analysis that the telephone company does a good job of processing accounts receivable. Its average cost per invoice is $3.80, whereas the cost in other companies that are considered world class is even higher—$4.60 per invoice. On the other hand, the cost of processing payroll cheques is significantly higher at the telephone company than at benchmark companies. The cost per payroll cheque at the telephone company is $7.30 versus $5.00 at Fortune 100 companies and $1.72 at world-class companies. This suggests that it may be possible to wring some waste out of this activity using TQM, process re-engineering, or some other method.

FOCUS *on Current Practice*

Tata Consultancy Services (TCS) is the largest consulting organization in India, serving both Indian and international clients. The company used activity-based management to identify problem areas in its software development business. An early finding was that "quality assurance, testing, and error-correction activities made up a significant chunk of the overall effort required to build a system, and this cost had to be kept under control to improve productivity and profitability." The company already had in place a quality management system that helped identify the types of errors that were occurring and the corrective action that would be required, but no costs were attached to these errors and actions. The activity-based management system provided this cost information, which allowed managers to set better priorities and to monitor the costs of error-detection and error-correction activities.

As another example of the usefulness of the system, 54 person-days in one software

12. Steve Coburn, Hugh Grove, and Cynthia Fukami, "Benchmarking with ABCM," *Management Accounting*, January 1995, pp. 56–60.

development project at TCS were charged to the activity "Waiting for client feedback"—a non-value-added activity. Investigation revealed that the client was taking a long time to review the graphical user interface (GUI) designed by TCS. The client was showing the GUI to various end users—often resulting in contradictory suggestions. The solution was to draw up guidelines for the GUI with the client, which were enforced. "As a result of this corrective action, subsequent client feedback was well within the time schedule. Most of our screens were accepted because they conformed to standards . . . ."

Source: Maha S. Mahalingam, Bala V. Balachandran, and Farooq C. Kohli, "Activity-Based Management for Systems Consulting Industry," *Journal of Cost Management*, May/June 1999, pp. 4–15.

ACTIVITY-BASED COSTING AND EXTERNAL REPORTS

Since activity-based costing generally provides more accurate product costs than traditional costing methods, why isn't it used for external reports? Some companies *do* use activity-based costing in their external reports, but most do not. There are a number of reasons for this. First, external reports are less detailed than internal reports prepared for decision making. On the external reports, individual product costs are not reported. Cost of goods sold and inventory valuations are disclosed, but there is no breakdown of these accounts by product. If some products are undercosted and some are overcosted, the errors tend to cancel each other when the product costs are added together.

Second, an ABC system such as the one described in this chapter does not conform to generally accepted accounting principles (GAAP). As discussed in Chapter 2, product costs computed for external reports must include all of the manufacturing costs and only manufacturing costs; however, in an ABC system as described in this chapter, product costs exclude some manufacturing costs and include some non-manufacturing costs. It is possible to adjust the ABC data at the end of the period to conform to GAAP, but that requires more work.

Third, auditors are likely to be uncomfortable with allocations that are based on interviews with the company's personnel. Such subjective data can easily be manipulated by management to make earnings and other key variables look more favourable.

For all of these reasons, most companies confine their ABC efforts to special studies for management, and they do not attempt to integrate activity-based costing into their formal cost accounting systems.

THE LIMITATIONS OF ACTIVITY-BASED COSTING

Implementing an activity-based costing system is a major project that requires substantial resources. And once implemented, an activity-based costing system is more costly to maintain than a traditional direct labour-based costing system—data concerning numerous activity measures must be collected, checked, and entered into the system. The benefits of increased accuracy may not outweigh these costs.

Activity-based costing produces numbers, such as product margins, that are at odds with the numbers produced by traditional costing systems. But managers are accustomed to using traditional costing systems to run their operations and traditional costing systems are often used in performance evaluations. Essentially, activity-based costing changes the rules of the game. It is a fact of human nature that changes in organizations, particularly those that alter the rules of the game, inevitably face resistance. This underscores the importance of top-management support and the full participation of line managers, as well as the accounting staff, in any activity-based costing initiative. If activity-based costing is viewed as an accounting initiative that does not have the full support of top management, it is doomed to failure.

In practice, most managers insist on fully allocating all costs to products, customers, and other costing objects in an activity-based costing system—including the costs of idle capacity and organization-sustaining costs. This results in overstated costs and understated margins and mistakes in pricing and other critical decisions.[13]

Activity-based costing data can easily be misinterpreted and must be used with care in making decisions. Costs assigned to products, customers, and other cost objects are only *potentially* relevant. Before making any significant decisions using activity-based costing data, managers must identify which costs are really relevant for the decision at hand. See the appendix to this chapter for more details.

As discussed in the previous section, reports generated by the best activity-based costing systems do not conform to generally accepted accounting principles. Consequently, an organization involved in activity-based costing should have two cost systems—one for internal use and one for preparing external reports. This is costlier than maintaining just one system and may cause confusion about which system is to be believed and relied on. However, the ERP systems illustrated in Exhibit 8–1 can effectively process alternative configurations of overhead information.

FOCUS *on Current Practice*

Bertch Cabinet Mfg., Inc. makes high-quality wooden cabinets, marble tops, and mirrors for bathrooms and kitchens. The company experimented with activity-based costing but found that it was too difficult to set up and maintain such a complex costing system. For example, 21 separate operations are required to make a single raised-panel cabinet door. The costs of keeping track of each of these operations would far exceed any conceivable benefit. Instead of building a complex ABC system, Bertch Cabinet adopted a variation of variable costing used in the theory of constraints. This simpler system required far less effort to build and maintain, and it was much easier to understand. In the Bertch Cabinet Mfg. variable costing system, 70% of the direct labour cost was classified as variable and the rest as fixed.

Source: John B. MacArthur, "From Activity-Based Costing to Throughput Accounting," *Management Accounting,* April 1996, pp. 30–38.

SUMMARY

Traditional cost accounting methods suffer from several defects that can result in distorted costs for decision-making purposes. All manufacturing costs—even those that are not caused by any specific product—are allocated to products, and non-manufacturing costs that are caused by products are not assigned to products. Traditional methods also allocate the costs of idle capacity to products. In effect, products are charged for resources that they don't use. And finally, traditional methods tend to place too much reliance on unit-level allocation bases such as direct labour and machine-hours. This results in overcosting high-volume products and undercosting low-volume products and can lead to mistakes when making decisions.

Activity-based costing estimates the costs of the resources consumed by cost objects such as products and customers. The approach taken in activity-based costing assumes that cost objects generate activities that in turn consume costly resources. Activities form the link between costs and cost objects. Activity-based costing is concerned with overhead—both manufacturing overhead and

13. Philip Beaulieu and Anila Lakra, "Coverage of the Criticism of Activity-Based Costing in Canadian Textbooks," *Canadian Accounting Perspectives,* vol. 4, 2005, pp. 87–109, provides relevant comments on the proper treatment of organization-sustaining activities and idle capacity based on earlier analysis in the literature.

selling, general, and administrative overhead. The accounting for direct labour and direct materials is usually unaffected.

To build an ABC system, companies typically choose a small set of activities that summarize much of the work performed in overhead departments. Associated with each activity is an activity cost pool. To the extent possible, overhead costs are directly traced to these activity cost pools. The remaining overhead costs are assigned to the activity cost pools in the first-stage allocation. Interviews with managers often form the basis for these allocations.

An activity rate is computed for each cost pool by dividing the costs assigned to the cost pool by the measure of activity for the cost pool. Activity rates provide useful information to managers concerning the costs of carrying out overhead activities. A particularly high cost for an activity may trigger efforts to improve the way the activity is carried out in the organization.

In the second-stage allocation, the activity rates are used to apply costs to cost objects such as products and customers. The costs computed under activity-based costing are often quite different from the costs generated by a company's traditional cost accounting system. While the ABC system is almost certainly more accurate, managers should nevertheless exercise caution before making decisions based on the ABC data. Some of the costs may not be avoidable and hence would not be relevant.

REVIEW PROBLEM: ACTIVITY-BASED COSTING

Ferris Corporation makes a single product—a fire-resistant commercial filing cabinet—that it sells to office furniture distributors. The company has a simple ABC system that it uses for internal decision making. The company has two overhead departments, for which the costs are listed below:

Manufacturing overhead	$500,000
Selling and administrative overhead	300,000
Total overhead costs	$800,000

The company's ABC system has the following activity cost pools and activity measures:

Activity Cost Pool	Activity Measure
Assembling units	Number of units
Processing orders	Number of orders
Supporting customers	Number of customers
Other	Not applicable

Costs assigned to the Other activity cost pool have no activity measure; they consist of the costs of unused capacity and organization-sustaining costs—neither of which are assigned to products, orders, or customers.

Ferris Corporation distributes the costs of manufacturing overhead and of selling and administrative overhead to the activity cost pools based on employee interviews, the results of which are reported below:

Distribution of Resource Consumption Across Activity Cost Pools

	Assembling Units	Processing Orders	Supporting Customers	Other	Total
Manufacturing overhead	50%	35%	5%	10%	100%
Selling and administrative overhead	10%	45%	25%	20%	100%
Total activity	1,000 units	250 orders	100 customers		

Required:

1. Perform the first-stage allocation of overhead costs to the activity cost pools as in Exhibit 8–5.
2. Compute activity rates for the activity cost pools as in Exhibit 8–6.

3. OfficeMart is one of Ferris Corporation's customers. Last year, OfficeMart ordered filing cabinets four different times. OfficeMart ordered a total of 80 filing cabinets during the year. Construct a table as in Exhibit 8–9 showing the overhead costs of these 80 units and four orders.
4. The selling price of a filing cabinet is $595. The cost of direct materials is $180 per filing cabinet, and direct labour is $50 per filing cabinet. What is the product margin on the 80 filing cabinets ordered by OfficeMart? How profitable is OfficeMart as a customer? See Exhibit 8–10 for an example of how to complete this report.

Solution to Review Problem

1. The first-stage allocation of costs to the activity cost pools is as follows:

	Activity Cost Pools				
	Assembling Units	Processing Orders	Supporting Customers	Other	Total
Manufacturing overhead*. .	$250,000	$175,000	$ 25,000	$ 50,000	$500,000
Selling and administrative overhead**	30,000	135,000	75,000	60,000	300,000
Total cost	$280,000	$310,000	$100,000	$110,000	$800,000

* .50 × $500,000 = $250,000; .35 × $500,000 = $175,000; and so on.
** .10 × $300,000 = $30,000; .45 × $300,000 = $135,000; and so on.

2. The activity rates for the activity cost pools are:

Activity Cost Pools	(a) Total Cost	(b) Total Activity	(a) ÷ (b) Activity Rate
Assembling units	$280,000	1,000 units	$ 280 per unit
Processing orders	$310,000	250 orders	$1,240 per order
Supporting customers	$100,000	100 customers	$1,000 per customer

3. The overhead cost for the four orders of a total of 80 filing cabinets would be computed as follows:

Activity Cost Pools	(a) Activity Rate	(b) Activity	(a) × (b) ABC Cost
Assembling units	$ 280 per unit	80 units	$22,400
Processing orders	$1,240 per order	4 orders	$ 4,960
Supporting customers	$1,000 per customer	Not applicable	

4. The product and customer margins can be computed as follows:

Filing Cabinet Product Margin		
Sales ($595 per unit × 80 units)		$47,600
Cost:		
Direct materials ($180 per unit × 80 units).	$14,400	
Direct labour ($50 per unit × 80 units)	4,000	
Volume-related overhead (above)	22,400	
Order-related overhead (above).	4,960	45,760
Product margin.		$ 1,840

Customer Profitability Analysis—OfficeMart	
Product margin (above)	$ 1,840
Less: Customer support overhead (above)	1,000
Customer margin	$ 840

APPENDIX 8A: ABC ACTION ANALYSIS

LEARNING OBJECTIVE 7
Prepare an action analysis report using activity-based costing data and interpret the report.

A conventional ABC analysis, such as the one presented in Exhibit 8–10 in the chapter, has several important limitations. Referring back to that exhibit, recall that the custom compass housing shows a negative product margin of $1,114. Because of this apparent loss, managers were considering dropping this product. However, as the discussion among the managers revealed, it is unlikely that all of the $1,764 cost of the product would be avoided if the product was dropped. Some of these costs would continue even if the product was totally eliminated. *Before* taking action, it is vital to identify which costs would be avoided and which costs would continue. Only those costs that can be avoided are relevant in the decision. Moreover, many of the costs are managed costs that would require explicit management action to eliminate. If the custom compass housing product was eliminated, the direct materials cost would be avoided without any explicit management action—the materials simply wouldn't be ordered. On the other hand, if the custom compass housing product was dropped, explicit management action would be required to eliminate the salaries of overhead workers that have been assigned to the product.

Simply shifting these managed costs to other products would not solve anything. These costs would have to be eliminated or the resources *shifted to the constraint* to be of any benefit to the company. Eliminating the cost is obviously beneficial. Redeploying a resource is beneficial only if the resource is shifted to the constraint in the process. If the resource is redeployed to a work centre that is not a constraint, it would have the effect of increasing the excess capacity in that work centre—which is of no direct benefit to the company.

In addition, if some overhead costs need to be eliminated as a result of dropping a product, specific managers must be held responsible for eliminating those costs or the reductions are unlikely to occur. If no one is specifically held responsible for eliminating the costs, they will almost certainly continue to be incurred. Without external pressure, managers usually avoid cutting costs in their areas of responsibility. The action analysis report developed in this appendix is intended to help top managers identify which costs are relevant in a decision and to place responsibility for the elimination of the costs on the appropriate managers.

Activity Rates—Action Analysis Report

Constructing an action analysis report begins with the results of the first-stage allocation, which is reproduced as Exhibit 8–12. In contrast to the conventional ABC analysis covered in the chapter, the calculation of the activity rates for an action analysis report is a bit more involved. In addition to computing an overall activity rate for each activity cost pool, an activity rate is computed for each cell in Exhibit 8–12. The computations of activity rates for the action analysis are carried out in Exhibit 8–13. For example, the $125,000 cost of indirect factory wages for the Customer Orders cost pool is divided by the total activity for that cost pool—1,000 orders—to arrive at the activity rate of $125 per customer order for indirect factory wages. Similarly, the $200,000 cost of indirect factory wages for the Product Design cost pool is divided by the total activity for that cost pool—200 designs—to arrive at the activity rate of $1,000 per design for indirect factory wages. Note that the totals at the bottom of Exhibit 8–13 agree with the overall activity rates in Exhibit 8–6 in the chapter. Exhibit 8–13, which shows the activity rates for the action analysis report, contains more detail than Exhibit 8–6, which contains the activity rates for the conventional ABC analysis.

Assignment of Overhead Costs to Products—Action Analysis Report

Similarly, computing the overhead costs to be assigned to products for an action analysis report involves more detail than for a conventional ABC analysis. The computations for Classic Brass are carried out in Exhibit 8–14. For example, the activity rate of $125 per customer order for indirect factory wages is multiplied by 2 orders for the standard stanchions to arrive at the cost of $250 for indirect factory wages in Exhibit 8–14. Instead of

EXHIBIT 8–12 First-Stage Allocations to Activity Cost Pools

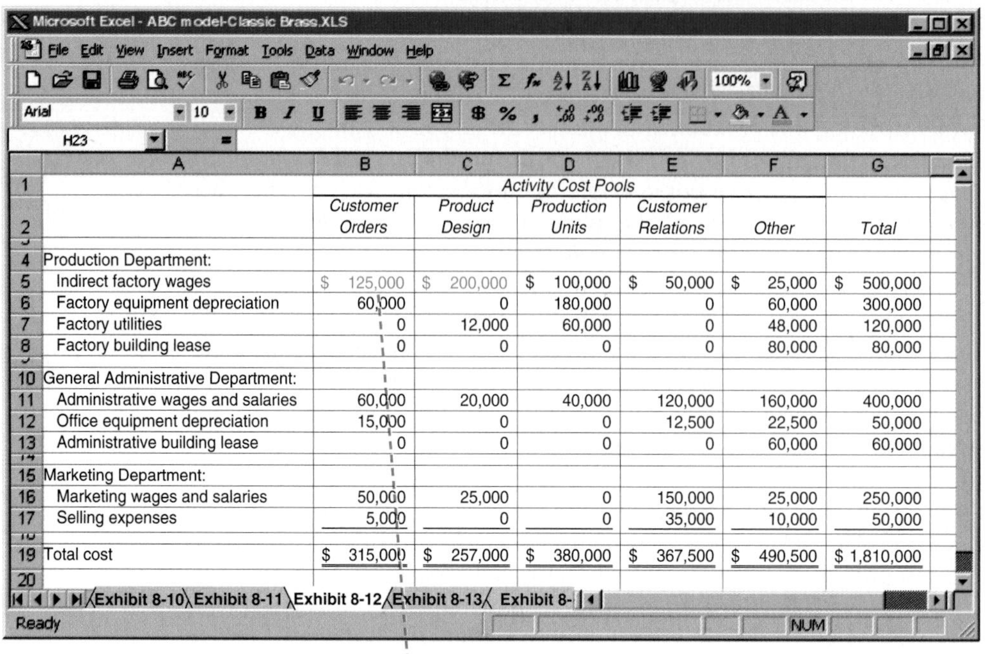

	Customer Orders	Product Design	Production Units	Customer Relations	Other	Total
	Activity Cost Pools					
Production Department:						
Indirect factory wages	$ 125,000	$ 200,000	$ 100,000	$ 50,000	$ 25,000	$ 500,000
Factory equipment depreciation	60,000	0	180,000	0	60,000	300,000
Factory utilities	0	12,000	60,000	0	48,000	120,000
Factory building lease	0	0	0	0	80,000	80,000
General Administrative Department:						
Administrative wages and salaries	60,000	20,000	40,000	120,000	160,000	400,000
Office equipment depreciation	15,000	0	0	12,500	22,500	50,000
Administrative building lease	0	0	0	0	60,000	60,000
Marketing Department:						
Marketing wages and salaries	50,000	25,000	0	150,000	25,000	250,000
Selling expenses	5,000	0	0	35,000	10,000	50,000
Total cost	$ 315,000	$ 257,000	$ 380,000	$ 367,500	$ 490,500	$ 1,810,000

EXHIBIT 8–13 Computation of the Activity Rates for the Action Analysis Report

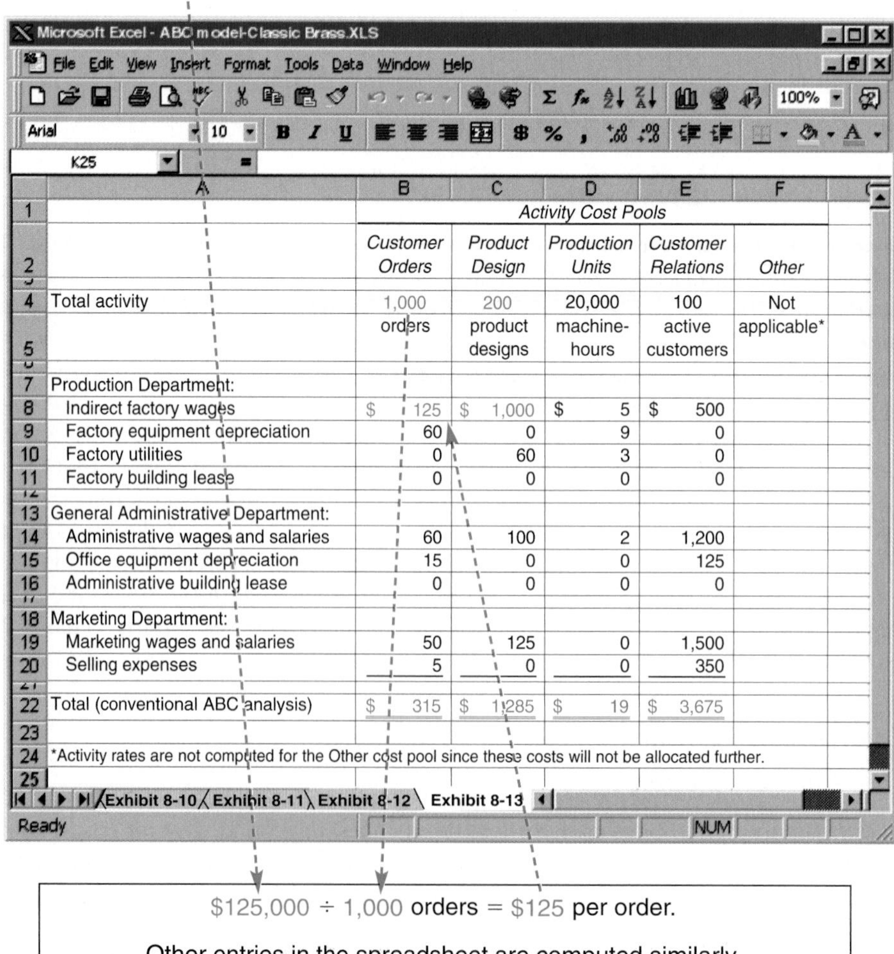

	Customer Orders	Product Design	Production Units	Customer Relations	Other
	Activity Cost Pools				
Total activity	1,000 orders	200 product designs	20,000 machine-hours	100 active customers	Not applicable*
Production Department:					
Indirect factory wages	$ 125	$ 1,000	$ 5	$ 500	
Factory equipment depreciation	60	0	9	0	
Factory utilities	0	60	3	0	
Factory building lease	0	0	0	0	
General Administrative Department:					
Administrative wages and salaries	60	100	2	1,200	
Office equipment depreciation	15	0	0	125	
Administrative building lease	0	0	0	0	
Marketing Department:					
Marketing wages and salaries	50	125	0	1,500	
Selling expenses	5	0	0	350	
Total (conventional ABC analysis)	$ 315	$ 1,285	$ 19	$ 3,675	

*Activity rates are not computed for the Other cost pool since these costs will not be allocated further.

$125,000 ÷ 1,000 orders = $125 per order.

Other entries in the spreadsheet are computed similarly.

EXHIBIT 8–14
Action Analysis Cost Matrices

Action Analysis Cost Matrix for Standard Stanchions

	Activity Cost Pools				
	Customer Orders	*Product Design*	*Production Units*	*Customer Relations*	*Total*
Total activity for stanchions	2 orders	0 product designs	200 machine-hours	Not applicable	
Production Department:					
Indirect factory wages	$ 250	$ 0	$ 1,000		$ 1,250
Factory equipment depreciation	120	0	1,800		1,920
Factory utilities	0	0	600		600
Factory building lease	0	0	0		0
General Administrative Department:					
Administrative wages and salaries	120	0	400		520
Office equipment depreciation	30	0	0		30
Administrative building lease	0	0	0		0
Marketing Department:					
Marketing wages and salaries	100	0	0		100
Selling expenses	10	0	0		10
Total (conventional ABC analysis)	$ 630	$ 0	$ 3,800		$ 4,430

From Exhibit 8–13, the activity rate for indirect factory wages for the Customer Orders cost pool is $125 per order.

$125 per order × 2 orders = $250

Other entries in the spreadsheet are computed in a similar way.

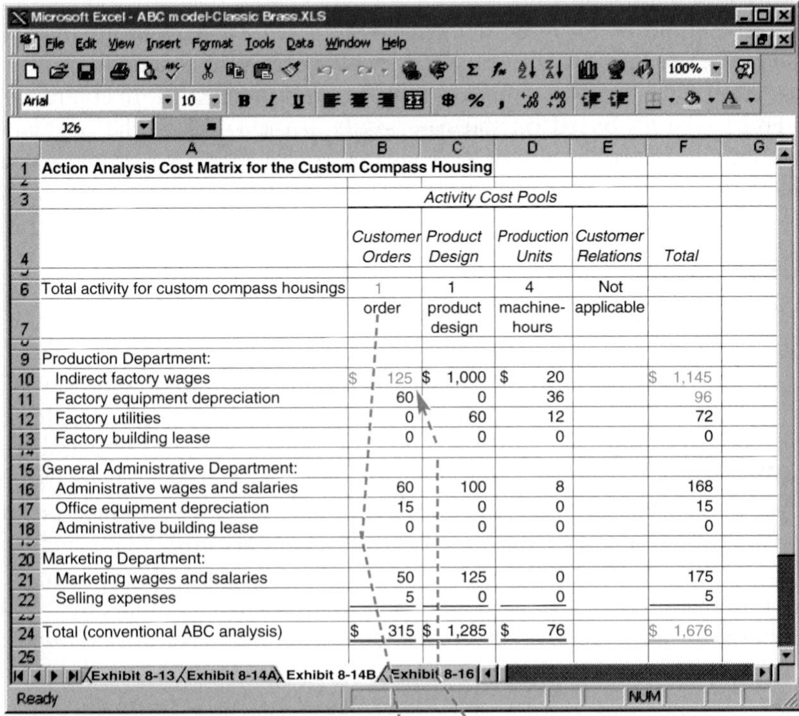

Action Analysis Cost Matrix for the Custom Compass Housing

	Activity Cost Pools				
	Customer Orders	*Product Design*	*Production Units*	*Customer Relations*	*Total*
Total activity for custom compass housings	1 order	1 product design	4 machine-hours	Not applicable	
Production Department:					
Indirect factory wages	$ 125	$ 1,000	$ 20		$ 1,145
Factory equipment depreciation	60	0	36		96
Factory utilities	0	60	12		72
Factory building lease	0	0	0		0
General Administrative Department:					
Administrative wages and salaries	60	100	8		168
Office equipment depreciation	15	0	0		15
Administrative building lease	0	0	0		0
Marketing Department:					
Marketing wages and salaries	50	125	0		175
Selling expenses	5	0	0		5
Total (conventional ABC analysis)	$ 315	$ 1,285	$ 76		$ 1,676

From Exhibit 8–13, the activity rate for indirect factory wages for the Customer Orders cost pool is $125 per order.

$125 per order × 1 order = $125

Other entries in the spreadsheet are computed in a similar way.

EXHIBIT 8–15 Ease of Adjustment Codes

Green: *Costs that adjust automatically to changes in activity without management action.*

- Direct materials
- Shipping costs

Yellow: *Costs that could, in principle, be adjusted to changes in activity, but management action would be required.*

- Direct labour
- Indirect factory wages
- Factory utilities
- Administrative wages and salaries
- Office equipment depreciation
- Marketing wages and salaries
- Selling expenses

Red: *Costs that would be very difficult to adjust to changes in activity and management action would be required.*

- Factory equipment depreciation
- Factory building lease
- Administrative building lease

just a single cost number for each cost pool as in the conventional ABC analysis, we now have an entire cost matrix showing much more detail. Note that the column totals for the cost matrix in Exhibit 8–14 agree with the ABC costs for stanchions in Exhibit 8–9. Indeed, the conventional ABC analysis of Exhibit 8–10 can be easily constructed using the column totals at the bottom of the cost matrices in Exhibit 8–14. In contrast, the action analysis report will be based on the row totals at the right of the cost matrices in Exhibit 8–14. In addition, the action analysis report will include a simple colour-coding scheme that will help managers identify how easily the various costs can be adjusted.

Ease of Adjustment Codes

The ABC team constructed Exhibit 8–15 to aid managers in the use of the ABC data. In this exhibit, each cost has been assigned an *ease of adjustment code*—Green, Yellow, or Red. The ease of adjustment code reflects how easily the cost could be adjusted to changes in activity.[14] Green costs are those costs that would adjust more or less automatically to changes in activity without any action by managers. For example, direct materials costs would adjust to changes in orders without any action being taken by managers. If a customer does not order stanchions, the direct materials for the stanchions would not be required and would not be ordered. Yellow costs are those costs that could be adjusted in response to changes in activity, but such adjustments require management action; the adjustment is not automatic. The ABC team believes, for example, that direct labour costs should be included in the Yellow category. Managers must make difficult decisions and

14. The idea of using colours to code how easily costs can be adjusted was suggested to us at a seminar held by Boeing and by an article by Alfred King, "Green Dollars and Blue Dollars: The Paradox of Cost Reduction," *Journal of Cost Management*, Fall 1993, pp. 44–52.

take explicit action to increase or decrease, in aggregate, direct labour costs—particularly since the company has a no lay-off policy. Red costs are costs that could be adjusted to changes in activity only with a great deal of difficulty, and the adjustment would require management action. The building leases fall into this category, since it would be very difficult and expensive to break the leases.

The Action Analysis View of the ABC Data

Looking at Exhibit 8–14, the totals on the right-hand side of the table indicate that the $1,676 of overhead cost for the custom housing consists of $1,145 of indirect factory wages, $96 of factory equipment depreciation, and so on. These data are displayed in Exhibit 8–16, which shows an action analysis of the custom compass housing product. An action analysis report is a report showing what costs have been assigned to the cost object, such as a product or customer, and how difficult it would be to adjust the cost if there is a change in activity. Note that the Red Margin at the bottom of Exhibit 8–16, ($1,114), is exactly the same as the Product Margin for the custom compass housing in Exhibit 8–10 in the chapter.

The cost data in the action analysis in Exhibit 8–16 are arranged by the colour-coded ease of adjustment. All of the Green costs—those that adjust more or less automatically to changes in activity—appear together at the top of the list of costs. These costs total $38 and are subtracted from the sales of $650 to yield a Green margin of $612. The same procedure is followed for the Yellow and Red costs. This action analysis indicates exactly what costs would have to be cut and how difficult it would be to cut them if the custom compass housing product was dropped. Prior to making any decision about dropping products, the managers responsible for the costs must agree to either eliminate the resources represented by those costs or to transfer the resources to an area in the organization that really needs the resources—namely, a constraint. If managers do not make such a commitment, it is likely that the costs would continue to be incurred. As a result, the company would lose the sales from the products without really saving the costs.

EXHIBIT 8–16
Action Analysis of Custom Compass Housing: Activity-Based Costing System

Microsoft Excel - ABC model-Classic Brass.XLS

	A	B	C	D
1	**Custom Compass Housing**			
2	Sales (from Exhibit 8-8)		$ 650	
3				
4	Green costs:			
5	Direct materials (from Exhibit 8-8)	$ 13		
6	Shipping costs (from Exhibit 8-8)	25	38	
7	Green margin		612	
8				
9	Yellow costs:			
10	Direct labour (from Exhibit 8-8)	50		
11	Indirect factory wages (from Exhibit 8-14)	1,145		
12	Factory utilities (from Exhibit 8-14)	72		
13	Administrative wages and salaries (from Exhibit 8-14)	168		
14	Office equipment depreciation (from Exhibit 8-14)	15		
15	Marketing wages and salaries (from Exhibit 8-14)	175		
16	Selling expenses (from Exhibit 8-14)	5	1,630	
17	Yellow margin		(1,018)	
18				
19	Red costs:			
20	Factory equipment depreciation (from Exhibit 8-14)	96		
21	Factory building lease (from Exhibit 8-14)	0		
22	Administrative building lease (from Exhibit 8-14)	0	96	
23	Red margin		$ (1,114)	
24				

Exhibit 8-14B | Exhibit 8-16 | Activity rates

MANAGERIAL ACCOUNTING IN ACTION

The Wrap-Up

After the action analysis was prepared by the ABC team, top management at Classic Brass met once again to review the results of the ABC analysis.

John: When we last met, we had discussed the advisability of discontinuing work like the custom compass housing for Windward Yachts. I understand that the ABC team has done some additional analysis to help us in making this decision.

Mary: That's right. The action analysis report we put together indicates how easy it would be to adjust each cost and where specific cost savings would have to come from if we were to drop jobs like the custom compass housing.

John: What's this red margin at the bottom of the action analysis? Isn't that a product margin?

Mary: Yes, it is. However, we call it a red margin because we should stop and think very, very carefully before taking any actions based on that margin.

John: Why is that?

Mary: We subtracted the costs of factory equipment depreciation to arrive at that red margin. We doubt that we could avoid any of that cost if we were to drop custom orders. We use the same machines on custom orders that we use on standard products. The factory equipment has no resale value, and it does not wear out through use.

John: What about this yellow margin?

Mary: Yellow means proceed with a great deal of caution. To get to the yellow margin we deducted from sales a lot of costs that could be adjusted only if the managers involved are willing to eliminate resources or shift them elsewhere in the organization.

John: If I understand the yellow margin correctly, the apparent loss of $1,018 on the custom compass housing is the result of the indirect factory wages of $1,145.

Susan: Right, that's basically the wages of our design engineers.

John: I wouldn't want to lay off any of our designers. Could we turn them into salespersons?

Tom: I'd love to have Shueli Park join our marketing team.

Susan: No way, she's our best designer.

John: Okay, I get the picture. We are not going to be cutting anyone's wages, we aren't going to be laying off anyone, and it looks like we may have problems agreeing about moving people around. Where does that leave us?

Mary: What about raising prices on our custom products?

Tom: We should be able to do that. We have been undercutting the competition to make sure we got custom work. We were doing that because we thought custom work was very profitable.

John: Why don't we just charge directly for design work?

Tom: Some of our competitors already charge for design work. However, I don't think we would be able to charge enough to cover our design costs.

John: What about design work? Can we do anything to make it more efficient so it costs us less? I'm not going to lay anyone off, but if we make the design process more efficient, we could lower the charge for design work and spread those costs across more customers.

Susan: That may be possible. I'll form a TQM team to look at it.

John: Let's get some benchmark data on design costs. If we set our minds to it, I'm sure we can be world-class in no time.

Susan: Okay. Mary, will you help with the benchmark data?

Mary: Sure.

Tom: There is another approach we can take too. Windward Yachts probably doesn't really need a custom compass housing. One of our standard compass housings would work just fine. If we start charging for the design work, I think they will see that it would be in their own best interest to use the lower-cost standard product.

John: Let's meet again in about a week to discuss our progress. Is there anything else on the agenda for today?

The points raised in the preceding discussion are extremely important. By measuring the resources consumed by products (and other cost objects), a "best practice" ABC system provides a much better basis for decision making than a traditional cost accounting system that spreads overhead costs around without much regard for what might be causing the overhead. A well-designed ABC system provides managers with estimates of potentially relevant costs that can be a very useful starting point for management analysis.

APPENDIX 8A SUMMARY

The action analysis report illustrated in this appendix is a valuable addition to the ABC tool kit. An action analysis report provides more information for decision making than a conventional ABC analysis. The action analysis report makes it clear where costs would have to be adjusted in the organization as a result of an action. In a conventional ABC analysis, a cost such as $315 for processing an order represents costs from many parts of the organization. If an order is dropped, there will be little pressure to actually eliminate the $315 cost unless it is clear where the costs are incurred and which managers would be responsible for reducing the cost. In contrast, an action analysis report traces the costs to where they are incurred in the organization and makes it much easier to assign responsibility to managers for reducing costs. In addition, an action analysis report provides information concerning how easily a cost can be adjusted. Costs that cannot be adjusted are not relevant in a decision.

Exhibit 8–17 summarizes all of the steps required to create both an action analysis report as illustrated in this appendix and an activity analysis as shown in the chapter.

EXHIBIT 8–17 Summary of the Steps to Produce an Action Analysis Report

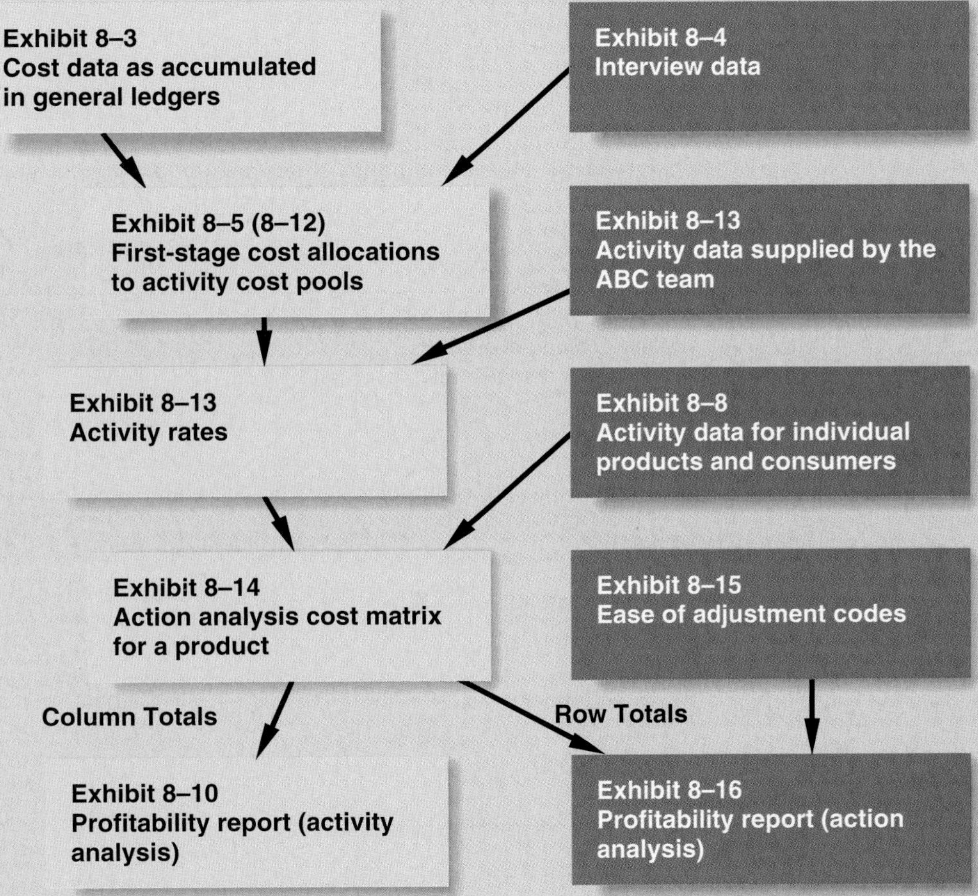

APPENDIX 8A REVIEW PROBLEM: ACTIVITY ANALYSIS REPORT

Refer to the data for Ferris Corporation in the Review Problem at the end of the chapter on pages 335–336.

Required:

1. Compute activity rates for Ferris Corporation as in Exhibit 8–13.
2. Using Exhibit 8–14 as a guide, construct a table showing the overhead costs for the Office-Mart orders described in requirement 3 of the Review Problem at the end of the chapter.
3. The management of Ferris Corporation has assigned ease of adjustment codes to costs as follows:

Cost	Ease of Adjustment Code
Direct materials	Green
Direct labour	Yellow
Manufacturing overhead	Yellow
Selling and administrative overhead	Red

Using Exhibit 8–16 as a guide, prepare an action analysis of the OfficeMart orders.

Solution to Appendix 8A Review Problem

1. The activity rates for the activity cost pools are:

	Assembling Units	Processing Orders	Supporting Customers
Total activity.	1,000 units	250 orders	100 customers
Manufacturing overhead	$250	$ 700	$ 250
Selling and administrative overhead	30	540	750
Total.	$280	$1,240	$1,000

2. The overhead cost for the four orders of a total of 80 filing cabinets would be computed as follows:

	Assembling Units	Processing Orders
Activity	80 units	4 orders
Manufacturing overhead.	$20,000	$2,800
Selling and administrative overhead.	2,400	2,160
Total	$22,400	$4,960

3. The action analysis of the four orders for 80 filing cabinets in total is:

Sales		$47,600
Green costs:		
Direct materials		14,400
Green margin.		33,200
Yellow costs:		
Direct labour.	$ 4,000	
Manufacturing overhead	22,800	26,800
Yellow margin.		6,400
Red costs:		
Selling and administrative overhead		4,560
Red margin		$ 1,840

Note: An action analysis report can also be prepared for OfficeMart as a customer. The first step would be to calculate the overhead costs for OfficeMart as follows:

	Assembling Units	Processing Orders	Supporting Customers	Total
Activity	80 units	4 orders	1 customer	
Manufacturing overhead	$20,000	$2,800	$ 250	$23,050
Selling and administrative overhead	2,400	2,160	750	5,310
Total	$22,400	$4,960	$1,000	$28,360

The action analysis report can then easily be prepared as follows:

Sales		$47,600
Green costs:		
Direct materials		14,400
Green margin		33,200
Yellow costs:		
Direct labour	$ 4,000	
Manufacturing overhead	23,050	27,050
Yellow margin		6,150
Red costs:		
Selling and administrative overhead		5,310
Red margin		$ 840

GLOSSARY

Visit the Online Learning Centre at http://www.mcgrawhill.ca/college/garrison/ for a review of key terms and definitions.

QUESTIONS

8–1 In what fundamental ways does activity-based costing differ from traditional costing methods such as those described in Chapters 2 and 3?

8–2 Why is direct labour a poor base for allocating overhead in many companies?

8–3 Why are overhead rates in activity-based costing based on the level of activity at capacity rather than on the budgeted level of activity?

8–4 Why is top-management support crucial when attempting to implement an activity-based costing system?

8–5 What are unit-level, batch-level, product-level, customer-level, and organization-sustaining activities?

8–6 What types of costs should not be assigned to products in an activity-based costing system?

8–7 Why are there two stages of allocation in activity-based costing?

8–8 Why is the first stage of the allocation process in activity-based costing often based on interviews?

8–9 How can the activity rates (i.e., cost per activity) for the various activities be used to target process improvements?

8–10 When activity-based costing is used, why are manufacturing overhead costs often shifted from high-volume products to low-volume products?

8–11 Why should an activity view of product margins, as in Exhibit 8–10, be supplemented with an action analysis, as in Exhibit 8–16, when making decisions about products or customers?

8–12 In what three ways does activity-based costing improve the costing system of an organization?

8–13 What are the two chief limitations of activity-based costing?

8–14 Can activity-based costing be used in service organizations?

EXERCISES

EXERCISE 8–1 ABC Cost Hierarchy [LO1]

The following activities occur at Greenwich Corporation, a company that manufactures a variety of products.

a. Receive raw materials from suppliers.
b. Manage parts inventories.
c. Do rough milling work on products.
d. Interview and process new employees in the personnel department.
e. Design new products.
f. Perform periodic preventive maintenance on general-use equipment.
g. Use the general factory building.
h. Issue purchase orders for a job.

Required:

Classify each of the activities above as either a unit-level, batch-level, product-level, or organization-sustaining activity.

EXERCISE 8–2 First Stage Allocation [LO2]

SecuriCorp operates a fleet of armoured cars that make scheduled pickups and deliveries in the Halifax area. The company is implementing an activity-based costing system that has four activity cost pools: Travel, Pickup and Delivery, Customer Service, and Other. The activity measures are kilometres for the Travel cost pool, number of pickups and deliveries for the Pickup and Delivery cost pool, and number of customers for the Customer Service cost pool. The Other cost pool has no activity measure. The following costs will be assigned using the activity-based costing system:

Driver and guard wages	$ 720,000
Vehicle operating expense	280,000
Vehicle depreciation	120,000
Customer representative salaries and expenses	160,000
Office expenses	30,000
Administrative expenses	320,000
Total cost	$1,630,000

The distribution of resource consumption across the activity cost pools is as follows:

	Travel	Pickup and Delivery	Customer Service	Other	Totals
Driver and guard wages	50%	35%	10%	5%	100%
Vehicle operating expense	70%	5%	0%	25%	100%
Vehicle depreciation	60%	15%	0%	25%	100%
Customer representative salaries and expenses	0%	0%	90%	10%	100%
Office expenses	0%	20%	30%	50%	100%
Administrative expenses	0%	5%	60%	35%	100%

Required:

Carry out the first stage allocations of costs to activity cost pools as illustrated in Exhibit 8–4.

EXERCISE 8–3 Compute Activity Rates [LO3]

Green Thumb Gardening is a small gardening service that uses activity-based costing to estimate costs for pricing and other purposes. The proprietor of the company believes that costs are driven primarily by the size of customer lawns, the size of customer garden beds, the distance to travel to customers, and the number of customers. In addition, the costs of maintaining garden beds depends on whether the beds are low maintenance beds (mainly ordinary trees and shrubs) or high maintenance beds (mainly flowers and exotic plants). Accordingly, the company uses the five activity cost pools listed below:

Activity Cost Pool	Activity Measure
Caring for lawn	Square feet of lawn
Caring for garden beds–low maintenance	Square feet of low maintenance beds
Caring for garden beds–high maintenance	Square feet of high maintenance beds
Travel to jobs	Kilometres
Customer billing and service	Number of customers

The company has already carried out its first stage allocations of costs and has summarized its annual costs and activity as follows:

Activity Cost Pool	Estimated Overhead Cost	Expected Activity
Caring for lawn	$72,000	150,000 square feet of lawn
Caring for garden beds–low maintenance	$26,400	20,000 square feet of low maintenance beds
Caring for garden beds–high maintenance	$41,400	15,000 square feet of high maintenance beds
Travel to jobs	$3,250	12,500 kilometres
Customer billing and service	$8,750	25 customers

Required:

Compute the activity rate for each of the activity cost pools.

EXERCISE 8–4 Compute ABC Product Costs [LO4]

Klumper Corporation is a diversified manufacturer of industrial goods. The company's activity-based costing system contains the following six activity cost pools and activity rates:

Activity Cost Pool	Activity Rates
Labour related	$6.00 per direct labour-hour
Machine related	$4.00 per machine-hour
Machine setups	$50.00 per setup
Production orders	$90.00 per order
Shipments	$14.00 per shipment
Product sustaining	$840.00 per product

Activity data have been supplied for the following two products:

	Total Expected Activity	
	K425	M67
Number of units produced per year	200	2,000
Direct labour-hours	80	500
Machine-hours	100	1,500
Machine setups	1	4
Production orders	1	4
Shipments	1	10
Product sustaining	1	1

Required:
Compute the total and average per unit cost of each of the products listed.

EXERCISE 8–5 Product and Customer Profitability Analysis [L04, LO5]
Thermal Rising, Inc., makes paragliders for sale through specialty sporting goods stores. The company has a standard paraglider model, but also makes custom-designed paragliders. Management has designed an activity-based costing system with the following activity cost pools and activity rates:

Activity Cost Pool	Activity Rate
Manufacturing volume	$26 per direct labour-hour
Order processing	$284 per order
Custom design processing	$186 per custom design
Customer service	$379 per customer

Management would like an analysis of the profitability of a particular customer, Big Sky Outfitters, which has ordered the following products over the last 12 months:

	Standard Model	Custom Design
Number of gliders	20	3
Number of orders	1	3
Number of custom designs	0	3
Direct labour-hours per glider	26.35	28.00
Selling price per glider	$1,850	$2,400
Direct materials cost per glider	$564	$634

The company's direct labour rate is $19.50 per hour.

Required:
Using the company's activity-based costing system, compute the profitability of each of the two products ordered by Big Sky Outfitters and the overall profitability of this customer.

EXERCISE 8–6 Contrasting Traditional and ABC Product Costs [LO6]
Superior Industrial Corporation makes two products—Model X100 and Model X200. Model X200 offers advanced features and is sold for a higher price than Model X100. Management expects to sell 50,000 units of Model X100 and 5,000 units of Model X200 next year. The company's total manufacturing overhead for the year is expected to be $1,920,000. A unit of Model X100 requires 0.2 direct labour-hours and a unit of Model X200 requires 0.4 direct labour-hours.

Required:
1. The company currently applies manufacturing overhead to products using direct labour-hours as the allocation base. If this method is followed, how much overhead cost would be applied to each product in total and per unit?
2. Management is considering an activity-based costing system and would like to know what impact this would have on product costs. Preliminary analysis suggests that under activity-based costing, a total of $1,340,000 in manufacturing overhead cost would be assigned to Model X100 and a total of $390,000 would be assigned to Model X200. In addition, a total of $160,000 in nonmanufacturing overhead would be applied to Model X100 and a total of $110,000 would be applied to Model X200. If this method is used, how much overhead cost would be applied to each product in total and per unit?
3. Explain the impact of switching from the traditional costing system based on direct labour-hours to the activity-based costing system on total and per unit overhead costs assigned to the two products.

EXERCISE 8–7 (Appendix 8A) Preparing an Action Analysis Report [LO7]
Hard Driver Corporation produces private label golf clubs for pro shops throughout North America. The company uses activity-based costing to evaluate the profitability of serving its customers. This analysis is based on categorizing the company's costs as follows, using the ease of adjustment colour coding scheme described in Appendix 8A:

	Ease of Adjustment Code
Direct materials	Green
Direct labour	Yellow
Indirect labour	Yellow
Factory equipment depreciation	Red
Factory administration	Red
Selling and administrative wages and salaries	Red
Selling and administrative depreciation	Red
Marketing expenses	Yellow

Management would like to evaluate the profitability of a particular customer—the Grouse Mountain Golf Club of Avon, PEI. Over the last 12 months, this customer submitted one order for 120 golf clubs that had to be produced in two batches due to differences in product labelling requested by the customer. Summary data concerning the order appear below:

Number of clubs	120
Number of orders	1
Number of batches	2
Direct labour-hour per club	0.4
Selling price per club	$49.00
Direct materials cost per club	$27.65
Direct labour rate per hour	$22.00

A cost analyst working in the controller's office at the company has already produced the action analysis cost matrix for the Grouse Mountain Golf Club that appears below:

Action Analysis Cost Matrix for Grouse Mountain Golf Club

	Activity Cost Pools				
	Volume	Batch Processing	Order Processing	Customer Service	Total
Activity	48 direct labour-hours	2 batches	1 order	1 customer	
Manufacturing overhead:					
Indirect labour	$57.60	$52.40	$3.40	$0.00	$113.40
Factory equipment depreciation	216.00	0.60	0.00	0.00	216.60
Factory administration	31.20	0.50	15.00	245.00	291.70
Selling and administrative overhead:					
Wages and salaries	21.60	0.00	42.00	324.00	387.60
Depreciation	0.00	0.00	7.00	21.00	28.00
Marketing expenses	268.80	0.00	65.00	376.00	709.80
Total	$595.20	$53.50	$132.40	$966.00	$1,747.10

Required:

Prepare an action analysis report showing the profitability of the Grouse Mountain Golf Club. Include direct materials and direct labour costs in the report. Use Exhibit 8–16 as a guide for organizing the report.

EXERCISE 8–8 Cost Hierarchy [LO1]

CD Express, Inc., provides CD duplicating services to software companies. The customer provides a master CD from which CD Express makes copies. An order from a customer can be for a single copy or for thousands of copies. Most jobs are broken down into batches to allow smaller jobs, with higher priorities, to have access to the machines.

Following are listed a number of activities carried out at CD Express.

a. Sales representatives' periodic visits to customers to keep them informed about the services provided by CD Express.

b. Ordering labels from the printer for a particular CD.
c. Setting up the CD duplicating machine to make copies from a particular master CD.
d. Loading the automatic labelling machine with labels for a particular CD.
e. Visually inspecting CDs and placing them by hand into protective plastic cases prior to shipping.
f. Preparation of the shipping documents for the order.
g. Periodic maintenance of equipment.
h. Lighting and heating the company's production facility.
i. Preparation of quarterly financial reports.

Required:
Classify each of the activities above as either a unit-level, batch-level, product-level, customer-level, or organization-sustaining activity. (An order to duplicate a particular CD is a product-level activity.) Assume the order is large enough that it must be broken down into batches.

EXERCISE 8–9 First-Stage Allocations [LO2]
The operations vice president of Security Home Bank has been interested in investigating the efficiency of the bank's operations. She has been particularly concerned about the costs of handling routine transactions at the bank and would like to compare these costs at the bank's various branches. If the branches with the most efficient operations can be identified, their methods can be studied and then replicated elsewhere. While the bank maintains meticulous records of wages and other costs, there has been no attempt thus far to show how those costs are related to the various services provided by the bank. The operations vice president has asked your help in conducting an activity-based costing study of bank operations. In particular, she would like to know the cost of opening an account, the cost of processing deposits and withdrawals, and the cost of processing other customer transactions.

The Westfield branch of Security Home Bank has submitted the following cost data for last year:

Teller wages	$160,000
Assistant branch manager salary	75,000
Branch manager salary	80,000
Total	$315,000

Virtually all of the other costs of the branch—rent, depreciation, utilities, and so on—are organization-sustaining costs that cannot be meaningfully assigned to individual customer transactions such as depositing cheques.

In addition to the cost data above, the employees of the Westfield branch have been interviewed concerning how their time was distributed last year across the activities included in the activity-based costing study. The results of those interviews appear below:

Distribution of Resource Consumption Across Activities

	Opening Accounts	Processing Deposits and Withdrawals	Processing Other Customer Transactions	Other Activities	Total
Teller wages	5%	65%	20%	10%	100%
Assistant branch manager salary	15%	5%	30%	50%	100%
Branch manager salary	5%	0%	10%	85%	100%

Required:
Prepare the first-stage allocation for the activity-based costing study. (See Exhibit 8–4 for an example of a first-stage allocation.)

EXERCISE 8–10 Computing and Interpreting Activity Rates [LO3]
(This exercise is a continuation of Exercise 8–9; it should be assigned *only* if Exercise 8–9 is also assigned.) The manager of the Westfield branch of Security Home Bank has provided the following data concerning the transactions of the branch during the past year:

Activity	Total Activity at the Westfield Branch
Opening accounts	500 new accounts opened
Processing deposits and withdrawals	100,000 deposits and withdrawals processed
Processing other customer transactions	5,000 other customer transactions processed

The lowest costs reported by other branches for these activities are displayed below:

Activity	Lowest Cost among All Security Home Bank Branches
Opening accounts	$26.75 per new account
Processing deposits and withdrawals	$1.24 per deposit or withdrawal
Processing other customer transactions	$11.86 per other customer transaction

Required:

1. Using the first-stage allocation from Exercise 8–9 and the above data, compute the activity rates for the activity-based costing system. (Use Exhibit 8–5 as a guide.) Round all computations to the nearest whole cent.
2. What do these results suggest to you concerning operations at the Westfield branch?

EXERCISE 8–11 Second-Stage Allocation to an Order [LO4]

Durban Metal Products, Ltd., of the Republic of South Africa makes specialty metal parts used in applications ranging from the cutting edges of bulldozer blades to replacement parts for Land Rovers. The company uses an activity-based costing system for internal decision-making purposes. The company has four activity cost pools as listed below:

Activity Cost Pool	Activity Measure	Activity Rate
Order size	Number of direct labour-hours	R16.85 per direct labour-hour
Customer orders	Number of customer orders	R320.00 per customer order
Product testing	Number of testing hours	R89.00 per testing hour
Selling	Number of sales calls	R1,090.00 per sales call

Note: The currency in South Africa is the Rand, denoted here by R.

The managing director of the company would like information concerning the cost of a recently completed order for heavy-duty trailer axles. The order required 200 direct labour-hours, 4 hours of product testing, and 2 sales calls.

Required:

Prepare a report showing the overhead cost of the order for heavy-duty trailer axles. (Use Exhibit 8–9 as a guide.) What is the total overhead cost assigned to the order?

EXERCISE 8–12 (Appendix 8A) Second-Stage Allocation to an Order Using the Action Analysis Approach [LO4, LO7]

This exercise should be assigned in conjunction with Exercise 8–11.

The results of the first-stage allocation of the activity-based costing system at Durban Metal Products, Ltd., in which the activity rates were computed, appear below:

	Order Size	Customer Orders	Product Testing	Selling
Manufacturing:				
Indirect labour	R 8.25	R180.00	R30.00	R 0.00
Factory depreciation	8.00	0.00	40.00	0.00
Factory utilities	0.10	0.00	1.00	0.00
Factory administration	0.00	48.00	18.00	30.00
Selling and administrative:				
Wages and salaries	0.50	80.00	0.00	800.00
Depreciation	0.00	12.00	0.00	40.00
Taxes and insurance	0.00	0.00	0.00	20.00
Selling expenses	0.00	0.00	0.00	200.00
Total overhead cost	R16.85	R320.00	R89.00	R1,090.00

Required:

1. Prepare a report showing the overhead cost of the order for heavy-duty trailer axles discussed in Exercise 8–11. (Use Exhibit 8–14 as a guide.) What is the total overhead cost of the order according to the activity-based costing system?
2. Explain the two different perspectives this report gives to managers concerning the nature of the overhead costs involved in the order. (Hint: Look at the row and column totals of the report you have prepared.)

EXERCISE 8–13 Activity Measures [LO1]

Listed below are activities that you have observed at Ming Corporation, a manufacturing company. Each activity has been classified as a unit-level, batch-level, product-level, or customer-level activity.

Activity	Level of Activity	Examples of Activity Measures
a. Direct labour workers assemble a product	Unit	
b. Products are designed by engineers	Product	
c. Equipment is set up	Batch	
d. Machines are used to shape and cut materials	Unit	
e. Monthly bills are sent out to regular customers	Customer	
f. Materials are moved from the receiving dock to production lines	Batch	
g. All completed units are inspected for defects	Unit	

Required:

Complete the table by providing examples of activity measures for each activity.

EXERCISE 8–14 Computing ABC Product Costs [LO3, LO4]

Fogerty Company makes two products, titanium Hubs and Sprockets. Data regarding the two products follow:

	Direct Labour-Hours per Unit	Annual Production
Hubs	0.80	10,000 units
Sprockets	0.40	40,000 units

Additional information about the company follows:

a. Hubs require $32 in direct materials per unit, and Sprockets require $18.
b. The direct labour wage rate is $15 per hour.
c. Hubs are more complex to manufacture than Sprockets and they require special equipment.
d. The ABC system has the following activity cost pools:

Activity Cost Pool	Activity Measure	Estimated Overhead Cost	Activity		
			Total	Hubs	Sprockets
Machine setups	Number of setups	$72,000	400	100	300
Special processing	Machine-hours	$200,000	5,000	5,000	—
General factory	Direct labour-hours	$816,000	24,000	8,000	16,000

Required:

1. Compute the activity rate for each activity cost pool.
2. Determine the unit cost of each product according to the ABC system, including direct materials and direct labour.

EXERCISE 8–15 Cost Hierarchy and Activity Measures [LO1]

Vapo Ingman Oy, a Finnish manufacturing company, makes a variety of products at its plant outside Helsinki. Listed below are activities that you have observed at the plant.

a. Machine settings are changed between batches of different products.
b. Parts inventories are maintained in the storeroom. (Each product requires its own unique parts.)
c. Products are milled on a milling machine.
d. New employees are hired by the personnel office.

e. New products are designed.
f. Periodic maintenance is performed on general-purpose production equipment.
g. A bill is sent to a customer who is late in making payments.
h. Yearly taxes are paid on the company's facilities.
i. Purchase orders are issued for materials to be used in production.

Required:

1. Classify each of the activities above as either a unit-level, batch-level, product-level, customer-level, or organization-sustaining activity.
2. Where possible, for each activity name one or more activity measures that might be used to assign costs generated by the activity to products or customers.

EXERCISE 8–16 Calculating and Interpreting Activity-Based Costing Data [LO3, LO4]

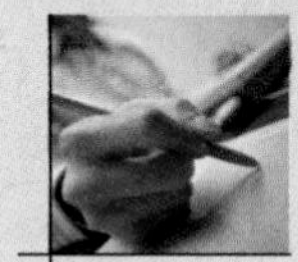

Hiram's Lakeside is a popular restaurant located on Lake Washington in British Columbia. The owner of the restaurant has been trying to better understand costs at the restaurant and has hired a student intern to conduct an activity-based costing study. The intern, in consultation with the owner, identified three major activities and then completed the first-stage allocations of costs to the activity cost pools. The results appear below.

Activity Cost Pool	Activity Measure	Total Cost	Total Activity
Serving a party of diners	Number of parties served	$33,000	6,000 parties
Serving a diner	Number of diners served	$138,000	15,000 diners
Serving drinks	Number of drinks ordered	$24,000	10,000 drinks

The above costs include all of the costs of the restaurant except for organization-sustaining costs such as rent, property taxes, and top-management salaries.

A group of diners who ask to sit at the same table are counted as a party. Some costs, such as the costs of cleaning linen, are the same whether one person is at a table or the table is full. Other costs, such as washing dishes, depend on the number of diners served.

Prior to the activity-based costing study, the owner knew very little about the costs of the restaurant. She knew that the total cost for the month (including organization-sustaining costs) was $240,000 and that 15,000 diners had been served. Therefore, the average cost per diner was $16.

Required:

1. According to the activity-based costing system, what is the total cost of serving each of the following parties of diners? (You can use the simplified approach described at the end of the chapter.)
   a. A party of four diners who order three drinks in total.
   b. A party of two diners who do not order any drinks.
   c. A lone diner who orders two drinks.
2. Convert the total costs you computed in (1) above to costs per diner. In other words, what is the average cost per diner for serving each of the following parties of diners?
   a. A party of four diners who order three drinks in total.
   b. A party of two diners who do not order any drinks.
   c. A lone diner who orders two drinks.
3. Why do the costs per diner for the three different parties differ from each other and from the overall average cost of $16 per diner?

EXERCISE 8–17 Activity-Based Costing as an Alternative to Traditional Product Costing [LO3, LO4, LO6]

This chapter emphasizes the use of activity-based costing in internal decisions. However, a modified form of activity-based costing can also be used to develop product costs for external financial reports. For this purpose, product costs include all manufacturing costs and exclude all nonmanufacturing costs. This problem illustrates such a costing system.

Harrison Company makes two products and uses a traditional costing system in which a single plantwide predetermined overhead rate is computed based on direct labour-hours. Data for the two products for the upcoming year follow:

	Rascon	Parcel
Direct materials cost per unit	$13.00	$22.00
Direct labour cost per unit	$6.00	$3.00
Direct labour-hours per unit	0.40	0.20
Number of units produced	20,000	80,000

These products are customized to some degree for specific customers.

Required:

1. The company's manufacturing overhead costs for the year are expected to be $576,000. Using the company's traditional costing system, compute the unit product costs for the two products.
2. Management is considering an activity-based costing system in which half of the overhead would continue to be allocated on the basis of direct labour-hours and half would be allocated on the basis of engineering design time. This time is expected to be distributed as follows during the upcoming year:

	Rascon	Parcel	Total
Engineering design time (in hours)	3,000	3,000	6,000

Compute the unit product costs for the two products using the proposed ABC system.

3. Explain why the product costs differ between the two systems.

EXERCISE 8–18 Second-Stage Allocation and Margin Calculations [LO4, LO5]

Foam Products, Inc., makes foam seat cushions for the automotive and aerospace industries. The company's activity-based costing system has four activity cost pools, which are listed below along with their activity measures and activity rates:

Activity Cost Pool	Activity Measure	Activity Rate
Volume	Number of direct labour-hours	$5.55 per direct labour-hour
Batch processing	Number of batches	$107.00 per batch
Order processing	Number of orders	$275.00 per order
Customer service	Number of customers	$2,463.00 per customer

The company just completed a single order from Interstate Trucking for 1,000 custom seat cushions. The order was produced in two batches. Each seat cushion required 0.25 direct labour-hours. The selling price was $20 per unit, the direct materials cost was $8.50 per unit, and the direct labour cost was $6.00 per unit. This was Interstate Trucking's only order during the year.

Required:

1. Prepare a report showing the product margin for this order from an activity viewpoint. (Use the product profitability analysis in Exhibit 8–9 as a guide.) At this point, ignore the customer service costs.
2. Prepare a report showing the customer margin on sales to Interstate Trucking from an activity viewpoint. (Use the customer profitability analysis in Exhibit 8–10 as a guide.)

EXERCISE 8–19 (Appendix 8A) Second-Stage Allocations and Margin Calculations Using the Action Analysis Approach [LO4, LO7]

Refer to the data for Foam Products, Inc., in Exercise 8–18 and the following additional details concerning the activity rates in the activity-based costing system:

	Activity Rates			
	Volume	Batch Processing	Order Processing	Customer Service
Manufacturing overhead:				
Indirect labour	$0.60	$ 60.00	$ 20.00	$ 0.00
Factory equipment depreciation	4.00	17.00	0.00	0.00
Factory administration	0.10	7.00	25.00	150.00
Selling and administrative overhead:				
Wages and salaries	0.40	20.00	160.00	1,600.00
Depreciation	0.00	3.00	10.00	38.00
Marketing expenses	0.45	0.00	60.00	675.00
Total	$5.55	$107.00	$275.00	$2,463.00

Management has provided their ease of adjustment codes for the purpose of preparing action analyses.

	Ease of Adjustment Code
Direct materials	Green
Direct labour	Yellow
Manufacturing overhead:	
Indirect labour	Yellow
Factory equipment depreciation	Red
Factory administration	Red
Selling and administrative overhead:	
Wages and salaries	Red
Depreciation	Red
Marketing expenses	Yellow

Required:

1. Using Exhibit 8–16 as a guide, prepare an action analysis report on the order from Interstate Trucking. Ignore customer service costs.
2. Management would like an action analysis report for the customer, Interstate Trucking, that is similar to those prepared for products, but is unsure of how this can be done. The customer service cost of $2,463 could be deducted directly from the product margin for the order, but this would obscure how much of the customer service cost consists of Green, Yellow, and Red costs. Prepare a report that clearly shows the adjustability of the various costs.

EXERCISE 8–20 Comprehensive Activity-Based Costing Exercise [LO2, LO3, LO4, LO5]
Advanced Products Corporation has supplied the following data from its activity-based costing system:

Overhead Costs	
Wages and salaries	$300,000
Other overhead costs	100,000
Total overhead costs	$400,000

Activity Cost Pool	Activity Measure	Total Activity for the Year
Volume related	Number of direct labour-hours	20,000 DLHs
Order related	Number of customer orders	400 orders
Customer support	Number of customers	200 customers
Other	These costs are not allocated to products or customers	Not applicable

Distribution of Resource Consumption Across Activities

	Volume Related	Order Related	Customer Support	Other	Total
Wages and salaries	40%	30%	20%	10%	100%
Other overhead costs	30%	10%	20%	40%	100%

During the year, Advanced Products completed one order for a new customer, Shenzhen Enterprises. This customer did not order any other products during the year. Data concerning that order follow:

Data concerning the Shenzhen Enterprises Order	
Units ordered	10 units
Direct labour-hours	2 DLHs per unit
Selling price	$300 per unit
Direct materials	$180 per unit
Direct labour	$50 per unit

Required:

1. Prepare a report showing the first-stage allocations of overhead costs to the activity cost pools. (Use Exhibit 8–5 as a guide.)
2. Compute the activity rates for the activity cost pools. (Use Exhibit 8–6 as a guide.)
3. Prepare a report showing the overhead costs for the order from Shenzhen Enterprises. (Use Exhibit 8–9 as a guide. Do not include the customer support costs at this point in the analysis.)
4. Prepare a report showing the product margin for the order and the customer margin for Shenzhen Enterprises. (Use Exhibit 8–10 as a guide.)

EXERCISE 8–21 (Appendix 8A) Comprehensive Activity-Based Costing Exercise [LO2, LO3, LO4, LO7]

Refer to the data for Advanced Products Corporation in Exercise 8–20.

Required:

1. Using Exhibit 8–12 as a guide, prepare a report showing the first-stage allocations of overhead costs to the activity cost pools.
2. Using Exhibit 8–13 as a guide, compute the activity rates for the activity cost pools.
3. Using Exhibit 8–14 as a guide, prepare a report showing the overhead costs for the order from Shenzhen Enterprises. Do not include customer support costs at this point in the analysis.
4. Using Exhibit 8–16 as a guide, prepare an activity analysis report showing the product margin for the order and the customer margin for Shenzhen Enterprises.
5. Using Exhibit 8–16 as a guide, prepare an action analysis report showing the product margin for the order and the customer margin for Shenzhen Enterprises. Direct materials should be coded as a Green cost, direct labour and wages and salaries as Yellow costs, and other overhead costs as a Red cost.
6. Using Exhibit 8–16 as a guide, prepare an action analysis report showing the customer margin for Shenzhen Enterprises. Direct materials should be coded as a Green cost, direct labour and wages and salaries as Yellow costs, and other overhead costs as a Red cost.
7. What action, if any, do you recommend as a result of the above analyses?

PROBLEMS

PROBLEM 8–22 Activity-Based Costing as an Alternative to Traditional Product Costing [LO3, LO4, LO5, LO6]

This chapter emphasizes the use of activity-based costing in internal decisions. However, a modified form of activity-based costing can also be used to develop product costs for external financial reports. For this purpose, product costs include all manufacturing overhead costs and exclude all nonmanufacturing costs. This problem illustrates such a costing system.

Siegel Company manufactures a product that is available in both a deluxe model and a regular model. The company has manufactured the regular model for years. The deluxe model was introduced several years ago to tap a new segment of the market. Since introduction of the deluxe model, the company's profits have steadily declined and management has become increasingly concerned about the accuracy of its costing system. Sales of the deluxe model have been increasing rapidly.

Manufacturing overhead is assigned to products on the basis of direct labour-hours. For the current year, the company has estimated that it will incur $900,000 in manufacturing overhead cost and produce 5,000 units of the deluxe model and 40,000 units of the regular model. The deluxe model requires two hours of direct labour time per unit, and the regular model requires one hour. Material and labour costs per unit are as follows:

	Model	
	Deluxe	Regular
Direct materials	$40	$25
Direct labour	$14	$7

Required:

1. Using direct labour-hours as the base for assigning overhead cost to products, compute the predetermined overhead rate. Using this rate and other data from the problem, determine the unit product cost of each model.
2. Management is considering using activity-based costing to apply manufacturing overhead cost to products for external financial reports. The activity-based costing system would have the following four activity cost pools:

Activity Cost Pool	Activity Measure	Estimated Overhead Cost
Purchasing	Purchase orders issued	$204,000
Processing	Machine-hours	182,000
Scrap/rework	Scrap/rework orders issued	379,000
Shipping	Number of shipments	135,000
		$900,000

Activity Measure	Expected Activity		
	Deluxe	Regular	Total
Purchase orders issued	200	400	600
Machine-hours	20,000	15,000	35,000
Scrap/rework orders issued	1,000	1,000	2,000
Number of shipments	250	650	900

Using Exhibit 8–6 as a guide, determine the predetermined overhead rate for each of the four activity cost pools.

3. Using the predetermined overhead rates you computed in part (2) above, do the following:
   a. Compute the total amount of manufacturing overhead cost that would be applied to each model using the activity-based costing system. After these totals have been computed, determine the amount of manufacturing overhead cost per unit of each model.
   b. Compute the unit product cost of each model (materials, labour, and manufacturing overhead).
4. From the data you have developed in parts (1) through (3) above, identify factors that may account for the company's declining profits.

PROBLEM 8–23 (Appendix 8A) Activity Rates and Activity-Based Management [LO2, LO3, LO7]

Aerotraiteur SA is a French company that provides passenger and crew meals to airlines operating out of the two international airports of Paris—Orly and Charles de Gaulle (CDG). The operations at Orly and CDG are managed separately, and top management believes that there may be benefits to greater sharing of information between the two operations.

To better compare the two operations, an activity-based costing system has been designed with the active participation of the managers at both Orly and CDG. The activity-based costing system is based on the following activity cost pools and activity measures:

Activity Cost Pool	Activity Measure
Meal preparation	Number of meals
Flight-related activities	Number of flights
Customer service	Number of customers
Other (costs of idle capacity and organization-sustaining costs)	Not applicable

The operation at CDG airport serves one million meals annually on 5,000 flights for 10 different airlines. (Each airline is considered one customer.) The annual cost of running the CDG airport operation, excluding only the costs of raw materials for meals, totals €2,940,000.

Note: The currency in France is the euro denoted by €.

Annual Cost of the CDG Operation	
Cooks and delivery personnel wages	€2,400,000
Kitchen supplies	30,000
Chef salaries	180,000
Equipment depreciation	60,000
Administrative wages and salaries	150,000
Building costs	120,000
Total cost	€2,940,000

To help determine the activity rates, employees were interviewed and asked how they divided their time among the four major activities. The results of employee interviews at CDG are displayed below:

Distribution of Resource Consumption Across Activities at the CDG Operation

	Meal Preparation	Flight Related	Customer Service	Other	Total
Cooks and delivery personnel wages . .	75%	20%	0%	5%	100%
Kitchen supplies	100%	0%	0%	0%	100%
Chef salaries	30%	20%	40%	10%	100%
Equipment depreciation	60%	0%	0%	40%	100%
Administrative wages and salaries	0%	20%	60%	20%	100%
Building costs	0%	0%	0%	100%	100%

Required:

1. Perform the first-stage allocation of costs to the activity cost pools. (Use Exhibit 8–12 as a guide.)
2. Compute the activity rates for the activity cost pools. (Use Exhibit 8–13 as a guide.) Do not round off.
3. The Orly operation has already concluded its activity-based costing study and has reported the following activity rates: €1.98 per meal for meal preparation; €115.60 per flight for flight-related activities; and €9,600 for customer service. Comparing the activity rates for the CDG operation you computed in part (2) above to the activity rates for Orly, do you have any suggestions for the top management of Aerotraiteur SA?

PROBLEM 8–24 Evaluating the Profitability of Services [LO2, LO3, LO4, LO5]
Gallatin Carpet Cleaning is a small, family-owned business operating out of Calgary, Alberta. For its services, the company has always charged a flat fee per hundred square feet of carpet cleaned. The current fee is $28 per hundred square feet. However, there is some question about whether the company is actually making any money on jobs for some customers—particularly those located on remote ranches that require considerable travel time. The owner's daughter, home for the summer from university, has suggested investigating this question using activity-based costing. After some discussion, a simple system consisting of four activity cost pools seemed to be adequate. The activity cost pools and their activity measures appear below:

Activity Cost Pool	Activity Measure	Activity for the Year
Cleaning carpets	Square feet cleaned (00s)	20,000 hundred square feet
Travel to jobs	Kilometres driven	60,000 kilometres
Job support	Number of jobs	2,000 jobs
Other (costs of idle capacity and organization-sustaining costs)	None	Not applicable

The total cost of operating the company for the year is $430,000, which includes the following costs:

Wages	$150,000
Cleaning supplies	40,000
Cleaning equipment depreciation	20,000
Vehicle expenses	80,000
Office expenses	60,000
President's compensation	80,000
Total cost	$430,000

Resource consumption is distributed across the activities as follows:

Distribution of Resource Consumption Across Activities	Cleaning Carpets	Travel to Jobs	Job Support	Other	Total
Wages	70%	20%	0%	10%	100%
Cleaning supplies	100%	0%	0%	0%	100%
Cleaning equipment depreciation	80%	0%	0%	20%	100%
Vehicle expenses	0%	60%	0%	40%	100%
Office expenses	0%	0%	45%	55%	100%
President's compensation	0%	0%	40%	60%	100%

Job support consists of receiving calls from potential customers at the home office, scheduling jobs, billing, resolving issues, and so on.

Required:

1. Prepare the first-stage allocation of costs to the activity cost pools. (Use Exhibit 8–5 as a guide.)
2. Compute the activity rates for the activity cost pools. (Use Exhibit 8–6 as a guide.)
3. The company recently completed a 5 hundred square foot carpet-cleaning job at the Flying N Ranch—a 75-kilometre round-trip journey from the company's offices in Bozeman. Compute the cost of this job using the activity-based costing system. (Use Exhibit 8–10 as a guide.)
4. The revenue from the Flying N Ranch was $140 (5 hundred square feet @ $28 per hundred square feet). Prepare a report showing the margin from this job. (Use Exhibit 8–10 as a guide. Think of the job as a product.)
5. What do you conclude concerning the profitability of the Flying N Ranch job? Explain.
6. What advice would you give the president concerning pricing jobs in the future?

PROBLEM 8–25 (Appendix 8A) Evaluating the Profitability of Services Using an Action Analysis [LO2, LO3, LO4, LO7]

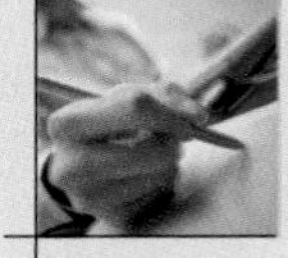

Refer to the data for Gallatin Carpet Cleaning in Problem 8–24.

Required:

1. Using Exhibit 8–13 as a guide, prepare the first-stage allocation of costs to the activity cost pools.
2. Using Exhibit 8–14 as a guide, compute the activity rates for the activity cost pools.
3. The company recently completed a 5 hundred square foot carpet-cleaning job at the Flying N Ranch—a 75-kilometre round-trip journey from the company's offices in Bozeman. Using Exhibit 8–14 as a guide, compute the cost of this job using the activity-based costing system.
4. The revenue from the Flying N Ranch was $140 (5 hundred square feet at $28 per hundred square feet). Using Exhibit 8–16 as a guide, prepare an action analysis report of the Flying N Ranch job. The president of Gallatin Carpet Cleaning considers all of the company's costs to be Green costs except for office expenses, which are coded Yellow, and his own compensation, which is coded Red. The people who do the actual carpet cleaning are all trained part-time workers who are paid only for work actually done.
5. What do you conclude concerning the profitability of the Flying N Ranch job? Explain.
6. What advice would you give the president concerning pricing jobs in the future?

PROBLEM 8–26 Activity-Based Costing as an Alternative to Traditional Product Costing [LO3, LO4, LO6]

This chapter emphasizes the use of activity-based costing in internal decisions. However, a modified form of activity-based costing can also be used to develop product costs for external financial reports. For this purpose, product costs include all manufacturing overhead costs and exclude all nonmanufacturing costs. This problem illustrates such a costing system.

Ellix Company manufactures two models of ultra-high fidelity speakers, the X200 model and the X99 model. Data regarding the two products follow:

Product	Direct Labour-Hours	Annual Production	Total Direct Labour-Hours
X200	1.8 DLHs per unit	5,000 units	9,000 DLHs
X99	0.9 DLHs per unit	30,000 units	27,000 DLHs
			36,000 DLHs

Additional information about the company follows:

a. Model X200 requires $72 in direct materials per unit, and model X99 requires $50.
b. The direct labour rate is $10 per hour.
c. The company has always used direct labour-hours as the base for applying manufacturing overhead cost to products.
d. Model X200 is more complex to manufacture than model X99 and requires the use of special equipment.
e. Because of the special work required in (d) above, the company is considering the use of activity-based costing to apply manufacturing overhead cost to products. Three activity cost pools have been identified as follows:

Activity Cost Pool	Activity Measure	Total Cost
Machine setups	Number of setups	$ 360,000
Special processing	Machine-hours	180,000
General factory	Direct labour-hours	1,260,000
		$1,800,000

	Expected Activity		
Activity Measure	Model X200	Model X99	Total
Number of setups	50	100	150
Machine-hours	12,000	0	12,000
Direct labour-hours	9,000	27,000	36,000

Required:

1. Assume that the company continues to use direct labour-hours as the base for applying overhead cost to products.
   a. Compute the predetermined overhead rate.
   b. Compute the unit product cost of each model.
2. Assume that the company decides to use activity-based costing to apply overhead cost to products.
   a. Compute the activity rate for each activity cost pool and determine the amount of overhead cost that would be applied to each model using the activity-based costing system.
   b. Compute the unit product cost of each model.
3. Explain why overhead cost shifted from the high-volume model to the low-volume model under activity-based costing.

PROBLEM 8–27 Activity-Based Costing and Bidding on Jobs [LO2, LO3, LO4]

Mercer Asbestos Removal Company removes potentially toxic asbestos insulation and related products from buildings. There has been a long-simmering dispute between the company's estimator and the work supervisors. The on-site supervisors claim that the estimators do not adequately distinguish between routine work such as removal of asbestos insulation around heating pipes in older homes and nonroutine work such as removing asbestos-contaminated ceiling plaster in industrial buildings. The on-site supervisors believe that nonroutine work is far more expensive than routine work and should bear higher customer charges. The estimator sums up his position in this way: "My job is to measure the area to be cleared of asbestos. As directed by top management, I simply multiply the square footage by $2.50 to determine the bid price. Since our average cost is only $2.175 per square foot, that leaves enough cushion to take care of the additional costs of nonroutine work that shows up. Besides, it is difficult to know what is routine or not routine until you actually start tearing things apart."

To shed light on this controversy, the company initiated an activity-based costing study of all of its costs. Data from the activity-based costing system follow:

Activity Cost Pool	Activity Measure	Total Activity
Job size	Thousands of square feet	800 thousand square feet
Estimating and job setup	Number of jobs	500 jobs
Working on nonroutine jobs	Number of nonroutine jobs	100 nonroutine jobs
Other (costs of idle capacity and organization-sustaining costs) . . .	Not applicable; these costs are not allocated to jobs	

Note: The 100 nonroutine jobs are included in the total of 500 jobs. Both nonroutine jobs and routine jobs require estimating and setup.

Costs for the Year	
Wages and salaries	$ 300,000
Disposal fees	700,000
Equipment depreciation	90,000
On-site supplies	50,000
Office expenses	200,000
Licensing and insurance	400,000
Total cost	$1,740,000

Distribution of Resource Consumption Across Activities

	Job Size	Estimating and Job Setup	Working on Nonroutine Jobs	Other	Total
Wages and salaries	50%	10%	30%	10%	100%
Disposal fees	60%	0%	40%	0%	100%
Equipment depreciation	40%	5%	20%	35%	100%
On-site supplies	60%	30%	10%	0%	100%
Office expenses	10%	35%	25%	30%	100%
Licensing and insurance	30%	0%	50%	20%	100%

Required:

1. Perform the first-stage allocation of costs to the activity cost pools. (Use Exhibit 8–5 as a guide.)
2. Compute the activity rates for the activity cost pools. (Use Exhibit 8–6 as a guide.)
3. Using the activity rates you have computed, determine the total cost and the average cost per thousand square feet of each of the following jobs according to the activity-based costing system.
   a. A routine 1,000-square-foot asbestos removal job.
   b. A routine 2,000-square-foot asbestos removal job.
   c. A nonroutine 2,000-square-foot asbestos removal job.
4. Given the results you obtained in (3) above, do you agree with the estimator that the company's present policy for bidding on jobs is adequate?

PROBLEM 8–28 Second Stage Allocations and Product Margins [LO4, LO5]

Pixel Studio, Inc., is a small company that creates computer-generated animations for films and television. Much of the company's work consists of short commercials for television, but the company also does realistic computer animations for special effects in movies.

The young founders of the company have become increasingly concerned with the economics of the business—particularly since many competitors have sprung up recently in the local area. To help understand the company's cost structure, an activity-based costing system has been designed. Three major activities are carried out in the company: animation concept, animation production, and contract administration. The animation concept activity is carried out at the contract proposal stage when the company bids on projects. This is an intensive activity that involves individuals from all parts of the company in creating story boards and prototype stills to be shown to the prospective client. Once a project is accepted by the client, the animation goes into production and contract administration begins. Almost all of the work involved in animation production is done by the technical staff, whereas the administrative staff is largely responsible for contract administration. The activity cost pools and their activity measures are listed below:

Activity Cost Pool	Activity Measure	Activity Rate
Animation concept	Number of proposals	$6,040 per proposal
Animation production	Minutes of completed animation	$7,725 per minute
Contract administration	Number of contracts	$6,800 per contract

These activity rates include all of the company' costs, except for the costs of idle capacity and organization-sustaining costs. There are no direct labour or direct materials costs.

Preliminary analysis using these activity rates has indicated that the local commercial segment of the market may be unprofitable. This segment is highly competitive. Producers of local commercials may ask three or four companies like Pixel Studio to bid, which results in an unusually low ratio of accepted contracts to bids. Furthermore, the animation sequences tend to be much shorter for local commercials than for other work. Since animation work is billed at fairly standard rates according to the running time of the completed animation, this means that the revenues from these short projects tend to be below average. Data concerning activity in the local commercial market appear below:

Activity Measure	Local Commercials
Number of proposals	25
Minutes of completed animation	5
Number of contracts	10

The total sales from the 10 contracts for local commercials was $180,000.

Required:

1. Using Exhibit 8–9 as a guide, determine the cost of the local commercial market. (Think of the local commercial market as a product.)
2. Using Exhibit 8–10 as a guide, prepare a report showing the margin of the local commercial market. (Remember, this company has no direct materials or direct labour costs.)
3. What would you recommend to management concerning the local commercial market?

PROBLEM 8–29 (Appendix 8A) Second Stage Allocations and Product Margins [LO4, LO7]

Refer to the data for Pixel Studio, Inc., in Problem 8–28. In addition, the company has provided the following details concerning its activity rates:

	Activity Rates		
	Animation Concept	Animation Production	Contract Administration
Technical staff salaries	$4,000	$6,000	$1,600
Animation equipment depreciation	360	1,125	0
Administrative wages and salaries	1,440	150	4,800
Supplies costs	120	300	160
Facility costs	120	150	240
Total	$6,040	$7,725	$6,800

Management has provided the following ease of adjustment codes for the various costs:

	Ease of Adjustment Code
Technical staff salaries	Red
Animation equipment depreciation	Red
Administrative wages and salaries	Yellow
Supplies costs	Green
Facility costs	Red

These codes created some controversy. In particular, some administrators objected to coding their own salaries Yellow, while the technical staff salaries were coded Red. However, the founders of the firm overruled these objections by pointing out that "our technical staff is our most valuable asset. Good animators are extremely difficult to find, and they would be the last to go if we had to cut back."

Required:

1. Using Exhibit 8–14 as a guide, determine the cost of the local commercials market. (Think of the local commercial market as a product.)
2. Using Exhibit 8–16 as a guide, prepare an action analysis report concerning the local commercial market. (This company has no direct materials or direct labour costs.)
3. What would you recommend to management concerning the local commercial market?

PROBLEM 8–30 Activity-Based Costing as an Alternative to Traditional Product Costing [LO3, LO4, LO6]

This chapter emphasizes the use of activity-based costing in internal decisions. However, a modified form of activity-based costing can also be used to develop product costs for external financial reports. For this purpose, product costs include all manufacturing overhead costs and exclude all nonmanufacturing costs. This problem illustrates such a costing system.

For many years, Zapro Company manufactured a single product called a mono-relay. Then three years ago, the company automated a portion of its plant and at the same time introduced a second product called a bi-relay which has become increasingly popular. The bi-relay is a more complex product, requiring one hour of direct labour time per unit to manufacture and extensive machining in the automated portion of the plant. The mono-relay requires only 0.75 hour of direct labour time per unit and only a small amount of machining. Manufacturing overhead costs are currently assigned to products on the basis of direct labour-hours.

Despite the growing popularity of the company's new bi-relay, profits have been declining steadily. Management is beginning to believe that there may be a problem with the company's costing system. Material and labour costs per unit are as follows:

	Mono-Relay	Bi-Relay
Direct materials	$35	$48
Direct labour (0.75 hour and 1.0 hour @ $12 per hour)	$9	$12

Management estimates that the company will incur $1,000,000 in manufacturing overhead costs during the current year and 40,000 units of the mono-relay and 10,000 units of the bi-relay will be produced and sold.

Required:

1. Compute the predetermined manufacturing overhead rate assuming that the company continues to apply manufacturing overhead cost on the basis of direct labour-hours. Using this rate and other data from the problem, determine the unit product cost of each product.
2. Management is considering using activity-based costing to apply manufacturing overhead cost to products for external financial reports. The activity-based costing system would have the following four activity cost pools:

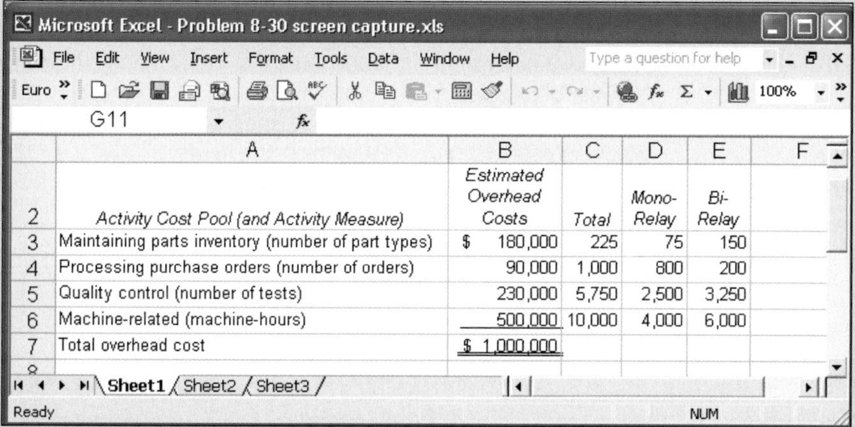

Activity Cost Pool (and Activity Measure)	Estimated Overhead Costs	Total	Mono-Relay	Bi-Relay
Maintaining parts inventory (number of part types)	$ 180,000	225	75	150
Processing purchase orders (number of orders)	90,000	1,000	800	200
Quality control (number of tests)	230,000	5,750	2,500	3,250
Machine-related (machine-hours)	500,000	10,000	4,000	6,000
Total overhead cost	$ 1,000,000			

Determine the predetermined overhead rate (i.e., activity rate) for each of the four activity cost pools.

3. Using the predetermined manufacturing overhead rates you computed in part (2) above, do the following:
   a. Determine the total amount of manufacturing overhead cost that would be applied to each product using the activity-based costing system. After these totals have been computed, determine the amount of manufacturing overhead cost per unit of each product.
   b. Compute the unit product cost of each product.
4. Look at the data you have computed in parts (1) through (3) above. In terms of manufacturing overhead costs, what factors make the bi-relay more costly to produce than the mono-relay? Is the bi-relay as profitable as management believes? Explain.

CASES

CASE 8–31 Activity-Based Costing and Pricing [LO3, LO4, LO5, LO6]

This chapter emphasizes the use of activity-based costing in internal decisions. However, a modified form of activity-based costing can also be used to develop product costs for external financial reports. For this purpose, product costs include all manufacturing overhead costs and exclude all nonmanufacturing costs. This problem illustrates such a costing system.

Java Source, Inc. (JSI), is a processor and distributor of a variety of blends of coffee. The company buys coffee beans from around the world and roasts, blends, and packages them for resale. JSI offers a large variety of different coffees that it sells to gourmet shops in one-kilogram bags. The major cost of the coffee is raw materials. However, the company's predominantly automated roasting, blending, and packing processes require a substantial amount of manufacturing overhead. The company uses relatively little direct labour.

Some of JSI's coffees are very popular and sell in large volumes, while a few of the newer blends sell in very low volumes. JSI prices its coffees at manufacturing cost plus a markup of 25%, with some adjustments made to keep the company's prices competitive.

For the coming year, JSI's budget includes estimated manufacturing overhead cost of $2,200,000. JSI assigns manufacturing overhead to products on the basis of direct labour-hours. The expected direct labour cost totals $600,000, which represents 50,000 hours of direct labour time. Based on the sales budget and expected raw materials costs, the company will purchase and use $5,000,000 of raw materials (mostly coffee beans) during the year.

The expected costs for direct materials and direct labour for one-kilogram bags of two of the company's coffee products appear below.

	Kenya Dark	Viet Select
Direct materials	$4.50	$2.90
Direct labour (0.02 hours per bag)	$0.24	$0.24

JSI's controller believes that the company's traditional costing system may be providing misleading cost information. To determine whether or not this is correct, the controller has prepared an analysis of the year's expected manufacturing overhead costs, as shown in the following table:

Activity Cost Pool	Activity Measure	Expected Activity for the Year	Expected Cost for the Year
Purchasing	Purchase orders	2,000 orders	$ 560,000
Material handling	Number of setups	1,000 setups	193,000
Quality control	Number of batches	500 batches	90,000
Roasting	Roasting hours	95,000 roasting hours	1,045,000
Blending	Blending hours	32,000 blending hours	192,000
Packaging	Packaging hours	24,000 packaging hours	120,000
Total manufacturing overhead cost			$2,200,000

Data regarding the expected production of Kenya Dark and Viet Select coffee are presented below.

	Kenya Dark	Viet Select
Expected sales	80,000 kilograms	4,000 kilograms
Batch size	5,000 kilograms	500 kilograms
Setups	2 per batch	2 per batch
Purchase order size	20,000 kilograms	500 kilograms
Roasting time per 100 kilograms	1.5 roasting hours	1.5 roasting hours
Blending time per 100 kilograms	0.5 blending hours	0.5 blending hours
Packaging time per 100 kilograms	0.3 packaging hours	0.3 packaging hours

Required:

1. Using direct labour-hours as the base for assigning manufacturing overhead cost to products, do the following:
   a. Determine the predetermined overhead rate that will be used during the year.

   b. Determine the unit product cost of one kilogram of the Kenya Dark coffee and one kilogram of the Viet Select coffee.
2. Using activity-based costing as the basis for assigning manufacturing overhead cost to products, do the following:
   a. Determine the total amount of manufacturing overhead cost assigned to the Kenya Dark coffee and to the Viet Select coffee for the year.
   b. Using the data developed in (2*a*) above, compute the amount of manufacturing overhead cost per kilogram of the Kenya Dark coffee and the Viet Select coffee. Round all computations to the nearest whole cent.
   c. Determine the unit product cost of one kilogram of the Kenya Dark coffee and one kilogram of the Viet Select coffee.
3. Write a brief memo to the president of JSI explaining what you have found in (1) and (2) above and discussing the implications to the company of using direct labour as the base for assigning manufacturing overhead cost to products.

(CMA, adapted)

CASE 8–32 Contrasting Activity-Based Costing and Traditional Costing [LO3, LO4, LO5]

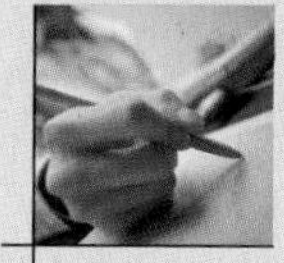

This chapter emphasizes the use of activity-based costing in internal decisions. However, a modified form of activity-based costing can also be used to develop product costs for external financial reports. For this purpose, product costs include all manufacturing overhead costs and exclude all nonmanufacturing costs. This problem illustrates such a costing system.

"Wow! Is that X-20 model ever a loser! It's time to cut back its production and shift our resources toward the new Y-30 model," said Darrel Karter, executive vice president of Cutler Products, Inc. "Just look at this income statement I've received from accounting. The Y-30 is generating four times as much profit as the X-20, and it has only about one-sixth as much in sales. I'm convinced that our future depends on the Y-30." The year-end statement to which Darrel was referring follows:

		Model	
	Total	X-20	Y-30
Sales	$7,250,000	$6,000,000	$1,250,000
Cost of goods sold	4,600,000	3,660,000	940,000
Gross margin	2,650,000	2,340,000	310,000
Less selling and administrative expenses	2,450,000	2,300,000	150,000
Net operating income	$ 200,000	$ 40,000	$ 160,000
Number of units produced and sold		30,000	5,000

"The numbers sure look that way," replied Karen Carpenter, the company's sales manager. "But why isn't the competition more excited about the Y-30? I know we've only been producing the model for three years, but I'm surprised that more of our competitors haven't recognized what a cash cow it is."

"I think it's our new automated plant," replied Darrel. "Now it takes only two direct labour-hours to produce a unit of the X-20 and three direct labour-hours to produce a unit of the Y-30. That's considerably less than it used to take us."

"I agree that automation is wonderful," replied Karen. "I suppose that's how we're able to hold down the price of the Y-30. Branson Company in Germany tried to bring out a Y-30 but discovered they couldn't touch our price. But Branson is killing us on the X-20 by undercutting our price with some of our best customers. I suppose they'll pick up all of our X-20 business if we move out of that market. But who cares? We don't even have to advertise the Y-30; it just seems to sell itself."

"My only concern about automation is how our manufacturing overhead rate has shot up," said Darrel. "Our total manufacturing overhead cost is $1,800,000. That comes out to be a hefty amount per direct labour-hour, but Darlene down in accounting has been using direct labour-hours as the base for computing overhead rates for years and doesn't want to change. I don't suppose it matters so long as costs get assigned to products."

"I've never understood that debit and credit stuff," replied Karen. "But I think you've got a problem in production. I had lunch with Joanne yesterday and she complained about how complex the Y-30 is to produce. Apparently they have to do a lot of setups, special soldering, and other work on the Y-30 just to keep production moving. And they have to inspect every single unit."

"It'll have to wait," said Darrel. "I'm writing a proposal to the board of directors to phase out the X-20. We've got to increase our bottom line or we'll all be looking for jobs."

Required:

1. Compute the predetermined overhead rate based on direct labour-hours that the company used during the year. (There was no under- or overapplied overhead for the year.)
2. Direct materials and direct labour costs per unit for the two products are as follows:

	X-20	Y-30
Direct materials	$50	$80
Direct labour	$24	$36

   Using these data and the rate computed in part (1) above, determine the unit product cost of each product under the company's traditional costing system.
3. Assume that the company's $1,800,000 in manufacturing overhead cost can be assigned to six activity cost pools, as follows:

Activity Cost Pool (and Activity Measure)	Estimated Overhead Costs	Expected Activity Total	X-20	Y-30
Machine setups (number of setups)	$ 208,000	1,600	1,000	600
Quality control (number of inspections)	360,000	9,000	4,000	5,000
Purchase orders (number of orders)	90,000	1,200	840	360
Soldering (number of solder joints)	450,000	200,000	60,000	140,000
Shipments (number of shipments)	132,000	600	400	200
Machine related (machine-hours)	560,000	70,000	30,000	40,000
	$1,800,000			

   Given these data, would you support a recommendation to expand sales of the Y-30? Explain your position.
4. From the data you have prepared in part (3) above, why do you suppose the Y-30 "just seems to sell itself"?
5. If you were president of Cutler Products, Inc., what strategy would you follow from this point forward to improve the company's overall profits?

CASE 8–33 (Appendix 8A) Comprehensive Activity-Based Costing Case [LO2, LO3, LO4, LO6, LO7]

Classic Windows is a small company that builds specialty wooden windows for local builders. For years the company has assigned overhead costs to products based on direct labour-hours (DLHs). However, the company's president became interested in activity-based costing after reading an article about activity-based costing in a trade journal. An activity-based costing design team was put together, and within a few months a simple system consisting of four activity cost pools had been created. The activity cost pools and their activity measures appear below:

Activity Cost Pool	Activity Measure	Activity for the Year
Making windows	Direct labour-hours	100,000 DLHs
Processing orders	Number of orders	2,000 orders
Customer relations	Number of customers	100 customers
Other (costs of idle capacity and organization-sustaining costs)	None	Not applicable

The Processing Orders activity cost pool includes order taking, job setup, job scheduling, and so on. Direct materials and direct labour are directly assigned to jobs in both the traditional and activity-based costing systems. The total overhead cost (both nonmanufacturing and manufacturing) for the year is $1,370,000 and includes the following costs:

Manufacturing overhead costs:		
Indirect factory wages	$400,000	
Production equipment depreciation	300,000	
Other factory costs	80,000	$ 780,000
Selling and administrative expenses:		
Administrative wages and salaries	300,000	
Office expenses	40,000	
Marketing expenses	250,000	590,000
Total overhead cost		$1,370,000

Based largely on interviews with employees, the distribution of resource consumption across the activities has been estimated as follows:

Distribution of Resource Consumption Across Activities

	Making Windows	Processing Orders	Customer Relations	Other	Total
Indirect factory wages	30%	40%	10%	20%	100%
Production equipment depreciation	90%	0%	0%	10%	100%
Other factory costs	30%	0%	0%	70%	100%
Administrative wages and salaries	0%	20%	30%	50%	100%
Office expenses	0%	30%	10%	60%	100%
Marketing expenses	0%	0%	60%	40%	100%

Management of the company is particularly interested in measuring the profitability of two customers. One of the customers, Kuszik Builders, is a low-volume purchaser. The other, Western Homes, is a relatively high-volume purchaser. Details of these two customers' orders for the year appear below:

	Kuszik Builders	Western Homes
Number of orders during the year	2 orders	3 orders
Total direct labour-hours	300 DLHs	2,000 DLHs
Total sales	$12,500	$68,000
Total direct materials	$4,200	$18,500
Total direct labour cost	$5,400	$36,000

Required:

1. The company's traditional costing system applies manufacturing overhead to jobs using direct labour-hours. Using this traditional approach, carry out the following steps:
   a. Compute the predetermined manufacturing overhead rate.
   b. Compute the total margin for all of the windows ordered by Kuszik Builders according to the traditional costing system. Do the same for Western Homes.
2. Using activity-based costing, do the following:
   a. Perform the first-stage allocation of costs to the activity cost pools. (Use Exhibit 8–5 as a guide.)
   b. Compute the activity rates for the activity cost pools. (Use Exhibit 8–6 as a guide.)
   c. Compute the overhead costs of serving each of the two customers. (You will need to construct a table like Exhibit 8–9 for each of the customers. However, unlike Exhibit 8–9, you should fill in the column for Customer Relations as well as the other columns. Exhibit 8–9 was constructed for a product; in this case we are interested in a customer.)
   d. Prepare an action analysis report showing the margin on business with Kuszik Builders. (The ease of adjustment codes follow.) Repeat for Western Homes.

	Ease of Adjustment Code
Direct materials	Green
Direct labour	Yellow
Indirect factory wages	Yellow
Production equipment depreciation	Yellow
Other factory costs	Yellow
Administrative wages and salaries	Red
Office expenses	Yellow
Marketing expenses	Yellow

3. Does Classic Windows appear to be losing money on either customer? Do the traditional and activity-based costing systems agree concerning the profitability of the customers? If they do not agree, which costing system do you believe? Why?

CASE 8–34 Activity-Based Costing as an Alternative to Traditional Product Costing [LO3, LO4, LO5, LO6]*

This chapter emphasizes the use of activity-based costing in internal decisions. However, a modified form of activity-based costing can also be used to develop product costs for external financial reports. For this purpose, product costs include all manufacturing overhead costs and exclude all nonmanufacturing costs. This problem illustrates such a costing system.

"A dollar of gross margin per briefcase? That's ridiculous!" roared Art Dejans, president of CarryAll, Inc. "Why do we go on producing those standard briefcases when we're able to make over $15 per unit on our specialty items? Maybe it's time to get out of the standard line and focus the whole plant on specialty work."

Mr. Dejans is referring to a summary of unit costs and revenues that he had just received from the company's Accounting Department:

	Standard Briefcases	Specialty Briefcases
Selling price per unit	$36	$40
Unit product cost	35	25
Gross margin per unit	$ 1	$15

CarryAll produces briefcases from leather, fabric, and synthetic materials in a single plant. The basic product is a standard briefcase that is made from leather lined with fabric. The standard briefcase is a high-quality item and has sold well for many years.

Last year, the company decided to expand its product line and produce specialty briefcases for special orders. These briefcases differ from the standard in that they vary in size, they contain the finest leather and synthetic materials, and they are imprinted with the buyer's name. To reduce labour costs on the specialty briefcases, automated machines do most of the cutting and stitching. These machines are used to a much lesser degree in the production of standard briefcases.

"I agree that the specialty business is looking better and better," replied Sally Henrie, the company's marketing manager. "And there seems to be plenty of specialty work out there, particularly since the competition hasn't been able to touch our price. Did you know that Armor Company, our biggest competitor, charges over $50 a unit for its specialty items? Now that's what I call gouging the customer!"

*Adapted from a case written by Harold P. Roth and Imogene Posey, "Management Accounting Case Study: CarryAll Company," *Management Accounting Campus Report*, Institute of Management Accountants, Fall 1991), p. 9. Used by permission.

A breakdown of the manufacturing cost for each of CarryAll's product lines is given below:

	Standard Briefcases	Specialty Briefcases
Units produced each month	10,000	2,500
Direct materials:		
Leather	$15.00	$ 7.50
Fabric	5.00	5.00
Synthetic	0	5.00
Total direct materials	20.00	17.50
Direct labour 0.5 DLH and 0.25 DLH @ $12 per DLH	6.00	3.00
Manufacturing overhead 0.5 DLH and 0.25 DLH @ $18 per DLH	9.00	4.50
Total cost per unit	$35.00	$25.00

Manufacturing overhead is applied to products on the basis of direct labour-hours. The rate of $18 per direct labour-hour is determined by dividing the total manufacturing overhead cost for a month by the direct labour-hours:

$$\frac{\text{Predetermined}}{\text{overhead rate}} = \frac{\text{Manufacturing overhead}}{\text{Direct labour-hours}} = \frac{\$101{,}250}{5{,}625 \text{ DLHs}} = \$18 \text{ per DLH}$$

The following additional information is available about the company and its products:

a. Standard briefcases are produced in batches of 200 units, and specialty briefcases are produced in batches of 25 units. Thus, the company does 50 setups for the standard items each month and 100 setups for the specialty items. A setup for the standard items requires one hour of time, whereas a setup for the specialty items requires two hours of time.
b. All briefcases are inspected to ensure that quality standards are met. A total of 300 hours of inspection time is spent on the standard briefcases and 500 hours of inspection time is spent on the specialty briefcases each month.
c. A standard briefcase requires 0.5 hour of machine time, and a specialty briefcase requires 2 hours of machine time.
d. The company is considering the use of activity-based costing as an alternative to its traditional costing system for computing unit product costs. Since these unit product costs will be used for external financial reporting, all manufacturing overhead costs are to be allocated to products and nonmanufacturing costs are to be excluded from product costs. The activity-based costing system has already been designed and costs allocated to the activity cost pools. The activity cost pools and activity measures are detailed below:

Activity Cost Pool	Activity Measure	Estimated Overhead Cost
Purchasing	Number of orders	$12,000
Material handling	Number of receipts	15,000
Production orders and setup	Setup hours	20,250
Inspection	Inspection-hours	16,000
Frame assembly	Assembly-hours	8,000
Machine related	Machine-hours	30,000
		$101,250

	Expected Activity		
Activity Measure	Standard Briefcase	Specialty Briefcase	Total
Number of orders:			
Leather	34	6	40
Fabric	48	12	60
Synthetic material	0	100	100
Number of receipts:			
Leather	52	8	60
Fabric	64	16	80
Synthetic material	0	160	160
Setup hours	?	?	?
Inspection-hours	?	?	?
Assembly-hours	800	800	1,600
Machine-hours	?	?	?

Required:

1. Using activity-based costing, determine the amount of manufacturing overhead cost that would be applied to each standard briefcase and each specialty briefcase.
2. Using the data computed in (1) above and other data from the case as needed, determine the unit product cost of each product line from the perspective of the activity-based costing system.
3. Within the limitations of the data that have been provided, evaluate the president's concern about the profitability of the two product lines. Would you recommend that the company shift its resources entirely to production of specialty briefcases? Explain.
4. Sally Henrie stated that "the competition hasn't been able to touch our price" on specialty business. Why do you suppose the competition hasn't been able to touch CarryAll's price?

GROUP AND INTERNET EXERCISES

GROUP EXERCISE 8–35 Dividing the Bill

Assume that you and your friends go to a restaurant as a group. At the end of the meal, you must decide how the bill for the group should be shared. One alternative is to figure out the cost of what each individual consumed and divide up the bill accordingly. Another alternative is to split the bill equally among the individuals.

Required:

Which system for dividing the bill is more equitable? Which system is easier to use? How does this issue relate to the material covered in this chapter?

GROUP EXERCISE 8–36 The Impact of Changing Cost Systems on Product Costs

A manufacturing company is thinking of changing its method of computing product costs for the purposes of making decisions. Under the company's traditional direct labour-based costing system, manufacturing overhead costs are applied to products on the basis of direct labour-hours. Under the proposed activity-based costing (ABC) system, manufacturing overhead costs would be applied to products using a variety of activity measures at the unit, batch, and product levels.

Required:

For each of the following products, indicate whether its unit product cost will increase or decrease when switching from a traditional direct labour-based costing system to an activity-based costing system.

1. A low-volume product that is produced in small batches.
2. A high-volume product that is produced in large batches with automated equipment and that requires very few direct labour-hours per unit.
3. A high-volume product that requires little machine work but a lot of direct labour.

INTERNET EXERCISE 8–37

As you know, the World Wide Web is a medium that is constantly evolving. Sites come and go, and change without notice. To enable the periodic updating of site addresses, this problem has been posted to the textbook Web site (www.mcgrawhill.ca/college/garrison). After accessing the site, enter the Student Centre and select this chapter. Select and complete the Internet Exercise.

CHAPTER 9

LEARNING OBJECTIVES

After studying Chapter 9, you should be able to:

1. Explain the importance of a business plan and the processes organizations use to create budgets.
2. Prepare a sales budget, including a schedule of expected cash collections.
3. Prepare a production budget.
4. Prepare a direct materials budget, including a schedule of expected cash disbursements for purchases of materials.
5. Prepare a direct labour budget.
6. Prepare a manufacturing overhead budget.
7. Prepare a selling and administrative expense budget.
8. Prepare a cash budget.
9. Prepare a budgeted income statement.
10. Prepare a budgeted balance sheet.
11. Describe variations in the master budget process when applying it to not-for-profit and activity-based situations.

BUDGETING

BUSINESS FOCUS

LILO & STITCH ON BUDGET

The full-length feature cartoon Tarzan grossed about $450 million worldwide for Walt Disney Company. However, production costs got out of control from focusing too much on meeting the planned release date. In the case of *Tarzan*, production fell behind schedule due to the tendency of animation teams to add more eye-dazzling complexity to each production. At one point, it was estimated that 190,000 individual drawings would be needed to complete the film in contrast to the 130,000 drawings needed to complete *The Lion King.* To meet *Tarzan*'s release date, workers were pulled off other productions and were often paid at overtime rates. The size of the film crew eventually reached 573, which was nearly twice the size of the crew that had made *The Lion King*. With animators earning salaries in the hundreds of thousands of dollars, the cost implications were staggering.

Thomas S. Schumacher, Disney's feature-animation chief, was charged with dramatically reducing the cost of future films while making sure that the audience wouldn't notice any decline in quality. *Lilo & Stitch* was the first film to be produced with this goal in mind. The process began by prioritizing where the money was to be spent. The budget for music was kept generous; animation costs were cut by controlling the small details that add big costs with little effect on the quality of the film. For example, animators wanted to draw cute designs on the skirts worn by Nani, Lilo's big sister. However, adding this level of detail on every frame in which Nani appears in the film would have added about $250,000 in cost. By controlling such details, *Lilo & Stitch* was finished on time and at a cost of about $80 million. This contrasted with a cost of over $150 million for Tarzan.

Source: Bruce Orwall, "Comics Stripped: At Disney, String of Weak Cartoons Leads to Cost Cuts," *The Wall Street Journal*, June 18, 2002, pp. A1 and A8.

Strategic planning is the term applied to the selection of policies, practices, and procedures by management in an attempt to achieve the long-term goals set for the organization. Such planning occurs in two phases: (1) deciding on the products to produce and/or the services to render, and (2) deciding on the marketing and/or manufacturing methods to employ in getting the intended products or services to the proper audience. Managerial accounting derives its relevance from its role in assisting strategic planning through the preparation of progress reports that provide feedback on the achievement of a set strategy. The types of information, the types of costs, and the systems used to provide useful information are all derived from an organization's objectives and strategies.

To focus the discussion to follow, we present a single organization, the Bestway Furniture Company, and look closely at this organization's objectives, strategy, and management, and at how these factors influence its need for managerial accounting data.

Setting Objectives

The Bestway Furniture Company is a corporation, and its owners have placed their money in the organization to earn a return on their investment. Thus, the first objective of the company is to earn a return on the money committed to it. This so-called *profit objective* is tempered by other objectives. The company is anxious to acquire and maintain a reputation for integrity, fairness, and dependability. It also wants to be a positive force in the social and ecological environment in which it operates.

The owners (shareholders) of the Bestway Furniture Company prefer not to be involved in the day-to-day operation of the company. Instead, they have outlined the broad objectives of the organization and have selected a president and other officers, collectively termed *management*, to oversee the implementation of these objectives. Although management should pursue the central objective of earning a return on the owners' investment, this must be done with a sensitivity to meeting other desired objectives.

The set of strategies emerging from strategic planning is often referred to as an organization's *policies*, and strategic planning itself is often referred to as *setting policy*.[1]

Phase 1: Product Strategy

In deciding on the products to sell or the services to render, there are several strategies that Bestway Furniture Company could follow. The company could specialize in office furniture, it could specialize in appliances, it could be a broad supermarket furniture outlet, or it could employ any one of a number of other product and/or service strategies.

After careful consideration of the various strategies available, Bestway's management has decided to sell only home furnishings, including appliances. For one reason or another, several other possible strategies were rejected. For example, management has decided not to service appliances and not to sell office furniture or to deal in institutional furnishings.

Phase 2: Marketing Strategy

Having made the decision to concentrate on home furnishings, the management of the Bestway Furniture Company is now faced with a second strategy decision. Some furniture dealers handle only the highest-quality home furnishings, thereby striving to maintain the image of a quality dealer. The markups of these dealers are usually quite high, their volume is quite low, and their promotional efforts are directed toward a relatively small segment of the public. Other furniture dealers operate volume outlets. They try to keep markups relatively low, with the thought that overall returns will be augmented by a

1. For an expanded discussion of strategic planning and its relationship to cost management, see Robert N. Anthony and Vijay Govindarajan, *Management Control Systems,* 11th ed. (Irwin McGraw-Hill, 2004)

larger number of units sold. Still other dealers may follow different strategies. The selection of a particular strategy is a matter of managerial judgement; some companies make a return by following one strategy, while other companies are rewarded by following another. Decisions are needed on the products, their price, their place, and their promotion. The words *products, price*, and *promotion* signify the product selection, their pricing rules, and the promotion strategy of the organization. The word *plac*e denotes quality, delivery, and service. The decision characteristics represent the "four Ps" of marketing strategy selection and implementation. The Bestway Furniture Company has decided to operate volume outlets and to maintain a discount image.

Every organization must make other strategic plans. The set of strategies may not be written down, but they exist nonetheless, and they are a central guiding force in the organization's activities and in its need for accounting information. A full discussion of the strategic planning process involves numerous considerations, such as the assessment of strengths, weaknesses, opportunities, and threats. Part of this process involves the consideration of five competitive forces: the power of their suppliers in negotiations, the power of their customers, the possible effects of substitutes, the entry of new competitors, and the threat of existing competitors. Each of the factors can impact on prices, costs, and investments made. Competitive advantages resulting from lower costs or product differentiation are combined with questions of how businesses are structured and conducted to provide an overall strategic plan.

Two directions that constitute the advantage organizations attempt to achieve are low cost and differentiation. Low cost provides the advantage in a competitive environment because the organization can underprice its competition. Differentiation involves, as the term suggests, a means of distinguishing the output of the organization in terms of function, service, or quality. Number of products, product complexity, service levels, and associated costs and cost classifications will be determined by the strategic directions set by the management of the organization. For example, what is direct labour and its behaviour depends on the employment practices, which in turn result from the competitive direction of the organization. Organizational structures depend on business location, size, and management practices that result from the strategic planning.

Information is being used as a means of achieving success. Information can be restricted so that it hinders competitors from entering the business. Information can be used to gain an advantage in many of the negotiations that must be conducted with customers and suppliers. Reservation systems used by the transportation or hospitality industries and purchasing systems employed in industries such as motor vehicle manufacture create dependencies among organizations that will assist business. Thus, information not only serves in developing and selecting strategies but it also serves as a means of achieving the results desired.

In summary, strategic planning to achieve the objectives of the organization sets the decision framework for managers and in turn these decisions provide the direction for the information providers and analysts.

THE BUSINESS PLAN

LEARNING OBJECTIVE 1
Explain the importance of a business plan and the processes organizations use to create budgets

New businesses typically formalize their strategic planning in the form of a business plan. A business plan consists of information about the company's basic product or service and about the steps to be taken to reach its potential market. The plan includes information about production methods, the competition, the management team, details on how the business will be financed and is a key document for the organization's internal management. It is also valuable for external use in attracting resources from potential creditors and investors. The answers to many of the questions raised by providers of funds can be found in the business plan.

Exhibit 9–1[2] shows a flow chart of the steps taken in a typical business plan. The 16-week time span is for illustrative purposes only. The actual length of the business plan

2. Adapted from Nicholas C. Siropolis, *Small Business Management: A Guide to Entrepreneurship*, 2nd ed. (Boston: Houghton Mifflin, 1982), pp. 138–41.

process varies with the nature and complexity of the venture and could span anywhere from a few weeks to several months. Note from the flow chart that it is essential for certain steps to be completed before others are begun. It makes no sense, for example, to talk about forecasting sales (step 5) until a product or service has been picked (step 3) and the market has been researched (step 4). Continuing businesses formalize part of the financial aspects of their strategy in their annual budgets. Although some steps clearly precede others the process is not entirely linear. Development of the business plan is an interactive process. In today's volatile, fast-paced, and complex business environment, the business plan must be flexible enough to adapt in response to market changes that require new estimates and forecasts. To work well, the business plan should encourage a shared vision with clear targets and well-defined performance measures such as those discussed later in Chapters 10 and 11 of this text.

Technology can help integrate these strategic processes through the use of compatible, linked applications with automatic updates and sophisticated architecture that allows for multi-dimensional reporting, what-if analysis, and performance management. By sharing real-time transaction data, predictive models, and trend analysis across the organization, senior and departmental management can create a clear link among strategic objectives, operational plans, and personal performance goals.

A business plan requires a knowledgeable person to write the report. Since most entrepreneurs are doers rather than report writers, the preparation of the plan required to start, expand, or downsize will usually be done by someone with capabilities in both financial and business affairs, using a variety of expertise from others.

A business plan report begins with a table of contents and an executive summary. Next, the company must be described, along with its products or services and its marketing plan. Operational plans, along with management personnel and the organizational structure, will provide the substance for the financial resources needed to understand the detailed financial plans. Attachments will include competitive analysis, revenue and profit breakdowns by product and customer, and a variety of legal agreements such as contracts, patents, and confidentiality agreements for outsiders who have access to the details as a result of their study of the report.[3]

EXHIBIT 9–1 Flow Chart of the Steps in Developing a Business Plan

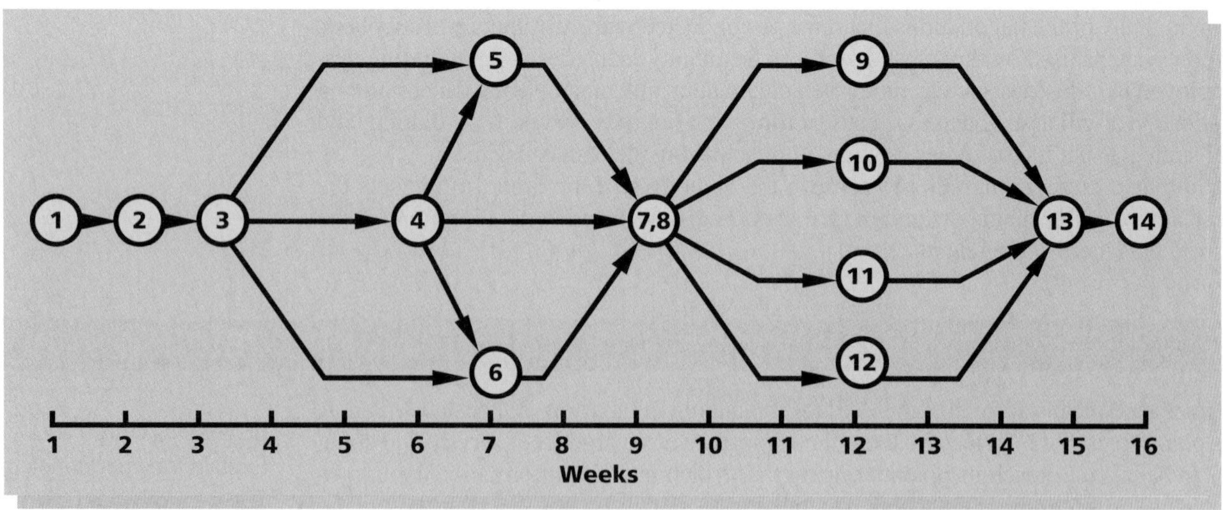

Key:
1. Decide to go into business.
2. Analyze yourself.
3. Pick product or service.
4. Research market.
5. Forecast sales revenues.
6. Pick site.
7. Develop production plan.
8. Develop marketing plan.
9. Develop personnel plan.
10. Decide whether to incorporate.
11. Explain need for records.
12. Develop insurance plan.
13. Develop financial plan.
14. Write summary overview.

3. Eric Siegel, Brian R. Ford, and Jay Bornstein, *The Ernst & Young Business Plan Guide,* 2nd ed. (Toronto, ON: John Wiley & Sons, Inc., 1993), provides a detailed description of the contents of a business plan, along with a specific example.

The focus of the remainder of this chapter will be on the financial plan portion of an established business. The discussion will provide a more complete financial plan than one associated with a new business, because existing assets, liabilities, and equities will be available to start the period. However, the procedures and principles of this chapter are relevant to the financial portion of a business plan. The aspects of a business plan that are omitted in the discussions that follow are nevertheless important as a foundation for the financial plans of both existing and new organizations. These details will of necessity have to be left for the reader to research.

FOCUS *on Current Practice*

BPM (Business Process Management) is a category of software that, according to Hyperion Company, enables companies to translate strategies into plans, monitor execution and provide insight to manage and improve financial and operational performance. Hyperion's BPM Suite delivers performance scorecarding, modelling, budgeting, planning and forecasting, consolidation and reporting, and business intelligence applications. Hyperion is targeted at companies with revenue greater than $100 million. Hyperion is fully compliant with U.S. GAAP, Canadian GAAP and international accounting standards. It is integrated with the leading ERP systems and includes validation controls in the extraction of data from source systems. Although Hyperion can't help eliminate internal control weaknesses in the source systems, it can be a big help in detecting and preventing control weaknesses once the consolidation process begins. However, its real advantage lies not in compliance but in improving financial and operational business processes so the right information is in the right hands when it's needed.

Source: Excerpted from Michael Burns, "Technology for 'Sarbanes-Oxley,'" *CA Magazine*, December 2003, vol. 136, iss. 10, p. 12. Reproduced by permission from *CA Magazine* produced by the Canadian Institute of Chartered Accountants, Toronto, Canada.

THE BASIC FRAMEWORK OF BUDGETING

Definition of Budgeting

A **budget** is a detailed plan for the acquisition and use of financial and other resources over a specified time period. It represents a plan for the future expressed in formal quantitative terms. The act of preparing a budget is called *budgeting*. The use of budgets to control a firm's activities is known as *budgetary control.*

Budget
A detailed plan for the acquisition and use of financial and other resources over a specified time period.

The **master budget** is a summary of a company's plans that sets specific targets for sales, production, distribution, and financing activities. It generally culminates in a cash budget, a budgeted income statement, and a budgeted balance sheet. In short, it represents a comprehensive expression of management's plans for the future and how these plans are to be accomplished.

Master budget
A summary of a company's plans in which specific targets are set for sales, production, distribution, and financing activities; generally culminates in a cash budget, budgeted income statement, and budgeted balance sheet.

Personal Budgets

Nearly everyone budgets to some extent. For example, people make estimates of their income and plan expenditures for food, clothing, housing, and daily life. As a result of this planning, people restrict their spending to some predetermined, allowable amount. While they may not be conscious of the fact, these people clearly go through a budgeting process. Income is estimated, expenditures are planned, and spending is restricted in accordance with the plan. Individuals also use budgets to forecast their future financial condition for purposes such as purchasing a home, financing college education, or setting aside funds for retirement. These budgets may exist only in the mind of the individual, but they are budgets nevertheless.

The budgets of a business or other organization serve much the same functions as the budgets prepared informally by individuals. Business budgets tend to be more detailed and to involve more work, but they are similar to the budgets prepared by individuals in most other respects. Like personal budgets, they assist in planning and controlling expenditures; they also assist in predicting operating results and financial condition in future periods.

Difference between Planning and Control

Planning
Developing objectives and preparing budgets to achieve these objectives.

Control
Those steps taken by management that attempt to increase the likelihood that the objectives set down at the planning stage are attained and to ensure that all parts of the organization function in a manner consistent with organizational policies.

The terms *planning* and *control* are often confused, and occasionally these terms are used in such a way as to suggest that they mean the same thing. Actually, planning and control are two quite distinct concepts. **Planning** involves developing objectives and preparing various budgets to achieve these objectives. **Control** involves the steps taken by management to increase the likelihood that the objectives set down at the planning stage are attained, and to ensure that all parts of the organization function in a manner consistent with organizational policies. To be completely effective, a good budgeting system must provide for *both* planning and control. Good planning without effective control is time wasted. On the other hand, unless plans are laid down in advance, there are no objectives toward which control can be directed.

Advantages of Budgeting

There is an old saying to the effect that "a man is usually down on what he isn't up on." Managers who have never tried budgeting are usually quick to state that budgeting is a waste of time. These managers may argue that even though budgeting may work well in *some* situations, it would never work well in their companies because operations are too complex or because there are too many uncertainties. These complexities and uncertainties provide one of the important justifications for budgeting: to analyze the situation on paper before consuming the resources necessary to try it in reality. Managers usually will have informal plans even before they become involved in writing their budgets. The difficulty they face is having a way of communicating their thoughts and plans to others, the only way their companies will ever attain the desired objectives.

Companies realize many benefits from a budgeting program including:

1. Budgets provide a means of *communicating* management's plans throughout the organization.
2. Budgets force managers to *think about* and plan for the future. Without a budget, managers' time would be consumed dealing with daily emergencies that might have been averted by the planning process. In the absence of the necessity to prepare a budget, too many managers would spend all of their time dealing with daily emergencies.
3. The budgeting process provides a means of *allocating resources* to those parts of the organization where they can be used most effectively.
4. The budgeting process can uncover potential **bottlenecks** before they occur.
5. Budgets *coordinate* the activities of the entire organization by *integrating* the plans of the various parts. Budgeting helps to ensure that everyone in the organization is pulling in the same direction.
6. Budgets define goals and objectives that can serve as *benchmarks* for evaluating subsequent performance.

Bottlenecks
The condition that retards or halts free movement in process.

In the past, some managers have avoided budgeting because of the time and effort involved in the budgeting process. It can be argued that budgeting is actually "free" in that the manager's time and effort are more than offset by greater profits. Moreover, with the advent of computer spreadsheet programs, *any* company—large or small—can implement and maintain a budgeting program at minimal cost. Budgeting lends itself well to readily available spreadsheet application programs.

Responsibility Accounting

Most of what we say in this chapter and in the next three chapters is concerned with *responsibility accounting*. The basic idea behind **responsibility accounting** is that a manager should be held responsible for those items—and *only* those items—that the manager can actually control to a significant extent. Each line item (i.e., revenue or cost) in the budget is made the responsibility of a manager, and that manager is held responsible for subsequent deviations between budgeted goals and actual results. In effect, responsibility accounting *personalizes* accounting information by looking at costs from a *personal control* standpoint. This concept is central to any effective profit planning and control system. Someone must be held responsible for each cost or else no one will be responsible, and the cost will inevitably grow out of control.

Responsibility accounting A system of accountability in which managers are held responsible for those items of revenue and cost—and *only* those items—over which the manager can exert significant control. The managers are held responsible for differences between budgeted and actual results.

Being held responsible for costs does not mean that the manager is penalized if the actual results do not measure up to the budgeted goals. However, the manager should take the initiative to correct any unfavourable discrepancies, should understand the source of significant favourable or unfavourable discrepancies, and should be prepared to explain the reasons for discrepancies to higher management. The point of an effective responsibility system is to make sure that nothing "falls through the cracks," that the organization reacts quickly and appropriately to deviations from its plans, and that the organization learns from the feedback it gets by comparing budgeted goals to actual results. The point is *not* to penalize individuals for missing targets.

Choosing a Budget Period

Operating budgets are ordinarily set to cover a one-year period. The one-year period should correspond to the company's fiscal year so that the budget figures can be compared with the actual results. Many companies divide their budget year into four quarters. The first quarter is then subdivided into months, and monthly budget figures are established. These near-term figures can often be established with considerable accuracy. The last three quarters are carried in the budget at quarterly totals only. As the year progresses, the figures for the second quarter are broken down into monthly amounts, then the third-quarter figures are broken down, and so forth. This approach has the advantage of requiring periodic review and reappraisal of budget data throughout the year.

Continuous or *perpetual budgets* are used by a significant number of organizations. A **continuous** or **perpetual budget** is a 12-month budget that rolls forward one month (or quarter) as the current month (or quarter) is completed. In other words, one month (or quarter) is added to the end of the budget as each month (or quarter) comes to a close. This approach keeps managers focused on the future at least one year ahead. Advocates of continuous budgets argue that with this approach there is less danger that managers will become too focused on short-term results as the year progresses.

Continuous or perpetual budget A 12-month budget that rolls forward one month as the current month is completed.

In this chapter, we will focus on one-year operating budgets. However, using basically the same techniques, operating budgets can be prepared for periods that extend over many years. It may be difficult to accurately forecast sales and required data much beyond a year, but even rough estimates can be invaluable in uncovering potential problems and opportunities that would otherwise be overlooked.

The Participative Budget

The success of a budget program will be determined in large part by the way in which the budget is developed. The most successful budget programs involve managers with cost control responsibilities in preparing their own budget estimates—rather than having a budget imposed from above. This approach to preparing budget data is particularly important if the budget is to be used to control and evaluate a manager's activities. If a budget is imposed on a manager from above, it may generate resentment and ill will rather than cooperation and increased productivity.

Participative budget A method of preparing budgets in which managers prepare their own budgets. These budgets are then reviewed by the manager's supervisor, and any issues are resolved by mutual agreement.

Self-imposed budget Same as *participative budget.*

A **participative budget** or **self-imposed budget** is a budget that is prepared with the full cooperation and participation of managers at all levels. Exhibit 9–2 illustrates this approach to budget preparation.

A number of advantages are commonly cited for such self-imposed budgets:

1. Individuals at all levels of the organization are recognized as members of the team whose views and judgements are valued by top management.
2. Budget estimates prepared by front-line managers are often more accurate and reliable than estimates prepared by top managers who have less intimate knowledge of market details and day-to-day operations.
3. Motivation is generally higher when individuals participate in setting their own goals than when the goals are imposed from above. Self-imposed budgets create commitment.
4. A manager who is not able to meet a budget that has been imposed from above can always say that the budget was unrealistic and impossible to meet. With a self-imposed budget, this excuse is not available.

Once self-imposed budgets are prepared, are they subject to any kind of review? The answer is yes. Budget estimates prepared by lower-level managers cannot necessarily be accepted without question by higher levels of management. If no system of checks and balances is present, self-imposed budgets may be too loose and allow too much "budgetary slack." The result will be inefficiency and waste. Therefore, before budgets are accepted, they must be carefully reviewed by immediate superiors. If changes from the original budget seem desirable, the items in question are discussed and modified as necessary by mutual consent.

In essence, all levels of an organization should work together to produce the budget. Since top management is generally unfamiliar with detailed, day-to-day operations, it should rely on subordinates to provide detailed budget information. On the other hand, top management has a perspective on the company as a whole that is vital in making broad policy decisions in budget preparation. Each level of responsibility in an organization should contribute in the way that it best can in a *cooperative* effort to develop an integrated budget document.

To be successful, a participative approach to setting budgets requires that all managers understand and agree with the organization's strategy. Otherwise, the budgets proposed by the lower-level managers will lack coherent direction. Differences in information can mean that different levels of managers do not operate consistently because they are working with different information. Certainly the individual managers can be expected to operate in a manner that optimizes their own interests, financial or otherwise.

An interesting, but unresolved, problem is how to design incentives to encourage subordinates to communicate accurate budget detail to top management. Subordinates can often control their own performance results by the nature of the budget information they feed through the system. This can be a problem for profit enterprises, not-for-profit enterprises, and government entities alike. Budgets can be used to set targets or quotas that in turn influence how top management allocates bonuses to managers and additional resources to the various units within the enterprise. Fundamentally, to provide incentives for a reward scheme, a designer needs to know what the alternative rewards will be from truthful forecasting rather than biased forecasting.[4] Unfortunately, these alternatives cannot be known beforehand, which is when the incentive scheme has to be set. Thus, to be effective, organizations must rely on a cooperative atmosphere among subordinates, not a competitive or self-serving one, and on the ability of top management to assess the reasonableness of forecasts obtained from subordinates.

4. Anthony A. Atkinson, "Truth-Inducing Schemes in Budgeting and Resource Allocation," *Cost and Management*, May–June, 1985, pp. 38–42. For a broader study of this issue, see Alan S. Dunk and Hossein Nouri, "Antecedents of Budgetary Slack: A Literature Review and Synthesis," *Journal of Accounting Literature*, 1998, pp. 72–96.

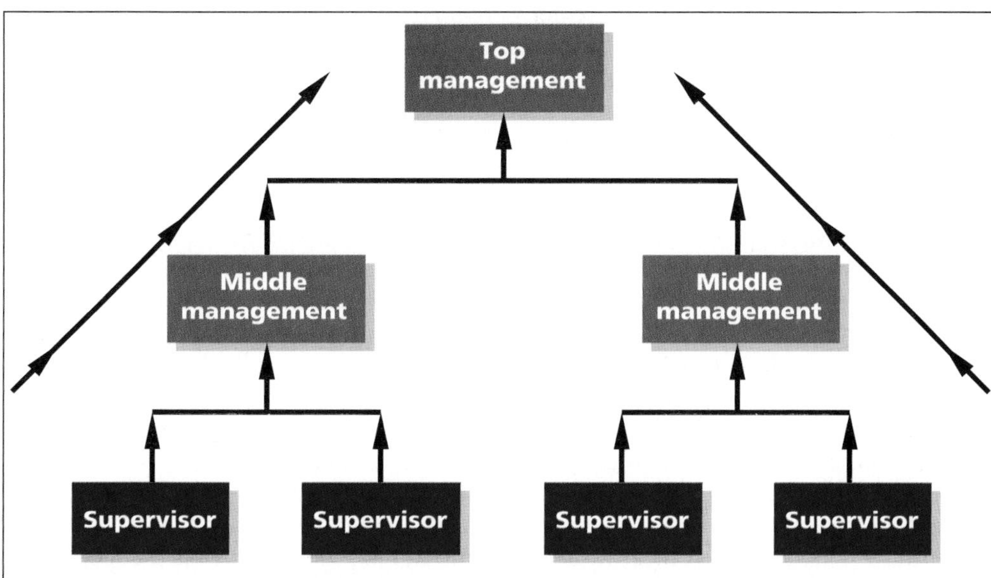

The initial flow of budget data in a participative system is from lower levels of responsibility to higher levels of responsibility. Each person with responsibility for cost control will prepare his or her own budget estimates and submit them to the next higher level of management. These estimates are reviewed and consolidated as they move upward in the organization.

EXHIBIT 9–2 The Initial Flow of Budget Data in a Participative Budgeting System

We have described an ideal budgetary process that involves self-imposed budgets prepared by the managers who are directly responsible for revenues and costs. Most companies deviate from this ideal. Typically, top managers initiate the budget process by issuing broad guidelines in terms of overall target profits or sales. Lower-level managers are directed to prepare budgets that meet those targets. The difficulty is that the targets set by top managers may be unrealistically high or may allow too much slack. If the targets are too high and employees know they are unrealistic, motivation will suffer. If the targets allow too much slack, waste will occur. Unfortunately, top managers are often not in a position to know whether the targets they have set are appropriate. Admittedly, however, in a pure participative budgeting system, lower-level managers may be tempted to build into their budgets a great deal of budgetary slack and there may be a lack of direction. Nevertheless, because of the motivational advantages of self-imposed budgets, top managers should be cautious about setting inflexible targets or otherwise imposing limits on the budgeting process.

The Matter of Human Relations

Whether or not a budget program is accepted by lower management personnel will be reflective of (1) the degree to which top management accepts the budget program as a vital part of the company's activities, and (2) the way in which top management uses budgeted data.

If a budget program is to be successful, it must have the complete acceptance and support of the persons who occupy key management positions. If lower or middle management personnel sense that top management is lukewarm about budgeting, or if they sense that top management simply tolerates budgeting as a necessary evil, then their own attitudes will reflect a similar lack of enthusiasm. Budgeting is hard work, and if top management is not enthusiastic about and committed to the budget program, then it is unlikely that anyone else in the organization will be either.

In administering the budget program, it is particularly important that top management not use the budget as a club to pressure employees or as a way to find someone to blame for a particular problem. This type of negative emphasis will simply breed hostility, tension, and mistrust rather than greater cooperation and productivity. Unfortunately, research suggests that the budget is often used as a pressure device and that great emphasis is placed on "meeting the budget" under all circumstances.

Management must recognize that the human aspects of budgeting are extremely important. It is easy to become preoccupied with the technical aspects of the budget to the exclusion of the human aspects. Indeed, the use of budget data in a rigid and inflexible manner is often the greatest single complaint of persons whose performance is evaluated using budgets. Management should remember that the purposes of the budget are to motivate employees and to coordinate their efforts. Preoccupation with cost reductions in the budget, or being rigid and inflexible is usually counterproductive and can lead to poor morale because people feel undervalued. An over-emphasis on cost reduction rather than value creation can lead to budget games by which managers skillfully time revenues, expenditures and investments. Administration of a budget program requires keen insight and sensitivity by management. An important objective is that the budget be designed as a positive aid in achieving both individual and company goals.

In establishing a budget, how challenging should budget targets be? If the targets are set too high, employees will know they are unrealistic and motivation will suffer. If the targets allow too much slack then waste will occur. Some experts argue that budget targets should be very challenging and should require managers to stretch to meet goals. Even the most capable managers may have to scramble to meet such a "stretch budget" and they may not always succeed. In practice, most companies set their budget targets at a "highly achievable" level. A highly achievable budget may be challenging, but it can almost always be met by competent managers exerting reasonable effort.

A 2001 study of the effect of fairness of imposed budgets examined the fairness of the budget target and the budget process on the performance of the budget recipient. When the target is deemed to be fair, the fairness of the budget process has no effect on performance. However, when the target is deemed to be unfair, then the fairness of the budget process is deemed to be important if the recipients of the budget are to be motivated to take efforts to reach the target. Thus, when a budget signals resource cutbacks that employees view as unfair, care must be taken to ensure that the budget implementation process is perceived as fair.[5]

Bonuses based on meeting and exceeding budgets are often an element of management compensation. Typically, no bonus is paid unless the budget is met. The bonus often increases when the budget target is exceeded, but the bonus is usually capped out at some level. For obvious reasons, managers who have such a bonus plan or whose performance is evaluated based on meeting budget targets usually prefer to be evaluated based on highly achievable budgets than on stretch budgets. Moreover, highly achievable budgets may help build a manager's confidence and generate greater commitment to the budget. And finally, highly achievable budgets may result in less undesirable behaviour at the end of budgetary periods by managers who are intent on earning their bonuses.

ZERO-BASE BUDGETING

In the traditional approach to budgeting, the manager starts with last year's budget and adds to it (or subtracts from it) according to anticipated needs. This is an incremental approach to budgeting in which the previous year's budget is taken for granted as a baseline.

Zero-base budgeting is an alternative approach that is sometimes used—particularly in the governmental and not-for-profit sectors of the economy. Under a **zero-base budget,** managers are required to justify *all* budgeted expenditures, not just changes in the budget from the previous year. The baseline is zero rather than last year's budget.

Zero-base budget
A method of budgeting in which managers are required to justify all costs as if the programs involved were being proposed for the first time.

5. Theresa Libby, "Reference Cognitions and Budgetary Fairness: A Research Note," *Journal of Management Accounting Research*, vol. 13, 2001, pp. 91–105.

A zero-base budget requires considerable documentation. In addition to all of the schedules in the usual master budget, the manager must prepare a series of "decision packages" in which all of the activities of the department are ranked according to their relative importance and the cost of each activity is identified. Higher-level managers can then review the decision packages and cut back in those areas that appear to be less critical or whose costs do not appear to be justified.

Nearly everyone would agree that zero-base budgeting is a good idea. The only issue is the frequency with which a zero-base review is carried out. Under zero-base budgeting, the review is performed every year. Critics of zero-base budgeting charge that properly executed zero-base budgeting is too time-consuming and too costly to justify on an annual basis. In addition, it is argued that annual reviews soon become mechanical and that the whole purpose of zero-base budgeting is then lost.

Whether or not a company should use an annual review is a matter of judgement. In some situations, annual zero-base reviews may be justified; in other situations, they may not because of the time and cost involved. However, most managers would at least agree that on occasion zero-base reviews can be very helpful.

The Budget Committee

A standing **budget committee** will usually be responsible for overall policy matters relating to the budget program and for coordinating the preparation of the budget itself. This committee generally consists of the president; vice presidents in charge of various functions such as sales, production, and purchasing; and the controller. Difficulties and disputes between segments of the organization in matters relating to the budget are resolved by the budget committee. In addition, the budget committee approves the final budget and receives periodic reports on the progress of the company in attaining budgeted goals.

Budget committee
A group of key management persons who are responsible for overall policy matters relating to the budget program and for coordinating the preparation of the budget.

Disputes can (and do) erupt over budget matters. Because budgets allocate resources, the budgeting process to a large extent determines which departments get more resources and which get relatively less. Also, the budget sets the benchmarks by which managers and their departments will be at least partially evaluated. Therefore, it should not be surprising that managers take the budgeting process very seriously and invest considerable energy and even emotion in ensuring that their interests, and those of their departments, are protected. Because of this, the budgeting process can easily degenerate into a dispute in which the ultimate goal of working together toward common goals is forgotten.

Running a successful budgeting program that avoids such disputes requires considerable interpersonal skills in addition to purely technical skills. But even the best interpersonal skills will fail if, as discussed earlier, top management uses the budget process inappropriately as a club or as a way to find blame.

THE MASTER BUDGET: AN OVERVIEW

The master budget consists of a number of separate but interdependent budgets. Exhibit 9–3 provides an overview of the various parts of the master budget and how they are related.

LEARNING OBJECTIVE 2
Prepare a sales budget, including a schedule of expected cash collections.

The Sales Budget A **sales budget** is a detailed schedule showing the expected sales for the budget period; typically, it is expressed in both dollars and units of product. An accurate sales budget is the key to the entire budgeting process. All of the other parts of the master budget are dependent on the sales budget in some way, as illustrated in Exhibit 9–3. Thus, if the sales budget is sloppily done, then the rest of the budgeting process is largely a waste of time.

Sales budget
A detailed schedule showing the expected sales for coming periods; these sales are typically expressed in both dollars and units.

The sales budget will help determine how many units will have to be produced. Thus, the production budget is prepared after the sales budget. The production budget in turn is used to determine the budgets for manufacturing costs including the direct materials budget, the direct labour budget, and the manufacturing overhead budget. These budgets are

EXHIBIT 9–3 The Master Budget Interrelationships

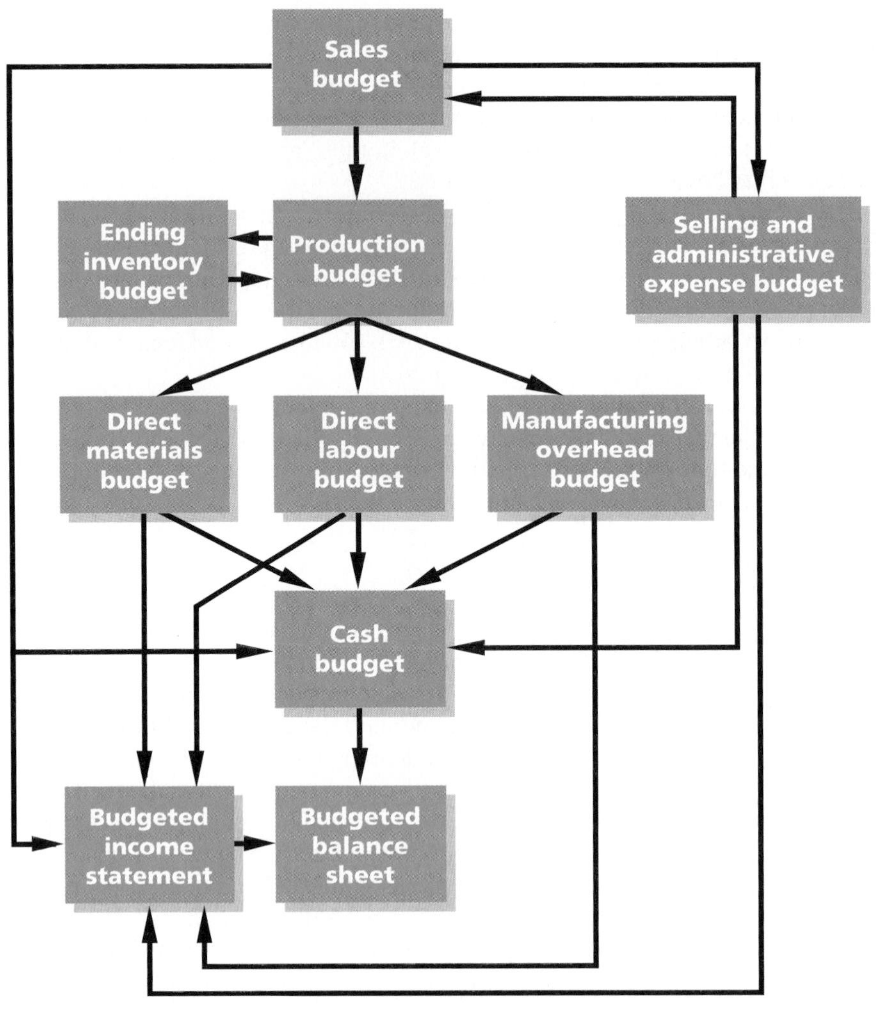

Source: Nicholas C. Siropolis, *Small Business Management: A Guide to Entrepreneurship,* Second Edition. Copyright © 1982 by Houghton Mifflin Company. Reprinted with permission.

then combined with data from the sales budget and the selling and administrative expense budget to determine the cash budget. In essence, the sales budget triggers a chain reaction that leads to the development of the other budgets.

As shown in Exhibit 9–3, the selling and administrative expense budget is both dependent on and a determinant of the sales budget. This reciprocal relationship arises because sales will in part be determined by the funds committed for advertising and sales promotion.

Cash budget
A detailed plan showing how cash resources will be acquired and used over some specific time period.

The Cash Budget Once the operating budgets (sales, production, and so on) have been established, the cash budget and other financial budgets can be prepared. A **cash budget** is a detailed plan showing how cash resources will be acquired and used over some specified time period. Observe from Exhibit 9–3 that all of the operating budgets have an impact on the cash budget. In the case of the sales budget, the impact comes from the planned cash receipts to be received from sales. In the case of the other budgets, the impact comes from the planned cash expenditures within the budgets themselves.

Sales Forecasting—A Critical Step

The sales budget is usually based on the company's *sales forecast.* Sales from prior years are commonly used as a starting point in preparing the sales forecast. In addition, the manager may examine the company's unfilled back orders, the company's pricing policy and marketing plans, trends in the industry, and general economic conditions. Sophisticated statistical tools may be used to analyze the data and to build models that are helpful in predicting key factors influencing the company's sales. The Focus on Current Practice feature below suggests how some companies are using computer simulations to enhance their marketing strategies and sales forecasts. We will not, however, go into the details of how sales forecasts are made.

Business intelligence is becoming an important means of gathering information for sales forecasting and cost estimation. For example, the Society of Competitive Intelligence Professionals, a U.S.-based group of 6,000 members, 100 of whom are in Québec, is used by Canadian companies such as Bell, the Royal Bank, Pratt and Whitney and Bombardier to gather information about competitors, opportunities, business practices, and personnel to better budget costs and sales.[6]

FOCUS on Current Practice

Borealis is a company headquartered in Copenhagen, Denmark, that produces polymers for the plastics industry. Thomas Boesen, the company's financial controller, felt that the traditional budgeting process has outlived its usefulness—markets were changing so fast that the budget was out of date within weeks of its publication. Moreover, since budgets were used to control and evaluate the performance of managers, they were subject to considerable gaming behaviour that reduced their accuracy and usefulness. So over a five-year period the company phased out its traditional budgets and replaced them with rolling forecasts and several other management tools. Instead of holding managers to a budget, targets based on competitors' performance were set for variable costs, fixed costs, and operating margins. Managers were given the freedom to spend money as needed to meet these competitive benchmarks. Since the rolling forecasts of financial results were not used to control spending or to evaluate managers' performance, managers had little incentive to "game the system," and hence the forecasts were more accurate than those obtained through the traditional budgeting process.

Source: Professor Bjorn Jorgensen, *Borealis*, Harvard Business School Case 9-102-048, Rev: May 9, 2002.

PREPARING THE MASTER BUDGET

MANAGERIAL ACCOUNTING IN ACTION

The Issue

Tom Wills is the majority shareholder and chief executive officer of Hampton Freeze, Inc., a company he started in 2005. The company makes premium popsicles using only natural ingredients and featuring exotic flavours such as tangy tangerine and minty mango. The company's business is highly seasonal, with most of the sales occurring in spring and summer.

In 2006, the company's second year of operations, there was a major cash crunch in the first and second quarters that almost forced the company into bankruptcy. In spite of this cash crunch, 2006 turned out to be overall a very successful year in terms of both cash flow and net income. Partly as a result of that harrowing experience, Tom decided toward the end of 2006 to hire a professional financial manager. Tom interviewed several promising candidates for the job and settled on Larry Giano, who had considerable experience in the packaged foods industry. In the job interview, Tom questioned Larry about the steps he would take to prevent a recurrence of the 2006 cash crunch:

6. Rene Lewandowski, "Corporate Confidential," *Financial Post Magazine,* March 1999, pp. 18–26. Also, a detailed discussion of this area of business intelligence gathering is provided in *Developing Comprehensive Competitive Intelligence*, *Management Accounting Guideline No. 39*, The Society of Management Accountants of Canada, 1996.

Tom: As I mentioned earlier, we are going to wind up 2006 with a very nice profit. What you may not know is that we had some very big financial problems this year.

Larry: Let me guess. You ran out of cash sometime in the first or second quarter.

Tom: How did you know?

Larry: Most of your sales are in the second and third quarter, right?

Tom: Sure, everyone wants to buy popsicles in the spring and summer, but nobody wants them when the weather turns cold.

Larry: So you don't have many sales in the first quarter?

Tom: Right.

Larry: And in the second quarter, which is the spring, you are producing like crazy to fill orders?

Tom: Sure.

Larry: Do your customers, the grocery stores, pay you the day that you make your deliveries?

Tom: Are you kidding? Of course not.

Larry: So in the first quarter, you don't have many sales. In the second quarter, you are producing like crazy, which eats up cash, but you aren't paid by your customers until long after you have paid your employees and suppliers. No wonder you had a cash problem. I see this pattern all the time in food processing because of the seasonality of the business.

Tom: So what can we do about it?

Larry: The first step is to predict the magnitude of the problem before it occurs. If we can predict early in the year what the cash shortfall is going to be, we can go to the bank and arrange for credit before we really need it. Bankers tend to be leery of panicky people who show up begging for emergency loans. They are much more likely to make the loan if you look like you know what you are doing, you have done your homework, and you are in control of the situation.

Tom: How can we predict the cash shortfall?

Larry: You can put together a cash budget. While you're at it, you might as well do a master budget. You'll find it is well worth the effort.

Tom: I don't like budgets. They are too confining. My wife budgets everything at home, and I can't spend what I want.

Larry: Can I ask a personal question?

Tom: What?

Larry: Where did you get the money to start this business?

Tom: Mainly from our family's savings. I get your point. We wouldn't have had the money to start the business if my wife hadn't been forcing us to save every month.

Larry: Exactly. I suggest you use the same discipline in your business. It is even more important here because you can't expect your employees to spend your money as carefully as you would.

Tom: I'm sold. Welcome aboard.

With the full backing of Tom Wills, Larry Giano set out to create a master budget for the company for the year 2007. In his planning for the budgeting process, Larry drew up the following list of documents that would be a part of the master budget:

1. A sales budget, including a schedule of expected cash collections.
2. A production budget (or merchandise purchases budget for a merchandising company).
3. A direct materials budget, including a schedule of expected cash disbursements for raw materials.
4. A direct labour budget.
5. A manufacturing overhead budget.
6. An ending finished goods inventory budget.
7. A selling and administrative expense budget.

8. A cash budget.
9. A budgeted income statement.
10. A budgeted balance sheet.

Larry felt it was important to get everyone's cooperation in the budgeting process, so he asked Tom to call a companywide meeting in which the budgeting process would be explained. At the meeting, there was initially some grumbling, but Tom was able to convince nearly everyone of the necessity for planning and getting better control over spending. It helped that the cash crisis earlier in the year was still fresh in everyone's minds. As much as some people disliked the idea of budgets, they liked their jobs even more.

In the months that followed, Larry worked closely with all of the managers involved in the master budget, gathering data from them and making sure that they understood and fully supported the parts of the master budget that would affect them. In subsequent years, Larry hoped to turn the whole budgeting process over to the managers and to take a more advisory role.

The interdependent documents that Larry Giano prepared for Hampton Freeze are Schedules 1 through 10 of his company's master budget. In this section, we will study these schedules.

The Sales Budget

The sales budget is the starting point in preparing the master budget. As shown earlier in Exhibit 9–3, all other items in the master budget, including production, purchases, inventories, and expenses, depend on it in some way.

The sales budget is constructed by multiplying the budgeted sales in units by the selling price. Schedule 1 on the next page contains the sales budget for Hampton Freeze for the year 2007, by quarters. Notice from the schedule that the company plans to sell 100,000 cases of popsicles during the year, with sales peaking in the third quarter.

A schedule of expected cash collections, such as the one that appears in Schedule 1 for Hampton Freeze, is prepared after the sales budget. This schedule will be needed later to prepare the cash budget. Cash collections consist of collections on sales made to customers in prior periods plus collections on sales made in the current budget period. At Hampton Freeze, experience has shown that 70% of sales is collected in the quarter in which the sale is made and the remaining 30% is collected in the following quarter. So, for example, 70% of the first quarter sales of $200,000 (or $140,000) is collected during the first quarter and 30% (or $60,000) is collected during the second quarter.

The Production Budget

LEARNING OBJECTIVE **3**
Prepare a production budget.

The production budget is prepared after the sales budget. The **production budget** lists the number of units that must be produced during each budget period to meet sales needs and to provide for the desired ending inventory. Production needs can be determined as follows:

Production budget
A detailed plan showing the number of units that must be produced during a period in order to meet both sales and inventory needs.

Budgeted sales in units	XXXX
Add desired ending inventory	XXXX
Total needs	XXXX
Less beginning inventory	XXXX
Required production	XXXX

Schedule 2, which appears on the next page, contains the production budget for Hampton Freeze.

Note that production requirements for a quarter are influenced by the desired level of the ending inventory. Inventories should be carefully planned. Excessive inventories tie up funds and create storage problems. Insufficient inventories can lead to lost sales or crash production efforts in the following period. At Hampton Freeze, management believes that an ending inventory equal to 20% of the next quarter's sales strikes the appropriate balance.

SCHEDULE 1

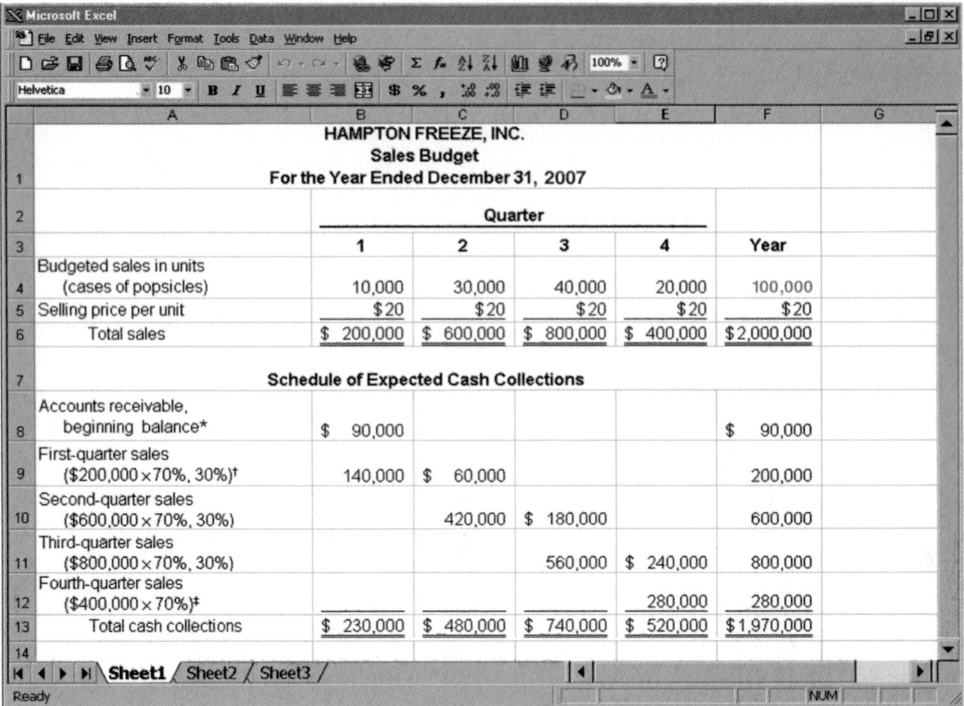

	Quarter 1	Quarter 2	Quarter 3	Quarter 4	Year
HAMPTON FREEZE, INC. Sales Budget For the Year Ended December 31, 2007					
Budgeted sales in units (cases of popsicles)	10,000	30,000	40,000	20,000	100,000
Selling price per unit	$20	$20	$20	$20	$20
Total sales	$ 200,000	$ 600,000	$ 800,000	$ 400,000	$2,000,000
Schedule of Expected Cash Collections					
Accounts receivable, beginning balance*	$ 90,000				$ 90,000
First-quarter sales ($200,000 × 70%, 30%)†	140,000	$ 60,000			200,000
Second-quarter sales ($600,000 × 70%, 30%)		420,000	$ 180,000		600,000
Third-quarter sales ($800,000 × 70%, 30%)			560,000	$ 240,000	800,000
Fourth-quarter sales ($400,000 × 70%)‡				280,000	280,000
Total cash collections	$ 230,000	$ 480,000	$ 740,000	$ 520,000	$1,970,000

*Cash collections from last year's fourth-quarter sales. See the beginning-of-year balance sheet on page 396.

†Cash collections from sales are as follows: 70% collected in the quarter of sale, and the remaining 30% collected in the following quarter.

‡Uncollected fourth-quarter sales appear as accounts receivable on the company's end-of-year balance sheet (see Schedule 10 on page 397).

SCHEDULE 2

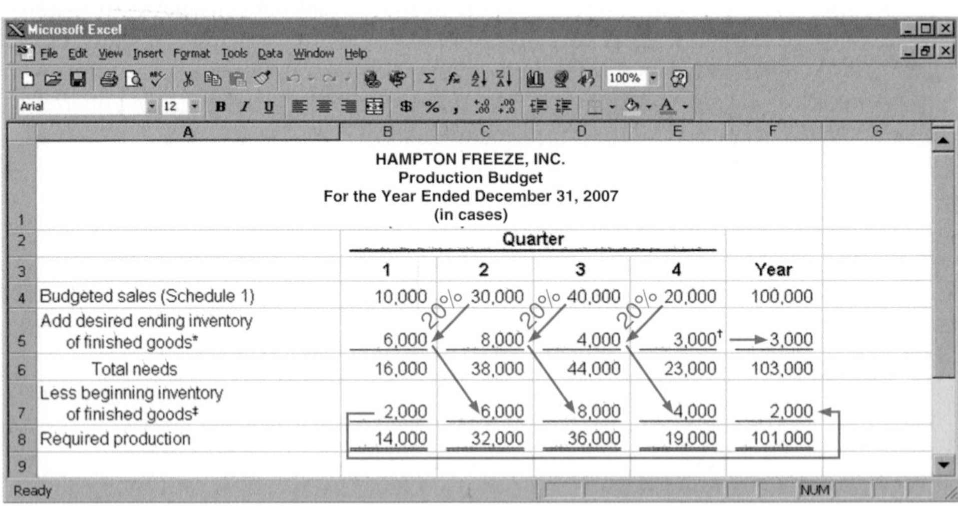

	Quarter 1	Quarter 2	Quarter 3	Quarter 4	Year
HAMPTON FREEZE, INC. Production Budget For the Year Ended December 31, 2007 (in cases)					
Budgeted sales (Schedule 1)	10,000	30,000	40,000	20,000	100,000
Add desired ending inventory of finished goods*	6,000	8,000	4,000	3,000†	3,000
Total needs	16,000	38,000	44,000	23,000	103,000
Less beginning inventory of finished goods‡	2,000	6,000	8,000	4,000	2,000
Required production	14,000	32,000	36,000	19,000	101,000

*Twenty percent of the next quarter's sales.

†Estimated.

‡The same as the prior quarter's *ending* inventory.

Merchandise purchases budget A budget used by a merchandising company that shows the amount of goods that must be purchased from suppliers during the period.

Inventory Purchases—Merchandising Firm

Hampton Freeze prepares a production budget, since it is a *manufacturing* firm. If it was a *merchandising* firm, then instead of a production budget, it would prepare a **merchandise purchases budget** showing the amount of goods to be purchased from its suppliers during the period. The merchandise purchases budget is in the same basic format as the production budget, except that it shows goods to be purchased rather than goods to be produced, as shown below:

Budgeted sales of goods sold (in units or in dollars)	XXXXX
Add desired ending merchandise inventory	XXXXX
Total needs	XXXXX
Less beginning merchandise inventory	XXXXX
Required purchases (in units or in dollars)	XXXXX

The merchandising firm would prepare a merchandise purchases budget such as the one above for each item carried in inventory. The merchandise purchases budget can be expressed in terms of either units or the purchase cost of those units. So, for example, the Budgeted sales shown in the above table can be expressed in terms of either the number of units sold or the purchase cost of the units sold. Some large retail organizations make such computations on a frequent basis (particularly at peak seasons) to ensure that adequate quantities are on hand to meet customer needs.

The Direct Materials Budget

LEARNING OBJECTIVE 4
Prepare a direct materials budget, including a schedule of expected cash disbursements for purchases of materials

Returning to Hampton Freeze's budget data, after the production requirements have been computed, a *direct materials budget* can be prepared. The **direct materials budget** details the raw materials that must be purchased to fulfil the production budget and to provide for adequate inventories. The required purchases of raw materials are computed as follows:

Raw materials needed to meet the production schedule	XXXXX
Add desired ending inventory of raw materials	XXXXX
Total raw materials needs	XXXXX
Less beginning inventory of raw materials	XXXXX
Raw materials to be purchased	XXXXX

Direct materials budget
A detailed plan showing the amount of raw materials that must be purchased during a period to meet both production and inventory needs.

Materials requirements planning (MRP)
An operations management tool that uses a computer to help manage materials and inventories.

Preparing a budget of this kind is one step in a company's overall **materials requirements planning (MRP).** MRP is an operations management tool that uses a computer to help manage materials and inventories. The objective of MRP is to ensure that the right materials are on hand, in the right quantities, and at the right time to support the production budget. The detailed operation of MRP is covered in most operations management books.

Schedule 3 on page 388 contains the direct materials budget for Hampton Freeze. The only raw material included in that budget is high fructose sugar, which is the major ingredient in popsicles other than water. The remaining raw materials are relatively insignificant and are included in variable manufacturing overhead. Notice that materials requirements are first determined in units (kilograms, litres, and so on) and then translated into dollars by multiplying by the appropriate unit cost. Also note that the management of Hampton Freeze desires to maintain ending inventories of sugar equal to 10% of the following quarter's production needs.

The first line in the direct materials budget contains the required production for each quarter, which is taken directly from the production budget (Schedule 2). Looking at the first quarter, since the production schedule calls for production of 14,000 cases of popsicles and each case requires 5 kilograms of sugar, the total production needs are 70,000 kilograms of sugar (14,000 cases × 5 kilograms per case). In addition, management wants to have ending inventories of 16,000 kilograms of sugar, which is 10% of the following quarter's needs of 160,000 kilograms. Consequently, the total needs are for 86,000 kilograms (70,000 kilograms for the current quarter's production plus 16,000 kilograms

SCHEDULE 3

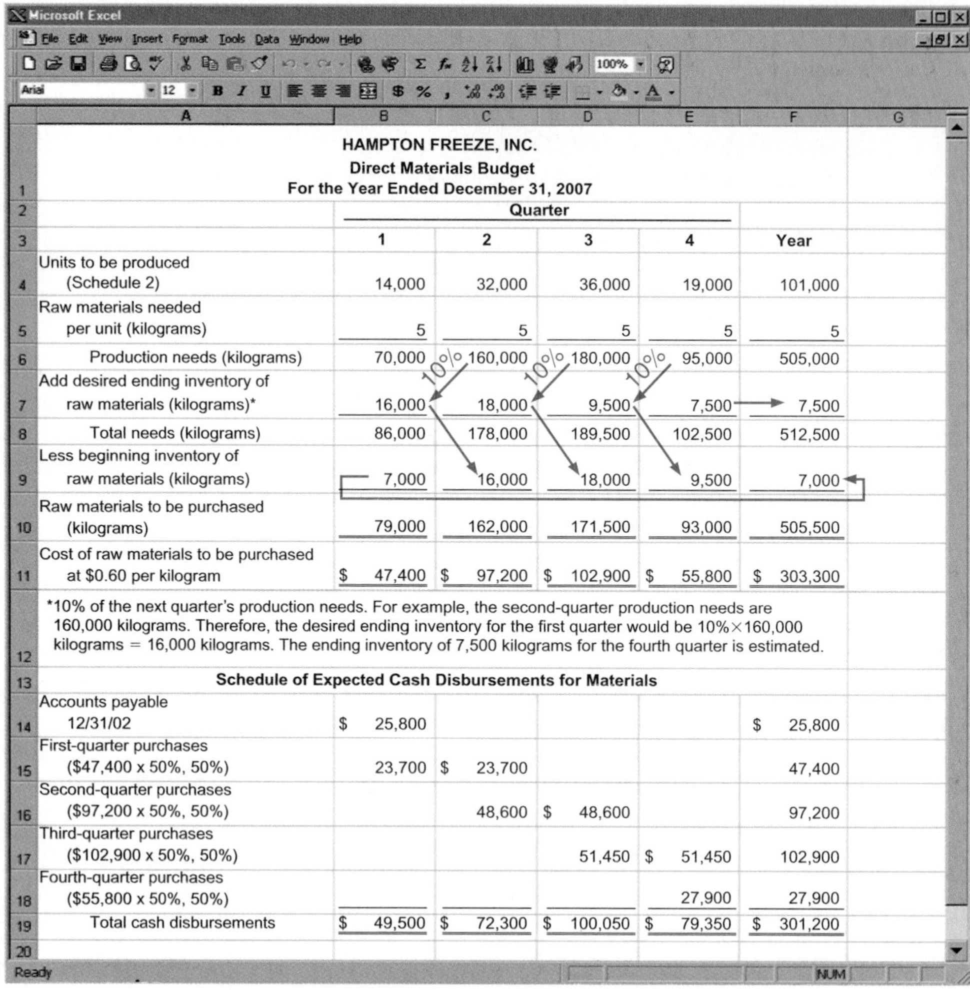

HAMPTON FREEZE, INC.
Direct Materials Budget
For the Year Ended December 31, 2007

	Quarter 1	Quarter 2	Quarter 3	Quarter 4	Year
Units to be produced (Schedule 2)	14,000	32,000	36,000	19,000	101,000
Raw materials needed per unit (kilograms)	5	5	5	5	5
Production needs (kilograms)	70,000	160,000	180,000	95,000	505,000
Add desired ending inventory of raw materials (kilograms)*	16,000	18,000	9,500	7,500	7,500
Total needs (kilograms)	86,000	178,000	189,500	102,500	512,500
Less beginning inventory of raw materials (kilograms)	7,000	16,000	18,000	9,500	7,000
Raw materials to be purchased (kilograms)	79,000	162,000	171,500	93,000	505,500
Cost of raw materials to be purchased at $0.60 per kilogram	$ 47,400	$ 97,200	$ 102,900	$ 55,800	$ 303,300

*10% of the next quarter's production needs. For example, the second-quarter production needs are 160,000 kilograms. Therefore, the desired ending inventory for the first quarter would be 10% × 160,000 kilograms = 16,000 kilograms. The ending inventory of 7,500 kilograms for the fourth quarter is estimated.

Schedule of Expected Cash Disbursements for Materials

	Quarter 1	Quarter 2	Quarter 3	Quarter 4	Year
Accounts payable 12/31/02	$ 25,800				$ 25,800
First-quarter purchases ($47,400 x 50%, 50%)	23,700	$ 23,700			47,400
Second-quarter purchases ($97,200 x 50%, 50%)		48,600	$ 48,600		97,200
Third-quarter purchases ($102,900 x 50%, 50%)			51,450	$ 51,450	102,900
Fourth-quarter purchases ($55,800 x 50%, 50%)				27,900	27,900
Total cash disbursements	$ 49,500	$ 72,300	$ 100,050	$ 79,350	$ 301,200

for the desired ending inventory). However, since the company already has 7,000 kilograms in beginning inventory, only 79,000 kilograms of sugar (86,000 kilograms – 7,000 kilograms) will need to be purchased. Finally, the cost of the raw materials purchased is determined by multiplying the amount of raw material to be purchased by the cost per unit of the raw material. In this case, since 79,000 kilograms of sugar will have to be purchased during the first quarter and sugar costs $0.60 per kilogram, the total cost will be $47,400 (79,000 kilograms × $0.60 per kilogram).

As with the production budget, the amounts listed under the Year column are not always the sum of the quarterly amounts. The desired ending inventory of raw materials for the year is the same as the desired ending inventory of raw materials for the fourth quarter. Likewise, the beginning inventory of raw materials for the year is the same as the beginning inventory of raw materials for the first quarter

The direct materials budget is usually accompanied by a schedule of expected cash disbursements for raw materials. This schedule is needed to prepare the overall cash budget. Disbursements for raw materials consist of payments for purchases on account in prior periods plus any payments for purchases in the current budget period. Schedule 3 contains such a schedule of cash disbursements.

Ordinarily, companies do not immediately pay their suppliers. At Hampton Freeze, the policy is to pay for 50% of purchases in the quarter in which the purchase is made and 50% in the following quarter, so while the company intends to purchase $47,400 worth of sugar in the first quarter, the company will only pay for half, $23,700, in the first quarter and the other half will be paid in the second quarter. The company will also pay $25,800 in the first quarter for sugar that was purchased on account in the previous quarter, but not yet paid for. This is the beginning balance in the accounts payable. Therefore, the total cash disbursements for sugar in the first quarter are $49,500 – the $25,800 payment for sugar acquired in the previous quarter plus the $23,700 payment for sugar acquired during the first quarter.

Inventory planning involves a series of questions, such as when to order, how much to order, and how much "safety" stock to carry. Three types of costs are associated with these decisions: ordering costs, carrying costs, and the cost of insufficient inventory. Essentially, the decision analysis determines the level of inventory that minimizes these three costs.

Economic order quantity (EOQ) and production lot sizes, safety stock, and reorder points are a major aspect of the study of operations management. Extensive discussions of various situations can be found by referring to operations management textbooks.[7] In addition, enterprise resource planning software programs such as SAP contain significant inventory management routines.

The Direct Labour Budget

LEARNING OBJECTIVE 5
Prepare a direct labour budget.

Direct labour budget
A detailed plan showing labour requirements over some specific time period.

The **direct labour budget** is also developed from the production budget. Direct labour requirements must be computed so that the company will know whether sufficient labour time is available to meet production needs. By knowing in advance just what will be needed in the way of labour time throughout the budget year, the company can develop plans to adjust the labour force as the situation may require. Firms that neglect to budget run the risk of facing labour shortages or having to hire and lay off at awkward times. Erratic labour policies lead to insecurity and inefficiency on the part of employees.

To compute direct labour requirements, the number of units of finished product to be produced each period (month, quarter, and so on) is multiplied by the number of direct labour-hours required to produce a single unit. Many different types of labour may be involved. If so, then computations should be by type of labour needed. The direct labour requirements can then be translated into expected direct labour costs. How this is done will depend on the labour policy of the firm. In Schedule 4 on page 390, the management of Hampton Freeze has assumed that the direct labour force will be adjusted as the work requirements change from quarter to quarter. In that case, the total direct labour cost is computed by simply multiplying the direct labour-hour requirements by the direct labour rate per hour. For example, 14,000 cases to be produced in the first quarter and each case requires 0.40 direct labour-hours, so a total of 5,600 direct labour-hours (14,000 cases × 0.40 direct labour-hours per case) will be required in the first quarter. The direct labour-hour requirement can then be translated into budgeted direct labour costs by multiplying the direct labour-hour requirement by the direct labour rate per hour. For example, the direct labour cost in the first quarter is $84,000 (5,600 direct labour-hours × $15 per direct labour-hour).

However, many companies have employment policies or contracts that prevent them from laying off and rehiring workers as needed. Suppose, for example, that Hampton Freeze has 25 workers who are classified as direct labour and each of them is guaranteed at least 480 hours of pay each quarter at a rate of $15 per hour. In that case, the minimum direct labour cost for a quarter would be as follows:

$$25 \text{ workers} \times 480 \text{ hours} \times \$15 = \$180,000$$

Note that in Schedule 4, the direct labour costs for the first and fourth quarters would have to be increased to a $180,000 level if Hampton Freeze's labour policy did not allow it to adjust the workforce at will.

7. Richard B. Chase, Nicholas J. Aquilano, and F. Robert Jacobs, *Operations Management for Competitive Advantage*, 9th ed. (New York, NY: McGraw-Hill Irwin, 2001), Chapter 13, and William J. Stevenson, *Operations Management*, 7th ed. (New York, NY: McGraw-Hill Irwin, 2002), Chapter 13.

SCHEDULE 4

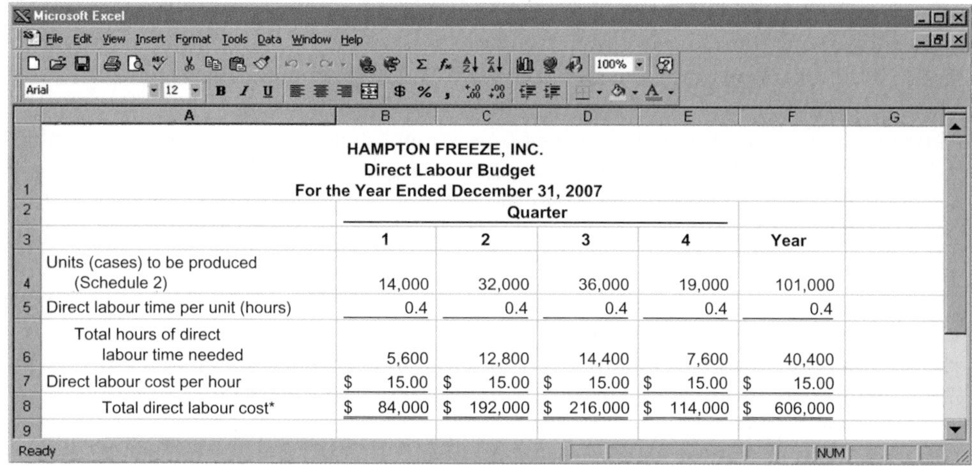

HAMPTON FREEZE, INC.
Direct Labour Budget
For the Year Ended December 31, 2007

	Quarter				
	1	2	3	4	Year
Units (cases) to be produced (Schedule 2)	14,000	32,000	36,000	19,000	101,000
Direct labour time per unit (hours)	0.4	0.4	0.4	0.4	0.4
Total hours of direct labour time needed	5,600	12,800	14,400	7,600	40,400
Direct labour cost per hour	$ 15.00	$ 15.00	$ 15.00	$ 15.00	$ 15.00
Total direct labour cost*	$ 84,000	$ 192,000	$ 216,000	$ 114,000	$ 606,000

*This schedule assumes that the direct labour workforce will be fully adjusted to the workload (i.e., "Total hours of direct labour time needed") each quarter.

FOCUS *on Current Practice*

A manager's compensation is often tied to the budget. Typically, no bonus is paid unless a minimum performance hurdle such as 80% of the budget target is attained. Once that hurdle is passed, the manager's bonus increases until a cap is reached. That cap is often set at 120% of the budget target.

This common method of tying a manager's compensation to the budget has some serious negative side effects. For example, a marketing manager for a big beverage company intentionally grossly understated demand for the company's products for an upcoming major holiday so that the budget target for revenues would be low and easy to beat. Unfortunately, the company tied its production to this biased forecast and ran out of products to sell during the height of the holiday selling season.

As another example, near the end of the year another group of managers announced a price increase of 10% effective January 2 of the following year. Why would they do this? By announcing this price increase, managers hoped that customers would order before year end, helping managers meet their sales targets for the current year. Sales in the following year would, of course, drop. What trick would managers pull to meet their sales targets next year in the face of this drop in demand?

Sources: Michael C. Jensen, "Corporate Budgeting is Broken—Let's Fix it," *Harvard Business Review,* November, 2001; and Michael C. Jensen, "Why Pay People to Lie?" *The Wall Street Journal,* January 8, 2001, p. A32.

The Manufacturing Overhead Budget

LEARNING OBJECTIVE **6**
Prepare a manufacturing overhead budget.

Manufacturing overhead budget A detailed plan showing the production costs, other than direct materials and direct labour, that will be incurred over a specified time period.

The **manufacturing overhead budget** provides a schedule of all costs of production other than direct materials and direct labour. Schedule 5 shows the manufacturing overhead budget for Hampton Freeze. Note how the production costs are separated into variable and fixed components. The variable component is $4 per direct labour-hour. The fixed component is $60,600 per quarter. Because the variable component of the manufacturing overhead depends on direct labour, the first line in the manufacturing overhead budget consists of the budgeted direct labour-hours from the direct labour budget (Schedule 4). The budgeted direct labour-hours in each quarter are multiplied by the variable overhead rate to determine the variable component of manufacturing overhead. For example, the variable manufacturing overhead for the first quarter is $22,400 (5,600 direct labour-hours × $4.00 per direct labour-hour). This is added to the fixed manufacturing

SCHEDULE 5

		Quarter				
	A	B	C	D	E	F
1	HAMPTON FREEZE, INC.					
2	Manufacturing Overhead Budget					
3	For the Year Ended December 31,					
6		1	2	3	4	Year
7	Budgeted direct labour-hours (Schedule 4)	5,600	12,800	14,400	7,600	40,400
8	Variable overhead rate	$ 4.00	$ 4.00	$ 4.00	$ 4.00	$ 4.00
9	Variable manufacturing overhead	$ 22,400	$ 51,200	$ 57,600	$ 30,400	$ 161,600
10	Fixed manufacturing overhead	60,600	60,600	60,600	60,600	242,400
11	Total manufacturing overhead	83,000	111,800	118,200	91,000	404,000
12	Less depreciation	15,000	15,000	15,000	15,000	60,000
13	Cash disbursements for manufacturing overhead	$ 68,000	$ 96,800	$ 103,200	$ 76,000	$ 344,000
15	Total manufacturing overhead (a)					$ 404,000
16	Budgeted direct labour-hours (b)					40,400
17	Predetermined overhead rate for the year (a)÷(b)					$ 10.00

overhead for the quarter to determine the total manufacturing overhead for the quarter. For example, the total manufacturing overhead for the first quarter is $83,000 ($22,400 + $60,600).

In most cases, fixed costs are the costs of supplying capacity to do things like make products, process purchase orders, handle customer calls, and so on. The amount of capacity that will be required depends on the expected level of activity for the period. If the expected level of activity is greater than the company's current capacity, then fixed costs may have to be increased. Or, if the expected level is appreciably below the company's current capacity, then it may be desirable to decrease fixed costs if that is possible. However, once the level of fixed costs has been determined in the budget, the costs really are fixed. The time to adjust fixed costs is during the budgeting process. To determine the appropriate level of fixed costs at budget time, an activity-based costing system can be very helpful. It can help answer questions like, "How many clerks will we need to hire to process the anticipated number of purchase orders next year?" For simplicity, we assume in all of the budgeting examples in this book that the appropriate levels of fixed costs have already been determined for the budget with the aid of activity-based costing or some other method.

The last line of Schedule 5 for Hampton Freeze shows its budgeted cash disbursements for manufacturing overhead. Since some of the overhead costs are not cash outflows, the total budgeted manufacturing overhead costs must be adjusted to determine the cash disbursements for manufacturing overhead. At Hampton Freeze, the only significant non-cash manufacturing overhead cost is depreciation, which is $15,000 per quarter. These non-cash depreciation charges are deducted from the total budgeted manufacturing overhead to determine the expected cash disbursements. Hampton Freeze pays all overhead costs involving cash disbursements in the quarter incurred. Note that the company's predetermined overhead rate for the year will be $10 per direct labour-hour, which is determined by dividing the total budgeted manufacturing overhead for the year by the total budgeted direct labour-hours for the year.

The Ending Finished Goods Inventory Budget

After completing Schedules 1–5, Larry Giano had all of the data he needed to compute unit product costs. This computation was needed for two reasons: first, to determine cost of goods sold on the budgeted income statement and second, to identify the amount to put on the balance sheet inventory account for unsold units. The carrying cost of the unsold units is computed on the **ending finished goods inventory budget.**

Ending finished goods inventory budget
A budget showing the dollar amount of cost expected to appear on the balance sheet for unsold units at the end of a period.

Larry Giano considered using variable costing in preparing Hampton Freeze's budget statements, but he decided to use absorption costing instead since the bank would very likely require that absorption costing be used. He also knew that it would be easy to convert the absorption costing financial statements to a variable costing basis later. At this point, the primary concern was to determine what financing, if any, would be required in the year 2007 and then to arrange for that financing from the bank.

The unit product cost computations are shown in Schedule 6. For Hampton Freeze, the absorption costing unit product cost is $13 per case of popsicles—consisting of $3 of direct materials, $6 of direct labour, and $4 of manufacturing overhead. For convenience, the manufacturing overhead is applied to units of product on the basis of direct labour-hours. The budgeted carrying cost of the expected ending inventory is $39,000.

The Selling and Administrative Expense Budget

LEARNING OBJECTIVE 7
Prepare a selling and administrative expense budget.

Selling and administrative expense budget
A detailed schedule of planned expenses that will be incurred in areas other than manufacturing during a budget period.

The **selling and administrative expense budget** lists the budgeted expenses for areas other than manufacturing. In large organizations, this budget would be a compilation of many smaller, individual budgets submitted by department heads and other persons responsible for selling and administrative expenses. For example, the marketing manager in a large organization would submit a budget detailing the advertising expenses for each budget period.

Schedule 7 contains the selling and administrative expense budget for Hampton Freeze. Like the manufacturing overhead budget, the selling and administrative expense budget is divided into variable and fixed cost components. For Hampton Freeze, the variable selling and administrative expense is $1.80 per case. Consequently, budgeted sales in cases for each quarter are entered at the top of the schedule. These data are taken from the sales budget (Schedule 1). The budgeted variable selling and administrative expenses are determined by multiplying the budgeted cases sold by the variable selling and administrative expense per case. For example, the budgeted variable selling and administrative expense for the first quarter is $18,000 (10,000 cases × $1.80 per case). The fixed selling and administrative expenses (all given data) are then added to the variable selling and administrative expenses to arrive at the total budgeted selling and administrative expenses. Finally, to determine the cash disbursements for selling and administrative items, the total budgeted selling and administrative expense is adjusted by subtracting any non-cash selling and administrative expenses (in this case, only depreciation).

The Cash Budget

LEARNING OBJECTIVE 8
Prepare a cash budget.

As illustrated in Exhibit 9–3 on page 382, the cash budget pulls together much of the data developed in the preceding steps. It is a good idea to restudy Exhibit 9–3 to get the big picture firmly in mind before moving on.

SCHEDULE 6

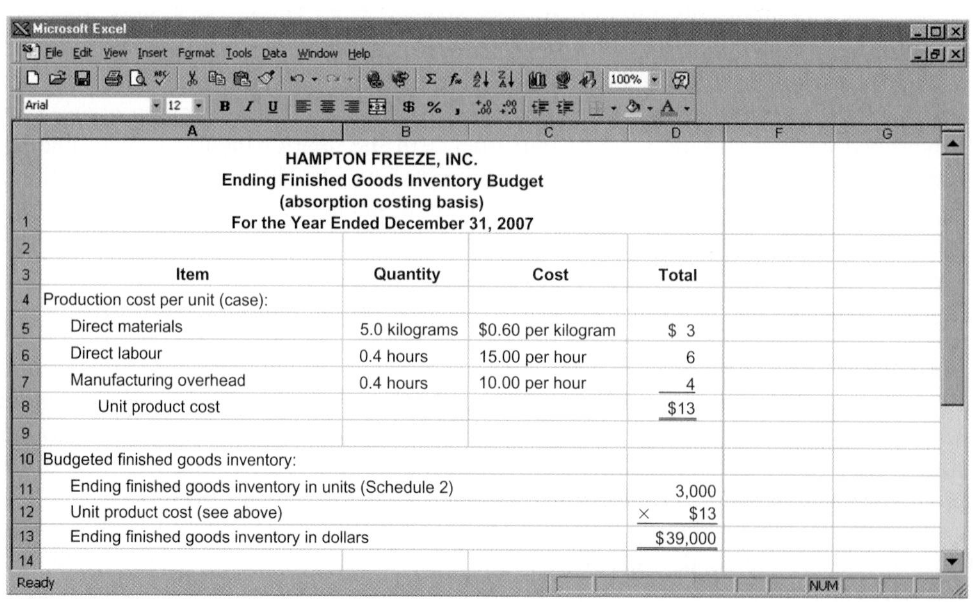

HAMPTON FREEZE, INC.
Ending Finished Goods Inventory Budget
(absorption costing basis)
For the Year Ended December 31, 2007

Item	Quantity	Cost	Total
Production cost per unit (case):			
Direct materials	5.0 kilograms	$0.60 per kilogram	$ 3
Direct labour	0.4 hours	15.00 per hour	6
Manufacturing overhead	0.4 hours	10.00 per hour	4
Unit product cost			$13
Budgeted finished goods inventory:			
Ending finished goods inventory in units (Schedule 2)			3,000
Unit product cost (see above)			× $13
Ending finished goods inventory in dollars			$39,000

SCHEDULE 7

	HAMPTON FREEZE				
	Selling and Administrative Expense Budget				
	For the Year Ended December 31, 2007				
			Quarter		
	1	**2**	**3**	**4**	**Year**
Budgeted sales in cases (Schedule 1)	10000	30000	40000	20000	100000
Variable selling and administrative expenses per case *	$1.80	$1.80	$1.80	$1.80	$1.80
Budgeted variable expense	$18,000	$54,000	$72,000	$36,000	$180,000
Budgeted fixed selling and administrative expenses					
Advertising	40000	40000	40000	40000	160000
Executive salaries	35000	35000	35000	35000	140000
Insurance	9912	9912	9912	9912	39648
Property taxes	4538	4538	4538	4538	18152
Depreciation	2000	2000	2000	2000	8000
Total budgeted fixed selling and administrative expenses	91450	91450	91450	91450	365800
Total budgeted selling and administrative expenses	109450	145450	163450	127450	545800
Less depreciation	(2,000)	(2,000)	(2,000)	(2,000)	(8,000)
less insurance expense	(9,912)	(9,912)	(9,912)	(9,912)	(39,648)
add insurance paid		1900	37750		39650
less property tax expense	(4,538)	(4,538)	(4,538)	(4,538)	(18,152)
add property tax paid				18150	18150
Cash disbursements for selling and administrative expenses	$93,000.00	$130,900.00	$184,750.00	$129,150.00	$537,800.00

*Commissions, clerical, and shipping.

The cash budget is composed of four major sections:

1. Receipts section.
2. Disbursements section
3. Cash excess or deficiency section.
4. Financing section.

The receipts section consists of a listing of all of the cash inflows, except for financing, expected during the budget period. Generally, the major source of receipts will be from sales.

The disbursements section consists of all cash payments that are planned for the budget period. These payments will include raw materials purchases, direct labour payments, manufacturing overhead costs, and so on, as contained in their respective budgets. In addition, other cash disbursements, such as equipment purchases, dividends, and other cash withdrawals by owners, are listed.

The cash excess or deficiency section is computed as follows:

Cash balance, beginning	XXXX
Add receipts	XXXX
Total cash available before financing	XXXX
Less disbursements	XXXX
Excess (deficiency) of cash available over disbursements	XXXX

If there is a cash deficiency during any budget period, the company will need to borrow funds. If there is a cash excess during any budget period, funds borrowed in previous periods can be repaid or the idle funds can be placed in short-term or other investments.

The financing section provides a detailed account of the borrowings and repayments projected to take place during the budget period. It also includes detail of interest payments that will be due on money borrowed. Banks are becoming increasingly insistent that firms in need of borrowed money give long advance notice of the amounts and times that funds will be needed. This permits the banks to plan and helps to assure that funds will be ready when needed. Moreover, careful planning of cash needs via the budgeting process avoids unpleasant surprises for companies as well. Few things are more disquieting to an organization than to run into unexpected difficulties in the Cash account. A well-coordinated budgeting program eliminates uncertainty as to what the cash situation will be in two months, six months, or a year from now.

Generally speaking, the cash budget should be broken down into time periods that are as short as feasible. There can be considerable fluctuations in cash balances that would be hidden by looking at a longer time period. While a monthly cash budget is most common, many firms budget cash on a weekly or even daily basis. Larry Giano has prepared a quarterly cash budget for Hampton Freeze that can be further refined as necessary. This budget appears in Schedule 8. The cash budget builds on the earlier schedules and on additional data that are provided as follows:

- The beginning cash balance is $42,500.
- Management plans to spend $50,000 during the year on equipment purchases: $30,000 in the first quarter and $20,000 in the second quarter.
- The board of directors has approved cash dividends of $17,500 per quarter.
- Management would like to have a cash balance of at least $40,000 at the beginning of each quarter for contingencies.

SCHEDULE 8

HAMPTON FREEZE, INC.
Cash Budget
For the Year Ended December 31, 2007

	Schedule	Quarter 1	Quarter 2	Quarter 3	Quarter 4	Year
Cash balance, beginning		$42,500	$40,000	$40,000	$40,500	$42,500
Add receipts:						
Collections from customers	1	230,000	480,000	740,000	520,000	1,970,000
Total cash available before current financing		272,500	520,000	780,000	560,500	2,012,500
Less disbursements:						
Direct materials	3	49,500	72,300	100,050	79,350	301,200
Direct labour	4	84,000	192,000	216,000	114,000	606,000
Manufacturing overhead	5	68,000	96,800	103,200	76,000	344,000
Selling and administrative*	7	93,000	130,900	184,750	129,150	537,800
Income taxes	9	10,500	10,500	10,500	10,500	42,000
Equipment purchases		30,000	20,000	—	—	50,000
Dividends*		17,500	17,500	17,500	17,500	70,000
Total disbursements		352,500	540,000	632,000	426,500	1,951,000
Excess (deficiency) of cash available over disbursements		(80,000)	(20,000)	148,000	134,000	61,500
Financing:						
Borrowings (at beginning)		120,000	60,000	—	—	180,000
Repayments (at ending)		—	—	(100,000)	(80,000)	(180,000)
Interest (at 10% per annum)†		—	—	(7,500)†	(6,500)†	(14,000)
Total financing		120,000	60,000	(107,500)	(86,500)	(14,000)
Cash balance, ending		$40,000	$40,000	$40,500	$47,500	$47,500

†The interest payments relate only to the principal being repaid at the time it is repaid. For example, the interest in quarter 3 relates only to the interest due on the $100,000 principal being repaid from quarter 1 borrowing, as follows: $100,000 × 10% × ¾ = $7,500. The interest paid in quarter 4 is computed as follows:

$20,000 × 10% × 1 year	$2,000
$60,000 × 10% × ¾	4,500
Total interest paid	$6,500

- Hampton Freeze has an open line of credit with a bank that enables the company to borrow at a 10% interest rate per year. All borrowing and repayments are in round $1,000 amounts. All borrowing would occur at the beginning of quarters and all repayments would be made at the end of quarters. Interest would be due when repayments are made and only on the amount of principal that is repaid.

The cash budget is prepared one quarter at a time, starting with the first quarter. Larry began the cash budget by entering the beginning cash balance of $42,500 for the first quarter. Receipts—in this case, just the $230,000 in cash collections from customers — are added to the beginning balance to arrive at the total cash available of $272,500. Since the total disbursements are $352,500 and the total cash available is only $272,500, there is a shortfall of $80,000. Since management would like to have a beginning cash balance of at least $40,000 for the second quarter, the company will need to borrow $120,000.

Required Borrowings at the End of the First Quarter	
Desired ending cash balance	$40,000
Plus deficiency of cash available over disbursements	80,000
Required borrowings	$120,000

The second quarter of the cash budget is handled similarly. Note that the ending cash balance for the first quarter is brought forward as the beginning cash balance for the second quarter. Also note that additional borrowing is required in the second quarter because of the continued cash shortfall.

Required Borrowings at the End of the Second Quarter	
Desired ending cash balance	$40,000
Plus deficiency of cash available over disbursements	20,000
Required borrowings	$60,000

In the third quarter, the cash flow situation improves dramatically and the excess of cash available over disbursements is $148,000. This makes it possible for the company to repay part of its loan from the bank, which now totals $180,000. How much can be repaid? The total amount of the principal and interest that can be repaid is determined as follows:

Total Maximum Feasible Loan Payments at the End of the Third Quarter	
Excess of cash available over disbursements	$148,000
Less desired ending cash balance	40,000
Maximum feasible principal and interest payment	$108,000

The next step—figuring out the exact amount of the loan payment – is tricky since interest must be paid on the principal amount that is repaid. In this case, the principal amount that is repaid must be less than $108,000, so we know that we would be paying off part of the loan that was taken out at the beginning of the first quarter. Since the repayment would be made at the end of the third quarter, interest would have accrued for three quarters. So the interest owed would be ¾ of 10%, or 7.5%. Either a trial-and-error or an algebraic approach will lead to the conclusion that the maximum principal repayment that can be made is $100,000. The interest payment would be 7.5% of this amount, or $7,500—making the total payment $107,500.

In the case of Hampton Freeze, all loans have been repaid by year-end. If all loans are not repaid and a budgeted income statement or balance sheet is being prepared, then interest must be accrued on the unpaid loans. This interest will *not* appear on the cash budget (since it has not yet been paid), but it will appear as part of interest expense on the budgeted income statement and as a liability on the budgeted balance sheet.

As with the production and raw materials budgets, the amounts under the Year column in the cash budget are not always the sum of the amounts for the four quarters. In particular, the beginning cash balance for the year is the same as the beginning cash balance for the first quarter and the ending cash balance is the same as the ending cash balance for the fourth quarter. Also, note that the beginning cash balance for any quarter is the same as the ending cash balance for the previous quarter.

The Budgeted Income Statement

LEARNING OBJECTIVE 9
Prepare a budgeted income statement.

A budgeted income statement can be prepared from the data developed in Schedules 1–8. *The budgeted income statement is one of the key schedules in the budget process.* It shows the company's planned profit for the upcoming budget period, and it stands as a benchmark against which subsequent company performance can be measured. Schedule 9 contains the budgeted income statement for Hampton Freeze.

The Budgeted Balance Sheet

LEARNING OBJECTIVE 10
Prepare a budgeted balance sheet.

The budgeted balance sheet is developed by beginning with the current balance sheet and adjusting it for the data contained in the other budgets. Hampton Freeze's budgeted balance sheet is presented in Schedule 10.

Some of the data on the budgeted balance sheet have been taken from the company's end-of-year balance sheet for 2006, which appears below:

HAMPTON FREEZE, INC.
Balance Sheet
December 31, 2006

Assets		
Current assets:		
Cash	$ 42,500	
Accounts receivable	90,000	
Raw materials inventory (7,000 kilograms)	4,200	
Finished goods inventory (2,000 cases)	26,000	
Total current assets		$162,700
Plant and equipment:		
Land	80,000	
Buildings and equipment	700,000	
Accumulated depreciation	(292,000)	
Plant and equipment, net		488,000
Total assets		$650,700
Liabilities and Shareholders' Equity		
Current liabilities:		
Accounts payable (raw materials)		$ 25,800
Shareholders' equity:		
Common shares, no par	$175,000	
Retained earnings	449,900	
Total shareholders' equity		624,900
Total liabilities and shareholders' equity		$650,700

SCHEDULE 9

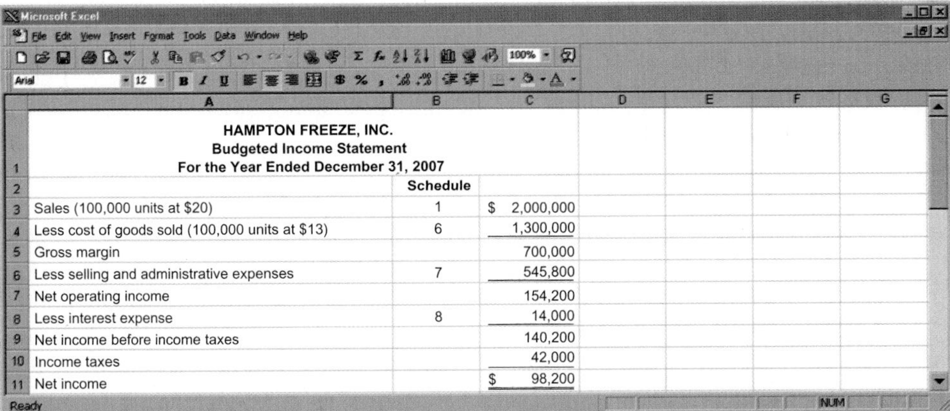

		A	B	C
1	HAMPTON FREEZE, INC. Budgeted Income Statement For the Year Ended December 31, 2007			
2		Schedule		
3	Sales (100,000 units at $20)	1	$ 2,000,000	
4	Less cost of goods sold (100,000 units at $13)	6	1,300,000	
5	Gross margin		700,000	
6	Less selling and administrative expenses	7	545,800	
7	Net operating income		154,200	
8	Less interest expense	8	14,000	
9	Net income before income taxes		140,200	
10	Income taxes		42,000	
11	Net income		$ 98,200	

SCHEDULE 10

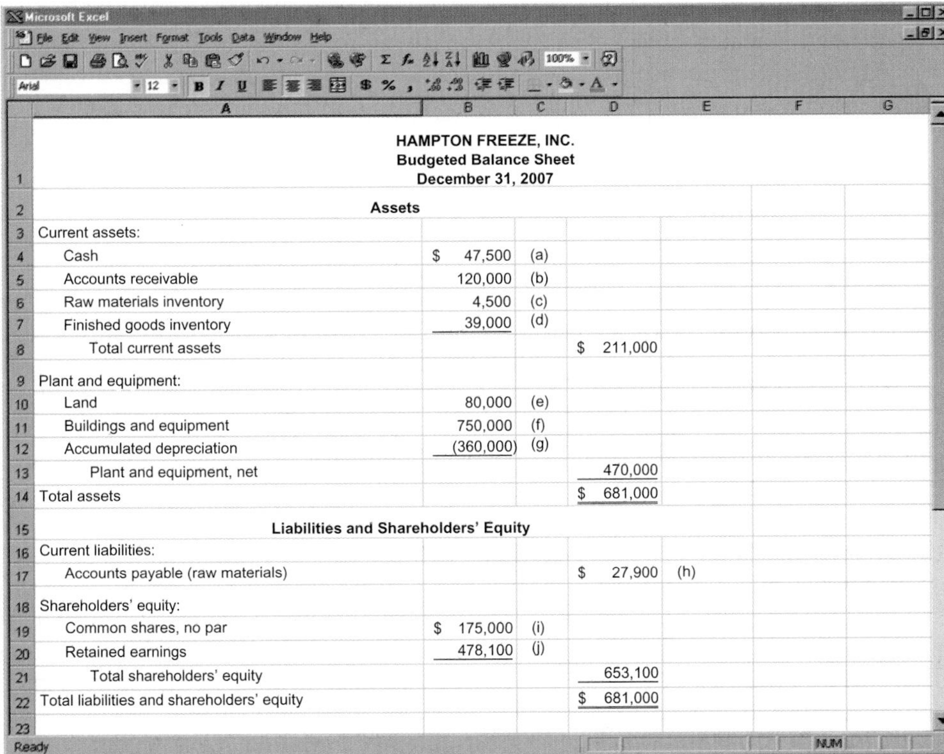

HAMPTON FREEZE, INC.
Budgeted Balance Sheet
December 31, 2007

		B	C	D	E
2	**Assets**				
3	Current assets:				
4	Cash	$ 47,500	(a)		
5	Accounts receivable	120,000	(b)		
6	Raw materials inventory	4,500	(c)		
7	Finished goods inventory	39,000	(d)		
8	Total current assets			$ 211,000	
9	Plant and equipment:				
10	Land	80,000	(e)		
11	Buildings and equipment	750,000	(f)		
12	Accumulated depreciation	(360,000)	(g)		
13	Plant and equipment, net			470,000	
14	Total assets			$ 681,000	
15	**Liabilities and Shareholders' Equity**				
16	Current liabilities:				
17	Accounts payable (raw materials)			$ 27,900	(h)
18	Shareholders' equity:				
19	Common shares, no par	$ 175,000	(i)		
20	Retained earnings	478,100	(j)		
21	Total shareholders' equity			653,100	
22	Total liabilities and shareholders' equity			$ 681,000	

Explanation of December 31, 2007, balance sheet figures:

a. The ending cash balance, as projected by the cash budget in Schedule 8.
b. Thirty percent of fourth-quarter sales, from Schedule 1 ($400,000 × 30% = $120,000).
c. From Schedule 3, the ending raw materials inventory will be 7,500 kilograms. This material costs $0.60 per kilogram. Therefore, the ending inventory in dollars will be 7,500 kilograms × $0.60 = $4,500.
d. From Schedule 6.
e. From the December 31, 2006, balance sheet (no change).
f. The December 31, 2006, balance sheet indicated a balance of $700,000. During 2007, $50,000 additional equipment will be purchased (see Schedule 8), bringing the December 31, 2007, balance to $750,000.
g. The December 31, 2006, balance sheet indicated a balance of $292,000. During 2007, $68,000 of depreciation will be taken ($60,000 on Schedule 5 and $8,000 on Schedule 7), bringing the December 31, 2007, balance to $360,000.
h. One-half of the fourth-quarter raw materials purchases, from Schedule 3.
i. From the December 31, 2006, balance sheet (no change).
j.

December 31, 2006, balance	$449,900
Add net income, from Schedule 9	98,200
	548,100
Deduct dividends paid, from Schedule 8	70,000
December 31, 2007, balance	$478,100

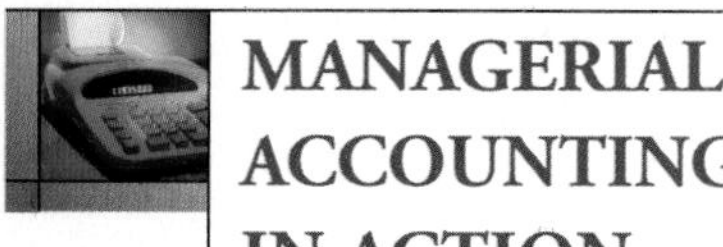

MANAGERIAL ACCOUNTING IN ACTION

The Wrap-Up

After completing the master budget, Larry Giano took the documents to Tom Wills, chief executive officer of Hampton Freeze, for his review. The following conversation took place:

Larry: Here's the budget. Overall, the net income is excellent, and the net cash flow for the entire year is positive.

Tom: Yes, but I see on this cash budget that we have the same problem with negative cash flows in the first and second quarters that we had last year.

Larry: That's true. I don't see any way around that problem. However, there is no doubt in my mind that if you take this budget to the bank today, they'll approve an open line of credit that will allow you to borrow enough to make it through the first two quarters without any problem.

Tom: Are you sure? They didn't seem very happy to see me last year when I came in for an emergency loan.

Larry: Did you repay the loan on time?

Tom: Sure.

Larry: I don't see any problem. You won't be asking for an emergency loan this time. The bank will have plenty of warning. And with this budget, you have a solid plan that shows when and how you are going to pay off the loan. Trust me, they'll go for it.

Tom: Fantastic! It would sure make life a lot easier this year.

Careful observation of the income statement (Schedule 9), the balance sheet (Schedule 10), and the cash budget (Schedule 8) would reveal that a significant item represented by income taxes has been simplified. Income taxes, while pertinent to budgets, have been simplified to avoid overdoing the complexity of the presentation. Given that income taxes can represent a significant percent of net income, this matter is serious.

In organizations, income taxes may not be administered at the level of the responsibility centre being budgeted. The specialized nature of the area means that taxes may require management by specialists at the headquarters level. In addition, income taxation is a companywide charge that may be difficult to break down by responsibility centre.

Some of the detail about income taxes is partially described in Chapter 14 when capital budgeting (long term) is presented. Here the complexity of capital cost allowance, capital gains and losses, recaptures, and terminal losses are an integral part of the required budgets. To introduce the full operational aspects of income taxes to the master budget requires the consideration of future tax liabilities and assets, instalments, and loss carryovers. Advanced discussions of budgeting can present these issues within the analysis after the necessary background study is made of the tax rules.

Expanding the Budgeted Income Statement

The master budget income statement in Schedule 9 focuses on a single level of activity and has been prepared using absorption costing. Some managers prefer an alternative format that focuses on a *range* of activity and that is prepared using the contribution approach. An example of a master budget income statement using this alternative format is presented in Exhibit 9–4.

A statement such as that in Exhibit 9–4 is *flexible,* since it is geared to more than one level of activity. If, for example, the company planned to sell 2,000 units during a period but actually sold only 1,900 units, then the budget figures at the 1,900-unit level would be used to compare against actual costs and revenues. Other columns could be added to the budget as needed by simply applying the budget formulas provided.

In short, a master budget income statement in this expanded format can be very useful in planning and controlling operations. The concepts underlying a flexible approach to budgeting are discussed in later chapters.

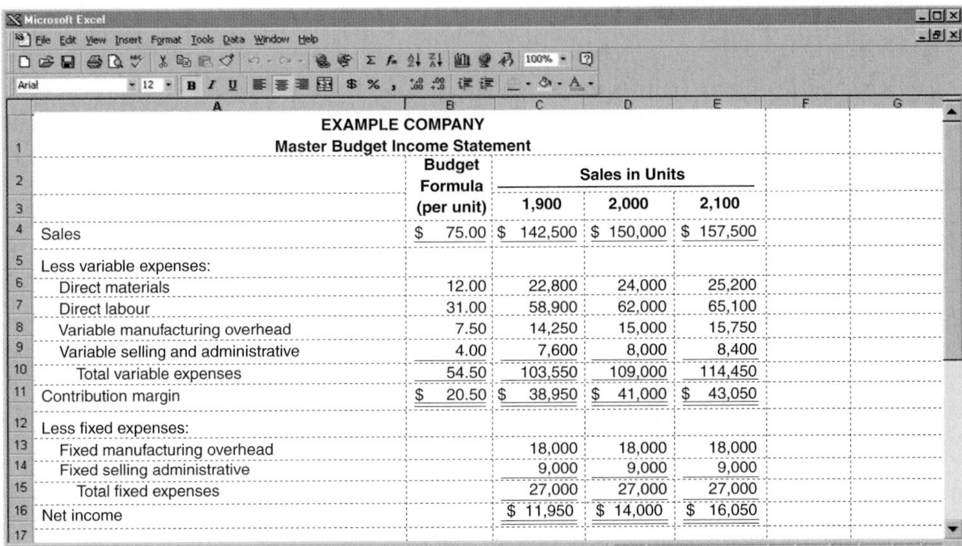

EXAMPLE COMPANY Master Budget Income Statement	Budget Formula (per unit)	Sales in Units		
		1,900	2,000	2,100
Sales	$ 75.00	$ 142,500	$ 150,000	$ 157,500
Less variable expenses:				
Direct materials	12.00	22,800	24,000	25,200
Direct labour	31.00	58,900	62,000	65,100
Variable manufacturing overhead	7.50	14,250	15,000	15,750
Variable selling and administrative	4.00	7,600	8,000	8,400
Total variable expenses	54.50	103,550	109,000	114,450
Contribution margin	$ 20.50	$ 38,950	$ 41,000	$ 43,050
Less fixed expenses:				
Fixed manufacturing overhead		18,000	18,000	18,000
Fixed selling administrative		9,000	9,000	9,000
Total fixed expenses		27,000	27,000	27,000
Net income		$ 11,950	$ 14,000	$ 16,050

EXHIBIT 9–4 Flexible Budget Income Statement

BUDGETING FOR NOT-FOR-PROFIT ENTITIES

LEARNING OBJECTIVE 11
Describe variations in the master budget process when applying it to not-for-profit and activity-based situations.

Up to this point, we have discussed budgeting in the context of profit-seeking enterprises. The sales estimate is the critical factor on which the rest of the master budget depends. Inaccurate sales estimates create additional inaccuracies in all other budgets. With profit-oriented bodies, there is an intricate relationship between expenses and revenues. With not-for-profit (NFP) entities, there is often no relationship between revenues expected to be received and expenditures expected to be incurred. Examples of NFP entities include municipal, provincial, and federal governmental units as well as hospitals, universities, voluntary associations, professional associations, and many others. The profit motive is replaced with a service orientation in NFP organizations. Budget information is gathered to assist in decisions regarding what programs and expenditures the entity will undertake. Subsequently the NFP entity estimates what revenues are needed to support these programs and anticipated expenditures. Revenue sources may be in the form of grants, donations, or special tax or membership levies. The very survival of NFP organizations such as art galleries depends on their ability to attract donors.

Accountability is of critical importance to most NFP entities. To ensure continued support from contributors, it is advantageous to have a budgeting process in place to assist in planning how resources are effectively and efficiently used. Budgets of NFP entities should be formally approved by the entity's governing body. A formally approved budget sends a signal to employees and volunteers alike that the governing body is committed to meeting revenue and expenditure goals.

A budget can be prepared either on an expenditure basis or on a program basis. An expenditure-based budget simply lists the total expected costs of such items as rent, insurance, salaries, and depreciation but does not detail how much of these various expenses relate to particular programs. For many NFP organizations there is a need to report information on the basis of programs rather than line-item expenses. Preparation of the budget on the basis of programs facilitates performance evaluation and allows for the comparison of budgeted with actual revenues and expenses of each program. This should aid decision making about resource allocation among various programs. Budgeting by program also facilitates a stewardship objective by providing information in a format permitting determination of whether designated funds are being spent as intended.

FOCUS on Current Practice

Given the importance of government budgets, the CICA's Public Sector Accounting Board (PSAB) commissioned a research report to survey the state of the union. The survey looks at the basis of accounting and accounting policies used by Canadian federal, provincial and territorial governments in their budgets and estimates (appropriations) as compared with those adopted in their summary financial statements. Planning, budgeting and reporting are elements of a government's performance management and accountability framework. The report discusses each of these elements. Traditionally, the approach begins with priority setting and planning, followed by the budgeting process and ending with reporting and auditing. The survey findings indicate a clear trend for senior governments in Canada: (1) to move to accrual-based accounting, (2) to prepare a summary budget, and (3) to change certain significant accounting policies to be in line with the recommendations set out in the Public Sector Accounting Handbook.

Source: Excerpted from J.Paul-Emile, "Accounting Bases Used in Canadian Government Budgeting," *CA Magazine*, Toronto, January/February 2005, vol. 138, iss. 1, p. 18. Reproduced by permission from *CA Magazine* produced by the Canadian Institute of Chartered Accountants, Toronto, Canada.

ACTIVITY-BASED BUDGETING

Activity-based budgeting A type of budgeting in which emphasis is placed on budgeting the costs of the activities needed to produce and market the firm's goods and services

In Chapter 8, we saw that activity-based costing has been developed to help provide the manager with more accurate product or service costs. More accurate costs should translate into better decision making and tighter control over costs. Activity-based costing principles can also be applied to budgeting. With **activity-based budgeting**, the emphasis is on budgeting the costs of the activities needed to produce and market the firm's goods and services.

Activity-based budgeting involves several stages. First, the budgeted cost of accomplishing each unit of activity is determined. Recall that an activity is a cost driver, such as machine set-up, a purchase order, a quality inspection, or a maintenance request. Next, sales and production targets are used to estimate the demand for these activities. The unit cost of each activity is then multiplied by the expected demand to determine the total cost of each activity. The result is a budget based on activities that drive costs rather than the traditional budget based on business functions and expense classifications.

For activity budgeting, costs within the responsibility centre are classified by activity, and activity drivers other than simple quantities produced or sold are identified. Activities such as quality inspections, materials handling, assembly, shipping, purchasing, and so on are identified, measured, and costed. These costs are then compiled to present the overall costs of the product or services if overall results are desired. The activity costing presented in Chapter 8 illustrates how activity budgets are presented.

The detail of applying activity-based costing techniques to budgeting technically requires reversal of the ABC approach. Instead of going from costs of resources, to activities, and then to the costs of outputs, activity-based budgeting goes from outputs to their costs, to the costs of the required activities, and then to the costs of procuring the required resources needed to produce the outputs. Such a reversal can result in inaccuracies in the budgets for the resources when the resources do not have a simple linear relationship to the outputs. Careful adjustments may be needed to compensate for the difficulties that this reversal of the costing process may cause.[8]

8. Robin Cooper and Regine Slagmulder, "Activity-Based Budgeting—Parts 1 and 2," *Strategic Finance*, September 2000, pp. 85–86, and October 2000, pp. 26–28.

INTERNATIONAL ASPECTS OF BUDGETING

A multinational company (MNC) faces special problems when preparing a budget. These problems arise because of fluctuations in foreign currency exchange rates, the high inflation rates found in some countries, and local economic conditions and governmental policies that affect everything from labour costs to marketing practices.

Fluctuations in foreign currency exchange rates create unique budgeting problems. Exporters may be able to predict with some accuracy their sales in the local foreign currency such as South African rands or euros. However, the amounts they eventually receive in their own currency will depend on the currency exchange rates that prevail at the time. If, for example, the currency exchange rates are less favourable than expected, the company will ultimately receive in its own currency less than it had anticipated.

Companies that are heavily involved in export operations often hedge their exposure to exchange rate fluctuations by buying and selling sophisticated financial contracts. These hedges ensure that if the company loses money in its exporting operations because of exchange rate fluctuations, it will make up that loss with gains on its financial contracts. The details of such hedging operations are covered in finance textbooks. When an MNC uses hedging operations, the costs of those activities should be budgeted along with other expenses.

Some MNCs have operations in countries with very high inflation rates—sometimes exceeding 100% a year. Such high inflation rates—called *hyperinflation*—can render a budget obsolete very quickly. A common budgeting tactic in such countries is to reduce the lead time for preparing the budget and to revise the budget frequently throughout the year in the light of the actual inflation experienced to date.

In addition to problems with exchange rates and inflation, MNCs must be sensitive to government policies in the countries in which they operate that might affect labour costs, equipment purchases, cash management, or other budget items.

FOCUS *on Current Practice*

"[In] 1985 the Toronto Blue Jays budgeted a loss for the season despite the fact that the team had the best win-loss record in the major leagues. The majority of team expenses were paid in U.S. dollars in contrast to their revenue, which was earned in Canadian dollars. To protect themselves against adverse changes in the exchange rate, the Blue Jays made forward purchases of U.S. dollars in late 1984 at 75 cents per Canadian dollar to cover a large portion of their budgeted 1985 U.S. dollar denominated expenses. In 1985, the Blue Jays profited on their hedged position when the Canadian dollar depreciated, which helped to offset losses on unhedged U.S. dollar denominated expenses during the same period."

Source: Paul V. Mannino and Ken Milani, "Budgeting for an International Business," *Management Accounting* 73, no. 8, February 1992, p. 37. Used by permission.

FOCUS *on Current Practice*

With the spread of smart cash registers, bar code readers and other new technologies, businesses have been able to operate more efficiently. Real time information can inform the budgeting process and provide companies with flexibility to make cost and price adjustments as needed. According to Grant Thornton LLP in Canada, these new technology tools are fascinating, exciting and powerful if properly used. But it is crucial to use them properly. First, always start with strategy. If you don't know where you're going and what specific measurable results you're after, don't be surprised when technology turns out to be a disappointment. Second, make sure you spend time to design robust, lean processes. Automating a bad process just gets you in trouble faster.

Source: www.grantthornton.ca

SUMMARY

Our purpose has been to present an overview of the budgeting process and to show how the various operating budgets relate to each other. We have seen how the sales budget forms the foundation for profit planning. Once the sales budget has been set, the production budget and the selling and administrative budget can be prepared since they depend on how many units are to be sold. The production budget determines how many units are to be produced, so after it is prepared, the various manufacturing cost budgets can be prepared. All of these various budgets feed into the cash budget and the budgeted income statement and balance sheet. There are many connections between these various parts of the master budget. For example, the schedule of expected cash collections, which is completed in connection with the sales budget, provides data for both the cash budget and the budgeted balance sheet.

The material in this chapter is just an introduction to budgeting and profit planning. In later chapters, we will see how budgets are used to control day-to-day operations and how they are used in performance evaluation.

REVIEW PROBLEM: BUDGET SCHEDULES

Mylar Company manufactures and sells a product that has seasonal variations in demand, with peak sales coming in the third quarter. The following information concerns operations for year 2—the coming year—and for the first two quarters of year 3:

a. The company's single product sells for $8 per unit. Budgeted sales in units for the next six quarters are as follows:

	Year 2 Quarter				Year 3 Quarter	
	1	2	3	4	1	2
Budgeted sales in units	40,000	60,000	100,000	50,000	70,000	80,000

b. Sales are collected in the following pattern: 75% in the quarter the sales are made, and the remaining 25% in the following quarter. On January 1, year 2, the company's balance sheet showed $65,000 in accounts receivable, all of which will be collected in the first quarter of the year. Bad debts are negligible and can be ignored.

c. The company desires an ending inventory of finished units on hand at the end of each quarter equal to 30% of the budgeted sales for the next quarter. This requirement was met on December 31, year 1, in that the company had 12,000 units on hand to start the new year.

d. Five kilograms of raw materials are required to complete one unit of product. The company requires an ending inventory of raw materials on hand at the end of each quarter equal to 10% of the production needs of the following quarter. This requirement was met on December 31, year 1, in that the company had 23,000 kilograms of raw materials on hand to start the new year.

e. The raw material costs $0.80 per kilogram. Purchases of raw materials are paid for in the following pattern: 60% paid in the quarter the purchases are made, and the remaining 40% paid in the following quarter. One January 1, year 2, the company's balance sheet showed $81,500 in accounts payable for raw materials purchases, all of which will be paid for in the first quarter of the year.

Required:

Prepare the following budgets and schedules for the year, showing both quarterly and total figures:

1. A sales budget and a schedule of expected cash collections.
2. A production budget.
3. A direct materials purchases budget and a schedule of expected cash payments for materials purchases.

Solution to Review Problem

1. The sales budget is prepared as follows:

	Year 2 Quarter				
	1	2	3	4	Year
Budgeted sales in units	40,000	60,000	100,000	50,000	250,000
Selling price per unit	× $8	× $8	× $8	× $8	× $8
Total sales	$320,000	$480,000	$800,000	$400,000	$2,000,000

Based on the budgeted sales above, the schedule of expected cash collections is prepared as follows:

	Year 2 Quarter				
	1	2	3	4	Year
Accounts receivable, beginning balance	$ 65,000				$ 65,000
First-quarter sales ($320,000 × 75%, 25%)	240,000	$ 80,000			320,000
Second-quarter sales ($480,000 × 75%, 25%)		360,000	$120,000		480,000
Third-quarter sales ($800,000 × 75%, 25%)			600,000	$200,000	800,000
Fourth-quarter sales ($400,000 × 75%)				300,000	300,000
Total cash collections	$305,000	$440,000	$720,000	$500,000	$1,965,000

2. Based on the sales budget in units, the production budget is prepared as follows:

	Year 2 Quarter					Year 3 Quarter	
	1	2	3	4	Year	1	2
Budgeted sales (units)	40,000	60,000	100,000	50,000	250,000	70,000	80,000
Add desired ending inventory of finished goods*	18,000	30,000	15,000	21,000†	21,000	24,000	
Total needs	58,000	90,000	115,000	71,000	271,000	94,000	
Less beginning inventory of finished goods	12,000	18,000	30,000	15,000	12,000	21,000	
Required production	46,000	72,000	85,000	56,000	259,000	73,000	

*30% of the following quarter's budgeted sales in units.

†30% of the budgeted year 3 first-quarter sales.

3. Based on the production budget figures, raw materials will need to be purchased as follows during the year:

	Year 2 Quarter					Year 3 Quarter
	1	2	3	4	Year 2	1
Required production (units)	46,000	72,000	85,000	56,000	259,000	73,000
Raw materials needed per unit (kilograms)	× 5	× 5	× 5	× 5	× 5	× 5
Production needs (kilograms)	230,000	360,000	425,000	280,000	1,295,000	365,000
Add desired ending inventory of raw materials (kilograms)*	36,000	42,500	28,000	36,500†	36,500	
Total needs (kilograms)	266,000	402,500	453,000	316,500	1,331,500	
Less beginning inventory of raw materials (kilograms)	23,000	36,000	42,500	28,000	23,000	
Raw materials to be purchased (kilograms)	243,000	366,500	410,500	288,500	1,308,500	

*10% of the following quarter's production needs in kilograms.

†10% of the year 3 first-quarter production needs in kilograms.

Based on the raw materials purchases above, expected cash payments are computed as follows:

	Year 2 Quarter 1	2	3	4	Year 2
Cost of raw materials to be purchased at $0.80 per kilogram	$194,400	$293,200	$328,400	$230,800	$1,046,800
Accounts payable, beginning balance	$ 81,500				$ 81,500
First-quarter purchases ($194,400 × 60%, 40%)	116,640	$ 77,760			194,400
Second-quarter purchases ($293,200 × 60%, 40%)		175,920	$117,280		293,200
Third-quarter purchases ($328,400 × 60%, 40%)			197,040	$131,360	328,400
Fourth-quarter purchases ($230,800 × 60%)				138,480	138,480
Total cash disbursements	$198,140	$253,680	$314,320	$269,840	$1,035,980

GLOSSARY

Visit the Online Learning Centre at http://www.mcgrawhill.ca/college/garrison/ for a review of key terms and definitions.

QUESTIONS

9–1 Some persons consider strategic planning to be the most important work that a manager performs. In what ways might this be true? In what ways might this be false?

9–2 Describe the four "P's" of strategic planning.

9–3 Outline the basis for deciding strategic decisions, in other words, the areas where the business can be challenged.

9–4 Besides using strategic information to make strategic decisions, information can serve a strategic purpose. Describe how information can serve a strategic objective.

9–5 What is a budget? What is budgetary control?

9–6 Discuss some of the major benefits to be gained from budgeting.

9–7 What is meant by the term *responsibility accounting?*

9–8 What is a master budget? Briefly describe its contents.

9–9 Why is the sales forecast the starting point in budgeting?

9–10 "As a practical matter, planning and control mean exactly the same thing." Do you agree? Explain.

9–11 Describe the flow of budget data in an organization. Who are the participants in the budgeting process, and how do they participate?

9–12 What is a participative budget? What are the major advantages of participative budgets? What caution must be exercised in their use?

9–13 How can budgeting assist a firm in its employment policies?

9–14 How does zero-base budgeting differ from traditional budgeting?

9–15 "The principal purpose of the cash budget is to see how much cash the company will have in the bank at the end of the year." Do you agree? Explain.

9–16 "Budgeting is designed primarily for organizations that have few complexities and uncertainties in their day-to-day operations." Do you agree? Why or why not?

9–17 Which is a better basis for judging actual results, budgeted performance or past performance? Why?

9–18 Is there any difference between a sales forecast and a sales budget? Explain.

9–19 "To a large extent, the success of a budget program hinges on education and good salesmanship." Do you agree? Explain.

9–20 "With profit, not-for-profit, and government entities, there is generally a direct relationship between revenues and expenditures." Do you agree with this statement? Why or why not?

9–21 Some people argue that budgets should be done away with by organizations facing stiff competition. Why would this be? Can the budgeting process be modified to cope with the pressures of competition?

EXERCISES

EXERCISE 9–1 Schedule of Expected Cash Collections [LO2]

Silver Company makes a product that is very popular as a Mother's Day gift. Thus, peak sales occur in May of each year. These peak sales are shown in the company's sales budget for the second quarter given below (all sales are on account):

	April	May	June	Total
Budgeted sales	$300,000	$500,000	$200,000	$1,000,000

From past experience, the company has learned that 20% of a month's sales are collected in the month of sale, another 70% are collected in the month following sale, and the remaining 10% are collected in the second month following sale. Bad debts are negligible and can be ignored. February sales totalled $230,000, and March sales totalled $260,000.

Required:

1. Prepare a schedule of expected cash collections from sales, by month and in total, for the second quarter.
2. Assume that the company will prepare a budgeted balance sheet as of June 30. Compute the accounts receivable as of that date.

EXERCISE 9–2 Production Budget [LO3]

Down Under Products, Ltd., of Australia has budgeted sales of its popular boomerang for the next four months as follows:

	Sales in Units
April	50,000
May	75,000
June	90,000
July	80,000

The company is now in the process of preparing a production budget for the second quarter. Past experience has shown that end-of-month inventory levels must equal 10% of the following month's sales. The inventory at the end of March was 5,000 units.

Required:

Prepare a production budget for the second quarter; in your budget, show the number of units to be produced each month and for the quarter in total.

EXERCISE 9–3 Direct Materials Budget [LO4]

Three grams of musk oil are required for each bottle of Mink Caress, a very popular perfume made by a small company in western Siberia. The cost of the musk oil is 150 roubles per kilogram. (Siberia is located in Russia, whose currency is the rouble.) Budgeted production of Mink Caress is given below by quarters for Year 2 and for the first quarter of Year 3.

	Year 2 Quarter				Year 3 Quarter
	First	Second	Third	Fourth	First
Budgeted production, in bottles	60,000	90,000	150,000	100,000	70,000

Musk oil has become so popular as a perfume ingredient that it has become necessary to carry large inventories as a precaution against stockouts. For this reason, the inventory of musk oil at the end of a quarter must be equal to 20% of the following quarter's production needs. Some 36,000 grams of musk oil will be on hand to start the first quarter of Year 2.

Required:

Prepare a direct materials budget for musk oil, by quarter and in total, for Year 2. At the bottom of your budget, show the amount of purchases in roubles for each quarter and for the year in total.

EXERCISE 9–4 Direct Labour Budget [LO5]

The production department of Rordan Corporation has submitted the following forecast of units to be produced by quarter for the upcoming fiscal year.

	1st Quarter	2nd Quarter	3rd Quarter	4th Quarter
Units to be produced	8,000	6,500	7,000	7,500

Each unit requires 0.35 direct labour-hours, and direct labourers are paid $12.00 per hour.

Required:

1. Construct the company's direct labour budget for the upcoming fiscal year, assuming that the direct labour work force is adjusted each quarter to match the number of hours required to produce the forecasted number of units produced.
2. Construct the company's direct labour budget for the upcoming fiscal year, assuming that the direct labour work force is not adjusted each quarter. Instead, assume that the company's direct labour work force consists of permanent employees who are guaranteed to be paid for at least 2,600 hours of work each quarter. If the number of required direct labour-hours is less than this number, the workers are paid for 2,600 hours anyway. Any hours worked in excess of 2,600 hours in a quarter are paid at the rate of 1.5 times the normal hourly rate for direct labour.

EXERCISE 9–5 Manufacturing Overhead Budget [LO6]

The direct labour budget of Yuvwell Corporation for the upcoming fiscal year contains the following details concerning budgeted direct labour-hours.

	1st Quarter	2nd Quarter	3rd Quarter	4th Quarter
Budgeted direct labour-hours	8,000	8,200	8,500	7,800

The company's variable manufacturing overhead rate is $3.25 per direct labour-hour and the company's fixed manufacturing overhead is $48,000 per quarter. The only non-cash item included in the fixed manufacturing overhead is depreciation, which is $16,000 per quarter.

Required:

1. Construct the company's manufacturing overhead budget for the upcoming fiscal year.
2. Compute the company's manufacturing overhead rate (including both variable and fixed manufacturing overhead) for the upcoming fiscal year. Round off to the nearest whole cent.

EXERCISE 9–6 Selling and Administrative Expense Budget [LO7]

The budgeted unit sales of Weller Company for the upcoming fiscal year are provided below:

	1st Quarter	2nd Quarter	3rd Quarter	4th Quarter
Budgeted unit sales	15,000	16,000	14,000	13,000

The company's variable selling and administrative expense per unit is $2.50. Fixed selling and administrative expenses include advertising expenses of $8,000 per quarter, executive salaries of $35,000 per quarter, and depreciation of $20,000 per quarter. In addition, the company will make insurance payments of $5,000 in the first quarter and $5,000 in the third quarter. Finally, property taxes of $8,000 will be paid in the second quarter.

Required:

Prepare the company's selling and administrative expense budget for the upcoming fiscal year.

EXERCISE 9–7 Cash Budget Analysis [LO8]

A cash budget, by quarters, is given below for a retail company. (000 omitted). The company requires a minimum cash balance of at least $5,000 to start each quarter.

Required:

Fill in the missing amounts in the following table.

	Quarter				
	1	2	3	4	Year
Cash balance, beginning	$ 6	$?	$?	$?	$?
Add collections from customers	?	?	96	?	323
Total cash available	71	?	?	?	?
Less disbursements:					
Purchase of inventory	35	45	?	35	?
Operating expenses	?	30	30	?	113
Equipment purchases	8	8	10	?	36
Dividends	2	2	2	2	?
Total disbursements	?	85	?	?	?
Excess (deficiency) of cash available over disbursements	(2)	?	11	?	?
Financing:					
Borrowings	?	15	—	—	?
Repayments (including interest)*	—	—	(?)	(17)	(?)
Total financing	?	?	?	?	?
Cash balance, ending	$?	$?	$?	$?	$?

*Interest will total $1,000 for the year.

PROBLEMS

PROBLEM 9–8 Evaluating a Company's Budget Procedures [LO1]
Springfield Corporation operates on a calendar-year basis. It begins the annual budgeting process in late August, when the president establishes targets for total sales dollars and net operating income before taxes for the next year.

The sales target is given to the Marketing Department, where the marketing manager formulates a sales budget by product line in both units and dollars. From this budget, sales quotas by product line in units and dollars are established for each of the corporation's sales districts.

The marketing manager also estimates the cost of the marketing activities required to support the target sales volume and prepares a tentative marketing expense budget.

The executive vice president uses the sales and profit targets, the sales budget by product line, and the tentative marketing expense budget to determine the dollar amounts that can be devoted to manufacturing and corporate office expense. The executive vice president prepares the budget for corporate expenses, and then forwards to the Production Department the product-line sales budget in units and the total dollar amount that can be devoted to manufacturing.

The production manager meets with the factory managers to develop a manufacturing plan that will produce the required units when needed within the cost constraints set by the executive vice president. The budgeting process usually comes to a halt at this point because the Production Department does not consider the financial resources allocated to it to be adequate.

When this standstill occurs, the vice president of finance, the executive vice president, the marketing manager, and the production manager meet to determine the final budgets for each of the areas. This normally results in a modest increase in the total amount available for manufacturing costs, while the marketing expense and corporate office expense budgets are cut. The total sales and net operating income figures proposed by the president are seldom changed. Although the participants are seldom pleased with the compromise, these budgets are final. Each executive then develops a new detailed budget for the operations in his or her area.

None of the areas has achieved its budget in recent years. Sales often run below the target. When budgeted sales are not achieved, each area is expected to cut costs so that the president's profit target can still be met. However, the profit target is seldom met because costs are not cut enough. In fact, costs often run above the original budget in all functional areas. The president is disturbed that Springfield has not been able to meet the sales and profit targets. He hired a consultant with considerable relevant industry experience. The consultant reviewed the budgets for the past four years. He concluded that the product-line sales budgets were reasonable and that the cost and expense budgets were adequate for the budgeted sales and production levels.

Required:

1. Discuss how the budgeting process as employed by Springfield Corporation contributes to the failure to achieve the president's sales and profit targets.
2. Suggest how Springfield Corporation's budgeting process could be revised to correct the problem.
3. Should the functional areas be expected to cut their costs when sales volume falls below budget? Explain your answer.

(CMA, adapted)

PROBLEM 9–9 Schedule of Expected Cash Collections; Cash Budget [LO2, LO8]

Herbal Care Corp., a distributor of herb-based sunscreens, is ready to begin its third quarter, in which peak sales occur. The company has requested a $40,000, 90-day loan from its bank to help meet cash requirements during the quarter. Since Herbal Care has experienced difficulty in paying off its loans in the past, the loan officer at the bank has asked the company to prepare a cash budget for the quarter. In response to this request, the following data have been assembled:

a. On July 1, the beginning of the third quarter, the company will have a cash balance of $44,500.

b. Actual sales for the last two months and budgeted sales for the third quarter follow (all sales are on account):

May (actual)	$250,000
June (actual)	$300,000
July (budgeted)	$400,000
August (budgeted)	$600,000
September (budgeted)	$320,000

Past experience shows that 25% of a month's sales are collected in the month of sale, 70% in the month following sale, and 3% in the second month following sale. The remainder is uncollectible.

c. Budgeted merchandise purchases and budgeted expenses for the third quarter are given below:

	July	August	September
Merchandise purchases	$240,000	$350,000	$175,000
Salaries and wages	$45,000	$50,000	$40,000
Advertising	$130,000	$145,000	$80,000
Rent payments	$9,000	$9,000	$9,000
Depreciation	$10,000	$10,000	$10,000

Merchandise purchases are paid in full during the month following purchase. Accounts payable for merchandise purchases on June 30, which will be paid during July, total $180,000.

d. Equipment costing $10,000 will be purchased for cash during July.

e. In preparing the cash budget, assume that the $40,000 loan will be made in July and repaid in September. Interest on the loan will total $1,200.

Required:

1. Prepare a schedule of expected cash collections for July, August, and September and for the quarter in total.
2. Prepare a cash budget, by month and in total, for the third quarter.
3. If the company needs a minimum cash balance of $20,000 to start each month, can the loan be repaid as planned? Explain.

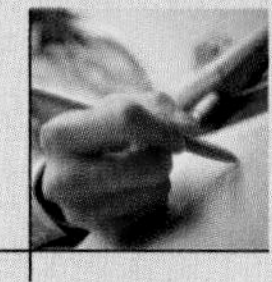

PROBLEM 9–10 Behavioural Aspects of Budgeting; Ethics and the Manager [LO1]

Norton Company, a manufacturer of infant furniture and carriages, is in the initial stages of preparing the annual budget for next year. Scott Ford has recently joined Norton's accounting staff and is interested to learn as much as possible about the company's budgeting process. During a recent lunch with Marge Atkins, sales manager, and Pete Granger, production manager, Ford initiated the following conversation.

Ford: Since I'm new around here and am going to be involved with the preparation of the annual budget, I'd be interested to learn how the two of you estimate sales and production numbers.

Atkins: We start out very methodically by looking at recent history, discussing what we know about current accounts, potential customers, and the general state of consumer spending. Then, we add that usual dose of intuition to come up with the best forecast we can.

Granger: I usually take the sales projections as the basis for my projections. Of course, we have to make an estimate of what this year's ending inventories will be, which is sometimes difficult.

Ford: Why does that present a problem? There must have been an estimate of ending inventories in the budget for the current year.

Granger: Those numbers aren't always reliable since Marge makes some adjustments to the sales numbers before passing them on to me.

Ford: What kind of adjustments?

Atkins: Well, we don't want to fall short of the sales projections so we generally give ourselves a little breathing room by lowering the initial sales projection anywhere from 5% to 10%.

Granger: So, you can see why this year's budget is not a very reliable starting point. We always have to adjust the projected production rates as the year progresses and, of course, this changes the ending inventory estimates. By the way, we make similar adjustments to expenses by adding at least 10% to the estimates; I think everyone around here does the same thing.

Required:

1. Marge Atkins and Pete Granger have described the use of what is sometimes called *budgetary slack.*
   a. Explain why Atkins and Granger behave in this manner and describe the benefits they expect to realize from the use of budgetary slack.
   b. Explain how the use of budgetary slack can adversely affect Atkins and Granger.
2. As a management accountant, Scott Ford believes that the behaviour described by Marge Atkins and Pete Granger may be unethical. By referring to the Standards of Ethical Conduct for Practitioners of Management Accounting and Financial Management in Chapter 1, explain why the use of budgetary slack may be unethical.

(CMA, adapted)

PROBLEM 9–11 Production and Direct Materials Budgets [LO3, LO4]

Pearl Products Limited of Shenzhen, China, manufactures and distributes toys throughout South East Asia. Three cubic centimetres (cc) of solvent H300 are required to manufacture each unit of Supermix, one of the company's products. The company is now planning raw materials needs for the third quarter, the quarter in which peak sales of Supermix occur. To keep production and sales moving smoothly, the company has the following inventory requirements:

a. The finished goods inventory on hand at the end of each month must be equal to 3,000 units of Supermix plus 20% of the next month's sales. The finished goods inventory on June 30 is budgeted to be 10,000 units.
b. The raw materials inventory on hand at the end of each month must be equal to one-half of the following month's production needs for raw materials. The raw materials inventory on June 30 is budgeted to be 54,000 cc of solvent H300.
c. The company maintains no work in process inventories.

A sales budget for Supermix for the last six months of the year follows.

	Budgeted Sales in Units
July	35,000
August	40,000
September	50,000
October	30,000
November	20,000
December	10,000

Required:

1. Prepare a production budget for Supermix for the months July, August, September, and October.
2. Examine the production budget that you prepared in (1) above. Why will the company produce more units than it sells in July and August, and fewer units than it sells in September and October?

3. Prepare a direct materials budget showing the quantity of solvent H300 to be purchased for July, August, and September, and for the quarter in total.

PROBLEM 9–12 Direct Materials and Direct Labour Budgets [LO4, LO5]
The production department of Zan Corporation has submitted the following forecast of units to be produced by quarter for the upcoming fiscal year.

	1st Quarter	2nd Quarter	3rd Quarter	4th Quarter
Units to be produced	5,000	8,000	7,000	6,000

In addition, the beginning raw materials inventory for the 1st Quarter is budgeted to be 6,000 grams and the beginning accounts payable for the 1st Quarter is budgeted to be $2,880.

Each unit requires 8 grams of raw material that costs $1.20 per gram. Management desires to end each quarter with an inventory of raw materials equal to 25% of the following quarter's production needs. The desired ending inventory for the 4th Quarter is 8,000 grams. Management plans to pay for 60% of raw material purchases in the quarter acquired and 40% in the following quarter. Each unit requires 0.20 direct labour-hour and direct labourers are paid $11.50 per hour.

Required:

1. Prepare the company's direct materials budget and schedule of expected cash disbursements for materials for the upcoming fiscal year.
2. Prepare the company's direct labour budget for the upcoming fiscal year, assuming that the direct labour workforce is adjusted each quarter to match the number of hours required to produce the forecasted number of units produced.

PROBLEM 9–13 Direct Labour and Manufacturing Overhead Budgets [LO5, LO6]
The Production Department of Hruska Corporation has submitted the following forecast of units to be produced by quarter for the upcoming fiscal year.

	1st Quarter	2nd Quarter	3rd Quarter	4th Quarter
Units to be produced	12,000	10,000	13,000	14,000

Each unit requires 0.2 direct labour-hour and direct labourers are paid $12.00 per hour.

In addition, the variable manufacturing overhead rate is $1.75 per direct labour-hour. The fixed manufacturing overhead is $86,000 per quarter. The only non-cash element of manufacturing overhead is depreciation, which is $23,000 per quarter.

Required:

1. Prepare the company's direct labour budget for the upcoming fiscal year, assuming that the direct labour work force is adjusted each quarter to match the number of hours required to produce the forecasted number of units produced.
2. Prepare the company's manufacturing overhead budget.

PROBLEM 9–14 Schedules of Expected Cash Collections and Disbursements [LO2, LO4, LO8]
You have been asked to prepare a December cash budget for Ashton Company, a distributor of exercise equipment. The following information is available about the company's operations:

a. The cash balance on December 1 is $40,000.
b. Actual sales for October and November and expected sales for December are as follows:

	October	November	December
Cash sales	$65,000	$70,000	$83,000
Sales on account	$400,000	$525,000	$600,000

Sales on account are collected over a three-month period as follows: 20% collected in the month of sale, 60% collected in the month following sale, and 18% collected in the second month following sale. The remaining 2% is uncollectible.

c. Purchases of inventory will total $280,000 for December. Thirty percent of a month's inventory purchases are paid during the month of purchase. The accounts payable remaining from November's inventory purchases total $161,000, all of which will be paid in December.

d. Selling and administrative expenses are budgeted at $430,000 for December. Of this amount, $50,000 is for depreciation.
e. A new Web server for the Marketing Department costing $76,000 will be purchased for cash during December, and dividends totalling $9,000 will be paid during the month.
f. The company maintains a minimum cash balance of $20,000. An open line of credit is available from the company's bank to bolster the cash position as needed.

Required:
1. Prepare a schedule of expected cash collections for December.
2. Prepare a schedule of expected cash disbursements for merchandise purchases for December.
3. Prepare a cash budget for December. Indicate in the financing section any borrowing that will be needed during the month.

PROBLEM 9–15 Cash Budget; Income Statement; Balance Sheet [LO2, LO4, LO8, LO9, LO10]

Minden Company is a wholesale distributor of premium European chocolates. The company's balance sheet as of April 30 is given below:

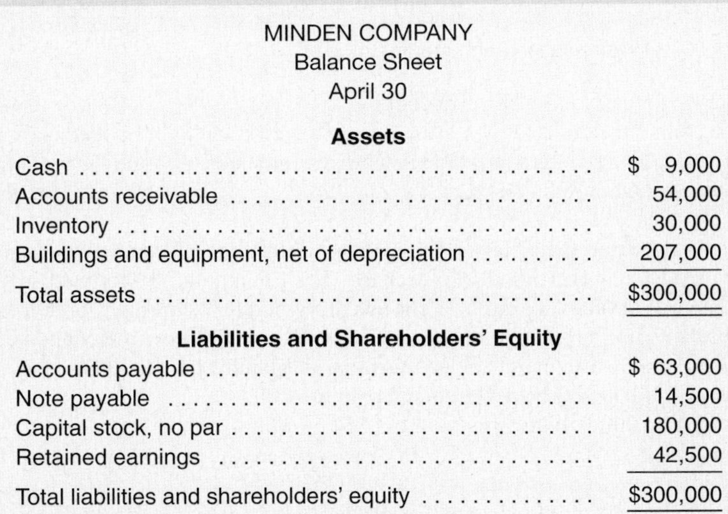

MINDEN COMPANY
Balance Sheet
April 30

Assets	
Cash	$ 9,000
Accounts receivable	54,000
Inventory	30,000
Buildings and equipment, net of depreciation	207,000
Total assets	$300,000
Liabilities and Shareholders' Equity	
Accounts payable	$ 63,000
Note payable	14,500
Capital stock, no par	180,000
Retained earnings	42,500
Total liabilities and shareholders' equity	$300,000

The company is in the process of preparing budget data for May. A number of budget items have already been prepared, as stated below:

a. Sales are budgeted at $200,000 for May. Of these sales, $60,000 will be for cash; the remainder will be credit sales. One-half of a month's credit sales are collected in the month the sales are made, and the remainder is collected in the following month. All of the April 30 accounts receivable will be collected in May.
b. Purchases of inventory are expected to total $120,000 during May. These purchases will all be on account. Forty percent of all purchases are paid for in the month of purchase; the remainder are paid in the following month. All of the April 30 accounts payable to suppliers will be paid during May.
c. The May 31 inventory balance is budgeted at $40,000.
d. Operating expenses for May are budgeted at $72,000, exclusive of depreciation. These expenses will be paid in cash. Depreciation is budgeted at $2,000 for the month.
e. The note payable on the April 30 balance sheet will be paid during May, with $100 in interest. (All of the interest relates to May.)
f. New refrigerating equipment costing $6,500 will be purchased for cash during May.
g. During May, the company will borrow $20,000 from its bank by giving a new note payable to the bank for that amount. The new note will be due in one year.

Required:
1. Prepare a cash budget for May. Support your budget with a schedule of expected cash collections from sales and a schedule of expected cash disbursements for merchandise purchases.
2. Prepare a budgeted income statement for May. Use the absorption costing income statement format as shown in Schedule 9.
3. Prepare a budgeted balance sheet as of May 31.

PROBLEM 9–16 Cash Budget with Supporting Schedules [LO2, LO4, LO8]

Garden Sales, Inc., sells garden supplies. Management is planning its cash needs for the second quarter. The company usually has to borrow money during this quarter to support peak sales of lawn care equipment, which occur during May. The following information has been assembled to assist in preparing a cash budget for the quarter:

a. Budgeted monthly absorption costing income statements for April–July are:

	April	May	June	July
Sales	$600,000	$900,000	$500,000	$400,000
Cost of goods sold	420,000	630,000	350,000	280,000
Gross margin	180,000	270,000	150,000	120,000
Less operating expenses:				
Selling expense	79,000	120,000	62,000	51,000
Administrative expense*	45,000	52,000	41,000	38,000
Total operating expenses	124,000	172,000	103,000	89,000
Net operating income	$ 56,000	$ 98,000	$ 47,000	$ 31,000

*Includes $20,000 of depreciation each month.

b. Sales are 20% for cash and 80% on account.

c. Sales on account are collected over a three-month period with 10% collected in the month of sale; 70% collected in the first month following the month of sale; and the remaining 20% collected in the second month following the month of sale. February's sales totalled $200,000, and March's sales totalled $300,000.

d. Inventory purchases are paid for within 15 days. Therefore, 50% of a month's inventory purchases are paid for in the month of purchase. The remaining 50% is paid in the following month. Accounts payable at March 31 for inventory purchases during March total $126,000.

e. Each month's ending inventory must equal 20% of the cost of the merchandise to be sold in the following month. The merchandise inventory at March 31 is $84,000.

f. Dividends of $49,000 will be declared and paid in April.

g. Land costing $16,000 will be purchased for cash in May.

h. The cash balance at March 31 is $52,000; the company must maintain a cash balance of at least $40,000.

i. The company can borrow from its bank as needed to bolster the Cash account. Borrowings and repayments must be in multiples of $1,000. All borrowings take place at the beginning of a month, and all repayments are made at the end of a month. The annual interest rate is 12%. Compute interest on whole months (1/12, 2/12, and so forth).

Required:

1. Prepare a schedule of expected cash collections for April, May, and June, and for the quarter in total.
2. Prepare the following for merchandise inventory:
   a. A merchandise purchases budget for April, May, and June.
   b. A schedule of expected cash disbursements for merchandise purchases for April, May, and June, and for the quarter in total.
3. Prepare a cash budget for April, May, and June as well as in total for the quarter. Show borrowings from the company's bank and repayments to the bank as needed to maintain the minimum cash balance.

PROBLEM 9–17 Integration of the Sales, Production, and Direct Materials Budgets [LO2, LO3, LO4]

Milo Company manufactures beach umbrellas. The company is preparing detailed budgets for the third quarter and has assembled the following information to assist in the budget preparation:

a. The Marketing Department has estimated sales as follows for the remainder of the year (in units):

July	30,000	October	20,000
August	70,000	November	10,000
September	50,000	December	10,000

The selling price of the beach umbrellas is $12 per unit.

b. All sales are on account. Based on past experience, sales are collected in the following pattern:

30% in the month of sale
65% in the month following sale
5% uncollectible

Sales for June totalled $300,000.

c. The company maintains finished goods inventories equal to 15% of the following month's sales. This requirement will be met at the end of June.

d. Each beach umbrella requires 1 metre of Gilden, a material that is sometimes hard to acquire. Therefore, the company requires that the ending inventory of Gilden be equal to 50% of the following month's production needs. The inventory of Gilden on hand at the beginning and end of the quarter will be:

June 30	18,000 metres
September 30	? metres

e. Gilden costs $3.20 per metre. One-half of a month's purchases of Gilden is paid for in the month of purchase; the remainder is paid for in the following month. The accounts payable on July 1 for purchases of Gilden during June will be $76,000.

Required:

1. Prepare a sales budget, by month and in total, for the third quarter. (Show your budget in both units and dollars.) Also prepare a schedule of expected cash collections, by month and in total, for the third quarter.
2. Prepare a production budget for each of the months July–October.
3. Prepare a direct materials budget for Gilden, by month and in total, for the third quarter. Also prepare a schedule of expected cash disbursements for Gilden, by month and in total, for the third quarter.

PROBLEM 9–18 Cash Budget with Supporting Schedules [LO2, LO4, LO7, LO8]

Westex Products is a wholesale distributor of industrial cleaning products. When the treasurer of Westex Products approached the company's bank late in the current year seeking short-term financing, he was told that money was very tight and that any borrowing over the next year would have to be supported by a detailed statement of cash collections and disbursements. The treasurer also was told that it would be very helpful to the bank if borrowers would indicate the quarters in which they would be needing funds, as well as the amounts that would be needed, and the quarters in which repayments could be made.

Since the treasurer is unsure as to the particular quarters in which bank financing will be needed, he has assembled the following information to assist in preparing a detailed cash budget:

a. Budgeted sales and merchandise purchases for next year, as well as actual sales and purchases for the last quarter of the current year, are:

Microsoft Excel - Problem 9-18 screen capture.xls

	A	B	C	D
1				
2		*Sales*	*Merchandise Purchases*	
3	Current year:			
4	Fourth quarter actual	$200,000	$126,000	
5	Next year:			
6	First quarter estimated	$300,000	$186,000	
7	Second quarter estimated	$400,000	$246,000	
8	Third quarter estimated	$500,000	$305,000	
9	Fourth quarter estimated	$200,000	$126,000	
10				

b. The company normally collects 65% of a quarter's sales before the quarter ends and another 33% in the following quarter. The remainder is uncollectible. This pattern of collections is now being experienced in the current year's fourth-quarter actual data.

c. Eighty percent of a quarter's merchandise purchases are paid for within the quarter. The remainder is paid for in the following quarter.

d. Operating expenses for next year are budgeted at $50,000 per quarter plus 15% of sales. Of the fixed amount, $20,000 each quarter is depreciation.

e. The company will pay $10,000 in dividends each quarter.
f. Equipment purchases of $75,000 will be made in the second quarter, and purchases of $48,000 will be made in the third quarter. These purchases will be for cash.
g. The Cash account contained $10,000 at the end of the current year. The treasurer feels that this represents a minimum balance that must be maintained.
h. Any borrowing will take place at the beginning of a quarter, and any repayments will be made at the end of a quarter at an annual interest rate of 10%. Interest is paid only when principal is repaid. All borrowings and all repayments of principal must be in round $1,000 amounts. Interest payments can be in any amount. (Compute interest on whole months, e.g., 1⁄12, 2⁄12.)
i. At present, the company has no loans outstanding.

Required:

1. Prepare the following by quarter and in total for next year:
   a. A schedule of expected cash collections.
   b. A schedule of expected cash disbursements for merchandise purchases.
2. Compute the expected cash disbursements for operating expenses, by quarter and in total, for next year.
3. Prepare a cash budget, by quarter and in total, for next year. Show clearly in your budget the quarter(s) in which borrowing will be necessary and the quarter(s) in which repayments can be made, as requested by the company's bank.

PROBLEM 9–19 Completing a Master Budget [LO2, LO4, LO7, LO8, LO9, LO10]

The following data relate to the operations of Shilow Company, a wholesale distributor of consumer goods:

Current assets as of March 31:	
Cash	$8,000
Accounts receivable	$20,000
Inventory	$36,000
Building and equipment, net	$120,000
Accounts payable	$21,750
Capital stock	$150,000
Retained earnings	$12,250

a. The gross margin is 25% of sales.
b. Actual and budgeted sales data:

March (actual)	$50,000
April	$60,000
May	$72,000
June	$90,000
July	$48,000

c. Sales are 60% for cash and 40% on credit. Credit sales are collected in the month following sale. The accounts receivable at March 31 are a result of March credit sales.
d. Each month's ending inventory should equal 80% of the following month's budgeted cost of goods sold.
e. One-half of a month's inventory purchases is paid for in the month of purchase; the other half is paid for in the following month. The accounts payable at March 31 are the result of March purchases of inventory.
f. Monthly expenses are as follows: commissions, 12% of sales; rent, $2,500 per month; other expenses (excluding depreciation), 6% of sales. Assume that these expenses are paid monthly. Depreciation is $900 per month (includes depreciation on new assets).
g. Equipment costing $1,500 will be purchased for cash in April.
h. The company must maintain a minimum cash balance of $4,000. An open line of credit is available at a local bank. All borrowing is done at the beginning of a month, and all repayments are made at the end of a month; borrowing must be in multiples of $1,000. The annual interest rate is 12%. Interest is paid only at the time of repayment of principal; figure interest on whole months (1⁄12, 2⁄12, and so forth).

Required:
Using the preceding data:
1. Complete the following schedule:

Schedule of Expected Cash Collections	April	May	June	Quarter
Cash sales	$36,000			
Credit sales	20,000			
Total collections	$56,000			

2. Complete the following:

Merchandise Purchases Budget	April	May	June	Quarter
Budgeted cost of goods sold	$45,000*	$54,000		
Add desired ending inventory	43,200†			
Total needs	88,200			
Less beginning inventory	36,000			
Required purchases	$52,200			

*For April sales: $60,000 sales × 75% cost ratio = $45,000.
†$54,000 × 80% = $43,200

Schedule of Expected Cash Disbursements—Merchandise Purchases	April	May	June	Quarter
March purchases	$21,750			$21,750
April purchases	26,100	$26,100		52,200
May purchases				
June purchases				
Total disbursements	$47,850			

3. Complete the following:

Schedule of Expected Cash Disbursements—Operating Expenses	April	May	June	Quarter
Commissions	$ 7,200			
Rent	2,500			
Other expenses	3,600			
Total disbursements	$13,300			

4. Complete the following cash budget:

Cash Budget	April	May	June	Quarter
Cash balance, beginning	$ 8,000			
Add cash collections	56,000			
Total cash available	64,000			

continued

	April	May	June	Quarter
Less cash disbursements:				
For inventory	47,850			
For expenses	13,300			
For equipment	1,500			
Total cash disbursements	62,650			
Excess (deficiency) of cash	1,350			
Financing:				
Etc.				

5. Prepare an absorption costing income statement, similar to the one shown in Schedule 9 in the text, for the quarter ended June 30.
6. Prepare a balance sheet as of June 30.

PROBLEM 9–20 Completing a Master Budget [LO2, LO4, LO7, LO8, LO9, LO10]
Hillyard Company, an office supplies specialty store, prepares its master budget on a quarterly basis. The following data have been assembled to assist in preparing the master budget for the first quarter:

a. As of December 31 (the end of the prior quarter), the company's general ledger showed the following account balances:

	Debits	Credits
Cash	$ 48,000	
Accounts Receivable	224,000	
Inventory	60,000	
Buildings and Equipment (net)	370,000	
Accounts Payable		$ 93,000
Capital Stock		500,000
Retained Earnings		109,000
	$702,000	$702,000

b. Actual sales for December and budgeted sales for the next four months are as follows:

December (actual)	$280,000
January	$400,000
February	$600,000
March	$300,000
April	$200,000

c. Sales are 20% for cash and 80% on credit. All payments on credit sales are collected in the month following sale. The accounts receivable at December 31 are a result of December credit sales.
d. The company's gross margin is 40% of sales. (In other words, cost of goods sold is 60% of sales.)
e. Monthly expenses are budgeted as follows: salaries and wages, $27,000 per month: advertising, $70,000 per month; shipping, 5% of sales; other expenses, 3% of sales. Depreciation, including depreciation on new assets acquired during the quarter, will be $42,000 for the quarter.
f. Each month's ending inventory should equal 25% of the following month's cost of goods sold.
g. One-half of a month's inventory purchases is paid for in the month of purchase; the other half is paid in the following month.
h. During February, the company will purchase a new copy machine for $1,700 cash. During March, other equipment will be purchased for cash at a cost of $84,500.
i. During January, the company will declare and pay $45,000 in cash dividends.
j. The company must maintain a minimum cash balance of $30,000. An open line of credit is available at a local bank for any borrowing that may be needed during the quarter. All borrowing is done at the beginning of a month, and all repayments are made at the end of a month. Borrowings and repayments of principal must be in multiples of $1,000. Interest is paid only at the time of payment of principal. The annual interest rate is 12%. (Figure interest on whole months, e.g., $\frac{1}{12}$, $\frac{2}{12}$.)

Required:
Using the data above, complete the following statements and schedules for the first quarter:

1. Schedule of expected cash collections:

	January	February	March	Quarter
Cash sales	$ 80,000			
Credit sales	224,000			
Total cash collections	$304,000			

2. *a.* Merchandise purchases budget:

	January	February	March	Quarter
Budgeted cost of goods sold	$240,000*	$360,000		
Add desired ending inventory	90,000†			
Total needs	330,000			
Less beginning inventory	60,000			
Required purchases	$270,000			

*$400,000 sales × 60% cost ratio = $240,000.
†$360,000 × 25% = $90,000.

b. Schedule of expected cash disbursements for merchandise purchases:

	January	February	March	Quarter
December purchases	$ 93,000			$ 93,000
January purchases	135,000	135,000		270,000
February purchases	—			
March purchases	—			
Total cash disbursements for purchases	$228,000			

3. Schedule of expected cash disbursements for operating expenses:

	January	February	March	Quarter
Salaries and wages	$ 27,000			
Advertising	70,000			
Shipping	20,000			
Other expenses	12,000			
Total cash disbursements for operating expenses	$129,000			

4. Cash budget:

	January	February	March	Quarter
Cash balance, beginning	$ 48,000			
Add cash collections	304,000			
Total cash available	352,000			
Less cash disbursements:				
Purchases of inventory	228,000			
Operating expenses	129,000			
Purchases of equipment	—			
Cash dividends	45,000			
Total cash disbursements	402,000			
Excess (deficiency) of cash	(50,000)			
Financing:				
Etc.				

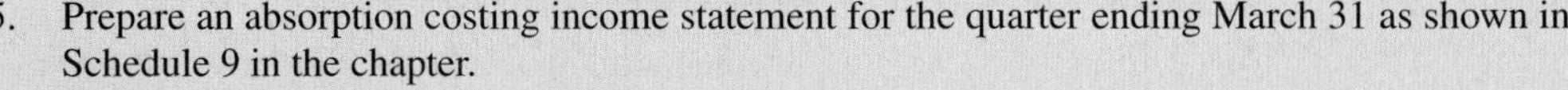

5. Prepare an absorption costing income statement for the quarter ending March 31 as shown in Schedule 9 in the chapter.
6. Prepare a balance sheet as of March 31.

PROBLEM 9–21 Cash Budget for One Month [LO2, LO4, LO6, LO8]

Wallace Products, Ltd., is planning its cash needs for July. Since the company will be buying some new equipment during the month, the treasurer is sure that some borrowing will be needed, but he is uncertain how much. The following data have been assembled to assist the treasurer in preparing a cash budget for the month:

a. Equipment will be purchased during July for cash at a cost of $45,000.
b. Selling and administrative expenses will be:

Advertising	$110,000
Sales salaries	$50,000
Administrative salaries	$35,000
Shipping	$2,100

c. Sales are budgeted at $800,000 for July. Customers are allowed a 2½% cash discount on accounts paid within 10 days after the end of the month of sale. Only 50% of the payments made in the month following the sale fall within the discount period. (All of the company's sales are on account.)
d. On June 30, the company will have the following accounts receivable outstanding:

Month	Sales	Accounts Receivable at June 30	Percentage of Sales Uncollected at June 30	Percentage to Be Collected in July
March	$430,000	$6,450	1½%	?
April	$590,000	$35,400	6%	?
May	$640,000	$128,000	20%	?
June	$720,000	$720,000	100%	?

Bad debts are negligible. All March receivables shown above will have been collected by the end of July, and the collection pattern implicit in the schedule above will be the same in July as in previous months.

e. Production costs are budgeted as follows for July:

Prime costs:		
Raw materials to be used in production		$342,000
Direct labour		95,000
Overhead costs:		
Indirect labour	$36,000	
Utilities	1,900	
Payroll benefits	14,800	
Depreciation	28,000	
Property taxes	1,100	
Fire insurance	1,700	
Amortization of patents	3,500	
Scrapping of obsolete goods	2,600	89,600
Total production costs		$526,600

f. The raw materials inventory is budgeted to increase by $18,000 during July; other inventories will not change.
g. Half of the raw materials purchased each month is paid for in the month of purchase; the other half is paid for in the following month. Accounts payable at June 30 for raw materials purchases will be $172,000.
h. All July payroll amounts will be paid for within the month of July.
i. Utilities costs are paid for within the month.

j. The $14,800 monthly charge above for "Payroll benefits" includes the following items:

Company pension plan, including 1/12 of a $9,600 special adjustment that was paid in April	$7,000
Group insurance (payable semiannually, with the last payment having been made in January)	$900
Employment insurance (payable monthly)	$1,300
Vacation pay, which represents 1/12 of the annual cost (July's vacations will require $14,100)	$5,600

k. Property taxes are paid in June of each year.
l. Fire insurance premiums were prepaid in January.
m. The company has an open line of credit with the Royal Calgary Bank. All borrowing from the bank must be in round $1,000 amounts.
n. The cash balance on June 30 is $78,000; the company must maintain a cash balance of at least $75,000.

Required:

1. Prepare a schedule of expected cash collections for July.
2. Compute (a) budgeted cash disbursements for raw materials purchases, and (b) budgeted cash disbursements for overhead for July.
3. Prepare a cash budget for July.
4. A member of the board of directors of Wallace Products stated, "The monthly cash budget shows the company's cash surplus or deficiency and assures us that an unexpected cash shortage will not occur." Comment on this statement.

(SMA, adapted)

PROBLEM 9–22 Integrated Operating Budgets [LO3, LO4, LO5, LO6]

The West Division of Vader Corporation produces an intricate component part used in Vader's major product line. The divisional manager has recently been concerned about a lack of coordination between purchasing and production personnel and believes that a monthly budgeting system would be better than the present system.

The manager of the West Division has decided to develop budget information for the third quarter of the current year as a trial before the budget system is implemented for an entire fiscal year. In response to the manager's request for data that could be used to develop budget information, the controller of the West Division accumulated the following data:

Sales Sales through June 30, the first six months of the current year, were 24,000 units. Actual sales in units for May and June and estimated unit sales for the next five months are detailed as follows:

May (actual)	4,000
June (actual)	4,000
July (estimated)	5,000
August (estimated)	6,000
September (estimated)	7,000
October (estimated)	7,500
November (estimated)	8,000

The West Division expects to sell 65,000 units during the year ending December 31.

Direct Materials Data regarding the direct materials used in the component are shown in the following schedule. Each month's ending direct materials inventory should equal 50% of the next month's production needs.

Direct Material	Units of Direct Materials per Finished Component	Cost per Unit	Inventory Level June 30
No. 101	6 grams	$2.40	35,000 grams
No. 211	4 kilograms	$5.00	30,000 kilograms

Direct Labour Each component must pass through three processes to be completed. Data regarding the direct labour are as follows:

Process	Direct Labour-Hours per Finished Component	Cost per Direct Labour-Hour
Forming	0.40	$16.00
Assembly	1.00	$11.00
Finishing	0.10	$15.00

Manufacturing Overhead The West Division produced 27,000 components and incurred the variable overhead costs shown below during the six-month period ended June 30. The controller of the West Division believes that the variable overhead costs will be incurred at the same rate during the last six months of the year.

Supplies	$ 59,400
Electricity	27,000
Indirect labour	54,000
Other	8,100
Total variable overhead	$148,500

The fixed manufacturing overhead costs incurred during the first six months amounted to $93,500. Fixed manufacturing overhead costs are budgeted for the full year as follows:

Supervision	$ 60,000
Taxes	7,200
Depreciation	86,400
Other	32,400
Total fixed manufacturing overhead . .	$186,000

Finished Goods Inventory The desired monthly ending finished goods inventory in units is 80% of the next month's estimated sales. There are 4,000 finished units in inventory on June 30.

Required:

1. Prepare a production budget for the West Division for the third quarter ending September 30. Show computations by month and in total for the quarter.
2. Prepare a direct materials budget for each type of material for the third quarter ending September 30. Again show computations by month and in total for the quarter.
3. Prepare a direct labour budget for the third quarter ending September 30. This time it is *not* necessary to show monthly figures; show quarterly totals only. Assume that the workforce is adjusted as work requirements change.
4. Assume that the company plans to produce a total of 65,000 units for the year. Prepare a manufacturing overhead budget for the six-month period ending December 31. (Do not compute a predetermined overhead rate.) Again, it is *not* necessary to show monthly figures.

(CMA, adapted)

CASES

CASE 9–23 Evaluating a Company's Budget Procedures [LO1]

Tom Emory and Jim Morris strolled back to their plant from the administrative offices of Ferguson & Son Mfg. Company. Tom is manager of the machine shop in the company's factory; Jim is the manager of the equipment maintenance department.

The men had just attended the monthly performance evaluation meeting for plant department heads. These meetings had been held on the third Tuesday of each month since Robert Ferguson, Jr., the president's son, had become plant manager a year earlier.

As they were walking, Tom Emory spoke: "Boy, I hate those meetings! I never know whether my department's accounting reports will show good or bad performance. I'm beginning to expect the worst. If the accountants say I saved the company a dollar, I'm called 'Sir,' but if I spend even a little too much—boy, do I get in trouble. I don't know if I can hold on until I retire."

Tom had just been given the worst evaluation he had ever received in his long career with Ferguson & Son. He was the most respected of the experienced machinists in the company. He had been with Ferguson & Son for many years and was promoted to supervisor of the machine shop when the company expanded and moved to its present location. The president (Robert Ferguson, Sr.) had often stated that the company's success was due to the high quality of the work of machinists like Tom. As supervisor, Tom stressed the importance of craftsmanship and told his workers that he wanted no sloppy work coming from his department.

When Robert Ferguson, Jr., became the plant manager, he directed that monthly performance comparisons be made between actual and budgeted costs for each department. The departmental budgets were intended to encourage the supervisors to reduce inefficiencies and to seek cost reduction opportunities. The company controller was instructed to have his staff "tighten" the budget slightly whenever a department attained its budget in a given month; this was done to reinforce the plant manager's desire to reduce costs. The young plant manager often stressed the importance of continued progress toward attaining the budget; he also made it known that he kept a file of these performance reports for future reference when he succeeded his father.

Tom Emory's conversation with Jim Morris continued as follows:

Emory: I really don't understand. We've worked so hard to meet the budget, and the minute we do so they tighten it on us. We can't work any faster and still maintain quality. I think my men are ready to quit trying. Besides, those reports don't tell the whole story. We always seem to be interrupting the big jobs for all those small rush orders. All that setup and machine adjustment time is killing us. And quite frankly, Jim, you were no help. When our hydraulic press broke down last month, your people were nowhere to be found. We had to take it apart ourselves and got stuck with all that idle time.

Morris: I'm sorry about that, Tom, but you know my department has had trouble making budget, too. We were running well behind at the time of that problem, and if we'd spent a day on that old machine, we would never have made it up. Instead we made the scheduled inspections of the forklift trucks because we knew we could do those in less than the budgeted time.

Emory: Well, Jim, at least you have some options. I'm locked into what the scheduling department assigns to me and you know they're being harassed by sales for those special orders. Incidentally, why didn't your report show all the supplies you guys wasted last month when you were working in Bill's department?

Morris: We're not out of the woods on that deal yet. We charged the maximum we could to other work and haven't even reported some of it yet.

Emory: Well, I'm glad you have a way of getting out of the pressure. The accountants seem to know everything that's happening in my department, sometimes even before I do. I thought all that budget and accounting stuff was supposed to help, but it just gets me into trouble. It's all a big pain. I'm trying to put out quality work; they're trying to save pennies.

Required:

1. Identify the problems that appear to exist in Ferguson & Son Mfg. Company's budgetary control system and explain how the problems are likely to reduce the effectiveness of the system.
2. Explain how Ferguson & Son Mfg. Company's budgetary control system could be revised to improve its effectiveness.

(CMA, adapted)

CASE 9–24 Master Budget with Supporting Schedules [LO2, LO4, LO8, LO9, LO10]

You have just been hired as a new management trainee by Earrings Unlimited, a distributor of earrings to various retail outlets located in shopping malls across the country. In the past, the company has done very little in the way of budgeting and at certain times of the year has experienced a shortage of cash.

Since you are well trained in budgeting, you have decided to prepare comprehensive budgets for the upcoming second quarter in order to show management the benefits that can be gained from an integrated budgeting program. To this end, you have worked with accounting and other areas to gather the information assembled below.

The company sells many styles of earrings, but all are sold for the same price—$10 per pair. Actual sales of earrings for the last three months and budgeted sales for the next six months follow (in pairs of earrings):

January (actual)	20,000	June (budget)	50,000
February (actual)	26,000	July (budget)	30,000
March (actual)	40,000	August (budget)	28,000
April (budget)	65,000	September (budget)	25,000
May (budget)	100,000		

The concentration of sales before and during May is due to Mother's Day. Sufficient inventory should be on hand at the end of each month to supply 40% of the earrings sold in the following month.

Suppliers are paid $4 for a pair of earrings. One-half of a month's purchases is paid for in the month of purchase; the other half is paid for in the following month. All sales are on credit, with no discount, and payable within 15 days. The company has found, however, that only 20% of a month's sales are collected in the month of sale. An additional 70% is collected in the following month, and the remaining 10% is collected in the second month following sale. Bad debts have been negligible.

Monthly operating expenses for the company are given below:

Variable:	
Sales commissions	4% of sales
Fixed:	
Advertising	$200,000
Rent	$18,000
Salaries	$106,000
Utilities	$7,000
Insurance	$3,000
Depreciation	$14,000

Insurance is paid on an annual basis, in November of each year.

The company plans to purchase $16,000 in new equipment during May and $40,000 in new equipment during June; both purchases will be for cash. The company declares dividends of $15,000 each quarter, payable in the first month of the following quarter.

A listing of the company's ledger accounts as of March 31 is given below:

Assets	
Cash	$ 74,000
Accounts receivable ($26,000 February sales; $320,000 March sales)	346,000
Inventory	104,000
Prepaid insurance	21,000
Property and equipment (net)	950,000
Total assets	$1,495,000
Liabilities and Shareholders' Equity	
Accounts payable	$ 100,000
Dividends payable	15,000
Capital stock	800,000
Retained earnings	580,000
Total liabilities and shareholders' equity	$1,495,000

The company maintains a minimum cash balance of $50,000. All borrowing is done at the beginning of a month; any repayments are made at the end of a month.

The annual interest rate is 12%. Interest is computed and paid at the end of each quarter on all loans outstanding during the quarter.

Required:

Prepare a master budget for the three-month period ending June 30. Include the following detailed budgets:

1. *a.* A sales budget, by month and in total.
   b. A schedule of expected cash collections from sales, by month and in total.
   c. A merchandise purchases budget in units and in dollars. Show the budget by month and in total.

   d. A schedule of expected cash disbursements for merchandise purchases, by month and in total.
2. A cash budget. Show the budget by month and in total. Determine any borrowing that would be needed to maintain the minimum cash balance of $50,000.
3. A budgeted income statement for the three-month period ending June 30. Use the contribution approach.
4. A budgeted balance sheet as of June 30.

CASE 9–25 Business Plan

Su Lam and Abel Brody are investigating the possibility of establishing a restaurant and lounge in a developing neighbourhood in Halifax. They have noticed a suitable location that can be leased from a realtor. The premises previously were used as a restaurant and lounge, so minimal improvements would be required. Lam and Brody have decided to cater to the ethnic food and entertainment tastes of the area's residents. Because of the developing nature of the neighbourhood, the initial clientele is expected to come from the immediate vicinity, with a marginal influx of people from outside the area. The potential to attract a wider clientele exists because of the location's proximity to the major office and entertainment area of mainland Halifax and the area improvements that are occurring. However, the focus for the initial start-up is on a local clientele.

Lam and Brody have done some preliminary investigation of their needs and the relative costs of various items. The capital cost estimates below include their leasehold improvements and various capital items they need to procure. Financing will be necessary for these items.

Capital Cost Estimates	
Cash	$ 5,000
Inventory	4,000
Tables, chairs, dishes, etc.	15,000
Kitchen	26,000
Alarms, signage	2,000
Leasehold improvements	3,000

Use life: Five years. Straight-line depreciation.

In addition to capital asset items, certain expenses were estimated, as shown below:

Operating Expenses Per Month	
Advertising	$ 200
Office costs, excluding wages	100
Utilities	600
Entertainment	1,200
Leasing—other than premises	200
Cleaning and maintenance	300

Operating Expenses Per Year	
Rent	$12 per square foot

Other data:

Capacity: 20 tables; 60 lounge seats, 20 square feet per table and 5 per lounge seat
Kitchen and entrance: 500 square feet
Stage and bar: 300 square feet

Salaries and wages are based on the usual practice of paying minimum wage and using a pool of tips to supplement these wages. The wages and an estimate of the hours of work are shown below:

Estimated Wages and Salaries	
Servers	$ 8.25 per hour
Bartender	9.20 per hour
Cooks	10.00 per hour
Hostess	8.00 per hour
Doorman	8.50 per hour
Cleaning	7.25 per hour
Manager	450.00 per week
Bookkeeping	100.00 per week

Other data:
Servers: One per five tables for the restaurant, average; one per 30 seats for the lounge, average.
Three cooks are necessary.
Bartender: One during dinner, one during lounge hours.
Employee benefits are estimated to be 9% of wages/salaries.

In addition to the costs, Lam and Brody determined a few of the essentials. First, they are assured of a licence by both the city and the province to operate a restaurant and lounge. Second, markups for food are expected to be 200% of the cost of food. This means that a plate of food costing $2 to purchase will sell for $6 on the menu. Liquor, beer, and wine have a variety of markups on cost but, on average, with an expected mix, they anticipate an 80% markup. Additional revenue will be obtained from a cover charge for late-night live entertainment three nights a week (not on Sunday).

Expected hours of operation for the restaurant will be from 5:00 p.m. to 9:00 p.m., seven days a week. Only one bartender will be needed during dinner hours. The lounge will operate only on Thursday, Friday, and Saturday, from 9:00 p.m. to 1:30 a.m., and Sunday, from 9:00 p.m. to 12:30 a.m. when live entertainment is provided. A cover charge of $5 seems appropriate. Only one bartender will be required for the lounge.

A number of key demographic data that Lam gathered to assist in the planning are shown below. Lam and Brody are unsure, however, whether the data are complete enough to serve as a base for analysis.

Demographics

Potential customers	19 to 39 years of age
Households in immediate vicinity	5,000
Spending on beverages per person per year in licensed premises	• $171.50 per person for 19–29 age group • $100.50 per person for 30–39 age group
Population of Metro Halifax	315,000, of which 69,610 are 19–29 and 52,815 are 30–39
Spending on food per year per household in restaurants	$630.00 for 93% of households

Assumption: 10% increase in sales in year 2.

Required:

You have been asked to provide a two-year financial forecast for operations beginning April 1, 2006, and broken into semi-annual segments. In addition, you are required to assess the feasibility of the operations. Your estimates will be used to obtain a five-year term loan at a 10% rate of interest for 10% of the required financing.

To protect your reputation, you will need to verify the information provided as much as possible. Where visual inspection is required, indicate this.

Prepared by G.R. Chesley. Permission to use this case was provided by the Accounting Case Institute.

CASE 9-26 Master Budget for a Manufacturer

Comeau Manufacturing Ltd. produces and distributes a special type of chemical compound called compound WX. The following information about Comeau's operations has been assembled to assist budget preparation. The company is preparing to build its master budget for the coming first quarter of 2007. The budget will detail each month's activity and the activity for the quarter in total. The master budget will be based on the following information:

1. Selling price is $60 per unit in 2006 and will not change for the first two quarters of 2007. Actual and estimated sales are as follows:
2. Unit sales by month are as follows:

2006 Actual		2007 Estimated				
Nov.	Dec.	Jan.	Feb.	Mar.	Apr.	May
10,000	12,000	11,000	10,000	13,000	11,000	10,000

3. The company produces enough units each month to meet that month's sales plus a desired inventory level equal to 20% of next month's estimated sales. Finished inventory at the end of 2006 consisted of 2,200 units at a variable cost of $33 each.
4. The company purchases enough raw materials each month for the current month's production requirement and 25% of next month's production requirement. Each unit of product requires 5 kilograms of raw material at $0.60 per kilogram. Comeau pays 40% of raw material purchases in the month of purchase and pays the remaining 60% in the following month.
5. Each unit of finished product requires 2 labour-hours. The average wage rate is $10 per hour.
6. Variable manufacturing overhead is 50% of the direct labour cost.
7. Credit sales are 60% of total sales. The company collects 50% of the credit sales during the first month following the month of sale and 50% during the second month.
8. Fixed overhead cost (per month)

Factory Supervisor's Salary	$75,000
Factory Insurance	1,400
Factory Rent	8,000
Depreciation of factory equipment	1,200

9. Total fixed selling and administrative expenses amount to the following:

Advertising	$ 300
Depreciation	9,000
Insurance	250
Salaries	4,000
Other	14,550

10. Variable selling and administrative expenses consist of $4 per unit for freight-out and sales commissions of 10% of sales.
11. The company is going to acquire assets for use in the sales office at a cost of $300,000 which will be paid at the end of January 2007. The monthly depreciation expense on the additional capital assets will be $6,000.
12. The balance sheet as of December 31, 2006, is as follows:

Assets		
Cash		$ 80,000
Accounts receivable		612,000
Inventory: Raw materials	8,100	
Finished goods	72,600	80,700
Plant and equipment	1,000,000	
Less: accumulated depreciation	(100,000)	900,000
Total assets		$1,672,700
Liabilities and Equity		
Accounts payable		$ 24,000
12% Long-term notes payable		900,000
Contributed capital		735,000
Retained earnings		13,700
Total liabilities and equity		$1,672,700

Additional Information:

- All cash payments except purchases of raw materials are made monthly as incurred.
- All loan repayments and borrowings, when appropriate, occur at the end of each month..
- All interest on borrowed funds is paid at the end of each month at the rate of 12% per year.
- Loan repayments and borrowings, when appropriate, may be made in any amount.
- A minimum cash balance of $30,000 is required at the end of each month.

Required:

1. Prepare the following budgets for *the first three months* of 2007:
   a. Sales budget
   b. Production budget
   c. Raw materials purchases budget
   d. Direct labour and manufacturing overhead budget
   e. Selling and administrative expense budget

f. Budgeted (pro forma) income statement (using variable costing)
g. Cash budget

2. Prepare a budgeted (pro forma) balance sheet as at March 31, 2007.
3. Compute the amount of conversion cost and direct materials cost assigned to units transferred out and to ending goods in inventory.

GROUP AND INTERNET EXERCISES

GROUP EXERCISE 9–27 Financial Pressures Hit Higher Education

In the late eighties and early nineties, public universities found that they were no longer immune to financial stress. Budget cuts were in the air across the land. When the budget axe hit, the cuts often came without warning and their size was sometimes staggering. Support for some institutions dropped significantly. Most university administrators had only experienced budget increases, never budget cuts. Also, the budget setbacks usually occurred at the most inopportune time—during the school year when contractual commitments with faculty and staff had been signed, programs had been planned, and students were enrolled and taking classes.

Required:

1. Should the university's administration be "fair" to all affected departments by declaring a round of across-the-board cuts whenever the government announces another subsidy reduction?
2. If not across-the-board cutbacks in programs, then would you recommend more focused reductions, and if so, what priorities would you establish for bringing spending in line with revenues?
3. Since these usually are not one-time-only cutbacks, how would you manage continuous, long-term reductions in budgets extending over a period of years?
4. Should the decision-making process be top-down (centralized with top administrators) or bottom-up (participative)? Why?
5. How should issues such as a protect-your-turf mentality, resistance to change, and consensus building be dealt with?

INTERNET EXERCISE 9–28

As you know, the World Wide Web is a medium that is constantly evolving. Sites come and go, and change without notice. To enable the periodic updating of site addresses, this problem has been posted to the textbook Web site (www.mcgrawhill.ca/college/garrison). After accessing the site, enter the Student Centre and select this chapter. Select and complete the Internet Exercise.

CHAPTER 10

LEARNING OBJECTIVES

After studying Chapter 10, you should be able to:

1. Explain how direct materials standards and direct labour standards are set.

2. Compute the direct materials price and quantity variances and explain their significance.

3. Complete the mix and yield variances for materials and explain their significance.

4. Compute the direct labour rate and efficiency variances and explain their significance.

5. Compute the variable manufacturing overhead spending and efficiency variances.

6. (Appendix 10A) Prepare journal entries to record standard costs and variances.

7. (Appendix 10B) Explain the concept of learning curves.

STANDARD COSTS

BUSINESS FOCUS

STANDARDS PUT TO THE TEST

A recent legal case against the federal government concerning the Canadian flags used for the 2003 Canada Day celebrations illustrates the complexity of the use of the idea of standards. The reported contention by Flag Connection Inc. was that the flags resulting from the $2.2 million contract awarded to Scythes Inc. did not meet the new standards set for the flag by the Canadian General Standards Board. Thus the winning and cheaper bid for the contract was given out for a product that was not up to "standard" so the bidding process for the contract was flawed.

Source: Glen McGregor, CanWest News Service, "Maple Leafs Not up to Standard: Flag-maker," *National Post*, January 20, 2005, p. A4.

Chapter 10 begins a three-chapter sequence whose focus is on performance measures and management control. Now we begin our study of management control and performance measures. Quite often, these terms carry with them negative connotations—we may have a tendency to think of performance measurement as something to be feared. Indeed, performance measurements can be used in very negative ways—to cast blame and to punish. However, that is not the way they should be used. As explained in the following quotation, performance measurement serves a vital function in both personal life and in organizations:

> Imagine you want to improve your basketball shooting skill. You know that practice will help, so you [go] to the basketball court. There you start shooting toward the hoop, but as soon as the ball gets close to the rim your vision goes blurry for a second, so that you cannot observe where the ball ended up in relation to the target (left, right, in front, too far back, inside the hoop?). It would be pretty difficult to improve under those conditions. . . . (And by the way, how long would [shooting baskets] sustain your interest if you couldn't observe the outcome of your efforts?)
>
> Or imagine someone engaging in a weight loss program. A normal step in such programs is to purchase a scale to be able to track one's progress: Is this program working? Am I losing weight? A positive answer would be encouraging and would motivate me to keep up the effort, while a negative answer might lead me to reflect on the process: Am I working on the right diet and exercise program? Am I doing everything I am supposed to?, etc. Suppose you don't want to set up a sophisticated measurement system and decide to forgo the scale. You would still have some idea of how well you are doing from simple methods such as clothes feeling looser, a belt that fastens at a different hole, or simply via observation in a mirror! Now, imagine trying to sustain a weight loss program without *any* feedback on how well you are doing.
>
> In these . . . examples, availability of quantitative measures of performance can yield two types of benefits: First, performance feedback can help improve the "production process" through a better understanding of what works and what doesn't; e.g., shooting this way works better than shooting that way. Secondly, feedback on performance can sustain motivation and effort, because it is encouraging and/or because it suggests that more effort is required for the goal to be met.[1]

Performance measurement can be helpful in an organization. It can provide feedback concerning what works and what does not work, and it can help motivate people to sustain their efforts. While we focus on performance, it is important to keep in mind that these performance measures can be used for planning and for decision making if we are careful to apply the logic of cost behaviour introduced in Chapters 5 through 8.

Our study of performance measurement begins in this chapter with the lowest levels in the organization. We work our way up the organizational ladder in subsequent chapters. In this chapter, we see how various measures are used to control operations and to evaluate performance. Even though we are starting with the lowest levels in the organization, keep in mind that the performance measures used should be derived from the organization's overall strategy. For example, a company like Samsung that bases its strategy on rapid introduction of innovative consumer products should use different performance measures than a company like Fed Ex, where on-time delivery, customer convenience, and low cost are key competitive advantages. Samsung may want to keep close track of the percentage of revenues from products introduced within the last year, whereas Fed Ex may want to closely monitor the percentage of packages delivered on time. In chapter 12 when we discuss the *balanced scorecard,* we will have more to say concerning the role of strategy in the selection of performance measures. But first we will see how *standard costs* are used by managers to help control costs.

Companies in highly competitive industries like Nortel, Fed Ex, WestJet, Hewlett-Packard, Imperial Oil, and Toyota must be able to provide high-quality goods and services at low cost. If they do not, they will perish. Stated in the starkest terms, managers must obtain inputs such as raw materials and electricity at the lowest possible prices and must use them as effectively as possible—while maintaining or increasing the quality of the output. If inputs are purchased at prices that are too high or more input is used than is really necessary, higher costs will result.

1. Soumitra Dutta and Jean-François Manzoni, *Process Reengineering, Organizational Change and Performance Improvement* (New York: McGraw-Hill, 1999), Chapter IV.

How do managers control the prices that are paid for inputs and the quantities that are used? They could examine every transaction in detail, but this obviously would be an inefficient use of management time. For many companies, the answer to this control problem lies at least partially in standard costs.

Budgeting, as described in Chapter 9, focuses on planning but is employed for control purposes where desired by management. Standards represent specific elements of budgets such as material requirements or labour requirements as well as overhead projections. Standards thus serve both a planning function and a control function. In addition, in some circumstances they can improve the accuracy of costs for inventory, for example a cost of a box of chocolates produced by Hershey. Whether or not organizations employ standard costs to formally cost jobs (Chapter 3) or processes (Chapter 4) is one of the decisions managers must make when implementing financial systems. If they decide to use actual costs for jobs or processes, they still can employ standard cost practices for budgeting and operational planning.

FOCUS *on Current Practice*

The Brass Products Division at Parker Hannifin Corporation, known as Parker Brass, is a world-class manufacturer of tube and brass fittings, valves, hose and hose fittings. Management at the company uses variances from its standard costing system to target problem areas for improvement. If a production variance exceeds 5% of sales, the responsible manager is required to explain the variance and to propose a plan of action to correct the detected problems. In the past, variances were reported at the end of the month—often several weeks after a particular job had been completed. Now, a variance report is generated the day after a job is completed and summary variance reports are prepared weekly. These more frequent reports help managers take more timely corrective action.

Source: David Johnsen and Parvez Sopariwala, "Standard Costing Is Alive and Well at Parker Brass," *Management Accounting Quarterly*, Winter 2000, pp. 12–20.

STANDARD COSTS—MANAGEMENT BY EXCEPTION

A *standard* is a benchmark or "norm" for measuring performance. Standards are found everywhere. Your doctor evaluates your weight using standards that have been set for individuals of your age, height, and gender. The food we eat in restaurants must be prepared under specified standards of cleanliness. The buildings we live in must conform to standards set in building codes. Standards are also widely used in managerial accounting, where they relate to the *quantity* and *cost* of inputs used in manufacturing goods or providing services.

Managers—often assisted by engineers and accountants—set quantity and cost standards for each major input such as raw materials and labour time. *Quantity standards* indicate how much of an input should be used in manufacturing a unit of product or in providing a unit of service. *Cost (price) standards* indicate what the cost, or purchase price, of the input should be. Actual quantities and actual costs of inputs are compared to these standards. If either the quantity or the cost of inputs departs significantly from the standards, managers investigate the discrepancy. The purpose is to find the cause of the problem and then eliminate it so that it does not recur. This process is called **management by exception.**

Management by exception
A system of management in which standards are set for various operating activities, with actual results then compared to these standards. Any differences that are deemed significant are brought to the attention of management as "exceptions."

In our daily lives, we operate in a management by exception mode most of the time. Consider what happens when you sit down in the driver's seat of your car. You put the key in the ignition, you turn the key, and your car starts. Your expectation (standard) that the car will start is met; you do not have to open the car hood and check the battery, the connecting cables, the fuel lines, and so on. If you turn the key and the car does not start, then you have a discrepancy (variance). Your expectations are not met, and you need to investigate why. Note that even if the car starts after a second try, it would be wise to investigate anyway. The fact that the expectation was not met should be viewed as an opportunity to uncover the cause of the problem rather than as simply an annoyance. If the underlying cause is not discovered and corrected, the problem may recur and become much worse.

This basic approach to identifying and solving problems is used in the *variance analysis cycle*, which is illustrated in Exhibit 10–1. The cycle begins with the preparation of standard cost performance reports in the Accounting Department. These reports highlight the variances, which are the differences between actual results and what should have occurred according to the standards. The variances raise questions. Why did the variance occur? Why is this variance larger than it was last period? The significant variances are investigated to discover their root causes. Corrective actions are taken, and then next period's operations are carried out. The cycle then begins again with the preparation of a new standard cost performance for the most recent period. The emphasis should be on flagging problems for attention, finding their root causes, and then taking corrective action. The goal is to improve operations—not to cast blame.

Who Uses Standard Costs?

Manufacturing, service, food, and not-for-profit organizations all make use of standards to some extent. Auto service centres like Canadian Tire, for example, often set specific

EXHIBIT 10–1 The Variance Analysis Cycle

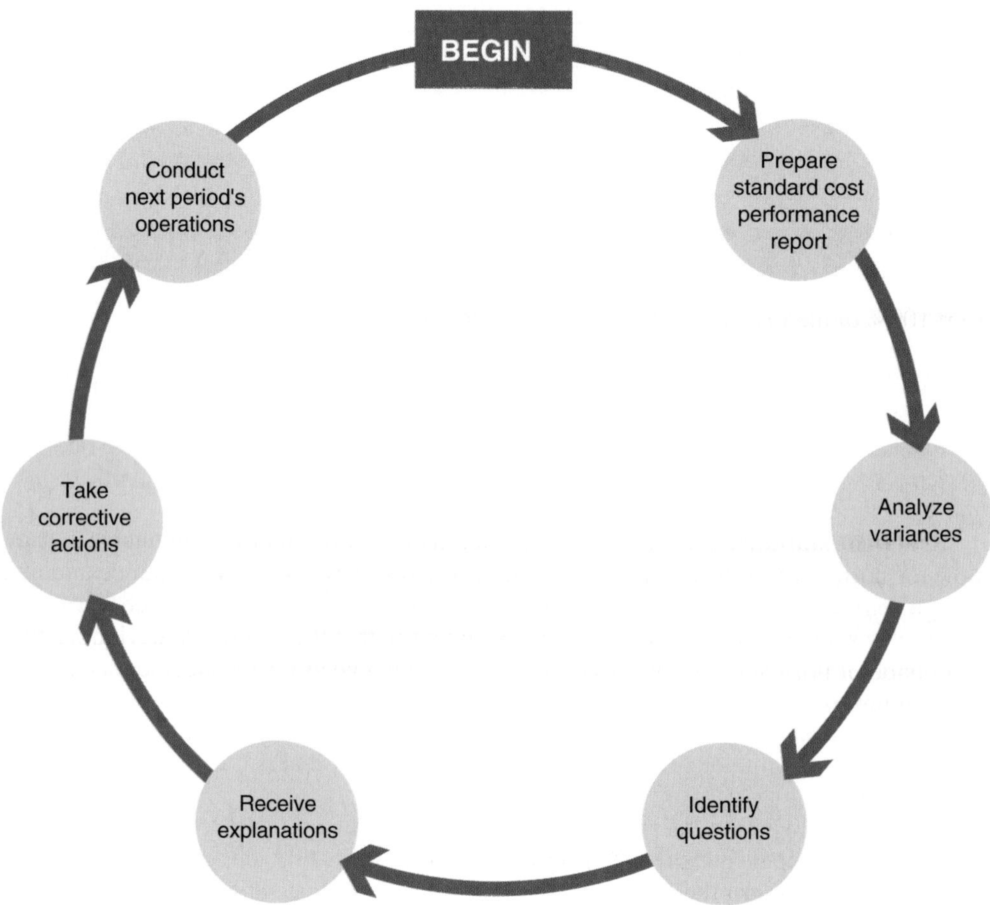

labour time standards for the completion of certain work tasks, such as installing a water pump or doing a valve job, and then measure actual performance against these standards. Fast-food outlets such as Harvey's have exacting standards as to the quantity of meat put into a sandwich, as well as standards for the cost of the meat. Hospitals have standard costs (for food, laundry, and other items) for each occupied bed per day, as well as standard time allowances for certain routine activities, such as laboratory tests. In short, you are likely to run into standard costs in virtually any line of business that you enter.

Manufacturing companies often have highly developed standard costing systems in which standards relating to materials, labour, and overhead are developed in detail for each separate product. These standards are listed on a **standard cost card** that provides the manager with a great deal of information concerning the inputs that are required to produce a unit and their costs. In the following section, we provide a detailed example of the setting of standard costs and the preparation of a standard cost card.

Standard cost card
A detailed listing of the standard amounts of materials, labour, and overhead that should go into a unit of product, multiplied by the standard price or rate that has been set for each cost element.

SETTING STANDARD COSTS

Setting price and quantity standards requires the combined expertise of all persons who have responsibility for input prices and for the effective use of inputs. In a manufacturing setting, this might include accountants, purchasing managers, engineers, production supervisors, line managers, and production workers. Past records of purchase prices and of input usage can be helpful in setting standards. However, the standards should be designed to encourage efficient *future* operations, not a repetition of *past* inefficient operations.

Ideal versus Practical Standards

Should standards be attainable all of the time, should they be attainable only part of the time, or should they be so tight that they become, in effect, "the impossible dream"? Opinions among managers vary, but standards tend to fall into one of two categories—either ideal or practical.

Ideal standards are those that can be attained only under the best circumstances. They allow for no machine breakdowns or other work interruptions, and they call for a level of effort that can be attained only by the most skilled and efficient employees working at peak effort 100% of the time. Some managers feel that such standards have a motivational value. These managers argue that even though employees know they will rarely meet the standard, it is a constant reminder of the need for ever-increasing efficiency and effort. Few firms use ideal standards. Most managers feel that ideal standards tend to discourage even the most diligent workers. Moreover, when ideal standards are used, variances from the standards have little meaning. Because of the ideal standards, large variances are normal and it is difficult to "manage by exception."

Ideal standards
Standards that allow for no machine breakdowns or other work interruptions and that require peak efficiency at all times.

Practical standards are defined as standards that are "tight but attainable." They allow for normal machine downtime and employee rest periods, and they can be attained through reasonable, although highly efficient, efforts by the average worker. Variances from such a standard are very useful to management in that they represent deviations that fall outside of normal operating conditions and signal a need for management attention. Furthermore, practical standards can serve multiple purposes. In addition to signalling abnormal conditions, they can also be used in forecasting cash flows and in planning inventory. By contrast, ideal standards cannot be used in forecasting and planning; they do not allow for normal inefficiencies, and therefore they result in unrealistic planning and forecasting figures.

Practical standards
Standards that allow for normal machine downtime and other work interruptions and that can be attained through reasonable, although highly efficient, efforts by the average worker.

Throughout the remainder of this chapter, we will assume the use of practical rather than ideal standards.

MANAGERIAL ACCOUNTING IN ACTION

The Issue

The Colonial Pewter Company was organized a year ago. The company's only product at present is a reproduction of an eighteenth-century pewter bookend. The bookend is made largely by hand, using traditional metal-working tools. Consequently, the manufacturing process is labour-intensive and requires a high level of skill.

Colonial Pewter has recently expanded its workforce to take advantage of unexpected demand for the bookends as gifts. The company started with a small cadre of experienced pewter workers but has had to hire less experienced workers as a result of the expansion. The president of the company, J.D. Wriston, has called a meeting to discuss production problems. Attending the meeting are Tom Kuchel, the production manager; Janet Warner, the purchasing manager; and Terry Sherman, the corporate controller.

J.D.: I've got a feeling that we aren't getting the production we should out of our new people.

Tom: Give us a chance. Some of the new people have been on board for less than a month.

Janet: Let me add that production seems to be wasting an awful lot of material—particularly pewter. That stuff is very expensive.

Tom: What about the shipment of defective pewter you bought a couple of months ago—the one with the iron contamination? That caused us major problems.

Janet: That's ancient history. How was I to know it was off-grade? Besides, it was a great deal.

J.D.: Calm down everybody. Let's get the facts before we start sinking our fangs into each other.

Tom: I agree. The more facts the better.

J.D.: Okay, Terry, it's your turn. Facts are the controller's department.

Terry: I'm afraid I can't provide the answers off the top of my head, but it won't take me too long to set up a system that can routinely answer questions relating to worker productivity, material waste, and input prices.

J.D.: How long is "not too long"?

Terry: I will need all of your cooperation, but how about a week from today?

J.D.: That's okay with me. What about everyone else?

Tom: Sure.

Janet: Fine with me.

J.D.: Let's mark it on our calendars.

Setting Direct Materials Standards

LEARNING OBJECTIVE 1
Explain how direct materials standards and direct labour standards are set.

Terry Sherman's first task was to prepare price and quantity standards for the company's only significant raw material, pewter ingots. The **standard price per unit** for direct materials should reflect the final, delivered cost of the materials, net of any discounts taken. After consulting with purchasing manager Janet Warner, Terry prepared the following documentation for the standard price of a kilogram of pewter in ingot form:

Standard price per unit
The price that should be paid for a single unit of materials, including allowances for quality, quantity purchased, shipping, receiving, and other such costs, net of any discounts allowed.

Purchase price, top-grade pewter ingots	$ 3.60
Freight, by truck, from the supplier's warehouse	0.44
Receiving and handling	0.05
Less purchase discount	(0.09)
Standard price per kilogram	$ 4.00

Notice that the standard price reflects a particular grade of material (top quality) delivered by a particular type of carrier (truck). Allowances have also been made for handling and discounts. If everything proceeds according to these expectations, the net standard price of a kilogram of pewter should therefore be $4.

Standard quantity per unit
The amount of materials that should be required to complete a single unit of product, including allowances for normal waste, spoilage, rejects, and similar inefficiencies.

The **standard quantity per unit** for direct materials should reflect the amount of material going into each unit of finished product, as well as an allowance for unavoidable waste, spoilage, and other normal inefficiencies. After consulting with the production manager, Tom Kuchel, Terry Sherman prepared the following documentation for the standard quantity of pewter going into a pair of bookends:

Material requirements as specified in the bill of materials for a pair of bookends, in kilograms	2.7
Allowance for waste and spoilage, in kilograms	0.2
Allowance for rejects, in kilograms	0.1
Standard quantity per pair of bookends, in kilograms	3.0

A **bill of materials** is a list that shows the type and quantity of each item of material going into a unit of finished product. It is a handy source for determining the basic materials input per unit, but it should be adjusted for waste and other factors, as shown above, when determining the standard quantity per unit of product. "Waste and spoilage" in the table above refers to materials that are wasted as a normal part of the production process or that spoil before they are used. "Rejects" refers to the direct material contained in units that are defective and must be scrapped.

Bill of materials
A listing of the quantity of each type of material required to manufacture a unit of product.

Although it is common to recognize allowances for waste, spoilage, and rejects when setting standard costs, this practice is now coming into question. Those involved in total quality management (TQM) and similar management approaches argue that no amount of waste or defects should be tolerated. If allowances for waste, spoilage, and rejects are built into the standard cost, the levels of those allowances should be periodically reviewed and reduced over time to reflect improved processes, better training, and better equipment.

Once the price and quantity standards have been set, the standard cost of material per unit of finished product can be computed as follows:

$$3.0 \text{ kilograms per unit} \times \$4 \text{ per kilogram} = \$12 \text{ per unit}$$

This $12 cost figure will appear as one item on the standard cost card of the product.

Setting Direct Labour Standards

Direct labour price and quantity standards are usually expressed in terms of a labour rate and labour-hours. The **standard rate per hour** for direct labour would include not only wages earned but also fringe benefits and other labour costs. Using last month's wage records and in consultation with the production manager, Terry determined the standard rate per hour at the Colonial Pewter Company as follows:

Standard rate per hour
The labour rate that should be incurred per hour of labour time, including employment taxes, fringe benefits, and other such labour costs.

Basic wage rate per hour	$10
Employment taxes at 10% of the basic rate	1
Fringe benefits at 30% of the basic rate	3
Standard rate per direct labour-hour	$14

Many companies prepare a single standard rate for all employees in a department. This standard rate reflects the expected "mix" of workers, even though the actual wage rates may vary somewhat from individual to individual due to differing skills or seniority. A single standard rate simplifies the use of standard costs and also permits the manager to monitor the use of employees within departments. More is said on this point a little later. According to the standard computed above, the direct labour rate for Colonial Pewter should average $14 per hour.

The standard direct labour time required to complete a unit of product (generally called the **standard hours per unit**) is perhaps the single most difficult standard to determine. One approach is to divide each operation performed on the product into elemental body movements (such as reaching, pushing, and turning over). Published tables of standard times for such movements are available. These times can be applied to the movements and then added together to determine the total standard time allowed per operation.

Standard hours per unit
The amount of labour time that should be required to complete a single unit of product, including allowances for breaks, machine downtime, clean-up, rejects, and other normal inefficiencies.

Another approach is for an industrial engineer to do a time and motion study, actually clocking the time required for certain tasks. As stated earlier, the standard time should include allowances for coffee breaks, personal needs of employees, clean-up, and machine downtime. After consulting with the production manager, Terry prepared the following documentation for the standard hours per unit:

Basic labour time per unit, in hours	1.9
Allowance for breaks and personal needs	0.1
Allowance for clean-up and machine downtime	0.3
Allowance for rejects	0.2
Standard labour-hours per unit of product	2.5

Once the rate and time standards have been set, the standard labour cost per unit of product can be computed as follows:

$$2.5 \text{ hours per unit} \times \$14 \text{ per hour} = \$35 \text{ per unit}$$

This $35 cost figure appears along with direct materials as one item on the standard cost card of the product.

Standard labour-hours have declined in relative importance for some organizations. This is particularly true in highly automated manufacturing firms. Service organizations and numerous other construction and processing organizations, however, still retain a major interest in labour and want to know how it performs. Standard labour-hours inform workers and managers what is expected and how labour should be used. Standard labour-hours assist in formulating, testing, and revising the plans of the organization. More specifically, standards and the resulting comparisons to actual labour-hours may serve to motivate workers and managers. Labour standards can influence individuals in setting their own goals. If standards are perceived as realistic and if the variances from these standards are used fairly and constructively, then employees will generally be motivated to work for the organizational objectives conveyed by the standards. Feelings of success or failure impact on performance, but pressure can invigorate or intimidate employees. Erosion of effort and performance levels can result when standards are set inappropriately and used incorrectly.

FOCUS *on Current Practice*

The Commissioner of Inland Revenue for New Zealand published national standard costs for raising livestock for Income Tax purposes. For example, to raise sheep for one year, the standard cost is given as $17. nz. To raise a beef animal for one year is given a standard cost of $152. nz. A pig raised for 10 to 17 weeks costs $53.40 nz. These standard costs are used for valuing the inventory of livestock if the producer chooses to follow them rather than use their own costs.

Source: www.ird.govt.nz, *IIB* vol. 13, February 2001.

Setting Variable Manufacturing Overhead Standards

As with direct labour, the price and quantity standards for variable manufacturing overhead are generally expressed in terms of rate and hours. The rate represents *the variable portion of the predetermined overhead rate* discussed in Chapter 3; the hours represent whatever hours base is used to apply overhead to units of product (usually machine-hours or direct labour-hours, as we learned in Chapter 3). At Colonial Pewter, the variable portion of the predetermined overhead rate is $3 per direct labour-hour. Therefore, the standard variable manufacturing overhead cost per unit is computed as follows:

$$2.5 \text{ hours per unit} \times \$3 \text{ per hour} = \$7.50 \text{ per unit}$$

This $7.50 cost figure appears along with direct materials and direct labour as one item on the standard cost card in Exhibit 10–2. Observe that the **standard cost per unit** is computed by multiplying the standard quantity or hours by the standard price or rate.

Standard cost per unit
The standard cost of a unit of product as shown on the standard cost card; it is computed by multiplying the standard quantity or hours by the standard price or rate for each cost element.

Are Standards the Same as Budgets?

Standards and budgets are very similar. The major distinction between the two terms is that a standard is a *unit* amount, whereas a budget is a *total* amount. The standard cost for materials at Colonial Pewter is $12 per pair of bookends. If 1,000 pairs of bookends are to be manufactured during a budgeting period, then the budgeted cost of materials would be $12,000. In effect, *a standard can be viewed as the budgeted cost for one unit of product.*

A GENERAL MODEL FOR VARIANCE ANALYSIS

An important reason for separating standards into two categories—price and quantity—is that different managers are usually responsible for buying and for using inputs and these two activities occur at different points in time. In the case of raw materials, for example, the purchasing manager is responsible for the price, and this responsibility is exercised at the time of purchase. In contrast, the production manager is responsible for the amount of the raw material used, and this responsibility is exercised when the materials are used in production, which may be many weeks or months after the purchase date. It is important, therefore, that we cleanly separate discrepancies due to deviations from price standards from those due to deviations from quantity standards. Differences between *standard* prices and *actual* prices and *standard* quantities and *actual* quantities are called **variances**. The act of computing and interpreting variances is called *variance analysis*.

Variance
The difference between standard prices and quantities and actual prices and quantities.

Price and Quantity Variances

A general model for computing standard cost variances for variable costs is presented in Exhibit 10–3. This model isolates price variances from quantity variances and shows how each of these variances is computed.[2] We will be using this model throughout the chapter to compute variances for direct materials, direct labour, and variable manufacturing overhead.

Three things should be noted from Exhibit 10–3. First, note that a price variance and a quantity variance can be computed for all three variable cost elements—direct materials, direct labour, and variable manufacturing overhead—even though the variance is not called by the same name in all cases. For example, a price variance is called a *materials price variance* in the case of direct materials but a *labour rate variance* in the case of direct labour and an *overhead spending variance* in the case of variable manufacturing overhead.

EXHIBIT 10–2 Standard Cost Card—Variable Production Cost

Inputs	(1) Standard Quantity or Hours	(2) Standard Price or Rate	(3) Standard Cost (1) × (2)
Direct materials	3.0 kilograms	$ 4.00	$12.00
Direct labour	2.5 hours	14.00	35.00
Variable manufacturing overhead . .	2.5 hours	3.00	7.50
Total standard cost per unit			$54.50

2. Variance analysis of fixed costs is described in Chapter 11.

EXHIBIT 10–3 A General Model for Variance Analysis—Variable Production Costs

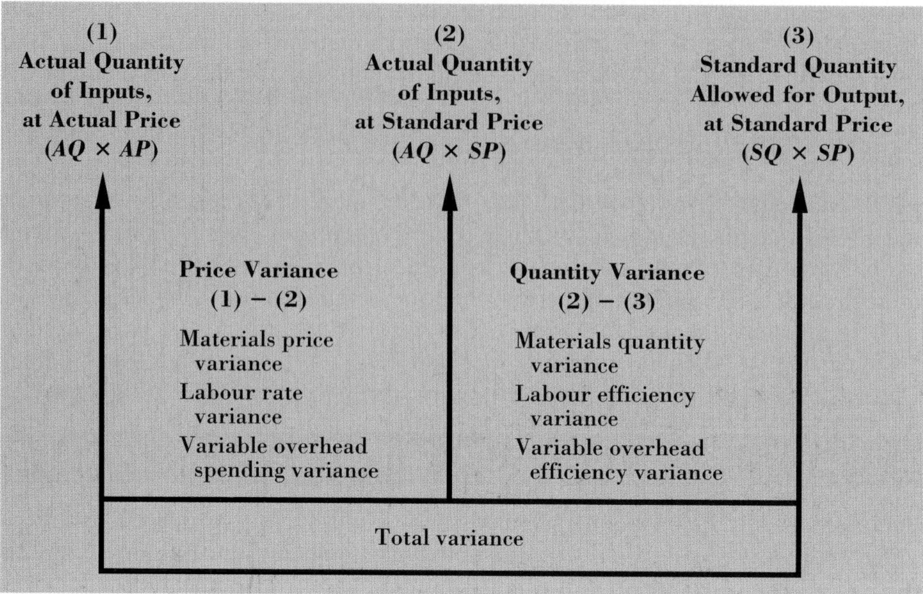

Second, note that even though a price variance may be called by different names, it is computed in exactly the same way, regardless of whether one is dealing with direct materials, direct labour, or variable manufacturing overhead. The same is true with the quantity variance.

Third, note that variance analysis is actually a type of input-output analysis. The inputs represent the actual quantity of direct materials, direct labour, and variable manufacturing overhead used; the output represents the good production of the period, expressed in terms of the *standard quantity (or the standard hours) allowed for the actual output* (see column 3 in Exhibit 10–3). By **standard quantity allowed** or **standard hours allowed,** we mean the amount of direct materials, direct labour, or variable manufacturing overhead *that should have been used* to produce the actual output of the period. This could be more or could be less materials, labour, or overhead than was *actually* used, depending on the efficiency or inefficiency of operations. The standard quantity allowed is computed by multiplying the actual output in units by the standard input allowed per unit.

Standard quantity allowed The amount of materials that should have been used to complete the period's output, as computed by multiplying the actual number of units produced by the standard quantity per unit.

Standard hours allowed The time that should have been taken to complete the period's output, as computed by multiplying the actual number of units produced by the standard hours per unit.

For the analysis of variances, it is key to note the difference between unit cost standards and total cost standards. For example, material has a standard unit cost of $4.00 per kilogram (Exhibit 10-2) but because 3 kilograms are used per pair of bookends, the production unit, the standard cost per pair is $12. However, when we look at the variances we need to consider the standard quantity for the period's production, 2,000 pairs. Thus we need to carefully determine what standard we are considering, unit of material, unit of production, or standard quantity for the actual amount of production for the period.

With this general model as a foundation, we will now examine the price and quantity variances in more detail.

USING STANDARD COSTS—DIRECT MATERIALS VARIANCES

LEARNING OBJECTIVE 2
Compute the direct materials price and quantity variances and explain their significance.

After determining Colonial Pewter Company's standard costs for direct materials, direct labour, and variable manufacturing overhead, Terry Sherman's next step was to compute the company's variances for June, the most recent month. As discussed in the preceding section, variances are computed by comparing standard costs to actual costs. To facilitate this comparison, Terry referred to the standard cost data contained in Exhibit 10–2. This exhibit shows that the standard cost of direct materials per unit of product is as follows:

3.0 kilograms per unit × $4 per kilogram = $12 per unit

Colonial Pewter's purchasing records for June showed that 6,500 kilograms of pewter were purchased at a cost of $3.80 per kilogram. This cost figure included freight and handling and was net of the quantity discount. All of the material purchased was used during June to manufacture 2,000 pairs of pewter bookends. Using these data and the standard costs from Exhibit 10–2, Terry computed the price and quantity variances shown in Exhibit 10–4.

The three arrows in Exhibit 10–4 point to three different total cost figures. The first, $24,700, refers to the actual total cost of the pewter that was purchased during June. The second, $26,000, refers to what the pewter would have cost if it had been purchased at the standard price of $4.00 per kilogram rather than the actual price of $3.80 per kilogram. The difference between these two figures, $1,300 ($26,000 − $24,700), is the price variance. It exists because the actual purchase price was $0.20 per kilogram less than the standard purchase price. Since 6,500 kilograms were purchased, the total amount of the variance is $1,300 ($0.20 per kilogram × 6,500 kilograms). This variance is labelled *favourable* (denoted by F), since the actual purchase price was less than the standard purchase price. A price variance is labelled *unfavourable* (denoted by U) if the actual price exceeds the standard price.

The third arrow in Exhibit 10–4 points to $24,000—the cost that the pewter would have been had it been purchased at the standard price and only the amount allowed by the standard quantity had been used. The standards call for 3 kilograms of pewter per unit. Since 2,000 pairs of bookends were produced, 6,000 kilograms of pewter should have been used. This is referred to as the *standard quantity allowed for the output*. If this 6,000 kilograms of pewter had been purchased at the standard price of $4.00 per kilogram, the company would have spent $24,000. The difference between this figure, $24,000, and the figure at the end of the middle arrow in Exhibit 10–4, $26,000, is the quantity variance of $2,000.

To understand this quantity variance, note that the actual amount of pewter used in production was 6,500 kilograms. However, the standard amount of pewter allowed for the actual output is only 6,000 kilograms. Therefore, a total of 500 kilograms too much of pewter was used to produce the actual output. To express this in dollar terms, the 500 kilograms is multiplied by the standard price of $4.00 per kilogram to yield the quantity variance of $2,000. Why is the standard price, rather than the actual price, of the pewter used in this calculation? The production manager is ordinarily responsible for the quantity variance. If the actual price was used in the calculation of the quantity variance, the production manager would be held responsible for the efficiency or inefficiency of the purchasing manager. Apart from being unfair, fruitless arguments between the production manager and purchasing manager would occur every time the actual price of an input is

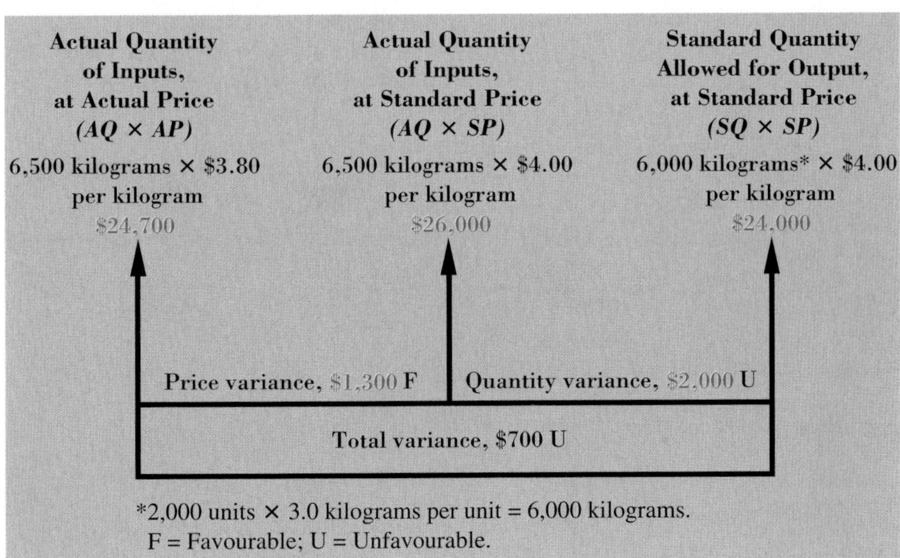

EXHIBIT 10–4 Variance Analysis—Direct Materials

above its standard price. To avoid these arguments, the standard price is used when computing the quantity variance.

The quantity variance in Exhibit 10–4 is labelled *unfavourable* (denoted by U). This is because more pewter was used to produce the actual output than is called for by the standard. A quantity variance is labelled *unfavourable* if the actual quantity exceeds the standard quantity and is labelled *favourable* if the actual quantity is less than the standard quantity.

The computations in Exhibit 10–4 reflect the fact that all of the material purchased during June was also used during June. How are the variances computed if a different amount of material is purchased than is used? To illustrate, assume that during June the company purchased 6,500 kilograms of materials, as before, but used only 5,000 kilograms of material during the month and produced only 1,600 units. In this case, the price variance and quantity variance would be as shown in Exhibit 10–5.

Most companies compute the materials price variance when materials are purchased rather than when they are used in production.[3] There are two reasons for this practice. First, delaying the computation of the price variance until the materials are used would result in less-timely variance reports. Second, by computing the price variance when the materials are purchased, the materials can be carried in the inventory accounts at their standard costs. This greatly simplifies bookkeeping. Note, however, that the problem of determining the purchase price variance at a different time than the materials usage variance would not occur in a strict JIT environment. See Appendix 10A at the end of the chapter for an explanation of how the bookkeeping works in a standard costing system where inventory of direct materials exists.

Note from Exhibit 10–5 that the price variance is computed on the entire amount of material purchased (6,500 kilograms), as before, whereas the quantity variance is computed only on the portion of this material used in production during the month (5,000 kilograms). A quantity variance on the 1,500 kilograms of material that were purchased during the month but *not* used in production (6,500 kilograms purchased − 5,000 kilograms used = 1,500 kilograms unused) will be computed in a future period when

EXHIBIT 10–5 Variance Analysis—Direct Materials, When the Amount Purchased Differs from the Amount Used

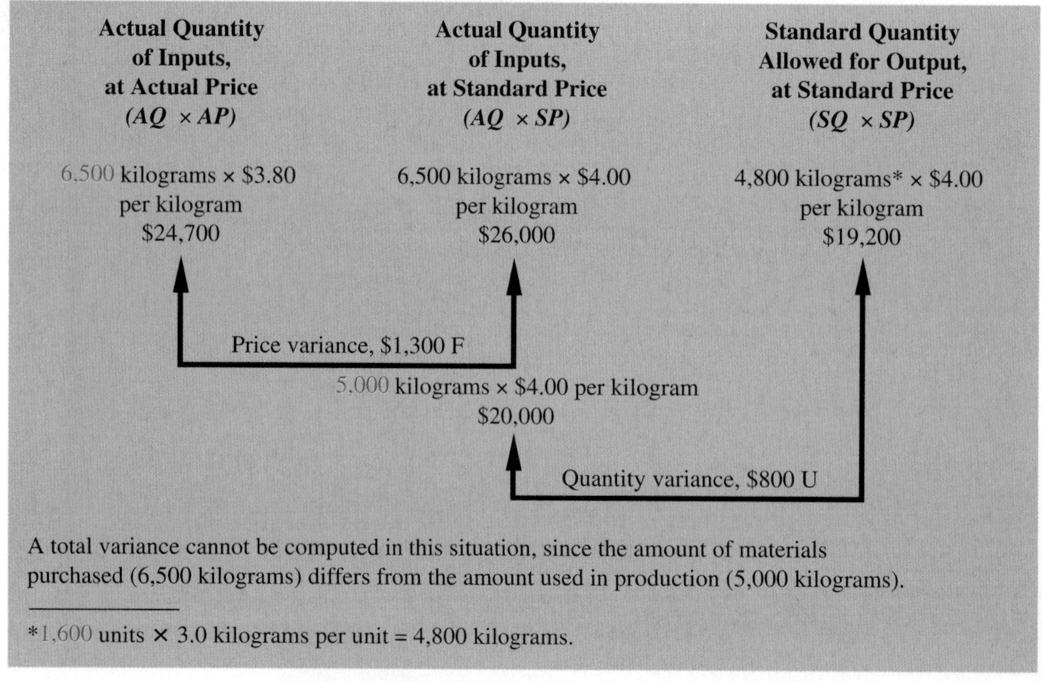

3. Max Laudeman and F. W. Schaeberle, "The Cost Accounting Practices of Firms Using Standard Costs," *Cost and Management* 57, no. 4, July–August 1983, p. 24.

these materials are drawn out of inventory and used in production. The situation illustrated in Exhibit 10–5 is common for companies that purchase materials well in advance of use and store the materials in warehouses while awaiting the production process.

Materials Price Variance—A Closer Look

A **materials price variance** measures the difference between what is paid for a given quantity of materials and what should have been paid according to the standard that has been set. From Exhibit 10–4, this difference can be expressed by the following formula:

Materials price variance A measure of the difference between the actual unit price paid for an item and the standard price, multiplied by the quantity purchased.

$$\text{Materials price variance} = (AQ \times AP) - (AQ \times SP)$$

(AQ = Actual Quantity; AP = Actual Price; SP = Standard Price)

The formula can be factored into simpler form as follows:

$$\text{Materials price variance} = AQ(AP - SP)$$

Some managers prefer this simpler formula, since it permits variance computations to be made very quickly. Using the data from Exhibit 10–4 in this formula, we have the following:

6,500 kilograms ($3.80 per kilogram − $4.00 per kilogram) = $1,300 F

Notice that the answer is the same as that yielded in Exhibit 10–4. Also note that a negative variance because of the order of the calculation is always labelled as *favourable* (F) and a positive variance is always labelled as *unfavourable* (U) when the formula approach is used. This will be true of all variance formulas in this and later chapters.

Variance reports are often issued in a tabular format that shows the details and explanation of particular variances. Following is an example of such a report that has been provided by the purchasing manager:

COLONIAL PEWTER COMPANY
Performance Report—Purchasing Department

Item Purchased	(1) Quantity Purchased	(2) Actual Price	(3) Standard Price	(4) Difference in Price (2) − (3)	(5) Total Price Variance (1) × (4)	Explanation
Pewter	6,500 kilograms	$3.80	$4.00	$0.20	$1,300 F	Bargained for an especially favourable price.

F = Favourable; U = Unfavourable.

Isolation of Variances At what point should variances be isolated and brought to the attention of management? The answer is, the earlier the better. The sooner deviations from standard are brought to the attention of management, the sooner problems can be evaluated and corrected. If long periods are allowed to elapse before variances are computed, costs that could otherwise have been controlled may accumulate to the point of doing significant damage to profits. Most firms compute the materials price variance, for example, when materials are *purchased* rather than when the materials are placed into production. This permits earlier isolation of the variance, since materials may remain in the warehouse before being used in production. Isolating the price variance in the inventory accounts when purchased also permits the company to carry its raw materials in the inventory at standard cost. This greatly simplifies the selection of the proper costs figure to use when raw materials are later placed into production.[4]

Once a performance report has been prepared, what does management do with the price variance data? The most significant variances should be viewed as "red flags," calling attention to the fact that an exception has occurred that will require some explanation and perhaps follow-up effort. Normally, the performance report itself will contain some explanation of the reason for the variance, as shown in the preceding table. In the case of Colonial Pewter Company, the purchasing manager, Janet Warner, said that the favourable price variance resulted from bargaining for an especially good price.

Responsibility for the Variance Who is responsible for the materials price variance? Generally speaking, the purchasing manager has control over the price paid for goods and is therefore responsible for any price variances. Many factors influence the prices paid for goods, including how many units are ordered in a lot, how the order is delivered, whether the order is a rush order, and the quality of materials purchased. A deviation in any of these factors from what was assumed when the standards were set can result in a price variance. For example, purchase of second-grade materials rather than top-grade materials may result in a favourable price variance, since the lower-grade materials would generally be less costly (but perhaps less suitable for production).

However, someone other than the purchasing manager could be responsible for a materials price variance. Production may be scheduled in such a way, for example, that the purchasing manager must request delivery by airfreight, rather than by truck. In these cases, the production manager would bear responsibility for the resulting price variances.

A word of caution is in order. Variance analysis should not be used as an excuse to assign blame. The emphasis must be on the control function in the sense of *supporting* the line managers and *assisting* them in meeting the goals that they have participated in setting for the company. In short, the emphasis should be positive rather than negative. Excessive dwelling on what has already happened, particularly in terms of trying to find someone to blame, can be destructive to the functioning of an organization.

Materials Quantity Variance—A Closer Look

Materials quantity variance A measure of the difference between the actual quantity of materials used in production and the standard quantity allowed, multiplied by the standard price per unit of materials.

The **materials quantity variance** measures the difference between the quantity of materials used in production and the quantity that should have been used, according to the standard that has been set. Although the variance is concerned with the physical usage of materials, it is generally stated in dollar terms, as shown in Exhibit 10–4. The formula for the materials quantity variance is as follows:

$$\text{Materials quantity variance} = (AQ \times SP) - (SQ \times SP)$$

Actual Quantity (AQ); Standard Price (SP); Standard Quantity Allowed for Output (SQ)

Again, the formula can be factored into simpler terms:

$$\text{Materials quantity variance} = SP(AQ - SQ)$$

Using the data from Exhibit 10–4 in the formula, we have the following:

$4.00 per kilogram(6,500 kilograms − 6,000 kilograms*) = $2,000 U

*2,000 units × 3.0 kilograms per unit = 6,000 kilograms.

4. See Appendix 10A at the end of this chapter for an illustration of journal entries in a standard cost system.

The answer, of course, is the same as that yielded in Exhibit 10–4. The data might appear as follows if a formal performance report was prepared:

COLONIAL PEWTER COMPANY
Performance Report—Production Department

Type of Materials	(1) Standard Price	(2) Actual Quantity	(3) Standard Quantity Allowed	(4) Difference in Quantity (2) − (3)	(5) Total Quantity Variance (1) × (4)	Explanation
Pewter	$4.00	6,500 kg	6,000 kg	500 kg	$2,000 U	Low-grade materials unsuitable for production

U = Unfavourable.

The materials quantity variance is best isolated at the time that materials are placed into production. Materials are drawn for the number of units to be produced, according to the standard bill of materials for each unit. Any additional materials are usually drawn with an excess materials requisition slip, which is different in colour from the normal requisition slips. This procedure calls attention to the excessive usage of materials *while production is still in process* and provides an opportunity for early control of any developing problem.

Excessive usage of materials can result from many factors, including faulty machines, inferior quality of materials, untrained workers, and poor supervision. Generally speaking, it is the responsibility of the production department to see that material usage is kept in line with standards. There may be times, however, when the *purchasing* department may be responsible for an unfavourable materials quantity variance. If the purchasing department obtains inferior-quality materials in an effort to economize on price, the materials may be unsuitable for use and may result in excessive waste. Thus, purchasing rather than production would be responsible for the quantity variance. At Colonial Pewter, the production manager, Tom Kuchel, said that low-grade materials were the cause of the unfavourable materials quantity variance for June.

FOCUS *on Current Practice*

Management at an unnamed breakfast cereal company became concerned about the apparent waste of raisins in one of its products. A box of the product was supposed to contain 300 grams of cereal and 50 grams of raisins. However, the production process had been using an average of 60 grams of raisins per box. To correct the problem, a bonus was offered to employees if the consumption of raisins dropped to 52.5 grams per box or less—which would allow for about 5% waste. Within a month, the target was hit and bonuses were distributed. However, another problem began to appear. Market studies indicated that customers had become dissatisfied with the amount of raisins in the product. Workers had hit the 52.5-grams per box target by drastically reducing the amount of raisins in rush orders. Boxes of the completed product are ordinarily weighed and if the weight is less than 350 grams, the box is rejected. However, rush orders aren't weighed since that would slow down the production process. Consequently, workers were reducing the raisins in rush orders so as to hit the overall target of 52.5 grams of raisins per box. This resulted in substandard boxes of cereal in rush orders and customer complaints. Clearly, managers need to be very careful when they set targets and standards. They may not get what they bargained for. Subsequent investigation by an internal auditor revealed that, due to statistical fluctuations, an average of about 60 grams of raisins must be used to ensure that every box contains at least 50 grams of raisins.

Source: Harper A. Roehm and Joseph R. Castellano, "The Danger of Relying on Accounting Numbers Alone," *Management Accounting Quarterly*, Fall 1999, pp. 4–9.

FURTHER ANALYSIS OF MATERIALS VARIANCES

LEARNING OBJECTIVE 3
Compute the mix and yield variances for materials and explain their significance.

A survey of the cost accounting practices of the 1,000 largest U.S. industrial companies[5] found that two other types of standard cost variances are frequently computed.[6] These are subcomponents of the material usage variance: a *materials mix* and *materials yield variance.* A representation of these variances is presented in Exhibit 10–6.

The production of most goods generally requires input from more than one material. Chemical firms, for example, may use varying proportions of interchangeable materials. The same is true with food processing companies. For example, a company that produces flour with a mixture of red and white wheat may, on occasion, substitute one kind of wheat for another. When legally permitted, a manufacturer of canned fruit may substitute peaches for pears and a manufacturer of sausages may substitute pork for beef. The calculation of mix and yield variances is appropriate only if different types of material can be substituted for one another. A **mix variance** results if the actual mix of materials differs from the budgeted mix of materials. The budgeted mix reflects a proportional mix of materials that is expected to be used to produce a given product. A mix variance is calculated to determine the effects of a change in the materials mix on the total materials cost. The mix variance is favourable if the actual mix is cheaper than the standard mix. This means that a greater proportion of less-expensive materials was used in the blend. The mix variance is unfavourable if the actual mix is more expensive than the standard mix because a greater proportion of more-expensive materials was used. Where a manager has control over the composition of the mix, the mix variance can be a useful measure of the manager's performance.

Mix variance
The dollar effect of a difference between the actual mix of materials and the budgeted mix of materials on total materials cost.

The amount of quantity variance remaining after deducting the mix variance from the total quantity variance is the **yield variance.** A yield variance occurs when the actual combination of inputs generates a different rate of output from what would have been produced by the input mix used in setting the standards. In other words, the actual yield differs from the standard yield expected from a given mix of inputs.

Yield variance
The portion of the efficiency variance that is not the mix variance. It occurs when the actual yield differs from the standard yield expected from a given mix of inputs.

To illustrate the calculation of the mix and yield variances, assume that Cape Breton Chemical Company combines secret ingredients A and B to make a product known as super-cleaner Bjax. The standard composition calls for a mix of 2 kilograms of A and 3 kilograms of B to produce one unit of Bjax. The standard mix for A and B is therefore ⅖ and ⅗, respectively. Assume that 150 units were produced using 350 kilograms of A and 450 kilograms of B. Material A has a standard unit price of $1.50 and material B has a standard price of $2.50 per unit.

For a given input, the mix variance can be calculated in two steps. First, multiply the budgeted mix percentage by the actual *total* input and subtract the actual quantity. This is the mix variance expressed in physical terms. Second, multiply your answer from step one by the standard cost of the input:

$$\text{Mix variance} = \left[\text{Actual quantity} - \left(\text{Budgeted \%} \times \text{Total input}\right)\right] \times \text{Standard price}$$

For material A, this would be:

$$[350 - \tfrac{2}{5}(350 + 450)] \times \$1.50 = \$45\ \text{U}$$

Similarly, for material B, the mix variance is:

$$[450 - \tfrac{3}{5}(350 + 450)] \times \$2.50 = \$75\ \text{F}$$

5. Max Laudeman and F. W. Schaeberle, "The Cost Accounting Practices of Firms Using Standard Costs," *Cost and Management,* July–August 1985, pp. 21–25.
6. Ibid.

EXHIBIT 10–6 Extended Model for Variance Analysis—Materials

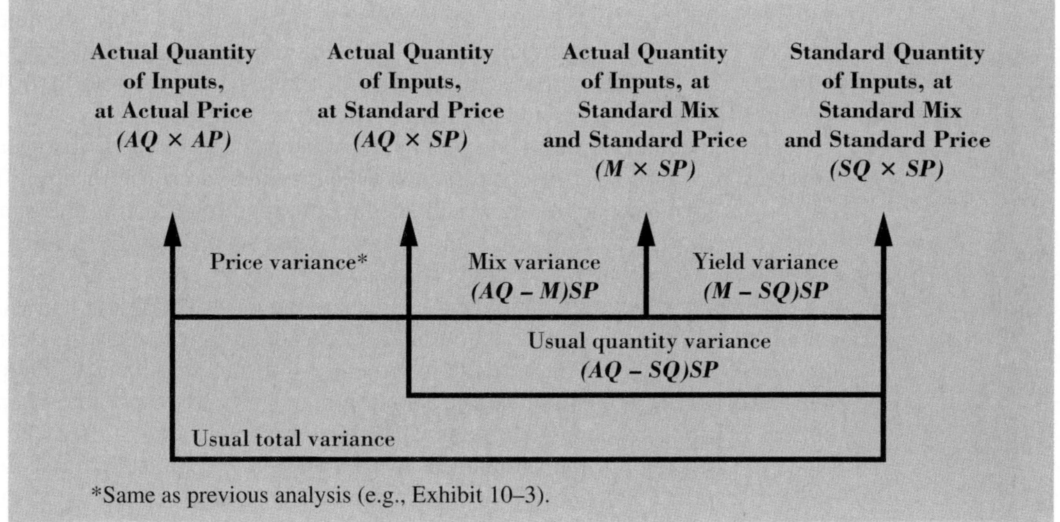

*Same as previous analysis (e.g., Exhibit 10–3).

The budgeted percent times the total input of material A is 320 [⅖(350 + 450)] kilograms. This is the amount of material A that would have been used if the budget had been adhered to. Since the amount of material used, 350 kilograms, exceeds the budgeted amount, the mix variance is unfavourable. If the budget had been adhered to in the case of material B, 480 [⅗(350 + 450)] kilograms would have been used. Since the actual usage of material B was only 450 kilograms, the material mix variance of material B is favourable.

Yield variance = [(Budgeted % × Total Input) – Standard Quantity] × Standard Price

Note the mix variance is always calculated before the yield variance so that the mix effect is isolated from the quantity or yield amount.

The variances can also be calculated using the following notation. For material A:

$$\text{Mix variance} = (AQ_A - M_A)SP_A$$
$$= [350 - \tfrac{2}{5}(350 + 450)]\$1.50 = \$45\text{ U}$$
$$\text{Yield variance} = (M_A - SQ_A)SP_A$$
$$= [\tfrac{2}{5}(350 + 450) - 150(2)]\$1.50 = \$30\text{ U}$$
$$\text{Total material quantity variance} = (AQ_A - SQ_A)SP_A$$
$$= (350 - 150(2))\$1.50 = \$75\text{ U}$$

or mix variance + yield variance

$45 U + $30 U = $75 U

where

AQ_A is the actual quantity used of material A.
M_A is the standard mix of material A actually used.
SQ_A is the standard quantity of material A.

For material B:

$$\text{Mix variance} = [450 - \tfrac{3}{5}(350 + 450)]\$2.50 = -\$75\text{ F}$$
$$\text{Yield variance} = [\tfrac{3}{5}(350 + 450) - 3(150)]\$2.50 = \$75\text{ U}$$
$$\text{Total material quantity variance} = [450 - 3(150)]\$2.50 = \$0.0$$

or

$$\$75\text{ F} - \$75\text{ U} = \$0.0$$

Labour efficiency variances, described in the section to follow, can be analyzed in a similar manner if the composition of a work group is provided in the standard. For example, if all junior staff members are assigned to other jobs, a public accounting firm might assign a senior staff member to a job that would normally be done by more junior personnel. The standard mix of employees can be applied to the total hours worked in the group to determine the standard mix for each employee group.

The calculation of mix and yield variances provides a means of separating the quantity variance into a set of constituents. This breakdown can be meaningful where managers are able to change the mix in production, thereby affecting the quantities of each type of material used. If the standard mix is the ideal, then departures from this mix should be made evident to statement users.

Managers, however, should carefully examine the effect of mix and yield variances to see how other costs, such as labour and overhead, are affected by the change in mix and its effect on yield. Often there are interrelationships among the mix, yield, and materials price variances. For example, a production manager may respond to changes in relative prices of inputs by changing the mix. The new mix may, in turn, affect the yield. If examined in isolation, the appropriateness of the decision to change the mix could not be properly assessed. This raises performance evaluation issues. The budgeted mix is no longer optimal and, therefore, cannot be used as a valid benchmark for evaluating the manager's performance.

One problem of mix and yield variances stems from its use of standard prices. When prices differ from standard, it is the change in actual relative prices within the composition of materials that may make changes in the mix and yield worthwhile. The fact that these price changes are held constant when calculating the mix and usage variances makes it difficult to interpret the effectiveness of managerial decisions to make changes in the mix of inputs. Conceptually, these variances can be left in physical units. Multiplying by standard prices is to facilitate aggregation by providing a common denominator.

USING STANDARD COSTS—DIRECT LABOUR VARIANCES

LEARNING OBJECTIVE 4
Compute the direct labour rate and efficiency variances and explain their significance.

Terry's next step in determining Colonial Pewter's variances for June was to compute the direct labour variances for the month. Recall from Exhibit 10–2 that the standard direct labour cost per unit of product is $35, computed as follows:

$$2.5 \text{ hours per unit} \times \$14 \text{ per hour} = \$35 \text{ per unit}$$

During June, the company paid its direct labour workers $74,250, including employment taxes and fringe benefits, for 5,400 hours of work. This was an average of $13.75 per hour. Using these data and the standard costs from Exhibit 10–2, Terry computed the direct labour rate and efficiency variances that appear in Exhibit 10–7.

Notice that the column headings in Exhibit 10–7 are the same as those used in the prior two exhibits, except that in Exhibit 10–7 the terms *hours* and *rate* are used in place of the terms *quantity* and *price.*

Labour Rate Variance—A Closer Look

Labour rate variance
A measure of the difference between the actual hourly labour rate and the standard rate, multiplied by the number of hours worked during the period.

As explained earlier, the price variance for direct labour is commonly termed a **labour rate variance.** This variance measures any deviation from standard in the average hourly rate paid to direct labour workers. The formula for the labour rate variance is expressed as follows:

$$\text{Labour rate variance} = (AH \times AR) - (AH \times SR)$$

Actual Hours — Actual Rate — Standard Rate

EXHIBIT 10–7 Variance Analysis—Direct labour

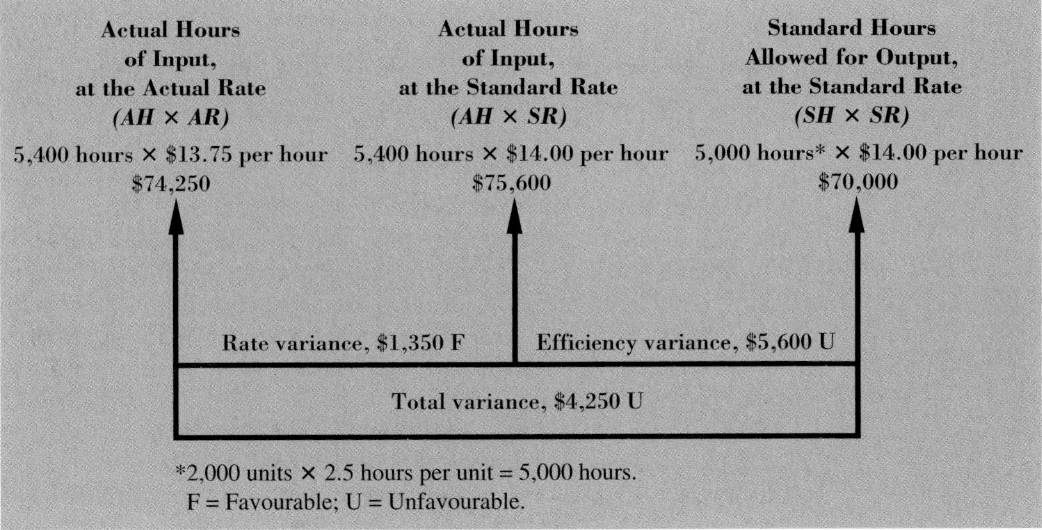

The formula can be factored into simpler form as follows:

$$\text{Labour rate variance} = AH(AR - SR)$$

Using the data from Exhibit 10–7 in the formula, we have the following:

$$5{,}400 \text{ hours } (\$13.75 \text{ per hour} - \$14.00 \text{ per hour}) = \$1{,}350 \text{ F}$$

It should be noted that the rate variance is calculated before the efficiency variance, left to right in Exhibit 10-7.

In most firms, the rates paid to workers are quite predictable. Nevertheless, rate variances can arise through the way labour is used. Skilled workers with high hourly rates of pay may be given duties that require little skill and call for low hourly rates of pay. This will result in unfavourable labour rate variances, since the actual hourly rate of pay will exceed the standard rate specified for the particular task being performed. A reverse situation exists when unskilled or untrained workers are assigned to jobs that require some skill or training. The lower pay scale for these workers will result in favourable rate variances, although the workers may be inefficient. Finally, unfavourable rate variances can arise from overtime work at premium rates if any portion of the overtime premium is added to the direct labour account.

Who is responsible for controlling the labour rate variance? Since rate variances generally arise as a result of how labour is used, supervisors bear responsibility for seeing that labour rate variances are kept under control.

Labour Efficiency Variance—A Closer Look

The quantity variance for direct labour, more commonly called the **labour efficiency variance,** measures the productivity of labour time. No variance is more closely watched by management, since it is widely believed that increasing the productivity of direct labour time is vital to reducing costs. The formula for the labour efficiency variance is expressed as follows:

Labour efficiency variance A measure of the difference between the actual hours taken to complete a task and the standard hours allowed, multiplied by the standard hourly labour rate.

$$\text{Labour efficiency variance} = (AH \times SR) - (SH \times SR)$$

(AH = Actual Hours; SR = Standard Rate; SH = Standard Hours Allowed for Output)

Factored into simpler terms, the formula is as follows:

$$\text{Labour efficiency variance} = SR(AH - SH)$$

Using the data from Exhibit 10–7 in the formula, we have the following:

$14.00 per hour (5,400 hours − 5,000 hours*) = $5,600 U

*2,000 units × 2.5 hours per unit = 5,000 hours.

Possible causes of an unfavourable labour efficiency variance include poorly trained or motivated workers; poor-quality materials, requiring more labour time in processing; faulty equipment, causing breakdowns and work interruptions; poor supervision of workers; and inaccurate standards. The managers in charge of production would generally be responsible for control of the labour efficiency variance. However, the variance might be chargeable to purchasing if the acquisition of poor materials resulted in excessive labour processing time.

Insufficient demand for the company's products may be another important cause of an unfavourable labour efficiency variance. Managers in some companies argue that it is difficult, and perhaps unwise, to constantly adjust the workforce in response to changes in the amount of work that needs to be done. In such companies, the direct labour workforce is essentially fixed in the short run. If demand is insufficient to keep everyone busy, workers are not laid off. In this case, if demand falls below the level needed to keep everyone busy, an unfavourable labour efficiency variance will often be recorded.

If customer orders are insufficient to keep the workers busy, the work centre manager has two options—either accept an unfavourable labour efficiency variance or build inventory.[7] A central lesson of the just-in-time (JIT) system is that building inventory with no immediate prospect of sale is a bad idea. Inventory—particularly work in process inventory—leads to high defect rates, obsolete goods, and generally inefficient operations. As a consequence, when the workforce is basically fixed in the short term, managers must be cautious about how labour efficiency variances are used. Some managers advocate dispensing with labour efficiency variances entirely in such situations—at least for the purposes of motivating and controlling workers on the shop floor.

USING STANDARD COSTS—VARIABLE MANUFACTURING OVERHEAD VARIANCES

LEARNING OBJECTIVE 5
Compute the variable manufacturing overhead spending and efficiency variances.

The final step in Terry's analysis of Colonial Pewter's variances for June was to compute the variable manufacturing overhead variances. The variable portion of manufacturing overhead can be analyzed using the same basic formulas that are used to analyze direct materials and direct labour. Recall from Exhibit 10–2 that the standard variable manufacturing overhead is $7.50 per unit of product, computed as follows:

2.5 hours per unit × $3.00 per hour = $7.50 per unit

Colonial Pewter's cost records showed that the total actual variable manufacturing overhead cost for June was $15,390. Recall from the earlier discussion of the direct labour variances that 5,400 hours of direct labour time were recorded during the month and that the company produced 2,000 pairs of bookends. Terry's analysis of this overhead data appears in Exhibit 10–8.

Notice the similarities between Exhibits 10–7 and 10–8. These similarities arise from the fact that direct labour-hours are being used as a base for allocating overhead cost to units of product; thus, the same hourly figures appear in Exhibit 10–8 for variable manufacturing overhead as in Exhibit 10–7 for direct labour. The main difference between the

7. For further discussion, see Eliyahu M. Goldratt and Jeff Cox, *The Goal,* 2nd rev. ed. (Croton-on-Hudson, NY: North River Press, 1992).

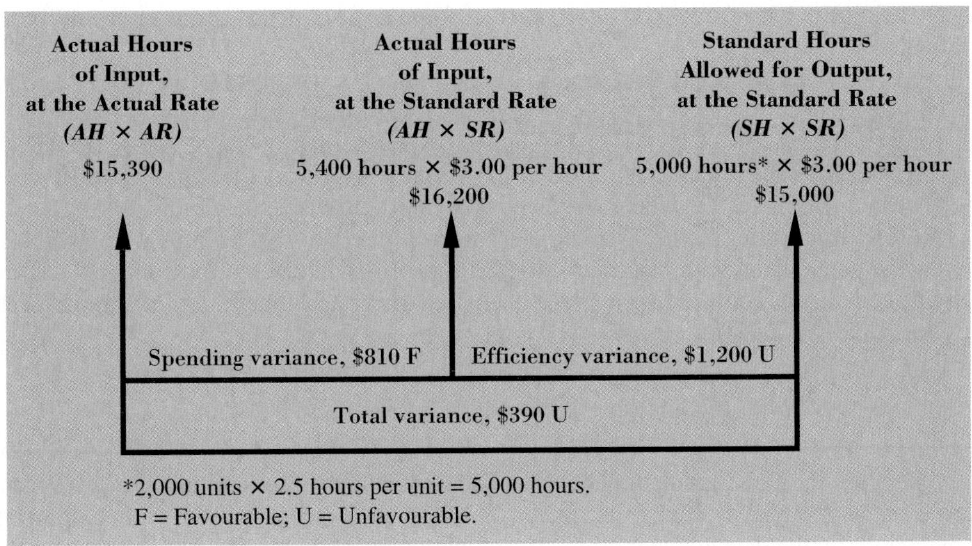

EXHIBIT 10–8 Variance Analysis—Variable Manufacturing Overhead

two exhibits is in the standard hourly rate being used, which in this company is much lower for variable manufacturing overhead. However, the format of the variance analysis for variable manufacturing overhead is the same if machine hours or material quantities or some other base were used.

Manufacturing Overhead Variances—A Closer Look

The formula for **variable overhead spending variance** is expressed as follows:

Variable overhead spending variance
The difference between the actual variable overhead cost incurred during a period and the standard cost that should have been incurred based on the actual activity of the period.

$$\text{Variable overhead spending variance} = (AH \times AR) - (AH \times SR)$$

(AH = Actual Hours; AR = Actual Rate; SR = Standard Rate)

Using the data from Exhibit 10-8, we have the following:

$$(5{,}400 \times \$2.85) - (5{,}400 \times \$3.00) = \$810\text{F}$$

Or, factored into simpler terms:

$$\text{Variable overhead spending variance} = AH(AR - SR)$$

Using the data from Exhibit 10–8 in the formula, we have the following:

$$5{,}400 \text{ hours } (\$2.85 \text{ per hour}^* - \$3.00 \text{ per hour}) = \$810 \text{ F}$$

*$15,390 ÷ 5,400 hours = $2.85 per hour.

The formula for the **variable overhead efficiency variance** is expressed as follows:

Variable overhead efficiency variance
The difference between the actual activity (direct labour-hours, machine-hours, or some other base) of a period and the standard activity allowed, multiplied by the variable part of the predetermined overhead rate.

$$\text{Variable overhead efficiency variance} = (AH \times SR) - (SH \times SR)$$

(AH = Actual Hours; SR = Standard Rate; SH = Standard Hours Allowed for Output)

Or, factored into simpler terms:

$$\text{Variable overhead efficiency variance} = SR(AH - SH)$$

Again using the data from Exhibit 10–8, the computation of the variance would be as follows:

$3 per hour(5,400 hours − 5,000 hours*) = $1,200 U

*2,000 units × 2.5 hours per unit = 5,000 hours.

We will reserve further discussion of the variable overhead spending and efficiency variances until Chapter 11, where overhead analysis is discussed in depth.

Before proceeding further, we suggest that you pause at this point and go back and review the data contained in Exhibits 10–2 through 10–8. These exhibits and the accompanying text discussion provide a comprehensive, integrated illustration of standard setting and variance analysis.

MANAGERIAL ACCOUNTING IN ACTION

The Wrap-Up

In preparation for the scheduled meeting to discuss her analysis of Colonial Pewter's standard costs and variances, Terry distributed Exhibits 10–2 through 10–8, with supporting explanations, to the management group of Colonial Pewter. This included J.D. Wriston, the president of the company; Tom Kuchel, the production manager; and Janet Warner, the purchasing manager. J.D. Wriston opened the meeting with the following question:

J.D.: Terry, I think I understand the report you distributed, but just to make sure, would you mind summarizing the highlights of what you found?

Terry: As you can see, the biggest problems are the unfavourable materials quantity variance of $2,000 and the unfavourable labour efficiency variance of $5,600.

J.D.: Tom, you're the production boss. What do you think is responsible for the unfavourable labour efficiency variance?

Tom: It pretty much has to be the new production workers. Our experienced workers shouldn't have much problem meeting the standard of 2.5 hours per unit. We all knew that there would be some inefficiency for a while as we brought new people on board.

J.D.: No one is disputing that, Tom. However, $5,600 is a lot of money. Is this problem likely to go away very soon?

Tom: I hope so. If we were to contrast the last two weeks of June with the first two weeks, I'm sure we would see some improvement.

J.D.: I don't want to beat up on you, Tom, but this is a significant problem. Can you do something to accelerate the training process?

Tom: Sure. I could pair up each of the new guys with one of our old-timers and have them work together for a while. It would slow down our older guys a bit, but I'll bet the new workers would learn a lot.

J.D.: Let's try it. Now, what about that $2,000 unfavourable materials quantity variance?

Tom: Are you asking me?

J.D.: Well, I would like someone to explain it.

Tom: Don't look at me. It's that iron-contaminated pewter that Janet bought on her "special deal."

Janet: We got rid of that stuff months ago.

J.D.: Hold your horses. We're not trying to figure out who to blame here. I just want to understand what happened. If we can understand what happened, maybe we can fix it.

Terry: Tom, are the new workers generating a lot of scrap?

Tom: Yeah, I guess so.

J.D.: I think that could be part of the problem. Can you do anything about it?

Tom: I can watch the scrap really closely for a few days to see where it's being generated. If it is the new workers, I can have the old-timers work with them on the problem when I team them up.

J.D.: Good. Let's reconvene in a few weeks and see what has happened. Hopefully, we can get those unfavourable variances under control.

STRUCTURE OF PERFORMANCE REPORTS

On preceding pages, we learned that performance reports are used in a standard cost system to communicate variance data to management. Exhibit 10–9 provides an example of how these reports can be integrated in a responsibility reporting system.

Note from the exhibit that the performance reports *start at the bottom and build upward,* with managers at each level receiving information on their own performance as well as information on the performance of each manager under them in the chain of responsibility. This variance information flows upward from level to level in a pyramid fashion, with the president finally receiving a summary of all activities in the organization. If the manager at a particular level (such as the production superintendent) wants to know the reasons behind a variance, she or he can ask for the detailed performance reports prepared by the various operations or departments.

In the following section, we turn our attention to the question of how a manager can determine which variances on these reports are significant enough to warrant further attention.

EXHIBIT 10–9 Upward Flow of Performance Reports

President's Report
The president's performance report summarizes all company data. The president can trace the variances downward through the company as needed to determine where top-management time should be spent.

	Budget	Actual	Variance
Responsibility centre:			
Sales manager	X	X	X
Production superintendent	$26,000	$29,000	$3,000 U
Engineering head	X	X	X
Personnel supervisor	X	X	X
Controller	X	X	X
	$54,000	$61,000	$7,000 U

Production Superintendent
The performance of each department head is summarized for the production superintendent. The totals on the superintendent's performance report are then passed upward to the next level of responsibility.

	Budget	Actual	Variance
Responsibility centre:			
Cutting department	X	X	X
Machining department . . .	X	X	X
Finishing department	$11,000	$12,500	$1,500 U
Packaging department . . .	X	X	X
	$26,000	$29,000	$3,000 U

Finishing Department Head
The performance report of each supervisor is summarized on the performance report of the department head. The department totals are then passed upward to the production superintendent.

	Budget	Actual	Variance
Responsibility centre:			
Sanding operation	X	X	X
Wiring operation	$ 5,000	$ 5,800	$ 800 U
Assembly operation	X	X	X
	$11,000	$12,500	$1,500 U

Wiring Operation Supervisor
The supervisor of each operation receives a performance report. The totals on these reports are then communicated upward to the next higher level of responsibility.

	Budget	Actual	Variance
Variable costs:			
Direct materials	X	X	X
Direct labour	X	X	X
Manufacturing overhead . .	X	X	X
	$ 5,000	$ 5,800	$ 800 U

VARIANCE ANALYSIS AND MANAGEMENT BY EXCEPTION

Variance analysis and performance reports are important elements of *management by exception*. Simply put, management by exception means that the manager's attention should be directed toward those parts of the organization where plans are not working out for one reason or another. Time and effort should not be wasted attending to those parts of the organization where things are going smoothly.

The budgets and standards discussed in this chapter and in the preceding chapter reflect management's plans. If all goes according to plan, there will be little difference between actual results and the results that would be expected according to the budgets and standards. If this happens, managers can concentrate on other issues. However, if actual results do not conform to the budget and to standards, the performance reporting system sends a signal to the manager that an "exception" has occurred. This signal is in the form of a variance from the budget or standards.

However, are all variances worth investigating? The answer is no. Differences between actual results and what was expected will almost always occur. If every variance was investigated, management would waste a great deal of time tracking down nickel-and-dime differences. Variances may occur for any of a variety of reasons—only some of which are significant and warrant management attention. For example, hotter-than-normal weather in the summer may result in higher-than-expected electrical bills for air conditioning. Or, workers may work slightly faster or slower on a particular day. Because of unpredictable random factors, one can expect that virtually every cost category will produce a variance of some kind.

How should managers decide which variances are worth investigating? One clue is the size of the variance. A variance of $5 is probably not big enough to warrant attention, whereas a variance of $5,000 might well be worth tracking down. Another clue is the size of the variance relative to the amount of spending involved. A variance that is only 0.1% of spending on an item is likely to be well within the bounds one would normally expect due to random factors. On the other hand, a variance of 10% of spending is much more likely to be a signal that something is basically wrong.

A more dependable approach is to plot variance data on a statistical control chart, as illustrated in Exhibit 10–10. The basic idea underlying a statistical control chart is that some random fluctuations in variances from period to period are normal and to be expected even when costs are well under control. A variance should be investigated only when it is unusual relative to that normal level of random fluctuation. Typically, only the standard deviation of the variances is used as the measure of the normal level of fluctuations. A rule of thumb is adopted such as "investigate all variances that are more than X standard deviations from zero." In the control chart in Exhibit 10–10, X is 1.0. That is, the rule of thumb in this company is to investigate all variances that are more than one standard deviation in

EXHIBIT 10–10 A Statistical Control Chart

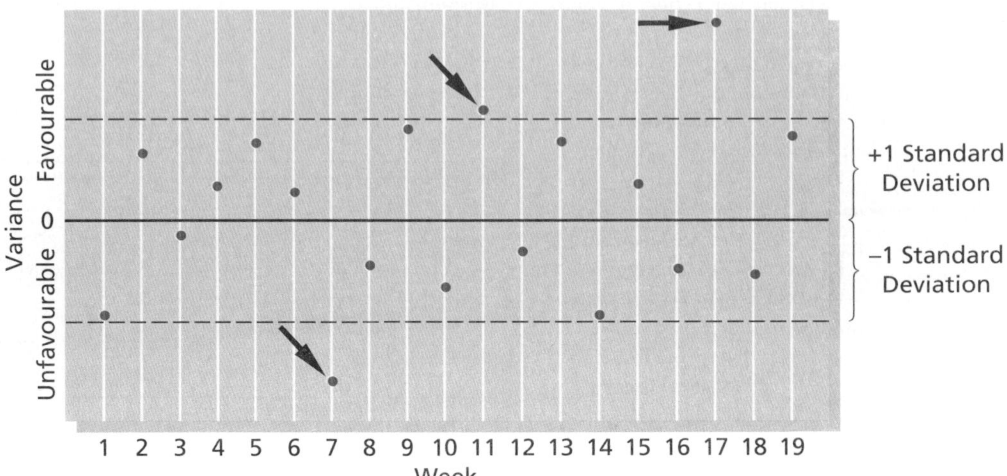

either direction (favourable or unfavourable) from zero. This means that the variances in weeks 7, 11, and 17 would have been investigated, but none of the others.

What value of *X* should be chosen? The greater the value of *X*, the wider the band of acceptable variances that would not be investigated. Thus, the greater the value of *X*, the less time will be spent tracking down variances, but the more likely it is that a real out-of-control situation would be overlooked. Ordinarily, if *X* is selected to be 1.0, roughly 30% of all variances will trigger an investigation even when there is no real problem. If *X* is set at 1.5, the figure drops to about 13%. If *X* is set at 2.0, the figure drops all the way to about 5%. Don't forget, however, that selecting a large value of *X* will result not only in fewer investigations but also in a higher probability that a real problem will be overlooked.

In addition to watching for unusually large variances, the pattern of the variances should be monitored. For example, a run of steadily mounting variances should trigger an investigation even though none of the variances is large enough by itself to warrant investigation.

FOCUS *on Current Practice*

Standard costs have a 100-year history in modern business practice. Modern computer systems have integrated standard cost practices on systems designed for a wide variety of organizations. Material requirements planning (MRP), supply chain management, and human resource management are a few of the terms used by modern computer systems that incorporate standard costs for planning, bidding, customer relationship management, inventory management and production planning.

One example of a modern application of standards is described by Nova Chemicals Corporation for the standardization of its maintenance practices for its 23 plants operating in Canada, United States and Europe. Nova claims the modern computer and management system they implemented provides standardization company wide, performance indicators and accurate data for the management of maintenance. Estimates by Nova suggest the new systems saved approximately 15% on their maintenance costs alone.

Source: Nova Chemicals, www.sap.com/industries.

INTERNATIONAL USES OF STANDARD COSTS

Standard costs are used by companies worldwide. A comparative study of cost accounting practices found that three-fourths of the companies surveyed in the United Kingdom, two-thirds of the companies surveyed in Canada, and 40% of the companies surveyed in Japan used standard cost systems.[8]

Standard costs were first introduced in Japan after World War II, with Nippon Electronics Company (NEC) being one of the first Japanese companies to adopt standard costs for all of its products. Many other Japanese companies followed NEC's lead after the war and developed standard cost systems. The ways in which these standard costs are used in Japan—and also in the other countries cited above—are shown in Exhibit 10–11.

Over time, the pattern of use shown in Exhibit 10–11 may change, but at present managers can expect to encounter standard costs in most industrialized nations. Moreover, the most important uses are for cost management and budgetary planning purposes.

8. Shin'ichi Inoue, "Comparative Studies of Recent Development of Cost Management Problems in U.S.A., U.K., Canada, and Japan," *Research Paper No. 29*, Kagawa University, March 1988, p. 17. The study included 95 United States companies, 52 United Kingdom companies, 82 Canadian companies, and 646 Japanese companies.

EXHIBIT 10–11 Uses of Standard Costs in Four Countries

	Canada	United States	United Kingdom	Japan
Cost management	2	1*	2	1
Budgetary planning and control†	1	2	3	3
Pricing decisions	3	3	1	2
Financial statement preparation	4	4	4	4

*The numbers 1 through 4 denote importance of use, from greatest to least.
†Includes management planning.

Source: Compiled from data in a study by Shin'ichi Inoue, "Comparative Studies of Recent Development of Cost Management Problems in U.S.A., U.K., Canada, and Japan," *Research Paper No. 29*, Kagawa University, March 1988, p. 20.

EVALUATION OF CONTROLS BASED ON STANDARD COSTS

Advantages of Standard Costs

Standard cost systems have a number of advantages:

1. As stated earlier, the use of standard costs is a key element in a management by exception approach. If costs remain within the standards, managers can focus on other issues. When costs fall significantly outside the standards, managers are alerted that there may be problems requiring attention. This approach helps managers focus on important issues.
2. Standards that are viewed as reasonable by employees can promote economy and efficiency. They provide benchmarks that individuals can use to judge their own performance.
3. Standard costs can greatly simplify bookkeeping. Instead of recording actual costs for each job, the standard costs for materials, labour, and overhead can be charged to jobs.
4. Standard costs fit naturally in an integrated system of "responsibility accounting." The standards establish what costs should be, who should be responsible for them, and whether actual costs are under control.

Potential Problems with the Use of Standard Costs

The use of standard costs can present a number of potential problems. Most of these problems result from improper use of standard costs and the management by exception principle or from using standard costs in situations in which they are not appropriate.

1. Standard cost variance reports are usually prepared on a monthly basis and often are released days or even weeks after the end of the month. As a consequence, the information in the reports may be so stale that it is almost useless. Timely, frequent reports that are approximately correct are better than infrequent reports that are very precise but out of date by the time they are released. As mentioned earlier, some companies are now reporting variances and other key operating data daily or even more frequently.
2. If managers are insensitive and use variance reports as a punishment, morale may suffer. Employees should receive positive reinforcement for work well done. Management by exception, by its nature, tends to focus on the negative. If variances are used as a punishment, subordinates may be tempted to cover up unfavourable variances or take actions that are not in the best interests of the company to make sure the variances are favourable. For example, workers may put on a crash effort to increase output at the end of the month to avoid an unfavourable labour efficiency variance. In the rush to produce output, quality may suffer.

3. Labour quantity standards and efficiency variances make two important assumptions. First, they assume that the production process is labour-paced; if labour works faster, output will go up. However, output in many companies is no longer determined by how fast labour works; rather, it is determined by the processing speed of machines. Second, the computations assume that labour is a variable cost. However, as discussed in earlier chapters, in many companies, direct labour may essentially be fixed. If labour is fixed, then an undue emphasis on labour efficiency variances creates pressure to build excess work in process and finished goods inventories.
4. In some cases, a "favourable" variance can be as bad or worse than an "unfavourable" variance. For example, McDonald's has a standard for the amount of hamburger meat that should be in a Big Mac. If there is a "favourable" variance, it means that less meat was used than the standard specifies. The result is a substandard Big Mac and possibly a dissatisfied customer.

5. There may be a tendency with standard cost reporting systems to emphasize meeting the standards to the exclusion of other important objectives, such as maintaining and improving quality, on-time delivery, and customer satisfaction. This tendency can be reduced by using supplemental performance measures that focus on these other objectives.
6. Just meeting standards may not be sufficient; continual improvement may be necessary to survive in the current competitive environment. For this reason, some companies focus on the trends in the standard cost variances—aiming for continual improvement rather than just meeting the standards. In other companies, engineered standards are being replaced either by a rolling average of actual costs, which is expected to decline, or by very challenging target costs.

In summary, managers should exercise considerable care in their use of a standard cost system. It is particularly important that managers go out of their way to focus on the positive, rather than just on the negative, and to be aware of possible unintended consequences.

Nevertheless, standard costs are still found in the vast majority of manufacturing companies and in many service companies, although their use is changing. For evaluating performance, standard cost variances may be supplanted in the future by a particularly interesting development known as the *balanced scorecard,* which is discussed in Chaper 12.

SUMMARY

A standard is a benchmark or "norm" for measuring performance. In business organizations, standards are set for both the cost and the quantity of inputs needed to manufacture goods or to provide services. Quantity standards indicate how much of a cost element, such as labour time or raw materials, should be used in manufacturing a unit of product or in providing a unit of service. Cost standards indicate what the cost of the time or the materials should be.

Standards are normally practical in nature, meaning that they can be attained by reasonable, although highly efficient, efforts. Such standards are generally felt to have a favourable motivational impact on employees.

When standards are compared to actual performance, the difference is referred to as a *variance.* Variances are computed and reported to management on a regular basis for both the price and the quantity elements of materials, labour, and overhead. Price and rate variances for inputs are computed by taking the difference between the actual and standard prices of the inputs and multiplying the result by the amount of input purchased. Quantity and efficiency variances are computed by taking the difference between the actual amount of the input used and the amount of input that is allowed for the actual output, and then multiplying the result by the standard price of the input.

Not all variances require management time or attention. Only unusual or particularly significant variances should be investigated—otherwise a great deal of time would be spent investigating unimportant matters. Additionally, it should be emphasized that the point of the investigation should not be to find someone to blame. The point of the investigation is to pinpoint the problem so that it can be fixed and operations improved.

Traditional standard cost variance reports should often be supplemented with other performance measures. Overemphasis on standard cost variances may lead to problems in other critical areas such as product quality, inventory levels, and on-time delivery.

REVIEW PROBLEM: STANDARD COSTS

Xavier Company produces a single product. Variable manufacturing overhead is applied to products on the basis of direct labour-hours. The standard costs for one unit of product are as follows:

Direct material: 6 grams at $0.50 per gram	$ 3
Direct labour: 1.8 hours at $10 per hour	18
Variable manufacturing overhead: 1.8 hours at $5 per hour	9
Total standard variable cost per unit	$30

During June, 2,000 units were produced. The costs associated with June's operations were as follows:

Materials purchased: 18,000 grams at $0.60 per gram	$10,800
Materials used in production: 14,000 grams	—
Direct labour: 4,000 hours at $9.75 per hour	39,000
Variable manufacturing overhead costs incurred	20,800

Required:

Compute the materials, labour, and variable manufacturing overhead variances.

Solution to Review Problem

Materials Variances

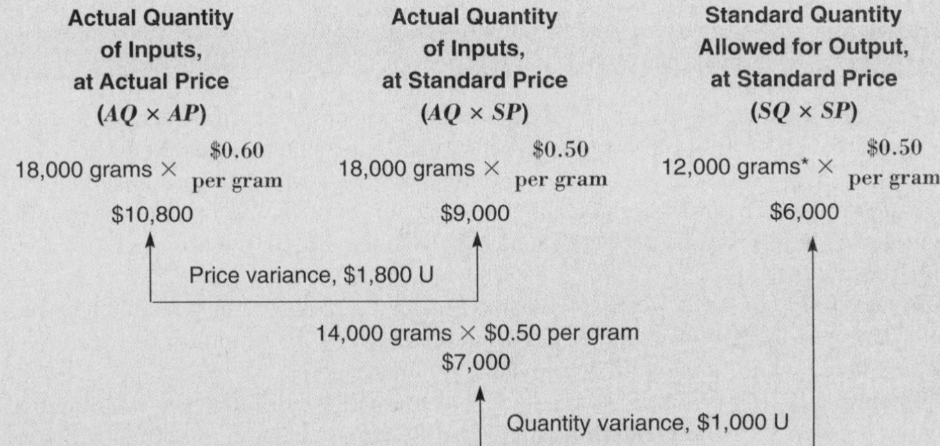

A total variance cannot be computed in this situation, because the amount of materials purchased (18,000 grams) differs from the amount of materials used in production (14,000 grams).

*2,000 units × 6 grams per unit = 12,000 grams.

Using the formulas in the chapter, the same variances would be computed as:

Materials price variance = $AQ(AP - SP)$
18,000 grams($0.60 per gram − $0.50 per gram) = $1,800 U

Materials quantity variance = $SP(AQ - SQ)$
$0.50 per gram(14,000 grams − 12,000 grams) = $1,000 U

Labour Variances

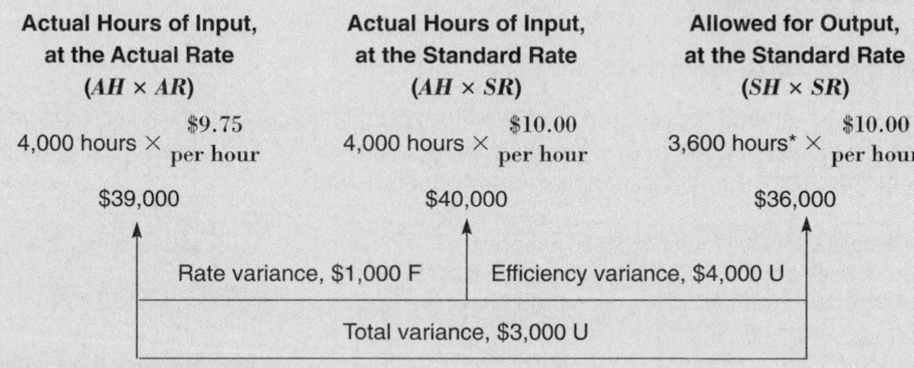

*2,000 units × 1.8 hours per unit = 3,600 hours.

Using the formulas in the chapter, the same variances would be computed as:

Labour rate variance = $AH(AR - SR)$
4,000 hours($9.75 per hour − $10.00 per hour) = $1,000 F

Labour efficiency variance = $SR(AH - SH)$
$10.00 per hour(4,000 hours − 3,600 hours) = $4,000 U

Variable Manufacturing Overhead Variances

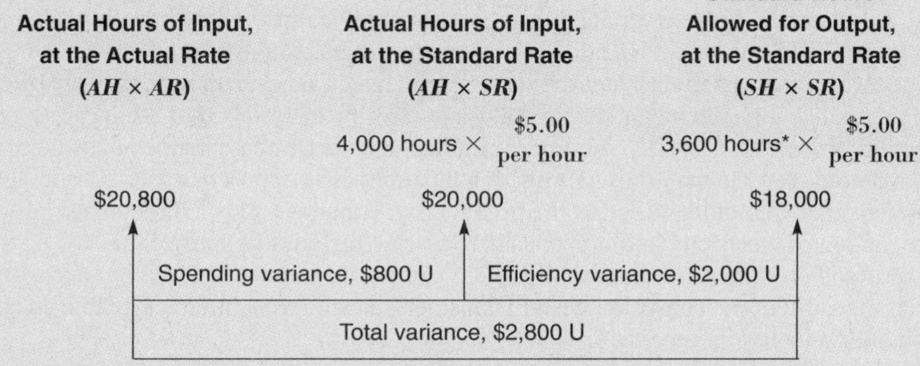

*2,000 units × 1.8 hours per unit = 3,600 hours.

Using the formulas in the chapter, the same variances would be computed as:

Variable overhead spending variance = $AH(AR - SR)$
4,000 hours($5.20 per hour* − $5.00 per hour) = $800 U

*$20,800 ÷ 4,000 hours = $5.20 per hour.

Variable overhead efficiency variance = $SR(AH - SH)$
$5.00 per hour(4,000 hours − 3,600 hours) = $2,000 U

APPENDIX 10A: GENERAL LEDGER ENTRIES TO RECORD VARIANCES

LEARNING OBJECTIVE 6
Prepare journal entries to record standard costs and variances.

Although standard costs and variances can be computed and used by management without being formally entered into the accounting records, most organizations prefer to make formal entries. Formal entry tends to give variances a greater emphasis than informal, off-the-record computations. This emphasis gives a clear signal of management's desire to keep costs within the limits that have been set. In addition, formal use of standard costs simplifies the bookkeeping process enormously. Inventories and cost of goods sold can be valued at their standard costs—eliminating the need to keep track of the actual cost of each unit.

Direct Materials Variances

To illustrate the general ledger entries needed to record standard cost variances, we will return to the data contained in the review problem at the end of the chapter. The entry to record the purchase of direct materials would be as follows:

Raw Materials (18,000 grams at $0.50 per gram)	9,000	
Materials Price Variance (18,000 grams at $0.10 per gram U)	1,800	
Accounts Payable (18,000 grams at $0.60 per gram)		10,800

Notice that the price variance is recognized when purchases are made, rather than when materials are actually used in production. This permits the price variance to be isolated early, and it also permits the materials to be carried in the inventory account at standard cost. As direct materials are later drawn from inventory and used in production, the quantity variance is isolated as follows:

Work in Process (12,000 grams at $0.50 per gram)	6,000	
Materials Quantity Variance (2,000 grams U at $0.50 per gram)	1,000	
Raw Materials (14,000 grams at $0.50 per gram)		7,000

Thus, direct materials enter into the Work in Process account at standard cost, in terms of both price and quantity.

Notice that both the price variance and the quantity variance above are unfavourable and are debit entries. If these variances had been favourable, they would have appeared as credit entries, as in the case of the direct labour rate variance below.

The term direct materials is not the same as raw materials even though they are often used interchangeably. Technically raw materials refer to materials that are basic to the production process and usually no processing has been done that changes their nature. Direct materials refer to materials identified in the product as opposed to indirect supplies or materials that are not identified in the product. For example, oil is a direct material for the production of electricity and it is considered a raw material by most. Steel is a direct material in the production of automobiles but a car seat is a direct material but not a raw material. Because of the confusion we will consider the two terms interchangeable unless an obvious distinction is necessary.

Direct Labour Variances

Referring again to the cost data in the review problem at the end of the chapter, the general ledger entry to record the incurrence of direct labour cost would be:

Work in Process (3,600 hours at $10.00 per hour)	36,000	
Labour Efficiency Variance (400 hours U at $10.00 per hour)	4,000	
Labour Rate Variance (4,000 hours at $0.25 per hour F)		1,000
Wages Payable (4,000 hours at $9.75 per hour)		39,000

Thus, as with direct materials, direct labour costs enter into the Work in Process account at standard, both in terms of the rate and in terms of the hours allowed for the actual production of the period.

Variable Manufacturing Overhead Variances

Variable manufacturing overhead variances generally are not recorded in the accounts separately but rather are determined as part of the general analysis of overhead, which is discussed in Chapter 11.

Cost Flows in a Standard Cost System

The flows of costs through the company's accounts are illustrated in Exhibit 10–12. Note that entries into the various inventory accounts are made at standard cost—not actual cost. The differences between actual and standard costs are entered into special accounts that accumulate the various standard cost variances. Ordinarily, these standard cost variance accounts are closed out to Cost of Goods Sold at the end of the period. Unfavourable variances increase Cost of Goods Sold, and favourable variances decrease Cost of Goods Sold.

EXHIBIT 10–12 Cost Flows in a Standard Cost System

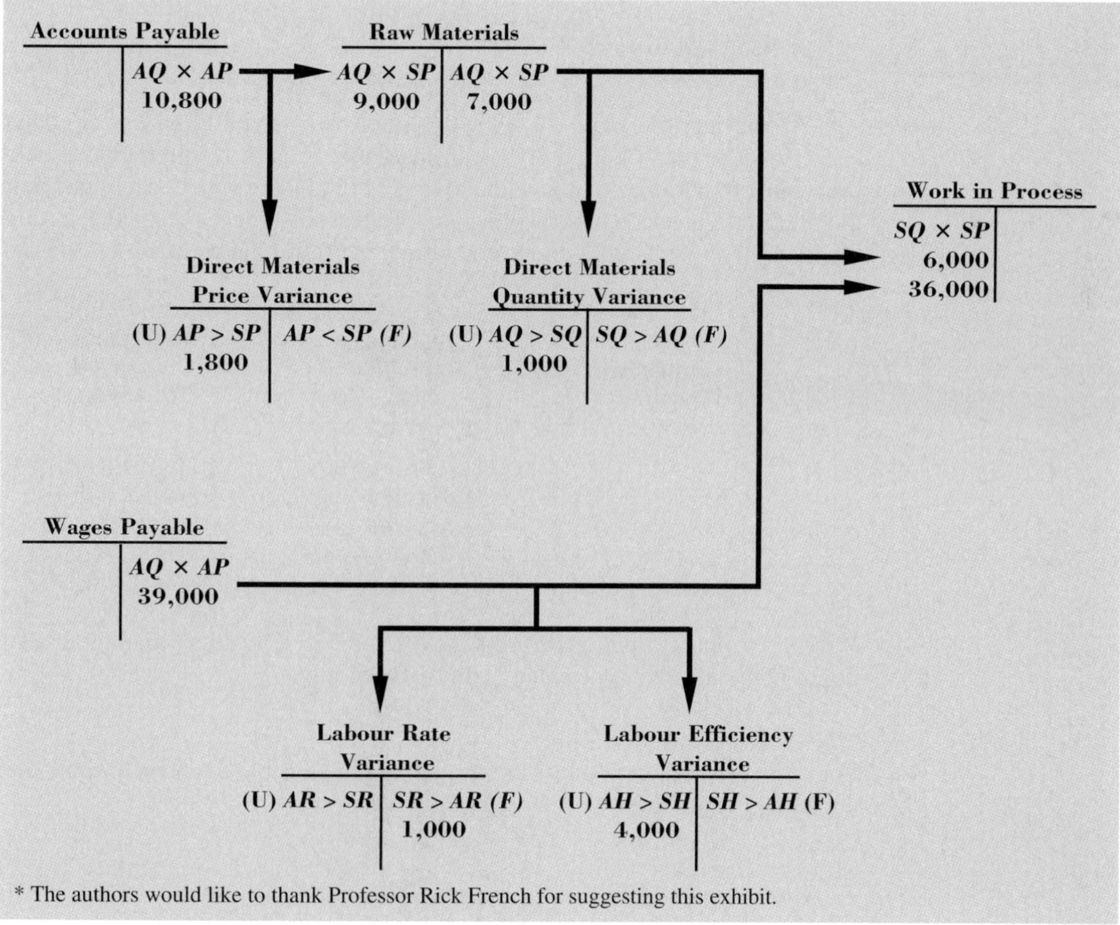

* The authors would like to thank Professor Rick French for suggesting this exhibit.

APPENDIX 10B: LEARNING CURVES

LEARNING OBJECTIVE 7
Explain the concept of learning curves.

Most workers become more proficient at their tasks the more they do them. Learning takes place especially through the early stages of a job. For example, contractors constructing a high-rise apartment building find the twenthieth storey goes on faster than the eighth storey. This effect means break-even analysis would have multiple break-even points when learning occurs, because the assumption of constant worker and machine productivity stated in Chapter 6 would be violated.[9] Studies of the learning of workers suggests the pattern illustrated in Exhibit 10–13.

The learning curve represents the fact that the time spent per unit declines by a constant percentage as the number of units produced doubles. This phenomenon has been observed where new long-term production activities are undertaken or where a long production cycle is conducted, such as building construction projects, airplane manufacture, and shipbuilding. Selling prices and workforce needs, as well as standards for time, can be assessed from such an analysis. Care is needed, however, because management practices, design, production technology, and quality requirements can interfere with the actual time spent by employees. Behaviour considerations can also affect learning. Factors such as peer pressure, union-imposed constraints, and the state of management-worker relationships can affect productivity and limit learning.

The functional form of the pattern in Exhibit 10–13 can be expressed as follows:

$$y = aQ^b$$

where

Q is the cumulative production in units.
b is a number representing the learning rate and expressed as follows: log (learning rate)/log 2
a is the hours required to produce the first unit.
y is the average time required to produce one unit.

If the learning rate is, say, 80%, then $b = \log .80/\log 2 = -.09691/.30103 = -.32193$. The pattern of an 80% learning curve is as shown in the table below. Note that every time experience doubles, the average hours to complete each unit drops to 80% of the preceding level. In other words, an 80% learning curve means that as cumulative production quantities double, the average time per unit falls by 20%.

Cumulative Quantity	Average Hours per Unit	Total Hours to Produce Cumulative Quantity
1	2	2
2	1.6(2 hours × .80)	3.2(2 × 1.6 hours)
4	1.3(1.6 hours × .80)	5.2(4 × 1.3 hours)
8	1.0(1.3 hours × .80)	8.0(8 × 1.0 hour)
16	0.8(1.0 hours × .80)	12.8(16 × 0.8 hour)
32	0.6(0.8 hour × .80)	19.2(32 × 0.6 hour)

With a computer, functional forms are often more convenient than tables. The total number of hours needed to produce Q units would be:

$$T = Q_y = Q_a Q^b = aQ^{b+1}$$

For a situation where T hours are available, the possible quantity of units that can be produced (Q) would be:

$$Q = (T/a)^x$$

9. Woody M. Liao, "The Effects of Learning on Cost-Volume-Profit Analysis," *Cost and Management,* November/December 1983, pp. 38–40, illustrates this issue.

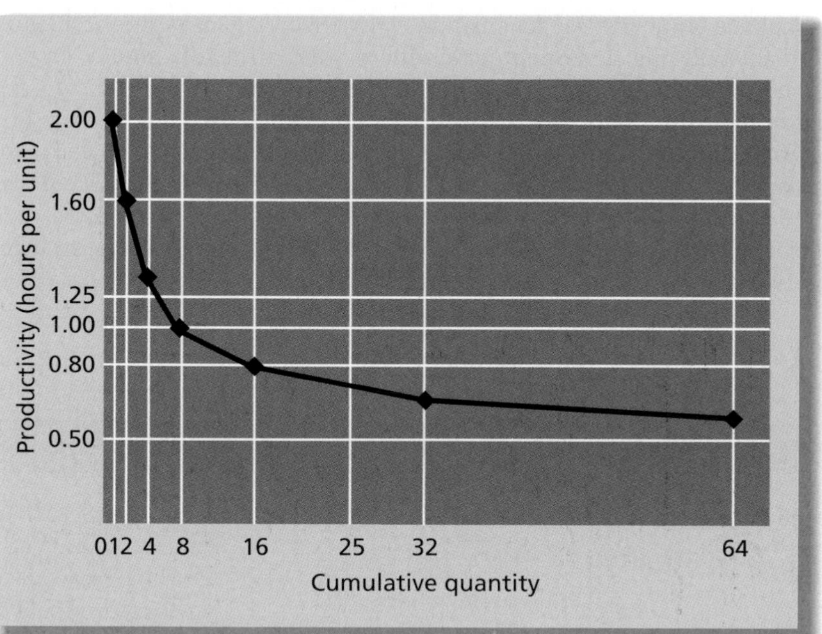

EXHIBIT 10–13 Learning Curve

where

$x = 1/(b + 1)$

Care is needed when using this formula. Assume, for example, a firm has produced 16 units already and wants to know the time required for another 16 units. By examining the earlier example, you can see the type of calculation required. Total time to produce 32 units is 19.2 hours. Total time to produce 16 units is 12.8 hours. Therefore, the last 16 units would take (19.2 − 12.8) or 6.4 hours; that is, 0.4 hours per unit. Mathematically, the exact answer can be determined by the following difference:

$$IT = a(Q_2)^{b+1} - a(Q_1)^{b+1}$$

where IT is the incremental time required, the 6.4 hours.

Interestingly, regression analysis, as described in Chapter 5, can be used to derive the parameters of a learning curve of the past history of an operation.

$$T = aQ^{b+1}$$

is the same as:

$$\log(T) = \log(a) + (b + 1)\log(Q)$$

If each T value and each Q amount is logged, a regression result can be calculated for the slope $(b + 1)$ and the intercept, log a. The regression value for log a can be converted to a by the following calculation, $10^{(\log a)}$, the y^x calculation on most standard hand calculators. The purpose of the log function is to convert the curved line displayed in Exhibit 10–13 into a straight line so that the linear regression gives an accurate result.

Learning curves can serve as a method of setting and revising standard labour hours in a repetitive task environment. The use of the approach would be most appropriate where many workers are learning a task over a reasonably extended period of time. Short-run learning effects can be dealt with within a single accounting period using an average performance rate. Individual employees can have labour efficiency variances occurring during their learning periods without serious inaccuracies being introduced to the standard cost variances. However, large groups functioning at the same stage, particularly early in a production sequence when the effects of learning are pronounced, need evaluation relative to their projected learning curve. Incorporating the learning curve times into the standard times should help avoid misleading standard cost variances.

It should be borne in mind that learning curve phenomena are applicable for labour-intensive manufacturing. Learning curve effects were originally studied in connection with aircraft manufacture in World War II. The learning curve has typically been employed in industries such as construction, shipbuilding, and electronics. In the new manufacturing environment, learning curves have less relevance. Automated manufacturing is unlikely to have much variation or to display a regular learning curve. In less-automated processes, however, where learning curves do occur, it is important to take the resulting decline in labour hours and costs into account in setting standards, determining prices, planning production, or setting up work schedules.

GLOSSARY

Visit the Online Learning Centre at http://www.mcgrawhill.ca/college/garrison/ for a review of key terms and definitions.

QUESTIONS

10–1 What is a quantity standard? What is a price standard?

10–2 Distinguish between ideal and practical standards.

10–3 If employees are chronically unable to meet a standard, what effect would you expect this to have on their productivity?

10–4 What is the difference between a standard and a budget?

10–5 What is meant by the term *variance*?

10–6 What is meant by the term *management by exception*?

10–7 Why are variances generally segregated in terms of a price variance and a quantity variance?

10–8 Who is generally responsible for the materials price variance? The materials quantity variance? The labour efficiency variance?

10–9 The materials price variance can be computed at what two different points in time? Which point is better? Why?

10–10 An examination of the cost records of the Sherbrook Furniture Company reveals that the materials price variance is favourable but that the materials quantity variance is unfavourable by a substantial amount. What might this indicate?

10–11 What dangers lie in using standards as punitive tools?

10–12 "Our workers are all under labour contracts; therefore, our labour rate variance is bound to be zero." Discuss.

10–13 What effect, if any, would you expect poor-quality materials to have on direct labour variances?

10–14 If variable manufacturing overhead is applied to production on the basis of direct labour-hours and the direct labour efficiency variance is unfavourable, will the variable overhead efficiency variance be favourable or unfavourable, or could it be either? Explain.

10–15 What is a statistical control chart, and how is it used?

10–16 Why can undue emphasis on labour efficiency variances lead to excess work in process inventories?

10–17 What is a mix variance?

10–18 Can standard costs be used for financial reporting purposes? Explain.

10–19 (Appendix 10A) What are the advantages of making formal journal entries in the accounting records for variances?

10–20 (Appendix 10B) What is a learning curve?

10–21 (Appendix 10B) If production workers perform according to an 80% learning curve, what pattern of labour times does this suggest?

10–22 (Appendix 10B) The cost function for CCM Co. reflects a 75% learning curve. The average time to complete a task with 50 units is 6 minutes. What is the projected time required for completion of the next 100 units?

EXERCISES

EXERCISE 10–1 Setting Standards; Preparing a Standard Cost Card [LO1]
Martin Company manufactures a powerful cleaning solvent. The main ingredient in the solvent is a raw material called Echol. Information concerning the purchase and use of Echol follows:

Purchase of Echol Echol is purchased in 60-litre containers at a cost of $115 per container. A discount of 2% is offered by the supplier for payment within 10 days, and Martin Company takes all discounts. Shipping costs, which Martin Company must pay, amount to $130 for an average shipment of 100 60-litre containers of Echol.

Use of Echol The bill of materials calls for 7.6 litres of Echol per bottle of cleaning solvent. About 5% of all Echol used is lost through spillage or evaporation (the 7.6 litres above is the *actual* content per bottle). In addition, statistical analysis has shown that every 41st bottle is rejected at final inspection because of contamination.

Required:
1. Compute the standard purchase price for one litre of Echol.
2. Compute the standard quantity of Echol (in litres) per salable bottle of cleaning solvent.
3. Using the data from (1) and (2) above, prepare a standard cost card showing the standard cost of Echol per bottle of cleaning solvent.

EXERCISE 10–2 Direct Materials Variances [LO2]
Bandar Industries Berhad of Malaysia manufactures sporting equipment. One of the company's products, a football helmet for the North American market, requires a special plastic. During the quarter ending June 30, the company manufactured 35,000 helmets, using 22,500 kilograms of plastic. The plastic cost the company RM 171,000. (The currency in Malaysia is the ringgit, which is denoted here by RM.)

According to the standard cost card, each helmet should require 0.6 kilograms of plastic, at a cost of RM 8 per kilogram.

Required:
1. What cost for plastic should have been incurred to make 35,000 helmets? How much greater or less is this than the cost that was incurred?
2. Break down the difference computed in (1) above into a materials price variance and a materials quantity variance.

EXERCISE 10–3 Direct Labour Variances [LO3]
SkyChefs, Inc., prepares in-flight meals for a number of major airlines. One of the company's products is grilled salmon in dill sauce with baby new potatoes and spring vegetables. During the most recent week, the company prepared 4,000 of these meals using 960 direct labour-hours. The company paid these direct labour workers a total of $9,600 for this work, or $10.00 per hour.

According to the standard cost card for this meal, it should require 0.25 direct labour-hours at a cost of $9.75 per hour.

Required:
1. What direct labour cost should have been incurred to prepare 4,000 meals? How much does this differ from the actual direct labour cost?
2. Break down the difference computed in (1) above into a labour rate variance and a labour efficiency variance.

EXERCISE 10–4 Variable Overhead Variances [LO4]

Logistics Solutions provides order fulfillment services for dot.com merchants. The company maintains warehouses that stock items carried by its dot.com clients. When a client receives an order from a customer, the order is forwarded to Logistics Solutions, which pulls the item from storage, packs it, and ships it to the customer. The company uses a predetermined variable overhead rate based on direct labour-hours.

In the most recent month, 120,000 items were shipped to customers using 2,300 direct labour-hours. The company incurred a total of $7,360 in variable overhead costs.

According to the company's standards, 0.02 direct labour-hours are required to fulfill an order for one item and the variable overhead rate is $3.25 per direct labour-hour.

Required:
1. What variable overhead cost should have been incurred to fill the orders for the 120,000 items? How much does this differ from the actual variable overhead cost?

2. Break down the difference computed in (1) above into a variable overhead spending variance and a variable overhead efficiency variance.

EXERCISE 10–5 (Appendix 10A) Recording Variances in the General Ledger [LO6]
Bliny Corporation makes a product with the following standard costs for direct material and direct labour:

Direct material: 2.00 metres at $3.25 per metre	$6.50
Direct labour: 0.40 hours at $12.00 per hour	$4.80

During the most recent month, 5,000 units were produced. The costs associated with the month's production of this product were as follows:

Material purchased: 12,000 metres at $3.15 per metre . .	$37,800
Material used in production: 10,500 metres	—
Direct labour: 1,975 hours at $12.20 per hour	$24,095

The standard cost variances for direct material and direct labour are:

Materials price variance: 12,000 metres at $0.10 per metre F	$1,200 F
Materials quantity variance: 500 metres at $3.25 per metre U	$1,625 U
Labour rate variance: 1,975 hours at $0.20 per hour U	$395 U
Labour efficiency variance: 25 hours at $12.00 per hour F	$300 F

Required:
1. Prepare the general ledger entry to record the purchase of materials on account for the month.
2. Prepare the general ledger entry to record the use of materials for the month.
3. Prepare the general ledger entry to record the incurrence of direct labour cost for the month.

EXERCISE 10–6 Setting Standards [LO1]
Victoria Chocolates, Ltd., makes premium handcrafted chocolate confections in London. The owner of the company is setting up a standard cost system and has collected the following data for one of the company's products, the Empire Truffle. This product is made with the finest white chocolate and various fillings. The data below pertain only to the white chocolate used in the product (the currency is stated in pounds denoted here as £):

Material requirements, kilograms of white chocolate per dozen truffles .	0.70 kilograms
Allowance for waste, kilograms of white chocolate per dozen truffles . .	0.03 kilograms
Allowance for rejects, kilograms of white chocolate per dozen truffles . .	0.02 kilograms
Purchase price, finest grade white chocolate	£7.50 per kilogram
Purchase discount	8% of purchase price
Shipping cost from the supplier in Belgium	£0.30 per kilogram
Receiving and handling cost	£0.04 per kilogram

Required:
1. Determine the standard price of a kilogram of white chocolate.
2. Determine the standard quantity of white chocolate for a dozen truffles.
3. Determine the standard cost of the white chocolate in a dozen truffles.

EXERCISE 10–7 Direct Materials and Direct Labour Variances [LO2, LO3]
Dawson Toys, Ltd., produces a toy called the Maze. The company has recently established a standard cost system to help control costs and has established the following standards for the Maze toy:

Direct materials: 6 microns per toy at $0.50 per micron
Direct labour: 1.3 hours per toy at $8 per hour

During July, the company produced 3,000 Maze toys. Production data for the month on the toy follow:

Direct materials: 25,000 microns were purchased at a cost of $0.48 per micron. 5,000 of these microns were still in inventory at the end of the month.
Direct labour: 4,000 direct labour-hours were worked at a cost of $36,000.

Required:

1. Compute the following variances for July:
   a. Direct materials price and quantity variances.
   b. Direct labour rate and efficiency variances.
2. Prepare a brief explanation of the possible causes of each variance.

EXERCISE 10–8 Working Backwards from Labour Variances [LO3]

The auto repair shop of Quality Motor Company uses standards to control the labour time and labour cost in the shop. The standard labour cost for a motor tune-up is given below:

Job	Standard Hours	Standard Rate	Standard Cost
Motor tune-up	2.5	$9	$22.50

The record showing the time spent in the shop last week on motor tune-ups has been misplaced. However, the shop supervisor recalls that 50 tune-ups were completed during the week, and the controller recalls the following variance data relating to tune-ups:

Labour rate variance	$87 F
Total labour variance	$93 U

Required:

1. Determine the number of actual labour-hours spent on tune-ups during the week.
2. Determine the actual hourly rate of pay for tune-ups last week.

(Hint: A useful way to proceed would be to work from known to unknown data either by using the variance formulas or by using the columnar format shown in Exhibit 10–7.)

EXERCISE 10–9 Direct Labour and Variable Manufacturing Overhead Variances [LO3, LO4]

Erie Company manufactures a small CD player called the Jogging Mate. The company uses standards to control its costs. The labour standards that have been set for one Jogging Mate CD player are as follows:

Standard Hours	Standard Rate per Hour	Standard Cost
18 minutes	$12.00	$3.60

During August, 5,750 hours of direct labour time were needed to make 20,000 units of the Jogging Mate. The direct labour cost totalled $73,600 for the month.

Required:

1. What direct labour cost should have been incurred to make 20,000 units of the Jogging Mate? By how much does this differ from the cost that was incurred?
2. Break down the difference in cost from (1) above into a labour rate variance and a labour efficiency variance.
3. The budgeted variable manufacturing overhead rate is $4 per direct labour-hour. During August, the company incurred $21,850 in variable manufacturing overhead cost. Compute the variable overhead spending and efficiency variances for the month.

EXERCISE 10–10 Direct Materials and Direct Labour Variances [LO2, LO3]

Huron Company produces a commercial cleaning compound known as Zoom. The direct materials and direct labour standards for one unit of Zoom are given near the top of the next page.

During the most recent month, the following activity was recorded:

a. Twenty thousand kilograms of material were purchased at a cost of $2.35 per kilogram.

b. All of the material purchased was used to produce 4,000 units of Zoom.
c. 750 hours of direct labour time were recorded at a total labour cost of $10,425.

	Standard Quantity or Hours	Standard Price or Rate	Standard Cost
Direct materials	4.6 kilograms	$2.50 per kilogram	$11.50
Direct labour	0.2 hours	$12.00 per hour	$2.40

Required:

1. Compute the direct materials price and quantity variances for the month.
2. Compute the direct labour rate and efficiency variances for the month.

EXERCISE 10–11 Direct Materials Variances [LO2]

Refer to the data in Exercise 10–10. Assume that instead of producing 4,000 units during the month, the company produced only 3,000 units, using 14,750 kilograms of material. (The rest of the material purchased remained in raw materials inventory.)

Required:

Compute the direct materials price and quantity variances for the month.

EXERCISE 10–12 (Appendix 10A) Direct Materials and Direct Labour Variances; Journal Entries [LO2, LO3, LO6]

Genola Fashions began production of a new product on June 1. The company uses a standard cost system and has established the following standards for one unit of the new product:

	Standard Quantity or Hours	Standard Price or Rate	Standard Cost
Direct materials	2.5 metres	$14 per metre	$35.00
Direct labour	1.6 hours	$8 per hour	$12.80

During June, the following activity was recorded regarding the new product:

a. Purchasing acquired 10,000 metres of material at a cost of $13.80 per metre.
b. Production used 8,000 metres of the material to manufacture 3,000 units of the new product.
c. Production reported that 5,000 direct labour-hours were worked on the new product at a cost of $43,000.

Required:

1. For direct materials:
   a. Compute the direct materials price and quantity variances.
   b. Prepare journal entries to record the purchase of materials and the use of materials in production.
2. For direct labour:
   a. Compute the direct labour rate and efficiency variances.
   b. Prepare a journal entry to record the incurrence of direct labour cost for the month.
3. Post the entries you have prepared to the following T-accounts:

Raw Materials

	Debit	Credit
	?	?
Bal.	?	

Work in Process

Debit	Credit
Materials used ?	
Labour cost ?	

Accounts Payable

Debit	Credit
	138,000

Wages Payable

Debit	Credit
	43,000

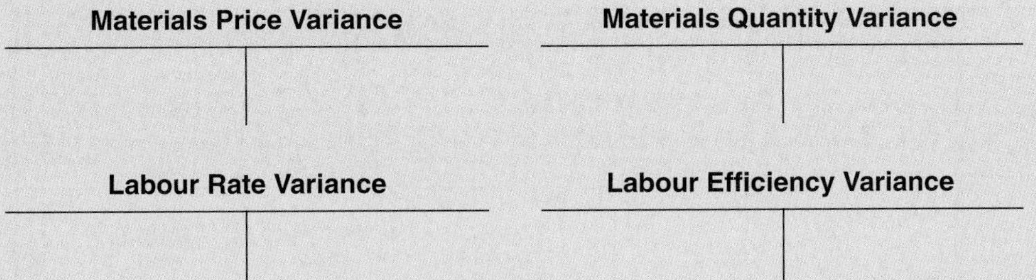

PROBLEMS

PROBLEM 10–13 Variance Analysis in a Hospital [LO2, LO3, LO4]

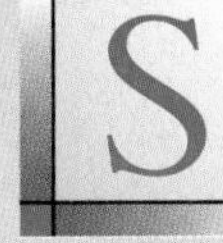

John Fleming, chief administrator for Valley View Hospital, is concerned about the costs for tests in the hospital's lab. Charges for lab tests are consistently higher at Valley View than at other hospitals and have resulted in many complaints. Also, because of strict regulations on amounts reimbursed for lab tests, payments received from governmental units have not been high enough to cover lab costs.

Mr. Fleming has asked you to evaluate costs in the hospital's lab for the past month. The following information is available:

a. Two types of tests are performed in the lab—blood tests and smears. During the past month, 1,800 blood tests and 2,400 smears were performed in the lab.

b. Small glass plates are used in both types of tests. During the past month, the hospital purchased 12,000 plates at a cost of $28,200. This cost is net of a 6% quantity discount. 1,500 of these plates were unused at the end of the month; no plates were on hand at the beginning of the month.

c. During the past month, 1,150 hours of labour time were recorded in the lab at a cost of $13,800.

d. The lab's variable overhead cost last month totalled $7,820.

Valley View Hospital has never used standard costs. By searching industry literature, however, you have determined the following nationwide averages for hospital labs:

Plates: Two plates are required per lab test. These plates cost $2.50 each and are disposed of after the test is completed.

Labour: Each blood test should require 0.3 hours to complete, and each smear should require 0.15 hours to complete. The average cost of this lab time is $14 per hour.

Overhead: Overhead cost is based on direct labour-hours. The average rate for variable overhead is $6 per hour.

Required:

1. Compute a materials price variance for the plates purchased last month and a materials quantity variance for the plates used last month.
2. For labour cost in the lab:
   a. Compute a labour rate variance and a labour efficiency variance.
   b. In most hospitals, one-half of the workers in the lab are senior technicians and one-half are assistants. In an effort to reduce costs, Valley View Hospital employs only one-fourth senior technicians and three-fourths assistants. Would you recommend that this policy be continued? Explain.
3. Compute the variable overhead spending and efficiency variances. Is there any relation between the variable overhead efficiency variance and the labour efficiency variance? Explain.

PROBLEM 10–14 Basic Variance Analysis [LO2, LO3, LO4]

Becton Labs, Inc., produces various chemical compounds for industrial use. One compound, called Fludex, is prepared using an elaborate distilling process. The company has developed standard costs for one unit of Fludex, as follows:

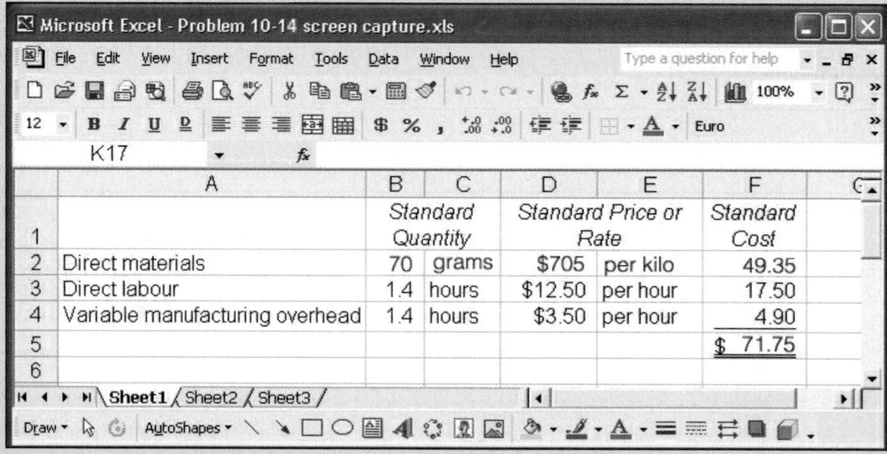

	A	B	C	D	E	F
1		Standard Quantity		Standard Price or Rate		Standard Cost
2	Direct materials	70	grams	$705	per kilo	49.35
3	Direct labour	1.4	hours	$12.50	per hour	17.50
4	Variable manufacturing overhead	1.4	hours	$3.50	per hour	4.90
5						$ 71.75
6						

During November, the following activity was recorded by the company relative to production of Fludex:

a. Materials purchased, 340.2 kilograms at a cost of $225,000.
b. There was no beginning inventory of materials; however, at the end of the month, 70.9 kilograms of material remained in ending inventory.
c. The company employs 35 lab technicians to work on the production of Fludex. During November, each worked an average of 160 hours at an average rate of $12 per hour.
d. Variable manufacturing overhead is assigned to Fludex on the basis of direct labour-hours. Variable manufacturing overhead costs during November totalled $18,200.
e. During November, 3,750 good units of Fludex were produced.

The company's management is anxious to determine the efficiency of the Fludex production activities.

Required:

1. For direct materials used in the production of Fludex:
   a. Compute the price and quantity variances.
   b. The materials were purchased from a new supplier who is anxious to enter into a long-term purchase contract. Would you recommend that the company sign the contract? Explain.
2. For direct labour employed in the production of Fludex:
   a. Compute the rate and efficiency variances.
   b. In the past, the 35 technicians employed in the production of Fludex consisted of 20 senior technicians and 15 assistants. During November, the company experimented with fewer senior technicians and more assistants in order to save costs. Would you recommend that the new labour mix be continued? Explain.
3. Compute the variable overhead spending and efficiency variances. What relation can you see between this efficiency variance and the labour efficiency variance?

PROBLEM 10–15 (Appendix 10A) Comprehensive Variance Analysis; Journal Entries [LO2, LO3, LO4, LO6]

Trueform Products, Inc., produces a broad line of sports equipment and uses a standard cost system for control purposes. Last year the company produced 8,000 varsity footballs. The standard costs associated with this football, along with the actual costs incurred last year, are given near the top of the next page (per football).

The president was elated when he saw that actual costs exceeded standard costs by only $0.27 per football. He stated, "I was afraid that our unit cost might get out of hand when we gave out those raises last year in order to stimulate output. But it's obvious our costs are well under control."

There was no inventory of materials on hand to start the year. During the year, 9,754 metres of materials were purchased and used in production.

Required:

1. For direct materials:
   a. Compute the price and quantity variances for the year.
   b. Prepare journal entries to record all activity relating to direct materials for the year.

2. For direct labour:
   a. Compute the rate and efficiency variances.
   b. Prepare a journal entry to record the incurrence of direct labour cost for the year.
3. Compute the variable overhead spending and efficiency variances.
4. Was the president correct in his statement that "our costs are well under control"? Explain.
5. State possible causes of each variance that you have computed.

	Standard Cost	Actual Cost
Direct materials:		
Standard: 1.13 metres at $16.40 per m	$18.53	
Actual: 1.22 metres at $15.74 per m		$19.20
Direct labour:		
Standard: 0.9 hour at $7.50 per hour	6.75	
Actual: 0.8 hour at $8.00 per hour		6.40
Variable manufacturing overhead:		
Standard: 0.9 hour at $2.50 per hour	2.25	
Actual: 0.8 hour at $2.75 per hour		2.20
Total cost per football	$27.53	$27.80

PROBLEM 10–16 Comprehensive Variance Analysis [LO2, LO3, LO4]

Miller Toy Company manufactures a plastic swimming pool at its Westwood Plant. The plant has been experiencing problems as shown by its June contribution format income statement below:

	Budgeted	Actual
Sales (15,000 pools)	$450,000	$450,000
Less variable expenses:		
Variable cost of goods sold*	180,000	196,290
Variable selling expenses	20,000	20,000
Total variable expenses	200,000	216,290
Contribution margin	250,000	233,710
Less fixed expenses:		
Manufacturing overhead	130,000	130,000
Selling and administrative	84,000	84,000
Total fixed expenses	214,000	214,000
Operating income	$ 36,000	$ 19,710

*Contains direct materials, direct labour, and variable manufacturing overhead.

Janet Dunn, who has just been appointed general manager of the Westwood Plant, has been given instructions to "get things under control." Upon reviewing the plant's income statement, Ms. Dunn has concluded that the major problem lies in the variable cost of goods sold. She has been provided with the following standard cost per swimming pool:

	Standard Quantity or Hours	Standard Price or Rate	Standard Cost
Direct materials	1.36 kilograms	$4.41 per kilogram	$ 6.00
Direct labour	0.8 hour	$6.00 per hour	4.80
Variable manufacturing overhead	0.4 hour*	$3.00 per hour	1.20
Total standard cost			$12.00

*Based on machine-hours.

Ms. Dunn has determined that during June the plant produced 15,000 pools and incurred the following costs:

a. Purchased 27,180 kilograms of materials at a cost of $4.30 per kilogram.
b. Used 22,288 kilograms of materials in production. (Finished goods and work in process inventories are insignificant and can be ignored.)
c. Worked 11,800 direct labour-hours at a cost of $7.00 per hour.
d. Incurred variable manufacturing overhead cost totalling $18,290 for the month. A total of 5,900 machine-hours was recorded.

It is the company's policy to close all variances to cost of goods sold on a monthly basis.

Required:

1. Compute the following variances for June:
   a. Direct materials price and quantity variances.
   b. Direct labour rate and efficiency variances.
   c. Variable overhead spending and efficiency variances.
2. Summarize the variances that you computed in (1) above by showing the net overall favourable or unfavourable variance for the month. What impact did this figure have on the company's income statement? Show computations.
3. Pick out the two most significant variances that you computed in (1) above. Explain to Ms. Dunn possible causes of these variances.

PROBLEM 10–17 Setting Standards [LO1]

Danson Company is a chemical manufacturer that supplies various products to industrial users. The company plans to introduce a new chemical solution, called Nysap, for which it needs to develop a standard product cost. The following information is available on the production of Nysap:

a. Nysap is made by combining a chemical compound (nyclyn) and a solution (salex), and boiling the mixture. A 20% loss in volume occurs for both the salex and the nyclyn during boiling. After boiling, the mixture consists of 9.6 litres of salex and 12 kilograms of nyclyn per 10-litre batch of Nysap.
b. After the boiling process is complete, the solution is cooled slightly before 5 kilograms of protet are added per 10-litre batch of Nysap. The addition of the protet does not affect the total liquid volume. The resulting solution is then bottled in 10-litre containers.
c. The finished product is highly unstable, and one 10-litre batch out of five is rejected at final inspection. Rejected batches have no commercial value and are thrown out.
d. It takes a worker 35 minutes to process one 10-litre batch of Nysap. Employees work an eight-hour day, including one hour per day for rest breaks and cleanup.

Required:

1. Determine the standard quantity for each of the raw materials needed to produce an acceptable 10-litre batch of Nysap.
2. Determine the standard labour time allowed to produce an acceptable 10-litre batch of Nysap.
3. Assuming the following purchase prices and costs, prepare a standard cost card for direct materials and direct labour for one acceptable 10-litre batch of Nysap:

Salex	$1.50 per litre
Nyclyn	$2.80 per kilogram
Protet	$3.00 per kilogram
Direct labour cost . . .	$9.00 per hour

(CMA, adapted)

PROBLEM 10–18 Variance Analysis with Multiple Lots [LO2, LO3]

Hillcrest Leisure Wear, Inc., manufactures men's clothing. The company has a single line of slacks that is produced in lots, with each lot representing an order from a customer. As a lot is completed, the customer's store label is attached to the slacks before shipment.

Hillcrest has a standard cost system and has established the following standards for a dozen slacks:

	Standard Quantity or Hours	Standard Price or Rate	Standard Cost
Direct materials	29.25 metres	$2.626 per m	$76.81
Direct labour	6 hours	$7.50 per hour	$45.00

During October, Hillcrest worked on three orders for slacks. The company's job cost records for the month reveal the following:

Lot	Units in Lot (dozens)	Materials Used (metres)	Hours Worked
48	1,500	43,953	8,900
49	950	27,427	6,130
50	2,100	61,198	10,270

The following additional information is available:

a. Hillcrest purchased 163,800 metres of material during October at a cost of $424,800.
b. Direct labour cost incurred during the month for production of slacks amounted to $192,280.
c. There was no work in process inventory on October 1. During October, lots 48 and 49 were completed, and lot 50 was 100% complete with respect to materials and 80% complete with respect to labour.

Required:

1. Compute the materials price variance for the materials purchased during October.
2. Determine the materials quantity variance for October in both metres and dollars:
   a. For each lot worked on during the month.
   b. For the company as a whole.
3. Compute the labour rate variance for October.
4. Determine the labour efficiency variance for the month in both hours and dollars:
   a. For each lot worked on during the month.
   b. For the company as a whole.
5. In what situations might it be better to express variances in units (hours, metres, and so on) rather than in dollars? In dollars rather than in units?

(CPA, adapted)

PROBLEM 10–19 Direct Materials and Direct Labour Variances; Computations from Incomplete Data [LO1, LO2, LO3]

Sharp Company manufactures a product for which the following standards have been set:

	Standard Quantity or Hours	Standard Price or Rate	Standard Cost
Direct materials	91.44 cm	$16.40 per metre	$15
Direct labour	? hours	? per hour	?

During March, the company purchased direct materials at a cost of $55,650, all of which were used in the production of 3,200 units of product. In addition, 4,900 hours of direct labour time were worked on the product during the month. The cost of this labour time was $36,750. The following variances have been computed for the month:

Materials quantity variance	$4,500 U
Total labour variance	$1,650 F
Labour efficiency variance	$800 U

Required:

1. For direct materials:
   a. Compute the actual cost per metre for materials for March.
   b. Compute the materials price variance and a total variance for materials.
2. For direct labour:
   a. Compute the standard direct labour rate per hour.
   b. Compute the standard hours allowed for the month's production.
   c. Compute the standard hours allowed per unit of product.

(Hint: In completing the problem, it may be helpful to move from known to unknown data either by using the columnar format shown in Exhibits 10–4 and 10–7 or by using the variance formulas.)

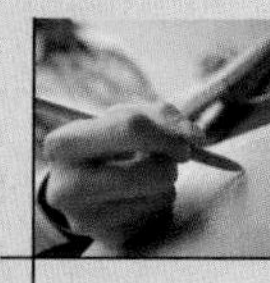

PROBLEM 10–20 (Appendix 10A) Comprehensive Variance Analysis with Incomplete Data; Journal Entries [LO2, LO3, LO4, LO6]

Maple Products, Ltd., manufactures a super-strong hockey stick. The standard cost of one hockey stick is:

	Standard Quantity or Hours	Standard Price or Rate	Standard Cost
Direct materials	? metres	$9.84 per metre	$?
Direct labour	2 hours	? per hour	?
Variable manufacturing overhead	? hours	$1.30 per hour	?
Total standard cost			$26.97

Last year, 8,000 hockey sticks were produced and sold. Selected cost data relating to last year's operations follow:

	Dr.	Cr.
Accounts payable—direct materials purchased (18,288 metres) . . .		$173,919
Wages payable (? hours)		$79,200*
Work in process—direct materials	$115,197	
Direct labour rate variance		$3,300
Variable overhead efficiency variance	$650	

*Relates to the actual direct labour cost for the year.

The following additional information is available for last year's operations:

a. No materials were on hand at the start of last year. Some of the materials purchased during the year were still on hand in the warehouse at the end of the year.

b. The variable manufacturing overhead rate is based on direct labour-hours. Total actual variable manufacturing overhead cost for last year was $19,800.

c. Actual direct materials usage for last year exceeded the standard by .064 metres per stick.

Required:

1. For direct materials:
   a. Compute the price and quantity variances for last year.
   b. Prepare journal entries to record all activities relating to direct materials for last year.
2. For direct labour:
   a. Verify the rate variance given above and compute the efficiency variance for last year.
   b. Prepare a journal entry to record activity relating to direct labour for last year.
3. Compute the variable overhead spending variance for last year and verify the variable overhead efficiency variance given above.
4. State possible causes of each variance that you have computed.
5. Prepare a standard cost card for one hockey stick.

PROBLEM 10–21 Comprehensive Variance Analysis [LO1, LO2, LO3, LO4]

Highland Company produces a lightweight backpack that is popular with college students. Standard variable costs relating to a single backpack are given below:

	Standard Quantity or Hours	Standard Price or Rate	Standard Cost
Direct materials	?	$6.77 per metre	$?
Direct labour	?	?	?
Variable manufacturing overhead	?	$3 per direct labour-hour	?
Total standard cost			$?

Overhead is applied to production on the basis of direct labour-hours. During March, 1,000 backpacks were manufactured and sold. Selected information relating to the month's production is given below:

	Materials Used	Direct Labour	Variable Manufacturing Overhead
Total standard cost allowed*	$16,800	$10,500	$4,200
Actual costs incurred	$15,000	?	$3,600
Materials price variance	?		
Materials quantity variance	$ 1,200 U		
Labour rate variance		?	
Labour efficiency variance		?	
Variable overhead spending variance			?
Variable overhead efficiency variance			?

*For the month's production.

The following additional information is available for March's production:

Actual direct labour-hours	1,500
Standard overhead rate per direct labour-hour	$3.00
Standard price of one metre of materials	$6.77
Difference between standard and actual cost per backpack produced during March	$0.15 F

Required:

1. What is the standard cost of a single backpack?
2. What was the actual cost per backpack produced during March?
3. How many metres of material are required at standard per backpack?
4. What was the materials price variance for March?
5. What is the standard direct labour rate per hour?
6. What was the labour rate variance for March? The labour efficiency variance?
7. What was the variable overhead spending variance for March? The variable overhead efficiency variance?
8. Prepare a standard cost card for one backpack.

PROBLEM 10–22 Variance Analysis and Internal Business Process Performance Measures [LO2, LO3, LO4, LO6]

"I've never seen such awful results," roared Ben Carrick, manufacturing vice president of Vorelli Industries. "I thought JIT and automation were supposed to make us more efficient, but just look at last month's efficiency report on Zets, our major product in this plant. The labour efficiency variance was $120,000 *unfavourable.* That's four times higher than it's ever been before. If you add on the $102,000 unfavourable materials price variance on Zets, that's over $220,000 down the drain in a single month on just one product. Have you people in purchasing and production lost control over everything?"

"Now take it easy, Ben," replied Sandi Shipp, the company's purchasing agent. "We knew when we adopted JIT that our material costs would go up somewhat. But we're locking onto the very best suppliers, and they're making deliveries three times a day for our Zets product. In a few months, we'll be able to offset most of our higher purchasing costs by completely vacating three rented warehouses."

"And I know our labour efficiency variance looks bad," responded Raul Duvall, the company's production superintendent, "but it doesn't tell the whole story. With JIT flow lines and our new equipment, we've never been more efficient in the plant."

"How can you say you're efficient when you took 90,000 direct labour-hours to produce just 30,000 Zets last month?" asked Ben Carrick. "That works out to be 3 hours per unit, but according to the standard cost card you should be able to produce a Zet in just 2.5 hours. Do you call that efficient?"

"The problem is that the president wants us to use JIT on the finished goods side of the plant as well as on the raw materials side," explained Raul. "So we're trying to gear production to demand, but at the moment we have to cut production back somewhat in order to work off our finished goods inventory of Zets. This will go on for several more months before we'll be able to get production completely in balance with current demand. And don't forget that our line people aren't just standing around when their machines are idle. Under the new system, they're doing their own inspections and they do maintenance on their own equipment."

"It had better *not* go on for several more months," roared Ben Carrick, "at least not if you people down in production want any bonuses this year. I've been looking at these reports for 30 years, and I know inefficiency when I see it. Let's get things back under control."

After leaving Ben Carrick's office, Raul Duvall has approached you for help in developing some performance measures that will show the actual efficiency of the company's production process. Working with Raul, you have gathered the following information:

a. The company manufactures several products in this plant. A standard cost card for Zets is given below:

	Standard Quantity or Hours	Standard Price or Rate	Standard Cost
Direct materials	5.4 metres	$10.00 per metre	$54.00
Direct labour	2.5 hours	$8.00 per hour	20.00
Variable manufacturing overhead	2.5 hours	$2.80 per hour	7.00
Total standard cost			$81.00

b. During June, the most recent month, the company purchased 155,450 metres of material for production of Zets at a cost of $10.50 per metre. All of this material was used in the production of 30,000 units during the month. A large part of the production process is now automated, and the company is experiencing less waste each month.

c. The company maintains a stable workforce to produce Zets. Persons who previously were inspectors and on the maintenance crew have been reassigned as direct labour workers. During June, 90,000 hours were logged by direct labour workers on the Zets flow lines. The average pay rate was $7.85 per hour.

d. Variable manufacturing overhead cost is assigned to products on the basis of direct labour-hours. During June, the company incurred $207,000 in variable manufacturing overhead costs associated with the manufacture of Zets.

e. Demand for Zets is increasing over time, and top management is discussing the possibility of constructing additional production facilities.

f. The following information has been gathered from computers located on the production line. This information is expressed in hours per unit of the Zets product.

   Processing: As workers have become more familiar with the new equipment and procedures, average processing time per unit has declined over the last three months, from 2.6 hours in April, to 2.5 hours in May, to 2.4 hours in June.

   Inspection: Workers are now directly responsible for quality control, which accounts for the following changes in inspection time per unit over the last three months: April, 1.3 hours; May, 0.9 hours; and June, 0.1 hours.

   Movement of goods: With the change to JIT flow lines, goods now move shorter distances between machines. Move time per unit over the past three months has been: April, 1.9 hours; May, 1.4 hours; and June, 0.6 hours.

   Queue time in cells: Better coordination of production with demand has resulted in less queue time as goods move along the production line. The data for the last three months are: April, 8.2 hours; May, 5.2 hours; and June, 1.9 hours.

Required:

1. Compute the materials price and quantity variances using traditional variance analysis. Is the decrease in waste apparent in this computation? Explain. If the company wants to compute the materials price variance, what should be done to make this computation more appropriate?
2. Compute the direct labour rate and efficiency variances using traditional variance analysis. Do you agree with Ben Carrick that the efficiency variance is still appropriate as a measure of performance for the company? Explain why you do or do not agree.
3. Compute the variable manufacturing overhead spending and efficiency variances using traditional variance analysis. Would you expect that a correlation still exists between direct labour and the incurrence of variable manufacturing overhead cost in the company? Explain, using data from your variance computations to support your position.

PROBLEM 10–23 Mix and Yield Variances [LO3]

The Moncton Company uses standard costs to account for its production of widgets. The standard cost of a widget is given as follows for materials and direct labour:

Material A	15 kilograms at 80 cents	$12.00
Material B	4 kilograms at $2.25	9.00
Direct Labour..................	5 hours at $12.00	60.00

Both material A and material B are added at the start of the process. Production data for June 2006 are as follows:

a. Beginning work process, 10,000 units, 30% complete.
b. Started during June, 40,000 units.
c. Ending work in process, 12,000 units, 60% complete.
d. No units were spoiled.
e. 620,000 kilograms of material A were issued to production.
f. 150,000 kilograms of material B were used during June.
g. Direct labour worked 212,000 hours at a cost of $2,597,000 for the month.

Required:
Determine all of the material and labour variances possible from the preceding data for the month of June.

PROBLEM 10–24 Mix and Yield Variances, [LO3]
Manitoba Division uses three materials. Alpha, Beta and Gamma, to produce its product Omega. The materials are mixed in the following standard proportions to yield 100 litres of Omega:

Material	Quantity (Litres)	Cost per Litre
Alpha............................	80	$ 2.00
Beta...............................	40	$ 4.00
Gamma	30	$10.00

It requires 50 hours of direct labour at $15.00 per hour to produce 100 litres of Omega.

On the average, the division can produce and sell 200,000 litres of Omega per month. In a recent month, the division used the following amounts of materials and labour to produce 175,000 litres of Omega:

Material	Quantity (Litres)	Total Actual Cost
Alpha	159,000	$ 323,565
Beta	72,000	$ 290,102
Gamma	44,000	$ 435,000
	275,000	$1,048,667
Direct labour	91,000 hours	$1,380,000

Required:

1. Calculate the following materials variances for Omega:
   a. Price.
   b. Usage.
   c. Mix.
   d. Yield.
2. The supervisor on the Omega product line argued that the workers were operating at standard, if not better, despite a large unfavourable labour efficiency variance of $52,500. Is the supervisor correct? Why or why not?

(SMAC, Adapted)

PROBLEM 10–25 Mix and Yield Variances [LO3]
The Sticky Division manufactures and sells two special purpose adhesives, Yum and Zob. The two products emerge from the same production process, which requires three materials: Amak, Brill, and Comad. The division developed standard costs for these two adhesives as shown on page 474.

Normal monthly volume is 11,000 kilograms of input materials processed or 10,000 kilograms of good output. Some variations of input quantities are permissible without affecting the quality of the finished products.

Joint Processing Costs		
Materials—Amak	6 kilograms at $2.40 per kilogram	$ 14.40
—Brill	4 kilograms at 4.20 per kilogram	16.80
—Comad	1 kilograms at 5.15 per kilogram	5.15
Total materials input	11 kilograms	36.35
Labour (applied at $5.60 per kilogram x 11 kilograms)		61.60
Overhead—Variable (applied at $2.80 per kilogram x 11 kilograms)		30.80
—Fixed (applied at $5.00 per kilogram x 11 kilograms)		55.00
Joint costs to produce 10 kilograms of good output		$183.75

Costs Assigned to the Two Joint Products Using Market Value

Product	Good Output	Per Kilogram	Total	Joint* Costs	Standard Cost Per Kilogram
Yum	7 kilograms	$20	$140	$105.00	$15.00
Zob	3 kilograms	35	105	78.75	26.25
	10 kilograms		$245	$183.75	

*Joint costs are allocated to the products on the basis of market value.

Materials are purchased from another division and are readily available; therefore, very little raw material stock is kept by Sticky Division. Material prices are negotiated annually between the divisions. All production is finished daily; therefore, there are no work in process inventories.

Actual production of good output amounted to 11,400 kilograms. The production costs were calculated as follows:

Materials input—Amak	7,500 kilograms at $2.40 per kilogram	$18,000
—Brill.	4,050 kilograms at 4.20 per kilogram	$17,010
—Comad	1,100 kilograms at 5.15 per kilogram	$ 5,665
Total Input	12,650 kilograms	$40,675
Labour for 12,650 kilograms processed		$70,840
Good output: Yum 7,900 kilograms		
Zob 3,500 kilograms		

Required:

Calculate the material and labour cost variances in as much detail as the data permit for the Sticky Division for the month of April. Comment on the performance of the production function of the Sticky Division during April by explaining the significance of the variances you calculated.

(SMAC, Adapted)

PROBLEM 10–26 (Appendix B) Standard Cost and Learning [LO7]

The Roune Co. Ltd. is concerned with its cost to produce a subassembly. The standard cost of material for the subassembly is $20 per unit. Budgeted set-up activity costs are $50 per set-up. Labour is a standard rate of $9 per hour and variable overhead is a standard predetermined rate of 140% of direct labour costs.

The subassembly production is a repetitive process that requires practice to reach usual productivity levels. Standards reflect a 90% learning rate. The initial subassembly requires five hours to produce.

Required:

1. Determine the average unit cost of eight units.
2. If the subassembly can be purchased for $120, how many units should be in a lot size to enable Roune Co. to save by producing internally?

PROBLEM 10–27 (Appendix B) Learning Curves [LO7]

Halifax Instruments has just completed the assembly of some 400 sonic buoys for the Canadian Forces; these buoys are especially equipped to detect undersea vessels. The company is now being asked to submit an estimate of the cost of an additional 800 units. Its management has noted that the direct labour-hours (DLH) on each unit seem to be declining. For the first 200 units produced, the average hours per unit were 2.1. For the assembly of the 400 units, however, the average hours per unit dropped to 1.68.

Required:

1. Using these values, calculate the total labour-hours required to assemble 1,600 units.
2. Suppose incremental costs (labour plus variable overhead costs) are $15 direct labour-hour. What would be the incremental assembly costs for a new order of 800 units?
3. Using the following data, determine the formula for total hours for various cumulative units produced using the high-low approach.

	Labour-Hours	
Cumulative units Produced	Average per Unit	Total
200	2.100	420.0
400	1.680	672.0
800	1.344	1,075.2

4. Halifax fills the order for the additional 800 units, and produces another 100 units for a second customer. Its cumulative experience with producing these 100 buoys shows 90 total direct labour-hours or an average of 0.90 DLH per buoy. Is this consistent with the learning curve you estimated? If not, suggest an explanation for the deviation.

PROBLEM 10–28 Comprehensive Variance Analysis [LO2, LO3, LO4]

Marvel Parts, Inc., manufactures auto accessories. One of the company's products is a set of seat covers that can be adjusted to fit nearly any small car. The company has a standard cost system in use for all of its products. According to the standards that have been set for the seat covers, the factory should work 2,850 hours each month to produce 1,900 sets of covers. The standard costs associated with this level of production are:

	Total	Per Set of Covers
Direct materials	$42,560	$22.40
Direct labour	$17,100	9.00
Variable manufacturing overhead (based on direct labour-hours)	$6,840	3.60
		$35.00

During August, the factory worked only 2,800 direct labour-hours and produced 2,000 sets of covers. The following actual costs were recorded during the month:

	Total	Per Set of Covers
Direct materials (10,920 metres)	$45,600	$22.80
Direct labour	$18,200	9.10
Variable manufacturing overhead	$7,000	3.50
		$35.40

At standard, each set of covers should require 5.0 metres of material. All of the materials purchased during the month were used in production.

Required:

Compute the following variances for August:

1. The materials price and quantity variances.
2. The labour rate and efficiency variances.
3. The variable overhead spending and efficiency variances.

PROBLEM 10–29 Developing Standard Costs [LO1]

ColdKing Company is a small producer of fruit-flavoured frozen desserts. For many years, ColdKing's products have had strong regional sales on the basis of brand recognition; however, other companies have begun marketing similar products in the area, and price competition has become increasingly intense. John Wakefield, the company's controller, is planning to implement a standard cost system for ColdKing and has gathered considerable information from his co-workers on production and material requirements for ColdKing's products. Wakefield believes that the use of standard costing will allow ColdKing to improve cost control and make better pricing decisions.

ColdKing's most popular product is raspberry sherbet. The sherbet is produced in 40-litre batches, and each batch requires 6 litres of good raspberries. The fresh raspberries are sorted by hand before they enter the production process. Because of imperfections in the raspberries and normal spoilage, 1 litre of berries is discarded for every 4 litres of acceptable berries. Three minutes is the standard direct labour time for the sorting that is required to obtain 1 litre of acceptable raspberries. The acceptable raspberries are then blended with the other ingredients; blending requires 12 minutes of direct labour time per batch. After blending, the sherbet is packaged in one-litre containers. Wakefield has gathered the following pricing information:

a. ColdKing purchases raspberries at a cost of $0.80 per litre. All other ingredients cost a total of $0.1125 per litre of sherbet.
b. Direct labour is paid at the rate of $9.00 per hour.
c. The total cost of direct material and direct labour required to package the sherbet is $0.38 per litre.

Required:

1. Develop the standard cost for the direct cost components (materials, labour, and packaging) of a 40-litre batch of raspberry sherbet. The standard cost should identify the standard quantity, standard rate, and standard cost per batch for each direct cost component of a batch of raspberry sherbet.
2. As part of the implementation of a standard cost system at ColdKing, John Wakefield plans to train those responsible for maintaining the standards on how to use variance analysis. Wakefield is particularly concerned with the causes of unfavourable variances.
   a. Discuss possible causes of unfavourable materials price variances and identify the individual(s) who should be held responsible for these variances.
   b. Discuss possible causes of unfavourable labour efficiency variances and identify the individual(s) who should be held responsible for these variances.

(CMA, adapted)

CASES

CASE 10–30 Ethics and the Manager; Rigging Standards [LO1]

Stacy Cummins, the newly hired controller at Merced Home Products, Inc., was disturbed by what she had discovered about the standard costs at the Home Security Division. In looking over the past several years of quarterly earnings reports at the Home Security Division, she noticed that the first-quarter earnings were always poor, the second-quarter earnings were slightly better, the third-quarter earnings were again slightly better, and the fourth quarter always ended with a spectacular performance in which the Home Security Division managed to meet or exceed its target profit for the year. She also was concerned to find letters from the company's external auditors to top management warning about an unusual use of standard costs at the Home Security Division.

When Ms. Cummins ran across these letters, she asked the assistant controller, Gary Farber, if he knew what was going on at the Home Security Division. Gary said that it was common knowledge in the company that the vice president in charge of the Home Security Division, Preston Lansing, had rigged the standards at his division in order to produce the same quarterly earnings pattern every year. According to company policy, variances are taken directly to the income statement as an adjustment to cost of goods sold.

Favourable variances have the effect of increasing operating income, and unfavourable variances have the effect of decreasing operating income. Lansing had rigged the standards so that there were always large favourable variances. Company policy was a little vague about when these variances have to be reported on the divisional income statements. While the intent was clearly to recognize variances on the income statement in the period in which they arise, nothing in the company's accounting manuals actually explicitly required this. So for many years Lansing had followed a practice of saving up the favourable variances and using them to create a nice smooth pattern of earnings growth in the first three quarters, followed by a big "Christmas present" of an extremely good fourth quarter. (Financial reporting regulations forbid carrying variances forward from one year to the next on the annual audited financial statements, so all of the variances must appear on the divisional income statement by the end of the year.)

Ms. Cummins was concerned about these revelations and attempted to bring up the subject with the president of Merced Home Products but was told that "we all know what Lansing's doing, but as long as he continues to turn in such good reports, don't bother him." When Ms. Cummins asked if the board of directors was aware of the situation, the president somewhat testily replied, "Of course they are aware."

Required:

1. How did Preston Lansing probably "rig" the standard costs—are the standards set too high or too low? Explain.
2. Should Preston Lansing be permitted to continue his practice of managing reported earnings?
3. What should Stacy Cummins do in this situation?

CASE 10–31 (Appendix 10A) Variances and Journal Entries from Incomplete Data [LO2, LO3, LO6]

You are employed by Olster Company, which manufactures products for the senior citizen market. As a rising young executive in the company, you are scheduled to make a presentation in a few hours to your superior. This presentation relates to last week's production of Maxitol, a popular health tonic that is manufactured by Olster Company. Unfortunately, while studying ledger sheets and variance summaries by poolside in the company's fitness area, you were bumped and dropped the papers into the pool. In desperation, you fished the papers from the water, but you have discovered that only the following fragments are readable:

Maxitol—Standard Cost Card

	Standard Quantity or Hours	Standard Price or Rate	Standard Cost
Material A	24 litres	$2 per litre	$
Material B		per litre	
Direct labour		per hour	
Standard cost per batch			$99.50

Maxitol—General Ledger Accounts

Raw Materials—Material A

Debit		Credit
Bal. 3/1	0	
Bal. 3/7	2,000	

Material B—Quantity Variance

Debit	Credit
100	

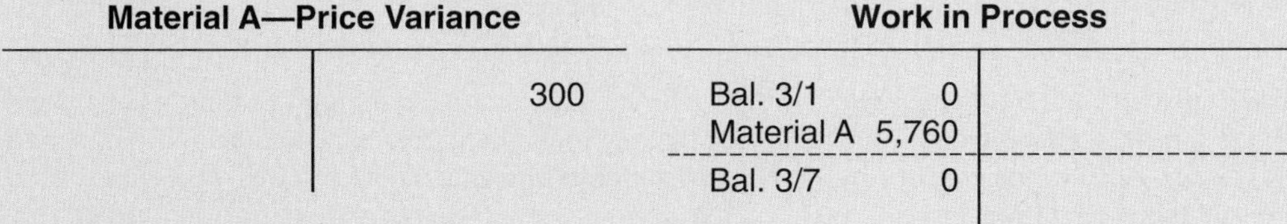

Material A—Price Variance

Debit	Credit
	300

Work in Process

Debit		Credit
Bal. 3/1	0	
Material A	5,760	
Bal. 3/7	0	

Raw Materials—Material B

Debit		Credit
Bal. 3/1	700	2,500
Bal. 3/7	1,400	

Wages Payable

Debit	Credit
	4,100

Labour Rate Variance		Accounts Payable	
500			11,460

You remember that the accounts payable are for purchases of both Material A and Material B. You also remember that only 10 direct labour workers are involved in the production of Maxitol and that each worked 40 hours last week. The wages payable above are for wages earned by these workers.

You realize that to be ready for your presentation, you must reconstruct all data relating to Maxitol very quickly. As a start, you have called purchasing and found that 4,000 litres of Material A and 800 kilograms of Material B were purchased last week.

Required:

1. How many batches of Maxitol were produced last week? (This is a key figure; be sure it's right before going on.)
2. For Material A:
   a. What was the cost of Material A purchased last week?
   b. How many litres were used in production last week?
   c. What was the quantity variance?
   d. Prepare journal entries to record all activity relating to Material A for last week.
3. For Material B:
   a. What is the standard cost per kilogram for Material B?
   b. How many kilograms of Material B were used in production last week? How many kilograms should have been used at standard?
   c. What is the standard quantity of Material B per batch?
   d. What was the price variance for Material B last week?
   e. Prepare journal entries to record all activity relating to Material B for last week.
4. For direct labour:
   a. What is the standard rate per direct labour-hour?
   b. What are the standard hours per batch?
   c. What were the standard hours allowed for last week's production?
   d. What was the labour efficiency variance for last week?
   e. Prepare a journal entry to record all activity relating to direct labour for last week.
5. Complete the standard cost card shown above for one batch of Maxitol.

CASE 10–32 Behavioural Impact of Standard Costs and Variances

Terry Travers is the manufacturing supervisor of Aurora Manufacturing Company, which produces a variety of plastic products. Some of these products are standard items that are listed in the company's catalogue, while others are made to customer specifications. Each month, Travers receives a performance report showing the budget for the month, the actual activity, and the variance between budget and actual. Part of Travers' annual performance evaluation is based on his department's performance against budget. Aurora's purchasing manager, Sally Christensen, also receives monthly performance reports and she, too, is evaluated in part on the basis of these reports.

The monthly reports for June had just been distributed when Travers met Christensen in the hallway outside their offices. Scowling, Travers began the conversation, "I see we have another set of monthly performance reports hand-delivered by that not very nice junior employee in the budget office. He seemed pleased to tell me that I'm in trouble with my performance again."

Christensen: I got the same treatment. All I ever hear about are the things I've done wrong. Now I'll have to spend a lot of time reviewing the report and preparing explanations. The worst part is that it's now the 21st of July so the information is almost a month old, and we have to spend all this time on history.

Travers: My biggest gripe is that our production activity varies a lot from month to month, but we're given an annual budget that's written in stone. Last month we were shut down for three days when a strike delayed delivery of the basic ingredient used in our plastic formulation, and we had already exhausted our inventory. You know about that problem, though, because we asked you to call all over the country to find an alternate source of supply. When we got what we needed on a rush basis, we had to pay more than we normally do.

Christensen: I expect problems like that to pop up from time to time—that's part of my job—but now we'll both have to take a careful look at our reports to see where the charges are reflected for that rush order. Every month I spend more time making sure I should be charged for each item reported than I do making plans for my department's daily work. It's really frustrating to see charges for things I have no control over.

Travers: The way we get information doesn't help, either. I don't get copies of the reports you get, yet a lot of what I do is affected by your department, and by most of our other departments. Why do the budget and accounting people assume that I should only be told about my operations even though the president regularly gives us pep talks about how we all need to work together as a team?

Christensen: I seem to get more reports than I need, and I am never asked to comment on them until top management calls me on the carpet about my department's shortcomings. Do you ever hear comments when your department shines?

Travers: I guess they don't have time to review the good news. One of my problems is that all the reports are in dollars and cents. I work with people, machines, and materials. I need information to help me solve *this* month's problems—not another report of the dollars expended *last* month or the month before.

Required:

1. Based on the conversation between Terry Travers and Sally Christensen, describe the likely motivation and behaviour of these two employees resulting from Aurora Manufacturing Company's standard cost and variance reporting system.
2. When properly implemented, both employees and companies should benefit from a system involving standard costs and variances.
   a. Describe the benefits that can be realized from a standard cost system.
   b. Based on the situation presented above, recommend ways for Aurora Manufacturing Company to improve its standard cost and variance reporting system so as to increase employee motivation.

(CMA, adapted)

PROBLEM 10-33 Standard and Budgets [LO1]

D. Hope, president of the Sun Company, is concerned about the company's lack of control over the cost of running its steno pool. Under their current system, the total staffing of the pool is determined at the beginning of the year by Hope and consultation with C. Count, manager of the steno pool, as to what additional work is expected and, therefore, how many additional workers are required. Hope does not feel that significant control is being applied over the total staff of the steno pool, but is unable to see how this can be improved. He vaguely recalls from a management accounting course that he completed years ago that there are several approaches to control of area like the steno pool such as:

a. Engineered variable-cost approach
b. Zero-base budgeting approach.

Unfortunately, Hope is unable to recall what these terms mean or how they might be applied to an area such as this. As a stating point, Hope has accumulated the following information on the steno pool for 2006:

a. Average typing speed of the typists on a test given prior to hiring was 100 words per minute with an average of two minutes required to set up the work (tabs, margins, etc.).
b. During 2006, the steno pool employed 24 typists at an average wage of $450 per week (5 days, 40 hours per week). The typists worked an average of 242 days in 2006.
c. Total output of the department in 2006 (including letters, financial statements, memos etc.) amounted to 184,500 documents with an average of 920 words each.

Required:

1. a. Use the engineered variable cost approach to estimate the cost of under- or overstaffing in 2006.
   b. What other things should be considered in using this approach to evaluate the performance of the steno pool?
2. Briefly describe how zero-base budgeting might be applied to controlling costs of the steno pool.

(SMAC Adapted)

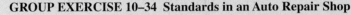

GROUP AND INTERNET EXERCISES

GROUP EXERCISE 10–34 Standards in an Auto Repair Shop

Make an appointment to meet with the manager of an auto repair shop that uses standards. In most cases, this would be an auto repair shop that is affiliated with a national chain such as Canadian Tire or the service department of a new-car dealer.

Required:

At the scheduled meeting, seek answers to the following questions:

1. How are standards set?
2. Are standards practical or ideal?
3. How are the standards used?
4. Is the actual time taken to complete a task compared to the standard time?
5. What are the consequences of unfavourable variances? Of favourable variances?
6. Do the standards and variances create any potential problems?

GROUP EXERCISE 10–35 Standards in Practice

Identify a company in your local area that is likely to use standards such as a commercial bakery, commercial printer, chain restaurant, or manufacturer. After verifying that the company uses standards, make an appointment to meet with the manager, controller, or chief financial officer of the organization.

Required:

At the scheduled meeting, seek answers to the following questions:

1. How are standards set?
2. Are standards practical or ideal?
3. How are the standards used?
4. What are the consequences of unfavourable variances? Of favourable variances?
5. Do the standards and variances create any potential problems?

INTERNET EXERCISE 10–36

As you know, the World Wide Web is a medium that is constantly evolving. Sites come and go, and change without notice. To enable the periodic updating of site addresses, this problem has been posted to the textbook Web site (www.mcgrawhill.ca/college/garrison). After accessing the site, enter the Student Centre and select this chapter. Select and complete the Internet Exercise.

CHAPTER 11

LEARNING OBJECTIVES

After studying Chapter 11, you should be able to:

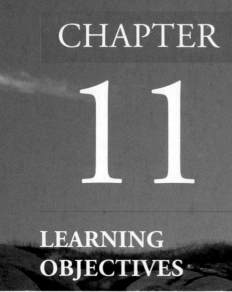

1. Prepare a flexible budget and explain the need for the flexible budget approach .
2. Prepare a performance report for both variable and fixed overhead costs using the flexible budget approach.
3. Prepare a variable overhead performance report.
4. Explain the significance of the denominator activity figure in determining the standard cost of a unit of product.
5. Apply overhead cost to units of product in a standard cost system.
6. Compute and interpret the fixed overhead budget and volume variances.

FLEXIBLE BUDGETS AND OVERHEAD ANALYSIS

HOW MUCH IS TOO MUCH?

BUSINESS FOCUS

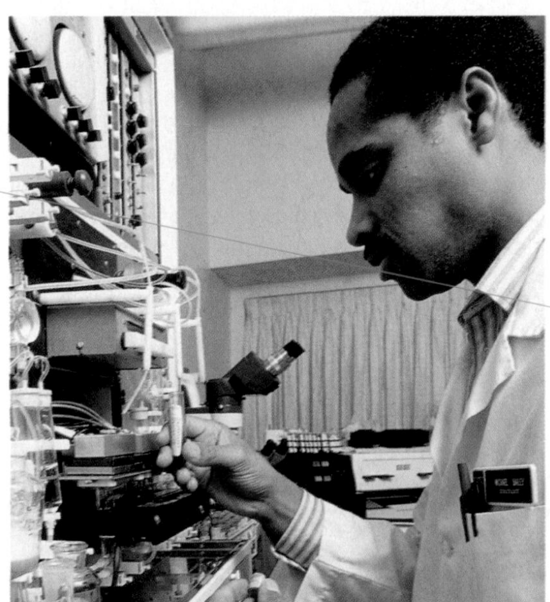

Dr. Salinas had just been unexpectedly appointed director of the Provincial Medical Centre. The previous director, who had instituted tight budgetary controls, was extremely unpopular with the centre's staff. This had led to his release by the centre's board of directors. Dr. Salinas suspected that he had been chosen for the job because of his popularity rather than any innate management ability. He thought of himself as a physician rather than as a manager.

Shortly after taking over as director, the centre's lab supervisor came into Dr. Salinas's office and stated: "Here, look at this report. It says we spent too much money in the Lab Department. We spent 5% more than had been authorized in the annual budget. Well, of course we did! Practically every department in the centre asked for more tests than they had predicted at budget time! What are we supposed to do, refuse to run tests once we run over budget?" Dr. Salinas responded: "Of course not. You have to run the tests. However, we also have to keep some control over our spending. On the other hand, I agree it isn't fair to hold you to the original budget. I don't see the solution right now, but I will work on it."

Controlling overhead costs is a major preoccupation of managers in business, in government, and in not-for-profit organizations. Overhead is a major cost, if not *the* major cost, in most large organizations. It costs Microsoft very little to download copies of its software onto CD's and to provide purchasers with software manuals; almost all of Microsoft's costs are in research and development and marketing—elements of overhead. Or consider the chain, Eastside Mario's. The only direct cost of serving a particular guest is the cost of the food the guest consumes; virtually all of the other costs of running the restaurant are overhead. At Bombardier, there are far more direct costs, but there are still huge amounts of overhead in the form of engineering salaries, buildings, insurance, administrative salaries, and marketing costs.

LEARNING OBJECTIVE 1
Prepare a flexible budget and explain the need for the flexible budget approach.

Control of overhead costs poses special problems. Costs like direct materials and direct labour are often easier to understand, and therefore to control, than overhead, which can include everything from the disposable coffee cup in the visitor's waiting area to the president's salary. Overhead is usually made up of many separate costs—many of which may be small. This makes it impractical to control them in the same way that costs such as direct materials and direct labour are controlled. And some overhead costs are variable, some are fixed, and some are a mixture of fixed and variable. These particular problems can largely be overcome by the use of flexible budgets—a topic that was briefly discussed in Chapter 9. In this chapter, we study flexible budgets in greater detail and learn how they can be used to control costs. We also expand the study of overhead variances that we started in Chapter 10.

FOCUS *on Current Practice*

Overhead costs now account for as much as 66% of the costs incurred by companies in service industries and up to 37% of the total costs of manufacturers. Consequently, overhead reduction is a recurring theme in many organizations. However, the extent of the reductions must be considered in light of competitive pressures to improve services and product quality. Managers must avoid cutting costs that add value to the organization.

Source: Nick Develin, "Unlocking Overhead Value," *Management Accounting*, December 1999, pp. 22–34.

FLEXIBLE BUDGETS

Characteristics of a Flexible Budget

Static budget
A budget designed for only one level of activity.

The budgets that we studied in Chapter 9 were *static budgets.* A **static budget** is prepared for only the planned level of activity. This approach is suitable for planning purposes, but it is inadequate for evaluating how well costs are controlled. If the actual activity during a period differs from what was planned, it would be misleading to simply compare actual costs to the static budget. If activity is higher than expected, the variable costs should be higher than expected; and if activity is lower than expected, the variable costs should be lower than expected.

Flexible budget
A budget that is designed to cover a range of activity and that can be used to develop budgeted costs at any point within that range to compare to actual costs incurred.

Flexible budgets take into account changes in costs that should occur as a consequence of changes in activity. A **flexible budget** provides estimates of what cost should be for any level of activity within a specified range. When a flexible budget is used in performance evaluation, actual costs are compared to what the *costs should have been for the actual level of activity during the period* rather than to the planned budgeted costs from the original budget. This is a very important distinction—particularly for variable costs.

If adjustments for the level of activity are not made, it is very difficult to interpret discrepancies between budgeted and actual costs.

Deficiencies of the Static Budget

To illustrate the differences between a static budget and a flexible budget we will consider the case of Rick's Hairstyling salon located in Toronto that is owned and managed by Rick Manzi. The salon has very loyal customers—many of whom are associated with the Toronto Blue Jays. Despite the glamour associated with the salon, Rick is a very shrewd businessperson. Recently he has been attempting to get better control over his overhead, and with the urging of his accounting and business advisor, Victoria Kho, he has begun to prepare monthly budgets. Victoria Kho is a public accountant and a certified management accountant in independent practice who specializes in small service-oriented businesses like Rick's Hairstyling.

At the end of February, Rick carefully prepared the March budget for overhead items that appears in Exhibit 11–1. Rick believes that the number of customers served in a month is the best way to measure the overall level of activity in his salon. Rick refers to these visits as *client-visits*. A customer who comes into the salon and has his or her hair styled is counted as one client-visit. After some discussion with Victoria Kho, Rick identified three major categories of variable overhead costs—hairstyling supplies, client gratuities, and electricity—and four major categories of fixed costs—support staff wages and salaries, rent, insurance, and utilities other than electricity. Client gratuities consist of small items that Rick gives to his customers while they are in the salon. Rick considers electricity to be a variable cost, since almost all of the electricity in the salon is consumed in running blow-dryers, curling irons, and other hairstyling equipment.

To develop the budget for variable overhead, Rick estimated that the average cost per client-visit should be $1.20 for hairstyling supplies, $4.00 for client gratuities, and $0.20 for electricity. Based on his estimate of 5,000 client-visits in March, Rick budgeted for $6,000 ($1.20 per client-visit × 5,000 client-visits) in hairstyling supplies, $20,000 ($4.00 per client-visit × 5,000 client-visits) in client gratuities, and $1,000 ($0.20 per client-visit × 5,000 client-visits) in electricity.

The budget for fixed overhead items was based on Rick's records of how much he had spent on these items in the past. The budget included $8,000 for support staff wages and salaries, $12,000 for rent, $1,000 for insurance, and $500 for utilities other than electricity.

EXHIBIT 11–1
Static Budget

RICK'S HAIRSTYLING
Static Budget
For the Month Ended March 31

Budgeted number of client-visits	5,000
Budgeted variable overhead costs:	
Hairstyling supplies (@$1.20 per client-visit)	$ 6,000
Client gratuities (@$4.00 per client-visit)	20,000
Electricity (@$0.20 per client-visit)	1,000
Total variable overhead cost	27,000
Budgeted fixed overhead costs:	
Support staff wages and salaries	8,000
Rent	12,000
Insurance	1,000
Utilities other than electricity	500
Total fixed overhead cost	21,500
Total budgeted overhead cost	$48,500

At the end of March, Rick prepared a report comparing actual to budgeted costs. That report appears in Exhibit 11–2. The problem with that report, as Rick immediately realized, is that it compares costs at one level of activity (5,200 client-visits) to costs at a different level of activity (5,000 client-visits). Since Rick had 200 more client-visits than expected, his variable costs *should* be higher than budgeted. The static budget performance report confuses control over activity and control over costs. From Rick's standpoint, the increase in activity was good and should be counted as a favourable variance, but the increase in activity has an apparently negative impact on the costs in the report. Rick knew that something would have to be done to make the report more meaningful, but he was unsure of what to do. So he made an appointment to meet with Victoria Kho to discuss the next step.

What is wrong with the overhead information presented in Exhibit 11–2 for performance evaluation? The static budget approach used to prepare the statement has a major deficiency in that it fails to distinguish between *activity* control and the *cost control* dimensions of a manager's responsibility. Activity control is involved with seeing that sales and production or service goals are met. Cost control is concerned with ensuring that sales and service or production are accomplished with the least possible costs consistent with quality standards. These are different responsibilities, and they must be kept separate in attempting to assess how well a manager is doing his or her job.

Of these two responsibilities, the static budget does a good job of determining whether or not activity control is being maintained. Look again at Exhibit 11–2. The data on the top line relate to service activity for the month. These data properly reflect the fact that activity control was exceeded since the business surpassed its goal of 5,000 client visits.

Notice in exhibits 11-1 and 11-2 that Rick's budget does not contain direct materials or direct labour. Rather all costs are treated as overhead. The reason for the change from the format seen in Chapter 10 is the nature of the business at Rick's. His operation does not make anything. Labour is fixed and variable costs such as hairstyling supplies that could be thought of as direct materials are not important enough to be directly traced to each client. The modifications seen in Rick's approach are a conscious choice of the designer of the system based on the cost benefit trade-offs of the situation.

EXHIBIT 11–2
Static Budget Performance Report

RICK'S HAIRSTYLING
Static Budget Performance Report
For the Month Ended March 31

	Actual	Budgeted	Variance
Client-visits	5,200	5,000	200 F
Variable overhead costs:			
Hairstyling supplies	$ 6,400	$ 6,000	$ 400 U*
Client gratuities	22,300	20,000	2,300 U*
Electricity	1,020	1,000	20 U*
Total variable overhead cost	29,720	27,000	2,720 U*
Fixed overhead costs:			
Support staff wages and salaries	8,100	8,000	100 U
Rent	12,000	12,000	0
Insurance	1,000	1,000	0
Utilities other than electricity	470	500	30 F
Total fixed overhead cost	21,570	21,500	70 U
Total overhead cost	$51,290	$48,500	$2,790 U*

*The cost variances for variable costs and for total overhead are useless for evaluating how well costs were controlled because they have been derived by comparing actual costs at one level of activity to budgeted costs at a different level of activity.

MANAGERIAL ACCOUNTING IN ACTION

The Issue

RICK'S

Victoria: How is the budgeting going?

Rick: Pretty well. I didn't have any trouble putting together the overhead budget for March. I also made out a report comparing the actual costs for March to the budgeted costs, but that report isn't giving me what I really want to know.

Victoria: Because your actual level of activity didn't match your budgeted activity?

Rick: Right. I know the level of activity shouldn't affect my fixed costs, but we had a lot more client-visits than I had expected and that had to affect my variable costs.

Victoria: So you want to know whether the actual costs are justified by the actual level of activity you had in March?

Rick: Precisely.

Victoria: If you leave your reports and data with me, I can work on it later today, and by tomorrow I'll have a report to show to you. Actually, I have a styling appointment for later this week. Why don't I move my appointment up to tomorrow, and I will bring along the analysis so we can discuss it.

Rick: That's great.

How a Flexible Budget Works

The basic idea of the flexible budget approach is that a budget does not have to be static. Depending on the actual level of activity, a budget can be adjusted to show what costs *should be* for that specific level of activity. To illustrate how flexible budgets work, Victoria prepared the report in Exhibit 11–3. It shows how overhead costs can be expected to change, depending on the monthly level of activity. Within the activity range of 4,900 to 5,200 client-visits, the fixed costs are expected to remain the same. For the variable overhead costs, Victoria multiplied Rick's per-client costs ($1.20 for hairstyling supplies, $4.00 for client gratuities, and $0.20 for electricity) by the appropriate number of client-

EXHIBIT 11–3 Flexible Budget

RICK'S HAIRSTYLING
Flexible Budget
For the Month Ended March 31

Budgeted number of client-visits	5,000				
	Cost Formula (per client-visit)	**Activity (in client-visits)**			
Overhead Costs		**4,900**	**5,000**	**5,100**	**5,200**
Variable overhead costs:					
Hairstyling supplies	$1.20	$ 5,880	$ 6,000	$ 6,120	$ 6,240
Client gratuities	4.00	19,600	20,000	20,400	20,800
Electricity (variable)	0.20	980	1,000	1,020	1,040
Total variable overhead cost	$5.40	26,460	27,000	27,540	28,080
Fixed overhead costs:					
Support staff wages and salaries		8,000	8,000	8,000	8,000
Rent		12,000	12,000	12,000	12,000
Insurance		1,000	1,000	1,000	1,000
Utilities other than electricity		500	500	500	500
Total fixed overhead cost		21,500	21,500	21,500	21,500
Total overhead cost		$47,960	$48,500	$49,040	$49,580

visits in each column. For example, the $1.20 cost of hairstyling supplies was multiplied by 4,900 client-visits to give the total cost of $5,880 for hairstyling supplies at that level of activity.

Using the Flexible Budgeting Concept in Performance Evaluation

LEARNING OBJECTIVE 2
Prepare a performance report for both variable and fixed overhead costs using the flexible budget approach.

To get a better idea of how well Rick's variable overhead costs were controlled in March, Victoria applied the flexible budgeting concept to create a new performance report (Exhibit 11–4.) Using the flexible budget approach, Victoria constructed a budget based on the *actual* number of client-visits for the month. The budget is prepared by multiplying the actual level of activity by the cost formula for each of the variable cost categories. For example, using the $1.20 per client-visit for hairstyling supplies, the total cost for this item *should be* $6,240 for 5,200 client-visits ($1.20 × 5,200). Since the actual cost for hairstyling supplies was $6,400, the unfavourable variance was $160.

Contrast the performance report in Exhibit 11–4 with the static budget approach in Exhibit 11–2. The variance for hairstyling supplies was $400 (unfavourable) using the static budget approach. In that exhibit, apples were being compared to oranges in the case of the variable cost items. Actual costs at one level of activity were being compared to budgeted costs at a different level of activity. Because actual activity was higher by 200 client-visits than budgeted activity, the total cost of hairstyling supplies *should* have been $240 ($1.20 per client-visit × 200 client-visits) higher than budgeted. As a result, $240 of the $400 unfavourable variance in the static budget performance report in Exhibit 11–2 was spurious.

In contrast, the flexible budget performance report in Exhibit 11–4 provides a more valid assessment of performance. Apples are compared to apples. Actual costs are compared to what costs should have been at the actual level of activity. When this is done, we see that the variance is $160 (unfavourable) rather than $400 (unfavourable) as it was in

EXHIBIT 11–4 Flexible Budget Performance Report

RICK'S HAIRSTYLING
Flexible Budget Performance Report
For the Month Ended March 31

Budgeted number of client-visits	5,000
Actual number of client-visits	5,200

Overhead Costs	Cost Formula (per client-visit)	Actual Costs Incurred for 5,200 Client-Visits	Budget Based on 5,200 Client-Visits	Variance
Variable overhead costs:				
Hairstyling supplies	$1.20	$ 6,400	$ 6,240	$ 160 U
Client gratuities	4.00	22,300	20,800	1,500 U
Electricity (variable)	0.20	1,020	1,040	20 F
Total variable overhead cost	$5.40	29,720	28,080	1,640 U
Fixed overhead costs:				
Support staff wages and salaries		8,100	8,000	100 U
Rent		12,000	12,000	0
Insurance		1,000	1,000	0
Utilities other than electricity		470	500	30 F
Total fixed overhead cost		21,570	21,500	70 U
Total overhead cost		$51,290	$49,580	$1,710 U

the original static budget performance report. In some cases, as with electricity in Rick's report, an unfavourable variance may be transformed into a favourable variance when an increase in activity is properly taken into account in a performance report.

If desired by the users, the difference between the flexible budget overhead cost of $49,580 and the fixed static budget overhead cost of $48,500 (Exhibit 11-1) could be computed and labelled an activity or planning variance of $1,050. Such a calculation would show the added costs of 200 more visits expressed in terms of budgeted costs. This amount could be a useful piece of information especially when compared to the added revenue of 200 visits. Regardless the performance of the unit should always be examined relative to the flexible budget for 5,200 actual visits as shown in Exhibit 11-4.

MANAGERIAL ACCOUNTING IN ACTION

The Wrap-Up

The following discussion took place the next day at Rick's salon.

Victoria: Let me show you what I've got. [Victoria shows Rick the report contained in Exhibit 11–4.] All I did was multiply the costs per client-visit by the number of client-visits you actually had in March for the variable costs. That allowed me to come up with a better benchmark for what the variable costs should have been.

Rick: That's what you labelled the "budget based on 5,200 client-visits"?

Victoria: That's right. Your original budget was based on 5,000 client-visits, so it understated what the variable overhead costs should be when you actually serve 5,200 customers.

Rick: That's clear enough. These variances aren't quite as shocking as the variances on my first report.

Victoria: Yes, but you still have an unfavourable variance of $1,500 for client gratuities.

Rick: I know how that happened. In March there was a big Conservative Party fund-raising dinner that I forgot about when I prepared the March budget. Everyone of political importance was there.

Victoria: Even Brian Mulroney?

Rick: Well, at any rate, to fit all of our regular clients in, we had to push them through here pretty fast. Everyone still got top-rate service, but I felt pretty bad about not being able to spend as much time with each customer. I wanted to give my customers a little extra something to compensate them for the less personal service, so I ordered a lot of flowers, which I gave away by the bunch.

Victoria: With the prices you charge, Rick, I am sure the gesture was appreciated.

Rick: One thing bothers me about the report. Why are some of my actual fixed costs different from what I budgeted? Doesn't *fixed* mean that they are not supposed to change?

Victoria: We call these costs *fixed* because they shouldn't be affected by *changes in the level of activity*. However, that doesn't mean that they can't change for other reasons. For example, your utilities bill, which includes natural gas for heating, varies with the weather.

Rick: I can see that. March was warmer than normal, so my utilities bill was lower than I had expected.

Victoria: The use of the term *fixed* also suggests to people that the cost can't be controlled, but that isn't true. It is often easier to control fixed costs than variable costs. For example, it would be fairly easy for you to change your insurance bill by adjusting the amount of insurance you carry. It would be much more difficult for you to have much of an impact on the variable electric bill, which is a necessary part of serving customers.

Rick: I think I understand, but it *is* confusing.

Victoria: Just remember that a cost is called *variable* if it is proportional to activity; it is called *fixed* if it does not depend on the level of activity. However, fixed costs can change for reasons having nothing to do with changes in the level of activity. And controllability has little to do with whether a cost is variable or fixed. Fixed costs are often more controllable than variable costs.

Using the flexible budget approach, Rick Manzi now has a much better way of assessing whether overhead costs are under control. The analysis is not as simple, however, in companies that provide a variety of products and services. The number of units produced or customers served may not be an adequate measure of overall activity. For example, does it make sense to count a floppy diskette, worth less than a dollar, as equivalent to a large-screen TV? If the number of units produced is used as a measure of overall activity, then the floppy diskette and the large-screen TV will be counted as equivalent. Clearly, the number of units produced (or customers served) may not be appropriate as an overall measure of activity when the organization produces a variety of products or services; a common denominator may be needed.

The Measure of Activity—A Critical Choice

What should be used as the measure of activity when the company produces a variety of products and services? At least three factors are important in selecting an activity base for an overhead flexible budget:

1. There should be a causal relationship between the activity base and variable overhead costs. Changes in the activity base should cause, or at least be highly correlated with, changes in the variable overhead costs in the flexible budget. Ideally, the variable overhead costs in the flexible budget should vary in direct proportion to changes in the activity base. For example, in a carpentry shop specializing in handmade wooden furniture, the costs of miscellaneous supplies such as glue, wooden dowels, and sandpaper can be expected to vary with the number of direct labour-hours. Direct labour-hours would therefore be a good measure of activity to use in a flexible budget for the costs of such supplies.
2. The activity base should not be expressed in dollars or other currency. For example, direct labour cost is often a poor choice for an activity base in flexible budgets. Changes in wage rates affect the activity base but do not usually result in a proportionate change in overhead. We would not ordinarily expect to see a 5% increase in the consumption of glue in a carpentry shop if the workers receive a 5% increase in pay. Therefore, it is normally best to use physical rather than financial measures of activity in flexible budgets.
3. The activity base should be simple and easily understood. A base that is not easily understood will probably result in confusion and misunderstanding. It is difficult to control costs if people don't understand the reports or do not accept them as valid.

FOCUS ***on Current Practice***

Understanding the difference between fixed and variable costs can be critical. Kennard T. Wing, of OMG Center for Collaborative Learning, reports that a large health care system made the mistake of classifying all of its costs as variable. As a consequence, when volume dropped, managers felt that costs should be cut proportionately and more than 1,000 people were laid off—even though "the workload of most of them had no direct relation to patient volume. The result was that morale of the survivors plummeted and within a year the system was scrambling to replace not only those it had let go, but many others who had quit. The point is, the accounting systems we design and implement really do affect management decisions in significant ways. A system built on a bad model of the business will either not be used or, if used, will lead to bad decisions."

Source: Kennard T. Wing, "Using Enhanced Cost Models in Variance Analysis for Better Control and Decision Making," *Management Accounting Quarterly*, Winter 2000, pp. 27–35.

VARIABLE OVERHEAD VARIANCES—A CLOSER LOOK

LEARNING OBJECTIVE 3
Prepare a variable overhead performance report.

A special problem arises when the flexible budget is based on *hours* of activity (such as direct labour-hours) rather than on units of product or number of customers served. The problem relates to whether actual hours or standard hours should be used to develop the flexible budget in the performance report.

The Problem of Actual versus Standard Hours

The nature of the problem can best be seen through a specific example. MicroDrive Corporation is an automated manufacturer of precision personal computer disk-drive motors. Data concerning the company's variable manufacturing overhead costs are shown in Exhibit 11–5 on page 490.

MicroDrive Corporation uses machine-hours as the activity base in its flexible budget. Based on the budgeted production of 25,000 motors and the standard of 2 machine-hours per motor, the budgeted level of activity was 50,000 machine-hours. However, actual production for the year was only 20,000 motors, and 42,000 hours of machine time were used to produce these motors. According to the standard, only 40,000 hours of machine time should have been used (40,000 hours = 2 hours per motor × 20,000 motors).

In preparing an overhead performance report for the year, MicroDrive could use the 42,000 machine-hours actually worked during the year *or* the 40,000 machine-hours that should have been worked according to the standard. If the actual hours are used, only a spending variance will be computed. If the standard hours are used, both a spending *and* an efficiency variance will be computed. Both of these approaches are illustrated in the following sections.

Spending Variance Alone

If MicroDrive Corporation bases its overhead performance report on the 42,000 machine-hours actually worked during the year, then the performance report will show only a spending variance for variable overhead. A performance report prepared in this way is shown in Exhibit 11–6 on page 490.

The formula for the spending variance was introduced in the preceding chapter. That formula is:

$$\text{Variable overhead spending variance} = (AH \times AR) - (AH \times SR)$$

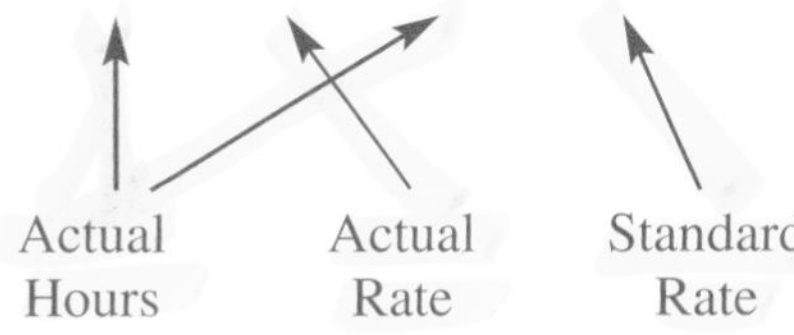

Or, in factored form:

$$\text{Variable overhead spending variance} = AH\,(AR - SR)$$

The report in Exhibit 11–6 is structured around the first, or unfactored, format.

Interpreting the Spending Variance The variable overhead spending variance is useful only if the cost driver for variable overhead really is the actual hours worked. Then the flexible budget based on the actual hours worked is a valid benchmark that tells us how much *should* have been spent in total on variable overhead items during the period. The actual overhead costs would be larger than this benchmark, resulting in an unfavourable

EXHIBIT 11–5 MicroDrive Corporation Data

Budgeted production	25,000	motors
Actual production	20,000	motors
Standard machine-hours per motor	2	machine-hours per motor
Budgeted machine-hours (2 × 25,000)	50,000	machine-hours
Standard machine-hours allowed for the actual production (2 × 20,000)	40,000	machine-hours
Actual machine-hours	42,000	machine-hours
Variable overhead costs per machine-hour:		
Indirect labour	$0.80	per machine-hour
Lubricants	0.30	per machine-hour
Power	0.40	per machine-hour
Actual total variable overhead costs:		
Indirect labour	$36,000	
Lubricants	11,000	
Power	24,000	
Total actual variable overhead cost	$71,000	

variance, if either (1) the variable overhead items cost more to purchase than the standards allow or (2) more variable overhead items were used than the standards allow. So the spending variance includes both price and quantity variances. In principle, these variances could be separately reported, but this is seldom done. Ordinarily, the price element in this

EXHIBIT 11–6 Variable Overhead Performance Report

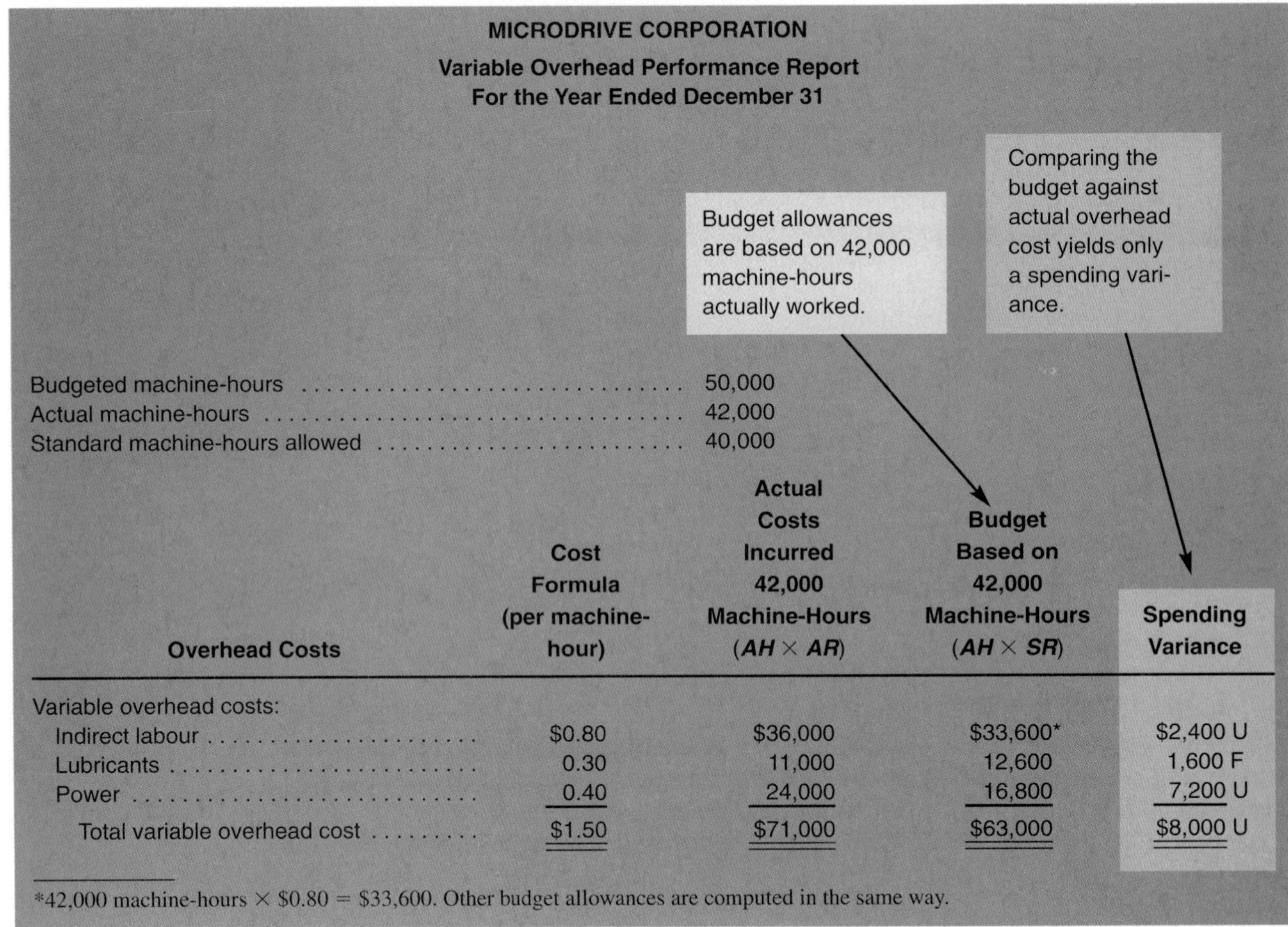

MICRODRIVE CORPORATION
Variable Overhead Performance Report
For the Year Ended December 31

Budget allowances are based on 42,000 machine-hours actually worked.
Comparing the budget against actual overhead cost yields only a spending variance.

Budgeted machine-hours	50,000
Actual machine-hours	42,000
Standard machine-hours allowed	40,000

Overhead Costs	Cost Formula (per machine-hour)	Actual Costs Incurred 42,000 Machine-Hours (*AH* × *AR*)	Budget Based on 42,000 Machine-Hours (*AH* × *SR*)	Spending Variance
Variable overhead costs:				
Indirect labour	$0.80	$36,000	$33,600*	$2,400 U
Lubricants	0.30	11,000	12,600	1,600 F
Power	0.40	24,000	16,800	7,200 U
Total variable overhead cost	$1.50	$71,000	$63,000	$8,000 U

*42,000 machine-hours × $0.80 = $33,600. Other budget allowances are computed in the same way.

variance will be small, so the variance will mainly be influenced by how efficiently variable overhead resources such as production supplies are used.

Both Spending and Efficiency Variances

If the management of MicroDrive Corporation wants both a spending and an efficiency variance for variable overhead, then it should compute flexible budget allowances for *both* the 40,000 machine-hour and the 42,000 machine-hour levels of activity. A performance report prepared in this way is shown in Exhibit 11–7.

Note from Exhibit 11–7 that the spending variance is the same as the spending variance shown in Exhibit 11–6. The performance report in Exhibit 11–7 has simply been expanded to include an efficiency variance as well. Together, the spending and efficiency variances make up the total variance.

Interpreting the Efficiency Variance Like the variable overhead spending, the variable overhead efficiency variance is useful only if the cost driver for variable overhead really is the actual hours worked. Then any increase in hours actually worked should result in additional variable overhead costs. Consequently, if too many hours were used to create the actual output, this is likely to result in an increase in variable overhead. The variable

EXHIBIT 11-7 Variable Overhead Performance Report—Efficiency Variance

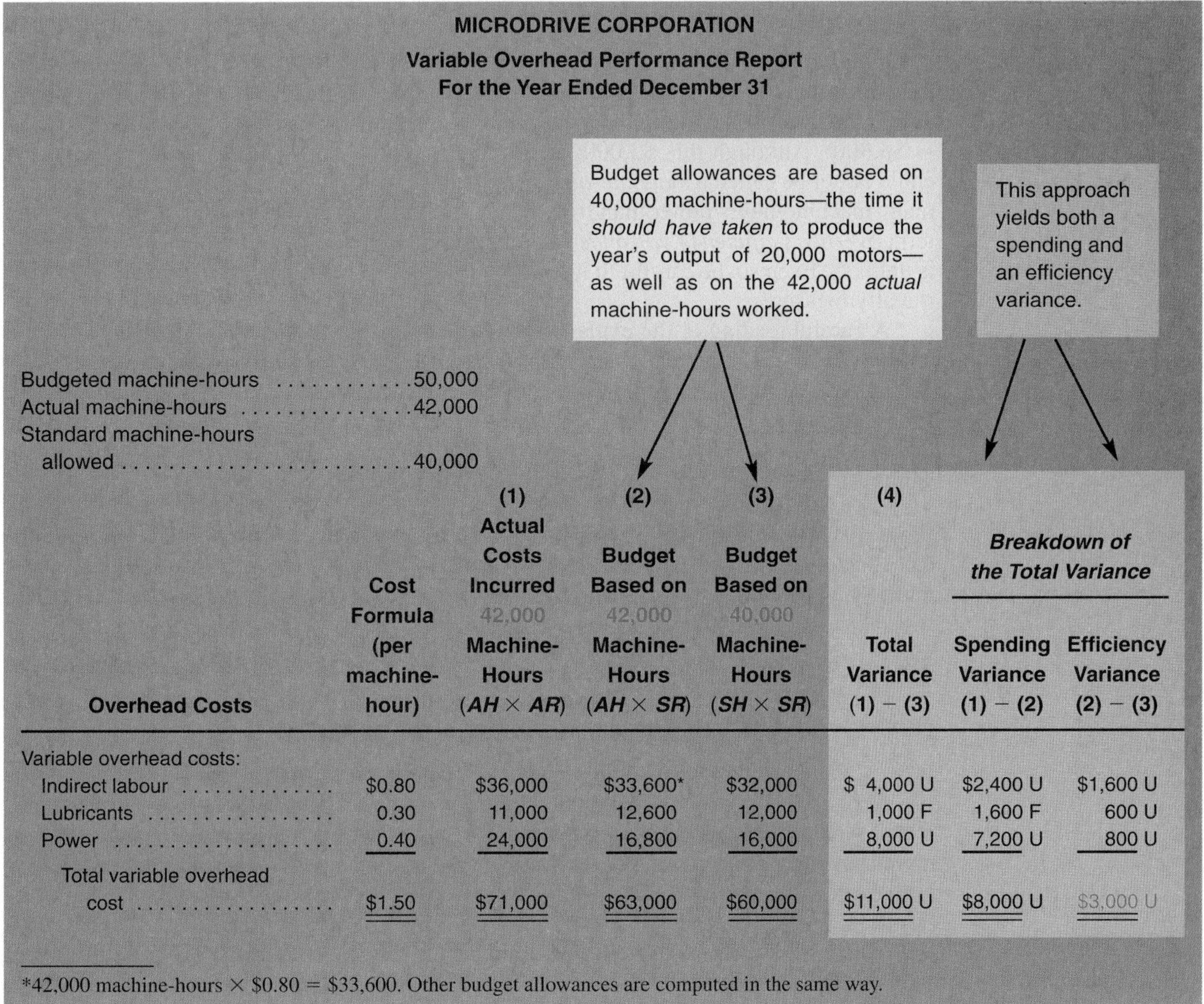

MICRODRIVE CORPORATION
Variable Overhead Performance Report
For the Year Ended December 31

Budget allowances are based on 40,000 machine-hours—the time it *should have taken* to produce the year's output of 20,000 motors—as well as on the 42,000 *actual* machine-hours worked.
This approach yields both a spending and an efficiency variance.

Budgeted machine-hours 50,000
Actual machine-hours 42,000
Standard machine-hours allowed 40,000

Overhead Costs	Cost Formula (per machine-hour)	(1) Actual Costs Incurred 42,000 Machine-Hours (*AH* × *AR*)	(2) Budget Based on 42,000 Machine-Hours (*AH* × *SR*)	(3) Budget Based on 40,000 Machine-Hours (*SH* × *SR*)	(4) Total Variance (1) − (3)	Breakdown of the Total Variance: Spending Variance (1) − (2)	Breakdown of the Total Variance: Efficiency Variance (2) − (3)
Variable overhead costs:							
Indirect labour	$0.80	$36,000	$33,600*	$32,000	$ 4,000 U	$2,400 U	$1,600 U
Lubricants	0.30	11,000	12,600	12,000	1,000 F	1,600 F	600 U
Power	0.40	24,000	16,800	16,000	8,000 U	7,200 U	800 U
Total variable overhead cost	$1.50	$71,000	$63,000	$60,000	$11,000 U	$8,000 U	$3,000 U

*42,000 machine-hours × $0.80 = $33,600. Other budget allowances are computed in the same way.

overhead efficiency variance is an estimate of the effect on variable overhead costs of inefficiency in the use of the base (i.e., hours). In a sense, the term *variable overhead efficiency variance* is a misnomer. It seems to suggest that it measures the efficiency with which variable overhead resources were used. It does not. It is an estimate of the indirect effect on variable overhead costs of inefficiency in the use of the activity base.

Recall from the preceding chapter that the variable overhead efficiency variance is a function of the difference between the actual hours incurred and the hours that should have been used to produce the period's output:

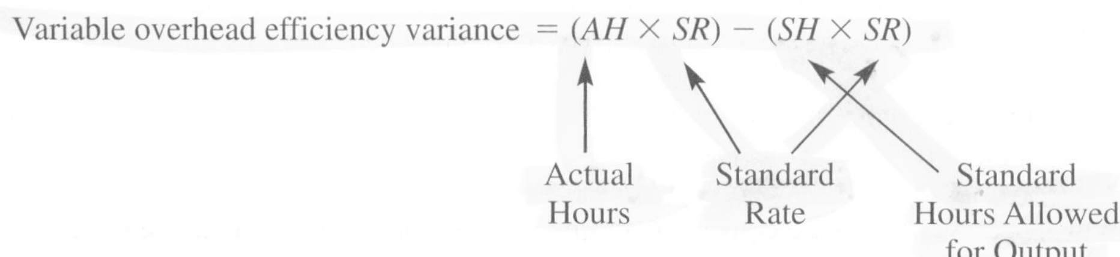

Variable overhead efficiency variance = (AH × SR) − (SH × SR)
Actual Hours
Standard Rate
Standard Hours Allowed for Output

Or, in factored form:

$$\text{Variable overhead efficiency variance} = SR(AH - SH)$$

If more hours are worked than are allowed at standard, then the overhead efficiency variance will be unfavourable. However, as discussed above, the inefficiency is not in the use of overhead *but rather in the use of the base itself.*

This point can be illustrated by looking again at Exhibit 11–7. Two thousand more machine-hours were used during the period than should have been used to produce the period's output. Each of these hours presumably required the incurrence of $1.50 of variable overhead cost, resulting in an unfavourable variance of $3,000 (2,000 hours × $1.50 = $3,000). Although this $3,000 variance is called an *overhead efficiency variance*, it could better be called a *machine-hours efficiency variance*, since it results from using too many machine-hours rather than from inefficient use of overhead resources. However, the term *overhead efficiency variance* is so firmly ingrained in day-to-day use that a change is unlikely. Even so, be careful to interpret the variance with a clear understanding of what it really measures.

A careful reading of the explanation of the efficiency variance for variable overhead will notice that an efficiency variance cannot be computed unless a standard base exists for the production level for the period. If, for example, units of production were the base for overhead, then 20,000 motors would be the base for overhead or $3 per unit. Thus there would not be a flexible budget for $63,000 because 20,000 motors is the base for the variable overhead regardless of the number of machine hours.

Control of the Efficiency Variance Who is responsible for control of the overhead efficiency variance? Since the variance really reflects efficiency in the utilization of the base underlying the flexible budget, whoever is responsible for control of this base is responsible for control of the variance. If the base is direct labour-hours, then the supervisor responsible for the use of labour time will be responsible for any overhead efficiency variance.

Activity-Based Costing and the Flexible Budget

It is unlikely that all of the variable overhead in a complex organization is driven by a single factor such as the number of units produced or the number of labour-hours or machine-hours. Activity-based costing provides a way of recognizing a variety of overhead cost drivers and thereby increasing the accuracy of the costing system. In activity-based costing, each overhead cost pool has its own measure of activity. The actual spending in each overhead cost pool can be independently evaluated using the techniques discussed in this chapter. The only difference is that the cost formulas for variable overhead costs will be stated in terms of different kinds of activities instead of all being stated in terms of units or a common measure of activity such as direct labour-hours or machine-hours. If done properly, activity-based costing can greatly enhance the usefulness of overhead performance reports by recognizing multiple causes of overhead costs. But the usefulness of overhead performance reports depends on how carefully the reports are done. In particular, managers must take care to separate the variable from the fixed costs in the flexible budgets.[1]

OVERHEAD RATES AND FIXED OVERHEAD ANALYSIS

The detailed analysis of fixed overhead differs considerably from the analysis of variable overhead, simply because of the difference in the nature of the costs involved. To provide a background for our discussion, we will first review briefly the need for, and computation of, predetermined overhead rates. This review will be helpful, since the predetermined overhead rate plays a major role in fixed overhead analysis. We will then show how fixed overhead variances are computed and make some observations as to their usefulness to managers.

Flexible Budgets and Overhead Rates

LEARNING OBJECTIVE 4
Explain the significance of the denominator activity figure in determining the standard cost of a unit of product.

Fixed costs come in large, indivisible pieces that by definition do not change with changes in the level of activity within the relevant range. As we learned in Chapter 3, this creates a problem in product costing, since a given level of fixed overhead cost spread over a small number of units will result in a higher cost per unit than if the same amount of cost is spread over a large number of units. Consider the data in the following table:

Month	(1) Fixed Overhead Cost	(2) Number of Units Produced	(3) Unit Cost (1) ÷ (2)
January	$6,000	1,000	$6.00
February	6,000	1,500	4.00
March	6,000	800	7.50

Notice that the large number of units produced in February results in a low unit cost ($4.00), whereas the small number of units produced in March results in a high unit cost ($7.50). This problem arises only in connection with the fixed portion of overhead, since by definition the variable portion of overhead remains constant on a per unit basis, rising and falling in total proportionately with changes in the activity level. Most managers feel that the fixed portion of unit cost should be stabilized so that a single unit cost figure can be used throughout the year. As we learned in Chapter 3, this stability can be accomplished through use of the predetermined overhead rate.

Throughout the remainder of this chapter, we will be analyzing the fixed overhead costs of MicroDrive Corporation. To assist us in that task, the flexible budget of the company—including fixed costs—is displayed in Exhibit 11–8. Note that the budgeted total fixed overhead costs amount to $300,000 within the relevant range of activity.

Denominator Activity The formula that we used in Chapter 3 to compute the predetermined overhead rate is as follows (MH: machine-hours; DLH: direct labour-hours):

$$\text{Predetermined overhead rate} = \frac{\text{Estimated total manufacturing overhead cost}}{\text{Estimated total units in the base (MH, DLH, etc.)}}$$

1. See Y.T. Mak and Melvin L. Roush, "Managing Activity Costs with Flexible Budgeting and Variance Analysis," *Accounting Horizons,* September 1996, pp. 141–46, for an insightful discussion of activity-based costing and overhead variance analysis.

EXHIBIT 11–8
Flexible Budget Schedule

MICRODRIVE CORPORATION
Flexible Budgets at Various Levels of Activity

Overhead Costs	Cost Formula (per machine-hour)	Activity (in machine-hours)			
		40,000	45,000	50,000	55,000
Variable overhead costs:					
Indirect labour	$0.80	$ 32,000	$ 36,000	$ 40,000	$ 44,000
Lubricants	0.30	12,000	13,500	15,000	16,500
Power	0.40	16,000	18,000	20,000	22,000
Total variable overhead cost	$1.50	60,000	67,500	75,000	82,500
Fixed overhead costs:					
Depreciation		100,000	100,000	100,000	100,000
Supervisory salaries		160,000	160,000	160,000	160,000
Insurance		40,000	40,000	40,000	40,000
Total fixed overhead cost		300,000	300,000	300,000	300,000
Total overhead cost		$360,000	$367,500	$375,000	$382,500

Denominator activity
The activity figure used to compute the predetermined overhead rate.

The estimated total units in the base in the formula for the predetermined overhead rate is called the **denominator activity.** Recall from our discussion in Chapter 3 that once an estimated activity level (denominator activity) has been chosen, it remains unchanged throughout the year, even if the actual activity turns out to be different from what was estimated. The reason for not changing the denominator is to maintain stability in the amount of overhead applied to each unit of product, regardless of when it is produced during the year.

Computing the Overhead Rate When we discussed predetermined overhead rates in Chapter 3, we didn't explain how the estimated total manufacturing cost was determined. This figure can be derived from the flexible budget. Once the denominator level of activity has been chosen, the flexible budget can be used to determine the total amount of overhead cost that should be incurred at that level of activity. The predetermined overhead rate can then be computed using the following variation on the basic formula for the predetermined overhead rate:

$$\text{Predetermined overhead rate} = \frac{\text{Overhead from the flexible budget at the denominator level of activity}}{\text{Denominator level of activity}}$$

To illustrate, refer to MicroDrive Corporation's flexible budget for manufacturing overhead shown in Exhibit 11–8. Suppose that the budgeted activity level for the year is 50,000 machine-hours (MH) and that this will be used as the denominator activity in the formula for the predetermined overhead rate. The numerator in the formula is the estimated total overhead cost of $375,000 when the activity is 50,000 machine-hours. This figure is taken from the flexible budget in Exhibit 11–8. Therefore, the predetermined overhead rate for MicroDrive Corporation will be computed as follows:

$$\frac{\$375{,}000}{50{,}000 \text{ MH}} = \$7.50 \text{ per machine-hour}$$

The company can also break its predetermined overhead rate down into variable and fixed elements rather than using a single combined figure:

$$\text{Variable element: } \frac{\$75{,}000}{50{,}000 \text{ MH}} = \$1.50 \text{ per machine-hour}$$

$$\text{Fixed element: } \frac{\$300{,}000}{50{,}000 \text{ MH}} = \$6 \text{ per machine-hour}$$

For every standard machine-hour of operation, work in process will be charged with $7.50 of overhead, of which $1.50 will be variable overhead and $6.00 will be fixed overhead. If a disk-drive motor takes two machine-hours to complete, then its cost will include $3 variable overhead and $12 fixed overhead, as shown on the following standard cost card:

Standard Cost Card—Per Motor	
Direct materials (assumed)	$14
Direct labour (assumed)	6
Variable overhead (2 machine-hours at $1.50)	3
Fixed overhead (2 machine-hours at $6)	12
Total standard cost per motor	$35

In summary, the flexible budget provides the estimated overhead cost needed to compute the predetermined overhead rate. Thus, the flexible budget plays a key role in determining the amount of fixed and variable overhead cost that will be charged to units of product.

Overhead Application in a Standard Cost System

LEARNING OBJECTIVE 5
Apply overhead cost to units of product in a standard cost system.

To understand the fixed overhead variances, it is necessary first to understand how overhead is applied to work in process in a standard cost system. In Chapter 3, recall that we applied overhead to work in process on the basis of actual hours of activity (multiplied by the predetermined overhead rate). This procedure was correct, since at the time we were dealing with a normal cost system.[2] However, we are now dealing with a standard cost system. In such a system, overhead is applied to work in process on the basis of the *standard hours allowed for the output of the period* rather than on the basis of the actual number of hours worked. This point is illustrated in Exhibit 11–9. In a standard cost system, every unit of product moving along the production line bears the same amount of overhead cost, regardless of any variations in efficiency that may have been involved in its production.

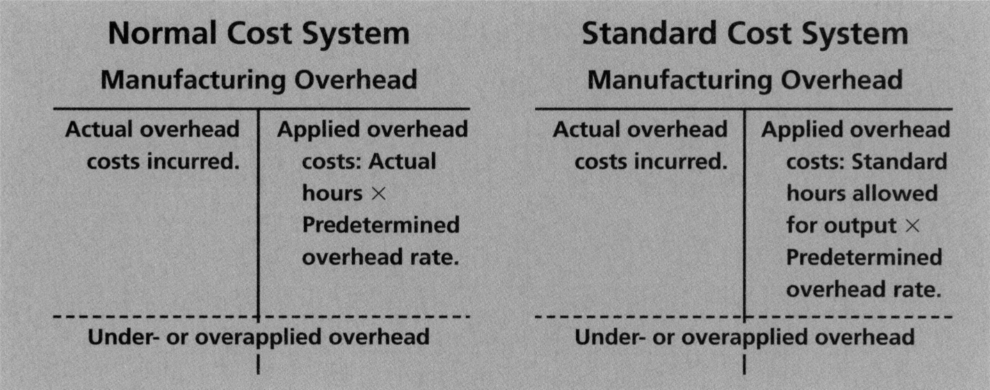

EXHIBIT 11–9 Applied Overhead Costs: Normal Cost System versus Standard Cost System

2. Normal cost systems are discussed in Chapter 3.

LEARNING OBJECTIVE 6
Compute and interpret the fixed overhead budget and volume variances.

The Fixed Overhead Variances

To illustrate the computation of fixed overhead variances, we will refer again to the data for MicroDrive Corporation:

Denominator activity in machine-hours	50,000
Budgeted fixed overhead costs	$300,000
Fixed portion of the predetermined overhead rate (computed earlier)	$6

Let us assume that the following actual operating results were recorded for the year:

Actual machine-hours	42,000
Standard machine-hours allowed*	40,000
Actual fixed overhead costs:	
Depreciation	$100,000
Supervisory salaries	172,000
Insurance	36,000
Total actual cost	$308,000

*For the actual production of the year.

From these data, two variances can be computed for fixed overhead—a *budget variance* and a *volume variance.* The variances are shown in Exhibit 11–10.

Notice from the exhibit that overhead has been applied to work in process on the basis of 40,000 standard hours allowed for the output of the year rather than on the basis of 42,000 actual hours worked. As stated earlier, this keeps unit costs from being affected by any variations in efficiency.

The Budget Variance—A Closer Look

Budget variance A measure of the difference between the actual fixed overhead costs incurred during the period and budgeted fixed overhead costs as contained in the flexible budget.

The **budget variance** is the difference between the actual fixed overhead costs incurred during the period and the budgeted fixed overhead costs as contained in the flexible budget. It can be computed as shown in Exhibit 11–10 or by using the following formula:

$$\text{Budget variance} = \text{Actual fixed overhead cost} - \text{Flexible budget fixed overhead cost}$$

EXHIBIT 11–10 Computation of the Fixed Overhead Variances

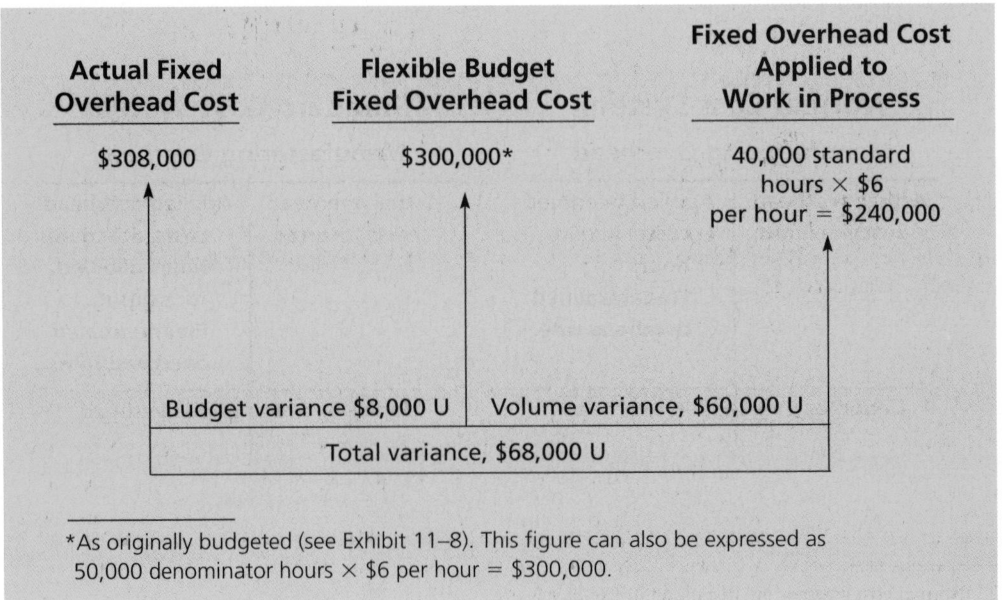

Applying this formula to MicroDrive Corporation, the budget variance would be as follows:

$$\$308{,}000 - \$300{,}000 = \$8{,}000 \text{ U}$$

The variances computed for the fixed costs at Rick's Hairstyling in Exhibit 11–4 are all budget variances, since they represent the difference between the actual fixed overhead cost and the budgeted fixed overhead cost from the flexible budget.

An expanded overhead performance report for MicroDrive Corporation appears in Exhibit 11–11. This report now includes the budget variances for fixed overhead as well as the spending variances for variable overhead that were in Exhibit 11–6.

The budget variances for fixed overhead can be very useful, since they represent the difference between how much *should* have been spent (according to the flexible budget) and how much was actually spent. For example, supervisory salaries has a $12,000 unfavourable variance. There should be some explanation for this large variance. Was it due to an increase in salaries? Was it due to overtime? Was another supervisor hired? If so, why was another supervisor hired? This was not included in the budget when activity for the year was planned.

The Volume Variance—A Closer Look

The **volume variance** is a measure of utilization of plant facilities. The variance arises whenever the standard hours allowed for the output of a period are different from the denominator activity level that was planned when the period began. It can be computed as shown in Exhibit 11–10 or by means of the following formula:

Volume variance The variance that arises whenever the standard hours allowed for the output of a period are different from the denominator activity level that was used to compute the predetermined overhead rate.

$$\text{Volume variance} = \begin{array}{c}\text{Fixed portion of}\\ \text{the predetermined}\\ \text{overhead rate}\end{array} \times \left(\begin{array}{c}\text{Denominator}\\ \text{hours}\end{array} - \begin{array}{c}\text{Standard hours}\\ \text{allowed}\end{array}\right)$$

EXHIBIT 11–11 Fixed Overhead Costs on the Overhead Performance Report

MICRODRIVE CORPORATION
Overhead Performance Report
For the Year Ended December 31

Budgeted machine-hours	50,000
Actual machine-hours	42,000
Standard machine-hours allowed	40,000

Overhead Costs	Cost Formula (per machine-hour)	Actual Costs 42,000 Machine-Hours	Budget Based on 42,000 Machine-Hours	Spending or Budget Variance
Variable overhead costs:				
Indirect labour	$0.80	$ 36,000	$ 33,600	$ 2,400 U
Lubricants	0.30	11,000	12,600	1,600 F
Power	0.40	24,000	16,800	7,200 U
Total variable overhead cost	$1.50	71,000	63,000	8,000 U
Fixed overhead costs:				
Depreciation		100,000	100,000	—
Supervisory salaries		172,000	160,000	12,000 U
Insurance		36,000	40,000	4,000 F
Total fixed overhead cost		308,000	300,000	8,000 U
Total overhead cost		$379,000	$363,000	$16,000 U

Applying this formula to MicroDrive Corporation, the volume variance would be computed as follows:

$$\$6 \text{ per MH } (50{,}000 \text{ MH} - 40{,}000 \text{ MH}) = \$60{,}000 \text{ U}$$

Note that this computation agrees with the volume variance shown in Exhibit 11–10. As stated earlier, the volume variance is a measure of utilization of available plant facilities. An unfavourable variance, as above, means that the company operated at an activity level *below* that planned for the period. A favourable variance would mean that the company operated at an activity level *greater* than that planned for the period.

It is important to note that the volume variance does not measure over- or underspending. A company normally would incur the same dollar amount of fixed overhead cost regardless of whether the period's activity was above or below the planned (denominator) level. Also note that fixed overhead does not have an efficiency variance because the fixed overhead budget for the actual machine-hours, 42,000, is the same as the fixed overhead budget for 40,000 standard machine-hours, namely $300,000. The volume variance only occurs as a result of the standard and denominator machine-hours difference, 10,000 machine-hours. In short, the volume variance is an activity-related variance. It is explainable only by activity and is controllable only through activity.

To summarize:

1. If the denominator activity and the standard hours allowed for the output of the period are the same, then there is no volume variance.
2. If the denominator activity is greater than the standard hours allowed for the output of the period, then the volume variance is unfavourable, signifying an underutilization of available facilities.
3. If the denominator activity is less than the standard hours allowed for the output of the period, then the volume variance is favourable, signifying a higher utilization of available facilities than was planned.

Graphic Analysis of Fixed Overhead Variances

Some insights into the budget and volume variances can be gained through graphic analysis. A graph containing these variances is presented in Exhibit 11–12.

As shown in the graph, fixed overhead cost is applied to work in process at the predetermined rate of $6 for each standard hour of activity. (The applied-cost line is the upward-sloping line on the graph.) Since a denominator level of 50,000 machine-hours was used in computing the $6 rate, the applied-cost line crosses the budget-cost line at exactly the 50,000 machine-hour point. Thus, if the denominator hours and the standard hours allowed for the output are the same, there can be no volume variance, since the applied-cost line and the budget-cost line will exactly meet on the graph. It is only when the standard hours differ from the denominator hours that a volume variance can arise.

In this case, the standard hours allowed for the actual output (40,000 hours) are less than the denominator hours (50,000 hours); the result is an unfavourable volume variance, since less cost was applied to production than was originally budgeted. If the situation had been reversed and the standard hours allowed for the actual output had exceeded the denominator hours, then the volume variance on the graph would have been favourable.

Cautions in Fixed Overhead Analysis

The reason we get a volume variance for fixed overhead is that the total fixed cost does not depend on activity; yet when applying the costs to work in process, we act *as if* the fixed costs were variable and depended on activity. This point can be seen from the graph in Exhibit 11–12. Notice from the graph that the fixed overhead costs are applied to work in process at a rate of $6 per hour *as if* they were variable. Treating these costs as if they were variable is necessary for product costing purposes, but there are some real dangers here. The manager can easily become misled and start thinking of the fixed costs as if they were *in fact* variable.

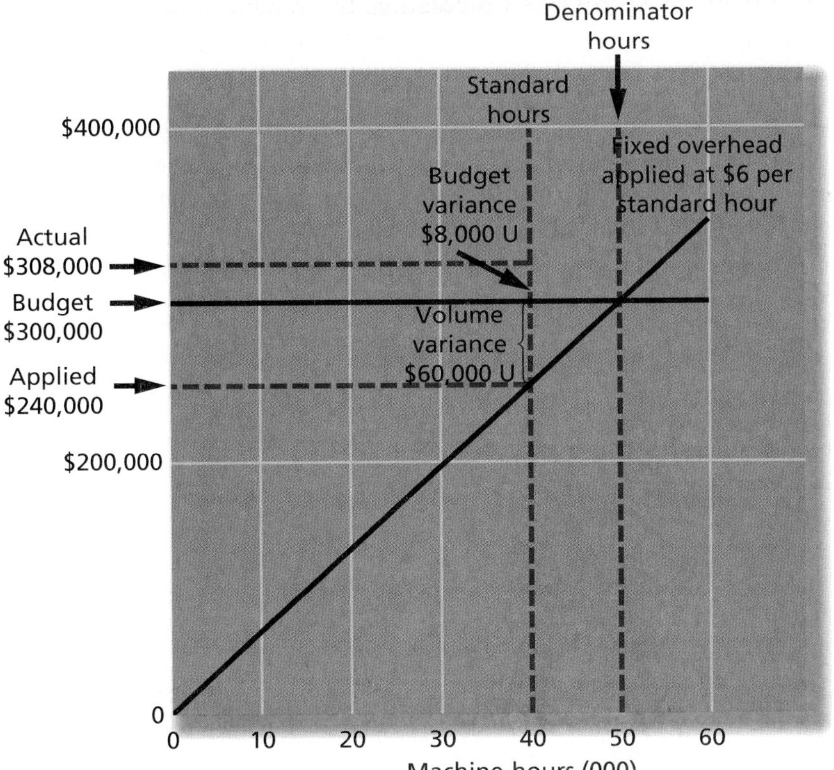

EXHIBIT 11–12 Graphic Analysis of Fixed Overhead Variances

The manager must keep clearly in mind that fixed overhead costs come in large, indivisible pieces. Expressing fixed costs on a unit or per hour basis, although necessary for product costing for external reports, is artificial. Increases or decreases in activity in fact have no effect on total fixed costs within the relevant range of activity. Even though fixed costs are expressed on a unit or per hour basis, they are *not* proportional to activity. In a sense, the volume variance is the error that occurs as a result of treating fixed costs as variable costs in the costing system.

Because of the confusion that can arise concerning the interpretation of the volume variance, some companies present the volume variance in physical units (hours) rather than in dollars. These companies feel that stating the variance in physical units gives management a clearer signal concerning the cause of the variance.

Overhead Variances and Under- or Overapplied Overhead Cost

Four variances relating to overhead cost have been computed for MicroDrive Corporation in this chapter. These four variances are as follows:

Variable overhead spending variance (p. 490) . . .	$ 8,000 U
Variable overhead efficiency variance (p. 491) . . .	3,000 U
Fixed overhead budget variance (p. 496)	8,000 U
Fixed overhead volume variance (p. 496)	60,000 U
Total overhead variance	$79,000 U

Recall from Chapter 3 that under- or overapplied overhead is the difference between the amount of overhead applied to products and the actual overhead costs incurred during a period. Basically, the overhead variances we have computed in this chapter break down the under- or overapplied overhead into variances that can be used by managers for control purposes. Consequently, *the sum of the overhead variances equals the under- or overapplied overhead cost for a period.*

Furthermore, in a standard cost system, unfavourable variances are equivalent to underapplied overhead and favourable variances are equivalent to overapplied overhead. Unfavourable variances occur because more was spent on overhead than the standards allow. Underapplied overhead occurs when more was spent on overhead than was applied to products during the period. But in a standard costing system, the standard amount of overhead allowed is exactly the same amount of overhead applied to products. Therefore, in a standard costing system, unfavourable variances and underapplied overhead are the same thing, as are favourable variances and overapplied overhead.

To record the overhead costs for MicroDrive, the data from Exhibit 11-11 will be used to illustrate.

Overhead costs		379,000	
Various credits such as accounts payable and accumulated depreciation			379,000
To record the actual overhead costs for the year ended December 31.			
Work in Progress		300,000	
Overhead costs			300,000
Variable $1.50 × 40,000 machine-hours	$ 60,000		
Fixed $6.00 ×40,000 machine-hour	240,000		
Total absorption cost overhead	$300,000		
Variable overhead spending variance		8,000	
Variable overhead efficiency variance		3,000	
Fixed overhead budget variance		8,000	
Fixed overhead volume variance		60,000	
Overhead costs			79,000
To record the standard cost variances for overhead.			

Overhead costs	
379,000	300,000
	79,000
Bal. 0	

For MicroDrive Corporation, the total overhead variance was $79,000 unfavourable. Therefore, its overhead cost was underapplied by $79,000 for the year. To solidify this point in your mind, *carefully study the review problem at the end of the chapter!* This review problem provides a comprehensive summary of overhead analysis, including the computation of under- or overapplied overhead cost in a standard cost system.

CAPACITY ANALYSIS FOR MANAGEMENT

Theoretical capacity
The volume of activity resulting from operations conducted 24 hours per day, 7 days per week, 365 days per year, with no downtime.

MicroDrive Corporation, discussed using the data in Exhibit 11–5, has a budgeted production level of 25,000 motors and an actual production of 20,000 motors. These activity levels were used earlier in this chapter to determine a standard cost per motor of $35 based on 25,000 motors or 50,000 machine-hours (see page 495).

If all of the production time was used and no waste occurred, MicroDrive could reach a level of capacity known as **theoretical capacity**. This level of capacity would require operations to be conducted around the clock, 365 days per year, with no downtime, similar to the definition of an ideal standard presented in Chapter 10. If the denominator level of 25,000 units or 50,000 machine-hours represented 60% of the theoretical capacity, then MicroDrive could produce 41,666 units (25,000 ÷ 0.60) in 83,333 hours.

Practical capacity represents what could be produced if unavoidable downtime was subtracted from theoretical capacity. Maintenance, breakdowns, and set-up times for new operations are considered to be unavoidable downtime. If the denominator level was 75% of practical capacity, then 33,333 units (25,000 ÷ 0.75) could be produced using 66,666 machine-hours.

Practical capacity The productive capacity of operations at a theoretical level less unavoidable downtime.

Capacity analysis could proceed by examining the cost at each level of capacity for overhead:

Theoretical	83,333 hrs × ($1.50) + $300,000 = $424,999
Practical	66,666 hrs × ($1.50) + $300,000 = $399,999
Denominator ...	50,000 hrs × ($1.50) + $300,000 = $375,000
Actual	40,000 hrs × ($1.50) + $300,000 = $360,000

If MicroDrive can sell all that it can produce at $40 per unit, then an indication of the opportunity loss by not operating at the various levels of capacity can be computed as follows:

Theoretical	41,666 units × ($40 – $20) – $424,999 = $408,321
Practical	33,333 units × ($40 – $20) – $399,999 = $266,661
Denominator ...	25,000 units × ($40 – $20) – $375,000 = $125,000
Actual	20,000 units × ($40 – $20) – $360,000 = $ 40,000

Note that $20 is composed of the standard materials cost of $14 per unit and the standard direct labour cost of $6 per unit shown on page 495. The remaining variable production cost of $3 for overhead is included in the overhead charges previously presented.

When management wants to consider what the cost of operating at 20,000 units is (a profit of $40,000), it needs to begin by looking at what additional profit would be possible at theoretical capacity: $408,321 – $40,000, or $368,321 in lost profits. By examining marketing possibilities for excess capacity of 21,666 units (41,666 units – 20,000 units), management might be able to significantly improve its profit picture. By refining the analysis to look at set-ups, maintenance, scrap levels, materials shortages, and other uses for capacity, either cost or profit implications can be obtained.

The use of theoretical or practical capacity as a means of analyzing overhead is typically performed outside of the costing for inventory and the income statement results as illustrated in Chapters 10 and 11. To reduce overhead to the unit cost of the theoretical level, for example, would under-cost ending inventory from the usual financial accounting perspective and create a large volume variance. As the denominator level used to compute the overhead rate increases, the unit overhead charge declines but the volume variance resulting from the difference between denominator and standard base allowed increases. This would create an excessive expense for the financial accountant but it would serve as a means of examining the costs of capacity for the management accountant.[3]

When budget planning, both short term as presented in Chapter 9 or long term as will be presented in Chapter 14, capacity analysis is an important strategic planning tool. Capacity costs and changes in capacity require time, so capacity utilization, bottlenecks, and marketing opportunities are important areas for investigation.

3 Ramji Balakrishnan and Geoffrey B. Sprinkle, "Integrating Profit Variance Analysis and Capacity Costing to Provide Better Managerial Information," *Issues in Accounting Education*, May 2002, pp. 149–162.

SUMMARY

When analyzing overhead costs, it is vital to distinguish between variable overhead and fixed overhead. Variable overhead costs vary in total in proportion to changes in activity, whereas total fixed costs do not change within the relevant range. This distinction is important when constructing flexible budgets and when computing variances for overhead.

A flexible budget shows what costs should be for various levels of activity. The flexible budget amount for a specific level of activity is determined differently, depending on whether a cost is variable or fixed. If a cost is variable, the flexible budget amount is computed by multiplying the cost per unit of activity by the level of activity specified for the flexible budget. If a cost is fixed, the original total budgeted fixed cost is used as the flexible budget amount.

The two variances for variable overhead discussed in the chapter are the variable overhead spending and variable overhead efficiency variances. These variances were also covered in the previous chapter.

Two variances for fixed overhead are covered in the chapter. One—the budget variance—is quite simple; the other—the volume variance—is considerably more complex. The budget variance is the difference between the actual total fixed overhead cost incurred and the total amount of fixed overhead cost that was originally budgeted. The volume variance is the difference between the amount of fixed overhead cost applied to inventory and the total amount of fixed overhead cost that was originally budgeted. The budget variance is a straightforward measure of the degree to which fixed overhead spending was under control. The volume variance is a consequence of treating a fixed cost as if it was variable and is more difficult to interpret meaningfully.

The sum of all four overhead variances equals the overhead over- or underapplied for the period. Unfavourable variances are equivalent to underapplied overhead and favourable variances are equivalent to overapplied overhead.

Capacity analysis extends the idea of a volume variance to an analysis of the implications of different levels of capacity, extending from actual activity to the extreme of theoretical capacity. Cost and profits for the various levels of capacity can project the implications of how capacity might be used. Given the tendency of fixed overhead to grow in relative importance as a manufacturing cost, such analysis is important.

REVIEW PROBLEM: OVERHEAD ANALYSIS

(This problem provides a comprehensive review of Chapter 11, including the computation of under- or overapplied overhead and its breakdown into the four overhead variances.)

Data for the manufacturing overhead of Aspen Company are given below:

Overhead Costs	Cost Formula (per machine-hour)	Machine-Hours 5,000	6,000	7,000
Variable overhead costs:				
Supplies	$0.20	$ 1,000	$ 1,200	$ 1,400
Indirect labour	0.30	1,500	1,800	2,100
Total variable overhead cost	$0.50	2,500	3,000	3,500
Fixed overhead costs:				
Depreciation		4,000	4,000	4,000
Supervision		5,000	5,000	5,000
Total fixed overhead cost		9,000	9,000	9,000
Total overhead cost		$11,500	$12,000	$12,500

Five hours of machine time are required per unit of product. The company has set denominator activity for the coming period at 6,000 machine-hours (or 1,200 units). The computation of the predetermined overhead rate would be as follows:

$$\text{Total: } \frac{\$12{,}000}{6{,}000 \text{ MH}} = \$2{,}00 \text{ per machine-hour}$$

$$\text{Variable element: } \frac{\$3{,}000}{6{,}000 \text{ MH}} = \$0.50 \text{ per machine-hour}$$

$$\text{Fixed element: } \frac{\$9{,}000}{6{,}000 \text{ MH}} = \$1.50 \text{ per machine-hour}$$

Assume the following *actual* results for the period:

Number of units produced	1,300 units
Actual machine-hours	6,800 machine-hours
Standard machine-hours allowed*	6,500 machine-hours
Actual variable overhead cost	$4,200
Actual fixed overhead cost	9,400

*1,300 units × 5 machine-hours per unit.

Therefore, the company's Manufacturing Overhead account would appear as follows at the end of the period:

Manufacturing Overhead

	Debit	Credit	
Actual overhead costs	13,600*	13,000†	Applied overhead costs
Underapplied overhead	600		

* $4,200 variable + $9,400 fixed = $13,600

† 6,500 standard hours × $2 per machine hour = $13,000. In a standard cost system, overhead is applied on the basis of standard hours, not actual hours.

Required:

Analyze the $600 underapplied overhead in terms of:

1. A variable overhead spending variance.
2. A variable overhead efficiency variance.
3. A fixed overhead budget variance.
4. A fixed overhead volume variance.

Solution to Review Problem

Variable Overhead Variances

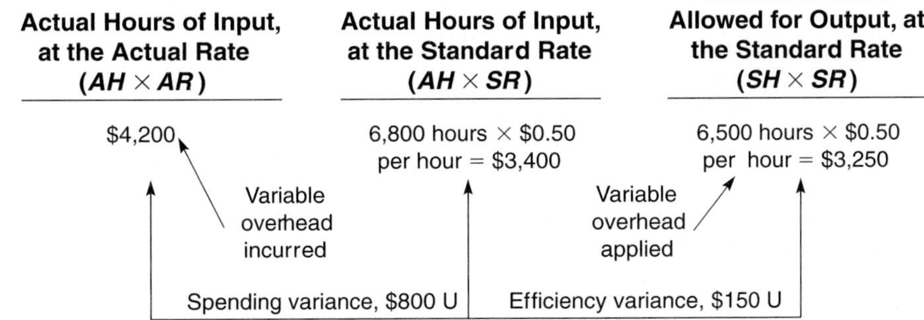

These same variances in the alternative format would be as follows:

Variable overhead spending variance:

$$\text{Spending variance} = (AH \times AR) - (AH \times SR)$$

$$(\$4{,}200^*) - (6{,}800 \text{ hours} \times \$0.50 \text{ per hour}) = \$800 \text{ U}$$

*$AH \times AR$ equals the total actual cost for the period.

Variable overhead efficiency variance:

$$\text{Efficiency variance} = SR(AH - SH)$$

$$\$0.50 \text{ per hour } (6{,}800 \text{ hours} - 6{,}500 \text{ hours}) = \$150 \text{ U}$$

Fixed Overhead Variances

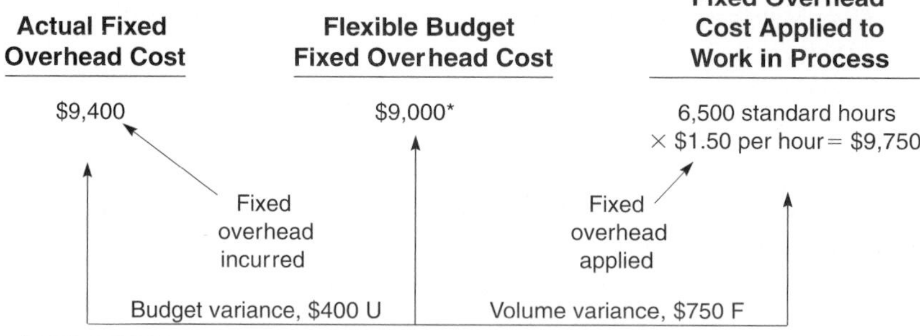

*Can be expressed as: 6,000 denominator hours × $1.50 per hour = $9,000

These same variances in the alternative format would be as follows:

Fixed overhead budget variance:

$$\text{Budget variance} = \text{Actual fixed overhead cost} - \text{Flexible budget fixed overhead cost}$$

$$\$9{,}400 - \$9{,}000 = \$400 \text{ U}$$

Fixed overhead volume variance:

$$\text{Volume variance} = \text{Fixed portion of the predetermined overhead rate} \times (\text{Denominator hours} - \text{Standard hours})$$

$$\$1.50 \text{ per hour } (6{,}000 \text{ hours} - 6{,}500 \text{ hours}) = \$750 \text{ F}$$

Summary of Variances

A summary of the four overhead variances is given below:

Variable overhead:		
Spending variance	$800	U
Efficiency variance	150	U
Fixed overhead:		
Budget variance	400	U
Volume variance	750	F
Underapplied overhead	$600	

Notice that the $600 summary variance figure agrees with the underapplied balance in the company's Manufacturing Overhead account. This agreement verifies the accuracy of our variance analysis.

Manufacturing overhead		13,600	
Various credits such as accounts payable and accumulated depreciation			13,600
Variable costs for overhead	$ 4,200		
Fixed costs for overhead	9,400		
Total actual overhead costs	$13,600		
Work in progress		13,000	
Manufacturing overhead			13,000
Applied:			
Variable 6,500 hours × $0.50 =	$ 3,250		
Fixed 6,500 hours × $1.50 =	9,750		
Total	$13,000		
Variable spending variance		800	
Variable efficiency variance		150	
Fixed budget variance		400	
Fixed volume variance			750
Manufacturing overhead			600
To record the overhead variance for the period.			

GLOSSARY

Visit the Online Learning Centre at http://www.mcgrawhill.ca/college/garrison/ for a review of key terms and definitions.

QUESTIONS

11–1 What is a static budget?

11–2 What is a flexible budget and how does it differ from a static budget?

11–3 What does the activity variance measure and how is it computed?

11–4 Name three criteria that should be considered in choosing an activity base on which to construct a flexible budget.

11–5 In comparing budgeted data with actual data in a performance report for variable overhead, what variance(s) will be produced if the budgeted data are based on actual hours worked? On both actual hours worked and standard hours allowed?

11–6 What is meant by the term *standard hours allowed?*

11–7 How does the variable manufacturing overhead spending variance differ from the materials price variance?

11–8 Why is the term *overhead efficiency variance* a misnomer?

11–9 In what way is the flexible budget involved in product costing?

11–10 What is meant by the term *denominator level of activity?*

11–11 Why do we apply overhead to work in process on the basis of standard hours allowed in Chapter 11 when we applied it on the basis of actual hours in Chapter 3? What is the difference in costing systems between the two chapters?

11–12 In a standard cost system, what two variances are computed for fixed manufacturing overhead?

11–13 What does the fixed overhead budget variance measure?

11–14 Under what circumstances would you expect the volume variance to be favourable? Unfavourable? Does the variance measure deviations in spending for fixed overhead items? Explain.

11–15 How might the volume variance be measured, other than in dollars?

11–16 What dangers are there in expressing fixed costs on a per unit basis?

11–17 In Chapter 3, you became acquainted with the concept of under- or overapplied overhead. The under- or overapplied overhead can be broken down into what four variances?

11–18 If factory overhead is overapplied for August, would you expect the total of the overhead variances to be favourable or unfavourable?

11–19 Capacity analysis extends beyond typical variance analysis of overhead. How are different definitions of capacity used as a starting point for capacity analysis?

EXERCISES

EXERCISE 11–1 Prepare a Flexible Budget [LO1]

The cost formulas for Emory Company's manufacturing overhead costs are given below. These cost formulas cover a relevant range of 15,000 to 25,000 machine-hours each year.

Overhead Costs	Cost Formula
Utilities	$0.30 per machine-hour
Indirect labour	$52,000 plus $1.40 per machine-hour
Supplies	$0.20 per machine-hour
Maintenance	$18,000 plus $0.10 per machine-hour
Depreciation	$90,000

Required:

Prepare a flexible budget in increments of 5,000 machine-hours. Include all costs in your budget.

EXERCISE 11–2 Preparing a Flexible Budget Performance Report [LO2]

Orcas Boat Charter Service rents boats for cruising in the Queen Charlotte Islands of British Columbia. The company bases its overhead cost budgets on the following data:

Variable overhead costs:	
Cleaning	$60.50 per charter
Maintenance	$35.25 per charter
Port fees	$15.75 per charter
Fixed overhead costs:	
Salaries and wages	$9,150 per month
Depreciation	$12,100 per month
Utilities	$860 per month
Moorage	$4,980 per month

Each time a boat is chartered, whether it is for one day or a week, certain costs must be incurred. Those costs are listed above under the variable overhead costs. For example, each time a boat returns from a charter, it must be thoroughly cleaned, which costs on average $60.50.

In July, the following actual costs were incurred for 160 charters:

Cleaning	$9,440
Maintenance	$5,980
Port fees	$2,670
Salaries and wages	$9,200
Depreciation	$12,800
Utilities	$835
Moorage	$5,360

Due to an unanticipated surge in demand for charters, the company purchased a new boat in July to add to its charter fleet.

Required:

1. Construct a Flexible Budget Performance Report for Orcas Boat Charter Service for July, following the format in Exhibit 11–4.
2. What is apparently the major cause of the overall variance for the month? Explain.

EXERCISE 11–3 Variable Overhead Performance Report with Just a Spending Variance [LO2, LO3]

Yung Corporation bases its variable overhead performance report on the actual direct labour-hours of the period. Data concerning the most recent year that ended on December 31 appear below:

Budgeted direct labour-hours	38,000
Actual direct labour-hours	34,000
Standard direct labour-hours allowed	35,000

Cost formula (per direct labour-hour):

Indirect labour	$0.60
Supplies	$0.10
Electricity	$0.05

Actual costs incurred:

Indirect labour	$21,200
Supplies	$3,200
Electricity	$1,600

Required:

Prepare a variable overhead performance report using the format in Exhibit 11–6. Compute just the variable overhead spending variances (do not compute the variable overhead efficiency variances).

EXERCISE 11–4 Variable Overhead Performance Report with Both Spending and Efficiency Variances [LO2, LO3]

Refer to the data for Yung Corporation in Exercise 11–3. Management would like to compute both spending and efficiency variances for variable overheads in the company's variable overhead performance report.

Required:

Prepare a variable overhead performance report using the format in Exhibit 11–7. Compute both the variable overhead spending variances and the overhead efficiency variances.

EXERCISE 11–5 Applying Overhead in a Standard Costing System [LO4, LO5]

Privack Corporation has a standard cost system in which it applies overhead to products based on the standard direct labour-hours allowed for the actual output of the period. Data concerning the most recent year appear below:

Variable overhead cost per direct labour-hour	$2.00
Total fixed overhead cost per year	$250,000
Budgeted standard direct labour-hours (denominator level of activity)	40,000
Actual direct labour-hours	39,000
Standard direct labour-hours allowed for the actual output	38,000

Required:

1. Compute the predetermined overhead rate for the year.
2. Determine the amount of overhead that would be applied to the output of the period.

EXERCISE 11–6 Fixed Overhead Variances [LO6]

Primara Corporation has a standard cost system in which it applies overhead to products based on the standard direct labour-hours allowed for the actual output of the period. Data concerning the most recent year appear below:

Total budgeted fixed overhead cost for the year	$250,000
Actual fixed overhead cost for the year	$254,000
Budgeted standard direct labour-hours (denominator level of activity)	25,000
Actual direct labour-hours	27,000
Standard direct labour-hours allowed for the actual output	26,000

Required:

1. Compute the fixed portion of the predetermined overhead rate for the year.
2. Compute the fixed overhead budget variance and volume variance.

EXERCISE 11–7 Preparing a Flexible Budget [LO1]

An incomplete flexible budget is given below for Lavage Rapide, a Swiss company that owns and operates a large automatic carwash facility near Geneva. The Swiss currency is the Swiss franc, which is denoted by SFr.

LAVAGE RAPIDE
Flexible Budget
For the Month Ended August 31

Overhead Costs	Cost Formula (per car)	Activity (cars) 8,000	9,000	10,000
Variable overhead costs:				
Cleaning supplies	?	?	7,200 SFr	?
Electricity	?	?	2,700	?
Maintenance	?	?	1,800	?
Total variable overhead cost	?	?	?	?
Fixed overhead costs:				
Operator wages		?	9,000	?
Depreciation		?	6,000	?
Rent		?	8,000	?
Total fixed overhead cost		?	?	?
Total overhead cost		?	? SFr	?

Required:

Fill in the missing data.

EXERCISE 11–8 Using a Flexible Budget [LO2]

Refer to the data in Exercise 11–7. Lavage Rapide's owner-manager would like to prepare a budget for August assuming an activity level of 8,800 cars.

Required:

Prepare a static budget for August. Use Exhibit 11–1 in the chapter as your guide.

EXERCISE 11–9 Flexible Budget Performance Report [LO2]

Refer to the data in Exercise 11–7. Lavage Rapide's actual level of activity during August was 8,900 cars, although the owner had constructed his static budget for the month assuming the level of activity would be 8,800 cars. The actual overhead costs incurred during August are given below:

	Actual Costs Incurred for 8,900 Cars
Variable overhead costs:	
Cleaning supplies	7,080 SFr
Electricity	2,460 SFr
Maintenance	1,550 SFr
Fixed overhead costs:	
Operator wages	9,100 SFr
Depreciation	7,000 SFr
Rent	8,000 SFr

Required:

Prepare a flexible budget performance report for both the variable and fixed overhead costs for August. Use Exhibit 11–4 in the chapter as your guide.

EXERCISE 11–10 Variable Overhead Performance Report [LO2, LO3]

The variable portion of Murray Company's flexible budget for manufacturing overhead is given below:

Variable Overhead Costs	Cost Formula (per machine-hour	Machine-Hours		
		10,000	12,000	14,000
Supplies	$0.20	$ 2,000	$ 2,400	$ 2,800
Maintenance	0.80	8,000	9,600	11,200
Utilities	0.10	1,000	1,200	1,400
Rework	0.40	4,000	4,800	5,600
Total variable overhead cost	$1.50	$15,000	$18,000	$21,000

During a recent period, the company recorded 11,500 machine-hours of activity. The variable overhead costs incurred were:

Supplies	$2,400
Maintenance	$8,000
Utilities	$1,100
Rework time	$5,300

The budgeted activity for the period had been 12,000 machine-hours.

Required:

1. Prepare a variable overhead performance report for the period. Indicate whether variances are favourable (F) or unfavourable (U). Show only a spending variance on your report.
2. Discuss the significance of the variances. Might some variances be the result of others? Explain.

EXERCISE 11–11 Variable Overhead Performance Report with Both Spending and Efficiency Variances [LO2, LO3]

The cheque-clearing office of Columbia National Bank is responsible for processing all cheques that come to the bank for payment. Managers at the bank believe that variable overhead costs are essentially proportional to the number of labour-hours worked in the office, so labour-hours are used as the activity base when preparing variable overhead budgets and performance reports. Data for September, the most recent month, appear below:

Budgeted labour-hours	3,080
Actual labour-hours	3,100
Standard labour-hours allowed for the actual number of cheques processed	3,200

	Cost Formula (per labour-hour)	Actual Costs Incurred in September
Variable overhead costs:		
Office supplies	$0.10	$ 365
Staff coffee lounge	0.20	520
Indirect labour	0.90	2,710
Total variable overhead cost	$1.20	$3,595

Required:

Prepare a variable overhead performance report for September for the cheque-clearing office that includes both spending and efficiency variances. Use Exhibit 11–7 as a guide.

EXERCISE 11–12 Predetermined Overhead Rate [LO4, LO5]

Operating at a normal level of 30,000 direct labour-hours, Lasser Company produces 10,000 units of product each period. The direct labour wage rate is $12 per hour. Two and one-half metres of direct materials go into each unit of product; the material costs $8.60 per metre. The flexible budget used to plan and control manufacturing overhead costs is given below (in condensed form):

Overhead Costs	Cost Formula (per direct labour-hour)	Direct Labour-Hours 20,000	30,000	40,000
Variable costs	$1.90	$ 38,000	$ 57,000	$ 76,000
Fixed costs		168,000	168,000	168,000
Total overhead cost		$206,000	$225,000	$244,000

Required:

1. Using 30,000 direct labour-hours as the denominator activity, compute the predetermined overhead rate and break it down into variable and fixed elements.
2. Complete the standard cost card below for one unit of product:

Direct materials, 2.5 metres at $8.60 per metre	$21.50
Direct labour, ?	?
Variable overhead, ?	?
Fixed overhead, ?	?
Total standard cost per unit	$?

EXERCISE 11–13 Using Fixed Overhead Variances [LO6]

The standard cost card for the single product manufactured by Cutter, Inc., is given below:

Standard Cost Card—per Unit	
Direct materials, 3 metres at $6 per metre	$ 18
Direct labour, 4 hours at $15.50 per hour	62
Variable overhead, 4 hours at $1.50 per hour	6
Fixed overhead, 4 hours at $5 per hour	20
Total standard cost per unit	$106

Manufacturing overhead is applied to production on the basis of standard direct labour-hours. During the year, the company worked 37,000 hours and manufactured 9,500 units of product. Selected data relating to the company's fixed manufacturing overhead cost for the year are shown below:

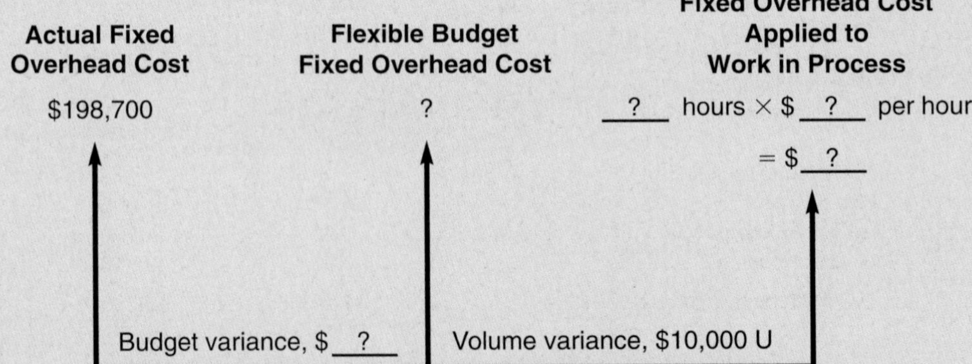

Required:

1. What were the standard hours allowed for the year's production?
2. What was the amount of fixed overhead cost contained in the flexible budget for the year?
3. What was the fixed overhead budget variance for the year?
4. What denominator activity level did the company use in setting the predetermined overhead rate for the year?

EXERCISE 11–14 Predetermined Overhead Rate; Overhead Variances [LO4, LO5, LO6]
Norwall Company's flexible budget for manufacturing overhead (in condensed form) is given below:

Overhead Costs	Cost Formula (per machine-hour)	Machine-Hours		
		50,000	60,000	70,000
Variable costs	$3	$150,000	$180,000	$210,000
Fixed costs		300,000	300,000	300,000
Total overhead cost		$450,000	$480,000	$510,000

The following information is available for a recent period:

a. The denominator activity of 60,000 machine-hours is used to compute the predetermined overhead rate.
b. At the 60,000 standard machine-hours level of activity, the company should produce 40,000 units of product.
c. The company's actual operating results were:

Number of units produced	42,000
Actual machine-hours	64,000
Actual variable overhead costs	$185,600
Actual fixed overhead costs	$302,400

Required:

1. Compute the predetermined overhead rate and break it down into variable and fixed cost elements.
2. Compute the standard hours allowed for the actual production.
3. Compute the variable overhead spending and efficiency variances and the fixed overhead budget and volume variances.

EXERCISE 11–15 Relations Among Fixed Overhead Variances [LO4, LO5, LO6]
Selected information relating to Yost Company's operations for the most recent year is given below:

Activity:	
Denominator activity (machine-hours)	45,000
Standard hours allowed per unit	3
Number of units produced	14,000
Costs:	
Actual fixed overhead costs incurred	$267,000
Fixed overhead budget variance	$3,000 F

The company applies overhead cost to products on the basis of standard machine-hours.

Required:

1. What were the standard machine-hours allowed for the actual production?
2. What was the fixed portion of the predetermined overhead rate?
3. What was the volume variance?

EXERCISE 11–16 Fixed Overhead Variances [LO6]

Selected operating information on three different companies for a recent year is given below:

	Company		
	A	B	C
Full-capacity machine-hours	10,000	18,000	20,000
Budgeted machine-hours*	9,000	17,000	20,000
Actual machine-hours	9,000	17,800	19,000
Standard machine-hours allowed for actual production	9,500	16,000	20,000

*Denominator activity for computing the predetermined overhead rate.

Required:

For each company, state whether the company would have a favourable or unfavourable volume variance and why.

PROBLEMS

PROBLEM 11–17 Comprehensive Standard Cost Variances [LO3, LO6]

"Wonderful! Not only did our salespeople do a good job in meeting the sales budget this year, but our production people did a good job in controlling costs as well," said Kim Clark, president of Martell Company. "Our $18,300 overall manufacturing cost variance is only 1.2% of the $1,536,000 standard cost of products made during the year. That's well within the 3% parameter set by management for acceptable variances. It looks like everyone will be in line for a bonus this year."

The company produces and sells a single product. The standard cost card for the product follows:

Standard Cost Card—per Unit of Product	
Direct materials, 2 metres at $8.45 per metre	$16.90
Direct labour, 1.4 direct labour-hours at $16 per direct labour-hour	22.40
Variable overhead, 1.4 direct labour-hours at $2.50 per direct labour-hour	3.50
Fixed overhead, 1.4 direct labour-hours at $6 per direct labour-hour	8.40
Standard cost per unit	$51.20

The following additional information is available for the year just completed:

a. The company manufactured 30,000 units of product during the year.

b. A total of 64,000 metres of material was purchased during the year at a cost of $8.55 per metre. All of this material was used to manufacture the 30,000 units. There were no beginning or ending inventories for the year.

c. The company worked 43,500 direct labour-hours during the year at a direct labour cost of $15.80 per hour.

d. Overhead is applied to products on the basis of standard direct labour-hours. Data relating to manufacturing overhead costs follow:

Denominator activity level (direct labour-hours)	35,000
Budgeted fixed overhead costs (from the overhead flexible budget)	$210,000
Actual variable overhead costs incurred	$108,000
Actual fixed overhead costs incurred	$211,800

Required:

1. Compute the direct materials price and quantity variances for the year.
2. Compute the direct labour rate and efficiency variances for the year.

3. For manufacturing overhead compute:
   a. The variable overhead spending and efficiency variances for the year.
   b. The fixed overhead budget and volume variances for the year.
4. Total the variances you have computed, and compare the net amount with the $18,300 mentioned by the president. Do you agree that bonuses should be given to everyone for good cost control during the year? Explain.

PROBLEM 11–18 Comprehensive Standard Cost Variances [LO3, LO4, LO5, LO6]

Flandro Company uses a standard cost system and sets predetermined overhead rates on the basis of direct labour-hours. The following data are taken from the company's budget for the current year:

Denominator activity (direct labour-hours)	5,000
Variable manufacturing overhead cost	$25,000
Fixed manufacturing overhead cost	$59,000

The standard cost card for the company's only product is given below:

Direct materials, 3 metres at $4.40 per metre	$13.20
Direct labour, 1 hour at $12 per hour	12.00
Manufacturing overhead, 140% of direct labour cost	16.80
Standard cost per unit	$42.00

During the year, the company produced 6,000 units of product and incurred the following costs:

Materials purchased, 24,000 metres at $4.80 per metre	$115,200
Materials used in production (in metres)	18,500
Direct labour cost incurred, 5,800 hours at $13 per hour	$75,400
Variable manufacturing overhead cost incurred	$29,580
Fixed manufacturing overhead cost incurred	$60,400

Required:

1. Redo the standard cost card in a clearer, more usable format by detailing the variable and fixed overhead cost elements.
2. Prepare an analysis of the variances for materials and labour for the year.
3. Prepare an analysis of the variances for variable and fixed overhead for the year.
4. What effect, if any, does the choice of a denominator activity level have on unit standard costs? Is the volume variance a controllable variance from a spending point of view? Explain.

PROBLEM 11–19 Preparing an Overhead Performance Report [LO2]

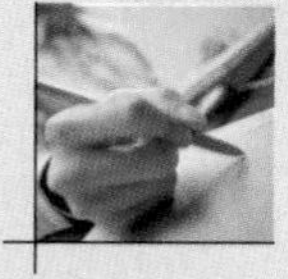

Several years ago, Westmont Company developed a comprehensive budgeting system for profit planning and control purposes. The line supervisors have been very happy with the system and with the reports being prepared on their performance, but both middle and upper management have expressed considerable dissatisfaction with the information being generated by the system. A typical manufacturing overhead performance report for a recent period follows:

WESTMONT COMPANY
Overhead Performance Report—Assembly Department
For the Quarter Ended March 31

	Actual	Budget	Variance
Machine-hours	35,000	40,000	
Variable overhead costs:			
Indirect materials	$ 29,700	$ 32,000	$2,300 F
Rework	7,900	8,000	100 F
Utilities	51,800	56,000	4,200 F
Machine setup	11,600	12,000	400 F
Total variable overhead cost	101,000	108,000	7,000 F

continued

Fixed overhead costs:			
Maintenance	79,200	80,000	800 F
Inspection	60,000	60,000	0
Total fixed overhead cost	139,200	140,000	800 F
Total overhead cost	$240,200	$248,000	$7,800 F

After receiving a copy of this overhead performance report, the supervisor of the Assembly Department stated, "These reports are super. It makes me feel really good to see how well things are going in my department. I can't understand why those people upstairs complain so much."

The budget data above are for the original planned level of activity for the quarter.

Required:

1. The company's vice president is uneasy about the performance reports being prepared and would like you to evaluate their usefulness to the company.
2. What changes, if any, should be made in the overhead performance report to give better insight into how well the supervisor is controlling costs?
3. Prepare a new overhead performance report for the quarter, incorporating any changes you suggested in (2) above. (Include both the variable and the fixed costs in your report.)

PROBLEM 11–20 Applying Overhead; Overhead Variances [LO3, LO4, LO5]

Chilczuk, S.A., of Gdansk, Poland, is a major producer of classic Polish sausage. The company uses a standard cost system to help control costs. Manufacturing overhead is applied to production on the basis of standard direct labour-hours. According to the company's flexible budget, the following manufacturing overhead costs should be incurred at an activity level of 35,000 labour-hours (the denominator activity level):

Variable manufacturing overhead costs	PZ 87,500
Fixed manufacturing overhead costs	210,000
Total manufacturing overhead cost	PZ 297,500

The currency in Poland is the zloty, which is denoted here by PZ.

During the most recent year, the following operating results were recorded:

Activity:	
Actual labour-hours worked	30,000
Standard labour-hours allowed for output	32,000
Cost:	
Actual variable manufacturing overhead cost incurred	PZ 78,000
Actual fixed manufacturing overhead cost incurred	PZ 209,400

At the end of the year, the company's Manufacturing Overhead account contained the following data:

Manufacturing Overhead

Actual	287,400	Applied	272,000
	15,400		

Management would like to determine the cause of the PZ 15,400 underapplied overhead.

Required:

1. Compute the predetermined overhead rate. Break the rate down into variable and fixed cost elements.
2. Show how the PZ 272,000 Applied figure in the Manufacturing Overhead account was computed.

3. Analyze the PZ15,400 underapplied overhead figure in terms of the variable overhead spending and efficiency variances and the fixed overhead budget and volume variances.
4. Explain the meaning of each variance that you computed in (3) above.

PROBLEM 11–21 Flexible Budget and Overhead Analysis [LO1, LO2, LO3, LO4, LO5, LO6]

Harper Company assembles all of its products in the Assembly Department. Budgeted costs for the operation of this department for the year have been set as follows:

Variable costs:	
Direct materials	$ 900,000
Direct labour	675,000
Utilities	45,000
Indirect labour	67,500
Supplies	22,500
Total variable cost	1,710,000
Fixed costs:	
Insurance	8,000
Supervisory salaries	90,000
Depreciation	160,000
Equipment rental	42,000
Total fixed cost	300,000
Total budgeted cost	$2,010,000
Budgeted direct labour-hours	75,000

Since the assembly work is done mostly by hand, operating activity in this department is best measured by direct labour-hours. The cost formulas used to develop the budgeted costs above are valid over a relevant range of 60,000 to 90,000 direct labour-hours per year.

Required:

1. Prepare a manufacturing overhead flexible budget for the Assembly Department using increments of 15,000 direct labour-hours. (The company does not include direct materials and direct labour costs in the flexible budget.)
2. Assume that the company computes predetermined overhead rates by department. Compute the rates that will be used to apply Assembly Department overhead costs to production. Break this rate down into variable and fixed cost elements.
3. Suppose that during the year the following actual activity and costs are recorded by the Assembly Department:

Actual direct labour-hours worked	73,000
Standard direct labour-hours allowed for the output of the year	70,000
Actual variable manufacturing overhead cost incurred	$124,100
Actual fixed manufacturing overhead cost incurred	$301,600

Complete the following:

a. A T-account for manufacturing overhead costs in the Assembly Department for the year is given below. Determine the amount of applied overhead cost for the year, and compute the under- or overapplied overhead.

Manufacturing Overhead

Actual cost	425,700	

b. Analyze the under- or overapplied overhead in terms of the variable overhead spending and efficiency variances and the fixed overhead budget and volume variances.

PROBLEM 11–22 Evaluating an Overhead Performance Report [LO2, LO3]

Frank Western, supervisor of the Machining Department for Freemont Company, was visibly upset after being reprimanded for his department's poor performance over the prior month. The department's performance report is given below:

FREEMONT COMPANY
Performance Report—Machining Department

	Cost Formula (per machine-hour)	Actual	Budget	Variance
Machine-hours		38,000	35,000	
Variable overhead costs:				
Utilities	$0.40	$ 15,700	$ 14,000	$ 1,700 U
Indirect labour	2.30	86,500	80,500	6,000 U
Supplies	0.60	26,000	21,000	5,000 U
Maintenance	1.20	44,900	42,000	2,900 U
Total variable overhead cost	$4.50	173,100	157,500	15,600 U
Fixed overhead costs:				
Supervision		38,000	38,000	0
Maintenance		92,400	92,000	400 U
Depreciation		80,000	80,000	0
Total fixed overhead cost		210,400	210,000	400 U
Total overhead cost		$383,500	$367,500	$16,000 U

"I just can't understand all the red ink," said Western to Sarah Mason, supervisor of another department. "When the boss called me in, I thought he was going to give me a pat on the back because I know for a fact that my department worked more efficiently last month than it has ever worked before. Instead, he tore me apart. I thought for a minute that it might be over the supplies that were stolen out of our warehouse last month. But they only amounted to a couple of thousand dollars, and just look at this report. *Everything* is unfavourable."

The budget for the Machining Department had called for production of 14,000 units last month, which is equal to a budgeted activity level of 35,000 machine-hours (at a standard time of 2.5 machine-hours per unit). Actual production in the Machining Department for the month was 16,000 units.

Required:

1. Evaluate the overhead performance report given above and explain why the variances are all unfavourable.
2. Prepare a new overhead performance report that will help Mr. Western's superiors assess efficiency and cost control in the Machining Department. (Hint: Exhibit 11–7 may be helpful in structuring your report; however, the report you prepare should include both variable and fixed costs.)
3. Would the supplies stolen out of the warehouse be included as part of the variable overhead spending variance or as part of the variable overhead efficiency variance for the month? Explain.

PROBLEM 11–23 Variable Overhead Performance Report [LO2, LO3]

The cost formulas for variable overhead costs in a machine shop are given at the top of page 517.

During August, the machine shop was scheduled to work 11,250 machine-hours and to produce 4,500 units of product. The standard machine time per unit of product is 2.5 hours. A strike near the end of the month forced a cutback in production. Actual results for the month were:

Actual machine-hours worked	9,250
Actual number of units produced	3,600

Variable Overhead Cost	Cost Formula (per machine-hour)
Power	$0.30
Setup time	0.20
Polishing wheels	0.16
Maintenance	0.18
Total variable overhead cost	$0.84

Actual costs for the month were:

Variable Overhead Cost	Total Actual Costs	Per Machine-Hour
Power	$2,405	$0.26
Setup time	2,035	0.22
Polishing wheels	1,110	0.12
Maintenance	925	0.10
Total variable overhead cost	$6,475	$0.70

Required:
Prepare an overhead performance report for the machine shop for August. Use column headings in your report as shown below:

					Breakdown of the Total Variance		
Overhead Item	Cost Formula (per machine-hour)	Actual Costs Incurred 9,250 Machine-Hours	Budget Based on ? Machine-Hours	Budget Based on ? Machine-Hours	Total Variance	Spending Variance	Efficiency Variance

PROBLEM 11–24 Standard Cost Card; Fixed Overhead Analysis; Graphing [LO4, LO5, LO6]

When planning operations for the year, Southbrook Company chose a denominator activity of 40,000 direct labour-hours. According to the company's flexible budget, the following manufacturing overhead costs should be incurred at this activity level:

Variable manufacturing overhead costs	$72,000
Fixed manufacturing overhead costs	$360,000

The company produces a single product that requires 2.5 hours to complete. The direct labour rate is $12 per hour. Eight metres of material are needed to complete one unit of product; the material has a standard cost of $4.50 per metre. Overhead is applied to production on the basis of standard direct labour-hours.

Required:

1. Compute the predetermined overhead rate. Break the rate down into variable and fixed cost elements.
2. Prepare a standard cost card for one unit of product using the following format:

Direct materials, 8 metres at $4.50 per metre	$36
Direct labour, ?	?
Variable manufacturing overhead, ?	?
Fixed manufacturing overhead ?	?
Standard cost per unit	$?

3. Prepare a graph with cost on the vertical (Y) axis and direct labour-hours on the horizontal (X) axis. Plot a line on your graph from a zero level of activity to 60,000 direct labour-hours for each of the following costs:
   a. Budgeted fixed overhead (in total).
   b. Applied fixed overhead [applied at the hourly rate computed in (1) above].
4. Assume that during the year actual activity is as follows:

Number of units produced	14,000
Actual direct labour-hours worked	33,000
Actual fixed manufacturing overhead cost incurred	$361,800

   a. Compute the fixed overhead budget and volume variances for the year.
   b. Show the volume variance on the graph you prepared in (3) above.
5. Disregard the data in (4) above. Assume instead that actual activity during the year is as follows:

Number of units produced	20,000
Actual direct labour-hours worked	52,000
Actual fixed manufacturing overhead costs incurred	$361,800

   a. Compute the fixed overhead budget and volume variances for the year.
   b. Show the volume variance on the graph you prepared in (3) above.

PROBLEM 11–25 Comprehensive Problem; Flexible Budget; Overhead Performance Report [LO1, LO2, LO3]

Gant Products, Inc., has recently introduced budgeting as an integral part of its corporate planning process. The company's first effort at constructing a flexible budget for manufacturing overhead is shown below:

Percentage of capacity	80%	100%
Machine-hours	4,800	6,000
Maintenance	$1,480	$ 1,600
Supplies	1,920	2,400
Utilities	1,940	2,300
Supervision	3,000	3,000
Machine setup	960	1,200
Total manufacturing overhead cost	$9,300	$10,500

The budgets above are relevant over a range of 80% to 100% of capacity. The managers who will be working under these budgets have control over both fixed and variable costs. The company applies manufacturing overhead to products on the basis of standard machine-hours.

Required:

1. Redo the company's flexible budget, presenting it in better format. Show the budget at 80%, 90%, and 100% levels of capacity. (Use the high-low method to separate fixed and variable costs.)
2. Express the flexible budget prepared in (1) above using a single cost formula for all overhead costs.
3. The company operated at 95% of machine-hour capacity during April. Five thousand six hundred standard machine-hours were allowed for the output of the month. Actual overhead costs incurred were:

Maintenance	$ 2,083
Supplies	3,420
Utilities	2,666
Supervision	3,000
Machine setup	855
Total overhead cost	$12,024

The fixed costs had no budget variances. Prepare an overhead performance report for April. Structure your report so that it shows only a spending variance for overhead. You may assume that the master budget for April called for an activity level during the month of 6,000 machine-hours.

4. Upon receiving the performance report you have prepared, the production manager commented, "I have two observations to make. First, I think there's an error on your report. You show an unfavourable spending variance for supplies, yet I know that we paid exactly the budgeted price for all the supplies we used last month. Pat Stevens, the purchasing agent, made a comment to me that our supplies prices haven't changed in over a year. Second, I wish you would modify your report to include an efficiency variance for overhead. The reason is that waste has been a problem in the factory for years and the efficiency variance would help us get overhead waste under control."
   a. Explain the probable cause of the unfavourable spending variance for supplies.
   b. Compute an efficiency variance for *total* variable overhead and explain to the production manager why it would or would not contain elements of overhead waste.

PROBLEM 11–26 Applying Overhead; Overhead Variances [LO3, LO4, LO5, LO6]

Lane Company manufactures a single product that requires a great deal of hand labour. Overhead cost is applied on the basis of standard direct labour-hours. The company's condensed flexible budget for manufacturing overhead is given below:

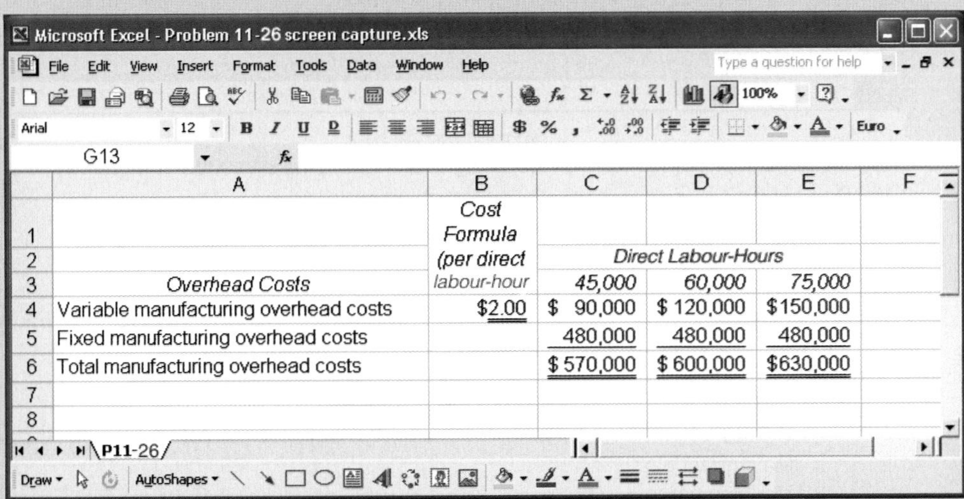

Microsoft Excel - Problem 11-26 screen capture.xls

	A	B	C	D	E
1		Cost Formula			
2		(per direct	Direct Labour-Hours		
3	Overhead Costs	labour-hour	45,000	60,000	75,000
4	Variable manufacturing overhead costs	$2.00	$ 90,000	$ 120,000	$150,000
5	Fixed manufacturing overhead costs		480,000	480,000	480,000
6	Total manufacturing overhead costs		$ 570,000	$ 600,000	$630,000

The company's product requires 3 kilograms of material that has a standard cost of $7 per kilogram and 1.5 hours of direct labour time that has a standard rate of $12 per hour.

The company planned to operate at a denominator activity level of 60,000 direct labour-hours and to produce 40,000 units of product during the most recent year. Actual activity and costs for the year were as follows:

Number of units produced	42,000
Actual direct labour-hours worked	65,000
Actual variable manufacturing overhead cost incurred	$123,500
Actual fixed manufacturing overhead cost incurred	$483,000

Required:

1. Compute the predetermined overhead rate for the year. Break the rate down into variable and fixed elements.
2. Prepare a standard cost card for the company's product; show the details for all manufacturing costs on your standard cost card.
3. Do the following:
   a. Compute the standard direct labour-hours allowed for the year's production.
   b. Complete the following Manufacturing Overhead T-account for the year:

Manufacturing Overhead

?	?
?	?

4. Determine the reason for any under- or overapplied overhead for the year by computing the variable overhead spending and efficiency variances and the fixed overhead budget and volume variances.
5. Suppose the company had chosen 65,000 direct labour-hours as the denominator activity rather than 60,000 hours. State which, if any, of the variances computed in (4) above would have changed, and explain how the variance(s) would have changed. No computations are necessary.

PROBLEM 11–27 Flexible Budget and Overhead Performance Report [LO1, LO2, LO3]
You have just been hired by FAB Company, the manufacturer of a revolutionary new garage door opening device. John Foster, the president, has asked that you review the company's costing system and "do what you can to help us get better control of our manufacturing overhead costs." You find that the company has never used a flexible budget, and you suggest that preparing such a budget would be an excellent first step in overhead planning and control.

After much effort and analysis, you are able to determine the following cost formulas for the company's normal operating range of 20,000 to 30,000 machine-hours each month:

Overhead Costs	Cost Formula
Utilities	$0.90 per machine-hour
Maintenance	$1.60 per machine-hour plus $40,000 per month
Machine setup	$0.30 per machine-hour
Indirect labour	$0.70 per machine-hour plus $130,000 per month
Depreciation	$70,000 per month

To show the president how the flexible budget concept works, you have gathered the following actual manufacturing overhead cost data for the most recent month, March, in which the company worked 26,000 machine-hours and produced 15,000 units:

Utilities	$ 24,200
Maintenance	78,100
Machine setup	8,400
Indirect labour	149,600
Depreciation	71,500
Total manufacturing overhead cost	$331,800

The only variance in the fixed costs for the month was with depreciation, which increased as a result of purchasing new equipment.

The company had originally planned to work 30,000 machine-hours during March.

Required:
1. Prepare a flexible budget for the company in increments of 5,000 hours.
2. Prepare an overhead performance report for the company for March. (Use the format illustrated in Exhibit 11–11.)
3. What additional information would you need to compute an overhead efficiency variance for the company?

PROBLEM 11–28 Selection of a Denominator; Overhead Analysis; Standard Cost Card [LO3, LO4, LO5, LO6]
Morton Company's condensed flexible budget for manufacturing overhead is given at the top of the next page.

The company manufactures a single product that requires two direct labour-hours to complete. The direct labour wage rate is $15 per hour. Four metres of raw material are required for each unit of product; the standard cost of the material is $8.75 per metre.

Although normal activity is 30,000 direct labour-hours each year, the company expects to operate at a 40,000-hour level of activity this year.

Overhead Costs	Cost Formula (per direct labour-hour)	Direct Labour-Hours		
		20,000	30,000	40,000
Variable manufacturing overhead costs	$4.50	$ 90,000	$135,000	$180,000
Fixed manufacturing overhead costs		270,000	270,000	270,000
Total manufacturing overhead cost		$360,000	$405,000	$450,000

Required:

1. Assume that the company chooses 30,000 direct labour-hours as the denominator level of activity. Compute the predetermined overhead rate, breaking it down into variable and fixed cost elements.
2. Assume that the company chooses 40,000 direct labour-hours as the denominator level of activity. Repeat the computations in (1) above.
3. Complete two standard cost cards as outlined below.

Denominator Activity: 30,000 Direct Labour-Hours

Direct materials, 4 metres at $8.75 per metre	$35.00
Direct labour ?	?
Variable overhead ?	?
Fixed overhead ?	?
Standard cost per unit	$?

Denominator Activity: 40,000 Direct Labour-Hours

Direct materials, 4 metres at $8.75 per metre	$35.00
Direct labour ?	?
Variable overhead ?	?
Fixed overhead ?	?
Standard cost per unit	$?

4. Assume that the company actually produces 18,000 units and works 38,000 direct labour-hours during the year. Actual manufacturing overhead costs for the year are:

Variable manufacturing overhead costs	$174,800
Fixed manufacturing overhead costs	271,600
Total manufacturing overhead cost	$446,400

Do the following:

a. Compute the standard direct labour-hours allowed for this year's production.

b. Complete the Manufacturing Overhead account below. Assume that the company uses 30,000 direct labour-hours (normal activity) as the denominator activity figure in computing predetermined overhead rates, as you have done in (1) above.

Manufacturing Overhead

Actual costs	446,400	?
?		?

c. Determine the cause of the under- or overapplied overhead for the year by computing the variable overhead spending and efficiency variances and the fixed overhead budget and volume variances.

5. Looking at the variances you have computed, what appears to be the major disadvantage of using normal activity rather than expected actual activity as a denominator in computing the predetermined overhead rate? What advantages can you see to offset this disadvantage?

PROBLEM 11–29 Activity-Based Costing and the Flexible Budget Approach [LO2]

The Little Theatre is a non-profit organization devoted to staging plays for children in Manchester, England. The theatre has a very small full-time professional administrative staff. Through a special arrangement with the actors' union, actors and directors rehearse without pay and are paid only for actual performances.

The costs of 2004's operations appear below. (The currency in England is the pound, denoted £.) During 2004, The Little Theatre had six different productions—each of which was performed 18 times. For example, one of the productions was Peter the Rabbit, which had the usual six-week run with three performances on each weekend.

THE LITTLE THEATRE
Cost Report
For the Year Ended 31 December 2004

Number of productions	6
Number of performances of each production	18
Total number of performances	108
Actual costs incurred:	
Actors' and directors' wages	£216,000
Stagehands' wages	32,400
Ticket booth personnel and ushers' wages	16,200
Scenery, costumes, and props	108,000
Theatre hall rent	54,000
Printed programs	27,000
Publicity	12,000
Administrative expenses	43,200
Total actual cost incurred	£508,800

Some of the costs vary with the number of productions, some with the number of performances, and some are relatively fixed and depend on neither the number of productions nor the number of performances. The costs of scenery, costumes, props, and publicity vary with the number of productions. It doesn't make any difference how many times Peter the Rabbit is performed, the cost of the scenery is the same. Likewise, the cost of publicizing a play with posters and radio commercials is the same whether there are 10, 20, or 30 performances of the play. On the other hand, the wages of the actors, directors, stagehands, ticket booth personnel, and ushers vary with the number of performances. The greater the number of performances, the higher the wage costs will be. Similarly, the costs of renting the hall and printing the programs will vary with the number of performances. Administrative expenses are more difficult to pin down, but the best estimate is that approximately 75% of these costs are fixed, 15% depend on the number of productions staged, and the remaining 10% depend on the number of performances.

At the end of 2004, the board of directors of the theatre authorized expanding the theatre's program in 2005 to seven productions, with 24 performances each. Not surprisingly, actual costs for 2005 were considerably higher than the costs for 2004. (Grants from donors and ticket sales were also correspondingly higher.) Data concerning 2005's operations appear at the top of page 523.

Even though many of the costs above may be considered direct costs rather than overhead, the flexible budget approach covered in the chapter can still be used to evaluate how well these costs are controlled. The principles are the same whether a cost is a direct cost or is overhead.

Required:

1. Use the actual results from 2004 to estimate the cost formulas for the flexible budget for The Little Theatre. Keep in mind that the theatre has two measures of activity—the number of productions and the number of performances.
2. Prepare a performance report for 2005 using the flexible budget approach and both measures of activity. Assume there was no inflation. (Note: To evaluate administrative expenses, first determine the flexible budget amounts for the three elements of administrative expenses. Then compare the total of the three elements to the actual administrative expense of £47,500.)

3. If you were on the board of directors of the theatre, would you be pleased with how well costs were controlled during 2005? Why or why not?
4. The cost formulas provide figures for the average cost per production and average cost per performance. How accurate do you think these figures would be for predicting the cost of a new production or of an additional performance of a particular production?

THE LITTLE THEATRE
Cost Report
For the Year Ended 31 December 2005

Number of productions	7
Number of performances of each production	24
Total number of performances	168
Actual costs incurred:	
Actors' and directors' wages	£341,800
Stagehands' wages	49,700
Ticket booth personnel and ushers' wages	25,900
Scenery, costumes, and props	130,600
Theatre hall rent	78,000
Printed programs	38,300
Publicity	15,100
Administrative expenses	47,500
Total actual cost incurred	£726,900

PROBLEM 11-30 Standard Cost Variances [LO3, LO4, LO5, LO6]

The Gaby Co. is a manufacturing company which has established the following standard cost per unit:

Materials	5 pieces at $4.00 =	$20.00
Direct Labour	2 hours at $8.00 =	16.00
Variable Overhead	2 hours at $3.00 =	6.00
Fixed Overhead	2 hours at $5.00 =	10.00
		$52.00

Normal activity of 60,000 hours was used as the denominator. Other possible denominators were:

Expected annual activity	55,000 hours
Practical capacity	75,000 hours

Actual activity during 2005 included the following:

Beginning inventory	0
Units produced	28,000
Materials used	$570,000
Direct Labour	$450,000
Variable Overhead	$170,000
Fixed overhead	$305,000
Ending inventory	7,000 units

Required:

Compute the cost of goods sold under each of the following sets of alternatives:

1. Absorption costing.
   Actual materials and labour and predetermined overhead.
   Normal activity used as denominator.
2. Direct costing.
   Standard costs.
3. Absorption costing.
   Standard costs.
   Practical activity used as denominator.

(CGAC, Adapted)

CASES

CASE 11–31 Ethics and the Manager [LO2]

Tom Kemper is the controller of the Winnipeg manufacturing facility of Prudhom Enterprises, Incorporated. Among the many reports that must be filed with corporate headquarters is the annual overhead performance report. The report covers the year ended December 31, and is due at corporate headquarters shortly after the beginning of the New Year. Kemper does not like putting work off to the last minute, so just before Christmas he put together a preliminary draft of the overhead performance report. Some adjustments would later be required for transactions that occur between Christmas and New Year's Day, but there are generally very few of these. A copy of the preliminary draft report, which Kemper completed on December 21, follows:

WINNIPEG MANUFACTURING FACILITY
Overhead Performance Report
December 21 Preliminary Draft

Budgeted machine-hours	200,000			
Actual machine-hours	180,000			
Overhead Costs	Cost Formula (per machine-hour)	Actual Costs 180,000 Machine-Hours	Budget Based on 180,000 Machine-Hours	Spending or Budget Variance
Variable overhead costs:				
Power	$0.10	$ 19,750	$ 18,000	$ 1,750 U
Supplies	0.25	47,000	45,000	2,000 U
Abrasives	0.30	58,000	54,000	4,000 U
Total variable overhead cost	$0.65	124,750	117,000	7,750 U
Fixed overhead costs:				
Depreciation		345,000	332,000	13,000 U
Supervisory salaries		273,000	275,000	2,000 F
Insurance		37,000	37,000	0
Industrial engineering		189,000	210,000	21,000 F
Factory building lease		60,000	60,000	0
Total fixed overhead cost		904,000	914,000	10,000 F
Total overhead cost		$1,028,750	$1,031,000	$ 2,250 F

Melissa Ilianovitch, the general manager at the Winnipeg facility, asked to see a copy of the preliminary draft report at 4:45 P.M. on December 23. Kemper carried a copy of the report to her office where the following discussion took place:

Ilianovitch: Ouch! Almost all of the variances on the report are unfavourable. The only thing that looks good at all are the favourable variances for supervisory salaries and for industrial engineering. How did we have an unfavourable variance for depreciation?

Kemper: Do you remember that milling machine that broke down because the wrong lubricant was used by the machine operator?

Ilianovitch: Only vaguely.

Kemper: It turned out we couldn't fix it. We had to scrap the machine and buy a new one.

Ilianovitch: This report doesn't look good. I was criticized last year when we had just a few unfavourable variances.

Kemper: I'm afraid the final report is going to look even worse.

Ilianovitch: Oh?

Kemper: The line item for industrial engineering on the report is for work we hired Ferguson Engineering to do for us on a contract basis. The original contract was for $210,000, but we asked them to do some additional work that was not in the contract. Under the terms of the contract, we have to reimburse Ferguson Engineering for the costs of the additional work. The

$189,000 in actual costs that appear on the preliminary draft report reflects only their billings up through December 21. The last bill they had sent us was on November 28, and they completed the project just last week. Yesterday I got a call from Laura Sunder over at Ferguson and she said they would be sending us a final bill for the project before the end of the year. The total bill, including the reimbursements for the additional work, is going to be . . .

Ilianovitch: I am not sure I want to hear this.

Kemper: $225,000

Ilianovitch: Ouch! Ouch! Ouch!

Kemper: The additional work we asked them to do added $15,000 to the cost of the project.

Ilianovitch: No way can I turn in a performance report with an overall unfavourable variance. They'll kill me at corporate headquarters. Call up Laura at Ferguson and ask her not to send the bill until after the first of the year. We have to have that $21,000 favourable variance for industrial engineering on the performance report.

Required:

What should Tom Kemper do? Explain.

CASE 11–32 Preparing a Performance Report Using Activity-Based Costing [LO2]

Can Del Courier Inc. offers an extensive delivery service in many areas throughout the province. For the convenience of its employees and administrative staff and to save costs, the company employs a supervisor to operate a motor pool. The motor pool operated with 20 vehicles until February, when an additional automobile was acquired. The motor pool furnishes gasoline, oil, and other supplies for its automobiles. A mechanic does routine maintenance and minor repairs. Major repairs are done at a nearby commercial garage.

Each year, the supervisor prepares an operating budget that informs the company administration of the funds needed for operating the motor pool. Depreciation (straight line) on the automobiles is recorded in the budget in order to determine the cost per kilometre of operating the vehicles.

The following schedule presents the operating budget for the current year, which has been approved by the company. The schedule also shows actual operating costs for March of the current year compared to one-twelfth of the annual operating budget.

CAN DEL COURIER INC.
Budget Report for March

	Annual Operating Budget	Monthly Budget*	March Actual	(Over) Under Budget
Gasoline	$ 78,750	$ 6,500	$ 9,040	$(2,540)
Oil, minor repairs, parts	4,000	333	380	(47)
Outside repairs	2,700	225	50	175
Insurance	6,000	500	525	(25)
Salaries and benefits	30,000	2,500	2,500	0
Depreciation of vehicles	26,400	2,200	2,310	(110)
Total cost	$147,850	$12,258	$14,805	$(2,547)
Total kilometres	1,000,000	84,000	105,000	
Cost per kilometre	$ 0.1485	$0.1459	$0.141	
Number of automobiles in use	20	20	21	

*Annual operating budget ÷ 12 months.

The annual operating budget was constructed on the following assumptions:

a. Twenty automobiles in the motor pool.
b. 50,000 thousand kilometres driven per year per automobile.
c. 10.5 litres per 100 kilometres per automobile.
d. $0.73 per litre of gasoline.
e. $0.004 cost per kilometre for oil, minor repairs, and parts.
f. $135 cost per automobile per year for outside repairs.
g. $300 cost per automobile per year for insurance.

The supervisor of the motor pool is unhappy with the monthly report comparing budget and actual costs for March, claiming it presents an unfair picture of performance. A previous employer used flexible budgeting to compare actual costs to budgeted amounts.

Required:

1. Prepare a new performance report for March showing budgeted costs, actual costs, and variances. In preparing your report, use flexible budgeting techniques to compute the monthly budget figures.
2. What are the deficiencies in the performance report presented above? How does the report that you prepared in (1) above overcome these deficiencies?

(CMA, adapted)

CASE 11–33 Working Backwards from Variance Data [LO3, LO4, LO5]

You have recently graduated from University and have accepted a position with Vitex, Inc., the manufacturer of a popular consumer product. During your first week on the job, the vice president has been favourably impressed with your work. She has been so impressed, in fact, that yesterday she called you into her office and asked you to attend the executive committee meeting this morning for the purpose of leading a discussion on the variances reported for last period. Anxious to favourably impress the executive committee, you took the variances and supporting data home last night to study.

On your way to work this morning, the papers were laying on the seat of your new, red convertible. As you were crossing a bridge on the highway, a sudden gust of wind caught the papers and blew them over the edge of the bridge and into the stream below. You managed to retrieve only one page, which contains the following information:

STANDARD COST CARD

Direct materials, 6 kilograms at $3 per kilogram	$18.00
Direct labour, 0.8 direct labour-hours at $15 per direct labour-hour	12.00
Variable manufacturing overhead, 0.8 direct labour-hours at $3 per direct labour-hour	2.40
Fixed manufacturing overhead, 0.8 direct labour-hours at $7 per direct labour-hour	5.60
Standard cost per unit	$38.00

	Total Standard Cost*	Variances Reported			
		Price or Rate	Spending or Budget	Quantity or Efficiency	Volume
Direct materials	$405,000	$6,900 F		$9,000 U	
Direct labour	$270,000	$14,550 U		$21,000 U	
Variable manufacturing overhead	$54,000		$1,300 F	$?[†] U	
Fixed manufacturing overhead	$126,000		$500 F		$14,000 U

*Applied to Work in Process during the period.
[†]Entry obliterated.

You recall that manufacturing overhead cost is applied to production on the basis of direct labour-hours and that all of the materials purchased during the period were used in production. Since the company uses JIT to control work flows, work in process inventories are insignificant and can be ignored.

It is now 8:30 A.M. The executive committee meeting starts in just one hour; you realize that to avoid looking like a bungling fool you must somehow generate the necessary "backup" data for the variances before the meeting begins. Without backup data it will be impossible to lead the discussion or answer any questions.

Required:

1. How many units were produced last period? (Think hard about this one!)
2. How many kilograms of direct material were purchased and used in production?
3. What was the actual cost per kilo of material?
4. How many actual direct labour-hours were worked during the period?
5. What was the actual rate paid per direct labour-hour?
6. How much actual variable manufacturing overhead cost was incurred during the period?
7. What is the total fixed manufacturing overhead cost in the company's flexible budget?
8. What were the denominator direct labour-hours for last period?

CASE 11–34 Comprehensive Variance Analysis; Incomplete Data [LO3, LO4, LO5]

Each of the cases below is independent. Each company uses a standard cost system and each company's flexible budget for manufacturing overhead is based on standard machine-hours.

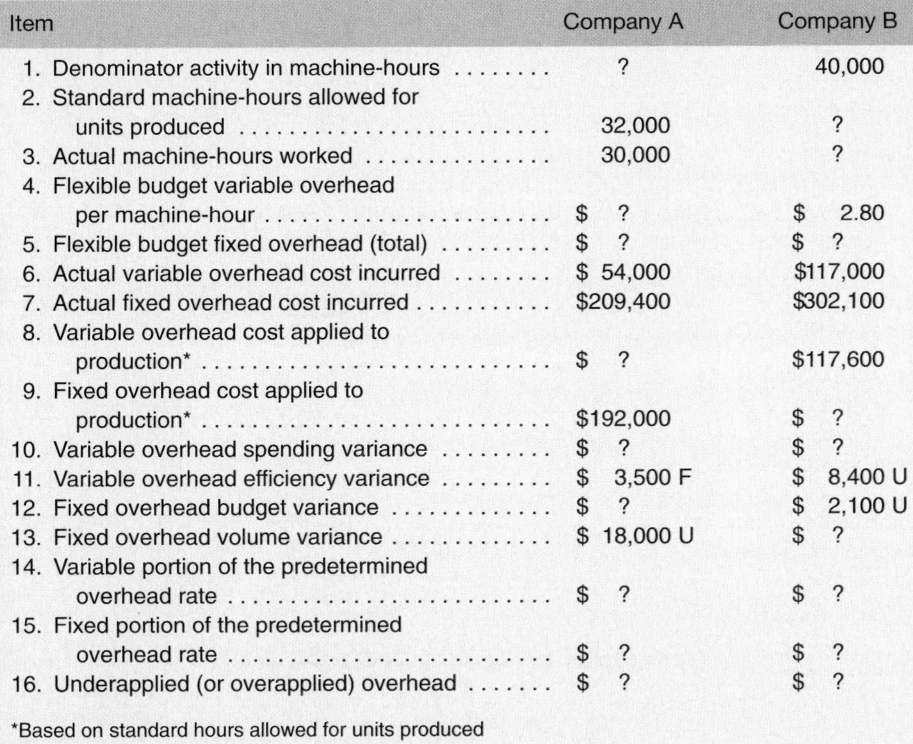

Item	Company A	Company B
1. Denominator activity in machine-hours	?	40,000
2. Standard machine-hours allowed for units produced	32,000	?
3. Actual machine-hours worked	30,000	?
4. Flexible budget variable overhead per machine-hour	$?	$ 2.80
5. Flexible budget fixed overhead (total)	$?	$?
6. Actual variable overhead cost incurred	$ 54,000	$117,000
7. Actual fixed overhead cost incurred	$209,400	$302,100
8. Variable overhead cost applied to production*	$?	$117,600
9. Fixed overhead cost applied to production*	$192,000	$?
10. Variable overhead spending variance	$?	$?
11. Variable overhead efficiency variance	$ 3,500 F	$ 8,400 U
12. Fixed overhead budget variance	$?	$ 2,100 U
13. Fixed overhead volume variance	$ 18,000 U	$?
14. Variable portion of the predetermined overhead rate	$?	$?
15. Fixed portion of the predetermined overhead rate	$?	$?
16. Underapplied (or overapplied) overhead	$?	$?

*Based on standard hours allowed for units produced

Required:

Compute the unknown amounts. (Hint: One way to proceed would be to use the format for variance analysis found in Exhibit 10–7 for variable overhead and in Exhibit 11–10 for fixed overhead.)

CASE 11-35 Full Variance Analysis: Direct Costing [LO3, LO4, LO5, LO6]

Ottawa Tech Limited manufactures and distributes intergrated circuits for electronics firms. In December 2003, Ottawa required a bank loan and the bank manager insisted that Christy Dasilva, Ottawa's president, prepare a budget for 2004. In January 2005 Ottawa needed an additional loan and Dasilva asked her accountant to prepare a budget for 2005 to show the bank manager. Dasilva was concerned because Ottawa's profit for 2004 was considerably less than the 2004 budget figure given the bank and she knew that the bank manager would want to know why. As a first step in analyzing the differences, Dasilva copied the 2004 actual figures onto a 2004 bank budget form shown at the top of the next page.

Required:

1. Redraft the budget to show the 2004 budget, flexible budget, actual, and variances from the flexible budget, with contribution margins separately identified.
2. Present quantitive analysis to demonstrate to management the main causes for the variance from the flexible budget, as a basis both for taking corrective action and for explaining the variance from the budget to the bank manager.
3. If anticipated 2005 operating results are similar to 2004, explain to the bank manager how much of the loan you would be able to repay from 2005 earnings. (Assume no changes in accounts receivable and accounts payable.)
4. If completion became intense in 2005, and Ottawa was operating well below capacity at 85,000 units, explain with calculation the minimum bid you would make on an order for 10,000 units.
5. What changes to the management accounting and reporting system for Ottawa Tech would you propose?

(CGAC, Adapted)

Ottawa Tech Limted
2004 Budget Prepared for Bank Loan

	Dollars in (000s)		
	Budget	Actual	Variance
Sales—units	110,000	105,000	5,000 U
Sales—dollars	$2,750	$2,520	$230 U
Cost of sales:			
Materials	440	421	19 F
Labour	880	845	35 F
Overhead	220	205	15 F
Fixed factory overhead	300	303	3 U
	1,840	1,774	66 F
Gross profit	910	746	164 U
Selling expenses:			
Variable	220	209	11 F
Fixed	100	102	2 U
Administration—fixed	200	197	3 F
	520	508	12 F
Profit before income tax	390	238	152 U
Income tax	156	95	61 F
Net earnings	$ 234	$ 143	$ 91 U

Standard Costs on Which Budget is Based

		Standard per Unit
Sales price		$25
Direct Material		$ 4
Labour 1/2 hour at $16 per hour		8
Overhead 1/2 hour at $4 per hour		2
Fixed factory overhead:		
Depreciation	$200,000	
Other	100,000	
	300,000	
Standard output 100,000 units at 1/2 hour = 50,000 direct labour hours ($300,000 ÷ 50,000) × 1/2 hour		3
Selling expenses:		
Variable		2
Fixed $100,000 ÷ 100,000 units		1
Administration Fixed:		
$200,000 ÷ 100,000 units		2
		$22

Standard costs were used for preparing bids whereas the cost accounting system recorded actual costs.

CASE 11-36 Absorption Costing Variance Report [LO1, LO2, LO3, LO6]
The data at the top of page 529 relates to Truro Company for 2005.

Required:

1. Prepare an absorption costing variance analysis report showing both activity and other spending, efficiency, and price variances.
2. Prepare a variable costing variance analysis report showing both activity and other spending, efficiency, and price variances.

	Master Budget	Actual
Sales volume	100,000 units	120,000 units
Selling price	$18 per unit	$17.50 per unit
Production volume	90,000 units	110,000 units
Direct materials:		
Quantity	1.0 kilogram per unit	1.1 kilogram per unit
Price	$2.00 per kilogram	$1.90 kilogram per unit
Direct labour:		
Time	0.5 hour per unit	0.4 hours per unit
Rate	$6.00 per hour	$6.20 per hour
Variable overhead	$1.50 per direct labour-hour	$1.60 per direct labour-hour
Fixed overhead	$45,000 (therefore standard cost rate = $1.00 per direct labour-hour)	$42,000
Work in process inventory:		
Beginning	10,000 equivalent units	10,000 equivalent units
Ending	5,000 equivalent units	5,000 equivalent units
Finished goods inventory:		
Beginning	8,000 units	8,000 units
Ending.	3,000 units	3,000 units
Selling and administration expenses:		
Variable.	$3.00 per unit sold	$2.80 per unit sold
Fixed.	$140,000	$150,000

GROUP AND INTERNET EXERCISES

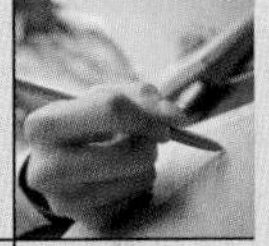

GROUP EXERCISE 11–37 Choice of Denominator Activity Level

American Widget, Inc., makes a number of high-volume standard products that are sold in highly competitive markets. As a result, its cost system stresses cost control. American uses a standard cost system and updates standards on a regular and timely basis. Until recently, expected annual capacity was the basis for determining predetermined factory overhead rates. This rate was used for internal planning and reporting and performance evaluation purposes, as well as for inventory valuation.

John Phillips, controller, has proposed changing the basis for internal planning and reporting from expected annual capacity to practical capacity. Since practical capacity remains relatively constant unless there is a plant expansion or purchase of new manufacturing machinery, Phillips believes this change would facilitate planning and budgeting.

Phillips has held one meeting with department managers and presented them with their new annual budgets prepared on the basis of the proposed practical capacity standard. There was little discussion. Later, a member of the cost accounting staff pointed out that the new standard for fixed manufacturing costs would be tighter than the old standard.

Required:

1. If the new annual budgets for American Widget reflect the implementation of tighter standards based on practical capacity:
   a. What negative behavioural implications for employees and department managers could occur as a result of this change?
   b. What could American Widget management do to reduce the negative behavioural effects?
2. Explain how tight cost standards within an organization could have positive behavioural effects.
3. Identify the individuals who should participate in setting standards and describe the benefits to an organization of their participation in the standard-setting process.

(CMA, adapted)

GROUP EXERCISE 11–38 Analyzing Your University's Budget

Obtain a copy of your college or university's budget and actual results for the most recently completed year.

Required:

1. Determine the major assumptions used in the last budget (e.g., number of students; tuition per student; number of employees; increases in wages, salaries, benefits; changes in occupancy costs; etc.).
2. Compare the budgeted revenue amounts with the actual results. Try to determine the reasons for any differences.
3. Compare budgeted expenses with the actual results using the basic approach shown in Exhibit 11–4. Try to determine the reasons for any differences.

INTERNET EXERCISE 11–39

As you know, the World Wide Web is a medium that is constantly evolving. Sites come and go, and change without notice. To enable the periodic updating of site addresses, this problem has been posted to the textbook Web site (www.mcgrawhill.ca/college/garrison). After accessing the site, enter the Student Centre and select this chapter. Select and complete the Internet Exercise.

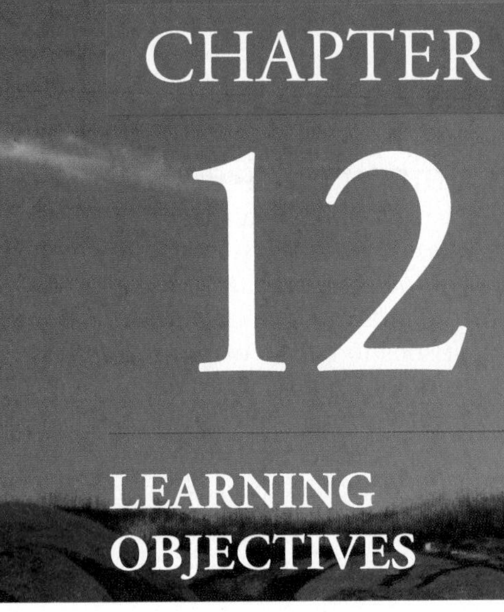

CHAPTER 12

LEARNING OBJECTIVES

After studying Chapter 12, you should be able to:

1. Differentiate among responsibility centres such as cost centres, profit centres, and investment centres, and explain how performance is measured in each.
2. Prepare a segmented income statement using the contribution format, and explain the difference between traceable fixed costs and common fixed costs.
3. Analyze variances from sales targets.
4. Analyze marketing expenses using cost drivers.
5. Analyze the return on investment (ROI).
6. Compute residual income and describe the strengths and weaknesses of this method of measuring performance.
7. Explain the use of balanced scorecards to assess performance.
8. (Appendix 12A) Determine the range, if any, within which a negotiated transfer price should fall.

REPORTING FOR CONTROL

BUSINESS FOCUS

STRATEGY, CONTROL AND UNANSWERED QUESTIONS

Academic accountants attempt to provide a rationale for performance reporting observed in the wider community. Changes in markets relevant to organizations are continuous and threaten to disrupt the control systems implemented by management. Strategies are forced to change and because control is part of strategy it too must change to be effective. Monitoring, anticipating, modifying contracts, renegotiating and implementing are suggested as roles important to managing the control function associated with strategy implementation for it to be effective. Foresight, vigilance, and creativity are considered to be necessary skills for control system's designers.

A more specific question that will become evident with the discussion to follow in this chapter is the role of allocated costs that appear in practice but contradict the economic principle of relevance for decisions. Economics argues that no benefit is derived from allocating non-incremental costs. The question of the relevance of allocated costs investigates the use of such allocations as a simplified way of providing information for capacity planning and pricing (a topic for discussion in Chapter 13). The full answer to this challenging question awaits further study because the question of suboptimal approaches contradicts the dominant historical view of the relevance of incremental costs presented by the very large literature from economics.

Sources: Shayan Sunder, "Management Control, Expectations, Common Knowledge and Culture," *Journal of Management Accounting Research*, 2002, pp. 173–187; and Ramji Balkrishnan and K. Sivaramakrishnan, "A Critical Review of the Use of Full-Costing Data for Planning and Pricing," *Journal of Management Accounting Research*, 2002, pp.3–31.

Managers of organizations determine the direction they wish the organization to take. *Strategic planning* is the term applied to this planning process. Budgeting is the financial expression of the plans. The short-term version of budgeting was presented in Chapter 9, while Chapter 14 describes long-term capital budgets. Planning, however, is only part of the management process. Through a combination of feedback of actual results, comparisons to budgets, comparisons to results of previous periods, and even comparisons to other organizations, managers attempt to ensure that the organization moves in the planned direction, termed performance assessment or control.

Managers control the organization using a variety of approaches. Accounting reports of financial results represent one important approach to controlling operations because such reports provide a means of obtaining comparisons to budgets, to previous results, and to the results of other organizations, as well as providing a knowledge of actual financial results. Such financial comparisons also serve as a base for reward schemes or contracts used to motivate managers to work toward the achievement of planned goals and objectives.

These financial performance reports can be constructed in various ways so that they better serve the specific control functions that management desires. As this chapter illustrates, segment reporting, profitability analysis, and investment performance are three commonly used reporting structures that provide somewhat different types of information. For each, it is important to understand what purpose is served by the report. Each presents information in a manner that permits a different view of the organization and a different aspect of organizational control. Understanding how the aspects change and why managers would want these changes will permit you to integrate the concepts of control with reports about standard cost variances, cost of production, and flexible budget analyses described in earlier chapters.

The modern manufacturing environment has promoted the need for flexibility in management to accompany flexibility in production. Flexibility in management requires timely and accurate decisions by members of the organization ranging from top management to the production worker. Timely and accurate decisions require timely and accurate control information appropriate to this wide range of organizational personnel. Providing information to operating or production workers so they can control their operations has posed an interesting challenge for accountants. Traditional reports have been considered too aggregated for operating workers. Accounting formats often represent approaches that are not well understood by production workers. Monthly reports, the common management accounting reporting period, are not timely enough to provide a review of operations that must change daily. Some accounting conventions, such as expensing items that are viewed as assets, can distort realities or misdirect attention so that incorrect control decisions can occur.

Study is ongoing to rectify some of the deficiencies. Focused indicators of performance such as scrap levels, rework efforts, market share, employee morale, pollutant discharges, and customer profitability are being used or refined. Some measures being developed are financial; some are physical. Aggregation of physical results is the focus of intense study because of the difficulty of having a meaningful total when financial numbers are not used.[1]

The process of collecting and presenting this vast array of data on a real-time basis is assisted by computer systems. Properly configured enterprise resource planning (ERP) systems enable the operational and financial data to be maintained consistently by using a common interactive database. A sufficiently large computer system with well-specified operational practices can provide the timely data needed for operational purposes. The term *balanced scorecard* is a best practice approach accepted by ERP system suppliers and others as a means of organizing and presenting this array of data.

1. "Developing Comprehensive Performance Indicators," *Management Accounting Guideline* 31 (Hamilton, ON: The Society of Management Accountants of Canada, 1994).

This chapter provides an explanation of common financial performance indicators. Reports based on these indicators represent the cornerstone of performance measurements to managers. Integrating material on performance from previous chapters with discussions in this and later chapters will provide you with a foundation for understanding developments in performance assessment.

DECENTRALIZATION IN ORGANIZATIONS

Once an organization grows beyond a few people, it becomes impossible for the top manager to make decisions about everything. For example, the CEO of the Delta Hotel chain cannot be expected to decide whether a particular hotel guest at the Delta Hotel on Vancouver Island should be allowed to check out later than the normal time. To some degree, managers have to delegate decisions to those who are at lower levels in the organization. However, the degree to which decisions are delegated varies from organization to organization.

A **decentralized organization** is one in which decision making is not confined to a few top executives but rather is spread throughout the organization, with managers at various levels making key operating decisions relating to their spheres of responsibility. Decentralization is a matter of degree, since all organizations are decentralized to some extent out of necessity. At one extreme, a strongly decentralized organization is one in which there are few, if any, constraints on the freedom of even the lowest-level managers and employees to make decisions. At the other extreme, in a strongly centralized organization, lower-level managers have little freedom to make decisions. Although most organizations fall somewhere between these two extremes, there is a pronounced trend toward more and more decentralization.

Decentralized organization An organization in which decision making is not confined to a few top executives but rather is spread throughout the organization.

Decentralization and Segment Reporting

Effective decentralization requires *segment reporting.* In addition to the companywide income statement, reports are needed for individual segments of the organization. A **segment** is a part or activity of an organization about which managers would like cost, revenue, or profit data. Examples of segments include divisions of a company, sales territories, individual stores, service centres, manufacturing plants, marketing departments, individual customers, and product lines. As we shall see, a company's operations can be segmented in many ways. For example, a grocery store chain like Loblaws or Sobeys can segment its business by geographic region, by individual store, by the nature of the merchandise (i.e., fresh foods, canned goods, paper goods), by brand name, and so on. In this chapter, we learn how to construct income statements for such business segments. These segmented income statements are useful in analyzing the profitability of segments and in measuring the performance of segment managers.

Segment Any part or activity of an organization about which the manager seeks cost, revenue, or profit data.

Cost, Profit, and Investment Centres

LEARNING OBJECTIVE 1 Differentiate among responsibility centres such as cost centres, profit centres, and investment centres, and explain how performance is measured in each.

Decentralized companies typically categorize their business segments into cost centres, profit centres, and investment centres—depending on the responsibilities of the managers of the segments.[2]

Cost Centre A **cost centre** is a business segment whose manager has control over costs but not over revenue or investment funds. Service departments, such as accounting,

Cost centre A business segment whose manager has control over cost but has no control over revenue or the use of investment funds.

2. Some companies classify business segments that are responsible mainly for generating revenue, such as an insurance sales office, as *revenue centres.* Other companies would consider this to be just another type of profit centre, since costs of some kind (salaries, rent, utilities) are usually deducted from the revenues in the segment's income statement.

finance, general administration, legal, personnel, and so on, are usually considered to be cost centres. In addition, manufacturing facilities are often considered to be cost centres. The managers of cost centres are expected to minimize cost while providing the level of services or the amount of products demanded by the other parts of the organization. For example, the manager of a production facility would be evaluated at least in part by comparing actual costs to how much the costs should have been for the actual number of units produced during the period.

Profit centre
A business segment whose manager has control over cost and revenue but has no control over the use of investment funds.

Profit Centre In contrast to a cost centre, a **profit centre** is any business segment whose manager has control over both cost and revenue. Like a cost centre, however, a profit centre generally does not have control over investment funds. For example, the manager in charge of one of six resorts would be responsible for both the revenues and costs, and hence the profits, of the resort but may not have control over major investments in the resort. Profit centre managers are often evaluated by comparing actual profit to targeted or budgeted profit.

Investment centre
A business segment whose manager has control over cost and over revenue and that also has control over the use of investment funds.

Investment Centre An **investment centre** is any segment of an organization whose manager has control over cost, revenue, and investments in operating assets. For example, the president of General Motors Canada would have a great deal of discretion over investments in the division. The president of the division would be responsible for initiating investment proposals, such as funding research into more fuel-efficient engines for sport-utility vehicles. Once the proposal has been approved by the top level of managers at General Motors Canada and the board of directors, the president of the division would then be responsible for making sure that the investment pays off. The manager and the board of GM Canada would still have to operate within the strategic plans set by GM world headquarters in the United States. Investment centre managers are usually evaluated using return on investment or residual income measures, as discussed later in the chapter.

Responsibility Centres

Responsibility centre
Any business segment whose manager has control over cost, revenue, or the use of investment funds.

Responsibility centre is broadly defined as any part of an organization whose manager has control over cost, revenue, or investment funds. Cost centres, profit centres, and investment centres are *all* known as responsibility centres.

A partial organization chart for Universal Foods Corporation, a company in the snack food and beverage industry, appears in Exhibit 12–1. This partial organization chart indicates how the various business segments of the company are classified in terms of responsibility. Note that the cost centres are the departments and work centres that do not generate significant revenues by themselves. These are staff departments such as finance, legal, and personnel, and operating units such as the bottling plant, warehouse, and beverage distribution centre. The profit centres are business segments that generate revenues and include the beverage, salty snacks, and confections product segments. The vice president of operations oversees allocation of investment funds across the product segments and is responsible for revenues and costs, and so is treated as an investment centre. And finally, corporate headquarters is an investment centre, since it is responsible for all revenues, costs, and investments.

SEGMENT REPORTING AND PROFITABILITY ANALYSIS

LEARNING OBJECTIVE 2
Prepare a segmented income statement using the contribution format, and explain the difference between traceable fixed costs and common fixed costs.

As previously discussed, a different kind of income statement is required for evaluating the performance of business segments—an income statement that emphasizes segments rather than the performance of the company as a whole. This point is illustrated in the following discussion.

EXHIBIT 12–1 Business Segments Classified as Cost, Profit, and Investment Centres

Investment centres

Universal Foods Corporation
Corporate Headquarters
President and CEO

Operations
Vice President

Finance
Chief Financial Officer

Legal
General Counsel

Personnel
Vice President

Profit centres

Salty Snacks Product Manager

Beverages Product Manager

Confections Product Manager

Cost centres

Bottling Plant Manager

Warehouse Manager

Distribution Manager

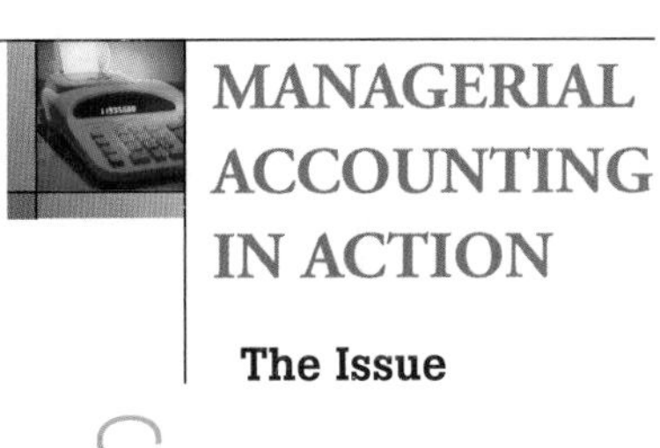

MANAGERIAL ACCOUNTING IN ACTION

The Issue

SoftSolutions Inc.

SoftSolutions, Inc. is a rapidly growing computer software company founded by Lori Saffer, who had previously worked in a large software company, and Marjorie Matsuo, who had previously worked in the hotel industry as a general manager. They formed the company to develop and market user-friendly accounting and operations software designed specifically for hotels. They quit their jobs, pooled their savings, hired several programmers, and got down to work.

The first sale was by far the most difficult. No hotel wanted to be the first to use an untested product from an unknown company. After overcoming this obstacle with persistence, good luck, dedication to customer service, and a very low introductory price, the company's sales burgeoned.

The company quickly developed similar business software for other specialized markets and then branched out into animation and computer games. Within four years of its founding, the organization had grown to the point where Saffer and Matsuo were no longer able to personally direct all of the company's activities. Decentralization had become a necessity.

Accordingly, the company was split into two divisions—Business Products and Consumer Products. By mutual consent, Matsuo took the title of president and Saffer took the title of vice president of the Business Products Division. Chris Worden, a programmer who had spearheaded the drive into the animation and computer games markets, was designated vice president of the Consumer Products Division.

Almost immediately, the issue arose of how best to evaluate the performance of the divisions. Matsuo called a meeting to consider this issue and asked Saffer, Worden, and the controller, Bill Carson, to attend. The following discussion took place at that meeting:

Matsuo: We need to find a better way to measure the performance of the divisions.

Worden: I agree. Consumer Products has been setting the pace in this company for the last two years, and we should be getting more recognition.

Saffer: Chris, we are delighted with the success of the Consumer Products Division.

Worden: I know. But it is hard to figure out just how successful we are with the present accounting reports. All we have are sales and cost of goods sold figures for the division.

Carson: What's the matter with those figures? They are prepared using generally accepted accounting principles.

Worden: The sales figures are fine. However, cost of goods sold includes some costs that really aren't the costs of our division, and it excludes some costs that are. Let's take a simple example. Everything we sell in the Consumer Products Division has to pass through the automatic bar-coding machine, which applies a unique bar code to the product.

Saffer: We know. Every item we ship must have a unique identifying bar code. That's true for items from the Business Products Division as well as for items from the Consumer Products Division.

Worden: That's precisely the point. Whether an item comes from the Business Products Division or the Consumer Products Division, it must pass through the automatic bar-coding machine after the software has been packaged. How much of the cost of the automatic bar coder would be saved if we didn't have any consumer products?

Matsuo: Since we have only one automatic bar coder and we would need it anyway to code the business products, I guess none of the cost would be saved.

Worden: That's right. And since none of the cost could be saved even if the entire Consumer Products Division was eliminated, how can we logically say that some of the cost of the automatic bar coder is a cost of the Consumer Products Division?

Saffer: Just a minute, Chris, are you saying that my Business Products Division should be charged with the entire cost of the automatic bar coder?

Worden: No, that's not what I am saying.

Matsuo: But Chris, I don't see how we can have sensible performance reports without making someone responsible for costs like the cost of the automatic bar coder. Bill, as our accounting expert, what do you think?

Carson: I have some ideas for handling issues like the automatic bar coder. The best approach would probably be for me to put together a draft performance report. We can discuss it at the next meeting when everyone has something concrete to look at.

Matsuo: Okay, let's see what you come up with.

Bill Carson, the controller of SoftSolutions, realized that segmented income statements would be required to evaluate more appropriately the performance of the two divisions. To construct the segmented reports, he would have to carefully segregate costs that are attributable to the two divisions from costs that are not. Since most of the disputes over costs would be about fixed costs such as the automatic bar-coding machine, he knew he would also have to separate fixed from variable costs. Under the conventional absorption costing income statement prepared for the entire company, variable and fixed production costs were being commingled in the cost of goods sold.

Largely for these reasons, Carson decided to use the contribution format income statement discussed in earlier chapters. Recall that when the contribution format is used: (1) the cost of goods sold consists only of the variable manufacturing costs; (2) the variable and fixed costs are listed in separate sections; and (3) a contribution margin is computed. When such a statement is segmented as in this chapter, fixed costs are broken down further into what are called *traceable* and *common costs,* as discussed later. This breakdown allows a *segment margin* to be computed for each segment of the company. The segment margin is a valuable tool for assessing the profitability of a segment and is also a much better tool for evaluating performance than the usual absorption costing reports.

Levels of Segmented Statements

A portion of the segmented report Carson prepared is shown in Exhibit 12–2. The contribution format income statement for the entire company appears at the very top of the exhibit under the column labelled Total Company. Immediately to the right of this column are two columns—one for each of the two divisions. We can see that the divisional segment margin is $60,000 for the Business Products Division and $40,000 for the Consumer Products Division. This is the portion of the report that was specifically requested by the company's divisional managers. They wanted to know how much each of their divisions was contributing to the company's profits.

However, segmented income statements can be prepared for activities at many levels in a company. To provide more information to the company's divisional managers, Carson has further segmented the divisions according to their major product lines. In the case of the Consumer Products Division, the product lines are animation and computer games. Going even further, Carson has segmented each of the product lines according to how they are sold—in retail computer stores or by Web sales. In Exhibit 12–2, this further segmentation is illustrated for the computer games product line. Notice that as we go from one segmented statement to another, we look at smaller and smaller pieces of the company. While not shown in Exhibit 12–2, Carson also prepared segmented income statements for the major product lines in the Business Products Division.

Substantial benefits are received from a series of statements such as those contained in Exhibit 12–2. By carefully examining trends and results in each segment, a manager is able to gain considerable insight into the company's operations viewed from many different angles. Advanced computer-based information systems make it easier to construct such statements and to keep them continuously current.

Sales and Contribution Margin

To prepare an income statement for a particular segment, variable expenses are deducted from the sales to yield the contribution margin for the segment. It is important to keep in mind that the contribution margin tells us what happens to profits as volume changes—holding a segment's capacity and fixed costs constant. The contribution margin is especially useful in decisions involving temporary uses of capacity, such as special orders. Decisions concerning the most effective uses of existing capacity often involve only variable costs and revenues, which of course are the very elements involved in contribution margin. Such decisions will be discussed in detail in Chapter 13.

Traceable and Common Fixed Costs

The most puzzling aspect of Exhibit 12–2 is probably the treatment of fixed costs. The report has two kinds of fixed costs—traceable and common. Only the *traceable fixed costs* are charged to the segments in the segmented income statements in the report. If a cost is not traceable to a segment, then it is not assigned to the segment.

A **traceable fixed cost** of a segment is a fixed cost that is incurred because of the existence of the segment—if the segment had never existed, the fixed cost would not have been incurred, and/or if the segment was eliminated, the fixed cost would disappear. Examples of traceable fixed costs include the following:

Traceable fixed cost
A fixed cost that is incurred because of the existence of a particular business segment.

- The salary of the Fritos product manager at PepsiCo is a *traceable* fixed cost of the Fritos business segment of PepsiCo.
- The maintenance cost for the building in which a Challenger jet is assembled is a *traceable* fixed cost of the Challenger business segment of Bombardier.

EXHIBIT 12–2 SoftSolutions, Inc.—Segmented Income Statements in the Contribution Format

Segments Defined as Divisions

	Total Company	Divisions: Business Products Division	Divisions: Consumer Products Division
Sales	$500,000	$300,000	$200,000
Less variable expenses:			
Variable cost of goods sold	180,000	120,000	60,000
Other variable expenses	50,000	30,000	20,000
Total variable expenses	230,000	150,000	80,000
Contribution margin	270,000	150,000	120,000
Less traceable fixed expenses	170,000	90,000	80,000*
Divisional segment margin	100,000	$ 60,000	$ 40,000
Less common fixed expenses not traceable to the individual divisions	85,000		
Operating income	$ 15,000		

Segments Defined as Product Lines of the Consumer Products Division

	Consumer Products Division	Product Line: Animation	Product Line: Computer Games
Sales	$200,000	$ 75,000	$125,000
Less variable expenses:			
Variable cost of goods sold	60,000	20,000	40,000
Other variable expenses	20,000	5,000	15,000
Total variable expenses	80,000	25,000	55,000
Contribution margin	120,000	50,000	70,000
Less traceable fixed expenses	70,000	30,000	40,000
Product-line segment margin	50,000	$ 20,000	$ 30,000
Less common fixed expenses not traceable to the individual product lines	10,000		
Divisional segment margin	$ 40,000		

Segments Defined as Sales Channels for One Product Line, Computer Games, of the Consumer Products Division

	Computer Games	Sales Channels: Retail Stores	Sales Channels: Web Sales
Sales	$125,000	$100,000	$ 25,000
Less variable expenses:			
Variable cost of goods sold	40,000	32,000	8,000
Other variable expenses	15,000	5,000	10,000
Total variable expenses	55,000	37,000	18,000
Contribution margin	70,000	63,000	7,000
Less traceable fixed expenses	25,000	15,000	10,000
Sales-channel segment margin	45,000	$ 48,000	$ (3,000)
Less common fixed expenses not traceable to the individual sales channels	15,000		
Product-line segment margin	$ 30,000		

*Notice that this $80,000 in traceable fixed expense is divided into two parts—$70,000 traceable and $10,000 common—when the Consumer Products Division is broken down into product lines. The reasons for this are discussed later in the section Traceable Costs Can Become Common Costs.

A **common fixed cost** is a fixed cost that supports the operations of more than one segment but is not traceable in whole or in part to any one segment. Even if a segment was entirely eliminated, there would be no change in a true common fixed cost. Note the following:

Common fixed cost A fixed cost that supports more than one business segment, but is not traceable in whole or in part to any one of the business segments.

- The salary of the CEO of General Motors Canada is a *common* fixed cost of the various divisions of General Motors Canada.
- The cost of the automatic bar-coding machine at SoftSolutions is a *common* fixed cost of the Consumer Products Division and of the Business Products Division.
- The cost of the receptionist's salary at an office shared by a number of doctors is a *common* fixed cost of the doctors. The cost is traceable to the office, but not to any one of the doctors individually.

Identifying Traceable Fixed Costs The distinction between traceable and common fixed costs is crucial in segment reporting, since traceable fixed costs are charged to the segments, whereas common fixed costs are not. In an actual situation, it is sometimes hard to determine whether a cost should be classified as traceable or common.

The general guideline is to treat as traceable costs *only those costs that would disappear over time if the segment itself disappeared.* For example, if the Consumer Products Division was sold or discontinued, it would no longer be necessary to pay the division manager's salary. Therefore, the division manager's salary should be classified as a traceable fixed cost of the division. On the other hand, the president of the company undoubtedly would continue to be paid even if the Consumer Products Division was dropped. In fact, he or she might even be paid more if dropping the division was a good idea. Therefore, the president's salary is common to both divisions. The same idea can be expressed in another way: *Treat as traceable costs only those costs that are added as a result of the creation of a segment.*

Activity-Based Costing Some costs are easy to identify as traceable costs. For example, the costs of advertising Crest toothpaste on television are clearly traceable to Crest. A more difficult situation arises when a building, machine, or other resource is shared by two or more segments. For example, assume that a multiproduct company leases warehouse space that is used for storing the full range of its products. Would the lease cost of the warehouse be a traceable or a common cost of the products? Managers familiar with activity-based costing might argue that the lease cost is traceable and should be assigned to the products according to how much space the products use in the warehouse. In like manner, these managers would argue that order processing costs, sales support costs, and other selling, general, and administrative (SG&A) expenses should also be charged to segments according to the segments' consumption of SG&A resources.

To illustrate, consider Holt Corporation, a company that manufactures concrete pipe for industrial uses. The company has three products—9-inch pipe, 12-inch pipe, and 18-inch pipe. Space is leased in a large warehouse on a yearly basis as needed. The lease cost of this space is $10 per square metre per year. The 9-inch pipe occupies 400 square metres of space, 12-inch pipe occupies 1,600 square metres, and 18-inch pipe occupies 2,000 square metres. The company also has an order-processing department that incurred $150,000 in order-processing costs last year. Management believes that order-processing costs are driven by the number of orders placed by customers in a year. Last year, 2,500 orders were placed, of which 1,200 were for 9-inch pipe, 800 were for 12-inch pipe, and 500 were for 18-inch pipe. Given these data, the following costs would be assigned to each product using the activity-based costing approach:

Warehouse space cost:	
9-inch pipe: $10 × 400 square metres	$ 4,000
12-inch pipe: $10 × 1,600 square metres	16,000
18-inch pipe: $10 × 2,000 square metres	20,000
Total cost assigned	$ 40,000

continued

Order-processing costs:	
$150,000 ÷ 2,500 orders = $60 per order	
9-inch pipe: $60 × 1,200 orders	$ 72,000
12-inch pipe: $60 × 800 orders	48,000
18-inch pipe: $60 × 500 orders	30,000
Total cost assigned	$150,000

This method of assigning costs combines the strength of activity-based costing with the power of the contribution approach and greatly enhances the manager's ability to measure the profitability and performance of segments. However, managers must still ask themselves if the costs would in fact disappear over time if the segment itself disappeared. In the case of Holt Corporation, it is clear that the $20,000 in warehousing costs for the 18-inch pipe would be eliminated if 18-inch pipes were no longer being produced. The company would simply rent less warehouse space the following year. However, suppose the company owns the warehouse. Then it is not so clear that $20,000 of the cost of the warehouse would really disappear if the 18-inch pipes were discontinued as a product. The company might be able to sublease the space or use it for other products, but then again the space might simply be empty while the costs of the warehouse continue to be incurred.

In assigning costs to segments, the key point is to resist the temptation to allocate costs (such as depreciation of corporate facilities) that are clearly common in nature and that would continue regardless of whether the segment exists or not. *Any allocation of common costs to segments will reduce the value of the segment margin as a guide to segment profitability and segment performance.* This point will be discussed at length later in the chapter.

FOCUS *on Current Practice*

Harris Corporation consolidated its division-level data centres into a centralized data centre called the Computing and Communication Services (CCS) Department. CCS is a cost centre that recovers its operating costs by charging other divisions within Harris for the use of its resources. To facilitate the "chargeback" process, CCS developed an activity-based costing system. Activities such as "test systems," "monitor network," "schedule jobs," "install software," "administer servers," and "print reports" were used to ensure that internal customers were only charged for the dollar value of the resources that they consumed.

Source: Peter Brewer, "Developing a Data Center Chargeback System Using ABC," *Journal of Cost Management*, May/June 1998, pp. 41–47.

Traceable Costs Can Become Common Costs

Fixed costs that are traceable to one segment may be a common cost of another segment. For example, an airline might want a segmented income statement that shows the segment margin for a particular flight from Montréal to London, further broken down into first-class, business-class, and economy-class segment margins. The airline must pay a substantial landing fee at Heathrow airport in London. This fixed landing fee is a traceable cost of the flight, but it is a common cost of the first-class, business-class, and economy-class segments. Even if the first-class cabin is empty, the entire landing fee must be paid. So the landing fee is not a traceable cost of the first-class cabin. But on the other hand, paying the fee is necessary in order to have any first-class, business-class, or economy-class passengers. So the landing fee is a common cost of these three classes.

The dual nature of some of the fixed costs can be seen in Exhibit 12–3. Notice from this exhibit that when segments are defined as divisions, the Consumer Products Division has $80,000 in traceable fixed expenses. Only $70,000 of this amount remains

		Segment	
	Total Company	Business Products Division	Consumer Products Division
Contribution margin	$270,000	$150,000	$120,000
Less traceable fixed expenses	170,000	90,000	80,000

	Consumer Products Division	Animation	Computer Games
Contribution margin	$120,000	$50,000	$70,000
Less traceable fixed expenses	70,000	30,000	40,000
Product-line segment margin	50,000	$20,000	$30,000
Less common fixed expenses	10,000		
Divisional segment margin	$ 40,000		

EXHIBIT 12–3
Reclassification of Traceable Fixed Expenses from Exhibit 12–2.

traceable, however, when we narrow the definition of a segment from divisions to product lines. Notice that the other $10,000 then becomes a common cost of the two product lines of the Consumer Products Division.

Why would $10,000 of traceable fixed cost become a common cost when the division is divided into product lines? The $10,000 is the monthly salary of the manager of the Consumer Products Division. This salary is a traceable cost of the division as a whole, but it is a common cost of the division's product lines. The manager's salary is a necessary cost of having the two product lines, but even if one of the product lines was discontinued entirely, the manager's salary would probably not be cut. Therefore, none of the manager's salary can really be traced to the individual products.

The $70,000 traceable fixed cost of the product lines consists of the costs of product-specific advertising. A total of $30,000 was spent on advertising animation software and $40,000 was spent on advertising computer games. These costs can clearly be traced to the individual product lines.

Segment Margin

Observe from Exhibit 12–2 that the **segment margin** is obtained by deducting the traceable fixed costs of a segment from the segment's contribution margin. It represents the margin available after a segment has covered all of its own costs. *The segment margin is the best gauge of the profitability of a segment,* since it includes only those costs that are caused by the segment. If a segment cannot cover its own costs, then that segment probably should not be retained (unless it has important side effects on other segments). Notice from Exhibit 12–2, for example, that Web Sales has a negative segment margin. This means that the segment is not covering its own costs; it is generating more costs than it collects in revenue.[3]

Segment margin The amount computed by deducting the traceable fixed costs of a segment from the segment's contribution margin. It represents the margin available after a segment has covered all of its own costs.

From a decision-making point of view, the segment margin is most useful in major decisions that affect capacity, such as dropping a segment. By contrast, as we noted

3. Retention or elimination of product lines and other segments is covered in more depth in Chapter 13.

earlier, the contribution margin is most useful in decisions relating to short-run changes in volume, such as pricing special orders that involve utilization of existing capacity.

MANAGERIAL ACCOUNTING IN ACTION

The Wrap-Up

Shortly after Bill Carson, the SoftSolutions, Inc. controller, completed the draft segmented income statement, he sent copies to the other managers and scheduled a meeting in which the report could be explained. The meeting was held on the Monday following the first meeting, and Marjorie Matsuo, Lori Saffer, and Chris Worden were in attendance.

Saffer: I think these segmented income statements are fairly self-explanatory. However, there is one thing I wonder about.

Carson: What's that?

Saffer: What is this common fixed expense of $85,000 listed under Total Company? And who is going to be responsible for it if neither Chris nor I have responsibility?

Carson: The $85,000 of common fixed expenses represents expenses like general administrative salaries and the costs of common production equipment such as the automatic bar-coding machine. Marjorie, do you want to respond to the question about responsibility for these expenses?

Matsuo: Sure. Since I'm the president of the company, I'm responsible for those costs. Some things can be delegated, others cannot be. It wouldn't make any sense for either you or Chris to make decisions about the bar coder, since it affects both of you. That's an important part of my job—making decisions about resources that affect all parts of the organization. This report makes it much clearer who is responsible for what. I like it.

Worden: So do I—my division's segment margin is higher than the operating income for the entire company.

Matsuo: Don't get carried away, Chris. Let's not misinterpret what this report means. The segment margins have to be big to cover the common costs of the company. We can't let the big segment margins lull us into a sense of complacency. If we use these reports, we all have to agree that our objective is to increase all of the segment margins over time.

Saffer: I'm willing to give it a try.

Worden: The reports make sense to me.

Matsuo: So be it. Then the first item of business would appear to be a review of catalogue sales of computer games, where we appear to be losing money. Chris, could you brief us on this at our next meeting?

Worden: I'd be happy to. I have been suspecting for some time that our catalogue sales strategy could be improved.

Matsuo: We look forward to hearing your analysis. Meeting's adjourned.

There Is More Than One Way to Segment a Company

SoftSolutions segmented its sales by division, by product line within each division, and by sales channel. An organization can be segmented in many ways. For example, two different ways of segmenting the sales of the Bombardier are displayed in Exhibit 12–4. In the first diagram, the company's sales are segmented by geographic region. In the second diagram, they are segmented by products. Note that each of the diagrams could be continued, providing progressively more detailed segment data. For example, the sales in Germany could be broken down by major product line, then by product. Similar breakdowns could be done of Bombardier's costs and segment margins, although that would require substantial additional analytical work to identify the segments to which various costs should be assigned.

Segment breakdowns such as those shown in Exhibit 12–4 give a company's managers the ability to look at the company from many different directions. With the increasing availability of companywide databases and sophisticated management information

EXHIBIT 12–4 Bombardier, Inc. Revenues Segmented by Geographic Region and Products

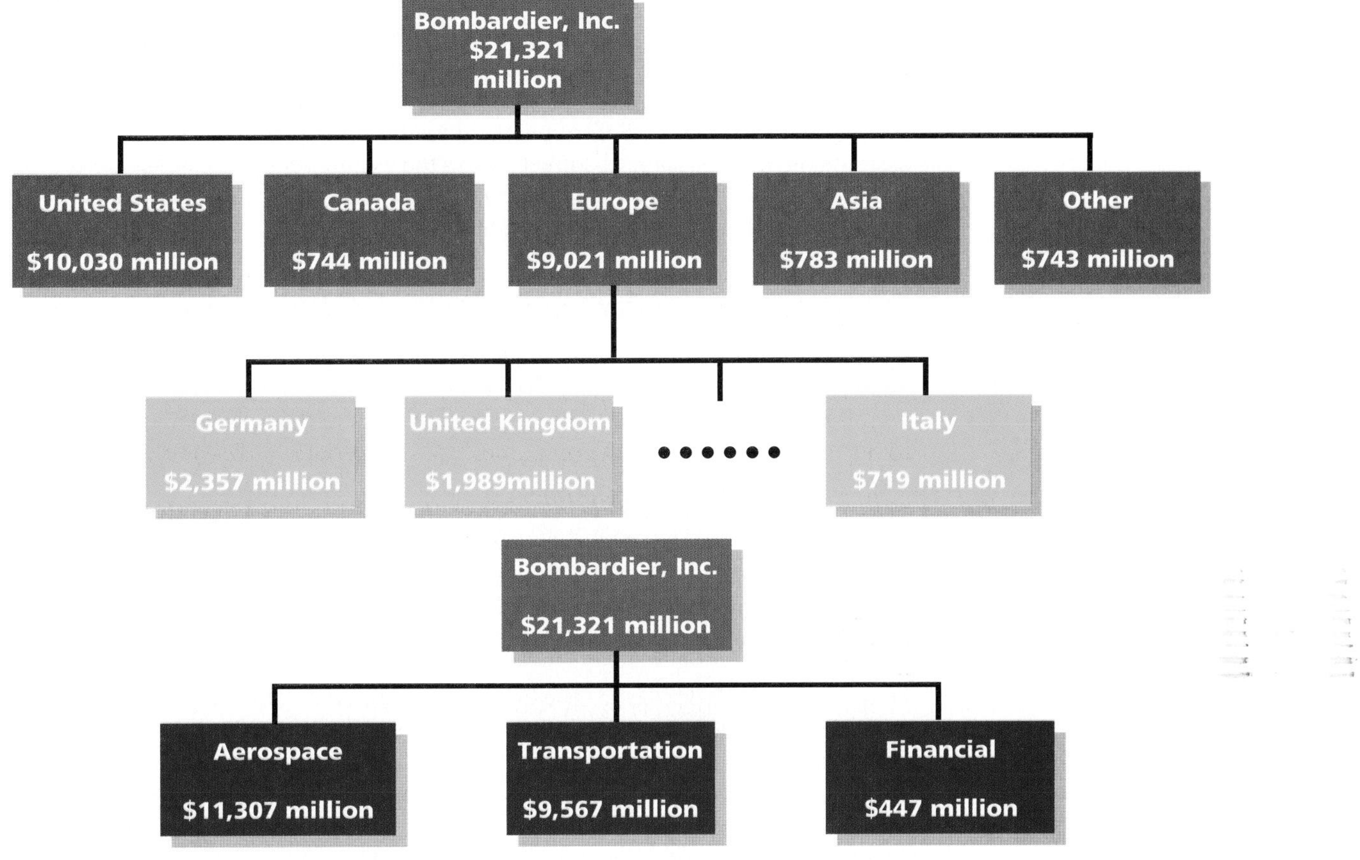

system software, detailed segment reports of revenues, costs, and margins are becoming much easier to do.

SEGMENT REPORTING FOR FINANCIAL ACCOUNTING

Conflicting reports between segment profits for internal management and those required for external statement users are now minimized as a result of the changes to section 1701 of the *CICA Handbook*. Segment profit or loss, segment assets, and certain specified items are required disclosures for public enterprises that have publicly traded debt or equity. The segmentation of profits is required to follow the practices of internal reporting to the chief operating officer or officers if the segment represents at least 10% of the revenues, profits, or assets, to an amount equal to 75% of the total. This harmonization of disclosures should help the conflict that can occur between the directions indicated by different segment profits. However, generally accepted accounting principles permit variations from the logic of segment reporting presented in this chapter even though the focus of segmentation is on products and services together with geographic areas. For example, interest expense is a required disclosure even though it would not be for the operating income presented here.[4]

4. Details of these specific disclosures can be found in section 1701 of the *CICA Handbook*, January 1998, paragraphs 29–34.

HINDRANCES TO PROPER COST ASSIGNMENT

For segment reporting to accomplish its intended purposes, costs must be properly assigned to segments. If the purpose is to determine the profits being generated by a particular division, then all of the costs attributable to that division—and only those costs—should be assigned to it. Unfortunately, three business practices greatly hinder proper cost assignment: (1) omission of some costs in the assignment process, (2) the use of inappropriate methods for allocating costs among segments of a company, and (3) assignment to segments of costs that are really common costs.

Inappropriate Methods for Allocating Costs among Segments

Cross-subsidization
A distortion of costs that occurs when costs are improperly assigned among a company's segments.

Cross-subsidization, or cost distortion, occurs when costs are improperly assigned among a company's segments. Cross-subsidization can occur in two ways: first, when companies fail to trace costs directly to segments in those situations where it is feasible to do so; and second, when companies use inappropriate bases to allocate costs.

Failure to Trace Costs Directly Costs that can be traced directly to a specific segment of a company should not be allocated to other segments. Rather, such costs should be charged directly to the responsible segment. For example, the rent for a branch office of an insurance company should be charged directly against the branch to which it relates rather than included in a companywide overhead pool and then spread throughout the company.

Inappropriate Allocation Base Some companies allocate costs to segments using arbitrary bases such as sales dollars or cost of goods sold. For example, under the sales dollars approach, costs are allocated to the various segments according to the percentage of company sales generated by each segment. Thus, if a segment generates 20% of total company sales, it would be allocated 20% of the company's *Selling, General and Administrative (SG&A)* expenses as its "fair share." This same basic procedure is followed if costs of goods sold or some other measure is used as the allocation base.

For this approach to be valid economically, the allocation base must actually drive the overhead cost, or at least the allocation base should be highly correlated with the cost driver of the overhead cost. For example, when sales dollars are used as the allocation base for SG&A expenses, it is implicitly assumed that SG&A expenses change in proportion to changes in total sales. If that is not true, the SG&A expenses allocated to segments will be misleading.

Arbitrarily Dividing Common Costs among Segments

The third business practice that leads to distorted segment costs is the practice of assigning non-traceable costs to segments. For example, some companies allocate the costs of the corporate headquarters building to products on segment reports. However, in a multiproduct company, no single product is likely to be responsible for any significant amount of this cost. Even if a product was eliminated entirely, there would usually be no significant effect on any of the costs of the corporate headquarters building. In short, there is no cause-and-effect relation between the cost of the corporate headquarters building and the existence of any one product. As a consequence, any allocation of the cost of the corporate headquarters building to the products must be arbitrary and thus not be an incremental cost for the segment.

Common costs like the costs of the corporate headquarters building are necessary, of course, to have a functioning organization. The common practice of arbitrarily allocating these costs to segments is often justified on the grounds that "someone" has to "cover the common costs." While it is undeniably true that the common costs must be covered, arbitrarily allocating common costs to segments does not ensure that this will happen. In fact, adding a share of common costs to the real costs of a segment may make an otherwise profitable segment appear to be unprofitable. If a manager erroneously eliminates the segment, the revenues will be lost, the real costs of the segment will be saved, but the common costs will still be there. The net effect will be to reduce the profits of the company as a whole and make it even more difficult to "cover the common costs."

In summary, the way many companies handle segment reporting results in cost distortion. This distortion results from three practices—the failure to trace costs directly to a specific segment when it is feasible to do so, the use of inappropriate bases for allocating costs, and the allocation of common costs to segments. These practices are widespread.

FOCUS *on Current Practice*

The Big Dig in Boston is a $14 billion-plus project to bury major roads underground in downtown Boston. Two companies—Bechtel and Parsons Brinckerhoff (PB)—manage the 20-year project, which is $1.6 billion over budget. The two companies will likely collect in excess of $120 million in fixed fees for their work on the project—not including reimbursements for overhead costs. Bechtel and PB have many projects underway at any one time and many common fixed costs. These common fixed costs are not actually caused by the Big Dig project and yet portions of these costs have been claimed as reimbursable expenses. "Bechtel and PB say they don't collect a penny more for overhead than they are entitled to." A Bechtel spokesman says, "Our allocation of overhead [on the Big Dig] is rigorously audited . . . " This is undoubtedly true; in practice, fixed common costs are routinely (and arbitrarily) allocated to segments for cost reimbursement and other purposes. Managers at Bechtel, PB, and other companies argue that someone must pay for these costs. While this too is true, who actually pays for these costs will depend on how the common fixed costs are arbitrarily allocated among segments. Massachusetts has lodged a number of complaints concerning Bechtel's cost recovery claims. Such complaints are almost inevitable when common fixed costs are allocated to segments. It might be better to simply set an all-inclusive fixed fee up front with no cost recovery and hence no issues concerning what costs are really attributable to the project.

Source: Nathan Vardi, *Forbes*, "Desert Storm," June 23, 2003, pp. 63–66.

Omission of Costs

The costs assigned to a segment should include all costs attributable to that segment from the company's entire *value chain*. The **value chain,** which is illustrated in Exhibit 12–5, consists of the major business functional activities that add value to a company's products and services. All of these functions, from research and development, through product design, manufacturing, marketing, distribution, and customer service, are required to bring a product or service to the customer and generate revenues.

Value chain
The major business functions that add value to a company's products and services. These functions consist of research and development, product design, manufacturing, marketing, distribution, and customer service.

However, as discussed in Chapters 2, 3, and 7, only manufacturing costs are included in product costs for financial reporting purposes. Consequently, when trying to determine product profitability for internal decision-making purposes, some companies deduct only manufacturing costs from product revenues. As a result, such companies omit from their profitability analysis part or all of the "upstream" costs in the value chain, which consist of research and development and product design, and the "downstream" costs, which consist of marketing, distribution, and customer service. Yet these non-manufacturing costs are just as essential in determining product profitability as are the manufacturing costs. These upstream and downstream costs, which are usually entitled *Selling, General, and Administrative*

EXHIBIT 12–5 Business Functions Making Up the Value Chain

Research and Development	Product Design	Manufacturing	Marketing	Distribution	Customer Service

(SG&A) on the financial accounting income statement, can represent half or more of the total costs of an organization. If either the upstream or downstream costs are omitted in profitability analysis, then the product is undercosted and management may unwittingly develop and maintain products that in the long run result in losses rather than profits for the company.

The functional organizational arrangement presented in the value chain represents a departure from the responsibility focus presented in the discussion to date. Both functional and responsibility are different classification schemes used to provide alternative views of the financial information. The responsibility view shown in Exhibits 12-1 and 12-2 focuses on what given managers control. A reclassification according to the value chain in Exhibit 12-5 could coincide with managerial responsibilities but may overlap specific responsibilities where different functions are the responsibility of a single manager or the opposite. While value chains may not present clear pictures of responsibility, they do demonstrate the activities or functions that serve to achieve the value goals of the organization. Thus they serve as a linkage between strategy and outcomes, something that is key to understanding the implementation process.

Life cycle costing
A costing approach that focuses on all costs along the value chain that will be generated throughout the entire life of a product.

Partly to avoid omitting costs that are an essential part of profitability analysis, some firms are turning to a concept known as *life cycle costing.* Essentially, **life cycle costing** focuses on all costs along the value chain that will be generated throughout the entire life of the product.

The focus on the entire life cycle means that more than one accounting period must usually be examined. Thus, costs for research that may be expensed before the product is produced would be considered along with marketing costs that for ordinary accounting might fall in a different period than the sales figures. The costs are matched to the life cycle from introduction to withdrawal rather than to arbitrary accounting periods, because profits tend to differ over different stages in the life cycle. This approach to costing helps ensure that no costs are omitted in profitability analysis.

Value chain analysis serves as a means of analyzing the internal operations or activities that contribute to the value of the product or service provided.[5] Separating the activities of an organization into those that contribute to the value perceived by the customer and those that do not provides an opportunity to focus management control on activities rather than responsibility departments, in much the same way that activity costing or activity management was presented in Chapters 8 and 9. Questions of spinning off non-strategic, non-value-added activities represent an additional part of the value chain analysis that will be discussed in Chapters 13 and 14. Nevertheless, the focus on activity analysis as part of value chains can provide an instructive look at what is important to customers and hopefully avoid inappropriate costing or allocation.

CUSTOMER PROFITABILITY ANALYSIS

In prior sections, we have noted that companies analyze profitability in many ways, including by product, by market segment, and by channel of distribution. One frequently overlooked way to analyze profitability is by customer. Although managers generally assume that a dollar of sales to one customer is just as profitable as a dollar of sales to any other customer, this assumption may not be correct. The reason is that customers have varying demands for resource-consuming activities, just as products, markets, or other segments of a company have varying demands. For example, some customers order in smaller lots and more frequently than other customers, requiring more paperwork and materials handling. Some customers order non-standard parts that require special engineering work, special machinery set-ups, and perhaps special packaging and handling. Other customers always seem to be in a hurry and want special expediting and delivery services. Customers who

5. Joseph G. Donelan and Edward A. Kaplan, "Value Chain Analysis: A Strategic Approach to Cost Management," *Journal of Cost Management,* March/April 1998. Also, "Value Chain Analysis for Assessing Competitive Advantage," *Management Accounting Guideline 41*, The Society of Management Accountants of Canada, 1996, provides an extensive discussion of the nature and role of value chains.

demand high levels of these resource-consuming activities should not be cross-subsidized by customers who demand little in the way of customized services, special packaging, and so forth. However, unless the activities that are provided for customer support are traced to the company's various customers, cross-subsidization almost certainly will occur.

After the various customer-support activities in a company have been identified, the costs of providing these activities should be charged to the customers who require them. Thus, a customer who requires special accounts receivable terms, many small orders and deliveries, the packing of goods in shop-ready containers, and specialized field service should be quoted a price that reflects these costly activities. This is why we stated in earlier chapters that suppliers who make deliveries to customers in a JIT environment frequently quote prices that are somewhat higher than prices charged by other suppliers. The higher prices are needed to compensate these suppliers for the special activities required on their part to support JIT customers.

Businesses that have analyzed customer profitability have been surprised to find that a fairly small number of customers are apparently responsible for most of their profits. It is also common to find that a small number of customers consume far more resources than are warranted by the revenue generated.

Sales Variance Analysis

LEARNING OBJECTIVE **3**
Analyze variances from sales targets.

Segmented profitability analysis combined with the variance analysis discussed in Chapters 10 and 11 can be used to generate a series of performance reports so that prices and volumes (quantities) can be compared to targets set by the budgeting process. The interaction of price and quantity represents important information for businesses to analyze to determine why the strategic goals and specific budgeted targets were not achieved. Managers want to know the effects of market volume changes, market penetration or share changes, sales mix changes, and price changes. Each of these elements can be isolated but the true test of management is to reconstitute the combination needed for a new marketing strategy. Variances from previous results can provide a valuable start for this process.

The ability to have segment revenue data for analysis depends on the coding attached to the revenue information. Geographic market, product line, customer, and sales personnel are common classifications. Managers, with the assistance of the accountant, must decide what they wish to know and what classifications can be realistically structured, given the degree of substitutes and complements that exist, the number of products that exist, and the nature of meaningful groupings.

To illustrate the nature of variance reporting in the revenue area, consider the following example for Ace Video Company.

Budget sales in units:	
Deluxe video game	10,000
Standard video game	5,000
Budget price:	
Deluxe	$20
Standard	$10
Market volume expected:	
Deluxe	70,000
Standard	90,000
Budget variable expense:	
Deluxe	$8
Standard	$5

The sales price for the deluxe video game was reduced to $18 from the anticipated $20. This resulted in a $16,000 increase in revenue. The standard video game price was increased by $1 per unit, resulting in a revenue decrease of $6,000. The reasoning behind the price and revenue changes is something marketing management should explain so that a new pricing strategy can be considered.

Actual results for the period were:

Unit sales:	
Deluxe	12,000
Standard	4,000
Sales prices:	
Deluxe	$18
Standard	$11
Market volume:	
Deluxe	75,000
Standard	85,000

Exhibit 12–6 presents a summary of the relationships among budgeted and actual results.

Analysis of revenue variances can proceed as follows:

Sales price variance Actual sales price minus budgeted sales price, all times actual sales quantity.

$$\textbf{Sales price variance} = \left(\text{Actual sales price} - \text{Budgeted sales price}\right) \times \text{Actual sales volume}$$

Deluxe	($18 − $20) × 12,000 units =	$24,000 U
Standard	($11 − $10) × 4,000 units =	4,000 F
	Total sales price variance =	$20,000 U

Note that the variance in contribution margin resulting from the change in sales price uses actual sales volume in units times the difference in sales price, actual versus budget.

Firms often wish to know how they are performing compared to the market for their product. If the market in total expands, they would like to see how their firm shares this expansion. *Market volume variances* and *market share variances* can provide a method of seeing the contribution margin effects of market volume changes or changes in the portion of the market, termed *market share* or *market penetration*, captured by the firm.

For Ace Video, market volume levels are tracked so we can show the variance analysis approach for Ace. We begin with market volume, holding market share constant.

Market volume variance Actual market volume minus budget market volume times anticipated market share, all times budgeted contribution margin.

$$\textbf{Market volume variance} = \left(\text{Actual market volume} - \text{Budget market volume}\right) \times \text{Anticipated market share percentage} \times \text{Budgeted contribution margin per unit}$$

Deluxe	(75,000 − 70,000) × (10,000/70,000) × ($20 − $8) =	$8,571 F
Standard	(85,000 − 90,000) × (5,000/90,000) × ($10 − $5) =	$1,389 U
Total		$7,182 F

Market volume variance presents the change in contribution margin as a result of the fact that the whole market unit sales were not what was anticipated. One example, Ace Video, converts changes in market quantities to Ace's portion using the anticipated market share. Ace's portion of market volume is converted to contribution margin using the budgeted contribution margin per unit.

Market share variance Actual sales volume minus the anticipated portion of the actual market volume, all times budgeted contribution margin per unit.

$$\textbf{Market share variance} = \text{Actual sales quantity} - \left[\text{Actual market volume} \times \text{Anticipated market share percentage}\right] \times \text{Budgeted contribution margin per unit}$$

Deluxe	{12,000 − [75,000 × (10,000/70,000)]} × ($20 − $8) =	$15,432 F
Standard	{4,000 − [85,000 × (5,000/90,000)]} × ($10 − $5) =	3,610 U
Total		$11,822 F

EXHIBIT 12–6 Actual and Budgeted Results: Ace Video Company

	Actual Results		Flexible Budget		Master Budget	
Revenue:						
Deluxe	(12,000 × $18)	$216,000	(12,000 × $20)	$240,000	(10,000 × $20)	$200,000
Standard	(4,000 × $11)	44,000	(4,000 × $10)	40,000	(5,000 × $10)	50,000
		260,000		280,000		250,000
Variable expenses:						
Deluxe	(12,000 × $8)	96,000	(12,000 × $8)	96,000	(10,000 × $8)	80,000
Standard	(4,000 × $5)	20,000	(4,000 × $5)	20,000	(5,000 × $5)	25,000
		116,000		116,000		105,000
Contribution margin		$144,000		$164,000		$145,000
		Sales Price Variance			**Sales Volume Variance**	
Total variances		$20,000 U			$19,000 F	

The market share variance shows what changes from the anticipated market share provided in terms of budgeted contribution margin. For example, if sales were 12,000 units of a total of 75,000 when management anticipated 10,000 of a total market of 70,000, then budgeted contribution would increase by $15,432, where the units are rounded to the nearest whole unit (1,286 units from 1285.71 units).

The market volume analysis and market share variances were calculated using the budget contribution margin. The use of the budget contribution numbers permits the isolation of volume effects from price effects, at least for purposes of presentation. Ultimately, managers may wish to consider the elasticity of the market in setting their future strategies, that is, they need to consider how sales volume will react to changes in sales price.

The market volume variance used contribution margins. This is a common approach so that the profit effect of volume changes can be viewed. Alternative valuations could be used, such as budgeted sales prices or budgeted gross margins, if managers find these values more relevant.

The total market volume variance and market share variance help to analyze why sales quantities were 12,000 deluxe and 4,000 standard instead of the anticipated 10,000 deluxe and 5,000 standard. These quantity shifts resulted in a change in budgeted contribution as follows:

Deluxe	(12,000 − 10,000) × ($20 − $8) =	$24,000 F
Standard	(4,000 − 5,000) × ($10 − $5) =	5,000 U
Total		$19,000 F
Composition:	Market volume =	$ 7,182 F
	Market share =	11,822 F
		$19,004 F*

*$4 due to rounding

An alternative view of sales volume variances can be generated by examining sales mix and sales quantity variances in terms of their relationship to the budgeted contribution margin. To be meaningful, management must be in a position to control the mix of products it sells in the market. While alternative formulations are possible using gross margins, sales prices, or weighted average contribution margins, the straightforward use of contributions will be employed in the illustration that follows so the principle can be understood.

Sales mix variance
Actual sales quantity minus actual sales quantity based on budgeted mix, all times budgeted contribution margin.

$$\text{Sales mix variance} = \left(\text{Actual sales quantity} - \text{Actual sales quantity at anticipated sales mix}\right) \times \text{Budgeted contribution margin per unit}$$

Deluxe	{[12,000 − 16,000 × (10/15)]} × ($20 − $8)	=	$15,996 F
Standard	{[4,000 − 16,000 × (5/15)]} × ($10 − $5)	=	6,665 U
Total sales mix variance		=	$ 9,331 F

Note: 16,000 units = (12,000 + 4,000) and 10/15 is the anticipated proportion of deluxe sales while 5/15 is the anticipated standard mix proportion.

Sales quantity variance
Actual sales quantity based on budgeted mix minus budgeted sales quantity, all times budgeted contribution margin.

$$\text{Sales quantity variance} = \left\{\left[\text{Actual sales quantity at anticipated sales mix}\right] - \text{Anticipated sales quantity}\right\} \times \text{Budgeted contribution margin per unit}$$

Deluxe	{[16,000 × (10/15)] − 10,000} × ($20 − $8)	=	$8,004 F
Standard	{[16,000 × (5/15)] − 5,000} × ($10 − $5)	=	1,665 F
Total sales quantity variance			$9,669 F

The total sales volume variance was $19,000 contribution, composed of the following:

Sales mix	$ 9,331 F
Sales quantity	9,669 F
Total	$19,000 F

MARKETING EXPENSE

LEARNING OBJECTIVE **4**
Analyze marketing expenses using cost drivers.

Knowledge of the nature and behaviour of marketing expenses provides managers with information about the costs of their marketing endeavours. Such information represents a significant aspect of marketing efforts, one that is needed to complement the pricing strategy previously discussed. Transport, warehousing, selling, advertising, and credit are some of the key factors managers need to consider in their marketing strategy. Accurate cost behaviour and allocation by the accounting function can assist marketing decision makers.

Accountants typically decompose marketing expense into two general categories, order-getting and order-filling. Order-getting costs are the pure marketing costs such as advertising, selling commissions, and travel. Order-filling includes the costs of warehousing, transportation, packing, and credit. Order-getting costs tend to be somewhat more discretionary than order-filling because order-filling occurs after the sale rather than to obtain the sale. Nevertheless, marketing managers need to understand the cost behaviour associated with both sets of costs so that analysis can be conducted to decide on what should be done and how. The simplified fixed variable analysis using sales dollars or sales units is too crude to provide suitable answers for many situations. Consider the following illustration:

Driver Analysis	Total for Period
Transport (kilometres to customer)	390 km
Jones Ltd.—30 km per shipment	
Smith Ltd.—60 km per shipment	
Selling (hours spent to call on per period)	150 hours
Jones Ltd.—50 hours	
Smith Ltd.—100 hours	
Advertising (relative cost of medium per period)	$4,000
Jones Ltd.—3 weight for mostly television	
Smith Ltd.—1 weight for mostly Internet	
Warehousing (space occupied)	5,880 m^3
Product A—50 cubic metres per unit	
Product B—80 cubic metres per unit	
Credit/Collection (invoice ratio per shipment—Jones requires more time to pay and line-item invoicing):	
Jones Ltd.—2 invoices per shipment, 10 units per invoice (4 of A, 6 of B)	5 shipments
Smith Ltd.—1 invoice per shipment, 10 units per invoice (6 of A, 4 of B)	4 shipments

	Costs for Period	
	Total	Unit
Transport	$ 1,950	$5 per km
Selling	7,500	$50 per hr
Advertising	4,000	—
Warehousing	6,500	$1.105 per m^3
Credit/Collection	750	$53.57 per invoice
Total	$20,700	

When costs for a period are associated with their drivers and drivers can be associated with customers, marketing costs demonstrate the costs associated with particular customers.

	Costs to Customer		
	Jones Ltd.	Smith Ltd.	Total
Transport:			
$5/km × 5 shipments × 30 km	$750		
$5/km × 4 shipments × 60 km		$1,200	$1,950
Selling:			
$50/hr × 50 hours	2,500		
$50/hr × 100 hours		5,000	7,500
Advertising: 3/4 × $4,000	3,000		
1/4 × $4,000		1,000	4,000
Warehousing:			
$1.105 m^3 × 5 × [(4 × 50) + (6 × 80)]	3,760*		
$1.105 m^3 × 4 × [(6 × 50) + (4 × 80)]		2,740	6,500
Credit/Collection:			
$53.57/invoice × 2 × 5	536		
$53.57/invoice × 1 × 4		214	750
	$10,546	$10,154	$20,700

*Rounded up. 5 shipments × m^3 per shipment.

	Costs to Products		
	Product A	Product B	Total
Transport—common	—	—	$1,950
Selling—common	—	—	7,500
Advertising—common	—	—	4,000
Warehousing:			
$1.105 m^3 \times [(4 \times 5) + (6 \times 4)] \times 50 m^3$	$2,431		
$1.105 m^3 \times [(6 \times 5) + (4 \times 4)] \times 80 m^3$		$4,069*	$6,500
Credit/Collection—common	—	—	750
	$2,431	$4,069	$20,700

*Rounded up. Cost per m^3 × units of product × space occupied per unit of A or B.

If the provided data are resegmented for the two products, A and B, then the marketing expense can be broken down for the warehousing. However, the other costs cannot be broken down because transport, selling, and advertising are independent of the type of product, and are treated as common costs for the product breakdown above. A similar situation exists for credit/collection since invoicing and collection costs are irrespective of the type of product. Only warehousing is a function of the product type and thus can be broken down by product type as well as by customer.

Marketing expense analysis uses the concepts of drivers to provide alternative views of the relationship of marketing costs to sales. The complexity of the analysis depends on the ability to define appropriate cost drivers for the marketing costs in a manner similar to the approach used with overhead costs as explained in Chapter 8. To avoid unnecessary arbitrary allocations, expenses that do not have suitable drivers should be treated as common costs that are not incremental for the particular categories of the breakdown attempted. Management may decide that further analysis of these common costs can result in refined driver definitions, which in turn will permit cause/effect allocations of common marketing costs.

CUSTOMER PROFITABILITY—A SUMMARY

Analysis of customer profitability by including drivers for marketing and administration can provide opportunities for important strategic decisions. Knowledge of the profitability of customers or customer classes can lead to decisions about not selling, surcharges for extra services, cross-selling opportunities, and changes in marketing approaches. Enterprise resource planning or similar computer systems can make the detailed analysis feasible and provide personnel with ratings of customer types so that the appropriate approach can be instituted for individual customers. With a wide variety of products and services, such analysis can be important, because all customers are not necessarily homogeneous and thus not equally profitable. Also, increases in sales value do not necessarily equate to increases in profitability because of the cost of providing the product services that customers demand.

RATE OF RETURN FOR MEASURING MANAGERIAL PERFORMANCE

LEARNING OBJECTIVE 5
Analyze the return on investment (ROI).

When a company is truly decentralized, segment managers are given a great deal of autonomy. So great is this autonomy that the various responsibility centres are often viewed as being virtually independent businesses, with their managers having about the same control over decisions as if they were in fact running their own independent firms. With this autonomy, competition often develops among managers, with each striving to make her or his segment the "best" in the company.

Competition between investment centres is particularly keen for investment funds. How do top managers in corporate headquarters go about deciding who gets new investment funds as they become available, and how do these managers decide which investment centres are most profitably using the funds that have already been entrusted to their care? One of the most popular ways of making these judgements is to measure the rate of return that investment centre managers are able to generate on their assets. This rate of return is called the *return on investment (ROI).*

The Return on Investment (ROI) Formula

The **return on investment (ROI)** is defined as operating income divided by average operating assets:

$$\text{ROI} = \frac{\text{Operating income}}{\text{Average operating assets}}$$

Return on investment (ROI) Operating income divided by average operating assets. ROI also equals margin multiplied by turnover.

There are some issues about how to measure operating income and average operating assets, but this formula seems clear enough. The higher the return on investment (ROI) of a business segment, the greater the profit generated per dollar invested in the segment's operating assets.

Operating Income and Operating Assets Defined

Note that *operating income,* rather than net income, is used in the ROI formula. **Operating income** is income before interest and taxes and is sometimes referred to as EBIT (earnings before interest and taxes). The reason for using operating income in the formula is that the income figure used should be consistent with the base to which it is applied. Notice that the base (i.e., denominator) consists of *operating assets.* Thus, to be consistent we use operating income in the numerator because no debt is included in the denominator, and interest expense is paid for by the profits from the operating assets and thus is a distribution of those profits rather than an expense.

Operating income Income before interest and income taxes have been deducted.

Operating assets include cash, accounts receivable, inventory, plant and equipment, and all other assets held for productive use in the organization. Examples of assets that would not be included in the operating assets category (i.e., examples of non-operating assets) would include land held for future use, an investment in another company, or a factory building rented to someone else. The operating assets base used in the formula is typically computed as the average of the operating assets between the beginning and the end of the year.

Operating assets Cash, accounts receivable, inventory, plant and equipment, and all other assets held for productive use in an organization.

Plant and Equipment: Net Book Value or Gross Cost?

A major issue in ROI computations is the dollar amount of plant and equipment that should be included in the operating assets base. To illustrate the problem involved, assume that a company reports the following amounts for plant and equipment on its balance sheet:

Plant and equipment	$3,000,000
Less accumulated depreciation	900,000
Net book value	$2,100,000

What dollar amount of plant and equipment should the company include with its operating assets in computing ROI? One widely used approach is to include only the plant and equipment's *net book value*—that is, the plant's original cost less accumulated depreciation ($2,100,000 in the example above). A second approach is to ignore depreciation and include the plant's entire *gross cost* in the operating assets base ($3,000,000 in the example above). Both of these approaches are used in actual practice, even though they will obviously yield very different operating asset and ROI figures.

The following arguments can be raised for using net book value to measure operating assets and for using gross cost to measure operating assets in ROI computation:

Arguments for Using Net Book Value to Measure Operating Assets in ROI Computations:

1. The net book value method is consistent with how plant and equipment are reported on the balance sheet (i.e., cost less accumulated depreciation to date).
2. The net book value method is consistent with the computation of operating income, which includes depreciation as an operating expense.

Arguments for Using Gross Cost to Measure Operating Assets in ROI Computations:

1. The gross cost method eliminates both the age of equipment and the method of depreciation as factors in ROI computations. (Under the net book value method, ROI will tend to increase over time as net book value declines due to depreciation.)
2. The gross cost method does not discourage replacement of old, worn-out equipment. (Under the net book value method, replacing fully depreciated equipment with new equipment can have a dramatic, adverse effect on ROI.)

Managers generally view consistency as the most important of the considerations above. As a result, a majority of companies use the net book value approach in ROI computations. In this text, we will also use the net book value approach unless a specific exercise or problem directs otherwise.

CONTROLLING THE RATE OF RETURN

When we first defined the return on investment, we used the following formula:

$$\text{ROI} = \frac{\text{Operating income}}{\text{Average operating assets}}$$

We can modify this formula slightly by introducing sales as follows:

$$\text{ROI} = \frac{\text{Operating income}}{\text{Sales}} \times \frac{\text{Sales}}{\text{Average operating assets}}$$

The first term on the right-hand side of the equation is the *margin,* which is defined as follows:

$$\text{Margin} = \frac{\text{Operating income}}{\text{Sales}}$$

Margin
Operating income divided by sales.

The **margin** is a measure of management's ability to control operating expenses in relation to sales. The lower the operating expenses per dollar of sales, the higher the margin earned.

FOCUS ***on Current Practice***

The release of the delayed financial reports of Nortel Networks Corp has presented an opportunity to analyze the results of its business. One analysis, namely BMO Nesbitt Burns, reports its concern over the use of lower depreciation rates than those used by Lucent, Cisco and Alcatel. In addition, the margin on Nortel's wireless business, earnings before taxes to revenue, was reported to be 13% in the latest quarter (2nd quarter 2004) rather than 18% as it has been even though revenues had increased in the quarter.

Source: Ian Karleff, "The Cracks in Nortel's Financials," *National Post*, February 3, 2005, p. IN1.

The second term on the right-hand side of the preceding equation is *turnover*, which is defined as follows:

$$\text{Turnover} = \frac{\text{Sales}}{\text{Average operating assets}}$$

Turnover is a measure of the sales that are generated for each dollar invested in operating assets.

Turnover
The amount of sales generated in an investment centre for each dollar invested in operating assets. It is computed by dividing sales by the average operating assets figure.

The following alternative form of the ROI formula, which we will use most frequently, combines margin and turnover:

$$\text{ROI} = \text{Margin} \times \text{Turnover}$$

Which formula for ROI should be used—the original one, stated in terms of operating income and average operating assets or this one, stated in terms of margin and turnover? Either can be used—they will always give the same answer. However, the margin and turnover formulation provides some additional insights.

Some managers tend to focus too much on margin and ignore turnover. To some degree at least, the margin can be a valuable indicator of a manager's performance. Standing alone, however, it overlooks one very crucial area of a manager's responsibility—the investment in operating assets. Excessive funds tied up in operating assets, which depresses turnover, can be just as much of a drag on profitability as excessive operating expenses, which depress margin. One of the advantages of ROI as a performance measure is that it forces the manager to control the investment in operating assets as well as to control expenses and the margin.

Du Pont pioneered the ROI concept and recognized the importance of looking at both margin and turnover in assessing the performance of a manager. The ROI formula is now widely used as the key measure of the performance of an investment centre. The ROI formula blends together many aspects of the manager's responsibilities into a single figure that can be compared to the returns of competing investment centres, the returns of other firms in the industry, and the past returns of the investment centre itself.

Du Pont also developed the diagram that appears in Exhibit 12–7. This exhibit helps managers understand how they can control ROI. An investment centre manager can increase ROI in basically three ways:

1. Increase sales.
2. Reduce expenses.
3. Reduce assets.

To illustrate how the rate of return can be improved by each of these three actions, consider how the manager of the Monthaven Burger Grill is evaluated. Burger Grill is a small chain of upscale casual restaurants that has been rapidly adding outlets via franchising. The Monthaven franchise is owned by a group of local surgeons who have little time to devote to management and little expertise in business matters. Therefore, they delegate operating decisions—including decisions concerning investment in operating assets such as inventories—to a professional manager they have hired. The manager is evaluated largely based on the ROI the franchise generates.

The following data represent the results of operations for the most recent month:

Operating income	$ 10,000
Sales	100,000
Average operating assets	50,000

The rate of return generated by the Monthaven Burger Grill investment centre is as follows:

$$\begin{aligned}\text{ROI} &= \text{Margin} \times \text{Turnover}\\ &= \frac{\text{Operating income}}{\text{Sales}} \times \frac{\text{Sales}}{\text{Average operating assets}}\end{aligned}$$

$$\frac{\$10{,}000}{\$100{,}000} \times \frac{\$100{,}000}{\$50{,}000}$$

$$10\% \times 2 = 20\%$$

As we stated previously, to improve the ROI figure, the manager can (1) increase sales, (2) reduce expenses, or (3) reduce the operating assets.

Approach 1: Increase Sales Assume that the manager of the Monthaven Burger Grill is able to increase sales from $100,000 to $110,000. Assume further that either because of good cost control or because some costs in the company are fixed, the operating income increases even more rapidly, going from $10,000 to $12,000 per period. The operating assets remain constant.

$$\text{ROI} = \frac{\$12{,}000}{\$110{,}000} \times \frac{\$110{,}000}{\$50{,}000}$$

$$10.91\% \times 2.2 = 24\% \text{ (as compared to 20\% above)}$$

Approach 2: Reduce Expenses Assume that the manager of the Monthaven Burger Grill is able to reduce expenses by $1,000 so that operating income increases from $10,000 to $11,000. Both sales and operating assets remain constant.

$$\text{ROI} = \frac{\$11{,}000}{\$100{,}000} \times \frac{\$100{,}000}{\$50{,}000}$$

$$11\% \times 2 = 22\% \text{ (as compared to 20\% above)}$$

EXHIBIT 12–7 Elements of Return on Investment (ROI)

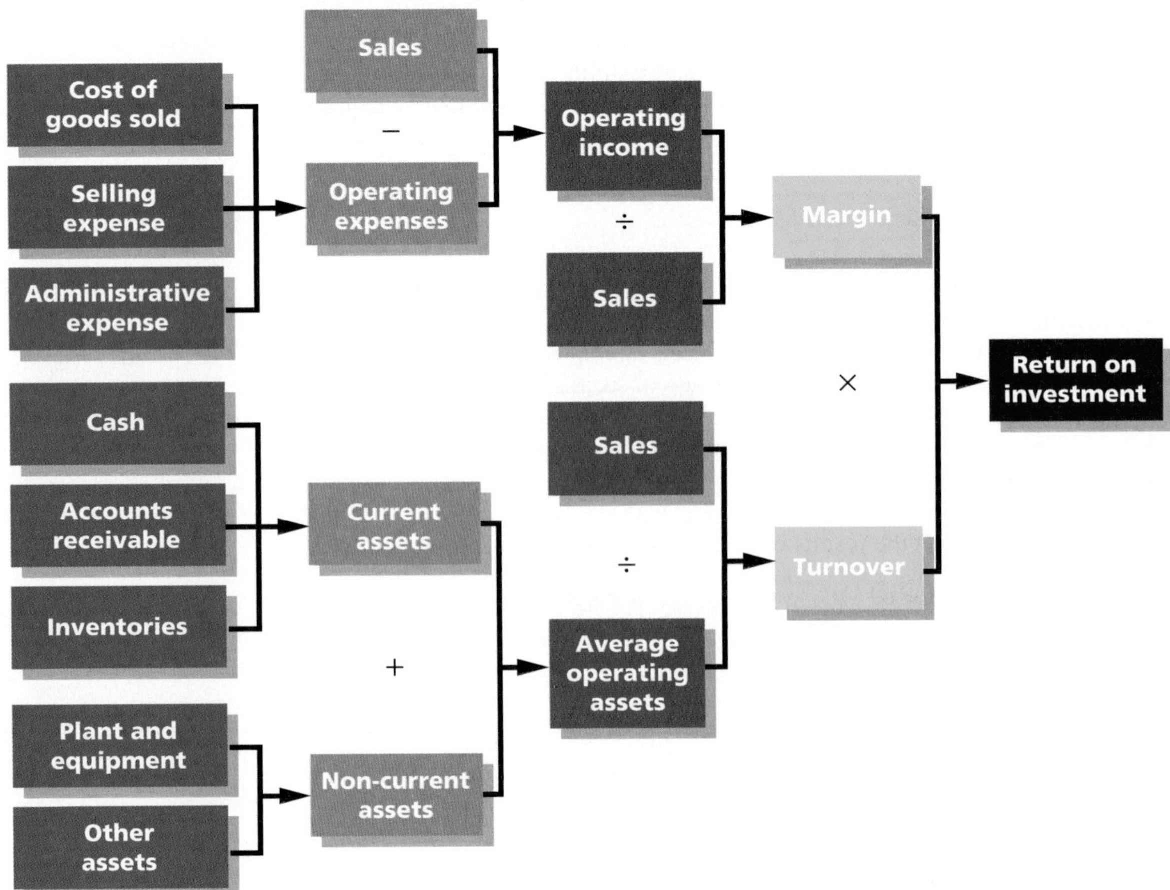

Approach 3: Reduce Operating Assets Assume that the manager of the Monthaven Burger Grill is able to reduce operating assets from $50,000 to $40,000. Sales and operating income remain unchanged.

$$\text{ROI} = \frac{\$10{,}000}{\$100{,}000} \times \frac{\$100{,}000}{\$40{,}000}$$

$$10\% \times 2.5 = 25\% \text{ (as compared to 20\% above)}$$

Note: The reduction in assets is included in the calculation for its whole amount.

A clear understanding of these three approaches to improving the ROI figure is critical to the effective management of an investment centre. We will now look at each approach in more detail.

Increase Sales

In first looking at the ROI formula, one is inclined to think that the sales figure is neutral, since it appears as the denominator in the margin computation and as the numerator in the turnover computation. We *could* cancel out the sales figure, but we do not do so for two reasons. First, this would tend to draw attention away from the fact that the rate of return is a function of *two* variables, margin and turnover. And second, it would tend to conceal the fact that a change in sales can affect both the margin and the turnover in an organization. To explain, a change in sales can affect the *margin* if expenses increase or decrease at a different rate than sales. For example, a company may be able to keep a tight control on its costs as its sales go up, with the result that operating income increases more rapidly than sales and increases the margin. Or a company may have fixed expenses that remain constant as sales go up, resulting in an increase in the operating income and in the margin. Either (or both) of these factors could have been responsible for the increase in the margin percentage from 10% to 10.91% illustrated in approach 1 above.

Further, a change in sales can affect the *turnover* if sales either increase or decrease without a proportionate increase or decrease in the operating assets. In the first approach above, for example, sales increased from $100,000 to $110,000, but the operating assets remained unchanged. As a result, the turnover increased from 2 to 2.2 for the period.

Reduce Expenses

Often the easiest route to increased profitability and to a stronger ROI figure is to simply cut the "fat" out of an organization through a concerted effort to control expenses. When margins begin to be squeezed, this is generally the first line of attack by a manager. Discretionary fixed costs usually come under scrutiny first, and various programs are either curtailed or eliminated in an effort to cut costs. Managers must be careful, however, not to cut out muscle and bone along with the fat. Also, they must remember that frequent cost-cutting binges can destroy morale. Most managers now agree that it is best to stay "lean and mean" all of the time.

Reduce Operating Assets

Managers have always been sensitive to the need to control sales, operating expenses, and operating margins. However, they have not always been equally sensitive to the need to control investment in operating assets. Firms that have adopted the ROI approach to measuring managerial performance report that one of the first reactions of investment centre managers is to trim their investment in operating assets. The reason, of course, is that these managers soon realize that an excessive investment in operating assets reduces turnover and hurts the ROI. As these managers reduce their investment in operating assets, funds are released that can be used elsewhere in the organization.

How can an investment centre manager control the investment in operating assets? One approach is to eliminate unneeded inventory. JIT purchasing and JIT manufacturing have been extremely helpful in reducing inventories of all types, with the result that ROI figures have improved dramatically in some companies. Another approach is to devise various methods of speeding up the collection of receivables. For example, many firms now employ Internet transfers by which customers in distant locations send their payments directly from their area. The funds are received and deposited by a local bank on behalf of the payee firm. This speeds up the collection process, since the payments are not delayed in the postal system. As a result of the speedup in collection, the accounts receivable balance is reduced and the asset turnover is increased.

FOCUS *on Current Practice*

Those who sell products and services to businesses are well aware that many potential customers look very carefully at the impact the purchase would have on ROI before making a purchase. Unfortunately, some salespersons make extravagant ROI claims. For example, businesspeople complain that software salespersons routinely exaggerate the impact that new software will have on ROI. Some of the tricks used by salespersons include: inflating the salaries of workers who are made redundant by productivity gains; omitting costs such as training costs and implementation costs; inflating expected sales increases; and using former clients as examples of ROI gains when the clients were given the software for free or for nominal cost. The message? Be skeptical of salespersons' claims with respect to ROI gains from purchasing their products and services.

Source: Scott Leibs, "All Hail the ROI," *CFO*, April 2002, pp. 27–28.

Criticisms of ROI

Although ROI is widely used in evaluating performance, it is not a perfect tool. The method is subject to the following criticisms:

1. Just telling managers to increase ROI may not be enough. Managers may not know how to increase ROI; they may increase ROI in a way that is inconsistent with the company's strategy; or they may take actions that increase ROI in the short run but harm the company in the long run (such as cutting back on research and development).
2. A manager who takes over a business segment typically inherits many committed costs over which the manager has no control. These committed costs may be relevant in assessing the performance of the business segment as an investment but make it difficult to fairly assess the performance of the manager relative to other managers.
3. As discussed in the next section, a manager who is evaluated based on ROI may reject profitable investment opportunities.

RESIDUAL INCOME—ANOTHER MEASURE OF PERFORMANCE

LEARNING OBJECTIVE 6
Compute residual income and describe the strengths and weaknesses of this method of measuring performance.

Another approach to measuring an investment centre's performance focuses on a concept known as *residual income.* **Residual income** is the operating income that an investment centre earns above the minimum required return on its operating assets. Thus we use operating income as defined with ROI but reduce it by a special charge computed as a percentage of average operating assets. In equation form, residual income is calculated as follows:

Residual income
The operating income that an investment centre earns above the required return on its operating assets.

$$\text{Residual Income} = \text{Operating Income} - \left(\text{Average operating assets} \times \text{Minimum required rate of return}\right)$$

Economic value added (EVA) is a similar concept that differs in some details from residual income.[6] For example, under the economic value added concept, funds used for research and development are treated as investments rather than as expenses.[7] However, for our purposes, we will not draw any distinction between residual income and economic value added. We will illustrate residual income because the adjustments for EVA are complex and would create more confusion than is appropriate for this introduction.

Economic value added (EVA) A concept similar to residual income.

When residual income or economic value added is used to measure performance, the purpose is to maximize the total amount of residual income or economic value added, not to maximize overall ROI. Organizations as diverse as Coca-Cola, Quaker Oats, Domtar, and Nortel have embraced some version of residual income in recent years.

For purposes of illustration, consider the following data for an investment centre—the Ketchican Division of Alaskan Marine Services Corporation.

ALASKAN MARINE SERVICES CORPORATION
Ketchican Division
Basic Data for Performance Evaluation

Average operating assets	$100,000
Operating income	$ 20,000
Minimum required rate of return	15%

Alaskan Marine Services Corporation has long had a policy of evaluating investment centre managers based on ROI, but it is considering a switch to residual income. The controller of the company, who is in favour of the change to residual income, has provided the following table that shows how the performance of the division would be evaluated under each of the two methods:

ALASKAN MARINE SERVICES CORPORATION
Ketchican Division
Alternative Performance Measures

	ROI	Residual Income
Average operating assets	$100,000 (a)	$100,000
Operating income	$ 20,000 (b)	$ 20,000
ROI, (b) ÷ (a)	20%	
Minimum required return (15% × $100,000)		15,000
Residual income		$ 5,000

The reasoning underlying the residual income calculation is straightforward. The company is able to earn a rate of return of at least 15% on its investments. Since the company has invested $100,000 in the Ketchican Division in the form of operating assets, the company should be able to earn at least $15,000 (15% × $100,000) on this investment. Since the Ketchican Division's operating income is $20,000, the residual income above and beyond the minimum required return is $5,000. If residual income is adopted as the performance measure to replace ROI, the manager of the Ketchican Division would be evaluated based on the growth from year to year in residual income.

6. The basic idea underlying residual income and economic value added has been around for more than a hundred years. In recent years, economic value added has been popularized and trademarked by the consulting firm Stern, Stewart & Co.
7. Over 100 different adjustments could be made for deferred taxes, LIFO reserves, provisions for future liabilities, mergers and acquisitions, gains or losses due to changes in accounting rules, operating leases, and other accounts, but most companies make only a few. For further details, see "Measuring and Managing Shareholder Value Creation," *Management Accounting Guideline 44*, The Society of Management Accountants of Canada, 1997.

Motivation and Residual Income

One of the primary reasons why the controller of Alaskan Marine Services Corporation would like to switch from ROI to residual income has to do with how managers view new investments under the two performance measurement schemes. The residual income approach encourages managers to make investments that are profitable for the entire company but that would be rejected by managers who are evaluated by the ROI formula.

To illustrate this problem, suppose that the manager of the Ketchican Division is considering purchasing a computerized diagnostic machine to aid in servicing marine diesel engines. The machine would cost $25,000 and is expected to generate additional operating income of $4,500 a year. From the standpoint of the company, this would be a good investment since it promises a rate of return of 18% ($4,500 ÷ $25,000), which is in excess of the company's minimum required rate of return of 15%.

If the manager of the Ketchican Division is evaluated based on residual income, she would be in favour of the investment in the diagnostic machine evaluated below:

ALASKAN MARINE SERVICES CORPORATION
Ketchican Division
Performance Evaluated Using Residual Income

	Present	New Project	Overall
Average operating assets	$100,000	$25,000	$125,000
Operating income	$ 20,000	$ 4,500	$ 24,500
Minimum required return	15,000	3,750*	18,750
Residual income	$ 5,000	$ 750	$ 5,750

*$25,000 × 15% = $3,750. $25,000 is assumed to represent an average asset for purposes of evaluation.

Since the project would increase the residual income of the Ketchican Division, the manager would want to invest in the new diagnostic machine.

Now suppose that the manager of the Ketchican Division is evaluated based on ROI. The effect of the diagnostic machine on the division's ROI is computed below:

ALASKAN MARINE SERVICES CORPORATION
Ketchican Division
Performance Evaluated Using ROI

	Present	New Project	Overall
Average operating assets (a)	$100,000	$25,000	$125,000
Operating income (b)	$ 20,000	$ 4,500*	$ 24,500
ROI, (b) ÷ (a)	20%	18%	19.6%

*$25,000 × 18% = $4,500.

The new project reduces the division's ROI from 20% to 19.6%. This happens because the 18% rate of return on the new diagnostic machine, while above the company's 15% minimum rate of return, is below the division's present ROI of 20%. Therefore, the new diagnostic machine would drag the division's ROI down, even though it would be a good investment from the standpoint of the company as a whole. If the manager of the division is evaluated based on ROI, she will be reluctant to even propose such an investment.

Basically, a manager who is evaluated based on ROI will want to reject any project whose rate of return is below the division's current ROI even if the rate of return on the project is above the minimum required rate of return for the entire company. In contrast, any project whose rate of return is above the minimum required rate of return for the company will result in an increase in residual income and thus add value for the shareholders. Since it is in the best interests of the company as a whole to accept any project whose rate of return is above the minimum required rate of return, managers who are evaluated based on residual income will tend to make better decisions concerning investment projects than managers who are evaluated based on ROI.

Divisional Comparison and Residual Income

The residual income approach has one major disadvantage. It cannot be used to compare the performance of divisions of different sizes. You would expect larger divisions to have more residual income than smaller divisions, not necessarily because they are better managed but simply because of the bigger numbers involved.

As an example, consider the following residual income computations for Division X and Division Y:

	Division	
	X	Y
Average operating assets (a)	$1,000,000	$250,000
Operating income	$ 120,000	$ 40,000
Minimum required return: 10% × (a)	100,000	25,000
Residual income	$ 20,000	$ 15,000

Observe that Division X has slightly more residual income than Division Y, but that Division X has $1,000,000 in operating assets as compared to only $250,000 in operating assets for Division Y. Thus, Division X's greater residual income is probably more a result of its size than the quality of its management. In fact, it appears that the smaller division is better managed, since it has been able to generate nearly as much residual income with only one-fourth as much in operating assets with which to work. This problem can be reduced to some degree by focusing on the percentage change in residual income from year to year rather than on the absolute amount of the residual income.

RI/EVA SUMMARY

Residual income and its derivative economic value added (EVA) include in the final result a composite picture of revenue, expenses, assets, and the cost of investment capital (debt and equity). This measure is suggested to be more closely related to share price activity than any of the individual or other composites such as revenue growth, net income however defined, or ROI. Thus, the advantage of the measure of performance is its focus on a key strategic objective: shareholder returns. Other suggested advantages include a more direct link to capital budgets similar to that shown in Chapter 14 when comparing ROI to net present value. The more direct relationship of EVA to share prices provides a base for senior executive bonuses that helps to direct these executives in a manner that is consistent with shareholder interests.

EVA and residual income are not without their detractors. Both are historically based, which means that particularly capital assets can suffer from being out of date in the manner mentioned with ROI. EVA/RI do not suggest whether the results achieved are the "best" that could have been achieved; thus, a means of comparison is needed to evaluate results. EVA requires numerous adjustments that can increase the cost of preparing the information. EVA and residual income provide a single composite result that lacks the comprehensiveness of balanced scorecards. However, regardless of the difficulties, EVA represents an example of the attempts to measure performance in a manner that focuses results on the strategic objectives of the firm.[8]

BALANCED SCORECARD

LEARNING OBJECTIVE 6
Understand how a balanced scorecard fits together and how it supports a company's strategy.

Simply exhorting managers to increase ROI is not sufficient. Managers who are told to increase ROI will naturally wonder how this is to be accomplished. The Du Pont scheme, which is illustrated in Exhibit 12–7, provides managers with *some* guidance. Generally speaking, ROI can be increased by increasing sales, decreasing costs, and/or decreasing investments in operating assets. However, it may not be obvious to managers *how* they are supposed to increase sales, decrease costs, and decrease investments in a way that is consistent with the company's strategy. For example, a manager who is given inadequate guidance may cut back on investments that are critical to implementing the company's strategy. A *balanced scorecard* represents a method of providing more explicit direction to managers as to how they should implement strategy.

Balanced scorecard
An integrated set of performance measures that is derived from and supports the organization's strategy.

A **balanced scorecard** consists of an integrated set of performance measures that is derived from the company's strategy and that supports the company's strategy throughout the organization.[9,10] A strategy is essentially a theory about how to achieve the organization's goals and deals with issues such as how to attract customers, what products or services to sell, what markets to enter, and how to compete with rivals. According to some experts, there are three potentially successful generic strategic approaches to outperforming competitors:[11]

1. **Cost leadership:** By maintaining low cost through efficiency relative to competitors, a company will be able to make superior profits at current industry prices. Alternatively, the company can become a price leader because other firms are unable to undercut its prices. Low costs may also serve as a barrier against potential new market entrants and thereby protect long-term profitability. However, technological change or imitation of low-cost techniques by rivals can threaten the success of this strategy.
2. **Differentiation:** For products or services that are perceived as unique, customers sometimes will pay premium prices, giving the company higher profit margins. This cushion of higher profits reduces the effect of supplier or buyer power. Brand loyalty, however, may fail if the cost differential between the firm and the cost leader in the industry becomes too wide.
3. **Focus or niche:** By serving a narrow, strategic target market more effectively than rivals who are competing more broadly, a firm may be able to achieve superior profitability. The risk of being overtaken by broad-target firms who have economies of scale is a constant threat to the success of this strategy.

---

8. For more technical discussions and alternative measures of EVA, see Michael Senyshen, "Touch of EVA," *CGA Magazine*, February 1999, pp. 20–27.
9. The balanced scorecard concept was promoted by Robert Kaplan and David Norton. For further details, see their articles "The Balanced Scorecard—Measures That Drive Performance," *Harvard Business Review*, January/February 1992, pp. 71–79; "Using the Balanced Scorecard as a Strategic Management System," *Harvard Business Review*, January/February 1996, pp. 75–85; "Why Does a Business Need a Balanced Scorecard?" *Journal of Cost Management*, May/June 1997, pp. 5–10; and their book *Translating Strategy into Action: The Balanced Scorecard* (Boston, MA: Harvard Business School Press, 1996).
10. In the 1960s, the French developed a concept similar to the balanced scorecard called *Tableau de Bord* or "dashboard." For details, see Michel Lebas, "Managerial Accounting in France: Overview of Past Tradition and Current Practice," *The European Accounting Review* 3, no. 3, 1994, pp. 471–87; and Marc Epstein and Jean-François Manzoni, "The Balanced Scorecard and the Tableau de Bord: Translating Strategy into Action," *Management Accounting*, August 1997, pp. 28–36.
11. Michael E. Porter, *Competitive Strategy: Creating and Sustaining Superior Performance* (New York, NY: Free Press, 1985).

To be successful in implementing either a cost leadership or differentiation strategy, the firm must be better than all of its industry rivals. Since only a few firms have enough resources to accomplish this, many firms adopt a focus strategy.

For example, Air Canada could adopt a strategy to offer passengers low prices and fun on short-haul jet service. The low prices result from the absence of costly frills such as meals, assigned seating, and interline baggage checking. The fun is provided by flight attendants who go out of their way to entertain passengers with their antics. This is an interesting strategy. The airline could consciously hire people who have a sense of humour and who enjoy their work. Hiring and retaining such employees probably costs no more—and may cost less—than retaining grumpy flight attendants who view their jobs as a chore. The purpose of this strategy is to build loyal customers through a combination of "fun"—which does not cost anything to provide—and low prices that are possible because of the lack of costly frills offered by competing airlines. The theory is that low prices and fun will lead to loyal customers, which, in combination with low costs, will lead to high profits.

Under the balanced scorecard approach, top management translates its strategy into performance measures that employees can understand and can do something about. For example, the length of time passengers have to wait in line to have their baggage checked might be a performance measure for the supervisor in charge of the Air Canada check-in counter at the Vancouver airport. This performance measure is easily understood by the supervisor, and can be improved by the supervisor's actions.

Common Characteristics of Balanced Scorecards

Performance measures used in the balanced scorecard approach tend to fall into the four groups illustrated in Exhibit 12–8: financial, customer, internal business processes, and learning and growth. Internal business processes are what the company does in an attempt to satisfy customers. For example, in a manufacturing company, assembling a product is an internal business process. For an airline, handling baggage is an internal business process. The basic idea is that learning is necessary to improve internal business processes; improving business processes is necessary to improve customer satisfaction; and improving customer satisfaction is necessary to improve financial results.

Note that the emphasis in Exhibit 12–8 is on *improvement*—not on just attaining some specific objective such as profits of $10 million. In the balanced scorecard approach, continual improvement is encouraged. In many industries, this is a matter of survival. If an organization does not continually improve, it will eventually lose out to competitors that do.

Financial performance measures appear at the top of Exhibit 12–8. Ultimately, most companies exist to provide financial rewards to owners. There are exceptions. Some companies—for example, The Body Shop—may have loftier goals, such as providing environmentally friendly products to consumers. However, even non-profit organizations must generate enough financial resources to stay in operation.

Ordinarily, top managers are responsible for the financial performance measures—not lower-level managers. The supervisor in charge of checking in passengers can be held responsible for how long passengers have to wait in line. However, this supervisor cannot reasonably be held responsible for the entire company's profit. That is the responsibility of the airline's top managers.

Exhibit 12–9 lists some examples of performance measures that can be found on the balanced scorecards of companies. However, few companies, if any, would use all of these performance measures, and almost all companies would add other performance measures. Managers should carefully select the performance measures for their company's balanced scorecard, keeping the following points in mind. First and foremost, the performance measures should be consistent with, and follow from, the company's strategy. If the performance measures are not consistent with the company's strategy, people will find themselves working at cross-purposes. Second, the scorecard should not have too many performance measures. This can lead to a lack of focus and confusion.

EXHIBIT 12–8 From Strategy to Performance Measures: The Balanced Scorecard

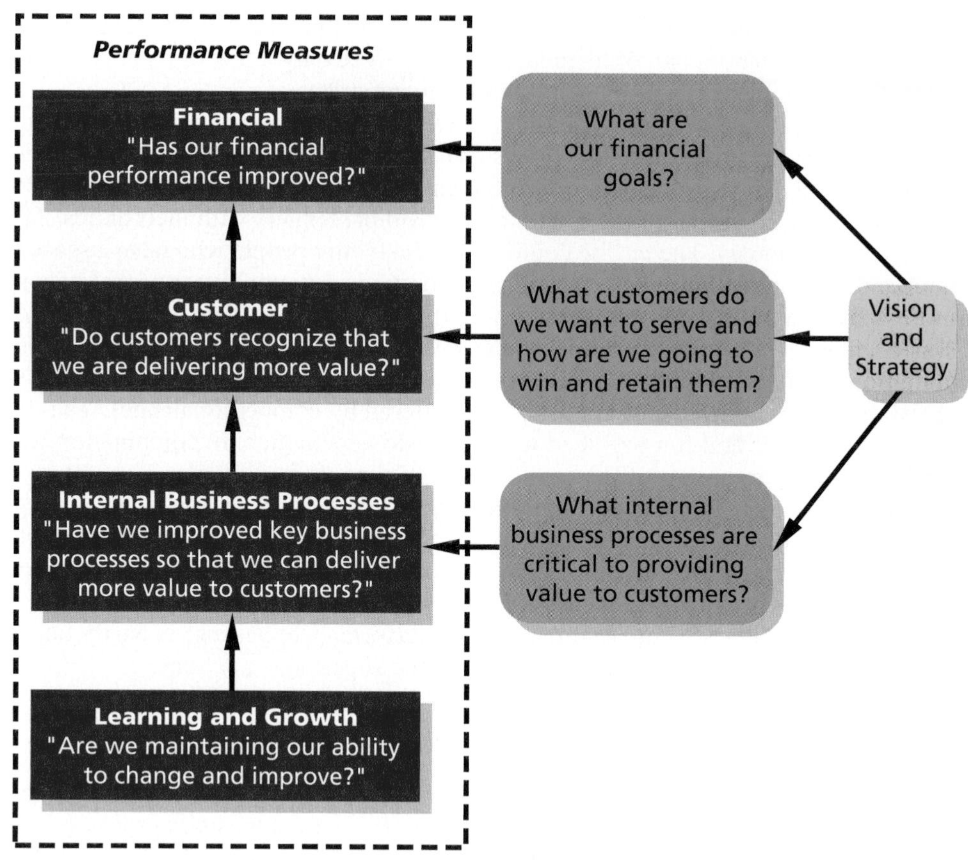

While the entire organization will have an overall balanced scorecard, each responsible individual will have his or her own personal scorecard as well. This scorecard should consist of items the individual can personally influence that relate directly to the performance measures on the overall balanced scorecard. The performance measures on this personal scorecard should not be overly influenced by actions taken by others in the company or by events that are outside of the individual's control.

With those broad principles in mind, we will now take a look at how a company's strategy affects its balanced scorecard.

A Company's Strategy and the Balanced Scorecard

Returning to the performance measures in Exhibit 12–8, each company must decide which customers to target and what internal business processes are crucial to attracting and retaining those customers. Different companies, having different strategies, will target different customers with different kinds of products and services. Take the automobile industry as an example. BMW stresses engineering and handling; Volvo, safety; Jaguar, luxury detailing; Corvette, racy styling; and Toyota, reliability. Because of these differences in emphases, a one-size-fits-all approach to performance measurement will not work even within this one industry. Performance measures must be tailored to the specific strategy of each company.

Suppose, for example, that Jaguar's strategy is to offer distinctive, richly finished luxury automobiles to wealthy individuals who prize handcrafted, individualized products. Part of Jaguar's strategy might be to create such a large number of options for details, such as leather seats, interior and exterior colour combinations, and wooden looking dashboards, that each car becomes virtually one of a kind. For example, instead

EXHIBIT 12–9 Examples of Performance Measures for Balanced Scorecards

Customer Perspective	
Performance Measure	**Desired Change**
Customer satisfaction as measured by survey results	+
Number of customer complaints	−
Market share	+
Product returns as a percentage of sales	−
Percentage of customers retained from last period	+
Number of new customers	+

Internal Business Processes Perspective	
Performance Measure	**Desired Change**
Percentage of sales from new products	+
Time to introduce new products to market	−
Percentage of customer calls answered within 20 seconds	+
On-time deliveries as a percentage of all deliveries	+
Work in process inventory as a percentage of sales	−
Unfavourable standard cost variances	−
Defect-free units as a percentage of completed units	+
Delivery cycle time*	−
Throughput time*	−
Manufacturing cycle efficiency*	+
Quality costs†	−
Set-up time	−
Time from call by customer to repair of product	−
Percent of customer complaints settled on first contact	+
Time to settle a customer claim	−

Learning and Growth Perspective	
Performance Measure	**Desired Change**
Suggestions per employee	+
Value-added employee‡	+
Employee turnover	−
Hours of in-house training per employee	+

*Explained later in this chapter.
†See Chapter 2.
‡Value-added is revenue less externally purchased materials, supplied, and services.

of just offering tan or blue leather seats in standard cowhide, the company may offer customers the choice of an almost infinite palette of colours in any of a number of different exotic leathers. For such a system to work effectively, Jaguar would have to be able to deliver a completely customized car within a reasonable amount of time—and without incurring more cost for this customization than the customer is willing to pay. Exhibit 12–10 suggests how Jaguar might reflect this strategy in its balanced scorecard.

If the balanced scorecard is correctly constructed, the performance measures should be linked together on a cause-and-effect basis. Each link can then be read as an hypothesis in the form "If we improve this performance measure, then this other performance measure should also improve." Starting from the bottom of Exhibit 12–10, we can read the links between performance measures as follows. If employees acquire the skills to install new options more effectively, then the company can offer more options and the options can be installed in less time. If more options are available and they are installed in less time, then customer surveys should show greater satisfaction with the range of

EXHIBIT 12–10 A Possible Strategy at Jaguar and the Balanced Scorecard

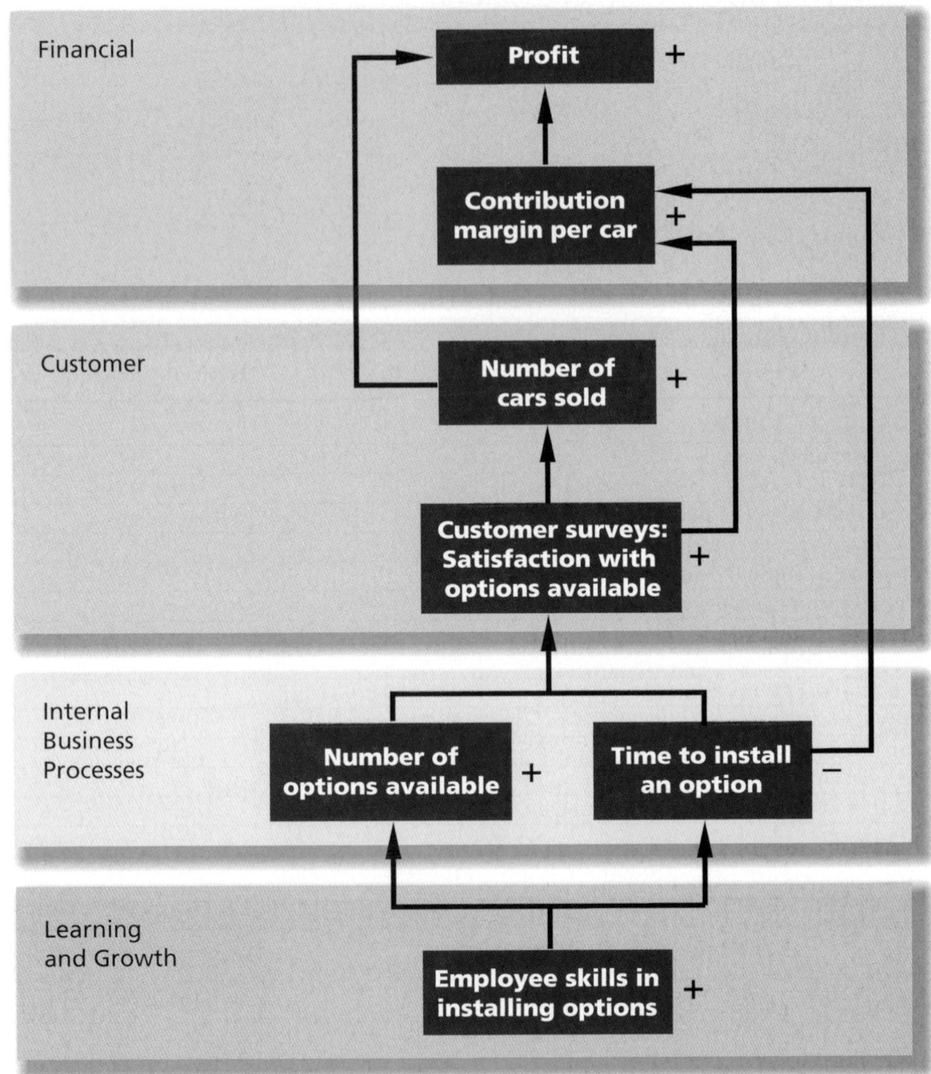

options available. If customer satisfaction improves, then the number of cars sold should increase. In addition, if customer satisfaction improves, the company should be able to maintain or increase its selling prices, and if the time to install options decreases, the costs of installing the options should decrease. Together, this should result in an increase in the contribution margin per car. If the contribution margin per car increases and more cars are sold, the result should be an increase in profits.

In essence, the balanced scorecard illustrates a theory of how the company can attain its desired outcomes (financial, in this case) by taking concrete actions. While the strategy laid out in Exhibit 12–10 seems plausible, it should be regarded as only a theory that should be discarded if it proves to be invalid. For example, if the company succeeds in increasing the number of options available and in decreasing the time required to install options and yet there is no increase in customer satisfaction, the number of cars sold, the contribution margin per car, or profits, the strategy would have to be reconsidered. One of the advantages of the balanced scorecard is that it continually tests the theories underlying management's strategy. If a strategy is not working, it should become evident when some of the predicted effects (i.e., more car sales) do not occur. Without this feedback, management may drift on indefinitely with an ineffective strategy based on faulty assumptions.

Advantages of Timely Feedback

Whatever performance measures are used, they should be reported on a frequent and timely basis. For example, data about defects should be reported to the responsible managers at least once a day so that action can be quickly taken if an unusual number of defects occurs. In the most advanced companies, any defect is reported *immediately*, and its cause is tracked down before any more defects can occur. Another common characteristic of the performance measures under the balanced scorecard approach is that managers focus on *trends* in the performance measures over time. The emphasis is on progress and *improvement* rather than on meeting any specific standard.

Some Measures of Internal Business Process Performance

Internal business process performance measures provide feedback needed for improving these processes. This information is essential for making cost and quality improvements that lead to greater profitability and customer satisfaction.

Most of the performance measures listed in Exhibit 12–9 are self-explanatory. However, three are not—*delivery cycle time*, *throughput time*, and *manufacturing cycle efficiency (MCE)*. These three important performance measures are discussed next.

Delivery Cycle Time

The amount of time from when an order is received from a customer to when the completed order is shipped is called **delivery cycle time.** This time is clearly a key concern to many customers, who would like the delivery cycle time to be as short as possible. Cutting the delivery cycle time may give a company a key competitive advantage—and may be necessary for survival—and therefore many companies would include this performance measure on their balanced scorecard.

Delivery cycle time
The amount of time required from receipt of an order from a customer to shipment of the completed goods.

Throughput (Manufacturing Cycle) Time

The amount of time required to turn raw materials into completed products is called **throughput time,** or *manufacturing cycle time*. The relationship between the delivery cycle time and the throughput (manufacturing cycle) time is illustrated in Exhibit 12–11.

Throughput time
The amount of time required to turn raw materials into completed products.

Note that, as shown in Exhibit 12–11, the throughput time, or manufacturing cycle time, is made up of process time, inspection time, move time, and queue time. *Process time* is the amount of time in which work is actually done on the product. *Inspection time* is the amount of time spent ensuring that the product is not defective. *Move time* is the time required to move materials or partially completed products from workstation to workstation. *Queue time* is the amount of time a product spends waiting to be worked on, to be moved, to be inspected, or in storage waiting to be shipped.

As shown at the bottom of Exhibit 12–11, the only one of these four activities that adds value to the product is process time. The other three activities—inspecting, moving, and queueing—add no value and should be eliminated as much as possible.

Manufacturing Cycle Efficiency (MCE)

Through concerted efforts to eliminate the *non-value-added* activities of inspecting, moving, and queueing, some companies have reduced their throughput time to only a fraction of previous levels. In turn, this has helped to reduce the delivery cycle time from months to only weeks or hours. The throughput time, which is considered to be a key measure in delivery performance, can be put into better perspective by computing the **manufacturing cycle efficiency (MCE).** The MCE is computed by relating the value-added time to the throughout time. The formula is as follows:

Manufacturing cycle efficiency (MCE)
Process (value-added) time as a percentage of throughput time.

$$\text{MCE} = \frac{\text{Value-added time}}{\text{Throughput (manufacturing cycle) time}}$$

EXHIBIT 12–11 Delivery Cycle Time and Throughput (Manufacturing Cycle) Time

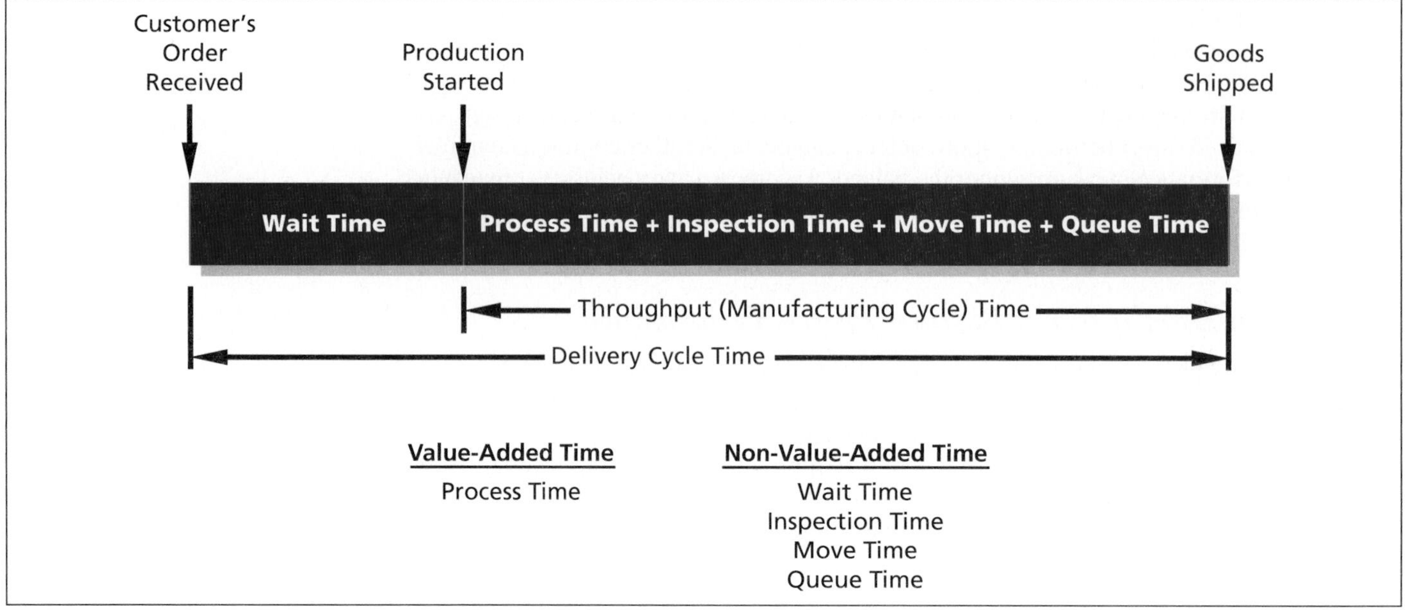

If the MCE is less than 1, then non-value-added time is present in the production process. An MCE of 0.5, for example, would mean that half of the total production time consisted of inspection, moving, and similar non-value-added activities. In many manufacturing companies, the MCE is less than 0.1 (10%), which means that 90% of the time a unit is in process is spent on activities that do not add value to the product.[12] By monitoring the MCE, companies are able to reduce non-value-added activities and thus get products into the hands of customers more quickly and at a lower cost.

To provide a numeric example of these measures, assume the following data for Novex Company:

Novex Company keeps careful track of the time relating to orders and their production. During the most recent quarter, the following average times were recorded for each unit or order:

	Days
Wait time	17.0
Inspection time	0.4
Process time	2.0
Move time	0.6
Queue time	5.0

Goods are shipped as soon as production is completed.

Required:

1. Compute the throughput time, or velocity of production.
2. Compute the manufacturing cycle efficiency (MCE).
3. What percentage of the production time is spent in non-value-added activities?
4. Compute the delivery cycle time.

12. Callie Berlinger and James A. Brimson, eds., *Cost Management for Today's Advanced Manufacturing* (Boston, MA: Harvard Business School Press, 1988), p. 4.

Solution

1. Throughput time = Process time + Inspection time + Move time + Queue time
   = 2.0 days + 0.4 days + 0.6 days + 5.0 days
   = 8.0 days
2. Only process time represents value-added time; therefore, the computation of the MCE would be as follows:

$$\text{MCE} = \frac{\text{Value-added time, 2.0 days}}{\text{Throughput time, 8.0 days}}$$
$$= 0.25$$

   Thus, once put into production, a typical unit is actually being worked on only 25% of the time.
3. Since the MCE is 25%, the complement of this figure, or 75% of the total production time, is spent in non-value-added activities.
4. Delivery cycle time = Wait time + Throughput time
   = 17.0 days + 8.0 days
   = 25.0 days

FOCUS *on Current Practice*

Banks ordinarily require three to four weeks to approve an application for a mortgage loan on a house. The application form includes the individual's employment history, income, and financial assets and liabilities. Personnel at the bank check credit references and review the entire application before granting the loan. A manager at one bank wondered why this process takes so long and asked employees to keep track of how much time they actually worked on processing an application. He discovered that processing an application took on average 26 days, but only about 15 minutes of this time was actual work. All of the rest of the time the application was waiting in someone's in-basket. The manufacturing cycle efficiency (MCE) was therefore only 0.0004 (15 minutes/[26 days × 24 hours per day × 60 minutes per hour]). By redesigning and automating the process, the cycle time was cut down to 15 minutes and the MCE rose to 1.0. Loan applicants can now have a cup of coffee while waiting for approval.

Source: Kaplan and Norton, *Translating Strategy into Action: The Balanced Scoreboard*, pp. 118–19.

Some Final Observations Concerning the Balanced Scorecard We would like to emphasize a few points concerning the balanced scorecard. First, the balanced scorecard should be tailored to the company's strategy; each company's balanced scorecard should be unique. The examples given in this chapter are just that—examples. They should not be interpreted as general templates to be fitted to each company. Second, the balanced scorecard reflects a particular strategy, or theory, about how a company can further its objectives by taking specific actions. The theory should be viewed as tentative and subject to change if the actions do not in fact lead to attaining the company's financial and other goals. If the theory (i.e., strategy) changes, then the performance measures on the balanced scorecard should also change. The balanced scorecard should be viewed as a dynamic system that evolves as the company's strategy evolves.

Balance scorecards provide a broader performance assessment and thus broader direction from ROI. These scorecards provide assessments of financial performance, customer performance, internal operational performance, and growth. The financial assessments include common measures such as ROI economic value added (residual income), or income. The customer focus would look at customer satisfaction and customer retention. Internal performance would examine the factors in the value chain such as research, new product sales, productivity, and efficiency of throughput. Growth would look at employee satisfaction, training, and turnover.

If such perspectives and measures are linked to the organization's strategies and are broken down into managerial segments, then clear direction is provided about what is expected of segment managers.[13] Because managers appear to use simplified decision rules in employing the diverse measures, questions do exist as to the quality of evaluations resulting from the use of balanced scorecards.[14]

SUMMARY

Segment reports can provide information for evaluating the profitability and performance of divisions, product lines, sales territories, and other segments of a company. Under the contribution approach to segment reporting, only those costs that are traceable are assigned to a segment. Fixed common costs and other non-traceable costs are not allocated to a segment. A cost is considered to be traceable to a segment only if the cost is caused by the segment and eliminating the segment would result in avoiding the cost.

Analysis provided by accountants can help managers view the important segment of marketing in a new light. Revenue and sales quantity analysis provide information about the effects of market changes or sales mix changes on profits. Association of marketing expenses with drivers that cause these expenses permits a review of how marketing activities cause expenses. Activity analysis is a powerful tool for assisting managers to understand marketing activities and their costs.

Costs that are traceable to a segment are further classified as either variable or fixed. The contribution margin is sales less variable costs. The segment margin is the contribution margin less the traceable fixed costs of the segment.

For purposes of evaluating the performance of managers, there are at least three kinds of business segments—cost centres, profit centres, and investment centres. Return on investment (ROI) is widely used to evaluate investment centre performance. However, there is a trend toward using residual income or economic value added instead of ROI. The residual income and economic value added approaches encourage profitable investments in many situations where the ROI approach would discourage investment.

The balanced scorecard is a promising approach to managing organizations. A balanced scorecard consists of an integrated system of performance measures that are derived from and support the company's strategy. Different companies will have different balanced scoreccards because they have different strategies. A well-constructed balanced scorecard provides a means for guiding the company and also provides feedback concerning the effectiveness of the company's strategy.

REVIEW PROBLEM 1: SEGMENTED STATEMENTS

The business staff of the legal firm Frampton, Davis & Smythe has constructed the report at the top of page 571, which breaks down the firm's overall results for last month in terms of its two main business segments—family law and commercial law.

However, this report is not quite correct. The common fixed expenses such as the managing partner's salary, general administrative expenses, and general firm advertising have been allocated to the two segments based on revenues from clients.

Required:

1. Redo the segment report, eliminating the allocation of common fixed expenses. Show both Amount and Percent columns for the firm as a whole and for each of the segments. Would the firm

---

13. Chris Moore, Beverly J. Rowe, and Sally K. Widener, "HCS: Designing a Balanced Scorecard in a Knowledge-Based Firm," *Issues in Accounting Education*, vol. 16, no. 4, Novermber 2001, pp. 569–81.
14. Marlys Gascho Lipe and Steven E. Salterio, "The Balanced Scoreccard: Judgmental Effects of Common and Unique Performance Measures," *The Accounting Review*, vol. 75, no. 3, July 2000, pp. 283–98.

	Total	Family Law	Commercial Law
Revenues from clients	$1,000,000	$400,000	$600,000
Less variable expenses	220,000	100,000	120,000
Contribution margin	780,000	300,000	480,000
Less traceable fixed expenses	670,000	280,000	390,000
Segment margin	110,000	20,000	90,000
Less common fixed expenses	60,000	24,000	36,000
Operating income	$ 50,000	$ (4,000)	$ 54,000

be better off financially if the family law segment was dropped? (Note: Many of the firm's commercial law clients also use the firm for their family law requirements, such as drawing up wills.)

2. The firm's advertising agency has proposed an ad campaign targeted at boosting the revenues of the family law segment. The ad campaign would cost $20,000, and the advertising agency claims that it would increase family law revenues by $100,000. The managing partner of Frampton, Davis & Smythe believes this increase in business could be accommodated without any increase in fixed expenses. What effect would this ad campaign have on the family law segment margin and on the overall operating income of the firm?

Solution to Review Problem 1

1. The corrected segmented income statement appears below:

	Total		Family Law		Commercial Law	
	Amount	Percent	Amount	Percent	Amount	Percent
Revenues from clients	$1,000,000	100%	$400,000	100%	$600,000	100%
Less variable expenses	220,000	22%	100,000	25%	120,000	20%
Contribution margin	780,000	78%	300,000	75%	480,000	80%
Less traceable fixed expenses	670,000	67%	280,000	70%	390,000	65%
Segment margin	110,000	11%	$ 20,000	5%	$ 90,000	15%
Less common fixed expenses	60,000	6%				
Operating income	$ 50,000	5%				

No, the firm would not be financially better off if the family law practice was dropped. The family law segment is covering all of its own costs and is contributing $20,000 to covering the common fixed expenses of the firm. While the segment margin as a percent of sales is much lower for family law than for commercial law, it is still profitable, and it is likely that family law is a service that the firm must provide to its commercial clients in order to remain competitive.

2. The ad campaign would be expected to add $55,000 to the family law segment as follows:

Increased revenues from clients	$100,000
Family law contribution margin ratio	× 75%
Incremental contribution margin	75,000
Less cost of the ad campaign	20,000
Increased segment margin	$ 55,000

Since there would be no increase in fixed expenses (including common fixed expenses), the increase in overall operating income should also be $55,000.

REVIEW PROBLEM 2: RETURN ON INVESTMENT (ROI) AND RESIDUAL INCOME

The Magnetic Imaging Division of Medical Diagnostics, Inc. has reported the following results for last year's operations:

Sales	$25 million
Operating income	3 million
Average operating assets	10 million

Required:

1. Compute the margin, turnover, and ROI for the Magnetic Imaging Division.
2. Top management of Medical Diagnostics, Inc. has set a minimum required rate of return on average operating assets of 25%. What is the Magnetic Imaging Division's residual income for the year?

Solution to Review Problem 2

1. The required calculations appear below:

$$\text{Margin} = \frac{\text{Operating income, \$3,000,000}}{\text{Sales, \$25,000,000}}$$
$$= 12\%$$

$$\text{Turnover} = \frac{\text{Sales, \$25,000,000}}{\text{Average operating assets, \$10,000,000}}$$
$$= 2.5$$

$$\text{ROI} = \text{Margin} \times \text{Turnover}$$
$$= 12\% \times 2.5$$
$$= 30\%$$

2. The residual income for the Magnetic Imaging Division is computed as follows:

Average operating assets	$10,000,000
Operating income	$ 3,000,000
Minimum required return (25% × $10,000,000)	2,500,000
Residual income	$ 500,000

APPENDIX 12A: TRANSFER PRICING

Transfer price The price charged when one division or segment provides goods or services to another division or segment of an organization.

There are special problems in evaluating the performance of business segments when goods or services are transferred from one division to another. The problems revolve around the question of what *transfer price* to charge between the segments. A **transfer price** is the price charged when one segment of a company provides goods or services to another segment of the company. For example, most companies in the oil industry, such as Imperial, Shell, and Petro-Canada, have petroleum refining and retail sales divisions that are evaluated on the basis of ROI or residual income. The petroleum refining division processes crude oil into gasoline, kerosene, lubricants, and other end products. The retail sales division takes gasoline and other products from the refining division and sells them through the company's chain of service stations. Each product has a price for transfers within the company. Suppose the transfer price for gasoline is $0.20 per litre. Then the refining division gets credit for $0.20 per litre of revenue on its segment report and the retailing division must deduct $0.20 per litre as an expense on its segment report. Clearly, the refining division would like the transfer price to be as high as possible, whereas the retailing division would like the transfer price to be as low as possible. However, the transaction has no direct effect on the entire company's reported profit. It is like taking money out of one pocket and putting it into the other.

Managers are intensely interested in how transfer prices are set, since they can have a dramatic effect on the apparent profitability of a division. Three common approaches are used to set transfer prices:

1. Allow the managers involved in the transfer to negotiate their own transfer prices.
2. Set transfer prices at cost using:
   a. Variable cost.
   b. Full (absorption) cost.
3. Set transfer prices at the market price.

We will consider each of these transfer pricing methods in turn, beginning with negotiated transfer prices. Throughout the discussion, we should keep in mind that *the fundamental objective in setting transfer prices is to motivate the managers to act in the best interests of the overall company.* In contrast, **suboptimization** occurs when managers do not act in the best interests of the overall company or even in the best interests of their own segment.

Suboptimization An overall level of profitability that is less than a segment or a company is capable of earning.

Negotiated Transfer Prices

LEARNING OBJECTIVE 8
Determine the range, if any, within which a negotiated transfer price should fall.

A **negotiated transfer price** is a transfer price that is agreed on between the selling and purchasing divisions. Negotiated transfer prices have several important advantages. First, this approach preserves the autonomy of the divisions and is consistent with the spirit of decentralization. Second, the managers of the divisions are likely to have much better information about the potential costs and benefits of the transfer than others in the company.

Negotiated transfer price A transfer price agreed on between buying and selling divisions.

When negotiated transfer prices are used, the managers who are involved in a proposed transfer within the company meet to discuss the terms and conditions of the transfer. They may decide not to go through with the transfer, but if they do, they must agree to a transfer price. Generally speaking, we cannot predict the exact transfer price to which they will agree. However, we can confidently predict two things: (1) the selling division will agree to the transfer only if the profits of the selling division increase as a result of the transfer, and (2) the purchasing division will agree to the transfer only if the profits of the purchasing division also increase as a result of the transfer. This may seem obvious, but it is an important point.

Clearly, if the transfer price is below the selling division's cost, a loss will occur on the transaction and the selling division will refuse to agree to the transfer. Likewise, if the transfer price is set too high, it will be impossible for the purchasing division to make any profit on the transferred item. For any given proposed transfer, the transfer price has both a lower limit (determined by the situation of the selling division) and an upper limit (determined by the situation of the purchasing division). The actual transfer price agreed to by the two division managers can fall anywhere between those two limits. These limits determine the **range of acceptable transfer prices**—the range of transfer prices within which the profits of both divisions participating in a transfer would increase.

Range of acceptable transfer prices The range of transfer prices within which the profits of both the selling division and the purchasing division would increase as a result of a transfer.

An example will help us to understand negotiated transfer prices. Harris & Louder, Ltd. owns fast-food restaurants and snack food and beverage manufacturers in the United Kingdom. One of the restaurants, Pizza Maven, serves a variety of beverages along with pizzas. One of the beverages is ginger beer, which is served on tap. Harris & Louder has just purchased a new division, Imperial Beverages, that produces ginger beer. The managing director of Imperial Beverages has approached the managing director of Pizza Maven about purchasing Imperial Beverages ginger beer for sale at Pizza Maven restaurants rather than its usual brand of ginger beer. Managers at Pizza Maven agree that the quality of Imperial Beverages' ginger beer is comparable to the quality of their regular brand. It is just a question of price. The basic facts are listed at the top of the next page.

Imperial Beverages:	
Ginger beer production capacity per month	10,000 barrels
Variable cost per barrel of ginger beer	£8 per barrel
Fixed costs per month	£70,000
Selling price of Imperial Beverages ginger beer on the outside market	£20 per barrel
Pizza Maven:	
Purchase price of regular brand of ginger beer	£18 per barrel
Monthly consumption of ginger beer	2,000 barrels

The Selling Division's Lowest Acceptable Transfer Price The selling division, Imperial Beverages, will be interested in a proposed transfer only if its profit increases. Clearly, the transfer price must not fall below the variable cost per barrel of £8. In addition, if Imperial Beverages has insufficient capacity to fill the Pizza Maven order, then it would have to give up some of its regular sales. Imperial Beverages would expect to be compensated for the contribution margin on these lost sales. In summary, if the transfer has no effect on fixed costs, then from the selling division's standpoint, the transfer price must cover both the variable costs of producing the transferred units and any opportunity costs from lost sales.

Seller's perspective:

$$\text{Transfer price} \geq \begin{matrix}\text{Variable cost}\\ \text{per unit}\end{matrix} + \frac{\text{Total contribution margin on lost sales}}{\text{Number of units transferred}}$$

The Purchasing Division's Highest Acceptable Transfer Price The purchasing division, Pizza Maven, will be interested in the proposal only if its profit increases. In cases like this where a purchasing division has an outside supplier, the purchasing division's decision is simple. Buy from the inside supplier if the price is less than the price offered by the outside supplier.

Purchaser's perspective:

$$\text{Transfer price} \leq \text{Cost of buying from outside supplier}$$

We will consider several different hypothetical situations and see what the range of acceptable transfer prices would be in each situation.

Selling Division with Idle Capacity Suppose that Imperial Beverages has sufficient idle capacity to satisfy the demand for ginger beer from Pizza Maven without cutting into sales of ginger beer to its regular customers. To be specific, let's suppose that Imperial Beverages is selling only 7,000 barrels of ginger beer per month on the outside market. That leaves unused capacity of 3,000 barrels per month—more than enough to satisfy Pizza Maven's requirement of 2,000 barrels per month. What range of transfer prices, if any, would make both divisions better off with the transfer of 2,000 barrels per month?

1. The selling division, Imperial Beverages, will be interested in the proposal only if:

$$\text{Transfer price} \geq \begin{matrix}\text{Variable cost}\\ \text{per unit}\end{matrix} + \frac{\text{Total contribution margin on lost sales}}{\text{Number of units transferred}}$$

Since Imperial Beverages has ample idle capacity, there are no lost outside sales. And since the variable cost per unit is £8, the lowest acceptable transfer price as far as the selling division is concerned is also £8:

$$\text{Transfer price} \geq £8 + \frac{£0}{2{,}000} = £8$$

2. The purchasing division, Pizza Maven, can buy similar ginger beer from an outside vendor for £18 per barrel. Therefore, Pizza Maven would be unwilling to pay more than £18 per barrel for Imperial Beverages' ginger beer:

$$\text{Transfer price} \leq \text{Cost of buying from outside supplier} = £18$$

3. Combining the requirements of both the selling division and the purchasing division, the acceptable range of transfer prices in this situation is:

$$£8 \leq \text{Transfer price} \leq £18$$

Assuming that the managers understand their own businesses and that they are cooperative, they should be able to agree on a transfer price within this range.

Selling Division with No Idle Capacity Suppose that Imperial Beverages has *no* idle capacity; it is selling 10,000 barrels of ginger beer a month on the outside market at £20 per barrel. To fill the order from Pizza Maven, Imperial Beverages would have to divert 2,000 barrels from its regular customers. What range of transfer prices, if any, would make both divisions better off transferring the 2,000 barrels within the company?

1. The selling division, Imperial Beverages, will be interested in the proposal only if:

$$\text{Transfer price} \geq \begin{matrix}\text{Variable cost}\\ \text{per unit}\end{matrix} + \frac{\text{Total contribution margin on lost sales}}{\text{Number of units transferred}}$$

Since Imperial Beverages has no idle capacity, there *are* lost outside sales. The contribution margin per barrel on these outside sales is £12 (£20 − £8):

$$\text{Transfer price} \geq £8 + \frac{(£20 - £8) \times 2{,}000}{2{,}000} = £8 + (£20 - £8) = £20$$

Thus, as far as the selling division is concerned, the transfer price must at least cover the revenue on the lost sales, which is £20 per barrel. This makes sense since the cost of producing the 2,000 barrels is the same whether they are sold on the inside market or on the outside. The only difference is that the selling division loses the revenue of £20 per barrel if it transfers the barrels to Pizza Maven.

2. As before, the purchasing division, Pizza Maven, would be unwilling to pay more than the £18 per barrel it is already paying for similar ginger beer from its regular supplier:

$$\text{Transfer price} \leq \text{Cost of buying from outside supplier} = £18$$

3. Therefore, the selling division would insist on a transfer price of at least £20, but the purchasing division would refuse any transfer price above £18. It is impossible to satisfy both division managers simultaneously; there can be no agreement on a transfer price and no transfer will take place. Is this good? The answer is yes. From the standpoint of the entire company, the transfer does not make sense. Why give up sales of £20 to save £18?

Basically, the transfer price is a mechanism for dividing between the two divisions any profit the entire company earns as a result of the transfer. If the company loses money on the transfer, there will be no profit to divide up, and it will be impossible for the two divisions to come to an agreement. On the other hand, if the company makes money on the transfer, there will be a potential profit to share, and it will always be possible for the two divisions to find a mutually agreeable transfer price that increases the profits of both divisions. If the pie is bigger, it is always possible to divide it up in such a way that everyone has a bigger piece.

Selling Division with Some Idle Capacity Suppose now that Imperial Beverages is selling 9,000 barrels of ginger beer per month on the outside market. Pizza Maven can sell only one kind of ginger beer on tap. It cannot buy 1,000 barrels from Imperial Beverages and 1,000 barrels from its regular supplier; it must buy all of its ginger beer from one source.

To fill the entire 2,000-barrel per month order from Pizza Maven, Imperial Beverages would have to divert 1,000 barrels from its regular customers who are paying £20 per barrel. The other 1,000 barrels can be made using idle capacity. What range of transfer prices, if any, would make both divisions better off transferring the 2,000 barrels within the company?

1. As before, the selling division, Imperial Beverages, will insist on a transfer price that at least covers its variable cost and opportunity cost:

$$\text{Transfer price} \geq \frac{\text{Variable cost}}{\text{per unit}} + \frac{\text{Total contribution margin on lost sales}}{\text{Number of units transferred}}$$

   Since Imperial Beverages does not have enough idle capacity to fill the entire order for 2,000 barrels, there *are* lost outside sales. The contribution margin per barrel on the 1,000 barrels of lost outside sales is £12 (£20 − £8):

$$\text{Transfer price} \geq £8 + \frac{(£20 - £8) \times 1{,}000}{2{,}000} = £8 + £6 = £14$$

   Thus, as far as the selling division is concerned, the transfer price must cover the variable cost of £8 plus the average opportunity cost of lost sales of £6.
2. As before, the purchasing division, Pizza Maven, would be unwilling to pay more than the £18 per barrel it pays its regular supplier:

$$\text{Transfer price} \leq \text{Cost of buying from outside suppliers} = £18$$

3. Combining the requirements for both the selling and purchasing divisions, the range of acceptable transfer prices is:

$$£14 \leq \text{Transfer price} \leq £18$$

   Again, assuming that the managers understand their own businesses and that they are cooperative, they should be able to agree on a transfer price within this range.

No Outside Supplier If Pizza Maven has no outside supplier for the ginger beer, the highest price the purchasing division would be willing to pay depends on how much the purchasing division expects to make on the transferred units—excluding the transfer price. If, for example, Pizza Maven expects to earn £30 per barrel of ginger beer after paying its own expenses, then it should be willing to pay up to £30 per barrel to Imperial Beverages. Remember, however, that this assumes Pizza Maven cannot buy ginger beer from other sources.

Evaluation of Negotiated Transfer Prices As discussed earlier, if a transfer within the company would result in higher overall profits for the company, there is always a range of transfer prices within which both the selling and purchasing division would also have higher profits if they agree to the transfer. Therefore, if the managers understand their own businesses and are cooperative, then they should always be able to agree on a transfer price if it is in the best interests of the company that they do so.

The difficulty is that not all managers understand their own businesses and not all managers are cooperative. As a result, negotiations often break down even when it would be in the managers' own best interests to come to an agreement. Sometimes that is the fault of the way managers are evaluated. If managers are pitted against each other rather than against their own past performance or reasonable benchmarks, a non-cooperative atmosphere is almost guaranteed. Nevertheless, it must be admitted that even with the best performance evaluation system, some people by nature are not cooperative.

Possibly because of the fruitless and protracted bickering that often accompanies disputes over transfer prices, most companies rely on some other means of setting transfer prices. Unfortunately, as we will see in the following sections, all of the alternatives to negotiated transfer prices have their own serious drawbacks.

FOCUS *on Current Practice*

Teva Pharmaceutical Industries Ltd. of Israel rejected the negotiated transfer price approach because senior executives believed that this approach would lead to endless, non-productive arguments. Instead, the company uses activity-based costing to set its transfer prices. Marketing divisions are charged for unit-level costs based on the actual quantities of each product they acquire. In addition, they are charged batch-level costs based on the actual number of batches their orders require. Product-level and facility-level costs are charged to the marketing divisions annually in lump sums—the details of this procedure are covered in Chapter 8. Essentially, Teva Pharmaceutical Industries sets its transfer prices at carefully computed variable costs. As long as Teva Pharmaceutical Industries has unused capacity, this system sends the marketing managers the correct signals about how much it really costs the company to produce each product. With this information, the marketing managers are much better equipped to make pricing and other decisions regarding the products.

Source: Robert S. Kaplan, Dan Weiss, and Eyal Desheh, "Transfer Pricing with ABC," *Management Accounting*, May 1997, pp. 20–28.

Transfers to the Selling Division at Cost

Many companies set transfer prices at either the variable cost or full (absorption) cost incurred by the selling division. Although the cost approach to setting transfer prices is relatively simple to apply, it has some major defects.

First, the use of cost—particularly full cost—as a transfer price can lead to bad decisions and thus suboptimization. Return to the example involving the ginger beer. The full cost of ginger beer can never be less than £15 per barrel (£8 per barrel variable cost + £7 per barrel fixed cost at capacity). What if the cost of buying the ginger beer from an outside supplier is less than £15—for example, £14 per barrel? If the transfer price was bureaucratically set at full cost, then Pizza Maven would never want to buy ginger beer from Imperial Beverages, since it could buy its ginger beer from the outside supplier at less cost. However, from the standpoint of the company as a whole, ginger beer should be transferred from Imperial Beverages to Pizza Maven whenever Imperial Beverages has idle capacity. Why? Because when Imperial Beverages has idle capacity, it costs the company only £8 in variable cost to produce a barrel of ginger beer, but it costs £14 per barrel to buy from outside suppliers.

Second, if cost is used as the transfer price, the selling division will never show a profit on any internal transfer. The only division that shows a profit is the division that makes the final sale to an outside party.

A third problem with cost-based prices is that they do not provide incentives to control costs. If the costs of one division are simply passed on to the next, then there is little incentive for anyone to work to reduce costs. This problem can be overcome to some extent by using standard costs rather than actual costs for transfer prices.

Despite these shortcomings, cost-based transfer prices are commonly used in practice. Advocates argue that they are easily understood and convenient to use.

Transfers at Market Price

Some form of competitive **market price** (i.e., the price charged for an item on the open market) is often regarded as the best approach to the transfer pricing problem—particularly if transfer price negotiations routinely become bogged down.

Market price
The price being charged for an item on the open (intermediate) market.

The market price approach is designed for situations in which there is an *intermediate market* for the transferred product or service. By **intermediate market,** we mean a market in which the product or service is sold in its present form to outside customers. If the selling division has no idle capacity, the market price in the intermediate market is the perfect choice for the transfer price. The reason for this is that if the selling division can

Intermediate market
A market in which a transferred product or service is sold in its present form to outside customers.

sell a transferred item on the outside market instead, then the real cost of the transfer as far as the company is concerned is the opportunity cost of the lost revenue on the outside sale. Whether the item is transferred internally or sold on the outside intermediate market, the production costs are exactly the same. If the market price is used as the transfer price, the selling division manager will not lose anything by making the transfer, and the purchasing division manager will get the correct signal about how much it really costs the company for the transfer to take place.

While the market price works beautifully when there is no idle capacity, difficulties occur when the selling division has idle capacity. Recalling once again the ginger beer example, the outside market price for the ginger beer produced by Imperial Beverages is £20 per barrel. However, Pizza Maven can purchase all of the ginger beer it wants from outside suppliers for £18 per barrel. Why would Pizza Maven ever buy from Imperial Beverages if Pizza Maven is forced to pay Imperial Beverages' market price? In some market price-based transfer pricing schemes, the transfer price would be lowered to £18, the outside vendor's market price, and Pizza Maven would be directed to buy from Imperial Beverages, as long as Imperial Beverages is willing to sell. This scheme can work reasonably well, but a drawback is that managers at Pizza Maven will regard the cost of ginger beer as £18 rather than the £8, which is the real cost to the company when the selling division has idle capacity. Consequently, the managers of Pizza Maven will make pricing and other decisions based on an incorrect cost.

Unfortunately, none of the possible solutions to the transfer pricing problem are perfect—not even market-based transfer prices.

International Aspects of Transfer Pricing

Transfer pricing is used worldwide to control the flow of goods and services between segments of an organization. However, the objectives of transfer pricing change when a multinational corporation (MNC) is involved and the goods and services being transferred must cross international borders. The objectives of international transfer pricing, as compared to domestic transfer pricing, are summarized in Exhibit 12–12.

As shown in the exhibit, the objectives of international transfer pricing focus on minimizing taxes, duties, and foreign exchange risks, along with enhancing a company's competitive position and improving its relations with foreign governments. Although domestic objectives such as managerial motivation and divisional autonomy are always desirable in an organization, they usually become secondary when international transfers are involved. Companies will focus instead on charging a transfer price that will slash its total tax bill or that will strengthen a foreign subsidiary.

EXHIBIT 12–12 Domestic and International Transfer Pricing Objectives[15]

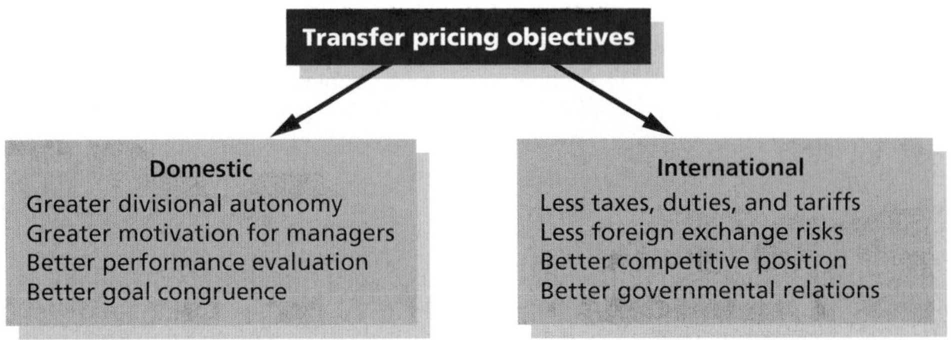

15. Exhibit 12–12 is adapted from Wagdy M. Abdallah, "Guidelines for CEOs in Transfer Pricing Policies," *Management Accounting* 70, no. 3, September 1988, p. 61.

For example, charging a low transfer price for parts shipped to a foreign subsidiary may reduce Customs duty payments as the parts cross international borders, or it may help the subsidiary to compete in foreign markets by keeping the subsidiary's costs low. On the other hand, charging a high transfer price may help an MNC draw profits out of a country that has stringent controls on foreign remittances, or it may allow an MNC to shift income from a country that has high income tax rates to a country that has low rates.

Transfer prices have a significant influence on a firm's duties and income taxes. Given that transfer prices are set by parties who are not independent of each other (non-arm's length), the opportunity exists to minimize taxes by shifting profit to low-tax jurisdictions or by minimizing duties paid. Canada Revenue Agency (CRA) seeks Canada's fair share of tax revenue by adopting policies and practices based on the principle of arm's length pricing. In simple cases, management simply needs to show CRA that the transfer price is comparable to an appropriately arm's length market price. In other cases, complex cost/profit allocation processes have to be documented by the company, together with the reasons for adopting such processes for determining the transfer price. Severe penalties exist for violations of the arm's length market price rule of the Income Tax Act, section 247, in foreign dealings with non-arm's length parties of an organization.[16]

In summary, managers need to be sensitive to legal rules in establishing transfer prices. In particular, the strict practices demonstrated with foreign transfer prices by the CRA rules illustrate the potential issues associated with provincial sales taxes, foreign trade practices under NAFTA and GATT, and the income tax provisions dealing with artificial tax-based transactions used to manipulate income taxes.

REVIEW PROBLEM 3: TRANSFER PRICING

Situation A

Collyer Products, Inc. has a Valve Division that manufactures and sells a standard valve as follows:

Capacity in units	100,000
Selling price to outside customers on the intermediate market	$30
Variable costs per unit	16
Fixed costs per unit (based on capacity)	9

The company has a Pump Division that could use this valve in the manufacture of one of its pumps. The Pump Division is currently purchasing 10,000 valves per year from an overseas supplier at a cost of $29 per valve.

Required:

1. Assume that the Valve Division has ample idle capacity to handle all of the Pump Division's needs. What is the acceptable range, if any, for the transfer price between the two divisions?
2. Assume that the Valve Division is selling all that it can produce to outside customers on the intermediate market. What is the acceptable range, if any, for the transfer price between the two divisions?
3. Assume again that the Valve Division is selling all that it can produce to outside customers on the intermediate market. Also assume that $3 in variable expenses can be avoided on transfers within the company, due to reduced selling costs. What is the acceptable range, if any, for the transfer price between the two divisions?

16. Stephanie de Breyne, "Transfer Pricing: Get It In Writing," *CMA Magazine*, February 1998, p. 36, and Hendrick Swaneveld and Martin Przysuski, "Transfer Pricing Now a Canadian Priority," *CMA Management*, April 2002, pp. 42–44.

Solution to Situation A

1. Since the Valve Division has idle capacity, it does not have to give up any outside sales to take on the Pump Division's business. Applying the formula for the lowest acceptable transfer price from the viewpoint of the selling division, we get:

$$\text{Transfer price} \geq \frac{\text{Variable cost}}{\text{per unit}} + \frac{\text{Total contribution margin on lost sales}}{\text{Number of units transferred}}$$

$$\text{Transfer price} \geq \$16 + \frac{\$0}{10{,}000} = \$16$$

The Pump Division would be unwilling to pay more than $29, the price it is currently paying an outside supplier for its valves. Therefore, the transfer price must fall within the range:

$$\$16 \leq \text{Transfer price} \leq \$29$$

2. Since the Valve Division is selling all that it can produce on the intermediate market, it would have to give up some of these outside sales to take on the Pump Division's business. Thus, the Valve Division has an opportunity cost that is the total contribution margin on lost sales:

$$\text{Transfer price} \geq \frac{\text{Variable cost}}{\text{per unit}} + \frac{\text{Total contribution margin on lost sales}}{\text{Number of units transferred}}$$

$$\text{Transfer price} \geq \$16 + \frac{(\$30 - \$16) \times 10{,}000}{10{,}000} = \$16 + \$14 = \$30$$

Since the Pump Division can purchase valves from an outside supplier at only $29 per unit, no transfers will be made between the two divisions.

3. Applying the formula for the lowest acceptable price from the viewpoint of the selling division, we get:

$$\text{Transfer price} \geq \frac{\text{Variable cost}}{\text{per unit}} + \frac{\text{Total contribution margin on lost sales}}{\text{Number of units transferred}}$$

$$\text{Transfer price} \geq (\$16 - \$3) + \frac{(\$30 - \$16) \times 10{,}000}{10{,}000} = \$13 + \$14 = \$27$$

In this case, the transfer price must fall within the range:

$$\$27 \leq \text{Transfer price} \leq \$29$$

Situation B

Referring to the original data in situation A above, assume the Pump Division needs 20,000 special high-pressure valves per year. The Valve Division's variable costs to manufacture and ship the special valve would be $20 per unit. To produce these special valves, the Valve Division would have to reduce its production and sales of regular valves from 100,000 units per year to 70,000 units per year.

Required:
As far as the Valve Division is concerned, what is the lowest acceptable transfer price?

Solution to Situation B

To produce the 20,000 special valves, the Valve Division will have to give up sales to outside customers of 30,000 regular valves. Applying the formula for the lowest acceptable price from the viewpoint of the selling division, we get:

$$\text{Transfer price} \geq \frac{\text{Variable cost}}{\text{per unit}} + \frac{\text{Total contribution margin on lost sales}}{\text{Number of units transferred}}$$

$$\text{Transfer price} \geq \$20 + \frac{(\$30 - \$16) \times 30{,}000}{20{,}000} = \$20 + \$21 = \$41$$

GLOSSARY

Visit the Online Learning Centre at http://www.mcgrawhill.ca/college/garrison/ for a review of key terms and definitions.

QUESTIONS

12–1 What is meant by the term *decentralization?*

12–2 Distinguish between a cost centre, a profit centre, and an investment centre.

12–3 Define a segment of an organization. Give several examples of segments.

12–4 How does the contribution approach assign costs to segments of an organization?

12–5 Distinguish between a traceable cost and a common cost. Give several examples of each.

12–6 Explain how the segment margin differs from the contribution margin.

12–7 Why aren't common costs allocated to segments under the contribution approach?

12–8 How is it possible for a cost that is traceable to a segment to become a common cost if the segment is divided into further segments?

12–9 What is meant by the terms *margin* and *turnover?*

12–10 What are the three basic approaches to improving return on investment (ROI)?

12–11 What is meant by residual income?

12–12 In what way can the use of ROI as a performance measure for investment centres lead to bad decisions? How does the residual income approach overcome this problem?

12–13 What is gained by examining costs from a life cycle perspective?

12–14 Why is value chain analysis an important viewpoint for revenue and cost analysis?

12–15 What is the advantage of examining a customer's profits over other segment analysis?

12–16 EVA provides a strategic focus for management. Analyze this statement.

12–17 Why do the measures used in a balanced scorecard differ from company to company?

12–18 Why does the balanced scorecard include financial performance measures as well as measures of how well internal business processes are doing?

12–19 What is the difference between delivery cycle time and throughput time? What four elements make up throughput time? Into what two classes can these four elements be placed?

12–20 If a company has a manufacturing cycle efficiency (MCE) of less than 1, what does it mean? How would you interpret an MCE of 0.40?

12–21 (Appendix 12A) What is meant by the term *transfer price,* and why are transfer prices needed?

12–22 (Appendix 12A) From the standpoint of a selling division that has idle capacity, what is the minimum acceptable transfer price for an item?

12–23 (Appendix 12A) From the standpoint of a selling division that has *no* idle capacity, what is the minimum acceptable transfer price for an item?

12–24 (Appendix 12A) What are the advantages and disadvantages of cost-based transfer prices?

12–25 (Appendix 12A) If a market price for a product can be determined, why isn't it always the best transfer price?

12–26 (Appendix 12A) What complexities exist when firms use transfer prices to conduct purchases and sales between different government jurisdictions?

EXERCISES

EXERCISE 12–1 Basic Segmented Income Statement [LO2]

Royal Lawncare Company produces and sells two packaged products, Weedban and Greengrow. Revenue and cost information relating to the products is at the top of page 562.

Common fixed expenses in the company total $33,000 annually. Last year the company produced and sold 15,000 units of Weedban and 28,000 units of Greengrow.

	Product	
	Weedban	Greengrow
Selling price per unit	$6.00	$7.50
Variable expenses per unit	$2.40	$5.25
Traceable fixed expenses per year	$45,000	$21,000

Required:
Prepare a contribution format income statement segmented by product lines. Show both Amount and Percent columns for the company as a whole and for each of the products.

EXERCISE 12–2 Compute the Return on Investment (ROI) [LO5]
Alyeska Services Company, a division of a major oil company, provides various services to the operators of the Arctic oil field. Data concerning the most recent year appear below:

Sales	$7,500,000
Operating income	$600,000
Average operating assets	$5,000,000

Required:
1. Compute the margin for Alyeska Services Company.
2. Compute the turnover for Alyeska Services Company.
3. Compute the return on investment (ROI) for Alyeska Services Company.

EXERCISE 12–3 Residual Income [LO6]
Juniper Design Ltd. of Manchester, England, is a company specializing in providing design services to residential developers. Last year the company had operating income of £600,000 on sales of £3,000,000. The company's average operating assets for the year were £2,800,000 and its minimum required rate of return was 18%. (The currency used in England is the pound sterling, denoted by £.)

Required:
Compute the company's residual income for the year.

EXERCISE 12–4 (Appendix 12A) Transfer Pricing Basics [LO8]
Sako Company's Audio Division produces a speaker that is used by manufacturers of various audio products. Sales and cost data on the speaker follow:

Selling price per unit on the intermediate market	$60
Variable costs per unit	$42
Fixed costs per unit (based on capacity)	$8
Capacity in units	25,000

Sako Company has a Hi-Fi Division that could use this speaker in one of its products. The Hi-Fi Division will need 5,000 speakers per year. It has received a quote of $57 per speaker from another manufacturer. Sako Company evaluates division managers on the basis of divisional profits.

Required:
1. Assume that the Audio Division is now selling only 20,000 speakers per year to outside customers.
   a. From the standpoint of the Audio Division, what is the lowest acceptable transfer price for speakers sold to the Hi-Fi Division?
   b. From the standpoint of the Hi-Fi Division, what is the highest acceptable transfer price for speakers acquired from the Audio Division?
   c. If left free to negotiate without interference, would you expect the division managers to voluntarily agree to the transfer of 5,000 speakers from the Audio Division to the Hi-Fi Division? Why or why not?
   d. From the standpoint of the entire company, should the transfer take place? Why or why not?
2. Assume that the Audio Division is selling all of the speakers it can produce to outside customers.

a. From the standpoint of the Audio Division, what is the lowest acceptable transfer price for speakers sold to the Hi-Fi Division?

b. From the standpoint of the Hi-Fi Division, what is the highest acceptable transfer price for speakers acquired from the Audio Division?

c. If left free to negotiate without interference, would you expect the division managers to voluntarily agree to the transfer of 5,000 speakers from the Audio Division to the Hi-Fi Division? Why or why not?

d. From the standpoint of the entire company, should the transfer take place? Why or why not?

EXERCISE 12–5 Segmented Income Statement [LO2]

Wingate Company, a wholesale distributor of videotapes, has been experiencing losses for some time, as shown by its most recent monthly contribution format income statement, which follows:

Sales	$1,000,000
Less variable expenses	390,000
Contribution margin	610,000
Less fixed expenses	625,000
Operating income (loss)	$ (15,000)

In an effort to isolate the problem, the president has asked for an income statement segmented by division. Accordingly, the Accounting Department has developed the following information:

	Division		
	East	Central	West
Sales	$250,000	$400,000	$350,000
Variable expenses as a percentage of sales	52%	30%	40%
Traceable fixed expenses	$160,000	$200,000	$175,000

Required:

1. Prepare a contribution format income statement segmented by divisions, as desired by the president. Show both Amount and Percent columns for the company as a whole and for each division.
2. As a result of a marketing study, the president believes that sales in the West Division could be increased by 20% if monthly advertising in that division were increased by $15,000. Would you recommend the increased advertising? Show computations.

EXERCISE 12–6 Effects of Changes in Sales, Expenses, and Assets on ROI [LO5]

CommercialServices.com Corporation provides business-to-business services on the Internet. Data concerning the most recent year appear below:

Sales	$3,000,000
Operating income	$150,000
Average operating assets	$750,000

Required:

Consider each question below independently. Carry out all computations to two decimal places.

1. Compute the company's return on investment (ROI).
2. The entrepreneur who founded the company is convinced that sales will increase next year by 50% and that operating income will increase by 200%, with no increase in average operating assets. What would be the company's ROI?
3. The chief financial officer of the company believes a more realistic scenario would be a $1,000,000 increase in sales, requiring a $250,000 increase in average operating assets, with a resulting $200,000 increase in operating income. What would be the company's ROI in this scenario?

EXERCISE 12–7 Working with a Segmented Income Statement [LO2]

Raner, Harris, & Chan is a consulting firm that specializes in information systems for medical and dental clinics. The firm has two offices—one in Toronto and one in Hamilton. The firm classifies the direct costs of consulting jobs as variable costs. A contribution format segmented income statement for the company's most recent year is given at the top of the next page.

	Total Company		Office			
			Toronto		Hamilton	
Sales	$450,000	100%	$150,000	100%	$300,000	100%
Less variable expenses	225,000	50%	45,000	30%	180,000	60%
Contribution margin	225,000	50%	105,000	70%	120,000	40%
Less traceable fixed expenses	126,000	28%	78,000	52%	48,000	16%
Office segment margin	99,000	22%	$ 27,000	18%	$ 72,000	24%
Less common fixed expenses not traceable to offices	63,000	14%				
Operating income	$ 36,000	8%				

Required:

1. By how much would the company's operating income increase if Hamilton increased its sales by $75,000 per year? Assume no change in cost behaviour patterns.
2. Refer to the original data. Assume that sales in Toronto increase by $50,000 next year and that sales in Hamilton remain unchanged. Assume no change in fixed costs.
   a. Prepare a new segmented income statement for the company using the format shown previously. Show both amounts and percentages.
   b. Observe from the income statement you have prepared that the contribution margin ratio for Toronto has remained unchanged at 70% (the same as in the previous data) but that the segment margin ratio has changed. How do you explain the change in the segment margin ratio?

EXERCISE 12–8 Working with a Segmented Income Statement [LO2]

Refer to the data in Exercise 12–7. Assume that Hamilton' sales by major market are:

	Hamilton		Market			
			Medical		Dental	
Sales	$300,000	100%	$200,000	100%	$100,000	100%
Less variable expenses	180,000	60%	128,000	64%	52,000	52%
Contribution margin	120,000	40%	72,000	36%	48,000	48%
Less traceable fixed expenses	33,000	11%	12,000	6%	21,000	21%
Market segment margin	87,000	29%	$ 60,000	30%	$ 27,000	27%
Less common fixed expenses not traceable to markets	15,000	5%				
Office segment margin	$ 72,000	24%				

The company would like to initiate an intensive advertising campaign in one of the two market segments during the next month. The campaign would cost $5,000. Marketing studies indicate that such a campaign would increase sales in the Medical market by $40,000 or increase sales in the Dental market by $35,000.

Required:

1. In which of the markets would you recommend that the company focus its advertising campaign? Show computations to support your answer.
2. In Exercise 12–7, Hamilton shows $48,000 in traceable fixed expenses. What happened to the $48,000 in this exercise?

EXERCISE 12–9 Effects of Changes in Profits and Assets on Return on Investment (ROI) [LO5]

Pecs Alley is a regional chain of health clubs. The managers of the clubs, who have authority to make investments as needed, are evaluated based largely on return on investment (ROI). The Springfield Club reported the following results for the past year:

Sales	$1,400,000
Operating income	$70,000
Average operating assets	$350,000

Required:

The following questions are to be considered independently. Carry out all computations to two decimal places.

1. Compute the club's return on investment (ROI).
2. Assume that the manager of the club is able to increase sales by $70,000 and that, as a result, operating income increases by $18,200. Further assume that this is possible without any increase in operating assets. What would be the club's return on investment (ROI)?
3. Assume that the manager of the club is able to reduce expenses by $14,000 without any change in sales or operating assets. What would be the club's return on investment (ROI)?
4. Assume that the manager of the club is able to reduce operating assets by $70,000 without any change in sales or operating income. What would be the club's return on investment (ROI)?

EXERCISE 12–10 Cost-Volume Profit Analysis and Return on Investment (ROI) [LO5]

Posters.com is a small Internet retailer of high-quality posters. The company has $1,000,000 in operating assets and fixed expenses of $150,000 per year. With this level of operating assets and fixed expenses, the company can support sales of up to $3,000,000 per year. The company's contribution margin ratio is 25%, which means that an additional dollar of sales results in additional contribution margin, and operating income, of 25 cents.

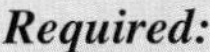

Required:

1. Complete the following table showing the relation between sales and return on investment (ROI).

Sales	Operating Income	Average Operating Assets	ROI
$2,500,000	$475,000	$1,000,000	?
$2,600,000	$?	$1,000,000	?
$2,700,000	$?	$1,000,000	?
$2,800,000	$?	$1,000,000	?
$2,900,000	$?	$1,000,000	?
$3,000,000	$?	$1,000,000	?

2. What happens to the company's return on investment (ROI) as sales increase? Explain.

EXERCISE 12–11 Return on Investment (ROI) [LO5]

Provide the missing data in the following table for a distributor of martial arts products:

	Division		
	Alpha	Bravo	Charlie
Sales	$?	$11,500,000	$?
Operating income	$?	$ 920,000	$210,000
Average operating assets	$800,000	$?	$?
Margin	4%	?	7%
Turnover	5	?	?
Return on investment (ROI)	?	20%	14%

EXERCISE 12–12 Evaluating New Investments Using Return on Investment (ROI) and Residual Income [LO5, LO6]

Selected sales and operating data for three divisions of different structural engineering firms are given below:

	Division A	Division B	Division C
Sales	$12,000,000	$14,000,000	$25,000,000
Average operating assets	$3,000,000	$7,000,000	$5,000,000
Operating income	$600,000	$560,000	$800,000
Minimum required rate of return	14%	10%	16%

Required:
1. Compute the return on investment (ROI) for each division using the formula stated in terms of margin and turnover.
2. Compute the residual income for each division.
3. Assume that each division is presented with an investment opportunity that would yield a 15% rate of return.
   a. If performance is being measured by ROI, which division or divisions will probably accept the opportunity? Reject? Why?
   b. If performance is being measured by residual income, which division or divisions will probably accept the opportunity? Reject? Why?

EXERCISE 12–13 Computing and Interpreting Return on Investment (ROI) [LO5]
Selected operating data for two divisions of Outback Brewing, Ltd., of Australia are given below:

	Division	
	Queensland	New South Wales
Sales	$4,000,000	$7,000,000
Average total operating assets	$2,000,000	$2,000,000
Operating income	$360,000	$420,000
Property, plant, and equipment (net)	$950,000	$800,000

Required:
1. Compute the rate of return for each division using the return on investment (ROI) formula stated in terms of margin and turnover.
2. Which divisional manager seems to be doing the better job? Why?

EXERCISE 12–14 Contrasting Return on Investment (ROI) and Residual Income [LO2, LO5, LO6]
Meiji Isetan Corp. of Japan has two regional divisions with headquarters in Osaka and Yokohama. Selected data on the two divisions follow (in millions of yen, denoted by ¥):

	Division	
	Osaka	Yokohama
Sales	¥3,000,000	¥9,000,000
Operating income	¥210,000	¥720,000
Average operating assets	¥1,000,000	¥4,000,000

Required:
1. For each division, compute the return on investment (ROI) in terms of margin and turnover. Where necessary, carry computations to two decimal places.
2. Assume that the company evaluates performance using residual income and that the minimum required rate of return for any division is 15%. Compute the residual income for each division.
3. Is Yokohama's greater amount of residual income an indication that it is better managed? Explain.

EXERCISE 12–15 (Appendix 12A) Transfer Pricing from the Viewpoint of the Entire Company [LO2, LO8]
Division A manufactures electronic circuit boards. The boards can be sold either to Division B of the same company or to outside customers. Last year, the following activity occurred in Division A:

Selling price per circuit board	$125
Production cost per circuit board	$90
Number of circuit boards:	
Produced during the year	20,000
Sold to outside customers	16,000
Sold to Division B	4,000

Sales to Division B were at the same price as sales to outside customers. The circuit boards purchased by Division B were used in an electronic instrument manufactured by that division (one board per instrument). Division B incurred $100 in additional cost per instrument and then sold the instruments for $300 each.

Required:

1. Prepare income statements for Division A, Division B, and the company as a whole.
2. Assume that Division A's manufacturing capacity is 20,000 circuit boards. Next year, Division B wants to purchase 5,000 circuit boards from Division A rather than 4,000. (Circuit boards of this type are not available from outside sources.) From the standpoint of the company as a whole, should Division A sell the 1,000 additional circuit boards to Division B or continue to sell them to outside customers? Explain.

EXERCISE 12–16 Return on Investment (ROI) and Residual Income Relations [LO5, LO6]

A family friend has asked your help in analyzing the operations of three anonymous companies operating in the same service sector industry. Supply the missing data in the table below:

	Company		
	A	B	C
Sales	$9,000,000	$7,000,000	$4,500,000
Operating income	$?	$ 280,000	$?
Average operating assets	$3,000,000	$?	$1,800,000
Return on investment (ROI)	18%	14%	?
Minimum required rate of return:			
Percentage	16%	?	15%
Dollar amount	$?	$ 320,000	$?
Residual income	$?	$?	$ 90,000

EXERCISE 12–17 (Appendix 12A) Transfer Pricing Situations [LO8]

In each of the cases below, assume that Division X has a product that can be sold either to outside customers or to Division Y of the same company for use in its production process. The managers of the divisions are evaluated based on their divisional profits.

	Case	
	A	B
Division X:		
Capacity in units	200,000	200,000
Number of units being sold to outside customers	200,000	160,000
Selling price per unit to outside customers	$90	$75
Variable costs per unit	$70	$60
Fixed costs per unit (based on capacity)	$13	$8
Division Y:		
Number of units needed for production	40,000	40,000
Purchase price per unit now being paid to an outside supplier	$86	$74

Required:

1. Refer to the data in case A above. Assume in this case that $3 per unit in variable selling costs can be avoided on intracompany sales. If the managers are free to negotiate and make decisions on their own, will a transfer take place? If so, within what range will the transfer price fall? Explain.
2. Refer to the data in case B above. In this case there will be no savings in variable selling costs on intracompany sales. If the managers are free to negotiate and make decisions on their own, will a transfer take place? If so, within what range will the transfer price fall? Explain.

EXERCISE 12–18 Creating a Balanced Scorecard [LO7]

Historically, the Mason Paper Company (MPC) has manufactured commodity grade papers for use in computer printers and photocopiers. MPC has reported operating losses for the last two years due to intense price pressure from much larger competitors. The MPC management team—including Kristen Townsend (CEO), Mike Martinez (vice president of Manufacturing), Tom Andrews (vice president of Marketing), and Wendy Chen (CFO)—is contemplating a change in strategy to save the company from impending bankruptcy. Excerpts from a recent management team meeting are shown below:

> **Townsend:** As we all know, the commodity paper manufacturing business is all about economies of scale. The largest competitors with the lowest cost per unit win. The limited capacity of our older machines prohibits us from competing in the high-volume commodity paper grades. Furthermore, expanding our capacity by acquiring a new paper-making machine is out of the question given the extraordinarily high price tag. Therefore, I propose that we abandon cost reduction as a strategic goal and instead pursue manufacturing flexibility as the key to our future success.
>
> **Chen:** Manufacturing flexibility? What does that mean?
>
> **Martinez:** It means we have to abandon our "crank out as many tonnes of paper as possible" mentality. Instead, we need to pursue the low-volume business opportunities that exist in the nonstandard, specialized paper grades. To succeed in this regard, we'll need to improve our flexibility in three ways. First, we must improve our ability to switch between paper grades. Right now, we require an average of four hours to change over to another paper grade. Timely customer deliveries are a function of changeover performance. Second, we need to expand the range of paper grades that we can manufacture. Currently, we can only manufacture three paper grades. Our customers must perceive that we are a "one-stop shop" that can meet all of their paper grade needs. Third, we will need to improve our yields (e.g., tonnes of acceptable output relative to total tonnes processed) in the nonstandard paper grades. I am certain that our percentage of waste within these grades will be unacceptably high unless we do something to improve our processes. Our variable costs will go through the roof if we cannot increase our yields!
>
> **Chen:** Wait just a minute! These changes are going to destroy our equipment utilization numbers!
>
> **Andrews:** You're right Wendy; however, equipment utilization is not the name of the game when it comes to competing in terms of flexibility. Our customers don't care about our equipment utilization. Instead, as Mike just alluded to, they want just-in-time delivery of smaller quantities of a full range of paper grades. If we can shrink the elapsed time from order placement to order delivery and expand our product offerings, it will increase sales from current customers and bring in new customers. Furthermore, we will be able to charge a premium price because of the limited competition within this niche from our cost-focused larger competitors. Our contribution margin per tonne should drastically improve!
>
> **Martinez:** Of course, executing the change in strategy will not be easy. We'll need to make a substantial investment in training. It is imperative that we do not shortchange our commitment to training because ultimately it is our people who create our flexible manufacturing capabilities.
>
> **Chen:** If we adopt this new strategy, it is definitely going to impact how we measure performance. We'll need to create measures that motivate our employees to make decisions that support our flexibility goals.
>
> **Townsend:** Wendy, you hit the nail right on the head. For our next meeting, could you pull together some potential measures that support our new strategy?

Later that same day, Wendy shared the essence of the above conversation with the employees of her Finance Department. She indicated that she would welcome suggested performance measures from anyone within the department. As an employee in the Finance Department, you have decided to pursue this opportunity to enhance your career prospects within the organization.

Required:

1. Contrast MPC's previous manufacturing strategy with its new manufacturing strategy.
2. Generally speaking, why would a company that changes its strategic goals need to change its performance measurement system as well? What are some examples of measures that would have been appropriate for MPC prior to its change in strategy? Why would those measures fail to support MPC's new strategy?
3. Using Exhibit 12–10 as a guide, construct a balanced scorecard that would support MPC's new manufacturing strategy. Use arrows to show the causal links between the performance measures and show whether the performance measure should increase or decrease over time. Feel free to create measures that may not be specifically mentioned in the chapter, but nonetheless make sense given the strategic goals of the company.
4. What hypotheses are built into MPC's balanced scorecard? Which of these hypotheses do you believe are most questionable and why?

EXERCISE 12–19 Measures of Internal Business Process Performance [LO7]
Management of Mittel Rhein AG of Köln, Germany, would like to reduce the amount of time between when a customer places an order and when the order is shipped. For the first quarter of operations during the current year the following data were reported:

	Days
Inspection time	0.3
Wait time (from order to start of production)	14.0
Process time	2.7
Move time	1.0
Queue time	5.0

Required:
1. Compute the throughput time.
2. Compute the manufacturing cycle efficiency (MCE) for the quarter.
3. What percentage of the throughput time was spent in non-value-added activities?
4. Compute the delivery cycle time.
5. If by use of just-in-time (JIT) all queue time during production is eliminated, what will be the new MCE?

EXERCISE 12–20 Creating a Balanced Scorecard [LO7]

Ariel Tax Services prepares tax returns for individual and corporate clients. As the company has gradually expanded to 10 offices, the founder Max Jacobs has begun to feel as though he is losing control of operations. In response to this concern, he has decided to implement a performance measurement system that will help control current operations and facilitate his growth plans of expanding to 20 offices.

Jacobs describes the keys to the success of his business as follows:

"Our only real asset is our people. We must keep our employees highly motivated and we must continually replenish our human capital by hiring the 'cream of the crop.' Interestingly, employee morale and recruiting success are both driven by the same two factors—compensation and career advancement. In other words, providing superior compensation relative to the industry average coupled with fast-track career advancement opportunities keeps morale high and makes us a very attractive place to work. It drives a high rate of job offer acceptances relative to job offers tendered.

"Hiring highly qualified people and keeping them energized ensures operational success, which in our business is a function of productivity, efficiency, and effectiveness. Productivity boils down to employees being billable rather than idle. Efficiency relates to the time required to complete a tax return. Finally, effectiveness is critical to our business in the sense that we cannot tolerate errors. Completing a tax return quickly is meaningless if the return contains errors.

"Our growth plans hinge upon acquiring new customers through word-of-mouth from satisfied repeat customers. We believe that our customers come back year after year because they value error-free, timely, and courteous tax return preparation. Common courtesy is an important aspect of our business! We call it service quality, and it all ties back to employee morale in the sense that happy employees treat their clients with care and concern.

"While sales growth is obviously important to our future plans, growth without a corresponding increase in profitability is useless. Therefore, we understand that increasing our profit margin is a function of cost-efficiency as well as sales growth. Given that payroll is our biggest expense, we must maintain an optimal balance between staffing levels and the revenue being generated. As I alluded to earlier, the key to maintaining this balance is employee productivity. If we can achieve cost-efficient sales growth, we should eventually have 20 profitable offices!"

Required:
1. Create a balanced scorecard for Ariel Tax Services. Link your scorecard measures using the framework from Exhibit 12–10. Indicate whether each measure is expected to increase or decrease. Feel free to create measures that may not be specifically mentioned in the chapter, but make sense given the strategic goals of the company.
2. What hypotheses are built into the balanced scorecard for Ariel Tax Services? Which of these hypotheses do you believe are most questionable and why?

3. Discuss the potential advantages and disadvantages of implementing an internal business process measure called *total dollar amount of tax refunds generated.* Would you recommend using this measure in Ariel's balanced scorecard?
4. Would it be beneficial to attempt to measure each office's individual performance with respect to the scorecard measures that you created? Why or why not?

PROBLEMS

PROBLEM 12–21 Segment Reporting and Decision Making [LO2]
Vulcan Company's contribution format income statement for June is given below:

VULCAN COMPANY Income Statement For the Month Ended June 30	
Sales	$750,000
Less variable expenses	336,000
Contribution margin	414,000
Less fixed expenses	378,000
Operating income	$ 36,000

Management is disappointed with the company's performance and is wondering what can be done to improve profits. By examining sales and cost records, you have determined the following:

a. The company is divided into two sales territories—Northern and Southern. The Northern territory recorded $300,000 in sales and $156,000 in variable expenses during June; the remaining sales and variable expenses were recorded in the Southern territory. Fixed expenses of $120,000 and $108,000 are traceable to the Northern and Southern territories, respectively. The rest of the fixed expenses are common to the two territories.
b. The company is the exclusive distributor for two products—Paks and Tibs. Sales of Paks and Tibs totalled $50,000 and $250,000, respectively, in the Northern territory during June. Variable expenses are 22% of the selling price for Paks and 58% for Tibs. Cost records show that $30,000 of the Northern territory's fixed expenses are traceable to Paks and $40,000 to Tibs, with the remainder common to the two products.

Required:

1. Prepare contribution format segmented income statements first showing the total company broken down between sales territories and then showing the Northern territory broken down by product line. Show both Amount and Percent columns for the company in total and for each segment.
2. Look at the statement you have prepared showing the total company segmented by sales territory. What insights revealed by this statement should be brought to the attention of management?
3. Look at the statement you have prepared showing the Northern territory segmented by product lines. What insights revealed by this statement should be brought to the attention of management?

PROBLEM 12–22 Comparison of Performance Using Return on Investment (ROI) [LO5]
Comparative data on three companies in the same service industry are given below:

	Company		
	A	B	C
Sales	$600,000	$500,000	$?
Operating income	$ 84,000	$ 70,000	$?
Average operating assets	$300,000	$?	$1,000,000
Margin	?	?	3.5%
Turnover	?	?	2
ROI	?	7%	?

Required:

1. What advantages are there to breaking down the ROI computation into two separate elements, margin and turnover?
2. Fill in the missing information above, and comment on the relative performance of the three companies in as much detail as the data permit. Make *specific recommendations* about how to improve the return on investment.

(Adapted from National Association of Accountants, *Research Report No. 35,* p. 34)

PROBLEM 12–23 Return on Investment (ROI) and Residual Income [LO5, LO6]

"I know headquarters wants us to add that new product line," said Dell Havasi, manager of Billings Company's Office Products Division. "But I want to see the numbers before I make any move. Our division's return on investment (ROI) has led the company for three years, and I don't want any letdown."

Billings Company is a decentralized wholesaler with five autonomous divisions. The divisions are evaluated on the basis of ROI, with year-end bonuses given to the divisional managers who have the highest ROIs. Operating results for the company's Office Products Division for the most recent year are given below:

Sales	$10,000,000
Less variable expenses	6,000,000
Contribution margin	4,000,000
Less fixed expenses	3,200,000
Operating income	$ 800,000
Divisional operating assets	$ 4,000,000

The company had an overall return on investment (ROI) of 15% last year (considering all divisions). The Office Products Division has an opportunity to add a new product line that would require an additional investment in operating assets of $1,000,000. The cost and revenue characteristics of the new product line per year would be:

Sales	$2,000,000
Variable expenses	60% of sales
Fixed expenses	$640,000

Required:

1. Compute the Office Products Division's ROI for the most recent year; also compute the ROI as it would appear if the new product line is added.
2. If you were in Dell Havasi's position, would you accept or reject the new product line? Explain.
3. Why do you suppose headquarters is anxious for the Office Products Division to add the new product line?
4. Suppose that the company's minimum required rate of return on operating assets is 12% and that performance is evaluated using residual income.
   a. Compute the Office Products Division's residual income for the most recent year; also compute the residual income as it would appear if the new product line is added.
   b. Under these circumstances, if you were in Dell Havasi's position, would you accept or reject the new product line? Explain.

PROBLEM 12–24 (Appendix 12A) Transfer Price with an Outside Market [LO8]

Hrubec Products, Inc., operates a Pulp Division that manufactures wood pulp for use in the production of various paper goods. Revenue and costs associated with a tonne of pulp follow:

Selling price		$70
Less expenses:		
Variable	$42	
Fixed (based on a capacity of 50,000 tonnes per year)	18	60
Operating income		$10

Hrubec Products has just acquired a small company that manufactures paper cartons. This company will be treated as a division of Hrubec with full profit responsibility. The newly formed Carton Division is currently purchasing 5,000 tonnes of pulp per year from a supplier at a cost of $70 per tonne, less a 10% quantity discount. Hrubec's president is anxious for the Carton Division to begin purchasing its pulp from the Pulp Division if an acceptable transfer price can be worked out.

Required:

For (1) and (2) below, assume that the Pulp Division can sell all of its pulp to outside customers for $70 per tonne.

1. Are the managers of the Carton and Pulp Divisions likely to voluntarily agree to a transfer price for 5,000 tonnes of pulp next year? Why or why not?
2. If the Pulp Division meets the price that the Carton Division is currently paying to its supplier and sells 5,000 tonnes of pulp to the Carton Division each year, what will be the effect on the profits of the Pulp Division, the Carton Division, and the company as a whole?

For (3)–(6) below, assume that the Pulp Division is currently selling only 30,000 tonnes of pulp each year to outside customers at the stated $70 price.

3. Are the managers of the Carton and Pulp Divisions likely to voluntarily agree to a transfer price for 5,000 tonnes of pulp next year? Why or why not?
4. Suppose that the Carton Division's outside supplier drops its price (net of the quantity discount) to only $59 per tonne. Should the Pulp Division meet this price? Explain. If the Pulp Division does *not* meet the $59 price, what will be the effect on the profits of the company as a whole?
5. Refer to (4) above. If the Pulp Division refuses to meet the $59 price, should the Carton Division be required to purchase from the Pulp Division at a higher price for the good of the company as a whole?
6. Refer to (4) above. Assume that due to inflexible management policies, the Carton Division is required to purchase 5,000 tonnes of pulp each year from the Pulp Division at $70 per tonne. What will be the effect on the profits of the company as a whole?

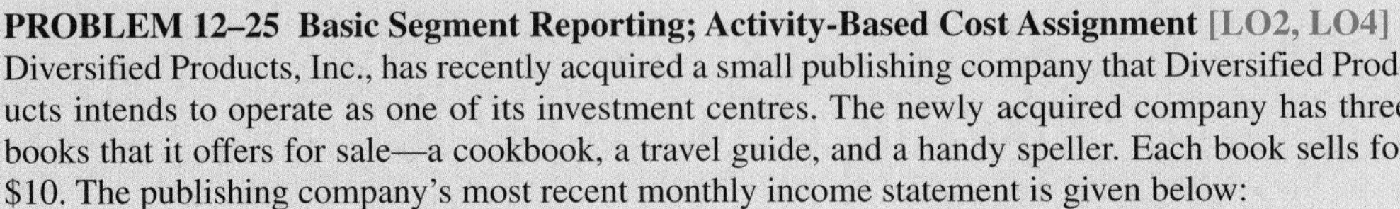

PROBLEM 12–25 Basic Segment Reporting; Activity-Based Cost Assignment [LO2, LO4]

Diversified Products, Inc., has recently acquired a small publishing company that Diversified Products intends to operate as one of its investment centres. The newly acquired company has three books that it offers for sale—a cookbook, a travel guide, and a handy speller. Each book sells for $10. The publishing company's most recent monthly income statement is given below:

	Total Company		Product Line: Cookbook	Product Line: Travel Guide	Product Line: Handy Speller
Sales	$300,000	100%	$90,000	$150,000	$60,000
Less expenses:					
Printing costs	102,000	34%	27,000	63,000	12,000
Advertising	36,000	12%	13,500	19,500	3,000
General sales	18,000	6%	5,400	9,000	3,600
Salaries	33,000	11%	18,000	9,000	6,000
Equipment depreciation	9,000	3%	3,000	3,000	3,000
Sales commissions	30,000	10%	9,000	15,000	6,000
General administration	42,000	14%	14,000	14,000	14,000
Warehouse rent	12,000	4%	3,600	6,000	2,400
Depreciation—office facilities	3,000	1%	1,000	1,000	1,000
Total expenses	285,000	95%	94,500	139,500	51,000
Operating income (loss)	$ 15,000	5%	$ (4,500)	$ 10,500	$ 9,000

The following additional information is available about the company:

a. Only printing costs and sales commissions are variable; all other costs are fixed. The printing costs (which include materials, labour, and variable overhead) are traceable to the three product lines as shown in the statement above. Sales commissions are 10% of sales for any product.

b. The same equipment is used to produce all three books, so the equipment depreciation cost has been allocated equally among the three product lines. An analysis of the company's activities indicates that the equipment is used 30% of the time to produce cookbooks, 50% of the time to produce travel guides, and 20% of the time to produce handy spellers.

c. The warehouse is used to store finished units of product, so the rental cost has been allocated to the product lines on the basis of sales dollars. The warehouse rental cost is $27 per square metre per year. The warehouse contains 5,334 square metres of space, of which 800 square metres is used by the cookbook line, 2,667 square metres by the travel guide line, and 1,867 square metres by the handy speller line.

d. The general sales cost above includes the salary of the sales manager and other sales costs not traceable to any specific product line. This cost has been allocated to the product lines on the basis of sales dollars.

e. The general administration cost and depreciation of office facilities both relate to overall administration of the company as a whole. These costs have been allocated equally to the three product lines.

f. All other costs are traceable to the three product lines in the amounts shown on the statement above.

The management of Diversified Products, Inc., is anxious to improve the new investment centre's 5% return on sales.

Required:

1. Prepare a new contribution format segmented income statement for the month. Show both an Amount column and a Percent column for the company as a whole and for each product line. Adjust allocations of equipment depreciation and of warehouse rent as indicated by the additional information provided.
2. After seeing the income statement in the main body of the problem, management has decided to eliminate the cookbook, since it is not returning a profit, and to focus all available resources on promoting the travel guide.
   a. Based on the statement you have prepared, do you agree with the decision to eliminate the cookbook? Explain.
   b. Based on the statement you have prepared, do you agree with the decision to focus all available resources on promoting the travel guide? Explain. (You may assume that an ample market is available for all three product lines.)
3. What additional points would you bring to the attention of management that might help to improve profits?

PROBLEM 12–26 Return on Investment (ROI) and Residual Income [LO5, LO6]

Financial data for Joel de Paris, Inc., for last year follow:

JOEL DE PARIS, INC. Balance Sheet	Ending Balance	Beginning Balance
Assets		
Cash	$ 120,000	$ 140,000
Accounts receivable	530,000	450,000
Inventory	380,000	320,000
Plant and equipment, net	620,000	680,000
Investment in Buisson, S.A.	280,000	250,000
Land (undeveloped)	170,000	180,000
Total assets	$2,100,000	$2,020,000
Liabilities and Shareholders' Equity		
Accounts payable	$ 310,000	$ 360,000
Long-term debt	1,500,000	1,500,000
Shareholders' equity	290,000	160,000
Total liabilities and shareholders' equity	$2,100,000	$2,020,000

JOEL DE PARIS, INC. Income Statement		
Sales		$4,050,000
Less operating expenses		3,645,000
Operating income		405,000
Less interest and taxes:		
Interest expense	$150,000	
Tax expense	110,000	260,000
Operating income		$ 145,000

The company paid dividends of $15,000 last year. The "Investment in Buisson, S.A.," on the balance sheet represents an investment in the shares of another company.

Required:

1. Compute the company's margin, turnover, and return on investment (ROI) for last year.
2. The board of directors of Joel de Paris, Inc., has set a minimum required rate of return of 15%. What was the company's residual income last year?

PROBLEM 12–27 (Appendix 12A) Basic Transfer Pricing [LO8]

Alpha and Beta are divisions within the same company. The managers of both divisions are evaluated based on their own division's return on investment (ROI). Assume the following information relative to the two divisions:

	Case			
	1	2	3	4
Alpha Division:				
Capacity in units	80,000	400,000	150,000	300,000
Number of units now being sold to outside customers	80,000	400,000	100,000	300,000
Selling price per unit to outside customers	$30	$90	$75	$50
Variable costs per unit	$18	$65	$40	$26
Fixed costs per unit (based on capacity)	$6	$15	$20	$9
Beta Division:				
Number of units needed annually	5,000	30,000	20,000	120,000
Purchase price now being paid to an outside supplier	$27	$89	$75*	—

*Before any quantity discount.

Managers are free to decide if they will participate in any internal transfers. All transfer prices are negotiated.

Required:

1. Refer to case 1 shown previously. Alpha Division can avoid $2 per unit in commissions on any sales to Beta Division. Will the managers agree to a transfer and if so, within what range will the transfer price be? Explain.
2. Refer to case 2 shown previously. A study indicates that Alpha Division can avoid $5 per unit in shipping costs on any sales to Beta Division.
   a. Would you expect any disagreement between the two divisional managers over what the transfer price should be? Explain.
   b. Assume that Alpha Division offers to sell 30,000 units to Beta Division for $88 per unit and that Beta Division refuses this price. What will be the loss in potential profits for the company as a whole?
3. Refer to case 3 shown previously. Assume that Beta Division is now receiving an 8% quantity discount from the outside supplier.
   a. Will the managers agree to a transfer? If so, what is the range within which the transfer price would be?
   b. Assume that Beta Division offers to purchase 20,000 units from Alpha Division at $60 per unit. If Alpha Division accepts this price, would you expect its ROI to increase, decrease, or remain unchanged? Why?

4. Refer to case 4 shown previously. Assume that Beta Division wants Alpha Division to provide it with 120,000 units of a *different* product from the one that Alpha Division is now producing. The new product would require $21 per unit in variable costs and would require that Alpha Division cut back production of its present product by 45,000 units annually. What is the lowest acceptable transfer price from Alpha Division's perspective?

PROBLEM 12–28 Restructuring a Segmented Income Statement [LO2]

Losses have been incurred at Millard Corporation for some time. In an effort to isolate the problem and improve the company's performance, management has requested that the monthly income statement be segmented by sales region. The company's first effort at preparing a segmented statement is given below. This statement is for May, the most recent month of activity.

	Sales Region		
	West	Central	East
Sales	$450,000	$800,000	$750,000
Less regional expenses (traceable):			
Cost of goods sold	162,900	280,000	376,500
Advertising	108,000	200,000	210,000
Salaries	90,000	88,000	135,000
Utilities	13,500	12,000	15,000
Depreciation	27,000	28,000	30,000
Shipping expense	17,100	32,000	28,500
Total regional expenses	418,500	640,000	795,000
Regional income (loss) before corporate expenses	31,500	160,000	(45,000)
Less corporate expenses:			
Advertising (general)	18,000	32,000	30,000
General administrative expense	50,000	50,000	50,000
Total corporate expenses	68,000	82,000	80,000
Operating income (loss)	$ (36,500)	$ 78,000	$(125,000)

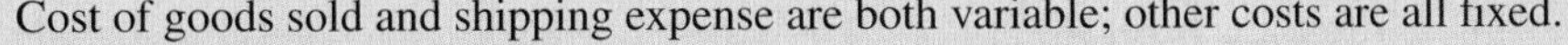

Cost of goods sold and shipping expense are both variable; other costs are all fixed.

Millard Corporation is a wholesale distributor of office products. It purchases office products from manufacturers and distributes them in the three regions given above. The three regions are about the same size, and each has its own manager and sales staff. The products that the company distributes vary widely in profitability.

Required:

1. List any disadvantages or weaknesses that you see to the statement format illustrated previously.
2. Explain the basis that is apparently being used to allocate the corporate expenses to the regions. Do you agree with these allocations? Explain.
3. Prepare a new contribution format segmented income statement for May. Show a Total column as well as data for each region. Include percentages on your statement for all columns.
4. Analyze the statement that you prepared in part (3) shown previously. What points that might help to improve the company's performance would you bring to management's attention?

PROBLEM 12–29 Segment Reporting; Activity-Based Cost Assignment [LO2, LO4]

"That commercial market has been dragging us down for years," complained Shanna Reynolds, president of Morley Products. "Just look at that anemic income figure for the commercial market. That market had three million dollars more in sales than the home market, but only a few thousand dollars more in profits. What a loser it is!"

The income statement to which Ms. Reynolds was referring is at the top of page 596.

"I agree," said Walt Divot, the company's vice president. "We need to focus more of our attention on the school market, since it's our best segment. Maybe that will bolster profits and get the shareholders off our backs."

	Total Company		Commercial Market	Home Market	School Market
Sales	$20,000,000	100.0%	$8,000,000	$5,000,000	$7,000,000
Less expenses:					
Cost of goods sold	9,500,000	47.5%	3,900,000	2,400,000	3,200,000
Sales support	3,600,000	18.0%	1,440,000	900,000	1,260,000
Order processing	1,720,000	8.6%	688,000	430,000	602,000
Warehousing	940,000	4.7%	376,000	235,000	329,000
Packing and shipping	520,000	2.6%	208,000	130,000	182,000
Advertising	1,690,000	8.5%	676,000	422,500	591,500
General management	1,310,000	6.6%	524,000	327,500	458,500
Total expenses	19,280,000	96.4%	7,812,000	4,845,000	6,623,000
Operating income	$ 720,000	3.6%	$ 188,000	$ 155,000	$ 377,000

The following additional information is available about the company:

a. Morley Products is a wholesale distributor of various goods; the cost of goods sold figures above are traceable to the markets in the amounts shown.

b. Sales support, order processing, and packing and shipping are variable costs. Warehousing, general management, and advertising are fixed costs. These costs have all been allocated to the markets on the basis of sales dollars—a practice that the company has followed for years.

c. You have compiled the following data.

Cost Pool and Allocation Base	Total Cost	Amount of Activity			
		Total	Commercial Market	Home Market	School Market
Sales support (number of calls)	$3,600,000	24,000	8,000	5,000	11,000
Order processing (number of orders)	$1,720,000	8,600	1,750	5,200	1,650
Warehousing (square metres of space)	$940,000	13,056	3,889	7,222	1,945
Packing and shipping (kilograms shipped)	$520,000	47,273	10,909	7,273	29,091

d. You have determined the following breakdown of the company's advertising expense and general management expense:

	Total	Market		
		Commercial	Home	School
Advertising:				
Traceable	$1,460,000	$700,000	$180,000	$580,000
Common	$230,000			
General management:				
Traceable—salaries	$410,000	$150,000	$120,000	$140,000
Common	$900,000			

The company is searching for ways to improve profit, and you have suggested that a contribution format segmented income statement in which costs are assigned on the basis of activities might provide some useful insights for management.

Required:

1. Refer to the data in part (c) shown previously. Determine a rate for each cost pool. Then, using this rate, compute the amount of cost assignable to each market.
2. Using the data from (1) above and other data from the problem, prepare a revised contribution format segmented income statement for the company. Show an Amount column and a Percent column for the company as a whole and for each market segment. Carry percentage figures to one decimal place. (Remember to include warehousing among the fixed expenses.)

3. What, if anything, in your segmented income statement should be brought to management's attention? Explain.

PROBLEM 12–30 Return on Investment (ROI) Analysis [LO5]

The contribution format income statement for Huerra Company for last year is given below:

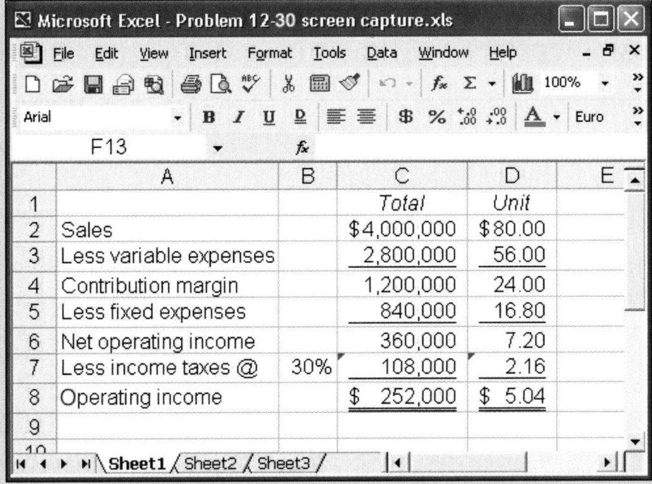

	A	B	C	D
1			Total	Unit
2	Sales		$4,000,000	$80.00
3	Less variable expenses		2,800,000	56.00
4	Contribution margin		1,200,000	24.00
5	Less fixed expenses		840,000	16.80
6	Net operating income		360,000	7.20
7	Less income taxes @	30%	108,000	2.16
8	Operating income		$ 252,000	$ 5.04

The company had average operating assets of $2,000,000 during the year.

Required:

1. Compute the company's return on investment (ROI) for the period using the ROI formula stated in terms of margin and turnover.

   For each of the following questions, indicate whether the margin and turnover will increase, decrease, or remain unchanged as a result of the events described, and then compute the new ROI figure. Consider each question separately, starting in each case from the data used to compute the original ROI in (1) above.
2. Using just-in-time (JIT), the company is able to reduce the average level of inventory by $400,000. (The released funds are used to pay off short-term creditors.)
3. The company achieves a cost savings of $32,000 per year by using less costly materials.
4. The company issues bonds and uses the proceeds to purchase $500,000 in machinery and equipment at the beginning of the period. Interest on the bonds is $60,000 per year. Sales remain unchanged. The new, more efficient equipment reduces production costs by $20,000 per year.
5. As a result of a more intense effort by salespeople, sales are increased by 20%; operating assets remain unchanged.
6. Obsolete inventory carried on the books at a cost of $40,000 is scrapped and written off as a loss.
7. The company uses $200,000 of cash (received on accounts receivable) to repurchase and retire some of its common stock.

PROBLEM 12–31 Return on Investment (ROI) and Residual Income; Decentralization [LO5, LO6]

Raddington Industries produces tool and die machinery for manufacturers. The company expanded vertically several years ago by acquiring Reigis Steel Company, one of its suppliers of alloy steel plates. Raddington decided to maintain Reigis' separate identity and therefore established the Reigis Steel Division as one of its investment centres.

Raddington evaluates its divisions on the basis of ROI. Management bonuses are also based on ROI. All investments in operating assets are expected to earn a minimum required rate of return of 11%.

Reigis' ROI has ranged from 14% to 17% since it was acquired by Raddington. During the past year, Reigis had an investment opportunity that would yield an estimated rate of return of 13%. Reigis' management decided against the investment because it believed the investment would decrease the division's overall ROI.

Last year's absorption costing income statement for Reigis Steel Division is given at the top of page 598. The division's operating assets employed were $12,960,000 at the end of the year, which represents an 8% increase over the previous year-end balance.

REIGIS STEEL DIVISION Divisional Income Statement For the Year Ended December 31		
Sales		$31,200,000
Cost of goods sold		16,500,000
Gross margin		14,700,000
Less operating expenses:		
Selling expenses	$5,620,000	
Administrative expenses	7,208,000	12,828,000
Operating income		$ 1,872,000

Required:

1. Compute the following performance measures for the Reigis Steel Division:
   a. ROI. (Remember, ROI is based on the *average* operating assets, computed from the beginning-of-year and end-of-year balances.) State ROI in terms of margin and turnover.
   b. Residual income.
2. Would the management of Reigis Steel Division have been more likely to accept the investment opportunity it had last year if residual income were used as a performance measure instead of ROI? Explain.
3. The Reigis Steel Division is a separate investment centre within Raddington Industries. Identify the items Reigis must be free to control if it is to be evaluated fairly by either the ROI or residual income performance measures.

(CMA, adapted)

PROBLEM 12–32 (Appendix 12A) Market-Based Transfer Price [LO8]

Stavos Company's Cabinet Division manufactures a standard cabinet for television sets. The cost per cabinet is:

Variable cost per cabinet	$ 70
Fixed cost per cabinet	30*
Total cost per cabinet	$100

*Based on a capacity of 10,000 cabinets per year.

Part of the Cabinet Division's output is sold to outside manufacturers of television sets and part is sold to Stavos Company's Quark Division, which produces a TV set under its own name. The Cabinet Division charges $140 per cabinet for all sales.

The costs, revenue, and operating income associated with the Quark Division's TV set is given below:

Selling price per TV set		$480
Less variable cost per TV set:		
Cost of the cabinet	$140	
Variable cost of electronic parts	210	
Total variable cost		350
Contribution margin		130
Less fixed costs per TV set		80*
Operating income per TV set		$ 50

*Based on a capacity of 3,000 sets per year.

The Quark Division has an order from an overseas source for 1,000 TV sets. The overseas source wants to pay only $340 per set.

Required:

1. Assume that the Quark Division has enough idle capacity to fill the 1,000-set order. Is the division likely to accept the $340 price or to reject it? Explain.

2. Assume that both the Cabinet Division and the Quark Division have idle capacity. Under these conditions, would it be advantageous for the company as a whole if the Quark Division rejects the $340 price? Show computations to support your answer.
3. Assume that the Quark Division has idle capacity but that the Cabinet Division is operating at capacity and could sell all of its cabinets to outside manufacturers. Compute the profit impact to the Quark Division of accepting the 1,000-set order at the $340 unit price.
4. What conclusions do you draw concerning the use of market price as a transfer price in intra-company transactions?

PROBLEM 12–33 Multiple Segmented Income Statements [LO2]

Companhia Bradesco, S.A., of Brazil, an industrial supply store chain, has two divisions. The company's contribution format income statement segmented by divisions for last year is given below (the currency in Brazil is the real, denoted here by R):

	Total Company	Division: Plastics	Division: Glass
Sales	R1,500,000	R900,000	R600,000
Less variable expenses	700,000	400,000	300,000
Contribution margin	800,000	500,000	300,000
Less traceable fixed expenses:			
Advertising	300,000	180,000	120,000
Depreciation	140,000	92,000	48,000
Administration	220,000	118,000	102,000
Total	660,000	390,000	270,000
Divisional segment margin	140,000	R110,000	R 30,000
Less common fixed expenses	100,000		
Operating income	R 40,000		

Top management doesn't understand why the Glass Division has such a low segment margin when its sales are only one-third less than sales in the Plastics Division. Accordingly, management has directed that the Glass Division be further segmented into product lines. The following information is available on the product lines in the Glass Division:

	Glass Division Product Lines		
	Flat Glass	Auto Glass	Specialty Glass
Sales	R200,000	R300,000	R100,000
Traceable fixed expenses:			
Advertising	R30,000	R42,000	R48,000
Depreciation	R10,000	R24,000	R14,000
Administration	R14,000	R21,000	R7,000
Variable expenses as a percentage of sales	65%	40%	50%

Analysis shows that R60,000 of the Glass Division's administration expenses are common to the product lines.

Required:

1. Prepare a contribution format segmented income statement for the Glass Division with segments defined as product lines. Show both an Amount column and a Percent column for the division in total and for each product line.
2. Management is surprised by Specialty Glass's poor showing and would like to have the product line segmented by market. The following information is available about the two markets in which Specialty Glass is sold:

	Specialty Glass Markets	
	Domestic	Foreign
Sales	R60,000	R40,000
Traceable fixed expenses:		
Advertising	R18,000	R30,000
Variable expenses as a percentage of sales	50%	50%

All of Specialty Glass's depreciation and administration expenses are common to the markets in which the product is sold. Prepare a contribution format segmented income statement for Specialty Glass with segments defined as markets. Show both Amount and Percent columns.

3. Refer to the statement prepared in (1) above. The sales manager wants to run a special promotional campaign on one of the products over the next month. A market study indicates that such a campaign would increase sales of Flat Glass by R40,000 or sales of Auto Glass by R30,000. The campaign would cost R8,000. Show computations to determine which product line should be chosen.

PROBLEM 12–34 (Appendix 12A) Cost-Volume-Profit Analysis; Return on Investment (ROI); Transfer Pricing [LO5, LO8]

The Valve Division of Bendix, Inc., produces a small valve that is used by various companies as a component part in their products. Bendix, Inc., operates its divisions as autonomous units, giving its divisional managers great discretion in pricing and other decisions. Each division is expected to generate a minimum required rate of return of at least 14% on its operating assets. The Valve Division has average operating assets of $700,000. The valves are sold for $5 each. Variable costs are $3 per valve, and fixed costs total $462,000 per year. The division has a capacity of 300,000 valves each year.

Required:

1. How many valves must the Valve Division sell each year to generate the desired rate of return on its assets?
   a. What is the margin earned at this level of sales?
   b. What is the turnover at this level of sales?
2. Assume that the Valve Division's current ROI equals the minimum required rate of 14%. In order to increase the division's ROI, the divisional manager wants to increase the selling price per valve by 4%. Market studies indicate that an increase in the selling price would cause sales to drop by 20,000 units each year. However, operating assets could be reduced by $50,000 due to decreased needs for accounts receivable and inventory. Compute the margin, turnover, and ROI if these changes are made.
3. Refer to the original data. Assume again that the Valve Division's current ROI equals the minimum required rate of 14%. Rather than increase the selling price, the sales manager wants to reduce the selling price per valve by 4%. Market studies indicate that this would fill the plant to capacity. In order to carry the greater level of sales, however, operating assets would increase by $50,000. Compute the margin, turnover, and ROI if these changes are made.
4. Refer to the original data. Assume that the normal volume of sales is 280,000 valves each year at a price of $5 per valve. Another division of the company is currently purchasing 20,000 valves each year from an overseas supplier, at a price of $4.25 per valve. The manager of the Valve Division has refused to meet this price, pointing out that it would result in a loss for his division:

Selling price per valve		$4.25
Cost per valve:		
Variable	$3.00	
Fixed ($462,000 ÷ 300,000 valves)	1.54	4.54
Operating loss per valve		$(0.29)

The manager of the Valve Division also points out that the normal $5 selling price barely allows his division to earn the required 14% rate of return. "If we take on some business at only $4.25 per unit, then our ROI is obviously going to suffer," he reasons, "and maintaining that ROI figure is the key to my future. Besides, taking on these extra units would require us to increase our operating assets by at least $50,000 due to the larger inventories and accounts receivable we would be carrying." Would you recommend that the Valve Division sell to the other division at $4.25? Show ROI computations to support your answer.

PROBLEM 12–35 (Appendix 12A) Negotiated Transfer Price [LO8]

Ditka Industries has several independent divisions. The company's Tube Division manufactures a picture tube used in television sets. The Tube Division's absorption costing income statement for last year, in which 8,000 tubes were sold, is given below:

	Total	Unit
Sales	$1,360,000	$170.00
Less cost of goods sold	840,000	105.00
Gross margin	520,000	65.00
Less selling and administrative expenses	390,000	48.75
Divisional operating income	$ 130,000	$ 16.25

As shown above, it costs the Tube Division $105 to produce a single tube. This figure consists of the following costs:

Direct materials	$ 38
Direct labour	27
Manufacturing overhead (75% fixed)	40
Total cost per tube	$105

The Tube Division has fixed selling and administrative expenses of $350,000 per year.

Ditka Industries has just formed a new division, called the TV Division, that will produce a television set that requires a high-resolution picture tube. The Tube Division has been asked to manufacture 2,500 of these tubes each year and sell them to the TV Division. As one step in determining the price that should be charged to the TV Division, the Tube Division has estimated the following cost for each of the new high-resolution tubes:

Direct materials	$ 60
Direct labour	49
Manufacturing overhead (2/3 fixed)	54
Total cost per tube	$163

To manufacture the new tubes, the Tube Division would have to reduce production of its regular tubes by 3,000 units per year. There would be no variable selling and administrative expenses on the intracompany business, and total fixed overhead costs would not change. Assume direct labour is a variable cost.

Required:

1. Determine the lowest acceptable transfer price from the perspective of the Tube Division for each of the new high-resolution tubes.
2. Assume that the TV Division has found an outside supplier that will provide the new tubes for $200 each. If the Tube Division meets this price, what will be the effect on the profits of the company as a whole?

PROBLEM 12-36 Variance Analysis [LO3]

The Leo company produces and sells two product lines with the budgeted revenues and expenses shown at the top of page 602.

	Spars	Masts
Expected total industry sales	48,000 units	85,000 units
Expected Leo Company sales	4,200 units	17,000 units
Expected selling price	$200 per unit	$300 per unit
Expected cost of manufacturing (40% fixed)	110 per unit	180 per unit
Expected selling and administration costs (70% fixed)	60 per unit	70 per unit
Expected product profit margin	$30 per unit	$ 50 per unit
Actual results for 2006 included:		
Actual total industry sales	60,000 units	100,000 units
Actual Leo Company sales	6,000 units	18,000 units
Actual selling price	$180 per unit	$300 per unit

All costs behaved exactly as expected.

W. Gallant, vice president of marketing and sales, has requested that the employees of his department be paid a bonus for the year based on the fact that they have been able to increase sales by 2,800 units over budget level for the year, an increase of over 13%.

Required:

1. Calculate the changes in overall company profits caused by the following factors:
   a. Sales price
   b. Sales mix
   c. Sales quanitity
   d. Market share
   e. Market size
2. Give two reasons why the marketing and sales employess should/should not receive the bonus suggested by Mr. Gallant.

(SMAC, adapted)

PROBLEM 12-37 Costing for Customers [LO4]

Brink Manufacturing and Distributing Ltd. distributes its preformed concrete slabs throughout eastern Canada to two classes of customers, wholesalers and contractors. In an effort to analyze its marketing expenses by distribution channel, the following statistics were obtained:

	Wholesalers	Contactors
Units sold	2,000	2,500
Kilometres travelled	30,000	42,000
Orders	1,200	1,500
Customers	38	160
Costs:		
Warehousing per unit	$10.00	$13.00
Transport	$1.20 per kilometre	
Credit and collection	$0.60 per order plus $150 per customer	
Selling	$2.00 per order	
Advertising	$100.00 per customer	

Required:

1. Analyze the marketing costs by customer class.
2. Brink is considering purchasing its own truck and hiring a driver for $36,000 per year. Determine how much it could afford to spend on a truck in year one to equal its current costs.

PROBLEM 12–38 Creating Balanced Scorecards that Support Different Strategies [LO7]

The Midwest Consulting Group (MCG) helps companies build balanced scorecards. As part of its marketing efforts, MCG conducts an annual balanced scorecard workshop for prospective clients. As MCG's newest employee, your boss has asked you to participate in this year's workshop by explaining to attendees how a company's strategy determines the measures that are appropriate for its balanced scorecard. Your boss has provided you with the excerpts below from the annual reports of two current MCG clients. She has asked you to use these excerpts as a basis for facilitating your portion of the workshop.

Excerpt from Applied Pharmaceuticals' annual report:

> The keys to our business are consistent and timely new product introductions and manufacturing process integrity. The new product introduction side of the equation is a function of research and development (R&D) yield (e.g., the number of marketable drug compounds created relative to the total number of potential compounds pursued). We seek to optimize our R&D yield and first-to-market capability by investing in state-of-the-art technology, hiring the highest possible percentage of the "best and the brightest" engineers that we pursue, and providing world-class training to those engineers. Manufacturing process integrity is all about establishing world-class quality specifications and then relentlessly engaging in prevention and appraisal activities to minimize defect rates. Our customers must have an awareness of and respect for our brand image of being "first to market and first in quality." If we deliver on this pledge to our customers, then our financial goal of increasing our return on shareholders' equity should take care of itself.

Excerpt from Destination Resorts International's annual report:

> Our business succeeds or fails based on the quality of the service that our front-line employees provide to customers. Therefore, it is imperative that we strive to maintain high employee morale and minimize employee turnover. In addition, it is critical that we train our employees to use technology to create one seamless worldwide experience for our repeat customers. Once an employee enters a customer preference (e.g., provide two extra pillows in the room, deliver fresh brewed coffee to the room at 8:00 A.M., etc.) into our database, our worldwide workforce strives to ensure that a customer will never need to repeat it at any of our destination resorts. If we properly train and retain a motivated workforce, we should see continuous improvement in our percentage of error-free repeat customer check-ins, the time taken to resolve customer complaints, and our independently assessed room cleanliness. This in turn should drive improvement in our customer retention, which is the key to meeting our revenue growth goals.

Required:

1. Based on the excerpts above, compare and contrast the strategies of Applied Pharmaceuticals and Destination Resorts International.
2. Select balanced scorecard measures for each company and link the scorecard measures using the framework from Exhibit 12–10. Use arrows to show the causal links between the performance measures and show whether the performance measure should increase or decrease over time. Feel free to create measures that may not be specifically mentioned in the chapter, but nonetheless make sense given the strategic goals of each company.
3. What hypotheses are built into each balanced scorecard? Why do the hypotheses differ between the two companies?

PROBLEM 12–39 Measures of Internal Business Process Performance [LO7]

DataSpan, Inc., automated its plant at the start of the current year and installed a flexible manufacturing system. The company is also evaluating its suppliers and moving toward a just-in-time (JIT) inventory system. Many adjustment problems have been encountered, including problems relating to performance measurement. After much study, the company has decided to use the performance measures below as part of its balanced scorecard, and it has gathered data relating to these measures for the first four months of operations.

	Month			
	1	2	3	4
Throughput time (days)	?	?	?	?
Delivery cycle time (days)	?	?	?	?
Manufacturing cycle efficiency (MCE)	?	?	?	?
Percentage of on-time deliveries	91%	86%	83%	79%
Total sales (units)	3,210	3,072	2,915	2,806

Management has asked for your help in computing throughput time, delivery cycle time, and MCE. The following average times have been logged over the last four months:

	Average per Month (in days)			
	1	2	3	4
Move time per unit	0.4	0.3	0.4	0.4
Process time per unit	2.1	2.0	1.9	1.8
Wait time per order before start of production	16.0	17.5	19.0	20.5
Queue time per unit	4.3	5.0	5.8	6.7
Inspection time per unit	0.6	0.7	0.7	0.6

Required:

1. For each month, compute the following:
   a. The throughput time.
   b. The MCE.
   c. The delivery cycle time.
2. Evaluate the company's performance over the last four months.
3. Refer to the move time, process time, and so forth, given above for month 4.
   a. Assume that in month 5 the move time, process time, and so forth, are the same as in month 4, except that through the use of JIT inventory methods the company is able to completely eliminate the queue time during production. Compute the new throughput time and MCE.
   b. Assume in month 6 that the move time, process time, and so forth, are again the same as in month 4, except that the company is able to completely eliminate both the queue time during production and the inspection time. Compute the new throughput time and MCE.

PROBLEM 12–40 Building a Balanced Scorecard [LO7]

Lost Peak ski resort was for many years a small, family-owned resort serving day skiers from nearby towns. Lost Peak was recently acquired by Western Resorts, a major ski resort operator. The new owners have plans to upgrade the resort into a destination resort for vacationers. As part of this plan, the new owners would like to make major improvements in the Powder 8 Lodge, the resort's on-the-hill cafeteria. The menu at the lodge is very limited—hamburgers, hot dogs, chili, tuna fish sandwiches, pizzas, french fries, and packaged snacks. With little competition, the previous owners of the resort had felt no urgency to upgrade the food service at the lodge. If skiers want lunch on the mountain, the only alternatives are the Powder 8 Lodge or a brown bag lunch brought from home.

As part of the deal when acquiring Lost Peak, Western Resorts agreed to retain all of the current employees of the resort. The manager of the lodge, while hardworking and enthusiastic, has very little experience in the restaurant business. The manager is responsible for selecting the menu, finding and training employees, and overseeing daily operations. The kitchen staff prepare food and wash dishes. The dining room staff take orders, serve as cashiers, and clean the dining room area.

Shortly after taking over Lost Peak, management of Western Resorts held a day-long meeting with all of the employees of the Powder 8 Lodge to discuss the future of the ski resort and the new management's plans for the lodge. At the end of this meeting, management and lodge employees created a balanced scorecard for the lodge that would help guide operations for the coming ski season. Almost everyone who participated in the meeting seemed to be enthusiastic about the scorecard and management's plans for the lodge.

The following performance measures were included on the balanced scorecard for the Powder 8 Lodge:

a. Weekly Powder 8 Lodge sales
b. Weekly Powder 8 Lodge profit
c. Number of menu items
d. Dining area cleanliness as rated by a representative from Western Resorts management
e. Customer satisfaction with menu choices as measured by customer surveys
f. Customer satisfaction with service as measured by customer surveys
g. Average time to take an order

h. Average time to prepare an order
i. Percentage of kitchen staff completing basic cooking course at the local community college
j. Percentage of dining room staff completing basic hospitality course at the local community college

Western Resorts will pay for the costs of staff attending courses at the local community college.

Required:

1. Using the above performance measures, construct a balanced scorecard for the Powder 8 Lodge. Use Exhibit 12–10 as a guide. Use arrows to show causal links and indicate with a + or − whether the performance measure should increase or decrease.
2. What hypotheses are built into the balanced scorecard for the Powder 8 Lodge? Which of these hypotheses do you believe are most questionable? Why?
3. How will management know if one of the hypotheses underlying the balanced scorecard is false?

PROBLEM 12–41 Perverse Effects of Some Performance Measures [LO7]

There is often more than one way to improve a performance measure. Unfortunately, some of the actions taken by managers to make their performance look better may actually harm the organization. For example, suppose the marketing department is held responsible only for increasing the performance measure "total revenues." Increases in total revenues may be achieved by working harder and smarter, but they can also usually be achieved by simply cutting prices. The increase in volume from cutting prices almost always results in greater total revenues; however, it does not always lead to greater total profits. Those who design performance measurement systems need to keep in mind that managers who are under pressure to perform may take actions to improve performance measures that have negative consequences elsewhere.

Required:

For each of the following situations, describe actions that managers might take to show improvement in the performance measure but which do not actually lead to improvement in the organization's overall performance.

1. Concerned with the slow rate at which new products are brought to market, top management of a consumer electronics company introduces a new performance measure—speed-to-market. The research and development department is given responsibility for this performance measure, which measures the average amount of time a product is in development before it is released to the market for sale.
2. The CEO of a telephone company has been under public pressure from city officials to fix the large number of public pay phones that do not work. The company's repair people complain that the problem is vandalism and damage caused by theft of coins from coin boxes—particularly in high-crime areas in the city. The CEO says she wants the problem solved and has pledged to city officials that there will be substantial improvement by the end of the year. To ensure that this is done, she makes the managers in charge of installing and maintaining pay phones responsible for increasing the percentage of public pay phones that are fully functional.
3. A manufacturing company has been plagued by the chronic failure to ship orders to customers by the promised date. To solve this problem, the production manager has been given the responsibility of increasing the percentage of orders shipped on time. When a customer calls in an order, the production manager and the customer agree to a delivery date. If the order is not completed by that date, it is counted as a late shipment.
4. Concerned with the productivity of employees, the board of directors of a large multinational corporation has dictated that the manager of each subsidiary will be held responsible for increasing the revenue per employee of his or her subsidiary.

PROBLEM 12–42 Internal Business Process Performance Measures [LO7]

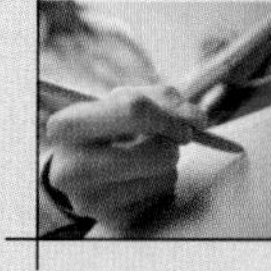

Tombro Industries is in the process of automating one of its plants and developing a flexible manufacturing system. The company is finding it necessary to make many changes in operating procedures. Progress has been slow, particularly in trying to develop new performance measures for the factory.

In an effort to evaluate performance and determine where improvements can be made, management has gathered the following data relating to activities over the last four months:

	Month			
	1	2	3	4
Quality control measures:				
Number of defects	185	163	124	91
Number of warranty claims	46	39	30	27
Number of customer complaints	102	96	79	58
Material control measures:				
Purchase order lead time	8 days	7 days	5 days	4 days
Scrap as a percent of total cost	1%	1%	2%	3%
Machine performance measures:				
Machine downtime as a percentage of availability	3%	4%	4%	6%
Use as a percentage of availability	95%	92%	89%	85%
Setup time (hours)	8	10	11	12
Delivery performance measures:				
Throughput time	?	?	?	?
Manufacturing cycle efficiency (MCE)	?	?	?	?
Delivery cycle time	?	?	?	?
Percentage of on-time deliveries	96%	95%	92%	89%

The president has read in industry journals that throughput time, MCE, and delivery cycle time are important measures of performance, but no one is sure how they are computed. You have been asked to assist the company, and you have gathered the following data relating to these measures:

	Average per Month (in days)			
	1	2	3	4
Wait time per order before start of production	9.0	11.5	12.0	14.0
Inspection time per unit	0.8	0.7	0.7	0.7
Process time per unit	2.1	2.0	1.9	1.8
Queue time per unit	2.8	4.4	6.0	7.0
Move time per unit	0.3	0.4	0.4	0.5

As part of its modernization process, the company is also moving toward a just-in-time (JIT) inventory system. Over the next year, the company hopes to have the bulk of its raw materials and parts on a JIT basis.

Required:

1. For each month, compute the following performance measures:
   a. Throughput time.
   b. MCE.
   c. Delivery cycle time.
2. Using the performance measures given in the main body of the problem and the performance measures computed in (1) above, do the following:
   a. Identify areas where the company seems to be improving.
   b. Identify areas where the company seems to be deteriorating.
3. Refer to the inspection time, process time, and so forth, given above for month 4.
   a. Assume that in month 5 the inspection time, process time, and so forth, are the same as for month 4, except that the company is able to completely eliminate the queue time during production. Compute the new throughput time and MCE.
   b. Assume that in month 6 the inspection time, process time, and so forth, are the same as in month 4, except that the company is able to eliminate both the queue time during production and the inspection time. Compute the new throughput time and MCE.

CASES

CASE 12–43 Segmented Statements; Product-Line Analysis [LO2, LO4]

"At last, I can see some light at the end of the tunnel," said Steve Adams, president of Jelco Products. "Our losses have shrunk from over $75,000 a month at the beginning of the year to only $26,000 for August. If we can just isolate the remaining problems with products A and C, we'll be in the black by the first of next year."

The company's absorption costing income statement for the latest month (August) is presented below:

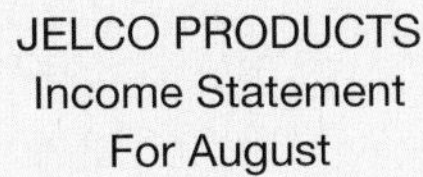

JELCO PRODUCTS
Income Statement
For August

	Total Company	Product A	Product B	Product C
Sales	$1,500,000	$600,000	$400,000	$500,000
Less cost of goods sold	922,000	372,000	220,000	330,000
Gross margin	578,000	228,000	180,000	170,000
Less operating expenses:				
Selling	424,000	162,000	112,000	150,000
Administrative	180,000	72,000	48,000	60,000
Total operating expenses	604,000	234,000	160,000	210,000
Operating income (loss)	$ (26,000)	$ (6,000)	$ 20,000	$ (40,000)

"What recommendations did that business consultant make?" asked Mr. Adams. "We paid the guy $100 an hour; surely he found something wrong." "He says our problems are concealed by the way we make up our income statements," replied Sally Warren, the executive vice president. "He left us some data on what he calls 'traceable' and 'common' costs that he says we should be isolating in our reports." The data to which Ms. Warren was referring are shown below:

	Total Company	Product A	Product B	Product C
Variable costs:*				
Manufacturing (materials, labour, and variable overhead)		18%	32%	20%
Selling		10%	8%	10%
Traceable fixed costs:				
Manufacturing	$376,000	$180,000	$36,000	$160,000
Selling	$282,000	$102,000	$80,000	$100,000
Common fixed costs:				
Manufacturing	$210,000	—	—	—
Administrative	$180,000	—	—	—

*As a percentage of sales.

"I don't see anything wrong with our income statements," said Mr. Adams. "Bill, our chief accountant, says that he has been using this format for over 30 years. He's also very careful to allocate all of our costs to the products."

"I'll admit that Bill always seems to be on top of things," replied Ms. Warren. "By the way, purchasing says that the X7 chips we use in products A and B are on back order and won't be available for several weeks. From the looks of August's income statement, we had better concentrate our remaining inventory of X7 chips on product B." (Two X7 chips are used in both product A and product B.)

The following additional information is available on the company:

a. Work in process and finished goods inventories are negligible and can be ignored.

b. Products A and B each sell for $250 per unit, and product C sells for $125 per unit. Strong market demand exists for all three products.

Required:

1. Prepare a new contribution format income statement for August, segmented by product. Show Amount and Percent columns for the company in total and for each product.
2. Assume that Mr. Adams is considering the elimination of product C due to the losses it is incurring. Based on the statement you prepared in (1) above, what points would you make for or against elimination of product C?
3. Do you agree with the company's decision to concentrate the remaining inventory of X7 chips on product B? Why or why not?
4. Product C is sold in both a vending and a home market with sales and cost data as follows:

	Market	
	Vending	Home
Sales	$50,000	$450,000
Variable costs:*		
Manufacturing	20%	20%
Selling	28%	8%
Traceable fixed costs:		
Selling	$45,000	$30,000

*As a percentage of sales.

The remainder of product C's fixed selling costs and all of product C's fixed manufacturing costs are common to the markets in which product C is sold.

a. Prepare a contribution format income statement showing product C segmented by market. Show both Amount and Percent columns for the product in total and for each market.

b. What insights revealed by this statement would you bring to management's attention?

CASE 12–44 (Appendix 12A) Transfer Pricing; Divisional Performance [LO8]

Weller Industries is a decentralized organization with six divisions. The company's Electrical Division produces a variety of electrical items, including an X52 electrical fitting. The Electrical Division (which is operating at capacity) sells this fitting to its regular customers for $7.50 each; the fitting has a variable manufacturing cost of $4.25.

The company's Brake Division has asked the Electrical Division to supply it with a large quantity of X52 fittings for only $5 each. The Brake Division, which is operating at 50% of capacity, will put the fitting into a brake unit that it will produce and sell to a large commercial airline manufacturer. The cost of the brake unit being built by the Brake Division follows:

Purchased parts (from outside vendors)	$22.50
Electrical fitting X52	5.00
Other variable costs	14.00
Fixed overhead and administration	8.00
Total cost per brake unit	$49.50

Although the $5 price for the X52 fitting represents a substantial discount from the regular $7.50 price, the manager of the Brake Division believes that the price concession is necessary if his division is to get the contract for the airplane brake units. He has heard "through the grapevine" that the airplane manufacturer plans to reject his bid if it is more than $50 per brake unit. Thus, if the Brake Division is forced to pay the regular $7.50 price for the X52 fitting, it will either not get the contract or it will suffer a substantial loss at a time when it is already operating at only 50% of capacity. The manager of the Brake Division argues that the price concession is imperative to the well-being of both his division and the company as a whole.

Weller Industries uses return on investment (ROI) to measure divisional performance.

Required:

1. Assume that you are the manager of the Electrical Division. Would you recommend that your division supply the X52 fitting to the Brake Division for $5 each as requested? Why or why not? Show all computations.
2. Would it be profitable for the company as a whole for the Electrical Division to supply the fittings to the Brake Division if the airplane brakes can be sold for $50? Show all computations, and explain your answer.

3. In principle, should it be possible for the two managers to agree to a transfer price in this particular situation? If so, within what range would that transfer price lie?
4. Discuss the organizational and manager behaviour problems, if any, inherent in this situation. What would you advise the company's president to do in this situation?

(CMA, adapted)

CASE 12–45 Service Organization; Segment Reporting [LO2, LO4]

Music Teachers, Inc., is an educational association for music teachers that has 20,000 members. The association operates from a central headquarters but has local membership chapters throughout the country. Monthly meetings are held by the local chapters to discuss recent developments on topics of interest to music teachers. The association's journal, *Teachers' Forum,* is issued monthly with features about recent developments in the field. The association publishes books and reports and also sponsors professional courses that qualify for continuing professional education credit. The association's statement of revenues and expenses for the current year is presented below:

MUSIC TEACHERS, INC.
Statement of Revenues and Expenses
For the Year Ended November 30

Revenues	$3,275,000
Less expenses:	
Salaries	920,000
Personnel costs	230,000
Occupancy costs	280,000
Reimbursement of member costs to local chapters	600,000
Other membership services	500,000
Printing and paper	320,000
Postage and shipping	176,000
Instructors' fees	80,000
General and administrative	38,000
Total expenses	3,144,000
Excess of revenues over expenses	$ 131,000

The board of directors of Music Teachers, Inc., has requested that a segmented income statement be prepared showing the contribution of each profit centre to the association. The association has four profit centres: Membership Division, Magazine Subscriptions Division, Books and Reports Division, and Continuing Education Division. Mike Doyle has been assigned responsibility for preparing the segmented income statement, and he has gathered the following data prior to its preparation.

a. Membership dues are $100 per year, of which $20 is considered to cover a one-year subscription to the association's journal. Other benefits include membership in the association and chapter affiliation. The portion of the dues covering the magazine subscription ($20) should be assigned to the Magazine Subscription Division.
b. One-year subscriptions to *Teachers' Forum* were sold to nonmembers and libraries at $30 per subscription. A total of 2,500 of these subscriptions were sold last year. In addition to subscriptions, the magazine generated $100,000 in advertising revenues. The costs per magazine subscription were $7 for printing and paper and $4 for postage and shipping.
c. A total of 28,000 technical reports and professional texts were sold by the Books and Reports Division at an average unit selling price of $25. Average costs per publication were $4 for printing and paper and $2 for postage and shipping.
d. The association offers a variety of continuing education courses to both members and nonmembers. The one-day courses had a tuition cost of $75 each and were attended by 2,400 students. A total of 1,760 students took two-day courses at a tuition cost of $125 for each student. Outside instructors were paid to teach some courses.
e. Salary costs and space occupied by division follow:

	Salaries	Space Occupied (square metres)
Membership	$210,000	222
Magazine Subscriptions	150,000	222
Books and Reports	300,000	334
Continuing Education	180,000	222
Corporate staff	80,000	111
Total	$920,000	1,111

Personnel costs are 25% of salaries in the separate divisions as well as for the corporate staff. The $280,000 in occupancy costs includes $50,000 in rental cost for a warehouse used by the Books and Reports Division for storage purposes.

f. Printing and paper costs other than for magazine subscriptions and for books and reports relate to the Continuing Education Division.
g. General and administrative expenses include costs relating to overall administration of the association as a whole. The company's corporate staff does some mailing of materials for general administrative purposes.

The expenses that can be traced or assigned to the corporate staff, as well as any other expenses that are not traceable to the profit centres, will be treated as common costs. It is not necessary to distinguish between variable and fixed costs.

Required:

1. Prepare a segmented income statement for Music Teachers, Inc. This statement should show the segment margin for each division as well as results for the association as a whole.
2. Give arguments for and against allocating *all* costs of the association to the four divisions.

(CMA, adapted)

CASE 12–46 Balanced Scorecard [LO7]

Haglund Department Store is located in the downtown area of a small city. While the store had been profitable for many years, it is facing increasing competition from large national chains that have set up stores on the outskirts of the city. Recently the downtown area has been undergoing revitalization, and the owners of Haglund Department Store are somewhat optimistic that profitability can be restored.

In an attempt to accelerate the return to profitability, management of Haglund Department Store is in the process of designing a balanced scorecard for the company. Management believes the company should focus on two key problems. First, customers are taking longer and longer to pay the bills they incur using the department store's charge card, and the company has far more bad debts than are normal for the industry. If this problem were solved, the company would have more cash to make much needed renovations. Investigation has revealed that much of the problem with late payments and unpaid bills results from customers disputing incorrect charges on their bills. These incorrect charges usually occur because salesclerks incorrectly enter data on the charge account slip. Second, the company has been incurring large losses on unsold seasonal apparel. Such items are ordinarily resold at a loss to discount stores that specialize in such distress items.

The meeting in which the balanced scorecard approach was discussed was disorganized and ineffectively led—possibly because no one other than one of the vice presidents had read anything about how to build a balanced scorecard. Nevertheless, a number of potential performance measures were suggested by various managers. These potential performance measures are:

a. Percentage of charge account bills containing errors.
b. Percentage of salesclerks trained to correctly enter data on charge account slips.
c. Average age of accounts receivables.
d. Profit per employee.
e. Customer satisfaction with accuracy of charge account bills from monthly customer survey.
f. Total sales revenue.
g. Sales per employee.
h. Travel expenses for buyers for trips to fashion shows.
i. Unsold inventory at the end of the season as a percentage of total cost of sales.
j. Courtesy shown by junior staff members to senior staff members based on surveys of senior staff.

k. Percentage of suppliers making just-in-time deliveries.
l. Sales per square metre of floor space.
m. Written-off accounts receivable (bad debts) as a percentage of sales.
n. Quality of food in the staff cafeteria based on staff surveys.
o. Percentage of employees who have attended the city's cultural diversity workshop.
p. Total profit.

Required:

1. As someone with more knowledge of the balanced scorecard than almost anyone else in the company, you have been asked to build an integrated balanced scorecard. In your scorecard, use only performance measures listed previously. You do not have to use all of the performance measures suggested by the managers, but you should build a balanced scorecard that reveals a strategy for dealing with the problems with accounts receivable and with unsold merchandise. Construct the balanced scorecard following the format used in Exhibit 12–10. Do not be concerned with whether a specific performance measure falls within the learning and growth, internal business process, customer, or financial perspective. However, use arrows to show the causal links between performance measures within your balanced scorecard and explain whether the performance measures should show increases or decreases.
2. Assume that the company adopts your balanced scorecard. After operating for a year, some performance measures show improvements, but not others. What should management do next?
3. *a.* Suppose that customers express greater satisfaction with the accuracy of their charge account bills but the performance measures for the average age of accounts receivable and for bad debts do not improve. Explain why this might happen.
   b. Suppose that the performance measures for the average age of accounts receivable, bad debts, and unsold inventory improve, but total profits do not. Explain why this might happen. Assume in your answer that the explanation lies within the company.

GROUP AND INTERNET EXERCISES

GROUP EXERCISE 12–47 College Segment Reports

Obtain a copy of your college or university's most recent financial report prepared for internal use.

Required:

1. Does the financial report break down the results into major segments such as schools, academic departments, intercollegiate sports, and so on? Can you determine the financial contribution (i.e., revenues less expenses) of each segment from the report?
2. If the report attempts to show the financial contribution of each major segment, does the report follow the principles for segment reporting in this chapter? If not, what principles are violated and what harm, if any, can occur as a result from violating those principles?

GROUP EXERCISE 12–48 (Appendix 12A) Transfer Pricing Role Playing

Divide your team into two groups—one will play the part of the managers of the Consumer Products Division of Highstreet Enterprises, Inc., and the other will play the part of the managers of the Industrial Products Division of the same company.

The Consumer Products Division would like to acquire an advanced electric motor from the Industrial Products Division that would be used to make a state-of-the-art sorbet maker. At the expected selling price of $89, the Consumer Products Division would sell 50,000 sorbet makers per year. Each sorbet maker would require one advanced electric motor. The only possible source for the advanced electric motor is the Industrial Products Division, which holds a critical patent. The variable cost of the sorbet maker (not including the cost of the electric motor) would be $54. The sorbet maker project would require additional fixed costs of $180,000 per year and additional operating assets of $3,000,000.

The Industrial Products Division has plenty of spare capacity to make the electric motors requested by the Consumer Products Division. The variable cost of producing the motors would be $13 per unit. The additional fixed costs that would have to be incurred to fill the order from the Consumer Products Division would amount to $30,000 per year and the additional operating assets would be $400,000.

The division managers of Highstreet Enterprises are evaluated based on residual income, with a minimum required rate of return of 20%.

Required:
The two groups—those representing the managers of the Consumer Products Division and those representing the managers of the Industrial Products Division—should negotiate the transfer price for the 50,000 advanced electric motors per year. (The groups may or may not be able to come to an agreement.) Whatever the outcome of the negotiations, each group should write a memo to the instructor justifying the outcome in terms of what would be in the best interests of their division.

INTERNET EXERCISE 12–49
As you know, the World Wide Web is a medium that is constantly evolving. Sites come and go, and change without notice. To enable the periodic updating of site addresses, this problem has been posted to the textbook Web site (www.mcgrawhill.ca/college/garrison). After accessing the site, enter the Student Centre and select this chapter. Select and complete the Internet Exercise.

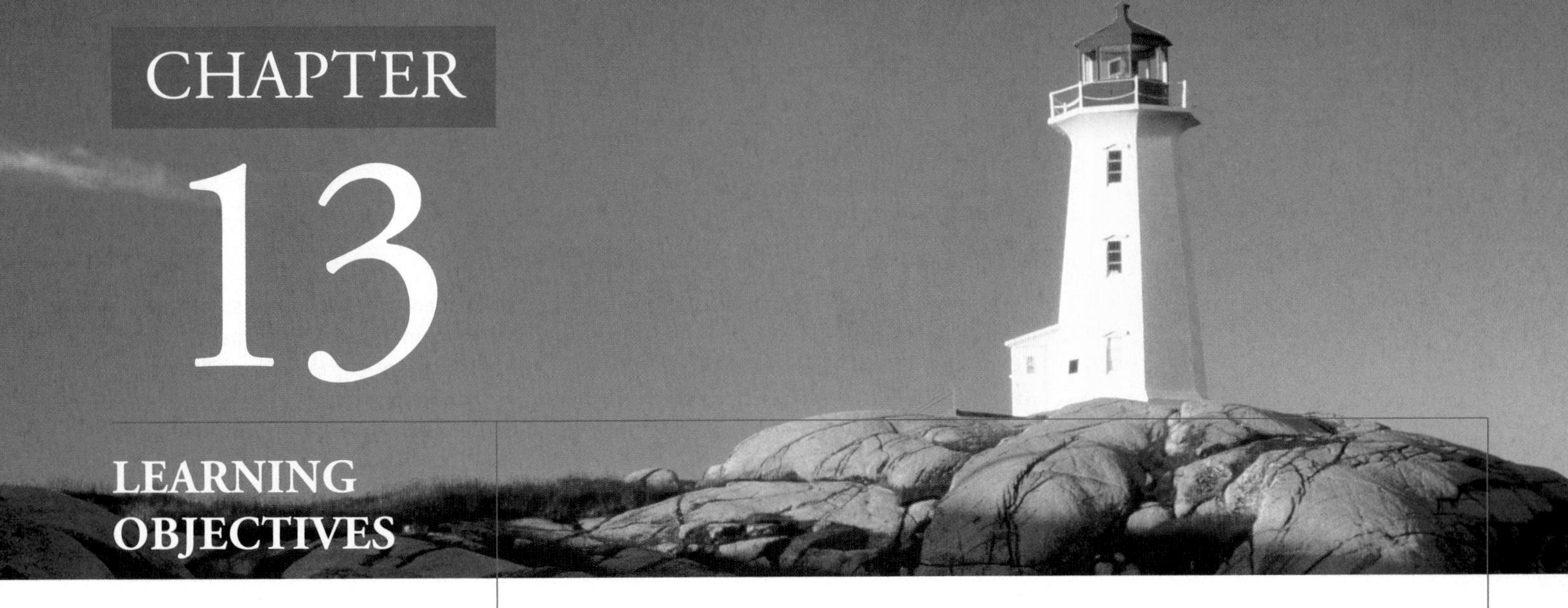

CHAPTER 13

LEARNING OBJECTIVES

After studying Chapter 13, you should be able to:

1. Distinguish between relevant and irrelevant costs in decision making.
2. Prepare analyses for various decision situations.
3. Determine the most profitable use of a constrained resource and the value of obtaining more of the constrained resource.
4. (Appendix 13A) Compute selling prices based on costs.
5. (Appendix 13A) Compute target costs based on selling prices.

RELEVANT COSTS FOR DECISION MAKING

BUSINESS FOCUS

CAN WASTE BE PROFITABLE?

A company located on the Gulf of St. Lawrence is a producer of soap products. Its six main soap product lines are produced from common inputs. Joint product costs up to the split-off point constitute the bulk of the production costs for all six product lines. These joint product costs are allocated to the six product lines on the basis of the relative sales value of each line at the split-off point.

The company has a waste product that results from the production of the six main product lines. Until a few years ago, the company loaded the waste onto trucks and took it to a landfill site since the waste was thought to have no commercial value. This was stopped, however, when the company's research division discovered that with some further processing the waste could be made commercially saleable as a fertilizer ingredient. The further processing was initiated at a cost of $175,000 per year. The waste was then sold to fertilizer manufacturers at a total price of $300,000 per year.

The accountants responsible for allocating manufacturing costs included the sales value of the waste product along with the sales value of the six main product lines in their allocation of the joint product costs at the split-off point. This allocation resulted in the waste product being allocated $150,000 in joint product cost. This $150,000 allocation, when added to the further processing costs of $175,000 for the waste, caused the waste product to show the net loss computed below:

Sales value of the waste product after further processing	$ 300,000
Less costs assignable to the waste product	325,000
Net loss	$ (25,000)

Based on this analysis it appears that the best course of action is to not process the waste further after all. However, an alternative analysis presented to company management ignores the $150,000 of allocated joint costs and shows incremental operating income of $125,000 ($300,000 – $175,000) if the waste is processed further. Management is now in a quandary. Which analysis represents the correct approach? Should they continue to process the waste further, or truck it to a landfill site?

Decision making is a critical aspect of managing an organization. Managers are constantly faced with problems of deciding which products or services to offer, what production methods to use, whether to make or buy component parts, what prices to charge, whether to accept special orders at special prices, how to allocate limited resources, and so on. In each case, the decision should lead to outcomes that contribute to achieving the performance goals identified as part of the organization's strategic objectives (e.g., grow revenues, reduce costs, improve return on investment, etc.). However, decision making is a complex process. Numerous alternatives may exist for each decision situation and large amounts of data must be analyzed, only some of which are relevant.

Relevant cost
A cost that differs between alternatives in a particular decision. In managerial accounting, this term is synonymous with avoidable cost and differential cost.

How can managers cope with these complexities in an effort to consistently make good decisions? The key is to identify and compare *only* the relevant costs and benefits for each alternative. **Relevant costs** are those that differ among the alternatives under consideration. A key challenge for managers, and fundamental to good decision making, is differentiating between relevant and irrelevant costs. This is critical because consideration of irrelevant costs wastes managers' time and effort, and can lead to the wrong decisions. Further complicating matters is the fact that the relevance of specific costs and benefits depends on the decision situation. For example, a product supervisor's salary is typically irrelevant in deciding whether or not to accept a special order from a customer but can be relevant when deciding whether to keep or drop that product line. The purpose of this chapter is to develop the skills necessary to distinguish between relevant and irrelevant costs by illustrating their use in a wide range of decision making situations.

We begin the chapter by developing a general framework for identifying relevant costs and benefits. We then apply this framework to a variety of non-recurring situations to illustrate how the relevance of a cost or benefit depends on the type of decision being made. Next we turn our attention to analyzing situations where managers must decide how to allocate a limited resource such as labour hours. Finally, the relation between relevant costs and pricing issues is further examined in the appendix.

Two aspects of the decision situations and the related analysis presented in this chapter are important to emphasize. First, none of the situations involve capital expenditures (e.g., replacing production equipment) where the time value of money is an important factor in the analysis. This type of analysis, termed *capital budgeting*, is covered in Chapter 14. Second, the key criterion used in the various decision situations presented in the chapter is the maximization of operating income. However, in practice managers may also consider qualitative factors when making decisions. For example, when deciding whether to keep or drop a product or segment, the effect on employee morale and the impact on the company's reputation may be important, but very difficult or costly to quantify. The extent to which qualitative factors influence a decision will vary from situation to situation but they are often taken into account.

COST CONCEPTS FOR DECISION MAKING

Four cost terms discussed in Chapter 2 are particularly applicable to this chapter. These terms are *differential costs, incremental costs, opportunity costs,* and *sunk costs.* You may find it helpful to turn back to Chapter 2 and review the concepts before reading on.

LEARNING OBJECTIVE 1
Distinguish between relevant and irrelevant costs in decision making.

Identifying Relevant Costs and Benefits

Because it is fundamental to the proper analysis of the various decision situations covered in this chapter, we begin by identifying the nature of relevant costs and beneifts. Only those costs and benefits that differ in total between alternatives are relevant in a decision. If a cost will be the same regardless of the alternative selected, then the decision has no effect on the cost and it can be ignored. For example, if you are trying to decide whether to go to a movie or to rent a videotape for the evening, the rent on your apartment is irrelevant. Whether you go to a movie or rent a videotape, the rent on your apartment will be exactly the same and is therefore irrelevant in the decision. On the other hand, the cost of the movie ticket and the cost of renting the videotape would be relevant in the decision because they are *avoidable costs.*

An **avoidable cost** is a cost that can be eliminated in whole or in part by choosing one alternative over another. By choosing the alternative of going to the movie, the cost of renting the videotape can be avoided. By choosing the alternative of renting the videotape, the cost of the movie ticket can be avoided. Therefore, the cost of the movie ticket and the cost of renting the videotape are both avoidable costs. On the other hand, the rent on the apartment is not an avoidable cost of either alternative. You would continue to rent your apartment under either alternative. Avoidable costs are relevant costs. Unavoidable costs are irrelevant costs.

Avoidable cost
Any cost that can be eliminated (in whole or in part) by choosing one alternative over another in a decision making situation. In managerial accounting, this term is synonymous with *relevant cost* and *differential cost.*

Two broad categories of costs are never relevant in decisions. These irrelevant costs are:

1. Sunk costs (e.g., previously owned video player).
2. Future costs that do not differ between the alternatives (e.g., apartment rent for movie decision).

As we learned in Chapter 2, a **sunk cost** is a cost that has already been incurred and that cannot be avoided, regardless of what a manager decides to do. Sunk costs are always the same, no matter what alternatives are being considered, and they are therefore always irrelevant and should be ignored. On the other hand, future costs that do differ between alternatives *are* relevant. For example, when deciding whether to go to a movie or rent a videotape, the cost of buying a movie ticket and the cost of renting a videotape have not yet been incurred. These are future costs that differ between alternatives when the decision is being made and therefore are relevant.

Sunk cost
Any cost that has already been incurred and that cannot be changed by any decision made now or in the future.

Along with sunk cost, the term **differential cost** was introduced in Chapter 2. In managerial accounting, the terms *avoidable cost, differential cost, incremental cost,* and *relevant cost* are often used interchangeably. To identify the costs and benefits that are relevant in a particular decision situation, these steps can be followed:

1. Eliminate costs and benefits that do not differ between alternatives. These irrelevant costs consist of (a) sunk costs and (b) future costs that do not differ between alternatives.
2. Use the remaining costs and benefits that do differ between alternatives in making the decision. The costs that remain are the differential, or avoidable, costs.

Differential cost
Any cost that differs between alternatives in a decision making situation. In managerial accounting, this term is synonymous with *avoidable cost* and *relevant cost.*

Different Costs for Different Purposes

We need to recognize from the outset of our discussion that costs that are relevant in one decision situation are not necessarily relevant in another. Simply put, this means that *the manager needs different costs for different purposes.* For one purpose, a particular group of costs may be relevant; for another purpose, an entirely different group of costs may be relevant. Thus, in *each* decision situation the manager must examine the data at hand and isolate the relevant costs. Otherwise, the manager runs the risk of being misled by irrelevant data.

The concept of "different costs for different purposes" is basic to managerial accounting; we will see its application frequently in the pages that follow.

An Example of Identifying Relevant Costs and Benefits

Cynthia is currently a student in an MBA program in Montréal and would like to visit a friend in Toronto over the weekend. She is trying to decide whether to drive or take the train. Because she is on a tight budget, she wants to carefully consider the costs of the two alternatives. If one alternative is far less expensive than the other, that may be decisive in her choice. By car, the distance between her apartment in Montréal and her friend's apartment in Toronto is 420 kilometres. Cynthia has compiled the list of items (shown in the table below) to consider.

Which costs and benefits are relevant in this decision? Remember, only those costs and benefits that differ between alternatives are relevant. Everything else is irrelevant and can be ignored.

Start at the top of the list with item (a): the original cost of the car is a sunk cost. This cost has already been incurred and therefore can never differ between alternatives. Consequently, it is irrelevant and can be ignored. The same is true of the accounting depreciation of $3,200 per year, which simply spreads the sunk cost across a number of years.

Automobile Costs

	Item	Annual Cost of Fixed Items	Cost per km (based on 16,000 km per year)
(a)	Annual straight-line depreciation on car [($20,000 original cost − $4,000 estimated resale value in 5 years)/5 years]	$3,200	$0.200
(b)	Cost of gasoline ($0.80 per litre ÷ 10 kilometres per litre)		0.080
(c)	Annual cost of auto insurance and licence	1,800	0.112
(d)	Maintenance and repairs		0.041
(e)	Parking fees at university ($45 per month × 8 months)	360	0.023
(f)	Tires ($900 to replace all 4 tires every 50,000 kilometres)		$0.018
(g)	Total average cost per kilometre		$0.474

Additional Data

	Item	
(h)	Cost of round-trip VIA ticket	$200
(i)	Benefit of relaxing and being able to study during the train ride rather than having to drive	?
(j)	Cost of putting the dog in a kennel while gone	$40
(k)	Benefit of having a car available in Toronto	?
(l)	Hassle of parking the car in Toronto	?
(m)	Cost of parking the car in Toronto	$25 per day

Move down the list to item (b): the cost of gasoline consumed by driving to Toronto would clearly be a relevant cost in this decision. If Cynthia takes the train, this cost would not be incurred. Hence, the cost differs between alternatives and is therefore relevant.

Item (c), the annual cost of auto insurance and licence, is not relevant. Whether

Cynthia takes the train or drives on this particular trip, her annual auto insurance premium and her auto licence fee will remain the same.[1]

Item (d), the cost of maintenance and repairs, is relevant. While maintenance and repair costs have a large random component, over the long run they should be more or less proportional to the amount the car is driven. Thus, the average cost of $0.041 per kilometre is a reasonable estimate to use.

Item (e), the monthly fee that Cynthia pays to park at her university during the academic year, would not be relevant in the decision of how to get to Toronto. Regardless of which alternative she selects—driving or taking the train—she will still need to pay for parking at school.

Item (f), the cost of replacing all four tires ($900) every 50,000 kilometres is relevant. The more often Cynthia uses her car the sooner she will have to replace the tires. Therefore, the $0.018 per kilometre for tires is appropriate to use in deciding whether to drive or take the train.

Item (g) is the total average cost of $0.474 per kilometre. As discussed above, some elements of this total are relevant, but some are not relevant. Since it contains some irrelevant costs, it would be incorrect to estimate the cost of driving to Toronto and back by simply multiplying the $0.474 by 840 kilometres (420 kilometres each way × 2). This erroneous approach would yield a cost of driving of $398.16. Unfortunately, such mistakes are often made in both personal life and in business. Since the total cost is stated on a per-kilometre basis, people are easily misled. Often people think that if the cost is stated as $0.474 per kilometre, the cost of driving 100 kilometres is $47.40. But it is not. Many of the costs included in the $0.474 cost per kilometre are sunk and/or fixed and will not increase if the car is driven another 100 kilometres. The $0.474 is an average cost, not an incremental cost. Study such unitized costs carefully (i.e., costs stated in terms of a dollar amount per unit, per kilometre, per direct labour-hour, per machine-hour, and so on)—they are often misleading.

Item (h), the $200 cost of a round-trip ticket on VIA, is clearly relevant in this decision. If Cynthia drives, she would not have to buy the ticket.

Item (i) is relevant to the decision, even if it is difficult to put a dollar value on relaxing and being able to study while on the train. It is relevant because it is a benefit that is available under one alternative but not under the other.

Item (j), the cost of putting Cynthia's dog in the kennel while she is gone, is clearly irrelevant in this decision. Whether she takes the train or drives to Toronto, she will still need to put her dog in a kennel.

Like item (i), items (k) and (l) are relevant to the decision even if it is difficult to measure their dollar impacts.

Item (m), the cost of parking in Toronto, is relevant to the decision.

Bringing together all of the relevant data, Cynthia would estimate the relative costs of driving and taking the train as follows:

Relevant financial cost of driving to Toronto:	
Gasoline (840 kilometres at $0.08 per kilometre)	$ 67.20
Maintenance and repairs (840 kilometres @ $0.041 per km)	34.44
Tires (840 kilometres @ $0.018 per km)	15.12
Cost of parking the car in Toronto (2 days @ $25 per day)	50.00
Total	$166.76
Relevant financial cost of taking the train to Toronto:	
Cost of round-trip VIA ticket from Montréal to Toronto	$200.00

What should Cynthia do? From a purely financial standpoint, it would be cheaper by $33.24 ($200 – $166.76) to drive. Cynthia has to decide whether being able to relax and

1. If Cynthia has an accident while driving to Toronto or back, this might affect her insurance premium when the policy is renewed. If the expected cost of the increase in the insurance premium could be estimated, it would be a relevant cost of this particular trip, but the normal amount of the insurance premium is not relevant in any case.

study on the train and avoiding the hassle of finding parking in the city justify the higher cost of taking the train.

In this example, we focused on identifying the relevant costs and benefits—everything else was ignored. In the next example, we will begin the analysis by including all of the costs and benefits—relevant or not. We will see that if we are very careful, we will still get the correct answer because the irrelevant costs and benefits will cancel out when we compare the alternatives.

Reconciling the Total and Differential Approaches

Oak Harbour Woodworks is considering a new labour-saving machine that rents for $3,000 per year. The machine will be used on the company's butcher block production line. Data concerning the company's annual sales and costs of butcher blocks with and without the new machine are shown in the table on this page.

Given the annual sales and the price and cost data in this table, the operating income for the product under the two alternatives can be computed as shown in Exhibit 13–1.

Note that the operating income is higher by $12,000 with the new machine, so that is the better alternative. Note also that the $12,000 advantage for the new machine can be obtained in two different ways. It is the difference between the $30,000 operating income with the new machine and the $18,000 net operating income for the current situation. It is also the sum of the differential costs and benefits as shown in the last column of Exhibit 13–1. A positive number in the Differential Costs and Benefits column indicates that the difference between the alternatives favours the new machine; a negative number indicates that the difference favours the current situation. A zero in that column simply means that the total amount for the item is exactly the same for both alternatives. Thus, since the difference in the operating incomes equals the sum of the differences for the individual items, any cost or benefit that is the same for both alternatives will have no impact on which alternative is preferred. This is the reason that costs and benefits that do not differ between alternatives are irrelevant and can be ignored. If we properly account for them, they will cancel out when we compare the alternatives.

	Current Situation	Situation with the New Machine
Units produced and sold	5,000	5,000
Selling price per unit	$ 40	$ 40
Direct materials cost per unit	14	14
Direct labour cost per unit	8	5
Variable overhead cost per unit	2	2
Fixed costs, other	62,000	62,000
Fixed costs, new machine	—	3,000

We could have arrived at the same solution more quickly by ignoring the irrelevant costs and benefits:

- The selling price per unit and the number of units sold do not differ between the alternatives. Therefore, the total sales revenues are exactly the same for the two alternatives as shown in Exhibit 13–1. Since the sales revenues are exactly the same, they have no effect on the difference in operating income between the two alternatives. That is shown in the last column in Exhibit 13–1, which indicates a $0 differential benefit.
- The direct materials cost per unit, the variable overhead cost per unit, and the number of units produced and sold do not differ between the alternatives. Consequently, the direct materials cost and the variable overhead cost will be the same for the two alternatives and can be ignored.
- The "other" fixed expenses do not differ between the alternatives, so they can be ignored as well.

Exhibit 13–1
Total and Differential Costs

	Current Situation	Situation with New Machine	Differential Costs and Benefits
Sales (5,000 units @ $40 per unit)	$200,000	$200,000	$ –0–
Less variable expenses:			
Direct materials (5,000 units @ $14 per unit)	70,000	70,000	–0–
Direct labour (5,000 units @ $8 and $5 per unit)	40,000	25,000	15,000
Variable overhead (5,000 units @ $2 per unit)	10,000	10,000	–0–
Total variable expenses	120,000	105,000	
Contribution margin	80,000	95,000	
Less fixed expenses:			
Other	62,000	62,000	–0–
Rent of new machine	–0–	3,000	(3,000)
Total fixed expenses	62,000	65,000	
Operating income	$ 18,000	$ 30,000	$12,000

Indeed, the only costs that do differ between the alternatives are direct labour costs and the fixed rental cost of the new machine. Hence, these are the only relevant costs. The two alternatives can be compared based on just these relevant costs:

Net advantage to renting the new machine:	
Decrease in direct labour costs (5,000 units at a cost savings of $3 per unit)	$15,000
Increase in fixed expenses (rent)	(3,000)
Net annual cost savings from renting the new machine	$12,000

Thus, if we focus on just the relevant costs and benefits, we get exactly the same answer that we got when we listed all of the costs and benefits—including those that do not differ between the alternatives and hence are irrelevant. We get the same answer because the only costs and benefits that matter in the final comparison of the operating incomes are those that differ between the two alternatives and hence are not zero in the last column of Exhibit 13–1. Those two relevant costs are both listed in the above analysis showing the net advantage to renting the new machine.

Why Isolate Relevant Costs?

In the preceding example, we used two different approaches to analyze the alternatives. First, we considered only the relevant costs; and second, we considered all costs, both those that were relevant and those that were not. We obtained the same answer under both approaches. It would be natural to ask, "Why bother to isolate relevant costs when total costs will do the job just as well?" Isolating relevant costs is desirable for at least two reasons.

First, only rarely will enough information be available to prepare a detailed income statement for both alternatives as we have done in the preceding examples. Assume, for example, that you are called on to make a decision relating to a *single operation* of a multidepartmental, multiproduct firm. Under these circumstances, it would be virtually impossible to prepare an income statement of any type. You would have to rely on your ability to recognize which costs are relevant and which are not in order to assemble the data necessary to make a decision.

Second, mingling irrelevant costs with relevant costs may cause confusion and distract attention from the matters that are really critical. Furthermore, the danger always exists that an irrelevant piece of data may be used improperly, resulting in an incorrect decision. Indeed, research shows that managers will often attempt to use *all* information provided, relevant and irrelevant, when making a decision.[2] The best approach is to discard irrelevant data and base the decision entirely on the relevant data.

Relevant cost analysis, combined with the contribution approach to the income statement, provides a powerful tool for making decisions. We will investigate various uses of this tool in the remaining sections of this chapter.

ANALYSIS OF VARIOUS DECISION SITUATIONS

LEARNING OBJECTIVE 2
Prepare analyses for various decision situations.

Periodically, managers are faced with making non-routine or special decisions. Should a product line or segment be kept or dropped? Should a product component be made internally or purchased from an external supplier (outsourced)? Should special orders be accepted or rejected? Should a product be sold as is, or processed further? While on the surface these may appear to be very different decision situations, the approach to the analysis is very similar in each case. For each of these situations, the relevant costs and benefits must be quantified, and the alternative with the most favourable impact on operating income selected. In some situations the analysis will consist only of a comparison of relevant costs (make versus buy) while in others both relevant benefits and relevant costs will be involved (keep or drop a product). As will be illustrated in the examples of each decision situation that follows, the challenge for managers is identifying and quantifying the relevant costs and benefits.

Adding and Dropping Product Lines and Other Segments

Decisions relating to whether old product lines or other segments of a company should be dropped and new ones added are among the most difficult that a manager has to make. In such decisions, many qualitative and quantitative factors must be considered. Ultimately, however, any final decision to drop an old segment or to add a new one is going to hinge primarily on the impact the decision will have on net operating income. To assess this impact, it is necessary to make a careful analysis of the costs involved.

Consider the three major product lines of the Discount Drug Company—drugs, cosmetics, and housewares. Sales and cost information for the preceding month for each separate product line and for the company in total are given in Exhibit 13–2.

What can be done to improve the company's overall performance? One product line—housewares—shows an operating loss for the month. Perhaps dropping this line would cause profits in the company as a whole to improve. In deciding whether the line should be dropped, management should reason as follows:

If the housewares line is dropped, then the company will lose $20,000 per month in contribution margin. By dropping the line, however, it may be possible to avoid some fixed costs by, for example, discharging certain employees or reducing advertising costs. If by dropping the housewares line the company is able to avoid more in fixed costs than it loses in contribution margin, then it will be better off if the line is eliminated, because overall operating income should improve. On the other hand, if the company is not able to avoid as much in fixed costs as it loses in contribution margin, then the housewares line should be retained. In short, the manager should ask, "What costs can I avoid if I drop this product line?"

2. K. Siegel-Jacobs and F. Yates, "Effects of Procedural and Outcome Accountability on Judgment Quality," *Organizational Behaviour and Human Decision Processes,* 1996, 65(1), pp. 7–17.

EXHIBIT 13–2 Discount Drug Company Product Lines

		Product Line		
	Total	**Drugs**	**Cosmetics**	**House-wares**
Sales	$250,000	$125,000	$75,000	$50,000
Less variable expenses	105,000	50,000	25,000	30,000
Contribution margin	145,000	75,000	50,000	20,000
Less fixed expenses:				
Salaries	50,000	29,500	12,500	8,000
Advertising	15,000	1,000	7,500	6,500
Utilities	2,000	500	500	1,000
Depreciation—fixtures	5,000	1,000	2,000	2,000
Rent	20,000	10,000	6,000	4,000
Insurance	3,000	2,000	500	500
General administrative	30,000	15,000	9,000	6,000
Total fixed expenses	125,000	59,000	38,000	28,000
Operating income (loss)	$ 20,000	$ 16,000	$12,000	$ (8,000)

As we have seen from our earlier discussion, not all costs are avoidable. For example, some of the costs associated with a product line may be sunk costs. Other costs may be allocated common costs that will not differ in total regardless of whether the product line is dropped or retained. As discussed in Chapter 8, an activity-based costing analysis may be used to help identify the relevant costs.

To show how the manager should proceed in a product-line analysis, suppose that the management of the Discount Drug Company has analyzed the costs being charged to the three product lines and has determined the following:

1. The salaries expense represents salaries paid to employees working directly in each product-line area. All of the employees working in housewares would be discharged if the line is dropped.
2. The advertising expense represents direct advertising of each product line and is avoidable if the line is dropped.
3. The utilities expense represents utilities costs for the entire company. The amount charged to each product line is an allocation based on space occupied and is not avoidable if the product line is dropped.
4. The depreciation expense represents depreciation on fixtures used for display of the various product lines. Although the fixtures are nearly new, they are custom-built and will have little resale value if the housewares line is dropped.
5. The rent expense represents rent on the entire building housing the company; it is allocated to the product lines on the basis of sales dollars. The monthly rent of $20,000 is fixed under a long-term lease agreement.
6. The insurance expense represents insurance carried on inventories within each of the three product-line areas.
7. The general administrative expense represents the costs of accounting, purchasing, and general management, which are allocated to the product lines on the basis of sales dollars. Total administrative costs will not change if the housewares line is dropped.

With this information, management can identify costs that can and cannot be avoided if the product line is dropped (see the top of page 622).

	Total Cost	Not Avoidable*	Avoidable
Salaries	$ 8,000		$ 8,000
Advertising	6,500		6,500
Utilities	1,000	$ 1,000	
Depreciation—fixtures	2,000	2,000	
Rent	4,000	4,000	
Insurance	500		500
General administrative	6,000	6,000	
Total fixed expenses	$28,000	$13,000	$15,000

*These costs represent either (1) sunk costs or (2) future costs that will not change if the housewares line is retained or discontinued.

To determine how dropping the line will affect the overall profits of the company, we can compare the contribution margin that will be lost to the costs that can be avoided if the line is dropped:

Contribution margin lost if the housewares line is discontinued (see Exhibit 13–2)	$(20,000)
Less fixed costs that can be avoided if the housewares line is discontinued (see above)	15,000
Decrease in overall company operating income	$ (5,000)

In this case, the fixed costs that can be avoided by dropping the product line are less than the contribution margin that will be lost. Therefore, based on the data given, the housewares line should not be discontinued unless a more profitable use can be found for the floor and counter space that it is occupying.

A Comparative Format

Some managers prefer to approach decisions of this type by preparing comparative income statements showing the effects on the company as a whole of either keeping or dropping the product line in question. A comparative analysis of this type for the Discount Drug Company is shown in Exhibit 13–3.

EXHIBIT 13–3
A Comparative Format for Product-Line Analysis

	Keep Housewares	Drop Housewares	Difference: Operating Income Increase or (Decrease)
Sales	$50,000	$ –0–	$(50,000)
Less variable expenses	30,000	–0–	30,000
Contribution margin	20,000	–0–	(20,000)
Less fixed expenses:			
Salaries	8,000	–0–	8,000
Advertising	6,500	–0–	6,500
Utilities	1,000	1,000	–0–
Depreciation—fixtures	2,000	2,000	–0–
Rent	4,000	4,000	–0–
Insurance	500	–0–	500
General administrative	6,000	6,000	–0–
Total fixed expenses	28,000	13,000	15,000
Operating income (loss)	$ (8,000)	$(13,000)	$ (5,000)

As shown by column 3 in the exhibit, overall company net operating income will decrease by $5,000 each period if the housewares line is dropped. This is the same answer, of course, as we obtained in our earlier analysis.

Beware of Allocated Fixed Costs

Our conclusion that the housewares line should not be dropped seems to conflict with the data shown earlier in Exhibit 13–2. Recall from the exhibit that the housewares line is showing a loss rather than a profit. Why keep a line that is showing a loss? The explanation for this apparent inconsistency lies at least in part with the common fixed costs that are being allocated to the product lines. As we observed in Chapter 12, one of the great dangers in allocating common fixed costs is that such allocations can make a product line (or other segment of a business) *look* less profitable than it really is. By allocating the common fixed costs among all product lines, the housewares line has been made to *look* as if it was unprofitable, whereas, in fact, dropping the line would result in a decrease in overall company operating income. This point can be seen clearly if we recast the data in Exhibit 13–2 and eliminate the allocation of the common fixed costs. This recasting of data—using the segmented approach from Chapter 12—is shown in Exhibit 13–4.

Exhibit 13–4 gives us a much different perspective of the housewares line than does Exhibit 13–2. As shown in Exhibit 13–4, the housewares line is covering all of its own traceable fixed costs and is generating a $3,000 segment margin toward covering the common fixed costs of the company. Unless another product line can be found that will generate a greater segment margin than this, the company would be better off keeping the housewares line. By keeping the line, the company's overall operating income will be higher than if the product line was dropped.[3]

Additionally, we should note that managers may choose to retain an unprofitable product line if the line is necessary to the sale of other products or if it serves as a "magnet" to attract customers. Bread, for example, is not an especially profitable line in food stores, but customers expect it to be available, and many would undoubtedly shift their buying elsewhere if a par-

DECISION *Aid*

KEEP OR DROP A PRODUCT/SEGMENT

Relevant Costs and Benefits

- Contribution margin (CM) lost if dropped
- Fixed costs avoided if dropped
- CM lost/gained on *other* products/segments

Irrelevant Costs

- Allocated common costs
- Sunk costs

Decision Rule:

Keep if: CM lost (*all* products/segments) > fixed costs avoided + CM gained (*other* products/segments)

Drop if: CM lost (*all* products/segments) < fixed costs avoided + CM gained (*other* products/segments)

3. An alternative way of formulating the analysis is to start with the housewares net loss of $(8,000) and add back the non-avoidable (irrelevant) expenses of $13,000 to arrive at the relevant benefit (segment margin) of $5,000 that would be forgone if the product line were to be discontinued.

EXHIBIT 13–4 Discount Drug Company Product Lines—Recast in Contribution Format (from Exhibit 13–2)

		Product Line		
	Total	**Drugs**	**Cosmetics**	**House-wares**
Sales	$250,000	$125,000	$75,000	$50,000
Less variable expenses	105,000	50,000	25,000	30,000
Contribution margin	145,000	75,000	50,000	20,000
Less traceable fixed expenses:				
Salaries	50,000	29,500	12,500	8,000
Advertising	15,000	1,000	7,500	6,500
Depreciation—fixtures	5,000	1,000	2,000	2,000
Insurance	3,000	2,000	500	500
Total	73,000	33,500	22,500	17,000
Product-line segment margin	72,000	$ 41,500	$27,500	$ 3,000*
Less common fixed expenses:				
Utilities	2,000			
Rent	20,000			
General administrative	30,000			
Total	52,000			
Operating income	$ 20,000			

*If the housewares line is dropped, this $3,000 in segment margin will be lost to the company. In addition, we have seen that the $2,000 depreciation on the fixtures is a sunk cost that cannot be avoided. The sum of these two figures ($3,000 + $2,000 = $5,000) would be the decrease in the company's overall profits if the housewares line was discontinued.

ticular store decided to stop carrying it. Accordingly, to the extent that dropping a product line or segment results in decreases (or increases) to sales of other products or segments, the related impact on contribution margin should be included in the keep versus drop analysis.

The Make or Buy Decision

Many steps may be involved in getting a finished product into the hands of a consumer. First, raw materials may have to be obtained through mining, drilling, growing crops, raising animals, and so forth. Second, these raw materials may have to be processed to remove impurities and to extract the desirable and usable materials. Third, the usable materials may have to undergo some preliminary fabrication so as to be usable in final products. For example, cotton must be made into thread and textiles before being made into clothing. Fourth, the actual manufacturing of the finished product must take place. And finally, the finished product must be distributed to the ultimate consumer. All of these steps taken together are called a *value chain* (see Chapter 12).

Vertical integration
The involvement by a company in more than one of the steps from production of basic raw materials to the manufacture and distribution of a finished product.

Separate companies may carry out each of the steps in the value chain or a single company may carry out several of the steps. When a company is involved in more than one of these steps in the entire value chain, it is following a policy of **vertical integration.** Vertical integration is very common. Some firms control *all* of the activities in the value chain from producing basic raw materials right up to the final distribution of finished goods. Other firms are content to integrate on a smaller scale by purchasing many of the parts and materials that go into their finished products.

Make or buy decision
A decision as to whether an item should be produced internally or purchased from an outside supplier.

A decision to produce a fabricated part internally, rather than to buy the part externally from a supplier, is called a **make or buy decision.** Actually, any decision relating to vertical integration is a make or buy decision, since the company is deciding whether to meet its own needs internally or to buy externally.

Strategic Aspects of the Make or Buy Decision

Integration provides certain advantages. An integrated firm is less dependent on its suppliers and may be able to ensure a smoother flow of parts and materials for production than a non-integrated firm. For example, a strike against a major parts supplier can interrupt the operations of a non-integrated firm for many months, whereas an integrated firm that is producing its own parts might be able to continue operations. Also, many firms feel that they can control quality better by producing their own parts and materials, rather than by relying on the quality control standards of outside suppliers.

The advantages of integration are counterbalanced by some advantages of using external suppliers. By pooling demand from a number of firms, a supplier may be able to enjoy economies of scale in research and development and in manufacturing. These economies of scale can result in higher quality and lower costs than would be possible if the firm was to attempt to make the parts on its own. A company must be careful, however, to retain control over activities that are essential to maintaining its competitive position. For example, Hewlett-Packard controls the software for a laser printer it makes in cooperation with Canon Inc. of Japan to prevent Canon from coming out with a competing product. The present trend appears to be toward less vertical integration, with some companies like Nokia Corp., the world's largest cellphone maker, focused on hardware while teaming up with companies such as Microsoft to acquire the email software used in its phones.[4] These factors suggest that the make or buy decision should be weighed very carefully.

An Example of Make or Buy

To provide an illustration of a make or buy decision, consider Mountain Goat Cycles. The company is now producing the heavy-duty gear shifters used in its most popular line of mountain bikes. The company's Accounting Department reports the following costs of producing the shifter internally:

	Per Unit	8,000 Units
Direct materials	$ 6	$ 48,000
Direct labour	4	32,000
Variable overhead	1	8,000
Supervisor's salary	3	24,000
Depreciation of special equipment	2	16,000
Allocated general overhead	5	40,000
Total cost	$21	$168,000

An outside supplier has offered to sell Mountain Goat Cycles 8,000 shifters per year at a price of only $19 each. Should the company stop producing the shifters internally and start purchasing them from the outside supplier? To approach the decision from a financial point of view, the manager should again focus on the differential costs. As we have seen, the differential costs can be obtained by eliminating those costs that are not avoidable—that is, by eliminating (1) the sunk costs and (2) the future costs that will continue regardless of whether the shifters are produced internally or purchased outside. The costs that remain after making these eliminations are the costs that are avoidable to the company by purchasing outside. If these avoidable costs are less than the outside purchase price, then the company should continue to manufacture its own shifters and reject the outside supplier's offer. That is, the company should purchase outside only if the outside purchase price is less than the costs that can be avoided internally as a result of stopping production of the shifters.

4. David Pringle, "Nokia, Microsoft Bury Hatchet," *The Globe and Mail,* February 2005, p. B14.

Looking at the data above, note first that depreciation of special equipment is listed as one of the costs of producing the shifters internally. Since the equipment has already been purchased, this depreciation is a sunk cost and is therefore irrelevant. If the equipment could be sold, its salvage value would be relevant. Or if the machine could be used to make other products, this could be relevant as well. However, we will assume that the equipment has no salvage value and that it has no other use except making the heavy-duty gear shifters.

Also note that the company is allocating a portion of its general overhead costs to the shifters. Any portion of this general overhead cost that would actually be eliminated if the gear shifters were purchased rather than made would be relevant in the analysis. However, it is likely that the general overhead costs allocated to the gear shifters are in fact common to all items produced in the factory and would continue unchanged even if the shifters are purchased from the outside. Such allocated common costs are not differential costs (because they do not differ between the make or buy alternatives) and should be eliminated from the analysis along with the sunk costs.

The variable costs of producing the shifters (materials, labour, and variable overhead) are differential costs, because they can be avoided by buying the shifters from the outside supplier. If the supervisor can be discharged and her salary avoided by buying the shifters, then it too will be a differential cost and relevant to the decision. Assuming that both the variable costs and the supervisor's salary can be avoided by buying from the outside supplier, then the analysis takes the form shown in Exhibit 13–5.

Since it costs $5 less per unit to continue to make the shifters, Mountain Goat Cycles should reject the outside supplier's offer. However, there is one additional factor that the company may wish to consider before coming to a final decision. This factor is the opportunity cost of the space now being used to produce the shifters.

Opportunity Cost

If the space now being used to produce the shifters *would otherwise be idle,* then Mountain Goat Cycles should continue to produce its own shifters and the supplier's offer should be rejected, as stated above. Idle space that has no alternative use has an opportunity cost of zero.

But what if the space now being used to produce shifters could be used for some other purpose? In that case, the space would have an opportunity cost that would have to

EXHIBIT 13–5 Mountain Goat Cycles Make or Buy Analysis

	Production "Cost" per Unit	Per Unit Differential Costs		Total Differential Costs—8,000 Units	
		Make	Buy	Make	Buy
Direct materials	$ 6	$ 6		$ 48,000	
Direct labour	4	4		32,000	
Variable overhead	1	1		8,000	
Supervisor's salary	3	3		24,000	
Depreciation of special equipment	2	—		—	
Allocated general overhead	5	—		—	
Outside purchase price			$19		$152,000
Total cost	$21	$14	$19	$112,000	$152,000
Difference in favour of continuing to make		$5		$40,000	

be considered in assessing the desirability of the supplier's offer. What would this opportunity cost be? It would be the segment margin that could be derived from the best alternative use of the space.

To illustrate, assume that the space now being used to produce shifters could be used to produce a new cross-country bike that would generate a segment margin of $60,000 per year. Under these conditions, Mountain Goat Cycles would be better off to accept the supplier's offer and to use the available space to produce the new product line:

	Make	Buy
Differential cost per unit (see Exhibit 13–5)	$ 14	$ 19
Number of units needed annually	× 8,000	× 8,000
Total annual cost	112,000	152,000
Opportunity cost—segment margin forgone on a potential new product line	60,000	
Total cost	$172,000	$152,000
Difference in favour of purchasing from the outside supplier	$ 20,000[5]	

Opportunity costs are not recorded in accounts of an organization because they do not represent actual dollar outlays. Rather, they represent economic benefits that are *forgone* as a result of pursuing some course of action. Because of this, opportunity costs are often erroneously ignored by managers when making decisions.[6] The opportunity costs of Mountain Goat Cycles are sufficiently large in this case to make continued production of the shifters very costly from an economic point of view.

FOCUS *on Current Practice*

Sometimes companies are forced to outsource in the short-run because of an unusually high demand for their product that exceeds their productive capacity. However, outsourcing can have negative consequences for the profitability of the organization if the costs of buying from the outside supplier exceed the costs of making the product internally.

Cott Corporation, based in Toronto, is the largest producer of retail-brand soft drinks. In 2004 their profit margin dropped to 17.2% versus 19.5% in 2003. According to chief executive officer John Sheppard, it was not lower demand that led to the reduced profit margin. He said that it was "pretty much the opposite. Our demand was so high it impacted our capacity." The result was the need to engage in an expensive outsourcing program because Cott could not meet the demand from its American customers. Because the per unit cost of buying from the outside supplier exceeded Cott's normal production costs, their profit margin declined in 2004 relative to 2003 when outsourcing did not occur. The challenge for organizations such as Cott is to find cost effective ways of increasing capacity to avoid the need to outsource in the future.

Source: Richard Bloom, "Cott Can't Handle High Demand, Sees Profit Fizzle," *The Globe and Mail*, February 3, 2005.

5. An alternative approach to the analysis is to add the incremental unit cost of continuing to make the shifters of $14 (see Exhibit 13-5) to the opportunity cost per unit of $7.50 ($60,000 opportunity cost ÷ 8,000 units), giving a total of $21.50. Since $21.50 is greater than the purchase price of $19 per unit, Mountain Goat Cycle should buy the shifter.
6. S. Vera-Munoz. "The Effects of Accounting Knowledge and Context on the Omission of Opportunity Costs in Resource Allocation Decisions," *The Accounting Review*, 1998, 73(1), pp. 47-72.

Special Orders

Special order A one-time order that is not considered part of the company's normal ongoing business.

Managers often must evaluate whether a *special order* should be accepted, and if the order is accepted, the price that should be charged. A **special order** is a one-time order that is not considered part of the company's normal ongoing business. The objective in setting a price for special orders is to achieve positive incremental operating income. To illustrate, Mountain Goat Cycles has just received a request from the Edmonton Police Department to produce 100 specially modified mountain bikes at a price of $179 each. The bikes would be used to patrol some of the more densely populated residential sections of the city. Mountain Goat Cycles can easily modify its City Cruiser model to fit the specifications of the Edmonton Police. The normal selling price of the City Cruiser bike is $249, and its unit product cost is $182 as shown below:

Direct materials	$ 86
Direct labour	45
Manufacturing overhead	51
Unit product cost	$182

The variable portion of the above manufacturing overhead is $6 per unit. The order would have no effect on the company's total fixed manufacturing overhead costs.

The modifications to the bikes consist of welded brackets to hold radios, nightsticks, and other gear. These modifications would require $17 in incremental variable costs. In addition, the company would have to pay a graphics design studio $1,200 to design and cut stencils that would be used for spray painting the Edmonton Police Department's logo and other identifying marks on the bikes.

This order should have no effect on the company's other sales. The production manager says that she can handle the special order without disrupting any of the regular scheduled production.

What effect would accepting this order have on the company's operating income?

Only the incremental costs and benefits are relevant. Since the existing fixed manufacturing overhead costs would not be affected by the order, they are not incremental costs and therefore are not relevant. The incremental operating income can be computed as follows:

	Per Unit	Total 100 Bikes
Incremental revenue	$179	$17,900
Incremental costs:		
Variable costs:		
Direct materials	86	8,600
Direct labour	45	4,500
Variable manufacturing overhead	6	600
Special modifications	17	1,700
Total variable cost	$154	15,400
Fixed cost:		
Purchase of stencils		1,200
Total incremental cost		16,600
Incremental operating income		$ 1,300

Therefore, even though the price on the special order ($179) is below the normal unit product cost ($182) and the order would require incurring additional costs, the order would result in an increase in operating income. In general, a special order is profitable as long as the incremental revenue from the special order exceeds the incremental costs of the order.

We must note, however, that it is important to make sure that there is indeed idle capacity and that the special order does not cut into normal sales. For example, what if Mountain Goat Cycle is already operating at 100% of capacity and normally sells all the bikes it can produce for $250 each? What is the opportunity cost of accepting the order? Should they accept the $179 price? If not, what is the minimum price they should accept? To answer these questions, the analysis can be conducted as follows:

	Per Unit
(a) Opportunity Costs:	
Normal selling price	$250
Less variable costs:	
Direct materials	86
Direct labour	45
Variable overhead	6
Total variable costs	$137
Contribution margin forgone	$113*
(b) Total relevant costs:	
Incremental costs:	
Variable	$154
Fixed ($1,200/100)	12
	$166
Opportunity costs	113
Total	$279

*If Mountain Goat Cycle is operating at 100% capacity, every bike they sell to the Edmonton Police Department means forgoing the contribution margin of $113 they would have earned on a sale to a regular customer. This is the per unit opportunity cost of accepting the special order.

Since the total relevant costs of $279 exceed the offer price of $179, Mountain Goat Cycle should decline the offer. Indeed, to be no worse off from a financial perspective, the minimum price that should be charged on the special order is $279 per bike. At this price, management should be indifferent between filling the special order and continuing to sell all it can produce to regular customers.

DECISION *Aid*

ACCEPT OR REJECT A SPECIAL ORDER

Relevant Costs and Benefits

- Incremental costs of filling the order (variable and fixed)
- Opportunity cost of filling the order
- Incremental revenues from the order

Irrelevant Costs

- Allocated common costs
- Sunk costs

Total Relevant Costs = incremental costs + opportunity costs

Decision Rule:

Accept if: incremental revenues > total relevant costs
Reject if: incremental revenues < total relevant costs

Joint Product Costs and The Sell or Process Further Decision

In some industries, a number of end products are produced from a single raw material input. A grisly, but apt, example is provided by the meat-packing industry. A great variety of end products—bacon, ham, spareribs, pork roasts, and so on—are produced from a single pig. Firms that produce several end products from a common input (e.g., a pig) are faced with the problem of deciding how the cost of that input is going to be divided among the end products. Firms must also decide whether to sell the end products as is, or to process them further. Before we address these problems, it will be helpful to define three terms—*joint products, joint product costs,* and *split-off point.*

Joint products
Two or more items that are produced from a common input.

Joint product costs
Costs that are incurred up to the split-off point in producing joint products.

Split-off point
That point in the manufacturing process where some or all of the joint products can be recognized as individual products.

Two or more products that are produced from a common input are known as **joint products.** The term **joint product costs** is used to describe those manufacturing costs that are incurred in producing joint products up to the split-off point. The **split-off point** is that point in the manufacturing process at which the joint products (bacon, ham, spareribs, and so on) can be recognized as separate products. At that point, some of the joint products will be in final form, ready to be marketed to the consumer. Others will still need further processing on their own before they are in marketable form. These concepts are presented graphically in Exhibit 13–6.

The Pitfalls of Allocation

Joint product costs are really common costs incurred to simultaneously produce a variety of end products. Traditional cost accounting books contain various approaches to allocating these common costs among the different products at the split-off point. A typical approach is to allocate the joint product costs according to the relative sales value of the end products.

Although allocation of joint product costs is needed for some purposes, such as balance sheet inventory valuation, allocations of this kind should be viewed with great caution *internally* in the decision making process. Unless a manager proceeds with care, he or she may be led into incorrect decisions as a result of relying on allocated common costs.

Sell or Process Further Decisions

Joint product costs are irrelevant in decisions regarding what to do with a product from the split-off point forward. The reason is that by the time one arrives at the split-off point, the joint product costs have already been incurred and therefore are sunk costs. In the case

EXHIBIT 13–6 Joint Products

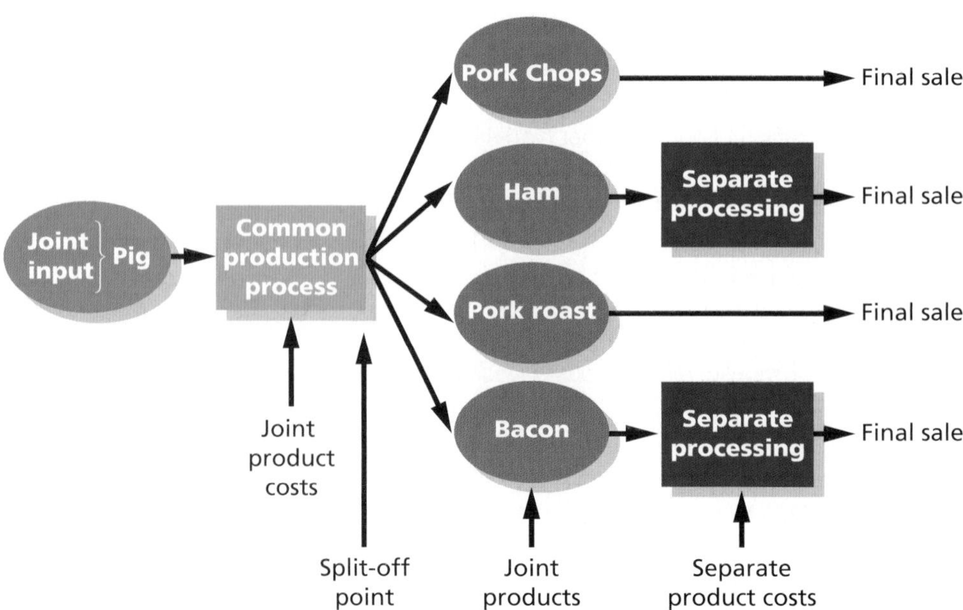

of the soap company in the chapter opener, the $150,000 in allocated joint costs should not have been permitted to influence what was done with the waste product from the split-off point forward. The "alternative" analysis was correct and is restated below:

	Send to Landfill	Process Further
Sales value	–0–	$300,000
Additional processing costs	–0–	175,000
Contribution margin	–0–	$125,000
Advantage of processing further	$125,000	

Decisions of this type are known as **sell or process further decisions.** It will always be profitable to continue processing a joint product after the split-off point *as long as the incremental revenue from such processing exceeds the incremental processing cost incurred after the split-off point.* Joint product costs that already have been incurred up to the split-off point are sunk costs, which are always irrelevant in decisions concerning what to do from the split-off point forward.

Sell or process further decision A decision as to whether a joint product should be sold at the split-off point or processed further and sold at a later time in a different form.

To provide a detailed example of a sell or process further decision, assume that three products are derived from a single raw material input. Cost and revenue data relating to the products are presented in Exhibit 13–7, along with an analysis of which products should be sold at the split-off point and which should be processed further. As shown in the exhibit, products B and C should both be processed further; product A should be sold at the split-off point.

EXHIBIT 13–7 Sell or Process Further Decision

	Product		
	A	B	C
Data:			
Sales value at the split-off point	$120,000	$150,000	$60,000
Sales value after further processing	160,000	240,000	90,000
Allocated joint product costs	80,000	100,000	40,000
Cost of further processing	50,000	60,000	10,000
Analysis of sell or process further:			
Sales value after further processing	$160,000	$240,000	$90,000
Sales value at the split-off point	120,000	150,000	60,000
Incremental revenue from further processing	40,000	90,000	30,000
Cost of further processing	50,000	60,000	10,000
Profit (loss) from further processing	$(10,000)	$ 30,000	$20,000

DECISION *Aid*

SELL OR PROCESS FURTHER

Relevant Costs and Benefits

- Incremental costs of further processing
- Incremental revenues from further processing

Irrelevant Costs

- Allocated joint product costs

Decision Rule:

Process further if: incremental revenues > incremental costs of further processing
Sell at split-off if: incremental revenues < incremental costs of further processing

UTILIZATION OF A CONSTRAINED RESOURCE

LEARNING OBJECTIVE 3
Determine the most profitable use of a constrained resource and the value of obtaining more of the constrained resource.

Constraint
A limitation under which a company must operate, such as limited machine time available or limited raw materials available, that restricts the company's ability to satisfy demand

Another decision situation managers often face is the problem of how to utilize a constrained resource. When a limited resource of some type restricts a company's ability to fully satisfy demand for its products or services, the company is said to have a **constraint**. A convenience store has limited shelf space so it must decide which products to sell. Manufacturing firms may have constraints on machine-hours, labour-hours or the amount of raw materials available for production. The challenge for managers is deciding how best to utilize the constrained resource in order to maximize the company's profits. As will be illustrated below, fixed costs are usually unaffected by the allocation of the constrained resource in the short-run, so the focus will be on analyzing and maximizing contribution margin.

Contribution Margin in Relation to a Constrained Resource

To maximize total contribution margin, a firm should not necessarily promote those products that have the highest *unit* contribution margins. Rather, total contribution margin will be maximized by promoting those products or accepting those orders that provide the highest unit contribution margin *in relation to the constrained resource.* To illustrate, Mountain Goat Cycles makes a line of panniers—a saddlebag for bicycles. There are two models of panniers—a touring model and a mountain model. Cost and revenue data for the two models of panniers are given below:

	Model	
	Mountain Pannier	Touring Pannier
Selling price per unit	$25	$30
Variable cost per unit	10	18
Contribution margin per unit	$15	$12
Contribution margin (CM) ratio	60%	40%

The mountain pannier appears to be much more profitable than the touring pannier. It has a $15 per unit contribution margin as compared to only $12 per unit for the touring model, and it has a 60% CM ratio as compared to only 40% for the touring model.

But now let us add one more piece of information—the plant that makes the panniers is operating at capacity. Ordinarily this does not mean that every machine and every person in the plant is working at the maximum possible rate. Because machines have different capacities, some machines will be operating at less than 100% of capacity. However, if the plant as a whole cannot produce any more units, some machine or process must be operating at capacity. The machine or process that is limiting overall output is called the **bottleneck**—it is the constraint.

Bottleneck
A machine or process that limits total output because it is operating at capacity.

At Mountain Goat Cycles, the bottleneck is a particular stitching machine. The mountain pannier requires two minutes of stitching time, and each unit of the touring pannier requires one minute of stitching time. Since this stitching machine already has more work than it can handle, something will have to be cut back. In this situation, which product is more profitable? To answer this question, the manager should look at the *contribution margin per unit of the constrained resource,* also known as the **profitability index**. This figure is computed by dividing the contribution margin by the amount of the constrained resource a unit of product requires. These calculations are carried out below for the mountain and touring panniers.

Profitability Index =
$$\frac{\text{Contribution margin per unit}}{\text{Quantity of constrained resource required per unit}}$$

	Model	
	Mountain Pannier	Touring Pannier
Contribution margin per unit (a)	$15.00	$12.00
Time on the stitching machine required to produce one unit (b)	2 min.	1 min.
Contribution margin per unit of the constrained resource, (a) ÷ (b)	$7.50/min.	$12.00/min.

Using the profitability index, it is easy to decide which product is less profitable and should be de-emphasized. Each minute of processing time on the stitching machine that is devoted to the touring pannier results in an increase of $12 in contribution margin and profits. The comparable figure for the mountain pannier is only $7.50 per minute. Therefore, the touring model should be emphasized. Even though the mountain model has the larger per unit contribution margin and the larger CM ratio, the touring model provides the larger contribution margin in relation to the constrained resource.

To verify that the touring model is indeed the more profitable product, suppose an hour of additional stitching time is available and that there are unfilled orders for both products. The additional hour on the stitching machine could be used to make either 30 mountain panniers (60 minutes ÷ 2 minutes) or 60 touring panniers (60 minutes ÷ 1 minute), with the following consequences:

	Model	
	Mountain Pannier	Touring Pannier
Contribution margin per unit (a)	$ 15	$ 12
Additional units that can be processed in one hour	× 30	× 60
Additional contribution margin	$450	$720

The analysis illustrated in this example generalizes well to situations where demand exceeds capacity and managers must allocate a constrained resource to three or more products. Demand should be fully satisfied for the product with the highest profitability index. Any capacity that remains should then be allocated to the product with the second highest profitability index, and so on until all available capacity has been utilized. Simply looking at unit contribution margins alone is not enough when constraints exist; contribution margin per unit of the scarce resource must guide decision making.

FOCUS *on Current Practice*

Indalex Aluminum Solutions Group is the largest producer of soft alloy extrusions in North America. The company has installed a new generation of business intelligence software created by pVelocity, Inc., of Toronto, Canada. The software "provides decision makers across our entire manufacturing enterprise with time-based financial metrics using TOC concepts to identify bottlenecks." And, it "shifts the focus of a manufacturing company from traditional cost accounting measurements to measuring the generation of dollars per unit of time." For example, instead of emphasizing products with the largest gross margins or contribution margins, the software helps managers to identify and emphasize the products that maximize the contribution margin per unit of the constrained resource.

Source: Mike Alger, "Managing a Business as a Portfolio of Customers," *Strategic Finance*, June 2003, pp. 54–57.

Managing Constraints

Profits can be increased by effectively managing the organization's constraints. One aspect of managing constraints is to decide how to best utilize them. As discussed above, if the constraint is a bottleneck in the production process, the manager should select the product mix that maximizes the total contribution margin. In addition, the manager should take an active role in managing the constraint itself. Management should focus efforts on increasing the efficiency of the bottleneck operation and on increasing its capacity. Such efforts directly increase the output of finished goods and will often pay off in an almost immediate increase in profits.

Relaxing (or elevating) the constraint
An action that increases the capacity of a bottleneck.

It is often possible for a manager to effectively increase the capacity of the bottleneck, which is called **relaxing (or elevating) the constraint.** For example, the stitching machine operator could be asked to work overtime. This would result in more available stitching time and hence more finished goods that can be sold. The benefits from relaxing the constraint in such a manner are often enormous and can easily be quantified. The manager should first ask, "What would I do with additional capacity at the bottleneck if it was available?" In the previous example, for touring (mountain) panniers, the additional capacity was worth $12 ($7.50) per minute or $720 ($450) per hour because adding an hour of capacity would generate an additional $720 ($450) of contribution margin if it were used solely to process more touring (mountain) panniers. Based on the profitability indices, additional capacity should first be allocated to production of touring panniers, followed by mountain panniers if any capacity remains. Since overtime pay for the operator is likely to be much less than $720 (or $450 for that matter!), running the stitching machine on overtime would be an excellent way to increase the company's profits while satisfying its customers at the same time.

The implications are clear: Managers should focus much of their attention on managing bottlenecks. As we have discussed, managers should emphasize products that most profitably utilize the constrained resource. They should also make sure that products are processed smoothly through the bottlenecks, with minimal lost time due to breakdowns and set-ups. And they should try to find ways to increase the capacity at the bottlenecks, which can be accomplished in a number of ways, including:

- Working overtime on the bottleneck.
- Subcontracting some of the processing that would be done at the bottleneck.
- Shifting workers from processes that are not bottlenecks to the process that *is* a bottleneck.
- Focusing business process improvement efforts such as TQM and business process re-engineering on the bottleneck.
- Reducing defective units. Each defective unit that is processed through the bottleneck and subsequently scrapped takes the place of a good unit that could be sold.

The last three methods of increasing the capacity of the bottleneck are particularly attractive, because they are low-cost interventions and may even yield additional cost savings.

Bottlenecks, as the name implies, represent restrictions to the productive capacity of an organization. As the discussions about capacity in Chapter 11 suggested, numerous types of restrictions can exist, thus preventing the organization from producing at practical capacity. Chapter 11 provided a discussion of how management may try to analyze the implications of various forms of capacity restrictions. The implications of administrative decisions about work shift numbers or maintenance practices, as well as available back-up capacity for breakdowns and other stoppages, can be analyzed to see what needs to be addressed by management to improve the economic performance of the organization.

The Problem of Multiple Constraints

What does a firm do if it has more than one potential constraint? For example, a firm may have limited raw materials, limited direct labour-hours available, limited floor space, and limited advertising dollars to spend on product promotion. How would it proceed to find the right combination of products to produce? The proper combination or "mix" of products can be found by use of a quantitative method known as *linear programming,* which is covered in quantitative methods and operations management courses.

FOCUS *on Current Practice*

It is often possible to elevate a constraint at very low cost. Western Textile Products makes pockets, waistbands, and other clothing components. The constraint at the company's branch plant in Greenville, South Carolina, was the slitting machines. These large machines slit huge rolls of textiles into appropriate widths for use on other machines. Management was contemplating adding a second shift to elevate the constraint. However, investigation revealed that the slitting machines were actually being run only one hour in a nine-hour shift. "The other eight hours were required to get materials, load and unload the machine, and do set-ups. Instead of adding a second shift, a second person was assigned to each machine to fetch materials and do as much of the setting up as possible off-line while the machine was running." This approach resulted in increasing the run time to four hours. If another shift had been added without any improvement in how the machines were being used, the cost would have been much higher and there would have been only a one-hour increase in run time.

Source: Eric Noreen, Debra Smith, and James T. Mackey, *The Theory of Constraints and Its Implications for Management Accounting* (Croton-on-Hudson, NY: The North River Press, 1995), pp. 84–85.

ACTIVITY-BASED COSTING AND RELEVANT COSTS

As discussed in Chapter 8, activity-based costing can be used to help identify potentially relevant costs for decision making purposes. Activity-based costing improves the traceability of costs by focusing on the activities caused by a product or other segment. Managers should exercise caution against reading more into this "traceability" than really exists. People have a tendency to assume that if a cost is traceable to a segment, then the cost is automatically an avoidable cost. That is not true. As emphasized in Chapter 8, the costs provided by a well-designed activity-based costing system are only *potentially* relevant. Before making a decision, managers must still decide which of the potentially relevant costs are actually avoidable. Only those costs that are avoidable are relevant and the others should be ignored.

To illustrate, refer again to the data relating to the housewares line in Exhibit 13–4. The $2,000 depreciation on fixtures is a traceable cost of the houseware lines because it relates to activities in that department. We found, however, that the $2,000 is not avoidable if the housewares line is dropped. The key lesson here is that the method used to assign a cost to a product or other segment does not change the basic nature of the cost. A sunk cost such as depreciation of existing equipment is still a sunk cost regardless of whether it is traced directly to a particular segment on an activity basis, allocated to all segments on the basis of labour-hours, or treated in some other way in the costing process. Regardless of the method used to assign costs to products or other segments, the manager still must apply the principles discussed in this chapter to determine the costs that are avoidable in each situation.[7]

7. For further discussion, see Douglas Sharp and Linda P. Christensen, "A New View of Activity-Based Costing," *Management Accounting* 73, no. 7, September 1991, pp. 32–34; and Maurice L. Hirsch, Jr., and Michael C. Nibbelin, "Incremental, Separable, Sunk, and Common Costs in Activity-Based Costing," *Journal of Cost Management* 6, no. 1, Spring 1992, pp. 39–47.

SUMMARY

The analysis presented for the various decision situations examined in this chapter illustrate one pervasive concept: When making decisions, managers should only consider those costs and benefits that will be incurred or realized in the future and that differ among the alternatives. Application of this concept ensures that only relevant costs, including opportunity costs, are considered and that irrelevant items such as sunk or common costs are ignored. Because technological advances have increased the availability of data for decision making, it is more important than ever that managers be able to consistently differentiate between relevant and irrelevant information. The examples in the chapter show that the relevance of particular costs and benefits depends on the type of decision situation and decision aids were provided in each case to summarize the appropriate approach to the analysis.

A simple approach was also illustrated for allocating a constrained resource when demand exceeds production capacity in the short-run. Use of the profitability index permits identification of the product that is most profitable per unit of the constrained resource and guides the resource allocation process.

Chapter 14 continues our examination of relevant costs in the context of long-run investment decisions.

REVIEW PROBLEM: RELEVANT COSTS

Charter Sports Equipment manufactures round, rectangular, and octagonal trampolines. Data on sales and expenses for the past month follow:

		Trampoline		
	Total	**Round**	**Rectangular**	**Octagonal**
Sales	$1,000,000	$ 140,000	$500,000	$360,000
Less variable expenses	410,000	60,000	200,000	150,000
Contribution margin	590,000	80,000	300,000	210,000
Less fixed expenses:				
Advertising—traceable	216,000	41,000	110,000	65,000
Depreciation of special equipment	95,000	20,000	40,000	35,000
Line supervisors' salaries	19,000	6,000	7,000	6,000
General factory overhead*	200,000	28,000	100,000	72,000
Total fixed expenses	530,000	95,000	257,000	178,000
Operating income (loss)	$ 60,000	$(15,000)	$ 43,000	$ 32,000

*A common cost that is allocated on the basis of sales dollars.

Management is concerned about the continued losses shown by the round trampolines and wants a recommendation as to whether or not the line should be discontinued. The special equipment used to produce the trampolines has no resale value. If the round trampoline model is dropped, the two line supervisors assigned to the model would be discharged.

Required:

1. Should production and sale of the round trampolines be discontinued? You may assume that the company has no other use for the capacity now being used to produce the round trampolines. Show computations to support your answer.
2. Recast the above data in a format that would be more usable to management in assessing the long-run profitability of the various product lines.

Solution to Review Problem

1. No, production and sale of the round trampolines should not be discontinued. Computations to support this answer follow:

Contribution margin lost if the round trampolines are discontinued		$(80,000)
Less fixed costs that can be avoided:		
Advertising—traceable	$41,000	
Line supervisors' salaries	6,000	47,000
Decrease in operating income for the company as a whole		$(33,000)

The depreciation of the special equipment represents a sunk cost, and therefore it is not relevant to the decision. The general factory overhead is allocated and will presumably continue regardless of whether or not the round trampolines are discontinued; thus, it also is not relevant to the decision.

Alternative Solution to Question 1

	Keep Round Units	Difference: Drop Round Units	Net Income Increase or (Decrease)
Sales	$140,000	$ –0–	$(140,000)
Less variable expenses	60,000	–0–	60,000
Contribution margin	80,000	–0–	(80,000)
Less fixed expenses:			
Advertising—traceable	41,000	–0–	41,000
Depreciation of special equipment	20,000	20,000	–0–
Line supervisors' salaries	6,000	–0–	6,000
General factory overhead	28,000	28,000	–0–
Total fixed expenses	95,000	48,000	47,000
Operating income (loss)	$(15,000)	$(48,000)	$ (33,000)

2. If management wants a clear picture of the profitability of the segments, the general factory overhead should not be allocated. It is a common cost and therefore should be deducted from the total product-line segment margin, as shown in Chapter 12. A more useful income statement format would be as follows:

		Trampoline		
	Total	Round	Rectangular	Octagonal
Sales	$1,000,000	$140,000	$500,000	$360,000
Less variable expenses	410,000	60,000	200,000	150,000
Contribution margin	590,000	80,000	300,000	210,000
Less traceable fixed expenses:				
Advertising—traceable	216,000	41,000	110,000	65,000
Depreciation of special equipment	95,000	20,000	40,000	35,000
Line supervisors' salaries	19,000	6,000	7,000	6,000
Total traceable fixed expenses	330,000	67,000	157,000	106,000
Product-line segment margin	260,000	$ 13,000	$143,000	$104,000
Less common fixed expenses	200,000			
Operating income (loss)	$ 60,000			

APPENDIX 13A: PRICING PRODUCTS AND SERVICES

LEARNING OBJECTIVE 4
Complete selling prices based on costs.

Our consideration of special orders in Chapter 13 focused on non-routine situations where companies receive an offer for a product or service at a specific price. By comparing the relevant costs that would be incurred if the offer were accepted to the offer price, managers can determine the incremental effect on operating income. In this appendix we expand our discussion of the relation between relevant costs and pricing issues to include two distinct pricing situations requiring on-going analysis by managers. First, we examine situations where companies are faced with the problem of setting their own prices for products or services. In this setting we present two approaches to setting prices based on costs. Second, we examine a setting where the company offers a product or service that competes with other identical products or services for which a market price already exists. In this setting, we introduce the concept of target costing. Importantly, in both settings managers must identify and use relevant cost information to make decisions that are in the best interests of the company. Setting prices is a critical decision for managers. If the price is set too high, customers will avoid purchasing the company's products. If the price is set too low, the company's costs may not be covered.

COST-PLUS PRICING

Markup
The difference between the selling price of a product or service and its cost. The markup is usually expressed as a percentage of cost.

Cost-plus pricing
A pricing method in which a predetermined markup is applied to a cost base to determine the target selling price.

The usual approach in pricing is to *mark up* cost.[8] A product's **markup** is the difference between its selling price and its cost. The markup is usually expressed as a percentage of cost. This approach is called **cost-plus pricing** because the predetermined markup percentage is applied to the cost base to determine a target selling price.

$$\text{Selling price} = \text{Cost} + (\text{Markup percentage} \times \text{Cost})$$

For example, if a company uses a markup of 50%, it adds 50% to the costs of its products to determine the selling price. If a product costs $10, then the company would charge $15 for the product.

There are two key issues when the cost-plus approach to pricing is used. First, what cost are relevant to the pricing decision? Second, how should the markup be determined? Several alternative approaches are considered in this appendix.

As discussed in Chapters 2 through 7 and Chapter 10, various definitions of cost exist, each of which could be used as the base for setting a selling price. To provide a coherent presentation of cost-plus pricing, absorption costing as described in Chapters 2, 3, 4, and 7 will be used. The approach presented in the discussion that follows can be applied to variable costing if it is used as a cost base for determining the selling price.

Setting a Target Selling Price Using the Absorption Costing Approach

To illustrate, let us assume that the management of Ritter Company wants to set the selling price on a product that has just undergone some design modifications. The Accounting Department has provided cost estimates for the redesigned product as shown below:

8. There are some legal restrictions on prices. Competition laws prohibit "predatory" prices, which are generally interpreted by the courts to mean a price below average variable cost. "Price discrimination"—charging different prices to customers in the same market for the same product or service—is also prohibited by the law.

	Per Unit	Total
Direct materials	$6	
Direct labour	4	
Variable manufacturing overhead	3	
Fixed manufacturing overhead	—	$70,000
Variable selling, general, and administrative expenses	2	
Fixed selling, general, and administrative expenses	—	60,000

The first step in the absorption costing approach to cost-plus pricing is to compute the unit product cost. For Ritter Company, this amounts to $20 per unit at a volume of 10,000 units, as shown in the first part of Exhibit 13–8.

Ritter Company has a general policy of marking up unit product costs by 50%. A price quotation sheet for the company prepared using the absorption approach is also presented in Exhibit 13–8. Note that selling, general, and administrative (SG&A) costs are not included in the cost base. Instead, the markup is supposed to cover these expenses. Let us see how some companies compute these markup percentages.

Determining the Markup Percentage

How did Ritter Company arrive at its markup percentage of 50%? This figure could be a widely used rule of thumb in the industry or just a company tradition that seems to work. The markup percentage may also be the result of an explicit computation. As we have discussed, the markup over cost ideally should be largely determined by market conditions. However, a popular approach is to at least start with a markup based on cost and desired profit. The reasoning goes like this: The markup must be large enough to cover SG&A expenses and provide an adequate return on investment (ROI)[9]. Given the forecasted unit sales, the markup can be computed as follows:

$$\frac{\text{Markup percentage}}{\text{on absorption cost}} = \frac{\begin{pmatrix}\text{Required ROI}\\ \times \text{ Investment}\end{pmatrix} + \text{SG\&A expenses}}{\text{Unit sales} \times \text{Unit product cost}}$$

To show how the formula above is applied, assume Ritter Company must invest $100,000 to produce and market 10,000 units of the product each year. The $100,000 investment covers purchase of equipment and funds needed to carry inventories and

Direct materials	$ 6
Direct labour	4
Variable manufacturing overhead	3
Fixed manufacturing overhead (based on 10,000 units)	7
Unit product cost	20
Markup to cover selling, general, and administrative expenses and desired profit—50% of unit manufacturing cost	10
Target selling price	$30

EXHIBIT 13–8 Price Quotation Sheet—Absorption Basis (10,000 Units)

9. Determining the markup percentage using total variable costs would proceed as follows: (a) the numerator would include the required ROI plus *all* fixed expenses (manufacturing overhead + SG & A); and (b) the denominator would include *all* variable costs (including variable SG & A expenses). Using the data for Ritter Company, the total amount in the numerator would be $150,000 ($20,000 + $70,000 + $60,000) and the total costs in the denominator would be: $15 ($6 + $4 + $3 + $2) × 10,000 units = $150,000. The result would be a 100% markup ($150,000/$150,000) based on total variable costs, which would result in the same $30 target selling price ($15 cost + $15 markup).

accounts receivable. If Ritter Company requires a 20% ROI, then the markup for the product would be determined as follows:

$$\text{Markup percentage on absorption cost} = \frac{\begin{pmatrix} 20\% \\ \times \$100{,}000 \end{pmatrix} + (\$2 \times 10{,}000) + \$60{,}000}{10{,}000 \times \$20}$$

$$\text{Markup percentage on absorption cost} = \frac{\$20{,}000 + \$80{,}000}{\$200{,}000} = 50\%$$

As shown earlier, this markup of 50% leads to a target selling price of $30 for Ritter Company. As shown in Exhibit 13–9, *if the company actually sells 10,000 units* of the product at this price, and actual costs are as expected, the company's ROI on this product will indeed be 20%. If it turns out that more than 10,000 units are sold at this price, the ROI will be greater than 20%. If fewer than 10,000 units are sold, the ROI will be less than 20%. *The required ROI will be attained only if the forecasted unit sales volume is attained,* and actual costs equal expected costs for that level of sales activity.

Problems with the Absorption Costing Approach

Using the absorption costing approach, the pricing problem looks deceptively simple. All you have to do is compute your unit product cost, decide how much profit you want, and then set your price. It appears that you can ignore demand and arrive at a price that will safely yield whatever profit you want. However, as noted above, the absorption costing approach relies on a forecast of unit sales. Neither the markup nor the unit product cost can be computed without such a forecast.

The absorption costing approach essentially assumes that customers *need* the forecasted unit sales and will pay whatever price the company decides to charge. However, customers have a choice. If the price is too high, they can buy from a competitor or they may choose not to buy at all. Suppose, for example, that when Ritter Company sets its price at $30, it sells only 7,000 units rather than the 10,000 units forecasted. As shown in Exhibit 13–10, the company would then have a loss of $25,000 on the prod-

EXHIBIT 13–9 Income Statement and ROI Analysis—Ritter Company Actual Unit Sales = 10,000 Units; Selling Price = $30

Direct materials	$ 6
Direct labour	4
Variable manufacturing overhead	3
Fixed manufacturing overhead ($70,000 ÷ 10,000 units)	7
Unit product cost	$20

RITTER COMPANY
Absorption Costing Income Statement

Sales ($30 × 10,000 units)	$300,000
Less cost of goods sold ($20 × 10,000 units)	200,000
Gross margin	100,000
Less selling, general, and administration expenses ($2 × 10,000 units +$60,000)	80,000
Operating income	$ 20,000

ROI

$$\text{ROI} = \frac{\text{Operating income}}{\text{Average operating assets}}$$

$$= \frac{\$20{,}000}{\$100{,}000}$$

$$= 20\%$$

EXHIBIT 13–10 Income Statement and ROI Analysis—Ritter Company Actual Unit Sales = 7,000 Units; Selling Price = $30

Direct materials	$ 6
Direct labour	4
Variable manufacturing overhead	3
Fixed manufacturing overhead ($70,000 ÷ 7,000 units)	10
Unit product cost	$23

RITTER COMPANY
Absorption Costing Income Statement

Sales ($30 × 7,000 units)	$210,000
Less cost of goods sold ($23 × 7,000 units)	161,000
Gross margin	49,000
Less selling, general, and administration expenses ($2 × 7,000 units + $60,000)	74,000
Operating income	$ (25,000)

ROI

$$\text{ROI} = \frac{\text{Operating income}}{\text{Average operating assets}}$$

$$= \frac{-\$25,000}{\$100,000}$$

$$= -25\%$$

uct instead of a profit of $20,000. Some managers believe that the absorption costing approach to pricing is safe. This is an illusion. The absorption costing approach is safe only as long as customers choose to buy at least as many units as managers forecasted they would buy.

Setting a Target Selling Price for Service Companies Using Time and Materials Pricing

A variation of cost-plus pricing used by some companies, particularly in service industries, is called **time and materials pricing**. Under this approach, two pricing rates are established, one based on direct labour time and the other based on the cost of direct material used.

Time and materials pricing A pricing method, often used in service firms, in which two pricing rates are established—one based on direct labour time and the other based on direct materials used

This pricing method is widely used in repair shops and printing shops, and by many professionals such as engineers and lawyers. The time and materials rates are usually market-determined. In other words, the rates are determined by the interplay of supply and demand and by competitive conditions in the industry. However, some companies set the rates using a process similar to the process followed in the absorption costing approach to cost-plus pricing. In this case, the rates include allowances for selling, general, and administrative expenses; for other direct and indirect costs; and for a desired profit. This section will show how the rates might be set using the cost-plus approach.

Time Component

The time component is typically expressed as a rate per hour of labour. The rate is computed by adding together three elements: (1) the direct costs of the employee, including salary and fringe benefits; (2) a pro rata allowance for selling, general, and administrative expenses of the organization; and (3) an allowance for a desired profit per hour of employee time. In some organizations (such as a repair shop), the same hourly rate will be charged regardless of which employee actually works on the job; in other organizations, the rate may vary by employee. For example, in a public accounting firm, the rate charged for a new assistant accountant's time will generally be less than the rate charged for an experienced senior accountant or for a partner.

Materials Component

Materials loading charge A markup applied to the cost of materials that is designed to cover the costs of ordering, handling, and carrying materials in inventory and to provide for some profit.

The materials component is determined by adding a **materials loading charge** to the invoice price of any materials used on the job. The materials loading charge is designed to cover the costs of ordering, handling, and carrying materials in inventory, plus a profit margin on the materials themselves.

An Example of Time and Materials Pricing

To provide a numerical example of time and materials pricing, assume the following data:

The Quality Auto Shop uses time and materials pricing for all of its repair work. The following costs have been budgeted for the coming year:

	Repairs	Parts
Mechanics' wages	$300,000	$ —
Service manager—salary	40,000	—
Parts manager—salary	—	36,000
Clerical assistant—salary	18,000	15,000
Retirement and insurance—16% of salaries and wages	57,280	8,160
Supplies	720	540
Utilities	36,000	20,800
Property taxes	8,400	1,900
Depreciation	91,600	37,600
Invoice cost of parts used	—	400,000
Total budgeted cost	$552,000	$520,000

The company expects to bill customers for 24,000 hours of repair time. A profit of $7 per hour of repair time is considered to be feasible, given the competitive conditions in the market. For parts, the competitive markup on the invoice cost of parts used is 15%.

Exhibit 13–11 shows the computation of the billing rate and the materials loading charge to be used over the next year. Note that the billing rate, or time component, is $30 per hour of repair time and the materials loading charge is 45% of the invoice cost of parts used. Using these rates, a repair job that requires 4.5 hours of mechanics' time and $200 in parts would be billed as follows:

Labour time: 4.5 hours × $30		$135
Parts used:		
Invoice cost	$200	
Materials loading charge: 45% × $200	90	290
Total price of the job		$425

Rather than using labour-hours as the basis for computing the time rate, a machine shop, a printing shop, or a similar organization might use machine-hours.

This method of setting prices is a variation of the absorption costing approach. As such, it is not surprising that it suffers from the same problem: Customers may not be willing to pay the rates that have been computed. If actual business is less than the forecasted 24,000 hours and $400,000 worth of parts, or actual costs exceed estimates, the profit objectives will not be met and the company may not even break even.

EXHIBIT 13–11 Time and Materials Pricing

	Time Component: Repairs		Parts: Material Loading Charge	
	Total	**Per Hour***	**Total**	**Percent†**
Cost of mechanics' time:				
Mechanics' wages	$300,000			
Retirement and insurance (16% of wages)	48,000			
Total cost	348,000	$14.50		
For repairs—other cost of repair service. For parts—costs of ordering, handling, and storing parts:				
Repairs service manager—salary	40,000		$ —	
Parts manager—salary	—		36,000	
Clerical assistant—salary	18,000		15,000	
Retirement and insurance (16% of salaries)	9,280		8,160	
Supplies	720		540	
Utilities	36,000		20,800	
Property taxes	8,400		1,900	
Depreciation	91,600		37,600	
Total cost	204,000	8.50	120,000	30%
Desired profit:				
24,000 hours × $7	168,000	7.00	—	
15% × $400,000	—		60,000	15%
Total amount to be billed	$720,000	$30.00	$180,000	45%

*Based on 24,000 hours.

†Based on $400,000 invoice cost of parts. The charge for ordering, handling, and storing parts, for example, is computed as follows: $120,000 cost ÷ $400,000 invoice cost = 30%.

TARGET COSTING

LEARNING OBJECTIVE 5
Compute target costs based on selling prices.

Our discussion so far has presumed that a product has already been developed, has been costed, and is ready to be marketed as soon as a price is set. In many cases, the sequence of events is just the reverse. That is, the company will already *know* what price should be charged, and the problem will be to *develop a product* that can be marketed profitably at the desired price. Even in this situation, where the normal sequence of events is reversed, cost is still a crucial factor. The company's approach will be to employ *target costing.* **Target costing** is the process of determining the maximum allowable cost for a new product and then developing a prototype that can be profitably made for that maximum target cost figure. Many companies use target costing, including DaimlerChrysler, Ford, ITT Automotive, NEC, Nissan, Sharp, Texas Instruments, and Toyota.

Target costing
The process of determining the maximum allowable cost for a new product and then developing a prototype that can be profitably manufactured and distributed for that maximum target cost figure.

The target cost for a product is computed by starting with the product's anticipated selling price and then deducting the desired profit, as follows:

$$\text{Target cost} = \text{Anticipated selling price} - \text{Desired profit}$$

The product development team is given the responsibility of designing the product so that it can be made for no more than the target cost.

Reasons for Using Target Costing

The target costing approach was developed in recognition of two important characteristics of markets and costs. The first is that many companies have less control over price than they would like. The market (i.e., supply and demand) really determines prices, and a company that attempts to ignore this does so at its peril. Therefore, the anticipated market price is taken as a given in target costing. The second observation is that most of the cost of a product is determined in the design stage. Once a product has been designed and has gone into production, not much can be done to significantly reduce its cost. Most of the opportunities to reduce cost come from designing the product so that it is simple to make, uses inexpensive parts, and is robust and reliable. If the company has little control over market price and little control over cost once the product has gone into production, then it follows that the major opportunities for affecting profit come in the design stage, where valuable features for which customers are willing to pay can be added and where most of the costs are really determined. So that is where the effort is concentrated—in designing and developing the product. The difference between target costing and other approaches to product development is profound. Instead of designing the product and then finding out how much it costs, the target cost is set first and then the product is designed so that the target cost is attained.

Effective target costing requires a detailed understanding of the customer; what is valued; the full costs of production, including long-term investments; and a detailed breakdown of the target cost. A management philosophy of customer focus and cost reduction (Kaizen costing) is part of the organizational package that will help a company to realize the full benefits of target costing.[10]

An Example of Target Costing

For a simple numerical example of target costing, assume the following situation: Handy Appliance Company feels that there is a market niche for a hand mixer with certain new features. Surveying the features and prices of hand mixers already on the market, the Marketing Department believes that a price of $30 would be about right for the new mixer. At that price, Marketing estimates that 40,000 of the new mixers could be sold annually. To design, develop, and produce these new mixers, an investment of $2,000,000 would be required. The company desires a 15% ROI. Given these data, the target cost to manufacture, sell, distribute, and service one mixer is $22.50, as shown below:

Projected sales (40,000 mixers × $30)	$1,200,000
Less desired profit (15% × $2,000,000)	300,000
Target cost for 40,000 mixers	$ 900,000
Target cost per mixer ($900,000 ÷ 40,000 mixers)	$22.50

This $22.50 target cost would be broken down into target costs for the various functions: manufacturing, marketing, distribution, after-sales service, and so on. Each functional area would be responsible for keeping its actual costs within the target.

Pricing and "The Law"

The federal Competition Act[11] restricts certain pricing practices to encourage competition and to protect consumers. For example, different prices cannot be charged for goods of like quality and quantity sold at the same time. In addition, a manufacturer can only suggest a list price; it cannot mandate this price to its retailers. Court proceedings represent only one of a variety of means used by the Industry Canada's Competition Bureau to enforce the Act. However, the bureau does list a number of settlements and fines in such diverse areas

10. A more detailed discussion of the use of target costing as a philosophy for strategic planning and control can be found in "Implementing Target Costing," *Management Accounting Guidelines*, The Society of Management Accountants of Canada, 1999.
11. Department of Justice Canada Web site: **http://laws.justice.gc.ca/**.

as scuba diving lessons, sunglasses, giftware, and jeans, and a large fine associated with the sale of sorbates (food preservatives) in Canada by three foreign suppliers.[12]

International restrictions on pricing appear in antidumping and subsidy laws. Prohibitions exist on the sale of products below cost (that is, full absorption cost) in international markets or the use of government subsidies to achieve the same end. GATT and NAFTA disputes provide obvious examples of the need for cost information to substantiate pricing.

FOCUS *on Current Practice*

Conventional target costing wisdom suggests that the approach is most beneficial when applied early in a product's life cycle. This is based on claims that approximately 80% of a product's costs are fixed (i.e., difficult to reduce) once the design phase has been completed. While many companies such as Toyota and Mitsubishi do employ target costing at the design stage of the product, others have found the approach can be successfully applied at the manufacturing stage. The Montclair Papers Division of Mohawk Forest Products is a good example.

After losing a bid to a key competitor on one of its paper products, management at Montclair began to question the validity of its standard costing system. Montclair's standard cost for the product on which they lost the bid was $2,900 per tonne, which was over $1,400 per tonne more than the *price* bid by its competitor! Spurred on by this vast difference in costs, management at Montclair adopted an aggressive target costing exercise in order to re-engineer the manufacturing process for product. Using the price bid by their competitor as the starting point, Montclair, then deducted the desired profit for the product to arrive at a target cost of $1,162. To achieve this target cost, management identified costing saving opportunities in each of the major activities involved in manufacturing and distributing the product. Eighteen months after adopting target costing, Montclair had reduced manufacturing costs to the target level, and through use of the Kaizen approach of continuous cost reductions, planned further reductions of $330 per tonne. Montclair's successful application of target costing provides evidence that the approach can yield benefits at the post-design phase of a product's life cycle.

Source: John K. Shank and Joseph Fisher, "Case Study: Target Costing as a Strategic Tool," *Sloan Management Review*, Fall 1999, 41(1), pp. 73–82.

APPENDIX 13A SUMMARY

This appendix extended our discussion of the relation between relevant costs and pricing issues. Companies offering products and services where a market price is not readily available often use cost-plus pricing. One approach to cost-plus pricing uses absorption unit product costs as the cost base with the markup calculated to cover both non-manufacturing costs and to provide an adequate return on investment. Companies in the service industry often use a variation of the cost-plus approach called time and materials pricing. Two pricing rates are established, one for direct labour time and the other for direct material costs. The degree to which either cost-plus pricing or time and materials pricing will lead to the desired profits critically depends on the accuracy of both the sales forecasts and the cost estimates.

Some companies develop and sell products or services for which an established market and price already exist. Target costing can be used in such situations. Desired profit is deducted from the estimated market price to determine the product's target cost. The product design and development team then has the responsibility of ensuring that the actual cost of the new product does not exceed the target cost.

12. Industry Canada's Competition Bureau Web site contains a listing of actions and fines: http://strategis.ic.gc.ca/.

GLOSSARY

Visit the Online Learning Centre at http://www.mcgrawhill.ca/college/garrison/ for a review of key terms and definitions.

QUESTIONS

13–1 What is a *relevant cost?*

13–2 Define the following terms: *incremental cost, opportunity cost,* and *sunk cost.*

13–3 Are variable costs always relevant costs? Explain.

13–4 The book value of a machine (as shown on the balance sheet) is an asset to a company, but this same book value is irrelevant in decision making. Explain why this is so.

13–5 "Sunk costs are easy to spot—they're simply the fixed costs associated with a decision." Do you agree? Explain.

13–6 "Variable costs and differential costs mean the same thing." Do you agree? Explain.

13–7 "All future costs are relevant in decision making." Do you agree? Why?

13–8 Prentice Company is considering dropping one of its product lines. What costs of the product line would be relevant to this decision? Irrelevant?

13–9 "If a product line is generating a loss, then that's pretty good evidence that the product line should be discontinued." Do you agree? Explain.

13–10 What is the danger in allocating common fixed costs among product lines or other segments of an organization?

13–11 How does opportunity cost enter into the make or buy decision?

13–12 A successful owner of a small business stated: "We have the best technology, the best products and the best people in the world. We have no constraints." Do you agree?

13–13 Give four examples of possible constraints.

13–14 How should the relative profitability of products be determined when trying to decide how to allocate a constrained resource such as machine hours?

13–15 Define the following terms: *joint products, joint product costs,* and *split-off point.*

13–16 From a decision-making point of view, what pitfalls are there in allocating common costs among joint products?

13–17 What guideline can be used in determining whether a joint product should be sold at the split-off point or processed further?

13–18 Airlines sometimes offer reduced rates during certain times of the week to members of a businessperson's family if they accompany him or her on trips. How does the concept of relevant costs enter into the decision to offer reduced rates of this type?

13–19 (Appendix 13–A) What is meant by cost-plus pricing?

13–20 (Appendix 13–A) When the absorption costing approach to cost-plus pricing is used, what is the markup supposed to cover?

13–21 (Appendix 13–A) What is target costing? How do target costs enter into the pricing decision?

13–22 (Appendix 13–A) What is time and materials pricing?

EXERCISES

EXERCISE 13–1 Identifying Relevant Costs [LO1]

A number of items that may be relevant in decisions faced by the management of Svahn, AB, a Swedish manufacturer of sailing yachts, are listed on the next page.

Required:

Copy the information above onto your answer sheet and place an X in the appropriate column to indicate whether each item is relevant or not relevant in the following situations. Requirement 1 relates to Case 1 above, and requirement 2 relates to Case 2.

1. The company chronically has no idle capacity and the old Model B100 machine is the company's constraint. Management is considering purchasing a Model B300 machine to use in

addition to the company's present Model B100 machine. The old Model B100 machine will continue to be used to capacity as before, with the new Model B300 machine being used to expand production. This will increase the company's production and sales. The increase in volume will be large enough to require increases in fixed selling expenses and in general administrative overhead, but not in the fixed manufacturing overhead.

2. The old Model B100 machine is not the company's constraint, but management is considering replacing it with a new Model B300 machine because of the potential savings in direct materials with the new machine. The Model B100 machine would be sold. This change will have no effect on production or sales, other than some savings in direct materials costs due to less waste.

	Case 1		Case 2	
Item	Relevant	Not Relevant	Relevant	Not Relevant
a. Sales revenue				
b. Direct materials				
c. Direct labour				
d. Variable manufacturing overhead				
e. Depreciation—Model B100 machine				
f. Book value—Model B100 machine				
g. Disposal value—Model B100 machine				
h. Market value—Model B300 machine (cost)				
i. Fixed manufacturing overhead (general)				
j. Variable selling expense				
k. Fixed selling expense				
l. General administrative overhead				

EXERCISE 13–2 Dropping or Retaining a Segment [LO2]

The St. Albert Cycle Company manufactures three types of bicycles—a dirt bike, a mountain bike, and a racing bike. Data on sales and expenses for the past quarter follow:

	Total	Dirt Bikes	Mountain Bikes	Racing Bikes
Sales	$300,000	$90,000	$150,000	$60,000
Less variable manufacturing and selling expenses	120,000	27,000	60,000	33,000
Contribution margin	180,000	63,000	90,000	27,000
Less fixed expenses:				
Advertising, traceable	30,000	10,000	14,000	6,000
Depreciation of special equipment	23,000	6,000	9,000	8,000
Salaries of product-line managers	35,000	12,000	13,000	10,000
Allocated common fixed expenses*	60,000	18,000	30,000	12,000
Total fixed expenses	148,000	46,000	66,000	36,000
Net operating income (loss)	$ 32,000	$17,000	$ 24,000	$ (9,000)

*Allocated on the basis of sales dollars.

Management is concerned about the continued losses shown by the racing bikes and wants a recommendation as to whether or not the line should be discontinued. The special equipment used to produce racing bikes has no resale value and does not wear out.

Required:

1. Should production and sale of the racing bikes be discontinued? Explain. Show computations to support your answer.

2. Recast the above data in a format that would be more usable to management in assessing the long-run profitability of the various product lines.

EXERCISE 13–3 Make or Buy a Component [LO2]
Wallace Engines, Ltd., manufactures a variety of engines for use in heavy equipment. The company has always produced all of the necessary parts for its engines, including all of the carburetors. An outside supplier has offered to sell one type of carburetor to Wallace Engines, Ltd., for a cost of $35 per unit. To evaluate this offer, management has gathered the following information relating to its own cost of producing the carburetor internally:

	Per Unit	15,000 Units per Year
Direct materials	$14	$210,000
Direct labour	10	150,000
Variable manufacturing overhead	3	45,000
Fixed manufacturing overhead, traceable	6*	90,000
Fixed manufacturing overhead, allocated	9	135,000
Total cost	$42	$630,000

*One-third supervisory salaries; two-thirds depreciation of special equipment (no resale value).

Required:

1. Assuming that the company has no alternative use for the facilities that are now being used to produce the carburetors, should the outside supplier's offer be accepted? Show all computations.
2. Suppose that if the carburetors were purchased, Wallace Engines, Ltd., could use the freed capacity to launch a new product. The segment margin of the new product would be $150,000 per year. Should Wallace Engines, Ltd., accept the offer to buy the carburetors for $35 per unit? Show all computations.

EXERCISE 13–4 Evaluating a Special Order [LO2]
Amherst Jewellers is considering a special order for 20 handcrafted gold bracelets to be given as gifts to members of a wedding party. The normal selling price of a gold bracelet is $189.95 and its unit product cost is $149.00 as shown below:

Direct materials	$ 84.00
Direct labour	45.00
Manufacturing overhead	20.00
Unit product cost	$149.00

Most of the manufacturing overhead is fixed and unaffected by variations in how much jewellery is produced in any given period. However, $4.00 of the overhead is variable with respect to the number of bracelets produced. The customer who is interested in the special bracelet order would like special filigree applied to the bracelets. This filigree would require additional materials costing $2.00 per bracelet and would also require acquisition of a special tool costing $250 that would have no other use once the special order is completed. This order would have no effect on the company's regular sales and the order could be fulfilled using the company's existing capacity without affecting any other order.

Required:
What effect would accepting this order have on the company's net operating income if a special price of $169.95 per bracelet is offered for this order? Should the special order be accepted at this price?

EXERCISE 13–5 Utilization of a Constrained Resource [LO3]
Canning Company manufactures three products: A, B, and C. The selling price, variable costs, and contribution margin for one unit of each product are shown at the top of the next page.

The same raw material is used in all three products. Canning Company has only 5,000 kilograms of raw material on hand and will not be able to obtain any more of it for several weeks due to a strike in its supplier's plant. Management is trying to decide which product(s) to concentrate on next week in filling its backlog of orders. The material costs $8 per kilogram.

	Product		
	A	B	C
Selling price	$180	$270	$240
Less variable expenses:			
Direct materials	24	72	32
Other variable expenses	102	90	148
Total variable expenses	126	162	180
Contribution margin	$ 54	$108	$ 60
Contribution margin ratio	30%	40%	25%

Required:

1. Compute the amount of contribution margin that will be obtained per kilogram of material used in each product.
2. Which orders would you recommend that the company work on next week—the orders for product A, product B, or product C? Show computations.
3. A foreign supplier could furnish Canning with additional stocks of the raw material at a substantial premium over the usual price. If there is unfilled demand for all three products, what is the highest price that Canning Company should be willing to pay for an additional kilogram of materials? Explain.

EXERCISE 13–6 Sell or Process Further [LO2]

Brampton Company manufactures three products from a common input in a joint processing operation. Joint processing costs up to the split-off point total $350,000 per quarter. The company allocates these costs to the joint products on the basis of their relative sales value at the split-off point. Unit selling prices and total output at the split-off point are as follows:

Product	Selling Price	Quarterly Output
A	$16 per kilogram	15,000 kilograms
B	$8 per kilogram	20,000 kilograms
C	$25 per litre	4,000 litres

Each product can be processed further after the split-off point. Additional processing requires no special facilities. The additional processing costs (per quarter) and unit selling prices after further processing are given below:

Product	Additional Processing Costs	Selling Price
A	$63,000	$20 per kilogram
B	$80,000	$13 per kilogram
C	$36,000	$32 per litre

Required:

Which product or products should be sold at the split-off point and which product or products should be processed further? Show computations.

EXERCISE 13–7 Identification of Relevant Costs [LO1]

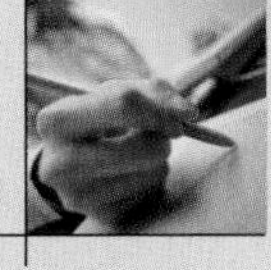

Hart Company sells and delivers office furniture in the Maritimes area.

The costs associated with the acquisition and annual operation of a delivery truck are given below:

Insurance	$1,600
Licenses	$250
Taxes (vehicle)	$150
Garage rent for parking (per truck)	$1,200
Depreciation ($9,000 ÷ 5 years)	$1,800*
Gasoline, oil, tires, and repairs	$0.07 per kilometre

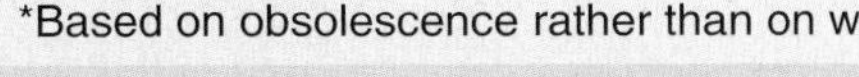

*Based on obsolescence rather than on wear and tear.

Required:

1. Assume that Hart Company has purchased one truck that has been driven 50,000 kilometres during the first year. Compute the average cost per kilometre of owning and operating the truck.
2. At the beginning of the second year, Hart Company is unsure whether to use the truck or leave it parked in the garage and have all hauling done commercially. (The government requires the payment of vehicle taxes even if the vehicle isn't used.) What costs from the previous list are relevant to this decision? Explain.
3. Assume that the company decides to use the truck during the second year. Near year-end an order is received from a customer over 1,000 kilometres away. What costs from the previous list are relevant in a decision between using the truck to make the delivery and having the delivery done commercially? Explain.
4. Occasionally, the company could use two trucks at the same time. For this reason, some thought is being given to purchasing a second truck. The total kilometres driven would be the same as if only one truck were owned. What costs from the previous list are relevant to a decision over whether to purchase the second truck? Explain.

EXERCISE 13–8 Dropping or Retaining a Segment [LO2]

Thalassines Kataskeves, S.A., of Greece makes marine equipment. The company has been experiencing losses on its bilge pump product line for several years. The most recent quarterly contribution format income statement for the bilge pump product line follows:

THALASSINES KATASKEVES, S.A.
Income Statement—Bilge Pump
For the Quarter Ended March 31

Sales		€850,000
Less variable expenses:		
Variable manufacturing expenses	€330,000	
Sales commissions	42,000	
Shipping	18,000	
Total variable expenses		390,000
Contribution margin		460,000
Less fixed expenses:		
Advertising	270,000	
Depreciation of equipment (no resale value)	80,000	
General factory overhead	105,000*	
Salary of product-line manager	32,000	
Insurance on inventories	8,000	
Purchasing department expenses	45,000†	
Total fixed expenses		540,000
Net operating loss		€ (80,000)

*Common costs allocated on the basis of machine-hours.
†Common costs allocated on the basis of sales dollars.

The currency in Greece is the euro, denoted here by €. Discontinuing the bilge pump product line would not affect sales of other product lines and would have no effect on the company's total general factory overhead or total Purchasing Department expenses. The bilge pump product manager would be laid off.

Required:

Would you recommend that the bilge pump product line be discontinued? Support your answer with appropriate computations.

EXERCISE 13–9 Make or Buy a Component [LO2]

Tanner Products manufactures 30,000 units of part S-6 each year for use on its production line. At this level of activity, the cost per unit for part S-6 is as follows:

Direct materials	$ 3.60
Direct labour	10.00
Variable manufacturing overhead	2.40
Fixed manufacturing overhead	9.00
Total cost per part	$25.00

An outside supplier has offered to sell 30,000 units of part S-6 each year to Tanner Products for $21 per part. If Tanner Products accepts this offer, the facilities now being used to manufacture part S-6 could be rented to another company at an annual rental of $80,000. However, Tanner Products has determined that two-thirds of the fixed manufacturing overhead being applied to part S-6 would continue even if part S-6 were purchased from the outside supplier.

Required:
Prepare computations showing how much profits will increase or decrease if the outside supplier's offer is accepted.

EXERCISE 13–10 Special Order [LO2]

Riley Company produces a single product. The cost of producing and selling a single unit of this product at the company's normal activity level of 60,000 units per year is:

Direct materials	$5.10
Direct labour	$3.80
Variable manufacturing overhead	$1.00
Fixed manufacturing overhead	$4.20
Variable selling and administrative expense	$1.50
Fixed selling and administrative expense	$2.40

The normal selling price is $21 per unit. The company's capacity is 75,000 units per year. An order has been received from a mail-order house for 15,000 units at a special price of $14 per unit. This order would not affect regular sales.

Required:
1. If the order is accepted, by how much will annual profits be increased or decreased? (The order will not change the company's total fixed costs.)
2. Assume the company has 1,000 units of this product left over from last year that are vastly inferior to the current model. The units must be sold through regular channels at reduced prices. What unit cost figure is relevant for establishing a minimum selling price for these units? Explain.

EXERCISE 13–11 Utilization of a Constrained Resource [LO3]
Spencer Company produces three products, A, B, and C. Data concerning the three products follow (per unit):

	Product		
	A	B	C
Selling price	$80	$56	$70
Less variable expenses:			
Direct materials	24	15	9
Other variable expenses	24	27	40
Total variable expenses	48	42	49
Contribution margin	$32	$14	$21
Contribution margin ratio	40%	25%	30%

Demand for the company's products is very strong, with far more orders each month than the company has raw materials available to produce. The same material is used in each product. The material costs $3 per kilogram with a maximum of 5,000 kilograms available each month.

Required:
Which orders would you advise the company to accept first, those for A, for B, or for C? Which orders second? Third?

EXERCISE 13–12 Sell or Process Further [LO2]
TB, Inc., produces several products from processing 1 tonne of clypton, a rare mineral. Material and processing costs total $60,000 per tonne, one-fourth of which is allocated to product X. Seven thousand units of product X are produced from each tonne of clypton. The units can either be sold at the split-off point for $9 each, or processed further at a total cost of $9,500 and then sold for $12 each.

Required:
Should product X be processed further or sold at the split-off point?

EXERCISE 13–13 Volume Trade-Off Decision [LO3]

Ancient Mariners makes reproductions of classic wooden boats. The bottleneck in the production process is fitting wooden planks to build up the curved sections of the hull. This process requires the attention of the shop's most experienced craftsman. A total of 1,800 hours is available per year in this bottleneck operation. Data concerning the company's four products appear below:

	Clipper	Lake Erie	Riser	Bluenose
Unit contribution margin	$485	$268	$385	$600
Annual demand (units)	80	120	100	140
Hours required in the bottleneck operation per unit	5	4	7	8

No fixed costs could be avoided by modifying how many units are produced of any product or even by dropping any one of the products.

Required:

1. Is there sufficient capacity in the bottleneck operation to satisfy demand for all products?
2. What is the optimal production plan for the year?
3. What would be the total contribution margin for the optimal production plan you have proposed?

EXERCISE 13–14 Identification of Relevant Costs [LO1]

Bill has just returned from a duck hunting trip in Northern Ontario. He has brought home eight ducks. Bill's friend, John, disapproves of duck hunting, and to discourage Bill from further hunting, John has presented him with the following cost estimates:

Camper and equipment:	
Cost, $12,000; usable for eight seasons; 10 hunting trips per season	$150
Travel expense (pickup truck):	
100 kilometres at $0.31 per kilometre (gas, oil, and tires—$0.21 per kilometre; depreciation and insurance—$0.10 per kilometre)	31
Shotgun shells (two boxes)	20
Boat:	
Cost, $2,320, usable for eight seasons; 10 hunting trips per season	29
Hunting license:	
Cost, $30 for the season; 10 hunting trips per season	3
Money lost playing poker:	
Loss, $24 (Bill plays poker every weekend)	24
Coffee beans:	
Cost, $15	15
Total cost of the trip	$272
Cost per duck ($272 ÷ 8 ducks)	$ 34

Required:

1. Assuming that the duck hunting trip Bill has just completed is typical, what costs are relevant to a decision as to whether Bill should go duck hunting again this season?
2. Suppose that Bill gets lucky on his next hunting trip and shoots 10 ducks in the amount of time it took him to shoot 8 ducks on his last trip. How much would it have cost him to shoot the last two ducks? Explain.
3. Which costs are relevant in a decision of whether Bill should give up hunting? Explain.

EXERCISE 13–15 Dropping or Retaining a Segment [LO2]

Home Computing, a retailing company, has two departments, Hardware and Software. A recent monthly contribution format income statement for the company follows:

		Department	
	Total	Hardware	Software
Sales	$4,000,000	$3,000,000	$1,000,000
Less variable expenses	1,300,000	900,000	400,000
Contribution margin	2,700,000	2,100,000	600,000
Less fixed expenses	2,200,000	1,400,000	800,000
Operating income (loss)	$ 500,000	$ 700,000	$ (200,000)

A study indicates that $340,000 of the fixed expenses being charged to Software are sunk costs or allocated costs that will continue even if the Software Department is dropped. In addition, the elimination of the Software Department will result in a 10% decrease in the sales of the Hardware Department.

Required:

If the Software Department is dropped, what will be the effect on the operating income of the company as a whole?

EXERCISE 13–16 Make or Buy a Component [LO2]

For many years Bouden Company has purchased the starters that it installs in its standard line of farm tractors. Due to a reduction in output, the company has idle capacity that could be used to produce the starters. The chief engineer has recommended against this move, however, pointing out that the cost to produce the starters would be greater than the current $8.40 per unit purchase price:

	Per Unit	Total
Direct materials	$3.10	
Direct labour	2.70	
Supervision	1.50	$60,000
Depreciation	1.00	40,000
Variable manufacturing overhead	0.60	
Rent	0.30	12,000
Total production cost	$9.20	

A supervisor would have to be hired to oversee production of the starters. However, the company has sufficient idle tools and machinery that no new equipment would have to be purchased. The rent charge above is based on space utilized in the plant. The total rent on the plant is $80,000 per period. Depreciation is due to obsolescence rather than wear and tear.

Required:

Prepare computations showing how much profits will increase or decrease as a result of making the starters.

EXERCISE 13–17 (Appendix 13A) Absorption Costing Approach to Setting a Selling Price [LO4]

Butler Limited is considering the introduction of a new product. Management has gathered the following information:

Number of units to be produced and sold each year	25,000
Unit product cost	$40
Projected annual selling and administrative expenses	$100,000
Estimated investment required by the company	$1,000,000
Desired return on investment (ROI)	20%

The company uses the absorption costing approach to cost-plus pricing.

Required:

1. Compute the markup the company will have to use to achieve the desired ROI.
2. Compute the target selling price per unit.

EXERCISE 13–18 (Appendex 13A) Target Costing [LO5]

Little River Cycles (LRC) produces and distributes carbon fiber road bikes. Management is eager to take advantage of the growing market for carbon fiber triathlon bikes. To be competitive, LRC's sales manager estimates that the triathlon bike can't be priced at more than $2,000. At this price management thinks they can sell 1,000 bikes per year. Producing the triathlon bikes will require an initial investment of $2,000,000 and the company's target ROI is 25%.

Required:

Calculate the target cost of one carbon fiber triathlon bike.

EXERCISE 13–19 (Appendix 13A) Time and Materials Pricing [LO4]

Ray's Repair Company provides repair services for small engines and uses time and materials pricing. The company has budgeted the following costs for next year:

Mechanic's wages and fringe benefits	$450,000
Other repair costs, except for parts-related costs	$225,000
Costs of ordering, handling, and storing parts	20% of invoice cost

In total, the company expects to log 25,000 hours of billable repair time next year. According to competitive conditions, the company believes it should aim for a profit of $4 per hour of each mechanic's time. The competitive markup on parts is 20% of invoice cost.

Required:

1. Compute the time rate and the material loading charge that would be used to bill jobs.
2. One of the company's mechanics has just completed a repair job that required six hours of time and $60 in parts (invoice cost). Compute the amount that would be billed for the job.

PROBLEMS

PROBLEM 13–20 Dropping or Retaining a Flight [LO2]

Profits have been decreasing for several years at Atlantic Airlines. In an effort to improve the company's performance, consideration is being given to dropping several flights that appear to be unprofitable.

A typical income statement for one such flight (flight 482) is given below (per flight):

Ticket revenue (175 seats × 40% occupancy × $200 ticket price)	$14,000	100.0%
Less variable expenses ($15 per person)	1,050	7.5
Contribution margin	12,950	92.5%
Less flight expenses:		
Salaries, flight crew	1,800	
Flight promotion	750	
Depreciation of aircraft	1,550	
Fuel for aircraft	5,800	
Liability insurance	4,200	
Salaries, flight assistants	1,500	
Baggage loading and flight preparation	1,700	
Overnight costs for flight crew and assistants at destination	300	
Total flight expenses	17,600	
Operating loss	$ (4,650)	

The following additional information is available about flight 306:

a. Members of the flight crew are paid fixed annual salaries, whereas the flight assistants are paid by the flight.
b. One-third of the liability insurance is a special charge assessed against flight 306 because in the opinion of the insurance company, the destination of the flight is in a "high-risk" area. The remaining two-thirds would be unaffected by a decision to drop flight 306.
c. The baggage loading and flight preparation expense is an allocation of ground crews' salaries and depreciation of ground equipment. Dropping flight 306 would have no effect on the company's total baggage loading and flight preparation expenses.
d. If flight 306 is dropped, Atlantic Airlines has no authorization at present to replace it with another flight.
e. Aircraft depreciation is due entirely to obsolescence. Depreciation due to wear and tear is negligible.
f. Dropping flight 306 would not allow Atlantic Airlines to reduce the number of aircraft in its fleet or the number of flight crew on its payroll.

Required:

1. Prepare an analysis showing what impact dropping flight 306 would have on the airline's profits.
2. The airline's scheduling officer has been criticized because only about 50% of the seats on Atlantic's flights are being filled compared to an industry average of 60%. The scheduling officer has explained that Atlantic's average seat occupancy could be improved considerably by eliminating about 10% of its flights, but that doing so would reduce profits. Explain how this could happen.

PROBLEM 13–21 Sell or Process Further [LO2]

(Prepared from a situation suggested by Professor John W. Hardy.) Valley Meat Processing Corporation is a major processor of beef and other meat products. The company has a large amount of T-bone steak on hand, and it is trying to decide whether to sell the T-bone steaks as is or to process them further into filet mignon and New York-cut steaks.

Management believes that a kilogram of T-bone steak would yield the following profit:

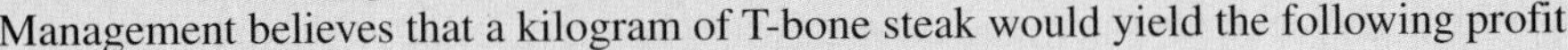

Wholesale selling price ($16.00 per kilogram)	$16.00
Less joint costs incurred up to the split-off point where T-bone steak can be identified as a separate product	12.00
Profit per kilogram	$4.00

As mentioned above, instead of being sold as is, the T-bone steaks could be further processed into filet mignon and New York-cut steaks. Cutting one side of a T-bone steak provides the filet mignon, and cutting the other side provides the New York cut. One 480-gram T-bone steak cut in this way will yield one 181-gram filet mignon and one 241-gram New York cut; the remaining grams are waste. The cost of processing the T-bone steaks into these cuts is $1.40 per kilogram. The filet mignon can be sold retail for $26 per kilogram, and the New York-cut can be sold wholesale for $22 per kilogram.

Required:

1. Determine the profit per kilogram from processing the T-bone steaks further into filet mignon and New York-cut steaks.
2. Would you recommend that the T-bone steaks be sold as is or processed further? Why?

PROBLEM 13–22 Close or Retain a Store [LO2]

Super Markets, Inc., operates three stores in a large metropolitan area. A segmented absorption costing income statement for the company for the last quarter is given below:

SUPER MARKETS, INC.
Income Statement
For the Quarter Ended September 30

	Total	Cambridge Store	Kitchener Store	Waterloo Store
Sales	$3,000,000	$720,000	$1,200,000	$1,080,000
Cost of goods sold	1,657,200	403,200	660,000	594,000
Gross margin	1,342,800	316,800	540,000	486,000
Operating expenses:				
Selling expenses	817,000	231,400	315,000	270,600
Administrative expenses	383,000	106,000	150,900	126,100
Total expenses	1,200,000	337,400	465,900	396,700
Operating income (loss)	$ 142,800	$(20,600)	$ 74,100	$ 89,300

The Cambridge Store has consistently shown losses over the past two years. For this reason, management is giving consideration to closing the store. The company has retained you to make a recommendation as to whether the store should be closed or kept open. The following additional information is available for your use:

a. The breakdown of the selling and administrative expenses is as shown near the top of page 574.
b. The lease on the building housing the Cambridge Store can be broken with no penalty.
c. The fixtures being used in the Cambridge Store would be transferred to the other two stores if it were closed.
d. The general manager of the Cambridge Store would be retained and transferred to another position in the company if it were closed. She would be filling a position that would otherwise be filled by hiring a new employee at a salary of $11,000 per quarter. The general manager of the Cambridge Store would be retained at her normal salary of $12,000 per quarter. All other employees in the store would be discharged.
e. The company has one delivery crew that serves all three stores. One delivery person could be discharged if the Cambridge Store were closed. This person's salary is $4,000 per quarter. The

delivery equipment would be distributed to the other stores. The equipment does not wear out through use, but does eventually become obsolete.

f. The company's employment taxes are 15% of salaries.

g. One-third of the insurance in the Cambridge Store is on the store's fixtures.

h. The "General office salaries" and "General office—other" relate to the overall management of Super Markets, Inc. If the Cambridge Store were closed, one person in the general office could be discharged because of the decrease in overall workload. This person's compensation is $6,000 per quarter.

	Total	Cambridge Store	Kitchener Store	Waterloo Store
Selling expenses:				
Sales salaries	$239,000	$ 70,000	$ 89,000	$ 80,000
Direct advertising	187,000	51,000	72,000	64,000
General advertising*	45,000	10,800	18,000	16,200
Store rent	300,000	85,000	120,000	95,000
Depreciation of store fixtures	16,000	4,600	6,000	5,400
Delivery salaries	21,000	7,000	7,000	7,000
Depreciation of delivery equipment	9,000	3,000	3,000	3,000
Total selling expenses	$817,000	$231,400	$315,000	$270,600

*Allocated on the basis of sales dollars.

	Total	Cambridge Store	Kitchener Store	Waterloo Store
Administrative expenses:				
Store management salaries	$ 70,000	$ 21,000	$ 30,000	$ 19,000
General office salaries*	50,000	12,000	20,000	18,000
Insurance on fixtures and inventory	25,000	7,500	9,000	8,500
Utilities	106,000	31,000	40,000	35,000
Employment taxes	57,000	16,500	21,900	18,600
General office—other*	75,000	18,000	30,000	27,000
Total administrative expenses	$383,000	$106,000	$150,900	$126,100

*Allocated on the basis of sales dollars.

Required:

1. Prepare a schedule showing the change in revenues and expenses and the impact on the company's overall operating income that would result if the Cambridge Store were closed.
2. Assuming that the store space can't be subleased, what recommendation would you make to the management of Super Markets, Inc.?
3. Disregard requirement 2. Assume that if the Cambridge Store were closed, at least one-fourth of its sales would transfer to the Waterloo Store, due to strong customer loyalty to Super Markets. The Waterloo Store has ample capacity to handle the increased sales. You may assume that the increased sales in the Waterloo Store would yield the same gross margin percentage as present sales in that store. What effect would these factors have on your recommendation concerning the Cambridge Store? Show all computations to support your answer.

PROBLEM 13–23 Make or Buy Analysis [LO2]

"In my opinion, we ought to stop making our own drums and accept that outside supplier's offer," said Wim Niewindt, managing director of Antilles Refining, N.V., of Aruba. "At a price of 18 florins per drum, we would be paying 5 florins less than it costs us to manufacture the drums in our own plant. (The currency in Aruba is the florin, denoted below by fl.) Since we use 60,000 drums a year, that would be an annual cost savings of 300,000 florins." Antilles Refining's present cost to manufacture one drum is given at the top of the next page (based on 60,000 drums per year):

Direct materials	fl10.35
Direct labour	6.00
Variable overhead	1.50
Fixed overhead (fl2.80 general company overhead, fl1.60 depreciation and, fl0.75 supervision)	5.15
Total cost per drum	fl23.00

A decision about whether to make or buy the drums is especially important at this time since the equipment being used to make the drums is completely worn out and must be replaced. The choices facing the company are:

Alternative 1: Rent new equipment and continue to make the drums. The equipment would be rented for fl135,000 per year.

Alternative 2: Purchase the drums from an outside supplier at fl18 per drum.

The new equipment would be more efficient than the equipment that Antilles Refining has been using and, according to the manufacturer, would reduce direct labour and variable overhead costs by 30%. The old equipment has no resale value. Supervision cost (fl45,000 per year) and direct materials cost per drum would not be affected by the new equipment. The new equipment's capacity would be 90,000 drums per year.

The company's total general company overhead would be unaffected by this decision.

Required:

1. To assist the managing director in making a decision, prepare an analysis showing the total cost and the cost per drum for each of the two alternatives given above. Assume that 60,000 drums are needed each year. Which course of action would you recommend to the managing director?
2. Would your recommendation in (1) above be the same if the company's needs were: (a) 75,000 drums per year or (b) 90,000 drums per year? Show computations to support your answer, with costs presented on both a total and a per unit basis.
3. What other factors would you recommend that the company consider before making a decision?

PROBLEM 13–24 Relevant Cost Analysis in a Variety of Situations [LO2]

Ovation Company has a single product called a Bit. The company normally produces and sells 60,000 Bits each year at a selling price of $32 per unit. The company's unit costs at this level of activity are given below:

Direct materials	$10.00	
Direct labour	4.50	
Variable manufacturing overhead	2.30	
Fixed manufacturing overhead	5.00	($300,000 total)
Variable selling expenses	1.20	
Fixed selling expenses	3.50	($210,000 total)
Total cost per unit	$26.50	

A number of questions relating to the production and sale of Bits follow. Each question is independent.

Required:

1. Assume that Ovation Company has sufficient capacity to produce 90,000 Bits each year without any increase in fixed manufacturing overhead costs. The company could increase its sales by 25% above the present 60,000 units each year if it were willing to increase the fixed selling expenses by $80,000. Would the increased fixed selling expenses be justified?
2. Assume again that Ovation Company has sufficient capacity to produce 90,000 Bits each year. A customer in a foreign market wants to purchase 20,000 Bits. Import duties on the Bits would be $1.70 per unit, and costs for permits and licenses would be $9,000. The only selling costs that would be associated with the order would be $3.20 per unit shipping cost. Compute the per unit break-even price on this order.
3. The company has 1,000 Bits on hand that have some irregularities and are therefore considered to be "seconds." Due to the irregularities, it will be impossible to sell these units at the

normal price through regular distribution channels. What unit cost figure is relevant for setting a minimum selling price? Explain.

4. Due to a strike in its supplier's plant, Ovation Company is unable to purchase more material for the production of Bits. The strike is expected to last for two months. Ovation Company has enough material on hand to operate at 30% of normal levels for the two-month period. As an alternative, Ovation could close its plant down entirely for the two months. If the plant were closed, fixed manufacturing overhead costs would continue at 60% of their normal level during the two-month period and the fixed selling expenses would be reduced by 20%. What would be the impact on profits of closing the plant for the two-month period?
5. An outside manufacturer has offered to produce Bits and ship them directly to Ovation's customers. If Ovation Company accepts this offer, the facilities that it uses to produce Bits would be idle; however, fixed manufacturing overhead costs would be reduced by 75%. Since the outside manufacturer would pay for all shipping costs, the variable selling expenses would be only two-thirds of their present amount. Compute the unit cost that is relevant for comparison to the price quoted by the outside manufacturer.

PROBLEM 13–25 Shutting Down or Continuing to Operate a Plant [LO2]

(Note: This type of decision is similar to dropping a product line.)

Kolbec Company normally produces and sells 30,000 units of RG-6 each month. RG-6 is a small electrical relay used as a component part in the automotive industry. The selling price is $22 per unit, variable costs are $14 per unit, fixed manufacturing overhead costs total $150,000 per month, and fixed selling costs total $30,000 per month.

Employment-contract strikes in the companies that purchase the bulk of the RG-6 units have caused Kolbec Company's sales to temporarily drop to only 8,000 units per month. Kolbec Company estimates that the strikes will last for two months, after which time sales of RG-6 should return to normal. Due to the current low level of sales, Kolbec Company is thinking about closing down its own plant during the strike, which would reduce its fixed manufacturing overhead costs by $45,000 per month and its fixed selling costs by 10%. Start-up costs at the end of the shutdown period would total $8,000. Since Kolbec Company uses just-in-time (JIT) production methods, no inventories are on hand.

Required:

1. Assuming that the strikes continue for two months, would you recommend that Kolbec Company close its own plant? Explain. Show computations in good form.
2. At what level of sales (in units) for the two-month period should Kolbec Company be indifferent between closing the plant or keeping it open? Show computations. (Hint: This is a type of break-even analysis, except that the fixed cost portion of your break-even computation should include only those fixed costs that are relevant [i.e., avoidable] over the two-month period.)

PROBLEM 13–26 Make or Buy Decision [LO2]

Sackville Industries, which manufactures and sells a highly successful line of summer lotions and insect repellents, has decided to diversify in order to stabilize sales throughout the year. A natural area for the company to consider is the production of winter lotions and creams to prevent dry and chapped skin.

After considerable research, a winter products line has been developed. However, Sackville's president has decided to introduce only one of the new products for this coming winter. If the product is a success, further expansion in future years will be initiated.

The product selected (called Chap-Off) is a lip balm that will be sold in a lipstick-type tube. The product will be sold to wholesalers in boxes of 24 tubes for $8 per box. Because of excess capacity, no additional fixed manufacturing overhead costs will be incurred to produce the product. However, a $90,000 charge for fixed manufacturing overhead will be absorbed by the product under the company's absorption costing system.

Using the estimated sales and production of 100,000 boxes of Chap-Off, the Accounting Department has developed the following cost per box:

Direct material	$3.60
Direct labour	2.00
Manufacturing overhead	1.40
Total cost	$7.00

The costs above include costs for producing both the lip balm and the tube that contains it. As an alternative to making the tubes, Sackville has approached a supplier to discuss the possibility of purchasing the tubes for Chap-Off. The purchase price of the empty tubes from the supplier would be $1.35 per box of 24 tubes. If Sackville Industries accepts the purchase proposal, direct labour and variable manufacturing overhead costs per box of Chap-Off would be reduced by 10% and direct materials costs would be reduced by 25%.

Required:

1. Should Sackville Industries make or buy the tubes? Show calculations to support your answer.
2. What would be the maximum purchase price acceptable to Sackville Industries? Explain.
3. Instead of sales of 100,000 boxes, revised estimates show a sales volume of 120,000 boxes. At this new volume, additional equipment must be acquired to manufacture the tubes at an annual rental of $40,000. Assuming that the outside supplier will not accept an order for less than 100,000 boxes, should Sackville Industries make or buy the tubes? Show computations to support your answer.
4. Refer to the data in (3) above. Assume that the outside supplier will accept an order of any size for the tubes at $1.35 per box. How, if at all, would this change your answer? Show computations.
5. What qualitative factors should Sackville Industries consider in determining whether they should make or buy the tubes?

(CMA, adapted)

PROBLEM 13–27 Accept or Reject a Special Order [LO2]

Reid Company manufactures and sells a single product called a Lop. Operating at capacity, the company can produce and sell 30,000 Lops per year. Costs associated with this level of production and sales are given below:

	Unit	Total
Direct materials	$15	$ 450,000
Direct labour	8	240,000
Variable manufacturing overhead	3	90,000
Fixed manufacturing overhead	9	270,000
Variable selling expense	4	120,000
Fixed selling expense	6	180,000
Total cost	$45	$1,350,000

The Lops normally sell for $50 each. Fixed manufacturing overhead is constant at $270,000 per year within the range of 25,000 through 30,000 Lops per year.

Required:

1. Assume that due to a recession, Reid Company expects to sell only 25,000 Lops through regular channels next year. A large retail chain has offered to purchase 5,000 Lops if Reid is willing to accept a 16% discount off the regular price. There would be no sales commissions on this order; thus, variable selling expenses would be slashed by 75%. However, Reid Company would have to purchase a special machine to engrave the retail chain's name on the 5,000 units. This machine would cost $10,000. Reid Company has no assurance that the retail chain will purchase additional units in the future. Determine the impact on profits next year if this special order is accepted.
2. Refer to the original data. Assume again that Reid Company expects to sell only 25,000 Lops through regular channels next year. The B.C. government would like to make a one-time-only purchase of 5,000 Lops. The government would pay a fixed fee of $1.80 per Lop, and it would reimburse Reid Company for all costs of production (variable and fixed) associated with the units. Since the government would pick up the Lops with its own trucks, there would be no variable selling expenses associated with this order. If Reid Company accepts the order, by how much will profits increase or decrease for the year?
3. Assume the same situation as that described in (2) above, except that the company expects to sell 30,000 Lops through regular channels next year. Thus, accepting the B.C. government's order would require giving up regular sales of 5,000 Lops. If the government's order is accepted, by how much will profits increase or decrease from what they would be if the 5,000 Lops were sold through regular channels?

PROBLEM 13–28 Utilization of a Constrained Resource [LO3]

The Fuhr Toy Company manufactures a line of dolls and a doll dress sewing kit. Demand for the dolls is increasing, and management requests assistance from you in determining an economical sales and production mix for the coming year. The company has provided the following data:

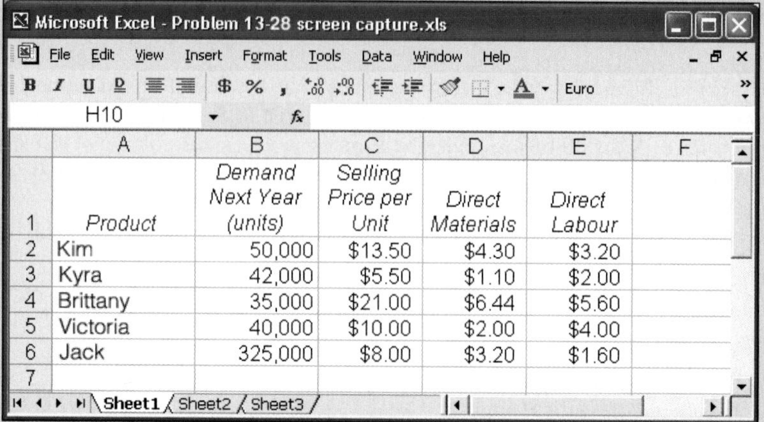

Microsoft Excel - Problem 13-28 screen capture.xls

	A	B	C	D	E	F
1	*Product*	*Demand Next Year (units)*	*Selling Price per Unit*	*Direct Materials*	*Direct Labour*	
2	Kim	50,000	$13.50	$4.30	$3.20	
3	Kyra	42,000	$5.50	$1.10	$2.00	
4	Brittany	35,000	$21.00	$6.44	$5.60	
5	Victoria	40,000	$10.00	$2.00	$4.00	
6	Jack	325,000	$8.00	$3.20	$1.60	
7						

Sheet1 / Sheet2 / Sheet3

The following additional information is available:

a. The company's plant has a capacity of 130,000 direct labour-hours per year on a single-shift basis. The company's present employees and equipment can produce all five products.
b. The direct labour rate of $8 per hour is expected to remain unchanged during the coming year.
c. Fixed costs total $520,000 per year. Variable overhead costs are $2 per direct labour-hour.
d. All of the company's nonmanufacturing costs are fixed.
e. The company's finished goods inventory is negligible and can be ignored.

Required:

1. Determine the contribution margin per direct labour-hour expended on each product.
2. Prepare a schedule showing the total direct labour-hours that will be required to produce the units estimated to be sold during the coming year.
3. Examine the data you have computed in (1) and (2) above. How would you allocate the 130,000 direct labour hours of capacity to Fuhr Toy Company's various products?
4. What is the highest price, in terms of a rate per hour, that Fuhr Toy Company would be willing to pay for additional capacity (that is, for added direct labour time)?
5. Assume again that the company does not want to reduce sales of any product. Identify ways in which the company could obtain the additional output.

(CPA, adapted)

PROBLEM 13–29 Volume Trade-Off Decision; Managing the Constraint [LO3]

Balmoral Brick, Inc., manufactures bricks using clay deposits on the company's property. Raw clays are blended and then extruded into molds to form unfired bricks. The unfired bricks are then stacked onto movable metal platforms and rolled into the kiln where they are fired until dry. The dried bricks are then packaged and shipped to retail outlets and contractors. The bottleneck in the production process is the kiln, which is available for 2,000 hours per year. Data concerning the company's four main products appear below. Products are sold by the pallet.

	Standard Brick	Quality Facing	Basic Block	Greco Brick
Gross revenue per pallet	$756	$1,356	$589	$857
Contribution margin per pallet	$472	$632	$376	$440
Annual demand (pallets)	90	110	100	120
Hours required in the kiln per pallet	8	8	4	5

No fixed costs could be avoided by modifying how much is produced of any product.

Required:

1. Is there sufficient capacity in the kiln to satisfy demand for all products?
2. What is the production plan for the year that would maximize the company's profit?
3. What would be the total contribution margin for the production plan you have proposed?

4. The kiln could be operated for more than 2,000 hours per year by running it after normal working hours. Up to how much per hour should the company be willing to pay in overtime wages, energy costs, and other incremental costs to operate the kiln additional hours?
5. The company is considering introducing a new product, glazed Sicilian bricks, whose variable cost would be $820 per pallet and that would require 10 hours in the kiln per pallet. What is the minimum acceptable selling price for this new product?
6. Salespersons are currently paid a commission of 5% of gross revenues. Will this motivate the salespersons to make the right choices concerning which products to sell most aggressively?

PROBLEM 13–30 Sell or Process Further [LO2]

Tidy Corporation produces a variety of cleaning compounds and solutions for both industrial and household use. While most of its products are processed independently, a few are related, such as the company's Grit 337 and its Sparkle silver polish.

Grit 337 is a coarse cleaning powder with many industrial uses. It costs $1.60 a kilogram to make, and it has a selling price of $2.00 a kilogram. A small portion of the annual production of Grit 337 is retained in the factory for further processing. It is combined with several other ingredients to form a paste that is marketed as Sparkle silver polish. The silver polish sells for $4.00 per jar.

This further processing requires one-fourth kilogram of Grit 337 per jar of silver polish. The additional direct costs involved in the processing of a jar of silver polish are:

Other ingredients	$0.65
Direct labour	1.48
Total direct cost	$2.13

Overhead costs associated with the processing of the silver polish are:

Variable manufacturing overhead cost	25% of direct labour cost
Fixed manufacturing overhead cost (per month):	
Production supervisor	$3,000
Depreciation of mixing equipment	$1,400

The production supervisor has no duties other than to oversee production of the silver polish. The mixing equipment, purchased two years ago, is special-purpose equipment acquired specifically to produce the silver polish. Its resale value is negligible and it does not wear out through use.

Direct labour is a variable cost at Tidy Corporation.

Advertising costs for the silver polish total $4,000 per month. Variable selling costs associated with the silver polish are 7.5% of sales.

Due to a recent decline in the demand for silver polish, the company is wondering whether its continued production is advisable. The sales manager feels that it would be more profitable to sell all of the Grit 337 as a cleaning powder.

Required:
1. What is the incremental contribution margin per jar from further processing of Grit 337 into silver polish?
2. What is the minimum number of jars of silver polish that must be sold each month to justify the continued processing of Grit 337 into silver polish? Explain. Show all computations in good form.

(CMA, adapted)

PROBLEM 13–31 Dropping or Retaining a Product [LO2]

Sally Robertson is the owner and managing director of Historic Garden Furniture, Ltd., a South African company that makes museum-quality reproductions of antique outdoor furniture. Ms. Robertson would like advice concerning the advisability of eliminating the model C3 lawnchair. These lawnchairs have been among the company's best-selling products, but they seem to be unprofitable.

A condensed absorption costing income statement for the company and for the model C3 lawnchair for the quarter ended June 30 is shown at the top of page 662.

	All Products	Model C3 Lawnchair
Sales	R2,900,000	R300,000
Cost of goods sold:		
Direct materials	759,000	122,000
Direct labour	680,000	72,000
Fringe benefits (20% of direct labour)	136,000	14,400
Variable manufacturing overhead	28,000	3,600
Building rent and maintenance	30,000	4,000
Depreciation	75,000	19,100
Total cost of goods sold	1,708,000	235,100
Gross margin	1,192,000	64,900
Selling and administrative expenses:		
Product managers' salaries	75,000	10,000
Sales commissions (5% of sales)	145,000	15,000
Fringe benefits (20% of salaries and commissions)	44,000	5,000
Shipping	120,000	10,000
General administrative expenses	464,000	48,000
Total selling and administrative expenses	848,000	88,000
Operating income (loss)	R 344,000	R (23,100)

The currency in South Africa is the rand, denoted here by R.

The following additional data have been supplied by the company:

a. Direct labour is a variable cost.
b. All of the company's products are manufactured in the same facility and use the same equipment. Building rent and maintenance and depreciation are allocated to products using various bases. The equipment does not wear out through use; it eventually becomes obsolete.
c. There is ample capacity to fill all orders.
d. Dropping the model C3 lawnchair would have no effect on sales of other product lines.
e. Work in process and finished goods inventories are insignificant.
f. Shipping costs are traced directly to products.
g. General administrative expenses are allocated to products on the basis of sales dollars. There would be no effect on the total general administrative expenses if the model C3 lawnchair were dropped.
h. If the model C3 lawnchair were dropped, the product manager would be laid off.

Required:

1. Given the current level of sales, would you recommend that the model C3 lawnchair be dropped? Prepare appropriate computations to support your answer.
2. What would sales of the model C3 lawnchair have to be, at minimum, in order to justify retaining the product? Explain. (Hint: Set this up as a break-even problem but include only the relevant costs.)

PROBLEM 13–32 (Appendix 13A) Standard Costs; Absorption Costing Approach to Setting Prices [LO4]

Corporate Clothing, Inc. has designed a business suit that is about to be introduced on the market. A standard cost card has been prepared for the new suit, as follows:

	Standard Quantity or Hours	Standard Price or Rate	Standard Cost
Direct materials	5.0 metres	$ 5.00 per metre	$25.00
Direct labour	2.0 hours	14.00 per hour	28.00
Manufacturing overhead (1/6 variable)	2.0 hours	12.00 per hour	24.00
Total standard cost per suit			$77.00

The following additional information relating to the new suit is available:

a. The only variable selling, general, or administrative costs will be $8 per suit for shipping. Fixed selling, general, and administrative costs will be (per year):

Salaries	$ 90,000
Advertising and other	400,000
Total	$490,000

b. Since the company manufactures many products, it is felt that no more than 20,000 hours of labour time per year can be devoted to production of the new suits.

c. An investment of $1,000,000 will be necessary to carry inventories and accounts receivable and to purchase some new equipment. The company desires a 20% return on investment (ROI) in new product lines.

d. Manufacturing overhead costs are allocated to products on the basis of direct labour-hours.

Required:

1. Assume that the company uses the absorption approach to cost-plus pricing.
   a. Compute the markup that the company needs on the suits to achieve a 20% ROI if it sells all of the suits it can produce using 20,000 hours of labour time.
   b. Using the markup you have computed, prepare a price quote sheet for a single suit.
   c. Assume that the company is able to sell all of the suits that it can produce. Prepare an income statement for the first year of activity, and compute the company's ROI for the year on the suits, using the ROI formula from Chapter 12.
2. After marketing the suits for several years, the company is experiencing a fall-off in demand due to an economic recession. A large retail outlet will make a bulk purchase of suits if its label is sewn in and if an acceptable price can be worked out. What is the minimum acceptable price for this order?

PROBLEM 13–33 (Appendix 13A) Target Costing [LO5]

Chef-Mate, Inc. sells restaurant equipment and supplies throughout most of Canada. Management is considering adding a gelato machine to its line of ice cream making machines. Management will negotiate the price of the gelato machine with its Greek manufacturer.

Management of Chef-Mate believes the gelato machines can be sold to its customers for $5,000 each. At that price, annual sales of the gelato machine should be 100 units. If the gelato machine is added to Chef-Mate's product lines, the company will have to invest $100,000 in inventories and special warehouse fixtures. The variable cost of selling the gelato machines would be $500 per machine.

Required:

1. If Chef-Mate requires a 15% return on investment (ROI), what is the maximum amount the company would be willing to pay the Greek manufacturer for the gelato machines?
2. After many hours of negotiations, management has concluded that the Greek manufacturer is unwilling to sell the gelato machine at a low enough price for Chef-Mate to earn its 15% required ROI. Apart from simply giving up on the idea of adding the gelato machine to Chef-Mate's product lines, what could management do?

PROBLEM 13–34 (Appendix 13A) Time and Material Pricing [LO4]

Laptop Repair, Inc. uses time and materials pricing, and each year it reviews its rates in light of the actual costs incurred in the prior year. Actual costs incurred last year in connection with repair work and in connection with the company's parts inventory are shown at the top of page 664.

Customers were billed for 20,000 hours of repair work last year.

The company has a target profit of $5 per hour of repair service time and a target profit of 20% of the invoice cost of parts used. During the past year, the company billed repair service time at $32 per hour and added a material loading charge of 40% to parts. Management feels these rates may now be inadequate, since costs have risen somewhat over the last year.

	Repairs	Parts
Repair technicians—wages	$300,000	
Repair service manager—salary	35,000	
Parts manager—salary		$40,000
Repairs and parts assistant—salary	18,000	5,000
Retirement benefits (20% of salaries and wages)	70,600	9,000
Health insurance (5% of salaries and wages)	17,650	2,250
Utilities	75,000	16,000
Truck operating costs	12,000	
Property taxes	5,800	3,600
Liability and fire insurance	4,200	2,000
Supplies	750	150
Rent—Building	24,000	22,000
Depreciation—trucks and equipment	37,000	
Invoice cost of parts used		400,000
Total costs for the year	$600,000	$500,000

Required:

1. Using the above data, compute the following:
   a. The rate that would be charged per hour of repair service time using time and materials pricing.
   b. The materials loading charge that would be used in billing jobs. The materials loading charge should be expressed as a percentage of the invoice cost.
2. Assume that the company adopts the rates that you have computed in (1) above. What should be the total price charged on a repair job that requires 3 hours of service time and parts with an invoice cost of $120?
3. If the company adopts the rates that you have computed in (1) above, would you expect the company's profits to improve?

CASES

CASE 13–35 Ethics and the Manager; Shut Down or Continue Operations [LO2]

Dana Porter had just been appointed vice president of the Rocky Mountain Region of the Bank Services Corporation (BSC). The company provides cheque processing services for small banks. The banks send cheques presented for deposit or payment to BSC, which records the data on each cheque in a computerized database. BSC then sends the data electronically to the nearest cheque-clearing centre where the appropriate transfers of funds are made between banks. The Rocky Mountain Region has three cheque processing centres, which are located in Edmonton, Red Deer, and Calgary. Prior to her promotion to vice president, Ms. Porter had been the manager of a cheque processing centre in Manitoba.

Immediately upon assuming her new position, Ms. Porter requested a complete financial report for the just-ended fiscal year from the region's controller, Joe Brigley. Ms. Porter specified that the financial report should follow the standardized format required by corporate headquarters for all regional performance reports. That report is shown at the top of page 665.

Upon seeing this report, Ms. Porter summoned Mr. Brigley for an explanation.

Porter: What's the story on Calgary? It didn't have a loss the previous year did it?

Brigley: No, the Calgary facility has had a nice profit every year since it was opened six years ago, but Calgary lost a big contract this year.

Porter: Why?

Brigley: One of our national competitors entered the local market and bid very aggressively on the contract. We couldn't afford to meet the bid. Calgary's costs—particularly their facility expenses—are just too high. When Calgary lost the contract, we had to lay off a lot of employees, but we could not reduce the fixed costs of the Calgary facility.

BANK SERVICES CORPORATION (BSC)
Rocky Mountain Region
Financial Performance

		Cheque Processing Centres		
	Total	Edmonton	Red Deer	Calgary
Sales	$50,000,000	$20,000,000	$18,000,000	$12,000,000
Operating expenses:				
Direct labour	32,000,000	12,500,000	11,000,000	8,500,000
Variable overhead	850,000	350,000	310,000	190,000
Equipment depreciation	3,900,000	1,300,000	1,400,000	1,200,000
Facility expense	2,800,000	900,000	800,000	1,100,000
Local administrative expense*	450,000	140,000	160,000	150,000
Regional administrative expense†	1,500,000	600,000	540,000	360,000
Corporate administrative expense‡	4,750,000	1,900,000	1,710,000	1,140,000
Total operating expense	46,250,000	17,690,000	15,920,000	12,640,000
Operating income	$ 3,750,000	$ 2,310,000	$ 2,080,000	$ (640,000)

*Local administrative expenses are the administrative expenses incurred at the cheque processing centres.

†Regional administrative expenses are allocated to the cheque processing centres based on sales.

‡Corporate administrative expenses are charged to segments of the company such as the Rocky Mountain Region and the cheque processing centres at the rate of 9.5% of their sales.

Porter: Why is Calgary's facility expense so high? It's a smaller facility than either Edmonton or Red Deer and yet its facility expense is higher.

Brigley: The problem is that we are able to rent suitable facilities very cheaply at Edmonton and Red Deer. No such facilities were available at Calgary; we had them built. Unfortunately, there were big cost overruns. The contractor we hired was inexperienced at this kind of work and in fact went bankrupt before the project was completed. After hiring another contractor to finish the work, we were way over budget. The large depreciation charges on the facility didn't matter at first because we didn't have much competition at the time and could charge premium prices.

Porter: Well we can't do that anymore. The Calgary facility will obviously have to be shut down. Its business can be shifted to the other two cheque processing centres in the region.

Brigley: I would advise against that. The $1,200,000 in depreciation at the Calgary facility is misleading. That facility should last indefinitely with proper maintenance. And it has no resale value; there is no other commercial activity around Calgary.

Porter: What about the other costs at Calgary?

Brigley: If we shifted Calgary's business over to the other two processing centres in the region, we wouldn't save anything on direct labour or variable overhead costs. We might save $90,000 or so in local administrative expense, but we would not save any regional administrative expense and corporate headquarters would still charge us 9.5% of our sales as corporate administrative expense.

In addition, we would have to rent more space in Edmonton and Red Deer in order to handle the work transferred from Calgary; that would probably cost us at least $600,000 a year. And don't forget that it will cost us something to move the equipment from Calgary to Edmonton and Red Deer. And the move will disrupt service to customers.

Porter: I understand all of that, but a money-losing processing centre on my performance report is completely unacceptable.

Brigley: And if you shut down Calgary, you are going to throw some loyal employees out of work.

Porter: That's unfortunate, but we have to face hard business realities.

Brigley: And you would have to write off the investment in the facilities at Calgary.

Porter: I can explain a write-off to corporate headquarters; hiring an inexperienced contractor to build the Calgary facility was my predecessor's mistake. But they'll have my head at headquarters if I show operating losses every year at one of my processing centres. Calgary has to go. At the next corporate board meeting, I am going to recommend that the Calgary facility be closed.

Required:

1. From the standpoint of the company as a whole, should the Calgary processing centre be shut down and its work redistributed to other processing centres in the region? Explain.
2. Do you think Dana Porter's decision to shut down the Calgary facility is ethical? Explain.
3. What influence should the depreciation on the facilities at Calgary have on prices charged by Calgary for its services?

CASE 13–36 Decentralization and Relevant Costs [LO2]

Hub Corporation consists of three decentralized divisions—Gulf Division, Shore Division, and Beach Division. The president of Hub has given the managers of the three divisions the authority to decide whether they will sell to outside customers on the intermediate market or sell to other divisions within the company. The divisions are autonomous in that each divisional manager has power to set selling prices to outside customers and to set transfer prices to other divisions. (A transfer price is a price one division charges another division of the same company for a product or service it supplies to that division.) Divisional managers are evaluated and compensated on the basis of their divisions' profits.

The manager of the Shore Division is considering two alternative orders. Data on the orders are provided below:

a. The Beach Division needs 2,000 motors that can be supplied by the Shore Division at a transfer price of $1,600 per motor. To manufacture these motors, Shore would purchase component parts from the Gulf Division at a transfer price of $400 per part. (Each motor would require one part.) Gulf would incur variable costs for these parts of $200 each. In addition, each part would require 2.5 hours of machine time at the Gulf Division's general fixed overhead rate of $38 per hour. Shore Division would then further process these parts, incurring variable costs of $450 per motor. The motors would require 5 hours of machine time each in Shore's plant at its general fixed overhead rate of $23 per hour.

   If the Beach Division can't obtain the motors from the Shore Division, it will purchase the motors from Bedford Corporation, which has offered to supply the same motors to Beach Division at a price of $1,500 per motor. To manufacture these motors, Bedford Corporation would also have to purchase a component part from Gulf Division. This would be a different component part than that needed by the Shore Division. It would cost Gulf $175 in variable cost to produce, and Gulf would sell it to Bedford Corporation for $350 per part on an order of 2,000 parts. Because of its intricate design, this part would also require 2.5 hours of machine time.

b. Spruce Corporation wants to place an order with the Shore Division for 2,500 units of a motor that is similar to the motor needed by the Beach Division. Spruce has offered to pay $1,200 per motor. To manufacture these motors, Shore Division would again have to purchase a component part from the Gulf Division. This part would cost Gulf Division $100 per part in variable cost to produce, and Gulf would sell it to Shore Division at a transfer price of $200 per part. This part would require 2 hours of machine time in Gulf's plant. Shore Division would further process these parts, incurring variable costs of $500 per motor. This work would require 4 hours of machine time in Shore Division.

The Shore Division's plant capacity is limited, and the division can accept only the order from the Beach Division or the order from Spruce, but not both. The president of Hub and the manager of the Shore Division both agree that it would not be beneficial to increase capacity at this time. The company's total general fixed overhead would not be affected by this decision.

Required:

1. If the manager of the Shore Division wants to maximize the division's profits, which order should be accepted—the order from the Beach Division or the order from Spruce Corporation? Support your answer with appropriate computations.
2. For the sake of discussion, assume that the Shore Division decides to accept the order from Spruce Corporation. Determine if this decision is in the best interests of Hub *as a whole*. Explain your answer. Support your answer with appropriate computations.

(CMA, adapted)

CASE 13–37 Sell or Process Further Decision [LO2]

The Cozy Sweater Company produces sweaters under the "Cozy" label. The company buys raw wool and processes it into wool yarn from which the sweaters are woven. One spindle of wool yarn is required to produce one sweater. The costs and revenues associated with the sweaters are given at the top of page 667.

		Per Sweater
Selling price		$30.00
Cost to manufacture:		
Raw materials:		
Buttons, thread, lining	$ 2.00	
Wool yarn	16.00	
Total raw materials	18.00	
Direct labour	5.80	
Manufacturing overhead	8.70	32.50
Manufacturing profit (loss)		$ (2.50)

Originally, all of the wool yarn was used to produce sweaters, but in recent years a market has developed for the wool yarn itself. The yarn is purchased by other companies for use in production of wool blankets and other wool products. Since the development of the market for the wool yarn, a continuing dispute has existed in the Cozy Sweater Company as to whether the yarn should be sold simply as yarn or processed into sweaters. Current cost and revenue data on the yarn are given below:

		Per Spindle of Yarn
Selling price		$20.00
Cost to manufacture:		
Raw materials (raw wool)	$7.00	
Direct labour	3.60	
Manufacturing overhead	5.40	16.00
Manufacturing profit		$ 4.00

The market for sweaters is temporarily depressed, due to unusually warm weather in the western provinces where the sweaters are sold. This has made it necessary for the company to discount the selling price of the sweaters to $30 from the normal $40 price. Since the market for wool yarn has remained strong, the dispute has again surfaced over whether the yarn should be sold outright rather than processed into sweaters. The sales manager thinks that the production of sweaters should be discontinued; she is upset about having to sell sweaters at a $2.50 loss when the yarn could be sold for a $4.00 profit. However, the production superintendent does not want to close down a large portion of the factory. He argues that the company is in the sweater business, not the yarn business, and that the company should focus on its core strength.

All of the manufacturing overhead costs are fixed and would not be affected even if sweaters were discontinued. Manufacturing overhead is assigned to products on the basis of 150% of direct labour cost. Materials and direct labour costs are variable.

Required:

1. Would you recommend that the wool yarn be sold outright or processed into sweaters? Support your answer with appropriate computations and explain your reasoning.
2. What is the lowest price that the company should accept for a sweater? Support your answer with appropriate computations and explain your reasoning.

CASE 13–38 Integrative Case: Relevant Costs; Pricing [LO1, LO2, LO4]

Greenco Incorporated's only product is a combination fertilizer-weed killer called GrowNWeed. GrowNWeed is sold nationwide to retail nurseries and garden stores.

Gomes Nursery plans to sell a similar fertilizer weed killer compound through its regional nursery chain under its own private label. Gomes does not have manufacturing facilities of its own, so it has asked Greenco (and several other companies) to submit a bid for manufacturing and delivering a 20,000-kilogram order of the private brand compound to Gomes. While the chemical composition of the Gomes compound differs from that of GrowNWeed, the manufacturing processes are very similar.

The Gomes compound would be produced in 1,000-kilogram lots. Each lot would require 25 direct labour-hours and the chemicals shown at the top of page 668.

Chemicals	Quantity in Kilograms
TH-1	300
SC-2	200
CE-3	150
WT-4	175

The first three chemicals (TH-1, SC-2, and CE-3) are all used in the production of GrowNWeed. WT-4 was used in another compound that Greenco discontinued several months ago. The supply of WT-4 that Greenco had on hand when the other compound was discontinued was not discarded. Greenco could sell its supply of WT-4 at the prevailing market price less $0.10 per kilogram selling and handling expenses.

Greenco also has on hand a chemical called AK-5, which was manufactured for use in another product that is no longer produced. AK-5, which cannot be used in GrowNWeed, can be substituted for TH-1 on a one-for-one basis without affecting the quality of the Gomes compound. The AK-5 in inventory has a salvage value of $600.

Inventory and cost data for the chemicals that can be used to produce the Gomes compound are shown below:

Raw Material	Kilograms in Inventory	Actual Price per Kilogram When Purchased	Current Market Price per Kilogram
TH-1	18,000	$1.15	$1.20
SC-2	6,000	$1.10	$1.05
CE-3	7,000	$1.35	$1.35
WT-4	3,000	$0.80	$0.70
AK-5	3,500	$0.90	(Salvage)

The current direct labour wage rate is $14 per hour. The predetermined overhead rate is based on direct labour-hours (DLH). The predetermined overhead rate for the current year, based on a two-shift capacity with no overtime, is as follows:

Variable manufacturing overhead	$ 3.00 per DLH
Fixed manufacturing overhead	10.50 per DLH
Combined predetermined overhead rate	$13.50 per DLH

Greenco's production manager reports that the present equipment and facilities are adequate to manufacture the Gomes compound. Therefore, the order would have no effect on total fixed manufacturing overhead costs. However, Greenco is within 400 hours of its two-shift capacity this month. Any additional hours beyond the 400 hours must be done in overtime. If need be, the Gomes compound could be produced on regular time by shifting a portion of GrowNWeed production to overtime. Greenco's direct labour wage rate for overtime is $21 per hour. There is no allowance for any overtime premium in the predetermined overhead rate.

Required:

1. Greenco has decided to submit a bid for the 20,000-kilogram order of Gomes's new compound. The order must be delivered by the end of the current month. Gomes has indicated that this is a one-time order that will not be repeated. Calculate the lowest price that Greenco could bid for the order without reducing its operating income.
2. Refer to the original data. Assume that Gomes Nursery plans to place regular orders for 20,000-kilogram lots of the new compound. Greenco expects the demand for GrowNWeed to remain strong. Therefore, the recurring orders from Gomes would put Greenco over its two-shift capacity. However, production could be scheduled so that 90% of each Gomes order could be completed during regular hours. As another option, some GrowNWeed production could be shifted temporarily to overtime so that the Gomes orders could be produced on regular time. Current market prices are the best available estimates of future market prices.

Greenco's standard markup policy for new products is 40% of the full manufacturing cost, including fixed manufacturing overhead. Calculate the price that Greenco, Inc., would quote Gomes Nursery for each 20,000-kilogram lot of the new compound, assuming that it is to be treated as a new product and this pricing policy is followed.

(CMA, adapted)

CASE 13–39 Make or Buy; Utilization of a Constrained Resource [LO1, LO2, LO3]
Store-It, Inc., sells a wide range of drums, bins, boxes, and other containers that are used in the chemical industry. One of the company's products is a heavy-duty corrosion-resistant metal drum, called the AUD drum, used to store toxic wastes. Production is constrained by the capacity of an automated welding machine that is used to make precision welds. A total of 2,000 hours of welding time is available annually on the machine. Since each drum requires 0.4 hour of welding time, annual production is limited to 5,000 drums. At present, the welding machine is used exclusively to make the AUD drums. The accounting department has provided the following financial data concerning the AUD drums:

AUD Drums		
Selling price per drum		$149.00
Cost per drum:		
Direct materials	$52.10	
Direct labour ($18 per hour)	3.60	
Manufacturing overhead	4.50	
Selling and administrative expense . . .	29.80	90.00
Margin per drum		$ 59.00

Management believes 6,000 AUD drums could be sold each year if the company had sufficient manufacturing capacity. As an alternative to adding another welding machine, management has considered buying additional drums from an outside supplier. Bentley Industries, Inc., a supplier of quality products, would be able to provide up to 4,000 AUD-type drums per year at a price of $138 per drum, which Store-It would resell to its customers at its normal selling price after appropriate relabelling.

Sharon Doane, Store-It's production manager, has suggested that the company could make better use of the welding machine by manufacturing bike frames, which would require only 0.5 hour of welding time per frame and yet sell for far more than the drums. Sharon believes that Store-It could sell up to 1,600 bike frames per year to bike manufacturers at a price of $239 each. The accounting department has provided the following data concerning the proposed new product:

Bike Frames		
Selling price per frame		$239.00
Cost per frame:		
Direct materials	$99.40	
Direct labour ($18 per hour)	28.80	
Manufacturing overhead	36.00	
Selling and administrative expense . . .	47.80	212.00
Margin per frame		$ 27.00

The bike frames could be produced with existing equipment and personnel. Manufacturing overhead is allocated to products on the basis of direct labour-hours. Most of the manufacturing overhead consists of fixed common costs such as rent on the factory building, but some of it is variable. The variable manufacturing overhead has been estimated at $1.35 per AUD drum and $1.90 per bike frame. The variable manufacturing overhead cost would not be incurred on drums acquired from the outside supplier.

Selling and administrative expenses are allocated to products on the basis of revenues. Almost all of the selling and administrative expenses are fixed common costs, but it has been estimated that variable selling and administrative expenses amount to $0.75 per AUD drum whether made or purchased and would be $1.30 per bike frame.

All of the company's employees—direct and indirect—are paid for full 40-hour workweeks and the company has a policy of laying off workers only in major recessions.

Required:

1. Given the margins of the two products as indicated in the reports submitted by the accounting department, does it make sense to consider producing the bike frames? Explain.
2. Compute the contribution margin per unit for:
   a. Purchased AUD drums.
   b. Manufactured AUD drums.
   c. Manufactured bike frames.
3. Determine the number of AUD drums (if any) that should be purchased and the number of AUD drums and/or bike frames (if any) that should be manufactured. What is the increase in operating income that would result from this plan over current operations?

   As soon as your analysis was shown to the top management team at Store-It, several managers got into an argument concerning how direct labour costs should be treated when making this decision. One manager argued that direct labour is always treated as a variable cost in textbooks and in practice and has always been considered a variable cost at Store-It. After all, "direct" means you can directly trace the cost to products. "If direct labour is not a variable cost, what is?" Another manager argued just as strenuously that direct labour should be considered a fixed cost at Store-It. No one had been laid off in over a decade, and for all practical purposes, everyone at the plant is on a monthly salary. Everyone classified as direct labour works a regular 40-hour workweek and overtime has not been necessary since the company adopted just-in-time techniques. Whether the welding machine is used to make drums or frames, the total payroll would be exactly the same. There is enough slack, in the form of idle time, to accommodate any increase in total direct labour time that the bike frames would require.
4. Redo requirements (2) and (3) above, making the opposite assumption about direct labour from the one you originally made. In other words, if you treated direct labour as a variable cost, redo the analysis treating it as a fixed cost. If you treated direct labour as a fixed cost, redo the analysis treating it as a variable cost.
5. What do you think is the correct way to treat direct labour cost in this situation—as variable or as fixed?

GROUP AND INTERNET EXERCISES

GROUP EXERCISE 13–40 Outsourcing May Be Hazardous to Your Health

In a *Focus on Current Practice* presented earlier in the chapter, Cott Corporation was reported to have suffered a decline in profit margin from 19.5% in 2003 to 17.2% in 2004. This was the result of having to outsource some of their production because of a shortfall in capacity during 2004.

Required:

1. Was deciding to outsource part of their production a bad decision by Cott? Why or why not?
2. What may have caused the shortfall in capacity at Cott Corporation in 2004?
3. In deciding which supplier to use for the outsourcing, what factors may Cott have considered?
4. What alternatives to outsourcing might Cott have considered in making this decision?

INTERNET EXERCISE 13–41

As you know, the World Wide Web is a medium that is constantly evolving. Sites come and go, and change without notice. To enable periodic updating of site addresses, this problem has been posted to the textbook Web site (www.mcgrawhill.ca/college/garrison). After accessing the site, enter the Student Centre and select this chapter. Select and complete the Internet Exercise.

CHAPTER 14

LEARNING OBJECTIVES

After studying Chapter 14, you should be able to:

1. Evaluate the acceptability of an investment project using the net present value method.
2. Evaluate the acceptability of an investment project using the internal rate of return method.
3. Evaluate an investment project that has uncertain cash flows.
4. Rank investment projects in order of preference.
5. Determine the payback period for an investment.
6. Compute the simple rate of return for an investment.
7. (Appendix 14A) Understand present value concepts and the use of present value tables.
8. (Appendix 14B) Explain the effect of inflation on capital budgeting decisions.
9. (Appendix 14C) Include income taxes in a capital budgeting analysis.

CAPITAL BUDGETING DECISIONS

BUSINESS FOCUS

CAPITAL BUDGETING AT SHELL CANADA

Shell Canada announced a $1.8 billion capital and exploration expenditure plan for 2005. Planned expenditures, up over 60% from 2004, will focus on growth in the upstream businesses and strengthening the retail network.

Plans include $220 million for exploration and $560 million for development projects. About 60% of the program is focused on maintaining current levels of natural gas production, $335 million in the Foothills area of Western Canada and approximately $150 million for the offshore Nova Scotia Sable gas project. The balance of the 2005 exploration and production planned expenditure program is related to growth opportunities, unconventional gas and Peace River in-situ oil sands in Western Canada, and the Mackenzie Gas Project in the far north. Construction on the Peace River expansion project could start in 2007.

The 2005 program for Oil Sands includes $135 million for Athabasca Oil Sands Project (AOSP) operations and profitability initiatives and $215 million for growth. Planned profitability initiatives are largely focused on reducing unit costs. The growth-related spending includes AOSP debottlenecking projects and front-end engineering for a 90,000 barrels per day expansion. The 2005 program also includes funding to capitalize a lease arrangement for large mobile equipment (trucks and shovels) at the Muskeg River Mine.

Approximately $110 million is earmarked for marketing and $370 million for manufacturing and distribution projects. Almost two-thirds of the planned manufacturing and distribution expenditure in 2005 is for distillate hydrotreater projects to meet ultra-low sulphur diesel requirements in 2006. More funds are also planned for marketing to boost the retail network in major urban areas.

Source: Excerpted from "Shell Canada Announces $1.8 Billion Capital Expenditure Program for 2005," **www.shell.ca**, November 18, 2004 Shell Canada Limited.

Capital budgeting The process of planning significant outlays on projects that have long-term implications, such as the purchase of new equipment or the introduction of a new product.

The term **capital budgeting** is used to describe how managers plan significant outlays on projects that have long-term implications, such as the purchase of new equipment and the introduction of new products. In a recent fiscal year, BCE Inc. had capital expenditures reaching $3.1 billion. Most companies have many more potential projects than can actually be funded. Hence, managers must carefully select those projects that promise the greatest future return. How well managers make these capital budgeting decisions is a critical factor in the long-run profitability of the company.

Capital budgeting involves *investment*—a company must commit funds now in order to receive a return in the future. Investments are not limited to stocks and bonds. Purchase of inventory or equipment is also an investment. For example, Tim Hortons makes an investment when it opens a new restaurant. McCain Foods makes an investment when it installs a new computer to handle customer billing. DaimlerChrysler makes an investment when it redesigns a product such as the Jeep Eagle and must retool its production lines. With a combination of public and private funding, universities such as UBC, U of T, McGill, Dalhousie, and Memorial make substantial investments in medical research. All of these investments are characterized by a commitment of funds today in the expectation of receiving a return in the future in the form of additional cash inflows or reduced cash outflows.

CAPITAL BUDGETING—PLANNING INVESTMENTS

Typical Capital Budgeting Decisions

What types of business decisions require capital budgeting analysis? Virtually any decision that involves an outlay now in order to obtain some return (increase in revenue or reduction in costs) in the future. Typical capital budgeting decisions include:

1. ***Cost-reduction decisions.*** Should new equipment be purchased to reduce costs?
2. ***Expansion decisions.*** Should a new plant, warehouse, or other facility be acquired to increase capacity and sales?
3. ***Equipment selection decisions.*** Which of several available machines would be the most cost-effective to purchase?
4. ***Lease or buy decisions.*** Should new equipment be leased or purchased?
5. ***Equipment replacement decisions.*** Should old equipment be replaced now or later?

Screening decision A decision as to whether a proposed investment meets some preset standard of acceptance.

Preference decision A decision as to which of several competing acceptable investment proposals is best.

Capital budgeting decisions tend to fall into two broad categories—*screening decisions* and *preference decisions.* **Screening decisions** are those relating to whether a proposed project meets some preset standard of acceptance. For example, a firm may have a policy of accepting projects only if they promise a return of, say, 20% on the investment. The required rate of return is the minimum rate of return a project must yield to be acceptable.

Preference decisions, by contrast, relate to selecting from among several *competing* courses of action. To illustrate, a firm may be considering five different machines to replace an existing machine on the assembly line. The choice of which machine to purchase is a *preference* decision.

In this chapter, we initially discuss ways of making screening decisions. Preference decisions are discussed toward the end of the chapter.

The Time Value of Money

As stated earlier, business investments commonly promise returns that extend over fairly long periods of time. Therefore, in approaching capital budgeting decisions, it is necessary to employ techniques that recognize the *time value of money.* A dollar today is worth more than a dollar a year from now. The same concept applies in choosing between investment projects. Projects that promise returns earlier in time are preferable to those that promise later returns.

The capital budgeting techniques that recognize these two characteristics of business investments most fully are those that involve *discounted cash flows.* We will spend most of this chapter illustrating the use of discounted cash flow methods in making capital budgeting decisions. If you are not already familiar with discounting and the use of present value tables, you should read Appendix 14A, The Concept of Present Value, at the end of this chapter before proceeding any further.

FOCUS *on Current Practice*

Sometimes a long-term decision does not have to involve present value calculations or any other sophisticated analytical technique. White Grizzly Adventures of Meadow Creek, British Columbia, needs two snowcats for its powder skiing operations—one for shuttling guests to the top of the mountain and one to be held in reserve in case of mechanical problems with the first. Bombardier of Canada sells new snowcats for $250,000 and used, reconditioned snowcats for $150,000. In either case, the snowcats are good for about 5,000 hours of operation before they need to be reconditioned. From White Grizzly's perspective, the choice is clear. Since both new and reconditioned snowcats last about 5,000 hours, but the reconditioned snowcats cost $100,000 less, the reconditioned snowcats are the obvious choice. They may not have all of the latest bells and whistles, but they get the job done at a price a small operation can afford.

Bombardier snowcats do not have passenger cabs as standard equipment. To save money, White Grizzly builds its own custom-designed passenger cab for about $15,000, using recycled Ford Escort seats and industrial-strength aluminum for the frame and siding. If purchased retail, a passenger cab would cost about twice as much and would not be as well suited for snowcat skiing.

Source: Brad and Carole Karafil, owners and operators of White Grizzly Adventures, www.whitegrizzly.com.

DISCOUNTED CASH FLOWS—THE NET PRESENT VALUE METHOD

LEARNING OBJECTIVE 1
Evaluate the acceptability of an investment project using the net present value method.

Two approaches to making capital budgeting decisions use discounted cash flows. One is the *net present value method,* and the other is the *internal rate of return method* (sometimes called the *time-adjusted rate of return method*). The net present value method is discussed in this section; the internal rate of return method is discussed in the following section.

The Net Present Value Method Illustrated

Under the net present value method, the present value of a project's cash inflows is compared to the present value of the project's cash outflows. The difference between the present value of these cash flows, called the **net present value,** determines whether or not the project is an acceptable investment. To illustrate, let us assume the following data:

Net present value
The difference between the present value of the cash inflows and the present value of the cash outflows associated with an investment project.

Example A

Harper Company is contemplating the purchase of a machine capable of performing certain operations that are now performed manually. The machine will cost $50,000, and it will last for five years. At the end of the five-year period, the machine will have a zero scrap value. Use of the machine will reduce labour costs by $18,000 per year. Harper Company requires a minimum return of 20% before taxes on all investment projects.[1]

1. For simplicity, we assume in this chapter that there is no inflation. The impact of inflation on discounted cash flow analysis is discussed in Appendix 14B to this chapter. Also, in this chapter we ignore income taxes. The impact of income taxes on capital budgeting decisions is discussed in Appendix 14C.

Should the machine be purchased? Harper Company must determine whether a cash investment now of $50,000 can be justified if it will result in an $18,000 reduction in cost each year over the next five years. It may appear that the answer is obvious since the total cost savings are $90,000 ($18,000 per year × 5 years). However, the company can earn a 20% return by investing its money elsewhere. It is not enough that the cost reductions cover just the original cost of the machine; they must also yield at least a 20% return or the company would be better off investing the money elsewhere.

To determine whether the investment is desirable, the stream of annual $18,000 cost savings is discounted to its present value, which is then compared to the cost of the new machine. Since Harper Company requires a minimum return of 20% on all investment projects, this rate is used in the discounting process and is called the *discount rate*. Exhibit 14–1 shows how this analysis is done.

According to the analysis, Harper Company should purchase the new machine. The present value of the cost savings is $53,838, as compared to a present value of only $50,000 for the investment required (cost of the machine). Deducting the present value of the investment required from the present value of the cost savings gives a *net present value* of $3,838. Whenever the net present value is zero or greater, as in our example, an investment project is acceptable. Whenever the net present value is negative (the present value of the cash outflows exceeds the present value of the cash inflows), an investment project is not acceptable. In summary:

If the Net Present Value Is . . .	Then the Project Is . . .
Positive	Acceptable, since it promises a return greater than the required rate of return.
Zero	Acceptable, since it promises a return equal to the required rate of return.
Negative	Not acceptable, since it promises a return less than the required rate of return.

A full interpretation of the solution would be as follows: The new machine promises more than the required 20% rate of return. This is evident from the positive net present value of $3,838. Harper Company could spend up to $53,838 for the new machine and still obtain the minimum required 20% rate of return. The net present value of $3,838, therefore, shows the amount of "cushion" or "margin of error." One way to look at this is that the company could underestimate the cost of the new machine by up to $3,838, or overestimate the net present value of the future cash savings by up to $3,838, and the project would still be financially attractive. If the present value of the cost savings was only $50,000 instead of $53,838, the project would still promise the required 20% return.

EXHIBIT 14–1
Net Present Value Analysis of a Proposed Project

Initial cost	$50,000
Life of the project (years)	5
Annual cost savings	$18,000
Salvage value	-0-
Required rate of return	20%

Item	Year(s)	Amount of Cash Flow	20% Factor	Present Value of Cash Flows
Annual cost savings	1–5	$ 18,000	2.991*	$ 53,838
Initial investment	Now	(50,000)	1.000	(50,000)
Net present value				$ 3,838

*From Exhibit 14–19 in Appendix 14A at the end of this chapter.

Emphasis on Cash Flows

In capital budgeting decisions, the focus is on cash flows and not on accounting net income. The reason is that accounting net income is based on accruals that ignore the timing of cash flows into and out of an organization. From a capital budgeting standpoint, the timing of cash flows is important, since a dollar received today is more valuable than a dollar received in the future. Therefore, even though the accounting net income figure is useful for many things, it is not used in discounted cash flow analysis. Instead of determining accounting net income, the manager must concentrate on identifying the specific cash flows associated with an investment project.

What kinds of cash flows should the manager look for? Although the specific cash flows will vary from project to project, certain types of cash flows tend to recur, as explained in the following paragraphs.

Typical Cash Outflows Most projects will have an immediate cash outflow in the form of an initial investment in equipment or other assets. Any salvage value realized from the sale of old equipment can be recognized as a cash inflow or as a reduction in the required investment. In addition, some projects require that a company expand its working capital. **Working capital** is current assets (cash, accounts receivable, and inventory) less current liabilities. When a company takes on a new project, the balances in the current asset accounts will often increase. For example, opening a new Bay department store would require additional cash in sales registers, increased accounts receivable for new customers, and more inventory to stock the shelves. These additional working capital needs should be treated as part of the initial investment in a project. Also, many projects require periodic outlays for repairs and maintenance and for additional operating costs. These should all be treated as cash outflows for capital budgeting purposes.

Working capital
The excess of current assets over current liabilities.

Typical Cash Inflows On the cash inflow side, a project will normally either increase revenues or reduce costs. Either way, the amount involved should be treated as a cash inflow for capital budgeting purposes. Notice that from a cash flows standpoint, a *reduction in costs is equivalent to an increase in revenues.*) Cash inflows are also frequently realized from salvage of equipment when a project is terminated, although the company may actually have to pay for the cost of disposing of some low-value or hazardous items. In addition, any working capital that was tied up in the project can be released for use elsewhere at the end of the project and should be treated as a cash inflow. Working capital is released, for example, when a company sells off its inventory or collects its receivables. (If the released working capital is not shown as a cash inflow at the termination of a project, then the project will go on being charged for the use of the funds forever!)

In summary, the following types of cash flows are common in business investment projects:

Cash outflows:

Initial investment (including installation costs).
Increased working capital needs.
Repairs and maintenance.
Incremental operating costs.

Cash inflows:

Incremental revenues.
Reduction in costs.
Salvage value.
Release of working capital.

Recovery of the Original Investment

When computing the present value of a project, depreciation is not deducted for two reasons. First, depreciation is not a current cash outflow.[2] As discussed previously, discounted cash flow methods of making capital budgeting decisions focus on *cash flows.* Although depreciation is used in computing net income for financial statements, it is not relevant in an analytical framework that focuses on cash flows.

A second reason for not deducting depreciation is that discounted cash flow methods *automatically* provide for return of the original investment, thereby making a deduction for depreciation unnecessary. To demonstrate this point, let us assume the following data:

Example B

Carver Dental Clinic is considering the purchase of an attachment for its X-ray machine that will cost $3,170. The attachment will be usable for four years, after which time it will have no salvage value. It will increase net cash inflows by $1,000 per year in the X-ray department. The clinic's board of directors has instructed that no investments are to be made unless they have an annual return of at least 10%.

A present value analysis of the desirability of purchasing the X-ray attachment is presented in Exhibit 14–2. Notice that the attachment promises exactly a 10% return on the original investment, since the net present value is zero at a 10% discount rate.

Each annual $1,000 cash inflow arising from use of the attachment is made up of two parts. One part represents a recovery of a portion of the original $3,170 paid for the attachment, and the other part represents a return on this investment. The breakdown of each year's $1,000 cash inflow between recovery *of* investment and return *on* investment is shown in Exhibit 14–3.

The first year's $1,000 cash inflow consists of a $317 interest return (10%) *on* the $3,170 original investment, plus a $683 return *of* that investment. Since the amount of the unrecovered investment decreases over the four years, the dollar amount of the interest return also decreases. By the end of the fourth year, all $3,170 of the original investment has been recovered.

Simplifying Assumptions

Two simplifying assumptions are usually made in net present value analyis.

The first assumption is that all cash flows other than the initial investment occur at the end of periods. This is somewhat unrealistic in that cash flows typically occur *throughout* a period—not only at year end. The purpose of this assumption is just to simplify computations.

EXHIBIT 14–2 Carver Dental Clinic—Net Present Value Analysis of X-Ray Attachment

Initial cost	$3,170
Life of the project (years)	4
Annual net cash inflow	$1,000
Salvage value	–0–
Required rate of return	10%

Item	Year(s)	Amount of Cash Flow	10% Factor	Present Value of Cash Flows
Annual net cash inflow	1–4	$ 1,000	3.170*	$ 3,170
Initial investment	Now	(3,170)	1.000	(3,170)
Net present value				$ –0–

*From Exhibit 14–19 in Appendix 14A.

2. Although depreciation itself is not a cash outflow, it does have an effect on cash outflows for income taxes. We will take a look at this effect in Appendix 14C when we discuss the impact of income taxes on capital budgeting.

EXHIBIT 14–3 Carver Dental Clinic—Breakdown of Annual Cash Inflows

Year	(1) Investment Outstanding during the Year	(2) Cash Inflow	(3) Return on Investment (1) × 10%	(4) Recovery of Investment during the Year (2) — (3)	(5) Unrecovered Investment at the End of the Year (1) — (4)
1	$3,170	$1,000	$317	$ 683	$2,487
2	2,487	1,000	249	751	1,736
3	1,736	1,000	173	827	909
4	909	1,000	91	909	–0–
Total investment recovered				$3,170	

The second assumption is that all cash flows generated by an investment project are immediately reinvested at a rate of return equal to the discount rate. Unless these conditions are met, the return computed for the project will not be accurate. To illustrate, we used a discount rate of 10% for the Carver Dental Clinic in Exhibit 14–2. Unless the funds released each period are immediately reinvested at a 10% return, the net present value computed for the X-ray attachment will be misstated.

Choosing a Discount Rate

A positive net present value means that the project's return exceeds the discount rate. A negative net present value indicates that the project's return is less than the discount rate. Therefore, if the company's minimum required rate of return is used as the discount rate, a project with a positive net present value is acceptable and a project with a negative net present value is unacceptable.

The firm's *cost of capital* is usually regarded as the most appropriate choice for the discount rate. The **cost of capital** is the average rate of return the company must pay to its long-term creditors and shareholders for the use of their funds. The cost of capital is the minimum required rate of return, because if a project's rate of return is less than the cost of capital, company earnings will not be enough to compensate its creditors and shareholders. Therefore, any rate of return less than the cost of capital should not be accepted.

Cost of capital
The overall cost to an organization of obtaining investment funds, including the cost of both debt sources and equity sources. (Same as *hurdle rate, cut-off rate,* and *required rate of return.*)

The mechanics involved in cost of capital computations are covered in finance texts and will not be considered here. The cost of capital is known by various names. It is sometimes called the *hurdle rate*, the *cut-off rate*, or the *required rate of return*.

Most finance specialists would agree that a before-tax cost of capital of 16–20% would be typical for an average industrial corporation. The appropriate after-tax figure would depend on the corporation's tax circumstances, but it would probably average around 10–12%. Among the top Canadian wealth producers, this cost of capital is comparatively high. For example, Barrick Gold Corp.'s 16.6% cost of capital, and Placer Dome Inc.'s 17.2% well outpace the 11% average cost of 300 ranked Canadian companies.[3]

An Extended Example of the Net Present Value Method

To conclude our discussion of the net present value method, we present an extended example of how it is used in analyzing an investment proposal, which will help to tie together (and to reinforce) many of the ideas developed so far.

3. "*Financial Post* MVA List," *Financial Post,* June 22/24, 1996, pp. 43–47

Example C

Under a special licensing arrangement, Swinyard Company has an opportunity to market a new product in western Canada for a five-year period. The product would be purchased from the manufacturer, with Swinyard Company responsible for all costs of promotion and distribution. The licensing arrangement could be renewed at the end of the five-year period at the option of the manufacturer. After careful study, Swinyard Company has estimated that the following costs and revenues would be associated with the new product:

Cost of equipment needed	$ 60,000
Working capital needed	100,000
Overhaul of the equipment in four years	5,000
Salvage value of the equipment in five years	10,000
Annual revenues and costs:	
Sales revenues	200,000
Cost of goods sold	125,000
Out-of-pocket operating costs (for salaries, advertising, and other direct costs)	35,000

At the end of the five-year period, the working capital would be released for investment elsewhere if the manufacturer decided not to renew the licensing arrangement. Swinyard Company's discount rate and cost of capital is 14%. Would you recommend that the new product be introduced?

This example involves a variety of cash inflows and cash outflows. The solution is given in Exhibit 14–4.

Notice particularly how the working capital is handled in this exhibit. It is counted as a cash outflow at the beginning of the project and as a cash inflow when it is released at the end of the project. Also notice how the sales revenues, cost of goods sold, and out-of-pocket costs are handled. **Out-of-pocket costs** are actual cash outlays for salaries, advertising, and other operating expenses. Depreciation would not be an out-of-pocket cost, since it involves no current cash outlay.

Since the overall net present value is positive, the new product should be added, assuming the company has no better use for the investment funds.

EXHIBIT 14–4 The Net Present Value Method—An Extended Example

Sales revenues	$200,000
Less cost of goods sold	125,000
Less out-of-pocket costs for salaries, advertising, etc.	35,000
Annual net cash inflows	$ 40,000

Item	Year(s)	Amount of Cash Flows	14% Factor	Present Value of Cash Flows
Purchase of equipment	Now	$ (60,000)	1.000	$ (60,000)
Working capital needed	Now	(100,000)	1.000	(100,000)
Overhaul of equipment	4	(5,000)	0.592*	(2,960)
Annual net cash inflows from sales of the product line	1–5	40,000	3.433†	137,320
Salvage value of the equipment	5	10,000	0.519*	5,190
Working capital released	5	100,000	0.519*	51,900
Net present value				$ 31,450

*From Exhibit 14–18 in Appendix 14A.

†From Exhibit 14–19 in Appendix 14A.

CASH FLOWS—THE INTERNAL RATE OF RETURN METHOD

The **internal rate of return** (or **time-adjusted rate of return**) can be defined as the interest yield promised by an investment project over its useful life. It is sometimes referred to simply as the **yield** on a project. The internal rate of return is computed by finding the discount rate that equates the present value of a project's cash outflows with the present value of its cash inflows. In other words, the internal rate of return is that discount rate that will cause the net present value of a project to be equal to zero.

LEARNING OBJECTIVE 2
Evaluate the acceptability of an investment project using the internal rate of return method.

Internal rate of return
The discount rate at which the net present value of an investment project is zero; thus, the internal rate of return represents the interest yield promised by a project over its useful life. This term is synonymous with *time-adjusted rate of return.*

Time-adjusted rate of return
Same as *internal rate of return.*

Yield
A term synonymous with *internal rate of return* and *time-adjusted rate of return.*

The Internal Rate of Return Method Illustrated

To illustrate the internal rate of return method, let us assume the following data:

Example D

Glendale School District is considering the purchase of a large tractor-pulled lawnmower. At present, the lawn is mowed using a small hand-pushed gas mower. The large, tractor-pulled mower will cost $16,950 and will have a useful life of 10 years. It will have only a negligible scrap value, which can be ignored. The tractor-pulled mower would do the job much more quickly than the old mower and would result in a labour savings of $3,000 per year.

To compute the internal rate of return promised by the new mower, we must find the discount rate that will cause the net present value of the project to be zero. How do we do this? The simplest and most direct approach *when the net cash inflow is the same every year* is to divide the investment in the project by the expected net annual cash inflow. This computation will yield a factor from which the internal rate of return can be determined. The formula is as follows:

$$\text{Factor of the internal rate of return} = \frac{\text{Investment required}}{\text{Net annual cash inflow}} \qquad (1)$$

The factor derived from this formula is then located in the present value tables to see what rate of return it represents. Using this formula and the data for Glendale School District's proposed project, we get:

$$\frac{\text{Investment required}}{\text{Net annual cash inflow}} = \frac{\$16{,}950}{\$3{,}000} = 5.650$$

Thus, the discount factor that will equate a series of $3,000 cash inflows with a present investment of $16,950 is 5.650. Now we need to find this factor in Exhibit 14–19 in Appendix 14A to see what rate of return it represents. We should use the 10-period line in Exhibit 14–19 since the cash flows for the project continue for 10 years. If we scan along the 10-period line, we find that a factor of 5.650 represents a 12% rate of return. Therefore, the internal rate of return promised by the mower project is 12%. We can verify this by computing the project's net present value using a 12% discount rate. This computation is shown in Exhibit 14–5.

Notice from Exhibit 14–5 that using a 12% discount rate equates the present value of the annual cash inflows with the present value of the investment required in the project, leaving a zero net present value. The 12% rate therefore represents the internal rate of return promised by the project.

Salvage Value and Other Cash Flows

The technique just demonstrated works very well if a project's cash flows are identical every year. But what if they are not? For example, what if a project will have some salvage value at the end of its life in addition to the annual cash inflows? Under these circumstances, a trial-and-error process is necessary to find the rate of return that will equate the cash inflows with the cash outflows. The trial-and-error process can be carried out by hand, or it can be

EXHIBIT 14–5 Evaluation of the Mower Purchase Using a 12% Discount Rate

Initial cost	$16,950
Life of the project (years)	10
Annual cost savings	$ 3,000
Salvage value	–0–

Item	Year(s)	Amount of Cash Flow	12% Factor	Present Value of Cash Flows
Annual cost savings	1–10	$ 3,000	5.650*	$ 16,950
Initial investment	Now	(16,950)	1.000	(16,950)
Net present value				$ –0–

*From Exhibit 14–20 in Appendix 14A.

carried out by means of computer software programs such as spreadsheets that perform the necessary computations in seconds. In short, erratic or uneven cash flows should not prevent a manager from determining a project's internal rate of return.

Using the Internal Rate of Return

Required rate of return The minimum rate of return that an investment project must yield to be acceptable.

Once the internal rate of return has been computed, what does the manager do with the information? The internal rate of return is compared to the company's *required rate of return.* The **required rate of return** is the minimum rate of return that an investment project must yield to be acceptable. If the internal rate of return is *equal* to or *greater* than the required rate of return, then the project is acceptable. If it is *less* than the required rate of return, then the project is rejected. Quite often, the company's cost of capital is used as the required rate of return. The reasoning is that if a project cannot provide a rate of return at least as great as the cost of the funds invested in it, then it is not profitable.

In the case of the Glendale School District example used earlier, let us assume that the district has set a minimum required rate of return of 15% on all projects. Since the large mower promises a rate of return of only 12%, it does not clear this hurdle and would therefore be rejected as a project.

THE COST OF CAPITAL AS A SCREENING TOOL

As we have seen in preceding examples, the cost of capital often operates as a *screening* device, helping the manager screen out undesirable investment projects. This screening is accomplished in different ways, depending on whether the company is using the internal rate of return method or the net present value method in its capital budgeting analysis.

When the internal rate of return method is used, the cost of capital is used as the *hurdle rate* that a project must clear for acceptance. If the internal rate of return of a project is not great enough to clear the cost of capital hurdle, then the project is ordinarily rejected. We saw the application of this idea in the Glendale School District example, where the hurdle rate was set at 15%.

When the net present value method is used, the cost of capital is the *discount rate* used to compute the net present value of a proposed project. Any project yielding a negative net present value is rejected unless other factors are significant enough to require its acceptance.

The use of the cost of capital as a screening tool is summarized in Exhibit 14–6.

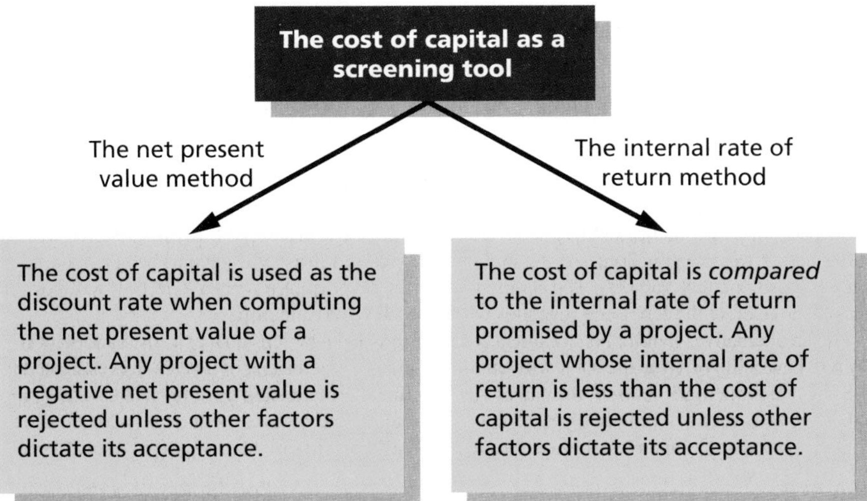

EXHIBIT 14–6 Capital Budgeting Screening Decisions

COMPARISON OF THE NET PRESENT VALUE AND THE INTERNAL RATE OF RETURN METHODS

The net present value method has several important advantages over the internal rate of return method.

First, the net present value method is often simpler to use. As mentioned earlier, the internal rate of return method may require using a trial-and-error process to find the discount rate that results in a net present value of zero. However, the process can be automated to some degree using a computer spreadsheet.

Second, the internal rate of return method makes a questionable assumption. Both methods assume that cash flows generated by a project during its useful life are immediately reinvested elsewhere. However, the two methods make different assumptions concerning the rate of return that is earned on those cash flows. The net present value method assumes that the rate of return is the discount rate, whereas the internal rate of return method assumes that the rate of return is the internal rate of return on the project. Specifically, if the internal rate of return of the project is high, this assumption may not be realistic. It is generally more realistic to assume that cash inflows can be reinvested at a rate of return equal to the discount rate—particularly if the discount rate is the company's cost of capital or an opportunity rate of return. For example, if the discount rate is the company's cost of capital, this rate of return can actually be realized by paying off the company's creditors and buying back the company's shares with cash flows from the project. In short, when the net present value method and the internal rate of return method do not agree concerning the attractiveness of a project, it is best to go with the net present value method. Of the two methods, it makes the more realistic assumption about the rate of return that can be earned on cash flows from the project.

EXPANDING THE NET PRESENT VALUE METHOD

So far all of our examples have involved only a single investment alternative. We will now expand the net present value method to include two alternatives. In addition, we will integrate the concept of relevant costs into the discounted cash flow analysis.

The net present value method can be used to compare competing investment projects in two ways. One is the *total-cost approach,* and the other is the *incremental-cost approach.* Each approach is illustrated in the following sections.

The Total-Cost Approach

The total-cost approach is the most flexible method for comparing competing projects. To illustrate the mechanics of the approach, let us assume the following data:

Example E

Halifax Ferry Company provides a ferry service across the Halifax Harbour. One of its ferryboats is in poor condition. This ferry can be renovated at an immediate cost of $200,000. Further repairs and an overhaul of the motor will be needed five years from now at a cost of $80,000. In all, the ferry will be usable for 10 years if this work is done. At the end of 10 years, the ferry will have to be scrapped at a salvage value of approximately $60,000. The scrap value of the ferry right now is $70,000. It will cost $300,000 each year to operate the ferry, and revenues will total $400,000 annually.

As an alternative, Halifax Ferry Company can purchase a new ferryboat at a cost of $360,000. The new ferry will have a life of 10 years, but it will require some repairs at the end of 5 years. It is estimated that these repairs will amount to $30,000. At the end of 10 years, it is estimated that the ferry will have a scrap value of $60,000. It will cost $210,000 each year to operate the ferry, and revenues will total $400,000 annually.

Halifax Ferry Company requires a return of at least 14% before taxes on all investment projects.

Should the company purchase the new ferry or renovate the old ferry? Using the total-cost approach, Exhibit 14–7 gives the solution.

Two points should be noted from the exhibit. First, *all* cash inflows and *all* cash outflows are included in the solution under each alternative. No effort has been made to isolate those cash flows that are relevant to the decision and those that are not relevant. The inclusion of all cash flows associated with each alternative gives the approach its name—the *total-cost* approach.

Second, notice that a net present value figure is computed for each of the two alternatives. This is a distinct advantage of the total-cost approach in that an unlimited number of alternatives can be compared side by side to determine the best action. For example, another alternative for Halifax Ferry Company would be to get out of the ferry business entirely. If management desired, the net present value of this alternative could be computed to compare with the alternatives shown in Exhibit 14–7. Still other alternatives might be open to the company. Once management has determined the net present value of each alternative that it wishes to consider, it can select the course of action that promises to be the most profitable. In this case, given only the two alternatives, the data indicate that the most profitable course is to purchase the new ferry.[4]

The Incremental-Cost Approach

When only two alternatives are being considered, the incremental-cost approach offers a simpler and more direct route to a decision. Unlike the total-cost approach, it focuses only on differential costs.[5] The procedure is to include in the discounted cash flow analysis only those costs and revenues that *differ* between the two alternatives being considered. To illustrate, refer again to the data in example E relating to Halifax Ferry Company. The solution using only differential costs is presented in Exhibit 14–8.

Two things should be noted from the data in this exhibit. First, notice that the net present value of $405,390 in favour of buying shown in Exhibit 14–8 agrees with the net present value shown under the total-cost approach in Exhibit 14–7. This agreement should be expected, since the two approaches are just different roads to the same destination.

Second, notice that the costs used in Exhibit 14–8 are just the differences between the costs shown for the two alternatives in the prior exhibit. For example, the $160,000 incremental investment required to purchase the new ferry in Exhibit 14–8 is the difference

4. The alternative with the highest net present value is not always the best choice, although it is the best choice in this case. For further discussion, see the section Preference Decisions—The Ranking of Investment Projects, later in this chapter.
5. Technically, the incremental-cost approach is misnamed, since it focuses on differential costs (that is, on both cost increases and decreases) rather than just on incremental costs. As used here, the term *incremental costs* should be interpreted broadly to include both cost increases and cost decreases.

EXHIBIT 14–7 The Total-Cost Approach to Project Selection

	New Ferry	Old Ferry
Annual revenues	$400,000	$400,000
Annual cash operating costs	210,000	300,000
Net annual cash inflows	$190,000	$100,000

Item	Year(s)	Amount of Cash Flows	14% Factor*	Present Value of Cash Flows
Buy the new ferry:				
Initial investment	Now	$(360,000)	1.000	$(360,000)
Repairs in five years	5	(30,000)	0.519	(15,570)
Net annual cash inflows	1–10	190,000	5.216	991,040
Salvage of the old ferry	Now	70,000	1.000	70,000
Salvage of the new ferry	10	60,000	0.270	16,200
Net present value				701,670
Keep the old ferry:				
Initial repairs	Now	$(200,000)	1.000	(200,000)
Repairs in five years	5	(80,000)	0.519	(41,520)
Net annual cash inflows	1–10	100,000	5.216	521,600
Salvage of the old ferry	10	60,000	0.270	16,200
Net present value				296,280
Net present value in favour of buying the new ferry				$405,390

*All factors are from Exhibits 14–19 and 14–20 in Appendix 14A.

between the $360,000 cost of the new ferry and the $200,000 cost required to renovate the old ferry from Exhibit 14–7. The other figures in Exhibit 14–8 have been computed in the same way.

Least-Cost Decisions

Revenues are not directly involved in some decisions. For example, a company that does not charge for delivery service may need to replace an old delivery truck, or a company may be trying to decide whether to lease or to buy its fleet of executive cars. In situations

EXHIBIT 14–8 The Incremental-Cost Approach to Project Selection

Item	Year(s)	Amount of Cash Flows	14% Factor*	Present Value of Cash Flows
Incremental investment required to purchase the new ferry	Now	$(160,000)	1.000	$(160,000)
Repairs in five years avoided	5	50,000	0.519	25,950
Increased net annual cash inflows	1–10	90,000	5.216	469,440
Salvage of the old ferry	Now	70,000	1.000	70,000
Difference in salvage value in 10 years	10	–0–	0.270	–0–
Net present value in favour of buying the new ferry				$405,390

*All factors are from Exhibits 14–18 and 14–19 in Appendix 14A.

such as these, where no revenues are involved, the most desirable alternative will be the one that promises the *least total cost* from the present value perspective. Hence, these are known as least-cost decisions. To illustrate a least-cost decision, assume the following data:

Example F

Val-Tek Company is considering the replacement of an old threading machine. A new threading machine is available that could substantially reduce annual operating costs. Selected data relating to the old and the new machines are presented below:

	Old Machine	New Machine
Purchase cost when new	$200,000	$250,000
Salvage value now	30,000	—
Annual cash operating costs	150,000	90,000
Overhaul needed immediately	40,000	—
Salvage value in six years	–0–	50,000
Remaining life	6 years	6 years

Val-Tek Company's cost of capital is 10%.

Exhibit 14–9 provides an analysis of the alternatives using the total-cost approach. As shown in the exhibit, the new machine has the lowest total cost when the present value of the net cash outflows is considered. An analysis of the two alternatives using the incremental-cost approach is presented in Exhibit 14–10. As before, the data in this exhibit represent the differences between the alternatives as shown under the total-cost approach.

EXHIBIT 14–9 The Total-Cost Approach (Least-Cost Decision)

Item	Year(s)	Amount of Cash Flows	10% Factor*	Present Value of Cash Flows
Buy the new machine:				
Initial investment	Now	$(250,000)	1.000	$(250,000)†
Salvage of the old machine	Now	30,000	1.000	30,000†
Annual cash operating costs	1–6	(90,000)	4.355	(391,950)
Salvage of the new machine	6	50,000	0.564	28,200
Present value of net cash outflows				(583,750)
Keep the old machine:				
Overhaul needed now	Now	$ (40,000)	1.000	$ (40,000)
Annual cash operating costs	1–6	(150,000)	4.355	(653,250)
Present value of net cash outflows				(693,250)
Net present value in favour of buying the new machine				$ 109,500

*All factors are from Exhibits 14–18 and 14–19 in Appendix 14A.

†These two items could be netted into a single $220,000 incremental-cost figure ($250,000 − $30,000 = $220,000).

EXHIBIT 14–10 The Incremental-Cost Approach (Least-Cost Decision)

Item	Year(s)	Amount of Cash Flows	10% Factor*	Present Value of Cash Flows
Incremental investment required to purchase the new machine	Now	$(210,000)	1.000	$(210,000)†
Salvage of the old machine	Now	30,000	1.000	30,000†
Savings in annual cash operating costs	1–6	60,000	4.355	261,300
Difference in salvage value in six years	6	50,000	0.564	28,200
Net present value in favour of buying the new machine				$109,500

*All factors are from Exhibits 14–18 and 14–19 in Appendix 14A.

†These two items could be netted into a single $180,000 incremental-cost figure ($210,000 − $30,000 = $180,000).

CAPITAL BUDGETING AND NON-PROFIT ORGANIZATIONS

Capital budgeting concepts can be applied in all types of organizations. Note, for example, the different types of organizations used in the examples in this chapter. These organizations include a dental clinic, a company working under a licensing agreement, a school district, a company operating a ferryboat service, and a manufacturing company. The diversity of these examples shows the range and power of discounted cash flow methods.

One problem faced by *non-profit* organizations in capital budgeting is determining the proper discount rate. Some non-profit organizations use, as their discount rate, the rate of interest that could be earned by placing money in an endowment fund rather than spending it on capital improvements, and others use discount rates that are set somewhat arbitrarily by governing boards.

The greatest danger lies in using a discount rate that is too low. Most government agencies, for example, at one time used the interest rate on government bonds as their discount rate. It is now recognized that this rate is too low and has resulted in the acceptance of many projects that should not have been undertaken.[6] The problem has not been resolved in Canada but in the United States, the Office of Management and Budget has specified that federal government units must use a discount rate of at least 10% on all projects.[7] For non-profit units such as schools and hospitals, it is generally recommended that the discount rate should "approximate the average rate of return on private sector investments."[8]

UNCERTAIN CASH FLOWS

LEARNING OBJECTIVE **3**
Evaluate an investment project that has uncertain cash flows.

The analysis to this point in the chapter has assumed that all of the future cash flows are known with certainty. However, future cash flows are often uncertain or difficult to estimate. A number of techniques are available for handling this complication. Some of these techniques are quite technical—involving computer simulations or advanced mathematical

6. See *Federal Capital Budgeting: A Collection of Haphazard Practices*, GAO, P.O. Box 6015, Gaithersburg, MD, PAD-81-19, February 26, 1981.
7. *Office of Management and Budget Circular No. A-94*, March 1972. The U.S. Postal Service is exempted from the 10% rate as are all water resource projects and all lease or buy decisions.
8. Robert N. Anthony and David W. Young, *Management Control in Nonprofit Organizations*, 5th ed. (Homewood, IL: Richard D. Irwin, Inc., 1994), p. 445.

skills—and some are beyond the scope of this book. However, we can provide some very useful information to managers without getting too technical.

An Example of Uncertain Cash Flows

As an example of difficult-to-estimate future cash flows, consider the case of investments in automated equipment. The up-front costs of automated equipment and the tangible benefits, such as reductions in operating costs and waste, tend to be relatively easy to estimate. However, the intangible benefits, such as greater reliability, greater speed, and higher quality, are more difficult to quantify in terms of future cash flows. These intangible benefits certainly affect future cash flows—particularly in terms of increased sales and perhaps higher selling prices—but the cash flow effects are difficult to estimate. What can be done?

A fairly simple procedure can be followed when the intangible benefits are uncertain and significant. Suppose, for example, that a company with a 12% cost of capital is considering purchasing automated equipment that would have a 10-year useful life. Also suppose that a discounted cash flow analysis of just the tangible costs and benefits shows a negative net present value of $226,000. Clearly, if the intangible benefits are large enough, they could turn this negative net present value into a positive net present value. In this case, the amount of additional cash flow per year from the intangible benefits that would be needed to make the project financially attractive can be computed as follows:

Net present value (negative)	$(226,000)
Factor for an annuity of 12% for 10 periods (from Exhibit 14–19 in Appendix 14A)	5.650

$$\frac{\text{Net present value, \$(226,000)}}{\text{Present value factor, 5.650}} = \$40{,}000$$

Thus, if intangible benefits such as greater flexibility, higher quality of output, and avoidance of capital decay are worth at least $40,000 per year to the company, then the automated equipment should be purchased. If, in the judgement of management, these intangible benefits are *not* worth $40,000 per year, then the automated equipment should not be purchased.

This technique can be used in other situations in which the future benefits of a current investment are uncertain or intangible. For example, this technique can be used when the salvage value is difficult to estimate. To illustrate, suppose that all of the cash flows from an investment in a supertanker have been estimated, other than its salvage value in 20 years. Using a discount rate of 12%, management has determined that the net present value of all these cash flows is a negative $1.04 million. This negative net present value would be offset by the salvage value of the supertanker. How large would the value have to be to make this investment attractive?

Net present value excluding salvage value (negative)	$(1,040,000)
Present value factor at 12% for 20 periods (from Exhibit 14–18 in Appendix 14A)	0.104

$$\frac{\text{Net present value to be offset, \$1,040,000}}{\text{Present value factor, 0.104}} = \$10{,}000{,}000$$

Thus, if the present value of the tanker is at least $10 million, its net present value would be positive and the investment would be made. However, if management believes the salvage value is unlikely to be as large as $10 million, the investment should not be made.

REAL OPTIONS

The analysis in this chapter has assumed that an investment cannot be postponed and that, once started, nothing can be done to alter the course of the project. In reality, investments can often be postponed. Postponement is a particularly attractive option when the net present value of the project is modest using current estimates of future cash flows, but the future cash flows involve a great deal of uncertainty that may be resolved over time.

Similarly, once an investment is made, management can often exploit changes in the business environment and take actions that enhance future cash flows. For example, buying a supertanker provides management with a number of options, some of which may become more attractive as time passes. Instead of operating the supertanker itself, the company may decide to lease it to another operator if the rental rates become high enough. Or, if a supertanker shortage develops, management may decide to sell the supertanker and take a gain. In the case of an investment in automated equipment, management may initially buy only the basic model without costly add-ons, but keep the option open to add more capacity and capability later.

The ability to delay the start of a project, to expand it if conditions are favourable, to cut losses if they are unfavourable, and to otherwise modify plans as business conditions change confers additional value on many investments. These advantages can be quantified using what is called *real option analysis*, but the techniques are beyond the scope of this book.

PREFERENCE DECISIONS—THE RANKING OF INVESTMENT PROJECTS

LEARNING OBJECTIVE 4
Rank investment projects in order of preference.

When considering investment opportunities, managers must make two types of decisions—screening decisions and preference decisions. Screening decisions, which come first, pertain to whether or not some proposed investment is acceptable. Preference decisions come *after* screening decisions and attempt to answer the following question: "How do the remaining investment proposals, all of which have been screened and provide an acceptable rate of return, rank in terms of preference? That is, which one(s) would be *best* for the firm to accept?"

Preference decisions are more difficult to make than screening decisions because investment funds are usually limited. This often requires that some (perhaps many) otherwise very profitable investment opportunities must be passed up.

Sometimes preference decisions are called *ranking decisions*, or *rationing decisions*, because they ration limited investment funds among many competing alternatives. Hence, the more reliable alternatives must be ranked. Either the internal rate of return method or the net present value method can be used in making preference decisions.

FOCUS *on Current Practice*

With an eye on environmental concerns, the board of directors of Royal Dutch/Shell, the Anglo-Dutch energy company, has decided that all large projects must explicitly take into account the likely future costs of abating carbon emissions. Calculations must assume a cost of $5 per tonne of carbon dioxide emission in 2005 through 2009, rising to $20 per tonne from 2010 onward. A Shell manager explains: "We know that $5 and $20 are surely the wrong prices, but everyone else who assumes a carbon price of zero in the future will be more wrong. This is not altruism. We see it as giving us a competitive edge."

Source: "Big Business Bows to Global Warming," *The Economist*, December 2, 2000, p. 1.

However, as discussed earlier, if the two methods are in conflict, it is best to use the more reliable net present value method.

Internal Rate of Return Method

When using the internal rate of return method to rank competing investment projects, the preference rule is: *The higher the internal rate of return, the more desirable the project.* An investment project with an internal rate of return of 18% is preferable to another project that promises a return of only 15%. Internal rate of return is widely used to rank projects.

Net Present Value Method

Unfortunately, the net present value of one project cannot be compared directly to the net present value of another project unless the investments in the projects are of equal size. For example, assume that a company is considering two competing investments, as shown below:

	Investment	
	A	B
Investment required	$(80,000)	$(5,000)
Present value of cash inflows	81,000	6,000
Net present value	$ 1,000	$ 1,000

Although each project has a net present value of $1,000, the projects are not equally desirable. The project requiring an investment of only $5,000 is much more desirable when funds are limited than the project requiring an investment of $80,000. To compare the two projects on a valid basis, the present value of the cash inflows should be divided by the investment required. The result is called the **profitability index**. The formula for the profitability index follows:

Profitability index
The ratio of the present value of a project's cash inflows to the investment required.

$$\text{Profitability index} = \frac{\text{Present value of cash inflows}}{\text{Investment required}} \qquad (2)$$

The profitability indexes for the two investments above would be computed as follows:

	Investment	
	A	B
Present value of cash inflows (a)	$81,000	$6,000
Investment required (b)	$80,000	$5,000
Profitability index, (a) ÷ (b)	1.01	1.20

When using the profitability index to rank competing investment projects, the preference rule is: *The higher the profitability index, the more desirable the project.* Applying this rule to the two investments above, investment B should be chosen over investment A.

The profitability index is an application of the techniques for utilizing scarce resources discussed in Chapter 13. In this case, the scarce resource is the limited funds available for investment, and the profitability index is similar to the contribution margin per unit of the scarce resource.

A few details should be clarified with respect to the computation of the profitability index. The "Investment required" refers to any cash outflows that occur at the beginning of the project, reduced by any salvage value recovered from the sale of old equipment. "Investment required" also includes any investment in working capital that the project may need.

Comparing the Preference Rules

The profitability index is conceptually superior to the internal rate of return as a method of making preference decisions. This is because the profitability index will always give the correct signal as to the relative desirability of alternatives, even if the alternatives have different lives and different patterns of earnings. By contrast, if lives are unequal, the internal rate of return method can lead the manager to make incorrect decisions. Assume the following situation:

Example G

Parker Company is considering two investment proposals, only one of which can be accepted. Project A requires an investment of $5,000 and will provide a single cash inflow of $6,000 in one year. Therefore, it promises an internal rate of return of 20%. Project B also requires an investment of $5,000. It will provide cash inflows of $1,360 each year for six years. Its internal rate of return is 16%. Which project should be accepted?

Although project A promises an internal rate of return of 20%, as compared to only 16% for project B, project A is not necessarily preferable over project B. It is preferable *only* if the funds released at the end of the year under project A can be reinvested at a high rate of return in some *other* project for the five remaining years. Otherwise, project B, which promises a return of 16% over the *entire* six years, is more desirable.

Let us assume that the company in this example has an after-tax cost of capital of 12%. The net present value method, with the profitability index, would rank the two proposals as follows:

	Project	
	A	B
Present value of cash inflows:		
$6,000 received at the end of one year at 12% factor (factor of 0.893)	$5,358 (a)	
$1,360 received at the end of each year for six years at 12% (factor of 4.111)		$5,591 (a)
Investment required	$5,000 (b)	$5,000 (b)
Profitability index, (a) ÷ (b)	1.07	1.12

The profitability index indicates that project B is more desirable than project A. This is in fact the case if the funds released from project A at the end of one year can be reinvested at only 12% (the cost of capital). Although the computations will not be shown here, in order for project A to be more desirable than project B, the funds released from project A would have to be reinvested at a rate of return *greater* than 14% for the remaining five years.

In short, the internal rate of return method of ranking tends to favour short-term, high-yield projects, whereas the net present value method of ranking (using the profitability index) tends to favour longer-term projects.

The internal rate of return method is problematic. It assumes that funds can be reinvested at a particular project's yield. The problem becomes apparent in the context of MacInnis Company of Kitchener, Ontario. If MacInnis has projects in Cambridge, Guelph, and Waterloo that have internal rates of return of 20%, 15%, and 10%, respectively, it is nonsense to differentiate among the cash flows and assume that a dollar returned from the Waterloo project will earn less than a dollar returned from the Cambridge project. Obviously, a dollar is a dollar regardless of the project from which it comes. The net present value method does not suffer from this flaw but assumes that funds can be reinvested at the firm's cost of capital. Because the net present value is conceptually superior, it should be used in ranking projects that are mutually exclusive. However, in choosing among projects that have the same net present values, the internal rates of return should be used to rank them. Projects should then be chosen based on the highest internal rates of return.

Although the net present value method is conceptually superior to the internal rate of return method, there are practical reasons for decision makers to choose the latter. Managers typically make project investment decisions within a four- or five-year planning horizon. Faced with this time constraint, projects will be ranked according to their terminal values at the end of the planning horizon. Estimated cash flows after the planning period may be perceived by managers to be too uncertain to be reliable. Projects with larger internal rate of return values will have cash flow patterns with higher short-term terminal values. In summary, although there are problems with the internal rate of return method over the entire life of a project, it will accurately evaluate projects within the planning horizon.

OTHER APPROACHES TO CAPITAL BUDGETING DECISIONS

LEARNING OBJECTIVE 5
Determine the payback period for an investment.

The net present value and internal rate of return methods are widely used as decision-making tools. Other methods of making capital budgeting decisions are also used, however, and are preferred by some managers. In this section, we discuss two such methods, known as *payback* and *simple rate of return.* Both methods have been used for many years but they are now declining in popularity.

The Payback Method

Payback period
The length of time that it takes for a project to recover its initial cost out of the cash receipts that it generates.

The payback method focuses on the *payback period.* The **payback period** is the length of time that it takes for a project to recoup its initial cost out of the cash receipts that it generates. This period is sometimes referred to as "the time that it takes for an investment to pay for itself." The basic premise of the payback method is that the more quickly the cost of an investment can be recovered, the more desirable is the investment.

The payback period is expressed in years. *When the net annual cash inflow is the same every year,* the following formula can be used to compute the payback period:

$$\text{Payback period} = \frac{\text{Investment required}}{\text{Net annual cash inflow*}} \quad (3)$$

*If new equipment is replacing old equipment, this becomes incremental net annual cash inflow.

To illustrate the payback method, assume the following data:

Example H

York Company needs a new milling machine. The company is considering two machines: machine A and machine B. Machine A costs $15,000 and will reduce operating costs by $5,000 per year. Machine B costs only $12,000 but will also reduce operating costs by $5,000 per year.

Which machine should be purchased according to the payback method?

$$\text{Machine A payback period} = \frac{\$15,000}{\$5,000} = 3.0 \text{ years}$$

$$\text{Machine B payback period} = \frac{\$12,000}{\$5,000} = 2.4 \text{ years}$$

According to the payback calculations, York Company should purchase machine B, since it has a shorter payback period than machine A.

Evaluation of the Payback Method

The payback method is not a true measure of the profitability of an investment. Rather, it simply tells the manager how many years will be required to recover the original investment. Unfortunately, a shorter payback period does not always mean that one investment is more desirable than another.

To illustrate, consider again the two machines used in the example above. Since machine B has a shorter payback period than machine A, it *appears* that machine B is more desirable than machine A. But if we add one more piece of data, this illusion quickly disappears. Machine A has a projected 10-year life, and machine B has a projected 5-year life. It would take two purchases of machine B to provide the same length of service as would be provided by a single purchase of machine A. Under these circumstances, machine A would be a much better investment than machine B, even though machine B has a shorter payback period. Unfortunately, the payback method has no inherent mechanism for highlighting differences in useful life between investments. Such differences can be very important, and relying on payback alone may result in incorrect decisions.

A further criticism of the payback method is that it does not adequately consider the time value of money. A cash inflow to be received several years in the future is weighed equally with a cash inflow to be received right now. To illustrate, assume that for an investment of $8,000 you can purchase either of the two following streams of cash inflows:

Year	0	1	2	3	4	5	6	7	8
Stream 1		–0–	–0–	–0–	$8,000	$2,000	$2,000	$2,000	$2,000
Stream 2		$2,000	$2,000	$2,000	$2,000	$8,000	–0–	–0–	–0–

Which stream of cash inflows would you prefer to receive in return for your $8,000 investment? Each stream has a payback period of 4.0 years. Therefore, if payback alone was relied on in making the decision, you would be forced to say that the streams are equally desirable. However, from the point of view of the time value of money, stream 2 is much more desirable than stream 1.

On the other hand, under certain conditions the payback method can be very useful. For one thing, it can help identify which investment proposals are in the "ballpark." That is, it can be used as a screening tool to help answer the question, "Should I consider this proposal further?" If a proposal doesn't provide a payback within some specified period, then there may be no need to consider it further. In addition, the payback period is often of great importance to new firms that are "cash poor." When a firm is cash poor, a project with a short payback period but a low rate of return might be preferred over another project with a high rate of return but a long payback period. The reason is that the company may simply need a faster return of its cash investment. And finally, the payback method is sometimes used in industries where products become obsolete very rapidly—such as consumer electronics. Since products may last only a year or two, the payback period on investments must be very short.

FOCUS *on Current Practice*

Investing in an energy solution can benefit hotels in many ways ranging from conservation to guest satisfaction (GSI) according to research conducted by Direct Energy Business Services. Hotels that have recently invested in total energy management solutions have also reduced their operating costs by as much as 24% per annum. With larger hotels, this equates to approximately $1.5 million per year, or an average of $644 per room per year.

The research, conducted with hotel properties across Canada whose energy management projects varied widely, shows that paying close attention to this back-of-house strategy that encompasses how a property buys, converts, uses and disposes of its energy, usually has a payback of three to five years and attractive ROI of up to 33%. For one hotel whose solution had a price tag of more than $3.7 million and resulted in savings of more than $650,000 per annum, when combined with incentives the simple payback was 5.6 years. In particular projects like lighting upgrades or automation can return investments in less than four years.

Source: Excerpted from "New Research Shows Managing Energy Benefits, ROI, Conservation and Guest Satisfaction," *Direct Energy Business Services*, Feb. 15, 2005.

An Extended Example of Payback

As shown by formula (3) given earlier, the payback period is computed by dividing the investment in a project by the net annual cash inflows that the project will generate. If new equipment is replacing old equipment, then any salvage value to be received on disposal of the old equipment should be deducted from the cost of the new equipment, and only the *incremental* investment should be used in the payback computation. In addition, any depreciation deducted in arriving at the project's net operating income must be added back to obtain the project's expected net annual cash inflow. To illustrate, consider the following data:

Example I

Goodtime Fun Centres, Inc. operates amusement parks. Some of the vending machines in one of its parks provide very little revenue, so the company is considering removing the machines and installing equipment to dispense soft ice cream. The equipment would cost $80,000 and have an eight-year useful life. Incremental annual revenues and costs associated with the sale of ice cream would be as follows:

Sales	$150,000
Less cost of ingredients	90,000
Contribution margin	60,000
Less fixed expenses:	
Salaries	27,000
Maintenance	3,000
Depreciation	10,000
Total fixed expenses	40,000
Net operating income	$ 20,000

The vending machines can be sold for a $5,000 scrap value. The company will not purchase equipment unless it has a payback period of three years or less. Does the equipment to dispense ice cream pass this hurdle?

An analysis of the payback period for the proposed equipment is given in Exhibit 14-11. Several things should be noted. First, depreciation is added back to net operating income to obtain the net annual cash inflow from the new equipment. Depreciation is not a cash outlay; thus, it must be added back to adjust net operating income to a cash basis. Second,

EXHIBIT 14–11 Computation of the Payback Period

Step 1: *Compute the net annual cash inflow.* Since the net annual cash inflow is not given, it must be completed before the payback period can be determined:

Net operating income (given above)	$20,000
Add: Noncash deduction for depreciation	10,000
Net annual cash inflow	$30,000

Step 2: *Compute the payback period.* Using the net annual cash inflow figure from above, the payback period can be determined as follows:

Cost of the new equipment	$80,000
Less salvage value of old equipment	5,000
Investment required	$75,000

$$\text{Payback period} = \frac{\text{Investment required}}{\text{Net annual cash inflow}}$$

$$= \frac{\$75{,}000}{\$30{,}000} = 2.5 \text{ years}$$

the payback computation deducts the salvage value of the old machines from the cost of the new equipment so that only the incremental investment is used in computing the payback period.

Since the proposed equipment has a payback period of less than three years, the company's payback requirement has been met.

Payback and Uneven Cash Flows

When the cash flows associated with an investment project change from year to year, the simple payback formula that we outlined earlier is no longer usable, and the computations involved in deriving the payback period can be fairly complex. Consider the following data:

Year	Investment	Cash Inflow
1	$4,000	$1,000
2		–0–
3		2,000
4	2,000	1,000
5		500
6		3,000
7		2,000
8		2,000

What is the payback period on this investment? The answer is 5.5 years, but to obtain this figure it is necessary to track the unrecovered investment year by year. The steps involved in this process are shown in Exhibit 14–12. By the middle of the sixth year, sufficient cash inflows will have been realized to recover the entire investment of $6,000 ($4,000 + $2,000).

The Simple Rate of Return Method

LEARNING OBJECTIVE **6**
Compute the simple rate of return for an investment.

Simple rate of return
The rate of return computed by dividing a project's annual accounting net income by the initial investment required.

The **simple rate of return** method is another capital budgeting technique that does not involve discounted cash flows. The method is also known as the *accounting rate of return,* or *the unadjusted rate of return.*

Unlike the other capital budgeting methods that we have discussed, the simple rate of return method does not focus on cash flows. Rather, it focuses on accounting net income. The approach is to estimate the revenues that will be generated by a proposed investment and then deduct from these revenues all of the projected operating expenses associated with the project. This net operating income figure is then related to the initial investment in the project, as shown in the following formula:

$$\text{Simple rate of return} = \frac{\text{Incremental revenues} - \text{Incremental expenses, including depreciation} = \text{Incremental net income}}{\text{Initial investment*}} \qquad (4)$$

*The investment should be reduced by any salvage from the sale of old equipment.

Or, if a cost reduction project is involved, the formula becomes:

$$\text{Simple rate of return} = \frac{\text{Cost savings} - \text{Depreciation on new equipment}}{\text{Initial investment*}} \qquad (5)$$

*The investment should be reduced by any salvage from the sale of old equipment.

EXHIBIT 14–12 Payback and Uneven Cash Flows

Year	(1) Beginning Unrecovered Investment	(2) Additional Investment	(3) Total Unrecovered Investment (1) + (2)	(4) Cash Inflow	(5) Ending Unrecovered Investment (3) − (4)
1	$4,000		$4,000	$1,000	$3,000
2	3,000		3,000	–0–	3,000
3	3,000		3,000	2,000	1,000
4	1,000	$2,000	3,000	1,000	2,000
5	2,000		2,000	500	1,500
6	1,500		1,500	3,000	–0–
7	–0–		–0–	2,000	–0–
8	–0–		–0–	2,000	–0–

Example J

Brigham Tea, Inc. is a processor of a low-acid tea. The company is contemplating purchasing equipment for an additional processing line. The additional processing line would increase revenues by $90,000 per year. Incremental cash operating expenses would be $40,000 per year. The equipment would cost $180,000 and have a nine-year life. No salvage value is projected.

The simple rate of return for this example is calculated as follows:

$$\text{Simple rate of return} = \frac{\begin{bmatrix}\$90{,}000\\ \text{Incremental}\\ \text{revenues}\end{bmatrix} - \begin{bmatrix}\$40{,}000 \text{ Cash operating expenses}\\ + \$20{,}000 \text{ Depreciation}\end{bmatrix}}{\$180{,}000 \text{ Initial investment}}$$

$$= \frac{\$30{,}000}{\$180{,}000}$$

$$= 16.7\%$$

Example K

Midwest Farms, Inc. hires people on a part-time basis to sort eggs. The cost of this hand-sorting process is $30,000 per year. The company is investigating the purchase of an egg-sorting machine that would cost $90,000 and have a 15-year useful life. The machine would have negligible salvage value, and it would cost $10,000 per year to operate and maintain. The egg-sorting equipment currently being used could be sold now for a scrap value of $2,500.

A cost reduction project is involved in this situation. By applying the formula for the simple rate of return found in equation (5), we can compute the simple rate of return as follows:

$$\text{Simple rate of return} = \frac{\$20{,}000^{*} \text{ Cost savings} - \$6{,}000 \text{ Depreciation on new equipment}}{\$90{,}000 - \$2{,}500}$$

$$= 16.0\%$$

*$30,000 − $10,000 = $20,000 cost savings.
†$90,000 ÷ 15 years = $6,000 depreciation.

Criticisms of the Simple Rate of Return

The most damaging criticism of the simple rate of return method is that it does not adequately consider the time value of money. The simple rate of return method considers a dollar received 10 years from now just as valuable as a dollar received today. Thus, the simple rate of return can be misleading if the alternatives being considered have different cash flow patterns. For example, assume that project A has a high simple rate of return but yields the bulk of its cash flows many years from now. Another project, B, has a somewhat lower simple rate of return but yields the bulk of its cash flows over the next few years. Project A has a higher simple rate of return than project B; however, project B might in fact be a much better investment if the time value of money was considered. In contrast, the net present value method provides a single result that summarizes all of the cash flows over the entire useful life of the project.

Behavioural Considerations

The chapter thus far has emphasized the technical aspects of capital budgeting. The management accountant should also be cognizant of important behavioural considerations. An understanding of the functional and dysfunctional consequences of human input provides deeper insight into the whole capital budgeting process.

Capital budgeting projects require creativity, judgement, and the ability to see ideas through to implementation. The entire capital budgeting process from idea generation to implementation can provide valuable training for managers. There may be non-financial reasons for accepting certain projects. Some marginal projects may be accepted because they provide good experience and training benefits.

Estimates of cash flows, discount rates, and salvage values may be affected by the attitudes of individual managers toward risk. Risk-averse managers tend to use more conservative figures in their estimates than those managers who tend to seek risk and take on more venturesome projects.

The micropolitics of organizations may also affect the capital budgeting process. Key managers may favour their own pet projects. Self-identification with projects may obscure management judgement of when to abandon a particular project. Obtaining truthful estimates may become problematic. Internal politics may also influence how projects are awarded. With only limited company funds available for capital investments, a division with several good investment proposals may be denied acceptance of some proposals for less profitable projects of other divisions. Such sharing of projects may be seen as necessary to maintain harmony and to give the appearance of fairness.

The capital budgeting process itself may create additional pressure on top management. Projects often have to go through several layers of approval before reaching top management. It may be difficult to reject projects already approved by managers at lower levels. On the other hand, some projects rejected at lower levels, and thus never to reach the purview of top management, may actually be acceptable to top management because they help diversify the firm's overall risk.

Projects involving employee safety, or environmental or consumer safety, or which impact heavily on the firm's social environment may have to be evaluated by non-financial criteria. Other projects that cannot be justified on financial grounds may have to be undertaken in order to conform to municipal, provincial, or federal laws.

Unethical behaviour involving nepotism or kickbacks sometimes occurs. The management accountant has an ethical responsibility to communicate information fairly and objectively. All relevant information, favourable or unfavourable, should be fully disclosed so as not to bias or undermine the decision-making process. Assumptions regarding cash flows, probabilities, salvage value, etc., should be clearly communicated. The management accountant is expected to act with full integrity and should avoid situations that could prejudice his or her ability to perform capital budgeting analysis in an ethical manner.

Capital budgeting can also be affected by the firm's performance reward system. If too much weight is given to short-term performance measures, there is little incentive for managers to devote time and effort to long-term capital budgeting projects.

In summary, the capital budgeting process involves more factors than first meet the eye. A purely quantitative approach to capital budgeting is not sufficient. Any model developed to solve capital budgeting problems is not broad enough to encompass all decision variables. Important qualitative factors imposed on the process by the political and social environment within the firm may strongly influence capital budgeting decisions. All levels of management should take a broad view, and reward systems within the firm should be flexible enough to encourage the acceptance of projects that lead to optimal capital investment decisions.

POST-APPRAISAL OF INVESTMENT PROJECTS

Post-appraisal
Following up on a project that has been approved to see if expected results are realized.

A *post-appraisal* should be conducted after an investment project has been approved and implemented. A **post-appraisal** involves checking whether or not expected results are actually realized. This is a key part of the capital budgeting process that helps keep managers committed to their investment proposals. Any tendency to inflate the benefits or downplay the costs in a proposal should become evident after the post-appraisal. The post-appraisal also provides an opportunity to reinforce and possibly expand successful projects and to cut losses on floundering projects.

The same technique should be used in the post-appraisal that was used in the original approval process. That is, if a project was approved on the basis of a net present value analysis, then the same procedure should be used in performing the post-appraisal. However, the data used in the post-appraisal analysis should be *actual observed data* rather than estimated data. This gives management an opportunity to make a side-by-side comparison to see how well the project has succeeded. It also helps assure that estimated data received on future proposals will be carefully prepared, since the persons submitting the data will know that their estimates will be given careful scrutiny in the post-appraisal process.

Monitoring of capital budgeting projects may also help improve the quality of similar investment proposals. Care should be exercised, however, when trying to use past experience as a guide to future decisions because assumptions about the business environment may no longer be valid.

FOCUS *on Current Practice*

The post-appraisal process can be applied in the context of *economic value creation* (EVA®). Economic value is a financial performance measure based on a firm's residual wealth calculated by deducting cost of capital from its net operating profit[1] after taxes as expressed by the following formula:

EVA = NOPAT – Capital charge

For example, assume that a firm employing $2,500,000 of capital with a 15% cost of capital reports a net operating profit after taxes of $1,000,000. EVA would equal $625,000.

EVA® = $1,000,000 – (15% × $2,500,000) = $625,000

1. It is common to adjust NOPAT for so called "accounting distortions" affecting inventory, deferred taxes and intangibles. Adjustments, for example, include capitalizing operating leases and adding back Research and Development cost and other intangible costs.

When considering strategic or major operating decisions, 15 (73%) of the respondents in a recent Canadian study indicated that they "always" or "often" explicitly use EVA to evaluate their decisions.

Supporters of EVA claim that it allows managers to measure actual value creation performance and that EVA tracks shareholder wealth better than traditional accounting measures such as net income or earnings per share. The Canadian study found inconclusive evidence on whether the effect of EVA actually brings about greater shareholder value. Of the companies surveyed 50% were underperforming their TSX sectoral indices. Of the other 50%, 36% are outperforming their TSX sectoral indices, and the remaining companies were at a similar level with comparable companies that did not use EVA.

Source: Howard Armitage, Ellen Wong, and Alan Douglas, "The Pursuit of Value," *CMA Management Accounting Magazine*, November 2003.

To avoid a liquidity crunch, the firm must respond quickly to significant overruns that require unplanned cash outflows. It may be necessary to arrange additional financing or to amend plans.

The post-appraisal should answer a variety of questions: Was the capital budgeting decision consistent with overall corporate strategy? Did the project meet the specifications that were set out in the appropriation request? Were the original specifications realistically and honestly determined? Were any additional expenditures properly authorized? A proper review may be tedious and time-consuming, and special care should be taken in making assertions about cause and effect. It is often difficult to relate particular costs and revenues to a specific project. This is especially true if there are several projects on-line simultaneously and is absolutely true if there is synergy among the projects.[9] A cost/benefit trade-off is necessary when deciding how many company sources are to be devoted to the post-appraisal.

To ensure objectivity, the post-appraisal should be performed by an individual or team that has not been directly involved in the actual project. The post-appraisal should not be a witch hunt aimed at placing blame, but should be an accountability process aimed at improving control and a learning process that will improve estimates of future projects.

In performing a post-appraisal, the same technique should be used as was used in the original approval process. That is, if a project was approved on a basis of a net present value analysis, then the same procedure should be used in performing the post-appraisal. However, the data going into the analysis should be *actual data* as observed in the actual operation of the project, rather than estimated data. This gives management an opportunity to make a side-by-side comparison to see how well the project has worked out. It also helps assure that estimated data received on future proposals will be carefully prepared, since the persons submitting the data know that their estimates will be given careful scrutiny in the post-appraisal process. Actual results that are far out of line with original estimates should be carefully reviewed by management, and corrective action taken as necessary. In accordance with the management by exception principle, those managers responsible for the original estimates should be required to provide a full explanation of any major differences between estimated and actual results.

9. Synergy occurs when the projects working together generate greater revenue than the sum of the revenues of all projects acting independently.

SUMMARY

Investment decisions should take into account the time value of money, since a dollar today is more valuable than a dollar received in the future. The net present value and internal rate of return methods both reflect this fact. In the net present value method, future cash flows are discounted to their present value so that they can be compared on a valid basis with current cash outlays. The difference between the present value of the cash inflows and the present value of the cash outflows is called the project's *net present value*. If the net present value of the project is negative, the project is rejected. The discount rate in the net present value method is usually a minimum required rate of return, such as the company's cost of capital.

The internal rate of return is the rate of return that equates the present value of the cash inflows and the present value of the cash outflows, resulting in a zero net present value. If the internal rate of return is less than the company's minimum required rate of return, the project is rejected.

After rejecting projects whose net present values are negative or whose internal rates of return are less than the minimum required rate of return, the company may still have more projects than can be supported with available funds. The remaining projects can be ranked using either the profitability index or their internal rates of return. The profitability index is computed by dividing the present value of the project's future net cash inflows by the required initial investment.

Some companies prefer to use either payback or the simple rate of return to evaluate investment proposals. The payback period is the number of periods required to recover the initial investment in the project. The simple rate of return is determined by dividing a project's accounting net income by the initial investment in the project.

After an investment proposal has been approved, a post-appraisal should be performed to see whether expected results are actually being realized. This is a key part of the capital budgeting process, since it tends to strengthen the quality of the estimates going into investment proposals and affords management with an early opportunity to recognize any developing problems or opportunities.

REVIEW PROBLEM: COMPARISON OF CAPITAL BUDGETING METHODS

Lamar Company is studying a project that would have an eight-year life and require a $2,400,000 investment in equipment. At the end of eight years, the project would terminate and the equipment would have no salvage value. The project would provide net operating income each year as follows:

Sales		$3,000,000
Less variable expenses		1,800,000
Contribution margin		1,200,000
Less fixed expenses:		
Advertising, salaries, and other fixed out-of-pocket costs	$700,000	
Depreciation	200,000	
Total fixed expenses		900,000
Net operating income		$ 300,000

The company's discount rate is 12%.

Required:

1. Compute the net annual cash inflow from the project.
2. Compute the project's net present value. Is the project acceptable?
3. Compute the project's internal rate of return.
4. Compute the project's payback period. If the company requires a maximum payback of three years, is the project acceptable?
5. Compute the project's simple rate of return.

Solution to the Review Problem

1. The net annual cash inflow can be computed by deducting the cash expenses from sales:

Sales	$3,000,000
Less variable expenses	1,800,000
Contribution margin	1,200,000
Less advertising, salaries, and other fixed out-of-pocket costs	700,000
Net annual cash inflow	$ 500,000

Or it can be computed by adding depreciation back to net operating income:

Net operating income	$300,000
Add: Non-cash deduction for depreciation	200,000
Net annual cash inflow	$500,000

2. The net present value can be computed as follows:

Item	Year(s)	Amount of Cash Flows	12% Factor	Present Value of Cash Flows
Cost of new equipment	Now	$(2,400,000)	1.000	$(2,400,000)
Net annual cash inflow	1–8	500,000	4.968	2,484,000
Net present value				$ 84,000

Yes, the project is acceptable since it has a positive net present value.

3. The formula for computing the factor of the internal rate of return is:

$$\text{Factor of the internal rate of return} = \frac{\text{Investment required}}{\text{Net annual cash inflow}}$$

$$= \frac{\$2,400,000}{\$500,000} = 4.800$$

Looking in Exhibit 14–19 in Appendix 14A at the end of the chapter and scanning along the 8-period line, we find that a factor of 4.800 represents a rate of about 13%:

4. The formula for the payback period is:

$$\text{Payback period} = \frac{\text{Investment required}}{\text{Net annual cash inflow}}$$

$$= \frac{\$2,400,000}{\$500,000}$$

$$= 4.8 \text{ years}$$

5. The formula for the simple rate of return is:

$$\text{Simple rate of return} = \frac{\text{Incremental revenues} - \text{Incremental expenses, including depreciation}}{\text{Initial investment}} = \text{Net income}$$

$$= \frac{\$300,000}{\$2,400,000}$$

$$= 8.3\%$$

APPENDIX 14A: THE CONCEPT OF PRESENT VALUE

LEARNING OBJECTIVE 7
Understand present value concepts and the use of present value tables.

The point was made in the main body of the chapter that a manager would rather receive a dollar today than a year from now. There are two reasons why this is true. First, a dollar received today is more valuable than a dollar received a year from now. The dollar received today can be invested immediately, and by the end of the year it will have earned some return, making the total amount in hand at the end of the year *greater* than the initial investment. The person receiving the dollar a year from now will simply have a dollar in hand at that time.

Second, the future involves uncertainty. The longer people have to wait to receive a dollar, the more uncertain it becomes that they will ever get the dollar. As time passes, conditions change. The changes may make future payments of the dollar impossible.

Since money has a time value, the manager needs a method of determining whether a cash outlay made now in an investment project can be justified in terms of expected receipts from the project in future years. That is, the manager must have a means of expressing future receipts in present dollar terms so that the future receipts can be compared *on an equivalent basis* with whatever investment is required in the project under consideration. The theory of interest provides managers with the means of making such a comparison.

The Theory of Interest

If a bank pays $105 one year from now in return for a deposit of $100 now, we would say that the bank is paying interest at an annual rate of 5%. The relationships involved in this notion can be expressed in mathematical terms by means of the following equation:

$$F_1 = P(1 + r) \tag{6}$$

where F_1 = the amount to be received in one year, P = the present outlay to be made, and r = the rate of interest involved.

If the present outlay is $100 deposited in a bank savings account that is to earn interest at 5%, then P = $100 and r = 0.05. Under these conditions, F_1 = $105, the amount to be received in one year.

Present value
The value now of an amount that will be received in some future period.

The $100 present outlay is called the **present value** of the $105 amount to be received in one year. It is also known as the *discounted value* of the future $105 receipt. The $100 figure represents the value in present terms of a receipt of $105 to be received a year from now when the interest rate is 5%.

Compound Interest What if the investor leaves her or his money in the bank for a second year? In that case, by the end of the second year, the original $100 deposit will have grown to $110.25:

Original deposit	$100.00
Interest for the first year:	
$100 × 0.05.	5.00
Amount at the end of the first year	105.00
Interest for the second year:	
$105 × 0.05.	5.25
Amount at the end of the second year	$110.25

Compound interest
The process of paying interest on interest in an investment.

Notice that the interest for the second year is $5.25, as compared to only $5 for the first year. The reason for the greater interest earned during the second year is that during the second year, interest is being paid *on interest.* That is, the $5 interest earned during the first year has been left in the account and has been added to the original $100 deposit in computing interest for the second year. This concept is known as **compound interest.** The compounding we have done is annual compounding. Interest can be compounded on a semi-annual, quarterly, or even more frequent basis. Many savings institutions are now compounding interest on a daily basis. The more frequently compounding is done, the more rapidly the invested balance will grow.

How is the concept of compound interest expressed in equation form? It is expressed by taking equation (6) and adjusting it to state the number of years, n, that a sum is going to be left deposited in the bank:

$$F_n = P(1 + r)^n \tag{7}$$

where n = years.

If $n = 2$ years, then our computation of the value of F in two years will be as follows:

$$F_2 = \$100(1 + 0.05)^2$$
$$F_2 = \$110.25$$

Present Value and Future Value Exhibit 14–13 shows the relationship between present value and future value as expressed in the theory of interest equations. As shown in the exhibit, if \$100 is deposited in a bank at 5% interest, it will grow to \$127.63 by the end of five years if interest is compounded annually.

Example L

A purchaser promises to pay \$96,800 two years from now for a lot of land. This amount includes interest at an annual rate of 10%. What is the selling price of the land today?

As indicated in Exhibit 14–18 (10% column, down two rows) the present value of \$1 is \$0.826. The present value of \$96,800 is \$79,956.80 (\$96,800 × .826). A more accurate answer is found as follows:

$$P = \$96{,}800(1 + .10)^{-2}$$
$$= \$80{,}000$$

Example M

A young woman in Vancouver plans to take a vacation trip four years from now. She estimates that she will need \$18,000. At an annual interest rate of 16%, compounded quarterly, how much must be deposited into a bank account today to accumulate the required \$18,000?

Because interest is compounded quarterly, the interest per period is 4% (the annual rate divided by four quarters). As shown in Exhibit 14–18, the present value of \$1 to be received 16 periods in the future at 4% interest is \$0.534. The present value of \$18,000

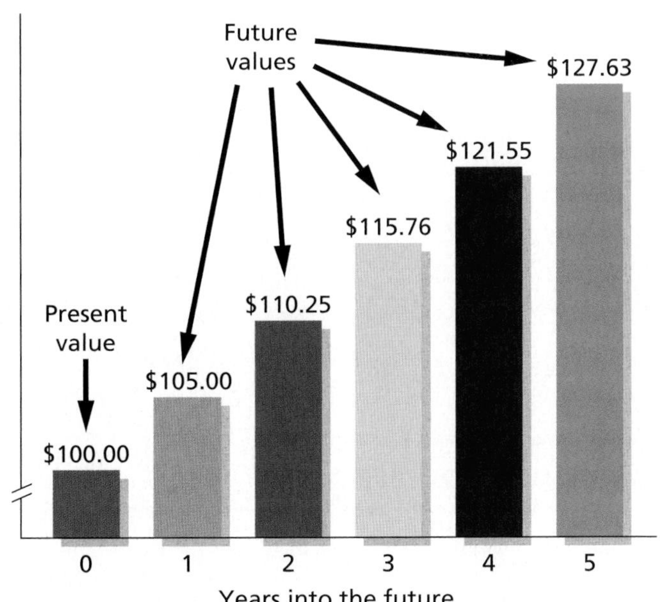

EXHIBIT 14–13
The Relationship between Present Value and Future Value

is, therefore, \$18,000 × .534, which is \$9,612. The calculator solution is \$18,000 × $(1 + 04)^{-16}$, which equals \$9,610.35.

Present Value of a Series of Cash Flows (Annuity)

Annuity
A series, or stream, of identical cash flows.

The present value of an **annuity** is the percent value of a series of equal payments or receipts discounted at compound interest and made at regular intervals. Stated differently, it is the sum that allows the withdrawal of a series of equal amounts at regular intervals if left at compound interest.

The present value of \$1 to be received at the end of each of four periods at 8% interest per period is shown graphically in Exhibit 14–14.

Two points are important in connection with Exhibit 14–14. First, notice that the farther we go forward in time, the smaller is the present value of the \$1 interest receipt. The present value of \$1 received a year from now is \$0.926, as compared to only \$0.735 for the \$1 interest payment to be received four periods from now. This point simply underscores the fact that money has a time value.

The second point is that even though the computations involved in Exhibit 14–14 are accurate, they have involved unnecessary work. The same present value of \$3.312 could have been obtained more easily by referring to Exhibit 14–19 (8% column, down four rows). Exhibit 14–19 contains the present value of \$1 to be received each year over a *series* of years at various interest rates. Exhibit 14–19 has been derived by simply adding together the factors from Exhibit 14–18.

The mathematical formula for the present value (P_n) of an annuity of \$1 per period compounded at the rate of r for n periods is:

$$P_n = \frac{1 - (1 + r)^{-n}}{r} \text{ or } \frac{1 - (1 + .08)^{-4}}{.08} = \$3.312$$

Example N

What is the present value of a series of six semi-annual payments of \$2,000 at 8% interest compounded annually? Assume that it is now January 1, 2000, and the first payment is made on June 30, 2000.

The purpose of solving this problem could be to determine (1) the sum that will provide for six semi-annual withdrawals of \$2,000 if invested at 4% per period (8% divided by two interest periods per year), and (2) the sum that is payable in settlement of a series of obligations of \$2,000 that are due at six semi-annual intervals and discounted at 4% per period. Using Exhibit 14–19 (4% column, down six periods) the value 5.242 is found.

EXHIBIT 14–14 Effect of Quality Costs on Quality of Conformance

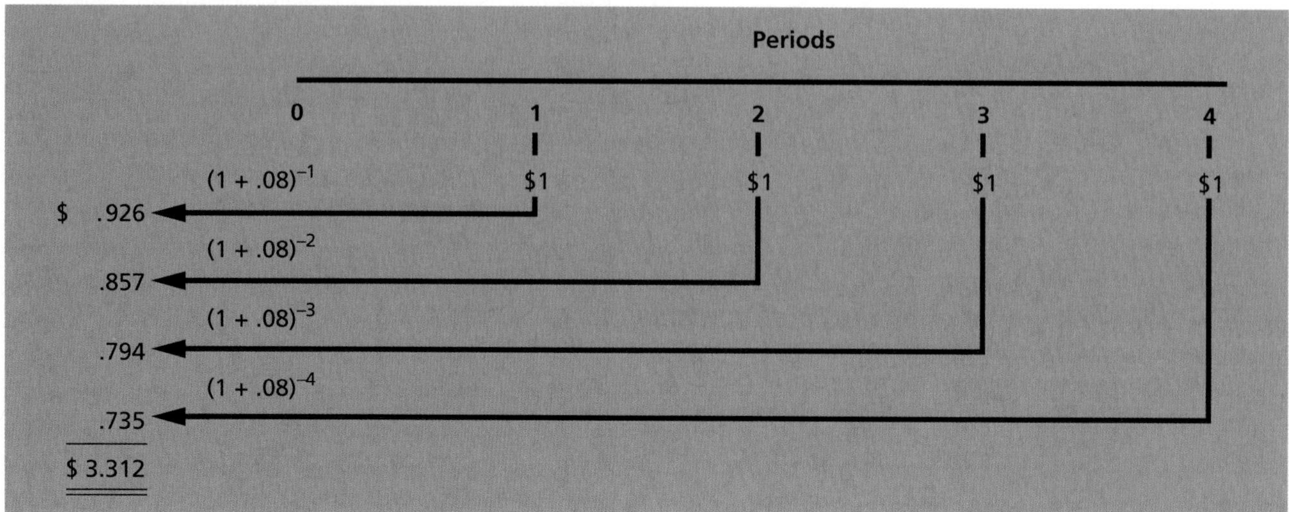

This present value of an annuity of $1 factor is then multiplied by $2,000 to give $10,484. Alternatively, using the present value of an ordinary annuity (annuity in arrears) formula:

$$P_n = \frac{1 - (1 + .04)^{-6}}{.04} \times \$2,000 = \$10,484.27$$

Example O

How much money would a company be willing to invest in a project that would return $3,000 every three months for three years, and in addition, a lump sum of $20,000 at the end of the third year? The receipts begin three months from now. Interest is 16% per annum.

The $3,000 to be received at the end of each three-month period is an ordinary annuity. The number of interest periods is 12 (4 per year for three years) and the quarterly interest rate is 4% (16%/4 periods). Using Exhibit 14–19 (4% column, down 12 rows) the value of 9.385 is found. The present value of this annuity is $28,155 (9.385 × $3,000). The present value of the single sum of $20,000 is .625 (Exhibit 14–18, 4% column, down 12 rows) × $20,000, or $12,500. The present value of the series of receipts and the single lump sum is, therefore, $28,155 + $12,500, which totals $40,655.

Present Value of an Annuity Due

An annuity due is one in which the payments or receipts occur at the *beginning* of each period. Exhibit 14–15 compares the present value of an ordinary annuity of $1 for four periods with the present value of an annuity due for $1 for four periods. The interest rate is assumed to be 8%.

Computation of Present Value

An investment can be viewed in two ways: either in terms of its future value or in terms of its present value. We have seen from our computations above that if we know the present value of a sum (such as our $100 deposit), it is a relatively simple task to compute the sum's future value in n years by using equation (7). But what if the tables are reversed, and we know the *future* value of some amount but we do not know its present value?

For example, assume that you are to receive $200 two years from now. You know that the future value of this sum is $200, since this is the amount that you will be receiving in two years. But what is the sum's present value—what is it worth *right now?* The present value of any sum to be received in the future can be computed by turning equation (7) around and solving for P:

$$P = \frac{F_n}{(1 + r)^n} \qquad (8)$$

In our example, F = $200 (the amount to be received in the future), $r = 0.05$ (the rate of interest), and $n = 2$ (the number of years in the future that the amount is to be received):

$$P = \frac{\$200}{(1 + 0.05)^2}$$

$$P = \frac{\$200}{1.1025}$$

$$P = \$181.40$$

As shown by the computation above, the present value of a $200 amount to be received two years from now is $181.40 if the interest rate is 5%. In effect, we are saying that $181.40 received *right now* is equivalent to $200 received two years from now if the rate of return is 5%. The $181.40 and the $200 are just two ways of looking at the same item.

EXHIBIT 14–15 Present Value of an Ordinary Annuity and an Annuity Due

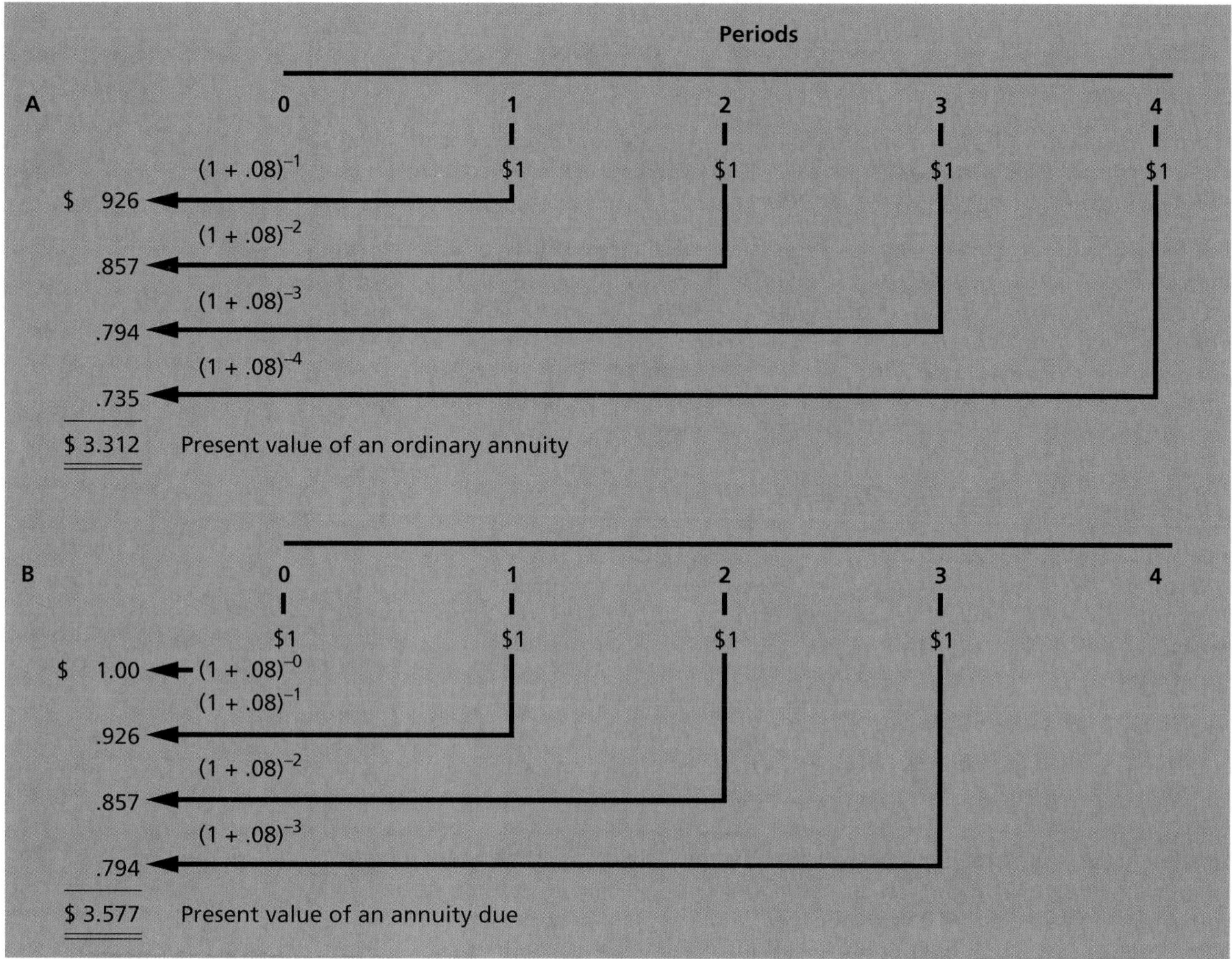

Discounting
The process of finding the present value of a future cash flow.

Discount rate
The rate of return that is used to find the present value of a future cash flow.

The process of finding the present value of a future cash flow, which we have just completed, is called **discounting.** We have *discounted* the $200 to its present value of $181.40. The 5% interest figure that we have used to find this present value is called the **discount rate.** Discounting of future sums to their present value is a common practice in business. A knowledge of the present value of a sum to be received in the future can be very useful to the manager, particularly in making capital budgeting decisions.

If you have a power key (y^x) on your calculator, the above calculations are fairly easy. However, some of the present value formulas we will be using are more complex and difficult to use. Fortunately, tables are available in which the calculations have already been done for you. For example, Exhibit 14–18 shows the discounted present value of $1 to be received at various periods in the future at various interest rates. The table indicates that the present value of $1 to be received two periods from now at 5% is 0.907. Since in our example we want to know the present value of $200 rather than just $1, we need to multiply the factor in the table by $200:

$$\$200 \times 0.907 = \$181.40$$

The answer we obtain is the same answer as we obtained earlier using the formula in equation (8).

Note that part B of Exhibit 14–15 can be interpreted as an ordinary annuity for $1 for three periods ($0.926 + $0.857 + $0.794) to which we add $1. We can calculate the present value of an annuity due by subtracting one period from n and calculating the present value of an ordinary annuity for $n - 1$ period. We then add \$1 to this annuity factor, which now gives the present value factor of an annuity due of \$1.

Example P

On February 1, 2005, Vacon Company signed an 18-month lease with Aucoin Leasing Company. The lease payments begin immediately. Calculate the present value of the lease, assuming that \$2,000 is paid each quarter and that the annual interest rate is 16%.

We can solve this problem by first determining the present value of an ordinary annuity for $n - 1$ periods, where n is equal to six periods (18 months = six quarters:)

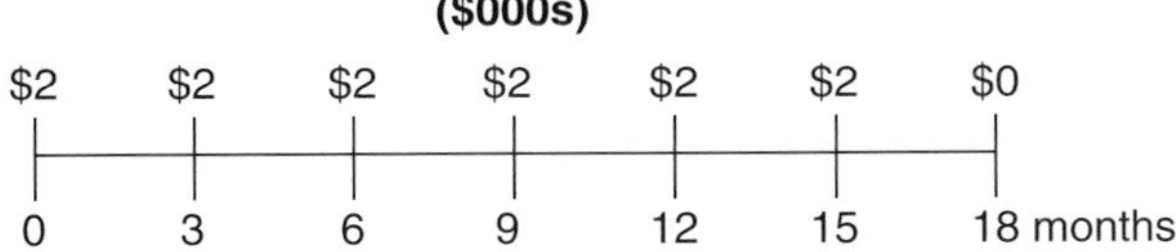

Using Exhibit 14–19, the present value of an annuity factor for five periods ($n - 1$) is 4.452 (4% column, five rows down). To this factor we add 1, resulting in an interest factor of 5.452. Next, we multiply the \$2,000 payments by 5.452 to arrive at \$10,904, the present value of the lease payments. Using the formula approach, the present value of an annuity due is as follows (calculator solution):

$$\begin{aligned} \text{PV(due)} &= \$2{,}000 \times \left[1 + \frac{(1 - (1 + .04)^{-5}}{.04}\right] \\ &= \$2{,}000 \times \ (1 + 4.4518223) \\ &= \$2{,}000 \times \ 5.4518223 \\ &= \$10{,}903.65 \end{aligned}$$

Deferred Annuities

A deferred annuity is one in which the first payment or receipt does not begin until more than one interest period has expired. This is common for capital expenditure decisions that may take several periods to become operational.

Example Q

What is the present value on January 1, 2005, of a series of five receipts of \$1,000, the first of which is expected to be received on January 1, 2008? The interest rate is 10% per annum.

A graphical representation of the problem is as follows:

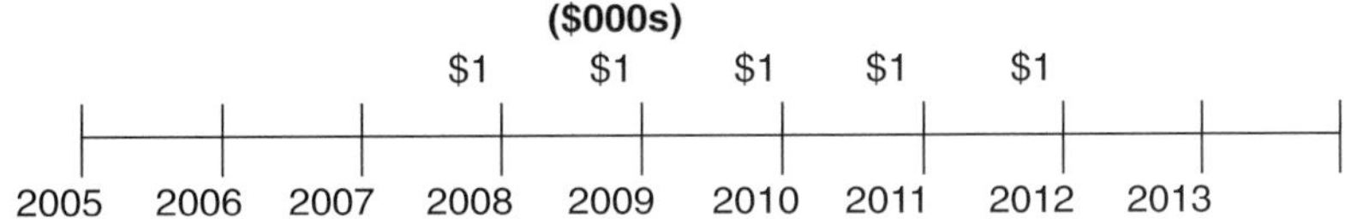

One way of solving this problem is by the following two-step procedure:

Step 1. Calculate the present value on January 1, 2007, of an ordinary annuity of a series of five receipts of \$1,000. This is \$1,000 times 3.791, or \$3,791.

Step 2. The problem is now translated into a simple present value problem, depicted as follows:

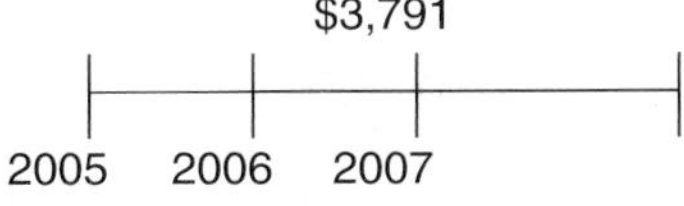

The present value on January 1, 2005, can now be computed by discounting the \$3,791 back two interest periods:

$$\text{PV (January 1, 2005)} = \$3{,}791(1 + .10)^{-2}$$
$$= \$3{,}133$$

This problem could have also been solved by adding fictitious receipts on January 1, 2006, and on January 1, 2007, and calculating the present value of an ordinary annuity on January 1, 2005, for seven periods and then subtracting the present value of the receipts that did not occur:

Step 1:

$$\$1{,}000 \times \frac{(1 - (1 + .10)^{-7})}{.10}$$
$$= \$4{,}868$$

Step 2:

$$\$4{,}868 - \left(\$1{,}000 \times \frac{(1 - (1 + .10)^{-2})}{.10}\right)$$
$$= \$4{,}868 - \$1{,}735$$
$$= \$3{,}133$$

Future Value of an Annuity

Business transactions often involve a series of equal payments spaced evenly apart. As discussed earlier in the chapter, a series of equal payments at regular intervals is known as an *annuity*. The total that becomes due immediately after the last payment is the amount of an ordinary annuity or an annuity in arrears. If the payments are made or received at the beginning of the first interest period, the annuity is termed an *annuity due* or an *annuity in advance*.

The distinction between an ordinary annuity and an annuity due is presented graphically as follows:

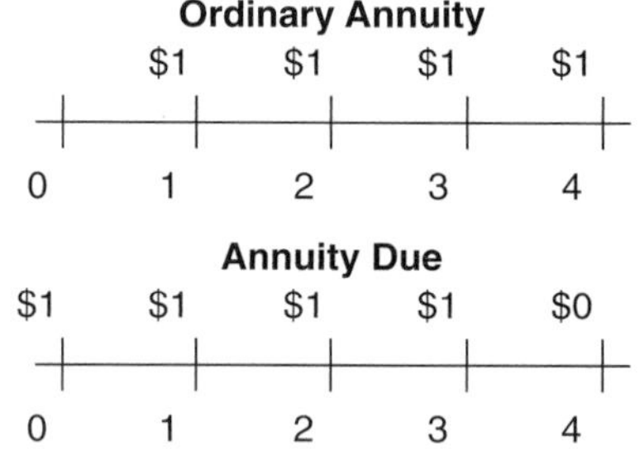

To illustrate how the future value of an ordinary annuity is determined, assume that $1 is deposited in a savings account at the end of each of four periods at 8% per period:

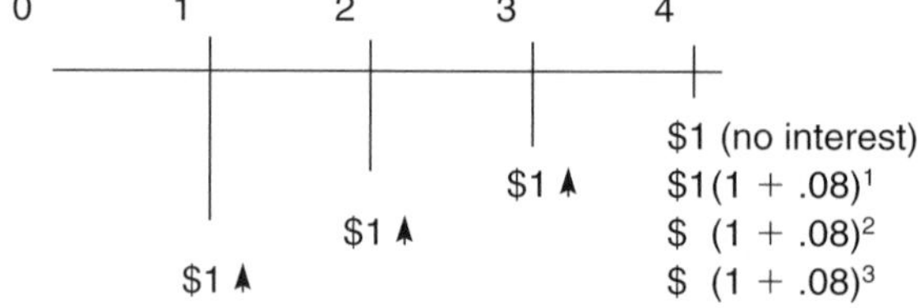

Thus, the value of an ordinary annuity of $1 due at the end of each period for four periods is:

$$\$1 + \$1\,(1 + .08)^1 + \$1(1 + .08)^2 + \$1(1 + .08)^3 =$$
$$\$1 + \quad \$1.08 \quad + \quad \$1.1664 \quad + \quad \$1.2597 \quad = \$4.5061$$

From the preceding illustration it can be seen that the $1 deposited at the end of the first year accumulates interest for a total of three periods, increasing to a value of $1.2597. The deposit at the end of the second year grows to $1.1664, and the $1 deposited at the end of the third period accumulates to \$1.08. The \$1 deposited at the end of the fourth period has not yet earned any interest. The series of four payments of \$1 each period grows to \$4.5061 at the end of the fourth period.

This problem can be solved quickly by using a mathematical expression based on a geometric progression. The future value of an annuity in arrears (F_n) compounded at an interest rate (r) for a given number of periods (n) is:

$$F_n = \frac{(1 + r)^n - 1}{r} \tag{9}$$

The value of a series of \$1 deposits made at the end of each of four years compounded at 8% annually is:

$$F_n = \$1 \times \frac{(1 + .08)^4 - 1}{.08} = \$4.5061$$

The same calculation, rounded at three decimal places, can be determined by referring to Exhibit 14–17 (8% column, down four rows) and multiplying this factor by the amount of each receipt (\$1).

It should be apparent that Exhibit 14–16 and 14–17 are related. We can treat each cash flow of the annuity separately and find the future value of each cash flow (Exhibit 14–16) and sum them. Alternatively, it is much faster to find the sum of the annuity using Exhibit 14–17.

To find the future value of an annuity of \$1 per period for four periods if each payment is made at the *beginning* of each period (an annuity due), we can modify the formula as follows:

$$F_n\,(\text{due}) = \frac{(1 + r)^n - 1}{r} \times (1 + r)$$

$$= \frac{(1 + .08)^4 - 1}{.08} \times (1 + .08)$$

$$= \$4,867$$

The same result can be reached by looking up the interest factor in Exhibit 14–17 for one additional interest period and then subtracting 1 from this factor (8% column, five rows down, deduct 1 from the factor 5.867 to give 4.867). This problem is illustrated by the following diagram:

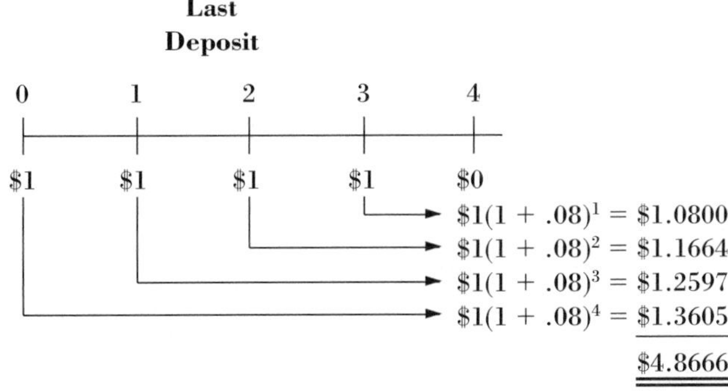

To summarize, the present value tables in Appendix A should be used as follows:

Exhibit 14–18: This table should be used to find the present value of a single cash flow (such as a single payment or receipt) occurring in the future.

Exhibit 14–19: This table should be used to find the present value of a series (or stream) of cash flows occurring in the future.

The use of these tables is illustrated in various exhibits in the main body of the chapter. *When a present value factor appears in an exhibit, the reader should take the time to trace*

EXHIBIT 14–16 Future Value of $1; $(1 + r)^n$

Periods	4%	5%	6%	7%	8%	9%	10%	11%	12%	13%	14%	15%	16%	17%	18%	19%	20%
1	1.040	1.050	1.060	1.070	1.080	1.090	1.100	1.110	1.120	1.130	1.140	1.150	1.160	1.170	1.180	1.190	1.200
2	1.082	1.103	1.124	1.145	1.166	1.188	1.210	1.232	1.254	1.277	1.300	1.323	1.346	1.369	1.392	1.416	1.440
3	1.125	1.158	1.191	1.225	1.260	1.295	1.331	1.368	1.405	1.443	1.482	1.521	1.561	1.602	1.643	1.685	1.728
4	1.170	1.216	1.262	1.311	1.360	1.412	1.464	1.518	1.574	1.630	1.689	1.749	1.811	1.874	1.939	2.005	2.074
5	1.217	1.276	1.338	1.403	1.469	1.539	1.611	1.685	1.762	1.842	1.925	2.011	2.100	2.192	2.288	2.386	2.488
6	1.265	1.340	1.419	1.501	1.587	1.677	1.772	1.870	1.974	2.082	2.195	2.313	2.436	2.565	2.700	2.840	2.986
7	1.316	1.407	1.504	1.606	1.714	1.828	1.949	2.076	2.211	2.353	2.502	2.660	2.826	3.001	3.185	3.379	3.583
8	1.369	1.477	1.594	1.718	1.851	1.993	2.144	2.305	2.476	2.658	2.853	3.059	3.278	3.511	3.759	4.021	4.300
9	1.423	1.551	1.689	1.838	1.999	2.172	2.358	2.558	2.773	3.004	3.252	3.518	3.803	4.108	4.435	4.785	5.160
10	1.480	1.629	1.791	1.967	2.159	2.367	2.594	2.839	3.106	3.395	3.707	4.046	4.411	4.807	5.234	5.695	6.192
11	1.539	1.710	1.898	2.105	2.332	2.580	2.853	3.152	3.479	3.836	4.226	4.652	5.117	5.624	6.176	6.777	7.430
12	1.601	1.796	2.012	2.252	2.518	2.813	3.138	3.498	3.896	4.335	4.818	5.350	5.936	6.580	7.288	8.064	8.916
13	1.665	1.886	2.133	2.410	2.720	3.066	3.452	3.883	4.363	4.898	5.492	6.153	6.886	7.699	8.599	9.596	10.699
14	1.732	1.980	2.261	2.579	2.937	3.342	3.797	4.310	4.887	5.535	6.261	7.076	7.988	9.007	10.147	11.420	12.839
15	1.801	2.079	2.397	2.759	3.172	3.642	4.177	4.785	5.474	6.254	7.138	8.137	9.266	10.539	11.974	13.590	15.407
16	1.873	2.183	2.540	2.952	3.426	3.970	4.595	5.311	6.130	7.067	8.137	9.358	10.748	12.330	14.129	16.172	18.488
17	1.948	2.292	2.693	3.159	3.700	4.328	5.054	5.895	6.866	7.986	9.276	10.761	12.468	14.426	16.672	19.244	22.186
18	2.026	2.407	2.854	3.380	3.996	4.717	5.560	6.544	7.690	9.024	10.575	12.375	14.463	16.879	19.673	22.901	26.623
19	2.107	2.527	3.026	3.617	4.316	5.142	6.116	7.263	8.613	10.197	12.056	14.232	16.777	19.748	23.214	27.252	31.948
20	2.191	2.653	3.207	3.870	4.661	5.604	6.727	8.062	9.646	11.523	13.743	16.367	19.461	23.106	27.393	32.429	38.338
30	3.243	4.322	5.743	7.612	10.063	13.268	17.449	22.892	29.960	39.116	50.950	66.212	85.850	111.065	143.371	184.675	237.376

EXHIBIT 14–17 Future Value of an Annuity of $1 in Arrears; $\frac{(1 + r)^n - 1}{r}$

Periods	4%	5%	6%	7%	8%	9%	10%	11%	12%	13%	14%	15%	16%	17%	18%	19%	20%
1	1.000	1.000	1.000	1.000	1.000	1.000	1.000	1.000	1.000	1.000	1.000	1.000	1.000	1.000	1.000	1.000	1.000
2	2.040	2.050	2.060	2.070	2.080	2.090	2.100	2.110	2.120	2.130	2.140	2.150	2.160	2.170	2.180	2.190	2.200
3	3.122	3.153	3.184	3.215	3.246	3.278	3.310	3.342	3.374	3.407	3.440	3.473	3.506	3.539	3.572	3.606	3.640
4	4.246	4.310	4.375	4.440	4.506	4.573	4.641	4.710	4.779	4.850	4.921	4.993	5.066	5.141	5.215	5.291	5.368
5	5.416	5.526	5.637	5.751	5.867	5.985	6.105	6.228	6.353	6.480	6.610	6.742	6.877	7.014	7.154	7.297	7.442
6	6.633	6.802	6.975	7.153	7.336	7.523	7.716	7.913	8.115	8.323	8.536	8.754	8.977	9.207	9.442	9.683	9.930
7	7.898	8.142	8.394	8.654	8.923	9.200	9.487	9.783	10.089	10.405	10.730	11.067	11.414	11.772	12.142	12.523	12.916
8	9.214	9.549	9.897	10.260	10.637	11.028	11.436	11.859	12.300	12.757	13.233	13.727	14.240	14.773	15.327	15.902	16.499
9	10.583	11.027	11.491	11.978	12.488	13.021	13.579	14.164	14.776	15.416	16.085	16.786	17.519	18.285	19.086	19.923	20.799
10	12.006	12.578	13.181	13.816	14.487	15.193	15.937	16.722	17.549	18.420	19.337	20.304	21.321	22.393	23.521	24.709	25.959
11	13.486	14.207	14.972	15.784	16.645	17.560	18.531	19.561	20.655	21.814	23.045	24.349	25.733	27.200	28.755	30.404	32.150
12	15.026	15.917	16.870	17.888	18.977	20.141	21.384	22.713	24.133	25.650	27.271	29.002	30.850	32.824	34.931	37.180	39.581
13	16.627	17.713	18.882	20.141	21.495	22.953	24.523	26.212	28.029	29.985	32.089	34.352	36.786	39.404	42.219	45.244	48.497
14	18.292	19.599	21.015	22.550	24.215	26.019	27.975	30.095	32.393	34.883	37.581	40.505	43.672	47.103	50.818	54.841	59.196
15	20.024	21.579	23.276	25.129	27.152	29.361	31.772	34.405	37.280	40.417	43.842	47.580	51.660	56.110	60.965	66.261	72.035
16	21.825	23.657	25.673	27.888	30.324	33.003	35.950	39.190	42.753	46.672	50.980	55.717	60.925	66.649	72.939	79.850	87.442
17	23.698	25.840	28.213	30.840	33.750	36.974	40.545	44.501	48.884	53.739	59.118	65.075	71.673	78.979	87.068	96.022	105.931
18	25.645	28.132	30.906	33.999	37.450	41.301	45.599	50.396	55.750	61.725	68.394	75.836	84.141	93.406	103.740	115.266	128.117
19	27.671	30.539	33.760	37.379	41.446	46.018	51.159	56.939	63.440	70.749	78.969	88.212	98.603	110.285	123.414	138.166	154.740
20	29.778	33.066	36.786	40.995	45.762	51.160	57.275	64.203	72.052	80.947	91.025	102.444	115.380	130.033	146.628	165.418	186.688
30	56.085	66.439	79.058	94.461	113.283	136.308	164.494	199.021	241.333	293.199	356.787	434.745	530.312	647.439	790.948	966.712	1181.882

EXHIBIT 14–18 Present Value of $1; $\frac{1}{(1 + r)^n}$

Periods	4%	5%	6%	7%	8%	9%	10%	11%	12%	13%	14%	15%	16%	17%	18%	19%	20%	21%	22%	23%	24%	25%
1	0.962	0.952	0.943	0.935	0.926	0.917	0.909	0.901	0.893	0.885	0.877	0.870	0.862	0.855	0.847	0.840	0.833	0.826	0.820	0.813	0.806	0.800
2	0.925	0.907	0.890	0.873	0.857	0.842	0.826	0.812	0.797	0.783	0.769	0.756	0.743	0.731	0.718	0.706	0.694	0.683	0.672	0.661	0.650	0.640
3	0.889	0.864	0.840	0.816	0.794	0.772	0.751	0.731	0.712	0.693	0.675	0.658	0.641	0.624	0.609	0.593	0.579	0.564	0.551	0.537	0.524	0.512
4	0.855	0.823	0.792	0.763	0.735	0.708	0.683	0.659	0.636	0.613	0.592	0.572	0.552	0.534	0.516	0.499	0.482	0.467	0.451	0.437	0.423	0.410
5	0.822	0.784	0.747	0.713	0.681	0.650	0.621	0.593	0.567	0.543	0.519	0.497	0.476	0.456	0.437	0.419	0.402	0.386	0.370	0.355	0.341	0.328
6	0.790	0.746	0.705	0.666	0.630	0.596	0.564	0.535	0.507	0.480	0.456	0.432	0.410	0.390	0.370	0.352	0.335	0.319	0.303	0.289	0.275	0.262
7	0.760	0.711	0.665	0.623	0.583	0.547	0.513	0.482	0.452	0.425	0.400	0.376	0.354	0.333	0.314	0.296	0.279	0.263	0.249	0.235	0.222	0.210
8	0.731	0.677	0.627	0.582	0.540	0.502	0.467	0.434	0.404	0.376	0.351	0.327	0.305	0.285	0.266	0.249	0.233	0.218	0.204	0.191	0.179	0.168
9	0.703	0.645	0.592	0.544	0.500	0.460	0.424	0.391	0.361	0.333	0.308	0.284	0.263	0.243	0.225	0.209	0.194	0.180	0.167	0.155	0.144	0.134
10	0.676	0.614	0.558	0.508	0.463	0.422	0.386	0.352	0.322	0.295	0.270	0.247	0.227	0.208	0.191	0.176	0.162	0.149	0.137	0.126	0.116	0.107
11	0.650	0.585	0.527	0.475	0.429	0.388	0.350	0.317	0.287	0.261	0.237	0.215	0.195	0.178	0.162	0.148	0.135	0.123	0.112	0.103	0.094	0.086
12	0.625	0.557	0.497	0.444	0.397	0.356	0.319	0.286	0.257	0.231	0.208	0.187	0.168	0.152	0.137	0.124	0.112	0.102	0.092	0.083	0.076	0.069
13	0.601	0.530	0.469	0.415	0.368	0.326	0.290	0.258	0.229	0.204	0.182	0.163	0.145	0.130	0.116	0.104	0.093	0.084	0.075	0.068	0.061	0.055
14	0.577	0.505	0.442	0.388	0.340	0.299	0.263	0.232	0.205	0.181	0.160	0.141	0.125	0.111	0.099	0.088	0.078	0.069	0.062	0.055	0.049	0.044
15	0.555	0.481	0.417	0.362	0.315	0.275	0.239	0.209	0.183	0.160	0.140	0.123	0.108	0.095	0.084	0.074	0.065	0.057	0.051	0.045	0.040	0.035
16	0.534	0.458	0.394	0.339	0.292	0.252	0.218	0.188	0.163	0.141	0.123	0.107	0.093	0.081	0.071	0.062	0.054	0.047	0.042	0.036	0.032	0.028
17	0.513	0.436	0.371	0.317	0.270	0.231	0.198	0.170	0.146	0.125	0.108	0.093	0.080	0.069	0.060	0.052	0.045	0.039	0.034	0.030	0.026	0.023
18	0.494	0.416	0.350	0.296	0.250	0.212	0.180	0.153	0.130	0.111	0.095	0.081	0.069	0.059	0.051	0.044	0.038	0.032	0.028	0.024	0.021	0.018
19	0.475	0.396	0.331	0.277	0.232	0.194	0.164	0.138	0.116	0.098	0.083	0.070	0.060	0.051	0.043	0.037	0.031	0.027	0.023	0.020	0.017	0.014
20	0.456	0.377	0.312	0.258	0.215	0.178	0.149	0.124	0.104	0.087	0.073	0.061	0.051	0.043	0.037	0.031	0.026	0.022	0.019	0.016	0.014	0.012
21	0.439	0.359	0.294	0.242	0.199	0.164	0.135	0.112	0.093	0.077	0.064	0.053	0.044	0.037	0.031	0.026	0.022	0.018	0.015	0.013	0.011	0.009
22	0.422	0.342	0.278	0.226	0.184	0.150	0.123	0.101	0.083	0.068	0.056	0.046	0.038	0.032	0.026	0.022	0.018	0.015	0.013	0.011	0.009	0.007
23	0.406	0.326	0.262	0.211	0.170	0.138	0.112	0.091	0.074	0.060	0.049	0.040	0.033	0.027	0.022	0.018	0.015	0.012	0.010	0.009	0.007	0.006
24	0.390	0.310	0.247	0.197	0.158	0.126	0.102	0.082	0.066	0.053	0.043	0.035	0.028	0.023	0.019	0.015	0.013	0.010	0.008	0.007	0.006	0.005
25	0.375	0.295	0.233	0.184	0.146	0.116	0.092	0.074	0.059	0.047	0.038	0.030	0.024	0.020	0.016	0.013	0.010	0.009	0.007	0.006	0.005	0.004
26	0.361	0.281	0.220	0.172	0.135	0.106	0.084	0.066	0.053	0.042	0.033	0.026	0.021	0.017	0.014	0.011	0.009	0.007	0.006	0.005	0.004	0.003
27	0.347	0.268	0.207	0.161	0.125	0.098	0.076	0.060	0.047	0.037	0.029	0.023	0.018	0.014	0.011	0.009	0.007	0.006	0.005	0.004	0.003	0.002
28	0.333	0.255	0.196	0.150	0.116	0.090	0.069	0.054	0.042	0.033	0.026	0.020	0.016	0.012	0.010	0.008	0.006	0.005	0.004	0.003	0.002	0.002
29	0.321	0.243	0.185	0.141	0.107	0.082	0.063	0.048	0.037	0.029	0.022	0.017	0.014	0.011	0.008	0.006	0.005	0.004	0.003	0.002	0.002	0.002
30	0.308	0.231	0.174	0.131	0.099	0.075	0.057	0.044	0.033	0.026	0.020	0.015	0.012	0.009	0.007	0.005	0.004	0.003	0.003	0.002	0.002	0.001
40	0.208	0.142	0.097	0.067	0.046	0.032	0.022	0.015	0.011	0.008	0.005	0.004	0.003	0.002	0.001	0.001	0.001	0.000	0.000	0.000	0.000	0.000

EXHIBIT 14–19 Present Value of an Annuity of $1 in Arrears; $\frac{1}{r}\left[1 - \frac{1}{(1 + r)^n}\right]$

Periods	4%	5%	6%	7%	8%	9%	10%	11%	12%	13%	14%	15%	16%	17%	18%	19%	20%	21%	22%	23%	24%	25%
1	0.962	0.952	0.943	0.935	0.926	0.917	0.909	0.901	0.893	0.885	0.877	0.870	0.862	0.855	0.847	0.840	0.833	0.826	0.820	0.813	0.806	0.800
2	1.886	1.859	1.833	1.808	1.783	1.759	1.736	1.713	1.690	1.668	1.647	1.626	1.605	1.585	1.566	1.547	1.528	1.509	1.492	1.474	1.457	1.440
3	2.775	2.723	2.673	2.624	2.577	2.531	2.487	2.444	2.402	2.361	2.322	2.283	2.246	2.210	2.174	2.140	2.106	2.074	2.042	2.011	1.981	1.952
4	3.630	3.546	3.465	3.387	3.312	3.240	3.170	3.102	3.037	2.974	2.914	2.855	2.798	2.743	2.690	2.639	2.589	2.540	2.494	2.448	2.404	2.362
5	4.452	4.329	4.212	4.100	3.993	3.890	3.791	3.696	3.605	3.517	3.433	3.352	3.274	3.199	3.127	3.058	2.991	2.926	2.864	2.803	2.745	2.689
6	5.242	5.076	4.917	4.767	4.623	4.486	4.355	4.231	4.111	3.998	3.889	3.784	3.685	3.589	3.498	3.410	3.326	3.245	3.167	3.092	3.020	2.951
7	6.002	5.786	5.582	5.389	5.206	5.033	4.868	4.712	4.564	4.423	4.288	4.160	4.039	3.922	3.812	3.706	3.605	3.508	3.416	3.327	3.242	3.161
8	6.733	6.463	6.210	5.971	5.747	5.535	5.335	5.146	4.968	4.799	4.639	4.487	4.344	4.207	4.078	3.954	3.837	3.726	3.619	3.518	3.421	3.329
9	7.435	7.108	6.802	6.515	6.247	5.995	5.759	5.537	5.328	5.132	4.946	4.772	4.607	4.451	4.303	4.163	4.031	3.905	3.786	3.673	3.566	3.463
10	8.111	7.722	7.360	7.024	6.710	6.418	6.145	5.889	5.650	5.426	5.216	5.019	4.833	4.659	4.494	4.339	4.192	4.054	3.923	3.799	3.682	3.571
11	8.760	8.306	7.887	7.499	7.139	6.805	6.495	6.207	5.938	5.687	5.453	5.234	5.029	4.836	4.656	4.486	4.327	4.177	4.035	3.902	3.776	3.656
12	9.385	8.863	8.384	7.943	7.536	7.161	6.814	6.492	6.194	5.918	5.660	5.421	5.197	4.988	4.793	4.611	4.439	4.278	4.127	3.985	3.851	3.725
13	9.986	9.394	8.853	8.358	7.904	7.487	7.103	6.750	6.424	6.122	5.842	5.583	5.342	5.118	4.910	4.715	4.533	4.362	4.203	4.053	3.912	3.780
14	10.563	9.899	9.295	8.745	8.244	7.786	7.367	6.982	6.628	6.302	6.002	5.724	5.468	5.229	5.008	4.802	4.611	4.432	4.265	4.108	3.962	3.824
15	11.118	10.380	9.712	9.108	8.559	8.061	7.606	7.191	6.811	6.462	6.142	5.847	5.575	5.324	5.092	4.876	4.675	4.489	4.315	4.153	4.001	3.859
16	11.652	10.838	10.106	9.447	8.851	8.313	7.824	7.379	6.974	6.604	6.265	5.954	5.668	5.405	5.162	4.938	4.730	4.536	4.357	4.189	4.033	3.887
17	12.166	11.274	10.477	9.763	9.122	8.544	8.022	7.549	7.120	6.729	6.373	6.047	5.749	5.475	5.222	4.990	4.775	4.576	4.391	4.219	4.059	3.910
18	12.659	11.690	10.828	10.059	9.372	8.756	8.201	7.702	7.250	6.840	6.467	6.128	5.818	5.534	5.273	5.033	4.812	4.608	4.419	4.243	4.080	3.928
19	13.134	12.085	11.158	10.336	9.604	8.950	8.365	7.839	7.366	6.938	6.550	6.198	5.877	5.584	5.316	5.070	4.843	4.635	4.442	4.263	4.097	3.942
20	13.590	12.462	11.470	10.594	9.818	9.129	8.514	7.963	7.469	7.025	6.623	6.259	5.929	5.628	5.353	5.101	4.870	4.657	4.460	4.279	4.110	3.954
21	14.029	12.821	11.764	10.836	10.017	9.292	8.649	8.075	7.562	7.102	6.687	6.312	5.973	5.665	5.384	5.127	4.891	4.675	4.476	4.292	4.121	3.963
22	14.451	13.163	12.042	11.061	10.201	9.442	8.772	8.176	7.645	7.170	6.743	6.359	6.011	5.696	5.410	5.149	4.909	4.690	4.488	4.302	4.130	3.970
23	14.857	13.489	12.303	11.272	10.371	9.580	8.883	8.266	7.718	7.230	6.792	6.399	6.044	5.723	5.432	5.167	4.925	4.703	4.499	4.311	4.137	3.976
24	15.247	13.799	12.550	11.469	10.529	9.707	8.985	8.348	7.784	7.283	6.835	6.434	6.073	5.746	5.451	5.182	4.937	4.713	4.507	4.318	4.143	3.981
25	15.622	14.094	12.783	11.654	10.675	9.823	9.077	8.422	7.843	7.330	6.873	6.464	6.097	5.766	5.467	5.195	4.948	4.721	4.514	4.323	4.147	3.985
26	15.983	14.375	13.003	11.826	10.810	9.929	9.161	8.488	7.896	7.372	6.906	6.491	6.118	5.783	5.480	5.206	4.956	4.728	4.520	4.328	4.151	3.988
27	16.330	14.643	13.211	11.987	10.935	10.027	9.237	8.548	7.943	7.409	6.935	6.514	6.136	5.798	5.492	5.215	4.964	4.734	4.524	4.332	4.154	3.990
28	16.663	14.898	13.406	12.137	11.051	10.116	9.307	8.602	7.984	7.441	6.961	6.534	6.152	5.810	5.502	5.223	4.970	4.739	4.528	4.335	4.157	3.992
29	16.984	15.141	13.591	12.278	11.158	10.198	9.370	8.650	8.022	7.470	6.983	6.551	6.166	5.820	5.510	5.229	4.975	4.743	4.531	4.337	4.159	3.994
30	17.292	15.372	13.765	12.409	11.258	10.274	9.427	8.694	8.055	7.496	7.003	6.566	6.177	5.829	5.517	5.235	4.979	4.746	4.534	4.339	4.160	3.995
40	19.793	17.159	15.046	13.332	11.925	10.757	9.779	8.951	8.244	7.634	7.105	6.642	6.233	5.871	5.548	5.258	4.997	4.760	4.544	4.347	4.166	3.999

it back in either Exhibit 14–18 or Exhibit 14–19 in order to get acquainted with the tables and how they work.

Using Microsoft Excel

You can also perform compound interest calculations using the following Microsoft Excel functions:

RATE(nper,pmt,pv,fv,type,guess)
NPER(rate,pmt,pv,fv,type)
PV(rate,nper,pmt,fv,type)
FV(rate,nper,pmt,pv,type)

where

- *rate* is the interest rate per period.
- *nper* is the total number of payment periods in an annuity.
- *pv* is the present value, the total amount that a series of future payments is worth now.
- *fv* is the future value, or a cash balance you want to attain after the last payment is made. If *fv* is omitted, it is assumed to be 0 (the future value of a loan, for example, is 0).
- *pmt* is the payment made each period and cannot change over the life of the annuity.
- *type* is the number 0 or 1 and indicates when payments are due. (0 or omitted, payment is at the end of the period; 1, it is at the beginning of the period).

Excel functions are particularly useful when you want to calculate compound interest when making regular payments, as for a mortgage or an annuity. They are powerful but are a little complex to use.

APPENDIX 14B: INFLATION AND CAPITAL BUDGETING

LEARNING OBJECTIVE 8
Explain the effect of inflation on capital budgeting decisions.

Doesn't inflation have an effect in a capital budgeting analysis? The answer is a qualified yes in that inflation does have an effect on the *numbers* that are used in a capital budgeting analysis, but it does not have an effect on the *results* of the analysis if certain conditions are satisfied. To show what we mean by this statement, we will use the following data:

Example R

Martin Company wants to purchase a new machine that costs $36,000. The machine would provide annual cost savings of $20,000, and it would have a three-year life with no salvage value. For each of the next three years, the company expects a 10% inflation rate in the cash flows associated with the new machine. If the company's cost of capital is 23.2%, should the new machine be purchased?

To answer this question, it is important to know how the cost of capital was derived. Ordinarily, it is based on the market rates of return on the company's various sources of financing—both debt and equity. This market rate of return includes expected inflation; the higher the expected rate of inflation, the higher the market rate of return on debt and equity. When the inflationary effect is removed from the market rate of return, the result is called a *real rate of return*. For example, if the inflation rate of 10% is removed from Martin's cost of capital of 23.2%, the "real cost of capital" is only 12%, as shown in Exhibit 14–20. (You cannot simply subtract the inflation rate from the market cost of capital to obtain the real cost of capital. The computations are a bit more complex than that.)

When performing a net present value analysis, you must be consistent. The market-based cost of capital reflects inflation. Therefore, if a market-based cost of capital is used to discount cash flows, then the cash flows should be adjusted upward to reflect the effects of inflation in forthcoming periods. Computations for Martin Company under this approach are given in solution B in Exhibit 14–20.

EXHIBIT 14–20 Capital Budgeting and Inflation

Reconciliation of the Market-Based and Real Costs of Capital

The real cost of capital	12.0%
The inflation factor.	10.0%
The combined effect (12% × 10% = 1.2%) . . .	1.2%
The market-based cost of capital	23.2%

Solution A: Inflation Not Considered

Item	Year(s)	Amount of Cash Flows	12% Factor	Present Value of Cash Flows
Initial investment	Now	$(36,000)	1.000	$(36,000)
Annual cost savings	1–3	20,000	2.402	48,040
Net present value				$ 12,040‡

Solution B: Inflation Considered

Item	Year(s)	Amount of Cash Flows	Price-Index Number*	Price-Adjusted Cash Flows	23.2% Factor†	Present Value of Cash Flows
Initial investment	Now	$(36,000)	1.000	$(36,000)	1.000	$(36,000)
Annual cost savings	1	20,000	1.100	22,000	0.812	17,864
	2	20,000	1.210	24,200	0.659	15,948
	3	20,000	1.331	26,620	0.535	14,242
Net present value						$ 12,054‡

*Computation of the price-index numbers, assuming a 10% inflation rate each year: year 1, $(1.10)^1 = 1.10$; year 2, $(1.10)^2 = 1.21$; and year 3, $(1.10)^3 = 1.331$.

†Discount formulas are computed using the formula $1/(1 + r)^n$, where r is the discount factor and n is the number of years. The computations are $1/1.232 = 0.812$ for year 1; $1/(1.232)^2 = 0.659$ for year 2; and $1/(1.232)^3 = 0.535$ for year 3.

‡These amounts are different only because of rounding error.

On the other hand, there is no need to adjust the cash flows upward if the "real cost of capital" is used in the analysis (since the inflationary effects have been taken out of the discount rate). Computations for Martin Company under this approach are given in solution A in Exhibit 14–20. Note that under solutions A and B, the answer will be the same (within rounding error) regardless of which approach is used, as long as you are consistent and all of the cash flows associated with the project are affected in the same way by inflation.

Several points should be noted about solution B, where the effects of inflation are explicitly taken into account. First, note that the annual cost savings are adjusted for the effects of inflation by multiplying each year's cash savings by a price-index number that reflects a 10% inflation rate. (Observe from the footnotes to Exhibit 14–20 how the index number is computed for each year.) Second, note that the net present value obtained in solution B, where inflation is explicitly taken into account, is the same, within rounding error, to that obtained in solution A, where the inflation effects are ignored. This result may seem surprising, but it is logical. The reason is that we have adjusted both the cash flows and the discount rate so that they are consistent, and these adjustments cancel each other out across the two solutions.

Throughout the chapter, we assume for simplicity that there is no inflation. In that case, the market-based and real costs of capital are the same, and there is no reason to adjust the cash flows for inflation since there is none. When there is inflation, the unadjusted cash flows can be used in the analysis if all of the cash flows are affected identically by inflation and the real cost of capital is used to discount the cash flows.

Otherwise, the cash flows should be adjusted for inflation and the market-based cost of capital should be used in the analysis.

APPENDIX 14C: INCOME TAXES IN CAPITAL BUDGETING DECISIONS

LEARNING OBJECTIVE 9
Include income taxes in a capital budgeting analysis.

In our discussion of capital budgeting, we ignored income taxes for two reasons. First, many organizations do not pay income taxes. Not-for-profit organizations, such as hospitals and charitable foundations, and governmental agencies are exempt from income taxes. Second, capital budgeting is complex and is best absorbed in small doses. Now that we have a solid groundwork in the concepts of present value and discounting, we can explore the effects of income taxes on capital budgeting decisions.

The Canadian income tax regulations are enormously complex. We only scratch the surface in this text. To keep the subject within reasonable bounds, we have made many simplifying assumptions about the tax regulations throughout this appendix. Among the most important of these assumptions are: (1) taxable income equals net income as computed for financial reports; and (2) the tax rate is a flat percentage of taxable income. The actual tax regulations are far more complex than this; however, the simplifications that we make throughout this appendix allow us to cover the most important implications of income taxes for capital budgeting without getting bogged down in details.

The Concept of After-Tax Cost

Businesses, like individuals, must pay income taxes. In the case of businesses, the amount of income tax that must be paid is determined by the company's net taxable income. Tax-deductible expenses (tax deductions) decrease the company's net taxable income and hence reduce the taxes the company must pay. For this reason, expenses are often stated on an *after-tax* basis. For example, if a company pays rent of $10 million per year but this expense results in a reduction in income taxes of $3 million, the after-tax cost of the rent is $7 million. An expenditure net of its tax effect is known as **after-tax cost.**

After-tax cost
The amount of net cash outflow resulting from a tax-deductible cash expense after income tax effects have been considered. The amount is determined by multiplying the tax-deductible cash expense by (1 – Tax rate).

To illustrate, assume that a company with a tax rate of 30% is contemplating a training program that costs $60,000. What impact will this have on the company's taxes? To keep matters simple, let's suppose the training program has no immediate effect on sales. How much does the company actually pay for the training program after taking into account the impact of this expense on taxes? The answer is $42,000 as shown in Exhibit 14–21. While the training program costs $60,000 before taxes, it would reduce the

EXHIBIT 14–21
The Computation of After-Tax Cost

	Without Training Program		With Training Program
Sales	$850,000		$850,000
Less tax-deductible expenses:			
Salaries, insurance, and other	700,000		700,000
New training program			60,000
Total expenses	700,000		760,000
Taxable income	$150,000		$ 90,000
Income taxes (30%)	$ 45,000		$ 27,000
Cost of new training program		$60,000	
Less: Reduction in income taxes ($45,000 – $27,000)		18,000	
After-tax cost of the new training program		$42,000	

company's taxes by $18,000, so its *after-tax* cost would be only $42,000. This $18,000 reduction in taxes can also be calculated directly by simply multiplying $60,000 by the 30% tax rate.

The after-tax cost of any tax-deductible cash expense can be determined using the following formula:[10]

$$\begin{array}{c}\text{After-tax cost}\\ \text{(net cash outflow)}\end{array} = (1 - \text{Tax rate}) \times \text{Tax-deductible cash expense}$$

We can verify the accuracy of this formula by applying it to the $60,000 training program expenditure:

$$(1 - 0.30) \times \$60{,}000 = \$42{,}000 \text{ after-tax cost of the training program}$$

This formula is very useful since it provides the actual amount of cash a company must pay after taking into consideration tax effects. It is this actual, after-tax, cash outflow that should be used in capital budgeting decisions.

Similar reasoning applies to revenues and other *taxable* cash inflows. Since these cash receipts are taxable, the company must pay out a portion of them in taxes. The **after-tax benefit,** or net cash inflow, realized from a particular cash receipt can be obtained by applying a simple variation of the cash expenditure formula used above:

After-tax benefit
The amount of net cash inflow realized from a taxable cash receipt after income tax effects have been considered. The amount is determined by multiplying the taxable cash receipt by (1 − Tax rate).

$$\begin{array}{c}\text{After-tax benefit}\\ \text{(net cash inflow)}\end{array} = (1 - \text{Tax rate}) \times \text{Taxable cash receipt}$$

We emphasize the term *taxable cash receipt* because not all cash inflows are taxable. For example, the release of working capital at the termination of an investment project would not be a taxable cash inflow. It is not counted as income for either financial accounting or income tax reporting purposes since it is simply a recovery of the initial investment.

Capital Cost Allowance (CCA) Tax Shield

Because capital cost allowance (CCA) is not a cash flow, it was ignored in this chapter in all discounted cash flow computations. However, CCA does affect the taxes that must be paid and therefore has an indirect effect on the company's cash flows.

To illustrate the effect of CCA deductions on tax payments, consider a company with annual cash sales of $500,000 and cash operating expenses of $310,000. In addition, the company has a depreciable asset on which the CCA deduction is $90,000 per year. The tax rate is 30%. As shown in Exhibit 14–22, the CCA deduction reduces the company's taxes by $27,000. In effect, the CCA deduction of $90,000 *shields* $90,000 in revenues from taxation and thereby *reduces* the amount of taxes that the company must pay. Because CCA deductions shield revenues from taxation, they are generally referred to as a **capital cost allowance tax shield.**[11] The reduction in tax payments made possible by the CCA tax shield is equal to the amount of the CCA deduction, multiplied by the tax rate as follows:

Capital cost allowance tax shield
A reduction in tax that results from capital cost allowance deductions. The reduction in tax is computed by multiplying the CCA deduction by the tax rate.

$$\begin{array}{c}\text{Tax savings from the}\\ \text{CCA tax shield}\end{array} = \text{Tax rate} \times \text{CCA deduction}$$

10. This formula assumes that a company is operating at a profit; if it is operating at a loss, the tax situation can be very complex. For simplicity, we assume in all examples, exercises, and problems that the company is operating at a profit.

11. The term *capital cost allowance tax shield* may convey the impression that there is something underhanded about capital cost allowance deductions—that companies are getting some sort of a special tax break. However, to use the CCA deduction, a company must have already acquired a depreciable asset—which typically requires a cash outflow. Essentially, the tax regulations require companies to delay recognizing the cash outflow as an expense until CCA charges are recorded.

EXHIBIT 14–22
The Effect of CCA Deductions on Tax Payments

	Without CCA Deduction	With CCA Deduction
Sales	$500,000	$500,000
Cash operating expenses	310,000	310,000
Cash flow from operations	190,000	190,000
Capital cost allowance	—	90,000
Taxable income	$190,000	$100,000
Income taxes (30%)	$ 57,000	$ 30,000

$27,000 lower taxes with the CCA deduction

Cash flow comparison:		
Cash flow from operations (above)	$190,000	$190,000
Income taxes (above)	57,000	30,000
Net cash flow	$133,000	$160,000

$27,000 greater cash flow with the CCA deduction

We can verify this formula by applying it to the $90,000 CCA deduction in our example:

$$0.30 \times \$90,000 = \$27,000 \text{ reduction in tax payments}$$

In this appendix, when we estimate after-tax cash flows for capital budgeting decisions, we will include the tax savings provided by the CCA tax shield.

Rules for CCA are complex and most companies take advantage of accelerated methods allowed under the tax regulations. These accelerated methods usually result in a reduction in current taxes and an offsetting increase in future taxes. This shifting of part of the tax burden from the current year to future years is advantageous from a present value point of view, since a dollar today is worth more than a dollar in the future. A summary of the concepts we have introduced so far is given in Exhibit 14–23.

Capital Cost Allowance for Depreciation

Capital cost allowance is the Canada Revenue Agency's counterpart to depreciation. Depreciation is the allocation of the cost of an asset over its useful life. The amount deducted each period for financial statement reporting purposes is based on generally accepted accounting principles (GAAP). For income tax purposes, however, depreciation is not an allowable expense. Instead, a capital cost allowance is permitted by regulations

EXHIBIT 14–23
Tax Adjustments Required in a Capital Budgeting Analysis

Item	Treatment
Tax-deductible cash expense*	Multiply by (1 − Tax rate) to get after-tax cost.
Taxable cash receipt*	Multiply by (1 − Tax rate) to get after-tax cash inflow.
CCA deduction	Multiply by the tax rate to get the tax savings from the CCA tax shield.

*Cash expenses can be deducted from the cash receipts and the difference multiplied by (1 − Tax rate). See the example at the top of Exhibit 14–24 on page 719.

that accompany the Canadian Income Tax Act. A CCA deduction is allowed for business-related capital property such as equipment and automobiles.

The income tax regulations group assets into classes and each class is then assigned a maximum capital cost allowance rate for tax reporting purposes. Maximum capital cost allowance rates are prescribed by the regulations in the Income Tax Act for 44 classes or pools of assets. A company has the option of deducting capital cost allowance for each asset class for any amount ranging from zero to the maximum amount prescribed by the Act. The CCA rate applicable to each class is usually intended to reflect the economic life of the assets of that class. Where the CCA rate is clearly in excess of that required to reflect the economic useful life, it can be considered to be an accelerated CCA.

These prescribed rates are subject to governmental change. Examples of these assets pools and prescribed rates follow:

Asset	Class	Prescribed Rate
Buildings	1	4%
Assets not included in other classes	8	20%
Computer equipment	10	30%
Machinery and Equipment used in manufacturing	43	30%

Capital cost allowance is calculated essentially by applying the prescribed rate to a declining balance called the **undepreciated capital cost** (UCC). For net additions to each asset class during the year, however, only one-half of the prescribed rate is permitted. Under this half-year rule, only half of the normal CCA for most assets is allowed as a tax-deductible expense in the year during which the asset is acquired. The management accountant may occasionally have to seek the advice of a tax expert to assist in capital budgeting analysis.

Undepreciated capital cost (UCC) The remaining book value of an asset class or pool of assets that is available for tax-deductible depreciation (capital cost allowance). The maximum amount of capital cost allowance that can be deducted in a taxation year of a particular CCA class is the UCC multiplied by the CCA rate for that asset class.

Example 1

Toronto Ltd. has obtained a $30,000 loan to acquire a truck. Assuming that the company will have a taxable income indefinitely into the future, calculate the present value of the capital cost allowance tax shield for the first three years if the cost of capital is 10% and the tax rate is 40%.

(1) Year	(2) Undepreciated Capital Cost	(3) CCA (2) × 30%	(4) Tax Savings (3) × 40%	(5) PV Factor at 10 %	(6) PV of Tax Savings (4) × (5)
1	$30,000	$4,500	$1,800	0.909	$1,636
2	25,500	7,650	3,060	0.826	2,528
3	17,850	5,355	2,142	0.751	1,609

Because the capital cost allowance is calculated on a declining balance of a pool of assets rather than on a single asset, a business is able to obtain tax savings from a project even after its disposition. As long as there are other assets in the pool and the proceeds from disposal are less than the UCC for the class, tax savings can be realized in perpetuity.

It can be shown mathematically that the present value of this infinite stream of tax savings from a declining balance capital cost allowance is calculated by what is referred to as the *CCA tax shield formula*:

$$PV = \frac{Cdt}{d + k} \times \frac{1 + 0.5k}{1 + k}$$

where

C = The capital cost of the asset added to the asset pool.
d = CCA rate.
t = The firm's marginal income tax rate.
k = The cost of capital.

$\frac{1 + 0.5k}{1 + k}$ = The correction factor to account for the provision that only one-half of the capital cost of an asset is included in UCC during the year of acquisition.

For the previous example, the present value of the CCA tax shield is:

$$\frac{\$30{,}000 \times 0.3 \times 0.4}{0.3 + 0.10} \times \frac{1 + 0.5 \times 0.10}{1 + 0.10} = \$9{,}000 \times 0.95455 = \$8{,}591$$

Example 2

Using the data in the previous example, calculate the present value of the CCA tax shield, assuming that other assets remain in the pool and the asset is disposed of for $6,000 after five years' use.

The sale of the asset results in a cash inflow at the end of year 5. This disposal results in the asset pool balance (UCC) being reduced by the $6,000 proceeds. The present value of the CCA tax shield is also reduced, because from the end of year 5 onward, CCA will be applied to a smaller UCC balance than it otherwise would have been without the asset disposal. If S represents salvage value, the CCA tax shield formula must be adjusted by deducting:

$$\frac{Sdt}{d + k} \times (1 + k)^{-n}$$

where

$$\frac{Sdt}{d + k}$$

calculates the present value of the lost tax shield at the end of year 5 ($n = 5$). This lost tax shield is then discounted to time period zero by multiplying it by $(1 + k)^{-n}$ or by using Exhibit 14–18. The present value of the tax shield is calculated to be $7,473.

FOCUS *on Current Practice*

Managers should be alert to income tax changes that could have an effect on the company's bottom line. For example, in the 2004 Federal Budget capital cost allowance changes were made that allowed companies to depreciate computers and computer infrastructure 50% more aggressively. The previous CCA rate of 30% was increased to 45% of the undepreciated value (UCC). The CCA rate for broadband, Internet and other data-network infrastructure equipment was increased from 20% to 30%.

Example of Income Taxes and Capital Budgeting

Armed with an understanding of after-tax cost, after-tax revenue, and the CCA tax shield, we are now prepared to examine a comprehensive example of income taxes and capital budgeting.

Holland Company owns the mineral rights to land that has a deposit of ore. The company is uncertain whether it should purchase equipment and open a mine on the property. After careful study, the following data have been assembled by the company:

Cost of equipment needed	$300,000
Working capital needed	75,000
Estimated annual cash receipts from sales of ore	250,000
Estimated annual cash expenses for salaries, insurance, utilities, and other cash expenses of mining the ore	170,000
Cost of road repairs needed in 6 years	40,000
Salvage value of the equipment in 10 years	100,000

The ore in the mine would be exhausted after 10 years of mining activity, at which time the mine would be closed. The equipment would then be sold for its salvage value. Holland Company uses a 20% rate, assuming no salvage value, to compute CCA deductions for tax purposes. The company's after-tax cost of capital is 12% and its tax rate is 30%.

Should Holland Company purchase the equipment and open a mine on the property? The solution to the problem is given in Exhibit 14–24. We suggest that you go through this solution item by item and note the following points:

Cost of new equipment. The initial investment of $300,000 in the new equipment is included in full, with no reductions for taxes. This represents an *investment,* not an expense, so no tax adjustment is made. (Only revenues and expenses are adjusted for the effects of taxes.) However, this investment does affect taxes through the CCA deductions that are considered below.

Working capital. Observe that the working capital needed for the project is included in full, with no reductions for taxes. Like the cost of new equipment, working capital is an investment and not an expense so no tax adjustment is made. Also observe that no tax adjustment is made when the working capital is released at the end of the project's life. The release of working capital is not a taxable cash flow, since it merely represents a return of investment funds back to the company.

EXHIBIT 14–24 Example of Income Taxes and Capital Budgeting

	Per Year
Cash receipts from sales of ore	$250,000
Less payments for salaries, insurance, utilities, and other cash expenses	170,000
Net cash receipts	$ 80,000

Items and Computations	Year(s)	(1) Amount	(2) Tax Effect*	After-Tax Cash Flows (1) × (2)	12% Factor	Present Value of Cash Flows
Cost of new equipment	Now	$(300,000)	—	$(300,000)	1.000	$(300,000)
Working capital needed	Now	(75,000)	—	(75,000)	1.000	(75,000)
Net annual cash receipts	1–10	180,000	1–0.30	56,000	5.650	316,400
Road repairs	6	(40,000)	1–0.30	(28,000)	.507	(14,196)
Salvage value of equipment	10	100,000	—	100,000	.322	32,200
Release of working capital	10	75,000	—	75,000	.322	24,150
Subtotal						$ (16,446)

Present value of CCA tax shield:

$$PV = \frac{Cdt}{d+k} \times \frac{(1+.5k)}{1+k} - \frac{S \times d \times t}{d+k} \times (1+k)^{-n}$$

$$PV = \frac{\$300{,}000 \times .3 \times .3}{.3 + .12} \times \frac{1.06}{1.12} - \frac{\$100{,}000 \times .3 \times .3}{.3 + .12} \times (1 + .12)^{-10}$$

$PV = \$64{,}285.71 \times .9464 - \$21{,}428.57 \times .322$

$PV = \$60{,}840.00 - \$6{,}900.00$ 53,940

Net present value .... $ 37,494

*Taxable cash receipts and tax-deductible cash expenses are multiplied by (1 − Tax rate) to determine the after-tax cash flow. CCA deductions are multiplied by the tax rate itself to determine the after-tax cash flow (i.e., tax savings from the CCA tax shield).

Net annual cash receipts. The net annual cash receipts from sales of ore are adjusted for the effects of income taxes, as discussed earlier in the chapter. Note at the top of Exhibit 14–23 that the annual cash expenses are deducted from the annual cash receipts to obtain the net cash receipts. This just simplifies computations.

Road repairs. Since the road repairs occur just once (in the sixth year), they are treated separately from other expenses. Road repairs would be a tax-deductible cash expense, and therefore they are adjusted for the effects of income taxes, as discussed earlier in the chapter.

Capital cost allowance deductions. The tax savings provided by CCA deductions are essentially an annuity that is included in the present value computations using the CCA tax shield formula.

Salvage value of equipment. The salvage value of $100,000 results in the present value inflow of $32,200. However, later in the analysis, note that the present value of the tax shield is reduced. The value of $6,900 is the present value at the end of year 10 of the lost tax shield from the salvage. This amount therefore must be discounted to *now* by multiplying it by the present value factor of $1 at the end of 10 periods $(1 + 0.12)^{-10}$.

Since the net present value of the proposed mining project is positive, the equipment should be purchased and the mine opened. Study Exhibit 14–24 thoroughly—*it is the key exhibit!*

APPENDIX 14C SUMMARY

Unless a company is a tax-exempt organization, such as a not-for-profit school or a governmental unit, income taxes should be considered in making capital budgeting decisions. Tax-deductible cash expenditures and taxable cash receipts are placed on an after-tax basis by multiplying them by (1 − Tax rate). Only the after-tax amount should be used in determining the desirability of an investment proposal.

Although CCA is not a cash outflow, it is a valid deduction for tax purposes and as such affects income tax payments. The CCA tax shield—computed by multiplying the CCA deduction by the tax rate itself—also results in savings in income taxes.

GLOSSARY

Visit the Online Learning Centre at http://www.mcgrawhill.ca/college/garrison/ for a review of key terms and definitions.

QUESTIONS

14–1 What is the difference between capital budgeting screening decisions and capital budgeting preference decisions?

14–2 What is meant by the term *time value of money?*

14–3 What is meant by the term *discounting?*

14–4 Why isn't accounting net income used in the net present value and internal rate of return methods of making capital budgeting decisions?

14–5 Why are discounted cash flow methods of making capital budgeting decisions superior to other methods?

14–6 What is net present value? Can it ever be negative? Explain.

14–7 Identify two simplifying assumptions associated with discounted cash flow methods of making capital budgeting decisions.

14–8 If a firm has to pay interest of 14% on long-term debt, then its cost of capital is 14%. Do you agree? Explain.

14–9 What is meant by an investment project's internal rate of return? How is the internal rate of return computed?

14–10 Explain how the cost of capital serves as a screening tool when dealing with (*a*) the net present value method and (*b*) the internal rate of return method.

14–11 As the discount rate increases, the present value of a given future cash flow also increases. Do you agree? Explain.

14–12 Refer to Exhibit 14–4. Is the return on this investment proposal exactly 14%, more than 14%, or less than 14%? Explain.

14–13 How is the profitability index computed, and what does it measure?

14–14 Can an investment with a profitability index of less than 1.00 be an acceptable investment? Explain.

14–15 What is meant by the term *payback period?* How is the payback period determined? How can the payback method be useful?

14–16 What is the major criticism of the payback and simple rate of return methods of making capital budgeting decisions?

14–17 (Appendix 14C) What is meant by after-tax cost and how is the concept used in capital budgeting decisions?

14–18 (Appendix 14C) What is a capital cost allowance tax shield and how does it affect capital budgeting decisions?

14–19 (Appendix 14C) Ludlow Company is considering the introduction of a new product line. Would an increase in the income tax rate tend to make the new investment more or less attractive? Explain.

14–20 (Appendix 14C) Assume that an old piece of equipment is sold at a loss. From a capital budgeting point of view, what two cash inflows will be associated with the sale?

14–21 (Appendix 14C) Assume that a new piece of equipment costs $40,000 and that the tax rate is 30%. Should the new piece of equipment be shown in the capital budgeting analysis as a cash outflow of $40,000, or should it be shown as a cash outflow of $28,000 [$40,000 × (1 − 0.30)]? Explain.

EXERCISES

EXERCISE 14–1 Net Present Value Method [LO1]

The management of Kunkel Company is considering the purchase of a $40,000 machine that would reduce operating costs by $7,000 per year. At the end of the machine's eight-year useful life, it will have zero scrap value. The company's required rate of return is 12% on all investment projects.

Required:

(Ignore income taxes.)

1. Determine the net present value of the investment in the machine.
2. What is the difference between the total, undiscounted cash inflows and cash outflows over the entire life of the machine?

EXERCISE 14–2 Internal Rate of Return [LO2]

S

Wendell's Doughnut Shoppe is investigating the purchase of a new $18,600 doughnut-making machine. The new machine would permit the company to reduce the amount of part-time help needed, at a cost savings of $3,800 per year. In addition, the new machine would allow the company to produce one new style of doughnut, resulting in the sale of at least 1,000 dozen more doughnuts each year. The company realizes a contribution margin of $1.20 per dozen doughnuts sold. The new machine would have a six-year useful life.

Required:

(Ignore income taxes.)

1. What would be the total annual cash inflows associated with the new machine for capital budgeting purposes?
2. Find the internal rate of return promised by the new machine to the nearest whole percent.

3. In addition to the data given previously, assume that the machine will have a $9,125 salvage value at the end of six years. Under these conditions, compute the internal rate of return to the nearest whole percent. (Hint: You may find it helpful to use the net present value approach; find the discount rate that will cause the net present value to be closest to zero. Use the format shown in Exhibit 14–4.)

EXERCISE 14–3 Present Value Potpourri [LO1, LO3]

Solve each of the following present value exercises independently:

Required:

(Ignore income taxes.)

1. The Cambro Foundation, a nonprofit organization, is planning to invest $104,950 in a project that will last for three years. The project will provide cash inflows as follows:

Year 1	$30,000
Year 2	$40,000
Year 3	?

   Assuming that the project will yield exactly a 12% rate of return, what is the expected cash inflow for Year 3?

2. Lukow Products is investigating the purchase of a piece of automated equipment that will save $400,000 each year in direct labour and inventory carrying costs. This equipment costs $2,500,000 and is expected to have a 15-year useful life with no salvage value. The company's required rate of return is 20% on all equipment purchases. Management anticipates that this equipment will provide intangible benefits such as greater flexibility and higher quality output. What dollar value per year would these intangible benefits have to have to make the equipment an acceptable investment?
3. The Matchless Dating Service has made an investment in video and recording equipment that costs $106,700. The equipment is expected to generate cash inflows of $20,000 per year. How many years will the equipment have to be used to provide the company with a 10% rate of return on its investment?

EXERCISE 14–4 Preference Ranking [LO4]

Information on four investment proposals is given below:

	Investment Proposal			
	A	B	C	D
Investment required	$(90,000)	$(100,000)	$(70,000)	$(120,000)
Present value of cash inflows	126,000	90,000	105,000	160,000
Net present value	$ 36,000	$ (10,000)	$ 35,000	$ 40,000
Life of the project	5 years	7 years	6 years	6 years

Required:

1. Compute the project profitability index for each investment proposal.
2. Rank the proposals in terms of preference.

EXERCISE 14–5 Payback Method [LO5]

The management of Unter Corporation is considering an investment with the following cash flows:

Year	Investment	Cash Inflow
1	$15,000	$1,000
2	$8,000	$2,000
3		$2,500
4		$4,000
5		$5,000
6		$6,000
7		$5,000
8		$4,000
9		$3,000
10		$2,000

Required:

1. Determine the payback period of the investment.
2. Would the payback period be affected if the cash inflow in the last year were several times as large?

EXERCISE 14–6 Simple Rate of Return Method [LO6]

The management of Ballard MicroBrew is considering the purchase of an automated bottling machine for $120,000. The machine would replace an old piece of equipment that costs $30,000 per year to operate. The new machine would cost $12,000 per year to operate. The old machine currently in use could be sold now for a scrap value of $40,000. The new machine would have a useful life of 10 years with no salvage value.

Required:

Compute the simple rate of return on the new automated bottling machine.

EXERCISE 14–7 (Appendix 14A) Basic Present Value Concepts [LO7]

Solve each of the following parts independently. (Ignore income taxes.)

1. The Atlantic Medical Clinic can purchase a new computer system that will save $7,000 annually in billing costs. The computer system will last for eight years and have no salvage value. Up to how much should the Atlantic Medical Clinic be willing to pay for the new computer system if the clinic's required rate of return is:
   a. 16%?
   b. 20%?
2. The Caldwell *Herald* newspaper reported the following story:
   Frank Ormsby of Caldwell is the province's newest millionaire. By choosing the six winning numbers on last week's provincial lottery, Mr. Ormsby has won the week's grand prize totalling $1.6 million. The Provincial Lottery Commission has indicated that Mr. Ormsby will receive his prize in 20 annual installments of $80,000 each.
   a. If Mr. Ormsby can invest money at a 12% rate of return, what is the present value of his winnings?
   b. Is it correct to say that Mr. Ormsby is the "province's newest millionaire"? Explain your answer.
3. Fraser Company will need a new warehouse in five years. The warehouse will cost $500,000 to build. What lump-sum amount should the company invest now to have the $500,000 available at the end of the five-year period? Assume that the company can invest money at:
   a. 10%.
   b. 14%.

EXERCISE 14–8 (Appendix 14C) After-Tax Costs [LO9]

Solve each of the following parts independently:

a. Neal Company would like to initiate a management development program for its executives. The program would cost $100,000 per year to operate. What would be the after-tax cost of the program if the company's income tax rate is 30%?

b. Smerk's Department Store has rearranged the merchandise display cases on the first floor of its building, placing fast turnover items near the front door. This rearrangement has caused the company's contribution margin (and taxable income) to increase by $40,000 per month. If the company's income tax rate is 30%, what is the after-tax benefit from this rearrangement of facilities?

c. Perfect Press, Inc., has just purchased a new binding machine at a cost of $210,000. For accounting purposes, the entire original cost of the machine will be depreciated over seven years using the straight-line method. Determine the yearly tax savings for the first three years from the CCA tax shield. Assume an 8% cost of capital and that the income tax rate is 30%.

EXERCISE 14–9 Basic Net Present Value Analysis [LO1]

Kathy Myers frequently purchases stocks and bonds, but she is uncertain how to determine the rate of return that she is earning. For example, three years ago she paid $13,000 for 200 shares of Malti Company's common shares. She received a $420 cash dividend on the shares at the end of each year for three years. At the end of three years, she sold the shares for $16,000. Kathy would like to earn a return of at least 14% on all of her investments. She is not sure whether the Malti Company shares provided a 14% return and would like some help with the necessary computations.

Required:
(Ignore income taxes.) Using the net present value method, determine whether or not the Malti Company stock provided a 14% return. Use the general format illustrated in Exhibit 14–4 and round all computations to the nearest whole dollar.

EXERCISE 14–10 Basic Payback Period and Simple Rate of Return Computations [LO5, LO6]
A piece of laboursaving equipment has just come onto the market that Mitsui Electronics, Ltd., could use to reduce costs in one of its plants in Japan. Relevant data relating to the equipment follow (currency is in thousands of yen, denoted by ¥):

Purchase cost of the equipment	¥432,000
Annual cost savings that will be provided by the equipment	¥90,000
Life of the equipment	12 years

Required:
(Ignore income taxes.)
1. Compute the payback period for the equipment. If the company requires a payback period of four years or less, would the equipment be purchased?
2. Compute the simple rate of return on the equipment. Use straight-line depreciation based on the equipment's useful life. Would the equipment be purchased if the company's required rate of return is 14%?

EXERCISE 14–11 Net Present Value Analysis of Two Alternatives [LO1]
Perit Industries has $100,000 to invest. The company is trying to decide between two alternative uses of the funds. The alternatives are:

	Project A	Project B
Cost of equipment required	$100,000	
Working capital investment required		$100,000
Annual cash inflows	$21,000	$16,000
Salvage value of equipment in six years	$8,000	
Life of the project	6 years	6 years

The working capital needed for project B will be released at the end of six years for investment elsewhere. Perit Industries' discount rate is 14%.

Required:
(Ignore income taxes.) Which investment alternative (if either) would you recommend that the company accept? Show all computations using the net present value format. Prepare separate computations for each project.

EXERCISE 14–12 Basic Net Present Value and Internal Rate of Return Analysis [LO1, LO2, LO3]
Consider each part below independently. Ignore income taxes.
1. Preston Company's required rate of return is 14% on all investments. The company can purchase a new machine at a cost of $84,900. The new machine would generate cash inflows of $15,000 per year and have a 12-year useful life with no salvage value. Compute the machine's net present value. (Use the format shown in Exhibit 14–1.) Is the machine an acceptable investment? Explain.
2. The Bedford *Daily News* is investigating the purchase of a new auxiliary press that has a projected life of 18 years. It is estimated that the new press will save $30,000 per year in cash operating costs. If the new press costs $217,500, what is its internal rate of return? Is the press an acceptable investment if the company's required rate of return is 16%? Explain.
3. Refer to the data above for the Bedford *Daily News.* How much would the annual cash inflows (cost savings) have to be for the new press to provide the required 16% rate of return? Round your answer to the nearest whole dollar.

EXERCISE 14–13 Payback Period and Simple Rate of Return [LO5, LO6]

Nick's Novelties, Inc., is considering the purchase of electronic pinball machines to place in amusement houses. The machines would cost a total of $300,000, have an eight-year useful life, and have a total salvage value of $20,000. The company estimates that annual revenues and expenses associated with the machines would be as follows:

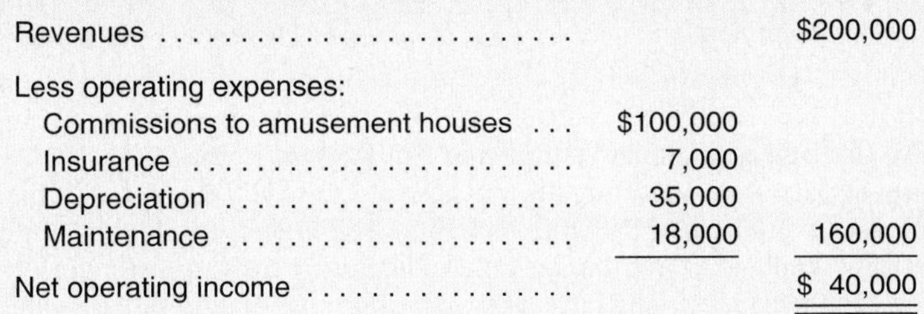

Revenues		$200,000
Less operating expenses:		
Commissions to amusement houses	$100,000	
Insurance	7,000	
Depreciation	35,000	
Maintenance	18,000	160,000
Net operating income		$ 40,000

Required:

(Ignore income taxes.)

1. Assume that Nick's Novelties, Inc., will not purchase new equipment unless it provides a payback period of five years or less. Would the company purchase the pinball machines?
2. Compute the simple rate of return promised by the pinball machines. If the company requires a simple rate of return of at least 12%, will the pinball machines be purchased?

EXERCISE 14–14 (Appendix 14A) Basic Present Value Concepts [LO7]

Consider each of the following situations independently. (Ignore income taxes.)

1. In three years, when he is discharged from the Air Force, Steve wants to buy an $8,000 power boat. What lump-sum amount must he invest now to have the $8,000 at the end of three years if he can invest money at:
   a. 10%?
   b. 14%?
2. Annual cash inflows that will arise from two competing investment projects are given below:

	Investment	
Year	A	B
1	$ 3,000	$12,000
2	6,000	9,000
3	9,000	6,000
4	12,000	3,000
	$30,000	$30,000

   Each investment project will require the same investment outlay. The discount rate is 18%. Compute the present value of the cash inflows for each investment.
3. Julie has just retired. Her company's retirement program has two options as to how retirement benefits can be received. Under the first option, Julie would receive a lump sum of $150,000 immediately as her full retirement benefit. Under the second option, she would receive $14,000 each year for 20 years plus a lump-sum payment of $60,000 at the end of the 20-year period. If she can invest money at 12%, which option would you recommend that she accept? Use present value analysis.

EXERCISE 14–15 Comparison of Projects Using Net Present Value [LO1]

Labeau Products, Ltd., of Perth, Australia, has $35,000 to invest. The company is trying to decide between two alternative uses for the funds as shown at the top of page 726.

The company's discount rate is 18%.

Required:

(Ignore income taxes.) Which alternative would you recommend that the company accept? Show all computations using the net present value approach. Prepare separate computations for each project.

	Invest in Project X	Invest in Project Y
Investment required	$35,000	$35,000
Annual cash inflows	$9,000	
Single cash inflow at the end of 10 years		$150,000
Life of the project	10 years	10 years

EXERCISE 14–16 Internal Rate of Return and Net Present Value [LO1, LO2]

Henrie's Drapery Service is investigating the purchase of a new machine for cleaning and blocking drapes. The machine would cost $130,400, including freight and installation. Henrie's has estimated that the new machine would increase the company's cash inflows, net of expenses, by $25,000 per year. The machine would have a 10-year useful life and no salvage value.

Required:

(Ignore income taxes.)

1. Compute the machine's internal rate of return to the nearest whole percent.
2. Compute the machine's net present value. Use a discount rate of 14% and the format shown in Exhibit 14–5. Why do you have a zero net present value?
3. Suppose that the new machine would increase the company's annual cash inflows, net of expenses, by only $22,500 per year. Under these conditions, compute the internal rate of return to the nearest whole percent.

EXERCISE 14–17 (Appendix 14C) After-Tax Cash Flows in Net Present Value Analysis [LO9]

Dwyer Company is considering two investment projects. Relevant cost and cash flow information on the two projects is given below:

	Project A	Project B
Investment in heavy trucks	$130,000	
Investment in working capital		$130,000
Net annual cash inflows	$25,000	$25,000
Life of the project	9 years*	9 years
CCA	30%	

*Useful life of the trucks

The trucks will have a $15,000 salvage value in nine years. For tax purposes, the company computes depreciation deductions assuming zero salvage value and uses straight-line depreciation. The trucks will be depreciated over five years. At the end of nine years, the working capital will be released for use elsewhere. The company requires an after-tax return of 12% on all investments. The tax rate is 30%.

Required:

Compute the net present value of each investment project. Round all dollar amounts to the nearest whole dollar.

EXERCISE 14–18 (Appendix 14C) Net Present Value Analysis Including Income Taxes [LO9]

The Midtown Cafeteria employs five people to operate antiquated dishwashing equipment. The cost of wages for these people and for maintenance of the equipment is $85,000 per year. Management is considering the purchase of a single, highly automated dishwashing machine that would cost $160,000 and have a useful life of 12 years. This machine would require the services of only three people to operate at a cost of $48,000 per year. A maintenance contract on the machine would cost an additional $2,000 per year. New water jets would be needed on the machine in six years at a total cost of $15,000.

The old equipment is fully depreciated and has no resale value. The new machine will have a salvage value of $9,000 at the end of its 12-year useful life. Management requires a 14% after-tax return on all equipment purchases. The company's tax rate is 30% and CCA is 20%.

Required:

1. Determine the before-tax net annual cost savings that the new dishwashing machine will provide.
2. Using the data from (1) above and other data from the exercise, compute the new dishwashing machine's net present value. Round all dollar amounts to the nearest whole dollar. Would you recommend that it be purchased?

PROBLEMS

PROBLEM 14–19 Basic Net Present Value Analysis [LO1]

Windhoek Mines, Ltd., of Namibia, is contemplating the purchase of equipment to exploit a mineral deposit on land to which the company has mineral rights. An engineering and cost analysis has been made, and it is expected that the following cash flows would be associated with opening and operating a mine in the area:

Cost of new equipment and timbers	R275,000
Working capital required	R100,000
Net annual cash receipts	R120,000*
Cost to construct new roads in three years	R40,000
Salvage value of equipment in four years	R65,000

*Receipts from sales of ore, less out-of-pocket costs for salaries, utilities, insurance, and so forth.

The currency in Namibia is the rand, denoted here by R.

It is estimated that the mineral deposit would be exhausted after four years of mining. At that point, the working capital would be released for reinvestment elsewhere. The company's required rate of return is 20%.

Required:

(Ignore income taxes.) Determine the net present value of the proposed mining project. Should the project be accepted? Explain.

PROBLEM 14–20 Net Present Value Analysis; Uncertain Cash Flows [LO1, LO3]

"I'm not sure we should lay out $500,000 for that automated welding machine," said Jim Alder, president of the Superior Equipment Company. "That's a lot of money, and it would cost us $80,000 for software and installation, and another $3,000 every month just to maintain the thing. In addition, the manufacturer admits that it would cost $45,000 more at the end of seven years to replace worn-out parts."

"I admit it's a lot of money," said Franci Rogers, the controller. "But you know the turnover problem we've had with the welding crew. This machine would replace six welders at a cost savings of $108,000 per year. And we would save another $6,500 per year in reduced material waste. When you figure that the automated welder would last for 12 years, I'm sure the return would be greater than our 16% required rate of return."

"I'm still not convinced," countered Mr. Alder. "We can only get $12,000 scrap value out of our old welding equipment if we sell it now, and in 12 years the new machine will only be worth $20,000 for parts. But have your people work up the figures and we'll talk about them at the executive committee meeting tomorrow."

Required:

(Ignore income taxes.)

1. Compute the net annual cost savings promised by the automated welding machine.
2. Using the data from (1) above and other data from the problem, compute the automated welding machine's net present value. (Use the incremental-cost approach.) Would you recommend purchasing the automated welding machine? Explain.
3. Assume that management can identify several intangible benefits associated with the automated welding machine, including greater flexibility in shifting from one type of product to another, improved quality of output, and faster delivery as a result of reduced throughput time. What dollar value per year would management have to attach to these intangible benefits in order to make the new welding machine an acceptable investment?

PROBLEM 14–21 Preference Ranking of Investment Projects [LO4]
The management of Revco Products is exploring five different investment opportunities. Information on the five projects under study follows:

	Project Number				
	1	2	3	4	5
Investment required . . .	$(270,000)	$(450,000)	$(400,000)	$(360,000)	$(480,000)
Present value of cash inflows at a 10% discount rate	336,140	522,970	379,760	433,400	567,270
Net present value	$ 66,140	$ 72,970	$ (20,240)	$ 73,400	$ 87,270
Life of the project	6 years	3 years	5 years	12 years	6 years
Internal rate of return . . .	18%	19%	8%	14%	16%

The company's required rate of return is 10%; thus, a 10% discount rate has been used in the present value computations above. Limited funds are available for investment, so the company can't accept all of the available projects.

Required:
1. Compute the project profitability index for each investment project.
2. Rank the five projects according to preference, in terms of:
   a. Net present value
   b. Project profitability index
   c. Internal rate of return
3. Which ranking do you prefer? Why?

PROBLEM 14–22 Simple Rate of Return; Payback [LO5, LO6]
Paul Swanson has an opportunity to acquire a franchise from The Yogurt Place, Inc., to dispense frozen yogurt products under The Yogurt Place name. Mr. Swanson has assembled the following information relating to the franchise:

a. A suitable location in a large shopping mall can be rented for $3,500 per month.
b. Remodelling and necessary equipment would cost $270,000. The equipment would have a 15-year life and an $18,000 salvage value. Straight-line depreciation would be used, and the salvage value would be considered in computing depreciation.
c. Based on similar outlets elsewhere, Mr. Swanson estimates that sales would total $300,000 per year. Ingredients would cost 20% of sales.
d. Operating costs would include $70,000 per year for salaries, $3,500 per year for insurance, and $27,000 per year for utilities. In addition, Mr. Swanson would have to pay a commission to The Yogurt Place, Inc., of 12.5% of sales.

Required:
(Ignore income taxes.)
1. Prepare a contribution format income statement that shows the expected net operating income each year from the franchise outlet.
2. Compute the simple rate of return promised by the outlet. If Mr. Swanson requires a simple rate of return of at least 12%, should he acquire the franchise?
3. Compute the payback period on the outlet. If Mr. Swanson wants a payback of four years or less, will he acquire the franchise?

PROBLEM 14–23 (Appendix 14C) Basic Net Present Value Analysis Including Income Taxes [LO9]
The Diamond Freight Company has been offered a seven-year contract to haul munitions for the government. Since this contract would represent new business, the company would have to purchase several new heavy-duty trucks at a cost of $350,000 if the contract were accepted. Other data relating to the contract are shown at the top of page 729.

With the motors being replaced after four years, the trucks will have a useful life of seven years. To raise money to assist in the purchase of the new trucks, the company will sell several old, fully depreciated trucks for a total selling price of $16,000. The company requires a 16% after-tax return on all equipment purchases. The tax rate is 30% and the CCA rate is 20%.

Net annual cash receipts (before taxes) from the contract	$105,000
Cost of replacing the motors in the trucks in four years	$45,000
Salvage value of the trucks at termination of the contract	$18,000

Required:
Compute the net present value of this investment opportunity. Round all dollar amounts to the nearest whole dollar. Would you recommend that the contract be accepted?

PROBLEM 14–24 Basic Net Present Value Analysis [LO1]

The Sweetwater Candy Company would like to buy a new machine that would automatically "dip" chocolates. The dipping operation is currently done largely by hand. The machine the company is considering costs $120,000. The manufacturer estimates that the machine would be usable for 12 years but would require the replacement of several key parts at the end of the sixth year. These parts would cost $9,000, including installation. After 12 years, the machine could be sold for $7,500.

The company estimates that the cost to operate the machine will be $7,000 per year. The present method of dipping chocolates costs $30,000 per year. In addition to reducing costs, the new machine will increase production by 6,000 boxes of chocolates per year. The company realizes a contribution margin of $1.50 per box. A 20% rate of return is required on all investments.

Required:
(Ignore income taxes.)
1. What are the net annual cash inflows that will be provided by the new dipping machine?
2. Compute the new machine's net present value. Use the incremental cost approach and round all dollar amounts to the nearest whole dollar.

PROBLEM 14–25 Net Present Value Analysis of a Lease or Buy Decision [LO1]

The Riteway Ad Agency provides cars for its sales staff. In the past, the company has always purchased its cars from a dealer and then sold the cars after three years of use. The company's present fleet of cars is three years old and will be sold very shortly. To provide a replacement fleet, the company is considering two alternatives:

Alternative 1: The company can purchase the cars, as in the past, and sell the cars after three years of use. Ten cars will be needed, which can be purchased at a discounted price of $17,000 each. If this alternative is accepted, the following costs will be incurred on the fleet as a whole:

Annual cost of servicing, taxes, and licensing	$3,000
Repairs, first year	$1,500
Repairs, second year	$4,000
Repairs, third year	$6,000

At the end of three years, the fleet could be sold for one-half of the original purchase price.

Alternative 2: The company can lease the cars under a three-year lease contract. The lease cost would be $55,000 per year (the first payment due at the end of Year 1). As part of this lease cost, the owner would provide all servicing and repairs, license the cars, and pay all the taxes. Riteway would be required to make a $10,000 security deposit at the beginning of the lease period, which would be refunded when the cars were returned to the owner at the end of the lease contract.

Required:
(Ignore income taxes.)
1. Riteway Ad Agency has an 18% required rate of return. Use the total-cost approach to determine the present value of the cash flows associated with each alternative. Round all dollar amounts to the nearest whole dollar. Which alternative should the company accept?

2. Using the data in (1) above and other data as needed, explain why it is often less costly for a company to lease equipment and facilities rather than to buy them.

S

PROBLEM 14–26 Internal Rate of Return; Sensitivity Analysis [LO2]

"In my opinion, a tanning salon would be a natural addition to our spa and very popular with our customers," said Stacey Winder, manager of the Lifeline Spa. "Our figures show that we could remodel the building next door to our spa and install all of the necessary equipment for $330,000. I have contacted tanning salons in other areas, and I am told that the tanning beds will be usable for about nine years. I am also told that a four-bed salon such as we are planning would generate a cash inflow of about $80,000 per year after all expenses."

"It does sound very appealing," replied Kevin Leblanc, the spa's accountant. "Let me push the numbers around a bit and see what kind of a return the salon would generate."

Required:

(Ignore income taxes.)

1. Compute the internal rate of return promised by the tanning salon to the nearest whole percent.
2. Assume that Ms. Winder will not open the salon unless it promises a return of at least 14%. Compute the amount of annual cash inflow that would provide this return on the $330,000 investment.
3. Although nine years is the average life of tanning salon equipment, Ms. Winder has found that this life can vary substantially. Compute the internal rate of return to the nearest whole percent if the life were (a) 6 years and (b) 12 years rather than 9 years. Is there any information provided by these computations that you would be particularly anxious to show Ms. Winder?
4. Ms. Winder has also found that although $80,000 is an average cash inflow from a four-bed salon, some salons vary as much as 20% from this figure. Compute the internal rate of return to the nearest whole percent if the annual cash inflows were (a) 20% less and (b) 20% greater than $80,000.
5. Assume that the $330,000 investment is made and that the salon is opened as planned. Because of concerns about the effects of excessive tanning, however, the salon is not able to attract as many customers as planned. Cash inflows are only $50,000 per year, and after eight years the salon equipment is sold to a competitor for $135,440. Compute the internal rate of return to the nearest whole percent earned on the investment over the eight-year period. (Hint: A useful way to proceed is to find the discount rate that will cause the net present value to be equal to, or near, zero.)

PROBLEM 14–27 Net Present Value; Uncertain Future Cash Flows; Postaudit [LO1, LO3]

Saxon Products, Inc., is investigating the purchase of a robot for use on the company's assembly line. Selected data relating to the robot are provided below:

Cost of the robot	$1,800,000
Installation and software	$900,000
Annual savings in labour costs	?
Annual savings in inventory carrying costs	$210,000
Monthly increase in power and maintenance costs	$2,500
Salvage value in 10 years	$70,000
Useful life	10 years

Engineering studies suggest that use of the robot will result in a savings of 25,000 direct labour-hours each year. The labour rate is $16 per hour. Also, the smoother work flow made possible by the use of automation will allow the company to reduce the amount of inventory on hand by $400,000. This inventory reduction will take place at the end of the first year of operation; the released funds will be available for use elsewhere in the company. Saxon Products has a 20% required rate of return on all purchases of equipment.

Shelly Martins, the controller, has noted that all of Saxon's competitors are automating their plants. She is pessimistic, however, about whether Saxon's management will allow it to automate. In preparing the proposal for the robot, she stated to a colleague, "Let's just hope that reduced labour and inventory costs can justify the purchase of this automated equipment. Otherwise, we'll never get it. You know how the president feels about equipment paying for itself out of reduced costs."

Required:

(Ignore income taxes.)

1. Determine the net *annual* cost savings if the robot is purchased. (Do not include the $400,000 inventory reduction or the salvage value in this computation.)

2. Compute the net present value of the proposed investment in the robot. Based on these data, would you recommend that the robot be purchased? Explain.
3. Assume that the robot is purchased. At the end of the first year, Shelly Martins has found that some items didn't work out as planned. Due to unforeseen problems, software and installation costs were $75,000 more than estimated and direct labour has been reduced by only 22,500 hours per year, rather than by 25,000 hours. Assuming that all other cost data were accurate, does it appear that the company made a wise investment? Show computations using the net present value format as in (2) above. (Hint: It might be helpful to place yourself back at the beginning of the first year with the new data.)
4. Upon seeing your analysis in (3) above, Saxon's president stated, "That robot is the worst investment we've ever made. And now we'll be stuck with it for years."
   a. Explain to the president what benefits other than cost savings might accrue from using the new automated equipment.
   b. Compute for the president the dollar amount of cash inflow that would be needed each year from the benefits in (a) above for the automated equipment to yield a 20% rate of return.

PROBLEM 14–28 Preference Ranking of Investment Projects [LO4]

Oxford Company has limited funds available for investment and must ration the funds among five competing projects. Selected information on the five projects follows:

Project	Investment Required	Net Present Value	Life of the Project (years)	Internal Rate of Return (percent)
A	$160,000	$44,323	7	18%
B	$135,000	$42,000	12	16%
C	$100,000	$35,035	7	20%
D	$175,000	$38,136	3	22%
E	$150,000	$(8,696)	6	8%

The net present values above have been computed using a 10% discount rate. The company wants your assistance in determining which project to accept first, second, and so forth.

Required:

1. Compute the project profitability index for each project.
2. In order of preference, rank the five projects in terms of:
   a. Net present value.
   b. Project profitability index.
   c. Internal rate of return.
3. Which ranking do you prefer? Why?

PROBLEM 14–29 Simple Rate of Return; Payback [LO5, LO6]

Sharkey's Fun Centre contains a number of electronic games as well as a miniature golf course and various rides located outside the building. Paul Sharkey, the owner, would like to construct a water slide on one portion of his property. Mr. Sharkey has gathered the following information about the slide:

a. Water slide equipment could be purchased and installed at a cost of $330,000. According to the manufacturer, the slide would be usable for 12 years after which it would have no salvage value.
b. Mr. Sharkey would use straight-line depreciation on the slide equipment.
c. To make room for the water slide, several rides would be dismantled and sold. These rides are fully depreciated, but they could be sold for $60,000 to an amusement park in a nearby city.
d. Mr. Sharkey has concluded that about 50,000 more people would use the water slide each year than have been using the rides. The admission price would be $3.60 per person (the same price that the Fun Centre has been charging for the old rides).
e. Based on experience at other water slides, Mr. Sharkey estimates that annual incremental operating expenses for the slide would be: salaries, $85,000; insurance, $4,200; utilities, $13,000; and maintenance, $9,800.

Required:

(Ignore income taxes.)

1. Prepare an income statement showing the expected net operating income each year from the water slide.

2. Compute the simple rate of return expected from the water slide. Based on this computation, would the water slide be constructed if Mr. Sharkey requires a simple rate of return of at least 14% on all investments?
3. Compute the payback period for the water slide. If Mr. Sharkey accepts any project with a payback period of five years or less, would the water slide be constructed?

PROBLEM 14–30 Net Present Value Analysis [LO1]

In eight years, Kent Duncan will retire. He is exploring the possibility of opening a self-service car wash. The car wash could be managed in the free time he has available from his regular occupation, and it could be closed easily when he retires. After careful study, Mr. Duncan has determined the following:

a. A building in which a car wash could be installed is available under an eight-year lease at a cost of $1,700 per month.
b. Purchase and installation costs of equipment would total $200,000. In eight years the equipment could be sold for about 10% of its original cost.
c. An investment of an additional $2,000 would be required to cover working capital needs for cleaning supplies, change funds, and so forth. After eight years, this working capital would be released for investment elsewhere.
d. Both a wash and a vacuum service would be offered with a wash costing $2.00 and the vacuum costing $1.00 per use.
e. The only variable costs associated with the operation would be 20 cents per wash for water and 10 cents per use of the vacuum for electricity.
f. In addition to rent, monthly costs of operation would be: cleaning, $450; insurance, $75; and maintenance, $500.
g. Gross receipts from the wash would be about $1,350 per week. According to the experience of other car washes, 60% of the customers using the wash would also use the vacuum.

Mr. Duncan will not open the car wash unless it provides at least a 10% return.

Required:

(Ignore income taxes.)

1. Assuming that the car wash will be open 52 weeks a year, compute the expected net annual cash receipts (gross cash receipts less cash disbursements) from its operation. (Do not include the cost of the equipment, the working capital, or the salvage value in these computations.)
2. Would you advise Mr. Duncan to open the car wash? Show computations using the net present value method of investment analysis. Round all dollar figures to the nearest whole dollar.

PROBLEM 14–31 Simple Rate of Return; Payback; Internal Rate of Return [LO2, LO5, LO6]

The Elberta Fruit Farm of Ontario has always hired transient workers to pick its annual cherry crop. Francie Wright, the farm manager, has just received information on a cherry picking machine that is being purchased by many fruit farms. The machine is a motorized device that shakes the cherry tree, causing the cherries to fall onto plastic tarps that funnel the cherries into bins. Ms. Wright has gathered the following information to decide whether a cherry picker would be a profitable investment for the Elberta Fruit Farm:

a. Currently, the farm is paying an average of $40,000 per year to transient workers to pick the cherries.
b. The cherry picker would cost $94,500, and it would have an estimated 12-year useful life. The farm uses straight-line depreciation on all assets and considers salvage value in computing depreciation deductions. The estimated salvage value of the cherry picker is $4,500.
c. Annual out-of-pocket costs associated with the cherry picker would be: cost of an operator and an assistant, $14,000; insurance, $200; fuel, $1,800; and a maintenance contract, $3,000.

Required:

(Ignore income taxes.)

1. Determine the annual savings in cash operating costs that would be realized if the cherry picker were purchased.
2. Compute the simple rate of return expected from the cherry picker. (Hint: Note that this is a cost reduction project.) Would the cherry picker be purchased if Elberta Fruit Farm's required rate of return is 16%?
3. Compute the payback period on the cherry picker. The Elberta Fruit Farm will not purchase equipment unless it has a payback period of five years or less. Would the cherry picker be purchased?

4. Compute (to the nearest whole percent) the internal rate of return promised by the cherry picker. Based on this computation, does it appear that the simple rate of return is an accurate guide in investment decisions?

PROBLEM 14–32 Net Present Value; Total and Incremental Approaches [LO1]

Bilboa Freightlines, S.A., of Panama, has a small truck that it uses for intracity deliveries. The truck is worn out and must be either overhauled or replaced with a new truck. The company has assembled the following information. (Panama uses the Canadian dollar as its currency):

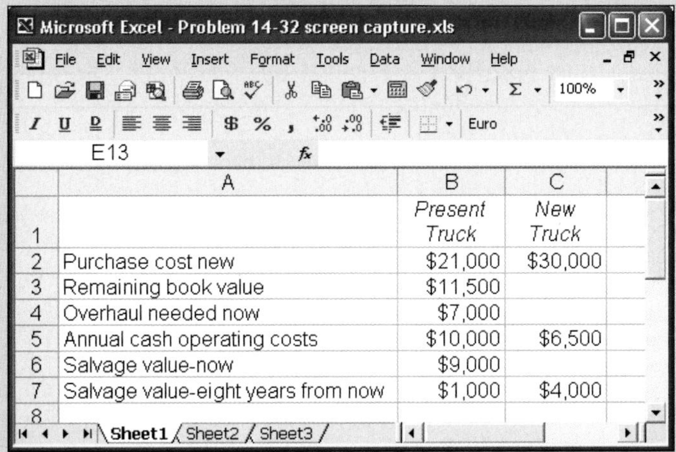

	A	B	C
1		*Present Truck*	*New Truck*
2	Purchase cost new	$21,000	$30,000
3	Remaining book value	$11,500	
4	Overhaul needed now	$7,000	
5	Annual cash operating costs	$10,000	$6,500
6	Salvage value-now	$9,000	
7	Salvage value-eight years from now	$1,000	$4,000

If the company keeps and overhauls its present delivery truck, then the truck will be usable for eight more years. If a new truck is purchased, it will be used for eight years, after which it will be traded in on another truck. The new truck would be diesel-operated, resulting in a substantial reduction in annual operating costs, as shown above.

The company computes depreciation on a straight-line basis. All investment projects are evaluated using a 16% discount rate.

Required:

(Ignore income taxes.)

1. Should Bilboa Freightlines keep the old truck or purchase the new one? Use the total-cost approach to net present value in making your decision. Round to the nearest whole dollar.
2. Redo (1) above, this time using the incremental-cost approach.

PROBLEM 14–33 (Appendix 14C) A Comparison of Investment Alternatives Including Income Taxes [LO9]

Julia Vanfleet is professor of mathematics. She has received a $225,000 inheritance from her father's estate, and she is anxious to invest it between now and the time she retires in 12 years. Professor Vanfleet is considering two alternatives for investing her inheritance.

Alternative 1. Corporate bonds can be purchased that mature in 12 years and that bear interest at 10%. This interest would be taxable and paid annually.

Alternative 2. A small retail business is available for sale that can be purchased for $225,000. The following information relates to this alternative:

a. Of the purchase price, $80,000 would be for fixtures and other depreciable items. The remainder would be for the company's working capital (inventory, accounts receivable, and cash). The fixtures and other depreciable items would have a remaining useful life of 12 years. At the end of 12 years these depreciable items would have a negligible salvage value; however, the working capital would be recovered (either through sale or liquidation of the business) for reinvestment elsewhere.
b. The store building would be leased. At the end of 12 years, if Professor Vanfleet could not find someone to buy the business, it would be necessary to pay $2,000 to the owner of the building to break the lease.
c. Store records indicate that sales have averaged $850,000 per year and out-of-pocket costs (including wages and rent on the building) have averaged $780,000 per year (*not* including income taxes). Management of the store would be entrusted to employees.
d. Professor Vanfleet's tax rate is 40%.

Required:
Advise Professor Vanfleet as to which alternative should be selected. Use the total-cost approach to net present value in your analysis, and a discount rate of 8%. Round all dollar amounts to the nearest whole dollar.

PROBLEM 14–34 Net Present Value Analysis of a New Product [LO1]
Matheson Electronics has just developed a new electronic device which, when mounted on an automobile, will tell the driver how many kilometres the automobile is travelling per litre of gasoline.

The company is anxious to begin production of the new device. To this end, marketing and cost studies have been made to determine probable costs and market potential. These studies have provided the following information:

a. New equipment would have to be acquired to produce the device. The equipment would cost $315,000 and have a 12-year useful life. After 12 years, it would have a salvage value of about $15,000.
b. Sales in units over the next 12 years are projected to be as follows:

Year	Sales in Units
1	6,000
2	12,000
3	15,000
4–12	18,000

c. Production and sales of the device would require working capital of $60,000 to finance accounts receivable, inventories, and day-to-day cash needs. This working capital would be released at the end of the project's life.
d. The devices would sell for $35 each; variable costs for production, administration, and sales would be $15 per unit.
e. Fixed costs for salaries, maintenance, property taxes, insurance, and straight-line depreciation on the equipment would total $135,000 per year. (Depreciation is based on cost less salvage value.)
f. To gain rapid entry into the market, the company would have to advertise heavily. The advertising program would be:

Year	Amount of Yearly Advertising
1–2	$180,000
3	$150,000
4–12	$120,000

g. Matheson Electronics' board of directors has specified a required rate of return of 14% on all new products.

Required:
(Ignore income taxes.)
1. Compute the net cash inflow (cash receipts less yearly cash operating expenses) anticipated from sale of the device for each year over the next 12 years.
2. Using the data computed in (1) above and other data provided in the problem, determine the net present value of the proposed investment. Would you recommend that Matheson accept the device as a new product?

PROBLEM 14–35 (Appendix 14C) Comparison of Total-Cost and Incremental-Cost Approaches Including Income Taxes [LO9]
Reliable Waste Systems provides a solid waste collection service in a large metropolitan area. The company is considering the purchase of several new trucks to replace an equal number of old trucks now in use. The new trucks would cost $650,000, but they would require only one operator per truck (compared to two operators for the trucks now being used), as well as provide other cost savings. A comparison of total annual cash operating costs between the old trucks that would be replaced and the new trucks is provided at the top of page 735.

If the new trucks are purchased, the old trucks will be sold to a company in a nearby city for $85,000. These trucks cost $300,000 when they were new and have a current book value of $120,000 and have been used for 4 years.

	Old Trucks	New Trucks
Salaries—operators	$170,000	$ 85,000
Fuel	14,000	9,000
Insurance	6,000	11,000
Maintenance	10,000	5,000
Total annual cash operating costs	$200,000	$110,000

If the new trucks are not purchased, the old trucks will be used for seven more years and then sold for an estimated $15,000 scrap value. However, to keep the old trucks operating, extensive repairs will be needed in one year that will cost $170,000. These repairs will be expensed for tax purposes in the year incurred.

The new trucks would have a useful life of seven years and would have an estimated $60,000 salvage value at the end of their useful life. The company's tax rate is 30%, and its after-tax cost of capital is 12%. For tax purposes, the company would depreciate the equipment over five years using straight-line depreciation and assuming zero salvage value. CCA is 30%.

Required:

1. Use the total-cost approach to net present value analysis to determine whether the new trucks should be purchased. Round all dollar amounts to the nearest whole dollar.
2. Repeat the computations in (1) above, this time using the incremental-cost approach to net present value analysis.

CASES

CASE 14–36 Ethics and the Manager

The Fore Corporation is an integrated food processing company that has operations in over two dozen countries. Fore's corporate headquarters is in Toronto, and the company's executives frequently travel to visit Fore's foreign and domestic facilities.

Fore has a fleet of aircraft that consists of two business jets with international range and six smaller turboprop aircraft that are used on shorter flights. Company policy is to assign aircraft to trips on the basis of minimizing cost, but the practice is to assign the aircraft based on the organizational rank of the traveller. Fore offers its aircraft for short-term lease or for charter by other organizations whenever Fore itself does not plan to use the aircraft. Fore surveys the market often in order to keep its lease and charter rates competitive.

William Earle, Fore's vice president of finance, has claimed that a third business jet can be justified financially. However, some people in the controller's office have surmised that the real reason for a third business jet was to upgrade the aircraft used by Earle. Presently, the people outranking Earle keep the two business jets busy with the result that Earle usually flies in smaller turboprop aircraft.

The third business jet would cost $11 million. A capital expenditure of this magnitude requires a formal proposal with projected cash flows and net present value computations using Fore's minimum required rate of return. If Fore's president and the finance committee of the board of directors approve the proposal, it will be submitted to the full board of directors. The board has final approval on capital expenditures exceeding $5 million and has established a firm policy of rejecting any discretionary proposal that has a negative net present value.

Earle asked Rachel Arnett, assistant corporate controller, to prepare a proposal on a third business jet. Arnett gathered the following data:

- Acquisition cost of the aircraft, including instrumentation and interior furnishing.
- Operating cost of the aircraft for company use.
- Projected avoidable commercial airfare and other avoidable costs from company use of the plane.
- Projected value of executive time saved by using the third business jet.
- Projected contribution margin from incremental lease and charter activity.
- Estimated resale value of the aircraft.

When Earle reviewed Arnett's completed proposal and saw the large negative net present value figure, he returned the proposal to Arnett. With a glare, Earle commented, "You must have made an error. The proposal should look better than that."

Feeling some pressure, Arnett went back and checked her computations; she found no errors. However, Earle's message was clear. Arnett discarded her projections that she believed were reasonable and replaced them with figures that had a remote chance of actually occurring but were more favourable to the proposal. For example, she used first-class airfares to refigure the avoidable commercial airfare costs, even though company policy was to fly coach. She found revising the proposal to be distressing.

The revised proposal still had a negative net present value. Earle's anger was evident as he told Arnett to revise the proposal again, and to start with a $100,000 positive net present value and work backwards to compute supporting projections.

Required:

1. Explain whether Rachel Arnett's revision of the proposal was in violation of the Standards of Ethical Conduct for Practitioners of Management Accounting and Financial Management.
2. Was William Earle in violation of the Standards of Ethical Conduct for Practitioners of Management Accounting and Financial Management by telling Arnett specifically how to revise the proposal? Explain your answer.
3. Identify specific internal controls that Fore Corporation could implement to prevent unethical behaviour on the part of the vice president of finance.

(CMA, adapted)

Case 14–37 Comparison of Alternatives Using Net Present Value Analysis [LO1]

Kingsley Products, Ltd., is using a model 400 shaping machine to make one of its products. The company is expecting to have a large increase in demand for the product and is anxious to expand its productive capacity. Two possibilities are under consideration:

Alternative 1. Purchase another model 400 shaping machine to operate along with the currently owned model 400 machine.

Alternative 2. Purchase a model 800 shaping machine and use the currently owned model 400 machine as standby equipment. The model 800 machine is a high-speed unit with double the capacity of the model 400 machine.

The following additional information is available on the two alternatives:

a. Both the model 400 machine and the model 800 machine have a 10-year life from the time they are first used in production. The scrap value of both machines is negligible and can be ignored. Straight-line depreciation is used.
b. The cost of a new model 800 machine is $300,000.
c. The model 400 machine now in use cost $160,000 three years ago. Its present book value is $112,000, and its present market value is $90,000.
d. A new model 400 machine costs $170,000 now. If the company decides not to buy the model 800 machine, then the old model 400 machine will have to be replaced in seven years at a cost of $200,000. The replacement machine will be sold at the end of the tenth year for $140,000.
e. Production over the next 10 years is expected to be:

Year	Production in Units
1	40,000
2	60,000
3	80,000
4–10	90,000

f. The two models of machines are not equally efficient. Comparative variable costs per unit are:

	Model	
	400	800
Direct materials per unit	$0.25	$0.40
Direct labour per unit	0.49	0.16
Supplies and lubricants per unit	0.06	0.04
Total variable cost per unit	$0.80	$0.60

g. The model 400 machine is less costly to maintain than the model 800 machine. Annual repairs and maintenance costs on a model 400 machine are $2,500.
h. Repairs and maintenance costs on a model 800 machine, with a model 400 machine used as standby, would total $3,800 per year.
i. No other costs will change as a result of the decision between the two machines.
j. Kingsley Products has a 20% required rate of return on all investments.

Required:

(Ignore income taxes.)

1. Which alternative should the company choose? Use the net present value approach.
2. Suppose that the cost of labour increases by 10%. Would this make the model 800 machine more or less desirable? Explain. No computations are needed.
3. Suppose that the cost of direct materials doubles. Would this make the model 800 machine more or less desirable? Explain. No computations are needed.

CASE 14–38 (Appendix 14C) Make or Buy Decision Including Income Taxes [LO9]

Jonfran Company manufactures three different models of paper shredders, including the waste container which serves as the base. While the shredder heads are different for all three models, the waste container is the same. The number of waste containers that Jonfran will need during the next five years is estimated as follows:

Year 1	50,000	Year 4	55,000
Year 2	50,000	Year 5	55,000
Year 3	52,000		

The equipment used to manufacture the waste containers must be replaced because it has broken and can't be repaired. The new equipment has a list price of $945,000 but will be purchased at a 2% discount. The freight on the equipment would be $11,000, and installation costs would total $22,900. The equipment would be purchased and placed into service in January of Year 1. The equipment would have a salvage value of $15,000 at the end of its useful life.

For tax reporting purposes, the cost of the new equipment net of discounts, but including freight and installation costs, would be depreciated using a 20% CCA.

The new equipment would be more efficient than the old equipment and it would slash both direct labour and variable overhead costs in half. However, the new equipment would require the use of a slightly heavier gauge of metal, which would increase direct material costs by 30%. The company uses JIT inventory methods, but the heavier gauge metal is sometimes hard to get so the company would have to keep a small quantity on hand, which would increase working capital needs by $20,000.

The old equipment is fully depreciated and is not included in the fixed overhead. The old equipment can be sold now for $1,500; Jonfran has no alternative use for the manufacturing space at this time, so if the new equipment is not purchased, the old equipment will be left in place.

Rather than replace the old equipment, one of Jonfran's production managers has suggested that the waste containers be purchased. One supplier has quoted a price of $28 per container. This price is $7 less than Jonfran's current manufacturing cost, which follows:

Direct materials		$10
Direct labour		8
Variable overhead		6
Fixed overhead:		
Supervision	$2	
Facilities	5	
General	4	11
Total cost per unit		$35

Jonfran uses a plantwide predetermined fixed overhead rate. If the waste containers are purchased outside, the salary and benefits of one supervisor, included in the fixed overhead at $45,000, would be eliminated. No other changes would be made in the other cash and noncash items included in fixed overhead except depreciation on the new equipment.

Jonfran is subject to a 40% tax rate and requires a 14% after-tax return on all equipment purchases.

Required:

Using net present value analysis, determine whether the company should purchase the new equipment and make the waste containers or purchase the containers from the outside supplier. Use the total-cost approach and round all dollar amounts to the nearest whole dollar.

(CMA, adapted)

CASE 14–39 Net Present Value Analysis of a Lease or Buy Decision [LO1]

Top-Quality Stores, Inc., owns a nationwide chain of supermarkets. The company is going to open another store soon, and a suitable building site has been located in an attractive and rapidly growing area. In discussing how the company can acquire the desired building and other facilities needed to open the new store, Sam Watkins, the company's vice president in charge of sales, stated, "I know most of our competitors are starting to lease facilities rather than buy, but I just can't see the economics of it. Our development people tell me that we can buy the building site, put a building on it, and get all the store fixtures we need for just $850,000. They also say that property taxes, insurance, and repairs would run $20,000 a year. When you figure that we plan to keep a site for 18 years, that's a total cost of $1,210,000. But then when you realize that the property will be worth at least a half million in 18 years, that's a net cost to us of only $710,000. What would it cost to lease the property?"

"I understand that Beneficial Insurance Company is willing to purchase the building site, construct a building and install fixtures to our specifications, and then lease the facility to us for 18 years at an annual lease payment of $120,000," replied Lisa Coleman, the company's executive vice president.

"That's just my point," said Sam. "At $120,000 a year, it would cost us a cool $2,160,000 over the 18 years. That's three times what it would cost to buy, and what would we have left at the end? Nothing! The building would belong to the insurance company!"

"You're overlooking a few things," replied Lisa. "For one thing, the treasurer's office says that we could only afford to put $350,000 down if we buy the property, and then we would have to pay the other $500,000 off over four years at $175,000 a year. So there would be some interest involved on the purchase side that you haven't figured in."

"But that little bit of interest is nothing compared to over 2 million bucks for leasing," said Sam. "Also, if we lease I understand we would have to put up an $8,000 security deposit that we wouldn't get back until the end. And besides that, we would still have to pay all the yearly repairs and maintenance costs just like we owned the property. No wonder those insurance companies are so rich if they can swing deals like this."

"Well, I'll admit that I don't have all the figures sorted out yet," replied Lisa. "But I do have the operating cost breakdown for the building, which includes $7,500 annually for property taxes, $8,000 for insurance, and $4,500 for repairs and maintenance. If we lease, Beneficial will handle its own insurance costs and of course the owner will have to pay the property taxes. I'll put all this together and see if leasing makes any sense with our required rate of return of 16%. The president wants a presentation and recommendation in the executive committee meeting tomorrow. Let's see, development said the first lease payment would be due now and the remaining ones due in years 1–17. Development also said that this store should generate a net cash inflow that's well above the average for our stores."

Required:

(Ignore income taxes.)

1. Using the net present value approach, determine whether Top-Quality Stores, Inc., should lease or buy the new facility. Assume that you will be making your presentation before the company's executive committee.
2. How will you reply in the meeting if Sam Watkins brings up the issue of the building's future sales value?

GROUP AND INTERNET EXERCISES

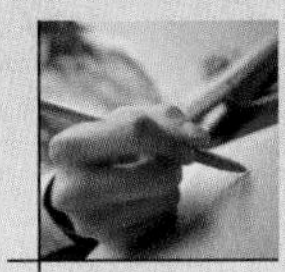

GROUP EXERCISE 14–40 Capital Budgets in Colleges

In recent years, your college or university has probably undertaken a capital budgeting project such as building or renovating a facility. Investigate one of these capital budgeting projects. You will probably need the help of your university's or college's accounting or finance office.

Required:

1. Determine the total cost of the project and the source of the funds for the project. Did the money come from provincial funds, gifts, grants, endowments, or the school's general fund?
2. Did the costs of the project stay within budget?
3. What financial criteria were used to evaluate the project?
4. If the net present value method or internal rate of return method was used, review the calculations. Do you agree with the calculations and methods used?
5. If the net present value method was not used to evaluate the project, estimate the project's net present value. If all of the required data are not available, make reasonable estimates for the missing data. What discount rate did you use? Why?
6. Evaluate the capital budgeting procedures that were actually used by your college or university.

GROUP EXERCISE 14–41 Complexities of Capital Cost

Canadian income tax regulations have become mind-numbingly complex. As a result, the Canada Revenue Agency issues interpretation bulletins to assist corporations and others to comply. Refer to IT-128R—Capital Cost Allowance—Depreciable Property by going to the CRC Web site at: http://www.cra-arc.gc.ca/E/pub/tp/it128r/it128r-e.html.

After accessing the site, find six guidelines listed in the bulletin for determining whether an expenditure is capital in nature because depreciable property was acquired or improved, or whether it is currently deductible because it is incurred for on-going maintenance or repair of a property.

Required:

List and briefly explain each guideline.

INTERNET EXERCISE 14–42

As you know, the World Wide Web is a medium that is constantly evolving. Sites come and go, and change without notice. To enable periodic updating of site addresses, this problem has been posted to the textbook Web site (www.mcgrawhill.ca/college/garrison). After accessing the site, enter the Student Centre and select this chapter. Select and complete the Internet Exercise.

After studying Appendix A, you should be able to:

1. Allocate service department costs to other departments using the direct method.
2. Allocate service department costs to other departments using the step method.
3. Allocate service department costs to other departments using the reciprocal method.
4. Allocate variable and fixed service department costs separately at the beginning of a period and at the end of the period.

SERVICE DEPARTMENT COSTING: AN ACTIVITY APPROACH

Departments within an organization can be divided into two broad classes: (1) operating departments and (2) service departments. **Operating departments** include those departments or units where the central purposes of the organization are carried out. Examples of such departments or units would include the Surgery Department at QEII Hospital; the undergraduate and graduate programs at Saint Mary's University; and producing departments such as Milling, Assembly, and Painting in a manufacturing company such as Bombardier.

Service departments, by contrast, do not engage directly in operating activities. Rather, they provide services or assistance to the operating departments. Examples of service departments include the cafeteria, internal auditing, human resources, cost accounting, and purchasing. Although service departments do not engage directly in the operating activities of an organization, the costs that they incur are generally viewed as being part of the cost of the final product or service, the same as are materials, labour, and overhead in a manufacturing company or medications in a hospital.

Operating department
A department or similar unit in an organization within which the central purposes of the organization are carried out.

Service department
A department that provides support or assistance to operating departments and that does not engage directly in production or in other operating activities of an organization.

Chapter 1 stated that most organizations have one or more service departments that provide services for the entire organization. In this appendix, we look more closely at service departments and consider how their costs are allocated to the units they serve. The major question we consider is: How much of a service department's cost is to be allocated to each of the units that it serves?

Service department costs are allocated to operating departments for a variety of reasons including:

- To encourage operating departments to make appropriate use of service department resources. If the services were provided for free, operating managers would be inclined to waste these resources.

- To provide operating departments with more complete cost data for making decisions. Actions taken by operating departments have impacts on service department costs. For example, hiring another employee will increase costs in the human resources department. Such service department costs should be charged to the operating departments, otherwise the operating departments will not take them into account when making decisions.
- To help measure the profitability of operating departments. Allocating service department costs to operating departments provides a more complete accounting of the costs incurred as a consequence of activities in the operating departments.
- To create an incentive for service departments to operate efficiently. Allocating service department costs to operating departments provides a system of checks and balances in the sense that cost-conscious operating departments will take an active interest in keeping service department costs low.
- To value inventory for external financial reporting purposes. Generally Accepted Accounting Principles (GAAP) require that all manufacturing overhead costs be assigned to products. Allocating service department costs to operating departments ensures that these manufacturing overhead costs are included in the operating departments' overhead rates, which are used to apply costs to products.
- When cost-plus pricing is used, service department costs are commonly allocated to the operating departments so as to include these costs in the cost base.

Several different allocation methods will be considered in this chapter. The method that is selected can have a significant impact on the computed costs of goods and services and can affect an operating department's performance evaluation.

Organizationally, managers are placed in charge of departments. For control purposes, costs are often collected by departments to permit the use of responsibility accounting. In Chapter 8, activities served as the basis of classifying costs. This permits an activity focus to cost management rather than the responsibility focus seen with departmental classification. When activities involve more than a single department, the specifics of classifications will differ between the two approaches. If activities remain within a single department, then the departmental and activities classifications can yield the same result. If departments involve both operating and support or service groupings, then the specifics of this appendix will be needed to allocate properly the costs to the output of the organization.

ALLOCATION OF SERVICE DEPARTMENT COSTS

Allocating service department costs begins with selecting the proper allocation base—the first topic in this section. After completing this discussion, we will move on to consider how to account for services that service departments provide to each other.

Selecting Allocation Bases

Many companies use a two-stage costing process. In the first stage, costs are assigned to the operating departments; in the second stage, costs are assigned from the operating departments to products and services. We focused on the second stage of this allocation process in Chapter 3 and reserved discussion of first-stage costing procedures to this appendix. On the following pages, we discuss the assignment of costs from service departments to operating departments, *which represents the first stage of the two-stage costing process.*

Costs are usually assigned from a service department to other departments using an allocation base, which is some measure of activity. The costs being allocated should be "driven" by the allocation base. Ideally, the total cost of the service department should be proportional to the size of the allocation base. Managers also often argue that the allocation base should reflect as accurately as possible the benefits that the various departments receive from the services that are being provided. For example, most managers would argue that the square metres of building space occupied by each operating department should be used as the allocation base for custodial services since both the benefits and costs of custodial services tend to be proportional to the amount of space occupied by a department. Examples of allocation bases for some service departments are listed in Exhibit A–1. A given service department's costs may be allocated using more than one base. For example, data processing costs may be allocated on the basis of CPU minutes for mainframe computers *and* on the basis of the number of personal computers used in each operating department.

Although the previous paragraph explains how to select an allocation base, another critical factor should not be overlooked: The allocations should be clear and straightforward and easily understood by the managers to whom the costs are being allocated.

Interdepartmental Services

Many service departments provide services for each other, as well as for operating departments. The Cafeteria Department, for example, provides food for all employees, including those assigned to other service departments. In turn, the Cafeteria Department may receive services from other service departments, such as from Custodial Services or from Human Resources. Services provided between service departments are known as **interdepartmental** or **reciprocal services.**

Interdepartmental services Services provided between service departments. Also called *reciprocal services.*

Reciprocal services Same as *interdepartmental services.*

Three approaches are used to allocate the costs of service departments to other departments. These are known as the *direct method,* the *step method,* and the *reciprocal method.* All three methods are discussed in the following paragraphs.

Direct Method The **direct method** is the simplest of the three cost allocation methods. It ignores the services provided by a service department to other service departments and allocates all costs directly to operating departments. Even if a service department (such as Human Resources) provides a large amount of service to another service department (such as the cafeteria), no allocations are made between the two departments. Rather, all costs are allocated *directly* to the operating departments. Hence the term *direct method.*

Direct method The allocation of all of a service department's costs directly to operating departments without recognizing services provided to other service departments.

LEARNING OBJECTIVE 1
Allocate service department costs to other departments using the direct method.

To provide an example of the direct method, assume that the QEII Hospital has two service departments and two operating departments as shown below:

	Service Departments		Operating Departments		
	Hospital Administration	Custodial Services	Laboratory	Daily Patient Care	Total
Departmental costs before allocation	$360,000	$90,000	$261,000	$689,000	$1,400,000
Employee hours	12,000	6,000	18,000	30,000	66,000
Space occupied—square metres	1,000	20	500	4,500	6,020

In the allocations that follow, Hospital Administration costs will be allocated on the basis of employee-hours and Custodial Services costs will be allocated on the basis of square metres occupied.

The direct method of allocating the hospital's service department costs to the operating departments is shown in Exhibit A–2. Several things should be carefully noted in this exhibit. First, even though there are employee-hours in both the Hospital Administration Department itself and in the Custodial Services Department, these employee-hours are ignored when allocating service department costs using the direct method. *Under the direct method, any of the allocation base attributable to the service departments themselves is ignored; only the amount of the allocation base attributable to the operating departments is used in the allocation.* Note that the same rule is used when allocating the costs of the Custodial Services Department. Even though the Hospital Administration and

EXHIBIT A–1 Examples of Bases Used in Allocating Service Department Costs

Service Department	Bases (cost drivers) Involved
Laundry	Kilograms of laundry
Airport Ground Services	Number of flights
Cafeteria	Number of employees; number of meals
Medical Facilities	Cases handled; number of employees; hours worked
Materials Handling	Hours of service; volume handled
Data Processing	CPU minutes; lines printed; disk storage used; number of personal computers
Custodial Services (building and grounds)	Square metres occupied
Cost Accounting	Labour-hours; clients or patients serviced
Power	Kilowatt-hours used; capacity of machines
Human Resources	Number of employees; employee turnover; training hours
Receiving, Shipping, and Stores	Units handled; number of requisitions; space occupied
Factory Administration	Total labour-hours
Maintenance	Machine-hours

Custodial Services departments occupy some space, this is ignored when the Custodial Services costs are allocated. Finally, note that after all allocations have been completed, all of the departmental costs are contained in the two operating departments. These costs will form the basis for preparing overhead rates for purposes of costing products and services produced in the operating departments.

Although the direct method is simple, it is less accurate than the other methods because it ignores interdepartmental services. This can lead to distorted product and service costs. Even so, many organizations use the direct method because of its simplicity.

LEARNING OBJECTIVE **2**
Allocate service department costs to other departments using the step method.

Step Method Unlike the direct method, the **step method** provides for allocation of a service department's costs to other service departments, as well as to operating departments. The step method is sequential. The sequence typically begins with the department that provides the greatest amount of service to other service departments. After its costs have been allocated, the process continues, step by step, ending with the department that provides the least amount of services to other service departments. This step procedure is illustrated in graphic form in Exhibit A–3, assuming that the Hospital Administration costs are allocated first at QEII Hospital.

Step method
The allocation of a service department's costs to other service departments, as well as to operating departments, in a sequential manner. The sequence starts with the service department that provides the greatest amount of service to other departments.

EXHIBIT A–2 Direct Method of Allocation

	Service Department		Operating Department		
	Hospital Administration	Custodial Services	Laboratory	Daily Patient Care	Total
Departmental costs before allocation	$ 360,000	$ 90,000	$261,000	$689,000	$1,400,000
Allocation:					
Hospital Administration costs ($^{18}/_{48}$, $^{30}/_{48}$)*	(360,000)		135,000	225,000	
Custodial Services costs ($^{5}/_{50}$, $^{45}/_{50}$)†		(90,000)	9,000	81,000	
Total costs after allocation	$ –0–	$ –0–	$405,000	$995,000	$1,400,000

*Based on the employee-hours in the two operating departments, which are 18,000 hours + 30,000 hours = 48,000 hours.

†Based on the space occupied by the two operating departments, which is 500 square metres + 4,500 square metres = 5,000 square metres.

EXHIBIT A–3 Graphic Illustration—Step Method

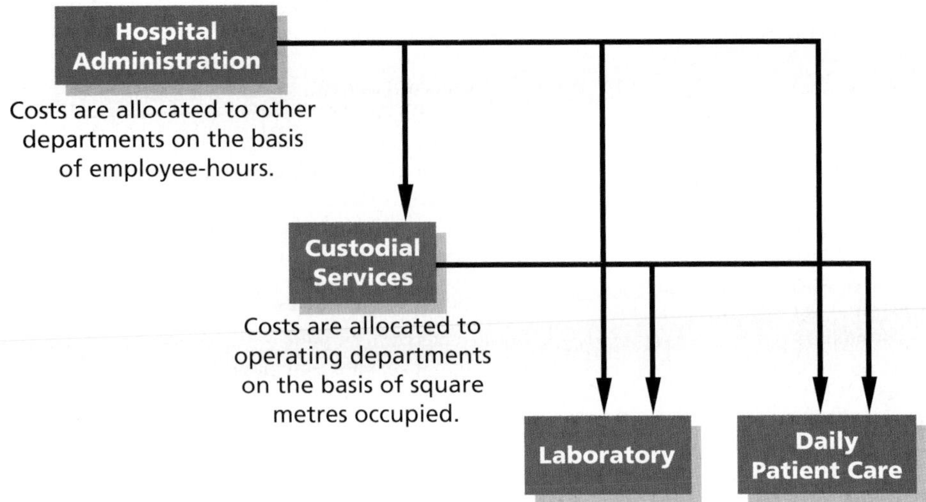

Exhibit A–4 uses the allocations of the QEII Hospital to show the details of the step method. Note the following three key points about these allocations. First, under the Allocation heading in Exhibit A–4, you see two allocations, or steps. In the step method, the first step allocates the costs of Hospital Administration to another service department (Custodial Services) as well as to the operating departments. The allocation base for Hospital Administration costs now includes the employee-hours for Custodial Services as well as for the operating departments. However, the allocation base still excludes the employee-hours for Hospital Administration itself. *In both the direct and step methods, any amount of the allocation base attributable to the service department whose cost is being allocated is always ignored.* Second, looking again at Exhibit A–4, note that in the second step under the Allocation heading, the cost of Custodial Services is allocated to the two operating departments, and none of the cost is allocated to Hospital Administration even though Hospital Administration occupies space in the building. *In the step method, any amount of the allocation base that is attributable to a service department whose cost has already been allocated is ignored.* After a service department's costs have been allocated, costs of other service departments are not reallocated back to it. Third, note that the

EXHIBIT A–4 Step Method of Allocation

	Service Department		Operating Department		
	Hospital Administration	Custodial Services	Laboratory	Daily Patient Care	Total
Departmental costs before allocation	$ 360,000	$ 90,000	$261,000	$ 689,000	$1,400,000
Allocation:					
Hospital Administration costs (6/54, 18/54, 30/54)*	(360,000)	40,000	120,000	200,000	
Custodial Services costs (5/50, 45/50)†		(130,000)	13,000	117,000	
Total costs after allocation	$ -0-	$ -0-	$394,000	$1,006,000	$1,400,000

*Based on the employee-hours in Custodial Services and the two operating departments, which are 6,000 hours + 18,000 hours + 30,000 hours = 54,000 hours.

†As in Exhibit A–2, this allocation is based on the space occupied by the two operating departments.

cost of Custodial Services allocated to other departments in the second step ($130,000) in Exhibit A–4 includes the costs of Hospital Administration that were allocated to Custodial Services in the first step in Exhibit A–4.

FOCUS *on Current Practice*

Computer software included as part of an overall system for enterprise resource planning or as an add-on to such a system can incorporate the routines necessary for overhead allocation either for activity-based costing or departmental overhead allocation. A recent addition to ABC software touted as a major advance is the inclusion of reciprocal allocation. This allows units such as information systems and human resources to incorporate their reciprocal relationships into the cost allocations. This feature is particularly important for banks, insurance companies, and government agencies that tend to have numerous reciprocal situations. The cost of such overhead software is reported to range from $2,000 to $30,000.

Source: Jim Gurowka, "Activity-Based Costing Software—The Market Explodes," *CMA Magazine*, May 1997, pp. 13–19.

LEARNING OBJECTIVE 3
Allocate service department costs to other departments using the reciprocal method.

Reciprocal method
A method of allocating service department costs that gives full recognition to interdepartmental services.

Reciprocal Method

The **reciprocal method** gives full recognition to interdepartmental services. Under the step method discussed above, only partial recognition of interdepartmental services is possible, since the step method always allocates costs forward—never backward. The reciprocal method, by contrast, allocates service department costs in *both* directions. Thus, since Custodial Services in the prior example provides service for Hospital Administration, part of Custodial Services' costs will be allocated *back* to Hospital Administration if the reciprocal method is used. At the same time, part of Hospital Administration's costs will be allocated *forward* to Custodial Services. This type of reciprocal allocation requires the use of simultaneous linear equations.

To illustrate reciprocal allocation, consider the following illustration in Exhibit A–5 based on Exhibit A–2 and the data provided about QEII Hospital (page 742).

Note that the amount allocated by Hospital Administration had to be determined outside the schedule before the allocation was made. Similarly the Custodial Services total costs of $132,453 include what was charged from Hospital Administration. These two new amounts include the effect of the reciprocal services each department performed for the other. Once the simultaneous solutions are determined, the allocations proceed as in the step method except that allocations can go backward rather than proceed in sequence as required by the step method. Once the allocations are completed, totals for the operating departments are checked to ensure that the total overhead of $1.4 million was actually allocated. If more than two service departments exist, the solution procedure to determine the amount to be allocated commonly uses matrix inversion, which is beyond the scope of this book.

The reciprocal method has not had a long history of use in practice for two reasons. First, the computations are relatively complex. Currently, this complexity issue can be overcome by the use of computers. Second, the step method usually provides results that are a reasonable approximation of the results that the reciprocal method would provide. Thus, companies have had little motivation to use the more complex reciprocal method.

Revenue-Producing Departments

To conclude our discussion of allocation methods, it is important to note that even though most service departments are cost centres and therefore generate no revenues, a few service departments such as the cafeteria may charge for the services they perform. If a service department generates revenues, these revenues should be offset against the department's costs, and only the net amount of cost remaining after this offset should be allocated to other departments within the organization. In this manner, the other departments will not be required to bear costs for which the service department has already been reimbursed.

EXHIBIT A–5 Reciprocal Allocation

Hospital Administration (HA)

$$HA = 360{,}000 + \tfrac{2}{12}\,CS$$

where HA denotes the costs to be allocated; that is, the direct costs plus those allocated [(1,000/(500 + 4,500 + 1,000)] = 1/6 or 2/12] from Custodial Services.

Custodial Services (CS)

$$CS = 90{,}000 + \tfrac{1}{9}\,HA$$

where CS denotes the costs to be allocated; that is, the direct costs plus those allocated [(6,000/(18,000 + 30,000 + 6,000)] = 1/9] from Hospital Administration.

To solve (1) $-360{,}000 = -HA + \tfrac{2}{12}\,CS$

(2) $-90{,}000 = \tfrac{1}{9}\,HA - CS$

Multiply (2) by 9 (1) $-360{,}000 = -HA + \tfrac{2}{12}\,CS$

(2) $\underline{-810{,}000} = \underline{HA - 9\,CS}$

Add (1) and (2) $-1{,}170{,}000 = 0 - 8\left(\tfrac{10}{12}\right) CS$

$CS = \$132{,}453$

Substitute in (1) $-360{,}000 = -HA + \tfrac{2}{12}(132{,}453)$

$HA = \$360{,}000 + \$22{,}076$

$HA = \$382{,}076$

	Service Department		Operating Department		
	Hospital Administration	Custodial Services	Laboratory	Daily Patient Care	Total
Departmental costs before allocation	$ 360,000	$ 90,000	$261,000	$ 689,000	$1,400,000
Allocation:					
Hospital Administration costs (1/9, 3/9, 5/9)	(382,076)	42,453	127,359	212,264	
Custodial Services costs (2/12, 1/12, 9/12)	22,076	(132,453)	11,038	99,339	
Totals	$ -0-	$ -0-	$399,397	$1,000,603	$1,400,000

ALLOCATING COSTS BY BEHAVIOUR

Whenever possible, service department costs should be separated into variable and fixed classifications and allocated separately. This approach is necessary to avoid possible inequities in allocation, as well as to provide more useful data for planning and control of departmental operations.

Variable Costs

Variable costs are direct costs of providing services that vary in total in proportion to fluctuations in the level of service provided. Food cost in a cafeteria would be a variable cost, for example, and one would expect this cost to vary proportionately with the number of persons using the cafeteria.

As a general rule, variable costs should be charged to consuming departments according to whatever activity causes the incurrence of the costs involved. If, for example, the variable costs of a service department such as maintenance are caused by the number of machine-hours worked in the producing departments, then variable maintenance costs should be allocated to the producing departments using machine-hours as the allocation basis. By this means, the departments directly responsible for the incurrence of servicing costs are required to bear them in proportion to their actual usage of the service.

Technically, the assigning of variable servicing costs to consuming departments can more accurately be termed *charges* than allocations, since the service department is actually charging the consuming departments at some fixed rate per unit of service provided. In effect, the service department is saying, "I'll charge you *X* dollars for every unit of my service that you consume. You can consume as much or as little as you desire; the total charge you bear will vary proportionately."

Fixed Costs

The fixed costs of service departments represent the costs of making capacity available for use. These costs should be allocated to consuming departments in *predetermined lump-sum amounts.* By predetermined lump-sum amounts we mean that the total amount charged to each consuming department is determined in advance and, once determined, does not change from period to period. The lump-sum amount charged to a department can be based either on the department's peak-period or long-run average servicing needs. The logic behind lump-sum allocations of this type is as follows:

When a service department is first established, its capacity will be determined by the needs of the departments that it will service. This capacity may reflect the peak-period needs of the other departments, or it may reflect their long-run average or "normal" servicing needs. Depending on how much servicing capacity is provided for, it will be necessary to make a commitment of resources to the servicing unit, which will be reflected in its fixed costs. These fixed costs should be borne by the consuming departments in proportion to the amount of capacity each consuming department requires. That is, if available capacity in the service department has been provided to meet the peak-period needs of consuming departments, then the fixed costs of the service department should be allocated in predetermined lump-sum amounts to consuming departments on this basis. If available capacity has been provided to meet only "normal" or long-run average needs, then the fixed costs should be allocated on this basis.

Once set, allocations should not vary from period to period, since they represent the cost of having a certain level of service capacity available and on line for each consuming department. The fact that a consuming department does not need a peak level or even a "normal" level of servicing every period is immaterial; if it requires such servicing at certain times, then the capacity to deliver it must be available. It is the responsibility of the consuming departments to bear the cost of that availability.

To illustrate this idea, assume that Novak Company has just organized a Maintenance Department to service all machines in the Cutting, Assembly, and Finishing departments. In determining the capacity of the newly organized Maintenance Department, the various producing departments estimated that they would have the following peak-period needs for maintenance:

Department	Peak-Period Maintenance Needs in Terms of Number of Hours of Maintenance Work Required	Percent of Total Hours
Cutting	900	30%
Assembly	1,800	60%
Finishing	300	10%
	3,000	100%

Therefore, in allocating the Maintenance Department fixed costs to the producing departments, 30% (i.e., 900/3,000 = 30%) should be allocated to the Cutting Department, 60% to the Assembly Department, and 10% to the Finishing Department. These lump-sum allocations *will not change* from period to period unless there is some shift in peak-period servicing needs.

Should Actual or Budgeted Costs Be Allocated?

Should the *actual* or *budgeted* costs of a service department be allocated to operating departments? The answer is that budgeted costs should be allocated. What's wrong with allocating actual costs? Allocating actual costs burdens the operating departments with any inefficiencies in the service department. If actual costs are allocated, then any lack of cost control on the part of the service department is simply buried in a routine allocation to other departments.

Any variance over budgeted costs should, in general, be retained in the service department and closed out at year-end against the company's revenues or against cost of goods sold, along with other variances. Operating department managers justifiably complain bitterly if they are forced to absorb service department inefficiencies.

A Summary of Cost Allocation Guidelines

To summarize the material covered in the preceding sections, we can note the following three guidelines to remember about allocating service department costs:

1. If possible, the distinction between variable and fixed costs in service departments should be maintained.
2. Variable costs should be allocated at the budgeted rate, according to whatever activity (kilometres driven, direct labour-hours, number of employees) causes the incurrence of the cost.
   a. If the allocations are being made at the beginning of the year, they should be based on the budgeted activity level planned for the consuming departments. The allocation formula would be:

   $$\text{Variable cost allocated at the beginning of the period} = \text{Budgeted rate} \times \text{Budgeted activity}$$

   b. If the allocations are being made at the end of the year, they should be based on the actual activity level that has occurred during the year. The allocation formula would be:

   $$\text{Variable cost allocated at the end of the period} = \text{Budgeted rate} \times \text{Actual activity}$$

   Allocations made at the beginning of the year would be to provide data for computing overhead rates for costing of products and billing of services in the operating departments. Allocations made at the end of the year would be to provide data for comparing actual performance to planned performance.
3. Fixed costs represent the costs of having service capacity available. Where feasible, these costs should be allocated in predetermined lump-sum amounts. The lump-sum amount going to each department should be in proportion to the servicing needs that gave rise to the investment in the service department in the first place. (This might be either peak-period needs for servicing or long-run average needs.) Budgeted fixed costs, rather than actual fixed costs, should always be allocated.

Implementing the Allocation Guidelines

We will now use specific examples to show how to implement the three guidelines given above. First, we focus on the allocation of costs for a single department.

LEARNING OBJECTIVE 4
Allocate variable and fixed service department costs separately at the beginning of a period and at the end of the period.

Basic Allocation Techniques Seaboard Airlines is divided into a Freight Division and a Passenger Division. The company has a single aircraft Maintenance Department that provides servicing to both divisions. Variable servicing costs are budgeted at $10 per flight-hour. The fixed costs of $750,000 for the Maintenance Department are budgeted based on the peak-period demand, which occurs during the month of December to the end of the New Year's holiday period. The airline wants to make sure that none of its aircraft are grounded during this key period due to unavailability of maintenance facilities. Approximately 40% of the maintenance during this period is performed on the Freight

Division's equipment, and 60% is performed on the Passenger Division's equipment. These figures and the budgeted flight-hours for the coming year appear below:

	Percent of Peak Period Capacity Required	Budgeted Flight-Hours
Freight Division	40%	9,000
Passenger Division ...	60%	15,000
Total	100%	24,000

Given these data, the amount of cost that would be allocated to each division from the aircraft Maintenance Department at the beginning of the coming year would be as follows:

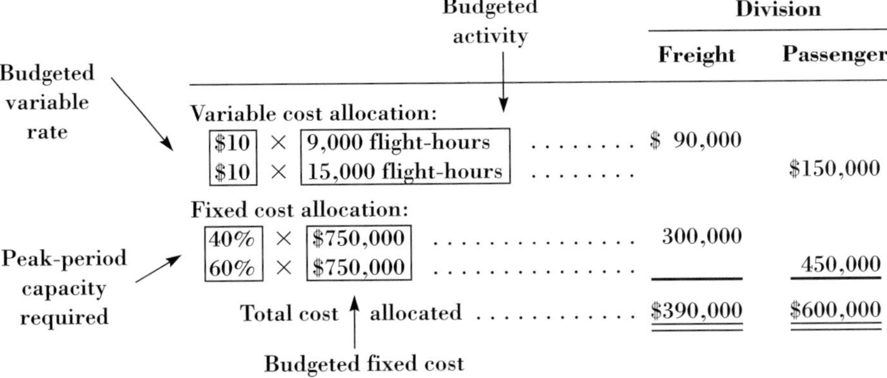

	Division: Freight	Division: Passenger
Variable cost allocation:		
$10 × 9,000 flight-hours	$ 90,000	
$10 × 15,000 flight-hours		$150,000
Fixed cost allocation:		
40% × $750,000	300,000	
60% × $750,000		450,000
Total cost allocated	$390,000	$600,000

As explained earlier, these allocated costs would be included in the flexible budgets of the respective divisions and included in the computation of divisional overhead rates.

At the end of the year, Seaboard Airlines' management may want to make a second allocation, this time based on actual activity, in order to compare actual performance for the year against planned performance. To illustrate, year-end records show that actual costs in the aircraft Maintenance Department for the year were variable costs, $260,000; and fixed costs, $780,000. One division logged more flight-hours during the year than planned, and the other division logged fewer flight-hours than planned, as shown below:

	Flight-Hours: Budgeted	Flight-Hours: Actual
Freight Division	9,000	8,000
Passenger Division	15,000	17,000
Total flight-hours	24,000	25,000

The amount of actual Maintenance Department cost charged to each division for the year would be as follows:

Actual Activity

Budgeted variable rate

Peak-period capacity required

	Division: Freight	Division: Passenger
Variable cost allocation:		
$10 × 8,000 flight-hours	$ 80,000	
$10 × 17,000 flight-hours		$170,000
Fixed cost allocation:		
40% × $750,000	300,000	
60% × $750,000		450,000
Total cost allocated	$380,000	$620,000

Budgeted fixed cost

Notice that variable servicing cost is charged to the operating divisions based on the budgeted rate ($10 per hour) and the *actual activity* for the year. In contrast, the charges for fixed costs are exactly the same as they were at the beginning of the year. Also note that the two operating divisions are *not* charged for the actual costs of the service department, which may be influenced by inefficiency in the service department and be beyond the control of the managers of the operating divisions. Instead, the service department is held responsible for the unallocated actual costs as shown below:

	Variable	Fixed
Total actual costs incurred	$260,000	$780,000
Costs allocated (above)	250,000*	750,000
Spending variance—not allocated . . .	$ 10,000	$ 30,000

*$10 per flight-hour × 25,000 actual flight-hours = $250,000

These variances will be closed out against the company's overall revenues for the year, along with any other variances that may occur.

EFFECT OF ALLOCATIONS ON OPERATING DEPARTMENTS

Once allocations have been completed, what do the operating departments do with the allocated service department costs? The allocations are typically included in performance evaluations of the operating departments and also included in determining their profitability.

In addition, if the operating departments are responsible for developing overhead rates for costing of products or services, then the allocated costs are combined with the other costs of the operating departments, and the total is used as a basis for rate computations. This rate development process is illustrated in Exhibit A–6.

The flexible budget serves as the means for combining allocated service department costs with operating department costs and for computing overhead rates. An example is presented in Exhibit A–7. Note from the exhibit that both variable and fixed service department costs have been allocated to Superior Company's Milling Department and are included on the latter's flexible budget. Since allocated service department costs become

EXHIBIT A–6 Effect of Allocations on Products and Services

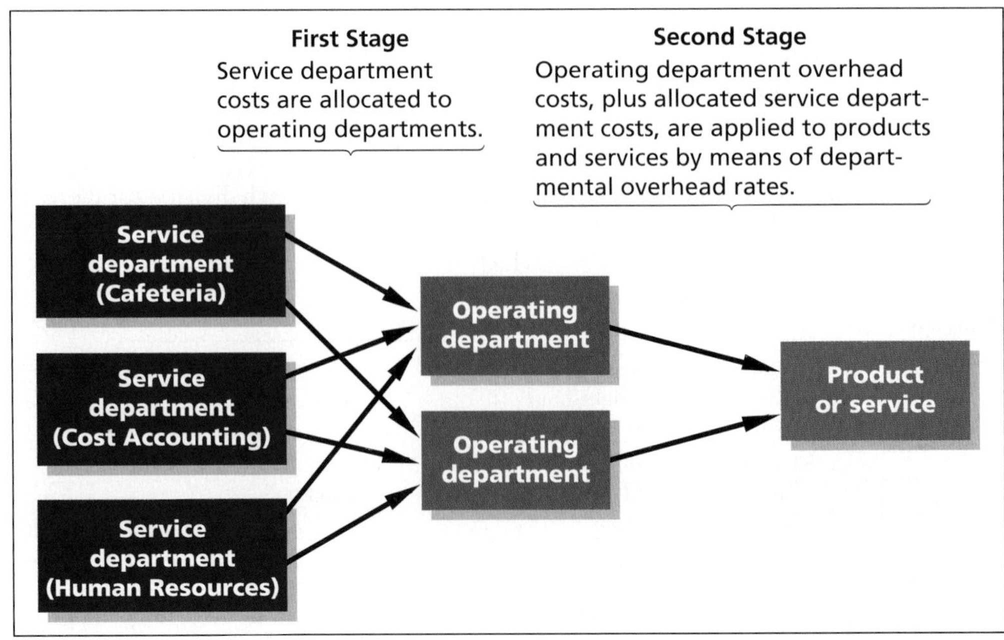

EXHIBIT A–7 Flexible Budget Containing Allocated Service Department Costs

SUPERIOR COMPANY
Flexible Budget—Milling Department

Budgeted direct labour-hours 50,000

Overhead Costs	Cost Formula (per direct labour-hour)	Direct Labour-Hours 40,000	50,000	60,000
Variable overhead costs:				
Indirect labour	$1.45	$ 58,000	$ 72,500	$ 87,000
Indirect material	0.90	36,000	45,000	54,000
Utilities	0.10	4,000	5,000	6,000
Allocation—Cafeteria	0.15	6,000	7,500	9,000
Total variable overhead cost	$2.60	104,000	130,000	156,000
Fixed overhead costs:				
Depreciation		85,000	85,000	85,000
Supervisory salaries		110,000	110,000	110,000
Property taxes		9,000	9,000	9,000
Allocation—Cafeteria		21,000	21,000	21,000
Allocation—Human Resources		45,000	45,000	45,000
Total fixed overhead cost		270,000	270,000	270,000
Total overhead cost		$374,000	$400,000	$426,000

$$\text{Predetermined overhead rate} = \frac{\$400{,}000}{50{,}000 \text{ DLH}} = \$8 \text{ per direct labour-hour}$$

an integral part of the flexible budget, they are automatically included in overhead rate computations, as shown at the bottom of the exhibit.

SOME CAUTIONS IN ALLOCATING SERVICE DEPARTMENT COSTS

Pitfalls in Allocating Fixed Costs

Rather than allocate fixed costs in predetermined lump-sum amounts, some firms allocate them by use of a *variable* allocation base that fluctuates from period to period. This practice can distort decisions and create serious inequities between departments. The inequities will arise from the fact that the fixed costs allocated to one department will be heavily influenced by what happens in *other* departments or segments of the organization.

To illustrate, assume that Kolby Products has an auto service centre that provides maintenance work on the fleet of autos used in the company's two sales territories. The auto service centre costs are all fixed. Contrary to good practice, the company allocates these fixed costs to the sales territories on the basis of actual kilometres driven (a variable base). Selected cost data for the last two years follow:

	Year 1	Year 2
Auto service centre costs (all fixed)	$120,000 (a)	$120,000 (a)
Western sales territory—kilometres driven	1,500,000	1,500,000
Eastern sales territory—kilometres driven	1,500,000	900,000
Total kilometres driven	3,000,000 (b)	2,400,000 (b)
Allocation rate per kilometre, (a) ÷ (b)	$0.04	$0.05

Notice that, in both years, the Western sales territory maintained an activity level of 1,500,000 kilometres driven. On the other hand, the Eastern sales territory allowed its activity to drop off from 1,500,000 kilometres in year 1 to only 900,000 kilometres in year 2. The auto service centre costs that would have been allocated to the two sales territories over the two-year span using actual kilometres driven as the allocation base are as follows:

Year 1:	
Western sales territory: 1,500,000 kilometres at $0.04	$ 60,000
Eastern sales territory: 1,500,000 kilometres at $0.04	60,000
Total cost allocated	$120,000
Year 2:	
Western sales territory: 1,500,000 kilometres at $0.05	$ 75,000
Eastern sales territory: 900,000 kilometres at $0.05	45,000
Total cost allocated	$120,000

In year 1, the two sales territories share the service department costs equally. However, in year 2, the bulk of the service department costs are allocated to the Western sales territory. This is not because of any increase in activity in the Western sales territory; rather, it is because of the *decrease* in activity in the Eastern sales territory. Even though the Western sales territory maintained the same level of activity in both years, the use of a variable allocation base has caused it to be penalized with a heavier cost allocation in year 2 because of what has happened in *another* part of the company.

This kind of inequity is almost inevitable when a variable allocation base is used to allocate fixed costs. The manager of the Western sales territory undoubtedly will be upset about the inequity forced on his territory, but he will feel powerless to do anything about it. The result will be a loss of confidence in the system and considerable ill feeling.

Beware of Sales Dollars as an Allocation Base

Over the years, sales dollars have been a favourite allocation base for service department costs. One reason is that a sales dollars base is simple, straightforward, and easy to work with. Another reason is that people tend to view sales dollars as a measure of well-being, or "ability to pay," and, hence, as a measure of how readily costs can be absorbed from other parts of the organization.

Unfortunately, sales dollars are often a very poor allocation base, for the reason that sales dollars vary from period to period, whereas the costs being allocated are often largely *fixed* in nature. As discussed earlier, if a variable base is used to allocate fixed costs, inequities can result between departments, because the costs being allocated to one department will depend in large part on what happens in *other* departments. For example, a let-up in sales effort in one department will shift allocated costs off that department and onto other, more productive departments. In effect, the departments putting forth the best sales efforts are penalized in the form of higher allocations, simply because of inefficiencies elsewhere that are beyond their control. The result is often bitterness and resentment on the part of the managers of the better departments.

Consider the following situation encountered by one of the authors:

A large men's clothing store has one service department and three sales departments—Suits, Shoes, and Accessories. The Service Department's costs total $60,000 per period and are allocated to the three sales departments according to sales dollars. A recent period showed the following allocation:

	Department			
	Suits	Shoes	Accessories	Total
Sales by department	$260,000	$40,000	$100,000	$400,000
Percentage of total sales	65%	10%	25%	100%
Allocation of service department costs, based on percentage of total sales	$ 39,000	$ 6,000	$ 15,000	$ 60,000

In a following period, the manager of the Suits Department launched a very successful program to expand sales by $100,000 in his department. Sales in the other two departments remained unchanged. Total service department costs also remained unchanged, but the allocation of these costs changed substantially, as shown below:

	Department			
	Suits	**Shoes**	**Accessories**	**Total**
Sales by department	$360,000	$40,000	$100,000	$500,000
Percentage of total sales	72%	8%	20%	100%
Allocation of service department costs, based on percentage of total sales	$ 43,200	$ 4,800	$ 12,000	$ 60,000
Increase (or decrease) from prior allocation	4,200	(1,200)	(3,000)	—

The manager of the Suits Department complained that as a result of his successful effort to expand sales in his department, he was being forced to carry a larger share of the Service Department costs. On the other hand, the managers of the departments that showed no improvement in sales were relieved of a portion of the costs that they had been carrying. Yet there had been no change in the amount of services provided for any department.

The manager of the Suits Department viewed the increased Service Department cost allocation to his department as a penalty for his outstanding performance, and he wondered whether his efforts had really been worthwhile after all in the eyes of top management.

Sales dollars should be used as an allocation base only in those cases where there is a direct causal relationship between sales dollars and the service department costs being allocated. In those situations where service department costs are fixed, they should be allocated according to the three guidelines discussed earlier in this appendix.

No Distinction Made between Fixed and Variable Costs

Unfortunately, many companies do not distinguish between fixed and variable costs in their service department allocations. An example of such an allocation was given earlier in Exhibit A–4, where we first illustrated the step method.

Should All Costs Be Allocated?

As a general rule, any service department costs that are incurred as a result of specific services provided to operating departments should be allocated back to these departments and used to compute overhead rates and to measure performance and profitability. The only time when this general rule is not followed is in those situations where, in the view of the management, allocation would result in an undesirable behavioural response from people in the operating departments. This is particularly a problem when, in violation of the principles stated earlier, fixed costs are allocated to operating units on the basis of their actual usage of a service. For example, in periods when departments are under pressure to cut costs, they may be reluctant to use the services of systems design analysts and internal consultants because of the charges that would be involved.

To avoid discouraging use of a service that is beneficial to the entire organization, some firms do not charge for the service at all. These managers feel that by making such services a free commodity, departments will be more inclined to take full advantage of their benefits.

Other firms take a somewhat different approach. They agree that charging according to usage may discourage utilization of such services as systems design, but they argue that such services should not be free. Instead of providing free services, these firms take what is sometimes called a **retainer fee approach.** This is essentially the predetermined lump-sum approach discussed earlier for fixed costs. Each department is charged a flat amount each year, regardless of how much or how little of the service it utilizes. If a department knows it is going to be charged a certain amount for systems design services, *regardless of usage,* then it is more likely to use the service.

Retainer fee approach
A method of allocating service department costs in which other departments are charged a flat amount each period regardless of usage of the service involved.

FOCUS on Current Practice

Hospitals in New Zealand, as elsewhere, are under considerable pressure to reduce costs. Consequently, managers are being held responsible for the costs of their departments and performance evaluations are often heavily influenced by cost control efforts. How these costs are computed can have a dramatic impact on evaluations. According to the accounting department of Waikato Hospital, the average cost per test in the hospital's pathology lab had increased from NZ$5.90 to NZ$7.29 over a three-year period. On the other hand, according to the management of the pathology lab, the cost per test had decreased from NZ$1.44 to NZ$1.42 over the same period. (NZ$ denotes a New Zealand dollar.) What accounts for this huge discrepancy in both the cost per test and the trend over time? The accounting department included allocations of the hospital's general overhead costs in the costs of the pathology lab; the managers of the pathology lab did not. The hospital's accounting staff conceded that the pathology laboratory was indeed more efficient in terms of its direct costs, but "Unfortunately, they're getting more indirect costs [allocated to them]." The manager of the pathology lab, who had taken aggressive steps to improve efficiency and control costs, was outraged.

Source: Necia France, Graham Francis, Stewart Lawrence, and Sydney Sacks, "Cost Counting and Comparability: Aspects of Performance Measurement in a Pathology Laboratory," *Pacific Accounting Review* 14, no. 2, December 2002, pp. 1–31.

SUMMARY

Service departments are organized to provide some needed service in a single, centralized place, rather than to have all units within the organization provide the service for themselves. Although service departments do not engage directly in production or other operating activities, the costs that they incur are vital to the overall success of an organization and therefore are properly included as part of the cost of its products and services.

Service department costs are charged to operating departments by an allocation process. In turn, the operating departments include the allocated costs within their flexible budgets, from which overhead rates are computed for purposes of costing of products or services.

Variable and fixed service department costs should be allocated separately. The variable costs should be allocated according to whatever activity causes their incurrence. The fixed costs should be allocated in predetermined lump-sum amounts according to either the peak-period or the long-run average servicing needs of the consuming departments. Budgeted costs, rather than actual costs, should always be allocated to avoid the passing on of inefficiency between departments. Any variances between budgeted and actual service department costs should be kept within the service departments for analysis purposes, then written off against revenues or against cost of goods sold, along with other variances.

FOCUS on Current Practice

Modelling the way products consume support services is a particular challenge. If different products draw on support services in different ways, then estimates of product costs can be significantly affected by how well the relationships among support services and with production activities are captured.

The use of step-down and reciprocal allocation methods attempt to better reflect these complex resource flows. The direct method of service department cost allocation and the activity-based costing method, for example, assume that service departments provide no support to each other. If this assumption is wrong, your estimates of the final costs of your products and services will be wrong, too.

Much of the current debate about overhead allocation is concerned with the way that products consume support services and other overhead resources. If you have only one product, or your products are produced in focused production facilities, or each of your products uses these resources in the same way, then simple overhead allocation methods will reasonably capture resource consumption. As your product diversity increases, and particularly as the volume of production and production techniques varies, it becomes important to develop more sophisticated overhead allocation systems.

A more sophisticated system will typically have more cost pools, cost pools that subdivide responsibility centres, non-volume-based allocation bases (e.g., batch, product-line level bases), and possibly non-linear allocation processes. Of course, all of these elaborations of the system add cost, so the earlier concern about the trade-off between cost and accuracy should be revisited.

Source: Excerpted from Alan J. Richardson, "Major League Decisions," *CGA Magazine*, March–April 2002, pp. 30–36, published by the Certified General Accountants Association of Canada © Alan J. Richardson, FCGA, 2002. Reprinted with permission. For the full article, see the magazine archives at www.cga-online.org.

REVIEW PROBLEM: DIRECT AND STEP METHODS

Kovac Printing Company has three service departments and two operating departments. Selected data for the five departments relating to the most recent period follow:

	Service Department			Operating Department		
	Training	**Custodial**	**Maintenance**	**Offset Printing**	**Lithography**	**Total**
Overhead costs	$360,000	$210,000	$96,000	$400,000	$534,000	$1,600,000
Number of employees	120	70	280	630	420	1,520
Square metres of space occupied	1,000	2,000	4,000	8,000	20,000	35,000
Press time hours	—	—	—	30,000	60,000	90,000

The company allocates service department costs in the following order and using the bases indicated: Training (number of employees), Custodial (space occupied), and Maintenance (hours of press time). The company makes no distinction between variable and fixed service department costs.

Required:

1. Use the direct method to allocate service department costs to the operating departments.
2. Use the step method to allocate service department costs to the operating departments.

Solution to Review Problem

1. Under the direct method, service department costs are allocated directly to the operating departments. Supporting computations for these allocations follow:

Allocation Bases

	Training		**Custodial**		**Maintenance**	
Offset Printing data	630 employees	3/5	8,000 square metres	2/7	30,000 hours	1/3
Lithography data	420 employees	2/5	20,000 square metres	5/7	60,000 hours	2/3
Total	1,050 employees	5/5	28,000 square metres	7/7	90,000 hours	3/3

Given these allocation rates, the allocations to the operating departments would be as follows:

	Service Department			Operating Department		
	Training	Custodial	Maintenance	Offset Printing	Lithography	Total
Overhead costs	$ 360,000	$ 210,000	$ 96,000	$400,000	$534,000	$1,600,000
Allocation:						
Training (3/5; 2/5)	(360,000)			216,000	144,000	
Custodial (2/7; 5/7)		(210,000)		60,000	150,000	
Maintenance (1/3; 2/3)			(96,000)	32,000	64,000	
Total overhead cost after allocations	$ –0–	$ –0–	$ –0–	$708,000	$892,000	$1,600,000

2. Under the step method, services rendered between service departments are recognized when costs are allocated to other departments. Starting with the training service department, supporting computations for these allocations follow:

	Allocation Bases					
	Training		Custodial		Maintenance	
Custodial data	70 employees	5%	—		—	
Maintenance data	280 employees	20%	4,000 square metres	1/8	—	
Offset Printing data	630 employees	45%	8,000 square metres	2/8	30,000 hours	1/3
Lithography data	420 employees	30%	20,000 square metres	5/8	60,000 hours	2/3
Total	1,400 employees	100%	32,000 square metres	8/8	90,000 hours	3/3

Given these allocation rates, the allocations to the various departments would be as follows:

	Service Department			Operating Department		
	Training	Custodial	Maintenance	Offset Printing	Lithography	Total
Overhead costs	$ 360,000	$ 210,000	$ 96,000	$400,000	$534,000	$1,600,000
Allocation:						
Training (5%; 20%; 45%; 30%)*	(360,000)	18,000	72,000	162,000	108,000	
Custodial (1/8; 2/8; 5/8)		(228,000)	28,500	57,000	142,500	
Maintenance (1/3; 2/3)			(196,500)	65,500	131,000	
Total overhead cost after allocations	$ –0–	$ –0–	$ –0–	$684,500	$915,500	$1,600,000

*Allocation rates can be shown either in percentages, in fractions, or as a dollar rate per unit of activity. Both percentages and fractions are shown in this problem for the sake of illustration. *It is better to use fractions if percentages would result in odd decimals.*

GLOSSARY

Visit the Online Learning Centre at http://www.mcgrawhill.ca/college/garrison/ for a review of glossary terms and definitions.

QUESTIONS

A–1 What are interdepartmental service costs? How are such costs allocated to other departments under the step method?

A–2 How are service department costs allocated to other departments under the direct method?

A–3 "A variable base should never be used in allocating fixed service department costs to operating departments." Explain.

A–4 Why might it be desirable not to allocate some service department costs to operating departments?

A–5 In what way are service department costs similar to costs such as lubricants, utilities, and factory supervision?

A–6 What criteria are relevant to the selection of allocation bases for service department costs?

A–7 How does the reciprocal method allocate interdepartmental services? How does the approach differ from the step method?

A–8 When is it proper to pass on variances from budget in a service department to departments using the services?

A–9 Why are arbitrary allocations a practice that should be avoided whenever possible?

A–10 When are arbitrary allocations necessary?

EXERCISES

EXERCISE A–1 Direct Method [LO1, LO3]

Western University has provided the following data to be used in its service department cost allocations:

	Service Departments		Operating Departments	
	Administration	Facility Services	Undergraduate Programs	Graduate Programs
Departmental costs before allocations	$2,400,000	$1,600,000	$26,800,000	$5,700,000
Student credit-hours			20,000	5,000
Space occupied—square metres	2,500	1,000	7,000	3,000

Required:

1. Using the direct method, allocate the costs of the service departments to the two operating departments. Allocate administrative costs on the basis of student credit-hours and facility services costs on the basis of space occupied.
2. Would the reciprocal method of allocation improve the overhead accuracy for Western? Comment and justify.

EXERCISE A–2 Step Method [LO2]

Arbon Company has three service departments and two operating departments. Selected data on the five departments are presented below:

	Service Department			Operating Department		
	X	Y	Z	1	2	Total
Overhead costs	$84,000	$67,800	$36,000	$256,100	$498,600	$942,500
Number of employees............	80	60	240	600	300	1,280
Square metres of space occupied	3,000	12,000	10,000	20,000	70,000	115,000
Machine-hours	—	—	—	10,000	30,000	40,000

The company allocates service department costs by the step method in the following order: X (number of employees), Y (space occupied), and Z (machine hours). The company makes no distinction between fixed and variable service department costs.

Required:

Using the step method, make the necessary allocations of service department costs.

EXERCISE A–3 Allocations by Cost Behaviour at the Beginning of the Period [LO4]
Hannibal Steel Company has a Transport Services Department that provides trucks to haul ore from the company's mine to its two steel mills—the Northern Plant and the Southern Plant. Budgeted costs for the Transport Services Department total $350,000 per year, consisting of $0.25 per tonne variable cost and $300,000 fixed cost. The level of fixed cost is determined by peak-period requirements. During the peak period, the Northern Plant requires 70% of the Transport Services Department's capacity and the Southern Plant requires 30%.

During the coming year, 120,000 tonnes of ore are budgeted to be hauled for the Northern Plant and 60,000 tonnes of ore for the Southern Plant.

Required:
Compute the amount of Transport Services Department cost that should be allocated to each plant at the beginning of the year for purposes of computing predetermined overhead rates. (The company allocates variable and fixed costs separately.)

EXERCISE A–4 Allocations by Cost Behaviour at the End of the Period [LO4]
Refer to the data in Exercise A-3. Assume that it is now the end of the year. During the year, the Transport Services Department actually hauled the following amounts of ore for the two plants: Northern Plant, 130,000 tonnes; Southern Plant, 50,000 tonnes. The Transport Services Department incurred $364,000 in cost during the year, of which $54,000 was variable cost and $310,000 was fixed cost.

Management wants end-of-year service department cost allocations in order to compare actual performance to planned performance.

Required:
1. Determine how much of the $54,000 in variable cost should be allocated to each plant.
2. Determine how much of the $310,000 in fixed cost should be allocated to each plant.
3. Should any of the $364,000 in the Transport Services Department cost not be allocated to the plants? Explain.

EXERCISE A–5 Step Method [LO2]
The Ferre Publishing Company has three service departments and two operating departments. Selected data from a recent period on the five departments follow:

	Service Departments			Operating Departments		
	Administration	Custodial	Maintenance	Binding	Printing	Total
Overhead costs	$140,000	$105,000	$48,000	$275,000	$430,000	$998,000
Number of employees	60	35	140	315	210	760
Square metres of space occupied	1,667	1,111	2,222	4,444	11,111	20,555
Hours of press time				30,000	60,000	90,000

The company allocates service department costs by the step method in the following order: Administration (number of employees), Custodial (space occupied), and Maintenance (hours of press time). The company makes no distinction between variable and fixed service department costs.

Required:
Using the step method, allocate the service department costs to the operating departments.

EXERCISE A–6 Direct Method [LO1]
Refer to the data for the Ferre Publishing Company in Exercise A–5.

Required:
Assuming that the company uses the direct method rather than the step method to allocate service department costs, how much overhead cost would be assigned to each operating department?

S 

EXERCISE A–7 Sales Dollars as an Allocation Base for Fixed Costs [LO4]
Konig Enterprises, Ltd., owns and operates three restaurants in Vancouver, B.C. The company allocates its fixed administrative expenses to the three restaurants on the basis of sales dollars. During 2004, the fixed administrative expenses totalled $2,000,000. These expenses were allocated as follows:

	Restaurants			
	Rick's Harbourside	Imperial Garden	Ginger Wok	Total
Total sales—2004	$16,000,000	$15,000,000	$9,000,000	$40,000,000
Percentage of total sales .	40%	37.5%	22.5%	100%
Allocation (based on the above percentages) ...	$800,000	$750,000	$450,000	$2,000,000

During 2005, the following year, the Imperial Garden restaurant increased its sales by $10 million. The sales levels in the other two restaurants remained unchanged. The company's 2005 sales data were as follows:

	Restaurants			
	Rick's Harbourside	Imperial Garden	Ginger Wok	Total
Total sales—2005	$16,000,000	$25,000,000	$9,000,000	$50,000,000
Percentage of total sales .	32%	50%	18%	100%

Fixed administrative expenses remained unchanged at $2,000,000 during 2005.

Required:

1. Using sales dollars as an allocation base, show the allocation of the fixed administrative expenses among the three restaurants for 2005.
2. Compare your allocation from (1) above to the allocation for 2004. As the manager of the Imperial Garden, how would you feel about the allocation that has been charged to you for 2005?
3. Comment on the usefulness of sales dollars as an allocation base.

EXERCISE A–8 Allocating Variable Costs at the End of the Year [LO4]

Westlake Hospital has a Radiology Department that provides X-ray services to the hospital's three operating departments. The variable costs of the Radiology Department are allocated to the operating departments on the basis of the number of X-rays provided for each department. Budgeted and actual data relating to the cost of X-rays taken last year are given below:

	Variable Costs	
	Budgeted	Actual
Radiology Department	$18 per X-ray	$20 per X-ray

The budgeted and actual number of X-rays provided for each operating department last year follow:

	Pediatrics	OB Care	General Hospital
Budgeted number of X-rays	7,000	4,500	12,000
Actual number of X-rays taken ..	6,000	3,000	15,000

Required:

Determine the amount of Radiology Department variable cost that should have been allocated to each of the three operating departments at the end of last year for purposes of comparing actual performance to planned performance.

EXERCISE A–9 Allocations of Fixed Costs [LO4]

Refer to Westlake Hospital in Exercise A–8. In addition to the Radiology Department, the hospital also has a Custodial Services Department that provides services to all other departments in the hospital. The fixed costs of the two service departments are allocated using the following bases:

Department	Basis for Allocation	
Custodial Services	Square metres of space occupied:	
	Radiology Department	667 square metres
	Pediatrics	3,333 square metres
	OB Care	2,667 square metres
	General Hospital	10,000 square metres
Radiology	Long-run average X-ray needs per year:	
	Pediatrics	9,000 X-rays
	OB Care	6,000 X-rays
	General Hospital	15,000 X-rays

Budgeted and actual fixed costs in the two service departments for the year follow:

	Custodial Services	Radiology
Budgeted fixed costs	$375,000	$590,000
Actual fixed costs	$381,000	$600,000

Required:

1. Show the allocation of the fixed costs of the two service departments at the beginning of the year. The hospital uses the step method of allocation.
2. Show the allocation of the fixed costs of the two service departments at the end of the year for purposes of comparing actual performance to planned performance.

PROBLEMS

PROBLEM A–10 Step Method versus Direct Method; Predetermined Overhead Rates [LO1, LO2]

The Sendai Co., Ltd., of Japan has budgeted costs in its various departments as follows for the coming year:

Factory Administration	¥270,000,000
Custodial Services	68,760,000
Human Resources	28,840,000
Maintenance	45,200,000
Machining—overhead	376,300,000
Assembly—overhead	175,900,000
Total cost	¥965,000,000

The Japanese currency is the yen, denoted by ¥. The company allocates service department costs to other departments in the order listed below.

Department	Number of Employees	Total Labour -Hours	Square Metres of Space Occupied	Direct Labour -Hours	Machine-hours
Factory Administration	12	—	556	—	—
Custodial Services	4	3,000	222	—	—
Human Resources	5	5,000	333	—	—
Maintenance	25	22,000	1,111	—	—
Machining	40	30,000	7,778	20,000	70,000
Assembly	60	90,000	2,222	80,000	10,000
	146	150,000	12,222	100,000	80,000

Machining and Assembly are operating departments; the other departments are service departments. The company does not make a distinction between fixed and variable service department costs. Factory Administration is allocated on the basis of labour-hours; Custodial Services on the basis of square metres occupied; Human Resources on the basis of number of employees; and Maintenance on the basis of machine-hours.

Required:

1. Allocate service department costs to consuming departments by the step method. Then compute predetermined overhead rates in the operating departments using a machine-hours basis in Machining and a direct labour-hours basis in Assembly.
2. Repeat (1) above, this time using the direct method. Again compute predetermined overhead rates in Machining and Assembly.
3. Assume that the company doesn't bother with allocating service department costs but simply computes a single plantwide overhead rate based on total overhead costs (both service department and operating department costs) divided by total direct labour-hours. Compute the plantwide overhead rate.
4. Suppose a job requires machine and labour time as follows:

	Machine-hours	Direct Labour-Hours
Machining Department	190	25
Assembly Department	10	75
Total hours	200	100

Using the overhead rates computed in (1), (2), and (3) above, compute the amount of overhead cost that would be assigned to the job if the overhead rates were developed using the step method, the direct method, and the plantwide method.

PROBLEM A–11 Allocating by Cost Behaviour [LO4]

Sharp Motor Company has two operating divisions—an Auto Division and a Truck Division. The company has a cafeteria that serves the employees of both divisions. The costs of operating the cafeteria are budgeted at $40,000 per month plus $3 per meal served. The company pays all the cost of the meals.

The fixed costs of the cafeteria are determined by peak-period requirements. The Auto Division is responsible for 65% of the peak-period requirements, and the Truck Division is responsible for the other 35%.

For June, the Auto Division has estimated that it will need 35,000 meals served, and the Truck Division has estimated that it will need 20,000 meals served.

Required:

1. At the beginning of June, how much cafeteria cost should be allocated to each division for planning purposes?
2. Assume that it is now the end of June. Cost records in the cafeteria show that actual fixed costs for the month totalled $42,000 and that actual meal costs totalled $128,000. Due to unexpected layoffs of employees during the month, only 20,000 meals were served to the Auto Division. Another 20,000 meals were served to the Truck Division, as planned. How much of the actual cafeteria costs for the month should be allocated to each division? (Management uses these end-of-month allocations to compare actual performance with planned performance.)
3. Refer to the data in (2) above. Assume that the company follows the practice of allocating *all* cafeteria costs to the divisions in proportion to the number of meals served to each division during the month. On this basis, how much cost would be allocated to each division for June?
4. What criticisms can you make of the allocation method used in (3) above?
5. If managers of operating departments know that fixed service costs are going to be allocated on the basis of peak-period requirements, what will be their probable strategy as they report their estimate of peak-period requirements to the company's budget committee? As a member of top management, what would you do to neutralize such strategies?

PROBLEM A–12 Allocating Costs Equitably Among Divisions [LO4]

"These allocations don't make any sense at all," said Bob Cosic, manager of National Airlines' Freight Division. "We used the maintenance hangar less during the second quarter than we did during the first quarter, yet we were allocated more cost. Is that fair? In fact, we picked up the lion's share of the hangar's cost during the second quarter, even though we're a lot smaller than the Domestic Passenger Division."

National Airlines established the maintenance hangar to service its three operating divisions. The company allocates the cost of the hangar to the divisions on the basis of the number of hours of use each quarter. Allocations for the first two quarters to which Mr. Cosic was referring are given below:

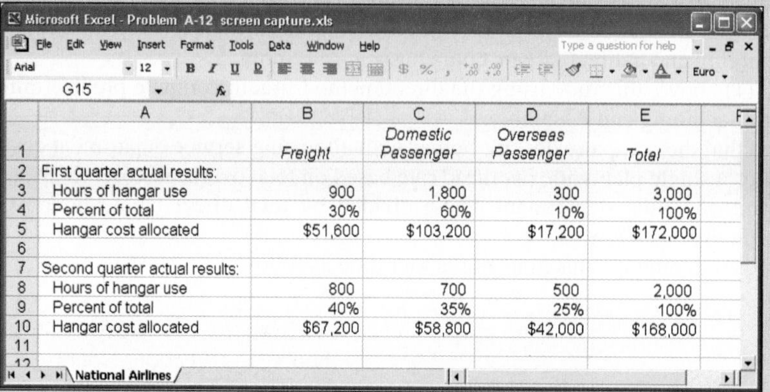

	A	B	C	D	E
1		Freight	Domestic Passenger	Overseas Passenger	Total
2	First quarter actual results:				
3	Hours of hangar use	900	1,800	300	3,000
4	Percent of total	30%	60%	10%	100%
5	Hangar cost allocated	$51,600	$103,200	$17,200	$172,000
6					
7	Second quarter actual results:				
8	Hours of hangar use	800	700	500	2,000
9	Percent of total	40%	35%	25%	100%
10	Hangar cost allocated	$67,200	$58,800	$42,000	$168,000

"Now don't get upset, Bob," replied Colleen Rogers, the controller. "Those allocations are fair. As you can see, your division used the hangar more than any other division during the second quarter and therefore it has been allocated the largest share of cost. Although use of the hangar was off somewhat during the second quarter, keep in mind that most of the hangar's costs are fixed and therefore continue regardless of how much the hangar is used. Also, remember that we built enough capacity into the hangar to handle the divisions' peak-period needs, and that cost has to be absorbed by someone. The fairest way to handle it is to charge according to usage from quarter to quarter. When you use the hangar more, you get charged more; it's as simple as that."

"That's just the point," replied Cosic. "I didn't use the hangar more, I used it less. So why am I charged more?"

The Freight Division requires 30% of the hangar's capacity during peak periods; the Domestic Passenger Division, 50%; and the Overseas Passenger Division, 20%. The peak period occurs in the fourth quarter of the year.

Required:

1. Is there any merit to Mr. Cosic's complaint? Explain.
2. Using the high-low method, determine the cost formula for the hangar in terms of a variable rate per hour and total fixed cost each quarter.
3. Reallocate the hangar costs for the first and second quarters in accordance with the cost allocation principles discussed in the chapter. Allocate the variable and fixed costs separately.

PROBLEM A–13 Step Method [LO2, LO4]

Woodbury Hospital has three service departments and three operating departments. Estimated cost and operating data for all departments in the hospital for the forthcoming quarter are presented in the table below:

	Service Departments			Operating Departments			
	Housekeeping Services	Food Services	Admin. Services	Laboratory	Radiology	General Hospital	Total
Variable costs	$ 0	$193,860	$158,840	$243,600	$304,800	$ 74,500	$ 975,600
Fixed costs	87,000	107,200	90,180	162,300	215,700	401,300	1,063,680
Total cost	$87,000	$301,060	$249,020	$405,900	$520,500	$475,800	$2,039,280
Meals served			800	2,000	1,000	68,000	71,800
Percentage of peak-period needs—Food Services			0.8%	2.4%	1.6%	95.2%	100%
Square metres of space	556	1,445	722	1,111	833	12,000	16,667
Files processed				14,000	7,000	25,000	46,000
Percentage of peak-period needs—Admin. Services				30%	20%	50%	100%

The costs of the service departments are allocated by the step method using the allocation bases and in the order shown in the following table:

Service Department	Costs Incurred	Allocation Bases
Housekeeping Services	Fixed	Square metres of space
Food Services	Variable	Meals served
	Fixed	Peak-period needs—Food Services
Administrative Services	Variable	Files processed
	Fixed	Peak-period needs—Admin. Services

All billing in the hospital is done through Laboratory, Radiology, or General Hospital. The hospital's administrator wants the costs of the three service departments allocated to these three billing centres.

Required:
Prepare the cost allocation desired by the hospital administrator. (Use the step method.) Include under each billing centre the direct costs of the centre, as well as the costs allocated from the service departments.

PROBLEM A–14 Beginning- and End-of-Year Allocations [LO4]

Tasman Products, Ltd., of Australia has a Maintenance Department that services the equipment in the company's Forming Department and Assembly Department. The cost of this servicing is allocated to the operating departments on the basis of machine-hours. Cost and other data relating to the Maintenance Department and to the other two departments for the most recent year are presented below. (The currency in Australia is the Australian dollar.)

Data for the Maintenance Department follow:

	Budget	Actual
Variable costs for lubricants	$96,000*	$110,000
Fixed costs for salaries and other	$150,000	$153,000

*Budgeted at $0.40 per machine-hour.

Data for the Forming and Assembly departments follow:

	Percentage of Peak-Period Capacity Required	Machine-Hours	
		Budget	Actual
Forming Department	70%	160,000	190,000
Assembly Department	30%	80,000	70,000
Total	100%	240,000	260,000

The company allocates variable and fixed costs separately. The level of fixed costs in the Maintenance Department is determined by peak-period requirements.

Required:
1. Assume that it is the beginning of the year. How much of the budgeted Maintenance Department cost would be allocated to each department?
2. Assume that it is now the end of the year. Management would like data to assist in comparing actual performance to planned performance in the Maintenance Department and in the other departments.
   a. How much of the actual Maintenance Department costs should be allocated to the Forming Department and to the Assembly Department? Show all computations.
   b. Should any portion of the actual Maintenance Department costs not be allocated to the other departments? If all costs should be allocated, explain why; if a portion should not be allocated, compute the amount and explain why it should not be allocated.

PROBLEM A–15 Step Method; Predetermined Overhead Rates [LO2, LO4]
Bombay Castings, Ltd., has two operating departments, Fabrication and Finishing, and three service departments. The service departments and the bases on which their costs are allocated to consuming departments are listed below:

Department	Cost	Allocation Bases
Building and Grounds	Fixed	Square metres occupied
Administration	Variable	Number of employees
	Fixed	Employees at full capacity
Equipment Maintenance	Variable	Machine-hours
	Fixed	40% to Fabrication 60% to Finishing

Indian currency is denominated in rupees, denoted here by R.

Service department costs are allocated to consuming departments by the step method in the order shown. The company has developed the cost and operating data given in the following table for purposes of preparing overhead rates in the two operating departments:

	Building and Grounds	Adminis-tration	Equipment Maintenance	Fabrication	Finishing	Total
Variable costs	R 0	R22,200	R16,900	R146,000	R320,000	R 505,100
Fixed costs	88,200	60,000	24,000	420,000	490,000	1,082,200
Total cost	R88,200	R82,200	R40,900	R566,000	R810,000	R1,587,300
Budgeted employees	6	4	30	450	630	1,120
Employees at full capacity	8	4	45	570	885	1,512
Square metres occupied	60	50	140	1,200	1,550	3,000
Budgeted machine-hours				70,000	105,000	175,000

Required:

1. Show the allocation of service department costs to operating departments for purposes of preparing overhead rates in Fabrication and Finishing.
2. Assuming that overhead rates are calculated using machine-hours as the allocation base, compute the overhead rate for each operating department.
3. Assume the following *actual* data for the year for the Administration Department:

Actual variable costs	R23,800
Actual employees for the year:	
Building and Grounds	6
Administration	4
Equipment Maintenance	32
Fabrication	460
Finishing	625
	1,127

Compute the amount of end-of-year Administration Department variable cost that should be allocated to each department. (Management uses these end-of-year allocations to compare actual performance to planned performance.)

PROBLEM A–16 Step Method [LO2, LO4]
The Bayview Resort has three operating units—the Convention Centre, Food Services, and Guest Lodging. These three operating units are supported by three service units—General Administration, Cost Accounting, and Laundry. The costs of the service units are allocated by the step method using the allocation bases and in the order shown below:

General Administration:
Fixed costs—allocated 10% to Cost Accounting, 4% to the Laundry, 30% to the Convention Centre, 16% to Food Services, and 40% to Guest Lodging.
Cost Accounting:
Variable costs—allocated on the basis of the number of items processed each period.
Fixed costs—allocated on the basis of peak-period requirements.
Laundry:
Variable costs—allocated on the basis of the number of kilograms of laundry processed each period.
Fixed costs—allocated on the basis of peak-period requirements.

Cost and operating data for all units in the resort for a recent quarter are given in the following table:

	Service Units			Operating Units			
	General Administration	Cost Accounting	Laundry	Convention Centre	Food Services	Guest Lodging	Total
Variable costs	$ 0	$ 70,000	$143,000	$ 0	$ 52,000	$ 24,000	$ 289,000
Fixed costs	200,000	110,000	65,900	95,000	375,000	486,000	1,331,900
Total overhead cost	$200,000	$180,000	$208,900	$95,000	$427,000	$510,000	$1,620,900
Kilograms of laundry processed				10,000	7,500	105,000	122,500
Percentage of peak-period requirements—Laundry				10%	6%	84%	100%
Number of items processed	1,000		800	1,200	3,000	9,000	15,000
Percentage of peak-period requirements—Cost Accounting	*		7%	13%	20%	60%	100%

*General administration is excluded from the computation of peak-period requirements due to the order in which the service unit costs are allocated.

Since all billing is done through the Convention Centre, Food Services, and Guest Lodging, the resort's general manager wants the costs of the three service units allocated to these three billing centres.

Required:
Prepare the cost allocation desired by the resort's general manager. Include under each billing centre the direct costs of the centre, as well as the costs allocated from the service units.

PROBLEM A–17 Comparison of Allocation Methods [LO4]

Madison Park Co-op, a whole foods grocery and gift shop, has provided the following data to be used in its service department cost allocations:

	Service Departments		Operating Departments	
	Administration	Custodial	Groceries	Gifts
Departmental costs before allocations	$150,000	$40,000	$2,320,000	$950,000
Employee-hours	320	160	3,100	740
Space occupied—square metres	250	100	4,000	1,000

Required:
1. Using the step method, allocate the costs of the service departments to the two operating departments. Allocate administrative costs first on the basis of employee-hours and then custodial costs on the basis of space occupied.

2. Use the reciprocal method to allocate the service departments.
3. Comment on the improvements in the overhead accuracy as a result of the two approaches.

CASES

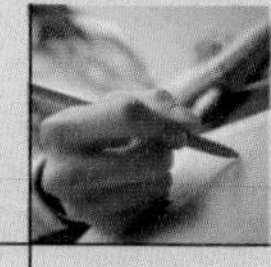

CASE A–18 Step Method versus Direct Method [LO1, LO2]

"This is really an odd situation," said Jim Carter, general manager of Highland Publishing Company. "We get most of the jobs we bid on that require a lot of press time in the Printing Department, yet profits on those jobs are never as high as they ought to be. On the other hand, we lose most of the jobs we bid on that require a lot of time in the Binding Department. I would be inclined to think that the problem is with our overhead rates, but we're already computing separate overhead rates for each department. So what else could be wrong?"

Highland Publishing Company is a large organization that offers a variety of printing and binding work. The Printing and Binding departments are supported by three service departments. The costs of these service departments are allocated to other departments in the order listed below. (For each service department, use the allocation base that provides the best measure of service provided, as discussed in the chapter.)

Department	Total Labour -Hours	Square Metres of Space Occupied	Number of Employees	Machine-Hours	Direct Labour-Hours
Human Resources . . .	20,000	400	10		
Custodial Services . . .	30,000	600	15		
Maintenance	50,000	2,000	25		
Printing	90,000	8,000	40	150,000	60,000
Binding	260,000	4,000	120	30,000	175,000
	450,000	15,000	210	180,000	235,000

Budgeted overhead costs in each department for the current year are shown below (no distinction is made between variable and fixed costs):

Human Resources	$ 360,000
Custodial Services	141,000
Maintenance	201,000
Printing	525,000
Binding	373,500
Total budgeted cost	$1,600,500

Because of its simplicity, the company has always used the direct method to allocate service department costs to the two operating departments.

Required:

1. Using the step method, allocate the service department costs to the consuming departments. Then compute predetermined overhead rates for the current year using machine-hours as the allocation base in the Printing Department and direct labour-hours as the allocation base in the Binding Department.
2. Repeat (1) above, this time using the direct method. Again compute predetermined overhead rates in the Printing and Binding departments.
3. Assume that during the current year the company bids on a job that requires machine and labour time as follows:

	Machine-hours	Direct Labour-Hours
Printing Department	15,400	900
Binding Department	800	2,000
Total hours	16,200	2,900

a. Determine the amount of overhead cost that would be assigned to the job if the company used the overhead rates developed in (1) above. Then determine the amount of overhead cost that would be assigned to the job if the company used the overhead rates developed in (2) above.

b. Explain to Mr. Carter, the general manager, why the step method provides a better basis for computing predetermined overhead rates than the direct method.

GROUP AND INTERNET EXERCISES

GROUP EXERCISE A–19 Understanding the Cost of Complexity

Service departments (or production support departments in the case of a manufacturer) make up a large and growing part of the cost structure of most businesses. This is as true in hospitals, financial institutions, universities, and other service industries as it is in manufacturing where production support department costs can average 40% or more of total manufacturing costs.

In an effort to reduce costs, many companies seek to reduce head count, which is a demoralizing experience not only for those who lose their jobs, but also for those who remain employed. One sure sign of problems with this head-count-reduction approach is that more than half of companies refill these positions within a year after eliminating them.

Required:

1. Choose an industry with which you are somewhat familiar (or with which someone you know is familiar) and list seven or eight major production support or service departments in the factory or other facility in this industry. What is the output of each of these support or service departments?
2. Assume a relatively uncomplicated factory (facility) where just a single, standard product (or service) is mass produced. Describe the activity or work being done in each of the service areas of this focused company.
3. Now assume a more complicated operation for another factory located close by where a wide range of products are made or services are offered—some are standard products/services while others are made to order, some are high-volume products/services while others are low volume, and some are fairly complex products/services while others are relatively simple. Describe the activity or work being done in the various service functions for this full-service company.
4. Which factory or facility has higher production support costs? Why?
5. Explain the relationship between the range of products produced and the size of the support departments. When does the output of each of these support departments increase? When does the cost of each of these support departments increase?
6. Most companies are under increasing pressure to reduce costs. How would you go about bringing the overall level of service department costs down?

INTERNET EXERCISE A–20

As you know, the World Wide Web is a medium that is constantly evolving. Sites come and go, and change without notice. To enable periodic updating of site addresses, this problem has been posted to the textbook Web site (www.mcgrawhill.ca/college/garrison). After accessing the site, enter the Student Centre and select this chapter. Select and complete the Internet Exercise.

Photo Credits

Chapter 1, Ryan McVay/Getty Images; Chapter 2, Skip Nall/Getty Images; Chapter 3, Steve Cole/Getty Images; Chapter 4, (c) Richard Hutchings; Chapter 5, Digital Vision/Getty Images; Chapter 6, Courtesy of Joie de Vivre Hospitality; Chapter 7, Steve Cole/Getty Images; Chapter 8, Ryan McVay/Getty Images; Chapter 9, Walt Disney Productions/PHOTOFEST; Chapter 10, PhotoLink/Getty Images; Chapter 11, © Digital Vision/Getty Images; Chapter 12, © Bruce Ayres/Getty Images; Chapter 13, Janis Christie/Getty Images; Chapter 14, © Creatus/PunchStock.

Company/Name Index

Subject Index

C

D

E

J

N

O

P

Q

R

S

T

U

V

W

Y

Z